THE HISTORY OF WORLD WAR II

Published by Prospero Books
a division of Chapters Inc.
90 Ronson Drive
Etobicoke
Ontario
Canada M9W 1C1

ISBN 1-55267-115-1

This revised and updated edition is based on material previously published
as part of the reference set World War II.

Editorial and design by Amber Books Ltd
Bradley's Close
74–77 White Lion Street
London N1 9PF

Editorial Consultant: Alexander Stilwell

Printed in Italy

CONTENTS

INTRODUCTION

▷ *American P-51 Mustangs fly in close formation. The black-and-white stripes on the fuselage are special markings for the invasion of France in 1944.*

Lieutenant-Colonel Eddy Bauer's history of World War II is a definitive and classic work: one of the most complete and objective accounts of the greatest conflict in world history. This revised edition's aim is to make the original work more concise and accessible without losing the essential character of the original text; new discoveries and revelations are covered by eminent military historians and linking synopses of lesser events provide a full and complete account of the events of World War II.

The Warning

On 25 January 1938, the last year in the reign of Pope Pius XI, two months before the Anschluss, or German annexation of Austria, an eerie light was seen in many parts of Europe, reaching as far south as Rome. Unexplained forest and building fires were also reported. Twenty-one years earlier, in 1917, three children from an obscure village called Fatima in the centre of Portugal had testified to a number of messages of world consequence given to them by none other than Mary, the Mother of Jesus Christ. One of these messages had warned that: "World War I will end soon. However, if humanity does not stop offending God, another, and worse war will break out in the reign of Pius XI." The sign for this impending

war was to be "a night illuminated by an unknown light".

However one wishes to interpret these strange events, and whether or not historians can agree that 1938 was the real beginning of World War II, containing as it did not only the Anschluss but the Munich crisis and the directive to the Wehrmacht for the final liquidation of Czecho-Slovakia, one thing can be certain: that World War II was indeed "worse" than its predecessor, World War I, which had been described as "the war to end war".

What immediately stands out from the casualty figures of the two world wars is that in World War II more civilians were killed than combatants, including well over five million Jews. The total of those who died in World War I was 8,538,315, while in World War II the military deaths on both sides in Europe alone numbered 19 million in contrast to six million in the war against Japan. In Poland 5,300,000 civilians died in addition to 120,000 combatants. A third of the civilian casualties were Jews.

Germany's Strengths

The build-up to World War II was characterised by the bullishness of the National Socialists and their skilful use of propaganda to compensate for areas of weakness. Their cause was aided by the reluctance of the major Western powers to confront them. That a powerful state with modern armaments like Czechoslovakia could have been absorbed by the Germans with barely a shot being fired demonstrated the true price of appeasement. Moreover, although sound defensive tactics had been enough to eventually turn the tide in the Allies favour in World War I, new circumstances and developments in tactics and armaments now favoured the aggressor. Men like General Heinz Guderian had been quick to take up new ideas on tank tactics which, although conceived by British thinkers such as Basil Liddell Hart, were rejected by conservative forces in the British high command. Thus the Germans developed the doctrine of the tank division used in conjunction with motorized artillery, motorised infantry divisions and dive bombers. The result was the "blitzkrieg" that literally took Europe by storm.

Naval Warfare

Although on the back foot militarily in 1939, Britain could still rely on naval ascendancy to keep it from disaster. What the Germans lacked by way of a powerful surface fleet was compensated for to some extent by the effectiveness of U-Boat tactics, enhanced by strategic Atlantic ports. But partly due to Hitler's reluctance to commit resources to U-Boat development and partly due to improved convoy tactics and increasing aid from the U.S.A., the tide began to turn in the Allies favour.

Mercurial German surface raiders occasionally slipped out like sharks from their lairs, notably the Admiral Graf Von Spee, which was famously cornered by British cruisers at the Battle of the River Plate, and the Bismarck which, tracked down by almost the entire British Home Fleet, spectacularly sank that emblem of British naval power, H.M.S. Hood, before meeting its own grisly end in the Atlantic. In the clash with Bismarck the Royal Navy launched from H.M.S. Victorious its first ever aircraft-carrier strike against a German battleship at sea. Although this barely caused a dent, a second strike from H.M.S. Ark Royal was enough to damage the rudder and allow pursuing battleships to catch up.

The most spectacular entrance for aircraft-carrier tactics in World War II, however, was made by the Japanese at Pearl Harbor on 7 December 1941. Thereafter the aircraft carrier superseded the battleship as the dominant vessel of the war. The U.S.A. demonstrated even greater command of carrier tactics at Midway Island, Coral Sea and Leyte Gulf.

Air Power

In 1939, the Germans could hold their own in terms of the quantity of aircraft produced and the quality was second to none. The Luftwaffe had also had the opportunity to practise air-to-ground support techniques in Spain. These tactics were anathema to senior British airmen and were only effectively employed by the British in 1942. Despite this, in the summer and autumn of 1940 the Royal Air Force achieved a victory over the Germans in the Battle of Britain which has become legendary. Here were knights of the air fighting the forces of evil over a land bathed in summer sunshine. Even the weapons they employed in the battle, notably the Supermarine Spitfire, seemed to be inspired.

After the Battle of Britain, it became apparent that the Germans, although starting the war with

▽ *Blitzkreig! An early German Panzer passes members of the Wehrmacht during the invasion of the Soviet Union.*

an impressive line up of aircraft, had made few plans for replacements in future years. By 1940, Britain alone was producing aircraft faster than Germany, and with the addition of U.S.A. resources, not to mention those of the Soviet Union, the imbalance in this vital arm of warfare became critical for Germany. By D-Day, the Germans had only 319 aircraft in the west against 12,837 for the Allies.

That the U.S.A. was in a position in 1945 not only to drop two atomic bombs on Japan more or less unopposed as well as launching raids as devastating as the Tokyo "fire raid" of 9 March 1945 shows to what extent Japanese air power, despite the excellence of fighters such as the Zero, had been eroded.

It was fortunate for the Western Allies that Hitler decided to turn on his erstwhile ally, the Soviet Union, and thus create a powerful enemy in the east that would eventually prove to be his Nemesis. In addition to the weapons they were

able to supply from their own factories, the Soviets also had the advantage of a massive supply of equipment from the Western powers. By the end of 1943, in the wake of epic battles such as Stalingrad and Kursk, the Germans had lost two thirds of the territory they had taken. By April 1945 the Red Army had reached Berlin. The major role the Soviet Union had played in defeating Nazi Germany, however, was now to be sullied by the institution of anti-democratic communist regimes in Eastern Europe.

Balance of Power

Japan's spectacular assault on the U.S. Navy and Hitler's decision to declare war upon the U.S.A. brought into the equation a country that was not only the most powerful nation in the world but which was more powerful at the end of the war than at the beginning. From now on the Allies could rely on steadily achieving their objectives through what Winston Churchill described as "the proper application of overwhelming force". In the West the U.S. factories were producing massive amounts of armaments and even in the East the Soviets had succeeded in moving whole factories from under German noses to the safety of their vast hinterlands. At the Battle of Kursk the Soviet Union was able to field 4,000 vehicles to the Germans' 2,700. The fundamental superiority in training of the German soldier and the excellence of German staff officers and NCOs could not make up for the growing imbalance in resources. The Axis powers were also increasingly overstretched and out-manouvred in the Intelligence game. Whereas the Germans were often at the mercy of flawed decisions made during the volatile mood swings of their supreme commander, the Japanese desire to fight to the death meant that they failed to take the opportunity to devise more effective tactics on the ground.

With the dropping of the two atomic bombs and the end of the war, the U.S.A. and the Soviet Union were the undisputed world powers, while Britain, although a victor and in command of much of its Empire, was bled white economically and at the end of an era in its history. Whereas Germany and Japan, despite being occupied, had no choice but to start completely afresh and begin to build powerful new economies, and whereas France succeeded in taking the initiative in European political experiments, Britain found itself caught between roles and with divided loyalties.

The message at the end of World War II was this: that if there was to be another, even worse war, it would probably mean the end of humanity. Man's technological genius had made the prospect unthinkable.

▽ *The Führer of Germany, Adolf Hitler, came to power in 1933. By 1945, only 12 years later, millions had died and Europe lay in ruins as a result on his actions.*

CHAPTER 1
POLAND'S AGONY

By the 17th day after France's proclamation of general mobilisation, Poland's existence as an independent state had been destroyed for the next five and a half years. There had been no precedent for such a catastrophe since Napoleon's destruction of Prussia at Jena in 1806. It was the result not so much of Poland's military weaknesses at the crucial moment as of the *matériel*, numerical, and strategic superiority of the German Army and of the Luftwaffe, helped by the fatal mistakes of the Polish High Command.

Within the frontiers which had been laid down by the Treaty of Versailles, Marshal Rydz-Smigly and his commanders had a difficult problem in planning the defence of Poland against Hitler's rearmed Germany. A glance at the map will show the reason for this. From Suwałki, on the frontier between East Prussia and Lithuania, to the Carpathians south of Przemyśl, the Polish frontier to be defended included the Slovak border and formed a huge salient with a front line of some 1,250 miles – excluding the defence requirements of Danzig and the Corridor. To defend this vulnerable salient, the Polish High Command had only 45 divisions at its disposal.

When the Germans examined the Polish Army archives after their victory in 1939, they found that the French had given several warnings to their Polish opposite numbers about the dangers of the situation. One of them, prepared by General Weygand, the French Chief-of-Staff, had advised the Poles "to base [their] defences behind the line formed by the Rivers Niemen, Bobr, Narew, Vistula, and San". And Weygand went on to add: "From the operational point of view this concept is the only sound one, for it disposes of every possibility of envelopment and places strong river barriers in the path of German armoured formations. More important, this line is only 420 miles long, instead of the 1,250-mile front from Suwałki to the Carpathian passes."

As early as the German reoccupation of the Rhineland, Gamelin had given Rydz-Smigly the same advice during a visit to

Throughout the summer of 1939, Europe waited with bated breath as Hitler put the Wehrmacht forces through their paces in rehearsal for their first real test–the invasion of Poland.

The role of the German infantry was crucial to Blitzkrieg strategy, and during the weeks and months prior to the September invasion the German infantrymen were thoroughly drilled on extensive exercises in preparation for the attack.

Countdown to War

March 16, 1935	Hitler announces German rearmament.
March 7, 1936	Germany reoccupies the Rhineland.
March 13, 1938	*Anschluss* – German annexation of Austria.
September 29, 1938	Munich Agreement between Britain, France, Germany and Italy in which the Sudetenland is surrendered to Germany.
October 21, 1938	Hitler issues directive to Wehrmacht calling for final liquidation "of the remainder of Czecho-Slovakia".
November 9-10, 1939	*Kristallnacht* – reprisals against Jews in Germany.
March 15, 1939	Total abdication of Czecho-Slovakia's sovereignty to Germany.
March 31, 1939	Britain announces guarantee of military aid to Poland in the event of a threat to her independence.
April 7, 1939	Italian expeditionary force lands on Albanian coast.
April 27, 1939	"Pact of Steel" signed between Italy and Germany.
August 23, 1939	Germany and Russia sign a Non-Aggression Pact (Molotov-Ribbentrop).
September 1, 1939	Germany invades Poland.
September 3, 1939	Britain and France declare war on Germany.

Warsaw, and he reiterated the point in his discussions with General Kasprzycki on May 16. The Polish High Command, however, replied to these French suggestions by pointing out that Poland could not continue to fight a prolonged war if she gave up the industrial regions of Upper Silesia and Łódź, and the rich agricultural regions of Kutno, Kielce, and Poznań without firing a shot. For this reason General Kutrzeba, according to the German examination of the Polish archives, proposed to include these regions in the defensive perimeter, but without stationing troops further west than the Warta river or cramming garrison forces into the Danzig Corridor, which would have meant that in the north the Polish troops were stationed where they had to face a two-front war, from German Pomerania and from East Prussia.

Whatever the reasons behind it, this was a rash plan. But when Rydz-Smigly stationed a full fifth of his resources around Poznań and in the Corridor itself it smacked of megalomania—and he did this despite the fact that his Intelligence department had provided him with extremely accurate figures for the forces massing against Poland. Moreover, general mobilisation was not proclaimed in Poland until 1100 hours on August 31, and this meant that on the first day of the German attack the Polish front was held by only 17 infantry divisions, three infantry brigades, and six cavalry brigades. Thirteen Polish divisions mobilised by the time of the German attack were still moving to their concentration areas, while another nine divisions were still mustering in barracks.

To crown everything, the Polish High Command was fatally vulnerable in its communications with the forces in the field. There was no adequate command structure between Rydz-Smigly and his eight army commanders, and the communication network on which he depended for control in battle was cut to ribbons by the Luftwaffe's precision attacks within the first few days of the campaign.

Blitzkrieg unleashed

This unbelievable combination of mistakes contributed greatly to the Wehrmacht's success, but nothing can detract from the thoroughness of the German preparation. Brauchitsch's plan of concentration for "Case White" was based on sound concepts of strategy, and had been explained clearly to the lower command levels. Ground and air missions were co-ordinated; every man knew what he had to do; and the result got the most out of the new concept of co-operation between an armoured army and a modern air force. Drawn up at the beginning of July, the O.K.H. Directive stated: "The objective of the operation is the destruction of the Polish armed forces. The political conduct of the war demands that it be fought with crushing, surprise blows to achieve rapid success.

"Intention of the Army High Command: to disrupt, by a rapid invasion of Polish territory, the mobilisation and concentration of the Polish Army, and to destroy the bulk of troops stationed to the west of the Vistula–Narew line by converging attacks from Silesia, Pomerania, and East Prussia."

The armoured and motorised divisions with which Germany attacked Poland totalled 55 divisions, including reserves, on "Y-Day", but by September 18 this figure had risen to 63. The front line divisions were divided into two large army groups with the following strengths and objectives:

1. **East Prussia and Pomerania**–Army Group North (Colonel-General Fedor von Bock).
   Left flank: 3rd Army (General Georg von Küchler), with eight infantry divisions, was to assist in the destruction of the Polish forces in the Corridor and drive south towards the Vistula and Warsaw.
   Right flank: 4th Army (General Günther Hans von Kluge), with six infantry divisions, two motorised divisions, and one Panzer division, was to attack from Pomerania and destroy the main body of Polish troops defending the Corridor, cutting off the Poznań-Kutno group from the north.
2. **Silesia and Slovakia**–Army Group South (Colonel-General Gerd von Rundstedt).
   Left flank: 8th Army (General Johannes Blaskowitz), with four infantry divisions and the S.S. motorised regiment *Leibstandarte Adolf Hitler*, was to engage the Polish forces in the Poznań-Kutno region and keep them from counter-attacking the central army of the group.
   Centre: 10th Army (General Walter von

△ *Tribute to Luftwaffe accuracy–a neatly bombed bridge. Pin-point attacks against communications formed one of the most effective elements in the pattern of the Blitzkrieg.*

▽ *Troops of a Maginot Line fortress, waiting for the war to come to them, while away the time playing cards.*

▽ *Offering courageous resistance against overwhelming odds, Polish Type 1 tanks move forward into attack.*

Reichenau), with six infantry divisions, two motorised divisions, three light divisions, and two Panzer divisions, was to drive north-east, straight for Wieluń, Łódź, and Warsaw.

Right flank: 14th Army (General Sigmund Wilhelm List), with one mountain division, six infantry divisions, one light division, two Panzer divisions, and the S.S. motorised regiment *Germania*, was to strike across the Carpathians from Slovakia and pin down the Polish forces around Kraków and Przemyśl.

Hitler, however, intervened and altered Army Group North's schedule. By switching its forces east of Warsaw, he made sure that any Polish forces which managed to cross the Vistula would be cut off to the east of the Capital.

For General Guderian, however, the opening of the German offensive started with near disaster. He was in command of XIX Panzer Corps and, a sound armour tactician, was well up with his forward troops. "The corps crossed the frontier simultaneously at 0445 hours on September 1," he later recalled. "There was a thick ground mist at first which prevented the Luftwaffe from giving us any support. I drove forward with the 3rd Panzer Brigade in the first wave [until it came into

action]. Contrary to my orders, the 3rd Panzer Brigade's heavy artillery felt itself compelled to fire into the mist. The first shell landed 50 yards in front of my command vehicle, the second 50 yards behind. I was sure that the next one would be a direct hit and ordered my driver to turn about and drive off. The unaccustomed noise had made him nervous, however, and he drove flat-out straight into a ditch. The front axle of the half-track was bent so that the steering mechanism was put out of action. This marked the end of my drive . . ."

The Blitzkrieg triumphant

The first stage of the campaign saw the Polish cavalry of the "Pomorze Army" (Pomeranian Army), under General Bortnowski, charge the tanks of Guderian's XIX Panzer Corps as they thrust across the Corridor towards the Vistula, which they crossed at Chełmno on September 6, making contact with 3rd Army on the far bank. As late as September 15–18, when the campaign was already lost, the Polish "Sosnkowski Group" (11th and 38th Divisions), marching by night and fighting by day, managed three times to break through

the ring which the German 14th Army was trying to close behind it. Fighting their way across the San river, the Sosnkowski divisions managed to capture 20 guns and 180 vehicles from 14th Army.

All this was achieved under non-stop bombing raids by the Luftwaffe. Although the Polish Air Force managed to keep up sporadic air attack up to September 17, the Luftwaffe dominated the air. *Luftflotten* (Air Fleets) I and IV, commanded by Generals Albert Kesselring and Alexander Löhr, concentrated their attacks on communication centres, pockets of resistance, and Polish forces on the move. *Luftflotte* I operated with Bock's Army Group North, *Luftflotte* IV with Rundstedt's Army Group South. Between them, the two air fleets totalled 897 bombers and 219 Stukas.

The advantage of unchallenged air power helped the German 10th Army to win rapid successes in its advance on Warsaw. It is true that on September 8 its 4th Panzer Division failed in its attempt to take Warsaw by surprise, but two days later 10th Army reached the Vistula at Góra Kalwaria and tore the Polish "Łódź Army" to shreds. At the same time the Polish "Prussian Army" had also been cut off, broken up, and destroyed in a battle against heavy odds. Marshal Rydz-Smigly's order for the Polish armies to

withdraw eastwards had gone out on September 6, but it was already too late.

This withdrawal led to one of the most dramatic episodes in the Polish campaign. Falling back on Warsaw, the "Pomorze" and "Poznań" Armies were challenged by the German 8th Army, coming up from Łódz, which tried to bar their retreat. The result was the hard-fought "Battle of the Bzura", which began on September 10. The Polish troops succeeded in capturing bridgeheads across the Bzura river near Łowicz, and drove back the German 30th Infantry Division. Thanks to Hitler's order to switch the advance east of Warsaw, Army Group North was unable to intervene fast enough to cover the flank of Army Group South. But Rundstedt rose to the crisis. While Stukas attacked the Bzura bridgeheads, the motorised and Panzer divisions of 10th Army wheeled north and caught the Polish forces in flank. There was vicious fighting around Lowicz and Sochaczew before the Poles pulled back; but at last, completely cut off and hemmed in about Kutno, General Bortnowski was forced to order the surrender of his 170,000 men on September 19.

While 8th Army closed the inner pincers of the German advance by investing Warsaw and Modlin, the plan imposed by

△ *The Poles dug a series of trenches round their capital before the siege. Despite a heroic defence during which large parts of Warsaw were devastated, the capital fell after two weeks.*

△ *For these Polish prisoners the war is over – but thousands of their compatriots escaped to the West through Rumania and carried on the fight from France and Britain.*

▽ *A comment on the Hitler/Stalin Pact by the famous Egyptian cartoonist Kem (Kimon Evan Marenjo): the two dictators are marching temporarily together, but each with a hand on his gun.*

Hitler aimed at a wider sweep to trap the remaining Polish fragments retreating east of the Vistula. This was achieved by a deep Panzer penetration led by Guderian. His XIX Panzer Corps had been transferred across East Prussia after its initial successes in the Corridor, and on September 9 it forced the Narew river upstream of Lomza. Six days later it had driven as far south as Brest Litovsk, and its 3rd Panzer Division, pressing south towards Włodawa, had made contact with advance units of 10th and 14th Armies from Army Group South. 14th Army, which had advanced eastwards as far as L'vov, had swung north-east to complete this link-up.

Until this time the Soviet Union had observed the letter of the Soviet–Polish Non-Aggression Pact of 1932, which, renewed on May 5, 1934, was intended to run until the end of 1945. But when it became obvious that the destruction of the Polish Army was imminent, Moscow decided to intervene in order to make sure of the territories (east of the line formed by the Narew, Vistula, and San rivers) conceded to the Soviet Union by the

secret protocol attached to the German–Soviet Non-Aggression Pact. At 0300 hours on September 17, Vladimir Potemkin, Deputy Commissar for Foreign Affairs, told Polish Ambassador Grzybowski that "the fact is that the Polish State and its Government have ceased to exist".

"For this reason," ran the note which Potemkin read to Grzybowski, "the treaties concluded between the Soviet Union and Poland have lost their validity. Abandoned to its own fate and deprived of its rulers, Poland has become an area in which could develop all manner of circumstances potentially dangerous to the Soviet Union. This is why, having maintained its neutrality up to now, the Soviet Union cannot remain neutral in the present situation.

"The Soviet Union can no longer remain indifferent to the sufferings of its blood-brothers the Ukrainians and Belorussians, who, inhabitants of Polish territory, are being abandoned to their fate and left defenceless. In consideration of this situation the Soviet Government has ordered the High Command of the Red Army to send its troops across the frontier and to take under their protection the lives and welfare of the populations of the western Ukraine and western Belorussia." The note had been drawn up with the full agreement of Germany, which had undertaken not to conclude an armistice with Poland.

The Polish Ambassador refused to accept this note, but a few hours later large Red Army forces crossed the frontier and pushed motorised and armoured columns westward towards Vilna, Brest-Litovsk, Kovel', and L'vov. Within days their spearheads had made contact with Wehrmacht troops in Galicia and along the River Bug.

The intervention of the Red Army ended the last vain hopes of the Polish High Command for prolonging resistance in a last-ditch campaign in eastern Galicia with their backs to the Rumanian frontier. On the morning of September 18, President Mościcki, Colonel Beck, and the remainder of the Polish Government, together with Marshal Rydz-Smigly, fled to Rumania and claimed political asylum. Poland's formal resistance was over.

Poland: erased from the map of Europe

During this 18-day campaign the German armies had largely over-run the demarcation line agreed between Stalin and Ribbentrop on August 23. This led to a new settlement between Moscow and Berlin: the "German-Soviet Treaty of Delimitation and Friendship", signed on September 28 by Ribbentrop after another journey to Moscow. The agreement, which split Poland in two, was made at Stalin's insistence, as he refused to countenance a German suggestion for the establishment of a Polish state of 15 million inhabitants.

In this partition agreement, Germany accepted the inclusion of Lithuania into the Soviet sphere of influence; in compensation, the parts of the province of Warsaw already conceded in the agreement of August 23, plus the entire province of Lublin, were conceded to Germany. In central Poland the new demarcation line connected the Vistula and Bug rivers; in Galicia it remained on the San river, for Stalin refused to give up the petroleum wells of Drohobycz and Boryslaw.

Another protocol declared that the

Soviet Union would not make any difficulties for citizens of Estonia, Latvia, and Lithuania who might wish to leave the Soviet zone of influence, taking their personal goods with them. In this agreement, Stalin and Hitler renewed the anti-Polish engagements which had bound together the Romanovs and Hohenzollerns in Imperial days. "The undersigned plenipotentiaries, on concluding the German-Soviet Treaty of Delimitation and Friendship, have declared their agreement on the following points:

"The two parties will tolerate in their territories no Polish agitation affecting the territory of the other party. They will suppress in their territories all beginnings of such agitation and inform each other concerning suitable measures for this purpose."

The same day, September 28, Warsaw surrendered after 14 days of heroic resistance. Luftwaffe bombing had set the city flourmills ablaze, and the filtration and pumping stations for the water supply had been more than half destroyed. A humane commander, General Blaskowitz of the German 8th Army allowed the honours of war to Warsaw's defenders, who had been galvanised by their leader, General Rommel, formerly the commander of the "Łódź Army". Among the prisoners-of-war was General Kutrzeba, who had broken out of the Kutno pocket with four divisions. Modlin capitulated a few hours before Warsaw.

The last shots of the campaign were fired in the Półwysep Hel peninsula, north of Danzig, where Admiral Unruh surrendered with 4,500 men on October 2.

When Hitler broadcast to the German people on September 30, he announced the number of Polish prisoners taken as 694,000, compared with German losses of 10,572 killed, 3,400 missing, presumed dead, and 30,322 wounded.

"On October 5," General von Manstein recalled, "a big military parade was held, which unfortunately ended with a disagreeable incident showing Hitler's bizarre attitude towards his generals. A table had been laid at which Hitler and his generals could sample some soup prepared by the field kitchens. But when he saw the white tablecloth and the flower decorations which had been provided in his honour, Hitler turned brusquely aside, tasted two or three mouthfuls of soup, chatted briefly with the soldiers, and got straight into his aeroplane. Apparently he wanted to show his close ties with the

▽ *A spoof "Wanted" poster from the London "Daily Mirror" of September 4, 1939, written by their famous columnist "Cassandra".*

people. But I doubt that this gesture was really to the taste of our brave grenadiers, who would have understood perfectly that if the Head of State chose to eat with his generals he would be paying equal homage to the troops."

For its part, the Red Army rounded up some 217,000 prisoners, many of whom were destined to die in Russia in circumstances that will be examined in due course. About 100,000 Poles managed to escape to the West via Rumania and carry on the fight against Germany from France and Britain.

All quiet on the Western Front . . .

On September 13, General Georges, commanding the French North-East Front, taking Poland's defeat as virtually completed, ordered General Prételat "not to advance beyond the objectives attained, but to strengthen your dispositions in depth and to arrange as soon as possible for replacement divisions to relieve your front-line divisions, in particular the motorised divisions".

So ended Operation "Saar", which had cost the French Army 27 killed, 22 wounded, and 28 missing. General Vuillemin's air force had lost nine fighters and 18 reconnaissance aircraft. Both Gamelin and Georges later justified this decision to halt operations against Germany on the following grounds. Everything suggested that with Poland annihilated, Hitler would turn against the West with his full strength, with the assurance of a superiority of about 100 divisions to 60. Moreover, it was possible that Mussolini, drawn by the ease with which Poland had been conquered, might attack France himself before the Alpine passes were snowed up and rendered impassable.

▽ *October 5, 1939: Hitler reviews his victorious troops in Warsaw. "He made a speech to his soldiers," recalled American journalist William L. Shirer, "the speech of a conquering Caesar."*

CHAPTER 2
BRITAIN: LIFE ON THE HOME FRONT

As was natural, the civilian population of Great Britain had certain preconceived ideas about the nature of the war to which they were committing themselves on September 3, 1939. These ideas were derived from a multitude of sources—experience in World War I, books, newspaper accounts of events such as the bombing of Guernica in the Spanish Civil War, and realistic, convincing films like "The Shape of Things to Come". Thus the people of Britain expected their declaration of war to unleash the hordes of German bombers waiting to raze London to the ground.

Nor were the civilians the only ones to predict an immense aerial bombardment: so too did the prophets and advocates of strategic air power in the armed forces.

But the British steeled themselves in vain. The bombers did not come. They were not to do so until the later stages of the Battle of Britain, for no nation in the world possessed a bomber fleet capable of dealing a decisive blow against a target such as London in a single night.

So the opening of hostilities was an anti-climax. Instead of cataclysmic and shattering total war there was only the crushing of Poland and then nothing, no action at all on the Western Front or over the embattled nations of Europe.

An American Senator, William Borah, dubbed it the "Phoney War".

▽ *Barrage balloons floating high over London, anchored in parks and other open spaces. Here they are being tested; within the year they were to provide an effective deterrent to low-flying bombers during the Blitz.*

Western Front: the Rival Plans

France and Great Britain rejected the "arrangement" for the partition of Poland proposed to Western powers by Hitler in a speech to the Reichstag on October 5.

Fall Gelb (Case Yellow): the original aim was to push through to gain Dunkirk and Boulogne as the basis of an offensive against England. Lt-Gen. Erich von Manstein called for the complete destruction of all enemy forces in the field. This views were largely shared by Hitler, who called for concentration on Army Group A in the south, which was to advance through the Ardennes and secure a bridgehead across the Meuse at Sedan.

The Dyle Plan: this was the Allied defensive position in Belgium which superseded the "Escaut" Plan, which had involved a longer front. In the Dyle Plan the 9th Army would advance to a line Mezieres-Namur with its units deployed west of the Meuse; the 1st Army would take up a position between Namur and Wavre, and the B.E.F. would hold the line between Wavre and Louvain, where it would establish contact with the Belgian Army. Giraud's 7th Army would be held in reserve west of Antwerp.

▽ *The German generals who were the architects of the defeat of France. Manstein, the Chief-of-Staff of Army Group "A", and Rundstedt, his commander, felt that the "right hook" plan for the invasion of France, as used in World War I, was not the right one to produce decisive results. Manstein was of the opinion that Army Group "A" should be made the main striking force, and that the German offensive should consist of a "left hook" through Sedan and up to the Channel coast.*

ARMY GROUP "A"

Rundstedt

Manstein

Busch

List

Battle of the River Plate

The German navy posed a considerable threat to Britain's maritime trade with its 11-inch pocket battleships, of which *Deutschland* (North Atlantic) and *Admiral Graf Spee* (South Atlantic and Indian Ocean) were in operation at the outbreak of war. After a feint into the Indian Ocean, *Admiral Graf Spee*, which was due back in Germany for running repairs, came upon the British Force "G" under the command of Commodore Harwood, comprising the heavy cruiser *Exeter* and the two light cruisers *Achilles* and *Ajax*. The British force was split in the hope of dividing the enemy fire, though in the event Captain Hans Langsdorf chose to concentrate his fire on the *Exeter*, which was forced to retire. Harwood's force disengaged and Langsdorf retreated into Montevideo harbour to lick his wounds. With a 72-hour time limit imposed by the Uruguayan authorities and reports of heavier British reinforcements, Langsdorf eventually scuttled his ship in neutral waters.

Chamberlain called it the "twilight war". To the Germans it was merely the "*Sitzkrieg*", the "sitting war".

In Britain, the people had a chance to prepare themselves for the bombing offensive, which though it had not come when first expected, was nevertheless thought to be inevitable. Air raid precautions were improved, prefabricated air raid shelters mushroomed in the gardens of the major cities, shop windows were taped in a dazzling variety of patterns to prevent them from shattering as a result of bomb blast, and most noticeable of all, the black-out was enforced stringently. In shops, offices, and private homes the windows had to be screened so that not a chink of light showed from the outside; many people constructed rigid screens to bolt on to the window-frame, which considerably simplified the nightly ritual of "putting up the blackout". Those who were careless or late risked the humiliat-

▷ *On the steps of St. Paul's Cathedral a giant blackboard proclaims the need for preparation through National Service.*

Finland: the Winter War

After the German-Soviet Treaty of September 28, 1939, the Soviet Government imposed "mutual defense agreements" upon Estonia, Latvia and Lithuania which they then wished to extend to Finland. On October 14, a Finnish delegate in Mosow listened to a number of requests by the Soviets, including the ceding of islands in the Gulf of Finland and the withdrawal of the frontier in Karelian Isthmus between the Baltic and the Lake Ladoga. There was deadlock in the discussions and on November 30 the Soviets invaded Finland with an estimated 19 rifle (infantry) divisions and five tank brigades. Marshal Carl Gustav Mannerheim, C-in-C of Finland's armed forces, had nine divisions at his disposal. This meant that 120,000 Finnish troops faced 300,000 Soviet troops who were supported by 800 aircraft. The Finns, however, were well equipped to operate in the terrain which gave them ample cover, while Soviet divisions were bogged down in impassable forests and lakelands. By the end of 1939 the Red Army had suffered a series of resounding and humiliating defeats. The Soviets lost about 27,500 dead against 2,700 Finnish dead and wounded.

The Soviets came back on February 1, 1940 with an estimated 45 divisions and an overall superiority of three to one over the Finns. Despite further heavy losses, the Soviets broke through Mannerheim's line on February 11, forcing him to retreat. The Finns sued for peace and on March 12 the Russo-Finnish Treaty was signed in Moscow by which Finland was to cede Viipuri district, lease Hango Peninsula, cede Salle district, cede her portion of Pybachiy Peninsula in Lapland and build a railway between Murmansk and Kemijarn.

There was support for Finland among the Allies, and Churchill, among others, saw the strategic advantage of cutting off the iron-ore supplies to Germany. Although the British and French put together an expeditionary force to land at Narvik on March 13, 1940, Sweden and Norway refused to allow them in. The Allied plan to mine the leads and land troops at Narvik was delayed by inter-Allied disagreements, allowing the Germans to take the initiative.

ing experience of a warden's stentorian voice roaring, for the whole street to hear, the words which quickly became a catch phrase: "Put that light out!" Nocturnal pedestrians were urged to wear white, men were told that they would be safer if they let their shirt-tails hang out, but accidents on the roads reached proportions so alarming that the government was forced to sanction dim street lighting to reduce them.

The novelty of such measures soon wore off, however. Within a few weeks it was estimated that at least a third of the boxes in which people were meant to carry their gas masks wherever they went were in fact being used to carry sandwiches, cosmetics, and the like.

All the while, children were evacuated from the major cities and sent to stay with families in safer areas, mostly the rural parts of the West Country. At the same time, able bodied girls were asked to volunteer for the Land Army, an organisation which it was hoped would free large numbers of men for war work by providing women to take their places on the farms.

The two most important measures, however, were the increase in conscription and the introduction of rationing. There was a list of reserved occupations, persons on which were exempted from conscription, but the exigencies of the war meant that the list had to be abridged considerably by the end of the year. Food rationing was introduced in early November. Each citizen was issued with a Ration Book containing a number of coupons for such items as sugar, bacon and butter, which the shopkeeper removed or marked each time a purchase was made. A large number of other foods were added to the list of rationed goods from time to time throughout the war.

But all this was only the thin end of the wedge. May 10, 1940 was to alter it all.

▽◁ *Members of the Eton College Officer Training Corps receiving instruction in rifle-drill. This corps formed part of the Local Defence Volunteers organisation, precursors of the Home Guard.*

Not only soldiers were issued with gas masks.
▽▽◁ *Dogs often tested experimental models before the war, and later were trained to wear them as messengers. The model on the right is being worn by the nurse ▽ who carries a baby in an all-enveloping gasproof suit.*

The Fate of Neutral Norway

The German Navy under Grand-Admiral Raeder were acutely aware of the strategic importance of Norwegian ports for U-Boat and surface raider operations. After the British stopped the German supply ship *Altmark* and liberated British prisoners in Norwegian territorial waters, Hitler issued two directives on February 26 and March 1, which stated that Norway must be dealt with before the Western Front offensive was launched. This would include the invasion of Denmark. The operation was named Weserubung and consisted of two army corps, an air force corps and every serviceable warship in the fleet. The attack went in on April 8, amidst Norwegian vacillation, and Narvik soon surrendered. Sola airfield and Stavenger were taken by German paratroops. In Denmark, King Christian X yielded to Hitler's ultimatum. The British Home Fleet under Admiral Forbes, consisting of two battleships, one battle cruiser and 21 destroyers, sailed from Scapa Flow on April 7 with the Admiralty prevaricating as to his real objective. Eventually Forbes was ordered to intercept the *Scharnhorst* and *Gneisenau*, taking him away from the main action on the Norwegian coast. Despite having lost the initiative, the British hit back heroically with an attack by the 2nd Destroyer Flotilla and Captain B.A.W. Warburton-Lee up the Vestfjord leading to Narvik. Warburton-Lee was killed but his force sank two German destroyers, damaged three others and went on to sink the vital German ammunition supply ship *Rauenfels*.

Badly equipped British troops proved to be no match for a well-balanced German force which made the most of its available resources and which was ably supported by the Luftwaffe in the form of X Fliegerkorps. On May 28, Narvik was taken by the 13th Foreign Legion Demi-Brigade reinforced by the Norwegian 6th Division but the Allies abandoned the campaign at the start of Fall Gelb in France and Narvik was left to fall back into German hands.

Chamberlain's Government fell in the face of the clear lack of support shown by its own members.

WOMEN OF BRITAIN
COME INTO THE FACTORIES
ASK AT ANY EMPLOYMENT EXCHANGE FOR ADVICE AND FULL DETAILS

HOLDING THE LINE!

CHAPTER 3
MANSTEIN'S MASTER PLAN

As we already know, the plan which was evolving painfully in Hitler's mind for the attack on France through the Low Countries had already been given an almost definitive form by General Erich von Manstein, Rundstedt's Chief-of-Staff at Army Group "A" H.Q. in Koblenz.

On January 12, with the offensive once again imminent, Manstein sent another memorandum to O.K.H., again with Rundstedt's approval. In this document he restated his doubts about the results which could be gained by the current plan, repeating his former arguments, but this time giving suggestions which he believed would result in the total destruction of the enemy.

Taking account of all that was known of the enemy strength and dispositions, Manstein argued that at best the current O.K.H. plan could only result in sterile and bloody trench warfare from the Somme estuary to the Maginot Line. This meant that the November 20 directive, which aimed at bringing Army Group "A" to the Meuse at Sedan, could only be considered an inadequate palliative. Manstein believed that the revised attack would only make sense if driven home on the left bank of the river. As he saw it, these were the objectives which should be given to Army Group "A":

"While one army on the south of the front acts as a flank guard to the whole operation by taking up an approximate position on the line Carignan-Thionville, it is essential that *another army*, having crossed the Meuse at Sedan, drives to the south-west. This attack will defeat any attempt by the enemy to re-establish himself between the Aisne and the Oise by counter-attacking. Throwing the enemy south of the Aisne might even prevent him from forming a continuous front on the line Thionville-Stenay-Aisne-Somme. This second attack would also assist the redeployment of the northern wing [Army Group "B"] towards the south.

"A *third army*, forcing the line of the Meuse between Dinant and Fumay, will drive towards Saint Quentin to take in flank the enemy forces retreating to the Somme before the advance of the northern wing. Even if this fails, it will clear the way to the Somme for the northern wing.

"Only the execution of this plan will result in a decisive victory over the French Army."

The transfer of the centre of gravity of the attack to the Meuse between Dinant and Sedan implied that Rundstedt's army group should be reinforced with more armoured units and an additional army; but O.K.H. did not reply to Manstein's memorandum of January 12 and refused to forward it to O.K.W. However, the question was soon raised again as a result of two war games. One of these was held at Koblenz on February 7; the other was held on the 14th at Mainz, the H.Q. of General List's 12th Army, with Halder present.

Given the known enemy strength in the

▽ *A master strategist at work– General Erich von Manstein, deviser of the tank thrust through the Ardennes, at work with his staff in the field.*

△ *Manstein (right) in earnest discussion with Field-Marshal Ewald von Kleist.*

▽ *A French patrol with horse-drawn equipment struggles along beside a barbed-wire fence at the Belgian frontier during the severe winter of 1939–40.*

Ardennes sector, the war game showed that Guderian's XIX Corps could reach the Meuse at Sedan on the fourth day of the attack. What should then be done? Cross the Meuse on the fifth day, was Guderian's opinion. "Absurd," noted Halder in his diary for February 7. O.K.H. would not be able to decide in which direction the offensive should be strengthened until the third day of the attack, which meant that a methodical attack could not be launched across the Meuse until the ninth or even the tenth day.

Several days before, however, Colonel Rudolf Schmundt, who had succeeded Hossbach as Hitler's aide, had been told by the Führer to make an inspection of the front.

On his way to Koblenz on January 30, Schmundt had occasion to hear of the objections which Manstein had been raising about the O.K.H. plan. Manstein's arguments impressed him so much that when he returned to Berlin his principal colleague, Captain Engel, noted: "Schmundt was very excited and told me that he had heard Manstein propose a plan identical to the one which the Führer was constantly proposing to us, but in a much more sophisticated form." Although there is no record of Schmundt's report to Hitler, there is no doubt that he passed on Manstein's idea to Hitler and that the latter received it with delight, as a specialist opinion which justified the prompting of his "intuition".

But this was the last personal inter-vention made by Manstein. On February 8 he left Koblenz to take command of the XXXVIII Corps, which was being formed at Stettin. To Manstein, this was "indubitable" proof that O.K.H. wanted to "rid themselves of an interloper" who had dared to oppose one of its plans. In *Panzer Leader*, Guderian echoes this opinion. But in fact this transfer–which carried promotion with it–had already been envisaged as far back as the preceding autumn; and it was Halder who, on February 26, put Manstein's name at the head of the list of suitable candidates to command the "armoured wedge" on which victory or defeat would depend.

On February 17, after a dinner which he had given in honour of the newly-appointed corps commanders, Hitler led Manstein into his office and invited him to speak freely about what he thought of the coming offensive. Manstein recalled that "with astonishing speed he grasped the points of view which the army group had been defending for months. He gave my ideas his full approval."

Hitler backs Manstein

Hitler accepted Manstein's plan so completely that on the following day he summoned Brauchitsch and Halder and gave them a summary of what he had heard on the previous evening, omitting nothing but Manstein's name. "One fine

The German
and Allied Plans

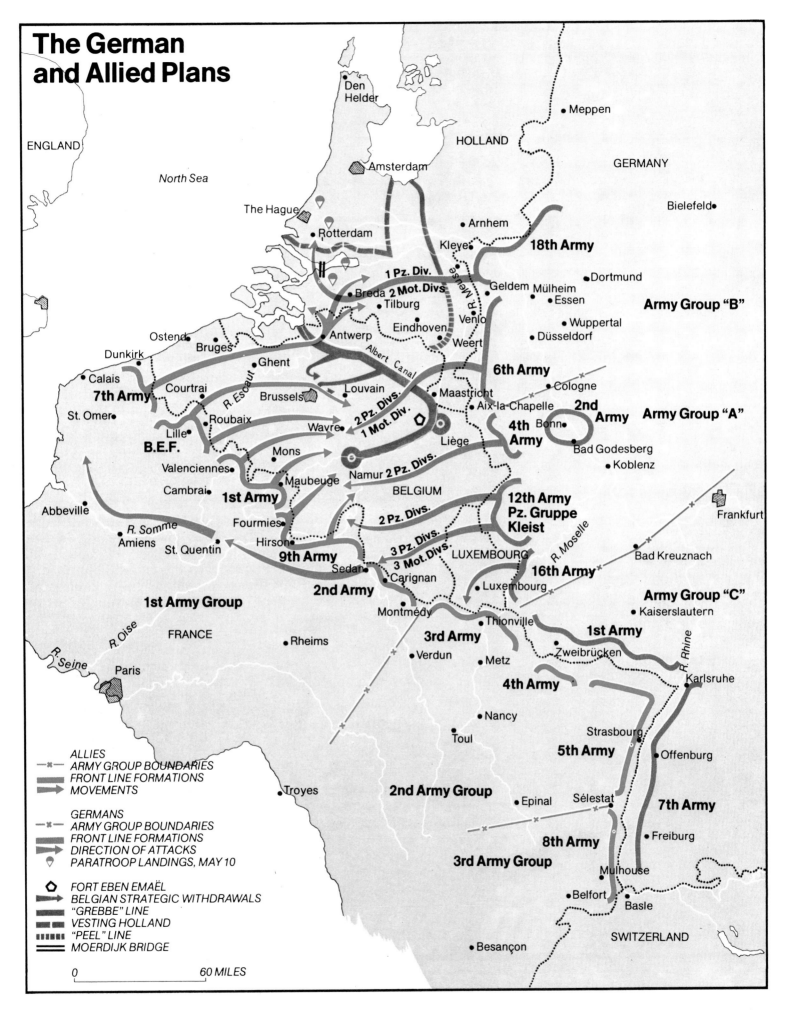

ENGLAND

North Sea

HOLLAND

GERMANY

Den Helder

Meppen

Amsterdam

The Hague

Bielefeld

Rotterdam

Arnhem

Kleve

18th Army

Dortmund

Geldern

Mülheim

1 Pz. Div.

Breda **2 Mot. Divs**

Tilburg

Venlo

Essen

Wuppertal

Eindhoven

Weert

Düsseldorf

Army Group "B"

Ostend

Bruges

Antwerp

R. Meuse

Albert Canal

6th Army

Dunkirk

Ghent

Louvain

Maastricht

Cologne

Calais

Courtrai

R. Escaut

Brussels

Aix-la-Chapelle

2nd Army

Army Group "A"

7th Army

St. Omer

Roubaix

2 Pz. Divs.

1 Mot. Div.

4th Army

Bonn

Lille

Wavre

Liège

Bad Godesberg

B.E.F.

Mons

Namur **2 Pz. Divs.**

Koblenz

Valenciennes

Maubeuge

BELGIUM

12th Army

Pz. Gruppe

Kleist

Cambrai

Frankfurt

1st Army

2 Pz. Divs.

R. Moselle

Abbeville

Fourmies

3 Pz. Divs.

3 Mot. Divs.

LUXEMBOURG

Bad Kreuznach

R. Somme

Hirson

16th Army

Amiens

St. Quentin

Sedan

9th Army

Carignan

Luxembourg

Army Group "C"

1st Army Group

2nd Army

Montmédy

Kaiserslautern

R. Oise

Thionville

1st Army

R. Seine

FRANCE

Rheims

3rd Army

Verdun

Metz

Zweibrücken

R. Rhine

Paris

4th Army

Karlsruhe

Nancy

Strasbourg

Toul

5th Army

Offenburg

2nd Army Group

Epinal

Sélestat

7th Army

Troyes

8th Army

Freiburg

3rd Army Group

Mulhouse

Belfort

Basle

SWITZERLAND

Besançon

ALLIES
ARMY GROUP BOUNDARIES
FRONT LINE FORMATIONS
MOVEMENTS

GERMANS
ARMY GROUP BOUNDARIES
FRONT LINE FORMATIONS
DIRECTION OF ATTACKS
PARATROOP LANDINGS, MAY 10

◇ *FORT EBEN EMAËL*
BELGIAN STRATEGIC WITHDRAWALS
"GREBBE" LINE
VESTING HOLLAND
"PEEL" LINE
MOERDIJK BRIDGE

0   60 MILES

Preparation for Defeat

In 1940 the French Army was insufficiently equipped for a defensive war, with a small number of mines and anti-tank weapons. French military doctrine during the inter-war years relied on the ideal of the "directed battle", carefully regulated by high command. The French High Command also showed little interest in the potential of modern technology like the tank. The French air force was poorly developed and incapable of giving French armour the necessary air cover.

On the German side, the Reichswehr carefully studied many of the successes and failures of German tactics in the First World War and Lt.-Col. Heinz Guderian, a disciple of Captain B.H. Liddell Hart, conducted extensive tactical training with dummy tanks. Guderian recommended that the armour should be organised in large mechanised units of all arms in order to overcome the hiatus between armour penetration and infantry support. Guderian had the support of Hitler in the creation of the Panzer divisions, which amounted to six when Germany went to war in 1934. Four more were formed soon after, along with four motorised infantry divisions of SS troops. This amounted to 17 divisions organised into three corps. They could depend on the close co-operation of the lethally accurate Ju 87 Stuka dive-bomber as well as an effective anti-aircraft arm.

▽ *King George VI, in his uniform of a Marshal of the R.A.F., visits an R.A.F. squadron in France during December 1939.*

day," wrote General von Lossberg, "during a conference at the Chancellery, Brauchitsch and Halder were surprised to see Hitler take a pencil and draw on the map the axis of advance suggested by Manstein in his project to drive towards Abbeville and the sea; and they heard Hitler declare that this direction looked very promising for the main effort! And everyone was astonished by Hitler's strategic brilliance–but it was the justification of Manstein's idea."

Brauchitsch and Halder raised no objections to the change of plan thus thrust upon them. They themselves had arrived at similar conclusions. In fact, the manoeuvre which O.K.W. had just accepted had been strongly recommended by Colonel Heusinger of the O.K.H. Operations Staff for several weeks. Heusinger, in turn, had been encouraging his colleague Schmundt to press for the plan's acceptance.

Events now moved quickly. On February 24 Brauchitsch put his signature to the new version of the *Fall Gelb* concentration plan. Kluge's 4th Army was now transferred from Army Group "B" to Army Group "A", which would also receive Weichs' 2nd Army, once the

Meuse had been crossed. The armour was reorganised as *Panzergruppe* Kleist–the armoured wedge or battering ram which was to punch through the Allied front in the Charleville-Sedan area and drive towards the Somme estuary. *Panzergruppe* Kleist contained the following units:

(a) XIX Panzer Corps (Guderian)–1st, 2nd, and 10th Panzer Divisions;
(b) XLI Panzer Corps (Reinhardt)–6th and 8th Panzer Divisions;
(c) XIV Motorised Corps (Wietersheim)– 2nd, 13th, and 29th Motorised Divisions.

In addition there were the 5th and 7th Panzer Divisions attached to 4th Army, which now came under Rundstedt's command. As a result, Army Group "A" now totalled 45½ divisions–seven of them Panzer divisions and three of them motorised. Bock, whose Army Group "B" had contained 42 divisions according to the original directive of October 29, was reduced to 29 divisions, and he protested against this severe weakening of his command. Would his two remaining armies be strong enough to carry out their missions–6th Army to force the Albert Canal, keystone of the Belgian

△ *A French patrol near the Belgian frontier, just south of the North Sea coast. The refusal of the Belgians to abandon their neutrality, even though it was obvious the Germans would not honour it, prevented any Allied soldiers advancing to take up a good defensive position on Belgian territory until the invasion.*

defences, and 18th Army's key mission, to conquer Holland?

Guderian speaks his mind

O.K.H. rejected the complaints from Army Group "B". However, not all the army commanders shared in the optimism which Guderian and Manstein had managed to instil into Halder and Brauchitsch. Guderian's memoirs contain a significant passage which reveals this.

On March 15 "a conference took place attended by the army and army group commanders of Army Group 'A', accompanied by General von Kleist and myself, in the Reich Chancellery. Hitler was there. Each of us generals outlined what his task was and how he intended to carry it out. I was the last to speak. My task was as follows: on the day ordered I would cross the Luxembourg frontier, drive through southern Belgium towards Sedan, cross the Meuse and establish a bridgehead on the far side so that the infantry corps following behind could get across. I explained briefly that my corps would advance through Luxembourg and south

Belgium in three columns; I reckoned on reaching the Belgian frontier posts in the first day and I hoped to break through them on that same day; on the second day I would advance as far as Neufchâteau; on the third day I would reach Bouillon and cross the Semois; on the fourth day I would arrive at the Meuse; on the fifth day I would cross it. By the evening of the fifth day I hoped to have established a bridgehead on the far bank.

"Hitler asked: 'And then what are you going to do?' He was the first person who had thought to ask me this vital question. I replied: 'Unless I receive orders to the contrary, I intend on the next day to continue my advance westwards. The supreme leadership must decide whether my objective is to be Amiens or Paris. In my opinion the correct course is to drive past Amiens to the English Channel.' Hitler nodded and said nothing more. Only General Busch, who commanded the 16th Army on my left, cried out: 'Well, I don't think you'll cross the river in the first place!' Hitler, the tension visible in his face, looked at me to see what I would reply. I said: 'There's no need for you to do so, in any case!'

"Hitler made no comment."

CHAPTER 4
ASSAULT ON THE LOW COUNTRIES

The German airborne assault on the Low Countries was launched at dawn on May 10. It was aimed at the key sectors of the Dutch front, at the Albert Canal bridges, and at Fort Eben Emael, and its effect was not limited to significant strategic advantages for Bock's Army Group "B". Because of their sensational nature, these airborne attacks helped to prolong Allied illusions as to where the main weight of the German offensive really lay, though they also achieved important results themselves.

The attack was made by 7th Airborne Division (Student), a Luftwaffe unit, and by 22nd Infantry Division (Sponeck), an army airborne division, with troops and equipment suited to their varying missions. They had

A House Divided

The Allies' Dyle Plan depended upon two major conditions if it was to succeed: sufficient advance warning of the German offensive and that General Giraud's 7th Army should not be committed prematurely on the extreme left of the Allied line. On March 20 it was decided to go ahead with a variant of the Dyle Plan, which involved the 7th Army moving into the line between the Schelde at Antwerp and the Maas, in order to cover the perceived extra threat to Holland. Dutch dispositions called for a readjustment of Belgian dispositions in order to close a gap between Hasselt and Weert, something which the Belgians rejected. The Belgians also refused to allow Allied armies into Belgium before the German attack actually began and provided little information about their plans and defences. Overall the French reserves were poorly disciplined, unready and susceptible to anti-British Communist propaganda.

Opposing Forces May 10, 1940

German

136 divisions available, including 10 armoured and seven motorised, for the Western offensive out of 157 in total.

3,634 front line aircraft of all types, 1,562 bombers and 1,016 fighters.

Allies

135 divisions (nine Dutch, 22 Belgian, 10 British and 94 French).

Belgian Air Force: 50 relatively modern fighters, including Hurricanes.

French Air Force: 418 Morane-Saulnier and 406 Curtiss Hawk fighters plus some bombers.

Royal Air Force: 130 fighters and 160 bombers as well as 60 reconnaissance aircraft.

(page 28) △ A Junkers Ju 52, backbone of the Luftwaffe transport fleet, over a Dutch coastal town.

▽ A German paratrooper, with stick grenade in his belt. The élite paratroop force, developed and commanded by General Kurt Student, played a vital part in the victory over Belgium and The Netherlands.

the all-important air support of Kesselring's *Luftflotte* II.

The 22nd Division had to take The Hague and if possible obtain the submission and co-operation of the Dutch Crown. As he was expecting to have to request an audience from Queen Wilhelmina, the divisional commander, General Graf von Sponeck, set out in full-dress uniform. The division's plan was to take the airfields at Valkenburg, Ypenburg, and Ockenburg–lying to the north, east, and south of The Hague respectively–and close in on the capital from there. But the Dutch I Corps, facing the North Sea, had been alerted in time. A furious battle ensued, in which 22nd Division lost the airfields which had been surprised by the paratroops; Sponeck himself was wounded, and by late evening about 1,000 German

prisoners were being shipped off to England from the North Sea port of IJmuiden.

The 7th Airborne Division, however, had much better luck. Its troops occupied part of Rotterdam and Waalhaven airport and held their positions in the face of Dutch counter-attacks, thanks to the close support of the aircraft of *Luftflotte* II. At Dordrecht the Germans held both banks of the Maas, although some troops had been dropped in the wrong places. Above all they had taken the Moerdijk bridges across the Maas estuary and so prevented their destruction. The 7th Airborne Division had therefore cleared a corridor which gave the German 18th Army access to the heart of the Dutch *Vesting Holland*. But would 18th Army be able to get to Moerdijk before the spearheads of the French 7th Army?

At dawn on May 10 the Dutch post guarding the bridge at Gennep spotted a patrol of Dutch-uniformed soldiers escorting a handful of German deserters. When the little column reached the bridge it opened fire on the Dutch guards and captured it. The men were all members of the *Brandenburg* Detachment, specially trained for this sort of mission. Similar attempts were made at Nijmegen and Roermond, but they failed. However, the success at Gennep opened the road to 's Hertogenbosch for the German 18th Army headed by 9th Panzer Division.

Dutch resistance was uneven. It was tougher on the Grebbe Line (defended by the II and IV Corps) than on the Peel Line, where the III Corps, as mentioned above, had only been intended to slow down the German advance before falling back. The

corps' withdrawal, although an orderly one, left the 1st Light Mechanised Division, the vanguard of Giraud's French 7th Army, exposed. Giraud's position had deteriorated even more by the evening of May 11, for the Belgian Army on his right flank was abandoning the Albert Canal and preparing to withdraw to the Antwerp-Louvain line. And by the evening of May 12 the 9th Panzer Division had made contact with the troops of the 7th Airborne Division holding the Moerdijk bridges.

By May 13 the situation along the Dutch front had become so grave that Queen Wilhelmina and her Government had resigned themselves to leaving the country. An appeal to Britain for help had produced no results, and could not have done. France, too, had been asked for help. But it would have been impossible for

△◁ *German troops, their eyes to the sky, pause beside their 37-mm. PAK36 anti-tank gun after taking a Dutch border post.*
◁ *A Dutch Fokker G-I destroyed, probably on the ground, by Luftwaffe air attack. Only 23 of these little-known, twin-boom, 3-seat fighter aircraft were serviceable at the time of the German invasion.*
△ *A German horse-drawn column on the move. Surprisingly, apart from the motorised and Panzer divisions, much of the German Army was to a great extent dependent on animal transport, which made for dangerous gaps between armour and support troops in the Battle of France.*

△ *German paratroopers in a drop zone on the Dutch frontier during the first hours of the invasion. A tripod-mounted MG 34 machine gun, retrieved from a weapons canister, is ready for action.*

Giraud to have sent his 60th and 68th Divisions into Zeeland. The Belgian retreat meant that he dare not push his left flank forward to Moerdijk and Dordrecht. In any case, his movements were hampered by the Stuka attacks of VIII *Fliegerkorps*.

Rotterdam blitzed; Holland surrenders

On the afternoon of May 14 the notorious "horror raid" on Rotterdam took place. The bombers came at the moment when the Dutch and Germans were parleying for the surrender of the city, and General Rudolf Schmidt, commanding XXXIX Panzer Corps, was not able to make contact with the aircraft of *Luftflotte* II and call off the attack.

Some 25,000 houses were razed, rendering 78,000 homeless. But instead of the figure of 35,000 killed which was announced at the time, today the Dutch claim only 900, and this is the figure which should be accepted.

Considering the situation of the Dutch troops who had been forced back from the Grebbe Line, and determined to spare Utrecht from Rotterdam's fate, General Winkelman made the decision to surrender. His army had lost 2,100 killed and 2,700 wounded. He signed the instrument of capitulation at 0930 hours on May 15, only surrendering the forces under his direct orders, which excepted Zeeland. But Queen Wilhelmina and the Dutch Government continued the struggle in exile, giving the Western Allies the benefit of the Dutch colonies and their resources, a merchant fleet of nearly three million tons, and the well-trained and battleworthy warships of the Dutch fleet.

At the time when General Winkelman ordered the cease-fire, the Belgian Army was preparing to give battle without further retreat, having fallen back to the sector of the Dyle Line agreed in the earlier discussions between King Léopold and Gamelin. It is true that the Belgian resistance along the Albert Canal had lasted barely 48 hours instead of the four or five days hoped for by the Belgian Government and the Allied High Command; but there was no connection between the surprise attacks which had forced this early withdrawal and the disaster on the Meuse on May 15.

The epic of Eben Emael

At dawn on May 10 the three regiments of the Belgian 7th Division were holding the line of the Albert Canal with their right flank anchored by the fortified complex of Eben Emael, which was armed with two 120-mm guns and 16 75-mm guns in armoured turrets and casemates. While General van Overstraeten was worried about possible sabotage of the demolition planned for the canal bridges, the Belgian dispositions seemed to be reassuring.

But no account had been taken of the imaginative flair of Adolf Hitler, who had taken a personal interest in the planning for surprise capture of the Albert Canal bridges, despite the scepticism of O.K.W.

The key factor in this daring enterprise was to be the glider. Paratroops would not have been able to land directly on their objectives with the same precision, and in any case the time needed to re-deploy them would have given the Belgian defenders plenty of warning. For

these reasons a special detachment of 42 gliders had been formed under the command of Captain Walter Koch, made up of 424 men (including pilots). For months, the Koch Detachment had undergone rigorous training under conditions of the strictest secrecy – training which included the specialised use of explosives.

On the left bank of the canal, the gliders of the Koch Detachment landed right in the middle of the defences covering the bridges at Veldwezelt and Vroenhoven. Profiting from the confusion caused by the appearance of these unfamiliar aircraft, which had seemed to the Belgians to be ordinary types in difficulties, the Germans cut the cables to the bridge demolition charges as well as the telephone lines, and then threw the explosive charges into the canal. At Canne, however, where the terrain prevented such an accurate landing, the Belgians had time to blow up the bridge, and then inflict heavy losses on the Germans. Meanwhile, 11 gliders had landed on top of Fort Eben Emael. Seventy-eight assault pioneers, equipped with two and a half tons of explosives, set about the turrets and casemates of the fort, according to the plans which had been worked out in great detail and rehearsed a hundred times during the previous months. Unlike the Maginot Line, Eben Emael was not protected by outer works – and within minutes many of its strong-points had been neutralised by explosive charges thrust into the gun-slits or by hollow-charge blocks applied to their armour.

Deployed along a front of 11¼ miles, the Belgian 7th Division was unable to launch any prompt counter-attacks against the

△ Reputedly the strongest fort of its time in the world – Fort Eben Emael, the capture of which was one of the first and most decisive blows dealt by the Wehrmacht forces in the Western Campaign. It was also the first sapper attack ever made from the air.

▽ In the attack on Eben Emael the German storm troops, led by Captain Walter Koch, took nine installations in the first ten minutes. Here sappers in a rubber dinghy under heavy fire cross the moat surrounding the fort.

bridgeheads won by the Koch Detachment at Vroenhoven and Veldwezelt. The least activity on the part of the Belgians provoked pitiless Stuka attacks. The Belgians fought back as best they could, but they could not prevent the Germans from bringing in reinforcements as planned. In the morning, machine gun sections were parachuted in; and about noon the advance units of 4th Panzer Divisions made contact. The latter had found the Maastricht bridges destroyed and had crossed the Maas as best they could.

At 0530 hours on May 11 the German pioneers opened a first 16-ton bridge to their traffic, which accelerated the arrival of 4th Panzer Division and XVI Panzer Corps, the spearhead of the German 6th Army (Reichenau). Towards noon, rendered helpless by neutralisation of its guns, the garrison of Fort Eben Emael surrendered to the 51st Pioneer Battalion under Lieutenant-Colonel Mikosch; and by the evening the Belgian 7th Division was out of the battle. These events caused King Léopold to issue the withdrawal order already mentioned. The Allies launched repeated air strikes against the Albert Canal bridges, the destruction of which would have cut off the bulk of Reichenau's advance units. But the fighters and anti-aircraft batteries of the Luftwaffe guarded their charges well. On May 11–12, 39 Belgian, French, and British bombers attacked the bridges. Of these, 17 were shot down and 11 were damaged beyond repair – and the Allied bombs caused virtually no damage at all.

The Belgian retreat caused a certain number of incidents of which the most unpleasant centered around the defence of Louvain – a disagreement between the commander of the Belgian 10th Division and Major-General B. L. Montgomery, commanding the British 3rd Division.

The Allies get under way

Despite all this, the withdrawal had been completed by the evening of the 13th; and King Léopold issued the following stirring order of the day: "Our position improves day by day; our ranks are tightening. In the decisive days which lie ahead do not spare yourselves; suffer every sacrifice to halt the invasion. As on the Yser in 1914, the French and British troops are relying on us; the safety and honour of the country demand it."

◁ *German paratroops paddle over the Meuse in inflatable rubber dinghies.*

At 0630 hours on May 10, Captain Beaufre, adjutant to General Doumenc at G.H.Q. Land Forces, Mantry, reported to Gamelin at Vincennes. The latter was about to set in motion the complicated Dyle-Breda manoeuvre, swinging the 1st Army Group into the Low Countries–a plan which would involve five armies, 13 corps, 41 divisions: a total of about 600,000 men. Beaufre found Gamelin in an optimistic mood, "pacing up and down the corridors of the barracks, humming audibly with a martial air . . ."

The day before, however, Paul Reynaud had been trying to obtain Gamelin's dismissal in a session of the French Cabinet. Failing because of the opposition of Daladier and his Radical Socialist colleagues, Reynaud had offered his resignation to President Lebrun, but withdrew it when the news of the German offensive broke. Gamelin, although under the shadow of imminent disgrace, faced the new crisis with confidence.

He held to his *War Plan 1940* of February 26, in which he had described how the Allied armies would respond to any German invasion of the Low Countries. "They [the Allies] will be well placed to go over to the counter-offensive, for the enemy will be venturing into open terrain. Only the battlefield of Luxembourg, Belgium, and southern Holland lends itself to a decisive battle in the country outside the fortified systems and lines of obstacles. If the Germans gain possession of the Albert-Meuse line upstream of Liège, a counter-offensive can be made by turning the Albert Canal from the north and by a thrust between the Ardennes and the Moselle, which would turn the Meuse."

Gamelin was obviously much less defensively-minded than is usually believed. But his projected "thrust between the Ardennes and the Moselle"–a spectre which was indeed to keep Hitler awake at nights–was a pipe-dream. To make it a reality, Gamelin would have had to have at his disposal on May 10 a standing reserve–and this did not exist and was not even being formed.

"There he [Gamelin] was," de Gaulle recalled, "in a setting which recalled a convent, attended by a few officers, working and meditating without mixing in day-to-day duties . . . In his *Thébaïde* [ivory tower] at Vincennes, General Gamelin gave me the impression of a savant, testing the chemical reactions of his strategy in a laboratory."

But even more serious was the multi-channelled chain of command. Gamelin's Vincennes H.Q. had no radio transmitter. Georges, Commander-in-Chief of the North-East Front, was 40 miles away from Vincennes at la Ferté-sous-Jouarre, while yet another key command area was Doumenc's G.H.Q. Land Forces, 22 miles from Vincennes at Mantry.

Another snag was that the French army commanders were far from unanimous in their attitude towards Gamelin's plan. When the bad news of the events on the Albert Canal came in on May 11, General René Prioux, whose cavalry corps had the task of covering the arrival of 1st Army in its new sector at Gembloux, told his army commander, General Blanchard that: "because of the weak Belgian resistance and the enemy superiority in the air, the Dyle manoeuvre seems difficult and it would be better to settle for the Escaut manoeuvre."

Blanchard agreed. He passed the message to his army group commander, Billotte, who telephoned Georges a few minutes later: "General Blanchard is pressing for the Escaut solution. I am leaving for 1st Army and will go on to General Prioux to see to the completion of the Dyle manoeuvre, which must be carried out."

In this difference of opinion the impetuous Billotte was in the right. The Dyle-Breda manoeuvre in course of execution could not have been adjusted to fit the Escaut solution, and in any case the rendezvous arranged with the Belgians had to be kept. As for the danger from the air, it was in fact less serious than Generals Prioux and Blanchard imagined–but for reasons which, if those generals had known them, would only have added to their worries. For to give the Ardennes venture its best chance of success, it suited Hitler not to impede the Franco-British advance into the Low Countries.

△ A German soldier storms through a French village not 50 miles from Dunkirk. As the racing German columns swung round to the north, the possibility that they could trap the Allied forces trying to hold Belgium began to look like an exciting reality.

First blood to the Allies

Although the Belgian retreat to the Antwerp-Louvain line was justified, it had been made earlier than envisaged, which meant that during the Allied advance into Belgium the brunt fell upon General Prioux's cavalry corps for a few days.

The corps consisted of the 2nd and 3rd Light Mechanised Divisions, commanded respectively by Generals Langlois and Bougrain. On the 13th the cavalry corps came to grips with XVI Panzer Corps in the

region of Merdorp, on the Liège-Namur road. German historians claim that the armoured units of 3rd Light Mechanised Division, mainly engaged with 4th Panzer Division, showed inferior manoeuvrability; furthermore, Major-General Stever's orders were transmitted more efficiently than those of General Bougrain.

But by the morning of the 15th the French 1st Army, thanks to the delaying actions fought by the cavalry corps, was in position between Namur and Wavre with six divisions in the line and one in reserve. Here it underwent the assault of the German 6th Army, driven home with heavy Stuka attacks. At Gembloux, where Bock had hoped to drive in the French line with the tanks of XVI Panzer Corps, the Germans were held and indeed repulsed by the French IV Corps under General Aymes. At 1630 hours Reichenau called off his troops, planning to resume his advance with a more orthodox, set-piece attack.

Meanwhile, Reichenau's XI Corps had tried to rush Louvain, but the German troops were promptly flung out by a timely counter-attack by the British 3rd Division under General Montgomery. All in all, north of Namur the Allies had the best of May 15. But to the south, at Sedan, matters were altogether different, causing Gort and Blanchard to issue orders for a retreat on the evening of the 15th.

The success of the Dyle manoeuvre depended on the firm holding of the Allied centre by the French 2nd and 9th Armies which, to the west of Longuyon and the south of Namur, blocked the exits from the Ardennes and held the line of the Meuse. All Huntziger's 2nd Army had to do was to hold the positions which it had occupied since September 1939; from Sedan to Givet the same applied to Corap's 9th Army, but his left and centre had to advance from the Rocroi-Fourmies region and take up defensive positions along the Belgian Meuse between Givet and Namur.

A crucial question: had General Billotte been given too much responsibility for one man to carry, dynamic though he was? In the Dyle-Breda manoeuvre he had naturally been more deeply concerned in the intricate manoeuvres of his 7th and 1st Armies than in the static sector of his front (9th and 2nd Armies). And to crown everything, a conference with Daladier, King Léopold, and Gort's Chief-of-Staff, Lieutenant-General H. R. Pownall, at Casteau near Mons on May 12, had charged Billotte with co-ordinating the activities of all Allied armies on Belgian territory. This meant that he had to direct six armies – seven, in fact, if a successful link-up with the Dutch could be achieved. To sum up, Billotte alone was the man who would have to handle the attacks made by the armies of Bock and Rundstedt.

Everything points to the fact that the French troops holding the central "hinge" of the Allied front should have been put under a tighter command, which would have kept them better in hand and compensated for many of their deficiencies.

Without exception, the troops holding the "hinge" were not only mediocre or worse, but also badly equipped and deployed on much too long a front. Facing the onslaught of Army Group "A" between Namur and Sedan were seven French divisions spread out along a sector of 85 miles. The current doctrines of defensive warfare demanded at least 12. Moreover, on May 13 only one out of these seven divisions was an active unit: the 5th Motorised Infantry Division on Corap's left flank. The rest were all reserve divisions, as were the 55th and 71st Infantry Divisions of 2nd Army, defending the Sedan sector.

These reserve divisions were appallingly short of anti-tank and anti-aircraft guns. The 55th and 71st Divisions had between them only 21 out of the 104 25-mm anti-tank guns which they should have had, and the 102nd and 61st Divisions of 9th Army were even worse off. As a result of the paucity of the anti-aircraft defences in the Sedan sector, the Stukas could operate virtually without opposition: 9th Army had only three groups of 75-mm and three batteries of 25-mm A.A. guns, despite the requests of General Corap, who required three times this number.

The ground defences had been neglected during the severe winter and had suffered even more from insufficient supplies of concrete and steel obstacles. In certain sectors of the French Meuse, sandbags had taken the place of proper obstacles. Anti-tank mines, which could have made up for many of these deficiencies, had only been supplied in pitifully small numbers. On the Belgian Meuse, fortifications were virtually non-existent.

The Ardennes drama

On the morning of May 10, Corap and Huntziger sent their cavalry divisions across the Franco-Belgian frontier into the Ardennes, to act as a screen while 9th Army took up its new positions. The 1st and 4th Light Cavalry Divisions, plus the 3rd Brigade of Spahis from 9th Army, managed to reach the Ourthe, but the 2nd and 5th Light Cavalry Divisions from 2nd Army engaged numerous German tanks near Arlon and fell back.

On the 11th, several cavalry engagements confirmed that the Germans were making a major effort in the Ardennes region. The 2nd and 5th Light Cavalry Divisions were thrown back with heavy losses and Corap was obliged to withdraw his cavalry to the left bank of the Meuse. The impression gained from these first skirmishes was confirmed by air observation: "The enemy seems to be preparing an energetic thrust in the direction of Givet," concluded General d'Astier de la Vigerie, commander-in-chief of the air forces attached to 1st Army Group, in his bulletin at noon on May 11.

Advancing against the four French light cavalry divisions and two cavalry brigades with their 300 tanks and armoured cars were no less than seven Panzer divisions totalling 2,270 armoured vehicles. Given these odds it is hardly surprising that the French cavalry units failed to sustain their delaying action for more than 48 hours, instead of the envisaged four days. But they retreated in good order and blew both bridges across the Meuse after they crossed in the afternoon of May 12.

On the evening of the same day, Major-General Erwin Rommel's 7th Panzer Division reached Houx lock, on the Meuse downstream of Dinant. Urged on by Rommel's enthusiasm, the 7th Motorcycle Battalion crossed the weir to the left bank and profited from a small gap between the French 5th Motorised Division and the 18th Division to infiltrate, scale the bank, and establish a provisional bridgehead. General Bouffet, commanding the II Corps in Corap's army, was well aware of this weakness in his front, but the battalion which he had sent that afternoon to cover the weir at Houx had completely failed to carry out its orders.

Rommel's tiny pocket on the left bank should have been pinched out on the following morning; but under Stuka bombardment the French infantry failed to co-ordinate with the tanks of the 4th Light Cavalry Division which headed the French counter-attack, and by the evening of the 13th the enterprising Rommel had gained enough ground for his sappers to begin bridging operations across the river.

It will be remembered that 7th Panzer Division, together with the 5th Panzer Division (Hartlieb) following in its tracks, formed Hoth's XV Panzer Corps, which in turn belonged to Kluge's 4th Army. During the night of May 12–13, the French in the sector of 102nd Division observed a heavy column of enemy traffic heading for Monthermé, slightly downstream of the junction of the Meuse and Semois rivers.

▽ *German infantry marshal a column of Belgian prisoners-of-war prior to marching them off to a camp in Germany.*

"It's an onrush, all lit up," reported a French airman – for the Germans, seeing the weakness in the Allied flank, were speeding forwards with all lights on.

Breakthrough at Sedan

The 6th and 8th Panzer Divisions (Kempff and Kuntzen), of Reinhardt's XLI Panzer Corps, formed the right-hand column of Kleist's *Panzergruppe*. They attacked at 1600 hours on May 13, only to meet furious resistance from the machine gunners of the 42nd Colonial Demi-Brigade. But all the courage of the latter was no substitute for anti-tank guns. The Pzkw IV tanks and self-propelled guns of the Panzer divisions took up position along the right bank of the Meuse and systematically blasted the French machine gun nests on the opposite bank.

When the latter had been silenced a German battalion crossed the Meuse on inflatable rafts and after bloody fighting took the little town of Monthermé. But they could get no further because of sustained resistance and awkward terrain. This setback at Monthermé was, however, largely eclipsed by the total victory of Guderian and his XIX Panzer Corps in the Sedan sector.

On hearing the alarming reports from the cavalry units, Huntziger had committed his reserve – 71st Division – to assist X Corps. On the morning of the 13th the 71st closed up on the right wing of the 55th Division on the Meuse. Yet the forces released by this move had not reached to their new sector when the Stukas of VIII *Fliegerkorps* launched a series of intensive attacks, pinning down the French troops where they stood.

On May 10 the XIX Panzer Corps – 1st Panzer Division in the lead, 2nd Panzer Division on the right, and 10th Panzer Division on the left – had surged forward at dawn. While crossing the Belgian-Luxembourg frontier some time was lost because of determined resistance from the *Chasseurs Ardennais* of Keyaerts Group and by extensive road demolitions. But by the evening of the 11th Guderian's leading Panzers had broken through to the Semois, having covered 60 miles in 48 hours. Considering the delay suffered by 2nd Panzer Division, Guderian had wanted to postpone a further advance from the 13th to the 14th, but Kleist, wanting to be sure of a close co-ordination between his two corps, would not agree. On the 12th, Guderian closed up his divisions and agreed with *Luftflotte* III (General Hugo Sperrle) on the measures to be taken to ensure close co-operation between the Luftwaffe and the ground troops.

From noon to 1600 hours the Stukas intensified their attacks, meeting no opposition at all. They concentrated on the artillery positions of 55th Division, while eight concentrations of 10.5-cm and 15-cm guns were pounding a front of 2,700 yards to speed the crossing of Kirchner's 1st Panzer Division. The French emplacements on the left bank of the Meuse were knocked out one by one by high velocity 8.8-cm A.A. guns.

About 1600 hours, when the French guns covering the Meuse had been silenced, the

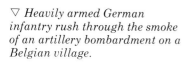

▽ *Heavily armed German infantry rush through the smoke of an artillery bombardment on a Belgian village.*

△ *German infantry firing from a wrecked railway bridge at a low-flying aircraft. They are armed with a Mauser Kar 98 carbine (left) and an MG 34 machine gun adapted for anti-aircraft use with a saddle drum magazine.*

S.S. Motorised Regiment *Grossdeutschland,* sent to help 1st Panzer Division, was ferried to the left bank in assault boats with outboard engines and on inflatable rafts, and was flung straight into the fray. The resistance of the French 55th Division fluctuated. Some units fought until the Germans broke into their positions; others gave up at the first shot. On the whole, however, the badly-trained reservists who made up the division broke and fled before the German infantry. Worse still, about 1800 hours at Bulson, five miles from Sedan, before any German tanks had crossed the Meuse, panic spread to a French regiment of heavy artillery and to the rear areas like a forest fire. Guns were blown up, telephone lines cut, and terrified troops took to their heels.

Guderian recalled the crossing in the following words: "I was now anxious to take part in the assault across the Meuse by the riflemen. The actual ferrying must be nearly over by now, so I went to St.

Menges and from there to Floing, which was the proposed crossing-place of 1st Panzer Division. I went over in the first assault boat. On the far bank of the river I found the efficient and brave commander of the 1st Rifle Regiment, Lieutenant-Colonel Balck, with his staff. He hailed me with the cheerful cry: 'Pleasure-boating on the Meuse is forbidden!' I had in fact coined the phrase myself during the training that we had had for this operation, since the attitude of some of the younger officers had struck me as too light-hearted. I now realised that they had judged the situation correctly."

By midnight, the German penetration south of Sedan was deep enough for Guderian's sappers to open their bridges to XIX Panzer Corps' heavy vehicles. On the right, the forward units of Veiel's 2nd Panzer Division had been halted in front of Donchery, while on the left Schaal's 10th Panzer Division had only gained a little ground around Wadelincourt on the

△ Mobile artillery of the Blitzkrieg–a Stuka begins to pull out of a dive after releasing its 1,100-lb. bomb.

left bank of the Meuse. But the French 55th Division had been scattered, leaving 500 dead; the 71st Division was on the brink of destruction and the French had lost 80 guns.

The following day Guderian headed his corps for Abbeville and the Channel, swinging to the west, sending 1st and 2nd Panzer Divisions across the River Bar and the Ardennes Canal. *Grossdeutschland* and 10th Panzer Division guarded the flank of the German penetration around Stonne. On the 14th and even on the 15th, an energetic counter-attack across the rear of 1st and 2nd Panzer Divisions by the 3rd Armoured and 3rd Motorised Divisions of Flavigny's XXI Corps would have had a very good chance of restoring the French front along the Meuse. But nothing was done. Flavigny was content to "contain" the south flank of the pocket. Meanwhile the German flak gunners defended the Sedan bridges with a high degree of skill; 170 bombers, most of them British, were flung against the bridges in near-suicidal missions, and 85 were shot down.

So it was that the 664 tanks of 1st and 2nd Panzer Divisions carved through the right flank of the French 9th Army. Corap tried to block their path by stationing his 3rd Brigade of Spahis and his 53rd Division between the Meuse and Poix-Terron; but the Spahis immolated themselves in a heroic but desperate engagement at La Horgne and the 53rd Division, a typically down-at-heel French reserve unit, went to pieces at the first encounter.

At the same time, further to the north, 8th Panzer Division crossed the Meuse at Nouzonville, midway between Monthermé and Mézières,. shouldering aside the French 61st Division. In the sector of the French XI Corps, covering Mariembourg and Philippeville, French resistance wilted on the 14th and collapsed on the 15th, for 5th Panzer Division had followed 7th Panzer across the Meuse, and their combined 654 fighting vehicles had caught the French 22nd and 18th Divisions in the act of installing themselves along an overstretched front of over 23 miles. Neither of these two French divisions was motorised; neither of them had more than 12 battalions apiece in the line on May 12; and both had been counting on at least 48 more hours to complete their redeployment. General Doumenc of G.H.Q. Land Forces, writing of the disorganisation of 9th Army after the German crossing of the Meuse, recalled: "The battlefield retained

its air of chaos until evening. These are the impressions of one staff officer: 'On the way, we passed through the swirling smoke of a fuel convoy which had been bombed and was burning beside the road. Further on, an artillery group had been attacked while still on the march. On the roadway and the verges a series of enormous shell craters and many dead horses showed that the attack must have been irresistible.'"

The fate of 1st Armoured Division only made matters worse. Billotte had put this division at the disposal of 9th Army; it had 156 tanks, of which 66 were the formidable Char B type, and prepared to counter-attack towards Dinant. But it was surprised while refuelling by the tanks of XV Panzer Corps and virtually wiped out. The technical reason was simple enough: French tanks were laboriously refuelled by tankers, while the Germans used the smaller, handier "Jerricans" for the job. To crown the disastrous events of May 15, 4th North African Infantry Division, going to the help of the French XI Corps, was cut to pieces as well.

In the morning of May 16 the advance units of XIX and XLI Panzer Corps, thrusting forwards from Poix-Terron and from Monthermé, joined hands at Montcornet–deep in the rear of the French XLI Corps. Further to the north the XV Panzer Corps –still subordinated to the German 4th Army–crossed the Franco-Belgian frontier near Fourmies.

In four days of battle *Panzergruppe* Kleist and XV Panzer Corps had destroyed eight divisions of 9th and 2nd Armies and had smashed open a breach of 81 miles in the front held by Billotte's 1st Army Group. And through that breach some 2,200 tanks and armoured cars were streaming towards the Channel. Were the French Government and High Command to blame for relying on a "defensive" front along the Dyle? That has always been the view of Paul Reynaud. But it is true to say that the defeat of this "defensive" army group had come about because it was not defensive enough. How would the story have turned out if, on May 13, the Germans had run into tough, well-prepared French troops waiting for them on the left bank of the Meuse? But to do this the French would have needed enough anti-tank guns to prevent the Panzers on the right bank from knocking out the French fortifications across the river, and enough anti-aircraft guns to break up the precision attacks of the deadly Stukas.

CHAPTER 5
THRUST TO THE CHANNEL

At 0300 hours on May 14, Captain Beaufre accompanied General Doumenc to G.H.Q. "North-East" for a conference with General Georges. With an emotion which 25 years had not dispelled, Beaufre recalled what took place.

"The atmosphere is that of a family keeping vigil over a dead member. Georges rises briskly and comes up to Doumenc. He is terribly pale: 'Our front has been pushed in at Sedan! There have been some failures . . .' He falls into an armchair and a sob stifles him. It was the first man that I had seen weep in this battle. I was to see many others, alas! It made a dreadful impression on me.

"Doumenc, surprised by this greeting, reacts at once. 'General, this is war, and this sort of thing always happens in war!' Then Georges, pale as ever, explains: two second rate divisions have fallen back after a terrible bombing

attack. The X Corps has signalled that its position has been overrun and that German tanks arrived in Bulson around midnight. Another sob. All the others in the room stand there, struck silent.

" 'Come, General,' says Doumenc, 'all wars have seen collapses like this! Let's look at the map. We'll see what can be done!' He speaks strongly in this encouraging vein and it does me good to hear it.

"Standing before the map, Doumenc sketches a manoeuvre: the gap must be closed, 'plugged' as they used to say in 1918."

Chaos on the roads

Doumenc's optimism was praiseworthy, but he was unaware of two elements of the situation which would ruin his hopes.

△ *Infantrymen of Bock's Army Group "B" tramp through a Belgian town to occupy territory recently overrun by armoured divisions. The infantry troops had to move fast to keep up with the rapidly advancing front line.*

Nor could he foresee the development of a third element, which would prove equally disastrous.

To start with, during the "collapses" of 1914 and 1918, neither Moltke nor Ludendorff had adequate means with which to keep up the pace of the German pursuit; large cavalry units were far too vulnerable, their endurance was poor, and no cavalry unit had as much fire-power as the infantry anyway. Second, neither Joffre in 1914 nor Pétain and Foch in 1918 had to worry about heavy enemy air attacks in their rear areas, which in 1940 wrought havoc among the troop columns and supply convoys, and the key road and railway junctions.

The third element which Doumenc had not foreseen was the flooding chaos of the refugee "exodus". Jean Vidalenc, who has made a special study of the phenomenon, has estimated that by August 13, 1940, some two and a half million refugees had reached the south, centre, and south-west of France. And this figure does not include the refugees who had found their way home after a brief flight, or who had made for Mayenne or Brittany. The same panic in Belgium also caused bottleneck jams on the roads, and badly disrupted the military operations of May-June 1940.

The whole grim story demonstrates the total failure of French propaganda, which had been entrusted to Jean Giraudoux at the beginning of hostilities. His concept of "psychological warfare" ended by making five million Frenchmen take to their heels.

The overall phenomenon of the civilian exodus put incredible problems in the way of the Allied conduct of military operations, and must be ranked with the other reasons for the Allied defeat. As Vidalenc puts it:

"Columns of refugees now struggled along the roads . . . In the grey light before the dawn, shadows appeared like pale ghosts, their features drawn by their march through the night, through the day before, perhaps through the day before that; the poor went on foot, pushing before them barrows laden with odds and ends. Their feet were raw with blisters; some would stop by the road-side and ease off their shoes. Horse-drawn vehicles, cars piled high with mattresses, suitcases, parcels tied with string, lashed together with straps or held by elastic cords, passed by the tramping pedestrians, their owners wearing the clothes selected as most useful or most valuable when the time came to leave home. The most harrowing sight was the children . . . It was frightful to hear their terrified young voices screaming: 'The planes, mummy, the planes!' and to know that they must already have seen death falling from the skies . . ."

"We have been defeated . . ."

At 0400 hours on May 15 Billotte telephoned Georges and made it clear that 9th Army was "on the brink of catastrophe". Billotte suggested that Giraud, a real leader of men, should take over; he would be able to create the "psychological shock" capable of stiffening 9th Army. Corap, as yet reproached with nothing, should take over 7th Army. By about 1600 hours Giraud, forcing his way along roads choked with refugees, had reached the H.Q. of 9th Army at Vervins – but he brought with him nothing but a solitary aide-de-camp, while he would have liked to hurl the motorised units of his former army against the flank of the Panzer breakthrough.

At 0730 on the 15th Winston Churchill had been jerked from his sleep by the news that Paul Reynaud was calling him by telephone. Churchill picked up the receiver and received Reynaud's message: "We have been defeated . . . the front is broken near Sedan; they are pouring through in great numbers with tanks and armoured cars." In his memoirs Churchill admits that he was unable to recall the precise words used by his French colleague. But he is clear enough about his own reply in which, like General Doumenc, he pointed to historical precedent:

"All experience shows the offensive will come to an end after a while. I remember the 21st of March, 1918. After five or six days they have to halt for supplies, and the opportunity for counter-attack is presented. I learned all this at the time from the lips of Marshal Foch himself."

There was equal astonishment at the French Ministry of National Defence. William Bullitt, the American Ambassador, was in the same room as Daladier when Gamelin telephoned with the news of the breakthrough at Sedan and the Panzer advance. Bullitt was so impressed by what he heard that on the 16th he did not hesitate to cable Washington: "It seems clear that without a miracle like the Battle of the Marne, the French Army

▽ Soldiers from a convoy of trucks on a dusty French road pause to fill their water-bottles with soup from a horse-drawn field kitchen. The German Army maintained the pace of its offensive with extraordinary efficiency. William L. Shirer, an American journalist in Germany, commented: "The chief impression you get from watching the German Army at work . . . is a gigantic, impersonal war machine, run as coolly and efficiently, say, as our automobile industry in Detroit."

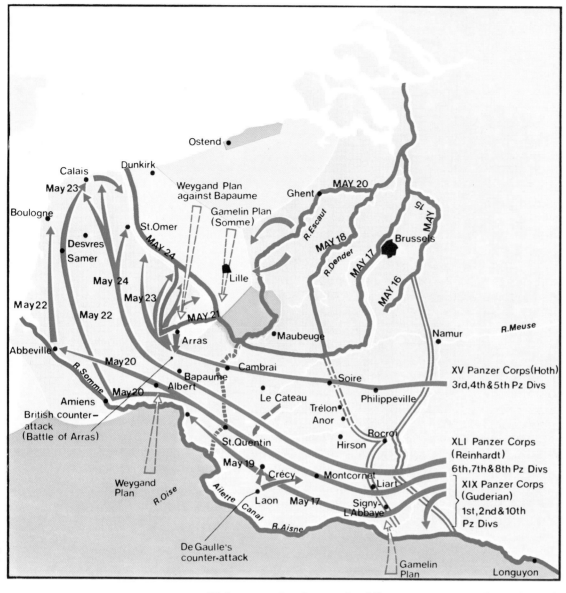

◁ *The "Panzer Corridor", the German armoured thrust to the English Channel, with their supporting infantry and logistic tail struggling forward many miles to the rear. It would have been a golden opportunity for the Allies, had they possessed an adequate reserve. The corridor could have been cut in several places, as the Allied plans indicate, but the two counter-attacks that did go in achieved only local success. ▷ The approach to and the crossing of the Meuse, and (inset) the breakthrough at Sedan. All along this sector the Germans broke through the weak French defences with ease, and then streamed out towards the Channel.*

▷ *Guderian keeps in touch with his advanced units, not from a headquarters in the rear, but from his command vehicle at the front. It was in this campaign that the merciless pressure he kept up on his Panzer crews earned him the grudging nickname of "Swift Heinz".*

will be completely crushed."

This is how Bullitt recalls the scene: "But the telephone rang from Vincennes; the Supreme Commander was calling the Minister. Suddenly Daladier shouted: 'No! That's not possible! You are mistaken!'

"Gamelin had told him that an armoured column had smashed through everything in its path and was at large between Rethel and Laon. Daladier was panting. He found the strength to shout: 'You must attack!' 'Attack? With what?' replied Gamelin. 'I have no more reserves.'

"Daladier's features crumpled more and more. He seemed to be shrinking as I watched.

"The grim conversation ended with the following exchange:

" 'So this means the destruction of the French Army?' 'Yes, this means the destruction of the French Army!' "

Bullitt added that there was already a certain amount of dissension between the French and the British. The latter considered the French attitude "defeatist"; and the analysis of Bullitt's despatch made by the American historian William L. Langer held that the British were showing reluctance to "risk their own fortunes in the common cause".

Churchill orders in more British reinforcements

None of this was in Churchill's mind when he arrived in Paris on the afternoon of May 16 for a meeting with Reynaud, Daladier, and Gamelin at the Quai d'Orsay. Within five minutes Churchill had been put in the picture and convinced of the gravity of the situation. "I then asked," says Churchill in *The Second World War*, 'Where is the strategic reserve?' and breaking into French, which

I used indifferently (in every sense): 'Où est la masse de manoeuvre?' General Gamelin turned to me and, with a shake of the head and a shrug, said 'Aucune.'" Churchill did not know that in Gamelin's "Breda" variant the Supreme Commander had ignored the repeated advice of his subordinates and, for political rather than for strategic reasons, had committed Giraud's 7th Army, which should have formed the "masse de manoeuvre". But this disastrous news did not prevent Churchill from agreeing to send ten more fighter squadrons to join Air-Marshal A. Barratt's force in France, which had already suffered considerable losses.

While these discussions were being held, the archives of the French Foreign Office were being burned by panic-stricken officials in the gardens of the Quai d'Orsay. But as evening drew on the tension eased. Near Rethel, a German colonel strayed into the French lines. He was captured, badly wounded, and was found to be carrying a map on which Arras and Abbeville were marked as the objectives for the Panzer forces, which had been expected to appear before Paris on the following day.

The breach widens

When the first reports of the disaster at Sedan came in, General Georges did what he could to restore continuity to the Allied front. On the eve of the German crossing of the Meuse he had ordered four divisions to head for the threatened sector. The following day, to ease the strain on Billotte, Georges took 2nd Army under his direct orders and diverted General Touchon's 6th Army, originally intended to cover the Swiss frontier, to the Aisne. On May 17 General Frère–not Corap–was given command of 7th Army and ordered to re-establish contact with 9th Army in the region of St. Quentin.

Thus between May 12–17 some 20 divisions were given new orders which would head them towards the breach in the Allied line–a redeployment which necessitated the smooth running of over 500 trains and 30,000 vehicles. But the plan was ruined from the outset by Luftwaffe attacks. During the same period, May 12–17, German bombers cut the French railway network in hundreds of places, isolating the sector exposed to the

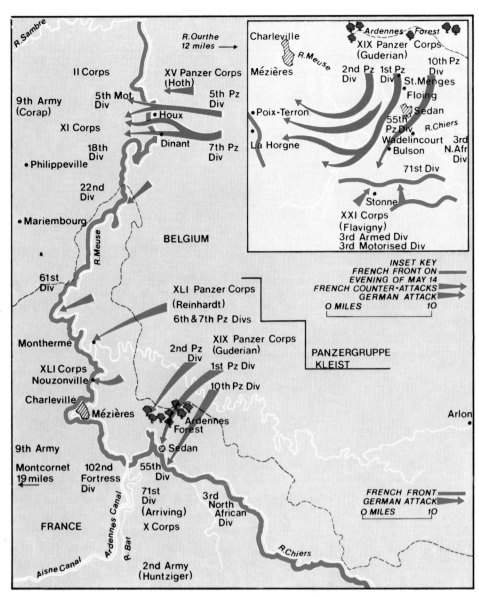

offensive of *Panzergruppe* Kleist.

This disruption caused a general delay of 24–36 hours before the first troops intended for the sectors of 6th and 7th Armies arrived on the scene. Some units were delayed by constant bombing, while others were forced to set out prematurely. The tracked vehicles of 2nd Armoured Division became pinned down on a stretch of railway 75 miles long between Tergnier and Hirson; the wheeled vehicles of the division, struggling along the roads, became separated from the tanks; and so 2nd Armoured Division was scattered into a shower of small, unco-ordinated detachments, and could not play its part in Georges's "plugging".

Up at the front the Germans made good use of the chaos in the Allied camp. As night fell on May 16, 7th Panzer Division forced the Franco-Belgian frontier near Solre-le-Château. Any commander other than Rommel would have been satisfied with this success, but he drove on through

△ Sedan in flames. The last time the Germans had broken through at Sedan had been in the Franco-Prussian war of 1870. Then they had marched on to Paris. Would they repeat the pattern now?

the darkness, surprised Avesnes at midnight, dashed past Landrecies, and arrived before Le Cateau at dawn on the 17th after a breath-taking advance of over 30 miles. He had scattered the surviving units of 18th Division and 1st Armoured Division, sweeping in thousands of prisoners, whom the Germans barely had time to disarm in their haste. Above everything else, Rommel had thrown the rear areas of 9th Army into inextricable confusion.

In his G.H.Q. at Münstereifel, however, Hitler did not share the optimism of his front-line commanders. Halder argued in vain that the Allies were not strong enough to launch a counter-attack towards Sedan, and that the Panzers could be allowed to thrust forwards without any unreasonable risk. Hitler remained paralysed with anxiety, and at noon on the 17th, after a visit to O.K.W. with Brauchitsch, Halder noted: "Apparently little mutual understanding. The Führer insists that he sees the main danger coming from the south. (In fact, I don't see any danger at all!) Therefore, infantry divisions must be brought up as quickly as possible to protect the southern flank; the armour will have to rely on its own resources to enlarge the breakthrough to the northwest."

And a few hours later the same subject arose after an intervention from O.K.W. by telephone: "2100 hours. A rather disagreeable day. The Führer is terribly nervous. Frightened by his own success, he fears to take risks and would prefer to curb our initiative. Reasons for this: his fears for the left flank. Keitel's telephone calls to the army groups and the Führer's personal visit to Army Group 'B' have produced nothing but trouble and doubt."

Next morning, the same problem . . .

This friction between O.K.W. and O.K.H. had its repercussions on the battlefield, resulting in order and counter-order. On the night of May 15–16 Guderian received a telephoned order from Kleist to postpone his advance until the supporting infantry had joined up. When Guderian protested vehemently he was authorised to resume the advance, but only for 48 hours. Despite a brilliant success on May 16, Guderian received a visit from Kleist on the morning of the 17th. Kleist had come to restate this unfortunate halt order to his impetuous subordinate, and he did so in terms which provoked Guderian to offer his resignation.

On Rundstedt's direct orders General List, commander of 12th Army, ended the dispute in the early afternoon. He settled it with a compromise which, made at the moment when every hour counted, saved the campaign from petering out. Guderian, restored to the command of XIX Panzer Corps, would obey Kleist's order to halt, which came from O.K.H. But he was authorised to continue with a "reconnaissance in force" towards the west. Seizing this loophole, Guderian chose to make his "reconnaissance in force" with the entire fighting strength of 1st and 2nd Panzer Divisions, pushing a first bridgehead across the Oise at Moy on the evening of the 17th. By noon on the 19th Guderian's tanks had taken Péronne.

Allied dislocation gets worse

Meanwhile, XVI Panzer Corps (Hoepner's 3rd and 4th Panzer Divisions) had also been transferred to Rundstedt's Army Group "A" and subordinated to 4th Army. This meant that nine Panzer divisions, followed by six motorised divisions, were now operating on Billotte's right flank and driving across his rear. Billotte's withdrawal to the Escaut Line was being hampered not only by the attacks of Army Group "B" but by Luftwaffe attacks and by the disorganised flood of refugees.

In this total confusion it was hardly surprising that all reinforcements for Giraud's army were sent in vain. Rendered meaningless by the course of events, his orders had either been drawn up for units which no longer existed, or only reached formations which were not yet in their correct position. On May 16

Giraud transferred his H.Q. from Vervins to Wassigny–but the break-up of 2nd Armoured Division after the destruction of 1st Armoured meant that he no longer had enough forces with which to counter-attack, while Rommel was driving towards Landrecies and Guderian's advance towards the Channel was being slowed down only by the untimely and cautious intervention of Kleist.

Giraud is captured

When Giraud decided to fall back from Wassigny to Le Catelet he found all the roads blocked before him. Abandoning his car for an armoured car, he tried in vain to get through the enemy lines–and at dawn on the 19th he himself became a prisoner of the Germans.

General Doumenc has described how it happened:

"General Giraud had left Wassigny at 1600 hours, taking only two officers with him. After moving to the H.Q. of 9th Division he passed through Busigny only to find that the enemy had armoured cars at every cross-roads on the main road from Cambrai to Le Catelet. By nightfall they had got to within seven miles of Le Catelet; the little group abandoned its vehicles and after a three-hour march by the compass had reached Le Catelet, part of which was burning . . . they ran into a German outpost and there was an exchange of shots, after which they took refuge in a wood. The General then ordered the party to separate. He himself was slowed down by an old wound and stopped behind a hedge at the side of the

(page 46) Stamp of the Blitzkrieg: German soldiers and local civilians stand amidst the wreckage of a smashed French horse-drawn transport column, while other horses graze quietly in the adjoining field. Constant Luftwaffe air strikes savaged the Allied supply lines, paralysing traffic and jamming the roads to the rear.

▽ *A canal bridge destroyed in the face of the oncoming German Army fails to deter these assault troops armed with rifles and flame-thrower.*

Cambrai road. Then he saw, coming from the south, a column of French trucks with a gun-carrier in the lead, which had by-passed Le Catelet. He climbed into the gun-carrier and knocked out the first German tank which they encountered, only to run into three more tanks. He then threw himself into a farmhouse which seemed isolated."

"Unhappily," runs Giraud's own account, "this farmhouse was filled with refugees who probably gave us away to the first Germans who questioned them. Within minutes three German tanks surrounded the farmhouse while a large column drew up on the road. We were rapidly discovered; I thought it would be useless to risk the life of the young troops there, and I ordered them not to fire. It was 6 o'clock; we were prisoners."

At about 2000 hours on May 20, Spitta's battalion from Veiel's 2nd Panzer Division was the first German unit to reach the Channel coast near Noyelles. Meanwhile, at Péronne, Corbie, Amiens, and Abbeville, other formations of XIX Panzer Corps had outrun the retreating French 7th Army and had established bridge-heads across the Somme.

Thus the "plugging" of the ruptured Allied front attempted by General Georges had failed completely. But did it ever have a chance of success? As Doumenc says, the breach could have been closed by a mass redeployment of the five infantry and three motorised divisions which were frittered away in vain attempts to assist 9th Army. But to have got this group of divisions into position (with its right on St. Quentin and its left on Le Cateau) by May 16 would have required it to have been set in motion on May 12, at the very moment when Rommel's motorcyclists reached the Meuse.

"This simple statement of dates," comments Doumenc, "shows the impossibility." Certainly, but there can be no denying that it was fatal to have committed 7th Army in the "Breda" variant of Gamelin's plan. If 7th Army had been retained as the mobile reserve for 1st Army Group, as Georges had originally recommended, it would probably have been a very different story. Instead, Giraud was forced, like General Soubise after the Battle of Rossbach in the old song, to go wandering about looking for his troops, lantern in hand . . .

Napoleon went further. He is quoted as having said: "In war, a major disaster always implies a major culprit."

CHAPTER 6
THE MIRACLE OF DUNKIRK

Thus when Gort ordered "Frankforce" to retire from Arras on the evening of the 23rd, and then, on the 25th, broke away from the manoeuvre laid down for 1st Army Group, he was not waiting on the course of events. But it was certainly a timely move. If Hitler had not intervened personally on the morning of the 24th and ordered that the Panzers were not to pass the Lens–Béthune–St. Omer–Gravelines line, it is clear that Guderian could have reached Dunkirk and Malo-les-Bains on the evening of the following day.

Hitler's celebrated "halt order" before Dunkirk has been interpreted in many ways, both by German generals and historians of the war. Some have held that Hitler wished to spare the B.E.F. the humiliation of total surrender in order to regain the favour of the British and make them more amenable to a settlement. This is hardly credible. Others have argued that Hitler wanted to give his friend and chosen successor, Hermann Göring, the chance of showing that no troops could retreat or embark under the bombs of the Luftwaffe. This explanation, however, is even thinner. The fact is that the order which spared nine British divisions and over 110,000 French troops from captivity was sent out to the German 4th Army by telephone, after a visit by Hitler to Rundstedt's H.Q. at Charleville, at 1231 hours on May 24.

According to the war diary of Army Group "A", published by the German historian Hans Adolf Jacobsen, it would appear that Hitler made this decision after a similar suggestion had been made to him by Rundstedt. It is hardly surpris-ing that after the event Rundstedt did not claim the credit for the "halt order".

The reasons given for the "halt order" were the danger involved in committing the Panzer forces in the swampy terrain around Dunkirk and the need to conserve them for Operation "Red", the second phase of the campaign. This decision, made at the top, drew the following bitter comments from Halder on May 25:

"The day began with one of those unfortunate quarrels between Brauchitsch and the Führer, over the closing stages of the battle of encirclement. The battle plan which I suggested requires Army Group 'B', by means of a heavy frontal attack, to force the enemy into an ordered retreat, while Army Group 'A', falling upon an already shaken enemy, cuts its communications and strikes the decisive blow –a job for our tanks. Now the political command has come up with the idea of fighting the decisive battle not on Belgian soil but in northern France. To cover up this political shift, the argument is that the terrain of Flanders, crossed by many water-courses, is unsuitable for a tank battle. As a result, all tanks and motorised troops must be moved quickly to the St. Omer–Béthune line.

"This is a complete reversal of our plan. I wanted to make Army Group 'A' the hammer and Army Group 'B' the anvil of the operation. Now 'B' will be the hammer and 'A' the anvil. But Army Group 'B' is facing a solid front; its progress will be slow and its losses high. Our air force, on which all hopes are pinned, is dependent upon the weather.

"This change means a stepping-up of

◁ *French and British troops withdraw into the Dunkirk perimeter, making for the beaches.*

the tempo which will need more energy than the actual plan of operations. For all that, the battle will be won, by this method or the other . . ."

On the following day, May 26, Hitler cancelled his decision and gave his tanks a free hand, but the time taken to get them on the move again meant that the chance of reaching Dunkirk before the British had been missed.

When Gort made his decision to retreat, he had already found himself obliged to keep close watch on his dwindling stocks of artillery ammunition. It is therefore difficult to find fault with his decision. Post-war memoirs by Gort's subordinates of 1940, such as Alanbrooke and Montgomery, conclude that Gort's decision had only one major fault, that of expecting too much from the French.

The fact remains that the French 1st Army, fighting at the bottom of the Allied pocket, was put in a difficult position by the British withdrawal; the British would have to cover only 47 miles from Arras to Dunkirk, but 1st Army, at Valenciennes, was over 62 miles from the port. When Weygand saw that his planned joint counter-attack, which should have been launched on the 26th, was now impossible, he still hoped that the 1st Army would be able to establish itself in a beach-head at

Dunkirk deep enough to save the port from German artillery fire. But by the 26th the situation had deteriorated so badly that Weygand cabled Blanchard: "We (that is to say Reynaud and myself) are fully aware of the situation. You must remain the only judge of what must be done to save what can be saved, above all the honour of the colours of which you are the guardian."

Belgian resistance fades

This was not optimistic language – but it took no account of the progressive decline of the Allied situation on the Belgian sector. The Belgian Army had been retreating from the Schelde to the Lys; when Antwerp and Brussels were surrendered on May 17 on the orders of the Belgian High Command, another segment of Belgian territory had been abandoned without a fight. Nevertheless the Belgians rallied to the call of their King, holding on valiantly along their front, which ran from the Léopold II Canal to the Lys Canal, along the line of the Lys, joining the left flank of the B.E.F. at Menin.

On May 24 the German 6th Army broke through the new position at Courtrai,

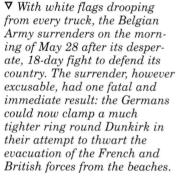

▽ *With white flags drooping from every truck, the Belgian Army surrenders on the morning of May 28 after its desperate, 18-day fight to defend its country. The surrender, however excusable, had one fatal and immediate result: the Germans could now clamp a much tighter ring round Dunkirk in their attempt to thwart the evacuation of the French and British forces from the beaches.*

The Weygand Gambit

On May 17 General Maxime Weygand, C-in-C Middle East, was ordered back to Paris from Beirut. After journeying to Belgium to assess the position, Weygand devised a plan which he presented to Reynaud and Churchill, among others: the Belgian Army should retire to the line of the Yser and the country should be flooded; the British and French should attack towards Bapaume and Cambrai with about eight divisions; the RAF should provide maximum support; the new French army group heading towards Amiens and forming a front along the Somme should thrust north to form a junction with British forces in the region of Bapaume. Britain sanctioned the movement of ten squadrons of fighters to France. Weygand believed the Allies must re-establish a continuous front between 1st Army Group and 3rd Army Group to form a "solid barrier" to prevent the Panzer forces that had ventured to the sea breaking out to the coast. Weygand's plans were wrecked, however, by a series of delays stemming from the death of General Billotte in a car accident. There was no attack by eight Allied divisions towards Bapaume and Cambrai on the 23rd or the 24th and the French 7th Army did not cross the Somme. On May 21 the British attacked at Arras with "Frankforce", the 5th and 50th divisions and 74 tanks of 1st Army Tank Brigade. Meeting with initial success, they were finally driven back, and Panzer forces headed north and north-west to besiege Calais and Boulogne.

revealing Reichenau's intention of driving towards Ypres and cutting off the Belgian Army from the B.E.F. The Belgians hit back as best they could; two reserve divisions had entered the line, and the fine showing of the 8th Division and the 2nd *Chasseurs Ardennais* Division limited the effect of the German breakthrough. On the 25th the 12th Division and the 1st *Chasseurs Ardennais* Division, on the Lys Canal and the Lys river respectively, launched timely and vigorous counter-attacks. But the Belgian reserves were rapidly used up, and the British refused to attack the flank of the German column thrusting towards Ypres, but continued their withdrawal to Dunkirk.

The Belgian surrender

On May 26 the Belgian Army was still fighting, but its right was bending under the renewed attacks by Reichenau, and its left was yielding ground before the German 18th Army advancing from the direction of Antwerp. The battle was renewed at dawn on the 27th; and at 1230 hours King Léopold informed Gort that: "The moment is rapidly approaching when our troops will no longer be able to fight. The King will be forced to capitulate to avoid a disaster." Two hours later the King gave General Champon, chief of the French Military Mission, a note which told the same story: "Belgian resistance is reaching the end of its tether. Our front is fraying like a worn-out, breaking rope."

▷ *German troops occupy the centre of Lille after the heroic stand by the French 1st Army under General Molinier. The battle for Lille, at the bottom of the Dunkirk pocket, enabled thousands of French and British troops to withdraw to the Dunkirk perimeter in time.*

In the centre of the front a breach, 3 to 4 miles wide, was opening in the Thielt area; on the left, the 17th Division was on the point of collapse. From above, the Stukas kept up a non-stop bombardment on the artillery positions and the emptying ammunition dumps. Behind the lines, among a population of 800,000, an equal number of refugees was wandering. At 1700 hours King Léopold overruled the advice of General van Overstraeten (who wanted to wait until the following day) and sent an envoy to the German lines to discuss the Belgian surrender. But the King did not do this without having first informed Colonels Hautcoeur and Haily of the French and British Military Mis-

Léopold had rejected the attempts of his ministers to persuade him to leave the battlefield and follow them into exile. King Léopold has been criticised for his conduct in not following the example of Queen Wilhelmina, but it is a false comparison. Under the Belgian constitution he was the Commander-in-Chief of the Belgian Army, a duty which did not apply in Queen Wilhelmina's case. While German propaganda proclaimed to the Allied troops in the Dunkirk pocket: "Your commanders have fled by aircraft. Lay down your arms!", Léopold had announced to his troops: "Whatever happens my fate will be yours." Should he have broken this promise at the very moment when he was

Camarades!

Telle est la situation!
En tout cas, la guerre est finie pour vous!
Vos chefs vont s'enfuir par avion
A bas les armes!

British Soldiers!

Look at this map: it gives your true situation!
Your troops are entirely surrounded —
stop fighting!
Put down your arms!

△ German propaganda leaflet urging the forces in the Dunkirk pocket to surrender. For once all the German propagandists had to do was to point out the true situation, correct in every detail but one: that the Luftwaffe had failed to seal off the sea approaches to Dunkirk.
◁ For the French civilian population, however, the fear of German air supremacy was stronger than ever.

sions. While waiting for the German reply, King Léopold provided for the French 60th Division which had been fighting on the left of the Belgian Army, transporting it in trucks to the Dunkirk sector to be put at the disposal of General Blanchard. In the same spirit he ordered the destruction of the Yser bridges and the blocking of the ports of Ostend and Zeebrugge.

At 2230 hours the Belgian envoy, Major-General Derousseaux, returned to the Belgian G.H.Q. with the message that Hitler was demanding unconditional surrender. The Belgian Army, having hidden or destroyed its standards and colours, ceased fire at 0400 hours on May 28. The following day the last Belgian troops surrendered and Belgium's 18-day battle came to an end. In this desperate battle against the invader, the unfortunate King

being informed of the "defection" of certain units, their morale undermined by the plotting of Flemish agitators in the pay of Hitler?

And how could the Dunkirk evacuation have met with the success it did if the Belgian Army, deprived of the commander in which it had confidence, had laid down its arms on May 26 or 27?

The Dunkirk perimeter

One fact at least is clear, however: the Belgian surrender sealed the fate of the French 1st Army around Lille. Both flanks of the 1st Army were now laid bare, and only 25 miles separated Hoth's *Panzergruppe* at la Bassée from Reichenau's forces at Menin on the French left. On

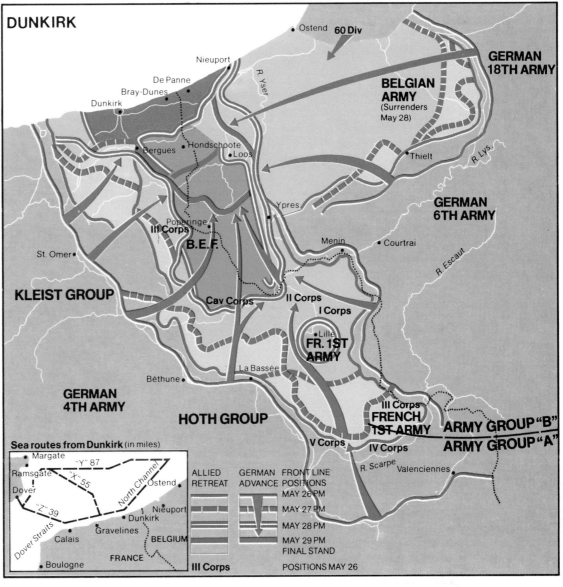

DUNKIRK

Ostend · 60 Div

GERMAN 18TH ARMY

Nieuport

De Panne

Bray-Dunes

Dunkirk

R. Yser

BELGIAN ARMY (Surrenders May 28)

Bergues · Hondschoote

· Loos

Thielt

R. Lys

Ypres

GERMAN 6TH ARMY

Poperinge

III Corps

B.E.F.

Menin · Courtrai

St. Omer ·

R. Escaut

KLEIST GROUP

Cav Corps

II Corps

I Corps

Lille

FR. 1ST ARMY

La Bassée

Béthune ·

GERMAN 4TH ARMY

HOTH GROUP

III Corps

FRENCH 1ST ARMY

ARMY GROUP "B"

ARMY GROUP "A"

V Corps

IV Corps

R. Scarpe · Valenciennes

Sea routes from Dunkirk (in miles)

Margate

"Y" 87

Ramsgate · "X" 55

Dover · Ostend

North Channel

"Z" 39

Nieuport

Dover Straits · Dunkirk

Calais · Gravelines

BELGIUM

· Boulogne

FRANCE

ALLIED RETREAT	GERMAN ADVANCE	FRONT LINE POSITIONS
		MAY 26 PM
		MAY 27 PM
		MAY 28 PM
		MAY 29 PM FINAL STAND
III Corps		POSITIONS MAY 26

△ Morbid comment by Le Rire.
Hitler redecorates the world –
with blood.

May 28, taking Cassel and the Monts des
Flandres, the Germans closed the ring
round the French IV and V Corps which
were dug in around Lille, Loos, and
Haubourdin. These forces put up such an
heroic resistance that when they surrendered, General Waeger, commander of the
German XXVIII Corps, honoured them
with a guard of honour from the 25th
Division. General Molinier, the French
commander, was allowed to retain his
staff car.

General Prioux would not abandon his
brave comrades of the IV and V Corps. He
hung on at his H.Q. at Steenwerck and
was captured there at 1245 hours on the
29th. General de la Laurencie, however,
urged his exhausted III Corps north
through Poperinge and Hondschoote and
saved them from captivity, in a 37-mile
night march along the incredibly choked
roads. On the morning of the 29th he
reported to Admiral Abrial, commanding
at Dunkirk, with his 12th and 32nd

Divisions and part of the 1st Motorised
Division. The survivors of the cavalry
corps did useful flank-guard service during this harrowing retreat.

Fagalde's XVI Corps was holding the
Dunkirk beach-head with the 60th and
68th Divisions; de la Laurencie's troops
came as a welcome reinforcement. Unfortunately, following the strict instructions laid down by the British High
Command, they had to abandon most of
their heavy weapons and a good deal of
ammunition before they were allowed to
withdraw into the Dunkirk zone, which
caused some recrimination between the
Allies. On the same day, May 29, the
embarkation of the B.E.F. reached an
encouraging figure. On that day 47,310
British troops were evacuated, while on
the 27th and 28th the total had been only
25,473. The credit for this success undoubtedly must go to Vice-Admiral Sir
Bertram Ramsay, Flag Officer, Dover.
Four years later, Ramsay's energy and

resourcefulness would be put to far better use than handling the details of an improvised evacuation under constant air bombardment: planning the Allied invasion of France in 1944.

Operation "Dynamo"

As early as May 20, Churchill had suggested that "as a precautionary measure the Admiralty should assemble a large number of small vessels in readiness to proceed to ports and inlets on the French coast". The War Cabinet agreed, and Ramsay was given the task of putting the scheme into operation. Ramsay took over everything that could float: small passenger ferry-boats from the Channel and the Irish Sea routes; coasters, trawlers, motor yachts and *schuyts*–flat-bottomed Dutch boats which had taken refuge in England.

In all some 850 commercial boats were taken over by the Admiralty, which agreed with some reluctance (in view of the needs of the Atlantic convoys) to detach 39 destroyers as escorts. But Ramsay did not content himself with putting the precious destroyers on purely defensive duties: in the teeth of the German bombers, magnetic mines, and torpedo-boats, he did not hesitate to send in the destroyers to embark troops from the port of Dunkirk and from the beaches of Malo-les-Bains, Bray-Dunes, and De Panne, just to the north of Dunkirk.

Operation "Dynamo", as the evacuation was called, formally went into operation at 1857 hours on May 26. Informed too late of the British intentions, the French were only able to make a comparatively feeble contribution. It was not until the 28th that Rear-Admiral Landriau was put in command of the Pas-de-Calais flotilla, which finally numbered some 300 vessels of every tonnage, including 15 destroyers and torpedo-boats, under the command of Captain Urvoy de Portzamparc.

If the British War Cabinet did take its time to inform the French of its decision to re-embark the B.E.F., Winston Churchill spared no effort to see that Operation "Dynamo" should take off as many French as possible. In his note to the Secretary of State for War on May 29, he wrote: "It is essential that the French should share in such evacuations from Dunkirk as may be possible. Nor must they be dependent only upon their own shipping resources. Arrangements must be concerted at once with the French Missions in this country, or, if necessary, with the French Government, so that no reproaches, or as few as possible, may arise . . ."

On May 30, 120,000 men, of which 6,000 were French, were embarked. On the 31st, when Gort received the order to hand over command of the beach-head to Lieutenant-General Alexander, first III Corps and

▽ German armoured car, the forward screen of every Panzer division. But at Dunkirk the Panzers lay helpless, paralysed by the orders of their own Supreme Command.

then II Corps – about 150,000 men – had been shipped back to England, together with 15,000 Frenchmen.

From June 1 the defence of the Dunkirk perimeter was taken over by the French XVI Corps. But it should be noted that the British spared no effort, without regard to risk, to spare their French comrades from imprisonment. By the time that Operation "Dynamo" ended on June 4, 113,000 French troops had been shipped to England out of a total of 338,226 Allied troops. That is to say that during the last four days of the evacuation 75,000 British and 98,000 French troops were embarked – and most of them on British ships.

The "miracle of Dunkirk" was only made possible by extremely difficult manoeuvres, one of which has been recalled by Alanbrooke:

"There was little possibility of sleep that night, as the 3rd Division were moving past and I repeatedly went out to see how they were progressing. They were travelling, as we had so frequently prac-tised for our night moves, with lights out and each driver watching the rear of the vehicle in front of him, which had the differential painted white and lit up by a tail-lamp under the vehicle. The 3rd Division through constant practice had become most proficient at this method of movement. However, with the congestion on the roads, road-blocks outside villages, and many other blocks caused by refugees and their carts, the division was frequent-ly brought to a standstill. The whole movement seemed unbearably slow; the hours of darkness were slipping by; should daylight arrive with the road crammed with vehicles the casualties from bombing might well have been disastrous.

"Our own guns were firing from the vicinity of Mount Kemmel, whilst German artillery was answering back, and the division was literally trundling slowly along in the darkness down a pergola of artillery fire, and within some 4,000 yards of a battle-front which had been fluctuat-ing all day somewhat to our disadvantage.

It was an eerie sight which I shall never forget. Before dawn came, the last vehicles had disappeared northwards into the darkness, and I lay down for a few hours' disturbed sleep, but kept wondering how the 3rd Division was progressing."

The resistance of the 12th Motorised Division and the 32nd and 68th Divisions was beyond praise; it lasted, contrary to all expectations, until dawn on June 4. General Janssen, commanding the 12th Motorised Division, was at the heart of the fighting and was killed by a bomb; General Fagalde, commanding XVI Corps, was taken prisoner with 40,000 men. Like Vice-Admiral Abrial, "Admiral North", and Rear-Admiral Platon, who embarked under orders at midnight on the 3rd, Fagalde had been the spirit of this battle without hope.

In the narrow sealane of the Straits of Dover, seven French destroyers and torpedo-boats and six British destroyers were sunk by Stukas and by attacks from E-boats (German motor torpedo-boats), together with a quarter of the small boats involved in the operation. In the air the fighters of the R.A.F. gave the Luftwaffe a hard time, greatly helping the embarkation of their comrades on the beaches; at the cost of 106 of their own machines, they accounted for most of the 156 German aircraft shot down during this phase of the campaign.

Hitler judges his enemies

Despite the undoubted setback represented by the Allied evacuations from Dunkirk, Hitler had scored a crushing victory.

For German losses put at 10,252 killed, 42,523 wounded, and 8,467 missing, he announced that 1,212,000 Dutch, Belgian, French, and British prisoners had been taken. In addition, his armies had captured an enormous booty: from the British Army alone, the spoils taken by the Germans amounted to 1,200 field guns, 1,250 anti-aircraft and anti-tank guns, 11,000 machine guns, and 75,000 vehicles. It is not surprising, therefore, that his letters to Mussolini were flushed with optimism; but setting aside the flamboyant boastfulness, four interesting points are to be found in the letter of May 25 in which Hitler passed judgement on his opponents:

△ Seen at low tide, an assortment of B.E.F. vehicles improvised as a pier for the little ships which plied between the beach and the disembarkation vessels.
▽ French and British walking wounded, who failed to get away. They are being marched off to hospital from a German checkpoint.

△ *French survivors survey the ruins of their town after the final evacuation and the German occupation of Dunkirk.*
▽ *From the German magazine* Signal: *curious German troops examine the shattered hull of the French destroyer* Bourrasque, *exposed at low tide.*

"As for the morale of our enemies, there is this to say:

1. *The Dutch.* They put up a much stronger resistance than we expected. Many of their units fought very bravely. But they had neither appropriate training nor experience of war. For this reason they were usually overcome by German forces which were often numerically very inferior.

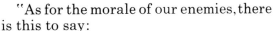

2. *The Belgians.* The Belgian soldier, too, has generally fought very bravely. His experience of war was considerably greater than that of the Dutch. At the beginning his tenacity was astounding. This is now decreasing visibly [written some three days before the Belgian surrender] as the Belgian soldier realises that his basic function is to cover the British retreat.

3. *The British.* The British soldier has retained the characteristics which he had in World War I. Very brave and tenacious in defence, unskilful in attack, wretchedly commanded. Weapons and equipment are of the highest order, but the overall organisation is bad.

4. *The French.* Very marked differences appear when it comes to assessing the military capacity of the French. Very bad units rub elbows with excellent units. In the overview, the difference in quality between the active and the reserve divisions is extraordinary. Many active divisions have fought desperately; most of the reserve divisions, however, are far less able to endure the shock which battle inflicts on the morale of troops. For the French, as with the Dutch and Belgians, there is also the fact that they know that they are fighting in vain for objectives which are not in line with their own interests. Their morale is very affected, as they say that throughout or wherever possible the British have looked after their own units and prefer to leave the critical sectors to their allies."

CHAPTER 7
ORDEAL ON THE SOMME

The disastrous course of events in Flanders had forced Weygand to abandon his plan of a joint counter-attack against the "Panzer Corridor". It was even more vital, however, that the bridgeheads won by the Germans on the left bank of the Somme should be destroyed. The outcome of the defensive battle which now had to be fought between Longuyon and Abbeville depended largely upon this.

To this end the French 7th Army and the forces under Altmayer (renamed 10th Army on May 28) were sent into action along the Somme while the retreat to Dunkirk and the evacuation were still in progress.

Upstream of Péronne, the efforts of General Toussaint's 19th Division, ably assisted by the tanks of 2nd Armoured Division under Colonel Perré, restored the French front along the Somme. Between Péronne and Amiens the Germans were also pushed back, but there they managed to hold on to their bridgehead across the river. It was hardly surprising that these counter-attacks were only partially successful. They were made by divisions which were flung into battle one by one and which, given their small

numbers, had to cover too wide a front.

The reduction of the Abbeville bridgehead was entrusted to de Gaulle's 4th Armoured Division, hastily re-formed since its raids on May 17 and 19, and reinforced with six infantry battalions. The division attacked on the afternoon of May 28. It struck at the positions held by a regiment of Lieutenant-General Blümm's 57th Division and caused much panic, for the German 3.7-cm anti-tank guns could not pierce the heavy armour of the French tanks. But because it was not promptly exploited, de Gaulle's success was fleeting. During the night of May 28–29, Blümm's force was reinforced by two 8.8-cm flak batteries, and their guns soon demonstrated, as they had done at Arras, their devastating power against tanks.

On May 29–30, the 4th Armoured Division made limited progress but failed to clear the crest of Mont Caubert; by the third day of the battle the division had taken some 500 prisoners, but it had been reduced to a mere 34 tanks. Finally called off on June 3, the counter-attack at Abbeville had achieved little – and on the 5th, Bock's army group attacked along the entire Somme front.

▽ *German infantry under bombardment during the advance on Paris. The French defence, inspired by the presence of Weygand, was improving steadily and taking a considerable toll of the invaders. This greatly surprised the Germans, who had expected their first quick advances to shatter the French defence beyond any hope of repair.*

Weygand's defence plan

Between the last embarkations from Dunkirk and the unleashing of Operation "Red" – the second and final phase of the Battle of France – there was a pause of little more than a single day.

Although Weygand was bombarded with a constant, bewildering stream of disastrous and disconcerting news, it must be said that he reacted with promptitude and energy throughout. Most of his decisions were sound, and above all there was the powerful, morale-boosting influence which he exerted on his subordinates. In a few days he had restored the spirit of the front-line troops to a remarkable degree. And the evidence for this can be found less on the French side than in the war diaries and memoirs of the Germans.

Weygand had shown his mettle as early as May 24, in a note laying down the measures to be taken against German armour supported by aircraft. On May 26, after his new defence plan had received the unanimous approval of the War Committee presided over by the President of the Republic, he issued the following "General Order of Operations":

"1. The battle on which the fate of the country depends will be fought without any idea of retreat from the positions which we occupy now. All commanders, from army commander to corporal, must be animated by the fierce resolve to stand and fight until death. If commanders set the example their troops will stand; and they will have the right to compel obedience if necessary.

2. To be certain of halting the enemy, constant aggressiveness is essential. If the enemy shows signs of attacking on any sector, we must reply with swift and brutal counter-methods.

If the enemy succeeds in establishing a bridgehead in our front which he can use for rushing in tanks and then moving on to an armoured attack, it is essential – no matter how insignificant the bridgehead may be – to drive the enemy back to his lines with artillery fire and air strikes, and to

▽ *Reconnaissance vehicles of a Panzer division enter the ruins of a northern French village, reduced to rubble by the Germans for the second time in 20 years.*

counter-attack. Infiltration must be countered with infiltration. If a unit believes that a neighbouring unit is wavering it must not at any cost fall back but must try to restore the situation. If this is impossible it must dig in and form a 'hedgehog' of resistance. This must apply to all units from divisional right down to company level.

3. The rear areas of the main defence line must be organised, in as great a depth as possible, into a checkerboard of centres of resistance, in particular on the main roads along which the Germans have always moved. Demolition charges must be prepared.

4. Every divisional general must be in constant touch with his colonels, the colonels with their battalion commanders, the battalion commanders with their company commanders, and the captains and lieutenants with their sections and their men.

Activity–Solidarity–Resolution."

Weygand's note of May 24 had anticipated the methods prescribed by this order. In the face of the "tank-aircraft tandem" attacks of the Blitzkrieg, it amounted to an improvised defensive tactic for which the French lacked sufficient means, but which nevertheless inflicted heavy losses on the victors of this first campaign in France.

Above all, Weygand believed, the Panzers must be cut off, decimated, and annihilated on a prepared battlefield. To do this meant, as he wrote: "substituting for the idea of the line the idea of control of communications", and this must be done by quartering the terrain, establishing the artillery in strongpoints and allocating a third of the artillery for anti-tank use, and by camouflaging all positions against air and ground observation.

A combination of these measures, he thought, would prevent the German infantry from following up as close support for those of their tanks which managed to infiltrate the French positions, while the tanks themselves, cut off from the trucks bringing up their fuel and ammunition, would fall victim to the crossfire of the French infantry and artillery. At this critical moment for the attacker, the defenders could send in their infantry to mop up, or to launch more ambitious counter-attacks backed by tanks.

On June 5, 1940, the French lacked sufficient forces to man such a front, as well as the thousands of anti-personnel

△ *Nothing was safe from the bombing of the Stukas: here a French church blazes in the aftermath of a raid.* ◁ *The newly promoted General de Gaulle about to set off for a meeting of the Council of Ministers on June 6, to which he had been summoned in his capacity of Under-Secretary for War by Reynaud.*

and anti-tank mines which it required. Apart from these fatal deficiencies, however, the type of front envisaged by Weygand was strikingly similar to the German defences which stopped the British and Americans in the Normandy *bocage* country after D-Day in 1944.

Could the plan have worked?

In his book *The Battle of France, 1940* Colonel Goutard condemned Weygand's plan for being "merely a return to the classical doctrine of a continuous front". But this ignores the fact that the front envisaged by Weygand was far more flexible than previous conceptions of a static defence line, and that without an armoured reserve, any other disposition than the one prescribed by Weygand on May 26 would have laid

France wide open to the onrush of the Panzers.

But when Weygand, with his forces diminished by a third, prepared to fight a defensive battle against an intact enemy, did such an armoured reserve exist? In his memoirs, de Gaulle says that it did. On June 1 he proposed the formation of two large armoured units from the 1,200 modern tanks still available for action. Supplied with infantry and artillery complements, he suggested that if the larger group were posted north of Paris and the other south of Rheims they could be used as an adequate mobile reserve. As de Gaulle put it, they would be able to strike at the flank "of any one of the German mechanised corps when, having broken through our front, they would be dislocated in width and extended in depth."

In his reply to General de Gaulle, prepared in 1955, Weygand excused himself for not remembering this suggestion. But he asserted that at the time he had no more

Paul Reynaud was born in 1878 and was trained as a lawyer. He served on the Western Front in World War I, and became a Deputy in 1919. In the early 1930's he held ministerial posts, but then fell out of favour until 1938, when he became Minister of Justice and later of Finance. He was a staunch advocate of tank warfare and opposition to Hitler. He was appointed Prime Minister on March 21, 1940, and resigned on June 16 when he failed to persuade his Cabinet to continue the war.

than 250 modern tanks at his disposal – not 1,200 – and this bears examination. A contemporary record gives only 86 tanks – Char B and Hotchkiss – to the 3rd Armoured Division, and 50 to the 4th Armoured. The figure for the 2nd Armoured Division on June 5 is not known, but it can hardly have been much higher than that of the other two. The 7th Light Mechanised Division was a recent formation, but even if it was at full strength it would have had only 174 tanks, of which half were Somua S-35's and half Hotchkiss H-35's. Even if the 2nd, 3rd, and 5th Light Cavalry Divisions had survived the disaster, they would have been reduced to skeleton strength.

Weygand's critics have argued that to attempt to defend both Paris and the Maginot Line could only have ended in disaster. This is a facile criticism. As far as Paris was concerned, calculations had been made to determine the effect on the French war effort of the loss of this or that line; and it was clear at the time that having already lost the industrial regions of the north, so vital to the production of tanks, it was essential to defend the line of the Somme and the Aisne.

As for the Maginot Line, it is true that shorter defensive fronts could have been

selected, but at best the advantages to be gained by abandoning the Maginot Line could only have been purely military ones. The Rhine basin would have been lost, together with the strongpoints between the Rhine and the Moselle which enabled a front of 220 miles to be defended by a mere 17 divisions, of which ten were "Series B" reserve ones.

The 3rd Army Group had been transferred from the Saône to the Somme. General Garchery had handed over the 8th Army to General Laure, and 8th Army was now attached to 2nd Army Group, with the task of coping with any German attempt to cross the Rhine between Basle and Strasbourg, or to violate neutral Swiss territory. From Sélestat to Bitche stood Bourret's 5th Army, and then, covering the Moselle valley, Condé's 3rd Army. As Weygand had redeployed many of its units to other sectors, 4th Army's strength was reduced to General Hubert's group covering the Saar. In view of the signs which hinted at a possible offensive by the German Army Group "C" on the Saar and across the Rhine at Neuf-Brisach, General Prételat found that his 2nd Army Group had really been reduced to a dangerous level.

Weygand had promoted Huntziger from

the command of 2nd Army to that of the new 4th Army Group. The 2nd Army, taken over by General Freydenberg, covered the passes of the Argonne; to the left of 2nd Army, General Réquin's 4th Army held the line of the Aisne between Attigny and Neufchâtel. The 12 divisions of the 4th Army Group had a front of 75 miles to cover; but although the Argonne forest favoured the defenders, the rolling chalk countryside of Champagne was so well adapted to tank warfare that it had been christened the "tankodrome" in French military circles.

Finally, the 150 miles of front between Neufchâtel-sur-Aisne and Abbeville were covered by General Besson's 3rd Army Group. This was made up of three armies: General Touchon's 6th Army on the Aisne; General Frère's 7th Army blocking the approaches to Compiègne and Beauvais; and General Altmayer's 10th Army on the lower Somme. With one division per $8\frac{1}{2}$ miles of front, General Besson's army group presented a very over-stretched network of strongpoints – while the Germans had seven bridgeheads on the left bank of the Somme.

Counting the 16 infantry divisions in army group or supreme command reserve, the seven armoured, mechanised, and cavalry divisions, and the four British and Polish divisions still in France, Weygand had at his disposal a force of 71 divisions.

But even to arrive at this unimpressive total he had had to draw upon the reserve armies in the Alps and North Africa, despite the increasing threat from Italy.

As a result of the disastrous opening phase of the campaign, some 25 infantry divisions had been destroyed. Thirteen out of the original 31 active infantry divisions had gone, and six out of the seven motorised divisions. Six out of the original 13 light cavalry, light mechanised, and armoured divisions which Gamelin had deployed on the morning of May 10 had also been removed from the board. Nevertheless, Weygand had managed to form three striking groups out of his surviving armoured units. On June 5, 1940, they were ready for the fight: the first, under General Pétiet, around Forges-les-Eaux, the second, under General Audet, in the Beauvais area, and the third, under General Buisson, in the Vouziers area. Weygand, therefore, cannot be accused of having failed to create an armoured reserve, albeit a sadly depleted one.

Reynaud's "Breton redoubt"

After Weygand's plan had been accepted by the War Committee on May 25, he had to reject an idea expressed by Reynaud in a note on the 29th; this had required him "to plan for the establishment of a national redoubt around a war port, allowing us to make use of the sealanes and above all to communicate with our allies. This national redoubt should be arranged and supplied, particularly with explosives, to make it *a veritable fortress*. It would consist of the Breton peninsula. The government would remain in the capital and would continue the war by making use of our naval and air forces in North Africa."

Attractive as this idea sounded on paper, the limited resources and the lack of time at the end of May 1940 made it an impossibility. Weygand put it in a nutshell: "The organisation of a 'veritable fortress' would need, after the construction of strongpoints along some 94 miles of front, the diverting of manpower and all kinds of war material, in particular anti-tank and anti-aircraft guns. All these resources were already insufficient to meet the needs of the defence line in process of organisation along the Somme and the Aisne; there could be no question of diverting even a small part of them; for even if it had been possible, there was not enough time."

◁ *A German officer briefs his men amid the ruins of Maubeuge.*

Assistance from the Allies

How much help did France receive from her allies?

In his 2nd Army Group, General Prételat had two divisions of Polish infantry who were soon to put up a magnificent fight under the most desperate conditions. So did the British 51st Division, on the left flank of 10th Army. But the British armoured division, under Major-General R. Evans, serving in the same sector, has been described by one of its officers as "a caricature of an armoured division," not even equipped with "half its official tank strength, no field guns, insufficient anti-tank and anti-aircraft guns, without infantry, without air cover, deprived of most of its auxiliary services, with part of its staff in a vehicle 'armoured' with plywood . . ."

So much for the actual forces in the field. As far as the future of the British co-operation in the Battle of France was concerned, the picture was not good. At a meeting of the Supreme War Council on May 31, Churchill held forth with his customary resolution – but when it came down to details he became reticent and vague. According to the minutes of the meeting, "Mr. Winston Churchill observed that the problem of the invasion of England had changed in appearance, and that yet again he could promise nothing before he knew what could be saved from the North.

"As far as air reinforcements were concerned, he did not have the authorisation of his Government to grant more than had been given."

When Reynaud tried to explain the "vital character" of the battle of the Somme to Churchill, he received the following reply, which Paul Baudouin has preserved: "M. Churchill finally declared that he would think over the French requests and reply to them soon. Perhaps a Canadian division might be ready by June 22; perhaps one of the divisions from Dunkirk.

"Fourteen British divisions were being trained, armed only with rifles and machine guns. He intended to draw upon the entire forces of the Empire for:

"eight Indian battalions;
"eight battalions from Palestine;
"14,000 Australians;
"the 2nd Canadian Division;
"one brigade from Narvik.
"But he returned to the necessity of guarding Britain . . ."

As far as the British land forces were concerned, post-war studies have indeed established these meagre figures as exact. But how sound were Churchill's motives for insisting that R.A.F. Fighter Command must be kept out of the battle for the Somme?

Where was the R.A.F.?

Churchill's supporters have endorsed the view that Britain would certainly have been invaded in September 1940, if the fighters of the R.A.F. had been sacrificed in the Battle of France. But this viewpoint needs examination. It implies that Churchill was in reality far more pessimistic about the French Army's capacity for resistance than he cared to admit, and that is why he refused to commit the Spitfires and Hurricanes in France. What are the facts? Could the large-scale intervention of British fighters have turned the scale of the Battle of France?

It could be argued that the total sacrifice of R.A.F. Fighter Command in France would have had punishing effects upon the Luftwaffe. The German air fleets might have suffered such heavy losses that they would have been unable to mount any large-scale air offensives against Britain during the autumn and winter of 1940. Moreover, had the 600-odd fighters at the R.A.F.'s disposal entered the fray, they would have been able to count on the aid of the 350–400 French fighters which were surrendered when the armistice was signed.

Against this, it could be claimed that a transfer to France of R.A.F. Fighter Command would have squandered Britain's trump card. For in France the Spitfires and Hurricanes would have been operating without the benefit of radar, a proper logistical backing and the tactical advantage of operating over their own territory, which gave them a considerable endurance advantage over the Germans in the Battle of Britain.

Shadow of disaster

When he presented his battle plan to the War Committee on May 25, Weygand did not conceal the possibility that the time could well come when the French Army, given only these forces and with no hope of reinforcement, would have suffered such heavy losses that it could no longer hold the Germans. He stressed that it was essential "to stand fast on the present Somme-Aisne line and fight to the last there. This line has several weak points, in particular the Crozat Canal and the Ailette. We could be broken there. If this should happen the surviving fragments will dig in. Every part of the army must fight until it drops for the honour of the country."

It was then that President Lebrun made an intervention which Reynaud has described as "disastrous", but which was natural enough at the time. What would happen, he asked, if the French armies should be scattered and destroyed? In such a crisis the government would have no liberty of action whatsoever, if proposals of peace came from the Germans. True, the agreements made with Britain on March

28 forbade France from concluding a separate peace; but if "relatively advantageous" conditions were offered by the Reich, they should be examined with care. With Reynaud's agreement, Weygand suggested that Britain should be sounded out on every question which would result from the total destruction of the French armies.

After the surrender of Belgium, Weygand once again raised the subject with Reynaud. Listing the reinforcements which France should request from Britain, he added: "It also seems necessary that the British Government be made aware of the fact that a time might come when France would find herself, against her will, unable to continue a military struggle to protect her soil."

It was this possibility which made Reynaud suggest the formation of a "Breton Redoubt". But as we have seen, it would have been impossible for Weygand to withdraw from the line the 12 or so divisions which this would entail. In any case, on June 5 Reynaud made yet another change in his cabinet. Baudouin replaced Daladier as Foreign Minister, Bouthillier replaced Lamoureux as Finance Minister – and Charles de Gaulle, promoted to the

◁ *A German squad at work in the ruins of Amiens, which had suffered very severe damage in the course of the German assault.* ◁▽ *An infantryman picks his way cautiously towards a burning house.* ▽ *One of the 92,000 dead that the French suffered in the course of the six-week German offensive.*

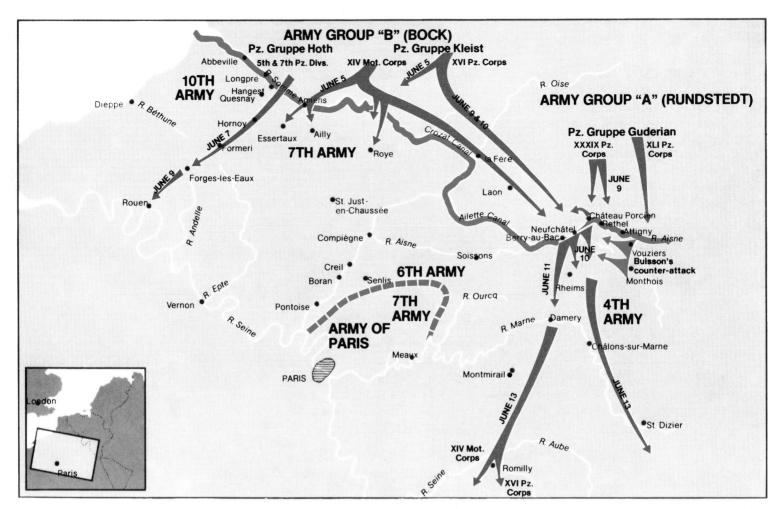

ARMY GROUP "B" (BOCK)

Pz. Gruppe Hoth
5th & 7th Pz. Divs.

Pz. Gruppe Kleist
XIV Mot. Corps   XVI Pz. Corps

ARMY GROUP "A" (RUNDSTEDT)

Pz. Gruppe Guderian
XXXIX Pz. Corps   XLI Pz. Corps

10TH ARMY

7TH ARMY

6TH ARMY

7TH ARMY

ARMY OF PARIS

4TH ARMY

△ The inexorable advance of the Germans southward in a gradual envelopment of Paris. Army Group "A" crossed the Aisne at Neufchâtel on June 9 and reached the Marne three days later. The 7th Panzer Division of Army Group "B" moved from the Somme to the Seine in three days, then turned north-west to trap 46,000 French and British troops against the Channel coast. Terrific resistance by the French around Amiens failed to prevent Strauss' 9th Army reaching Soissons by the evening of June 6. The German entry into Paris was barely a week away.

▷ German artillery crosses a pontoon bridge over the Marne, the furthest extent of their advance into France in 1914. The gun is the standard 10.5 cm field howitzer. Most of the German artillery at this point of the war was horse-drawn.

temporary rank of brigadier-general, became Under-Secretary for War.

The last act begins

Facing Weygand's 71 divisions, the German commander of Operation "Red" had massed 143 divisions – seven more than on May 10. Three of them had come from the German-Soviet frontier zone, thanks to the benevolent attitude of Stalin and Molotov since the Norwegian campaign. Three others had been diverted from the *Ersatzheer* or training army. And the single infantry division which had been occupying Denmark was also transferred to France. For the coming battle, Hitler and the O.K.W. staff installed themselves in the Belgian village of Brûly-de-Pesche, not far from the O.K.H. headquarters at Chimay.

The French 3rd Army Group was about to be attacked by a new and formidable German concentration under Bock. As the woods and steep gradients of the Chemin-des-Dames were unfavourable for armour, the new mass Panzer assault with its usual air support was to be made on the plain of Picardy: Kleist's *Panzergruppe* striking from Péronne and Amiens, and XV Panzer Corps debouching from Longpré, where Rommel's 7th Panzer Division held the railway-bridge. The battle was to rage for 48 hours without the French showing any signs of breaking. In fact, on the evening of June 5 Colonel-General von Bock noted in his war diary: "The French are defending themselves stubbornly."

Certainly, the new tactics which the French were using would not keep the Panzers at bay for long. "For the moment," wrote Hans-Adolf Jacobsen, "[the French tactics] had the following advantage: around Amiens and Péronne, our armoured divisions were able to push their tanks into the gaps between the enemy strongpoints, but our infantry, caught by the flanking fire from the villages, could not follow up. For this reason it was not possible to commit our motorised divisions on the first day."

Strauss' 9th Army, on the Laon sector, also scored mediocre successes on the first day. At Army Group "B" H.Q., the first impression was that this would be a long, hard fight. At Ablaincourt, Captain Jungenfeld, commanding a tank battalion of the 4th Panzer Division, had nine tanks knocked out within minutes. Shortly afterwards his battalion suffered new losses and by noon had only penetrated some $6\frac{1}{4}$ miles into the French positions. Jungenfeld described the situation in the following words: "In front of us, every village and wood – one might even say every clump of trees – is literally stuffed with guns and defences; even small artillery detachments can put us under direct fire. Behind us is the glare of a vicious battle where one fights not only for each village, but for each house. We are not therefore surprised to find ourselves under fire from all quarters, and one could say: 'Nobody knows which is the front and which is the rear.' "

And resistance like this was being put up by the French 19th Division, covering seven miles of front and faced by two German corps. On June 6, Bock noted in his diary: "A serious day, rich in crises. It seems that we are in trouble." But at the moment when, "with a heavy heart", he was about to order XIV Motorised Corps to break off the action at Amiens to reinforce the attack of XVI Panzer Corps, he heard of the successes of his 9th and 4th Armies.

On the left of the German front, 9th Army had thrust across the Chemin des Dames and had reached the Aisne at Soissons. Better still, on the German right, XV Panzer Corps had broken through the French 10th Army, and Rommel's 7th Panzer Division surged forward to Formerie and Forges-les-Eaux on June 7, scattering the 17th Light Division.

This situation forced General Besson to order General Frère to pull back 7th Army into alignment with 6th Army on its right and 10th Army on its left. But this withdrawal amounted to the total sacrifice of the divisions which had defended the line of the Somme so valiantly, and certainly resulted in the loss of most of their heavy weapons. The 7th Panzer Division, exploiting its successes on the 7th, thrust towards Elbeuf, where the Seine bridges were destroyed at the approach of his first tanks, then swung north-west to reach the Channel at Fécamp. This move trapped General Ihler's IX Corps (which included the French 31st and 40th Divisions and part of the British 51st Division, which had been transferred from the Maginot Line) plus the survivors of 2nd and 5th Light Cavalry Divisions, trapped with their backs to the sea. On June 12, 46,000 French and British troops surrendered at St. Valéry-en-Caux, while 3,300 succeeded in breaking through the German ring.

Winston Churchill was born in 1874, the son of a distinguished English politician and an American mother. At Harrow School and at the Royal Military Academy Sandhurst, he displayed little of the brilliance he was to reveal later in many fields.

During his early twenties he gained a reputation as a war correspondent in Cuba, South Africa and (as a serving officer) in India and Egypt; he subsequently became a prolific writer of biography, history, and war memoirs. In India he served on the North-West Frontier, and in Egypt took part in the Battle of Omdurman. In South Africa his escape from a Boer prison camp in 1899 brought him further notoriety. At the age of 26 he entered Parliament. He became Home Secretary in 1910, and First Lord of the Admiralty a year later, resigned in 1915 after the failure of the Dardanelles offensive, but before the war ended was appointed Minister of Munitions. In 1919 he organised the British Expedition against the Bolsheviks. From 1924 to 1929 he was Chancellor of the Exchequer, but all through the thirties he held no office. He became instead a lone voice against British complacency in the face of the rising European dictatorships, and was an untiring campaigner for rearmament. At the outbreak of war he returned to office as First Lord of the Admiralty, and after the fall of the appeaser Neville Chamberlain in May 1940 he was, even at the age of 65, the obvious and popular choice for Prime Minister.

CHAPTER 8
THE DRIVE TO PARIS

In the evening of June 10, on hearing the news that the Germans were crossing the Seine at Andelys and Vernon, President Lebrun and Reynaud's Cabinet left Paris and headed for Tours. Following the example given in 1914 by his predecessor, Myron T. Herrick, U.S. Ambassador William Bullitt stayed on in Paris. There is a case for the arguments of de Gaulle and the American historian Langer that Bullitt was wrong to do so, for his voice would have carried much weight both in the last French government talks at Bordeaux and in the final inter-Allied discussions. For their part, Generals Weygand and Georges withdrew to Briare with their staffs.

On the 9th, after issuing a vibrant appeal to his troops for continued resistance, Weygand had drawn up a note for the French Government. In it he warned, without yet abandoning hope of stabilising the situation, that the "decisive break-through" could come at any moment. He ended: "If this should happen our armies will fight on until they are exhausted, to the last round, but their dispersion will only be a matter of time."

At about 1000 hours on June 10, having listened to the opening paragraphs of Doumenc's report, Weygand sent a note detailing the ever-worsening situation to Reynaud, who had returned to his idea of a "Breton Redoubt" in a directly-argued appeal. Although the word "armistice" had not yet been pronounced, the basic differences between the French Government and High Command were deepening.

The solution to the conflict could have been – and should have been – the replacement of Weygand. Reynaud wanted this, and he had sounded out General Huntziger via de Gaulle, his Under-Secretary for War. According to de Gaulle, Huntziger would have agreed readily if the proposition had been put to him. Henri Massis, however, who was serving at the time in the 4th Army Group, takes the opposite

▽ On June 14 Paris surrendered, and the victors marched in triumph through the capital.

France's Agony

On June 9 Rundstedt's Army Group "A" entered the battle against General Requin's 4th Army between Neufchatel and Attigny and the French VII Corps. The French 14th Division fought superbly on the Aisne against the German XXIII Corps. Guderian's Panzergruppe managed to cross the river, however, and the 10th XXXIX Panzer Corps struck out for the south. On June 12 Guderian reached Chalons-sur-Marne. After the battle on the Somme, the battle for Champagne was lost. By June 11 Weygand had only 27 divisions to cover a front of some 280 miles between the Maginot line and the Seine estuary. Weygand ordered the withdrawal to a line Geneva-Dole-Avallon-Cosen (Loire)-Tours-Argentan-Caen-Mouth of the Orne. This longer line was to be covered by only 45 divisions.

On June 10, 1940, Italy went to war, mobilising 73 divisions. Of these 19 were complete, 34 usable, 20 at a state of low efficiency. The Italian divisions were under-strength. The Italian navy had two battleships, 19 cruisers, 126 destroyers and torpedo boats and 117 submarines. Four other battleships were completing trials. However, the fleet was low on oil and had no aircraft carriers. Italy did not have fighter aircraft capable of defending her cities.

France: the Fatal Decision

On June 13, Churchill and Lord Beaverbrook met Reynaud at Tours. On June 16 the British Government agreed to France seeking a separate armistice with Germany on the condition that the French sailed forthwith to British harbours. The British also asked for the evacuation of all Polish, Czech and Belgian troops fighting with the French Army. In the event, 24,300 Poles and 5,000 Czechs were embarked for England. After the British proposal for a Franco-British Union had been rejected, Reynaud's Government fell on June 16-17. Petain formed a new Government on June 16, including Weygand, as Chief of National Defence, and Admiral Darlan, who retained command of the Navy. The new Government agreed an armistice at 0100 hours on the 17th. General de Gaulle flew to London.

▽ *Mounted trumpeters of a ceremonial unit about to play a fanfare.*

view; and considering the personal friendship between Huntziger and Massis his opinion is probably nearer the mark. The affair went no further, Reynaud deciding to leave things as they were; and this is why (if we replace with "armistice" the word "peace", which he uses incorrectly) de Gaulle was right when he wrote that in taking this decision Reynaud was following "the idea of taking the road of war with a supreme commander who wanted to take the road of peace".

In the meeting of the Supreme War Council held at Briare on the evening of June 11 and on the morning of the 12th, Churchill brought the entire French delegation, including Reynaud, round against him. Resolute and optimistic as to the final outcome of the war, but remote from the actual conflict, he gave a definite "no" to the French request for immediate air aid.

No less than 20–25 British divisions would be fighting beside the French by the following spring; but in the meantime the only British troops in France were the 52nd Division, which had just crossed the Channel, and the 1st Canadian Division, which was disembarking at Brest. A third division would follow on about June 20. At the time of the Briare conference, what more could Churchill offer? It is clear that the R.A.F., entering the fray above the land battles which were developing on the lower Somme and in Champagne, would have been unable to redress the balance, while the French Air Force, left to its own resources, had been largely destroyed as a fighting force. In addition to this, one

particular suggestion by Churchill aroused the unanimous opposition of the French leaders: "Will not the mass of Paris and its suburbs present an obstacle dividing and delaying the enemy as in 1914, or like Madrid?"

Quite apart from the fact that Churchill did not apply this argument in the case of the Channel Islands but had them evacuated on the signing of the armistice, his suggestion that Paris be defended was an empty one because neither O.K.H. nor Hitler intended to fight a costly battle for Paris, although this was not known at the French High Command. The French divisions which had been earmarked for the defence of Paris therefore remained inactive, a complete loss to the defence which Weygand was trying to improvise on the Loire.

The day of June 12, when the debate on these grave matters continued, began with a comical incident which might have influenced Churchill's good humour in the morning discussions. According to Benoist-Méchin: "All was calm at the Château du Muguet where Churchill passed the night. Two officers on Weygand's staff were having their breakfast in the dining room (converted into a conference room the day before). Suddenly the door of the room was flung open. In the doorway there appeared a strange sight, a sort of Japanese demon swathed in an ample red silk kimono held in with a white silk belt, a bulky figure with disordered hair who bellowed angrily: *'Uh ay ma bain?'*"

It was Churchill, finding that the service in the château left much to be desired. The French officers were paralysed by the apparition and took several moments to recover themselves; but, as the British liaison officer, General Spears, noted: "The Prime Minister, as usual, got his way, and efforts were made to satisfy him." When Spears arrived at Muguet he found Churchill dressing in his room. "He was in a very bad humour."

The Panzers flood south

At Briare on June 12, Weygand repeated that he hoped to hold on with British help. But on the afternoon of the same day he declared in the French Council: "I will continue to resist, if the Council orders me to do so. But as of this moment I have to make this clear: the ending of hostilities must be considered soon."

On the 13th, driving through the shattered French armies on the lower Somme and in Champagne, the Panzers fanned out in their southward advance: Hoth's group headed for Normandy; Kleist, using the bridges at Nogent and Romilly-sur-Seine, made for the Massif Central and Burgundy; and Guderian swung east, heading for the flank and rear areas of Prételat's 2nd Army Group.

At this point, from the Siegfried Line, Leeb unleashed Operation "Tiger", sending seven divisions from General von Witzleben's 1st Army against the French Saar Detachment under General Hubert. The latter consisted only of General Echard's 52nd Division and General Duch's 1st Polish Division; but despite the fire of 229 artillery batteries and an entire Luftwaffe *Fliegerkorps*, the Germans made no notable progress on the 14th. During the night, however, General Hubert had to retreat in accordance with the order intended to realign 2nd Army Group along the Geneva–Dôle front.

This movement favoured the attack of General Dollmann's German 7th Army which, launching Operation "Bear", crossed the Rhine at Markolsheim and Neuf-Brisach at dawn on the 15th. The XXVII Corps under General Brandt succeeded in gaining only 1¼ miles on the left bank of the Rhine that day, despite the fact that he was faced merely by fortress troops; but further bridging operations by the German sappers allowed 7th Army to expand into the plain of Alsace and to swing towards Mulhouse for a link-up with *Panzergruppe* Guderian.

Although he complains in his memoirs of having been given contradictory orders, Guderian had lived up to the nickname of "Swift Heinz" which his troops had given him. On the evening of the 12th he had been at Châlons-sur-Marne. By noon on the 14th he had reached St. Dizier, which fell to the 1st Panzer Division, urged on by Guderian towards Langres. Langres fell on the 15th, after an advance of 66 miles, and the division pressed on towards Besançon. On June 17 – his 51st birthday – Guderian joined his 29th Motorised Division (which had been advancing on the right of 1st Panzer Division) at Pontarlier on the Swiss frontier. When the news of this exploit came in, Hitler thought that a mistake had been made and that Guderian meant Pontailler-sur-Saône, 50 miles back.

This astonishing raid by XXXIX Panzer Corps indicates clearly enough that after St. Dizier the Germans found no further organised resistance to their advance, apart from some improvised shellfire at the entrances to towns. The same applied to XLI Panzer Corps. Having taken Verdun and Bar-le-Duc on June 15, XLI Corps found itself, 48 hours later, in the region of Vesoul-Port-sur-Saône and Bourbonne-les-Bains. On June 17 an O.K.H. order subordinated *Panzergruppe* Guderian and the 16th Army on its left to

▽ *At the march-past in the Place de la Concorde, von Bock takes the salute surrounded by his staff officers. It was the second time that Paris had fallen to the Germans in 70 years.*

The Partition of France

At Rethondes on June 24, 1940, France surrendered to Germany. The suspension of hostilities between France, Italy and Germany was set for 0035 hours on Tuesday, June 25. Mussolini's attack on south-eastern France was a failure and threw a blinding spotlight on the weaknesses of Italy's land forces in 1940. The German casualty figures after the battle for France reveal that the Germans suffered much more heavily after Weygand had taken command.

The armistice meant that Germany occupied the industrial northern regions of France while the south was to be left unoccupied under an 'independent' French government. Thanks to the superb fighting skills of the French Army of the Alps, Mussolini's clumsy attempt to overrun south-eastern France was a complete failure.

Army Group "C". Without losing a moment, the impetuous Guderian swung his Panzer corps through 90 degrees and gave them the following new objectives: XXXIX Panzer Corps – from Pontarlier and Besançon towards Belfort; and XLI Panzer Corps – from Vesoul and Bourbonne-les-Bains towards Epinal and Charmes.

As the 29th Motorised Division was approaching the Swiss frontier, XVI Panzer Corps on the left of *Panzergruppe* Kleist was entering the suburbs of Dijon. The day before, in a battle near Saulieu and Semur-en-Auxois, XVI Panzer Corps had smashed the last resistance put up by the remnants of the French 3rd Armoured Division and by Major-General Maczek's Polish 10th Armoured Brigade, which was fighting its first engagement. As soon as the armistice negotiations began Maczek marched his brigade across France from east to west and embarked it for England. In 1944 he and his compatriots would return to France in the battle for Normandy.

The southward flood of the Panzer advance cut off the line of retreat of all French forces east of the Argonne – 2nd Army Group and the 2nd Army on its left – between Longuyon and Vouziers. General Prételat, who had preceded his troops to their new sector, found himself cut off from them, and General Condé, commander of 3rd Army, took command of this last bastion of resistance. But before it became clear whether he would break out of the encirclement or fight and die where he stood, a wide gap, some 50 miles across, opened between the Swiss frontier and the Massif du Morvan, clearing the road to Grenoble, Toulon, and Marseilles for the invader.

Similar catastrophe had enveloped the opposite end of the front. On June 16, having reduced the pocket at St. Valéry-en-Caux, XV Panzer Corps crossed the Seine with Rommel in the van. In front of XV Panzer Corps was 4th Army, whose XXXVIII Corps, led by Manstein, had just reached la Ferté-Vidame, 49 miles south of the bridgehead which he had won. Weygand tried to form a new 10th Army from the survivors of the Somme battle and troops evacuated from Dunkirk, but these forces were mere debris, thrown piecemeal into the fray as soon as they disembarked and lacking all their heavy weapons.

On June 14 the leading troops of the German 18th Army entered Paris, declared an open city and evacuated the day before on the orders of General Héring. His forces, designated the "Army of Paris" had recently been formed between the right of 6th Army and the left of the 7th, both of them now falling back to the Loire.

Should France surrender?

In these conditions – made worse by the refugee exodus and German air attacks – discussions continued between the Allied governments and within Reynaud's Cabinet. It was no longer a question of continuing the fight or of defending metropolitan France: the question now was how to bring about an end of hostilities in conditions which would prove the least damaging for the permanent interests of defeated France.

The debate was still conducted according to the terms of the reciprocal undertakings exchanged by France and Britain in London on March 28, on the occasion of Reynaud's first visit, as Prime Minister, to London. These undertakings pledged the two powers not to conclude any peace treaty or armistice convention without the agreement of the other party. And at Tours on June 13 Churchill gave his formal refusal to release France from the undertaking which she had given.

Certain Frenchmen claimed after the event that as the agreement of March 28 had not been ratified by the French parliament it could not be considered as official. This, surely, is a technical quibble; it was certainly not cited by anyone at the time. But there are no grounds for claiming – as did Reynaud, Georges Mandel, César Campinchi, Jules Jeanneney, Edouard Herriot and others, both at Tours and at Bordeaux – that armistice negotiations blackened the national honour of France. The expression "When matters are impossible, nothing is binding" is not only common sense but a principle of right which is always valid.

In July 1945 the former President of the Republic, Lebrun, was examined as a witness in the trial of Marshal Pétain. His reply to M. Isorni, one of the defence advocates, was unambiguous: "From the moment when one of the two countries which signed a convention like that of March 28 retains part of its forces for its own defence, instead of risking it in the common battle – as the British Empire did – it can always keep a paper to recall us to the obligations written on it. But it no longer has the moral authority to say: I will not release you from your obligations."

It is perfectly true that in mid-June 1940 the Hurricanes and Spitfires of the R.A.F., which until then had played only a sporadic part in the battle, represented the main defence of the British Empire; more than that, considering the lack of military preparation of the United States, R.A.F. Fighter Command was in fact the champion of the entire free world, including defeated nations and neutrals. But this does not change the fact that the circumstances of 1940 speak strongly in favour of Lebrun's later argument.

In its appalling situation, with no hope of help from Britain, the French Government therefore had the right to claim its freedom of decision. But this does not necessarily imply that Reynaud's successor made the best decision in preferring an armistice to capitulation.

Armistice or capitulation?

Given this tragic alternative, opinions were divided at the time and remain so today. Hundreds of books have been written on the fall of Reynaud, his replacement by Marshal Pétain, the conclusion of the armistice, and the establishment of the Vichy régime.

A fair analysis can only be made by considering the facts which influenced the key personalities at the time in making their decisions, or the conjectures which could

have influenced their reading of the situation. It is misleading, therefore, to refer to documents later discovered in the German archives, which the victors examined after the German surrender in May 1945, in judging the events of June 1940.

While trying to get Weygand to open negotiations with the Germans for the capitulation of the armies entrusted to him, Reynaud wanted to keep the alliance with Britain intact and continue hostilities against Germany. If it crossed to Algiers, his Government would have been able to use the entire French Navy, what could be saved of the Army and Air Force, and the human and material resources of the French Empire. But the counterpart of this plan meant the total surrender of the army – captivity for every man wearing French uniform. And when the Armistice was signed, the Germans announced that they had taken 1,450,000 prisoners. Moreover, Reynaud and his supporters consented to the total occupation of France, not only by the German victors but also by the Italians, who had been unable to make

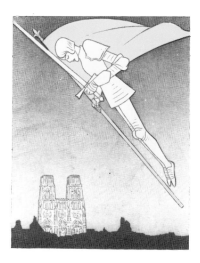

△ *German comment on the politics of the war from the magazine "Simplicissimus": Joan of Arc prays that it will be the last time that France has to shed her blood for England.*
▽ *German soldiers stand before Joan's statue at the site of her first great victory at Orléans shortly after taking the town on June 24.*

△ Apparently indifferent to their fate, these French prisoners lie stretched out in the sun, the image of resignation.

good their claims by force. Finally installed at Toulon, Marseilles, and Port-Vendres, the Axis powers would have been able to carry the war to North Africa.

General Noguès, French C.-in-C. in North Africa, had already been required to send a large proportion of his troops and most of his modern weapons to reinforce the armies in France. On May 20 he had had under his orders 11 infantry divisions, a light division, and two cavalry brigades; a month later he was reduced to eight divisions – three of them territorial – with considerable patrolling and policing duties.

In Libya, Marshal Italo Balbo had mobilised 14 divisions, of which nine were concentrated west of Tripoli. In the west, across the Moroccan frontier, French Intelligence had identified no less than five Spanish divisions, stationed between Ceuta and Larache. How would Spain react if there were no armistice and Hitler decided to carry the war into North Africa? At the very least it seemed that General Franco, who had just occupied Tangier in defiance of international statute, might well open Spain to the passage of the Wehrmacht.

Could the French have reinforced North Africa with troops withdrawn from metropolitan France? This had been thought of, but too late. Nor was this surprising, for according to Navy calculations it would

have taken a fortnight to collect sufficient tonnage to transport several hundreds of thousands of men and their equipment. This means that if the project were to have been possible a decision would have had to have been taken around June 1.

On that date it would have been impossible for the French Government to have made the deliberate decision to abandon the whole of France before the crucial battle had been fought – the battle on whose outcome Weygand was far from pessimistic.

In any case, the Germans would have been hard on the heels of the retiring French; and considering the enormous breach which opened on the French right flank, there is every reason to believe that the French defenders of the Loire would have been cut off from the Mediterranean.

The day before the armistice came into being XVI Panzer Corps, which had reached Valence, was ordered by O.K.H. to prepare for an advance against Toulon and Marseilles. At the same time Guderian was ordered to gather his *Panzergruppe* near Montluçon and head for Toulouse, Bordeaux, and the Atlantic coast. Pétain and Weygand were without a shadow of doubt unaware of these orders when they made their decision in favour of an armistice, but a simple look at the map told them that a new encircling move by the Germans could be started at any moment.

The French and Royal Navies could have intercepted any attempts to land Axis troops on the central sector of the Algerian coast; but the bitter experience of Norway had shown that sea power was of no avail in narrow waters without supremacy in the air. It would have been possible for the Spaniards, reinforced by the Germans, to have attacked Morocco across the Strait of Gibraltar, while the Italians, with the aid of the Luftwaffe, attacked Tunis across the Sicilian Channel. As for the numerous French aircraft which landed in Algeria during the last days of the campaign, the question of their supply and replacement only raised new problems.

Faced with all these difficulties, General Noguès ended by rallying, with a heavy heart, to the idea of an armistice. He lamented that American aid had not been requested but at this stage, this was more symbolic than real, for Roosevelt's policy had sadly disarmed the United States.

All this reasoning can be criticised on the grounds that Hitler in fact had no intentions of the kind. This is true, but in war one very rarely has the enemy's plans before one, and every possible enemy move must be considered. And the possibility of Hitler choosing to exploit his victory on the far shore of the Mediterranean could not be taken lightly at the time. This was made clear when, on June 19, the Germans asked the beaten French for the use of certain air bases in North Africa and for the authority to set up meteorological bases there. The fact that the request was dropped when the Vichy Government refused to make any concessions of this kind does not make it any the less significant.

Such were the pros and cons of the choice of policy which Reynaud recommended to his colleagues. But he did not fight for it to the bitter end. It seems clear that he had offered his resignation to President Lebrun before the majority of his colleagues had opposed his plans, knowing (none better) that at this crucial moment there was no alternative but an armistice.

First and foremost among the advantages of the latter solution was the fact that a government would be preserved in France at the moment when, invaded, her communications were cut by German air raids and the demolitions of retreating troops, and when 15 per cent of her population consisted of homeless refugees. The appalling fate of Poland, administered by *Reichkommissare* selected for their Nazi Party fanaticism, had become known to the world by 1940. For France in 1940, it

seemed better to spare the population a similar fate, despite the rigours of a military occupation which, it was hoped, would apply to as small a part of the country as possible.

Moreover, an armistice would leave France with an army. Certainly, nobody who supported an armistice believed that the victors would leave the French Army the military necessities to resume the struggle with any chance of success. But the example of the German Army after Versailles spoke for itself. If even a part French Army survived, it could also serve as the basis of future hopes. Meanwhile the Army would demobilise itself, concealing as much war material from the German commissions of inquiry as it could, and retaining the documentation which would make a future remobilisation possible. In addition, in their habitual secrecy, the Intelligence sections of the Army, Navy, and Air Force, together with the counter-espionage department, would continue to function.

It was clear that Germany and Italy

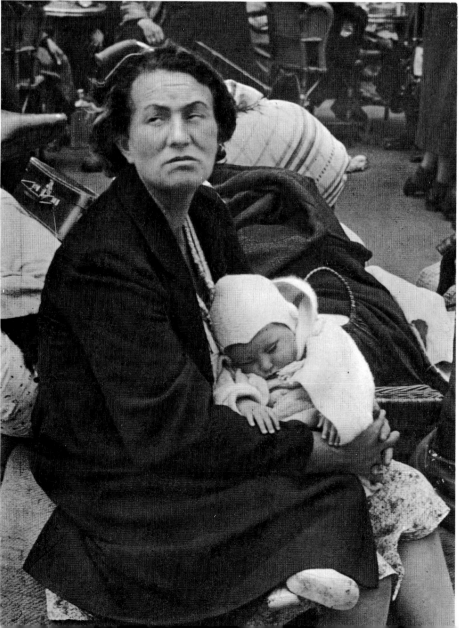

△ Exhaustion did not hit only the losers in the Battle of France, as this photograph of weary German gunners indicates. In the six weeks of almost continual campaigning, the non-motorised infantry divisions covered great distances trying to keep up with the Panzers.

◁ △ The flood of refugees (it eventually swept up 15 per cent of the population) streams towards the south, further complicating the already over-burdened supply system.

◁ ▽ Utterly dejected by the situation, a French mother clutches her child and waits in vain for a train away from the fighting.

would not agree to any arrangement which, suspending hostilities in metropolitan France, would not also apply to the fleet and to the Empire. For this reason Weygand, on June 13, had proposed that the fleet be sent to Britain to prevent it falling into enemy hands. This solution had met with the approval of both Churchill and Roosevelt. But how could the French fleet have quitted Toulon, Bizerta, and Mers el Kébir without exposing North Africa, Corsica, and possibly even Provence to Italian naval attacks, and perhaps even landings? This suggestion, too, was rejected by the French Council of Ministers.

Despite all this, even though neutralised, the French Empire and its fleet remained trump cards of the French régime set up after the armistice. If Hitler and Mussolini tried to go too far, they could be made to understand that if they were obdurate the Empire and the fleet would go over to the Allies. This naturally worked the other way: Hitler and Mussolini could make it equally clear that the existence of unoccupied France could depend on the submission of the Empire and the fleet.

Pétain's problems

When Marshal Pétain replaced Reynaud late on June 16, he estimated that the sup-

porters of an armistice would be outnumbered by those who wanted to continue the war, which meant that the army would eventually have to surrender. But Weygand believed that the honour of the army which he still commanded must prevent him from sending envoys to ask for terms. He had violently rejected similar propositions which Reynaud had made to him, even when the latter had offered to absolve him from responsibility by giving him written orders.

If the choice of an armistice proved to be the less disastrous alternative, one good reason was that General de Gaulle had joined the "dissidents", as they were known during the summer of 1940. Among those who heard de Gaulle's appeal on June 17 – "France has lost a battle! But France has not lost the war!" – were Hitler and Mussolini. German and Italian diplomatic documents prove how attentive they were to every manifestation of "Free France", and this restrained them in the two separate armistice negotiations at Rethondes and the Villa Incisa. Future months would prove this; as Hitler complained to Mussolini in January 1941, without de Gaulle and his Free French, the "Weygand blackmail" would have been much more difficult, if not impossible.

In the meantime, the Axis still had to be persuaded to agree to French rearmament in North Africa.

CHAPTER 9

BATTLE OF BRITAIN

As in the days of Philip of Spain, Louis XIV, and Napoleon, Britain's chances of resisting an invasion from the Continent depended on retaining control of the Channel and the North Sea.

For an attack on Britain in 1940, Hitler was considerably weaker than Napoleon had been in 1805. The heavy naval losses suffered in the Norwegian campaign had reduced the German fleet to the strength of one pocket-battleship, four cruisers, and a dozen destroyers. But the enormous superiority of the British Home Fleet, based on Scapa Flow, was countered by the numerical strength of the Luftwaffe, plus the danger represented by U-boats and torpedo-boats. This triple threat would have made Home Fleet operations in the Narrow Seas far too hazardous, and the Admiralty, in the light of the experience of Dunkirk, was unwilling to risk the fleet further south than the Wash.

Thus the Channel and the southern approaches to the North Sea became a sort of naval no-man's-land. In the skies above these waters victory or defeat for the Luftwaffe would decide whether or not Germany risked an invasion attempt.

Britain's weaknesses after Dunkirk

Would a defeat for the R.A.F. have permitted the Wehrmacht to land—as envisaged by the O.K.H. Directive of July 27, 1940—on the coasts of Kent, Sussex, the Isle of Wight, and Dorset? At the time of the French armistice at Rethondes on June 22, the British Army in Britain totalled some 26 divisions, of which 12 had been formed recently and were not yet fully trained or equipped. The 13–14 divisions which had seen action in France had lost most of their artillery and anti-tank weapons, and had brought back only 25 out of their 600 tanks. Nor had the troops been assigned equal sectors of the south coast to defend. Around Brighton, Montgomery's 3rd Division had some 30 miles of coastline to watch; between western Sussex and Wales, Sir Alan Brooke's Southern Command consisted of

a corps staff and a mere three divisions, of which two were Territorial.

On June 26, Brooke wrote gloomily: "The main impression I had was that the Command had a long way to go to be put on a war footing . . . The more I see of conditions at home, the more bewildered I am as to what has been going on in this country since the war started. It is now ten months, and yet the shortage of trained men and equipment is appalling . . . There are masses of men in uniform, but they are mostly untrained: why, I cannot think after ten months of war. The ghastly part of it is that I feel certain that we can only have a few more weeks before the *boche* attacks."

This was hardly an exaggeration. On

Britain at Bay

On June 17 Churchill ordered the establishment of Force H under the Command of Admiral Sir James Somerville, based at Gibraltar and centred on the battle-cruiser *Hood* and aircraft carrier *Ark Royal*. On July 3 at 0700 hours, an officer from Force H delivered an ultimatum to Admiral Gensoul, commanding the French fleet at Mers el Kebir. At 1656 hours on July 13th, Force H opened fire on the four French warships in the harbour. Only the *Strasbourg* escaped. French losses were 1,297. At Alexandria the British Admiral Cunningham and French Admiral Godfroy overrode their orders and came to an agreement whereby the French Force X stationed there would be disabled.

△ *The Luftwaffe strikes against British shipping in the Channel–a turbulence of white water marks a near miss on a freighter.*

July 19 General Ironside, C.-in-C., Home Forces, had been relieved of his post. Although he was promoted to field-marshal and given a seat in the House of Lords, this was still seen as a disgrace, since it was only two months since he had been replaced as Chief of the Imperial General Staff by General Sir John Dill. But was Ironside alone responsible for the weaknesses of the British Army? In his memoirs, Eden says not. He refers to the "surprising bitterness" with which Dill criticised Hore-Belisha, former Secretary of State for War. "He had done damage to the army that could not be repaired in years, Dill said, commanders had come to look over their shoulders."

Passing Southern Command to General Auchinleck, who had done so well at Narvik, Brooke took over from Ironside and threw himself into intense and timely activity as commander of the Home Forces. Making lavish use of aircraft transport, he was everywhere, countermanding the strict defensive prescribed to all sectors and releasing mobile reserves for counter-attacks. But this was not enough: he also had to order that the areas in which such counter-attacks might have to be made were cleared for action, by demolishing the concrete obstacles which had studded village streets since May.

Brooke's responsibilities were far greater than the resources at his disposal. In the diary which he kept for his wife, he occasionally gave vent to the anguish which the immediate future caused him. On September 15 he wrote:

"Still no move on the part of the Germans. Everything remains keyed up for an early invasion, and the air war goes on unabated. This coming week must remain a critical one, and it is hard to see how Hitler can retrace his steps and stop the invasion. The suspense of waiting is very trying, especially when one is familiar with the weaknesses of one's defences. Our exposed coast line is just twice the length of the front that we and the French were holding in France with about eighty divisions and the Maginot Line. Here we have twenty-two divisions of which only about half can be looked upon as in any way fit for any form of mobile operations. Thank God the spirit is now good and the defeatist opinions expressed after Dunkirk are no longer prevalent. But I wish I could have six months more to finish equipping and training the forces under my command. A responsibility such as that of the defence of this country under existing conditions is one that weighs on one like a ton of bricks, and it is hard at times to retain the hopeful and confident exterior which is so essential to retain the confidence of those under one and to guard against their having any doubts as regards final success."

The organisation responsible for the defence of the island was not likely to soothe Brooke's worries. If the Germans had tried an invasion they would have encountered no inter-service high command capable of co-ordinating the efforts of the British Army, Navy, and Air Force. The First Sea Lord had no less than six "commanders-in-chief" under his orders, while the Chief of the Air Staff had three. And Brooke had no authority to give orders to any of them.

"This system," he wrote after the war, "presented grave dangers. If a landing had taken place I fear that Churchill, as Minister of Defence, would have tried to co-ordinate the activity of the different commands himself. This would have been a perilous mistake, for with his impulsive nature he would have tended to take decisions according to his intuition and not from a logical perspective."

It was no less urgent to replace the *matériel* lost at Dunkirk as soon as possible, to raise the divisions still training to battle-worthiness, and to arm the Home Guard, which in August 1940 contained one million volunteers. To this end, guns were taken from military museums and war memorials; the Drury Lane Theatre contributed a dozen rusty old rifles; shotguns and ammunition were commandeered; and even cutlasses from the navy of Nelson's day were distributed to the local defence volunteers.

Stepping up production

Meanwhile, the arms factories were accelerating their production all the time. On June 8 there were 72 infantry and cruiser tanks in Britain; this rose to 200 by August, and there were 438 by September 29. The production rate was expected to rise to 12–15 per week for infantry tanks and nine per week for cruiser tanks. But these tanks, although brand new, were – as Rommel was to prove in Libya – already obsolescent for modern armoured warfare.

Britain took over from France the military contracts which the latter had signed with the United States and which had not been completed by the time of the armistice. But, most important of all, Roosevelt agreed to provide Britain with 500,000 rifles and 900 75-mm guns, each supplied with 1,000 shells. By the "cash and carry" principle still in force, the British Merchant Navy was responsible for bringing these precious cargoes home, and this was done with no losses to U-boat attacks. Churchill commented that certain generals turned up their noses at these 900 guns, which dated from the end of World War I. But the British were desperately short of artillery: on June 8 there were only 420 field guns and 163 heavy guns, with 200 and 150 rounds per gun respectively. And during the second phase of the Battle of France the 75-mm gun had proved its worth as a tank-killer. On June 8 the British Home Forces had only 54 2-pounder (40-mm) guns which could be used against tanks.

By September 17 Brooke had the following resources for the defence of Great Britain and Northern Ireland: 29 divisions and eight independent brigades, six of which were armoured. These forces included two Canadian divisions, the 1st and 2nd, of which only the 1st Division had suffered at all (one man killed and five missing) during its recent excursion to France. This little army, faced with invasion, was outnumbered by an estimated four to one – and on top of that it was still not ideally deployed.

Raeder prepares for a Channel crossing . . .

During the winter of 1939–40, not wishing to be caught unprepared by a sudden demand from Hitler, Grand-Admiral Raeder had ordered his staff to make a study of the many problems which would have to be settled if he were ordered to transport the German Army across the Channel.

On May 21, 1940, at the moment when the Panzers were driving onwards from Abbeville towards Boulogne and Calais, Raeder told Hitler of the conclusions reached by these studies. But the information fell upon preoccupied ears. As late as June 20 Raeder had still received no reaction from Hitler on the subject: when he made his report and asked for instructions, all he got from the Führer were some vague suggestions for a scheme to transport Jews to Madagascar.

. . . and Hitler dallies

Hitler's indifference to Raeder's invasion suggestions on May 21 was not surprising: his attention was focussed on the battle in hand. He was apprehensive that the temerity of his generals would allow the French to stage a new "Miracle of the Marne", recovering as they had done in 1914. Later, on the eve of the arrival of the French armistice delegates at Rethondes, Hitler's dilatory attitude towards Raeder was the result of his uncertainty about the

best road to take now that France had been crushed. At Munich on the 18th, Ciano had seen Hitler as an actor preparing to play the part of Charlemagne, "the gambler who has made a big scoop and would like to get up from the table risking nothing more", and wondering if there were any real advantage in overthrowing the awesome mass of the British Empire. Would Churchill see sense? Would he fall? Either of the two would make an invasion of England unnecessary.

From June 25 to July 5 Hitler remained with a small group of consultants aboard his special train *Tannenberg* at Kniebis, near Freudenstadt in the Black Forest, waiting for the situation to become clarified one way or the other. On July 2 a landing in England was certainly the object of an order – but it was only a hypothetical case, together with several others, and no preparations were to be made yet.

It was on July 16, in Berlin, that Hitler signed his famous Directive No. 16 – *Seelöwe* (Operation "Sea Lion"). But the preamble to this document shows that even at this date the invasion was not regarded as inevitable. It stated: "Since England, in spite of her apparently hopeless military situation, shows no sign of coming to terms, I have decided to prepare a landing operation against England, and if necessary to carry it out.

"The aim of this operation is to eliminate the British homeland as a base for the further prosecution of the war against Germany, and, if necessary, to occupy it completely."

This was not, therefore, Hitler's final word. But a month had passed since the fall of Paul Reynaud's government and France's request for an armistice, and those 30 days had not been wasted by the British aircraft industry, ably stimulated by Lord Beaverbrook. Allowing for two more months of preparations and preliminary moves, an invasion would not be possible until September 16 – on the eve of the period of boisterous early autumn weather which would make the Channel impassable to light landing-craft.

From the Reichstag on July 19 Hitler addressed an ultimatum, dressed up as an offer of peace, to Winston Churchill. Churchill was recommended, in all conscience, to make the British people see reason, for he, Hitler, could see no reason for the struggle to continue. He would not be responsible for any further shedding of blood. London made no reply to this in-

solent harangue; and Hitler was forced to go ahead with the build-up for "Sea Lion". On July 27 Brauchitsch – recently promoted to Field-Marshal, together with 12 other Army and Luftwaffe generals – submitted a preliminary invasion plan to O.K.W. With 41 divisions, six of them armoured and three motorised, plus the Luftwaffe's 7th Parachute Division and the 22nd Airborne Division, the plan read as follows:

On D-Day (set at shortly after August 25) Rundstedt's Army Group "A" would cross the Channel with two armies:

Right flank: 16th Army (Busch), concentrated between Ostend and the Somme, would land between Ramsgate and Hastings; and

Left flank: 9th Army (Strauss), concentrated between the Somme and the Orne, would land between Brighton and Littlehampton, with a detachment on the Isle of Wight.

The Gravesend–Reigate–Portsmouth line was designated as the first objective for Rundstedt's army group.

Simultaneously, or after a short delay, depending on circumstances, Bock's Army Group "B" would launch Reichenau's 6th Army from the Cherbourg Peninsula against the Dorset coast. Landing between Weymouth and Lyme Regis it would strike towards Bristol, pushing a detachment across Devon.

At this moment the 9th Army would break the British defences along the North Downs, cross the Thames at Reading, and encircle London from the west. The second objective for Rundstedt and Bock was to be the line connecting Maldon on the North Sea with Gloucester on the Severn.

As the man responsible for the land forces during the assault crossing, and for their supply during the campaign, Raeder denounced the whole ambitious scheme as impracticable. Even by requisitioning every available vessel from the inland waterways and the fishing fleets – which would have serious results on war production and civilian food supplies – he would not be able to assure the landing

△ △ *Battle is joined: British machine gun bullets converge on a Heinkel 111 (left) and a Messerschmitt 110. Luftwaffe pilots were astonished by the manoeuvrability of the British fighters and the pulverising fire-power of their eight-gun batteries, four guns in each wing. This larger cone of fire did much to compensate for the fact that the German cannon caused more destructive hits; and, moreover, less accuracy was required than with cannon.*
△ *Direct hits on a Heinkel 111 (left) envelop the aircraft in smoke and flames; the starboard undercarriage leg has swung down. The picture at bottom right shows fragments flying from a Junkers 88, whose starboard engine is on fire.*

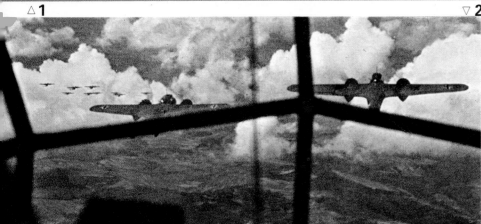

△ 1

▽ 2

The rival forces.
1. A Hurricane patrol in "fin-ger-four" formation. The British soon abandoned their rigid "vic" formations of three aircraft for this more flexible "finger-four" pattern, with each leader shielded by a wing-man.
2. Air-to-air view of a Dornier bomber formation.
3. A Staffel *(squadron) of Heinkel 111's in flight.*
4. Men of the British Observer Corps sent in vital reports of the German bomber formation.
5. A Schwarm *(unit of four) of Messerschmitt 109 fighters flies low over St. Margaret's Bay on the Channel Coast.*

▽ 3

▽ 4

▽ 5

of a first wave of 13 divisions, even if their numbers were considerably reduced.

The Navy also condemned the idea of a landing on the wide front envisaged by Brauchitsch, stating that adequate protection could not be guaranteed and recommending a crossing in the Pas-de-Calais sector. But Brauchitsch and Halder in turn refused to consider feeding troops into the narrow Ramsgate-Folkestone sector suggested by Raeder and his chief-of-staff, Admiral Schniewind.

The result was a compromise. The 6th Army venture from Cherbourg was dropped completely, and O.K.H. agreed to concentrate its right flank between Ramsgate and Folkestone. But the plan for 9th Army remained unchanged, and Rundstedt would still have a sufficiently wide front for his break-out. This adjustment lowered the invasion force to 27 divisions, nine of them in the first wave, each of which would land 6,700 men on D-Day, now set for September 21. A feint landing against the Norfolk coast was also planned, to draw off the British reserves from immediately behind the landing beaches.

As there was no German battle fleet to give heavy gunfire support, and as the Luftwaffe would be unable to provide total coverage for the assault, it was decided to give the landing troops the benefit of tank fire-power. To do this, some 128 Pzkw III and IV tanks were converted to allow them to be landed offshore and descend to the sea

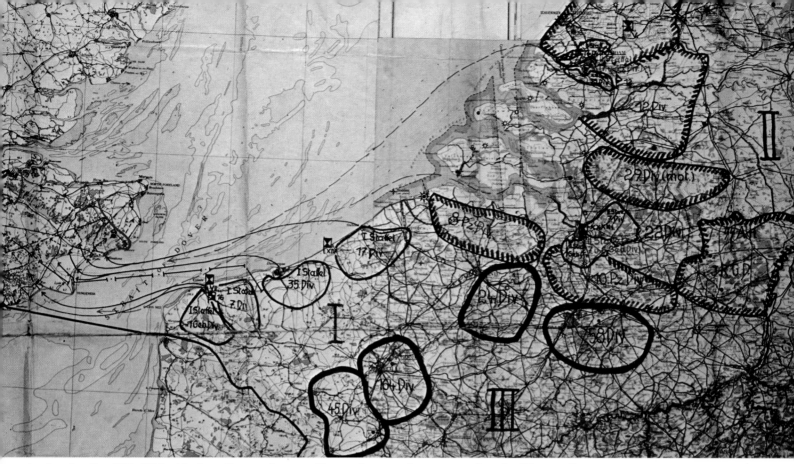

bed, a depth of 25–30 feet below the surface. Because of the extra 0.8 atmospheres pressure created at this depth, careful waterproofing was needed: the turret ring of each tank was sealed with an inflatable tube; and the crew and the engine got their air supply via a long, flexible snorkel tube supported on the surface, while a special valve coped with the exhaust problem. Special landing-craft with hinged ramps, and their bottoms reinforced with concrete to bear the weight of the tanks, would carry the tanks to their launch points off the British coast.

Experiments carried out by Reinhardt's XLI Panzer Corps off the island of Sylt in the North Sea proved that these submarine tanks were perfectly capable of carrying out this task. Finally, long-range artillery support was provided by coastal batteries which could reach the British coast between Ramsgate and Dungeness: four batteries between Sangatte and the north of Boulogne, with four 28-cm, three 30.5-cm, four 38-cm, and three 40.6-cm guns, with ranges of between 28 and 37 miles.

Onus on the Luftwaffe

Above all, the Royal Navy and the R.A.F. had to be prevented from attacking the sealanes which the 16th and 9th Armies would use. These extended eastward to Rotterdam and westward to le Havre. In view of the enfeebled state of the German Navy, this task fell squarely on the Luft-waffe. The latter would have to replace naval firepower on D-Day with massive Stuka attacks to neutralise the British coastal defences. But the whole operation depended on the preliminary removal from the board of the R.A.F. as a fighting force, and especially its fighter formations.

Hitler was well aware of this: his Directive No. 17 of August 1 ordered the intensification of naval and air operations against England, and the first paragraph read:

"Using all possible means, the German air forces will smash the British air forces in as brief a period of time as possible. Its attacks will be directed in the first instance against formations in flight, their ground facilities, and their supply centres, then against the British aircraft industry, in-cluding factories producing anti-aircraft guns."

When this had been done, the Luftwaffe was to turn against Britain's ports, crush-ing those on which the country depended for its supplies, but sparing the south coast ports which would be needed for supplying the invasion after the first landings. Finally there was to be no "terror-bombing" of open cities without the express order of the Führer: the whole weight of the Luftwaffe was to be used only on Britain's military potential.

△ *How the Germans planned to invade Britain. This O.K.W. map illustrates the rôle of 16th Army, which was to land in the sector between Hastings and Folkestone.*

Hermann Göring, as C.-in-C. of the Luftwaffe, made two fatal errors during the Battle. He called off the attacks on the British radar stations when they were on the verge of success, and ordered the fighters to stay with the slow, ungainly bomber streams in a defensive rôle, where they were helpless against British fighters.

Field-Marshal Hugo Sperrle was commander of *Luftflotte* III, which officially "opened" the Battle with heavy raids on August 13–*Adlertag* or "Eagle Day". Sperrle and Kesselring, commander of *Luftflotte* II, were the two principal German operational commanders in France and the Low Countries during the Battle of Britain.

Lieutenant-Colonel Werner Mölders was the greatest German ace and fighter tactician of the early years of World War II. He was the first fighter pilot to score over 100 "kills", and the first Luftwaffe pilot to be decorated with the Knight's Cross with Oak Leaves, Swords, and Diamonds–Germany's highest award.

Major Adolf Galland, like Mölders, was a veteran of the "Condor Legion" in the Spanish Civil War. After the Battle of Britain he stepped into Mölders's shoes as Germany's leading fighter ace, replacing Mölders as General of Fighters when the latter died in a crash in November 1941, and scored a total of 104 victories.

▽ *Britain's "eyes" during the Battle were the "Chain Home" radar stations which could detect the build-up of the big German bomber formations over France. This enabled Fighter Command to have squadrons brought to the alert and directed to their targets when the bombers crossed the English coast.*

The point of balance

Was the Battle of Britain lost before it began? Or did Hitler and Göring fail to make a thorough and methodical use of their advantages?

On August 13, 1940–*Adlertag*, the "Day of the Eagle"–the losses of the Battle of France had not yet been recouped by the Luftwaffe. (The French Air Force alone had caused the loss of 778 German aircraft.) To tackle England, the Luftwaffe was deployed in three air fleets:

Norway and Denmark: *Luftflotte* V (Stumpff);

Belgium and Holland: *Luftflotte* II (Kesselring); and

Northern France: *Luftflotte* III (Sperrle).

On August 13 the Luftwaffe deployed 2,422 aircraft against Britain: 969 bombers, 336 Ju 87 dive-bombers, 869 Bf 109 single-engined fighters and 268 twin-engined Bf 110 "destroyer" fighters.

The British, however, had come a long way since the days of the "Phoney War". Fighter production–157 in January 1940, 325 in May, 446 in June, and 496 in July–was no longer a serious worry. The supply of trained pilots was far more serious. On July 13 Fighter Command, led by Air Chief-Marshal Sir Hugh Dowding, had only 1,341 trained pilots; it would have to draw heavily upon the pilots of Coastal Command and the Fleet Air Arm, as well as forming four Polish and one Czech squadron in a few weeks.

This meant, on the surface, that this decisive battle would pit 1,137 German fighters against 620 R.A.F. Hurricanes and Spitfires–but the comparison is not as simple as that. The Messerschmitt Bf 110 twin-engined "destroyer" fighter– "Göring's folly"–was too slow and too sluggish to hold its own against the British fighters. On the other hand the Messerschmitt Bf 109E single-seat fighter was

1st Phase: Attacks on shipping and coastal ports (July 10 to August 7). German fighter tactics prove definitely superior, while the British Defiant turret-fighter is shown to be useless. The British concentrate on raising pilot strength and building up for the battle ahead. Losses: Fighter Command 169; Luftwaffe: 192 (+77 damaged).

2nd Phase: Attacks on radar stations and forward fighter bases (August 8 to 23). The climax of this phase occurs on August 15. Attacks from Scandinavia are repulsed with heavy losses, but in the south Fighter Command suffers heavy losses and pilots begin to show signs of extreme fatigue. Göring spares the R.A.F. by deciding to abandon attacks on radar stations. Losses: Fighter Command 303; Luftwaffe 403 (+127 damaged).

3rd Phase: Attacks on aircraft production and inland fighter bases (August 24 to September 6) with strong fighter escort to

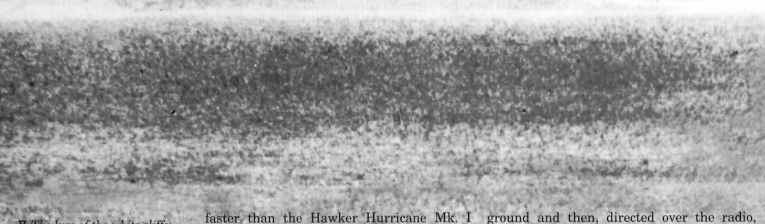

▽ The lure of the white cliffs: Goring (sixth from right) and his staff officers gaze across the Channel towards the British coast, 20-odd miles away. As the Battle went on and it became increasingly apparent that the R.A.F. had not been eliminated, Goring began to turn against his own pilots and accuse them of not giving of their best.

faster than the Hawker Hurricane Mk. I and about as fast as the Supermarine Spitfire Mks. I and II, although the latter machine had only begun to appear with the front-line squadrons of R.A.F. Fighter Command. The Bf 109 could climb faster than the British fighters; the British fighters were more manoeuvrable, and their batteries of eight machine guns gave

ground and then, directed over the radio, to intercept the enemy, often surprising him.

Second came the fact that Fighter Command was operation largely over British soil and could recover most of its shot-down pilots. German aircraft shot down over Britain almost always meant the loss of their crews as well as their machines. On

tempt British fighters up. The Bf 110 and Stuka have proved easy meat for the Spitfires and Hurricanes, but British pilot losses and fatigue have reached desperately high levels. Losses: Fighter Command 262; Luftwaffe: 378 (+115 damaged).

4th Phase: Attacks on London (September 7 to 30) in a final effort to destroy British air power after the realisation that Fighter Command is still a force to be reckoned with. Battle reaches climax on the 15th. "Sea Lion" postponed in definitely, and Germans switch tactics to high-level fighter-bomber raids. Losses: Fighter Command: 380; Luftwaffe: 435 (+161 damaged).

5th Phase: The aftermath (October 1 to 31). German fighter-bomber sweeps and preparation for the Blitz. Fighter Command reserves in aircraft and pilots increase rapidly. Losses: Fighter Command 265; Luftwaffe: 325 (+163 damaged).

them a bigger, though lighter, cone of fire that the German fighters.

Two paramount elements favoured the R.A.F. First was the defence radar network extending from the Shetland Islands to Land's End At the western extremity of Cornwall. Radar information enabled the British commanders to get their fighters off in sufficient time to avoid attack on the August 15, for example, the R.A.F. destroyed 70 German fighters and bombers. Some 28 Spitfires and Hurricanes were shot down that day – but half their pilots eventually rejoined their squadrons.

For some 25 years the accepted idea has been that the German air offensive reached its peak on Sunday, September 15; during a series of German attacks on London, the

Air Vice-Marshal Keith Park, commander of No. 11 Group, R.A.F. Fighter Command, responsible for the South-East. This group, under Park's brilliant leadership, bore the brunt of the fighting in the Battle. But after the Battle, Park was relegated to Training Command.

Wing-Commander Robert Stanford Tuck led No. 257 Squadron—the "Burma" Squadron— into action on September 15, the climax of the Battle. He scored two "kills" on this day, raising his personal tally to 16. He achieved a final score of 29 before being shot down in 1942.

Wing-Commander Douglas Bader, legless, opinionated, and aggressive, led the three squadrons of the "Duxford wing". His pleas for the use of fighters *en masse* caused much controversy in R.A.F. Fighter Command. Bader's final tally was 23. He was shot down in 1941 and captured.

Sergeant-Pilot "Ginger" Lacey (later commissioned) flew with 501 Squadron during the Battle. He was credited with shooting down the plane which bombed Buckingham Palace on September 13. Subsequently, Lacey served in the Far East, and finished the war with 28 confirmed victories.

British defence claimed to have shot down 185 German aircraft, a total lowered to 56 by the official post-war figures. In fact, although the British came close to defeat on the 15th they had already won, as much because of the mistakes of the German high command as the courage of the R.A.F. fighter pilots. The Luftwaffe's offensive had begun badly: in five days of operations between August 13 and August 17, the Germans lost 255 aircraft to the R.A.F.'s 184. As a result Göring withdrew *Luftflotte* V and the Stuka formations from the battle—*Luftflotte* V because it was badly placed to make worthwhile attacks on targets in northern England, and the Stukas because they were too vulnerable.

However, as long as the Luftwaffe kept up its attacks on the Fighter Command bases in southern England it was close to winning set and match. Many British aircraft were destroyed on the ground, and their essential runways riddled with bomb craters. Far more serious, however, was the fact that the operations centres, unfortunately sited on the airfields themselves and insufficiently protected against bombs, suffered heavy damage, which caused additional difficulties in co-ordinating the formations in the air.

During this phase—August 24 to September-6—the scales tilted heavily in favour of the Luftwaffe, which lost 378 aircraft as opposed to 262 British planes shot down or destroyed on the ground. On paper this suggests that the R.A.F. still had an advantage of 45 per cent—but in fact these figures were far more favourable to the Luftwaffe than might be imagined, because the German losses were shared between the fighters and the bombers. On the British side the brunt fell on Fighter Command, now reduced to under 1,000 pilots, constantly in action and desperately in need of rest.

With casualties of 15 to 20 pilots killed and wounded every day, Fighter Command was nearing its last gasp when suddenly the whole picture changed.

▽ *Hurricane patrol. As the Battle progressed the Hurricanes came to be reserved for the German bomber streams while the Spitfires tackled the Messerschmitt fighter escorts. The Hurricane was the R.A.F.'s mainstay in the Battle: there were 29 Hurricane squadrons as compared with 19 Spitfire squadrons on August 8, 1940.*

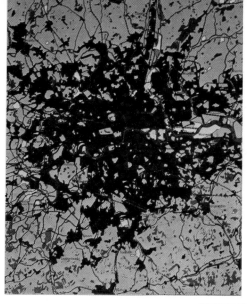

▷ △ *The navigator of a Heinkel searches for landmarks.*
△ *German Intelligence map of the London area, with principal military targets outlined in red.*
▽ *The Battle of Britain. Note how the British had the interior position, which gave their fighters a distinct advantage over those of their opponents.*

Turning-point: the London Blitz

Late in the evening of August 24, a German bomber formation accidentally bombed some non-military targets in London. Churchill's immediate response was to order a reprisal raid on Berlin. The following night, 81 twin-engined bombers took off for the German capital, but only 29 reached Berlin; the others got lost on the way. This modest raid cost the British eight men killed and 28 wounded – but this time it was Hitler's turn to lose control. Forgetting that he had formerly regarded "terror bombing" as a dangerous distraction from the main effort, he immediately ordered that London be given the same treatment as Warsaw and Rotterdam. On September 7 the first heavy "Blitz" raid broke on London, with some 330 tons of bombs being dropped.

The bombing of London continued for 57 consecutive nights – but it meant that Hitler and Göring had abandoned the principal objective of the directive of August 1. The Luftwaffe was unable to smother London with terror raids without relaxing the grinding pressure which it had been inflicting on the British fighters. Fighter Command recovered rapidly: between September 7 and September 30 the British gained the upper hand over the Luftwaffe, destroying some 380 aircraft for a loss of 178 of their own.

By October 31 the Luftwaffe had lost 1,733 fighters and bombers to the R.A.F.'s 1,379 fighters – but the R.A.F. had lost only 414 pilots killed (of whom 44 were Allied, mainly Poles). Churchill, therefore, was not exaggerating when he proclaimed the R.A.F.'s victory in the House of Commons with the immortal sentence: "Never in the field of human conflict has so much been owed by so many to so few." The same praise was repeated when he wrote *The Second World War* after 1945. But at the time he was far less satisfied with the results obtained. The brilliant C.-in-C., Fighter Command, Air Chief-Marshal Sir

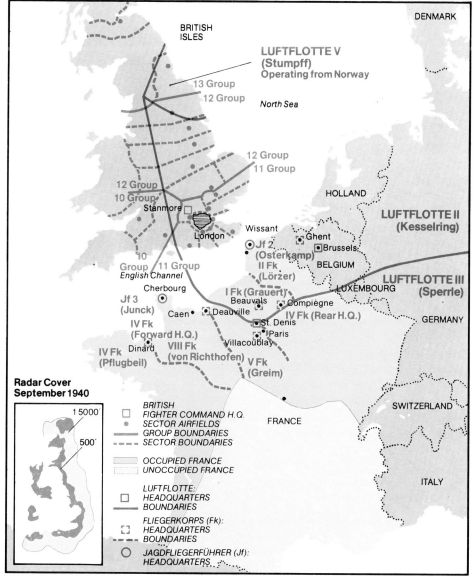

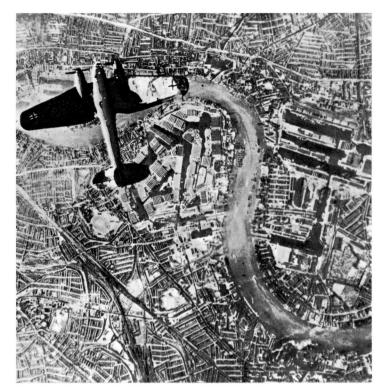

Hugh Dowding, and the commander of Fighter Command's No. 11 Group, Air Vice-Marshal Keith Park, the real brains behind the victory, were deprived of their commands within weeks and relegated to secondary posts. The ostensible reason was that there had been far too many faults in the field of radio communications and that the battle had been fought too much on the defensive, using "penny-packet" tactics.

The invasion postponed

Across the Channel the final preparations for Operation "Sea Lion" were being pushed ahead at an uneven pace. On shore, the troops of 16th and 9th Armies were concentrated around their embarkation points. At sea, however, the mine-laying and mine-sweeping programme intended to secure the invasion lanes from British attacks had suffered badly from attacks by Coastal Command—and Göring had failed to smash the R.A.F. Against the German invasion fleet—2,500 transports, barges, tugs, lighters, and light craft massed in the invasion ports between Rotterdam and Le Havre—R.A.F. Bomber Command was intensifying its attacks. True, the losses of the invasion fleet were under ten per cent, but they still had to be replaced.

On September 11 Hitler announced his intention of beginning the count-down for "Sea Lion" on the 14th, which would place the landing at dawn on Tuesday, September 24. But on the 14th he decided to take three more days to decide whether or not to give the final order.

In 1940, September 27 was the last day in which the tides were favourable for such a venture. From then on into October, the high seas and strong winds which could be expected in the Channel would be too much for the inland craft to risk the crossing; they would have stood a good chance of foundering. On the 17th, Hitler ordered "Sea Lion" to be postponed. Two days later he gave the order for the invasion fleet to be dispersed in order to protect it from British bombing, but in such a way that it could be readily re-assembled as soon as he needed it.

But the real implications ran far deeper. On October 12, while the ravages of the German Blitz were being extended across England, Keitel issued the following order from O.K.W.:

"The Führer has decided that until next spring the preparations for *Seelöwe* are to be continued with the sole intention of maintaining political and military pressure on Britain . . .

"Should the projected landing be resumed in spring or early summer, orders will be given for new preparations. In the meantime, it is necessary to shape conditions in the military sphere to suit a final invasion."

△ *The German switch of objective from the British fighter bases to mass daylight raids on London lost them the Battle.*

Air Chief-Marshal Sir Hugh Dowding has by far the strongest claim to being the victor of the Battle of Britain. Before World War II he spared no effort in building up Fighter Command into the magnificent weapon which it was in the vital summer of 1940. He stoutly resisted the demand to fling Britain's last reserve of fighter squadrons into the Battle of France, and so preserved the metropolitan fighter force which met and defeated the German attempt to gain day and night control of the air over Britain.

Hitler faces east

This order of October 12 reflects all the conditional uncertainty expressed in the "Sea Lion" Directive, No. 16, of July 16. Why did Hitler abandon the invasion? Was it because of the defeat which the inconstancy and presumption of Göring had brought upon the German air arm?

Certainly he had accepted that the whole idea of a landing in England had to be re-thought. On January 11, 1941, developing the subject during a visit by Ciano, Hitler compared himself with a marksman, only one cartridge in his gun, who wanted to make quite sure that he would hit the mark. But was he telling Ciano the whole truth? Or rather–having signed the "Barbarossa" Directive, No. 21, for the invasion of Soviet Russia three weeks before–was he disguising his real intentions for 1941?

To answer these questions we must examine Hitler's changing attitudes between his supervision of *Fall Gelb* in late 1939 and early 1940 and his postponement of "Sea Lion" in September 1940.

From the end of October 1939 until the end of June 1940, Hitler had been deeply involved in the planning for the invasion of France, in consultation with O.K.H. This was not all wrong: without Hitler's supervision, Manstein's suggestions would certainly have been suppressed and the outcome of the campaign would probably have been quite different. It also shows Hitler's strong desire to live up to his title of "Leader" by assuming total responsibility for the conduct of the war, and to impose his wishes on everyone.

None of this shows through between the signing of the armistice at Rethondes and the suspension of "Sea Lion". Obviously, this was a far more difficult operation for Hitler to dictate: an amphibious invasion without precedent in history. But his repeated retreats to Kniebis and Berchtesgaden, broken by a fortnight's stay in Berlin, show a certain uncertainty on Hitler's part as to the political and military decisions to be taken to assure the perpetual supremacy of the Third Reich.

No document has survived which allows us to unravel the thread of his solitary meditations. But on July 29, 1940, he spoke out.

On the afternoon of that day Jodl, head of the O.K.W. Operations Staff, returned from a visit to Hitler in the Obersalzberg.

Aboard his special train *Atlas*, which served him as a mobile command post, he summoned his deputy, Colonel Warlimont, and representatives from the three services: Lieutenant-Colonel von Lossberg, Lieutenant-Commander Junge, and Luftwaffe Major von Falkenstein. Under cover of the strictest secrecy, Jodl revealed the message which, like Moses, he had brought down from the mountain.

The Führer intended to launch an armed invasion of the Soviet Union in the following spring. As this news was received with shocked dismay by his listeners, Jodl followed with this argument:

"The elimination of the Bolshevik menace which constantly weighs on Germany renders this clash of arms inevitable. For this reason the best solution is to introduce it into the course of the present war."

Here was a singular argument, to say the least. But how had Hitler arrived at this fatal decision? Here again, documents are of little help. On June 19 at Munich, as we know from Ciano's diary, Hitler made absolutely no mention of his intention to attack Russia, although Moscow had finally put an end to the independence of Estonia, Latvia, and Lithuania a few days before.

Shortly after the armistice at Rethondes, Molotov summoned the Rumanian Ambassador to the Kremlin and gave him a 48-hour ultimatum to cede Bessarabia–a former province of Tsarist Russia–to the Soviet Union. The Rumanian Government appealed to Germany, but all it received from the Wilhelmstrasse was the advice to accede to Moscow's wishes.

The ensuing Soviet-Rumanian treaty not only restored to Soviet Russia Bessarabia–a territory which the Tsars had ruled since 1812 in defiance of the nationalist principle–but the Bukovina as well. The latter, on the north side of the Carpathians, had once been a province of the Austrian Empire, and the Kremlin had no historical claim whatsoever to it.

Was it the latter demand which precipitated Hitler's decision, being as it was a demonstration of insatiable Soviet imperialism which even a blind man could appreciate? In pushing westward the Soviet-Rumanian frontier from the Dniestr to the Prut, Soviet Russia had advanced 125 miles further to the southwest, putting its bombers within a 30-minute flight of the petroleum wells and refineries at Ploieşti–and Hitler's obsession with war economy, and liquid fuel in particular, is well known.

(page 87) *R.A.F. reconnaissance pictures show the ominous massing of German invasion barges in the cross-Channel ports. Bomber Command did its utmost to sink as many as possible–but after September 19 the pictures told a very different story. Hitler's invasion fleet was being broken up and dispersed to less vulnerable target areas. The threat of immediate invasion had clearly passed.*

All the same, following former Rumanian Foreign Minister Grigore Gafencu and his captivating book *The Origins of the War in the East*, one is bound even today to return to the view that it was the failure of "Sea Lion" which provoked this total change of direction. Just as Napoleon, abandoning the idea of reducing Britain by a direct attack, recoiled eastwards and set off on the road through Ulm, Austerlitz, Tilsit, and Moscow to Waterloo, so Hitler sought in the destruction of the Soviet Union the means of compensation for his helplessness on the Straits of Dover.

It is possible that as early as the end of June 1940 Hitler had been considering the idea of an attack on Russia, but that he shelved it as his attention became more

length upon the short-sightedness of both Hitler and Göring; for at this period their illusions were shared by every expert on strategic air power. When 36 British Wellington bombers dropped 36 tons of bombs on Turin, London announced that the Fiat factories had ceased to exist . . .

Although it was incapable of doing any serious damage to Britain's war production, the Luftwaffe's Blitz sowed fire and destruction across England and claimed over 40,000 victims, including 16,000 civilian dead. So it was that on Hitler's initiative the war was embarked on the course which between December 1940 and February 1945 would ravage Europe, from the fire raids on London to the destruction of Dresden.

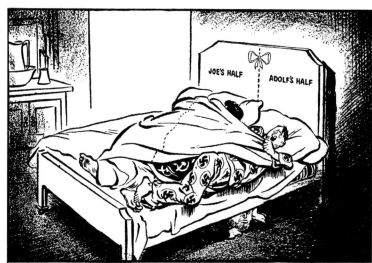

△ Evening Standard *cartoonist David Low ridicules Hitler's dilemma over the invasion of England, and (right) his relations with Stalin's Russia.*

and more focussed on the technical problems of "Sea Lion". He could hardly send the Wehrmacht across the Channel to knock out Britain, the last combatant left, while husbanding all his resources for a trial of strength with Stalin.

Hence Hitler's uncertainties in the summer of 1940. With one eye on London and the other on Moscow, hoping until the beginning of September for an arrangement with the British which would free his armies for an assault on the east, he directed the battle on too loose a rein, and left far too much to Göring. The idea of adopting night bombing instead of a direct attack in order to bring Britain to her knees was totally unreal, considering the losses suffered by the Luftwaffe. Even allowing for new aircraft construction, the Luftwaffe's strength now consisted of:

898 level bombers instead of 969;
375 dive-bombers instead of 346;
730 Bf 109 fighters instead of 869; and
174 Bf 110 fighters instead of 260.

But it is unfair to dwell exclusively at

Still in the ring

By autumn 1940 all neutral powers and the occupied countries knew that the Anglo-German struggle had not ended, and that this fight to the death would not be resumed until spring. What would happen then? On July 15 Weygand had said to Colonel P. A. Bourget, who had followed him from Beirut to Bordeaux; "although British victory is still not certain, neither is that of Germany". If Weygand was talking in this fashion only 20 days after the signing of the armistice, it is easy to imagine the tremendous encouragement given three months later to the early resistance networks forming in France, Belgium, and Holland by the postponement of "Sea Lion". Now the defeat of May-June 1940 had been proved to be provisional; Hell had become Purgatory; cruel sufferings lay ahead, but they would not last for ever . . .

CHAPTER 10
THE DUCE'S AMBITIONS

Fascist Italy had entered World War II at what seemed to her leaders to be her hour of destiny. But the total and unforeseen collapse of the Allied armed forces resulted in crippling problems for Ciano and Mussolini.

What was Hitler planning next? At the time of the conference at Munich on June 19, Ciano got the impression that Hitler did not wish to risk losing his winnings. If he maintained his current attitude, would he hesitate to sacrifice the international claims of Fascist Italy on the altar of a German-British agreement, to restore the racial solidarity, so to speak, of the

Teutonic race? The Italian régime believed that a premature peace settlement would hardly suit Italy's interests, as was proved by the fact that the French-Italian armistice had yielded Mussolini nothing more than Menton and two or three Alpine villages.

But although the Fascist leaders were not eager to see a rapid end to hostilities, they certainly did not want to associate with their German allies in any military ventures upon which Italy might embark in pursuit of her claims in the Balkans and the Mediterranean. This would only have meant offering Hitler a share of the

△ *Italian bomber crewmen by their aircraft. Despite its convincing numerical superiority in the Mediterranean theatre the Italian Air Force soon proved its inadequacies. During the first brush between the British and Italian fleets the Italian bombers did virtually no damage to the enemy – and they launched as many attacks on their own warships as against the British.*

spoils, and as the past history of the Axis had revealed that Germany always desired at least 50 per cent of the cake it is not hard to understand the Italian doubts.

Hitler's contempt for weaker members of the Fascist Party – men like "that swine", as he called Minister of Justice Count Dino Grandi – extended to King Victor Emmanuel III and the House of Savoy, the Pope and the Vatican, and to the entire aristocracy and bourgeoisie of the country. If, as he believed, "traitors" abounded in the most secret councils of his friend Mussolini, there was all the more reason to reveal only the sketchiest hints of his projects to the Duce, and even then to do it as late as possible.

In his distrustful attitude towards Italy Hitler found no opposition from his generals. Quite the contrary: all of them had fought in World War I and remembered what they called Italy's "defection" from the alliance of the Central Powers to the Allied *Entente* in May 1915. Nor were these professional soldiers in the least impressed by Mussolini's martial swaggering. They strongly suspected that although Fascist Italy's military structure looked impressive, it was built of plaster rather than marble.

As we have seen, the German Army High Command had opposed the suggestion to employ an Italian army in Alsace during the last stage of the Battle of France. While armistice negotiations were still in progress, a suggestion from General Mario Roatta, Deputy Chief-of-Staff of the Italian Army, caused great indignation in his colleague Halder, who noted in his diary on June 24: "The Italians are halted before the French fortifications and are getting nowhere. But in the armistice negotiations they still want to secure an occupied zone of French territory which will be as big as they can get. To this end they have proposed sending to List's front a certain number of Italian battalions to be flown in by air, either by way of Munich or direct to Lyons, and to have them occupy the areas to which Italy wants to extend her right of occupation. All this is nothing more or less than a piece of the most vulgar deception. I have stated that I refused to be associated with the whole business."

Marshal Badoglio, however, also refused to put his name to this sordid project, drawing from Halder the complimentary statement: "According to all appearances, he is the only real soldier among this whole delegation of negotiators."

There can be no doubt that the forthright opinions expressed in Halder's diary were shared by every general close to Hitler and capable of influencing the Führer's decisions.

With all this political and psychological friction there could be no question of the two Axis partners co-ordinating their

△ *Cartoon by Lino Palacia of* La Razón *shows that the flaws in the Axis relationship were visible even in Buenos Aires.*
Hitler: *'Want a push?'*
Mussolini: *'Okay, but not too hard. I'm frightened of getting seasick . . .'*
▷ *Italian Army spit and polish:* Bersaglieri *parade with 47-mm anti-tank guns – an arm in which most Italian units were pitifully weak. Reforms in basic equipment and supply were long overdue when Mussolini went to war – and the man who suffered was the Italian soldier.*

efforts with a common objective in view, as Britain and the United States would do after Pearl Harbor. Still less was there any chance of creating an Axis counterpart to the Allied Combined Chiefs-of-Staff in Washington, where, although discussions were often acrimonious, the final decisions reached were religiously carried out.

Rome and Berlin therefore followed a system of "parallel war", but with astonishing mutual concealment and even double-dealing. Both General Efisio Marras, for all his title of "Italian Liaison General at O.K.W.", and his opposite number attached to the *Comando Supremo*, General von Rintelen, were scantily, badly, and tardily informed of the intentions of the two dictator-warlords.

The Germans were understandably incensed when, on October 28, 1940, they found that Mussolini had concealed his intention to invade Greece until the last moment. "Shocking and stupid!" exclaimed Keitel, when he heard the news of the first Italian defeats on the Albanian front. Certainly Keitel had a point, for all the harshness of its expression. But what did Keitel say when Hitler made his decision to make a total reversal of his policy and invade Soviet Russia, without informing Mussolini?

Germany's anger about Mussolini's Greek campaign is well attested. "In November I went to Innsbruck to meet the German Chief-of-Staff, Marshal Keitel," wrote Badoglio. "He immediately pointed out that we had launched an offensive against Greece without having made the least notification to the German Command. The Führer was adamant that the situation in the Balkans must not be disturbed. Germany was receiving important supplies from those countries, which she now seemed in danger of losing. 'If I had known,' said Keitel, 'I would soon have come to Rome to halt this campaign.'

"I had to tell him the truth, that I had been ordered by Mussolini to say nothing to Germany. He had in fact given me this order, and when I commented that an alliance put certain obligations on us, Mussolini replied furiously: 'Did they ask us anything before attacking Norway? Did they ask our opinion when they wanted to start the offensive in the West? They have acted precisely as if we did not exist. I'll pay them back in their own coin.'"

One would certainly have expected an operation aiming at the conquest of

Greece, and above all of the Greek archipelago, to have been on the agenda of Mediterranean strategy at the Brenner Pass conference on October 4, 1940. No operation of the scale of Operation "Barbarossa", the invasion of Russia, was mentioned – a venture which could have been only prejudicial to Italy's interests in the immediate future.

In attacking the Soviet Union, Hitler proposed to deprive Britain of the last ally which she could win on the Continent. But the relaxation of the pressure of the combined forces of the Wehrmacht on Britain could mean only that the joint enemy of the Axis would be able to recover a certain freedom of action.

Such was the system of "parallel war" which Mussolini congratulated himself upon having established against the wishes of his ally and friend. He was confirmed in his euphoria by another factor: when Churchill ignored Hitler's "peace offer" at the end of June 1940, it meant that the war would continue. And

△ *Fascist propaganda in Rome: "Mussolini is always right". Was it true that in Italy the man in the street went reluctantly to war in 1940? Sir David Hunt, then an Intelligence officer, thinks not. "I believe, on the contrary, that the war of 1940 was the most popular war the Italians were ever engaged in ... For the first five months of the war at least, all the prisoners we and the Greeks took spoke with great confidence of a successful outcome and boasted of the future greatness of Italy, victorious at the side of Germany."*

▷*Fascist propaganda in Rome: "Mussolini is always right". Was it true that in Italy the man in the street went reluctantly to war in 1940? Sir David Hunt, then an Intelligence officer, thinks not. "I believe, on the contrary, that the war in 1940 was the most popular war the Italians were ever engaged in ... For the first five months of the war at least, all the prisoners we and the Greeks took spoke with great confidence of a successful outcome and boasted of the future greatness of Italy, victorious at the side of Germany."*

as Mussolini said to Badoglio on September 22: "I am happy that the war will not end quickly, for that would be to our total disadvantage. A rapid peace would be a setback for us."

Mussolini, warlord

But again the Duce was forgetting the enormous deficiencies in armaments with which Fascist Italy had gone to war, and the impossibility of making them good in a prolonged war because of Italy's lack of adequate raw materials. It was only a few months since the plain facts had been put before him and he had said to his Chief of the General Staff: "This time I will declare war, but I will not wage it. This way I will get big results for using little effort."

On assuming supreme command, however, Mussolini was soon to give the most obvious proof of his lack of military talent. Before his contemporaries, Benito Mussolini, with his strutting stance, jutting chin, hand on hip or thumb hooked in belt, certainly acted the part of a dynamic and resolute commander. Even today, he is represented by the conformist and ill-informed historical viewpoint as a despot who imposed his inexorable will upon the Italian people, after deep and inhuman meditation. But eye-witness accounts and documents show his weathercock nature, his inability to make a decision and stick to it, his lack of method, his ignorance of the basic problems of organisation and command. No Napoleon, in fact.

An important source is the diary of General Quirino Armellini, Badoglio's main colleague at *Comando Supremo*. Despite the fact that Armellini was opposed to the Fascist régime, the notes which he took between May 11, 1940 and January 26, 1941 – when he was disgraced – are not totally malevolent and tell an eloquent story.

The Alpine offensive had not yet begun when he wrote, on June 21: "The longer I stay at this post, the more I see of the disorder, lack of preparation, and muddle in every sphere, which seriously delay or completely prevent the functioning of the High Command; the more I believe that military necessities are being completely overlooked; and the more I am convinced that everything has yet to be done, or must be done again."

On August 15 he was more bitter still. "What once seemed an interesting prospect today disgusts me! We continue in the greatest disorder and complete chaos. In *Comando Supremo*, everyone commands. The last man to speak is always right. Strategic conceptions are regularly reversed with an astonishing lack of logic.

"Someone will say: 15 days from now we must be ready to march against Yugoslavia; or, in eight days we will attack Greece from Albania – as easily as saying, let's have a cup of coffee. The Duce hasn't the least idea of the differences between preparing for war on flat terrain or in mountains, in summer or in winter. Still less does he worry about the fact that we lack weapons, ammunition, equipment, animals, raw materials."

Armellini's laments are typical of many, and all would be disastrously confirmed on the battlefield. But when blaming Mussolini and the Fascist régime, how much of the military chaos can be laid at the door of Marshal Badoglio, and, in more general terms, of the Italian Army? In 1946, Badoglio stated that his resignation "would not have resolved the situation", for Mussolini would never have gone back on his pact with Hitler; and Badoglio added: "By retaining my position, I could at least prevent some disastrous move from being made; for this was all which could have been expected from Mussolini, who was completely lacking in any military knowledge."

Badoglio had not invented this explanation to defend himself. On August 15, 1940, he had said to Armellini: "Although it may be a small thing, perhaps I can do more with him than someone else. We

PRE RAGIONE

must carry on, saving what can be saved, and trying to avoid sudden moves which could lead to more serious consequences."

Writing on St. Helena after Waterloo, Napoleon had thought very differently. "A commander-in-chief cannot take as an excuse for his mistakes in warfare an order given by his minister or his sovereign, when the person giving the order is absent from the field of operations and is imperfectly aware or wholly unaware of the latest state of affairs.

"It follows that any commander-in-chief who undertakes to carry out a plan which he considers defective is at fault; he must put forward his reasons, insist on the plan being changed and finally tender his resignation rather than be the instrument of his army's downfall."

No sooner, however, had Italy entered the war than setbacks assailed her in all theatres of operations.

The air and sea offensive ordered by Mussolini never truly got under way. What was worse, by June 29 the Italian Navy had lost ten out of the 117 submarines with which it had entered the war, sunk in the Red Sea and the Mediterranean. There was a very good reason for the losses (4 boats) of Italian submarine flotilla based on Massawa in the Red Sea: far too often, when submerged, the accumulator batteries of the submarines gave off poisonous fumes which rendered the crew unconscious.

In Libya, as mentioned above, Marshal Balbo had been ordered to remain on the defensive. If the reports of *Comando Supremo*'s military Intelligence can be taken as correct this was a somewhat odd decision, for 14 centrally-based Italian divisions were opposed by only eight French and five British divisions. But the situation was complicated by an exaggerated interpretation of Allied strength made by the *Servizio Informazioni Militari*. This did not dissuade Mussolini from going to war, but it did paint the strategic picture in excessively pessimistic colours.

On June 10, 1940, the French C.-in-C., North Africa, General Noguès, did have eight divisions under his command; but apart from the fact that three of them were not operational, they were deployed between the Libyan frontier and Spanish Morocco. The *Servizio* on the other hand, reported the French divisions as being massed between Bizerta and the Mareth Line, ready for an invasion of Libya.

General Sir Archibald Wavell, the British Commander-in-Chief, Middle East, had a total strength of five divisions (about 100,000 men), but of these only 36,000 were in Egypt. They were formed into two incomplete divisions: Major-General M. O'Moore Creagh's 7th Armoured Division and Major-General P. Neame's (from August Major-General N. M. Beresford-Peirse's) 4th Indian Division.

In Libya, the Italian forces were disposed as follows:
West: 5th Army (General Italo Gariboldi), consisting of X, XX, and XXIII Corps, with six infantry divisions and two Black Shirt divisions;
East: 10th Army (General Francesco Berti) consisting of XXI and XXII Corps, with three infantry divisions, one Black Shirt division, and one Libyan native division.

A fourth division (the 2nd Libyan Division) was moving up from Tripoli to Benghazi.

All in all, there were in Italian North Africa slightly over 236,000 officers, N.C.O.'s and other ranks, 1,811 guns, 339 light tanks, 8,039 trucks and 151 first line aircraft. The Italian air strength was comparatively weak, but even so was far stronger than that of the British.

The armistice with France was a bitter disappointment to Marshal Balbo. He had hoped that the occupation of Tunisia would put the port of Bizerta at his disposal, allowing him to draw on the material and military supplies in the province. Instead of this, he had to content himself with the demilitarisation of the Mareth Line.

The Italians were kept off balance for another reason: the British 7th Armoured Division did not imitate the action of the Italian 10th Army and remain on the defensive. Instead, it launched daily armoured and motorised raids across the Libyan frontier, which led the Italians to believe that their weapons were inferior. On June 20 Balbo wrote to Badoglio: "Our light tanks, already old and armed only with machine guns, are completely outclassed. The machine guns of the British armoured cars pepper them with bullets which pierce their armour easily. We have no armoured cars. Our anti-tank defences are largely a matter of make-do; our modern weapons lack adequate ammunition. Thus the conflict has taken on the character of steel against flesh, which only too easily explains certain episodes which are luckily of little importance."

There was nothing surprising about the

failure of the Italian L-3-33/5 3-ton light tank in Libya, for the "sardine-can", as Franco's men had dubbed it, had cut a sorry figure as early as the Spanish Civil War. One is, however, surprised to read that on June 25 Badoglio announced to Balbo that 70 "magnificent" M-11 tanks were on their way to Libya. In fact this 11-ton tank could be knocked out by any gun with a calibre larger than 20-mm. The standard British anti-tank gun was the 2-pounder (40-mm), and no one in Italy could have been unaware of the fact.

The threat to Egypt

On June 28, on hearing the news that French North Africa would remain loyal to the Government of Marshal Pétain, *Comando Supremo* ordered Balbo to invade Egypt with his total force, even if this meant "cannibalising" the 5th Army. But Balbo never got the order. On the same day he was shot down over Tobruk by his own gunners during the confusion of an alert.

Marshal Rodolfo Graziani, Army Chief-of-Staff, took over Balbo's command and mission, and D-Day was fixed for July 15, 1940.

In the post which he had just left, Graziani had constantly urged Balbo to take the initiative; but as soon as he arrived in Libya he too began to raise the same arguments against an advance which his predecessor had used. His task was not an easy one. There was only one supply-route across the desert between the Libyan frontier and Alexandria, on which were the British bases of Sidi Barrani and Marsa Matrûh. Graziani was not prepared to advance until he had received sufficient trucks and water tankers to supply his transport and the needs of the troops. Moreover, considering the heat of the African summer, he would have preferred to delay the conquest of Egypt until October.

But Mussolini would not hear of this. He wanted to launch the offensive on the same day as the first Germans landed in England. This led to painful scenes between Graziani and *Comando Supremo*, a visit by Graziani to Rome, and, on August 19, a peremptory telegram from Mussolini which concluded: "Marshal Graziani, as I have already told you since our last discussion, time is working against us. The loss of Egypt will be the

△ and ▽ *Motorised warfare, Italian style. After weeks of wrangling and procrastination, Marshal Graziani's invasion finally got under way on September 13. On the 16th, after a 60-mile advance, the Italians reached Sidi Barrani and dug in. The trucks in the photograph below are carrying field artillery en portée. Note the immaculate tropical uniforms of the officers in the front seats.*

◁ *Mussolini's pride: the Italian fleet, dressed for a peace-time review. In the summer of 1940 the Italian fleet, with its bases dominating the central Mediterranean, was a crucial factor. Would it cause the fall of Malta by striking at the British supply convoys? And could the British, only slightly out-numbered ship for ship but forced to operate from Gibraltar and Alexandria, keep Malta's lifeline open?*

coup de grace for Great Britain, while the conquest of that rich country, necessary for our communications with Ethiopia, will be the great reward for which Italy is waiting. That you will procure it, I am certain."

Nevertheless, 10th Army's offensive did not get under way until September 13. Four divisions and an armoured group crossed the frontier, commanded by General Annibale Bergonzoli, C.-in-C. XXIII Corps. Difficult terrain, temperatures at times over 50 degrees Centigrade, sand storms, and anti-tank mines slowed the Italian advance to a bare 12½ miles per day. In the afternoon of September 16 the "23rd of March" Black Shirt Division occupied Sidi Barrani. This advance had cost the Italians 120 dead and 410 wounded; the British 7th Armoured Division, which had been ordered to fall back before the advance, had lost 50 men.

In taking Sidi Barrani, Graziani had covered 60 of the 315 miles between the Libyan frontier at Sollum and Alexandria, and was 75 miles from his next objective, Marsa Matrûh. But before moving on Matrûh, Graziani was determined to halt until the damage done by the retreating British had been repaired; until the *Via Balbia*, the main road which ran across Libya along the coast, had been extended to Sidi Barrani, where the road to Alexandria began; to set up a fresh-water pipeline; and to stock Sidi Barrani with provisions, ammunition, and fuel. Graziani, a veteran colonial general, was entirely correct in taking all these precautions, for Wavell was hoping to see the Italian forces over-extend themselves by a premature dash on Matrûh.

Mussolini was disappointed by the pause in the offensive. But he consoled himself by reflecting that although the Italians had not passed Sidi Barrani, the Germans had not crossed the Channel.

Hitler restrains Mussolini

Mussolini had nobody but himself to blame for the sluggishness and delays of Graziani. If Mussolini had not kept the greater part of the resources which had been released by the Franco-Italian armistice in Italy, things might have turned out very differently during the invasion of Egypt. But at the beginning of July he had decided to smash Yugoslavia, that "creation of Versailles" which had to disappear like the others.

As a result three armies, totalling some 37 divisions, were concentrated in north-eastern Italy. But Hitler was anxious that peace should not be disturbed in this corner of the Continent. On August 17 Ribbentrop, via Ambassador Dino Alfieri, informed Ciano of the Führer's opposition to any venture against Yugoslavia or Greece. Mussolini had to yield, but what was he to do with the armies which were now left without a mission? For reasons of economy, 600,000 soldiers were demobilised and sent home, to be remobilised a few weeks later.

In the summer of 1940, as far as circumstances permitted, the maritime honours went to the Royal Navy, which more than lived up to its aggressive tradition.

Is it fair to blame the Italian admirals for their lack of offensive spirit? They were certainly kept on a far shorter rein by the Italian High Command in Rome – *Supermarina* – than were their opponents. But one reason for *Supermarina*'s reticence was the early realisation that the Italian Air Force was not to be relied upon, whether for reconnaissance missions or for combat.

This was shown clearly during the action off Cape Spartivento on the Calabrian coast on July 9, 1940. The Italian fleet, under Admiral Campioni, was returning to base after having escorted an important convoy carrying troops and material to Benghazi. The British Mediterranean Fleet, under Admiral Cunningham, was also at sea; it was well informed about the movements of the Italian fleet, by aircraft operating from Malta and from the aircraft-carrier *Eagle*; and Cunningham planned to intercept the Italians during their return to Taranto.

Cunningham did not succeed, but the battleship *Warspite* managed to hit the Italian battleship *Giulio Cesare* at a range of 26,000 yards. Campioni broke away under the cover of a smoke screen, and Cunningham, having closed to within 25 miles of the Italian coast, also withdrew. On this occasion the Italian Air Force showed all its weaknesses; no dive-bombing or torpedo attacks were made during the encounter, and only one of the 1,000 bombs dropped scored a hit – on the cruiser *Gloucester*.

This inaccuracy did have its good side: it spared the Italian fleet from heavy losses, when Campioni's ships were enthusiastically bombed by the Savoia-Marchetti 79's of the Italian Air Force. On July 13 Ciano noted in his diary: "The real controversy in the matter of naval armament is not between us and the British, but between our Air Force and our Navy."

Nevertheless, Mussolini announced with a straight face that within three days half the British naval potential in the Mediterranean had been eliminated. On July 19 there was another encounter in the Antikithera Channel off the northwest coast of Crete. The Italian light cruisers *Bartolomeo Colleoni* and *Bande Nere*, which were heading for Leros in the Dodecanese, fell in with the Australian light cruiser *Sydney* and five destroyers. Hit in her engine-rooms, the *Colleoni* was

immobilised and sunk by torpedoes, while the *Bande Nere* escaped. This was a clear indication of combat weaknesses of these light warships, in which protection had been sacrificed for the sake of speed.

In early August, however, the naval balance in the Mediterranean appeared to shift heavily in Italy's favour. The battleships *Littorio*, *Vittorio Veneto*, *Caio Duilio*, and *Andrea Doria* joined the Italian fleet. The first two were powerful,

▽ *Aboard the* Cesare *after the clash off Cape Spartivento: an Italian damage party surveys the havoc wrought by a shell from the* Warspite.

modern warships displacing over 41,000 tons, with a main armament of nine 15-inch guns and a top speed of 28 knots. The others were battleships which had been launched in 1913 and completely overhauled in the late 1930's. The two *Doria*-class battleships were each armed with ten 12.6-inch guns and could make 26 knots.

From its central position this formidable battle fleet outnumbered the combined squadrons of Admirals Somerville and Cunningham by six capital ships to five, the British squadrons being separated at opposite ends of the Mediterranean. The British still had a slight advantage in firepower, but none of the battleships in the Mediterranean Fleet was faster than 24 knots. After the affair off Calabria, the British Admiralty sent to the eastern

△ *The last minutes of the Italian cruiser* Bartolomeo Colleoni, *sunk on July 19. The Australian cruiser* Sydney *landed repeated hits on the* Colleoni *and wrecked her engine room. Dead in the water and defenceless, the* Colleoni *was finished off by torpedoes from the destroyers* Hyperion *and* Ilex.

forcements anchored at Alexandria on September 5.

During the operation the veteran aircraft-carrier *Argus*, having steamed to the south of Sardinia, flew off 12 Hurricanes to strengthen the threadbare defences of Malta. It is surprising to note that after the neutralisation of Bizerta with the signing of the armistice, the Italians had made no attempt to take Malta. The defences of the "island fortress" were pitifully weak: there were only 68 light and heavy A.A. guns instead of the 156 guns which had been envisaged in a pre-war programme, and the one radar set on the island functioned only sporadically. When Italy entered the war on June 10 Malta's air defences consisted of five Swordfish torpedo-bombers and four Sea Gladiators; one of the latter was soon damaged beyond repair, and the remaining three were christened "Faith", "Hope", and "Charity". These were later joined by nine Swordfish and nine Hurricanes.

Admiral Cunningham had protested against the running-down of Malta's defences which the British Government and the Imperial General Staff had countenanced, but his complaints had not been taken up. London had decided that in the event of a war with Italy the Middle East theatre would be supplied by the sea route round the Cape of Good Hope. But in view of the timidity of *Comando Supremo* and the weaknesses of the Italian Air Force it was decided to restore to Malta the offensive rôle which had seemed impossible because of the menace of the bomber.

But to do this it would be necessary to proceed by very careful and easy stages while the defences of the island remained as weak as they were. Cunningham saw this very clearly. He wrote at the time: "If we are to avoid a serious threat to Malta itself, it appears necessary that in any given period the scale of attack drawn down should not be disproportionate to the state of the defences it has been possible to install. It is only logical therefore to expect the full weight of Italian attack if our light forces work effectively."

In the long run, the offensive action of the light surface forces and the bombers which would be based on Malta would depend on the parallel development of Malta's defences (fighters, anti-aircraft guns, and radar). This was obvious; it was confirmed by experience. But it did not appeal to Churchill, who reproached Cunningham on September 9 for not being sufficiently offensively minded.

Mediterranean the battleship *Valiant* (fresh from a refit), the anti-aircraft cruisers *Calcutta* and *Coventry*, and, most important of all, the new aircraft-carrier *Illustrious*, which carried 34 aircraft, of which 12 were Fulmar fighters. With this reinforcement Cunningham's battle fleet could defend itself adequately against the Italian bombers. *Illustrious* and *Valiant* had the additional advantage of being equipped with radar.

Thus the Royal Navy had reacted promptly and skilfully: these new rein-

Meanwhile, a local conflict with no direct connection with the war between the major powers was about to become a matter of great importance. Soon it would impinge upon the joint interests of Germany and Italy–with fateful results.

We have already mentioned that neither the Hungarian Regent, Admiral Horthy, the various governments at Budapest, nor Hungarian national opinion had accepted the territorial restrictions imposed upon Hungary by the Treaty of Trianon in 1920. After Munich, Hungary had obtained substantial frontier rectifications at the expense of Czechoslovakia; later, in March 1939, the Prague coup had enabled her to occupy and annex Sub-Carpathian Ruthenia. But Hungary had other claims to make, against both Yugoslavia and Rumania.

For many years the region of Transylvania had been a source of discord between Rumania and Hungary. With the defeat of Austria-Hungary in 1918, Hungary had been forced to cede Transylvania to Rumania, the latter country being one of the victorious Allies. It was a fair enough decision, considering that the majority of the population was Rumanian and that it had endured harsh treatment while under Hungarian rule. But along the bend of the Carpathians there was a compact bloc of Magyars, known as Szeklers or Sicules. There were around two million of them, and they were cut off from their fellow Magyars on the Danubian plain. When they became Rumanian citizens, they had no reason to be pleased with their change of nationality.

△ *Admiral Horthy, Regent of Hungary, enters Nagyvárad in triumph.*
▽ *Ribbentrop talks with the Rumanian leaders Manoïlescu (centre) and Gafencu.*

The Axis verdict

After the crushing of France, the Hungarian Government once again raised the question of Transylvania. But although King Carol II of Rumania and his Prime Minister, Gigurtu, were prepared to consider certain concessions, no complete agreement between the rival countries seemed possible. They would have gone to war but for the intervention of Hitler, who, as we have seen, feared the consequences of any outbreak of trouble in the Balkans, and Mussolini, who always tended to favour the cause of the Hungarians. Rumania and Hungary submitted to Axis arbitration, which was presided over by Ciano and Ribbentrop in the Belvedere Palace in Vienna. On August 30, 1940, the Axis verdict was delivered.

Under the terms of the Axis arbitration, Rumania would retain the western part of Transylvania. Hungary recovered the region of the Szeklers, but in order to extend her 1920 frontier to the Moldavian Carpathians she was also granted territory occupied by some three million Rumanians, plus the important towns of Cluj and Oradea, which for the next four years were known by the Magyar names of Kolozsvar and Nagyvárad.

This high-handed partition of Transylvania still did not satisfy the Hungarian claims in full. On the other hand, coming as it did two months after the loss of Bessarabia and the Bukovina to Soviet Russia, it sparked off deep feelings of resentment among the Rumanians. On September 4 General Ion Antonescu seized power, forced King Carol to abdicate in favour of his son Prince Michael, and, taking the title of "Conducator", set up a dictatorship.

German patronage for Rumania

As Italy, of the two Axis partners, had always supported Hungary's cause, it was not surprising that both King Carol and Antonescu had thought it advisable to seek German patronage. Hitler was extremely anxious not to be cut off from the output of the Rumanian oil wells at Ploieşti, and to safeguard them from possible Allied attempts at sabotage. As a result, he welcomed eagerly the request made to him by a Rumanian military mission which visited him on September 2. And on October 7, Lieutenant-General Hansen and his staff, together with the first elements of the 13th Motorised Division, arrived in Bucharest.

This move, coming as it did after the guarantee of territorial integrity which had been given to Rumania after the Vienna arbitration, could only be interpreted as a clear-cut anti-Soviet move by Hitler. Stalin and Molotov, however, showed no outward reaction. But the effect on Mussolini was totally different.

Mussolini turns on Greece

On October 12 Ciano visited Mussolini in the Palazzo Venezia. He found the Duce "indignant", claiming that the occupation of Rumania by German troops had had a very bad impression on Italian public opinion. He had made his decision. "Hitler always faces me with a *fait accompli*. This time I am going to pay him back in his own coin. He will find out from the papers that I have occupied Greece. In this way the equilibrium will be re-established."

No other decision of Mussolini's could have been more welcome to Ciano, who had always pressed for imperialist Italian policies in the eastern Mediterranean. Nevertheless he thought it necessary to ask if Mussolini had discussed the matter with Marshal Badoglio. "Not yet," he replied, "but I shall send in my resignation as an Italian if anyone objects to our fighting the Greeks."

On the 15th Badoglio and Roatta, appalled, heard of Mussolini's decision. Three weeks before, acting on his orders, they had demobilised 600,000 men. Now he was asking them to attack Greece within 12 days, D-Day being set as dawn on October 26.

Without objecting to the operation in principle, Badoglio undertook to attack with 20 Italian divisions on condition that the Bulgarians would undertake to tie down six to eight Greek divisions. But General Sebastiano Visconti-Prasca, commanding in Albania, only had eight Italian divisions under his orders. It would therefore be necessary to remobilise 12 more divisions, send them across the Adriatic, and set up the necessary depôts and reserves for them on the spot. Considering the inadequacies of the Albanian ports of

Valona and Durazzo, all this needed at least three months.

Mussolini could not accept these arguments: everything suggested that such a delay would allow Hitler to interpose a new veto. Ciano, Jacomoni (Lieutenant-General of Albania), and Visconti-Prasca all supported the idea. During the discussions on October 15 at the Palazzo Venezia they destroyed the objections of Badoglio and Roatta; and they were backed by Admiral Cavagnari and General Pricolo, respectively Under-Secretary of State and Chief-of-Staff of the Navy, and Chief-of-Staff of the Air Force.

As Ciano saw it, the political situation was favourable. Neither Turkey nor Yugoslavia would support Greece, their ally in the Balkan Pact, and Bulgaria's attitude would be favourable to Italy. But above all, the political situation in Athens gave cause for reasonable optimism. Only the Court and the plutocracy remained hostile to Fascist Italy, and a well-organised system of bribery was laying the groundwork for a change of régime.

For his part, Jacomoni claimed that the

Admiral Miklos Horthy de Nagybánya was born in 1868 in eastern Hungary. When 14 he entered the Austro-Hungarian naval academy. Between 1909 and 1914 Horthy was the Emperor Franz Joseph's naval aide-de-camp, and during World War I was noted as a daring and able leader. He was promoted Admiral in January 1918. After the war Horthy returned to Hungary and led the counter-revolution which ousted the Communists from power. He became Regent in March 1920, but refused to surrender the office in 1921. His policies were based on a desire to maintain the current social order and extend Hungary's borders. Though on bad terms with Hitler, Horthy joined the Axis in 1941, chiefly so that he could continue his struggle against Communism. He tried to secure a separate peace in 1944, but was imprisoned by the Nazis. He died in Portugal in 1957.

entire population of Albania was anxious to settle accounts with Greece, its hereditary enemy. "One can even state," he declared proudly, "that the enthusiasm is so great that it [the Albanian people] has recently given signs of disillusionment that the war has not already begun." Asked to present his plan of operations, Visconti-Prasca declared that he foresaw no difficulty in opening the campaign with his current forces in Albania. Leaving a covering force on the Pindus Mountains on the eastern sector, he undertook to conquer Epirus in 10 to 15 days, throwing 70,000 Italians against 30,000 Greeks. Then, reinforced from Italy and from the Ionian Islands through the captured port of Préveza, he would march on Athens, whose fall would end the campaign before the close of the year.

Faced with these arguments, particularly the political explanations of Ciano and Jacomoni, Badoglio gave way. He contented himself with saying that the Peloponnese and Crete should be included as objectives, for otherwise the British would move in. He has been blamed –

▽ *Hitler and General Franco meet at Hendaye, on the Spanish frontier. For once Hitler's magnetism failed completely: the Spanish dictator refused to join the Axis partnership.*

correctly – for the exaggerated military promises which he made. But at the time he had no idea of the extent to which the claims of Ciano and Jacomoni were totally mistaken.

Nevertheless, Mussolini granted his generals a deadline extension of two days; and he impressed on all parties that the whole affair was to be kept a strict secret from the Germans.

Hitler and the Mediterranean

While the preliminary studies for an invasion of Soviet Russia were still under way, Hitler, on the urging of Grand-Admiral Raeder and the suspension of Operation "Sea Lion", was showing signs of interest in a strategic project which could have lessened the weakening effects of the "parallel war" and allowed the Axis partners to co-operate more directly in their fight against the common enemy. This was Operation "Felix", aimed at the conquest of Gibraltar.

If the Wehrmacht could establish itself on the Strait of Gibraltar it could close the Mediterranean to the Royal Navy and give the Italian fleet access to the Atlantic. It would also enable the Axis to put French North Africa, where Weygand had just installed himself, under pressure similar to that already being imposed on Unoccupied France. It would no longer be possible for Vichy France to fend off Hitler's demands by pleading the possible defection of Morocco, Algeria, and Tunisia.

Overtures to Franco

Such an operation would require the co-operation of Spain. When it seemed likely that Hitler was about to invade Britain, the Spanish Government had raised the question of Spain's claims to Oran and the French zone of the Moroccan protectorate. In mid-September Serrano Suñer, Spanish Minister of the Interior and Franco's brother-in-law, met Hitler and Ribbentrop for a series of talks. According to his account, which, it is true, was written after the war, he was disappointed – not to say shaken – by the German reaction to these overtures.

Ciano's diary confirms Suñer's version. On October 1 it records "Serrano's colourful invectives against the Germans for their absolute lack of tact in dealing with Spain. Serrano is right." Hitler and Ribbentrop wanted the Atlantic coast of Morocco for Germany, plus an air and naval base in the Canary Isles. Moreover, they were still uncertain about the economic aid which Germany could send to Spain, for the moment she entered the war Spain would instantly be cut off from her important imports of cereals and fuel, and would then become dependent on Germany.

On October 4 the same question was raised at the Brenner Pass conference between Hitler, Mussolini, Ribbentrop, and Ciano. At the same time the eventual dispatch of a German armoured detachment to North Africa was discussed. But Mussolini, who was still waiting from day to day for Graziani to resume his offensive in Egypt, cold-shouldered the idea. In his opinion, Panzer troops should only be sent to North Africa after the third phase of the operation: when the Italian 10th Army moved east from Marsa Matrûh on Alexandria and Cairo. There can be no doubt, however, that he hoped to be able to avoid German help.

If the Italians had taken Cairo by October 22, Franco could well have acted very differently. As it was, on that day he met Hitler at Hendaye on the Spanish frontier. Franco believed that the war would in fact be a long one and that without firm guarantees of corn and fuel supplies it would only impose further bitter sacrifices on the Spanish people.

As Hitler continued to speak in general terms, affirming that Britain was already beaten, Franco turned down the invitation to enter the war on the day that the Wehrmacht attacked Gibraltar, provisionally set for January 10, 1941.

Interpreter Paul Schmidt was an eyewitness at this discussion. "To put it bluntly, I was most interested to hear Franco's reply to Hitler's declaration that from the jumping-off point of Gibraltar, Africa could be rid of the British by armoured troops." This was quite possible along the fringe of the great desert, said Franco, "but central Africa is protected against any large-scale land offensive by the desert belt, which defends it as the sea defends an island. I have fought a great deal in Africa and I am certain of it."

Schmidt's account continues: "Even Hitler's hopes of eventually conquering Britain might turn out to be hollow. Franco thought it possible that the British Isles could be conquered. But if this

△ *Another moral defeat for Hitler: his meeting with Pétain at Montoire on October 24, 1940. "Pétain listened in silence," recalled interpreter Schmidt. "Not once did he offer a single friendly word for Hitler or for Germany."*

happened the British Government and fleet would carry on the struggle from Canada, with American aid.

"While Franco talked on in a calm, monotonous, sing-song voice like an Arabic muezzin, Hitler began to grow more and more restless. The discussion was clearly fraying his nerves. At one stage he even got up and said that further discussion would be useless, but he soon sat down and continued his attempt to change Franco's mind. Franco declared that he was prepared to conclude a treaty but, in view of the supplies of food and armaments Hitler was prepared to offer from the moment Spain went to war, that the offer was only a hollow sham."

Franco was using the technique which can loosely be described as "yes, but", and it was not at all to the liking of Hitler. Ribbentrop, too, was receiving the same treatment from Serrano Suñer, who had only lately become the Spanish Minister of Foreign Affairs. Ribbentrop's latest proposal had not been well received by Suñer: "Spain will receive territories from the French colonial empire, for which France can be compensated in equal measure by territories from the British colonial empire."

This was very different to what had been said to Suñer during his visit to Berlin; but Ribbentrop, too, was infuriated by the caution of the Spaniards. Schmidt, who flew to Montoire with Ribbentrop, has described him as "fuming with rage", and spending the journey in invective against "that ungrateful rogue" Franco and "that Jesuit" Suñer.

Pétain refuses to help Hitler

If Hitler's meeting with Franco at Hendaye was a definite setback for German policies, his meeting with Pétain at Montoire did nothing to compensate for it. Hitler wanted to induce the Vichy French Government to go to war with Britain. Pétain, however, left Hitler in no doubt as to his refusal to allow France to be drawn into a war with her former ally, even on the pretext of reconquering the colonies which had gone over to de Gaulle.

Once again, Schmidt has provided an account of the Montoire meeting.

"As darkness fell on October 24, 1940, it was difficult at first to tell the victor from the vanquished in the feeble lights on the platform of the little station. Standing very straight, despite his great age, in his plain uniform, Pétain put out his hand to the dictator with an almost royal gesture, while fixing him with a quizzical, icy, and penetrating glance. I knew how he felt about Hitler, Göring, and other prominent National Socialists. To most Germans he himself stood for all the military virtues of France, and this was very clear in Hitler's attitude when they met. He was no longer the triumphal victor shown by certain photographs of 1940. Nor was he a corporal intimidated in the presence of a marshal, as certain French publications have since claimed. He behaved without haughtiness and without harshness.

"With a gesture, Hitler invited the Marshal to enter his railway car. I myself was seated before Pétain and was admirably placed to observe him throughout the talk. His complexion, which had seemed pale to me on the platform, became faintly pink. No emotion or interior tension could be seen behind his mask of impassivity. Ribbentrop, a mute and almost tolerated witness, together with Laval, who was wearing his inevitable white tie, assisted the conversation.

"Pétain listened in silence. Not once did he offer a single friendly word for Hitler or for Germany. His attitude conveyed a vaguely haughty impression, rising above the situation of France in this autumn of 1940."

▽ German propaganda directed at potential French collaborators, warning that subversive Jewish activities could wreck the Franco-German agreement reached at Montoire.

COLLABORATION ?

Comment on l'envisageait après Montoire entre la France et l'Allemagne

Ce qu'ils en ont fait

Finira-t-elle ainsi ?

CHAPTER 11
ALBANIA, TARANTO, SIDI BARRANI

(page 104) ▷ Italian transport halts beside a road in Albania which has been churned into a swamp by the wheels of previous vehicles ▷ ▷ A Bersagliere *motor-cyclist in difficulties. Torrential rains at the beginning of November proved a blessing to the Greek army.*

▷ Although Mussolini was never a convincing military figure, that was the image which he loved to present to the world. Here he proudly reviews his troops as they parade under a canopy of gun barrels.

Hitler had hardly left Montoire after his uncomfortable meeting with Pétain when a message from the German Ambassador in Rome threw him into the deepest consternation: his ally was on the brink of invading Greece. In the hope of staving off this dangerous venture, he went straight to Italy instead of returning to Berlin. At 1000 hours on October 28, he was greeted at the station in Florence by Mussolini, all smiles: "Führer, we are on the march! At dawn this morning our Italian troops victoriously crossed the Albanian-Greek frontier!"

Koritsa, Taranto, and Sidi Barrani were three decisive defeats for Italian arms which severely darkened the prospects of the Axis. They gave the suppressed peoples of Western Europe their first glimmer of hope since June 25, 1940. From the moment the attack began, Mussolini and Ciano watched while the political assumptions on which the war with Greece had been founded began to collapse. They already knew that King Boris of Bulgaria would stay on the sidelines until events had run their course. They had grossly underestimated the patriotism of the Greek nation, which closed its ranks under the feeble Italian bombing raids when it heard that King George II and the Prime Minister, General Joannis

Metaxas, had indignantly rejected the Italian ultimatum and had immediately decreed general mobilisation.

The fact was that Italy was violently unpopular in Greece. Quite apart from the historical legacy of the Venetian rule in Crete, the Morea, and the Ionian Islands, the Fascist methods brought to bear on the people of Rhodes and the Dodecanese by Count Cesare de Vecchi had resulted in the unanimous hostility of all sectors of Greek opinion against Mussolini, his régime, and his country.

Italians crossed the frontier in torrential rain which converted every brook into a torrent and every road into a sea of clinging mud. In these conditions the demolitions carried out by the Greeks added still

▽ *Greek soldiers–their natural toughness and fighting spirit was lent added strength by the animosity felt against the Fascist oppression of Rhodes and the Dodecanese.*

The Greeks hit back

General mobilisation gave the Greek commander, General Alexandros Papagos, 15 infantry divisions, four infantry brigades, and a cavalry division, formed into five army corps. On paper the Greek divisions were definitely inferior to the Italian divisions, but this disparity was largely balanced by the chronic difficulties of the terrain and of communications, which favoured the defenders.

In the Italian plan the initial assault would be carried out by four divisions attacking in Epirus, with another two divisions covering the main attack by advancing against the Morova massif. Visconti-Prasca planned a breakthrough which would surprise Papagos before he could concentrate his forces. But the weather was on the side of the Greeks: the

In the autumn of 1940 there was world-wide speculation as to the outcome of Italy's ventures in the Balkans and North Africa; and Axis, Allied, and neutral cartoonists each had their own interpretations of the pattern of events.

As had happened when the Soviet Union attacked Finland in December 1939, the free world rang with applause when the Greeks not only stood up to Italy's invasion but won victory after victory over the Duce's armies. This cartoon, by Punch, is entitled, quite simply, "Trophies of the mountains".

further to the slowing-up of the Italian advance.

Nevertheless, Visconti-Prasca's left-hand column, formed by the "Julia" Alpine Division, broke through the advanced Greek positions, then their main position, pushed up the Aóos valley and took the village of Vovoússa on November 2. Here the division found itself at the foot of the important Métzovon pass, crossed by the Lárisa–Yanina road, having covered some 25 miles of mountain terrain under an icy rain. On the following day a Greek counter-attack down from the heights forced the Italians into a retreat that was as hasty as it was disastrous.

In the centre, the 23rd "Ferrana" Infantry Division and the 131st "Centauro" Armoured Division, which had Yanina as their first objective, were held up by the Greek forward positions and completely halted by their main position, largely as a result of the action fought by the Greek 8th Division, acting as covering force.

In the coastal sector, the "Siena" Division was luckier. It took Filiates, crossed the raging River Thíamis, and reached Paramithia with the intention of encircling the Greek position at Yanina. At sea, appalling conditions forced Comando Supremo to abandon its projected amphibious operation against Corfu, while bad weather prevented the Italian Air Force from bringing its superiority to bear.

The Italians had lost all the advantage of surprise: the Italian bombers were not able to slow down the mobilisation and concentration of the Greek forces; and all the weaknesses of the plan adopted on the recommendation of Visconti-Prasca were now obvious. By November 12 General Papagos had at the front over 100 infantry battalions fighting in terrain to which they were accustomed, compared with less than 50 Italian battalions.

Visconti-Prasca was dismissed on November 9 and was replaced by General Ubaldo Soddu, Under-Secretary of State for War and Deputy Chief-of-Staff of the Army. He now found two armies under his command: on the right, General Carlo Gelosa's 11th Army, and on the left General Mario Vercellino's 9th Army. But until the remobilised divisions could be shipped across the Adriatic these units were armies only in name.

On the Greek side, General Papagos did not content himself with the success of his defensive strategy; in this war, with 45 million Italians attacking seven million

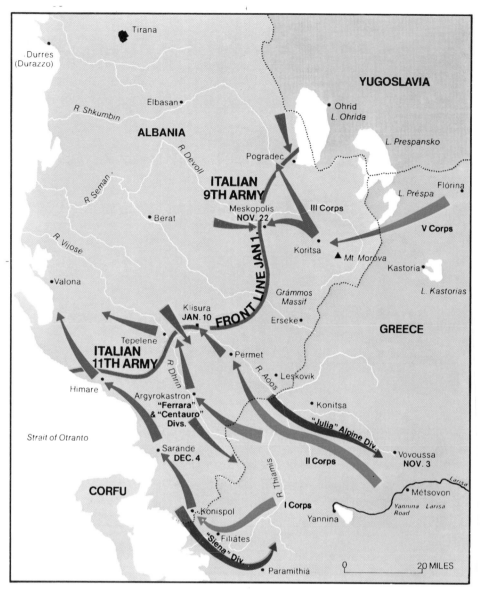

△ *The Italian invasion of Greece and the Greek counter-attacks. The Greek commander, General Papagos, timed his counter-stroke perfectly.*
▽ *The Italian commander in Albania: General Soddu. He liked to spend his evenings with his somewhat unmilitary hobby of composing music for films.*

On November 21 the II Corps under General Papadopoulos also crossed the Albanian frontier, despite the formidable obstacle of the Grámmos massif, and took Ersekë and Leskovik. This gave the Greek High Command an excellent front between the Koritsa plateau and the valley of the Aóos. On December 5, a gallant action gave the II Corps Përmet, 23 miles inside Albania. On the left, the I Corps under General Kosmas crossed the Thíamis on the heels of the retreating 11th Army. Pushing down the Dhrin valley, the Greek advance guards were greeted enthusiastically by the population of Argyrokastron – which says much for the deep Albanian feelings of loyalty towards Italy which Jacomoni had described to Mussolini. Two days before, the left-flank division under General Kosmas had taken Sarandë, formerly Santi Quaranta, which the Italian Fascist régime had rechristened Porto Edda.

After December 5 the Greek offensive began to peter out. The Greek Army's lack of tanks and its poverty in anti-tank weapons forced it to shun the plains and valleys in its attacks, and so the excellent Greek infantrymen concentrated on the mountain heights for their operations. But by the beginning of December temperatures in the mountains were falling as low as 15 and even 20 degrees Centigrade below zero, and these were rendered even more unbearable by severe snowstorms.

Lacking tanks, lacking even sufficient transport vehicles, the Greeks now began to experience the sufferings of their enemy. The British had no material which they could spare for their new allies. On the other hand, no less than eight Italian divisions had been shipped to Albania between October 28 and the end of December. Far too often, however, the demands of the front led General Soddu to use up his reinforcements piecemeal to plug local breakthroughs. But quite apart from this, the supply of Italian reinforcements was badly organised.

However, the comparatively rapid supply of Italian reinforcements only raised fresh problems with regard to their supplies. On December 4 the Quartermaster-General, Scuero, described the depôt and magazine supplies as almost completely exhausted.

No one could deny the victor's laurels to the Greek soldier. But under conditions like these one can only say that the Italian soldier had earned the martyr's crown a thousand times over.

Greeks, a "wait and see" policy would have been tantamount to an admission of defeat. Papagos determined to exploit the errors committed by the Italians and to counter-attack before the enormous numerical and material superiority of the Italian Army could be brought into play. On November 14 the Greek Army went over to the offensive along the entire front from Lake Prespa to the Ionian Sea.

On the Greek right, V Corps under General Tzolakoglou, fielding at first three and finally five divisions, broke through at Mount Morova and after eight days' fighting had destroyed the Italian 9th Army at Koritsa, taking 2,000 prisoners, 80 field guns, 55 anti-tank guns and 300 machine guns from the "Tridentina" Mountain Division and the "Arezzo", "Parma", and "Piemonte" Infantry Divisions. This brilliant success was exploited further to the north, and on December 4 the Greek III Corps occupied Pogradec on Lake Ohrida.

Taranto

Meanwhile, the British Mediterranean Fleet had struck as deadly a blow as the Greek Army. From the moment when the aircraft-carrier *Illustrious* joined his command, Cunningham detected a certain lack of offensive spirit in the Italian squadron based on Taranto. This led to

the preparation of a British torpedo-bombing attack, to be known as Operation "Judgement".

The first idea of Rear-Admiral Lyster, commanding the British carrier force in the Mediterranean, had been to attack on the night of October 21, the anniversary of Trafalgar; but an accident aboard *Illustrious* forced him to postpone "Judgement" until November 11, when the phase of the moon would next favour the venture.

△△ Mainstay of the Italian bomber arm: the Savoia-Marchetti S.M.-79, unattractive but effective.
△ Italian Air Force briefing photograph for bombing raids on Malta, with the key forts, gun batteries, arsenals, reservoirs, and fuel dumps all carefully identified and numbered. Malta's vital airfields at Hal Far and Luqa are at the top right of the picture, numbered 24 and 25.

Then he had to operate without the aircraft-carrier *Eagle*, which transferred some of her Swordfish aircraft to *Illustrious*, however. Despite all this, Cunningham put to sea on November 6 to co-operate with a sortie by Force H, which was escorting the battleship *Barham* on its journey to the eastern Mediterranean.

On the evening of November 11 an air reconnaissance from Malta carried out by Martin Marylands and Short Sunderlands established that all six of the Italian battleships were in port. Having steamed to within 190 miles of Taranto, Lyster flew off his 21 Swordfish in two waves. Eleven of them were fitted with torpedoes and the other ten with bombs and flares.

Several circumstances favoured the attackers. A few days before, a heavy storm had driven down several balloons from the barrage protecting the Taranto anchorage. The anti-torpedo nets surrounding the warships only extended 26 feet down while the British torpedoes, set to detonate either on contact or by magnetic proximity, ran at 30 feet. Finally, when the alert was sounded, the Italians did not activate the harbour smoke-screens, in order not to impair the fire of the anti-aircraft guns. Nevertheless, the

Fleet Air Arm crews needed all their dash and gallantry to penetrate the fire of the 21 100-mm batteries and the 200 light A.A. guns, quite apart from the guns aboard the warships, mark their targets, and drop their torpedoes accurately.

Eleven torpedoes were launched, and six scored hits: three on the *Littorio*, two on the *Duilio*, and one on the *Cavour*. The last Swordfish returned to *Illustrious* at about 0300 hours. The British lost only two aircraft. In reply, the Italian land batteries alone had fired some 8,500 shells. Of the aircraft crews, one was killed and three others were taken prisoner. *Littorio* and *Duilio* were out of action for the next six months and needed considerable repairs. The older *Cavour* was raised, towed from Taranto to Trieste, and abandoned there. Until the summer of 1941 *Supermarina*'s battle fleet was reduced to three battleships, which permitted Admiral Cunningham to release the elderly British battleships *Ramillies* and *Malaya* for much-needed escort duties on the Atlantic convoy routes.

This series of disasters caused near chaos in the Italian High Command. Refusing to put the blame where it belonged – on his own vanity – Mussolini decided to make a scapegoat of Marshal Badoglio. But as the Commander-in-Chief of the Italian Armed Forces could hardly level a public indictment against his own Chief of General Staff, Mussolini opened his campaign against Badoglio with a vicious editorial aimed at the Marshal by Roberto Farinacci, editor of the official paper *Regime Fascista*. Badoglio demanded a public retraction of this allegation that he was not only incompetent but had also betrayed Mussolini's trust by ignorance or deliberate treachery. When he was refused all satisfaction, Badoglio resigned on November 26.

General Ugo Cavallero stepped into his place. Apart from the torrent of defamation poured on his character in Ciano's diary, it must be said that Cavallero was a much-discussed figure among his fellow generals, and that a period of involvement in the arms industry had not added to his prestige. Admiral Cavagnari was dismissed as head of *Supermarina* and Under-Secretary of State for the Navy and was replaced by Admiral Arturo Riccardi, a fact which publicly branded the former as the man responsible for the Taranto fiasco. Finally, de Vecchi resigned and was replaced by General Ettore Bastico as Governor of the Aegean.

▽ *Aftermath of the Taranto raid: a reconnaissance photograph of the inner harbour, where the cruisers were anchored, on the day after the raid. Oil fuel lies thick on the water; a tug fusses about the stern of a* Bolzano-*class heavy cruiser (4). The other crippled heavy cruiser (5) belongs to the* Trento-*class. A second* Trento-*class vessel (3) has been moved from the quayside. The three large ships still moored by the quay are* Zara-*class heavy cruisers, which escaped without damage. In the outer harbour, the battleships* Littorio *and* Caio Duilio *were put out of action for six months, and the* Cavour *so badly damaged that she never put to sea again.*

Although Hitler was infuriated by the disasters which his friend and ally had brought down on himself, the interests of the Reich nevertheless made it essential for the Wehrmacht to retrieve the situation. On November 18, at the Berghof, Hitler made himself clear to Ciano: he had only sent German troops into Rumania to safeguard the Ploieşti oil wells from Soviet machinations, and now they would be within range of R.A.F. bombers if the British set up air bases in Greece. He therefore proposed to invade Greece via Bulgaria, and set the provisional date at around March 15.

But this new plan of Hitler's meant that Mussolini must reverse his entire policy towards Yugoslavia. Instead of the aggressive attitude which Mussolini had always kept up, it was now essential to bring Yugoslavia into the Axis. Ciano, however, had reservations about the political decisions which governed Hitler's military intervention in the Balkans. It was clear to him that from now on Italy would not be waging a war aimed at her own interests, and that the future relations between Mussolini and Hitler would be those of vassal and lord.

The day after Ciano's departure from Berchtesgaden, Hitler and Ribbentrop put their cards on the table before the Spanish Foreign Minister, Serrano Suñer. On November 12 Hitler had ordered the preliminary moves for Operation "Felix", which was to capture Gibraltar. It was vital to waste no further time in establishing Franco's final intentions.

Suñer restated the arguments which had been put forward at Hendaye. The capture of Gibraltar, he declared, would not pay full dividends until the Italians had taken Port Said, the key to the other entrance to the Mediterranean. Moreover, Spain would need nearly 400,000 tons of cereals and two months to prepare for war. For all his powers of persuasion, Hitler failed to get Suñer to modify this point of view. Suñer left the Berghof without having accepted anything, but – and this was probably even more important – without having issued a flat refusal.

The Italian defeats at Koritsa and Taranto had certainly done much to influence Franco's decision. In less than a month, the further defeat at Sidi Barrani would confirm the Caudillo in his policy of non-belligerence.

△ *"Taranto" by Bagley. A dramatic reconstruction of the action that wrested numerical superiority from the Italian Navy at the end of 1940.*

△ *First taste of the agony to come: reinforcements for the British forces in Egypt, fresh from their long journey round the Cape of Good Hope, and with "their knees not yet brown", parade in the arid and scorching heat of a transit camp.*

More arms for Egypt

In December 1940 Wavell not only abandoned the defensive to which he had been confined since June 25, but launched an offensive which won such a total success that Hitler was forced to send yet more German forces to help his tottering ally, facing ruin after only six months of war.

Certain aspects of this episode would still be unknown were it not for the surprising information contained in the memoirs of Sir Anthony Eden. He was Secretary of State for War at the time, and what he has to say on the preparation for Wavell's attack on Sidi Barrani throws a very different light on the story told by Churchill's *The Second World War*.

"A good average colonel and would make a good chairman of a Tory associa-

tion." That was how Churchill described Wavell after a visit by the latter to London between August 8–15, 1940. Worse still, he did not feel in him, as he wrote to Eden, "the sense of mental vigour and resolve to overcome obstacles, which was indispensable to successful war." Moreover, Churchill's readiness to scrutinise Wavell's dispositions left Wavell "clearly upset". He even considered resignation.

In *The Second World War* Churchill chose to play down this clash, in which he was proved utterly wrong by the course of events. But whatever one thinks of Churchill's account, written years after the event, nothing can detract from the heroic decision he made at the time. Thirty days before the invasion which was anticipated for mid-September 1940, it was decided to weaken the British Home Forces in order to reinforce Wavell's command in Egypt.

The British Carrier, Universal Number 1, Mark II

Weight: $4\frac{1}{4}$ tons.
Crew: 4.
Armament: one .55-inch Boys anti-tank rifle, two .303-inch Bren machine guns, and one 2-inch mortar.
Armour: 7-mm minimum, 10-mm maximum.
Engine: Ford V-8, 85-hp. **Speed:** 30 mph. **Range:** 160 miles.
Length: 12 feet 4 inches. **Width:** 6 feet 11 inches. **Height:** 5 feet 3 inches.

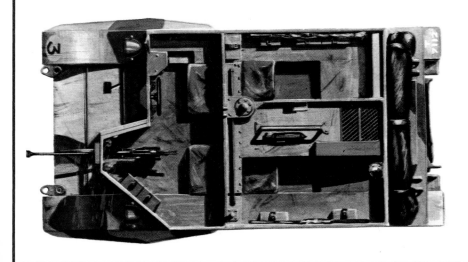

▽ *The king of the desert beats a hasty retreat: Berlin's* Lustige Blätter *exults over Britain's withdrawal from British Somaliland, effected in the face of overpowering Italian pressure in August.*

In all there were three tank regiments (154 armoured vehicles), 48 anti-tank guns, 48 25-pounder field guns, and other infantry weapons which Churchill wanted to send to Egypt through the Mediterranean. As the Admiralty refused to accept responsibility, the risk being too great, these reinforcements were sent out round the Cape. On September 19 they entered the Red Sea, finding no challenge from the Italian naval forces based on Massawa. The British air forces in the Middle East were also being reinforced. Between the end of August and the end of December 1940, 107 Hurricane fighters and Blenheim bombers were taken by sea to Takoradi on the Gold Coast and flown across Africa by devious stages to Khartoum on the Nile. When French Equatorial Africa, and particularly the important staging-post of

Fort Lamy, went over to de Gaulle's cause, it became possible to build up the Takoradi air route into a key supply line.

Wavell's opportunities

"What would happen if the Italians were not to attack?" asked Eden on October 15, when he visited Wavell in Cairo. By way of reply Wavell brought in General Sir Henry Maitland Wilson, commanding the British forces in Egypt, and asked him to explain to Eden the plan of attack – or rather of strategic envelopment – which had been prepared against the Italian forces dug in at Sidi Barrani.

At this time, it should be noted the Italian attack on Greece had led to more tension between London and G.H.Q. Cairo.

The British War Cabinet demanded effective aid for the Greeks; and very unwillingly, as their own resources were weak, Wavell and Air Chief-Marshal Sir Arthur Longmore, Air Officer Commanding Mediterranean and Middle East, agreed to send 63 fighters and 46 bombers to Greece in two months.

There was equal friction and conflict of interests between Rome and Tripoli. Mussolini was pressing Graziani to march on Marsa Matrûh without further delay, while Graziani wanted to wait until he had been supplied with three more motorised battalions, with armoured cars, and with water trucks. Exasperated, Mussolini warned Graziani on October 21 that if any further objections were raised he would not hesitate to accept Graziani's resignation. Nothing came of this, doubtless

▷ *As a result of the fighting around Sidi Barrani, the port of Sollum fell to the British forces in mid-December. In the background is the desert escarpment that marks the end of the coastal region.*

because of the catastrophe on the Greek front.

The Greek venture and its disastrous results for Italy rebounded as far as the Western Desert, for the emergency transport of supplies to the Albanian front which it necessitated cut down the reserves of mobile forces which might reasonably have been sent to North Africa before the resumption of the campaign. Thus Mussolini's share of the blame for the defeat of December 9 was great, but it did not excuse the mistakes of Graziani, Berti, and Gariboldi.

Battle at Sidi Barrani

The Italian forces around Sidi Barrani had severe weaknesses in their deployment. In the first line, General Gallina's Libyan Corps held the 19 miles between Maktila on the coast and Nibeiwa in the desert. In reserve, General Merzari's "3rd of January" Black Shirt Division, occupying Sidi Barrani itself, was some 12 miles back from the units which it would be required to support. In the second line, XXI Corps (General Dalmazzo) had its "Cirene" Division dug in on the escarpment, 20 miles west of Nibeiwa. The area between the two points was only weakly patrolled.

Such a strung-out disposition was fatally vulnerable to an armoured attack. As it could not be adjusted within 24 hours it exposed the Italian Army, "motorised on foot", as a wag referred to it, to piecemeal destruction. In addition, the rocky terrain had prevented an anti-tank ditch from being dug, and there were not enough mines and too few 47-mm anti-tank guns to repel an armoured advance.

Matters were worsened by Italian Intelligence's failure to grasp British plans. Graziani believed that the British were over 200,000 strong – a wildly exaggerated figure. But it did not prevent him giving permission for General Berti to go to Italy at the end of November. At the front, there was the impression that something was afoot, but the increase in British motorised patrols had not caused the Italians to change their dispositions before December 9.

By then it was too late. At dawn on the 9th, surging forward from their concentration-point in the desert (which had been christened "Piccadilly Circus") the British 7th Armoured Division and 4th Indian Division struck through the gap in

◁ *Their first desert victory before them, British infantry vault from their transport for the surprise south-flank assault on the Italian positions around Sidi Barrani.*
▽ *The moment of truth: anxious infantry wait for Vickers Mark VI light tanks to open the onslaught against the Italians.*

the Italian front, while a brigade under Brigadier A. R. Selby attacked Maktila on the coast road. The entire force, soon to be known as XIII Corps, was under the command of Lieutenant-General Richard O'Connor, and consisted of only 36,000 men and 225 armoured vehicles; among the latter were 57 Infantry tanks known as "Matildas", whose massive armour was proof against the Italian shells.

The 4th Indian Division and the Matilda tank battalion attacked Nibeiwa, which was defended by the Maletti Motorised Group. Surprise was complete, for the uproar of the artillery and air bombardment drowned the noise of engines and tank tracks, and the British were attacking from the south-west and even from the west. Badly wounded, General Maletti fought on until he was killed at the head of his troops, but by 0830 it was all over. For the price of 56 dead, Major-General Beresford-Peirse, commanding 4th Indian Division, had taken 2,000 prisoners.

Encamped at Tummar, General Pescatori of the 2nd Libyan Division planned to march to the sound of the guns as soon as the British attack began. But 4th Indian Division and the Matildas saved him the trouble. Thrown back, Pescatori counterattacked with spirit, but his forces were broken up by crushing British artillery fire. Tummar West fell in the afternoon while Tummar East did not surrender until dawn on the 10th.

In the evening of December 9, Brigadier J. A. L. Caunter's 7th Armoured Division reached the sea, cutting off the retreat of the survivors of the 2nd Libyan Division. Facing Sidi Barrani, Selby Force had thrown General Sibille's 1st Libyan Division (not without some trouble) out of its position at Maktila. The Italian pocket thus formed at Maktila was cleaned up with the assistance of British naval bombardment, a task which had been completed by the evening of the 11th.

During the same day Graziani ordered XXI Corps to fall back immediately to the Halfaya–Sollum–Capuzzo line on the frontier. The "Cirene" Division got the order in time and fell back without trouble. But this was not the case with General Spinelli's "Catanzaro" Division, thanks to an error in transmission. It was caught on the move between Buqbuq and Sollum and half annihilated.

This last defeat raised the losses of the Italian 10th Army to 38,000 prisoners, 237 guns, and 73 tanks, while the British losses amounted to only 624 killed, wounded, and missing. But O'Connor's

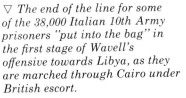

▽ *The end of the line for some of the 38,000 Italian 10th Army prisoners "put into the bag" in the first stage of Wavell's offensive towards Libya, as they are marched through Cairo under British escort.*

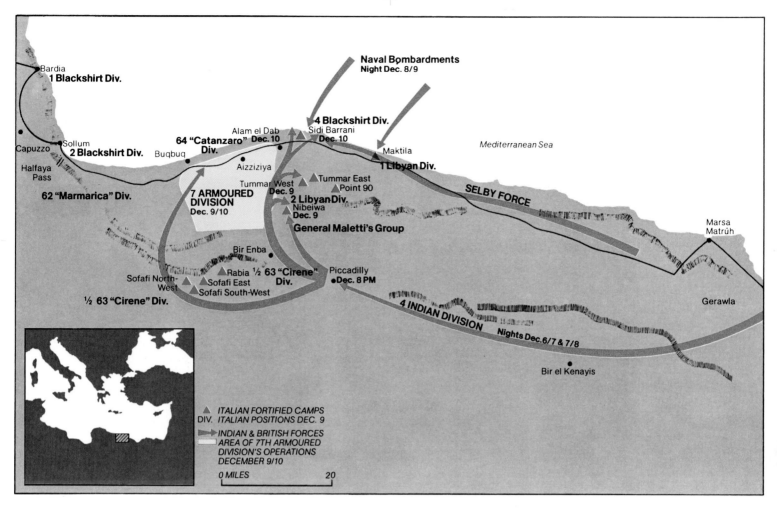

force had no sooner won this glorious and virtually painless victory than it was seriously weakened by the withdrawal of the excellent 4th Indian Division, which was earmarked for the campaign against the Italians in Eritrea.

It is now clear that this was a mistake. In Italian East Africa the Duke of Aosta, Viceroy of Abyssinia, was already so weak that the Anglo-Egyptian Sudan had nothing to fear from his forces, and the same applied to Kenya. The 4th Indian Division was badly missed in the Western Desert.

Was Wavell to blame? Certainly, the original scope of Operation "Compass", the attack on the Italians at Sidi Barrani, was limited to a five-day raid after which O'Connor was to fall back on Marsa Matrûh. But the real responsibility lay much higher. The British War Cabinet was deeply concerned with Abyssinia, and Churchill was at the same time trying to interest the Imperial General Staff in a venture called Operation "Workshop", directed against the Italian island of Pantelleria in the Mediterranean.

The 6th Australian Division (Major-General I. G. Mackay) replaced 4th Indian Division in XIII Corps. But General O'Connor did not wait for its arrival before launching an all-out pursuit against the beaten and disorganised Italian forces. On December 14 he crossed the frontier south of Capuzzo, swung his armoured and motorised forces to the north, and invaded Bardia on the 18th. The Bardia perimeter, 24 miles in extent, was defended by General Bergonzoli's XXIII Corps, with the survivors of the "Catanzaro" and "Cirene" Divisions from Egypt, General Tracchia's "Marmarica" Division, and General Antonelli's "23rd of March" Black Shirt Division – a total force of 45,000 men and 430 guns.

On December 18, General Mackay's 6th Australian Division joined XIII Corps. Prospects for the Axis darkened with the fall of Bardia right at the beginning of 1941; not even the first major fire raid on London on the night of December 30–31 did much to redress the balance. In the occupied or threatened countries of Europe there was a widespread feeling that the defeat of Mussolini would only be a matter of time, and that that of Hitler would follow.

But in view of the military weakness of Great Britain and her Empire, this was very far from the truth . . .

△ The unexpected counter-stroke: Wavell's surprise attack, which took the Italian defences of Sidi Barrani in flank and left the British poised for a deep thrust into the Italian colony of Libya.

△ *Italian prisoners taken at Tobruk march towards a temporary prison camp.*

After receiving this reassuring confirmation of Greece's intentions, the British Government made no attempt to influence the Greek Government. On January 21, the very day of the attack on Tobruk, London, now free from any urgent Greek commitments, ordered G.H.Q. Cairo to resume its offensive towards Benghazi without further delay.

After the surprise attack on Sidi Barrani, Marshal Graziani had given his opinion that Cyrenaica could no longer be defended and that it would be advisable to withdraw to Tripoli, putting the Sirte Desert between his 10th Army and the Army of the Nile. When the Italian High Command recommended him to be more optimistic, Graziani set to work to improvise the defence of Cyrenaica – but it must be admitted that he did not make a very good job of it. His 10th Army was divided into three defensive groups: XXIII Corps at Bardia, XXII Corps at Tobruk, and the XX Corps (General Cona) holding the Mechili-Derna line. This disposition meant that it was highly likely that 10th Army could be defeated piece-

meal by an enemy who was greatly inferior in overall numbers.

On January 9, despite the destruction of XXIII Corps in the battle for Bardia, Graziani was now showing optimism instead of his previous pessimism. In fact the Jebel Akhdar, the massif between Mechili and Derna which rises to a height of about 1,650 feet, was quite unsuitable for an attack by mechanised forces.

By putting an infantry division into the Derna position and the armoured brigade of General Babini into Mechili, Graziani thought he would have an excellent chance of halting the British advance towards Benghazi. But he was forgetting that those two formations would have to fight independently as they were separated by the Jebel Akhdar hills and could not reinforce one another.

On January 24 the 6th Australian Division approached the Derna position, while the 7th Armoured Division fell upon Babini's armoured brigade, in spite of the extremely poor state of the British tanks. The Italian 14-ton tanks were fighting the same number of 12.5-ton British cruiser tanks, and the battle ended badly for the Italians. They retreated into the Jebel Akhdar to avoid encirclement – but in so doing they gave the British a clear road to the main Italian supply-line along the Gulf of Sirte. For this reason Graziani decided to abandon western Cyrenaica on February 1. General Gariboldi was sent to Tripoli to organise the defence of the province, and General Tellera succeeded him as commander of 10th Army.

The distance between Mechili and Beda Fomm, near the Gulf of Sirte, is about 140 miles. Along the coast road between Derna and Beda Fomm the distance is about 225 miles. But the retreating Italians had the advantage of using the *Via Balbia*, the excellent coast road; the British, advancing from Mechili towards Beda Fomm, had only a poorly reconnoitred track, which was not clearly marked and which crossed a desert consisting either of soft sand or of areas strewn with large rocks.

"War is won with leftovers", Marshal Foch had once said. It is hardly likely that Generals O'Connor and O'Moore Creagh, commander of 7th Armoured Division, had ever heard of this dictum, but now they put it into practice with a vengeance. At 1500 hours on February 4 the 11th Hussars (Colonel Combe) were at Msus, only 60 miles from the *Via Balbia*. At

dawn on the 5th, after they had been reinforced with some artillery, they took the track leading to Antelat and at noon reached their objective at Beda Fomm, half an hour before the first Italian column retreating from Benghazi down the *Via Balbia*. Confused engagements were fought throughout February 6, with the Italians hitting out wildly as they came up against the British blocking their retreat.

Finally, at 0900 hours on February 7, O'Connor sent an uncoded signal for the information of Wavell and the edification of Mussolini: "Fox killed in the open." Badly wounded, General Tellera died a few hours later; the H.Q. of 10th Army, and Generals Cona and Babini, had been captured. General Bergonzoli had also been captured: he had managed to make his way through the Australian lines when Bardia fell. About 20,000 Italians were also captured, and the final count of the equipment seized by the British after this last battle amounted to 112 11- and 14-ton M11 and M13 medium tanks, 216 guns, and 1,500 vehicles.

On February 3 the British had reached El Agheila at the bottom of the Gulf of Sirte. This was a very important position, for there was only a narrow gap about 15-20 miles wide through which tanks could pass between the desert and the sea.

△ *Marshal Graziani, relieved of his command on February 10.*

Atlantic 1940

Between January 1 and March 31, 1940 only 108 merchantmen totalling 343,610 tons were sunk by U-boats. Eight U-boats were sunk during the same period. From November, no German surface raider had penetrated the Royal Navy's blockade extending between Iceland and the Orkney Islands. The threat of the magnetic mine had also largely been neutralised. By the end of June 1940, Grand-Admiral Raeder could dispose of every Atlantic port between Tromso and St. Jean-de-Luz while a third of the Royal Navy's capital ships were now committed to the Mediterranean. The Germans, lacked a powerful surface fleet with which to take advantage of the strategically placed ports, which were also within easy range of R.A.F. bombers. The Atlantic ports did, however, allow the U-boats an extra week of operations. Admiral Dönitz set up an HQ at Kerneval where he used powerful radio communications to direct U-boat packs towards Allied convoys. Between July and December 1940, 285 ships were sunk. Britain needed more destroyers and eventually obtained 50 from the United States in return for leasing strategic bases to the U.S.A. The Germans were slow in expanding their U-boat production and had insufficient air support: the tide began to turn in Britain's favour.

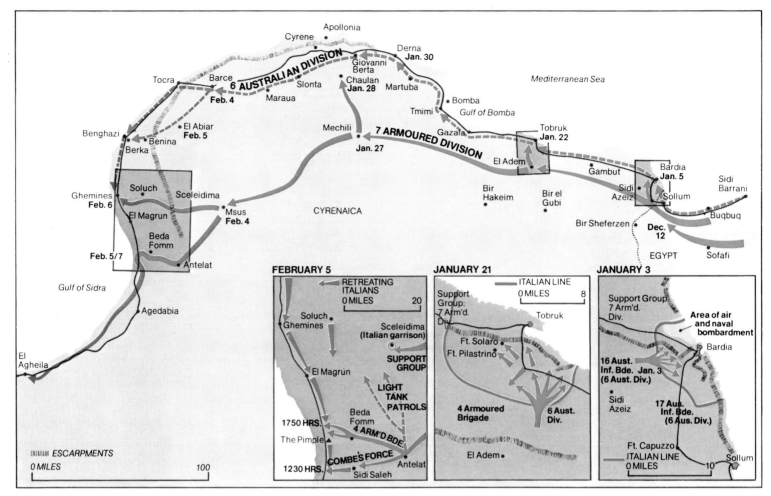

As the British XIII Corps now commanded this position, it was well placed to invade Tripolitania or defend Cyrenaica as required.

Wavell's original five-day raid had developed into a two-month campaign. In four pitched battles O'Connor had advanced 560 miles from his starting position. Although he never had more than two divisions under his command, he had destroyed one Italian army (four corps, or nine divisions) at a cost of only 500 dead, 1,373 wounded, and 56 missing. The "bag" of Italian prisoners amounted to 130,000 men, including 22 generals and one admiral, and O'Connor had seized or destroyed 845 guns and 380 tanks. For the third time in the war Guderian's words to Hitler had been proved true: "Tanks are a life-saving weapon".

Graziani steps down

On February 10 Marshal Graziani was ordered to hand over his command to General Gariboldi and to return to Italy. His conduct of operations was carefully examined by a commission of enquiry, which came to highly equivocal conclusions about them. But it was hard to assign him the total responsibility for this catastrophe without implicating the Duce himself. Undoubtedly, Graziani had not excelled himself; possibly, also, he still suffered from the effects of the hand-grenade which had been thrown at him in Addis Ababa in 1938. But above all he had been hampered by his shortage of modern weapons, just as had Gamelin in the French campaign a few months earlier.

The Luftwaffe strikes

On December 27, after the battle of Sidi Barrani, Graziani had attempted to explain matters to Mussolini. "From the harsh experience of these bitter days," he wrote, "we must conclude that in this theatre of war a single armoured division is more powerful than a whole army."

Coming events would prove these to be prophetic words.

The Wehrmacht's intervention in the Mediterranean theatre began when the German High Command transferred X *Fliegerkorps* to Sicily and Calabria.

Admiral Sir Andrew Cunningham was born in 1883. In 1939 he was C.-in-C., Mediterranean, and when Italy entered the war he soon found himself outnumbered and in difficult straits strategically and logistically. He quickly wrested command from the Italians, however, in several actions at sea and at Taranto, and thus secured the army's right flank. Cunningham became Allied Naval C.-in-C. under Eisenhower in 1943, and First Sea Lord in October of the same year.

At the end of December 1940, General Geissler of the Luftwaffe set up his H.Q. at Taormina. His squadrons were divided between the airfields at Catania, Comiso, Marsala, Trápani, Palermo, and Reggio di Calabria, along with 45 Italian bombers and 75 Italian fighters. Together with the 70 bombers and 25 fighters of the *Regia Aeronautica* based in Sardinia, the number of Axis aircraft capable of operating in the central Mediterranean, which narrows to under 90 miles between Cape Bon in Tunisia and Marsala in Sicily, was approximately 400.

Such a force should normally have been under the command of *Superaero*, the High Command of the Italian Air Force. But Göring had no intention of permitting this, for he deliberately kept "his" airmen under his own control and reserved to himself the right to give them orders. Thus it is fairly certain that he was responsible for continual interference and fraction in the conduct of operations.

The strength of the R.A.F. on Malta was far smaller. When X *Fliegerkorps* moved south, the British air defences of Malta consisted of a dozen Swordfish, 16 Hurricanes, 16 Wellington twin-engine bombers, and a few Martin Maryland bomber/ reconnaissance aircraft built in the United States. Admittedly a new shipload of 16 Hurricanes was expected with the next convoy from Gibraltar, but this was still a drop in the ocean.

General Geissler and his aircrews got their first chance to distinguish themselves with the British Operation "Excess", which started on January 6. Admiral Somerville's task was to convoy four merchantmen (one for Malta, the others for Greece) from Gibraltar to the central Mediterranean. Admiral Cunningham in Alexandria would make use of the appearance of Force H in the Western Mediterranean to send two merchantment into Malta. At the same time,

two cruisers from his light forces would take troops there. After that he would take charge of the ships making for Greece from Gibraltar.

While the two British convoys converged on Malta from east and west, the Malta-based bombers struck at Naples on the night of January 8–9. Their target was the Italian battleships which had survived the Taranto raid. The *Giulio Cesare* suffered a leak as the result of a bomb explosion on the bottom of the harbour and had to steam to Genoa for repairs. The *Vittorio Veneto* escaped untouched, but *Supermarina* decided to transfer her to La Spezia, where she would be out of range of the Malta-based bombers. This, however, would prevent *Vittorio Veneto* from taking any useful action in the narrows between Tunisia and Sicily.

Force H completed its mission without incident. Somerville passed to the south of Sardinia on the evening of January 9 and returned to Gibraltar with the battleship *Malaya*, the battle-cruiser *Renown*, and the aircraft-carrier *Ark Royal*, leaving his charges under the protection of an A.A. cruiser, two heavy cruisers (*Gloucester* and *Southampton*, which had joined him after landing the troops they had

△◁ *The advance from Sidi Barrani to El Agheila.* ▽ *Two British soldiers inspect the gutted wreckage of a FIAT C.R. 42 fighter. This, the best such aircraft available to the Italians in North Africa, was no match for the Hurricanes of the R.A.F. and about equal to the Gladiator.* ▽ ▽ *Australian artillery in action before Derna, which was evacuated by the Italians on January 30.*

Help for Mussolini

The Italian defeats in Albania, at Taranto and in Libya were a cause of deep concern for the Germans. The Luftwaffe's X *Fliegerkorps* was sent to bases in Sicily at the end of December 1940 to close the Mediterranean to the British between Sicily and Tunisia and to fight British aircraft based on Malta.

On January 3, 1941, Australian forces took Bardia in Libya. On January 21 the British captured Tobruk. Having made these important inroads into Mussolini's North American Empire, the British now turned their attention to the support of Greece. It was estimated that the Germans had at least 12 divisions in Rumania and the Greek General Papagos believed that the Greeks would need to be reinforced with nine British divisions. The British offer was more modest, amounting to little more than two or three divisions along with an air formation.

brought from Alexandria in Malta), and five destroyers. At dawn on January 10 the *Gloucester* and *Southampton* sank the Italian torpedo-boat *Vega* which had tried heroically to attack them. During this action, the destroyer *Gallant* hit a mine and had to be towed to Malta. Repairs proved impossible, however, because of Axis air attacks.

Ordeal of the *Illustrious*

But Cunningham's Mediterranean Fleet did not get off so easily. Towards 1230 hours Junkers Ju 87 and Ju 88 bombers appeared over the British fleet, which had joined the convoy soon after the sinking of the *Vega*. They launched a fierce attack on the aircraft-carrier *Illustrious*, in spite of sustained fire from the battleships *Warspite* and *Valiant*.

"There was no doubt we were watching complete experts," wrote Admiral Cunningham in his memoirs. "Formed roughly in a larger circle over the fleet they peeled off one by one when reaching the attacking position. We could not but admire the skill and precision of it all. The attacks were pressed home to point-blank range, and as they pulled out of their dives some of them were seen to fly along the flight deck of the *Illustrious* below the level of her funnel."

Illustrious was struck by two 550-lb and four 1,100-lb bombs in under 10 minutes, and but for her armoured flight deck she would most likely have suffered the same fate as many American and British aircraft-carriers in the Far East. Nevertheless she was badly damaged; her steering-gear was out of action and she had to steer with her propellers. Admiral Cunningham therefore ordered her to return to Malta for repairs.

On its return voyage the following day Cunningham's force was again attacked by the dive-bombers of X *Fliegerkorps*. The luckless *Southampton* was disabled and set on fire; she had to be abandoned by her crew and was sunk by torpedoes.

At Malta, workers and engineers laboured frantically to get *Illustrious* ready for action again. But on January 16 she received more damage from German bombs, which was patched up, after a fashion. On the night of January 23 *Illustrious* left the Grand Harbour and returned to Alexandria, making the remarkable speed of 28 knots. Nevertheless, she had to be completely overhauled and set out on a long voyage to the American yards at Norfolk, Virginia, which undertook the work with the sympathetic agreement of President Roosevelt.

In the absence of *Illustrious* the Admiralty decided that the carrier *Formidable*, which was in the Atlantic, should proceed to Alexandria round the Cape of Good Hope. Without fleet air cover, Admiral Cunningham was unable to take any action in the waters south of Sicily until *Formidable* joined his flag, which she did, in spite of the Luftwaffe's attempts to mine the Suez Canal and the approaches to Alexandria, on March 10.

Meanwhile the German bombers based in Sicily kept Malta under constant air bombardment. Heavy losses were inflicted on the island's aircraft, which were under the command of Air Vice-Marshal H. P. Lloyd. At the end of February the surviving Wellington bombers had to be brought back to Egypt; the fighters had been suffering similar losses, and on March 11 the Hurricanes, the only aircraft on Malta capable of tackling the Messerschmitt 109's and 110's on anything like equal terms, were reduced to eight battle-worthy machines.

From March 1941, however, the need for air support for the Afrika Korps and for Operation "Marita" in the Balkans compelled General Geissler to divert a large number of his squadrons to these new operational theatres. The inevitable result was a slackening of the pressure put on Malta by X *Fliegerkorps*. Between April 3 and May 21 Force H was able to supply Malta with 82 Hurricanes, flown from the carriers *Ark Royal* and *Furious*.

Rome and Berlin reinforce North Africa

It is true that the German High Command and the Italian *Comando Supremo* failed to take full advantage of the temporary local superiority in all neighbouring waters achieved by the transfer of X *Fliegerkorps* to Sicily. Nevertheless, the actions of X *Fliegerkorps* gave the Axis three months in which to transfer troops to North Africa for the defence of Tripolitania against the British, which was done with very little loss. From this point of view, the air and sea engagements between Sicily and Tunisia on January 10–11 had much more serious consequences than the destruction of the *Southampton* and the temporary disablement of the *Illustrious*.

Between February 1 and June 30, 1941, no less than 81,785 Axis troops were landed at Tripoli with approximately 450,000 tons of weapons, fuel, and ammunition. In February and March, with the temporary neutralisation of Malta, the troops were shipped with very few casualties. These increased slightly from April onwards, but until June 30 casualties totalled only 4.8 per cent of all the troops embarked.

First to arrive were the Italian "Ariete" and "Trento" Divisions, together with the German 5th Light Division, which was the first contingent of the *Deutsches Afrika Korps* or D.A.K.

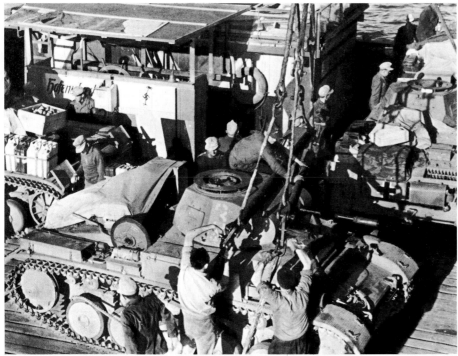

△ ◁ *Two curious British soldiers inspect a portrait of the "warlord" Mussolini, whose armies they had just defeated.*

△ ▷ *The spoils of war lined up for inspection. At Benghazi alone, the Italians had abandoned 112 tanks, 216 guns, and 1,500 vehicles. Even if their morale had not been completely broken, the Italians had lost so much* matériel *in their precipitate retreat that they would have been unable to launch a counter-offensive.* △ *Advent of the new order: tanks of the German 5th Light Division are unloaded from an Italian ship.*

Rommel arrives in Tripoli

On February 6, 1941, Lieutenant-General Erwin Rommel was received by Brauchitsch, who gave him instructions for his new mission. He was appointed to command the expeditionary corps which was to be sent to Africa, and received orders to proceed to Africa as soon as possible. Rommel's intention, as he noted in his diary, was to examine the possibilities of using the new formation. It was anticipated that the first German troops would arrive in mid-February and that the last unit of the 5th Light Division would be landed in mid-April. By the end of May the last detachments of the 15th Panzer Division should be in position, and the D.A.K. ready to move.

In his new rôle Rommel was to take his orders from Marshal Graziani. This was decided only after O.K.W. and *Comando Supremo* had agreed that the original plan for a close defence of Tripoli should be abandoned. The Italian and German forces, under Rommel's immediate command, would move further down the Gulf of Sirte and base their defence of Tripoli on Buerat. Rommel was authorised to appeal to the German Army High Command over Graziani's head, if the latter's orders looked like endangering the safety of the expeditionary force or the honour of the German Army.

In the afternoon of the same day, Hitler received Rommel and told him that he would be accompanied to Africa by Colonel Schmundt, the Führer's personal aide-de-camp. On February 11, Rommel presented himself to General Guzzoni, acting Chief of the General Staff in the absence of General Cavallero at the Albanian front. After a quick review of the situation with General Roatta, Italian Army Chief-of-Staff, Rommel set off for North Africa via Catania, where he conferred with Geissler. On February 12 he arrived at Tripoli and reported to General Gariboldi, who had just relieved Graziani.

And thus this remarkable commander began his military career in North Africa.

CHAPTER 13
ENTER ROMMEL

For 18 months, between March 1941 and September 1942, Erwin Rommel displayed outstanding ability to attack and to manoeuvre, learning to combine cunning with force. There is no doubt that the man who managed to rebound from a decisive defeat before Tobruk into an advance which took him to the gates of Alexandria must be counted among the truly great commanders of all time.

But was his brilliance as a tactician matched by his strategic ability? This is not so clear. One firm criterion of sound strategy is that it must combine the different interests of land, sea, and air forces into a framework which Churchill described with the ugly word "triphibian". And Rommel repeatedly failed to do this.

During the summer of 1942, for example, Rommel constantly blamed *Comando Supremo* for the frequent breakdowns in his supply system, forgetting that after taking Tobruk on June 21 he had assured Cavallero that he would be able to reach the Nile with the help of the fuel and transport captured in Tobruk. He also forgot that although he was keeping Luftwaffe squadrons from the task of neutralising Malta, the British bombers, torpedo-bombers, and submarines based on the island were exacting a merciless toll on the Italian merchant tonnage in the central Mediterranean. In fact, it was on Rommel's urgent request – despite the protests of Kesselring and Cavallero – that Hitler and Mussolini gave up Operation "Hercules", which could and should

have presented the Axis with Malta and Gozo.

Whatever one may think of Rommel in a historical context, his former subordinates and opponents all pay tribute to his nobility of character and his high moral code. Undoubtedly his task in fighting a "clean war" in the African desert was easier than that of his colleagues on the Eastern Front, who had the partisans and Hitler to deal with. But when slight scuffles broke out between his troops and Arab tribesmen, whom British agents were trying to enlist against the Italians, Rommel noted in his diary on September 16, 1942: "There is nothing so unpleasant as partisan warfare. It is perhaps very important not to make reprisals on hostages at the first outbreak of partisan warfare, for these only create feelings of revenge and serve to strengthen the *franc-tireurs*. It is better to allow an incident to go unavenged than to hit back at the innocent. It only agitates the whole neighbourhood, and hostages easily become martyrs."

In 1944 Rommel protested to Hitler in the same spirit of humanity, good sense, and true German patriotism against the appalling massacre of French civilians at Oradour-sur-Glane perpetrated by the S.S. *Das Reich* Panzer Division, and demanded exemplary punishment for those responsible for the crime. (The result was a coarse and violent rebuff.) The honourable treatment which Rommel offered to the Free French prisoners taken at Bir

The War Transformed

It was only when Hitler invaded Russia on June 22, 1941 and when Japan entered the war in December 1941 the Second World War truly became a world war.

▽ *New factor in the Desert War– Afrika Korps Panzer units move up to the front on the* Via Balbia–*the lifeline along the Libyan coast which the Italians built before the war.*

The German Panzerkampfwagen III Ausführung F

Weight: 19¼ tons.
Crew: 5.
Armament: one 5-cm KwK 39 L/42 with 99 rounds plus two 7.92-mm MG34 machine guns with 3,750 rounds.
Armour: 30-mm maximum, 16-mm minimum.
Engine: one Maybach HL 120 TRM 12-cylinder, 300-hp.
Speed: 25 mph.
Range: 105 miles.
Length: 18 feet.
Width: 9 feet 9 inches.
Height: 8 feet 1 inch.

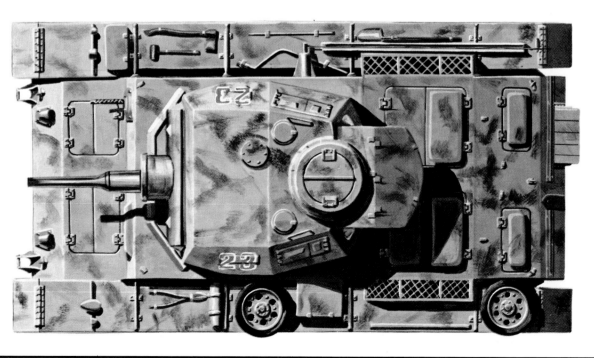

△ Help for the Italians: Afrika Korps *armour reaches the quayside at Tripoli. In the light of Rommel's later spectacular successes it is often hard to remember that the original purpose of the German desert army was nothing more than the defence of the Libyan capital.*

"February 6, 1941
"Dearest Lu,
"Landed at Staaken 12.45. First to C.in-C. Army, who appointed me to my new job, and then to Führer. Things are moving fast. My kit is coming on here. I can only take barest necessities with me. Perhaps I'll be able to get the rest out soon. I need not tell you that my head is swimming with all the many things there are to be done. It'll be months before anything materialises.

"So 'our leave' was cut short again. Don't be sad, it had to be. The new job is very big and important."

"February 7, 1941.
"Slept on my new job last night. It's one way of getting my rheumatism treatment. I've got a lot to do, in the few hours that remain, getting together all I need."

This was typical of Rommel. And one can only conclude that when his widow and his son, Manfred, chose the title *War Without Hate* for the collection of letters and memoirs which he left, it was a perfectly appropriate decision.

The British and the Greeks

While the advance units of the *Afrika Korps* were leaving Italy for Africa General Wavell in Cairo was carrying out the orders he had received from London. The 6th Australian Division, the 2nd New Zealand Division (Major-General B.C. Freyberg) and over half the 2nd Armoured Division (Major-General M. D. Gambier-Parry), which had just arrived from England, were to be sent to help the Greeks.

Brigadier E. Dorman-Smith, an officer of G.H.Q. Middle East in Cairo, who had been at the front with O'Connor from Mechili to Beda Fomm, returned to Cairo to see Wavell at 1000 hours on February 12 (a few hours, in fact, before Rommel called on Gariboldi in Tripoli), and heard about this new change of front from Wavell, Dorman-Smith remarked that while he had been away from G.H.Q. the usual maps of the Western Desert on the walls had been replaced by maps of Greece, and that Wavell commented sardonically: "You see, Eric, I'm starting my spring campaign."

On the previous day Wavell had in fact cabled Churchill after receiving a message from Lieutenant-General Sir Henry Maitland Wilson in Tobruk, informing him that the Italian forces were in a state

Hakeim in June 1942 should also be noted. It ignored the fact that the Franco-German armistice of 1940, according to the rules and usages of war, had deprived de Gaulle's Free French adherents of the status and privileges of regular combatants.

Rommel was also an attentive husband, who wrote to his wife every day to keep her in touch with his fortunes. The following extracts come from two successive letters (the second contains a thinly-veiled reference to his new assignment in Africa).

of collapse. At the front, O'Connor stated that he was ready to move forward into Tripolitania if all available troops were sent to reinforce his 7th Armoured Division, and if the R.A.F. and Admiral Cunningham's Inshore Squadron (one monitor and three gunboats) could harass the Italian-held coastline and give him the necessary support. On the latter assumption he had planned amphibious operations against Buerat and subsequently against Misurata, further along the coast.

O'Connor's optimism was matched in Tripoli by Rommel's initial pessimism. The latter had just received a discouraging report from Lieutenant Heggenreiner, a German liaison officer in North Africa. Rommel noted that Heggenreiner "described some very unpleasant incidents which had occurred during the retreat, or rather the rout which it had become. Italian troops had thrown away their weapons and ammunition and clambered on to overloaded vehicles in a wild attempt to get away to the west. This had led to some ugly scenes, and even to shooting. Morale was as low as it could be in all military circles in Tripoli. Most of the Italian officers had already packed their bags and were hoping for a quick return trip to Italy."

General Gariboldi now had only five divisions under his orders: the "Bologna", "Brescia", "Pavia", "Sabratha", and "Savona" Divisions. Even on June 10, 1940, these were considered "inefficient",

△ *Rommel's desert flank: an oasis reconnaissance force.*
▷ *The left-hand prong of Rommel's triple advance was the thrust along the coast road to Benghazi. This tank belongs to Rommel's principal unit in his first desert offensive – General Streich's 5th Light Division.*

and had since had orders to give up part of their equipment to the recently-destroyed 10th Army. But for the formal orders of the British War Cabinet, nothing could have kept O'Connor and the victors of Sidi Barrani, Bardia, Tobruk, Mechili, and Beda Fomm from driving through to Tripoli.

But Churchill had already made his decision, and it was adhered to. For once Sir John Dill, the C.I.G.S., supported the Prime Minister's view. But Brooke, still C.-in-C., Home Forces, believed that Churchill's decision overreached the possibilities of British strategy, considering the means then available. Brooke later wrote: "This is one of the very few occasions on which I doubted Dill's advice and judgement, and I am not in a position to form any definite opinion as I was not familiar with all the facts. I have, however, always considered from the very start that our participation in the operations in Greece was a definite strategic blunder. Our hands were more than full at that time in the Middle East, and Greece could only result in the most dangerous dispersal of force."

Brooke's fears were certainly proved correct by the course of events. But the British felt themselves bound to go to the aid of the Greeks, quite apart from the fact that a refusal to do so would have been a gift for the Axis propagandists. There was always the possibility that without British help the Greeks might have been tempted to negotiate some arrangement with Hitler. On the other hand, the sending of a British expeditionary force to Greece proved to the world that Britain was not pursuing a policy of national self-interest. Despite the defeats in Greece and Crete, the attempt did much to save British prestige – more so than if it had not been made. The same cannot be said for projects such as Operation "Mandible", which compelled Wavell to keep the 7th Australian Division in the Nile Delta for a possible attack on Rhodes and Leros.

The desert front

As G.H.Q. Cairo was forced to give up the troops for this expeditionary force, it was left with only skeleton forces to "consolidate" its position in western Cyrenaica, according to orders. These forces consisted mainly of the rump of the 2nd

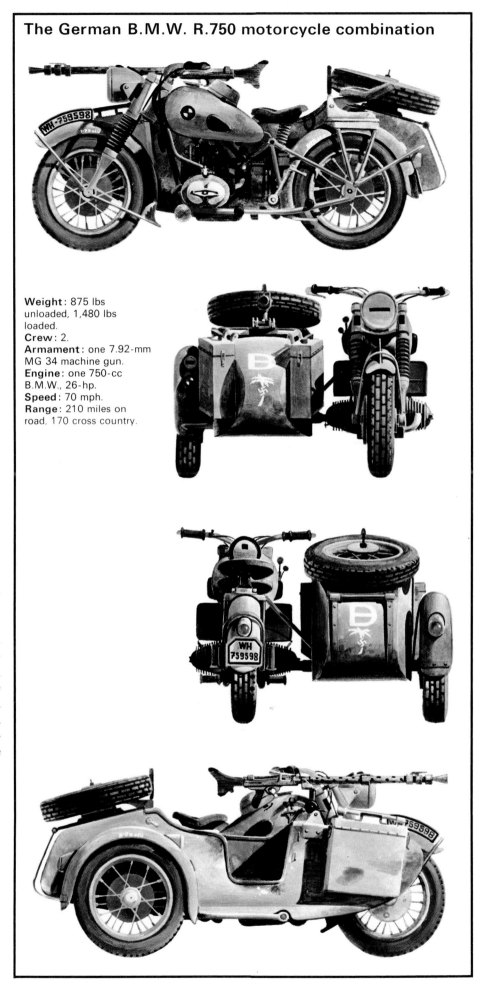

The German B.M.W. R.750 motorcycle combination

Weight: 875 lbs unloaded, 1,480 lbs loaded.
Crew: 2.
Armament: one 7.92-mm MG 34 machine gun.
Engine: one 750-cc B.M.W., 26-hp.
Speed: 70 mph.
Range: 210 miles on road, 170 cross country.

△ Afrika Korps *artillery in action. In a later note on the rules of desert warfare, Rommel wrote: "The artillery must have great range and must, above all, be capable of great mobility and of carrying with it ammunition in large quantities." Here, however, the* Afrika Korps *was at a disadvantage. General Fritz Bayerlein, who in time became commander of the* Afrika Korps, *put the problem in a nutshell: "A long arm is decisive–and here the British had the best of it. It was not pleasant to be exposed to the fire of their 25-pounder guns at extreme range and be unable to make an effective reply."*

Armoured Division, which had been equipped with captured Italian vehicles to replace the tanks sent to Greece. But the Italian tanks were so poor that even good British crews could not improve their performance. The 9th Australian Division (Major-General L. J. Morshead) should have reinforced this so-called armoured formation, but because of supply difficulties its foremost units had not got beyond Tobruk. The 3rd Indian Motorised Brigade completed this mediocre force.

After the capture of Benghazi, Wavell had appointed General Maitland Wilson as military governor of Cyrenaica. But the latter was recalled to Cairo and put in charge of the Greek expeditionary force immediately after taking up his command. He was succeeded by Lieutenant-General Philip Neame, V.C., a newcomer to the desert theatre, who only had a few days to accustom himself to the terrain.

The 7th Armoured Division, which had been the spearhead of XIII Corps, had been brought back to the Delta by Wavell to be completely refitted. Churchill had protested violently against this decision, and it is clear that if the division's repair shops could have been set up in Tobruk

after its fall, Rommel's task would have been much harder. But it must be remembered that this first British desert offensive had been the result of successive improvisations. On December 9, 1940, O'Connor had set out on a five-day raid. By February 6, 1941, he was over 500 miles further west, at El Agheila. It was not surprising that in these totally unexpected circumstances the base facilities had not kept up with the advance of the tanks.

In any event the dispositions made by Wavell show clearly that he believed that any large-scale counter-offensive by Rommel was highly improbable. Brauchitsch and Halder also believed that Rommel's attack on Agedabia could not take place until the end of May, after the last units of 15th Panzer Division had joined his force. Again, on March 19 Hitler, decorating Rommel with the Oak Leaves to the Knight's Cross, gave him no other instructions. According to his diaries this left Rommel, eager for action, "not very happy". Benghazi, the objective given him for his spring campaign, appeared to him to be indefensible by itself. The whole of Cyrenaica must therefore be recovered to ensure its security.

Rommel strikes

At dawn on March 24 the reconnaissance group of Rommel's 5th Light Division attacked El Agheila in Libya, and the British units defending this key position pulled back. They took up new positions at Marsa Brega, between the Gulf of Sirte and salt marsh impassable to tanks, about 50 miles south-west of Agedabia.

Rommel felt that he could not stick to the letter of his orders and so leave the British with enough time to reorganise while he waited for the whole of the 15th Panzer Division to reach the front. If he attacked again without delay he had a chance of surprising the British with his small mobile forces and of dislodging them from what was an extremely strong defensive position.

He therefore attacked again on March 31. The British did put up some resistance at Marsa Brega, but, outflanked on the desert front, they were forced to give up the place to the 5th Light Division. By the evening of April 2 the German forces, followed by the "Ariete" Armoured Division and the "Brescia" Infantry Division, occupied the Agedabia region two months ahead of the schedule set by O.K.H. About 800 British prisoners were taken during this engagement. Rommel's cunning use of dummy tanks had added to the confusion of the British as they retreated; German reconnaissance aircraft saw disorganised columns streaming back towards Benghazi and Mechili.

Rommel has often been criticised for acting incorrectly; but any subordinate is entitled to pursue his own objectives if he discovers that the ones he has been given by his superiors have been based on an incorrect appreciation of the situation. And this was precisely the position when Rommel and the *Afrika Korps* reached Marsa Brega at the end of March 1941.

But in such a situation a subordinate is also supposed to inform his superiors without a moment's delay of the steps he feels himself obliged to take. Rommel failed to do so, and for days he played hide and seek with his Italian and German superiors while he breathlessly exploited his initial success.

In his book on the war in Africa General Pietro Maravigna makes this quite clear. "The covering enemy troops were surprised by the attack and withdrew. They abandoned Bir es-Suera and Marsa Brega,

which Rommel's advanced forces occupied on April 1, while the main body of the 5th Light Division took up its position to the east of El Agheila.

"In Tripoli, and even more so in Rome, this news came like thunder in a clear sky. Mussolini, who was very much put out, asked Rintelen for information. Rintelen had none to give. He then asked Gariboldi to explain matters. Gariboldi replied that Rommel had evaded all authority and was acting entirely on his own initiative. Moreover, Gariboldi disclaimed all responsibility, as he had only authorised Rommel to make a surprise attack on the

△ *"The* Feldherr *of the front line"–Rommel, in an armoured car, with his men.*

British forces west of Marsa Brega to improve our own defences; the German general, carried away by his initial success, had exceeded his authority."

Gariboldi subsequently set off after Rommel with the intention of stopping him, but he was very abruptly received by his impetuous subordinate, especially as fresh successes had provided further justification for his actions; and the German High Command in Berlin signalled its approval. In fact, on the night of April 3–4 the reconnaissance group of the 5th Light Division entered Benghazi, and its main body drove onwards towards Mechili.

In Cairo the news of Rommel's escapade caused as much bewilderment as it had to *Comando Supremo*. Neame had been ordered not to let his position be endangered if the Axis forces attacked but to make a fighting retreat; but Wavell quickly realised that Neame had been overtaken by the sudden speed of events, and that the organised retreat he had had in mind was turning into a rout.

▽ *"There'll be no Dunkirk here!": Major-General Morshead* (centre), *commander of the 9th Australian Division—the defender of Tobruk.*
▽ ▽ *Overwhelmed by the speed of Rommel's advance—British prisoners of the* Afrika Korps.

British generals in the bag

Wavell therefore decided to call upon the services of O'Connor, but the latter had not had time to take stock of the situation before suffering an appalling stroke of ill luck. O'Connor and Neame, accompanied by General Carton de Wiart of Narvik fame, were on their way to Tmimi for a staff conference when they were captured by a German patrol near Derna.

"He was half asleep when his driver braked suddenly," writes Anthony Heckstall-Smith. "An *Afrika Korps* soldier shone his torch inside the car and could not suppress a cry of astonishment. Perhaps the generals could have escaped in that fraction of a second, but the soldier was rapidly joined by his comrades from the machine gun battalion commanded by Lieutenant-Colonel Ponath. O'Connor realised, too late, that his driver had veered to the north instead of steering eastward towards Tmimi.

"A few months later people in Egypt were telling the story of O'Connor's arrival at Rommel's field H.Q., when Rommel was having breakfast with his staff. O'Connor looked them up and down and asked: 'Does anyone here speak English?

"A bespectacled officer leapt to his feet, clicked his heels, bowed deeply, and said 'I do, sir.'

"'Well, get lost.'

"The story is probably apocryphal, but the soldiers in the desert army are very proud of it."

At Mechili General Gambier-Parry, commander of the 2nd Armoured Division, was also captured, along with most of his 3rd Armoured Brigade and large numbers of the 3rd Indian Motorised Brigade.

When he thrust from Agedabia to Mechili, and from Mechili to Derna, Rommel was executing the reverse of

O'Connor's manoeuvre at Beda Fomm. But he was not so fortunate as O'Connor had been; when the advanced German units reached the Gulf of Bomba, the rearguard of the Australian brigade retreating from Benghazi had already fallen back on Tobruk and was strengthening the garrison. The Allies had escaped from the Axis net.

Decision to hold Tobruk

The decision to defend Tobruk at all costs was taken by Wavell on the advice of Air Chief-Marshal Longmore and Admiral Cunningham. The garrison consisted of the 9th Australian Division, reinforced by a brigade of the 7th, an armoured regiment with 45 armoured cars, and an A.A. brigade with 16 heavy and 59 light guns. All in all, there were about 36,000 men within the Tobruk perimeter.

The assault on January 21, in which Major-General Mackay had captured Tobruk, had been so rapid that the fortifications had fallen into the hands of the British almost untouched. The strongpoints, which were laid out in alternating rows, were protected by 3-foot thick concrete slabs which were proof against the heaviest guns (15-cm) the *Afrika Korps* had at this time. The anti-tank ditch was also intact and was still completely camouflaged with sand-covered planks.

But above all – if it is true that an army is as good as its commander – the strongest part of the Tobruk defences was Major-

▽ *The miseries of a desert sandstorm – "khamseen" to the British, "ghibli" to the Germans – here experienced by two* Afrika Korps *soldiers.*
▽▽ *A German magazine illustration reflects the pride caused by the surprise capture of the British Generals O'Connor and Neame during Rommel's offensive into Cyrenaica.*

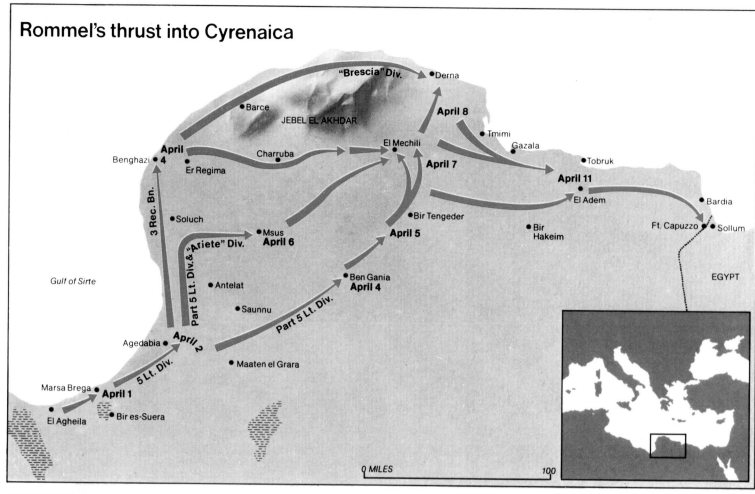

Rommel's thrust into Cyrenaica

General (later Field-Marshal) Erwin Rommel was born in Heidenheim in 1891. He served with distinction in World War I. In 1938 Rommel was selected to command Hitler's escort battalion in Czechoslovakia and later in Poland, and he was appointed to the command of 7th Panzer Division in February 1940. Rommel led 7th Panzer with such success during the campaign in France that it became known as the "Ghost Division", confirming Hitler's confidence in Rommel as a daring and resourceful commander.

General Leslie Morshead, commander of 9th Australian Division. "There'll be no Dunkirk here!" he told his men. "If we should have to get out, we shall have to fight our way out. No surrender and no retreat."

Morshead, who had fought in World War I, had risen to the command of an infantry battalion at 28. For his bravery under fire he had been awarded the C.M.G., the D.S.O., and the *Légion d'Honneur,* and had been six times mentioned in despatches. His soldiers called him "Ming the Merciless" because of his iron discipline. Another factor favouring the defenders was the comparative narrowness of the battlefield, which prevented Rommel from making his customary surprise manoeuvres.

Rommel halted at Tobruk

On April 10 Rommel tried to storm Tobruk by launching a motorised detachment under General von Prittwitz, commander of the 15th Panzer Division, to cut the coast road. But the detachment was repulsed by heavy gunfire and its com-

mander was killed by a shell. During the night of April 13–14, a battalion of the 5th Light Division succeeded in finding a way through the minefields and crossing the anti-tank ditch. Rommel stated, however, that:

"The division's command had not mastered the art of concentrating its strength at one point, forcing a breakthrough, rolling up and securing the flanks on either side, and then penetrating like lightning, before the enemy had time to react, deep into his rear." For this reason the Panzer regiment of the 5th Light Division was overwhelmed by the concentrated fire of the Australian artillery and was unable to support the battalion which had made a "fingerprobe" advance into the defences. The latter battalion was counter-attacked and virtually destroyed, leaving 250 prisoners in the hands of the Australians. Rommel was incensed by this failure, which he punished by sacking General Streich.

The Italian divisions (the "Brescia" Infantry Division, "Trento" Motorised Division, and "Ariete" Armoured Division) were even less fortunate. On the other hand, the *Afrika Korps* units covering the rear of the troops attacking

Tobruk reoccupied the former Axis frontier positions at Sollum, Halfaya, and Capuzzo and now stood on the Egyptian frontier. But they were considerably dispersed, and although 15th Panzer Division had now joined him, Rommel realised at last that he would only be able to capture Tobruk with a well-organised attack. He lacked the resources to do this, and the regrets he expressed to O.K.H. met with a chilly reception on the part of Brauchitsch and Halder.

Rommel is called to heel

Halder's note dated April 23 shows this clearly. "I have a feeling that things are in a mess. He [Rommel] spends his time rushing about between his widely-scattered units and sending out reconnaissance raids in which he fritters away his strength ... no one knows exactly how his troops are deployed, nor the strength of their fighting capacity ... He has had heavy losses as a result of piecemeal attacks. In addition his vehicles are in a bad state because of the wear and tear caused by the desert sand and many of the tank engines need replacing. Our air transport can't meet Rommel's crazy demands; we haven't enough petrol anyway, and the planes sent to North Africa wouldn't have enough fuel for the return flight."

But whatever Halder thought, he could only express it in his private diary, as Hitler retained full confidence in Rommel. In these circumstances, and with the approval of Brauchitsch, he merely sent Lieutenant-General Paulus, the Quartermaster-General of O.K.H., out to the North African front to obtain first-hand information.

Paulus, Halder thought, because of his

△△ *Life in the desert:* Afrika Korps *armoured car crews establish themselves in new positions.*
△ *First check for Rommel's men. His headlong charge at the strongest sector of the Tobruk defences caused heavy casualties for little gain. Here an Australian sentry guards German prisoners.*

Malta Submarines

*During the first period of
Luftwaffe ascendancy over Malta
the main attack force based on
the island consisted of the
submarine flotilla, which made
constant patrols against the Axis
supply-lines to Tripoli. The odds
were stacked heavily against the
British submarines, and between
April-August 1941 five of them
were sunk. But between January
and May of that year they
accounted for 16 out of the 31
Axis ships sunk while carrying
supplies and reinforcements to
North Africa–a striking
achievement. Simultaneous
patrols were made by the
destroyer flotillas based on
Gibraltar and Alexandria.*

◁ *Submarines of the Malta
flotilla. In early 1941 the smaller,
"U-class" submarines hunted in
the shallow waters off the North
African coast while the larger
boats worked the deeper, offshore
waters.*
▷▷ *More teeth for the offensive-
one of the Malta submarines
takes on torpedoes. To keep the
Malta submarines, among other
offensive weapons, supplied
with fuel and torpedoes was a
vital but difficult task.*

old friendship for Rommel, would
"perhaps be capable of exerting some
influence to head off this soldier who has
gone stark mad". The special envoy of the
German Army High Command carried out
his delicate mission satisfactorily–but a
few weeks later the entire North African
theatre was transferred from O.K.H. to
O.K.W. This change of the command
structure eliminated any further causes of
friction between the impulsive Rommel
and the methodical Halder. Halder has
been criticised for being unduly cautious,
because his fears did not materialise. But
he had no way of knowing how small were
the reserve forces at the disposal of the
British C.-in-C. Halder was relying on the
information of his Intelligence experts,
who estimated that Wavell had 21 divisions, six of which were actually fighting
or in the area between Tobruk, Sollum,
and Halfaya.

As already mentioned, the Axis convoys
which carried the 5th Light Division to
North Africa had suffered insignificant
losses. But the ships which carried 15th
Panzer Division had a harder time.

From the time of his first meeting with
General Geissler of X *Fliegerkorps*,
Rommel had asked that the efforts of the
German bombers should be concentrated
against the port of Benghazi. Later, X
Fliegerkorps had given very efficient air
cover to the advance of the *Afrika Korps*
between Agedabia and Tobruk, making
up to a large extent for the heavy artillery
which Rommel lacked.

The inevitable result of this was that
the former pressure being applied to
Malta by these air forces became considerably lighter. Admiral Cunningham
was not slow to exploit this welcome and
unexpected respite. Early in April he
transferred a flotilla of the most modern
destroyers from Alexandria to Valletta.
This small force, commanded by Captain
P. J. Mack, scored its first success on the
night of April 14–15. It surprised an Axis
convoy of five merchantmen escorted by
three destroyers about 35 miles off Sfax.
The convoy was silhouetted against the
moon while Mack's ships were in darkness. Surprise was complete. The
merchantmen were reduced to wrecks

Lieutenant-Commander Malcolm David Wanklyn (*second from left*) and fellow submarine officers. Wanklyn rapidly emerged as the most prominent British submarine ace in the Mediterranean. The *Upholder* sailed on her first patrol against the Axis supply-lines to North Africa in January 1941, and Wanklyn scored his first success by sinking the German transport *Duisburg* in the early morning of January 28. His greatest success in 1941 was the sinking of the large Italian liner *Conte Rosso* on May 25, for which he was awarded the Victoria Cross. In the desperate course of the Mediterranean War there was little respite for the submarine crews. Wanklyn and his crew were eventually lost when *Upholder* was depth-charged on April 14, 1942. He was on his twenty-third patrol and had sunk two submarines, two destroyers, and 94,900 tons of merchant shipping.

within a few minutes; 350 men, 300 vehicles, and 3,500 tons of equipment for the *Afrika Korps* were lost. The Italian destroyer *Baleno* was sunk, but Captain de Cristoforo of the *Tarigo*, with a leg shot off by a British shell, managed to launch three torpedoes before sinking with his ship. Two of these torpedoes hit and sank the British destroyer *Mohawk*.

The third Italian escort destroyer, the *Lampo*, was totally disabled and stranded on the shoals of the Kerkenna Bank, together with the German merchantman *Arta*. *Lampo* was recovered by the Italians in August and subsequently recommissioned – but in the meantime a group of French Resistance men from Tunisia had searched the derelicts by night, seized the ships' papers, and had passed on all information about the *Afrika Korps'* order of battle to Malta.

The work of the British destroyers was supplemented by that of the British submarines based on Malta and Alexandria. On February 25 the *Upright* (Lieutenant E. D. Norman) had scored a direct hit on the Italian light cruiser *Armando Diaz*, which sank in four minutes with three-quarters of her crew. In a space of four months the British submarines in the Mediterranean sank at least a dozen Axis merchantmen, tankers, and transports between Messina and Tripoli.

The submarine *Upholder*, commanded by Lieutenant-Commander Malcolm Wanklyn, a brilliant submariner, particularly distinguished herself in these actions, on which the outcome of the Desert War so much depended. On the evening of May 25 *Upholder* sank the large Italian liner *Conte Rosso* (17,879 tons), and only 1,520 out of the 2,732 sailors and soldiers aboard were saved. In recognition of this Wanklyn received the Victoria Cross.

Cunningham's troubles

Yet another consequence of the first offensive of the *Afrika Korps* was to create serious tension between the Admiralty and Admiral Cunningham.

Cunningham was ordered to bombard

△ Afrika Korps *scout car in the desert. Despite the failure to take Tobruk, Rommel's reconquest of Cyrenaica meant that the initiative in the Desert War had been wrested from the British. Once again, Axis troops stood on the Egyptian frontier.*

▽ *From the* Gazzetta del Popolo *of Turin: Neptune wonders when the British Admiralty will announce the latest bump on his head in the sinkings column of* The Times.

the port installations of Tripoli with his battle fleet, but he doubted whether the fleet's guns would be able to inflict any serious damage. He pressed for the transfer of long-range heavy bombers to Egypt, to smash the installations from the air. But this would be impossible in the immediate future. Seeking a drastic solution to the problem of Tripoli, the War Cabinet and the Admiralty decided that Cunningham should sacrifice the battleship *Barham* and an A.A. cruiser. Manned by skeleton crews, these would be deliberately scuttled in the entrance to Tripoli harbour.

When Cunningham received this message on April 15 he reacted with an immediate objection. If he obeyed he would not only lose one of his three vital battleships: it was also to be feared that the *Barham* and the cruiser would be sunk by the Italians before reaching their objective. Nor was there any guarantee that the crews, however small, could be recovered, and this would mean the additional loss of about 1,000 highly-trained officers, petty officers, and ratings. But Cunningham was ready to make a compromise. Reconsidering his first objections, he stated that he was prepared to bombard Tripoli.

The Admiralty agreed, and at dawn on April 21 the battleships *Barham*, *Valiant*, and *Warspite*, with the cruiser *Gloucester*, battered Tripoli harbour for three-quarters of an hour while Swordfish from the carrier *Formidable* and aircraft from Malta assisted the warships by bombing and illuminating the port. As Cunningham had anticipated, the actual damage inflicted was not severe and had no lasting effect; but the Italians were so slow to sound the alarm that the British squadron completed its hazardous mission without suffering any harm.

Churchill's own account in *The Second World War* suggests that the responsibility for this venture rested with Sir Dudley Pound. This, however, seems unlikely. Pound would hardly have issued such a drastic order without first referring it to the Minister of Defence, Churchill. Much more likely, the initiative for the idea to scuttle the *Barham* came from Churchill. And the fact that Pound retracted his order so promptly suggests that he was being influenced by Churchill again.

CHAPTER 14
THE BALKAN FRONT

On December 29, 1940, General Ugo Cavallero, the new Chief-of-Staff of the *Comando Supremo*, was sent over by Mussolini to relieve General Ubaldo Soddu of his command and to take control of the Italian armed forces in Albania. The Duce defined Cavallero's task in a letter dated January 1: his forces were to move over to the offensive and prove, by their energy and resolve, that doubts abroad about Italian military prestige were baseless. "Germany," the letter went on, "is ready to send a mountain division into Albania and at the same time is preparing an army to attack Greece through Bulgaria in March. I am expecting, nay, I am certain, that your intervention and the bravery of your men will show that any direct support by Germany on the Albanian front will prove to be unnecessary. The Italian nation is impatiently waiting for the wind to change."

After the war General Halder drew attention to the vexing question of German reinforcements in Albania, on which Hitler and his generals never agreed:

"When the Italians got into trouble in Albania, Hitler was inclined to send help. The Army Commander-in-Chief managed to stop the plan from being put into action, as it would have been fruitless. It was a different matter when the German forces, which were actually intended for an attack on the Greeks, were ordered into Greece from Bulgaria to throw the British back into the sea. Hitler then ordered major units into northern Albania. This eccentric operation could have thrown into jeopardy any lightning success against Greece. But Hitler refused to give up his plan and his political will overrode all military objections. No harm was done, however, as the German High Command evaded executing the order, and events proved that they were right."

War in the mountains

Before Cavallero could meet the Duce's wishes he had to prevent the Greeks reaching Valona and Durazzo. At this date, to cover a front of 156 miles, he had

16 divisions, some in very bad shape and most of them poorly supplied on account of Albania's virtually non-existent communications. It is true that the opposing forces, the Greeks, who had been on the offensive since November 14, had lost a

△ *The Duce with his new High Command Chief-of-Staff, General Ugo Cavallero, who now had the unenviable task of trying to avert complete disaster for the Italian forces on the Albanian front.*

fair number of men and had only 13 divisions or their equivalent. Until such time as they could make up their strength and repair communications, General Papagos decided to abandon temporarily any idea of an all-out attack and restricted himself to limited-objective offensives. It was during one of these operations that the Greek II Corps, working as usual in the mountains, captured the important crossroads at Klisura on January 9. In a heavy snowstorm they inflicted a severe defeat on the *"Lupi di Toscana"* (Wolves of Tuscany) Division (General Ottavio Bollea), which had been force-marched to its objective. Papagos grouped his I and II Corps together under General Drakos as the Army of Epirus, but this was defeated at Telepenë in February. Not that the Greek troops lacked keenness or endurance (in his diary Cavallero says that their attacks were "frenzied"): they simply had no means of waging modern offensive warfare. This is clearly explained in the former Greek Commander-in-Chief's book on his army's operations:

"The presence among the Italian troops of a considerable number of tanks, and the fact that we had none at all and very few anti-tank guns, forced us to keep well clear of the plains, which would allow rapid movement, and to manoeuvre only in the mountains. This increased the fatigue of the men and the beasts of burden, lengthened and delayed our convoys and brought additional difficulties in command, supplies and so on. The enemy, on the other hand, thanks to the means at his disposal, was able to fall back rapidly on the plains and take up new positions without much difficulty. Taking advantage of the terrain, he was then able to hold up our advance in the mountains with a relatively small number of men. Also, the fresh troops which the Italians brought up during this phase of the war came to the front in lorries, whereas ours had to move on foot, reaching the front tired and frequently too late to be of any use. As a final point I must mention the difficulties we had in restoring the works of art which had been damaged by the enemy, and the superiority of the Italian Air Force which, after the limited daily sorties by Greek and British planes, were able to attack with impunity both our forward and our rear areas." General Cavallero's success in these defensive operations gave him enough respite to reinforce and rest his troops so as to go over to the offensive as Mussolini had ordered.

From December 29, 1940, to March 26, 1941, no fewer than ten divisions, four machine gun battalions, together with three legions and 17 battalions of Black Shirts crossed the Adriatic. When spring came the Italian land forces in Albania thus comprised: the 9th and the 11th Armies, the 9th now under General Pirzio-Biroli and the 11th still under General Geloso: six corps, with 21 infantry divisions, five mountain divisions and the "Centauro" Armoured Division. The Greeks, on the other hand, had only 13 to 14 divisions, all of them suffering from battle fatigue.

This goes to show that, though denied the Mediterranean, the Italian Navy still controlled the Adriatic. Only one difficulty faced General Cavallero: was he to give priority to bringing up reinforcements or to supplying his troops at the front, given that all the Albanian ports together, whatever might be done to increase their capacity, could only handle 4,000 tons a day? One of the few units lost during these operations was the hospital ship *Po*, torpedoed in error in Valona harbour. Countess Edda Ciano, who was serving on board as a nurse, escaped with no more than a ducking.

▽ *A Greek supply column moves through hair-raising terrain in in the Devoll river valley. These troops are on the Greek right flank, which swept forward to take Pogradec on December 4, 1940. After this the centre of gravity of the Greek offensive switched to the coastal sector, where the Greeks made gallant but unavailing efforts to take the Italian base at Valona.*
▷ *March 1941: Mussolini visits the Albanian front. By this time the situation was well in hand, and the reinforced Italian armies were on the offensive again. The Greeks held out gallantly against massive attacks, but their losses were heavy.*

Another Italian offensive

As he had re-established numerical superiority, General Cavallero now set about his offensive operations. On March 9, 1941, watched by Mussolini, the 9th Army began attacking in the sector between the river Osum (called the Apsos by the Greeks) in the north-east and the Vijosë or the Aóos in the south-west. The area is dominated by the Trebesina mountains. General Geloso put in his IV, VIII and XXV Corps (Generals Mercalli, Gambara and Carlo Rossi respectively), comprising 11 infantry divisions and the "Centauro" Armoured Division. On D-day the Greeks had three divisions and the equivalent of a fourth, all from the II Corps (General Papadopoulos). At dawn the Greek positions were heavily shelled and bombed. From their observation point, at 0830, Mussolini and Cavallero could see the infantry moving up to their objectives over territory not unlike the Carso, where so many Italians had fallen in fruitless attacks between June 1915 and August 1917 during the First World War.

The Trebesina offensive did not restore the Duce's prestige. Not because the Greek defenders equalled the Italian attacking force in strength, as Cavallero wrote in his diary in the evening of March 9, but because they were well organised and their morale was high. He went on:

"The Greek artillery is powerfully deployed. All the elements of the defending forces are well organised in depth, using positions of strength which enable them to contain the offensive and to counter-attack immediately and vigorously."

Forty-eight hours later, not only had there not been the expected breakthrough, but losses were mounting, the 11th Alpini Regiment alone reporting 356 killed and wounded, including 36 officers. Should the plan be abandoned after this discouraging start? Mussolini did not think so. That very day he said to General Geloso: "The directives of the plan must be adhered to at all costs. Between now and the end of the month a military victory is vital for the prestige of the Italian Army."

And he added, with an unusual disregard for his responsibilities in the matter of Italian military unpreparedness:

General Alexander Papagos was born in 1883, and was Commander-in-Chief of the Greek forces when Italy invaded Greece on October 28, 1940. Papagos's forces not only repulsed the Italians, but also counter-attacked into Albania. His forces held the renewed Italian offensive in March 1940, but the German offensive proved too much for them in April. He was arrested and taken to Germany, where he was freed by the Americans in 1945.

△ Armoured help from the British: a Cruiser Mark IIA (A-10). "They were ponderous, square things," wrote Bob Crisp, a South African tank commander who went to Greece with Wavell's B.E.F.; "like mobile pre-fab houses and just about as flimsy. By far their worst failing was their complete inability to move more than a mile without breaking a track, or shedding one on a sharp turn." Crisp added: "Of the 60-odd tanks 3rd RTR had taken to Greece at the beginning of the year, not half a dozen were casualties of direct enemy action. All the others had been abandoned with broken tracks or other mechanical breakdowns. They littered the passes ... stripped of their machine-guns, but otherwise intact. They were of no help to the enemy; no other army would have contemplated using them ..."

"I have always done my best to maintain the fame and the prestige of the Italian Army, but today it is vital to drive on with the offensive." They drove on, therefore, but attacks were followed by counter-attacks and General Papagos having, so to speak, thrown two divisions into the fray, the Italians were no further forward on the 15th than they had been on the 9th. When General Gambara was asked by Mussolini about the morale of his corps he replied, tactfully: "It cannot be said to be very high, but it remains firm. Losses, no territorial gains, few prisoners; this is hardly encouraging. All the same, morale is good enough not to prejudice the men's use in battle."

Mussolini and Cavallero finally drew the right conclusions from the situation and called off the attack. Mussolini returned to Rome without increasing his reputation. The three corps engaged in

this unhappy affair lost 12,000 dead and wounded, or some 1,000 men per division. When it is realised that most of these losses were borne by the infantry it cannot be denied that they fought manfully.

The Greeks, on their side, however, suffered enormously and this defensive success, however honourable it might have been for their army, left them with only 14 divisions against 27.

Britain aids Greece

Meanwhile, on January 29, 1941, General Metaxas, who had forged the victories in Epirus and Albania, died suddenly in Athens and King George nominated Petros Koryzis as his successor. Events were soon to bring tragic proof that the new Greek Prime Minister could not match his predecessor in strength of character. He was, however, no less resolved to oppose with force the Germans' aggressive intentions in Rumania, as he made known in a letter to London dated February 8. This led to the departure from Plymouth on the 14th in a Sunderland flying boat bound for Cairo of Anthony Eden and Dill, the Chief of the Imperial General Staff. General Wavell raised no objections in principle to aid for Greece, in spite of the serious risks involved. Eden was thus in a position to cable the Prime Minister on February 21:

"Dill and I have exhaustively reviewed situation temporarily [sic] with Commanders-in-Chief. Wavell is ready to make available three divisions, a Polish brigade and best part of an armoured division, together with a number of specialized troops such as anti-tank and anti-aircraft units. Though some of these ... have yet to be concentrated, work is already in hand and they can reach Greece as rapidly as provision of ships will allow. This programme fulfils the hopes expressed at Defence Committee that we could make available a force of three divisions and an armoured division.

"Gravest anxiety is not in respect of army but of air. There is no doubt that need to fight a German air force, instead of Italian, is creating a new problem for Longmore. My own impression is that all his squadrons are not quite up to standard of their counterpart at home . . . . . We should all have liked to approach Greeks tomorrow with a suggestion that we

should join with them in holding a line to defend Salonika, but both Longmore and Cunningham are convinced that our present air resources will not allow us to do this ."

The truth is that the R.A.F. would find itself having to face not the Italian Air Force but the Luftwaffe, and that is why both Air Chief-Marshal Longmore and Admiral Cunningham doubted if the ex-

△ *Italian heavy artillery rumbles towards the front.*
▽ *Greek mountain gunners hit back at the Italians.*

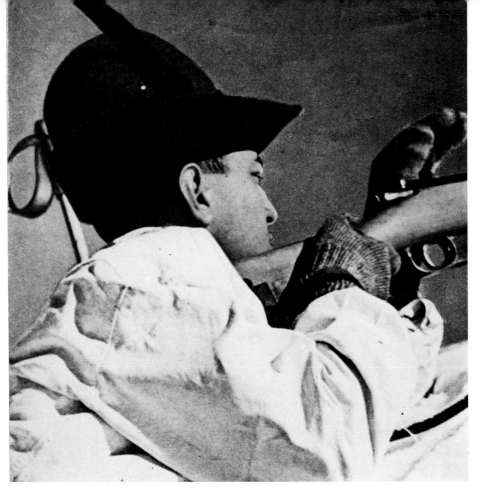

△ *In preparation for the new offensive: one of the Italian Alpini in training, from the German magazine* Signal. *But when the offensive went in, the Greeks held the high ground and the Italians were compelled to attack at a disadvantage. The Alpini suffered very heavy losses.*

General Count Ugo Cavallero, born in 1880, was appointed Under-Secretary of War by Mussolini in 1925 and later became Chief-of-Staff to the Duke of Aosta in Abyssinia. He became Chief of the Italian General Staff on Badoglio's resignation in 1940, a post which he held until Mussolini's overthrow in 1943. After a spell in prison he was released, but committed suicide shortly afterwards.

peditionary force could fight on a front covering Salonika. These doubts were shared also by Sir John Dill. However, the matter was to be discussed with the Greeks at a secret conference on the following day (February 22) at the Royal Palace at Tatoi, near Athens. The results were to prove very dangerous.

The Greek viewpoint

The conference was attended by King George II, Anthony Eden, Prime Minister Koryzis, the British Ambassador in Athens, Generals Dill and Wavell, Air Chief-Marshal Longmore, and the heads of the British Military Missions in Greece. General Papagos was asked to report on the latest situation.

After giving an account of the latest Intelligence information, he put forward the solution he would advocate if Yugoslavia were to remain neutral and refuse to allow German troops to cross her territory. In this hypothesis the defence of western Thrace and eastern Macedonia would seem to be inadvisable. Troops defending the Metaxas Line, the main bulwark against Bulgaria, would therefore be given the task of slowing down the enemy advance, holding out to the last

round, but the troops supporting them opposite Yugoslavia (three divisions) would fall back on a position between the lower Aliákmon river and the Vérmion and Kaïmakchalán mountains, which rise, respectively, to 6,725 and 8,375 feet. If all went well this operation should take about 20 days. But Papagos thought that the German forces in Rumania would need only a fortnight to get to the Bulgarian-Greek frontier from the left bank of the Danube.

Yugoslav reactions

This is where General Papagos's version disagrees with that of Eden. According to Papagos, no firm decision was taken at the end of the Tatoi conference concerning the eventual evacuation of the two provinces mentioned above. "I emphasised, however," he writes, "that after taking such a grave decision as to withdraw our troops from Thrace and eastern Macedonia and to leave this whole sector of our national territory at the mercy of the enemy without even defending it, we had to be absolutely sure about the attitude of Yugoslavia and I suggested informing the Yugoslavs about the decisions we intended to take and which would depend on their reaction."

"The British delegation," he adds, "seemed to agree and it was decided that Eden would inform H.M. Ambassador in Belgrade by urgent coded telegram. The Greek Commander-in-Chief would define his position according to the reply received. Whereupon Anthony Eden and Generals Dill and Wavell flew off to Ankara."

Eden's version is very different, though he affirms his statement on the evidence of General Wavell who died, it is true, in 1950. But, for all that, it appears that on this point, like many others, Eden's record is at variance with the events. When he got back from his fruitless journey to Ankara he sent a telegram to the Prime Minister on March 4, in which he said, among other things:

"General Papagos had on the last occasion insisted strongly that the withdrawal of all troops in Macedonia to the Aliákmon line was the only sound military solution. We expected that this withdrawal to the Aliákmon line had already begun. Instead we found that no movement had in fact commenced, Papa-

gos alleging that it had been agreed that the decision taken at our last meeting was dependent on the receipt of an answer from Yugoslavia as to their attitude."

As we see, if this text establishes the good faith of Anthony Eden, it also shows that General Papagos's version was not thought up after the event. There was therefore a misunderstanding at Tatoi. However this may be, one thing is clear: the premature evacuation of Salonika, Yugoslavia's only possible access to the Aegean Sea, could only have a discouraging effect on Belgrade.

Bulgaria joins the Tripartite Pact

On March 1, 1941 Bulgaria joined the Tripartite Pact and the German 12th Army under Field-Marshal List crossed the Danube on pontoon bridges. In line with undertakings given on the previous January 18, this event decided the Athens Government to allow the entry into Greece of the expeditionary force organised in Cairo and put under the command of Sir Henry Maitland Wilson. But however strongly the British might have insisted, General Papagos refused to begin the anticipated withdrawal from Thrace and eastern Macedonia. It was already March 4 and everything inclined to the belief that if his three divisions on the Metaxas Line were given the order, they would now be caught in full movement.

From March 7 onwards the British Expeditionary Force began to land at the ports of Piraeus and Vólos. It was transported in 25 ships and no untoward incident occurred, as the Italian air forces based in the Dodecanese were not up to strength. Altogether 57,577 men and about 100 tanks were landed to form the 1st Armoured Brigade, the 6th Australian Division (Maj.-Gen. Sir Iven Mackay) and the 2nd New Zealand Division,

△ *Italian bombing strike: Savoia-Marchetti S.M.-79's head out to the attack. Heavy bombing attacks heralded the abortive Trebesina offensive on March 9.*

▽ *Greek machine gunners get ready to hit back at the next bombing raid.*

the latter being under Major-General Bernard Freyberg, V.C., a hero of the Dardanelles and the Somme.

At the end of the month Maitland Wilson's troops were in position behind the Aliákmon and the Vérmion mountains. On the other hand, after negotiations which, in a telegram dated March 4, Eden describes somewhat testily as "bargaining more reminiscent of oriental bazaars", the Greek High Command put under the B.E.F. three divisions (the 12th, the 20th, and the 19th Motorised) with seven battalions withdrawn from the Turkish border after reassurances from Ankara. The British expected more of their allies, but it should be noted on the other hand, that the 7th Australian Division (Major-General J. D. Lavarack) and the 1st Polish Brigade (General Kopanski), which should have been sent to Greece, never left the Middle East.

Joint plans

On February 14 at Merano, Grand-Admiral Raeder had recommended Admiral Riccardi to be more active. The transportation of the expeditionary force to Greece gave *Supermarina* the chance of intervening in the Eastern Mediterranean. The German and Italian G.H.Q.'s encouraged these impulses towards an offensive all the more keenly because on March 16 the X *Fliegerkorps* announced, wrongly as it turned out, that its planes had torpedoed two of the three battleships of the Mediterranean Fleet and put them out of action.

The plan was to sweep the Aegean and Mediterranean on D-day with two detachments as far as the island of Gávdhos, 31 miles south of Crete. The task force was put under the command of Rear-Admiral Angelo Iachino and consisted of the battleship *Vittorio Veneto*, six heavy and two light cruisers, and 13 destroyers. The operation also required considerable air support, both for reconnaissance and for defence against British bombers and torpedo-carrying aircraft.

Agreement was reached on joint air support with both the Italian Air Force and the Luftwaffe's X *Fliegerkorps*, but there was no time to test the arranged procedures in exercises. It is true that there were German and Italian liaison officers on board the *Vittorio Veneto*, but on the whole Admiral Iachino was sceptical of the results to be expected from this improvised collaboration, particularly concerning fighter support.

The Battle of Matapan

In the afternoon of March 27 a Sunderland flying boat spotted the squadron, which was then steaming through the Ionian Sea. The British had thus been alerted, as decoded messages subsequently confirmed, and it was now unlikely that any of their convoys could be intercepted. Yet the only offensive orders countermanded by *Supermarina* were those concerning the area north of Crete. That same evening Cunningham slipped out of Alexandria with three battleships and the aircraft-carrier *Formidable*, which had 37 aircraft on board. He had arranged a rendezvous south-east of Gávdhos with Vice-Admiral H. D. Pridham-Wippell's squadron of four cruisers from Piraeus.

First contact, at about 0800 hours, was between Admiral Sansonetti's three heavy cruisers and Pridham-Wippell's light cruisers. Though the British ships mounted only 6-inch guns against the Italian vessels' 8-inchers, their evasive

△ Squelching through the mud of the spring thaw, Greek supplies are brought up by mule train.

▷ △ Battle is joined off Cape Matapan: a Bolzano-class cruiser under Swordfish attack. This photograph, taken from the second Swordfish, shows the leading aircraft just after dropping its torpedo, the splash of which can be seen on the left of the picture.
▷ ▽ All sunk at Matapan: top to bottom: Italian heavy cruisers Zara and Pola, with the Oriani-class destroyer Giosue Carducci.

action, contrary to the Royal Navy's tradition of aggressiveness, led Iachino to think that they might be acting as bait for a large ship as yet out of sight. He therefore recalled Sansonetti. Pridham-Wippell then gave chase, only to find himself being fired on by the *Vittorio Veneto*'s 15-inch guns. The Italians loosed off 94 rounds but failed to score a hit. Then at about mid-day torpedo-carrying aircraft from the *Formidable* launched a first attack, but without success. Admiral Iachino thereupon headed back to base.

At 1510 hours, the Fleet Air Arm launched its second attack. At the cost of his life, Lieutenant-Commander J. Dalyell-Stead dropped his torpedo at very short range and severely damaged the *Vittorio Veneto*, causing her to ship 4,000 tons of water and putting her two port engines out of action. Thanks to the efforts of her crew the damaged battleship got under way again at a speed of first 17, then 19 knots.

By this time Cunningham, with the main body of his fleet, was about 87 miles away. The *Formidable*'s planes kept him fully informed of the Italian movements, whereas Iachino was in complete ignorance of Cunningham's, and was no better informed than he had been defended by the exiguous Axis air support. In des-

pair, and relying on a radio bearing from *Supermarina*, Iachino admitted that he was being chased by an aircraft-carrier and a cruiser some 170 miles away.

As daylight faded he gathered about the damaged flagship his 1st and 3rd Cruiser Squadrons and the destroyers in case another attack was made by British aircraft. These had, in fact, been ordered to delay the *Vittorio Veneto* so that the British battleships could finish her off. Iachino's defensive tactics, including the use of smoke screens, prevented this, but towards 1925 hours the heavy cruiser *Pola* was torpedoed. Iachino ordered Admiral Cattaneo to stay with the *Pola*, taking her in tow if possible and scuttling her if this proved impracticable. The decision was later criticised, but was justified in the light of Iachino's estimate of the British position. However this may be, the luckless cruiser then came up on the *Ajax*'s radar screen. Pridham-Wippell took her for the *Vittorio Veneto* and signalled to Cunningham, who was closing with the *Warspite*, *Valiant*, and *Barham*. At about 2200 hours *Valiant*'s radar picked up Cattaneo's cruisers sailing blindly forward into the darkness. Some 30 minutes later the British squadron's 24 15-inch guns blasted them out of the water at point-blank range. The

Fiume went down at 2315 hours, the *Zara*, which was sinking more slowly, was scuttled by her commander and the destroyers *Alfieri* and *Carducci* met a similar fate. Finally a British destroyer sank *Pola* after picking up her survivors.

That night and the morning after the battle, which took place 112 miles southwest of Cape Matapan, the British, with the aid of some Greek destroyers, picked up just over a thousand survivors. The rescue operations were hampered by a Luftwaffe attack, but Cunningham generously signalled Rome, giving the area where further survivors might still be found. The hospital ship *Gradisca* subsequently picked up another 160. Altogether 2,400 Italian seamen were lost, including Admiral Cattaneo and the commanders of the cruisers *Zara* and *Fiume*, Captains Giorgis and Corsi respectively. The only British loss was that of the heroic Dalyell-Stead.

Although Admiral Cunningham was not altogether satisfied with the outcome of the battle, since the *Vittorio Veneto* had got away and reached Taranto, Cape Matapan was a heavy defeat for the Italian Navy, which had lost at one blow three of its 12,000-ton cruisers, a loss which could not be made good overnight. This was what Mussolini had in mind when he received Admiral Iachino at the Palazzo Venezia.

"The operation promised well and might have been successful had it not been for the total lack of co-operation from the air arm. During the whole time you never had a single Italian or German plane over you. All the aircraft you saw were the enemy's. They chased you, attacked you, overpowered you. Your ships were like blind invalids being set upon by several armed killers."

Naval operations, then, were impossible in British-controlled waters without proper reconnaissance and fighter support. Mussolini concluded, with what Iachino describes as the true journalist's capacity for summing things up: "And as fighter aircraft have a limited range, the ships must take their escorts with them. In a word, all naval forces must always be accompanied by at least one aircraft-carrier."

And so, the Duce was going back on the point of view he had expressed in 1930, but rather belatedly, after a defeat which weighed heavily on Italian strategy. To alleviate the consequences it was decided to convert two liners, *Roma* and *Augustus*, into aircraft-carriers and rename them *Aquila* and *Sparviero*. Until they came into service the fleet was forbidden to sail outside land-based fighter range.

The exploit of Lieutenant Faggioni and his five men in the battle of Cape Matapan deserves not to be forgotten. During the night of March 25–26 they managed to get into Suda Bay, on the north coast of Crete, in boats loaded with explosives. There they effectively crippled the cruiser *York* and the oil-tanker *Pericles*.

▽ *Italy's belated attempt to match the superiority given to the Mediterranean Fleet by the activity of the Fleet Air Arm: the aircraft-carrier Aquila. The decision to build a carrier for the Italian Navy was finally taken after Matapan. The passenger liner SS* Roma *was taken over for complete conversion. She was given the 4-shaft turbine engines from the unfinished light cruisers* Cornelio Silla *and* Paolo Emilio, *which were intended to enable her to make 30 knots. The hull was armoured with a bulge of reinforced concrete 600-mm thick. Twin catapults were installed for launching her air group, which would have consisted of a maximum of 51 Reggiane 2001 fighters. Aquila was virtually ready for sea trials when Italy signed the armistice with the Allies in 1943. She was captured by the Germans, who scuttled her in 1945.*

CHAPTER 15

ASSAULT ON CRETE

▽ *The British cruiser, York, which was attacked by Italian explosive motor boats on the morning of March 26, 1941. York was badly damaged and had to be beached. Salvage operations were abandoned because of subsequent bomb damage.*

▽▽ *Paratroops race into action as another "stick" comes down.*

With Greece evacuated, should the Allies have continued to cling on to Crete? British critics of Churchill's war strategy have said on more than one occasion that the island should have been abandoned. Yet a glance at the map will show that whereas Crete is 500 miles from Alexandria, it is only 200 from Tobruk. Tobruk, the bastion of British resistance in the Middle East, could only be supplied by sea and the great danger was that it might be starved out if the Luftwaffe controlled the aerodromes at Máleme and Heraklion. If Churchill is to be criticised for wanting to fight the war on every front with insufficient means, this is not a front which should be held against him.

Hitler drew similar conclusions. His aims were defensive as well as offensive. Within a few weeks the unleashing of "Barbarossa" would deprive him (only temporarily he hoped) of Russian oil. What would happen if the R.A.F. on Crete were to wipe out all the production of Ploieşti? That is why, on April 25, 1941, his Directive No. 28 ordered the three armies in Greece to prepare Operation "Mercury", which was to secure Crete for Germany.

Brauchitsch, Göring, and Raeder set to work with great energy. And it was no small matter to plan an operation of the size required in a country with such limited resources as Greece where, in particular, air bases had to be improvised.

German preparations for operation "Mercury"

The task of planning the operation fell to General Kurt Student, the commander of XI *Fliegerkorps*, which included the 7th Paratroop Division, reinforced by three infantry regiments from 5th and 6th Mountain Divisions. Air support was to be provided by VIII *Fliegerkorps*, commanded by General Wolfram von Richthofen, 18 fighter and reconnaissance *Gruppen*, that is 228 bombers, 205 dive bombers, 119 single-engined and 114 twin-engined fighters, and 50 reconnaissance aircraft.

The first wave of paratroops was to be carried in 493 three-engined Ju 52's and 72 gliders, but the mountain troops who were to reinforce the paratroops would be ferried over in 63 motorised sailing ships and seven small steamers hastily requisitioned by Rear-Admiral Schuster. This flotilla was to be escorted by two destroyers

△ *Focal point of the assault on Crete: Máleme airfield, where the battle hung in the balance until the defenders were forced back from the perimeter. This picture shows the litter of wrecked and damaged Ju 52's on the airfield – by the end of the battle there were 80 of them. The Germans used a captured British tank to bulldoze the wrecks off the single runway. Allied shells can be seen bursting on the left of the picture.*

and twelve torpedo-boats of the Italian Navy under Captain Peccori-Giraldi.

The defence of Crete

On the island itself, the defence on paper comprised 42,500 men, of whom 10,300 were Greeks. Its core was the A.N.Z.A.C. force, 6,540 Australians and 7,700 New Zealanders who had escaped from Greece but had had to abandon a great deal of material on the beaches of Attica and the Peloponnese. They were thus very short of vehicles, artillery, infantry weapons, ammunition, entrenching tools, barbed wire, blankets, and mess-tins, and were likely to remain so. They had only 68 heavy and light A.A. guns, which were clearly not enough to cover the 162-mile front from the eastern to the western end of the island. On May 1, 1941, the R.A.F. had 35 operational aircraft; on the 19th, after incessant bombardment by the Luftwaffe, it had only four Hurricanes and three Gladiators left in a state good enough to take off for Egypt. Abandoned

aerodromes were merely obstructed and not put out of use, as it was intended to reoccupy them as soon as possible.

On April 30, Sir Archibald Wavell entrusted the command of this severely weakened defence force to General Freyberg. Whatever the eminent qualities of this commander, whose 27 wounds testified to his bravery in World War I, he was nevertheless the seventh British commander the island had had in six months and, when he arrived, he had only three weeks in which to familiarise himself with the situation.

Operation "Tiger", which had brought 238 tanks across the Mediterranean, had given the Admiralty the chance of reinforcing the Alexandria naval squadron with the battleship *Queen Elizabeth* and the cruisers *Fiji* and *Naiad*. London thought that this naval force would thus be in a better position to oppose Axis landings on the island from the continent. But Cunningham's only aircraft-carrier, the *Formidable*, had only a handful of Fulmar fighters which, even if there had been more of them, would have been no match for the Germans' crack Messerschmitts.

△ *German troops take a welcome opportunity for a quick cigarette and a drink.*

German paratroops land

The German invasion of Crete began early on May 20, when airborne troops of the 7th *Fliegerdivision* were dropped around Máleme, Réthimnon and Heraklion. The defenders had been expecting them for 48 hours and so the fighting was bitter. At Máleme General Meindl, gravely wounded, had to hand over his command to Colonel Ramcke; at Réthimnon the paratroops landed with no commander at all as the glider carrying General Sussman had crashed on the island of Aegina. The battle might have swung in General Freyberg's favour had he had time to reinforce the brigade defending Máleme airstrip against Ramcke, and if the Mediterranean Fleet had been able to destroy completely the convoys bringing in Lieutenant-General Ringel's mountain troops. But, for the few losses they inflicted on the Germans, the Royal Navy lost, in rapid succession from aerial bombardment by Stukas, the cruisers *Gloucester* and *Fiji* together with four destroyers, while the *Warspite* and the aircraft-carrier *Formidable* were so badly damaged that they had to be sent for repair in the United States.

In spite of pressure from London, Admiral Cunningham had to give up

The Defeat of Yugoslavia

March 27 1940, after King Peter's majority was proclaimed and General Simons had assumed power, Hitler declared that Yugoslavia must be regarded as an enemy: "The military revolt in Yugoslavia has changed the political position in the Balkans. Yugoslavia, even if it makes initial professions of loyalty, must be regarded as an enemy and beaten down as soon as possible." He went on to the means of execution. Two strategic groups, one from the Fiume-Graz front and the other from the Sofia area, would converge on Belgrade and wipe out the Yugoslav Army. A third group would attack Serbian Macedonia to secure a base for the Italo-German attack on Greece.

The Germans had to draw heavily on their preparations for "Barbarossa" against the Soviet Union in order to conduct operation "Marita" against Yugoslavia under Field-Marshal List. Support for the Germans would be received from Italy and Hungary. The defeat of Yugoslavia took 12 days. On April 24, 1941, after a valiant resistance, the Greeks were forced to sign a surrender document. Their spirit, however, was unbroken.

operations north of Crete, where he was suffering heavy losses. On May 25, with admirably controlled air support, the 5th Mountain Division managed to break out of the Máleme perimeter held by the 2nd New Zealand Division and push on through Canea. The German breakthrough decided General Freyberg on May 27 to begin the evacuation of the island and to ask for help from the Mediterranean Fleet. This help was not refused him.

The evacuation of Crete

In spite of the risks involved and the losses already sustained, the Commander-in-Chief Mediterranean, Admiral Cunningham, did not hesitate a moment.

"We cannot let [the army] down," he signalled to the ships of his fleet which had been designated for this mission, and when one member of his staff seemed pessimistic he retorted, with a just sense of realities: "It takes the Navy three years

to build a ship. It would take 300 years to re-build a tradition."

The evacuation of Crete, begun on the night of May 28–29, was carried out through the small harbour at Sphakia on the south coast and was completed by dawn on June 2. During the operation the A.A. cruiser *Calcutta* and the destroyers *Hereward* and *Imperial* were lost. But the heaviest losses of life were on board the cruiser *Orion*, Vice-Admiral Pridham-Wippell's flagship. One single German bomb killed 260 men and wounded 280.

British Empire losses were nearly 1,800 killed and about 12,000 captured out of 32,000 men engaged. The Royal Navy lost 1,828 killed and 183 wounded. 18,000 troops were evacuated to Egypt. But the losses of General Student and XI *Fliegerkorps* had not been slight in spite of this. Though the Germans' casualties could not have reached the 15,000 given by Churchill in his memoirs, statistics published since the war show that, with 3,714 killed and missing and 2,494 wounded, the eight days of fighting on Crete had cost the Germans, particularly in the loss of experienced

△ *New Zealand recruiting poster. Freyberg's New Zealanders fought superbly – but their courage was not enough to overcome the Germans.*

▽ *The German conquest of Crete. Despite their losses, the German airborne units proved that they could deal with the conventional forces of the Allies.*

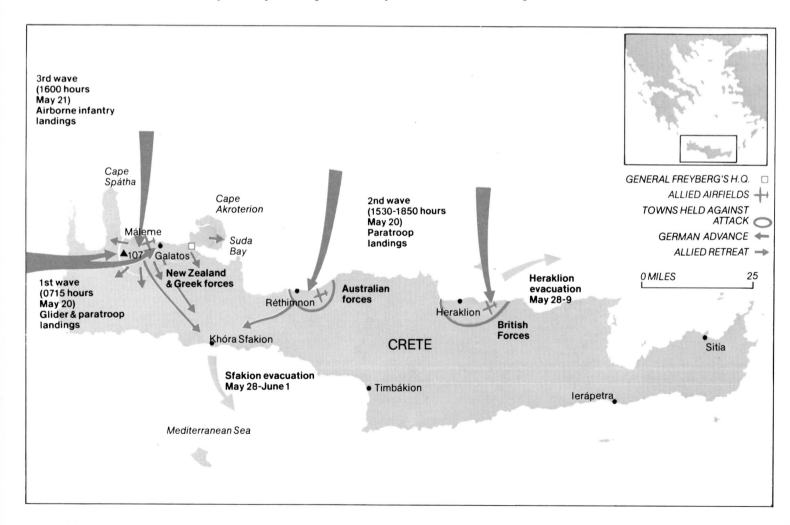

△ △ *After the defeat of Crete the British used this picture of Germans questioning a Cretan village headman for propaganda purposes. "Their brutal faces press round him as they demand information. This can happen here . . ."*
△◁ *and* △▷ *Rounding up the prisoners. British and Empire P.O.W.s taken on Crete totalled 11,835.*

airborne troops, more than the whole three weeks of the Balkans campaign.

Was it because of these German losses that Hitler rejected General Student's suggestion to follow up the victory on Crete by capturing Cyprus? We do not know. But the memory of this blood-bath admittedly encouraged Hitler to abandon his operation "Hercules" (the capture of Malta from the air) in late June 1942, when Rommel thought he had convinced him that the Axis forces could get to the Nile and Suez. In any case, the British forces in Libya, in Macedonia, and in the Aegean Sea had suffered heavy reverses which more than balanced the losses

accountable to Italian strategy in the previous winter. Did the War Cabinet's decisions and the orders of the Imperial General Staff "lamentably" fail to appreciate the situation, as Lord Cunningham of Hyndhope claims in his *A Sailor's Odyssey*? It is difficult to dispute the validity of this statement by one of the great commanders of the war, yet in the end, we cannot always do as we would wish in war and sometimes the only choice left lies between two very great disadvantages. Churchill's solution was not necessarily the wrong one, therefore. Fifteen years of disarmament had reduced Britain to this level of impotence.

CHAPTER 16
THE ARMIES FACE TO FACE

Russia's time runs out

Hitler's decision to attack the Soviet Union was made at Berchtesgaden between July 20 and 29, 1940. He was motivated partly by the vulnerability of the indispensable Ploiesti oil fields to Soviet Bombers.

On June 22, 1941, at dawn, 3,400,000 Germans launched a surprise attack on the Soviet Union, defended by the 4,700,000 men of the Red Army, as Russia's army was called. In the numbers engaged and the losses suffered on both sides, this titanic struggle, unprecedented in human history, had no equal in any other theatre of operations in World War II. It would go on until the annihilation of the Wehrmacht, expressed in the smoking ruins of Berlin, and the signing of the instrument of unconditional surrender by Field-Marshal Keitel, followed by Grand-Admiral von Friedeburg and Colonel-General Stumpff of the Luftwaffe, in the presence of Marshal of the U.S.S.R. Georgi Zhukov, General Carl Spaatz of the United States Army Air Force, Air Chief-Marshal Sir Arthur Tedder of the R.A.F., and General de Lattre de Tassigny of France.

It must be stated in introduction that there are many aspects of this tragic struggle which, even today, have not been clarified. There is an abundant German bibliography on the Eastern Front operations, in the form of memoirs, general or specialised histories, monographs and published documents, but nothing of the kind is available on the other side of the Iron Curtain. Historical research, which suffered under Stalin, was also weak in the period of "destalinisation", and the disgrace of Nikita Kruschev was reflected in new instructions as imperious as those of previous epochs.

But does the quality of Soviet historical publication compensate for its lack of quantity? Not in the opinion of Alexander Werth, who was the *Sunday Times* correspondent in Moscow throughout the war. In the introduction to his book *Russia at War* he writes:

". . . but even the longest of them, the vast six-volume Russian *History of the Great Patriotic War of the Soviet Union* running to over two million words, and trying to cover not only the military operations, but 'everything', is singularly unsatisfactory in many ways. It contains an immense amount of valuable information which was not available under Stalin; but it is overburdened with names of persons, regiments and divisions and an endless variety of military and economic details. It is full of ever-recurring 'heroic' clichés."

Whatever their differences, all the Soviet authors consulted in German translation are in agreement on one point, or rather one dogma, summarised neatly by Colonel-General P. A. Kurochkin in his conclusion to the collective work entitled *The Most Important Operations of the Great Patriotic War*:

"The colossal victory of the Soviet armed forces in the Great Patriotic War proves indisputably the progressive nature of Soviet military skill and its incontestable superiority over the military art of bourgeois armies."

This condemnation evidently includes not only the defeated in that merciless war, but also Russia's British and American allies. And as the statement is "indisputable", those who dare to question it prove, by doing so, their incurable ignorance or cynical bad faith. Such doubters are anathematised as "bourgeois falsifiers of history".

German armour

After the problem of Soviet sources, the armed forces of the two giants who clashed on June 22 must be analysed.

As has already been described, the decisive stroke had been allotted to the armour. It is essential, then, to consider briefly the growth of this arm between May 10, 1940 and June 22, 1941, with the aid of the following table:

	1940	1941
Panzergruppen	1	4
Panzer or motorised corps	5	11
Panzer divisions	10	21
Motorised divisions	7	14

The number of armoured divisions had thus risen from 17 to 35, but this is not all: as a result of their battle experience in 1939 and 1940, the Germans had ceased production of the Pzkw I and II light tanks and up-gunned most of their 965 Pzkw III medium tanks with 5-cm guns. This tank and the Pzkw 38(t) formed the backbone of the *Panzerwaffe* or Armoured Forces. The number of Pzkw IV heavy tanks armed with the short 7.5-cm gun had been increased from 278 to 517.

The introduction of tracked cross-country vehicles should have allowed an infantry battalion and a pioneer company to be attached to each armoured division, but this stage had not been reached by all units on June 22. In the German Army there were also 250 self-propelled guns, and these were to give excellent service in infantry support and anti-tank operations.

German weaknesses

These many improvements do not, however, hide the fact that German war industry, under Göring, had not adapted itself properly to meet the huge effort needed to equip these formations. The year before, the ten Panzer divisions in the army had shared 35 battalions of tanks. To maintain 21 Panzer divisions at the same strength, it would have been necessary to equip another 40 or so battalions, but only 22 had in fact been formed, and six of these were not combat-ready. Because of this, the average strength of the Panzer divisions had dropped from 258 to 196 tanks during the period in question.

Thus even before going into action the number of tanks available had fallen to a dangerously low level. And during the campaign itself, a further toll was taken as the summer dust, autumn mud, and winter snows decimated the Panzer divisions' equipment. In these circumstances, it would have seemed sensible to bring under-strength units up to establishment before attempting to win a quick victory. But Hitler had other ideas, and the combat troops waited in vain for replacements as Hitler, back in Germany, constantly ordered the creation of new divisions, which were still untried and not available for service.

This great effort to increase armoured strength, combined with the insufficiency of German production, obliged the German High Command to make up its vehicle stocks with booty from Poland and France, requisitions from occupied countries, and deliveries under the terms of the Rethondes armistice. Both Hoth and Guderian concur, however, in saying that these French vehicles were too light and delicate to survive in the face of the Russian climate and Soviet roads. The situation soon became more serious as the problem of spare parts

reared its ugly head.

The German infantry, including mountain troops, totalled 129 divisions at the end of the French campaign. By June 22, 1941, it had increased to 162 divisions made up into 47 corps. Luckily, the 27 corps which were to invade Russia on the 22nd had also been able to stock their motor pools with vehicles captured in 1939 and 1940. But as with the armoured forces, this was to cause serious trouble after several months of campaigning. Finally, the standard 3.7-cm infantry anti-tank gun was gradually being superseded by the newer 5-cm gun.

But Russia's strength of resistance lay

△ *The eternal trio at the head of the German Armed Forces High Command: Hitler, Keitel, and Jodl. In the summer of 1941 the Führer's moral ascendancy over the German armed forces was at its height. Openly contemptuous of the Soviet régime and the Red Army, he radiated complete confidence: "We have only to kick in the door and the whole rotten structure will come tumbling down."*

Diplomatic Prelude

During the last months of 1940, Hitler's intention to attack Russia grew firmer, his belligerent attitudes reinforced by the failure of the negotiations with Molotov in November. At the foot of each of the nine copies of his Directive No. 21 "Barbarossa", he wrote, "The German armed forces must be prepared, even before the conclusion of the war against England, to crush Soviet Russia in a rapid campaign." During this intended campaign, the task of keeping up activity against Great Britain would be delegated chiefly to the German Navy. The Luftwaffe would aid the navy in blockade operations, while maintaining a solid defence against attacks by the R.A.F. on the industrial centres of the Reich and occupied Europe.

The plan for Operation "Barbarossa" was to launch an offensive against the bulk of the Soviet forces deployed in Western Russia, which were to be dislocated by savage armoured thrusts, pushing right into Russia in order to prevent Russian forces regrouping. By the end of February 1941 there were 25 divisions in the concentration area; seven more arrived in March, 13 in April, 30 in May, and 51 between June 1st and 22nd. A further 19 moved up into battle after the outbreak of hostilities. The Luftwaffe concentrated some 2,000 first line aircraft. On April 6, the Soviet Union and Yugoslavia signed a Pact of Non-Aggression and Friendship. On the same day the Luftwaffe conducted a savage air attack on Belgrade.

▽ *The job of breaking up the Russian masses was left to the foot-slogging infantry, who trudged forwards in the dust of the Panzers.*

not only with her regular armed forces. From information received by German Intelligence it was known that Moscow, if Russia were invaded, could also hurl the civil population of any areas overrun, organised into guerrilla units, against the flanks and communications of the invader. To combat this threat, O.K.H. formed nine Security Divisions (*Sicherungsdivisionen*) and allotted three to each army group. Though not capable of fighting regular troops in open country, they were nevertheless useful auxiliaries to front line troops, whom they relieved of the necessity of attending to their own security. The task of these divisions became more and more onerous as the Germans plunged deeper into Russian territory.

Germany's deployment

Including one cavalry division (1st Cavalry Division), which was removed from the front at the end of the year to be converted into an armoured division, the German Army could muster no less than 208 divisions in all theatres of war. Three-quarters of them, 153 to be exact, were engaged on the Eastern Front on June 22. Brauchitsch commanded 148 between the Black Sea and the Baltic deployed as follows:

1. *Right flank:* Army Group "South" (Rundstedt) with 42 divisions, including five Panzer and three motorised, divided between three armies and one *Panzergruppe*;
2. *Centre:* Army Group "Centre" (Bock), between Lublin and Suwałki, with 49 divisions, including nine Panzer, six motorised, and one cavalry, divided between two armies and two *Panzergruppen*; and
3. *Left flank:* Army Group "North" (Leeb) with 29 divisions, including three Panzer and two motorised, divided between two armies and one *Panzergruppe*.

In greater detail, these army groups broke down thus:

1. Army Group "South":
   Moldavia: 11th Army (Colonel-General E. von Schobert); Carpathians–Lublin area: 17th Army (Colonel-General K. H. von Stülpnagel), *Panzergruppe* I (Colonel-General von Kleist) with 750 tanks, and 6th Army (Field-Marshal von Reichenau);
2. Army Group "Centre":
   from south to north: *Panzergruppe* II (Colonel-General Guderian) with 930

tanks, 4th Army (Field-Marshal von Kluge), 9th Army (Colonel-General Strauss), and *Panzergruppe* III (Colonel-General Hoth) with 840 tanks; and

3. Army Group "North":
East Prussia: 16th Army (Colonel-General E. Busch), *Panzergruppe* IV Colonel-General Hoeppner) with 570 tanks, and 18th Army (Colonel-General G. von Küchler).

Thus the front line forces contained 120 divisions, including 17 of the 21 Panzer divisions (3,090 tanks), and 12 of the 14 motorised divisions. In reserve, O.K.H. had 2nd Army (Colonel-General von Weichs) with five corps made up of the 2nd and 5th Panzer Divisions, two motorised divisions, and no less than 24 infantry divisions.

In contrast, the German forces in Finland came under O.K.W. command and totalled five divisions or their equivalent.

In its struggle against the Soviet Union, the Third Reich could count on the help of Rumania, Hungary, and Slovakia, as well as the collaboration of Finland which, though she never signed any formal agreement with Germany, waged war at her side in order to recover the territory which she had lost to Russia by the terms of the

treaty of March 12, 1940.

Marshal Antonescu put the Rumanian 3rd and 4th Armies at the service of his ally. These totalled 12 infantry divisions and her mountain, cavalry, and tank brigades, the equivalent of another two divisions. Admiral Horthy, the Regent of Hungary, played a more modest part, for Hungary had no bone to pick with Russia. Only one Hungarian corps, composed of a motorised brigade and two cavalry brigades, took part in the first phase of the campaign. Slovakia could not remain neutral in such a conflict, and put a motorised brigade and two small infantry divisions under the command of Rundstedt, who also controlled the Hungarian and Rumanian contingents.

Between the Arctic Circle and the Gulf of Finland, Marshal Mannerheim took the field within 18 divisions, all eager for revenge after the Winter War.

It was not until the evening of June 21 that the Führer communicated his decision to invade Russia to his friend Mussolini in a long letter. Although Hitler made no request for aid, Mussolini proclaimed that the dignity of Fascist Italy would not allow her to surrender her share in the "Crusade against Bolshevism".

△ *German assault engineers poised to attack, minutes before the opening of the attack on the Soviet Union. In offensive operations, the assault engineers carried out the vital role of destroying enemy strongpoints and fortifications that might inflict heavy casualties on attacking infantry. They were normally equipped with flamethrowers to help them in this task.*

The *Corpo di spedizione italiano in Russia* (C.S.I.R.) was immediately formed under General Giovanni Messe with three infantry divisions: the partially motorised "Pasubio" and "Torino", and the "Celere". The corps formed part of the German 11th Army and went into battle on August 7, 1941.

At the news of the split between the allies of the Treaty of Moscow, General Franco authorised the recruitment of a Spanish infantry division, which was to repay the debt he had owed to Hitler since the Civil War. Composed of volunteers and named the *División Azul* (Blue Division), it went into line on the Novgorod front at the end of the summer of 1941 under General Muñoz Grande, who was later replaced by General Esteban Infantes.

Thus new satellites or associates had put about 50 divisions and brigades in the service of Germany. Nevertheless, with the exception of the Finnish Army, which did not belie its previous superb reputation, these allied forces were far less efficient than those of the Reich, in training, leadership, organisation, and equipment. Experience showed that three satellite units were required to complete a mission for which only two German units were necessary.

△ *Guard of honour for General Gariboldi, inspecting troops of the Italian expeditionary force destined for service on the Eastern Front.*
▽ *German sappers repair a damaged bridge. The enormous length of the Wehrmacht's* lines of communication demanded strenuous efforts of the rear area troops: bridge-building, road-making, and converting the Russian railway gauge to standard European gauge to keep supplies flowing to the front lines.

The Luftwaffe's part

The major ground offensive was also to be supported from the air, the four air fleets involved being allocated as follows:
1. *Luftflotte* IV (Colonel-General Alexander Löhr) to Army Group "South";
2. *Luftflotte* II (Field-Marshal Albert Kesselring) to Army Group "Centre";
3. *Luftflotte* I (Colonel-General Alfred Keller) to Army Group "North"; and
4. *Luftflotte* V (Colonel-General Hans-Jürgen Stumpff) to the mountain corps attacking Murmansk.

The Luftwaffe performed its tasks brilliantly. By the end of the first day of the invasion it had wiped out the Red Air Force as a fighting force for months to come, leaving the skies open for the Stukas to repeat the successes of Poland, France, the Balkans, and Crete against minimal opposition. The question was, however, whether the techniques of Blitzkrieg, already used so effectively in Europe, would have the same success on the almost endless Russian plains, against the vast reserves of the Red Army.

The Red Army

More than a quarter of a century after the unconditional surrender of the Third Reich, the initial deployment of the Soviet armed forces, as well as their structure and composition, are still much of a mystery. And since the secrecy which surrounds the subject has no relation, in view of the tremendous development of all arms, to present day security, the only conclusion that can be reached is that for reasons of domestic and international politics and propaganda, Moscow wishes to draw a veil over certain aspects of the great struggle.

The result is that, whereas with the aid of documents published in West Germany the German order of battle is known in detail down to divisional and even lower level, the semi-official *History of the Great Patriotic War of the Soviet Union* describes the Soviet forces, on the day of confrontation, only down to army level.

Between the Arctic and the Black Sea, the Red Army was deployed in five major groups:

1. Leningrad Military District (Rybachiy Peninsula to Vyborg, latterly Viipuri, some 750 miles), under Lieutenant-General M. M. Popov, was made up of:
   a. 14th Army (Lieutenant-General V. A. Frolov);
   b. 7th Army (Lieutenant-General F. D. Gorelenko); and
   c. 23rd Army (Lieutenant-General P. S. Pshennikov);
2. Baltic Special Military District (Polanga to the southern frontier of Lithuania, some 200 miles), under Colonel-General F. I. Kuznetsov, was made up of:
   a. 8th Army (Major-General P. P. Sobennikov); and
   b. 11th Army (Lieutenant-General V. I. Morozov);
3. West Special Military District (southern frontier of Lithuania to northern frontier of the Ukraine, some 280 miles), under General D. G. Pavlov, was made up of:
   a. 3rd Army (Lieutenant-General V. I. Kuznetsov);
   b. 10th Army (Major-General K. D. Golubev); and
   c. 4th Army (Major-General A. A. Korobkov);
4. Kiev Special Military District (northern frontier of the Ukraine to Lipkany, some 500 miles), under Colonel-General

M. P. Kirponos, was made up of:
   a. 5th Army (Major-General of Armoured Forces M. I. Potapov);
   b. 6th Army (Lieutenant-General I. N. Muzychenko);
   c. 26th Army (Lieutenant-General F. Ya. Kostenko); and
   d. 12th Army (Major-General P. D. Ponedelin); and
5. Odessa Military District (Lipkany to the Black Sea, some 300 miles), under General I. V. Tyulenev, which shortly after the opening of hostilities divided its forces into:
   a. 18th Army (Lieutenant-General A. K. Smirnov) and
   b. 9th Army (Lieutenant-General Ya. T. Cherevichenko).

The Soviet dispositions formed a long, undulating line along the western frontier. The organisation within the Military Districts was poor (with reserve units too far back to give effective support to the front line troops) and there was little real coordination between the Districts.

Although considerable effort had been invested in the construction of field fortifications in strategically vital areas (over 200,000 men were engaged in the task), the results failed to live up to expectations. In what was supposedly an interlocking system of defence, gaps 10 to 80 kilometres wide were apparent.

A further problem facing the Soviet commanders was Stalin's own curious attitude towards the possibility of war. Because of Stalin's refusal to heed the warnings of impending invasion he forbade his generals to mobilise their forces in anticipation of attack. He maintained that any sizeable troop movements would be construed by the Germans as "provocation".

The most serious flaw in the Russian dispositions was their forward deployment which made it quite impossible for the Soviet commanders to react effectively to the swiftness of the German invasion. The reasoning behind the decision to defend the frontier line of the Soviet Union was based on two erroneous assumptions: firstly, that a formal declaration of war would precede offensive operations, so that the Red Army would not be surprised, and secondly, that the enemy offensive would be opened with limited forces, thereby giving the army time to fight holding actions and allow a full mobilisation. The folly of these assumptions would soon be fully exposed.

If we consider the Red Army in more de-

Marshal Klimenti Voroshilov, born in 1881, was People's Commissar for Defence during the Anglo-French negotiations for a Soviet alliance during the summer of 1939, in which he insisted that if the Red Army should go to Poland's aid it must be permitted to enter Polish territory. In the reshuffle of the Red Army after the bitter lessons of the Winter War against Finland, he became Deputy Premier and Chairman of the Defence Committee. On July 3, 1941, Stalin set up a State Defence Committee: himself, Voroshilov, Molotov, Beria, and Malenkov, and Voroshilov was given the job of defending Leningrad from the advance of Army Group "North". Stalin was forced to replace him with Zhukov, however, and remove Voroshilov from active command. Later in the war Voroshilov acted with much greater success as a military spokesman in discussions with the Allied leaders and commanders. His real talent lay in statesmanship and diplomacy rather than in military command. His stature in the Soviet High Command was considerable, however, and he gave his initials to the formidable "KV" heavy tank.

△ *A Russian T-35 heavy tank in a parade in Red Square, Moscow. Although heavily armoured, T-35s proved clumsy in action, and were rarely used after the battle for Moscow in December 1941.*

tail we see that it was quite unprepared for modern war. A fundamental problem acting against military efficiency was the absence of effective communications. Radio equipment was in short supply, especially so in the armoured formations and the air force. Basic communication was carried out through the civilian network so that in one instance, noted by Professor Erickson, the signals of the 22nd Tank Division were sent through a local post-office, the unit "plugging-in" to the civilian network and telegraph service!

Similarly in the fields of transport and supply the Russian armed forces were woefully deficient. The Motorised Transport branch was another victim of administrative ineptitude: its independent status was removed, being reassigned to the armoured forces. However, the armoured units proved incompetent in this additional role.

As Professor Erickson explains, within the Red Army there was a general failure to put theory into practise:

"Throughout the whole of the Soviet military sector, from research and development to tactical training, the pressure was on, but its application was uneven, uncoordinated and in parts uncomprehending."

Soviet armour

In terms of size, the Soviet tank force, was unchallengeable: the total mechanised force facing the Wehrmacht was 13 motorised divisions and 34 tank divisions. But by 1941 many of its tanks were obsolete and grossly unreliable.

How good were Soviet tanks?

In a weapon as complicated as the tank, technical qualities are naturally more significant than in the infantry.

From this point of view, the numerous lessons learnt in the Spanish Civil War justify the belief that the Soviet T-26 and BT-7 light tanks, derived from original designs by Vickers of Great Britain and Christie of the United States, were superior to German machines of the same class and far better than Italian ones. On the other hand, they were greatly inferior to the medium and heavy tanks in service with the German Army.

The small number of T-35 and KV-2 heavy tanks, weighing 49 and 52 tons respectively, were to give the Germans some very unpleasant surprises in Lithuania and Galicia, but they were so clumsy that once the German infantry had got over their initial shock at the size of the tanks, they rapidly learned how to immobilise them with grenades before going in to attack them directly.

In contrast, M. I. Koshkin, A. A. Morozov, and N. A. Kucherenko had achieved in the T-34 the best combination of the three factors important in armour at the time: armament, armour, and mobility. The rate of fire of its 76.2-mm gun was superior to that of the 7.5-cm gun mounted by the heaviest German tank, the Pzkw IV, and its armour, in places 65-mm thick and well sloped, made it impervious to German anti-tank shells. Its mobility came from its 500-hp engine, wide tracks, and improved Christie-type suspension, and enabled it to tackle marshy or snow-covered ground in which its opponents bogged down.

At the same time as Soviet tacticians readopted Marshal Tukhachevsky's theories, they kept the infantry tank, constructing the KV-1 for this purpose. Its speed was only 21 mph, compared with the 33 mph of the T-34, but this was not the disadvantage it might have been as the KV-1 was an infantry support weapon, and its lack of speed was compensated for by its massive hull, which gave it a weight of 43.5 tons, compared with the 26.3 tons of the T-34.

With 967 T-34's and 508 KV-1's, the Red Army had an enormous *matériel* superiority over the Germans who, on June 22, could put only 439 20-ton Pzkw IV's into the field. Yet this advantage was cancelled by several circumstances. Firstly, Stalin's blindness about Hitler's intentions had obliged the Soviet High Command to adopt unsuitable strategic plans. Secondly, Russian equipment was badly maintained: according to the *History of the Great Patriotic War*, only 29 per cent of the Russian tanks were ready to move out at a minute's notice because of the shortage of spare parts. Lastly, radio equipment was in extremely short supply and functioned only poorly.

The remarkable development of Soviet armour had escaped Hitler's eyes entirely, and had raised no more than unformulated doubts at O.K.H. But in his book *Panzer*

Leader, General Guderian records the "curious incident" about Germany's possible enemy which led him to entertain doubts about the Third Reich's alleged invincibility:

"In the spring of 1941 Hitler had specifically ordered that a Russian military commission be shown over our tank schools and factories; in this order he had insisted that nothing be concealed from them. The Russian officers in question firmly refused to believe that the Panzer IV was in fact our heaviest tank. They said repeatedly that we must be hiding our newest models from them, and complained that we were not carrying out Hitler's order to show them everything. The military commission was so insistent on this point that eventually our manufacturers and Ordnance Office officials concluded: 'It seems that the Russians must already possess

better and heavier tanks than we do.' It was at the end of July, 1941, that the T-34 tank appeared at the front and the riddle of the new Russian model was solved."

The Red Air Force

Whatever the numerical superiority of the Red Air Force over the Luftwaffe, it merits only a brief mention in the calculation of Russian forces, since most of its few modern aircraft were surprised and destroyed on the ground in the first few hours of the campaign. In May 1941, Luftwaffe Intelligence estimated that the Red Air Force had 7,300 aircraft of all types, 4,000 of them first line, deployed in the west. It was later admitted that the figures were in error, greatly underestimating Soviet air

△ *Heavy metal: German artillery in position on the Eastern Front. "Barbarossa" would be launched with a mammoth artillery barrage extending from the Black Sea to the Baltic at dawn on June 22, 1941 . . .*

△ *Cavalry was also used by the Germans in Russia. The regular army's East Prussian cavalry division was earmarked for Army Group Centre; these men belong to one of the two* Waffen-S.S. *cavalry regiments which were formed into a brigade in August 1941.*

this submarine fleet was the largest in the world.

Its size was not, however, matched by its successes. Between June 22, 1941 and May 8, 1945, it sank only 292,000 tons of shipping, compared with Germany's 14.5 million tons, the United States' 5.5 million tons, and Great Britain's 1.8 million tons. It is true that the Arctic, Baltic, and Black Sea offered far less in the way of prey than the North Atlantic, Pacific, and Mediterranean, but all the same, not until the end of 1944 were Soviet submarines able to interfere significantly with the seaborne supply or evacuation of German troops, and with imports of Swedish iron ore.

It must be admitted, however, that Germany's main lines of communication lay on land, and thus even had they been more efficient, there would have been little that the submarines could do.

Airborne troops

The Soviet High Command had been the first in the world to recognise the value of airborne troops for operations in the enemy's rear, destroying his communications and cutting front line units off from their supplies and reinforcements. Under Tukhachevsky's aegis, the first parachute units in the Red Army had been raised in 1935. But at the beginning of the Russian campaign such troops were hardly used, possibly because of the devastating losses suffered by the Red Air Force. Another reason is that after Tukhachevsky's downfall Stalin and his military advisers had lost interest in the arm supported so ardently by their late victim, and its establishment and efficiency had declined.

Surprise on the side of the Germans

Such were the strengths and weakness of the Soviet land, sea, and air forces. But the defeats which the Russians suffered in four continuous months, and the German's advance to the suburbs of Moscow, cannot be explained without mentioning the factor of surprise, of which the invaders made full use right from the beginning of the campaign. Naturally, Hitler and O.K.H. had camouflaged as best they could the 153 German divisions which would go into the

strength.

Nevertheless, the Red Air Force would need at least a year to recover from the stunning blow inflicted on it by the Luftwaffe. In the interim, the Stukas of the Luftwaffe could attack Soviet armour and positions without hindrance, while the German A.A., now unemployed, could concentrate on anti-tank action, where its 8.8-cm guns achieved notable successes.

Soviet naval strength

We have already noted Stalin's desire to build up a strong navy in the chapter on German military aid to Russia. On June 22, 1941, the Soviet Navy possessed no fewer than 139 submarines, distributed thus: Arctic Ocean 14; the Baltic 74; and the Black Sea 51. In other classes of vessel the Russian Navy was weak, having only a few modern cruisers and destroyers, but

attack on June 22, and they had also made several diversionary feints.

"For two days," writes Paul Carell, "they had been lying in the dark pine-woods with their tanks and their vehicles. They had arrived, driving with masked head-lights, during the night of June 19–20. During the day they lay silent. They must not make a sound. At the mere rattle of a hatch cover the troop commanders would have fits. Only when dusk fell were they allowed to go to the stream in the clearing to wash themselves, a troop at a time.

"The regiment was bivouacking in the forest in full battle order. Each tank, moreover, carried ten jerricans of petrol strapped to its turret and had a trailer in tow with a further three drums. These were the preparations for a long journey, not a swift battle. 'You don't go into battle with jerricans on your tank,' the experienced tankmen were saying.

"A fantastic rumour swept through the field kitchens. 'Stalin has leased the Ukraine to Hitler and we're just going to occupy it.'"

Hitler himself had had his command post carefully concealed. "This great H.Q.," recalls Paul Schmidt, "was hidden in a thick forest near Rastenburg in East Prussia. One recalled the old tales of witches. Not without reason was the H.Q. known by the code-name of *Wolfsschanze* (Wolf's lair).

"The atmosphere of the post in the dark Prussian forest was depressing for people coming from sunnier parts.

"The rooms were tiny. You always felt constricted. The humidity which came from masses of concrete, the permanent electric light, the constant hum of the air-conditioning imposed an air of unreality on the atmosphere in which Hitler, growing paler and more flabby every day, received the foreign visitors. The whole place might easily have been the mystic retreat of some legendary spirit of evil."

Nevertheless, since the coming of spring, London, Vichy, Berne, Stockholm, Tokyo, and Washington had been expecting a decisive split between the signatories of the German-Soviet Non-Aggression Pact of August 23, 1939, and were already calculating the effect this immense extension of the war would have.

Only the Kremlin refused until the last moment to admit that Hitler was about to cross his Rubicon. Stalin took none of the measures which were clearly required if Russia was to be prepared for the imminent change in the political and military situation. The *Great Patriotic War* explains his strange blindness in this way:

"One of the reasons for the error made in the appreciation of the situation is that J. V. Stalin, who alone decided the most important political and military questions, was of the opinion that Germany would not break the Non-Aggression Pact in the near future. Therefore he considered all the reports of German troop movements merely as evidence of provocations, intended to force the Soviet Union into counter-measures.

"If he took such measures, Stalin feared he might furnish the Hitlerian clique with a good pretext for accusing the U.S.S.R. of having broken the treaty and attacking Germany treacherously. For the same reasons, certain commanders of military districts who wanted to place their troops in defensive positions and have them ready for combat, had their requests refused.

◁ *Help from the Spaniards: a colour-bearer of the "Blue Division" sent by Franco to fight on the Eastern Front under the command of General Muñoz-Grande.*

▽ *"Schnell Heinz" Guderian, the Panzer virtuoso. His initial reaction to the idea of invading Soviet Russia was unequivocal. "When they spread out a map of Russia before me I could scarcely believe my eyes . . . I made no attempt to conceal my disappointment and disgust . . . All the men of the O.K.W. and the O.K.H. with whom I spoke evinced an unshakable optimism and were quite impervious to criticism or objections."*

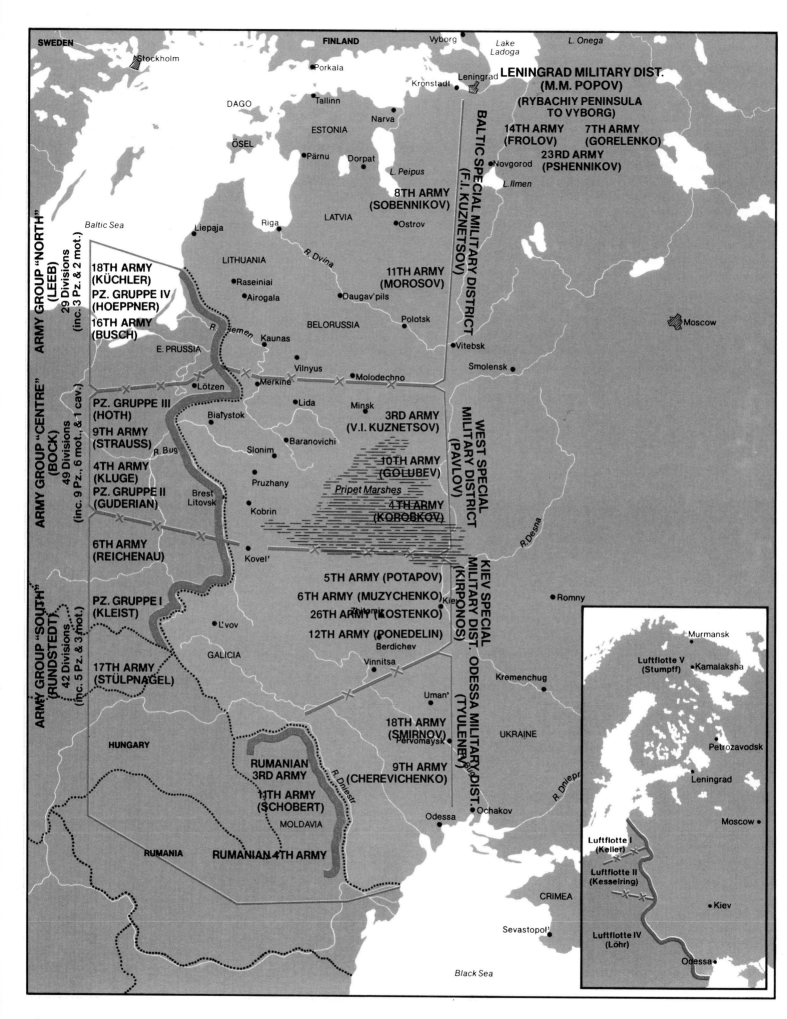

SWEDEN

FINLAND

Stockholm

Porkala

Vyborg

Lake Ladoga

L. Onega

Kronstadt

Leningrad

LENINGRAD MILITARY DIST.
(M.M. POPOV)

(RYBACHIY PENINSULA TO VYBORG)

14TH ARMY **7TH ARMY**
(FROLOV) **(GORELENKO)**

23RD ARMY
(PSHENNIKOV)

Tallinn

Narva

DAGO

ESTONIA

ÖSEL

Pärnu

Dorpat

L. Peipus

Novgorod

L. Ilmen

8TH ARMY
(SOBENNIKOV)

Moscow

Baltic Sea

Liepaja

Riga

LATVIA

Ostrov

R. Dvina

11TH ARMY
(MOROSOV)

LITHUANIA

Raseiniai

Airogala

Daugav'pils

Polotsk

BELORUSSIA

ARMY GROUP "NORTH"
(LEEB)
29 Divisions
(inc. 3 Pz. & 2 mot.)

18TH ARMY
(KÜCHLER)

PZ. GRUPPE IV
(HOEPPNER)

16TH ARMY
(BUSCH)

R. Niemen

Kaunas

Vitebsk

Smolensk

E. PRUSSIA

Vilnyus

Merkine

Molodechno

Lötzen

BALTIC SPECIAL MILITARY DISTRICT
(F.I. KUZNETSOV)

ARMY GROUP "CENTRE"
(BOCK)
49 Divisions
(inc. 9 Pz., 6 mot., & 1 cav.)

PZ. GRUPPE III
(HOTH)

9TH ARMY
(STRAUSS)

4TH ARMY
(KLUGE)

PZ. GRUPPE II
(GUDERIAN)

6TH ARMY
(REICHENAU)

R. Bug

Białystok

Lida

Minsk

3RD ARMY
(V.I. KUZNETSOV)

Slonim

Baranovichi

10TH ARMY
(GOLUBEV)

Pruzhany

Pripet Marshes

Brest Litovsk

Kobrin

4TH ARMY
(KOROBKOV)

R. Desna

WEST SPECIAL MILITARY DISTRICT
(PAVLOV)

Kovel'

5TH ARMY (POTAPOV)

6TH ARMY (MUZYCHENKO)

26TH ARMY (KOSTENKO)

Zhitomir

Kiev

Romny

ARMY GROUP "SOUTH"
(RUNDSTEDT)
42 Divisions
(inc. 5 Pz. & 3 mot.)

PZ. GRUPPE I
(KLEIST)

L'vov

12TH ARMY (PONEDELIN)

Berdichev

GALICIA

Vinnitsa

KIEV SPECIAL MILITARY DIST.
(KIRPONOS)

R. Dnie...

Kremenchug

17TH ARMY
(STÜLPNAGEL)

Uman'

18TH ARMY
(SMIRNOV)

Pervomaysk

UKRAINE

HUNGARY

RUMANIAN 3RD ARMY

R. Dniestr

9TH ARMY
(CHEREVICHENKO)

R. Bug

ODESSA MILITARY DIST.
(TYULENEV)

11TH ARMY
(SCHOBERT)

MOLDAVIA

Ochakov

R. Dniepr

RUMANIA

RUMANIAN 4TH ARMY

Odessa

Black Sea

Sevastopol'

CRIMEA

Murmansk

Luftflotte V
(Stumpff)

Kamalaksha

Petrozavodsk

Leningrad

Luftflotte I
(Keller)

Moscow

Luftflotte II
(Kesselring)

Kiev

Luftflotte IV
(Löhr)

Odessa

"The People's Defence Commissar, Marshal of the Soviet Union Timoshenko, and G. K. Zhukov, Chief-of-Staff, bear a heavy burden of responsibility for the unpreparedness of the Red Army to resist a surprise attack. They had not appreciated the military and political situation clearly enough and had not understood that immediate measures to put the armed forces into combat readiness were essential."

There is nothing surprising in Stalin's refusal to believe Churchill's warning about an imminent German attack. The message that the British Prime Minister sent him on April 3 and which, for various reasons, was not handed him until the 22nd was not explicit enough to have made him change his views:

"*Prime Minister to Sir Stafford Cripps* [British Ambassador in Moscow]

"Following from me to M. Stalin, *provided it can be personally delivered by you:*

"I have sure information from a trusted agent that when the Germans thought they had got Yugoslavia in the net–that is to say, after March 20–they began to move three out of the five Panzer divisions from Rumania to southern Poland. The moment they heard of the Serbian revolution this movement was countermanded. Your Excellency will readily appreciate the significance of these facts."

Stalin did nothing, fearing that Churchill, using all kinds of forged information, was trying to create a split between Berlin and Moscow and to divert the weight of German arms from Great Britain to the Soviet Union. Though history has shown these suspicions to be groundless, the man in the Kremlin cannot be blamed for being on his guard.

Soviet spies at work

The fact remains, however, that the British message of April 3 was soon corroborated by a deluge of information which ought to have found more credence in Moscow, since it originated from Soviet spy networks in the Far East and Central Europe.

At the outbreak of war the *Frankfurter Zeitung*'s Far East correspondent, Richard Sorge, long in the pay of the Soviet Secret Service, had been sent as Press Attaché to the German Embassy in Tokyo. General Eugen Ott, Hitler's envoy to the Mikado, was well connected in Japanese circles and kept no secrets from Sorge.

So, on May 19, this informer, an old hand at his calling and particularly well placed, reported the concentration of nine armies (which was correct) and 150 German divisions (he underestimated by three) facing the Soviet frontiers. On June 1, he described the strategy the Nazis would use; and on June 15, he gave June 22 as the date of attack. "Too good to be true," it might have been thought, when the first revelations of Richard Sorge's exploits appeared some 20 years ago. The fact that in 1964 the Kremlin awarded him posthumously the title of "Hero of the Soviet Union" and issued a commemorative postage stamp, indicates the importance of his services to Russia.

In Switzerland there was a network known to the *Abwehr* as the "Red Trio" (or "Lucy Ring") because of the three clandestine transmitters which it used to communicate from Lausanne and Geneva.

The three "musicians", as they were known in Moscow, were led by the German Rudolf Rössler, known under the codename "Lucy", a German refugee of Christian Progressive hue who lived, ostensibly, as a bookseller in Lucerne. Where did this agent obtain the information that he communicated to Moscow? Even today this question is difficult to answer. From the value of the information he gathered and the three or four days he took to obtain it each time, it is reasonable to conclude that he got it from someone who took part in the most secret conferences of O.K.W.

A proof of this, in respect of Operation "Barbarossa", is the description of Rössler's information given by General Otto Heilbrunn in the book he wrote about the Soviet Secret Service. "Not only had the 'Red Trio' given the date of the attack to its Moscow control, but it had also supplied the German plan of campaign, the composition and numbers of Army Groups "North", "Centre", and "South", with precise details of the number of tanks and their distribution between the groups. What is more, Moscow now knew the intentions of the enemy, his directions of attack, and his precise objectives. Lastly Moscow was told the names of all senior officers down to the corps commanders."

Never had a state been better informed than Russia about the aggressive intent of another. Never had the accuracy of the information been so highly guaranteed, since there could have been no collusion

◁◁ *The deployment of the German, Rumanian and Russian armies along the Eastern Front for the offensive of June 22, 1941. The inset shows the allocation of the four Luftwaffe fleets which supported the ground offensive and virtually wiped out the Red Air Force.*

between Sorge and Rössler. But never had an army been so ill-prepared to meet the initial onslaught of its enemy than the Red Army on June 22, 1941.

With 138 infantry divisions and 40 motorised and armoured divisions under arms between the frozen Arctic Ocean and the Danube delta, the Red Army could have been expected to hold the attack of some 200 German and satellite divisions, had it been properly deployed for a defensive campaign. But it was not. The troops of the Baltic Special Military District were dispersed between the Niemen and the Dvina to a depth of nearly 200 miles. It was worse in the West Special Military District where General Pavlov had placed divisions along the whole 300 mile line between Białystok and Minsk.

This dispersal of Soviet Forces was the pattern the length of the German-Russian demarcation line. There is no getting away from the fact that the fronts were too long for the divisions detailed to garrison them. For instance, according to the *Great Patriotic War*, the Russians had only the 125th Division covering a 25-mile front facing *Panzergruppe* IV which, on June 22, put two infantry divisions and three armoured divisions into the field. The situation was the same in the sectors awaiting the onslaught of Hoth and

Guderian, powerfully supported by Colonel-General von Richthofen's Stukas.

On June 18, a German deserter crossed into the Russian lines near Kovel' and reported the attack as coming on June 22. But this extra proof provoked no greater reaction from the Kremlin than the information it had previously received. Nevertheless, on the night of June 21, after midnight, the penny dropped and at 0030 hours the commanders of the military districts concerned were ordered to occupy their front line positions, disperse and camouflage their aircraft, and put the A.A. on full alert. But they were not to take "any other steps without special orders". This instruction, however, insufficient as it was, had not reached all commanders before they found themselves at grips with forces which were very much greater in numbers and in armament. Furthermore, the Russian communications with the rear had been cut by the German artillery bombardment, which began at 0335 hours that morning and destroyed the Russian telephone networks. At 0415 the barrage of shells was followed by the wide-ranging destruction of Russian barbed wire by German sappers. The Stukas, diving from high in the sky, alternated with the artillery in pounding the bewildered Soviet Union.

△ *June 22, 1941: Ribbentrop formally announces the invasion of Russia to the press, hours after the actual attack had gone in. "When Barbarossa begins the world will hold its breath and make no comment," Hitler boasted. He was wrong on one count. The assault on Russia provoked an immediate declaration of alliance from Churchill, who for decades had been as outspoken a critic of Communism as Hitler himself. "If Hitler invaded Hell," Churchill commented, "I should at least make a favourable reference to the Devil in the House of Commons."*

CHAPTER 17

BARBAROSSA: THE STORM BREAKS

On the evening of June 22, in the head-quarters which German G.H.Q. had just taken over at Lötzen in East Prussia, Halder observed in his invaluable diary:

"The enemy has been taken unawares by our attack. His forces were not tactically in position for defence. In the frontier zone his troops were widely dispersed and his frontier defence was weak overall.

"Because of our tactical surprise, enemy resistance on the frontier has been weak and disorganised. We have been able to seize bridges over the border rivers and, slightly further on, to overwhelm enemy positions fortified by deep earthworks."

Stalin's failure to react until the very eve of the German attack is astonishing. Some validity can be given to the explanation given by one of the best-informed biographers of the Russian leader:

"At dawn on June 22, 1941," writes Emmanuel d'Astier de la Vigerie, "on the day before the anniversary of Napoleon's crossing of the Niemen, 120 divisions speed towards Kiev, Leningrad, and Moscow, where the theatre is performing *A Midsummer Night's Dream*.

"Stalin, living in a dream world of hope, has spurned warnings and refused advice.

During the first hours of the attack he issued orders that German firing is not to be answered. He would like to think he is faced by nothing more than a provocative act from a few ill-disciplined German units. On June 21, a German Communist worker deserted and revealed the date and time of the attack. Stalin is told but refuses to believe the evidence. Fifteen years later Nikita Khruschev recounts the episode; and another historian adds that Stalin ordered Korpik, the deserting worker, who could in his view only be an *agent provocateur*, to be shot."

Soviet resistance in chaos

To the north of the Pripet Marshes, Soviet resistance had, from the early hours of that warm summer morning, been surprised and overcome more or less everywhere. The same fate had overcome reinforcements moving up to the front to obey People's Defence Commissar Marshal Timoshenko's broadcast message of 0715 hours:

"Our troops must hurl themselves with

▽ *Field-Marshal Fedor von Bock, commander of Army Group "Centre", the strongest of the three army groups, whose task it was to destroy the Soviet armoured and motorised forces in the triangle Vilnyus–Smolensk–Brest.*

▷ *Safe from air attack, German trucks and dispatch riders wait in a traffic jam on the borders of the Soviet Union.*

△ *German troops double towards a burning farm house. Resistance on the frontier was disorganised and weak, but following Stalin's speech of July 3 the defence stiffened and the "scorched earth" policy was carried out ruthlessly.*

all their means and energy against the enemy and annihilate them in all places where they have violated our frontiers."

In Army Group "Centre's" area, Colonel-General Guderian had taken the bridges over the River Bug, above and below Brest-Litovsk, by storm, and by the evening his XXIV Panzer Corps (General Geyr von Schweppenburg) was in Kobrin and his XLVII Panzer Corps (General Lemelsen) in Pruzhany, 41 and 47 miles respectively from their jump-off points.

This enormous success by *Panzergruppe* II was equalled and even surpassed by that of *Panzergruppe* III. Not only had Colonel-General Hoth penetrated deeply into the Russian defences but his LVII Panzer Corps (General Kuntzen) and his XXXIX Panzer Corps (General R. Schmidt) had taken the bridges over the Niemen at Merkine and Olyta intact. The XXXIX Corps was in fact 59 miles over the demarcation line.

This ultra-rapid war of movement led at times to comic incidents such as this adventure of General Guderian:

"I next visited the front line in Slonim and then drove in a Panzer IV through no-man's-land to the 18th Panzer Division. At 15.30 hrs I was back in Slonim having ordered the 18th Panzer Division to push

on in the direction of Baranovichi, while the 29th (Motorised) Infantry Division was instructed to hasten its advance towards Slonim. I then returned to my Group command post. This drive took me unexpectedly through the middle of Russian infantry, which had come up in lorries to the very outskirts of Slonim and was on the point of dismounting. I ordered my driver, who was next to me, to go full speed ahead and we drove straight through the Russians; they were so surprised by this unexpected encounter that they did not even have time to fire their guns. All the same they must have recognised me because the Russian press later announced my death; I felt bound to inform them of their mistake by means of the German wireless."

In Army Group "North", Field-Marshal von Leeb had no reason to be any less satisfied with the results of the first day of the campaign. *Panzergruppe* IV (Colonel-General Hoeppner) had also thrown the Russians into disorder; in particular, at about 1900 hours, the LVI Panzer Corps (General von Manstein) had boldly seized the important viaduct which crosses the Doubissa gorges at Airogala. He was about 50 miles from his starting point.

As for the Soviet Air Force, those planes

which had not been destroyed on the ground in the first hour made a rather pitiful impression on General Kesselring:

"From the second day onward I watched the battle against the aircraft which were arriving from the depths of Russia. It seemed almost criminal to me that they should use formations which were so ridiculous from the point of view of aerial tactics, and machines obviously incapable of getting out of trouble in the air. In they came, one squadron after the other, at regular intervals, and one after the other they crashed, easy prey to our fighters. 'This is the massacre of the innocents,' I thought. So completely did we manage to crush the basis of any future bomber fleet that Russian bombers never appeared again throughout the whole campaign!"

In contrast, south of the Pripet Marshes, the achievements of Field-Marshal von Rundstedt had been no greater than what German military theorists call an "ordinary victory", and it had not been possible to split off units from *Panzergruppe* I (Colonel-General von Kleist) to exploit the success.

The designs of the Third Reich on the Ukraine were known to all and so Stalin had emphasised the defence of the approaches to that territory. It was defended by 68 divisions, including ten armoured and five motorised, while Rundstedt had only 54 divisions under him, including 12 Rumanian, five Panzer, and three motorised divisions. Furthermore, following an order from Hitler, the German 11th Army (seven divisions), which had been concentrated in Moldavia, did not join battle on June 22. This allowed the Russians to assemble part of the forces they had aligned along the Rumanian frontier and use them profitably in Galicia.

The performance of Soviet officers and men

Looking at the Soviet Army and the performance of its officers and men, the testimony of General Fedyuninsky, who was fighting in Kovel' that day, may be useful. As his memoirs have not been translated into any Western language, they will be quoted in the translation given by Alexander Werth:

"Railway junctions and lines of communication were being destroyed by German planes and diversionist groups. There was a shortage of wireless sets at army headquarters, nor did any of us know how to use them . . . Orders and instructions were slow in arriving, and sometimes did not arrive at all . . . The liaison with the neighbouring units was often completely absent, while nobody tried to establish it. Taking advantage of this, the enemy would often penetrate into our rear, and attack the Soviet headquarters. . . Despite German air supremacy, our marching columns did not use any proper camouflage. Sometimes on narrow roads, bottlenecks were formed by troops, artillery, motor vehicles, and field kitchens, and then the Nazi planes had the time of their life." In such conditions the higher levels of the front line command often performed rather poorly. Certain commanders, such as General Boldin, performed heroically; he managed to blast his

▽ *Crouching in a shell hole an N.C.O. of the* Waffen-S.S. *primes his hand grenade before going in to mop up a party of Russians. Well supplied with modern equipment, the S.S. came to serve as a "fire brigade" on the Eastern Front, blocking counterattacks and heading offensives.*

way through the German lines with 2,000 men of his XIII Corps; others, such as General D. G. Pavlov, who was shot, together with his chief-of-staff and General Korobkov of the 10th Army, lost their heads. Opposite *Panzergruppe* III a Lithuanian division went over to the Germans and, as Fedyuninsky points out, at first cannon shot many Ukrainian partisans rebelled against their September 1939 "liberators". In contrast, the Brest-Litovsk garrison, surrounded on the evening of June 22, held out to July 24, under a hail of bombs and artillery fire, among which were monster 2.2-ton shells

fired by the 61.5-cm mortar *Karl*.

In many other sectors, once he had overcome his initial shock, the Russian soldier fought with a stubbornness and bravery admitted by most German combatants who have written about the campaign:

"The Russians again proved their mastery in forest fighting. With sure instinct they moved among the impenetrable undergrowth. Their positions, not on the forest's edge but deep inside, were superbly camouflaged. Their dugouts and foxholes were established with diabolical cunning, providing a field of fire only to the rear. From the front and from above they were invisible. The German infantrymen passed them unsuspecting, and were picked off from behind.

"The Russians were also very good at infiltrating into enemy positions. Moving singly, they communicated with each other in the dense forest by imitating the cries of animals, and after trickling through the German positions they rallied again and reformed as assault units. The headquarters staff of 247th Infantry Regiment fell victim to these Russian tactics.

"In the night, at 0200, the shout went up, 'Action Stations!' There was small-arms fire. The Russians were outside the regimental head-quarters. They had surrounded it. With fixed bayonets they broke into the officers' quarters. The regimental adjutant, the orderly officer, and the regimental medical officer were cut down in the doorway of their forest ranger's hut. N.C.O.s and headquarters personnel were killed before they could reach their pistols or carbines.

"Lieutenant-Colonel Brehmer, the regimental commander, succeeded in barricading himself behind a woodpile and defending himself throughout two hours with his sub-machine-gun."

In Moscow, on June 22, the Praesidium of the Supreme Soviet announced the mobilisation of the reserves of the years 1925 to 1938, thus recalling 15 million men to the colours. The next day, Supreme Headquarters began work. Stalin, assisted by Molotov, took control. General Zhukov, and later General Shaposhnikov, served as Chiefs-of-Staff. Marshals Voroshilov, Timoshenko, and Budenny played their parts until they were called to direct field operations, Voroshilov in the Baltic countries, Timoshenko in Belorussia, and Budenny in the Ukraine. In their new posts they used the services of Comrades

The Panzers drive east. The wear on men and machines became a considerable problem with the huge distances and almost non-existent roads.
△ *Tanks of* Panzergruppe *Kleist spread out either side of a dust track that would dissolve into a mud bath by autumn.*

Zhdanov, Bulganin, and also Khruschev as political advisers.

Timoshenko gave up his position as People's Defence Commissar and was succeeded by Stalin who, on August 7, had himself appointed to the post of Supreme Commander of the Soviet Armed Forces.

The general running of the war fell to the National Defence Committee. This was presided over by Stalin, and its members were Molotov, Voroshilov, Malenkov, and the sinister L. P. Beria in his capacity as head of the Soviet Secret Service or N.K.V.D.

On July 3, 1941, Stalin broadcast:

"Comrades, citizens, brothers and sisters, men of our Army and Navy! I speak to you, my friends!"

This sort of language from the tongue of the cruel master of the "purges" of previous years was unfamiliar, but nevertheless, as Alexander Werth has pointed out, it evoked an enormous response.

"A serious threat hangs over our country," he went on. "It can only be dispersed by the combined efforts of the military and industrial might of the nation. There is no room for the timid or the coward, for deserters or spreaders of panic, and a merciless struggle must be waged against such people. We must destroy spies, *agents provocateurs*, and enemy parachutists . . . On the spot court-martials will try anyone who, through panic or cowardice, hinders our defence,

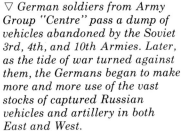

▽ *German soldiers from Army Group "Centre" pass a dump of vehicles abandoned by the Soviet 3rd, 4th, and 10th Armies. Later, as the tide of war turned against them, the Germans began to make more and more use of the vast stocks of captured Russian vehicles and artillery in both East and West.*

whatever his post or rank."

Stalin expressed himself in this way not only because he had to consider a possible Fifth Column, but also because he was hinting at anybody who might have been tempted to ask him to justify his policies over the previous two years. Whatever his intentions, he gave the order that, if the enemy push became stronger, the Russians should abandon only "scorched earth" to the invader:

"The enemy must not find a single railway-engine, not a wagon, not a pound of bread or a glassful of petrol. All the *Kolkhozes* [collective farms] must bring in their herds and hand their stocks of wheat over to official bodies to be sent to the rear. Everything that is usable but cannot be sent back (such as wheat, petrol, or non-ferrous metals) must be destroyed."

Lastly, he decreed the setting-up of partisan units which would take the war into the enemy rearguard and destroy his communications.

There was also a change in military organisation. The corps (the formation between the army and the division) was abandoned and, as already mentioned, the armoured, motorised, and mechanised brigades were no longer to be formed into divisions. Furthermore, infantry divisions were required to give up one of their artillery regiments. This enabled Russian G.H.Q. to organise large artillery units as the High Command's reserve of firepower.

The Germans reach the Black Sea

Operation "Barbarossa" had begun very successfully for the Germans, and in the days following June 22 their offensive movements developed at frightening speed, to the disadvantage and dismay of the Russians.

From the Black Sea to the Pripet Marshes, Army Group "South" had finally overcome Soviet resistance. L'vov fell on June 30 and on July 2, the German 11th Army, which included the Rumanian 3rd Army (General Dumitrescu), went over to the attack. Three days later, the German 6th Army (Field-Marshal von Reichenau) succeeded in punching a hole through the fortified positions constructed by the Russians near the old Polish-Soviet frontier; *Panzergruppe* I drove into the breach along the Berdichev-Zhitomir line and it is possible that its III Panzer Corps (General von Mackensen) would have taken Kiev and the Dniepr bridges if a sudden order from Hitler had not forbidden him to risk his tanks in the city.

He was forced to wait outside Kiev to be replaced by the German 6th Army, and then wheel from the east to the south-east. On August 2, near Pervomaysk, on the Bug, the 6th Army linked forces with Colonel-General von Stülpnagel's 17th Army, which had arrived after forced marches from Vinnitsa.

The Soviet 6th, 12th, and part of the 18th Armies had their lines of retreat cut off and were wiped out. The victors captured 103,000 prisoners, 317 tanks, and 858 guns, all that remained of seven corps (22 divisions). Rapidly exploiting their success, the Germans reached the Black Sea near Ochakov.

Army Group "Centre" takes 328,000 prisoners

This success was notable but not as remarkable as that of Field-Marshal von Bock. By June 25, Guderian had arrived at Baranovichi and Hoth had reached Lida and Molodechno, both more than 125 miles east of Białystok, where the unfortunate Pavlov was still bottled up. On the next

△ *During a break in the fighting a German officer summons his N.C.O.s to the lee of a Pzkw III. When the fighting was going their way, German officers had a freedom of movement that would be lost with later "stand and fight" orders from Hitler.*
◁ *A Pzkw III drives past a burning BT-7. Of the 29 Russian armoured divisions, 20 had been practically eliminated by the beginning of July.*

day the two *Gruppen* established first contact at Slonim, and at Minsk on the 29th the pincers closed behind the Russians, who had left the decision to retreat until too late. On July 8, according to Halder's diary, of the 43 divisions in the Soviet 3rd, 4th, 10th Armies, 32 could be taken as annihilated. The Germans counted close on 290,000 prisoners, as well as 2,585 tanks, 1,449 guns, and 246 aircraft captured or destroyed.

A second pincer movement was closed at Smolensk on July 16, when *Panzergruppe* II, which had advanced to Elnia after forcing the bridges over the Berezina and the Dniepr, met *Panzergruppe* III, which had sped from Polotsk to Vitebsk and then wheeled south to meet Guderian. Here O.K.H. amalgamated the two *Gruppen* as the 4th *Panzerarmee* (Tank Army), with Kluge as its commander.

Unfortunately, Kluge could not get on with his impetuous subordinates, who accused him of failing to understand the tactical possibilities of tanks and restricting their initiative to an intolerable degree. Whatever the effect of this friction, the Smolensk sector was the centre of a furious struggle until August 8. The Russians trapped in the pocket tried to break through the perimeter which hemmed them in. From outside, Timoshenko and Lieutenant-General A. I. Eremenko tried to break through to the besieged Russian forces.

In the final analysis, all was in vain. Marshal Timoshenko was defeated at Roslavl' and Guderian took 38,000 prisoners, 300 tanks, and 300 guns. When fighting ceased in the "cauldron" of Smolensk, a communiqué from O.K.H. announced the capture of 310,000 prisoners and the capture or destruction of more than 3,000 armoured vehicles and 3,000 pieces of artillery. At Elnia, the Panzers were 200 miles from Moscow but, since June 22, they had travelled 440 miles, mostly on unmetalled roads, in dust which had scored their pistons and cylinders mercilessly.

The Gulf of Riga occupied

In Army Group "North", *Panzergruppe* IV was counter-attacked strongly near Raseiniai on June 24 by the Soviet XII Armoured Corps, which launched 100 immense KV-1 tanks against the Germans. Even so, the Russians were cut to pieces and this success allowed LVI Panzer Corps to take Daugav'pils during the course of 26th without the Russians having time to destroy the bridges over the Dvina. Kaunas and Vilnyus fell to the 16th Army, Liepāja and Riga to the 18th. The Lithuanians and Letts welcomed the Germans as liberators, but Hitler had no intention of restoring their independence.

Beginning his push on July 2, Hoeppner reassembled his *Panzergruppe* on the right bank of the Dvina, moved up to the fortified Russo-Latvian frontier and forced it at Ostrov, opening the way for his XLI Panzer Corps (General Reinhardt) to capture the important centre of Pskov on the eastern shore of Lake Peipus on July 8, and his comrade Manstein to manoeuvre in the direction of Novgorod. Meanwhile, the 16th Army had established links with the 9th Army (Army Group "Centre") near Vitebsk and the 18th had established itself along a line from Lake Peipus, through Dorpat, to Pärnu on the Gulf of Riga.

From now on, the operations of Army Group "North" would slow down markedly, because of Soviet resistance and counter-attacks and also as a result of the swampy nature of the area and the heavy rain. Another reason was that Leeb had given different objectives to his *Panzergruppe* IV. Its LVI Panzer Corps was to drive on Novgorod while its XLI Panzer Corps moved towards Narva.

Halder surveys the results of the assault

Though not everything had gone according to plan during this first phase of the campaign, the German Chief-of-Staff was nevertheless satisfied with the results that had been achieved. On July 3, he wrote in his diary:

"All in all, I can already say that we have carried out the task entrusted to us, which was to crush the mass of the Russian Army between the Dvina and the Dniepr rivers."

On July 8 his optimism was confirmed by the figures of Russian losses that were submitted to him:

"Of the 164 infantry divisions which the Red Army mobilised, 89 have been completely or partially destroyed. Forty-six Russian divisions are still fighting and in reasonable condition. Eighteen are in

other sectors (14 in Finland and four in the Caucasus) and a maximum of 11 are in reserve in the interior of the Soviet Union. Of the 29 armoured divisions mobilised, 20 have been completely or partially destroyed and nine are still fully fit for combat. The Russians can no longer offer a continuous front even using the best defensive positions."

In spite of the hecatombs of Minsk,

△ *Pioneers operate a ferry with two inflatable assault boats, while engineers examine a demolished trestle bridge.*

▽ *Russian industry was switched to a war footing as soon as possible after June 22. Here, women assemble automatic weapons in a factory near Moscow.*

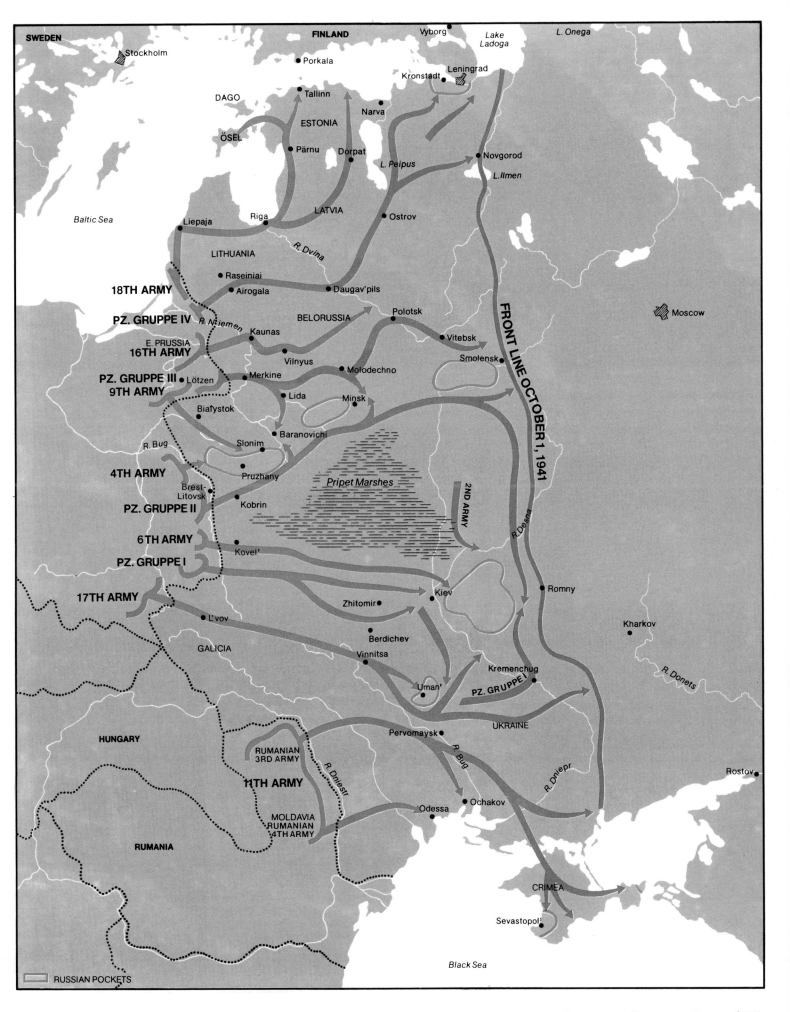

SWEDEN

FINLAND

Stockholm

Porkala

Vyborg

Lake Ladoga

L. Onega

DAGO

Tallinn

Narva

Kronstadt

Leningrad

ESTONIA

ÖSEL

Pärnu

Dorpat

L. Peipus

Novgorod

L. Ilmen

Baltic Sea

Liepaja

Riga

LATVIA

Ostrov

R. Dvina

LITHUANIA

Raseiniai

Airogala

Daugav'pils

18TH ARMY

PZ. GRUPPE IV

R. Niemen

Kaunas

BELORUSSIA

Polotsk

Vitebsk

E. PRUSSIA

16TH ARMY

Vilnyus

Molodechno

Smolensk

PZ. GRUPPE III

Lötzen

Merkine

9TH ARMY

Lida

Minsk

Białystok

Baranovichi

R. Bug

Slonim

Pruzhany

4TH ARMY

Brest-Litovsk

Kobrin

PZ. GRUPPE II

6TH ARMY

PZ. GRUPPE I

Kovel'

Pripet Marshes

2ND ARMY

R. Desna

FRONT LINE OCTOBER 1, 1941

Moscow

17TH ARMY

L'vov

Zhitomir

Kiev

Romny

Kharkov

GALICIA

Berdichev

Vinnitsa

Kremenchug

R. Donets

Uman'

PZ. GRUPPE I

HUNGARY

RUMANIAN 3RD ARMY

UKRAINE

Pervomaysk

R. Bug

Rostov

R. Dnlestr

11TH ARMY

R. Dnlepr

MOLDAVIA RUMANIAN 4TH ARMY

Odessa

Ochakov

RUMANIA

CRIMEA

Sevastopol'

Black Sea

RUSSIAN POCKETS

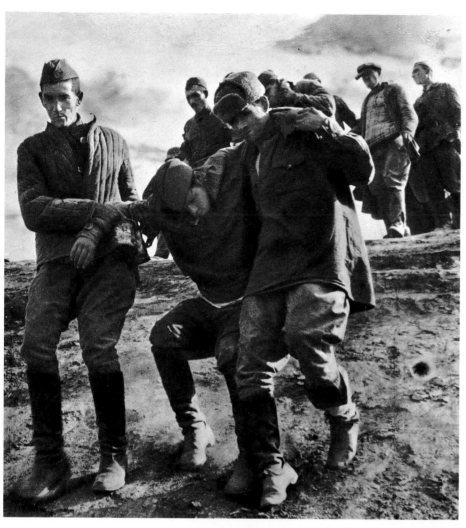

Bialystok, Uman', and Smolensk, it is true that, on August 8, O.K.H. had identified 143 Russian divisions arrayed against the 136 German divisions, but many of them existed in name and number only. By August 13, the 53rd day of the campaign, German losses had reached the total of 389,924 officers, N.C.O.'s, and men, of whom 98,600 had been posted killed or missing. Yet between September 1, 1939 and May 31, 1941, the Polish, Norwegian, French, North African, and Balkan campaigns had cost the Wehrmacht 218,109 casualties of whom 97,000 were killed.

The figures for the Russian campaign indicated losses of 11 per cent of the effectives engaged on June 22, 1941. However, this did not yet dishearten Colonel-General Halder, who wrote on August 8, after listing the figures given above and estimating that 70 of the 143 Russian divisions were still barring the invaders' road to Moscow:

"This confirms my original belief that 'North' (Leeb) has sufficient forces to carry out its task, that all forces in the 'Centre' (Bock) must concentrate to crush the main mass of the enemy and that 'South' (Rundstedt) is strong enough to carry out its mission with success. It might even be able to help 'Centre'."

△ *Faces drawn with fatigue and shock – some of the 290,000 prisoners taken by Army Group "Centre" by July 8. Russian losses were so heavy that few Germans believed that they could continue the war.*
▷ *In some villages in the Ukraine German troops were welcomed as liberators, but the insane political concept of the "Slavic sub-human" denied the Germans the opportunity of tapping this good will.*
(page 173): The map shows the extent of German advances into the Soviet Union after the offensive of June 22, 1941, and the new Front Line of October 1.

CHAPTER 18
TARGET MOSCOW

Planned for September 15, Operation "Typhoon", the attack on Moscow, was delayed until October 2. Army Group "Centre" was reinforced to the strength of 78 divisions, with 14 armoured and eight motorised divisions over and above the 19 and 11 of these units which it already possessed. These units were by now quite depleted and the Panzers had less than half the regulation number of tracked vehicles; the Army group however, was expected to wipe out the Bryansk Front (General Eremenko) and the West Front (General Konev), which contained, according to German information, 14 armies with 77 divisions, of which six were armoured and six cavalry.

The manoeuvre included a double pincer movement.

Panzergruppe II and the 2nd Army formed the southern pincer. The 4th and 9th Armies, which included *Panzergruppen* III and IV, formed the northern claw. *Luftflotten* I and II, reinforced with all of Richthofen's Stukas, would support this attack, as a result of which Moscow would fall to the Germans.

Emerging from the area of Glukhov, Guderian swept aside everything in his path. He sped through the gap made on October 1, and his XXIV Panzer Corps drove 90 miles north in two days to take Orel. This achievement allowed the XLVII Panzer Corps, which followed Guderian, to veer north-west, take Bryansk from the rear and link up with the 2nd Army, which had forced the Russian positions along the Desna. In this way, two encircling pockets were formed on either side of the city. Both had surrendered by October 25th.

On the first day of Operation "Typhoon", the 4th Army and *Panzergruppe* IV concentrated near Roslavl', attacked the left wing of Konev's army and soon made a breakthrough. On the next day Colonel-General Hoeppner began to advance north-east to exploit his success. On October 7, his XL Motorised Corps (General Stumme) entered the city of Vyaz'ma to meet the spearhead of LVI Panzer Corps, which had come under the command of General Schaal as a result of General von Manstein's promotion. To the left of Army Group "Centre", the joint 9th Army and *Panzergruppe* III poured

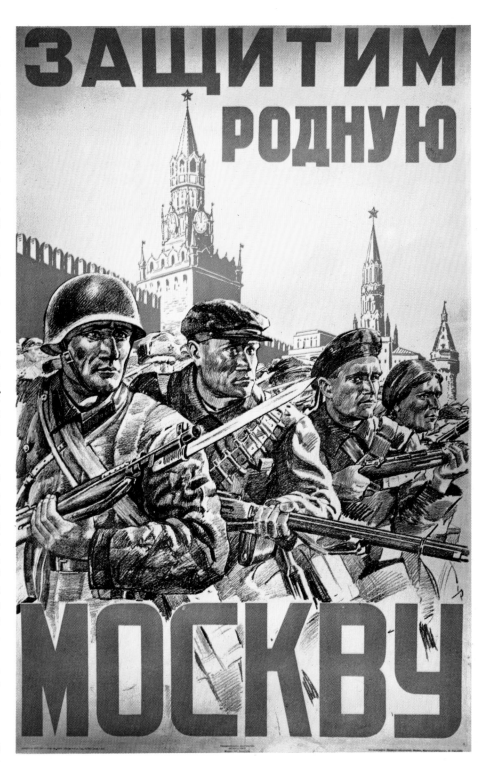

out of the zone north of Smolensk and easily pierced the right of the Russian West Front. So Colonel-General Hoth was immediately able to unleash his tanks, which reached Vyaz'ma by the date mentioned, after cutting round through Kholm. According to the Germans, the Bryansk and Vyaz'ma pockets yielded

△ *The old appeal to patriotism. A poster showing a soldier, militiaman, sailor, and woman, pledges Russia's determination to shield Moscow.*

Moscow or Kiev

Hitler did not remain faithful to the plan he had accepted the previous winter, which was to take Smolensk first, then Leningrad and finally Moscow. His new orders, as expressed on August 18, were that the essential target to be achieved before the winter was not the capture of Moscow but the conquest of the Crimea and the Donets coal and industrial basin together with the interruption of oil supplies from the Caucasus. In the north, Leningrad was to be invested and German forces to link up with the Finns. On August 23, 1941, General Guderian, whose Panzergruppe, diverted from its original objective of Moscow, was to be launched against the line defending the Dniepr, visited Hitler in the presence of Field-Marshal Keitel, General Jodl, and Colonel Schmundt. Guderian protested in vain that the operation as now planned would force him to make a detour of 600 miles when he was now less than 220 miles from Red Square: "My generals understand nothing of the theory of war", was Hitler's unpleasant retort. Guderian chose not to resign. Guderian's Second Panzer Group moved south behind the Dniepr and the met with Kleist's spearhead 125 miles east of Kiev. Stalin forbade the Soviet army under General Kirponos from breaking out and the Germans took 665,000 prisoners.

663,000 prisoners from 67 infantry divisions, six cavalry divisions, and various armoured units, as well as 1,242 tanks and 5,412 guns. As usual, Soviet historians contest these figures and Marshal A. I. Eremenko does so in terms which are particularly insulting ("pure and simple lies") to the memory of Colonel-General Guderian, his direct adversary in those tragic October days.

It is only fair to admit that Eremenko's 50th Army was not totally annihilated in the pocket which had been formed to the north of Bryansk. Yet the truth is that, in order to regroup and cause some trouble to the 2nd *Panzerarmee* (ex *Panzergruppe* II) near Epifan on November 21, it had had to retreat 170 miles.

The 4th Army exploited the situation even more successfully. Leaving Roslavl' on October 2, three weeks later Kluge found himself outside Naro-Fominsk, nearly 200 miles from his starting point. So, without claiming absolute reliability for the German figures quoted above, it may safely be concluded that the Red Army had undergone a defeat of incalculable magnitude as a result of "Typhoon."

The Soviet Government abandons Moscow

That was the conclusion reached in Moscow by Stalin, Molotov, Voroshilov, and Malenkov, who constituted the National Defence Council. And so, on October 10, a new West Front, barring the way to Moscow, was established and General G. K. Zhukov was called on to command it. He was given a first-class Chief-of-Staff in the person of Lieutenant-General Sokolovsky; as political adviser, the authorities appointed N. A. Bulganin. Some days later, the Soviet Government and the main organs of administration left the capital and set up house at Kuybyshev on the left bank of the Volga.

As is clear, in October 1941 there was less optimism in the Kremlin about the situation than would appear from Soviet historiography 20 years later. The state of affairs was even more serious because the departure of the authorities had given rise to serious disorder in Moscow. In referring to this, the evidence of the German writer Paul Carell or the testimony of the British journalist Alexander Werth is not being cited lest it be alleged, using current Soviet terminology, that they are "bourgeois falsifiers of the truth". The evidence comes from A. M. Samsonov's work entitled *The Great Battle of Moscow*, in a version supplied in 1959 by the East German Ministry of Defence.

State of siege

Speaking about the period from October 16 to October 20, Samsonov describes the Soviet capital thus:

"Those days also witnessed isolated difficulties among the population. There were those who spread panic, abandoned their places of work and fled hastily from the city. There were traitors who took advantage of the situation to pillage Soviet property and to try to sap the strength of the Soviet state, but everywhere these attempts were blocked by the resistance of the population."

The truth of this is not doubted for a moment, but the Soviet author continues:

"On October 18, the Executive Committee of the Moscow Soviet published a decree aimed at assuring order as rigorously as possible, maintaining normal commercial and public services, and providing for the feeding of the inhabitants of the city."

Does the decreeing of such measures prove their insufficiency? In any case, Samsonov writes:

"On October 20, following the decision of the National Defence Committee, a state of siege was declared in Moscow and the surrounding districts."

This decree ordered that those guilty of offences against public order should be tried without delay by military courts and also prescribed immediate execution for *provocateurs*, spies, and other enemies who incited the people to acts of disorder.

"The National Defence Committee," the decree reads, "appeals to all the workers of Moscow to observe order, remain calm and give their entire support to the Red Army in defence of the capital."

Moscow's defence organised

There is no reason to suppose that the powers decreed on October 20, 1941 were not applied with implacable rigour under Stalin's personal control, for the Russian

(Overleaf): The advance of German matériel from the Front Line for Operation "Typhoon", of October 2, 1941.
▽ A burning T-34. With tough, well-sloped armour, they could withstand fire from low calibre anti-tank weapons, and the only certainty of scoring a kill was a shot from the 8·8-cm Flak gun. Though lacking the finish of western tanks, the T-34 represented the beginning of a new era in the design of armoured vehicles. It was to see action throughout World War II and the Korean War. The German Panther tank, which with the T-34 ranks as one of the great weapons of the war, was directly inspired by the T-34, and many of its design features were the result of the study of captured T-34s. The Germans even used these tanks—well marked with national insignia—against their former owners.

Marshal Semyon Budenny, was born in 1883. A spectacular figure with his moustaches and mahogany-butt revolvers, he had Patton's showy glamour with little of his ability. After the invasion of Russia he was appointed C.-in-C. of the armies in the Ukraine and Bessarabia. Outmanoeuvred at Kiev, he was responsible for the loss of more than half a million men. Relieved of command, he was given the job of training recruits for the rapidly expanding Red Army.

Marshal Boris Shaposhnikov was born in 1882 and passed out from the Tsarist military academy in 1910. During World War I he rose to the rank of colonel on the general staff. Despite his background, he served with great distinction on the Red Army staff in the Civil War, afterwards commanding the Moscow and Leningrad districts. He was Chief of General Staff from 1937 to 1942, after which he acted as Stalin's military adviser. His main contribution was in planning, not command.

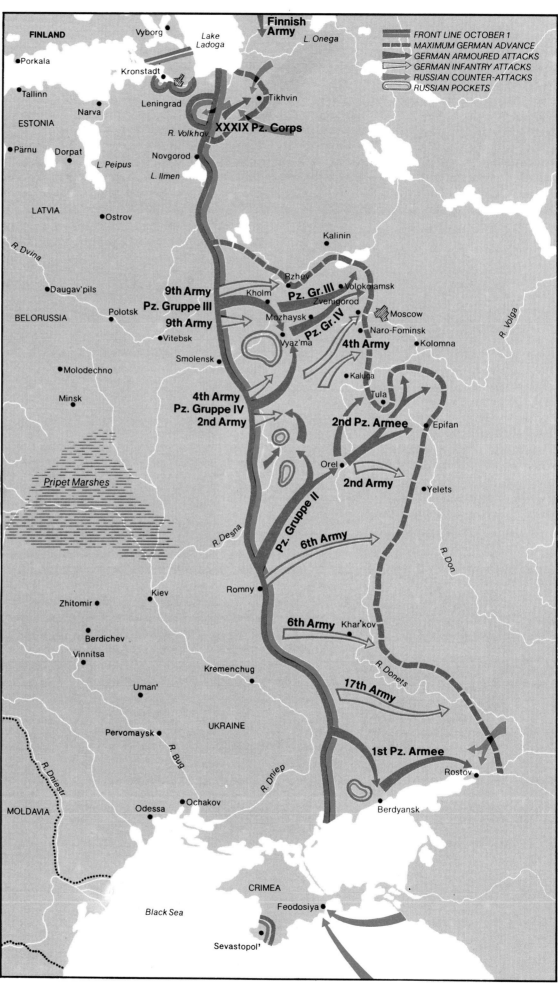

leader had decided to stay on in Moscow.

The Soviet capital organised its defence at a speed that astounded the invaders. Five divisions were improvised from the factories of Moscow. In addition, 500,000 men and women, workmen, clerks, students, secondary school pupils, and housewives were conscripted to improvise a system of fortifications nine miles deep. Without repeating all Samsonov's figures, it may be noted that there were 62 miles of anti-tank ditches and 5,000 miles of trenches; 177 miles of barbed wire were laid and 45 miles of barricades were thrown up.

Rain and mud check the German offensive

Two circumstances came to the aid of the defenders of Moscow.

The quite magnificent weather which favoured the offensive at dawn on October 2 was followed, a few days later, by a long period of rain, sometimes mixed with snow. From October 20 onward, the German armies were literally wading in the mud of the steppes which, in Poland at the end of December 1806, Napoleon had described as the "fifth element". Off the roads, the terrain was generally impassable and, with rare exceptions, the roads themselves were dreadful sloughs where vehicles were seen to disappear completely. All the rivers were in flood, which made it a long and difficult operation to

repair the countless bridges that the Russians had destroyed in their retreat.

Under these conditions, the motorised supply columns were able to cover only 20 miles a day, or even less. The German units had to be amalgamated more and more frequently because of their losses. At the end of October, outside Kalinin, the 36th Motorised Division of *Panzergruppe* III had only one quarter of its regulation reserve of ammunition and the 6th Panzer Division had lost all its tractors. In the 2nd *Panzerarmee*, mud and the wear resulting from the Ukraine offensive combined to produce an even worse situation. On November 14, by grouping together all the tanks of XXIV Panzer Corps which were still functioning, General Guderian was able to improvise a "brigade" of only 50 machines, yet on June 22, 1941, the 3rd and 4th Panzer Divisions, which formed the XXIV Corps, must have totalled 350 tanks. Taken as a whole, the Panzers had lost the use of about half their effectives. In spite of this, Army Group "Centre" had taken the towns of Kaluga, Mozhaysk, and Rzhev and, by the end of October, it was fighting along the line Yelets–Tula–Naro-Fominsk –Volokolamsk–Kalinin.

Soviet historians of World War II have always rejected unanimously the view that mud played any part in the final check of the German attack on Moscow. It cannot be denied that the massing of brigades of T-34 tanks at the front slowed down the Panzer advance but, on the other hand, there is abundant photographic evidence to illustrate this phase of the

△ *General Erich von Manstein, who started as the commander of LVI Panzer Corps and rose to the rank of Field-Marshal, fighting the enormous defensive battles in the latter part of the war.*
▽ *A factory rolls east. The Russians evacuated most of the plant and machinery which might be of value to the Germans, and re-established their factories beyond the Ural mountains, well out of range of German bombers. Here they concentrated on mass production of weapons, from tanks to sub-machine guns, notable for their simplicity and robustness. Like the machinery, the workers who produced these weapons were taken east from the industrial areas of central and southern Russia. Between July and November 1941 no fewer than 1,523 industrial enterprises, including 1,360 large war plants, were moved.*

▽ Armed with a variety of weapons of Russian and German origin, partisans rest in one of the vast forests of central Russia. Though the whole conflict in the East was seen by both sides as an ideological struggle, the battles with the partisans were particularly savage. An O.K.W. order stated: "For the life of one German soldier, a death sentence of from 50 to 100 Communists must be generally deemed commensurate." But these terror methods only served to drive more and more men and women into the forests and service with the partisans. The nine Sicherungsdivisionen, whose duty was to maintain order in the rear, could not cope and regular units were later drafted into the fight against the partisans.

▷ △ Showing signs of wear after the drive from the borders of Poland to the gates of Moscow, German tanks halt in a Russian town.
▷ ▽ Only 60 miles from Moscow. The frosts had come and the Panzers were on the move again. Could they recapture the impetus of the early days and punch through to the nerve centre of the nation?

campaign and this shows mud up to the hubs of German vehicles, up to the bellies of their horses, and over the knees of their soldiers. This speaks for itself.

Alexander Werth's opinion is more balanced but, despite the distinction of this author, it cannot be advanced as true. Quoting Guderian's recollections, he writes:

"Guderian's argument that rain and mud interfered with the success of the first German offensive against Moscow seems futile, since it affected the Russians as much as the Germans."

This argument seems to ignore the fact that the Russians had all the resources of their railway network, while their adversaries were at a great disadvantage since the Soviets had carried out wide-scale demolitions and evacuated their rolling-stock. Furthermore, the bridges behind them were intact and they could draw supplies from depôts in the rear as they moved back. The pursuing Germans, on the other hand, were getting further from their logistic bases every day. Finally, as Kesselring remarks, in that season of torrential rain, the Luftwaffe was able to fly very few missions in support of the ground troops. Because of their losses, the Russians were in the same position.

Stalin calls on his Siberian reserves

However, by now a vitally important piece of news had reached Moscow. On September 14, Richard Sorge, the spy, had revealed that the Japanese Government had no intention of taking advantage of the military situation to associate itself actively with the German attack. Stalin had learned, from Sorge's warning about the attack of June 22, 1941, to appreciate the value of his information. Therefore he felt secure enough to draw freely from the garrisons in eastern Siberia, calculated at 20 to 25 divisions. As early as October 13, near Borodino, *Panzergruppe* IV had come up against the 32nd Division, which had left Vladivostok the previous month. In his diary on November 21, Colonel-General Halder noted the intervention in the Tula sector of "new Siberian divisions".

Such was the last but not the least of the services which Richard Sorge rendered the cause of the Soviet Union. He served Russia from the shadows for close on 15 years but, on October 18, 1942, he was

arrested by the redoubtable Japanese counter-espionage service, which was not deterred by Sorge's status as Press Attaché in the German Embassy in Tokyo. He and his Japanese accomplice were condemned to death and executed in the autumn of 1943.

As autumn wore on, the ground hardened with frost, to the satisfaction of the German generals, who thought that they could get the offensive going again at the speed it had reached at the beginning of October. But the drop in temperature was far greater than was tolerable for the tasks required of Army Group "Centre". On November 12, the temperature was −12 degrees Centigrade, the following day −13 degrees and, on December 4, the mercury fell to −35 degrees and a strong north-east wind made the biting cold even more painful. Winter equipment had been ordered too late, because of intervention by Hitler, but even that which had been manufactured had not crossed the Russo-German demarcation line. Even though the Russian railways had been relaid on the European gauge, the equipment was delayed on its way to the front by the effect of the cold on German locomotives

△ The "flying tank" in action. The heavily armoured Ilyushin Il-2 Shturmovik made its appearance in 1941. Though later models had a rear gunner, they all served as ground attack aircraft. In this role they carried 880 pounds of bombs or eight 56-lb rockets. The pilot and engine were enclosed in an armoured box that made the aircraft very difficult to shoot down, as it was proof against machine gun fire. The aircraft were used in train-busting missions and attacks on tanks.

▽ Breaking from cover, a section of German soldiers dashes forward during the opening stages of Operation "Typhoon". Despite their successes, they were unable to capture Moscow, though advanced units reached the outlying suburbs. Had Hitler followed the advice of his staff and concentrated the main thrust of "Barbarossa" on the capital, he might have severed the Russian north/south communications.

and the ever more numerous and daring Russian partisan raids.

Badly worn by five months in the field, the clothing of the German soldier was, in any case, not at all suitable for the rigours of the Russian winter. It did not include a Balaclava helmet, earflaps, a padded tunic, fur gloves, or camouflage overalls. The infantryman's boots had room for only one pair of socks whereas, when Marshal Mannerheim inspected the 163rd Division in Helsinki, he observed to its commander that, to face the Finnish winter, each man should have boots two sizes too large. For these reasons there was a great increase in the number of men evacuated with serious frostbite: 400 in each infantry regiment in the 112th Division, Guderian noted on November 17.

For lack of anti-freeze, engines had to be left running all the time, which meant a considerable increase in fuel consumption. Crampons for the tank tracks had not yet reached the front, and the tracks were too narrow to carry the tanks over deep snow. Automatic arms jammed during combat and guns did not recoil properly after firing. Parts made of artificial rubber (Buna) became friable and took on the consistency of wood. Lastly, the army's livestock suffered terribly. The German horse does not have the same resistance to the harsh Russian climate as his Russian cousin who is accustomed to scratching out grass with his hoof.

Hitler's new offensive plans

Since the beginning of November, Hitler had been forced to recognise that the final objectives of Operation "Barbarossa" would not be achieved by the end of the year. He was thus compelled to fall back on a far more modest programme. According to the new plan:
1. Rundstedt would take Sevastopol' and Rostov, throw his armour across the Don, and conquer Maykop and the Kuban' oil areas;
2. Bock would bring about the fall of Moscow by a pincer attack; and
3. Leeb would push east as far as Tikhvin, then wheel north and link up with the Finns on the Svir'; this would solve the problem of Leningrad.

The final objectives of the original plan had been to reach the Volga between Astrakhan and Gor'ky, and the Northern Dvina between Kotlas and Archangel, but this goal now became the target of a new attack to be launched in 1942 as soon as weather permitted. In spite of the delay, Hitler still felt optimistic. Though the enemy had not been literally annihilated, he had been decisively defeated. Hitler's optimism was misplaced. Although the Red Army had suffered a blow of staggering proportions, sustaining heavier numerical losses in six months

than any other army in history, it was not finished. Stalin's ruthless control of the Soviet war effort and the fighting spirit of the Red Army had enabled Russia to survive the German onslaught.

The plans were now prepared for the offensive against Moscow, to be carried out by Army Group 'Centre' under von Bock.

In the fulfilment of its task, Army Group "Centre" put six armies into the field:

1. Covered on the right by the 2nd Army, the 2nd *Panzerarmee* would push north along the Tula-Kolomna line;
2. In the centre, the 4th Army would attack the Russians directly opposite in order to hold them and prevent them escaping encirclement; and
3. Covered on their left by the 9th Army, *Panzergruppen* IV and III would force a passage over the canal connecting Moscow with the Volga. Then turning south-east, they would meet Guderian as he fanned out from Kolomna.

Though he did not issue his generals with a peremptory order, the Führer's aim was to see his armies solidly installed along a line running from Ryazan', through Vladimir and Yaroslavl', to Rybinsk from where, with the spring, they would move towards Gor'ky, the ancient city previously known as Nizhny-Novgorod.

In carrying out his task, Bock displayed energy that Keitel describes in his diary as "incredible". The fact remains, nevertheless, that by December 5, 1941, his army group had reached, in the words of the famous military theoretician Karl von Clausewitz, its "limit of strategic consumption". Any fresh movement forward was out of the question, as much because of the exhaustion of the troops as through the obstinate resistance of the Russians.

Russian revenge

Unable to take the great industrial city of Tula, the 2nd *Panzerarmee* had tried to bring it to its knees by cutting it off, but the Germans had spread themselves over a front of 200 miles. In the centre, the 4th Army had been held up at Zvenigorod. The 2nd Panzer Division of *Panzergruppe* IV had reached Krasnaya Polyana, 22 miles from Red Square but, on December 4, a young artillery officer in

the 2nd Motorised Division *Das Reich*, belonging to the *Waffen*-S.S., wrote to his mother:

"These Russians seem to have an inexhaustible supply of men. Here they unload fresh troops from Siberia every day; they bring up fresh guns and lay mines all over the place. On the 30th we made our last attack – a hill known to us as Pear Hill, and a village called Lenino. With artillery and mortar support we managed

to take all of the hill and half of the village. But at night we had to give it all up again in order to defend ourselves more effectively against the continuous Russian counter-attacks. We only needed another eight miles to get the capital within gun range – but we just could not make it."

The view of this junior officer is in accord with that expressed by Colonel-General Guderian, who wrote to his wife on November 9:

"We have seriously underestimated the Russians, the extent of the country and

△ *Gloves, felt boots, and scarves, part of the essential winter clothing lacked by the Germans at the beginning of the winter, have reached these two soldiers enjoying a rare hot meal on the trail of their 10·5-cm howitzer. Some were still fighting in lightweight uniforms in which they had begun the campaign in the east, because Hitler believed that German industry should not produce winter clothing as this would overload its capacity.*

the treachery of the climate. This is the revenge of reality."

A last effort by the 7th Panzer Division, once Rommel's division and now part of the *Panzergruppe* III, under the command of General Reinhardt since the end of October, brought it not only up to the Moscow – Volga canal, but also across it near Dmitrov. A vigorous counter-attack threw it back to the west bank and Reinhardt did not try to regain the lost ground. Besides, with the reversal of fortune, he and his comrade Hoeppner were in a dangerously exposed position and liable to possible flanking attacks.

During the Stalin epoch, Communist sources claimed that this last offensive by Army Group "Centre" had cost it more than 55,000 dead between November 16 and December 6. However the statistics of O.K.H., preserved in Halder's diary, quote losses from November 16 to December 10 as less than 66,000 officers, N.C.O.s and men for the whole of the Eastern Front, and of these only 15,435 were killed or missing. It is true that these losses threw a terrible burden on the already seriously undermanned German units. For example, in the 7th Division, the infantry regiments consisted of about 400 men each by the end of November, and were commanded by lieutenants.

The Russians attack on the Moscow front

Whatever its mental anguish after the catastrophes of Bryansk and Vyaz'ma, the Soviet High Command had not given up the idea of taking the offensive. During October and November, no less than nine armies, totalling about 50 divisions, were being organised in the rear. On December 1, the Russians estimated that they had reached numerical par with their adversary. Though the Germans were still better equipped with armoured vehicles, they had nothing capable of emerging successfully from a clash with the redoubtable T-34 and KV-1 tanks. This is illustrated by an episode recounted by Colonel Pavel Guds, then a lieutenant and tank commander:

"Our target was a base outside Volokolamsk. The battalion commander ordered me to support the infantry attack with fire from my KV-1 tank. When our infantry were some way forward, the enemy

unleashed a counter-attack, spearheaded by 18 tanks. Our men stopped, wavered, and broke in disorder. They needed help. I ordered my driver to move forward towards the German tanks and my gunner to open fire. Methodically, the Soviet tank destroyed its opponents one after the other. A few minutes later, ten mutilated and burning German tanks lay on the battlefield and the eight survivors were fleeing. On the same occasion, our machines rolled several anti-tank guns flat into the ground.

"When we had finished, we inspected our tank. It bore the marks of 29 impacts and yet it was in first-class condition."

It was also evident that the defenders of Moscow, and the reserves which came flowing in to reinforce them, were perfectly equipped to face the rigours of the climate. A few examples suffice for illustration of this point. The factories of Moscow alone delivered 326,700 pairs of Russian-style boots and 264,400 pairs of fur gloves. The only shortage was in transport, for the 8,000 lorries that the Russians possessed were not sufficient to supply the needs of the attack. The lack was made good by using long columns of trailers and sledges.

The troops who launched the attack on the Germans on December 5 and 6 seem to have had excellent morale. On November 7, the twenty-fourth anniversary of the November Revolution, Stalin had appealed to the patriotic glory of ancient Mother Russia. One after the other he rolled off the names of Alexander Nevsky, who defied the German knights on the frozen Lake Peipus in 1242, Dmitri Donskoy, who crushed the Tartars at Kulikovo in 1380, Minin the Butcher and Pozharsky the Boyar, who raised Moscow against the Poles in 1612, Alexander Suvorov, conqueror of Ismail, Warsaw, and Cassano, and of Mikhail Kutusov, who forced Bonaparte, the victor of Europe, to begin his retreat from Moscow in 1812.

The Soviet offensive on the Moscow front was part of a pattern of movement which aimed at destroying the three German army groups fighting between Lake Ladoga and the Kerch' Strait, which separates the Crimea from Kuban'. For the sake of clarity, and because of its great importance, the great battle which began on December 5 and 6, 1941, will be described first. It began, according to High Command orders, on the immense, 500-mile front which twisted and turned from Kalinin to Yefremov.

Georgi Zhukov, born in 1896, made his reputation as a military commander by defeating the Japanese 6th Army in Mongolia in 1939. When Germany attacked in 1941 he served with distinction at Smolensk. On September 11 he replaced Voroshilov in the North and conducted the defence of Leningrad. On October 10 he was appointed C.-in-C. of the West Front. He held the front against two German autumn offensives, and on December 6, 1941 directed the Russian counter-offensive. His next great battle was at Stalingrad, where in mid-November 1942 the Russians trapped the 6th Army.

Bock's order of battle has already been described and had not been changed to any great extent since about November 15, so there is no need to outline it again.

The thin grey line

However, on account of the considerable losses suffered by the German infantry, the line was thinly held and nowhere were there sufficient troops to cover the front adequately. Army Group "Centre" had spent all its reserves and was by now, to use the expression applied by General Laffargue to the deployment that General Gamelin had tried to organise on May 10, 1940, in a state of "pre-rupture". Furthermore, the Germans, abandoning their attack on December 4, had only 24 or, at most, 48 hours, according to the sector, to carry out a defensive reorganisation of their newly-won positions. If this were not enough, a temperature of 34 degrees below zero made the ground so hard that no real fortification work was possible.

This last observation draws attention to the fact that the success of the first Soviet winter offensive can be partially explained by the speed with which the Red Army was able to put its plans into effect. On November 30, Stalin and Shapo-

▽ Dead in the mud and slush of the East. German soldiers died from the cold as much as from enemy action during this first winter in Russia.

shnikov approved the plans drawn up by Zhukov, nicknamed "vinegar-face" or "cropped-head". The plans' first effects became apparent less than one week later.

According to John Erickson in his book *The Road to Stalingrad*, Konev's Kalinin Front comprised 15 rifle divisions, one motorised rifle brigade, two tank batallions and one cavalry division; Zhukov's West Front 48 rifle divisions (plus three forming in the rear), three motorised rifle divisions, three tank divisions (two without tanks), 15 cavalry divisions, 18 rifle brigades, 15 tank brigades and a parachute corps; Timoshenko's South-West Front (right wing) 11 rifle divisions, one motorised rifle division, six cavalry divisions, one rifle brigade, two tank brigades and a motor-cycle regiment; a grand total of 718,000 men, 7,985 guns and 720 tanks. The Soviet Army's main advantage lay not in numbers, but in fresh, well-clad troops where the Germans were exhausted, ill-fed, demoralised and freezing.

The disappearing general

The *History of the Great Patriotic War* quotes the names of 12 of the 13 army commanders who led the Soviet flag to final victory. Yet the name of the commander of the 20th army is missing. Is this an accident? On the contrary, the reason for this reticence is both curious and significant for, in his summary of the performance of the 20th Army, the historian A. M. Samsonov uses a form of expression which is very interesting:
"On the evening of December 11, this was the situation:
  a. General Lelyushenko's forces . . .
  b. General Kuznetsov's forces . . .
  c. The forces whose Chief-of-Staff was General Sandalov, in pursuit of the 2nd Panzer Division and the 106th Division, took Solnechnogorsk."
But the original text of the communiqué that Stalin triumphantly broadcast on December 11 contains the name of the commander of the 20th Army:
"Lieutenant-General Lelyushenko . . .
"Lieutenant-General Kuznetsov . . .
"Lieutenant-General A. A. Vlasov defeated the 2nd Panzer Division and the 106th Infantry Division and took Solnechnogorsk."
Vlasov went over to the Germans in the spring of 1942, and because of this he has been expunged from Russian history.

Like Operation "Typhoon" of October 2, 1941, the Soviet attack launched on December 5 consisted of two pincers designed to crush the flanks of Army Group "Centre". When this result had been achieved, Bock's army group, trapped in front by holding attacks, would be cut off from its communications with Smolensk, surrounded, and annihilated.

To the north-west of Moscow, the salient bounded by the Zvenigorod–Krasnaya-Polyana – Dmitrov – Kalinin line, against which the last efforts of *Panzergruppen* IV and III and the German 9th Army had spent themselves, would undergo the concentrated assault of the 5th, 16th, and 20th Armies, the 1st Shock Army and the 30th Army of the Moscow Front, as well as the 31st and 29th Armies of the Kalinin Front, under the command of Generals L. A. Govorov, K. K. Rokossovsky, A. A. Vlasov, V. I. Kuznetsov, D. D. Lelyushenko, I. I. Maslennikov, and Y. Yushkevich respectively.

On the southern side, the forces in the 200-mile salient pushed through the Soviet line by the 2nd *Panzerarmee*, bordered by Tula, Kashira, Mikhaylov, and Yefremov, would be cut off from their base and crushed by the concentrated attacks of the

50th and 10th Armies (Generals I. V. Boldin and F. I. Golikov), of the Guard Cavalry Corps and the 13th Army (General Gorodnyansky), the latter forming the right wing of the South-West Front.

The Germans were surprised as much by their adversary's initiative as by the vigour and scale of its execution. In effect, by nightfall on D-Day, December 6, General Lelyushenko had penetrated 12 miles into the depleted lines of *Panzergruppe* III and, on the 11th, a special Kremlin communiqué was able to give details of 400 villages liberated around Moscow, including the small towns of Yakhroma, Solnechnogorsk, and Istra, and the defeat of 17 German divisions, seven of which were armoured and three motorised.

The Volga was secured and would no longer hinder General Konev's forces. In spite of this advantage, they were less fortunate than those of the West Front in their attacks against the German 9th Army. Not till December 16 did they manage to retake Kalinin and fan out south-west. As a result the pincer did not grip the left wing of the German Army Group "Centre", as Moscow had hoped. But, though Hoeppner, Hoth, and Strauss managed to elude the encirclement that threatened them, they did so at the price of losing a large part of their equipment.

Guderian's heavy losses

When Generals Boldin, Golikov, and Belov were concentrating their attacks on the 2nd *Panzerarmee*, Colonel-General Guderian was trying to get out of the exposed position in which he had been left by the halt of the German offensive. To some extent he succeeded, but not without being forced to make painful sacrifices. In the course of their retreat, the 3rd and 4th Panzer Divisions abandoned most of their combat and transport vehicles in the deep snow, and the rout of the 10th Panzer was echoed even in the rarefied realms of the German Supreme Command, as Halder's diary records.

Worse was to come; under the blows of the converging thrusts of his adversaries, who retook Stalinogorsk and Venev on December 13, Guderian had to pull in his forces, which obliged him to break contact with his right (2nd Army) and his left (4th Army). And so enormous gaps appeared in the German line, which Bock could not fill for lack of men and which the Russians resolutely exploited towards both Kaluga and Kursk. Army Group "Centre" was now in great danger. The situation was even more serious for, though the fighting units retreated in as good an order as circumstances permitted, outbreaks of panic could be observed in the rear services not to mention the Luftwaffe ground crews, who left an enormous amount of material behind.

More German reverses

At the northern and southern ends of the immense Eastern Front, just as Leeb was not successful in carrying out the mission entrusted to him, Rundstedt, after having overrun the Eastern Ukraine and the Crimea, was also gradually forced onto the defensive by Soviet counter-attacks, which his troops, worn out by five months of sustained effort, could not withstand.

In Army Group "North", the XXXIX Panzer Corps forced the River Volkhov on October 16 near Chudovo and took Tikhvin on November 8, being hampered in its

◁ △ Armed with M38 semi-automatic rifles, but equipped with caps that date back to the Russian Civil War, Soviet cavalry of General Belov's corps move up to the front.
◁ ▽ Dressed in quilted jackets and fur hats and inured to the cold, Siberian troops arrived at the Moscow front in December 1941. They were to turn the scales in the battle for the capital.
▽ Soldiers of a ski battalion march through the streets of Moscow. The Russians learnt the value of such troops in their attack on Finland in 1939. These men are dressed in snow suits and armed with PPSh sub-machine guns. The Russians favoured automatic weapons and whole units were equipped with the PPSh, giving them a fearful volume of close-range firepower.

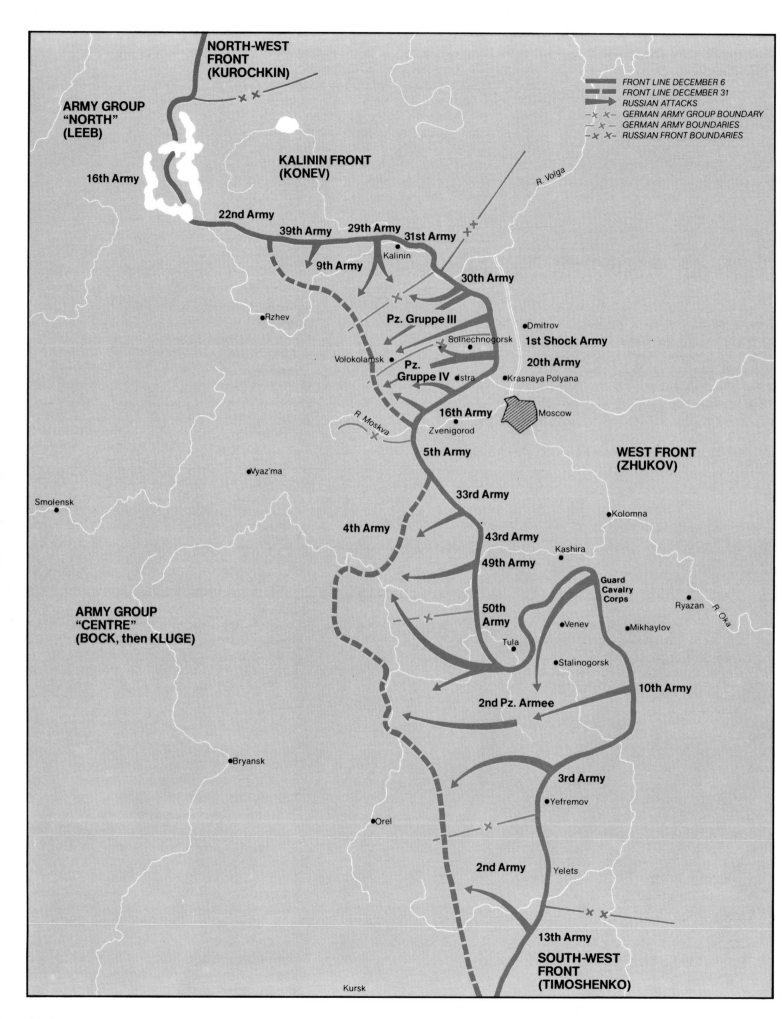

NORTH-WEST
FRONT
(KUROCHKIN)

ARMY GROUP
"NORTH"
(LEEB)

KALININ FRONT
(KONEV)

16th Army

R. Volga

22nd Army

39th Army   29th Army
                        31st Army

9th Army   Kalinin

30th Army

Rzhev

Pz. Gruppe III

Dmitrov

Solnechnogorsk   1st Shock Army

Volokolamsk   20th Army
                Pz.
                Gruppe IV   Istra   Krasnaya Polyana

R. Moskva   16th Army   Moscow

Zvenigorod

Vyaz'ma

5th Army   WEST FRONT
                                (ZHUKOV)

Smolensk   33rd Army

4th Army   Kolomna

                        43rd Army

                        49th Army   Kashira

ARMY GROUP
"CENTRE"   Ryazan   R. Oka
(BOCK, then KLUGE)   50th
                               Army   Venev
                                              Mikhaylov
                                   Tula
                                          Stalinogorsk

                                   Guard
                                   Cavalry
                                   Corps

                                                      10th Army

                        2nd Pz. Armee

Bryansk   3rd Army

                                        Yefremov

                        2nd Army

Orel   Yelets

                                        13th Army

                                   SOUTH-WEST
                                   FRONT
                                   (TIMOSHENKO)

Kursk

FRONT LINE DECEMBER 6
FRONT LINE DECEMBER 31
RUSSIAN ATTACKS
GERMAN ARMY GROUP BOUNDARY
GERMAN ARMY BOUNDARIES
RUSSIAN FRONT BOUNDARIES

advance less by Russian action than by bad weather and soft ground. The corps did not manage to consolidate its position and less still to link up with the Finns. On December 8, suitably reinforced, the Soviet 54th, 4th, and 52nd Armies, under the command of Generals Fedyuninsky, Meretskov, and Klykov, forced the Germans to evacuate the salient. The Russians now crossed the Volkhov and established a 30-mile deep bridgehead on the left bank of the river. Of course the victors of Tikhvin had not achieved their ultimate purpose, which was to lift the siege of Leningrad, but henceforward the besiegers were to find themselves in a highly exposed position at Petrokrepost'.

Because so many units had been removed from his army group for Operation "Typhoon", Rundstedt's forces were reduced to 40 German divisions, to which four divisions and eight brigades of Germany's allies provided a rather feeble backing. However, the Kiev disaster had weakened the Russians so greatly between the Dniepr and the Don that for nearly two months, Army Group "South" did not feel the loss of its transferred units.

Manstein overruns the Crimea

On September 12, Colonel-General von Schobert, commanding the 11th Army, was killed when his aircraft landed in a minefield, and Manstein was appointed to succeed him. The first exploit of the new commander, using the 1st *Panzerarmee* and the Rumanian 3rd Army, was to annihilate the Russian 18th Army (Lieutenant-General Smirnov); a pocket was created between Bol'shoy-Tokmak and Berdyansk on October 10. In it were trapped 100,000 men, 212 tanks, and 672 guns. Then the German 11th Army turned its attention to the strong position of the Perekop Isthmus which joins the Crimea to the Russian land mass and, on October 29, with the aid of the Stukas, battered the Russian 51st Army (Colonel-General F. I. Kuznetsov). Though he possessed no tanks, Manstein still conducted the Crimean campaign at Blitzkrieg pace. On November 16, his XLII Corps (General von Sponeck) was overlooking the Kerch' Strait and the bulk of the 11th Army was besieging Sevastopol', right at the south of the Crimea.

Hoth attacks the Donets Basin

Meanwhile, the 1st *Panzerarmee* had arrived from Mariupol. Skirting the shores of the Sea of Azov, it took Rostov on November 21, while the 17th Army, now under Colonel-General Hoth, overran the western half of the Donets industrial and mining basin. To Halder's disappointment, the 5th Army's progress was less spectacular, for by the same date it had advanced only 30 miles from the great city of Khar'kov, abandoned by the Russians on October 24. These were notable successes all the same, however, for between the Don at Rostov and the junction of Army Groups "Centre" and "South", Field-Marshal von Rundstedt was operating on a front of some 525 miles with only 32 German divisions, including only three armoured and two motorised.

The Russians parry

The Russian High Command in Moscow now tried to use the situation to its best advantage. While the South Front (General Cherevichenko) took Rostov and pursued the invader back to the Dniepr, the Transcaucasus Front (General Kozlov) would send two armies into the Crimea, lift the siege of Sevastopol' and, crossing the Perekop Isthmus, spread out

◁◁ *The Russian two-pronged attack launched along the Eastern Front, on December 6, against Army Group "Centre".*
▽ *Wearing hoods beneath their helmets Soviet soldiers pass abandoned German vehicles. The Finns were shocked to see that the Germans wore steel helmets and studded boots in the sub-zero temperatures of the Eastern Front, the steel freezing the head and feet. The Russians received British greatcoats during the winter and these they knew affectionately as "a present from the King of England".*

△ *The first liberators of the war. Red Army soldiers are welcomed in a village they have just recaptured on the Moscow front.*

and harry the retreating Germans. On November 30, the 9th Army (General Kharitonov), the 17th Army (General Lopatin), and the 18th Army (General Kolpakchy), totalling 22 infantry divisions, nine cavalry divisions, and six armoured brigades (about 330 tanks), took Rostov after a grim struggle with Colonel-General von Kleist. Hitler ordered Rundstedt to stem the retreat of the 1st *Panzerarmee* in front of the Mius line. Rundstedt promptly requested to be relieved of his command. He was replaced by Reichenau, who made exactly the same arrangements as his predecessor and, what is more, had them accepted by higher authority. All the efforts of the Russian South Front to break the line failed with heavy losses.

The operations order issued for the Transcaucasus Front included two landings in the Crimea: the 51st Army (General Lvov) at Kerch', and the 44th Army (General Chernyak) at Feodosiya. On December 26, only 3,000 Russians were locked in combat with the 46th Division in the Kerch' Peninsula. At dawn on the 29th there were more than 17,000 Russians with 47 guns and 12 tanks, while at the same time advance units of the 44th Army were throwing the Germans into confusion at Feodosiya. Disobeying the express orders of his army commander, General von Sponeck, with his communications in peril, ordered his 46th Division to abandon its positions at Kerch'. When the order was obeyed, all the divisional equipment was left behind. But Generals Lvov and Chernyak, doubtless inhibited by over-rigid orders, were slow to take up fortune's favours and their hesitation gave Manstein time to bar their road over the Kamenskoye Isthmus. However, to do this he had been obliged to abandon the attack on Sevastopol', with all its consequences. Relieved of his command, Sponeck was court-martialled on Hitler's orders. Without regard for his daring exploits at Rotterdam, where he had led the 22nd Airborne Division, he was sentenced to death. The Führer commuted the sentence to imprisonment in the fortress of Rastatt, where agents of Heinrich Himmler murdered him in the confusion at the end of March 1945.

Guderian gives us the following picture of the winter battle. He noted it at Tula, but it is true for the whole front:

"On the actual day of the offensive, the thermometer fell from −20 to −40 degrees. The sufferings of the troops were ghastly. All the automatic arms ceased to work because the oil in them froze. On the afternoon of the 5th all the armies called a spontaneous halt.

"There is nothing more dramatic in military history than the stunning assault of the cold on the German Army. The men had greatcoats and jackboots. The only additional clothing they had received consisted of a scarf and a pair of gloves. In the rear, the locomotives had seized up with cold. In the line, weapons were unserviceable and, according to General Schaal, the tank motors had to be warmed up for 12 hours before the machines could get going. One hideous detail is that many men, while satisfying the calls of nature, died when their anuses froze."

On December 20, General Guderian left for the Führer's H.Q. to try and obtain his consent to cease operations. All he got were renewed orders to attack:

"So greatly had the cold disorganised the army that the Führer's orders could not be obeyed. The Russians counterattacked as often as they could, for their own men were suffering badly, but they managed to endanger our forward lines which they trapped by circling round them from behind. Our communications were interrupted and our radio-transmitters put out of action by the snow and the cold. Our casualties were enormous, as the slightest wound meant death. The battle fell silent everywhere, without orders, and in spite of the efforts of the officers."

Changes in the German command

On December 16, 1941, quite exhausted in mind and body, Field-Marshal von Bock asked to be relieved. The Führer granted his request and appointed Kluge to succeed him as commander of Army Group "Centre". On December 19, Field-Marshal von Brauchitsch, who had suffered a severe heart attack on the night of November 6/7, left O.K.H., where he was succeeded by the Führer and Reich Chancellor, who remained in command of O.K.W. also. Hitler ordered Colonel-General Halder to stay at his post. These changes brought others in their wake between the second fortnight of December 1941 and the end of January 1942:

1. In Army Group "South", the sudden death of Field-Marshal von Reichenau on January 18, 1942 brought Bock back into active service, though the 6th Army was entrusted to General Paulus,

△ After their experiences in the East and North Africa, the Germans stopped production of motorcycle combinations as they were too vulnerable to cold and dirt. ▽ Luftwaffe men dig their vehicle out of the snow. The Russians were able to operate from heated hangars around Moscow, while the Luftwaffe had to face the winter on improvised or captured airfields after bringing up their equipment and personnel from the borders of Poland.

who thus left O.K.H. In addition, General Ruoff replaced Colonel-General Hoth at the head of the 17th Army;

2. In Army Group "Centre", Field-Marshal von Kluge's appointment brought in General Heinrici to command the 4th Army while General Model, with swift promotion, relieved Colonel-General Strauss in the 9th Army. Colonel-General Hoeppner, who had had the temerity to order the 4th *Panzerarmee* (from January 1, 1942) to disengage, without first asking Hitler, was dismissed from the *Wehrmacht* and was forbidden to wear uniform. On December 26 Guderian was relieved in his turn. He was replaced by General Rudolf Schmidt while Colonel-General Hoth was ordered to replace the unfortunate Hoeppner.

3. In Army Group "North", Field-Marshal von Leeb requested and obtained permission to go into retirement. Colonel-General von Küchler took command of the group and was replaced in the 18th Army by General Lindemann.

By December 31, German losses on land had reached 830,903 officers, N.C.O.s, and men, or about a quarter (25.9 per cent) of the forces which had been allotted to Operation "Barbarossa" the preceding June. Of this total, 173,722 were dead and 35,875 were missing. But in spite of all these sacrifices, the objectives of the campaign as laid down in the order of December 18, 1940 had not been achieved, on the political, the economic, or the strategic level, for the Soviet Union had not collapsed, the Red Army was counterattacking and, though the Germans held the rich wheatlands and mineral wealth of the Ukraine, the indispensable oil of the Caucasus still eluded them. Operation "Barbarossa" had failed.

A solid Soviet defence

Between June 22 and December 6, 1941, Soviet losses in prisoners alone were of the order of 2,800,000 officers, N.C.O.s, and men. From Brest-Litovsk to the suburbs of Moscow, the Germans had covered a distance equivalent to that

▽ *The fighter pilot Boris Safonov, a Hero of the Soviet Union, talks with two British Flight-Sergeants, part of the Hurricane wing sent at Churchill's instigation. No. 151 Wing comprised two new squadrons, Nos. 81 and 134.*

between London and Prague. But to help it withstand the blows that hammered it, the Red Army possessed two elements lacked by the nations which had been overrun in 1940: depth and resources. Regarding the latter, on December 1, 1941, Stalin is thought to have had at his disposal 200 infantry divisions, 35 cavalry divisions, and 40 armoured brigades (2,600 tanks) at the front, and another 80 formations (63 infantry divisions, six cavalry divisions, and 11 armoured brigades) in the rear. In spite of the difficulties inherent in an operation of that size, the evacuation of war industries to the other side of the Urals was successful and would begin to bear fruit in the spring of 1942. The Soviet Union was now no longer alone. The day after the Germans attacked, President Roosevelt announced that Russia would enjoy the benefits of "Lend-Lease". Winston Churchill shipped no less than 500 Hurricane fighters to his ally on Arctic convoys during the summer and winter of 1941. These supplies would be increased in the following year, in spite of heavy losses suffered by both merchantmen and warships in the convoys.

War on two fronts

From the operational aspect, although the Imperial General Staff, however much Churchill insisted, was not able at this stage to open the "Second Front", it is none the less true that British activities in Libya and the Straits of Messina forced Hitler to issue his order No. 38 on December 2, 1941, in which he appointed Field-Marshal Kesselring "Supreme Commander South" and ordered the transfer of a *Fliegerkorps* from the Eastern Front to come under Kesselring's orders in his North African and Italian bases.

This transfer of forces from east to west was tiny, yet it signified that Hitler now faced war on two fronts. Moreover Hitler's rash and foolish declaration of war on the United States after the Japanese attack on Pearl Harbor inevitably meant that Germany would now have to face America's enormous war potential. However, the three Allied powers were deeply suspicious of each other and it was not until May 1942 that the U.S.S.R., Britain and the U.S.A. formed a triple alliance against the Axis forces.

◁ *A Russian village burns in mid-winter.*

CHAPTER 20
PEARL HARBOR: THE PLAN

On July 2, 1941, the Imperial Council of Japan decided to avail itself at once of the opportunity it now had to extend Japanese dominion over the whole of Indo-China; and on July 14, Kato, Japanese Ambassador in Paris, informed Admiral Darlan, then head of the Vichy Government, of a request to this effect from the Prime Minister, Prince Konoye. It was a case of organising the "joint defence" of the colony and this, Tokyo asserted, involved its entire occupation by an unlimited number of troops and, in addition, the right for the occupying force to set up bases wherever it pleased.

Within 24 hours, Darlan alerted Admiral Leahy, United States Ambassador in the capital of Unoccupied France. But from documents which have been published on the subject, it appears that, while encouraging Darlan and Marshal Pétain to resist this pressure on the part of Tokyo, Leahy, contrary to reliable sources of information, gave them no effective guarantee of aid in the eventuality of French intransigence resulting in the invasion of Indo-China.

According to the wording of a memorandum from Vichy to Washington, dated August 5, President Roosevelt's Ambassador, earlier on July 16, "in the course of conversations with Marshal Pétain informed him that there were no grounds for thinking that the American Government was disposed to reconsider the passive attitude adopted by the State Department following the first Japanese intervention in 1940."

In these conditions, Vichy bowed to the inevitable, and on July 29, 1941 an exchange of letters between Kato and Darlan ratified the agreement which had been signed in Hanoi by Admiral Decoux and the Japanese negotiators.

Just when Prince Konoye was trying to come to an agreement with Washington, and had in fact, in the hope of a settlement, sacrificed Matsuoka and installed Admiral Toyoda in his place, the news of the occupation of Saigon hit the United States with the force of a thunderbolt and obviated all Konoye's efforts.

And, indeed, if the establishment of Japanese bases in Cochin-China hardly constituted an act of war, it was none-theless an act preparatory to war which threatened at one and the same time the British positions in Burma and Malaya, the Dutch in Indonesia, and the American in the Philippines. President Roosevelt's reaction was to freeze Japanese assets in the United States as from July 26 and to place an embargo on exports of oil to Japan. A few days later, the United Kingdom, Canada, and the Dutch Government in exile followed suit, thus straightway depriving Japan of any access to the Sumatra, Borneo, and Burma oilfields.

Negotiations with the United States

Nevertheless, these new developments had no effect on the Japanese Government's attempts to restart negotiations, and, as has already been observed, President Roosevelt, who wanted to give his British allies time to strengthen Singapore, was not unwilling to talk. To this end, Prince Konoye proposed a meeting with President Roosevelt in Honolulu, but he was informed by Washington that it was desirable first to prepare the ground by diplomatic negotiation.

And indeed, with the embargo on oil, Franklin Roosevelt and Cordell Hull possessed a most effective means of exerting pressure, since it was estimated that Japanese stocks of oil would not last more than two years. But, in fact, this was a double-edged weapon; for it was idle to think that the exchange of diplomatic notes between Tokyo and Washington would be allowed to continue indefinitely at a time when the fleet of the Rising Sun might find itself incapacitated for lack of fuel oil. Especially when Tarakan and Balikpapan in Borneo and Palembang in Sumatra, not to mention the Burmese installations of Burmah Oil, might all be within striking distance. And so, Japan's military leaders, without rejecting attempts to obtain a negotiated settlement out of hand, insisted on a time limit being set to the negotiations, for it would not do to submit to the considerable advantage the other party would obtain, if negotia-

△ Joseph Clark Grew, American Ambassador in Tokyo. As Roosevelt's man on the spot he had the unenviable task of trying to obtain a diplomatic solution from a Japanese Government bent on war.
▷ Japanese aircrew in training. In 1941 Japan's air power was hopelessly under-estimated by the Allies. In this picture the two aircraft in the background are Avro 504 trainers, originally of British design. Memories of large-scale Japanese orders, and the granting of permission to build aircraft under licence, lulled the Allies into believing that the Japanese were incapable of producing anything as formidable as the Spitfire or Messerschmitt. They were soon to realise their mistake.

tions were broken off, simply by constant temporising.

On September 6, upon the covert refusal of President Roosevelt to meet the Japanese Prime Minister either in Honolulu or even in Juneau (Alaska), the Imperial Council met again to consider the situation; there was no avoiding the arguments that have just been summarised and the following conclusions were drawn:

1. Japan, "determined not to reject the possibility of a conflict", was likely to have completed her preparations for war between that time and the end of October;

2. "Parallel to and in tune with this", she would endeavour, "by all diplomatic means", to reach agreement with the United States and Great Britain on the basis of the programme which had been drawn up in Tokyo; and

3. "If, at the beginning of October, there was no longer any appearance of our demands being able to be met by means of negotiation, it would be resolved to go to war with the United States, Great Britain, and the Netherlands."

Accordingly, while the Japanese Foreign Minister was informing Ambassador Grew of his government's intentions, Admiral Nomura, the Japanese Ambassador in Washington, was conveying them on September 28 to Secretary of State Cordell Hull, who gave him a somewhat cold reception as it transpired from a reading of his memorandum of October 2.

The military gain the upper hand

The date fixed by the Imperial Council on September 6 passed with absolutely no solution to the diplomatic *impasse* and, on October 12, Prince Konoye summoned his Minister of Foreign Affairs, Admiral Toyoda, War Minister, General Tojo Navy Minister, Admiral Okawa, and General Suzuki, the head of military planning, to his villa on the outskirts of Tokyo. According to the account of this meeting which has come down to us from Giuglaris, words ran high between the head of the Japanese Government and his Minister of War:

Tojo: "Negotiations cannot succeed. In order for them to succeed, there must be concessions on both sides. Till now, it is

Atlantic Charter

February 8, 1941, the U.S. House of Representatives adopts the text of the Lend-Lease bill. Through Lend-Lease the U.S.A. produced, among other material, 17 million rifles, 315,000 guns, 878,000 tanks, 2,434,000 motor vehicles and 296,000 planes.

August 9, 1941, President Roosevelt and Winston Churchill meet at Placentia Bay, Newfoundland for the Atlantic Conference. It was agreed that the U.S. Navy should assume responsibility for the sector of the Atlantic between Newfoundland and Iceland. An Atlantic Charter was also signed which set out various joint principles such as the self-determination of nations and the destruction of Nazi tyranny.

On September 11, 1941, Roosevelt announced he had ordered the U.S. armed forces to fire on sight at Axis 'Pirates', both surface and submarine vessels. On October 9 he requested Congress to amend the Act of Neutrality regarding the arming of merchant ships and authorising them to navigate in waters declared to be within the zone of hostilities. This move received only 50 votes as against 37 in the Senate, and 212 as against 194 in the House of Representatives. The changes were enacted on November 7, 1941.

Japan that has made the concessions, the Americans who have not budged an inch."

Okawa: "We're precisely balanced between peace and war. It is up to the Prime Minister to decide and to stand by his decision."

Tojo: "It's not as simple as that. It's not the Prime Minister alone who counts, there are the army and the navy."

Konoye: "We can contemplate a one- or two-year war with equanimity, but not so a war that might last more than two years."

Tojo: "That reflection is the Prime Minister's personal opinion."

Konoye: "I would rather a diplomatic solution than war."

Tojo: "The question of the Prime Minister's confidence in going to war should have been discussed in the Imperial Council. The Prime Minister attended that Council, did he not? There can be no question now of his evading his responsibilities."

Konoye: "Not only do I have no confidence in going to war but I refuse to take responsibility for doing so. The only action taken by the Imperial Council was to determine the measures to be taken should all diplomatic means fail. I still have confidence in a diplomatic solution."

With the benefit of the hindsight afforded the historian as compared with those who direct the course of events, one is at liberty to point out that both men were wrong on October 12, 1941. General Hideki Tojo was in error in assuming that, given the maximum effect of surprise, the military potential of the Japanese Empire would in one fell swoop inflict a fatal blow on the American colossus. And, on his side, Prince Fumimaro Konoye was under a delusion in thinking that the country with which he was trying to reach agreement, invigorated by the anticipated effect of the oil embargo she had imposed, would lift it merely for Japan's assurance not to use Indo-China as a springboard for the conquest of South-East Asia.

Be that as it may, General Tojo was uttering no empty threat when he called his Prime Minister's attention to the state of opinion in the Army and the Navy, for, under the terms of the Japanese constitution, the ministers responsible for national defence were appointed by the Emperor and so escaped the rule of ministerial solidarity, and could at any time within the cabinet voice the censure of the military. In which case, the Prime Minister must tender his resignation; this in effect occurred on October 16, 1941, the

△ *Young, tough and battle-hardened Japanese soldiers on parade.*

instigator of the crisis then being called upon to resolve it.

As Prince Konoye's successor, Tojo kept the portfolio of War and entrusted Foreign Affairs to Shinegori Togo, who had previously been Japan's Ambassador in Moscow, and who had no post at the time.

The United States still remain unworried

At the time, this latest ministerial crisis in Japan caused no disquiet in the American Embassy in Tokyo; the military attaché, Lieutenant-Colonel Cresswell, commenting on the fact, wrote to the Secretary for War: "The composition of the new government is the very image of conservatism, but it is not thought that the resignation of the government led by Konoye will mark an abrupt change, at least not for the present. Certainly, General Tojo puts Japan before all else, but he is said to have a breadth of view which goes against his embarking on an extreme course."

Instancing the Emperor's pressing for a peaceful settlement, Ambassador Grew held approximately the same view as his military attaché. Nevertheless, on November 3, he put Secretary of State Cordell Hull on guard against imagining that Tojo would direct his conduct according to the norms of self-interest generally accepted in the West. "Make no mistake," he cabled, "the Japanese are capable of launching a suicide war with the United States. Self-interest should prevent them doing so; but Japanese national self-interest cannot be assessed according to the canons of our logic." The new Minister of Foreign Affairs in the Tojo Cabinet declared his earnest intention of enabling negotiations between Japan and America to succeed as soon as he took up office, and, on October 20, his Prime Minister declared that the maintenance of world peace was the first concern of his government's policy. But time was running out: throughout the Empire, stocks of liquid fuel were dwindling slowly but surely; moreover, the weather conditions prevailing in South-East Asia argued for action before December 15. The military necessities of the situation were now forcing the politicians' hands.

▽ *Emperor Hirohito inspects a surrealist, Wagnerian battery of sound detectors, designed to pick up the engine noises of incoming enemy bombers. In the right background can be seen a battery of the guns of the Tokyo A.A. barrage.*

A month's grace

Confronted with these problems, Tojo called a cabinet meeting on November 1, to which were summoned the Chiefs-of-Staff of the Army (General Sugiyama) and of the Navy (Admiral Nagano) as well as their deputies. That day the debate was yet stormier than on October 12, witness the following extract of the proceedings taken from Giuglaris' book:

Togo (Foreign Affairs): "It is unlikely that the Germans will succeed in effecting a landing in England, even with our assistance. And, in any case, we should not delude ourselves about the contribution that collaboration between Germany and Italy can make to our cause."

Sugiyama: "We need the help of no one to achieve our objectives in our campaign in the south. Once that is over, China will be isolated and will capitulate. Next spring we shall turn our attention to the Soviet Union."

Kaya (Finance): "We have confidence in a war lasting two years. But not beyond."

Tojo: "Anyway, that gives us two years."

Togo: "Why take such a risk? The Western powers won't attack us, they have enough on their plate with the war in Europe. It is to our advantage to maintain peace."

Nagano: "After two years at war, we shall have made all the conquered territory in the south impregnable. We shall not fear America, however strong she then is."

Kaya: "Defence is not the way to victory. When and how will victory come?"

Nagano: "Now. At once. We shall never have a chance like this again."

Sugiyama: "The first half of December is the right time to start active operations. We can temporise no longer with only a month to go. Let us break off diplomatic negotiations now and prepare unequivocally for war."

Tsukada (Deputy Chief-of-Staff, Army): "The decision to go to war should be taken at once."

Togo: "2,600 years of Japanese history cannot be dismissed so glibly."

Tsukada: "The Army must have an immediate decision."

Ito (Deputy Chief-of-Staff, Navy): "The Navy will be ready by November 20. Why not continue negotiations till then?"

Tsukada: "The Army cannot wait longer than November 13. After that date the Government may be overturned. I propose that as from November 13 military action takes priority over diplomatic action."

Shimada (Navy): "Why not continue negotiating to within 24 hours of launching an attack?"

The debate concluded with the decision to let the military chiefs take command of the situation at midnight on November 30. Nevertheless, Togo had gained an ultimate respite of four weeks within which he hoped to get agreement by the United States for new compromise proposals that were to be submitted by Ambassador Kurusu. Kurusu, who was married to an American, was thought to have a better chance of being listened to in Washington. He arrived there on November 16 with Admiral Nomura. In fact, with the proposals contained in Plan B, the Tokyo cabinet made a few concessions to the American negotiators. These included the undertaking to withdraw the troops who

Admiral Isoroku Yamamoto was C.-in-C. of the Imperial Japanese Navy when war came in 1941. Born in 1884, he was no stranger to the United States. He had studied at Harvard and had served in the U.S.A. as a naval attaché. He was one of the first "air-minded" naval strategists of the 20th Century, and had been instrumental in seeing to it that the powerful Japanese Combined Fleet was equipped with a strong force of aircraft-carriers. Faced with the pressure for war with the United States which came from the army leaders, Yamamoto always argued that in the long run Japan must lose any protracted war because her industrial potential could not match that of the Americans. When he was argued down he based his naval strategy on swift, knock-out blows, of which the first and most important was the attack on Pearl Harbor to annihilate the U.S. Pacific Fleet. Despite the brilliant successes gained at Pearl Harbor, and the fact that by January 1942 every Allied battleship in the Pacific was out of action or sunk, Yamamoto's basic plan had not succeeded: the all-important American carrier fleet in the Pacific escaped to fight again.

Japan's Road to War

Japan's air forces had as many as 4,000 planes; the navy ten battleships, ten aircraft carriers, 38 cruisers (18 heavy and 20 light), 112 fleet destroyers and 65 submarines; the Imperial Army 51 divisions in service, 27 of which were involved against China, 13 facing the Red Army.

had recently established themselves in the south of Indo-China to Tonkin, provided that Washington agreed to annul the economic sanctions decreed on the previous July 26. A further demand was that the United States should cease to supply arms to Chiang Kai-shek.

The U.S. conditions

The last stipulation in the Japanese offer of November 20 was in fact unacceptable to the government and public opinion in America. But the counter-proposals for a *modus vivendi* that Cordell Hull handed to the two envoys, Kurusu and Nomura, on November 26, were for Japan still more unacceptable: the American Secretary of State posed as a prerequisite the evacuation not only of Indo-China, but of all China, the disowning of the puppet governments in Mukden and Nanking, the recognition of the sovereignty over China of Chungking alone, and finally an agreement between Japan and America whereby Japan covertly abrogated the *casus foederis* as defined by the Tripartite Pact.

Were the American President and his Secretary of State so far from a true appreciation of the situation as to think that their ten articles of November 26 could really lead to a revival of peaceful intentions on the part of the Japanese? It is hardly credible, there being clear evidence that Japanese diplomatic correspondence was an open book to them. It cannot have escaped their notice that as the days passed and his anxieties grew, Togo notified his embassy in Washington that beyond a certain date limit, finally fixed for November 29, relations between Japan and America, in view of the inability to find a compromise, "would disintegrate in chaos", or that "events would occur of their own accord."

Preparations for war

However, on November 25, the day before the American counter-proposals for a *modus vivendi* were handed to the Japanese envoys, the Defense Committee, presided over by President Roosevelt, and attended by the Secretaries of State, of War, and of the Navy, the Chief of the General Staff and the Chief of Naval Operations, held its weekly meeting. Afterwards, Harry Stimson, the Secretary of War, made this entry in his diary: "How could the Japanese be got

▷ *General Tojo (centre) with his Cabinet. Stormy discussions preceded its decision for war. Finance Minister Kaya said on November 1: "We have confidence in a war lasting two years. But not beyond." "Anyway, that gives us two years," was Tojo's reaction.*

into a situation where they would have to fire the first shot, and without leaving ourselves too exposed? That was the question."

And that is not all, because, on November 27, Knox, Secretary of the Navy, in a communication to his department heads, wrote:

"This dispatch is to be considered a war warning. Negotiations with Japan looking toward stabilization of conditions in the Pacific have ceased and an aggressive move by Japan is expected within the next few days."

Certainly, at the time that he sent out this warning, Knox might have been in possession of the decoded despatch which Kurusu and Nomura had sent to Togo the previous day, at the conclusion of which they made known the degree of amazement they felt at the Secretary of State's latest proposals. But it was not till the day following the warning reproduced above that the Japanese Minister of Foreign Affairs announced the imminent rupture of negotiations.

From the texts quoted above it appears that the American administration applied the "semi-positive" method in its relations with Japan, forcing on Japan responsibility for the last word which, in the view of President Roosevelt's entourage, would be war. And certainly in Washington this contingency was contemplated with complete optimism. Stimson, the Secretary of War, indeed wrote on October 21: "An extraordinarily favourable strategic situation has just developed in the South-West Pacific. All the strategic options open to us during the last 20 years have been totally transformed in the last six months. Whereas we were unable before to change the course of events, suddenly we find ourselves possessed of enormous potential, whose full possibilities we are as yet unable to appreciate."

Pearl Harbor orders go out

At all events, the ten articles of the *modus vivendi* proposed to Japan by the State Department played into the hands of General Tojo and those of his cabinet who were urging war against the United States, Great Britain, and the Netherlands. On November 29 an "Imperial Conference" assembled, consisting of ministers in office and the leading Japanese politicians of the past few years. The fateful decision was approved by a majority on a count of everyone present; Emperor Hirohito gave tacit consent, and on December 2 somewhere between the Kurile Islands and Hawaii, Admiral Nagumo, commanding the Air Attack and Support Forces, received the message agreed upon: "Climb Mount Niitaka", signifying the order to attack the fleet anchored at Pearl Harbor at dawn on Sunday, December 7, 1941.

Did the U.S. know?

Quite apart from the strictly military enquiries, the "mystery of Pearl Harbor" or, perhaps better, the mystery of the surprise at Pearl Harbor, has been the subject of a congressional enquiry in Washington whose proceedings, published in 1946, fill 40 volumes.

In regard to the controversy produced by Rear-Admiral R. A. Theobald's book, referred to above, use has been made of Volume III of the *History of United States Naval Operations in World War II,* whose author, Professor Samuel Eliot Morison, of Harvard University, enlisted in the United States Navy in 1942 as a historiographer with the rank of Lieutenant-Commander. In spite of its official character, it is a work which is totally objective and can be recommended both on account of the abundance and the reliability of its information.

More recently, in 1962, Mrs. Roberta Wohlstetter published a large volume at the University of Stanford, California, devoted to the same question. *Pearl Harbor* is a masterpiece of critical analysis, every significant document is examined, and the conclusions drawn are quite unbiased. The author is fully conversant with the different questions relating to the political and military information services, how they functioned, the constraints imposed upon them, and the extent and limit of their possibilities.

The question that is most pertinent could be put briefly as follows: bearing in mind that Colonel William S. Friedmann and his team of cipher experts in Washington had managed to "break" the Japanese diplomatic codes within the required time, how did it come about that the Pacific Fleet at Pearl Harbor did not receive warning of the stratagem that was being prepared to take them by surprise there where they lay at anchor?

Prince Fumimaro Konoye, born in 1891, became Prime Minister of Japan in June 1937. A somewhat tragic figure, he failed to prevent the Chinese war or to bring it to a speedy end; he failed to restrain the extreme militarists; and he failed to reach agreement with the United States. Konoye was the main hope of all Japanese moderates but he was never able to prevail over War Minister Tojo, and resigned two months before the attack on Pearl Harbor. His successor was Tojo. He held office after the war, but killed himself when about to be tried as a war criminal.

Was Roosevelt to blame?

To this, Rear-Admiral R. A. Theobald's reply is: because President Roosevelt and his advisers (principally, General Marshall and Admiral Stark) had made up their minds that the fleet should play the part of the goat that is left tethered to the post as bait for the Japanese tiger, and that the risk to which it was thereby exposed was the one means of provoking the attack which would bring the United States irrevocably into the war.

It is perfectly true that none of the five electronic machines built to decipher the "Purple Code" of the Japanese was allocated to Pearl Harbor, nor was Rear-

▽ Grotesque war preparations in Japan: two Buddhist monks, snouted and goggled in their gas masks, practise their stretcher drill.

◁◁ Chief-of-Staff of the Imperial Japanese Navy, Admiral Nagano. When would be the best moment for Japan to strike? "Now. At once," was Nagano's opinion, "We shall never have a chance like this one again."

Admiral Kimmel among those who received the "Magic" messages which recorded the transcription of Japanese secret despatches. But it is common knowledge that the secrecy surrounding the activity of decoding services is, in every country in the world, the most jealously guarded of all; increasing the circulation of "Magic" messages would have involved a serious risk of disclosure, which was at all costs to be avoided, and it is a fact that in July and August 1945, the "purple machine" was still unscrambling radio correspondence between the Japanese Ministry of Foreign Affairs and its representatives in Moscow, Stockholm, and Berne.

Besides, Togo's despatches contained nothing relating to Pearl Harbor for the excellent reason that he had no knowledge whatsoever of the operation en-

trusted to Admiral Nagumo. On the other hand, it would have been of use to Kimmel to know that, after the end of September, the Japanese consul in Honolulu received the order to communicate the exact moorings of all major American warships.

But this clue, which seems so obvious to us today, was just one among a host of others which singled out Malaya and the Dutch colonies as the single objective of Japanese aggression, and with such conclusiveness that some sources in Washington even forecast that the Philippines would be spared.

On the afternoon of December 6, the Navy's "purple machine" decoded Togo's final instructions to his envoys in Washington. They were followed by a message containing 13 points to be completed by a fourteenth on the following morning. The complete document was to be handed to the Secretary of State at 1300 hours on December 7; when it was shown to President Roosevelt, it drew from him the exclamation: "This is war!" And, in fact, the thirteenth paragraph included the statement:

"The (American) Proposal menaces the Empire's existence itself and disparages its honor and prestige. Therefore, viewed in its entirety, the Japanese Government regrets that it cannot accept the proposal as a basis for negotiation."

Yet nothing was done to alert the Pacific Fleet of the imminence of hostilities. But if Rear-Admiral R. A. Theobald interprets this silence as supporting his thesis, it can be advanced against him that the fleet had already, on November 27, been placed on the alert by the Chief of Naval Operations.

The attack is planned

And this brings us to Pearl Harbor itself. There, on the previous March 31, a report drawn up by two senior officers, one Army, one Navy, drew attention to the danger to which the base was exposed from a carrier-borne aircraft attack. But this prediction was disregarded, Japanese naval concentration seeming to converge on points in South-East Asia. And this thesis appeared to receive confirmation in the "ultimatum" of November 27, according to which Siam, the Kra isthmus (the narrowest part of the Malay peninsula), North Borneo, and the Philippines seemed to be the particular points of possible attack. And, doubtless, it was thought that the huge Japanese aircraft-carriers, which had been out of radio contact for several weeks past, were to cover an amphibious campaign.

Within the Pacific Fleet, to have maintained a permanent state of readiness would have impaired the action training programme, and on that point Admiral Kimmel was not prepared to compromise, because the operational order *Rainbow 5* that it was his task to execute required him to lead his forces to attack the Marshall, then the Caroline, Islands.

In the Army Air Force, Major-General W. Short, commanding the military district of Hawaii had, on sight of the "ultimatum", been concerned above all to prevent acts of sabotage which were to be expected on the part of enemy agents introduced into the archipelago's large Japanese colony, and this led him to order his planes to be close-packed on airfields, rather than dispersed. Furthermore, reconnaissance patrols round Oahu Island suffered from the fact that the intensive training programme for fighters and bombers had left insufficient stocks of fuel for reconnaissance.

Finally, liaison between the naval and air force information services was insufficient and unreliable, while within the Pacific Fleet and the military district of Hawaii, radio communications left a lot to be desired.

But rather than adopt Rear-Admiral Theobald's argument concerning Washington's responsibilities in the Pearl Harbor disaster, one is inclined to give credence rather to Professor Morison. He points out that the commanders of the U.S. armed forces may have fallen into a very simple but dangerous trap: that of considering what they thought the enemy was likely to do and formulating contingency plans based upon that, rather than assessing all the possibilities open to the enemy and being prepared for any eventuality. Though often pointed out, this is an error all too simple to fall into.

Seen in this light, the surprise attack on December 7, 1941 is the exact replica of that in the Ardennes on May 10, 1940. It follows, however, that Morison's judgement embraces Admiral Stark and General Marshall in Washington as well as Kimmel and Short in Honolulu.

Pearl Harbor's fate was set.

▽ *Grim scenes, soon to be repeated on airfields around Pearl Harbor: Chinese aircraft are shot out of the sky while the Japanese assert their mastery at Wangchang airfield in China.*

Battleship Row transformed. After the attack smoke belches from the blazing Tennessee. *At the right of the picture can be seen the tall lattice-masts of the* California, *which settled to the harbour bed on an even keel.*

CHAPTER 21
PEARL HARBOR

It was early in January 1941 that Admiral Yamamoto, commanding the Combined Fleet, instructed a small group of staff officers to make a study of a surprise attack on Pearl Harbor, which would be made by carrier-borne aircraft. Until then, the Japanese Admiralty had contemplated adopting a defensive posture towards the American Pacific forces. But it became apparent that only a single devastating blow dealt at the enemy's principal naval formation at the beginning of hostilities would guarantee Japan the smooth conquest of her objectives in South-East Asia. Was the idea for such an enterprise suggested to her by the remarkable success of the Fleet Air Arm's attack on Taranto on November 11 of the previous year? It seems highly probable, in view of the fact that at the end of May 1941, a mission from the Japanese Naval Air Force visited Taranto and was given a detailed account of the course of events in Operation "Judgement".

In the following August, a series of strategic map exercises carried out under the supervision of Admiral Yamamoto provided the basis for Operational Order No. 1, which was signed on November 1. In the meantime, he had converted his colleagues to his plan, some of them having

at first found it too risky, others objecting that the expeditionary corps destined for South-East Asia was being excessively weakened; but further and most important, Yamamoto had made his aircrews undergo a period of intensive training.

Under the orders of Vice-Admiral Chuichi Nagumo, the task force given the mission of attacking Pearl Harbor included six aircraft carriers (*Kaga, Akagi, Hiryu, Soryu, Zuikaku,* and *Shokaku*) with a total complement of 432 planes; two fast battleships (*Hiei* and *Kirishima*); three cruisers (two heavy and one light); nine destroyers; three submarines, which were to patrol the itinerary plotted; and eight tankers to refuel the squadron at sea.

In the eventuality of Japan's deciding on war, the attack would take place at dawn on December 7, a Sunday, when the American fleet was normally at its moorings. In the words of Rear-Admiral Matome Ugaki, chief-of-staff of the task force, addressing his unit commanders, the attack on Pearl Harbor would be the Waterloo of the war that was to follow. Furthermore, the damage from the air attacks would be added to by those delivered by midget submarines carried

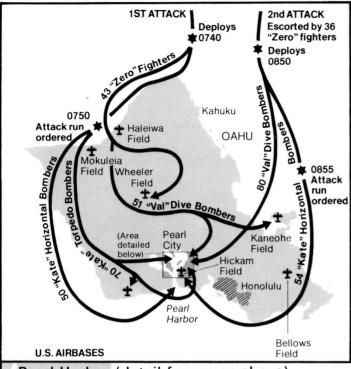

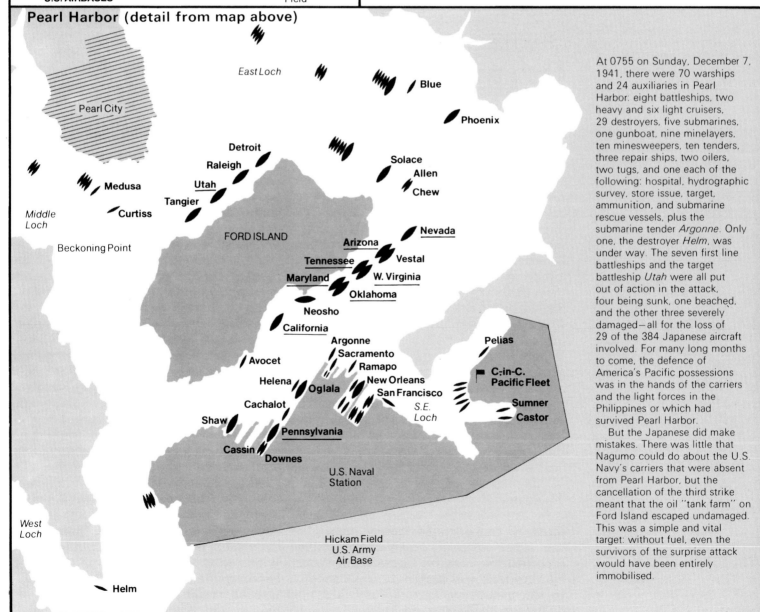

U.S. AIRBASES

◁ Details of Japanese air deployment and ▽ grouping of American matériel during the attack on Pearl Harbor.

Heard at Pearl Harbor:
"All hands, general quarters! Air raid! This is no drill!"
"Padre, there's planes out there and they look like Japs."
"Hell, I didn't even know they were sore at us."
"We're not giving up this ship yet!"
"To hell with fuse settings—shoot!"
"TORA-TORA-TORA!"

Pearl Harbor (detail from map above)

At 0755 on Sunday, December 7, 1941, there were 70 warships and 24 auxiliaries in Pearl Harbor: eight battleships, two heavy and six light cruisers, 29 destroyers, five submarines, one gunboat, nine minelayers, ten minesweepers, ten tenders, three repair ships, two oilers, two tugs, and one each of the following: hospital, hydrographic survey, store issue, target, ammunition, and submarine rescue vessels, plus the submarine tender *Argonne*. Only one, the destroyer *Helm*, was under way. The seven first line battleships and the target battleship *Utah* were all put out of action in the attack, four being sunk, one beached, and the other three severely damaged—all for the loss of 29 of the 384 Japanese aircraft involved. For many long months to come, the defence of America's Pacific possessions was in the hands of the carriers and the light forces in the Philippines or which had survived Pearl Harbor.

But the Japanese did make mistakes. There was little that Nagumo could do about the U.S. Navy's carriers that were absent from Pearl Harbor, but the cancellation of the third strike meant that the oil "tank farm" on Ford Island escaped undamaged. This was a simple and vital target: without fuel, even the survivors of the surprise attack would have been entirely immobilised.

to Oahu by ocean-going submarines.

On November 22, the 31 units commanded by Vice-Admiral Nagumo assembled in a deserted bay on the island of Etorofu, the southernmost of the Kurile chain. On the 26th, the Japanese task force set sail, but, as has been said, the order to attack was to be communicated in a coded message and this came on December 2. The course charted ran east along the 43rd Parallel, thus, with the fog that prevails in those Pacific latitudes, rendering any accidental encounter with other ships unlikely.

On December 6, after nightfall, the formation set course for its objective. The news that no aircraft-carrier was present in Pearl Harbor caused some disappointment among the Japanese pilots. On the other hand, listening to the light-hearted radio programmes coming from Hawaii, it seemed quite clear that the Americans suspected nothing.

Nagumo launches his first strike

The following day, Sunday December 7, at 0615, Nagumo, who was by then 230 miles from Pearl Harbor, despatched a first wave of 214 machines, including 50 conventional bombers, 51 dive-bombers and 70 torpedo planes. One hour later, this formation appeared on a training radar screen, at a range of approximately 160 miles. But this information, which would have given 30 minutes warning to the Pacific Fleet, was not reported by the young air force officer to whom it had been passed because of the coincidence that a formation of Flying Fortresses coming from California was expected at the same time and from the same direction.

Lieutenant-Commander Nakaya, who was leading the fighters in the first wave, saw Pearl Harbor at about 0750:

"Pearl Harbor was still asleep in the morning mist. It was calm and serene inside the harbor, not even a trace of smoke from the ships at Oahu. The orderly group of barracks, the wriggling white line of the automobile road climbing up to the mountain-top; fine objectives of attack in all directions. In line with these, inside the harbor, were important ships of the Pacific Fleet, strung out and anchored two ships side by side in an orderly manner."

A few minutes later, two radio messages crossed: at 0753, Captain Fuchida signalled *Akagi:* "Surprise successful"; at 0758, Rear-Admiral Patrick Bellinger from his H.Q. on Ford Island sent out in plain language: "Air raid, Pearl Harbor – this is no drill."

△ *Pearl Harbor under Japanese attack, showing Ford Island and the American battleships moored two by two in "Battleship Row". A Japanese aircraft can be seen banking away after making its attack, while the camera has caught the stalagmite-plume of water thrown up by an exploding torpedo.*

The Japanese aircraft-carrier *Kaga*

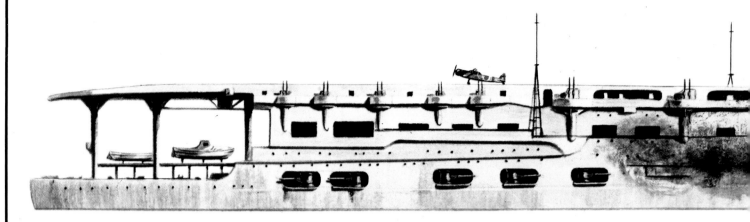

Displacement: 38,200 tons.
Armament: ten 7.9-inch, sixteen 5-inch, and twenty-two 25-mm A.A. guns, plus up to 90 aircraft.
Armour: 11-inch belt. **Speed:** 28⅓ knots.
Length: 812⅓ feet. **Beam:** 106¾ feet.
Draught: 30 feet.
Complement: 2,019.

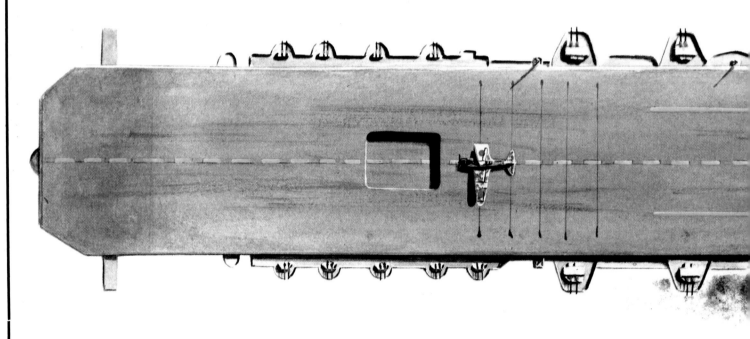

First objective: seven battleships

Of the 127 ships under the command of Rear-Admiral Husband E. Kimmel, 94 were at berth and preparing for the ceremony of the colours. But the Japanese concentrated their efforts on the seven battleships moored in pairs alongside Ford Island, which stands in the middle of the roadstead. One 1,760-pound bomb blew up the forward magazine of *Arizona,* while another dropped down the funnel and exploded in the engine room. The ship settled quickly and went down with Rear-Admiral Isaac C. Kidd and 1,106 officers, petty officers, and other ranks out of a crew of 1,511. Struck by three torpedoes, *Oklahoma* capsized almost instantaneously, trapping below decks 415 men, some of whom survived until Christmas Eve. Had it not been for the extraordinary presence of mind of their crews in taking action to right the two ships, *West Virginia* and *California* would have met the same

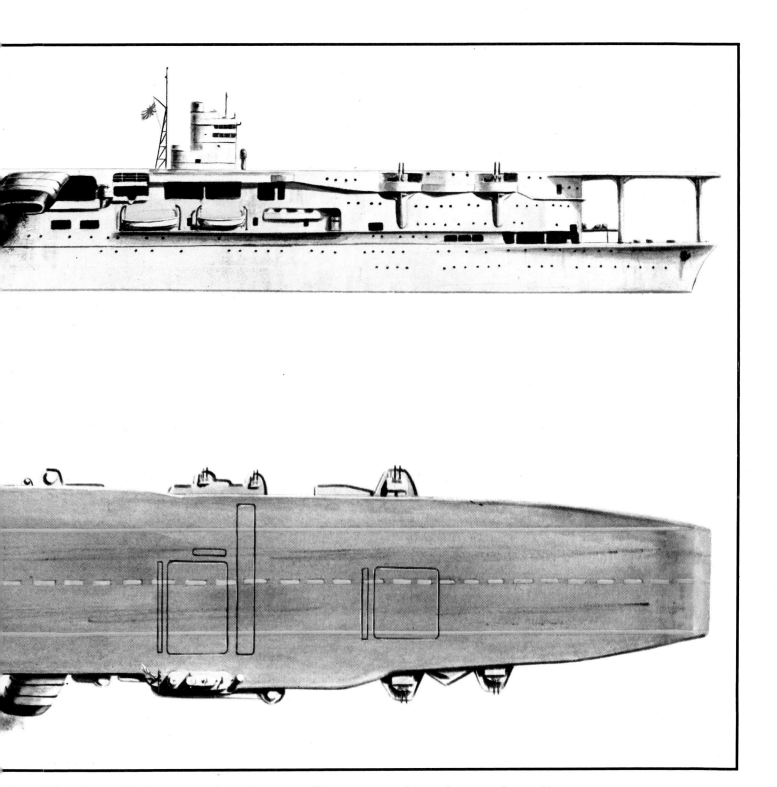

fate; *Nevada* was hit by a torpedo and two bombs but shot down three of her attackers. *Maryland* and *Tennessee* escaped relatively lightly and were able, after December 20, to leave Oahu for an American dockyard, together with *Pennsylvania,* which had been in dry-dock, and thus out of reach of torpedoes. Three cruisers and three destroyers also suffered damage.

The Japanese pilot Nuzo Mori gives the following account of his feelings as he flew his torpedo plane in to attack an American battleship:

"I manoeuvred in order to make my line of approach absolutely right, knowing that the depth of water in the harbour was rarely more than 35 feet. The slightest error in speed or altitude when firing might upset the mechanism of the torpedo and make it go to the bottom or break surface, undoing all my efforts either way.

"At the time, I was hardly aware of my actions. I acted like an automaton through force of habit which my long training had given me.

"The battleship appeared to leap suddenly into view across the front of my

"A Farewell on a Carrier" by the Japanese artist Shuri Arai depicts a strike wave of Zeros warming-up for take-off.

machine, looming huge like a vast grey mountain.

"Stand by! . . . Fire! . . .

"All the while, I completely forgot the enemy fire and the throbbing of my own engine, totally absorbed by my manoeuvre. At the right moment, I pulled with all my strength on the release lever. The machine jolted violently as shells hit the wings and fuselage. My head was flung back, and I felt as though I'd just hit an iron bar head-on. But I'd made it! The torpedo-launching was perfect! My plane still flew and responded to my control. The torpedo was going to score a direct hit. I suddenly became conscious of where I was and of the intensity of the enemy fire."

The second wave attacks

At 0715, Nagumo launched his second strike, consisting of 54 bombers, 80 dive-bombers, and 36 fighters. Led by Lieutenant-Commander Shimazaki, it completed the work of the first wave in the harbour, then turned its attention to the naval installations on Ford Island, Wheeler and Hickham Fields (the air force bases), and the flying boat station at Kaneohe, destroying 65 aircraft out of the 231 on Oahu. In men, American losses for the day totalled 2,403 killed and 1,178 wounded.

Japan's losses: a mere fleabite

This tremendous success cost Nagumo 29 planes and 55 airmen. After recovering the aircraft of the second strike, Nagumo set course north at 1300. The midget submarine attack was a complete failure, however, and on December 10 one of the transport submarines was sent to the bottom by an aircraft from the carrier *Enterprise*. Moreover, the Japanese omitted to attack the vast oil storage tanks at Pearl Harbor, whose destruction would have incapacitated the U.S. fleet for months. American soldiers and sailors had acted so swiftly to re-establish the situation that Nagumo abandoned a third assault, as he thought that its cost in aircraft would be prohibitive – conclusive enough proof that Kimmel had shown energy and intelligence in training his crews.

Yamamoto – if one may be forgiven an analogy from boxing – had flattered himself that he would knock out the U.S. Navy in the first round; in fact, he had merely left it groggy but upright. The destruction of two battleships and the damage sustained by six others did not deprive it of its main striking force: its three aircraft-carriers were intact and with them 20 cruisers and 65 destroyers. Above all, the attack on December 7 mobilised all American resources and raised a mighty wave of indignation across the United States which with steadily mounting strength would break on Japan with colossal force.

Vengeance is sworn

"A date which will live in infamy," said Roosevelt, giving an account of the events before Congress. And, on the bridge of *Enterprise* as she headed back to Pearl Harbor on December 9, Rear-Admiral William F. Halsey echoed him when, at the sight of the wrecks obstructing the fairway at Ford Island he made this, less academic, utterance: "Before we're through with 'em, the Japanese language will be spoken only in hell!"

▽ *Fuel tanks explode at the wrecked seaplane base at Kaneohe Bay on the east coast of Oahu. There were 33 long-range Catalina flying-boats at Kaneohe before the Japanese struck; the loss of these indispensable "eyes of the fleet" was in itself a serious blow.*

CHAPTER 22
JAPAN'S BLITZKRIEG

△ "And there was I thinking it was only a footprint," says a myopic Axis Robinson Crusoe in this Punch cartoon. The thinking behind cartoons such as this – that U.S. power in the Far East was an impregnable shield behind which other nations could expect safety – was misplaced by December 1941, however. The Japanese surprise attack on Pearl Harbor and their rapid advances in the Pacific showed that a new power had emerged on the world stage, and that the days of the white monopoly of world power were past.

In the spring of 1939, with the threat of war in Europe posed by Germany and Italy, the case of Japanese intervention on the side of the Axis powers was examined in the course of conversations between the British and French staff officers who drew up the Allied war plans. If Japan joined in the war, the French Navy was to assume responsibility for operations throughout the Mediterranean while the British naval forces based on Alexandria sailed to reinforce those at Singapore.

The armistice signed at Rethondes on June 22, 1940 caused reverberations as far as the Far East, because it was now out of the question for the British Mediterranean Fleet to abandon the Mediterranean to the Italian Navy. Thus the naval defence of South-East Asia against the emergent threat by Japan was reduced to an absolute minimum, even allowing for the small Dutch force based on the East Indies, which effectively took its orders from the British War Cabinet. Graver still, while in 1939 the British could still consider French Indo-China as the bastion of Malaya, two years later, the agreements forced on Vichy by Tokyo turned Saigon into a Japanese pistol aimed at Singapore; and already Japanese technical missions were finding their way into Siam.

It is clear that, faced with the defence of the Far East, on which in the last analysis depended that of Australia and New Zealand, the Imperial General Staff and the War Cabinet found themselves with an extremely difficult problem, in spite of the fact that Roosevelt, at the Atlantic Conference, had given Churchill his guarantee that he would consider any new Japanese violation of territory in this global sector as a ground for war and that he would inform the Tokyo Government accordingly.

The right decision?

In view of this threat and of the choice of measures it required, did the British Premier give evidence of somewhat impulsive, dilettante decision-making rather than the sober appreciation of military reality that was called for? In his book

The Fall of Singapore, Captain Russell Grenfell gives a clearly affirmative answer to this question, taking Churchill very severely to task in fact. The substance of his accusation is that with full knowledge of the deficiency in aircraft in the bastion of empire that was Singapore, Churchill, who had accepted the loss of 209 planes in Greece, nevertheless sent another 593 to the Soviet Union during the second half of 1941. Grenfell concludes:

"It follows that had the aircraft given or utilised for the benefit of foreign countries been sent to Singapore, the A.O.C. Malaya could by autumn have had a total of 802 modern aircraft instead of 141 old crocks. It is true that many of the 802 would have been fighters. But more and better fighters were Malaya's principal need."

To this it could apparently be replied that the failure to give due recognition to the technical and tactical capacity of the Japanese air forces was not only Churchill's but that of the highest ranking officers in the R.A.F. We have already seen that to confront the estimated 713 planes of his adversaries the unfortunate Pulford expressed himself content with 336. It is true that he did not receive even these and that as the crisis loomed he was far less optimistic. Furthermore, it could be objected that by sending Stalin hundreds of Hurricane fighters, the British Premier acted in the conviction that he was defending Britain in the Russian sky. The real danger in the summer of 1941 was that the Red Army might collapse under the assault by the Wehrmacht, and that in the spring following the Wehrmacht would turn its full power against Great Britain. In that event her chances of survival would be slender, and Singapore would inevitably follow her into defeat.

It will also be recalled that, in the previous March, the British and American Governments had agreed to assume certain strategic risks *vis-à-vis* Japan in order the better to fight the Third Reich. There is therefore no doubt but that the transfer of war material to the Soviet Union agreed by the War Cabinet met with the approval of the White House. These, in the main are the reasons that would militate against total acceptance of the point of view expressed by Captain Russell Grenfell.

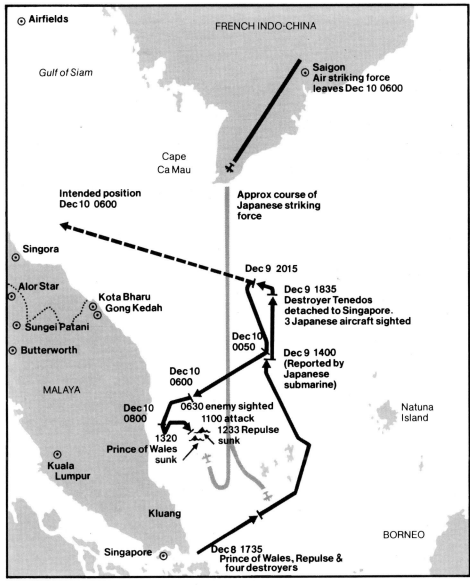

Airfields (legend symbol)

FRENCH INDO-CHINA

Gulf of Siam

Saigon
Air striking force
leaves Dec 10 0600

Cape
Ca Mau

Intended position
Dec 10 0600

Approx course of
Japanese striking
force

Singora

Alor Star

Kota Bharu
Gong Kedah

Sungei Patani

Butterworth

MALAYA

Dec 9 2015

Dec 9 1835
Destroyer Tenedos
detached to Singapore.
3 Japanese aircraft sighted

Dec 10
0050

Dec 9 1400
(Reported by
Japanese
submarine)

Dec 10
0600

Dec 10
0800

0630 enemy sighted
1100 attack

1233 Repulse
sunk

1320

Prince of Wales
sunk

Natuna
Island

Kuala
Lumpur

Kluang

BORNEO

Singapore

Dec 8 1735
Prince of Wales, Repulse &
four destroyers

Churchill sends reinforcements

Nevertheless, Russell Grenfell would seem to be entirely justified in the criticism he brings to bear on another initiative of Winston Churchill's: the despatch to Malayan waters of the new battleship *Prince of Wales* and the elderly battle-cruiser *Repulse*.

On returning from his meeting with President Roosevelt in Newfoundland waters, the Prime Minister, on August 25, made a suggestion to Pound which in his view would lead to an improvement in the situation in the Far East:

"I felt strongly that it should be possible in the near future to place a deterrent squadron in the Indian Ocean, and that this should consist of the smallest number of the best ships", including *Duke of York*, which was finishing her trials, a battle-cruiser, and an aircraft-carrier.

But the First Sea Lord did not believe in the "deterrent" effect such a formation might have and, from a strategic point of view, advised that a strike force, composed of the two *Nelsons, Renown,* and two or three aircraft-carriers, should be based on Trincomalee, the four old "R" Class battleships being assigned to escort duties in the Indian Ocean.

Churchill nevertheless was obdurate.

△ *The loss of* Prince of Wales *and* Repulse *on December 10, 1941. The sinking of these two capital ships, one new and one old, was yet again a clear indication that the day of the unprotected capital ship was over – it was now the aircraft that was to dominate naval warfare. In the short term, too, the sinking of the two vessels left Malaya with no powerful maritime defence – the Japanese Navy could operate around the peninsula with almost complete impunity.*
▷ *The last moments of* Prince of Wales. *Despite the speed and precision with which she was sunk, most of her crew was saved: 90 out of 110 officers and 1,195 out of 1,502 ratings. Unfortunately, however, neither Admiral Phillips, commander of Force Z (*Prince of Wales *and* Repulse) *nor Captain Leach, the former ship's captain, was among those rescued.*

In his view, *Resolution* and the others of her class were no more than "floating coffins", and Pound took insufficient account of the effect on the enemy of the detachment of one of the *King George V* class; and Churchill repeated on August 29:

"It exercises a vague general fear and menaces all points at once. It appears, and disappears, causing immediate reactions and perturbations on the other side."

The Foreign Office supported this argument which, it should be noted, went further than purely "preventive" measures, and the First Sea Lord deferred to Winston Churchill's evidently imperious wishes, prevailing upon him only to the extent of replacing *Duke of York* by *Prince of Wales,* whose crew was more highly trained. Admiral Sir Tom Phillips, hitherto Deputy Chief-of-Staff (Operations) at the Admiralty, was appointed C.-in-C. of this reduced squadron, which left the Clyde on October 25. On November 11, *Repulse* was ordered to join *Prince of Wales* in Ceylon. But, in the meantime, there was an unfortunate accident: the carrier *Indomitable,* which was to join the two capital ships, ran aground during a training exercise in the Caribbean.

Sir Tom Phillips arrived in Singapore on December 2; on December 5 he met General MacArthur and Admiral Hart, commanding the United States Asiatic Fleet, in Manila, and the three agreed that in the circumstances Singapore could not serve as the main base. From London, the Admiralty instructed Phillips to consider falling back on Port Darwin in Australia. Already, Winston Churchill's strategic conceptions were beginning to crumble.

The rest of the story is well known. On December 7 Japanese bombs fell on Singapore, proclaiming the beginning of hostilities. Could Admiral Phillips decently slink away when only a few days earlier it had been announced, with less concern for the truth than for flag-waving, that *"Prince of Wales* and other battleships"* had arrived at Singapore to participate in the defence of this great bastion of the British Empire? However, on hearing the news that the Japanese had set foot in Singora on Siamese territory, not far from the Malayan frontier, he decided to try to take them by surprise while landing troops and supplies. Leaving his chief-of-staff in Singapore to try to arrange the vital fighter cover needed, Phillips weighed anchor at nightfall on December 8.

Japanese aircraft sink *Repulse* and *Prince of Wales*

However, the following afternoon, he abandoned his plans when the appearance of Japanese planes in the sky overhead led him to believe that the enemy knew of his intentions. In fact this was not so, but

▷ ▷ *Japanese fighter planes take off from a captured airfield in the Philippines.*

▽ *The first wave of the Japanese invasion of the Philippines heads in towards its beach on northern Luzon. General Homma hoped to pin down the American and Filipino defences of the island here while other landings further to the south outflanked them and cut them off from their bases near Manila. But Lieutenant-General Douglas MacArthur was too quick for him. The moment it became clear that the first assault was only a pinning attack, MacArthur pulled back onto the Bataan peninsula, from which he could prevent the Japanese using Manila.*

General Douglas Mac-Arthur, Supreme Commander of the United States Forces in Australia and the South-West Pacific and Allied Supreme Commander in the Pacific at the end of the war, was born in 1880. He served with the American Expeditionary Force in France at the end of World War I. In 1941 MacArthur was military adviser to the Philippine Government, but was recalled to active service with the U.S. Army in July. He was appointed commander of the U.S. land forces in the Far East, which also included the Philippine Army. He conducted the defence of the area until pulled out by President Roosevelt to take command of the U.S. forces in Australia in March 1942. MacArthur decided that the defence of Australia hinged on that of New Guinea, and so made Port Moresby his main base. Here he slowly built up his forces and developed the strategy of cutting off large Japanese forces and then leaving them to rot, rather than attacking them head on and destroying them, suffering heavy losses himself in the process. With these tactics MacArthur was able to start pushing back towards the Philippines in 1943. The Philippines were reached in late 1944 and largely overrun in 1945. The surrender of Japan was accepted by MacArthur on September 2, 1945.

his movements had been observed and signalled by two submarines, and even before dawn on December 10, Rear-Admiral Matsunaga despatched 11 reconnaissance planes, 52 torpedo planes, and 34 level bombers, belonging to his 22nd Air Flotilla, from Saigon.

At the same instant, the two British capital ships, escorted by three destroyers, were on course for Kuantan. Phillips had abandoned his plan to attack the Japanese landing force at Singora when his chief-of-staff had informed him that fighter cover was impossible, and decided to return to Singapore. *En route* he had been informed of possible enemy landings at Kuantan and concluded that he should investigate. Having ascertained that all was normal and that nothing untoward was happening, Sir Tom Phillips headed back for Singapore. At about 1100 hours, when he had Kuantan on his beam, the first enemy planes appeared in the sky. The fire from the British ships was as poor as the aim of the Japanese bombers, who managed to get only three out of 57 bombs on target;

◁ Manila under aerial
bombardment on December 24–
the day on which it was declared
an open city. Bombing was
almost daily until the Japanese
occupied the city on January 2–3.

but the torpedo planes attacked with consummate skill, setting up a crossfire of torpedoes to defeat any attempt at avoiding action on the part of *Repulse* and *Prince of Wales*. The former sank half an hour after noon, the latter less than an hour later.

What can be more tragic for a commanding officer than to witness his ship's agony? The following account by a British naval officer vividly conveys the intense personal drama of *Repulse*'s captain, W. G. Tennant, after he had given the order to abandon ship:

"As she heeled rapidly over, Captain Tennant clambered over the side of the bridge on to what had previously been a vertical surface and was walking unsteadily along it when the sea seemed to come up and engulf him. The ship must have rolled right over on top of him, for everything at once became pitch dark, telling him he was a long way down under water. The defeatist part of the mind that we all possess whispered to him that this was the end of things and that he might as well take in water and get it over. But another part of his brain bade him react against this advice, and he decided to hang on to life as long as possible; though he wondered if he could possibly hold his breath long enough to come up again. Lumps of wood hit him in the darkness. After what seemed a long, long time the water began to show a faint lightening, and suddenly he was on the surface in swirling water, luckily close to a Carley float, the occupants of which hauled him on board still wearing his steel helmet. The destroyers *Vampire* and *Electra* were coming up to pick up survivors and soon had them on board."

Of the 2,921 officers and other ranks who manned the two capital ships, 2,081 were picked up by the destroyers who went to their rescue with no concern for the risk to themselves; Admiral Sir Tom Phillips, however, went down with *Prince of Wales* as did her commanding officer, Captain J. C. Leach who, on May 24 of the same year, had been one of two survivors out of the 11 men on the bridge of his vessel when it was struck by a shell from *Bismarck*. Just as rescue operations were being completed, nine R.A.F. fighter planes from the Singapore base appeared in the sky. In enumerating the causes of this disaster, unprecedented in the annals of the Royal Navy, Captain Russell Grenfell indicts principally:

"The presence in London of a Minister of Defence so convinced of his own individual competence as a master of naval strategy that he was prepared to ignore the advice of his professional naval experts and force upon them measures for the naval defence of Malaya which they clearly did not like."

And one is left no choice but to confirm this opinion. As for the initiative taken by the ill-fated Sir Tom Phillips, it was that to be expected of a British sailor, bred in the tradition of taking the offensive and promoted to his high command by virtue of this very fighting spirit.

△ Air Chief-Marshal Sir
Robert Brooke-Popham, British
Commander-in-Chief Far East.
Admittedly, the forces at his
disposal were entirely
inadequate, but the dispositions
he made were nonetheless not
the best he could have made.
He handed over his command to
Lieutenant-General Sir Henry
Pownall on December 23, 1941.

American submarines powerless

The loss of *Prince of Wales* and of *Repulse* was a considerable relief to the 2nd and 3rd Japanese Fleets which, under the command of Vice-Admirals Kondo and

△ *President Roosevelt stares aghast at the awful shadow cast before him by Japan's rising sun.*

▷ *Japan's first tide of conquest. Covered by their navy's fast, powerful, and almost unopposed striking forces, the Japanese struck swiftly at the Allies' far-flung islands and mainland possessions right round the perimeter of the "Greater East Asia Co-Prosperity Sphere".*

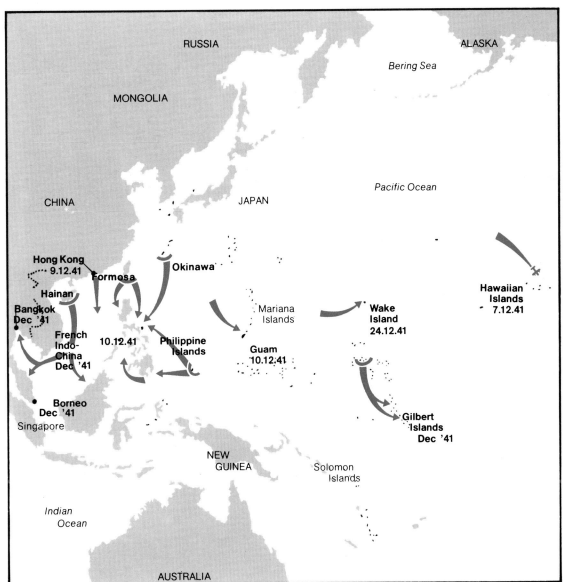

Takahashi, had the task of protecting, then supplying the 14th and 25th Armies, which would go on to conquer respectively the Philippines and the Malayan peninsula, including Singapore.

If the American, Dutch, and British cruisers and destroyers in this theatre of operations on December 10, 1941 were ineffective, being old and open to attack from the air, the 42 submarines under the orders of Admirals Helfrich at Surabaja and Thomas Hart at Manila did not perform much better; certainly, the Dutch registered some successes, but the Americans had the bitter experience of finding that their magnetic detonators worked no better than those carried by U-boats in 1940; this extract from a series of reports collected by Captain Edward L. Beach provides evidence of this:

"Fired three torpedoes, bubble tracks of two could plainly be seen through the periscope, tracked by sight and sound

right through target. They looked like sure hits from here. No explosions. Cannot understand it."

In such advantageous conditions, it is hardly surprising that the amphibious operation set in motion by the Japanese High Command on December 8 proceeded as planned.

In the Philippines, General Douglas MacArthur disposed of rather more than 31,000 men (19,000 Americans) against General Homma's 14th Army, which began the assault with two divisions. It was the same story in the air, the attacking force having 750 planes, the defence 300, at the moment, that is, when Clark Field was bombed, involving a loss of 17 out of 36 Flying Fortresses and several fighters destroyed on the ground. The lack of spare runways has been put forward as explaining the success of this operation, carried out only a few hours after Manila had received the news of Pearl Harbor.

Japan's flood-tide of conquest

On December 10, 1941, General Homma established a first beach-head at Aparri in the north of Luzon, with the intention of engaging the defence at this spot while effecting a second landing in the bay of Lingayen in order to outflank and destroy it. But MacArthur was too quick for him. At the first sign of the enemy's second manoeuvre, he disengaged, but far from trying to block the Japanese advance on Manila, he side-stepped, so to speak, placing his troops across the peninsula of Bataan, which shuts off the bay of Cavite, in positions prepared beforehand. When, on December 27, Homma got over his surprise, the Americans and Filipinos were so well dug in that it took the Japanese five months

to drive them out of their last stronghold.

Hong Kong was the objective of General Sakai's 23rd Army. The defence of the island city of Victoria and Kowloon on the mainland devolved upon Major-General C. M. Maltby with 12,000 men, a force which was hardly to be adequate for the task.

On the night of December 9–10 the Japanese stormed the defence of Kowloon peninsula and forced the British troops to fall back on to the island after three days' severe fighting. On the 18th, again under cover of darkness, the Japanese 38th Division crossed the strait separating Victoria from the continent. In spite of vastly superior enemy forces, Major-General Maltby continued to resist until shortage of ammunition obliged him to accede to the third call to surrender. The cease-fire came on Christmas Day 1941.

On the day that the first Japanese landings took place at Singora, Air Chief-Marshal Sir Robert Brooke-Popham

△ *A grimly determined machine gun crew covers the landing of Japanese troops at Guam in this painting by Kohei Esaki. The Type 99 machine gun seen here is fitted with its 1½ magnification sight. Also of note is the strict personal camouflage: even while Japan had control in the air her troops maintained a standard of camouflage discipline unrivalled by her enemies. When America turned to attack in the "island hopping" campaign, she would find that this same ingenuity was applied to fixed emplacements, which would be so well camouflaged that they were invisible except at very close range.*

△ *Bren-gun carriers force their way through swampy jungle en route to the north. The Japanese also used light armoured vehicles in their advance, but they relied for the most part on infiltration and speed through the jungle to bypass the Allied positions, rather than engaging them head on with armour.*

served.) Advancing by means of constant infiltration and outflanking movements, he forced Percival to abandon position after position, never leaving him time to entrench himself; many times, in order to further his objective, he "mixed" (his own description) his own commandos in with retreating British troops with the aim of preventing a "scorched earth" policy being carried out.

By the end of the year General Yamashita was ahead of schedule. The fall of Kota Bharu provided him with an excellent base for air attacks on Singapore, as well as an easy path to the Indian Ocean. Once there, he commandeered everything that would float, and, with a barrage of tiny amphibious operations prodding at the British rear areas, unnerved the British completely.

In Siam, General Iida, commanding the 15th Army, found every door opened for him by a collaborator government. By the end of December, after what may be described as a "route march", he reached the frontier with Burma to whose defence Lieutenant-General T. J. Hutton had just been appointed. The means at hand to do so were exiguous to say the least, and will be covered in a later chapter.

With the exception of Guam, the Mariana group of islands was transferred from Germany to become a Japanese mandate by the Treaty of Versailles in 1919. Hence the American island of Guam was left virtually indefensible and surrendered on December 10.

It remained for Wake Island, half way between Guam and Midway, to inflict a first reverse on the Japanese, whose offensive in other sectors was so successful and auspicious. An exceptionally timely reinforcement had arrived on December 4 in the shape of a squadron of Grumman F4F "Wildcat" fighter-bombers, and the atoll's garrison repelled a first assault, even managing to sink two Japanese destroyers. Exasperated by this humiliating setback, Yamamoto ordered Nagumo to detach the carriers *Hiryu* and *Soryu,* two cruisers, and two destroyers so as to contrive a fresh assault.

On December 21, the last Wildcat was shot down, but not before it had itself disposed of two Zero fighters. Then the dive bombers destroyed the batteries defending the island, reducing them one by one. On December 23, overwhelmed by the Japanese landings, the heroic garrison at Wake at last surrendered.

was C.-in-C. of combined British forces in the Far East. The planes at his disposal were woefully inadequate, as has already been observed. If the state of his troops, under the command of General Percival, was somewhat better, it was still far from satisfactory: no tanks, little artillery, and the infantry a mixture of British, Indian, Australian and Malay. In training and tactics Percival's forces could not compete with the enemy. Neither had the troops been positioned in the most effective manner.

The Japanese 25th Army's mission was to fly the Rising Sun over Singapore on D-Day plus 100, counting from the first landing, that is to say March 16, 1942. With three, subsequently four divisions (27, then 36 battalions), its numerical superiority over the British was only slight. The Japanese forces, however, were crack formations and had the initial advantage of surprise. Furthermore, their abundant aircraft support would thwart British attempts to reform and regain the initiative. To this end, the numerous airfields in the Malay peninsula which the R.A.F. had put into service proved invaluable. And the army had at its head an outstandingly dynamic and resourceful leader in General Yamashita – "Rommel of the jungle" as he was known. (Yamashita had a reputation for cruelty, but in other respects the resemblance was fully de-

CHAPTER 23

"BATTLEAXE": STRUGGLE ON THE FRONTIER

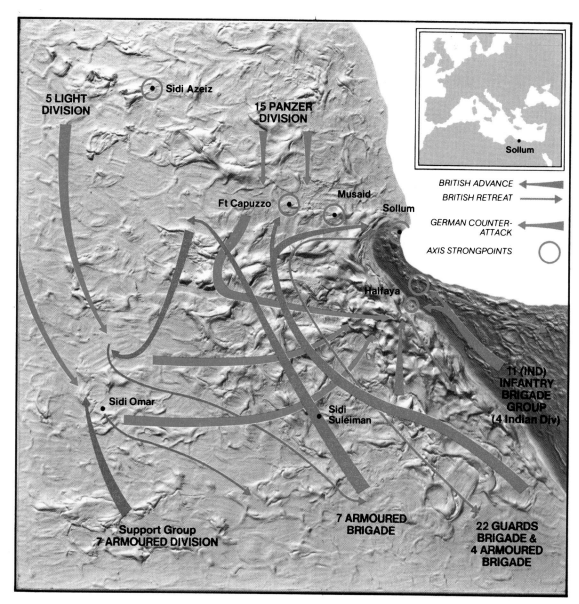

5 LIGHT DIVISION

15 PANZER DIVISION

Sidi Azeiz

Ft Capuzzo

Musaid

Sollum

Halfaya

Sidi Omar

Sidi Suleiman

Support Group 7 ARMOURED DIVISION

7 ARMOURED BRIGADE

22 GUARDS BRIGADE & 4 ARMOURED BRIGADE

11 (IND) INFANTRY BRIGADE GROUP (4 Indian Div)

BRITISH ADVANCE
BRITISH RETREAT
GERMAN COUNTER-ATTACK
AXIS STRONGPOINTS

Sollum

△ *Troops of the* Afrika Korps *move forward on motor-cycle combinations.*
◁ *Operation "Battleaxe", the ill-starred offensive that was to cost General Wavell his command.*

Until Pearl Harbor, developments in the North African campaign depended on the course of the naval/air war in the Mediterranean. This was affected to a great extent by the defensive and offensive capabilities of Malta, which relied on supplies sent from England and Egypt. It was a case of "triphibious" warfare, as Winston Churchill called it. The Italian Navy, whose task was to keep open the sealanes to the forces fighting in Libya and Egypt, was faced, from mid-July 1941, with an increasingly difficult situation. Already at a disadvantage as it lacked any naval airpower worthy of the name, its shortage of oil fuel was now assuming tragic proportions. It had entered the war with reserves of 1,880,000 tons, 600,000 of which had been consumed in the first six months of operations. Monthly consumption was reduced to 75,000 tons. But when it became clear that supplies from Germany would not exceed 50,000 tons a month, this meant, recorded *Supermarina*, that it would be impossible "to maintain forces in a state that was already inadequate for waging war".

But even these supplies could not be relied on, for when the yearly figures were established it was shown that supplies from Germany amounted to barely 254,000 tons, instead of the 600,000 tons expected. One can understand why, just before El Alamein, the Chief-of-Staff of the Italian *Comando Supremo*, Marshal Cavallero, wrote in his diary on October

Wavell Recovers Abyssinia

On June 10, 1940, Mussolini's empire included the old Italian colonies of Eritrea on the Red Sea, Somaliland on the Indian Ocean, and also the ancient empire of Abyssinia, wrested from Emperor Haile Selassie in spite of the League of Nations and its inoperative sanctions. Forming enclaves within this empire were the colonies of British and French Somaliland. The latter's capital, Djibouti, was linked to Addis Ababa by a narrow-gauge railway.

In July 1940 the Duke of Aosta captured Kassala, Galabat and Kurmuk in the Sudan, and took the Moyale salient in Kenya. On August 1, Lieutenant-General Guglielmo Nasi began the invasion of British Somaliland. From January 15, 1941, Italian forces retreated to take a strong defensive position at Keren. By March 24, however, British forces were able to break through to Aguara. Lieutenant-General Cunningham broke the Italian line along the Juba and went on to Mogadishu, arriving at Addis Ababa on April 5.

23, 1942: "I have two major pre-occupations—oil and Malta."

Thus it is clear that in this and many other respects Operation "Barbarossa" damaged the Axis potential in the Mediterranean.

The success of Operation "Tiger"

The arrival in Africa of the 15th Panzer Division in the latter part of April caused alarm in G.H.Q. Cairo and in the British War Cabinet. General Wavell expected a strong force of German infantry to move up the line, and on April 20 he signalled to the C.I.G.S., Sir John Dill:

"I have just received disquieting intelligence. I was expecting another German colonial division, which disembarked at Tripoli early this month, to appear in the fighting line about the end of the month. Certain units have already been identified. I have just been informed that latest evidence indicates this is not a colonial but an *armoured* division. If so, the situation is indeed serious, since an armoured division contains over 400 tanks, of which 138 are medium. If the enemy can arrange supply it will take a lot of stopping."

It is now known that Wavell over-estimated considerably the strength of the Panzer division in the spring of 1941. Instead of the three or four tank battalions at the disposal of the large armoured units in action in the Balkans at this time, the 15th Panzer Division had only two, which comprised 168 tanks and 30 reconnaissance vehicles. It must be recognised, however, that this distinguished soldier was basing his assessment on reports not only from the British Intelligence service but also from its French, Belgian, and Swiss counterparts. These sources gave the Panzer strength as 488, including 122 heavy tanks.

In any case, once he had "digested" the information, Wavell informed Dill that he attached the highest priority to immediate reinforcement of his armoured strength. He had in reserve sufficient personnel to man six armoured regiments, and was insistent that the tanks he needed should be delivered before the 15th Panzer Division was in position and ready for action. Churchill overruled the objections of the C.I.G.S., who was reluctant to weaken the home front while there was still a possibility of a German invasion, excluded the Cape route in view of the urgency of the problem, and insisted that the First Lord of the Admiralty order delivery by the Mediterranean route. At the same time, the battleship *Queen Elizabeth* and the cruisers *Fiji* and *Naiad* were transferred from home waters to Alexandria. Two hundred and ninety-five tanks and 53 Hurricane fighters were loaded aboard five fast 15-knot merchant ships.

This convoy was escorted by Force H between Gibraltar and Cape Bon. During the night of May 7–8 one merchant ship struck a mine in the dangerous Sicilian Narrows, but the next day, 55 miles south of Malta, the convoy was taken over by Admiral Cunningham who, while he was about it, shelled Benghazi and sent three tankers and four supply ships to Malta. A few days later, the four remaining ships unloaded at Alexandria 43 Hurricanes and 238 tanks–135 Matildas, 82 cruisers, and 21 Mark VI's, small 5½-ton machines of relatively little value in battle. Apparently, the transfer of X *Fliegerkorps* from Sicily to Rommel in Africa had contributed considerably to the success of this daring operation–"Tiger" as it was named by Churchill.

Rommel maintains his advantage

The War Cabinet had learned from intercepts of "Enigma" signals that Rommel had various weaknesses. Wavell was therefore urged to attack with minimum delay, and to relieve the tired garrison of Tobruk. He had under his command XIII Corps, under Lieutenant-General Sir Noel Beresford-Peirse, including the 4th Indian Division (Major-General F. W. Messervy), the 7th Armoured Division (Major-General Sir Michael O'Moore Creagh), and the 22nd Guards Brigade (Brigadier J. Marriot).

However, recent engagements at Halfaya Pass had made him aware of a number of "black spots". In a message to the C.I.G.S. on May 28 he said:

"Our armoured cars are too lightly armoured to resist the fire of enemy fighter aircraft, and, having no gun, are powerless against the German eight-wheeled armoured cars, which have guns and are faster. This makes reconnaissance difficult. Our Infantry tanks are really too slow for a battle in desert, and have been suffering considerable casualties from the fire of the powerful enemy anti-tank guns. Our cruisers have little advantage in power or speed over German medium tanks. Technical breakdowns are still too numerous. We shall not be able to accept battle with perfect confidence in spite of numerical inferiority, as we could against Italians. Above factors

▽ *On the British side: a fox-hole of the 4th Indian Division, facing the key position of Halfaya. The Great Libyan Escarpment, which dominated the frontier battles of summer 1941, looms in the background. These men are watching a shell bursting in the background, on the left.*

△ *Replaced after "Battleaxe": Wavell (right) and Air Chief-Marshal Longmore.*
▽ *A "Battleaxe" casualty; a British cruiser tank, heading for the repair workshops in the rear areas aboard a recovery vehicle.*

may limit our success. They also make it imperative that adequate flow of armoured reinforcements and reserves should be maintained."

Did General Wavell exaggerate the weakness of his armoured forces? It is unlikely, since Rommel's account completely supports Wavell. Discussing his successful defensive action of June 15–17, 1941, Rommel wrote:

"But [Wavell] was put at a great disadvantage by the slow speed of his heavy Infantry tanks, which prevented him from reacting quickly enough to the moves of our faster vehicles. Hence the slow speed of the bulk of his armour was his soft spot, which we could seek to exploit tactically."

He also reveals that the Matilda tanks, which were supposed to sweep a path for the infantry through enemy defences, had only anti-tank armour-piercing shells.

Against troops that were widely spread and well dug in one might as well have used the iron cannon ball of the Napoleonic wars. Finally, the *Afrika Korps'* commander used 8·8-cm anti-aircraft guns as anti-tank weapons. This 21-pounder gun was highly accurate, firing 15 to 20 rounds a minute at a velocity of over 2,600 feet per second. It thus outclassed all British armour, which could be knocked out even before the Germans were within range of their 40-mm guns. After the battle the British said they had been taken by surprise, but it was really nothing new. Colonel de Gaulle had been through the experience at the Abbeville bridgehead on May 30, 1940.

In these circumstances it was not surprising that the British offensive, Operation "Battleaxe", was a failure. Wavell had not even had the advantage of surprise. The plan was to take the

conscripted in 1939, aided by Major Pardi of the Italian artillery, offered a determined and courageous resistance. Their gallantry gave Rommel the time to bring the whole of his forces to bear. By June 16 he had stabilised the situation, bringing the British to a halt with considerable casualties. But he was not the man to be satisfied with a merely defensive success. Assembling as much of his *Afrika Korps* as possible he struck south, reaching Sidi Omar, then east, hoping to surround and wipe out XIII Corps. The British managed to withdraw, however, before their last lines of communication were cut, and on June 17 all was quiet again on the Halfaya escarpment.

Of the 25,000 men in the engagement, British casualties were 122 killed, 588 wounded, and 259 missing, most of whom were taken prisoner. Wavell's fears on May 28 were justified if one considers the losses in his armoured units. Of the 180 tanks which had set off at dawn on June 15, about 100 were lost. As for Rommel, he recorded the loss of 12 tanks totally destroyed and 675 men, including 338 dead or missing. His success was timely as he had many critics in O.K.H. and especially since on June 22 O.K.W. was to assume complete control over this theatre of operations.

Halfaya position in an encircling movement, with the 7th Armoured Division attacking the rear and the 4th Indian Division making the frontal assault. After an initial success by the 7th Armoured Division, which took Capuzzo, the whole operation went wrong.

For one thing, General Beresford-Peirse's command was apparently too remote and inflexible. Also, at Halfaya Pass, the battalion of the 15th Panzer holding the position put up a remarkable fight although almost completely surrounded. Its commander, Captain Wilhelm Bach, formerly a priest in Baden and

Auchinleck replaces Wavell

The defeat of XIII Corps at Halfaya led to the removal of its commander. In London, Churchill decided that the G.H.Q. Cairo needed new inspiration and strength and so replaced Wavell by General Sir Claude Auchinleck, formerly Commander-in-Chief, India. Was Wavell really "exhausted", as Churchill claimed? He certainly had more responsibilities than he would have liked, in view of the lack of resources at his disposal. But nevertheless his successor, who took over on July 5, later told the British historian Correlli Barnett: "Wavell showed no signs of tiredness at all. He was always the same. I think he was first class; in spite of his silences, he made a tremendous impact on his troops. I have a very great admiration for him . . . but he was given impossible tasks."

Perhaps it should be noted that Auchinleck, after his own misfortune in 1942, was not enamoured of Churchill. And Sir Alan Brooke, C.-in-C., Home Forces, wrote in his diary on June 17, 1941 that he entirely disapproved of Churchill's strategy:

"The P.M. began with a survey of the world situation which was interesting. To my horror he informed us that the present Libyan operation is intended to be a large-scale operation! How can we undertake offensive operations on two fronts in the Middle East when we have not got sufficient for one? From the moment we decided to go into Syria we should have put all our strength in the front to complete the operation with the least possible delay. If the operation is not pressed through quickly, it may well lead to further complications."

In fact, Wavell's thinking corresponded exactly with Brooke's concerning orders to move troops to various foreign theatres (Balkans, Crete, Iraq, and Syria), with complete disregard for the principle of concentration of force, as applied in the main areas of Tobruk and Halfaya. Whereas Brooke could only write in his diary at his London H.Q. in St. Paul's School, Wavell would have been failing in his duty as commanding officer if he had not put before Churchill all the dangers involved in the latter's strategy. This is exactly what he did, even offering to resign, in the hope of calling off the operation intended to win Syria from the

△ *Unchallenged masters of the Western Desert after "Battleaxe" – Rommel and his armour.*
◁ Afrika Korps *soldiers in their encampment. After "seeing off" Wavell's ill-starred attack, Rommel drew in his siege lines around Tobruk and prepared for a decisive attack on the perimeter.*

Vichy régime. At the same time he was ordered to speed up preparations for "Battleaxe", of which the government expected no less than the rapid destruction of the *Afrika Korps*. As we know, Wavell finally gave in to Churchill and launched the operation, although disapproving of it in principle. His professional military judgement was, however, entirely vindicated.

It is worth noting that it took over a month for Lieutenant-General Maitland Wilson to overcome the resistance of General Henri Dentz who, in any case, had no intention of fighting to the last man. But the two divisions employed in this Syrian operation could well have been employed in the Western Desert. What would have happened if they had been in position at Sidi Omar to face Rommel? It is, of course, a matter of conjecture, but Rommel's flanking tactics on June 16 and 17 might have ended in failure.

Air Chief Marshal Longmore, commanding the British air forces in the Middle East, was recalled to London and was then given the post of Inspector-General of the R.A.F. His place was taken by Air-Marshal Sir Arthur Tedder, later chosen by Eisenhower to be his Deputy C.-in-C. just before the Normandy landings. Also, the War Cabinet appointed Oliver Lyttelton, formerly President of the Board of Trade, as resident Minister of State in the Middle East. More fortunate than his predecessor, General Auchinleck, relieved of a host of political and administrative duties, was to be able to devote himself entirely to military matters in his own province.

Before examining Auchinleck's operations, we should look briefly at events in Iraq and Syria.

The Iraqi rebellion

At the end of March 1941, the Emir Abdul Illah, Regent of Iraq and a strong supporter of friendship with Britain, had to leave his capital after a rebellion by his premier, Rashid Ali, and a mutiny in the army. On May 2 his partisans attacked Habbānīyah, the large air base on the right bank of the Euphrates some 30 miles from Baghdad. Were the rebels going to cut the pipeline taking oil from the Mosul fields to Haifa? Were they going to occupy Basra, within reach of the Kuwait oil wells and the Abadan refinery? It was a critical time for the British, but the events seemed to have taken both Hitler and Mussolini by surprise. Not until May 23 did the Führer sign his Directive Number 30, ordering the organisation and despatch to Baghdad of a military mission commanded by

▽ Mopping up in Syria after the heavy fighting against the Vichy French defenders: Australians jump from their Bren-gun carrier among the ruins of Palmyra. The Syrian campaign had a tragedy of its own: it saw Frenchman fight Frenchman, Gaullist troops versus Vichy French.
▷ The new rivals in the Middle East: Rommel and Auchinleck. On taking over from Wavell, Auchinleck set himself to the task of proving, in his own words, that Rommel did not represent "anything more than an ordinary German general".

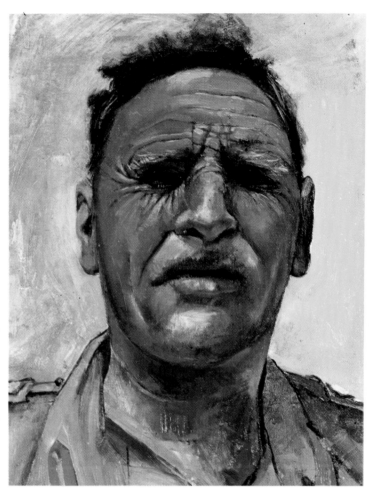

General Hellmuth Felmy. Its task was to prepare for action a unit each of Messerschmitt Bf 109 fighters and of Heinkel He 111 bombers. Mussolini's contribution was a promise to send a few fighters to Iraq.

But by this time Churchill had already seized the initiative. He was aware of Wavell's doubts in Cairo, but in India the Viceroy, Lord Linlithgow, and General Auchinleck diverted to Basra an Indian division previously intended for Malaya. On May 19 a motorised division from Palestine arrived at Habbānīyah, where the rebel siege had been abandoned. On the rebels' surrender, a cease-fire was declared on May 30, and Rashid Ali left for Germany, by way of Iraq and Turkey.

The Syrian affair

Vichy had allowed German aircraft bound for Iraq to refuel at Beirūt, Damascus, and Aleppo. It was expected that the Germans, having taken Crete, would begin the invasion of Cyprus, and so it was not surprising that Churchill decided to force a solution to the Syrian problem.

General de Gaulle supported the proposed operation and provided General Legentilhomme's brigade, comprising six infantry battalions, one field battery, and a light tank company.

For the reasons already mentioned, Wavell was much less forthcoming. Having finally given in to Churchill he ordered into Syria an expeditionary force, commanded by General Maitland Wilson and composed of the 7th Australian Division, the 1st Cavalry Division, the 5th Indian Brigade Group, and the Legentilhomme brigade. Since General Henri Dentz, Vichy commander in Syria, had two divisions, the British force could not be considered a strong one.

In these circumstances, it was not surprising that the operation progressed slowly. It was launched at dawn on June 8, back by a barrage of radio and other propaganda. Engagements took place at Sidon, El Quneitra, on the Damascus road, and around the Palmyra Oasis. The Vichy French troops proved a determined foe. To prevail, Wavell had to draw on some of his last reserves, two brigades of the British 6th Division and the motorised group he had sent to help the defenders of the Habbānīyah base. With these rein-

General Sir Claude Auchinleck had commanded in northern Norway during the abortive campaign of spring 1940. After a spell as G.O.C., Southern Command, in England, he went to India as C.-in-C. in 1941. His prompt despatch of an Indian division to help put down the Iraqi revolt earned him Churchill's approval, and he was the man selected by Churchill to replace Wavell in late June 1941. After settling the problem posed by Vichy Syria, Auchinleck turned to the paramount task of beating Rommel in the Western Desert and resuming the advance on Tripoli begun with so much promise by "Wavell's Thirty Thousand" in December 1940. Forced by his other heavy duties to work from Cairo, he did not hesitate to fly up to the front and take over personal control when the 8th Army found itself in trouble – as it did during "Crusader", its first offensive, in November 1941. But he fell foul of Churchill and was replaced in August 1942.

▷ *General Legentilhomme, who commanded the Gaullist French brigade which advanced into Vichy Syria with the Allied expeditionary force. The Australian troops and Legentilhomme's Free French occupied Damascus on June 21.*

forcements, the Australians and Free French occupied the Syrian capital on June 21.

In his memoirs, General de Gaulle recalls this unhappy campaign:

"The memories evoked in me by the campaign we have been obliged to open are cruel ones. I can still see myself coming and going between Jerusalem, where I had fixed my head-quarters, and our brave troops as they advanced towards Damascus, or else going to visit the wounded in the Franco-British ambulance unit of Mrs. Spears and Dr. Fruchaut. And I heard, gradually, how many of our men, and of the best, were left on the field– how, for instance, General Legentilhomme had been severely wounded, how Colonel Génin and Lieutenant-Commander Détroyat had been killed, how Majors de Chevigné, de Boissoudy, and de Villontreys had been badly hit – and how, on the other side, many good officers and men were falling under our fire – how, on the Litani on June 9th and 10th, before Kiswe on the 12th, and round Quneitra and Izra' on the 15th and 16th, violent fighting had mingled French dead from both camps and those of their British Allies. I felt, towards those who were opposing us on a point of honour, mixed emotions of esteem and commiseration. At a time when the enemy held Paris under his boot, was attacking in Africa, and was infiltrating into the Levant, this courage shown and the losses borne in the fratricidal struggle imposed by Hitler upon leaders who had fallen under his yoke made on me an impression of horrible waste."

Surrender at Acre

On July 10 Dentz, who had lost 6,500 men, most of his aircraft, the destroyer *Chevalier Paul* and the submarine *Souffleur,* sent General de Verdillac to Maitland Wilson, who offered the French representative very honourable terms. The surrender agreement was signed at Acre on July 14, but not without vigorous protest from General de Gaulle, who considered that he had been cheated of his share of the victory. An addition to the agreement, on July 24, gave him the right to the French forces' equipment in the Levant and facilities for recruiting among the 30,000 men who had surrendered. One hundred and twenty-seven officers and 6,000 men were thus induced to join de Gaulle's Free French forces. Writing of this division among the beaten French, de Gaulle said:

"But 25,000 officers, N.C.O.s and men of the French Army and Air Force were finally torn away from us, whereas the great majority would without any doubt have decided to join us if we had had the time to enlighten them. For those Frenchmen who were returning to France with the permission of the enemy, so giving up the possibility of returning there as fighters, were, I knew, submerged in doubt and sadness. As for me, it was with my heart wrung that I gazed at the Vichy transports lying in the harbour and saw them, once loaded, disappear out to sea, taking with them one of the chances of our country."

General de Gaulle had appointed General Catroux his "Delegate-General and Plenipotentiary in the Levant", giving him instructions to negotiate, with the Syrian and Lebanese authorities, a new statute granting the two countries independence and sovereignty but ensuring that they remained allies of France. But propaganda, intrigues and money were already being employed by, among others, Glubb "Pasha" at Palmyra, Commodore Bass in the Jebel ed Drūz, and the chief British liaison officer, General Spears, at Damascus and Beirūt to supplant Vichy and Free France alike. This caused new quarrels between Oliver

Un tank britannique en action dans le Désert Occidental

British field-guns smash a German tank attack at point-blank range in Libya

LA CHUTE DES DICTATEURS EST ASSUREE

BACK THEM UP!

Lyttelton and General de Gaulle. But there was nothing the French could do to prevent the appointment, in January 1942, of General Spears as Minister Plenipotentiary in Syria and the Lebanon. Spears was a former friend of de Gaulle and there is little doubt that what he had to do was not his own personal responsibility but attributable to the Prime Minister and Anthony Eden. In 1945 it was thought in London that the celebrated Colonel T. E. Lawrence's dream of undivided British influence throughout the Arab world was about to become a reality. It did not take long for events to prove that there was no substance in this dream.

Relations between the new C.-in-C. Middle East and Churchill differed very little from those in Wavell's time. On his arrival in Cairo on July 1, Auchinleck received a letter from Churchill apparently giving him complete freedom of action in his own sphere of responsibility. But this

was no more than a façade; Churchill neither expected the C.-in-C. in Cairo to have any other criteria with which to judge the situation than those applied in Downing Street, nor did he envisage any other plans than his own.

And no sooner had Auchinleck demanded three months of preparations and three or four extra divisions (two or three of them armoured), than these two equally determined men found themselves in violent disagreement. At the end of July, Auchinleck was summoned to London to explain his views. His arguments were sound enough to win over the General Staff and the War Cabinet, but, as Churchill's memoirs show, he did not alter the Prime Minister's basic convictions. Nevertheless, Churchill had to bow to the majority and accept that Operation "Crusader", aimed at expelling Rommel from Cyrenaica, should be postponed until the period between September 15 and November 1.

△ By the autumn of 1941, with the Germans driving deeper and deeper into Soviet Russia and Japan on the brink of war, the Middle East was the only theatre where the Allies could hit back at the Axis with any effect. But even so the fighting of 1941 in the Middle East was largely defensive for the Allies; and although the poster on the left proclaimed that "The Downfall of the Dictators is Assured", it certainly did not look imminent as the winter of 1941 approached.

CHAPTER 24
TOBRUK AND MALTA

Before zero hour on the desert front, the British and Australian Governments were involved in an incident with unfortunate consequences. Defeated in Parliament, Mr. Menzies' Liberal Government gave way to a Labour administration headed first by Mr. Fadden, then by Mr. Curtin. Australian opinion had become extremely sensitive following all kinds of alarmist rumours about Tobruk. Anxious to appease public feeling, the new cabinet demanded the immediate relief of the Australians in the garrison.

Whatever he said or did, the Prime Minister had to fall in with this demand, which was put forward in a most truculent manner, for however loyal the Dominions were to the United Kingdom, their relationship was between equals and decisions had to be negotiated, not imposed by Westminster.

Therefore, using periods of the new moon in September and October, a shuttle operation was organised, bringing into Tobruk General S. Kopanski's Polish 1st Carpathian Brigade and the British 70th Division, commanded by Major-General R. M. Scobie, and evacuating to Alexandria the 9th Australian Division and the 18th Australian Infantry Brigade

Group. In spite of the loss of the fast minelayer *Latona,* the operation was completely successful.

Owing to the late arrival in Egypt of the 22nd Armoured Brigade, Auchinleck found that he was obliged to postpone his attack from November 1 to November 18. Churchill has been criticised for his irritation at the delay, but seen in the context of the overall situation, there was some rational justification on his side. He wanted Rommel attacked, beaten, and eliminated in Cyrenaica before a likely German victory in Russia permitted Hitler to drive his Panzers across the Caucasus towards the Persian Gulf and the Red Sea. This is precisely what the Wehrmacht was planning to do.

Malta reinforced

The new delay to "Crusader" had no adverse effect on the progress of the operations, thanks to the pressure exerted on Axis communications in the Mediterranean by the sea and naval air forces of Admirals Cunningham and Somerville. No harm can be done to these remarkable

▽ *A picture from one of a series of posters on the rôle of the Merchant Navy in the war. It claimed that out of every 200 ships that sailed in convoy, 199 arrived safely. In the Mediterranean, however, where shipping came under attack from the air and from Italian and German submarines, the losses were so high that Tobruk had to be supplied by fast warships at night, and organising convoys for Malta became a major naval operation.*

△ Afrika Korps *transport
moves forward over a typically
rugged stretch of the desert. In
these conditions, both sides
encountered grave problems in
trying to organise sufficient
land transport to supply the
front line troops and armoured
units.*

commanders' reputations by pointing out
two circumstances which made their task
easier. In the first place, after the Balkans
campaign X *Fliegerkorps* did not return
to its bases in Sicily but served with
Rommel. In the second place, the Italian
fleet was not permitted to operate beyond
coastal waters. In these conditions, the
three convoys sent to Malta during 1941
lost only one merchant ship out of the
40 which left Gibraltar. Force H came
well out of these dangerous operations,
losing only the cruiser *Southampton* and
the destroyer *Fearless,* though the battleship *Nelson* was seriously damaged on
the "Halberd" convoy in a torpedo attack
by an audacious Italian pilot.

In the same period the aircraft-carrier
Ark Royal, sometimes accompanied by
the *Victorious,* despatched to Malta nearly
300 fighters, most of which reached their
destination. Also, during the summer,
the island's airfields were reoccupied
by a small attacking force of Blenheim
and Wellington bombers. Finally, on
October 21, Captain W. G. Agnew's
Force K–the light cruisers *Aurora* and
Penelope, from Scapa Flow–anchored
in the Grand Harbour. The situation
around Malta now seemed sufficiently
under control for the Admiralty to send
the cruisers *Ajax* and *Neptune* to join
them a few weeks later.

This succession of reinforcements explains why, from August onwards, supplies to the Axis forces in Libya became
more and more unreliable. During
September, 94,000 tons of equipment and
fuel were loaded in Italy, but 26,000 tons
of it went to the bottom. Submarines
operating from Malta took the lion's
share of this destruction. For example, on
September 18 Commander Wanklyn in
Upholder sank with five torpedoes the
two 19,500 ton ships *Oceania* and
Neptunia. Also taking part in this sea
offensive were the Alexandria and
Gibraltar flotillas, including two Dutch
vessels.

The Italian defence was at a disadvantage in this fighting since their
vessels had no asdic of the type used by
British escorts. A few dozen sets were
obtained from Germany during the
summer of 1941, but it took time for them
to be installed and crews trained to use
them, time which was not wasted by their
opponents. On the other hand, minefields
in waters around Malta and Tripoli
accounted for five of the eight British
submarines lost in the Mediterranean in
1941.

In October, losses of supplies between
Italian ports and Tripolitania amounted
to one fifth of the cargoes loaded, and of
12,000 tons of fuel bound for the Axis
forces, 2,500 tons disappeared into the sea.
November was even worse, and for a while
it was thought that Rommel would be
brought to a standstill. In fact, out of a

total of 79,208 tons of supplies loaded in Italy, he lost 62 per cent (49,365 tons). Every episode in the first battle of the convoys cannot be described here, but the disaster of November 9 does deserve mention in some detail.

Nine sinkings in ten minutes

The convoy "*Duisburg*", composed of six merchant ships and a tanker, left from Messina on the afternoon of November 8. It was closely escorted by six destroyers, backed up by the 3rd Cruiser Squadron commanded by Vice-Admiral Brivonesi (*Trento, Trieste,* and four destroyers). At 1645 the convoy was sighted and reported to Malta by a Maryland on patrol. At nightfall Captain Agnew set out with his cruisers and the destroyers *Lance* and *Lively*. Other aircraft, in constant radar contact with the enemy, guided him to the convoy.

Towards 0100, about 155 miles east of Syracuse, the convoy appeared on the radar screens of the British ships, them-

△ *Australian troops embus at dawn in Alexandria after the night trip from Tobruk. Their evacuation was the result of demands from Australia's new Prime Minister, Mr. John Curtin. The increasing independence of the Dominions enabled them to dictate the tactical employment of their expeditionary forces. This strict control had been impossible in World War I.*
▷ *Polish troops of General S. Kopanski's 1st Carpathian Brigade embark in Alexandria for Tobruk. During periods of the new moon in September and October they were shipped with the British 70th Division. The 9th Australian Division and the 18th Infantry Brigade Group were evacuated.*

selves still unseen by the Italians. Less than ten minutes later it was all over, after a barrage of shellfire and torpedoes. The seven merchant ships were sinking, and the destroyer *Fulmine* was going down with them, shattered by a salvo from the *Aurora*. The attack had been so rapid that the 3rd Cruiser Squadron, in any case badly equipped for battle at night, had not time to intervene. On top of all this, near dawn, the destroyer *Libeccio* was sunk by the tireless *Upholder*.

With losses mounting, *Supermarina* tried to ensure delivery of the fuel vital to the Libyan operations by using very fast light cruisers. As a result of this decision, there was another disaster during the night of December 13. Loaded with drums of oil, the cruisers *Alberico da Barbiano* and *Alberto di Guissano* had sailed for Tripoli from Palermo. They were sighted by Malta-based aircraft which transmitted the information to Commander G. H. Stokes, leading four destroyers, including the Dutch vessel *Isaac Sweers,* from Gibraltar to Alexandria. Stokes surprised the two Italian ships off Cape Bon. Their cargo caught fire immediately and most of their crews, including Admiral Toscano, perished. And as if this were not enough, during the same night two brand new merchant ships, *Filzi* and *Del Greco,* were sunk.

In short, post-war statistics show that in the second half of 1941 Italy lost no less than 189 merchant vessels totalling 500,000 tons. On June 10, 1940, taking into account 500,000 tons of Italian shipping frozen in American ports, the Italian merchant fleet had totalled 3,300,000 tons. As a result of these losses, the situation for the Italians by the middle of December was, to say the least, very serious.

Was *Supermarina* betrayed?

When one considers these events, so disastrous for the Axis, the question arises whether they were due to treason committed by a member of *Supermarina* in a key position. This question caused violent arguments in Italy, and ended in the courts. In his book *The Foxes of the Desert,* Paul Carell supports this view, but such serious naval historians as Bragadin and Admiral Bernotti refute it. Methodical modern techniques of enquiry, using evidence from continuous monitoring of enemy radio communica-

tions, tend to leave one sceptical of the theory. Moreover, there were one or more British submarines permanently on the watch outside every port where convoys were formed. Finally, the two incidents already described are proof of the excellent work done by reconnaissance aircraft, operating from Malta with complete impunity.

The French contribution

Italian ships bound for Tripoli had been used to hugging the Tunisian coast in order to avoid the perils waiting for them in the open sea. Thus they were spotted by French observers, who had already carefully recorded the wreckage of Axis units washed ashore at Kerkenna after the battle on April 15 and had also been the first to report the movement of the 15th Panzer Division to Africa. General de Gaulle's men were no longer the only ones passing information to the British. General Weygand, in his memoirs, reveals that Major Navarre, his head of Intelligence, had organised a secret Intelligence system to transmit as quickly as possible the information about Axis convoy movements to Tripolitania obtained on the Tunisian coast by air and naval observers. He was to continue this activity although General Weygand was relieved of his post as the government's Delegate-General in Africa and replaced by General Juin on November 18, 1941.

Cavallero seeks to occupy Tunisia

Marshal Cavallero, Chief-of-Staff at *Comando Supremo,* had not waited until disaster was inevitable before grasping the importance of the port of Bizerta and Tunisian lines of communication. At a meeting at Brenner on June 2 he made his views known to Field-Marshal Keitel. His German colleague was very cool on this question, considering that Cavallero's inclination for strong action would result in the secession of the French Empire, whereas by bargaining with prisoners-of-war and by negotiation, Vichy should be amenable to further concessions. This was also Hitler's view.

▷ Sinking slowly by the stern, an Italian freighter is caught in the shadow of a circling British aircraft. She was sunk by aircraft based at Malta as she worked along the Tunisian coast towards Tripoli.
▽ Life boats are swung out, and a sailor jumps overboard (bottom right) as R.A.F. Blenheims scream in over an Italian timber vessel. Post-war figures showed that Italy lost 189 merchant vessels totalling 500,000 tons, much of it to the fatally efficient team of submarines, surface vessels, and aircraft based on Malta.

Count Ciano met Admiral Darlan at Turin on December 9 and gave no support to the *Comando Supremo*. When Darlan brought up the question of the Tunisian ports the Duce's son-in-law cut him short. He wrote: "I interrupted him to say that I had no intention of talking about this subject and had no instructions to do so." There is no satisfactory explanation for Ciano's negative attitude, so clearly prejudicial to the campaign then being fought.

Rommel's secrecy

Since his victory at Sollum-Halfaya, Rommel had nurtured plans to capture Tobruk. The successes of Force K and Malta-based R.A.F. operations, however, forced him to postpone the attack from week to week. By November 4 everything was at last ready, and he revealed his plans to Marshal Cavallero in Rome.

To take advantage of the full moon, the operation would begin between November 20 and December 4. The evening before the chosen day, the "Brescia" Division would make a strong diversionary attack on the south-west front, thus drawing the defence's reinforcements. The following dawn Rommel would attack the fortress from the south-east with General Crue-well's *Afrika Korps* and General Navar-rini's Italian XXI Corps. He calculated that it would be all over in 48 hours.

After the meeting, Cavallero wrote: "I asked Rommel if he thought the enemy might be able to launch a full-scale attack. He thought not because the enemy would not want to expose their lines of communication to easier interception by the German and Italian divisions. He expected defensive action by relatively few ground forces but with air support."

Was Rommel unaware of General Auchinleck's offensive preparations or did he conceal them from the Italian Chief-of-Staff in case he should be ordered to remain on the defensive? In 1949 this was still an open question, and in the Italian official account we read:

"There was a striking difference in the information supplied by the German and Italian Intelligence services. For reasons that were not very clear, the Germans insisted that the British had no intention of taking the offensive, and considered their Italian colleagues to be 'excessively nervous Latins'." Again, on November 11, Major von Mellenthin, chief of Rommel's Intelligence, discussing the matter with an Italian liaison officer, said: "Major Revetria (chief of Italian Intelligence) is too jumpy. Tell him to calm down, because the British are not going to attack."

In 1955, however, Mellenthin, in his war memoirs, gave the key to the enigma, writing quite candidly: "To allay the fears of the Italians and prevent inter-ference with his plans, Rommel instructed his staff to adopt a confident tone in all discussions with Italian officers, and in November – as the date of our attack drew nearer – I deliberately minimised the possibilities of a British offensive whenever I spoke to our allies."

CHAPTER 25

OPERATION "CRUSADER"

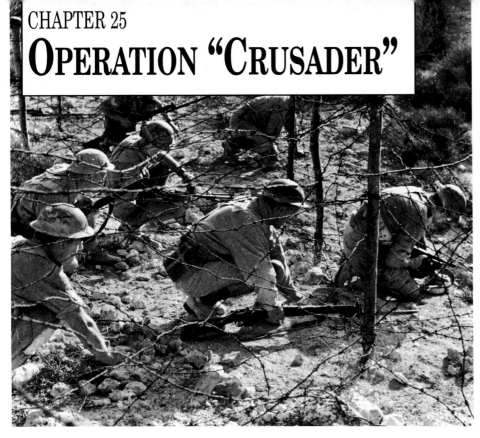

Sir Claude Auchinleck had organised the troops taking part in "Crusader" into the 8th Army, commanded by Lieutenant-General Sir Alan Cunningham, who had just achieved fame for his lightning defeat of the Italians in Abyssinia. Auchinleck had thus some justification for giving him precedence over his colleague Sir Henry Maitland Wilson, in spite of Churchill's disagreement. He had no idea that Cunningham would not be equal to the strain involved in directing a battle between armoured forces. On the day of the battle the 8th Army was deployed as follows:

Tobruk:

70th Division (Major-General R. M. Scobie, who also commanded the whole garrison); Polish 1st Carpathian Infantry Brigade Group (Major-General S. Kopanski); and 32nd Army Tank Brigade (Brigadier A. C. Willison);

Right flank:

XIII Corps (Lieutenant-General A. R.

△ *A fighting patrol returns through the Tobruk perimeter wire. The aggressive garrison was a constant irritant to Rommel, who was preparing to attack the fortress when Operation "Crusader" broke on his main front on November 18, 1941. Many of the defences at Tobruk had been built by the Italians and were captured intact in the early months of the desert war. They were soundly built and resisted both their former owners and the Afrika Korps.*

▷ *Italian anti-aircraft guns in action near Tobruk. Though the garrison had no aircraft of its own, support missions were flown from the main British lines, and the Royal Navy brought in the essential supplies that kept the men alive and fighting.*

Godwin-Austen), made up of:

1. New Zealand Division (Major-General B. C. Freyberg);
2. 4th Indian Division (Major-General F. W. Messervy); and
3. 1st Army Tank Brigade (Brigadier H. R. B. Watkins);

Left flank:

XXX Corps (Lieutenant-General C. W. M. Norrie), made up of:

1. 7th Armoured Division (Major-General W. H. E. Gott);
2. 4th Armoured Brigade Group (Brigadier A. H. Gatehouse);
3. 1st South African Division (Major-General G. L. Brink); and
4. 22nd Guards Brigade (Brigadier J. C. O. Marriott).

This was a completely motorised and partially armoured force, spearheaded by the 7th Armoured Division, which had 469 tanks; this total included 210 Crusaders and 165 American M3 Stuarts.

The British had by no means given up using tanks as infantry support weapons, so the Tobruk garrison and XIII Corps each included an independent brigade equipped with either cruiser or Matilda tanks. In all, 8th Army had 713 gun-armed tanks and could count on over 200 more in reserve to replace any losses.

In the air, Air Vice-Marshal H. Coningham provided the 8th Army with support from the Western Desert Air Force's 16 fighter, eight bomber, and three reconnaissance squadrons. Finally there was Sir Andrew Cunningham, whose fleet's guns were there to give direct support to his brother's operations. This explains the British soldier's characteristically humorous nickname for the operation– "Cunningham, Cunningham, and Coningham".

The Axis deployment might give the impression that Rommel's armour was under the command of General Ettore Bastico and that the "Italian Supreme Commander in North Africa" could control General Gambara's XX Corps. But the impetuous *Panzergruppe Afrika* commander had no intention whatsoever of respecting this chain of command, and went over Bastico's head to appeal directly to the *Comando Supremo,* or even to Hitler, when he did not agree with Cavallero's decisions. The deployment was as follows, under Bastico's overall command:

1. Italian XX Mobile Corps (General Gambara), made up of:
   a. "Ariete" Armoured Division

(General Balotta) and
   b. "Trieste" Motorised Division (General Piazzoni); and
2. *Panzergruppe Afrika* (Rommel), made up of:
   i *Afrika Korps* (Lieutenant-General Ludwig Cruewell), composed of:
      a. 15th Panzer Division (Major-General Walther Neumann-Silkow);
      b. 21st Panzer Division (Major-General Johann von Ravenstein);
      c. *Afrika* Division (Major-General Sommermann); and
      d. "Savona" Division (General de Giorgis); and
   ii Italian XXI Corps (General Enea Navarrini), composed of:
      a. "Brescia' Division (General Zambon);
      b. "Trento" Division (General de Stefanis);
      c. "Bologna" Division (General Gloria); and
      d. "Pavia' Division (General Franceschini).

Panzergruppe Afrika was formed on August 15 and this enabled Rommel to hand over command of the *Afrika Korps* to General Cruewell. The 5th Light Division was renamed 21st Panzer Division, but retained its original composition. The *Afrika* Division comprised only two infantry battalions, recruited from former German volunteers in the French Foreign Legion, to whom Hitler

△ *Major-General Ronald Scobie, garrison commander at Tobruk.*

▷ *Lieutenant-General Ludwig Cruewell, who assumed command of the* Afrika Korps *with Rommel's promotion to the command of* Panzergruppe Afrika. *During the chaotic fighting that took place in the "Crusader" operation he lost contact with Rommel, and narrowly escaped capture by the 6th New Zealand Brigade, but the documents, headquarters equipment, and most of the staff of the* Afrika Korps *were captured on the dawn of November 23.*

▷ *The opening of Operation "Crusader".*

was offering a chance to "make good". At the beginning of December it was renamed the 90th Light Division.

While the Italian XXI Corps was to overrun Tobruk, the *Afrika Korps*–some German units and the whole "Savona" Division–would make contact with the British on the Sidi Omar–Capuzzo–Halfaya–Sollum front. Ready for any eventuality, the 15th and 21st Panzer Divisions were stationed in the Gambut area and further south. Finally, Gambara had placed the "Ariete" Armoured Division around the Bir el Gubi watering place and the "Trieste" Motorised Division around Bir Hakeim.

The Axis forces thus amounted to ten divisions, against the 8th Army's six divisions. But it should not be overlooked that the large Italian units were considerably under-strength and that Rommel's supplies of food and fuel were more and more uncertain. As for the armoured forces, General Cunningham had 713

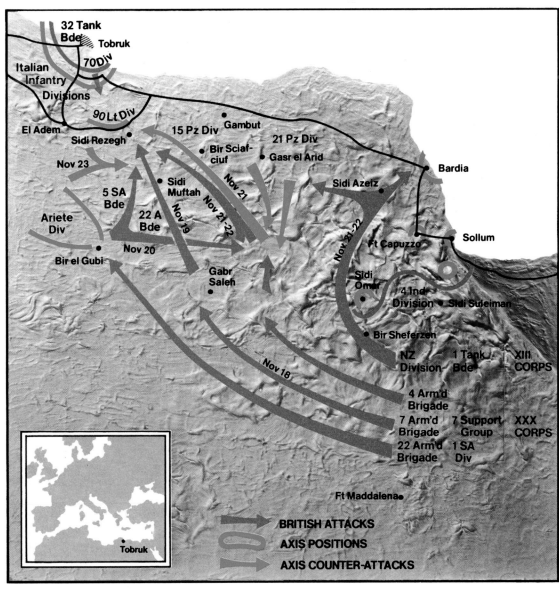

BRITISH ATTACKS
AXIS POSITIONS
AXIS COUNTER-ATTACKS

gun-armed tanks, the Italians 146, and the Germans 174.

These are the approximate figures of the forces involved. But when one gets down to brass tacks the British superiority was reduced by certain technical factors. The Matilda had well-known defects and the Crusaders and other cruisers were subject to frequent mechanical faults. In addition the Stuart or M3, driven by an aero engine requiring a high octane fuel, displayed an alarming tendency to catch fire.

But this is not all. Whereas none of the British tanks had weapons more powerful than 40-mm (37-mm for the American M3), half of the *Afrika Korps'* 139 Pzkw III's were fitted with a 5-cm rather than 3.7-cm gun, and their 35 Pzkw IV's already had a 7.5-cm. Ballistically, the heavier the projectile the more consistent its speed, giving it a longer range and a greater armour-piercing potential. With their 4½-pounder (5-cm) and 15-pounder (7.5-cm)

shells, the Germans had an important advantage over their opponents' 40-mm shells, weighing only two pounds.

On the tactical level, it appears that the Germans had struck a better balance between tanks, infantry, and artillery than the 8th Army, and that their radio communications were more reliable. One should also remember Rommel's formidable defensive weapon–the 8·8-cm anti-aircraft gun. Used in an anti-tank role, it soon became a decisive factor on the battlefields of the Western Desert. The "88" as it was called by the British was notorious, and assumed the status of an all-purpose wonder weapon, which could destroy any British tank at any range. One British officer, captured and under interrogation, expressed the opinion that it was unfair to use anti-aircraft guns against tanks. His captors replied that it was equally unfair for the British to use tanks whose armour nothing but the "88" would penetrate!

▽ *Pzkw III's on the move in the desert. Their 5-cm guns gave them a distinct advantage in the tank versus tank contests fought at long range in North Africa. Such battles resembled naval actions in which the opponents met and manoeuvred over a vast level area. In fighting in which there was no real "front line", commanders needed good communications and a reliable supply of fuel and ammunition–they were also in danger of being captured by advanced enemy units.*

A British Crusader Mk. 1 stops by a burning German Pzkw IV tank during the opening stages of Operation "Crusader". Though the Crusader was admired by the Germans for its high speed (it could reach, and sometimes better, 27 m.p.h.) it was mechanically unreliable, while its armour, unlike that on German tanks, was not face-hardened.

Cunningham's preparations

According to Cunningham's planning, the leading rôle in "Crusader" was to be played by XXX Corps, which would cross the Egyptian-Libyan border near Fort Maddalena and deploy at Gabr Saleh. It was expected that while this was happening, Rommel would have arrived, and a tank battle would then take place, in which the more numerous and better equipped British and South Africans would have the upper hand. Meanwhile, from the south-east, XIII Corps would overrun the frontier position at Sollum– Sidi Omar. With the *Afrika Korps* toppled, XXX Corps would push on vigorously to Sidi Rezegh to join up with the Tobruk garrison, which, on the signal, would break out of the Italian XXI Corps' partial encirclement to meet the British forces advancing from the south-east.

Between Cunningham's two columns, however, there was a 20-mile gap, which would widen as Godwin-Austen's XIII Corps moved north and Norrie's XXX Corps headed north-west. Fearing an outflanking movement on his left, Godwin-Austen therefore demanded, and secured, an intermediary column, which was

drawn, however, from Norrie's force. Norrie was far from pleased with this decision which, in the event, was an unfortunate one. The resulting diversion of the 4th Armoured Brigade meant that the 7th Armoured Division lost a third of its strength, 165 Stuarts, and was thus weakened in what was intended to be its decisive rôle.

This was the first setback to the operation, even before it had begun. When the attack got under way at dawn on November 18, in torrential rain, Rommel's reaction caused a second setback. Ready to attack Tobruk, he saw the British move as no more than a reconnaissance in strength and kept his armoured forces around Gambut, whereas Cunningham was waiting for him at Gabr Saleh. On top of all this, a third setback occurred with the capture of no less than the 8th Army operations orders, carelessly brought to the front by a British officer. This happened on November 19 when the 22nd Armoured Brigade, equipped with the new Crusader tanks (7th Armoured Division) was defeated in its attempt to take Bir el Gubi, bitterly defended by the "Ariete" Armoured Division. This fourth setback cost the British about 50 tanks.

XXX Corps did, however, reach Sidi

Rezegh, although weakened for the reasons already explained. There it met a counter-attack by the *Afrika Korps*, strengthened by the Italian XXI Corps, ordered in by Mussolini himself at Rommel's direct request. Saturday, November 22 was a black day for Willoughby Norrie. His 7th Armoured Brigade was reduced to 10 effective tanks, and the 22nd Armoured Brigade was little better off with only 34. On the next day, the German onslaught smashed into the 5th South African Brigade, the 22nd Armoured Brigade was reduced to some 12 tanks, and Sidi Rezegh was lost.

If Rommel had followed up this important success against XXX Corps he could probably have wiped it out. But this chance was not enough for him; he was after the destruction of the whole of 8th Army. To do this, he brought 15th and 21st Panzer Divisions under his direct command, left Lieutenant-Colonel Siegfried Westphal, head of the operations section, in charge of the *Panzergruppe* H.Q., and set off with his Chief-of-Staff, Major-General Alfred Gause, and 100 tanks to reach the Mediterranean by way of Sidi Omar and strike the British in the rear.

▽ *A dead German crewman lies beside a captured Pzkw IV. Rommel lost 142 of the 174 tanks which he commanded at the beginning of "Crusader". 32,000 prisoners, 9,000 of them Germans, were taken in two months by the 8th Army, which itself lost 18,000 men. It was a victory for the 8th Army, but one which they were unable to follow up. Another two years of thrust and parry would be needed before the Afrika Korps finally surrendered at Cape Bon.*

◁ *Huddled in a shell scrape (a shallow and very temporary weapon pit) the crew of a Vickers machine gun opens fire in the chilly desert dawn. The Vickers machine gun was nearly 57 years old in 1939, and with some small modifications it would soldier on to 1965. It was awkward, heavy, and cumbersome, but utterly reliable. It needed 7½ pints of water to cool the barrel, and this presented an additional supply problem in the desert.*

Auchinleck perseveres

For Cunningham, in his Maddalena H.Q., the reversals occurring since November 19 were an immense strain, and seemed to offer sufficient justification for an order to retreat. But in the evening of the 23rd, Sir Claude Auchinleck appeared in his mobile caravan H.Q. and ordered him to continue the attack. Auchinleck later wrote: "My opinion was different from Cunningham's. I thought Rommel was probably in as bad shape as we were, especially with Tobruk unvanquished behind him, and I ordered the offensive to continue. I certainly gambled (in fact, by going on we might have lost all) and Cunningham might very well have proved to be right and I wrong!"

At the same moment, his opponent, writing to his wife, claimed to be "well, in excellent spirits and full of confidence." In spite of this, Rommel's raid in the British rear did not succeed in upsetting Auchinleck. "He is making a desperate effort but he won't get very far," he said to Cunningham on November 24. At the end of his order of the day to his troops he told them:

"His position is desperate, and he is trying by lashing out in all directions to distract us from our object, which is to destroy him utterly. We will NOT be distracted and he WILL be destroyed. You have got your teeth into him. Hang on and bite deeper and deeper and hang on till he is finished. Give him NO rest. The general situation in NORTH AFRICA is EXCELLENT. There is only one order: ATTACK AND PURSUE. ALL OUT EVERYONE."

But as he suspected that Cunningham was in no condition to carry out this aggressive plan, he replaced him, on November 26, by his own Deputy Chief-of-Staff, Major-General Neil Methuen Ritchie. The former chief of Intelligence in the *Panzergruppe Afrika,* in his book *Panzer Battles,* said of this action by Auchinleck at this most critical moment: "This was certainly one of the most important decisions of the war. Auchinleck's will to attack and his strategy of penetration saved 'Crusader' and much else besides." This is a sound judgement.

Although Ritchie took over from Cunningham it was Auchinleck who directed the battle.

A 15-cm gun in action. The siege of Tobruk absorbed much of the Axis heavy artillery then available in North Africa.
▷ △ Victors in Operation "Crusader", a group of British and French soldiers display a tattered Swastika flag on top of a captured Pzkw IV.
▷ ▽ A 15-cwt truck of the 8th Army's XXX Corps reaches the Libyan border with Egypt. Both sides used captured armoured and soft-skinned vehicles.

On November 25 Scobie received a telegram informing him that the New Zealand Division would attempt to take Sidi Rezegh the next day. The garrison was then expected to occupy El Duda. Scobie launched a new attack on the morning of November 26. After a fierce struggle his infantry overcame the final centre of resistance called "Wolf". But there was still no sign of the arrival of the New Zealanders. At 1300 hours the garrison saw tanks on the horizon, and from one of their turrets three red rockets soared into the blue sky.

The troops cheered wildly, for it was the recognition signal of the 8th Army. Reinforcements were at last in sight!

Rommel decides to retreat

Writing to his wife on their silver anniversary, Rommel described his action behind the British lines as a "magnificent success" calling for a "special communiqué" from O.K.W. But he was undoubtedly alone in this view. For not only

had he not overcome the 4th Indian Division's stubborn resistance or captured the 8th Army's supply dumps, but he had also left the *Panzergruppe* without orders for four days, unconcerned that a few hours after his reckless departure he had lost his mobile radio, broken down in the desert.

Liddell Hart's description of this incident in his presentation of Rommel's notebooks gives some idea of the life led in the desert by the commanders themselves:

"A wireless signal from Rommel summoned the commander of the Afrika Korps to the Panzer Group's forward H.Q., which was said to be located near Gambut. After searching for a long time in the darkness they finally discovered a British lorry, which General Cruewell's command car approached with great caution. Inside it, to his good fortune, were no British troops, but Rommel and his Chief-of-Staff, both of whom were unshaven, worn with lack of sleep and caked with dust. In the lorry was a heap of straw as a bed, a can of stale water to drink and a few tins of food. Close by were two wireless trucks and a few dispatch riders. Rommel now gave his instructions for next day's operations."

Meanwhile, XIII Corps had succeeded where XXX Corps had failed. The New Zealand Division, moving through Belhamed, had made contact with the Tobruk garrison, which itself had broken out at El Duda.

With the situation becoming more critical, Lieutenant-Colonel Westphal took it upon himself to pass over the head of his untraceable chief and recall to the Tobruk sector the 21st Panzer Division, which was unattached south of Sollum. When he returned to his H.Q. on November 27, Rommel tacitly endorsed this initiative and without any pause mounted a new operation designed to bring him victory. Some very confused engagements followed, during which the New Zealand Division was cut in two and part of it thrown back to Tobruk. The Germans were becoming exhausted, however, and the 21st Panzer Division's commander, General von Ravenstein, was captured in the confusion.

Auchinleck's reinforcement of the 8th Army had been timely, and the rapidly reorganised XXX Corps again made its presence felt in the battle. Rommel, on the other hand, had to rely on a mere

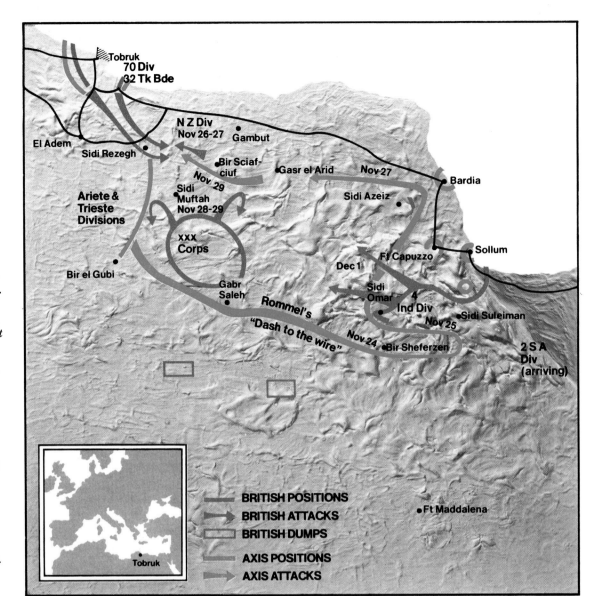

The map includes the following labels: Tobruk, 70 Div, 32 Tk Bde, El Adem, Sidi Rezegh, N Z Div Nov 26-27, Gambut, Bir Sciaf-ciuf, Gasr el Arid, Nov 27, Bardia, Ariete & Trieste Divisions, Sidi Muftah Nov 28-29, Nov 29, Sidi Azeiz, XXX Corps, Ft Capuzzo, Sollum, Dec 1, Sidi Omar, 4 Ind Div, Sidi Suleiman, Bir el Gubi, Gabr Saleh, Rommel's "Dash to the wire", Nov 25, Nov 24, Bir Sheferzen, 2 S A Div (arriving), Ft Maddalena, Tobruk

BRITISH POSITIONS
BRITISH ATTACKS
BRITISH DUMPS
AXIS POSITIONS
AXIS ATTACKS

▷ *Rommel's unsuccessful attempt to prevent the relief of Tobruk by attacking the rear of Auchinleck's army in November 1941.*

▷ △ *A Bf 110 fighter lands in a cloud of sand on an Italian-built airfield in North Africa. All engines suffered from the sand and heat, but aero engines were particularly vulnerable and needed special filters.*

▷ ▽ *A standard bearer of Jagdgeschwader 27 at a ceremonial parade. It was in this wing that Hans-Joachim Marseille scored most of his 158 kills. Marseille was the 30th ranking German ace.*

▽ *Luftwaffe medical orderlies operating a water purification plant. Fresh water was needed for both men and vehicles and little was available for washing. Only sea bathing gave them a chance for a complete clean-up.*

handful of tanks in the decisive days that lay ahead. He had been warned that no supplies of any consequence could be delivered before the latter half of December. So on December 5 he withdrew his forces attacking east of Tobruk, and the next day, after a counter-attack had failed, gave the order for a general retreat. He left to the "Savona" Division the honour of holding out as long as possible in the Bardia–Sollum–Halfaya area.

Axis disagreement

The previous summer, while waiting for a British offensive, the Germans and Italians had agreed to make an all-out defensive stand on the heights of Aïn el Gazala if it became impossible to hold the frontier. General Bastico now wanted to stick to this plan, as it had the advantage of covering Benghazi. Rommel, how-

ever, insisted that to stand on this line would risk the loss of Tripolitania without even saving Cyrenaica. In his view, as a result of British superiority, the retreat should be extended to Derna–Mechili; but he really wanted to move back to the area of Mersa Brega, which he had left on March 31.

On December 8, 14, and 17 these differences of opinion led to dramatic exchanges between the two commanders and their general staffs. During the first of these Rommel became excited and, according to the testimony of Lieutenant-Colonel Ravajoli exclaimed "that he had fought to win for three weeks, and that now he had decided to take his divisions to Tripoli and seek internment in Tunisia."

In order to win over the Italians to his argument in favour of a retreat he had no hesitation in using false information – now 2,000 or 3,000 motor vehicles sighted south of Sidi Barrani, now a convoy reported in Tobruk waters. On December 17 he succeeded in obtaining freedom of action from Cavallero, who had arrived with Field-Marshal Kesselring from Rome. They both strongly opposed the retreat from Derna; Rommel, however, said that his orders had already been issued, and in some cases were actually being carried out.

The British enter Benghazi

Whatever judgement one makes about Rommel's methods, the basic soundness of his decision must be admitted. Moreover he conducted the retreat in a masterly fashion, dealing sharp blows to the British whenever they became too hurried in pursuit. On Christmas Day, General Ritchie's advance guard entered Benghazi. But as the year ended, the 8th Army had not succeeded in intercepting

Rommel, although desert patrols had occupied the Jalo oasis. He was now securely in position behind the El Agheila–Marada strongpoint, leaving behind him 340 tanks destroyed since November 18. On January 17 the "Savona" Division, its food and ammunition exhausted, surrendered to General Villiers, commander of the 2nd South African Division, which had relieved the 4th Indian Division. 32,000 prisoners, 9,000 of them Germans, were taken by the 8th Army in two months. The 8th Army itself had lost 18,000 in killed, wounded and prisoners.

In Washington, Churchill was jubilant over this limited, but undeniable, victory. In a few weeks' time, he thought, Auchinleck would begin Operation "Acrobat", which would complete the destruction of the Axis forces in North Africa and take Ritchie from El Agheila to the Tunisian frontier. Then, under the agreement just reached with President Roosevelt, Operation "Gymnast" would be launched. With or without the consent of the Vichy Government, an Anglo-American expeditionary force would invade Morocco and Algeria.

Hitler reinforces the Mediterranean

For various reasons, the Mediterranean situation then changed, upsetting British plans.

First, Hitler was rightly concerned about the way things were developing and decided to send a submarine force there, just at the time when he seemed in sight of success in the battle of the Atlantic. From the outset, this move proved to be profitable, since on November 13 *U-81* (Lieutenant Guggenberger) sank the aircraft-carrier *Ark Royal* near

Gibraltar just after she had despatched another load of fighters to Malta. As *Illustrious, Formidable,* and *Indomitable* were still undergoing repairs in the United States, the only modern vessel in this class the Admiralty had was *Victorious.* Some 60 miles north of Sollum, *U-331* (Lieutenant von Tiesenhausen) succeeded in hitting the battleship *Barham* with three torpedoes, and this proud veteran of the Battle of Jutland disappeared in a terrible explosion, with 861 officers, petty officers, and men. Destroyers picked up 450 survivors, including Vice-Admiral Pridham-Wippell, who had distinguished himself at Cape Matapan. Finally, on December 14, not far from Alexandria, the light cruiser *Galatea* was destroyed by *U-557* (Lieutenant Paulsen).

Enter Kesselring

Hitler's assistance to his ally did not stop there. With the Italians' agreement he signed Directive No. 38 on December 2, ordering a unified command of the Axis forces in the central Mediterranean under a Supreme Commander "South" (*Oberbefehlshaber Süd*).

This was Field-Marshal Kesselring, commander of *Luftflotte* II. He was given a three-fold task:

"To win mastery of the air and sea in the area between Southern Italy and North Africa in order to ensure communications with Libya and Cyrenaica, and particularly to neutralise Malta. Secondly, to co-operate with the German and allied forces operating in North Africa. Thirdly, to paralyse enemy movements in the Mediterranean, including supplies to Tobruk and Malta, working in close co-operation with the available German and Italian naval forces."

Kesselring took command of the Luftwaffe air and anti-aircraft units already in the Mediterranean, and was reinforced by II *Fliegerkorps* (General Loerzer), withdrawn from the Eastern Front. So the Soviet allies obtained some benefit from British strategy between Malta and Suez.

But these were only half measures by Hitler, for the Supreme Commander "South", or O.B.S. as he was abbreviated, was nowhere in the same class as Eisenhower, Nimitz, or MacArthur when it came to commanding a whole theatre of war. In fact, *Panzergruppe Afrika* refused to acknowledge his supreme authority, thus very likely prejudicing the outcome of Axis operations. It remained to be proved that this Bavarian, a former artilleryman turned pilot, had a better overall conception of modern combined operations than the Württemberger, a former mountain infantryman converted to tanks. In addition, subordinate to the *Comando Supremo*, O.K.W., and even *Reichsmarschall* Göring, Kesselring's position was a most ambiguous one. In spite of all this, he was still able to redress the balance in the central Mediterranean for a time.

▽ *A British 6-inch howitzer in action near Tobruk. It was not until the battle of El Alamein that British artillery would be used in numbers sufficient to allow centralised control: the 25-pounder was called upon to act as a long range anti-tank gun, while the communication and location system that allowed gunners to conduct effective counter-battery fire was dismantled. Artillery regiments were parcelled out to brigades, and batteries to defended localities.*

Aid from Japan

Japan's entry into World War II, especially the invasion of Malaya and the threat to Singapore, also played its part in the change in the Mediterranean balance. In Washington, the American President and the British Premier decided that, in spite of the Pearl Harbor and the Kuantan disasters, Germany was still to be considered as the prime enemy. Therefore, until Germany was beaten, the Allies would adopt an opportunist, wait-and-see policy in the Far East war. The Australian Government did not share this view. If Roosevelt could impose his own policy on Admiral Nimitz and General MacArthur, it did not follow that Churchill could do likewise with Mr. Curtin's troublesome government.

So the 6th and 7th Australian Divisions, which it had been hoped would take part in Operation "Acrobat", left the Middle East for good, and the British 70th Division embarked for Singapore. Again, the formation of a new squadron, to defend communications in the Indian Ocean against possible action by the Japanese fleet, prevented the Admiralty from making good the considerable losses sustained by the Mediterranean Fleet.

The naval balance begins to swing

During the night of December 18 and 19, Force K was pursuing an Italian convoy heading for North Africa when it ran into a minefield. *Neptune* struck four

△ *Field-Marshal Albert Kesselring, who as Supreme Commander "South" or O.B.S., was Rommel's superior. In his dealings with the Italians and the defence of southern Italy he was to prove himself both a diplomat and strategist; but Panzergruppe Afrika was reluctant to acknowledge his supreme authority. He is seen here leaving a Dornier Do 17 on a visit to Luftwaffe units in North Africa.*

△ *"December 1941: All's well . . ." so reads the caption to this Illingworth cartoon. The attack on Pearl Harbor, which would give Japan temporary dominance in the Pacific, is discreetly shown in the bottom right of the globe. Even the German defeats in North Africa and Russia would be redressed in the spring offensives of 1942. But the supply of arms from the United States would grow with the defeat of the U-boat menace.*

mines in succession and sank with all her crew except one leading seaman. *Aurora* and *Penelope* survived, but were so badly damaged that they remained unseaworthy for many long weeks. The destroyer *Kandahar* made a courageous attempt to help *Neptune* but her stern was blown off by another mine and she sank on the spot.

Italian human torpedoes

Also on December 18, at 2100 hours, with admirable precision, the Italian submarine *Sciré* (Lieutenant Valerio Borghese) managed to launch three manned torpedoes less than one and a half miles from the lighthouse overlooking Alexandria's main channel. Seated astride their machines, in pairs, the six daring

men slipped in behind a returning group of destroyers and aimed for their allotted targets: De la Penne and Bianchi for *Valiant,* Marceglia and Schergat for *Queen Elizabeth,* and Martellota and Marino for the large tanker *Sagona.* Once under the hulls of their targets, they removed the explosive warheads of their torpedoes, suspended them from the bottom of the vessels and set the detonators. All this was done in pitch darkness over 30 feet below the surface.

Sagona blew up first, at dawn on December 20. Then came *Valiant,* with De la Penne and Bianchi aboard. They had been picked up during the night but had uttered no word about their mission, of which they might have been the first victims. At about 0625 hours, Admiral Cunningham was on the rear deck of *Queen Elizabeth* inspecting the damage to *Valiant* when the explosion from Marceglia and Schergat's torpedo flung him four or five feet in the air.

As Roskill points out, "both battleships were seriously flooded and incapacitated for many months. Fortunately it was possible to keep them on even keels and the enemy's . . . air reconnaissance failed to reveal the full measure of success achieved." But it would be months before they rejoined the fleet, and meanwhile, apart from destroyers Cunningham had no more than four light cruisers under his command, including the old anti-aircraft cruiser *Carlisle.* The Italian Navy, thanks to its mines and midget submarines, had gained, in a single night, a considerable advantage in the Mediterranean. It is true, however, that it did not have enough supplies of oil fuel to make use of this advantage, and so the situation continued to deteriorate in 1942.

Crisis point for Allied seapower

Taking a general view of all the theatres of operations, it can be concluded that between November 25 and December 20, 1941, the Anglo-American forces had lost five of their 33 major vessels, and eight others were out of commission for some months. It may be argued that aircraft-carriers were taking the place of battleships. This is no doubt true, but Japan led the field in this category, with ten to her nearest rival's eight.

CHAPTER 26

THE RAIDERS RETURN

In his memoirs, Winston Churchill sums up the strategic situation as he saw it at the end of 1941 thus:

"Amid the torrent of violent events one anxiety reigned supreme. Battles might be won or lost, enterprises might succeed or miscarry, territories might be gained or quitted, but dominating all our power to carry on the war, or even keep ourselves alive, lay our mastery of the ocean routes and the free approach and entry to our ports."

Though written after the war, these words are not the product of hindsight, but express exactly the feelings of the wartime British leader as he prepared to face up to the menace of the U-boats and the four-engined Focke-Wulf Fw 200 Condor; although this does not mean to say that all the measures he took to eliminate the threat were equally effective, as we shall have occasion to point out later. But Churchill was never the one to commit himself half-heartedly.

Churchill and the "Battle of the Atlantic"

Proof of this is contained in his order of March 6, 1941, concerning the conduct of what he called "The Battle of the Atlantic", for the purpose of waging which he established that same day a standing committee. This brought together three times a week representatives of the Transport Department of the Admiralty, and of the Ministries of Transport and Shipping. To this new body fell the task of recommending measures necessary "to defeat the attempt to strangle our food supplies and our connection with the United States."

The Prime Minister naturally expected that among the means that Germany would use to attain these objectives, would figure prominently the renewed bombing by the Luftwaffe of Clydeside, Merseyside, and the Bristol Channel, since this was where American war supplies were being landed – and where the unloading and distribution operations were falling further and further behind schedule. Furthermore, one and a half million tons of merchant shipping were lying idle for lack of repair. Churchill therefore ordered the immediate strengthening of anti-aircraft defences in all the west coast ports.

Germany's answer to "Lend-Lease"

And indeed, during the early days of March, it certainly looked as if Hitler and Göring were going to follow this strategy. The results were sobering.

On March 13 and 14, Clydeside, which up till then had got off rather lightly, was subjected to the merciless attacks of the Luftwaffe; in fact, so fierce were the attacks upon Greenock and Glasgow that some shipyards remained closed until June, and others even until November. This "second edition" of the Blitz reached its height between May 1 and May 7, when, for seven successive nights, German bombers implacably pounded Liverpool and the adjoining Merseyside ports. Not only were there 3,000 dead and wounded as a result; in addition, 69 of the 144 mooring bays were put out of action, and the unloading capacity of the area reduced by 75 per cent for some weeks after.

Thus the shattering effects of this aerial bombardment of western port installations, combined with the successes achieved on the high seas by U-boats, Focke-Wulf Condors, and the surface raiders, added up to an effective reply to the "Lend-Lease" law promulgated by President Roosevelt on March 11, 1941. And yet, from May 13 onwards, after one last massive attack on London, the Luftwaffe relaxed the pressure it had – especially over the past few months, when the western ports had been the chief victims – been exerting on Britain. Some 43,381 civilians had been killed and 50,856 seriously injured; but the respite thus granted by the calling-off of the bombing was to last more than three years, until the launching of the first V-1 flying bombs on June 13, 1944.

It is of course, true that the implementation of Operation "Barbarossa" inevitably entailed the transfer of the bulk of the Luftwaffe from the West to the East, if the Russian giant was to be laid low before the onset of winter. Nevertheless, writing about this piece of good fortune in his memoirs, Churchill affirmed that if the Germans had continued their attacks against Britain, the Battle of the Atlantic would have been even more tightly fought. And in 1954, discussing this aspect of the conflict, Captain S. W. Roskill, the Royal

△ *Britain's Admiral Sir Percy Noble, who became C.-in-C., Western Approaches, in February 1941. His Admiralty brief was "the protection of trade, the routing and control of the outward and homeward-bound ocean convoys and measures to combat any attacks on convoys by U-boats or hostile aircraft within his command".*
▽ *Germany's Admiral Karl Dönitz.*

Navy's official historian, asked this question:

"If Hitler, instead of attacking Russia, had concentrated the full weight of his air power against our commercial ports, our docks and dockyards, our unloading and storage facilities, our coastal shipping and river estuaries, and had he kept the might of the Luftwaffe so directed for months on end if need were, could this country have survived?"

British defences strengthened

At all events, the Prime Minister, confronted with the growing menace of the Focke-Wulf aircraft, gave top priority to equipping the Merchant Navy with anti-aircraft weapons, the Admiralty providing the necessary gun crews. In addition, Fighter Command was given orders to release 50 fighters and pilots for convoy escort duty; these planes were to be installed on catapults on board merchantmen, from which they would take off on sighting a Condor; they would shoot it down and then ditch in the sea themselves, there to wait until one of the escort vessels came to pick them up—a procedure which inevitably resulted in the loss of the aircraft, and, very often, in that of the pilot's life. When escort aircraft-carriers, intended for convoy duty, came into operation, these expensive Catapult Aircraft Merchantmen were abandoned.

Facing up to Admiral Dönitz's U-boats in June 1941, the British defences were better equipped than a year earlier, thanks to the successful carrying out of the war production programme, and also to the additional help of the U.S.A. At his Liverpool base, where he had taken over command of Western Approaches on February 17, Sir Percy Noble had available for convoy escort duties 248 destroyers (59 of which were, in fact, being refitted and therefore unusable), 99 corvettes (small ships of 950 tons, admirably suited to this task, but the last word in discomfort), 48 sloops (ten of which had just been given to Britain by Washington under the recent "Lend-Lease" Act, for the duration of hostilities), and 300 miscellaneous small craft. It should be noted, however, that as a result of the arduous tasks they were called upon to perform, a large proportion of them were out of

The Short Sunderland flying-boats flown by R.A.F. Coastal Command were invaluable tools in the Battle of the Atlantic. The Sunderland had a normal range of 2,980 miles and could carry up to 2,000 lbs of bombs. It also bristled with defensive armament, so much so that it earned the respectful Luftwaffe nickname of fliegende Stachelschwein – "flying porcupine".
◁ *A Sunderland circles protectively over a stricken merchantman.*

Bismarck's Agony

The German battleship *Bismarck's* armament consisted of eight 15-inch guns in four two-gun turrets and excellent ranging equipment. Secondary armament consisted of twelve 5.9-inch, sixteen 4.1-inch A.A., and sixteen 3.7cm A.A. guns. On the evening of May 20 *Bismarck*, accompanied by the heavy cruiser *Prinz Eugen*, passed through the Kattegat and emerged into the North Sea. On the evening of May 21, Vice-Admiral L.E. Holland's Battle-Cruiser Squadron consisting of the battle-cruiser *Hood*, battleship *Prince of Wales* and six destroyers, was ordered to sail from Scapa Flow to Hvalfjord. On May 22 the main British fleet sailed from Scapa Flow under Admiral Tovey, consisting of the battleship *King George V*, aircraft carrier *Victorious*, four cruisers and seven destroyers. The battle-cruiser *Repulse* joined them later. On May 23 the Battle-Cruiser squadron sighted *Bismarck* and *Prinz Eugen*. At 0600 *Hood* was hit by a 15-inch salvo from *Bismarck* and blew up. Captain Leach of the *Prince of Wales* broke off the engagement and 0613 after being fired upon. His ship was not in full running order when ordered to sail.

action at any one time.

The escort vessels were fitted with the first radar equipment, which, though rather primitive, was quite effective in countering the enemy submarines' favourite tactic – the night surface attack. We are thus poised on the threshold of that escalation of this campaign, in which the final word went to the Allies.

Coastal Command's task

Though still part of the R.A.F., Coastal Command was placed under the operational control of the Admiralty from April 1941: a hybrid solution which goes far to explaining why Coastal Command was always at the end of the queue when it came to receiving new equipment, whether produced at home or supplied by the United States. A second explanation is

and the North Sea, to observe and harry German ships sheltering in Brest harbour, to lay mines, and to weed out raiders operating in the Atlantic. In short, July 1941 saw Air Chief-Marshal Sir Philip Joubert de la Ferté, who had just taken over from Sir Frederick Bowhill as the head of Coastal Command, having to carry out a great variety of tasks with insufficient resources.

At the same time, R.A.F. Coastal Command's Short Sunderland and Consolidated PBY Catalina flying boats, as well as Lockheed Hudson bombers, were being fitted with radar, sometimes combined with a searchlight.

The wrong targets

While Bomber Command made futile efforts to knock out German submarines

(page 250) △ *A U-boat commander sweeps the horizon through his periscope.*
(page 250) ▽ *Dönitz and his staff ponder their next move. Apart from co-ordinating the movements of the U-boats at sea into an overall strategy, Dönitz fought a constant and unsuccessful battle with the Luftwaffe for more long-range patrolling aircraft.*

▽ *In the U-boat base at Lorient on the Biscay coast, one of the "grey wolves" is overhauled on the slip.*

that top priority was being given to Bomber Command, which was expected by the Chief of Air Staff, Sir Charles Portal, by the Air Minister, Sir Archibald Sinclair, and by the Prime Minister to cripple German industrial production, especially the submarine shipyards, in an impossibly short space of time.

In any case, the fight against the U-boat menace, though a high priority, was only one of the tasks which Coastal Command had to carry out. It had also to attack enemy shipping in the Channel

lying at their bases – Bremen, Hamburg, and Kiel – it proceeded to ignore the U-boat shelters then being built at Lorient, Saint Nazaire, Brest, la Pallice, and Bordeaux, which might have been more profitable targets. When, via the Free French "Rémy" network, Lieutenant Philippon sent a message from Brest to London, pointing out the magnitude of the work being carried out, and how important it was to attack these sites, London loftily replied, according to Jacques Mordal: "These bases will be attacked when they are finished." In Mordal's opinion, this was a woeful error of judgement, since the horizontal protection to these pens comprised two 12-feet thick layers of concrete, and as the pens themselves were also well-protected with A.A. guns, they stood up to all that the British and American air forces could throw at them.

Britain's losses

From a consideration of Great Britain's defences, let us now look at her losses, especially as we have the memoirs of Admirals Raeder and Dönitz, and also the historical works of Vice-Admiral Assmann and Captain Gerhard Bidlingmaier to help us.

Statistics published after the war, in the British official history, *The War at Sea*, demonstrate that the year 1941 cost Allied and neutral shipping 1,299 ships, displacing 4,328,558 tons, an increase of 240 ships and some 340,000 tons over 1940. If we split up these figures according to the way the losses were incurred, we find that losses to submarine action were down slightly, to 2,171,754 tons, as against the 2,186,158 tons of 1940. On the other hand the Luftwaffe considerably increased its total of tonnage destroyed, from 580,074 to over one million, though it has to be remembered that in April and May the evacuation of Greece, and then of Crete, had cost British shipping dear. This makes it easier to understand why, until the Stukas could be eliminated, the British High Command was so reserved in discussing plans for a European second front, which Harry Hopkins and General Marshall had submitted for its consideration, with the enthusiastic backing of President Roosevelt, as early as the spring of 1942.

The tonnage sunk by surface warships, including camouflaged surface raiders, was almost the same for both years, and the menace of the magnetic mine, which made its first appearance in November 1939, was greatly reduced and no longer represented a real threat: 13 per cent of all ships destroyed in 1940, but only $5\frac{1}{2}$ per cent in 1941.

Since Admiral Raeder's staff calculated that British and Canadian shipyards produced 1,600,000 tons annually, Allied shipping thus sustained for 1941 a net loss of 2,700,000 tons, excluding ships that were out of service for repair. However,

the Japanese attack on Pearl Harbor and the declaration of war by Germany and Italy on the U.S.A. on December 11, 1941, placed the enormous resources of the American shipyards, estimated by the Germans at more than 5,000,000 tons for 1942, at the disposal of Great Britain–a major turning-point in the Battle.

Now that the weight of American industry was tipping the scale in Britain's favour, the task of the U-boats became commensurately more difficult. The amount of shipping they had to sink to sever Britain's supply lines suddenly rose to a far higher figure.

The wolf-packs attack

At the beginning of 1942, Admiral Dönitz, from his command post at Kernével near Lorient, had 22 submarines operating under his orders, while another 67, based on Gotenhafen, as the Germans now called Gdynia, were carrying out their trials in the Baltic. For the first two months of the year, the heavy storms which lashed the North Atlantic severely limited the number of U-boat successes, just as they made it impossible for the British convoy escorts to sink a single submarine. March enabled the two adversaries to resume the struggle in more normal conditions; 41 British and Allied vessels (243,021 tons) were torpedoed and sunk by Dönitz's wolf packs.

This success was, however, dearly bought. Five U-boats were sunk, three of them by the five destroyers and two corvettes which, under the command of Captain Donald Macintyre, were escorting convoy H.X. 112. Besides these, on March 18, *U-47*, commanded by Günther Prien, famous for his Scapa Flow exploit and credited with 28 ships sunk as well as *Royal Oak*, was lost with all hands to an attack by the destroyer *Wolverine*. The first attack on the submerged submarine had bent its propeller shafts. According to Captain Macintyre's account:

"Surfacing after dark in the hope of escaping the destroyer, which had clung persistently to an intermittent asdic contact, the submarine's propellers emitted a rattle clearly to be heard on *Wolverine*'s asdic, leading her accurately to the target. Further depth-charge attacks shattered *U-47*'s hull. A vivid flash and an explosion from the depths told of her end, confirmed as wooden debris floated to the surface."

Disastrous losses

During the night of March 15–16, U-boats succeeded in sinking five of convoy H.X. 112's merchantmen and tankers. But the destroyer *Vanoc*, thanks to her radar, managed to locate, ram, and sink *U-100*, whose captain, Joachim Schepke, was killed in the collision. A particularly aggressive submarine commander, Schepke had been credited with the sinking of 39 ships totalling 159,130 tons. Almost simultaneously, the destroyer *Walker*, under Captain Macintyre, depth-charged *U-99*, which had used all its torpedoes; completely crippled, the German submarine was able to remain on the surface just long enough for its crew to escape. Wearing his officer's peaked cap and with his binoculars slung round his neck – the binoculars had been presented to him by Admiral Dönitz – Otto Kretschmer was the last man to be hoisted aboard *Walker*. With 44 ships totalling 266,629 tons to his credit, Kretschmer was the U-boat "ace of aces", and as such had been decorated with the Oak Leaves to his Knight's Cross of the Iron Cross. He spent the first stage of his captivity in Captain Macintyre's cabin, showing himself to be a fine bridge player.

May, with 58 ships sunk, a total of 325,492 tons, was the worst month for Great Britain in the Battle of the Atlantic; and if we add to this the losses incurred in the Aegean and Mediterranean Seas during the campaign in the Balkans we find that Allied shipping had lost nearly 1,200,000 tons in two months; Germany was within an ace of the figures Raeder and Dönitz had calculated as being necessary to bring Britain to her knees, without

(page 251)

◁△ *A U-boat on the surface of the Atlantic.*

◁◁ *Survivors from a sunk merchantman are hauled alongside a U-boat for questioning.*

◁▽ *A narrow escape. This U-boat is limping back to base after being rammed.*
▽ *The last moments of a merchantman.*

△ Innocent-looking but deadly: one of Germany's fleet of disguised merchant raiders which operated with conspicuous success in 1940 and 1941. This is Kormoran, *armed with six 5.9-inch guns, four 21-inch torpedo tubes, and carrying two aircraft. She was out for 352 days and sank or captured 11 ships with a total tonnage of 68,264. Her end was a dramatic one: on November 19, 1941, she encountered the Australian cruiser* Sydney *and in a furious battle the two ships sank each other.*

undertaking any other military action.

However, the second half of the year, as a simple comparison with the first half shows, was far from justifying the optimism felt in Dönitz's Kernével H.Q.: between July and December, for various political and strategic reasons, the monthly average of shipping sunk by the U-boats slumped by 50 per cent, to only 120,000 tons.

Firstly, the posting of American naval forces near Greenland and Iceland, and the inclusion of the North Atlantic between Iceland and eastern Newfoundland in the American security zone enabled the British Admiralty to release ships in that area for the strengthening of escorts in the eastern Atlantic. This was especially important; as we have mentioned earlier, Hitler had given strict instructions to avoid any trouble with the U.S.A. The U-boats had stuck to them, despite the fact that on September 11, 1941 the U.S. Navy ships in the Atlantic had been told to shoot on sight.

Secondly, although the number of submarines operational had increased from 22 in January to 65 in July, and to 91 by the end of the year, not all of them were employed on this vital task of destroying enemy shipping, despite Dönitz's frenzied pleas; with the increase in submarine numbers, Hitler seemed to think he could post them anywhere. Some of his decisions were correct, others much less so.

Thus the beginning of hostilities against the Russians seemed to him to demand the sending of four submarines to the Arctic. Because they found no targets there worthy of their torpedoes, they were recalled, but were not posted back to their essential task, for the Führer had decreed

that Norway constituted a "zone of destiny", and would probably be Churchill's first objective. Dönitz thought such an enterprise out of the question. He was probably right, but it still remains a fact that Churchill gave Sir Alan Brooke, Commander-in-Chief, Home Forces, express instructions to cease all other activity and prepare a plan to attack Trondheim. It was only after a week's polite but steadfast objections that Brooke was able to note in his diary on October 12: "The meeting finished shortly after 8.30 p.m. and for the second time Winston had been ridden off Trondheim." All of which would seem to indicate that, in this case at least, Hitler was right and Dönitz wrong.

Dönitz's forces were further weakened by the continually worsening situation in the central Mediterranean. On the orders of O.K.W., six submarines passed through the Straits of Gibraltar at the end of September, being joined in Eleusis harbour by four more in November. In the last chapter we saw the useful contribution they made to the Italians' strategy, just when the southern theatre of operations was being gravely threatened. However, it had been agreed that once their mission had been accomplished, they would return to service in the Atlantic. But this was a meaningless phrase: the current in the middle of the Strait flows very rapidly from the Atlantic to the Mediterranean, which prevented the U-boats from returning underwater, while one night was not long enough to allow them to return on the surface. At the end of December the German Navy had no fewer than 23 U-boats in the Mediterranean, unable to play any part in the battle of the Atlantic (to say nothing of four submarines which had been lost while entering the Mediterranean).

Lastly, expecting an "Anglo-Gaullist" landing in French North Africa, Hitler sent an order to Admiral Dönitz on November 29 to post 15 U-boats on either side of the Strait of Gibraltar. Dönitz thought that the rumours upon which Hitler had based his decision were quite false, but when, at the end of December, Churchill and Roosevelt met in Washington for the "Arcadia" Conference, this was the very plan they agreed on: as soon as Operation "Crusader", then being carried out, had completed the destruction of Axis forces in Cyrenaica, General Auchinleck would implement Operation "Acrobat", bringing the British 8th Army quickly up to the

Returning to this question in the light of the extra information available after the war, Captain S. W. Roskill comes down, with slight reservations, in favour of Dönitz's arguments:

"But the transfer [of U-boats] from the Atlantic brought us a most welcome easement in that vital theatre. The German Staff, when it ordered the U-boats to the Mediterranean, did not know of the Japanese intention to attack on the 7th of December, and could not therefore have foretold that a new ally would assist greatly towards propping up Italy and saving the Axis armies in North Africa. But, in the long view, it may be doubted whether the redistribution of the enemy's U-boat strength brought him any advan-

Tunisian border; after which an expeditionary force, Anglo-American rather than Anglo-Gaullist as first envisaged, would carry out Operation "Gymnast", appearing unexpectedly on the Atlantic coast of Morocco and at suitable points in Algeria and Tunisia. The local French authorities and the Vichy Government would thus be given a last chance to choose between "a blessing or a cursing", as Churchill put it in a note of December 16. We know what happened to this plan, but it is clear that Hitler was right to be concerned about such an eventuality, and about the means of countering it.

On December 31, therefore, there were 91 U-boats available, split up as follows:

Mediterranean	26
West of Gibraltar	6
Norway	4
Available to Dönitz	55

tage, because of the decline in his Atlantic offensive which it made inevitable."

With 55 U-boats at his disposal for the blockade of Britain, Dönitz would have done much better if he had been able to use them in co-operation with air and surface forces. He could of course rely on Lieutenant-Colonel Martin Harlinghausen, commanding *Kampfgeschwader 40* at Bordeaux, equipped with Focke-Wulf 200 Condors, adequate maritime reconnaissance/bomber machines. But the immense enthusiasm and intelligence of this former naval officer could not compensate for the very limited serviceability rate of his unit's aircraft—only two per day at the most, instead of the 12 that Dönitz would have liked. And yet, each time that aircraft and U-boats were able to co-operate, the results proved most encouraging, and this tiny handful of four-engined German

△ *The* Gneisenau *copes easily with the Atlantic swell during her successful raiding cruise with* Scharnhorst. *Both ships were launched at the end of 1936 and worked as an efficient team, sinking between them 115,622 tons of shipping. It was the success of this operation that prompted the Germans to launch* Bismarck *and the* Prinz Eugen *on Operation "Rheinübung". The new operation would bring all four ships together to harass the Atlantic sealanes.*

Hitler salutes the newest addition to his battle fleet: the battleship Bismarck, *pride of the German Navy*. Grand-Admiral Raeder planned to unleash her on the North Atlantic convoy routes as the natural culmination of over a year of highly successful operations by surface raiders.

bombers produced considerable consternation among Allied convoys.

With a little more diplomacy, would Dönitz have been able to bring home to the vindictive and presumptuous Hermann Göring a more accurate realisation of what was really needed for naval and air forces to co-operate successfully? This is most unlikely because, on Hitler's express instructions, Göring combined responsibility for the Wehrmacht's air operations with the industrial dictatorship of the Third Reich and the occupied countries, and flitted from one sphere of activity to the other with the most disconcerting frivolity, apparently quite incapable of setting his mind to a problem and carrying it through to a reasonable conclusion.

Another factor militating against the effective waging of the battle of the Atlantic was the pitifully small number of maintenance personnel available to Dönitz. And even these could not do all that they might have done as a result of several unforeseeable circumstances.

On March 23, 1941, at the end of a lightning raid, the battle-cruisers *Scharnhorst* and *Gneisenau* put in at Brest, being joined

there on June 1 by the heavy cruiser *Prinz Eugen*, which had succeeded, in circumstances related below, in escaping from the battle which had resulted in the sinking of *Bismarck*. The concentration of three such powerful units in one place provoked a violent reaction from the R.A.F.

On April 6, an R.A.F. pilot succeeded in hitting *Gneisenau* with a torpedo, and after she had been towed back to harbour, she was hit again, this time by four bombs. On July 1 a British bomber hit *Prinz Eugen*, putting her out of commission for four months. Lastly, *Scharnhorst* was hit by five bombs while on trials off la Pallice.

In order to repair these surface warships as soon as possible, maintenance crews, despite Dönitz's strongest protests, were taken off submarine work in considerable numbers, and the overhaul and repair of U-boats consequently suffered.

Thus, at the end of the year, 60 per cent of Dönitz's U-boats were out of action, and of the 22 left, ten were in transit, leaving only 12 for operations over the whole theatre of operations from Cape Farewell in Greenland to the Azores.

Meanwhile, Admiral Sir Percy Noble's

anti-submarine forces had increased both in quantity and quality. This is clearly shown by the results of the battle, from Gibraltar to Ushant, between U-boats and the escort for the 32 merchantmen of convoy H.G. 76 between December 14–23. The British Admiralty had gone to great lengths to protect this convoy, giving Captain F. J. Walker, commanding the escort force, an escort carrier, three destroyers, four sloops, and no fewer than ten corvettes.

After nine days of relentless combat, the losses were these:
1. Britain: escort carrier *Audacity*, lost to *U-751* (Lieutenant Bigalk) and destroyer *Stanley*;
2. Germany: two Focke-Wulf Condors, shot down by *Audacity*'s fighters, and five of the ten submarines involved. One of these was *U-567*, commanded by Lieutenant Endrass, whose total tonnage sunk was very close to the record set shortly before by Otto Kretschmer.

In short, the British had had the best of the engagement, especially as 30 of the 32 merchantmen reached their destination.

1941 had cost the Germans 35 U-boats, of which three had been lost in the Baltic and five in the Mediterranean. During the first half of the year, however, the shipyards of the Reich had been producing new U-boats at the rate of 13 a month, a figure that increased to 20 in the second half of the year. Thus the U-boat arm gained a total of 163 boats during the year (a production of 198 minus 35 boats lost). Dönitz therefore had no reason to be pessimistic, especially as the German and Italian declarations of war on the United States on December 11, 1941 left his boats free to attack American shipping. To complete the picture, it should be noted that the Italians lost eight boats in the battle of the Atlantic.

During the same period, Germany's surface warships destroyed 427,000 tons of Allied shipping, slightly less than one-fifth of the tonnage despatched by the U-boats. By this activity, however, the surface raiders tied down ships that could profitably have been used elsewhere. Battleships, for example, had to be escorted by four destroyers, and this weakening of the anti-submarine effort made Dönitz's task that much easier.

On January 1, 1941, there were six German disguised surface raiders (con-verted cargo or banana boats) at large on the high seas: two in the Pacific, two in the Indian Ocean, and two in the South Atlantic. Operating either singly or in pairs, they scuttled their prey after taking off supplies for their own use or sent them off with a skeleton crew to one of the French Atlantic ports if their cargoes of food or industrial supplies could be of use to the Reich.

There were, for example, three Norwegian whaling factory ships captured by *Pinguin* off the Antarctic ice-pack on January 14–15. Slipping through the British patrols, they managed to reach Bordeaux. *Pinguin* had left Germany on June 22, 1940 and had sunk 28 merchantmen (137,000 tons) when she was surprised and sunk by the cruiser *Cornwall* on May 8, 1941, off Somaliland.

On November 19, 1941, another German raider, *Kormoran*, was sunk off the coast of Western Australia by the cruiser *Sydney*. But before going down with most of her crew, she torpedoed her attacker, which sank with all hands. *Kormoran* had been at sea for more than ten months and had 11 ships (68,000 tons) to her credit.

Three days later Germany lost a further raider. *Atlantis* was caught while transferring supplies to a U-boat half way between Guinea and Brazil. She was sunk quickly by the 8-inch guns of the cruiser *Devonshire* after a cruise that had brought her 22 victims (146,000 tons) in 1½ years.

The three remaining raiders, *Komet*, *Thor*, and *Orion*, were luckier, and managed to get back to Germany under the very noses of the Allies. The most noteworthy of their cruises was probably that of *Komet*, commanded by Captain Eyssen, who was promoted to Rear-Admiral on the last day of 1940. *Komet* left Hamburg on June 6, 1940 and returned there on April 30, 1941, after cruising right round the world. With the aid of Russian ice-breakers she had made the North-East Passage, skirted Siberia, and entered the Pacific via the Bering Strait. After taking her toll of Allied shipping in the Pacific in conjunction with *Orion*, she returned to Hamburg via the Cape of Good Hope, her whole cruise having taken her something like 100,000 miles.

From figures released after the war, it seems that *Komet*, *Thor*, and *Orion* accounted for 33 merchantmen totalling about 183,000 tons. In addition to these, *Thor* met and sank the British auxiliary cruiser *Voltaire* on April 4, 1941, picking up 196 survivors.

△ *Captain Bernhard Rogge of the* Atlantis, *the "top-scoring" disguised merchant raider commander with 22 ships.*

△ *Captain Otto Kähler of the* Thor. *He fought three extremely punishing battles against British auxiliary cruisers –* Alcantara, Carnarvon Castle, *and* Voltaire.
▽ *Captain Helmuth von Rückteschell of the* Widder.

CHAPTER 27
RUSSIA HITS BACK

△ *Huddled in their greatcoats, these German infantrymen stumble forward over Russia's frozen steppe. Under such terrible conditions, Russian reinforcements, many of them Siberians used to the cold, were doubly effective.*

On January 1, 1942, between Feodosiya, on the south side of the Crimea, and Oranienbaum on the Gulf of Finland, 12 German armies (with 141 divisions, six of them from satellite countries, plus five Hungarian and Rumanian brigades) were locked in combat with 22 Soviet armies (a total of 328 divisions or their equivalent).

The temperatures of 30 and even 40 degrees below zero, recorded from one end to the other of the front, and 1,000 miles difference in latitude, did not force the Russians to seek winter quarters. On the contrary, during the month of January, Stalin would extend his offensive to the left and right flanks of the front, no longer limiting himself to Army Group "Centre", against which Generals Konev and Zhukov continued to struggle, with 165 divisions confronting Kluge's 68.

In the face of this first Soviet winter offensive, Hitler, who had taken over control of O.K.H. and the Eastern Front from Field-Marshal von Brauchitsch, issued the following order to his armies on December 28.

"The abandonment without struggle of positions, even if they have been only cursorily prepared, leads, under present weather conditions, to intolerable losses in material and munitions. It weakens our fighting capacities and allows the enemy ever-growing freedom of action."

In order to exploit to the full the defensive situation to which he was for the moment reduced, he ordered every village and even every farmhouse to be made into a stronghold, with garrisons drawn from all fighting arms and also from the service échelons. Over a wide expanse of territory, this "quartering" of the terrain–to use General Weygand's expression from the end of May 1940 – would force the enemy to bivouac in the open, prevent him using his road and rail network, and finally reduce him to impotence and famine.

Nevertheless, to redeploy in depth, as the order required, the heavily-stretched German units, who were already fighting on an excessively long front, were obliged to spread their resources even more thinly. And so the enemy was able to filter through the gaps which inevitably opened in their lines. In fact the Russians were able to penetrate the German front even more easily than they would have been able to do in summer, because the extreme temperatures had frozen the lakes and rivers to the extent that they no longer formed obstacles. Their ice was so thick that it could even support 52-ton heavy tanks.

To stiffen the German line, which was buckling and threatening to break at any moment, Hitler called on troops from Occupied France and others who had just finished their training in Germany. Between the end of December 1941 and the end of March 1942, no less than 22 infantry divisions were moved from West to East for this purpose.

Moreover, the situation was so dangerous in certain sectors that they were thrown into action just as soon as they arrived, in small groups and without time to distribute equipment and clothing to withstand the climate. For its part, the Red Army was reinforced in the first six months of 1942 by the addition of about 60 new divisions.

The offensive against Army Group "Centre"

In a directive dated January 7, 1942, the Soviet High Command ordered Generals Konev and Zhukov, in command of the Kalinin and West Fronts respectively, to go over once more to the attack, with the intention of annihilating Army Group "Centre".

For this purpose the forces of the Kalinin Front would move forward along the Ostashkov–Volga line, attacking in a general south-westerly direction and, to the west of Vyaz'ma, would cut the road and railway between Minsk and Moscow, the life-lines of Army Group "Centre". Furthermore, using the gap which had been formed during the retreat to the south of Kaluga between the right wing of the German 4th Army and the left wing of 2nd *Panzerarmee*, the West Front would make its main effort in the direction of Vyaz'ma. This gigantic pincer-movement, aimed at bringing about the encirclement of the whole of Army Group "Centre", would be covered on its right by attacks by troops of the North-West Front and on its left by offensives by the Bryansk Front.

The offensive so planned made an excellent beginning on January 9 and 10, 1942. For three weeks, O.K.H. was seriously concerned that Konev and Zhukov should meet in the region of Dorogobuzh, some 16 miles south of the Moscow–Minsk railway.

Eremenko pushes through

In the north, the 4th Shock Army (General A. I. Eremenko), which formed the right of the Kalinin Front, took advantage of the thick ice on Lake Seliger, the boundary between Army Groups "Centre" and "North", to break through the German lines which, in this sector, were no more than skeletal. Eremenko pushed straight as far as Velikiye-Luki, more than 115 miles from his starting-point, replenishing his supplies from depôts which the

△ *A Russian poster of 1942: "Defend Mother Volga". But the Soviet winter and spring offensives meant that this vital river barrier, which Hitler had intended his armies to reach in their first thrust into Russia, would now be safe until the end of August 1942–and then the river's major town, Stalingrad, was to prove the graveyard of Germany's Russian adventure.*

◁ *The negation of modern war: where motors would not run, both sides had recourse to the old Russian methods of transport–trains of sledges pulled by horses.*

▷ *Although the Soviets made hard-won gains along the Front Line from December 1941 to March 1942, they were to fail in their ultimate objective of isolating and destroying Army Group "Centre".*

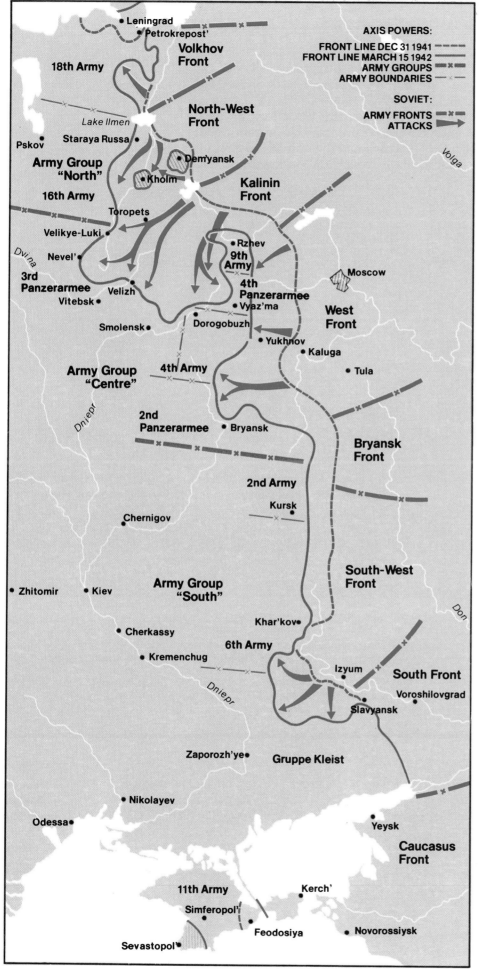

AXIS POWERS:
FRONT LINE DEC 31 1941 ----
FRONT LINE MARCH 15 1942 ────
ARMY GROUPS ✕✕✕
ARMY BOUNDARIES ─ ∙ ─

SOVIET:
ARMY FRONTS ✕✕✕
ATTACKS ➤

Germans had built up at Toropets. In this way the Russians made up for the defects of the Soviet supply services, which had failed to keep up with the front line units. On February 1, however, 3rd *Panzerarmee* (Colonel-General Reinhardt) retook the line Demidov–Velizh–Nevel'–Velikiye-Luki and blocked the Russians' potentially dangerous advance to Vitebsk and Smolensk.

29th Army cut off

In the centre of the Kalinin Front, General Konev separated his 29th, 39th, and 30th Armies which, to the west of Rzhev, had succeeded in splitting the German 9th Army and isolating its left wing, which consisted of the XXIII Corps (General Schubert). The Soviet 29th Army exploited its breakthrough to the full, and, on January 27, was within tactical reach of the Minsk–Moscow road. But General Walther Model, who had just taken over command of 9th Army, was an astonishing military improviser. Ignoring the various concentrated offensives against Rzhev from the north and east, he counter-attacked vigorously in a westerly direction and established contact with XXIII Corps at the end of the month. Now it was the turn of the Soviet 29th Army to find its communications cut. In the course of the subsequent furious battles, it lost 27,000 dead and 5,000 prisoners. Only 5,000 men, 800 of whom were wounded, managed to break out of the pocket and reach Soviet lines on February 15.

"German casualties, too, had been heavy," Paul Carell notes. "On February 18, when *Obersturmbannführer* Otto Kumm reported at his divisional headquarters, Model happened to be there. He said to Kumm: 'I know what your regiment has been through – but I still can't do without it. What is its present strength?'

"Kumm gestured towards the window. *'Herr Generaloberst*, my regiment is on parade outside.' Model glanced through the window. Outside, 35 men had fallen in."

Model's gift for manoeuvre and his prompt decision had therefore carried the day against Russian doggedness, for the Russian 39th Army was as sore-hit as the Germans. Nevertheless, Model's army was trapped in a tube-shaped pocket nearly 125 miles long and, in the region of Sychevka, barely 40 miles in width.

It was now vital that Rzhev be evacuated, if only to allow the 12 or so divisions earmarked for the summer offensive the chance to recuperate. Yet before he would consent, Hitler delayed until the reverse at Stalingrad set the seal on his defeat.

Hitler consents to a retreat

On the other hand, on January 15, in view of the speedy and dangerous advances by the 49th, 50th, and 10th Armies of the West Front into the breach which had been opened south of Kaluga, Hitler authorised Kluge to order the necessary withdrawals to permit the left of 2nd *Panzerarmee* to link-up firmly again with the right of 4th Army:

"This is the first time in the war," his order concluded, "that I have ordered a withdrawal over a sizable section of the front. I expect the movement to be carried out in a manner worthy of the German Army. Our men's confidence in their innate superiority and their absolute determination to cause the enemy as much damage as possible must also condition the way in which this withdrawal is carried out."

In order to slow down enemy pursuit, the Germans, just as the Russians had done previously, applied a scorched earth policy to the areas they abandoned. Villages were razed, and even the stoves used to heat the Russian dwellings were destroyed at Hitler's express order.

Zhukov's advance blocked

General Zhukov's offensive followed a pattern similar to Konev's. A lightning jump-off took I Guard Cavalry Corps almost to Dorogobuzh, but there the advance was checked, causing a stabilised front to develop. At the end of February, Field-Marshal von Kluge had redeployed

▽ *The pattern of Russian attacks: intense artillery bombardment and close co-operation by aircraft such as the Shturmoviks seen flying over this gun.*
▽ ▽ *Winter war in Russia – temperatures dropping to 40 degrees below zero Centigrade and logistics based on horse and sledge.*

General von Seydlitz-Kurzbach, whose drive from Staraya Russa lifted the siege of the Dem'yansk pocket. The successful defence and air supply of the pocket was hailed as a considerable success at the time – and so it was, tactically. But it led the Germans to believe that it could be repeated on a larger, strategic level, and thus sowed the seeds of the terrible defeat at Stalingrad.

after his withdrawal and re-established a continuous front along the Kirov–Yukhnov line. As a result, General Pliev's I Guard Cavalry Corps was trapped and, slightly more to the north, a similar fate overtook the 33rd Army. Russian G.H.Q. in Moscow tried to get the operation moving again by parachuting two brigades behind the German lines and extending General Zhukov's authority to include the Kalinin Front. But Army Group "Centre" still maintained its positions along the Minsk–Vyaz'ma and Vyaz'ma–Rzhev lines.

The *History of the Great Patriotic War* does not conceal the slowing down of this winter offensive, from which Stalin had expected a decisive victory. It blames its failure on to the fact that the armies of the West Front wasted their shock value by attacking over fronts which were too long. This is very likely, but the question must be considered at a higher level than the one set by the *Great Patriotic War*. It would appear that the principles of concentration of force and convergence of effort were both insufficiently understood in the highest councils of *Stavka*, as Russian G.H.Q. was called.

Beginning on January 8, to the north of the Kalinin Front, General Kurochkin, commander of the North-West Front, badly mauled the German 16th Army, which formed the right wing of Army Group "Centre". The 16th Army broke under the assault of the 3rd Shock Army (General Purkaev) emerging from the Lake Seliger region, and the 11th Army (General Morosov), which swept over the frozen Lake Ilmen.

Certainly the latter, in spite of five furious attacks, was halted before Staraya Russa, but working its way up the Lovat' it succeeded, on February 8, in closing the trap around the German II Corps. This formed a 200 mile pocket around Dem'yansk, which was defended by five badly worn divisions. But, under the command of General Brockdorff-Ahlefeldt, they repelled every enemy attack, even when the Russians parachuted two brigades into the centre of the pocket. To supply the 96,000 men and their 20,000 horses, the Luftwaffe organised an airlift. At a rate of 100 to 150 aircraft daily, it brought the besieged men more than 65,000 tons of foodstuffs, forage, munitions, and fuel, also flying out over 34,500 wounded and sick.

The Kholm pocket

On March 21, General Seydlitz-Kurzbach moved out of Staraya Russa and attacked with four divisions in the direction of Dem'yansk. An unexpected thaw hampered this movement and not till April 21 was he able to re-establish contact with II Corps across the Lovat'. Some 65 miles south-west of Dem'yansk, the little town of Kholm and its garrison, commanded by Major-General Scherer, was cut off by the 3rd Shock Army. The pocket was relieved just as it was about to fall.

The actions at Kholm and Dem'yansk must be put very much on the debit side of the Red Army's account book. And furthermore, the operation laid down for the Volkhov Front (General Meretskov) ended in disaster for the 2nd Shock Army.

Failure before Leningrad

Under the command of General Vlasov, 2nd Shock Army, six divisions strong, crossed the Volkhov on January 22 and pushed north-east, reaching the Leningrad–Novgorod railway. The attack was to take place at the same time as an offensive by the 54th Army, emerging from the area south-east of Petrokrepost'. If the manoeuvre had succeeded, the salient formed here by the German 18th Army would have been liquidated and Leningrad relieved at the same time. But the 54th Army failed in the face of the resistance of I Corps (March 10, 1942).

From that moment on, Vlasov, who had been reinforced by the XIII Cavalry Corps and three armoured brigades and had deployed his forces fanwise, found himself in a very risky situation, for the handle of the fan was only 13 miles wide while his forward troops were 50 miles from the Volkhov. From March 15 to March 19, furious combat, in which the Spanish volunteers of the *División Azul* distinguished themselves, allowed the German 18th Army to sever the line which joined the 2nd Shock Army to the main Soviet line. The mopping-up operations lasted until the end of May. Vlasov himself was not captured until the end of July.

Success in the south

In the southern theatre of operations, the sudden death of Field-Marshal von Reichenau led Hitler to entrust the command of Army Group "South" to Field-Marshal von Bock. As he entered his office at Poltava on January 18, the new commander of German operations in the Ukraine and the Crimea was received with two pieces of news. One was good: Feodosiya had been recaptured by General von Manstein, who had also taken 10,000 prisoners. This would allow the siege of Sevastopol' to continue without fear of being surprised by Russian attack. The other news was disturbing: the 17th Army's front had been pierced near Izyum.

General von Manstein recalls the difficulties which arose at the time of the recapture of Feodosiya and also his attitude about the treatment of Russian P.O.W.s:

"Everything seemed to have conspired against us. Extremely severe frosts affected the airfields at Simferopol' and Yevpatoriya, which were used by our Stukas and bombers, and often prevented aircraft taking off in the morning to attack Feodosiya. The Kerch' Strait was frozen over and allowed free passage to enemy units.

"In spite of the difficulties, the army did its best to feed–sometimes even reducing its own rations–the prisoners whom we had not sufficient transport to transfer north. Consequently, the mortality rate among the prisoners averaged only two per cent. This was an extremely low figure, considering that most of them were seriously wounded or absolutely exhausted at the time of their capture. One incident may serve to illustrate their feelings towards us. There was a camp for 8,000 prisoners close to Feodosiya when the Russians made their landing. The camp guards fled, but the prisoners, instead of running towards their 'liberators', set off, without guards, towards Simferopol', towards us, that is."

On the Donets, Marshal Timoshenko, in command of the South-West Front, had attacked seven German divisions with his 37th, 57th, and 6th Armies, totalling 21 infantry divisions, 11 cavalry divisions, and ten armoured brigades (about 650 tanks). The long-range object of this operation was Khar'kov and the railway between Dniepropetrovsk and Donetsk (Stalino), which supplied the German 17th Army and 1st *Panzerarmee*. In temperatures of 40 degrees below zero the Russians spread out behind the German line and, by January 26, were restocking their supplies from the stores which the 17th Army had established at Lozovaya. Two days later they reached Sinel'nikovo and Grishino, which were within gunshot of the railway they hoped to cut. Several days later they were thrown back by *Gruppe* von Kleist which was an amalgamation of Kleist's own 1st *Panzerarmee* and the 17th Army.

The Russian attack then folded up. Army Group "South" had indeed had a nasty shock, but Timoshenko had not been able to widen the breach he had made on the Donets front on January 18. The Izyum salient, about 60 miles deep, would cause him the same tragic disaster as the Volkhov salient had brought on Vlasov.

▽ *The mud of the spring thaw which effectively ended large-scale movement over the whole front, as vehicles could hardly be moved. Both sides prepared for the summer campaign.*

△ *A column of German infantry on the move. The improved weather of late spring gave the Germans the opportunity to use their superior tactical skills to halt the Russian offensive.*

▽ *The ever-present threat to German communications – "Partisans, fight the enemy without pity!"*

The weather forces a truce

From March 21, mud steadily replaced snow between the shores of the Baltic and the Black Sea, making any significant operations impossible for close on two months. This relative truce allowed the two adversaries to consider their achievements and lay their plans for the coming summer campaign.

According to statistics calculated by O.K.H., over the entire Eastern Front the Germans had lost, between January 1 and March 20, a little more than 240,000 men, of whom 51,837 had been killed and 15,086 were missing. This brought their losses since June 22, 1941 to 1,073,006 officers, N.C.O.s, and men, that is just under one-third of the effectives who had attacked on that date. It is true that the Wehrmacht had escaped the disaster which had just threatened it, but only just, and, to a large extent, because of the fact that *Stavka* had not been able to concentrate its efforts to destroy Army Group "Centre".

And so Colonel-General Halder, not

exhibiting at this time any sign of pessimism in general, recommended prudence to the new Commander-in-Chief of the German Army. But it was not for lack of caution that Hitler had dismissed Brauchitsch. Since the Soviet winter offensive had been more or less checked, all risks appeared laudable to the Führer and, for six months, he could be heard shouting as he stared at the campaign maps: "*Der Russe ist tot! Der Russe ist tot!* (Russia is dead! Russia is dead!)".

Even today information on Soviet losses in this period is unavailable. However, everything seems to indicate that these were considerable, even more so as the rear-guard services of the Red Army functioned very badly and the Russians were not so insensitive to the cold as their opponents thought. As Lieutenant Goucharov noted:

"January 25. 'You know, Comrade Lieutenant,' one of my men said to me yesterday, 'when one gets really cold one becomes indifferent to freezing to death or being shot. One only has one wish – to die as quickly as possible.' That's the exact truth. The cold drains the men of the will to fight."

CHAPTER 28
JAVA SEA AND SINGAPORE

△ Fleet Admiral Ernest J. King, who replaced Stark as C.-in-C., Navy. Despite his concern for the Pacific war, he endorsed the "Germany First" principle.

On September 11, 1941, General Marshall and Admiral Stark sketched out to President Roosevelt the "main lines of the military policy" which they thought should be adopted, and proposed that these should be implemented without delay. In this extensive document they drew the President's attention to the enormous danger that the Third Reich would be to America if it were given the time to re-organise the continent of Europe as it liked. They therefore both agreed:

"The principal strategic method employed by the United States in the immediate future should be the material support of present military operations against Germany, and their reinforcement by active participation in the war by the United States while holding Japan in check pending future developments."

For this purpose, the "maintenance of an active front in Russia" appeared extremely important to them, and it was also imperative to "prevent Axis penetration into North Africa and the islands of the Atlantic" (Cape Verdes, Canaries, Madeira, and Azores).

These proposals, which were accepted by the President, also met the wishes of the British cabinet. In effect, Hitler and Mussolini, by declaring war on the United States, had saved Roosevelt the difficulty of persuading Congress that the best way to avenge Pearl Harbor would be to have two more new enemies on America's hands. Nevertheless, just when Churchill was preparing to put the case for Operation "Gymnast" (an American landing in Algeria in conjunction with an 8th Army drive into Tunisia) to the men responsible for American strategy, it was already apparent to the latter that their forces were unable to keep Japan at bay anywhere in the Far East.

But this order of priorities, in which the defeat of Germany would take priority over that of Japan, was not questioned by Roosevelt, Marshall, and Stark at the "Arcadia" Conference in Washington at the end of 1941. On the contrary, Marshall and Stark (the latter of whom was later replaced by Admiral Ernest J. King) took up an unequivocal position on the matter from the time of their first meeting with their British colleagues:

". . . notwithstanding the entry of Japan into the war, our view remains that Germany is still the prime enemy and her defeat is the key to victory. Once Germany is defeated the collapse of Italy and the defeat of Japan must follow."

Agreement was reached on the principle of such a landing on January 12, whereupon the plan was reworked as "Super-Gymnast". According to this new version, three British and three American divisions were to land in Morocco and Algeria from April 15 onwards. At the same time, three more American divisions would cross the Atlantic and relieve three British divisions in Northern Ireland. The latter

The Production Race

United States War Production

	Forecast	1942	1943
Warplanes	31,250	45,000	100,000
Tanks	29,550	45,000	75,000
Anti-aircraft guns	8,900	20,000	35,000
Anti-tank guns	11,700	14,000	Not fixed
Machine guns	238,000	500,000	Not fixed

Aircraft Production in 1942

AXIS	ALLIES
Germany – 15,556	United States – 45,000
Italy – 2,818	Great Britain – 17,385
Japan – 2,700	Soviet Union – 12,000
Total – 21,074	Total – 74,385

On June 22, 1941, of his 208 divisions, Hitler had 55 left in occupied Europe and Libya between the North Cape and Halfaya Pass. On June 5, 1944, though German land forces had increased to 304 divisions, 108 were taken up in Norway, the low countries, France, Italy, the Balkans, Crete and Rhodes. On the day of Operation "Overlord", O.K.H. could deploy only 30 armoured and motorised divisions between the Black Sea and the Baltic while O.K.W. controlled 12 in France and six in Italy.

▷ *Japanese troops land from their transports. The Allied naval forces in the Dutch East Indies were powerless to stop the Japanese "leap-frog" advance to the south.*

▽ *Japanese paratroops go in to establish yet another foot-hold during the fight for the Dutch East Indies.*

would then be available for active operations.

It was maintained among General Douglas MacArthur's staff that this decision had been wrung from Roosevelt by Churchill's plausible eloquence. This was not in fact so; the American Chiefs-of-Staff, quite independently of the British and for purely national reasons, were already entirely in favour of the "Germany first" principle. However, it must be noted that in his memoirs MacArthur, the defender of the Philippines, claims that he was kept in ignorance of this important decision, and it is understandable that as a result of this omission he remained somewhat bitter against Marshall.

On the other hand, no great importance need be attached to the criticism MacArthur made of Admiral King, the new Chief of Naval Operations, when he wrote:

"Although Admiral King felt that the fleet did not have sufficient resources to proceed to Manila, it was my impression that our Navy depreciated its own strength and might well have cut through to relieve our hard-pressed forces. The Japanese blockade of the Philippines was to some extent a paper blockade. Mindanao was still accessible and firmly held by us. The bulk of the Japanese Navy, operating on tight schedules, was headed south for the seizure of Borneo, Malaya and Indonesia. American carriers having escaped destruction at Pearl Harbor could have approached the Philippines and unloaded planes on fields in Mindanao."

Writing about Pearl Harbor shortly before his death in 1966, Admiral Chester W. Nimitz, who must share with MacArthur the credit for the final defeat of Japan, said:

"No one regrets more than I our 3,000 dead when the Japanese attacked Pearl Harbor. But if Admiral Husband Kimmel, who at that time commanded the American forces at Pearl Harbor, had had information of the attack 24 hours in advance, he would have sent off all our forces to meet the Japanese.

"We had not one aircraft-carrier capable of opposing Admiral Nagumo's aircraft-carrier formation, and the Japanese would have sunk all our ships on the high seas.

"We would have lost 6,000 men and almost all our Pacific Fleet."

This was the position on the day of the attack. But on the next day, when the aircraft-carriers *Lexington* and *Enterprise* reached Pearl Harbor, there was no question of sending them out on an operation against six other carriers without the advantage of surprise. Moreover, the six aircraft-carriers of the Japanese striking force each carried at least 60 planes, all superior in performance to the 80 machines on each of the American carriers.

MacArthur's proposed operation would therefore in all probability have led to a second Pearl Harbor, but this time in mid-ocean, with no hope of rescue.

Joint efforts in South-East Asia

Faced with Japanese aggression that had been prepared and worked out at leisure, the "Arcadia" Conference hastily formed the A.B.D.A. command, the initials standing for the American, British, Dutch, and Australian forces fighting the Japanese in the Philippines, Malaya, Burma, and the Dutch East Indies. The establishment and appointments for this unified command, which Churchill cheerfully compared with Marshal Foch's appointment as Allied generalissimo on March 26, 1918, gave rise to hard talking among the conference delegates at the White House.

The Americans wanted the commander-in-chief to be British and expressed a preference for Sir Archibald Wavell; the British refused to accept any responsibility for this, giving somewhat unconvincing reasons for their hesitation.

Though Churchill remained optimistic about the fate of Singapore, Sir John Dill, in a letter to Sir Alan Brooke, introducing him to his new duties as C.I.G.S., gave his views on the subject and put forward an argument, which he could obviously not pursue at an inter-Allied conference. He wrote, not mincing his words:

"It would, I think, be fatal to have a British commander responsible for the disasters that are coming to the Americans as well as ourselves . . . Never was a soldier given a more difficult task . . . It is of the first importance that we should not be blamed for the bloody noses that are coming to them."

However, General Marshall and President Roosevelt carried the day, with the result that on January 15, 1942, General Wavell started to set up his A.B.D.A. headquarters at Batavia. He was assigned three deputy commanders: General H. ter Poorten, a Dutch officer, for the land forces; Admiral Thomas Hart, C.-in-C. U.S. Asiatic Fleet, for the naval forces; and Air-Marshal Sir Richard Peirse for the air forces. Although the command struc-

▽ *The victory march through Malaya: a Japanese infantry column, complete with flag, fords a creek. The British strategy of defending the key roads and relying on jungle and swamp to guard their flanks was foiled by the skill shown by the Japanese at jungle infiltration. They found, for example, that "impassable" mangrove swamps could be crossed by treading on the roots of the trees, and they bypassed the British positions time and again.*

ture appeared logical and workable, Wavell, seeing that the *matériel* resources of his command were poor and obsolete, noted sarcastically: "I had been handed not just a baby but quadruplets."

Malaya in danger

The Japanese offensive, making full use of its considerable *matériel* superiority, particularly at sea and in the air, was now in full spate, with its right wing threatening Burma and its left Australia. Success followed success.

Lieutenant-General A. E. Percival, G.O.C. Malaya, had III Indian Corps with which to try to oppose the Japanese advance. This corps, under the command of Lieutenant-General Sir Lewis Heath, disposed of three divisions, the 9th and 11th Indian in the line and the 8th Australian in reserve. Percival, faced with the problem of defending the Malay Peninsula, at places 175 miles wide, was forced to deploy his forces to cover the main axial roads, while the Japanese either infiltrated the British line through the jungle or bypassed the British positions by carrying out amphibious landings in their rear.

British weaknesses

Although the British forces enjoyed a slight superiority in numbers over their opponents (88,000 allied troops to 70,000 Japanese), their formations were inferior in training. The crack Japanese divisions were more than a match for those troops facing them. The British, moreover, had deployed well forward in northern Malaya to cover airfields for which, in the event, no air cover could be found. To reinforce these stretched dispositions, it is true that convoys were bringing in considerable reinforcements: an Indian brigade on January 3, the 53rd Brigade of the 18th Division from Britain on the 13th, a second Indian brigade on the 22nd, and the rest of the 18th Division on the 29th. But the training of the Indian troops was entirely inadequate, and the British division, which had originally been intended for the Middle East and diverted to Malaya at the Cape of Good Hope, had declined in efficiency during its long sea passage.

◁ *Japanese infantry double forwards to the attack.*
▽ *A scene during the furious battle for Kuala Lumpur in Malaya. The town finally fell to the Japanese on January 11.*

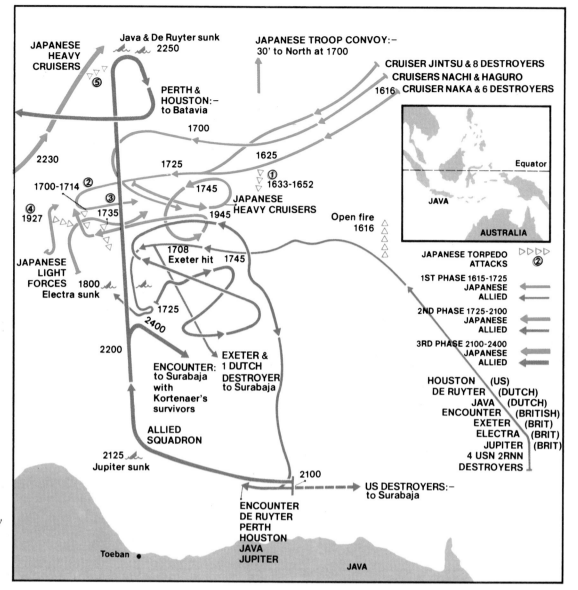

Java & De Ruyter sunk
2250

JAPANESE HEAVY CRUISERS

⑤

PERTH & HOUSTON:– to Batavia

JAPANESE TROOP CONVOY:– 30' to North at 1700

CRUISER JINTSU & 8 DESTROYERS
CRUISERS NACHI & HAGURO
1616 CRUISER NAKA & 6 DESTROYERS

1700

2230

1725

1625

1700-1714 ②

1745

1633-1652 ①

③

JAPANESE HEAVY CRUISERS

④ 1927

1735

1945

Open fire 1616

2400

1708 Exeter hit

1745

1745

JAPANESE LIGHT FORCES 1800 Electra sunk

1725

2200

ENCOUNTER: to Surabaja with Kortenaer's survivors

EXETER & 1 DUTCH DESTROYER to Surabaja

ALLIED SQUADRON

2125 Jupiter sunk

2100

US DESTROYERS:– to Surabaja

ENCOUNTER DE RUYTER PERTH HOUSTON JAVA JUPITER

Toeban •

JAVA

Equator

JAVA

AUSTRALIA

JAPANESE TORPEDO ATTACKS ②

1ST PHASE 1615-1725
JAPANESE
ALLIED

2ND PHASE 1725-2100
JAPANESE
ALLIED

3RD PHASE 2100-2400
JAPANESE
ALLIED

HOUSTON (US)
DE RUYTER (DUTCH)
JAVA (DUTCH)
ENCOUNTER (BRITISH)
EXETER (BRIT)
ELECTRA (BRIT)
JUPITER (BRIT)
4 USN 2RNN DESTROYERS

▷ *The Battle of the Java Sea, in which the last Allied attempt to counter the Japanese invasion of Java was broken. Rear-Admiral Karel Doorman of the Royal Netherlands Navy sailed with an ill-assorted American-British-Dutch-Australian squadron to intercept and destroy the Japanese invasion convoy, but his force was relentlessly ground down and destroyed by the covering Japanese cruiser squadrons.*

THE DUTCH FIGHT ON TO VICTORY

The new Japanese objectives

Meanwhile, the Japanese Navy had also been moving forward, stretching out its tentacles to seize the bases it coveted, as Admiral Morison puts it. These tentacles consisted of the 2nd Scouting Fleet, 3rd Blockade and Transport Fleet, and 4th Mandate Fleet. The 2nd Scouting Fleet, commanded by Vice-Admiral Kondo, was to assist in the capture of Malaya and the reduction of the "impregnable" fortress of Singapore; the 3rd Blockade and Transport Fleet, under Vice-Admiral Takahashi, was ordered to gain possession of the Philippines, Borneo, and Celebes and then to join forces with the 2nd Scouting Fleet in order to take the Dutch East Indies, with their coveted oilfields; and the 4th Mandate Fleet,

commanded by Vice-Admiral Inouye, was to take Guam and Wake. The attainment of these objectives would secure the perimeter of the Greater South-East Asia Co-Prosperity Sphere.

It should also be noted here that the Japanese land-based air forces co-operated very efficiently with the 2nd and 3rd Fleets, which had no carriers. From December 15, 1941 they operated from the base at Davao on the island of Mindanao; Kendari airfield, in the south of Celebes, was captured in record time on January 17 and was soon in full swing as a Japanese advanced base; Amboina, in the Moluccas, was captured on February 3. From these bases, the Japanese could wreak havoc over the whole area of operations assigned to the 2nd and 3rd Fleets.

Besides being better trained than the Allied pilots opposing them, the Japanese had a distinct advantage in numbers and *matériel*. Most of the Hawker Hurricanes which had reached Singapore on January

14 were quickly overwhelmed in the air or destroyed on the ground, and a second consignment of these fighters, the only Allied aircraft in the theatre capable of taking on the Zero at anything like even terms, was diverted to Java. And thus the Japanese bombers had a field day at little cost. On February 3, Surabaja in Java was bombed for the first time; the next day the American cruisers *Houston* and *Marblehead* were both hit, the second badly enough to have to return to Australia for repairs.

Borneo and Sumatra invaded

The first Japanese landing on Borneo occurred at Miri, on December 16. The oil port of Tarakan, near the entrance to the Makassar Strait, and Manado, at the northern tip of Celebes, both fell on the same day, January 11, 1942. During the night of January 24, a division of American destroyers surprised the Japanese as they were landing an invasion force at Balik-papan, where most of Borneo's oil was refined, and sank four merchantmen, but this success could not alter the course of events. Without even taking into account the fall of Kendari and Amboina, or waiting for the capture of Singapore, the Japanese invaded Sumatra, on February 14, and Timor on the 20th, without making any distinction between the Portuguese and Dutch parts of the island. This advance was of great strategic import, as it breached the "Malay barrier" and thus gave the Japanese the opportunity of cutting communications with Australia.

The situation was now beyond any hope of remedy, and on February 25 Wavell received orders to move his headquarters back to Ceylon, to which he had been preceded, on February 14, by Admiral

△ *The whirling chaos of an air/sea battle, captured by a Japanese artist. In the Java Sea campaign the Japanese did not need Nagumo's carriers. Land-based aircraft gave them virtually unchallenged air superiority.*

△ *A column of Japanese tanks rumbles across the Causeway from the mainland to Singapore Island.*

Hart. Command of the Allied naval forces still operating against the Japanese had devolved upon the Dutch Vice-Admiral C. E. L. Helfrich, who was later to show exceptional courage in a disastrous situation.

Battle of the Java Sea

Meanwhile, the Allied advanced headquarters at Bandung in Java had received information that two convoys, totalling 97 transports and with powerful escorts, had been observed off the Malay Peninsula and leaving the Makassar Strait. These were in fact the convoys carrying the Japanese 16th Army to the invasion of Java. With three divisions and one brigade, this force was far superior to the 30,000 trained troops with which General ter Poorten had to conduct the defence of Java.

Java's only hope lay in the destruction of the two convoys before they reached the island. To this end, the Allied naval forces in the area were dispatched under the Dutch Rear-Admiral Karel Doorman to the decisive Battle of the Java Sea. The Allied force, however, was at a distinct disadvantage as it had not had the time to learn to co-ordinate its efforts properly and to work out a common signalling code. Doorman's command consisted of two heavy cruisers, the British *Exeter* and American *Houston*; three light cruisers, the Dutch *De Ruyter* and *Java*, and the Australian *Perth*; and nine destroyers, four American, three British, and two Dutch.

On February 27, at 1500, Doorman was at sea off Surabaja when he received orders to intercept the Japanese convoy heading from the Makassar Strait towards Surabaja. Contact was made at about 1615 between the Allied force and the Japanese escort under Rear-Admiral Nishimura: the heavy cruisers *Nachi* (Rear-Admiral Takagi) and *Haguro*, the light cruisers *Naka* (Nishimura) and *Jintsu*, and 13 destroyers.

Though the Allies thus had a numerical superiority in cruisers, the range at which the action opened, more than 13 miles, meant that it was the numbers of 8-inch guns involved that was the critical factor. And here the Japanese prevailed, with 20 such weapons against the Allies' 12 (it should be remembered that *Houston* had been hit by bombs on February 4, and this had knocked out her after turret). The battle was to continue for almost seven hours without achieving concrete results, partly because the Japanese were more concerned with the safety of their convoy than sinking Allied vessels, and partly because the Allied warships had no reconnaissance aircraft, and were thus forced, as Morison puts it, to play a kind of blind man's bluff.

During the first engagement, *Exeter* was hit in her engine room at 1708 and hauled out of the line, the cruisers following her doing the same under the impression that such a manoeuvre had been ordered by Doorman in *De Ruyter*, leading the Allied line. While the crippled British cruiser made for Surabaja, the Japanese launched a wave of 72 torpedoes, only one of which, remarkably, hit an Allied warship, the Dutch destroyer *Kortenaer*, which exploded and sank. While covering the retirement of *Exeter*, the British destroyer *Electra* was stopped by gunfire and hammered into a blazing wreck. During the night, Doorman searched in vain for the Japanese convoy, which had been ordered by Nishimura to retreat to the north during the action, without finding it. He was also forced to release his American destroyers, which had expended all their torpedoes and were running drastically short of fuel.

During his fruitless search for the Japanese transports, however, Doorman once again ran into their escort, in the form of the cruiser *Jintsu* and her seven destroyers, at 1930. Turning away from the Japanese cruiser, Doorman inadvertently led his force over a newly-laid Dutch minefield, which cost him the British destroyer *Jupiter*. But time was running out for the Allied ships, for Japanese seaplanes had been keeping their cruisers informed of the Allied survivors' movements, and *Nachi* and *Haguro* were moving in for the kill. During the subsequent engagement, *De Ruyter* and *Java* were both hit and sunk by Japanese torpedoes. Doorman went down with his flagship. Immediately afterwards *Perth* and *Houston* broke off the action and returned to Batavia.

The crisis in Allied naval fortunes had yet further to run, however. After refuelling at Batavia, *Perth* and *Houston* received orders to retire southwards through the Sunda Strait. Here they ran into the second of the Japanese convoys mentioned above. This had sailed from Indo-China and was in the process of landing the first units of the Japanese 2nd Division in Banten Bay. The two Allied cruisers immediately went into the attack, and managed to sink one transport and force three others to beach themselves, as well as damaging one cruiser and three destroyers, before being sunk by the rest of the Japanese escort.

A few hours later, *Exeter* sailed from Surabaja with two destroyers to try to pass through the Sunda Strait. They were spotted by Japanese reconnaissance aircraft and sunk by four cruisers and three destroyers on March 1.

Defeat in Java

The naval defeat of February 27 sealed the fate of Java. The two vital centres of Batavia and Surabaja fell into Imamura's hands, and General ter Poorten asked the Japanese commander for armistice terms. As was to be expected, the victor demanded unconditional surrender, which he received at Bandung on March 10. Sherwood notes at this time:

"Churchill, who had won his greatest Parliamentary triumph a scant three weeks before, now faced the worst predicament of his career as Prime Minister. He made a broadcast speech in which he attributed the whole series of misfortunes in the Far East to the fact that America's shield of sea power had been 'dashed to the ground' at Pearl Harbor. There were

△ *Japanese troops march into surrendered Singapore.*

numerous expressions of irritation at this statement in Washington, as though Churchill were attempting to escape censure by blaming it all on the U.S. Navy, but it did not bother Roosevelt at all. He merely remarked: 'Winston had to say *something*.''

Retreat to Singapore

Under the keen and vigorous command of Lieutenant-General Tomoyuki Yamashita, the Japanese 25th Army smashed its way through the British defences in the north of Malaya. On January 1, 1942 Kuantan, on the east coast, fell to the swiftly-advancing Japanese, while on the other side of the country Kuala Lumpur, on the Slim river, succumbed on the 11th, after a period of fierce resistance. Seeing

his reserves melting away, Percival ordered his forces to fall back on Singapore on January 29, after asking for and receiving Wavell's authorisation. On January 30 the causeway linking the island fortress and the mainland was blown up.

But Singapore's garrison, its back to the wall, was in no position to offer a solid resistance for the great imperial base, which was intended to close the Indian Ocean to attack from the east and to ensure the safety of Britain's sea link with Australia and New Zealand. The Committee of Imperial Defence had recognised since the mid-1930's that the survival of Singapore in the face of a land attack depended upon the successful defence of the jungles of the Malayan hinterland – and that a Japanese attack via Malaya was quite probable. But now that the British defence of Malaya had collapsed, Singapore was practically indefensible.

In his memoirs, Churchill tells us of the "feelings of painful surprise" he had when reading Wavell's message of January 16,

▷ *The "Tiger of Malaya"– General Yamashita, a tough, thrusting commander who brooked no delay to his lightning campaign in Malaya and Singapore.*
▽ *British prisoners in Singapore await their transfer to prison camp–first in the comparative comfort of Changi Jail, but later, for thousands, amid the horrors of the "Death Railway" in Siam.*

which emphasised Singapore's weakness as a fortress. Churchill adds:

"Moreover, even more astounding, no measures worth speaking of had been taken by any of the commanders since the war began, and more especially since the Japanese had established themselves in Indo-China, to construct field defences. They had not even mentioned the fact they did not exist." He summed up as follows:

"I do not write this in any way to excuse myself. I ought to have known. My advisers ought to have known and I ought to have been told, and ought to have asked. The reason I had not asked about this matter, amid the thousands of questions I put, was that the possibility of Singapore having no landward defences no more entered into my mind than that of a battleship being launched without a bottom." It should be added, however, that Churchill had been a member of the Conservative cabinet in the 1920's when the Singapore base was planned and begun. There is, therefore, no reason why he should not have known the details then.

The fall of Singapore

In the circumstances, it was not difficult for General Yamashita, on the night of February 8–9, to get his forces across the Strait of Johore and win a beach-head north-west of the city of Singapore. Immediately afterwards, the Japanese captured Tengah airfield and the reservoirs supplying the city's million inhabitants with water.

On February 15, the advanced guard of the Japanese 5th Division ran into the British delegation sent out to seek terms for surrender. General Yamashita refused to discuss terms, but insisted that General Percival come to see him personally. The Japanese commander told Percival that his forces "respect the valour of your army and will honour your dead", but then insisted on unconditional surrender. Percival hesitated for nearly an hour, and then signed the British surrender.

One of Yamashita's staff then asked if he was to prepare for a victory parade through the streets of Singapore, to which he received the dry reply:

"No. The war isn't finished. We have lost 3,300 men in the campaign. What have the survivors done to deserve it? We must first honour our dead. Then we'll prepare for future campaigns."

The disaster in Malaya provoked another crisis between the irritable Mr. Curtin and Churchill, following on their earlier disagreement about Tobruk.

Curtin had a majority of two in the Australian parliament and stubbornly refused to introduce the conscription necessary for the defence of Australia. This did not, however, prevent him from abusing Churchill for his lack of zeal in calling the home country to the defence of her Pacific dominions. On December 27, 1941, for example, the following virtual ultimatum appeared over Curtin's signature in the *Melbourne Herald*:

"Without any inhibitions of any kind, I make it quite clear that Australia looks to America, free of any pangs as to our traditional links with the United Kingdom.

"We know the problems that the United Kingdom faces. We know the constant threat of invasion. We know the dangers of dispersal of strength. But we know too that Australia can go, and Britain can still hold on.

"We are therefore determined that Australia shall not go, and we shall exert all our energies towards the shaping of a plan, with the United States as its keystone, which will give to our country some confidence of being able to hold out until the tide of battle swings against the enemy.

"Summed up, Australian external policy will be shaped towards obtaining Russian aid, and working out, with the United States, as the major factor, a plan of Pacific strategy, along with British, Chinese, and Dutch forces."

The reader will be spared the details of the somewhat acrimonious correspondence which followed. In the course of this the Australian Prime Minister went so far as to inform his British opposite number that after all the assurances that had been given to various Canberra governments for years: "the evacuation of Singapore would be regarded here and elsewhere as an inexcusable betrayal."

But it must be emphasised that Churchill, for all his normal impetuosity, made no attempt to modify his attitude to placate the Australian Prime Minister. Faced with the daily-growing threat of the Japanese advance, it was decided to withdraw the 6th and 7th Australian Divisions from the Middle East and incorporate them into the defence of Java and what British and American strategists called the "Malay barrier", separating the Indian Ocean from the Pacific.

△ *Berlin's* Lustige Blätter *jibes at Anglo-Australian discord. "This blighter's really getting me down," grumbles the Australian kangaroo; "I'll have to kick him out."*

▽ Travaso *of Rome salutes the new conquests of Italy's Japanese partner: "Delicacies of the season— yellow sweetbreads."*

CHAPTER 29
BATAAN AND CORREGIDOR

Meanwhile, the defence of the Philippines had been concentrated in the Bataan Peninsula, west of Manila Bay. Here MacArthur had 15,000 Americans and 65,000 Filipinos, although only 10,000 of the latter could be considered as fully trained soldiers. MacArthur's foresight had provided the garrison with ample ammunition, but the position with food supplies was a problem right from the beginning of the siege as the provisions for the garrison itself had to be spread to feed the thousands of refugees who had fled the Japanese advance and now seriously jeopardised the defence of Bataan. Notwithstanding, the American and Filipino forces on the peninsula held out for a very creditable period, not surrendering until April 9, 1942 after a siege of 98 days.

Bataan holds out

On January 10, Lieutenant-General Homma, the commander of the Japanese 14th Army, sent the following message to MacArthur:

"Sir,

You are well aware that you are doomed. The end is near. The question is how long you will be able to resist. You have already cut rations by half. I appreciate the fighting spirit of yourself and your troops who have been fighting with courage. Your prestige and honour have been upheld.

"However, in order to avoid needless bloodshed and to save the remnants of your divisions and your auxiliary troops, you are advised to surrender."

When this summons remained unanswered, the 14th Army attacked the American lines during the night of the 11th. After ten days of fruitless frontal attacks, the Japanese infiltrated the American lines across the slopes of Mount Natib, which the defenders had thought inaccessible, and thus forced the Americans to fall back to their second defence line across the peninsula. The retreat was conducted in an orderly fashion, however, and the American forces did not lose their cohesion. Homma, to his extreme chagrin, had to ask Tokyo for reinforcements.

On February 22, MacArthur received a message from the White House ordering him to quit Bataan, organise the defence of Mindanao to the south, and then proceed to Australia. MacArthur delayed in executing these orders, claiming that his departure would result in the immediate collapse of resistance in the Philippines. On March 10, however, Roosevelt cabled him: "Proceed immediately to Melbourne." General MacArthur could no longer ignore this direct order, and on the night of the 11th, he and his staff sailed from his command post on the island of Corregidor in four PT boats (motor torpedo boats). After an eventful three days at sea, MacArthur landed at Cagayan de Oro in Mindanao, flying from there to Australia on board a B-17 bomber. On this occasion he made his celebrated promise to the journalists waiting for him: "I shall return!"

Major-General J. M. Wainwright, who succeeded MacArthur as commander in the Philippines, visited his superior just before he left. Their conversation has been preserved by John Toland:

"' Jonathan,' [MacArthur] said as they shook hands, 'I want you to understand my position very plainly.' He was leaving he said, only because of insistent, repeated orders from Roosevelt. At first he had told his staff he would refuse, but they convinced him that defying the President's direct order would bring disciplinary action. 'I want you to make it known throughout all elements of your command that I'm leaving over my repeated protests.'

"'Of course I will, Douglas,' said Wainwright.

"'If I get through to Australia, you know I'll come back as soon as I can with as much as I can.' Then he warned of the necessity of greater defense in depth. 'And be sure to give them everything you've got with your artillery. That's the best arm you have.'

"The two men were quiet for a moment. In the distance the dull rumble of battle from Bataan could be heard. Wainwright was thinking of the dwindling ammunition and food supply, his air force of two battered P-40's, of the spreading malaria and dysentery and lack of medicine. He

△ One of the last discussions between Wainright and MacArthur (right) before the latter handed over the defence of Bataan and set off for Australia. MacArthur's famous promise "I shall return" was fulfilled in time–but years too late for the defenders of Bataan.

▽ MacArthur's triumphant arrival in Australia after an eventful voyage by PT boat. After the traumatic experience of the Philippine campaign, it was hardly surprising that he became the champion of all Allied ventures intended to bring the war home to Japan rather than to Germany or Italy.

said, 'You'll get through.'

"'And back,' MacArthur added with determination. He gave Wainwright a box of cigars and two large jars of shaving cream. 'Good-bye Jonathan.' They shook hands warmly. 'If you're still on Bataan when I get back, I'll make you a Lieutenant-General.'

"'I'll be on Bataan if I'm still alive.' Wainwright turned and slowly started back to his lunch."

MacArthur: the right man?

Lieutenant-General Douglas MacArthur had a strong and somewhat theatrical personality. He was the object of passionate disagreement in his own country, not only in political circles, where he was regarded as a possible rival to Roosevelt, but also among his peers in the army and navy, among whom he aroused feelings of great admiration or great animosity. To describe him we may quote the evidence of a British officer who was far from indulgent when assessing the great American military commanders. On leaving Tokyo on November 22, 1945, where he had visited MacArthur, Lord Alanbrooke noted in his diary:

"MacArthur was the greatest general and best strategist that the war produced. He certainly outshone Marshall, Eisenhower and all the other American and British generals including Montgomery. As a fighter of battles and as a leader of men Montgomery was hard to beat, but I doubt whether he could have shown the same strategic genius had he been in MacArthur's position."

Alanbrooke believed that MacArthur, apart from his outstanding qualities as a war leader, also showed great political and diplomatic ability, and this view may certainly be correct. In fact, MacArthur succeeded in keeping the loyalty of the Filipinos during the Japanese occupation, remained on good terms with the intractable Curtin, and after the war won the friendship of Emperor Hirohito and helped the Japanese get over their defeat.

Surrender on Bataan

When he arrived in Australia, General MacArthur, who had been eating at the same mess as his men, noted that he had lost nearly two stones in weight at Bataan. It is thus clear that the American garrison was severely weakened when Homma launched his final assault. Added to this physical debilitation was the loss of morale of the troops, to whom it was now abundantly clear that there was no possibility of a relief force reaching them. These facts, then, make it clear why General Wainwright was unable to galvanise his men to action. Moreover, the Japanese 14th Army had been reinforced with another division and brigade, and had improved its tactics, from now on combining frontal assaults with small-scale landings in the Americans' rear.

On April 1 Wainwright ignored a fresh summons from Homma to surrender and accept an "honourable defeat". The final Japanese attack started two days later, and three days after that the American defences were finally breached. After the failure of one counter-attack, General King, commanding on Bataan, considered that his men were at the end of their tether and sent emissaries to the Japanese to discuss terms on April 9. The surrender was signed the next day; 64,000 Filipinos and 12,000 Americans were taken prisoner.

The Bataan "Death March"

There then followed the notorious "Death March", when the prisoners taken on Bataan were marched from Mariveles 55 miles to the railhead at San Fernando, under the most inhuman conditions. During the march, 2,330 Americans and between 7–10,000 Filipinos died. As the officer responsible, General Homma was tried after the war, found guilty, and executed. General MacArthur, turning down a final appeal for Homma, said: "I am again confronted with the repugnant duty of passing final judgement on a former adversary in a major military campaign ... I approve the finding of guilt and direct the Commanding General, United States Forces in the Western Pacific to execute the sentence."

But the American historian John Toland examined all the documents pertaining to the case and did not come to such definite conclusions about Homma's guilt, attaching blame more to the 14th Army's general staff for their irresponsibility than to Homma himself for criminal intent. The Japanese had expected to find 30,000 prisoners and got 76,000, all of them in poor physical condition. Twenty miles from Mariveles, transport had been provided for the rest of the journey, but only 230 trucks were available. Moreover, the behaviour of the Japanese guards towards their prisoners varied considerably: in some cases it was relatively humane, in others completely abominable. This seems to indicate that these guards were not obeying a general directive from their superiors.

The end in the Philippines

The Japanese now controlled all of Luzon except the island fortress of Corregidor and the islets surrounding it. While the Americans held these, the Japanese were denied the use of Manila harbour. On May 4, the Japanese poured a barrage of 16,000 shells on to the island, and under the cover so provided landed a powerful assault force, which managed to secure a small beach-head. The American garrison numbered 15,000, but of these only 1,300 could be considered battleworthy. Homma

urged Wainwright to surrender, but insisted that if he did so, the capitulation must also apply to all other American forces in the Philippines archipelago. The Japanese would thus be able to secure Mindanao and the islands around the Visayan Sea without firing a shot.

▽ *With his assault forces safely established ashore, General Homma lands on Luzon.*
▽▽ *The Japanese did not have things all their own way in the Philippines, witness these Japanese prisoners taken in an over-confident attack.*

△ *"Toul Pocket, Bataan" by Stanley Dersh. The painting depicts the desperate American-Filipino counter-attack in mid-February 1942 which wiped out the Japanese salients pushed into the American front and postponed the struggle on Bataan for another two months. (This painting was later used for propaganda purposes on a U.S. Department of the Army poster.)*

After a painful mental struggle, and despite MacArthur's intervention, Wainwright finally ordered his subordinates to terminate their resistance. The latter at first protested, but all American resistance finally ended on May 6, 1942. Wainwright was not condemned for ordering the capitulation by the American Government, General Marshall, and MacArthur. Indeed, with General Percival, who had surrendered Singapore, he was one of those invited to the Japanese surrender ceremony on September 2, 1945.

The turn of Burma

According to Churchill, it was not expected in London that the Japanese would invade Burma until they had finished with Malaya and conquered Singapore. As a result of this lack of foresight, the defences of this wealthy colony were extremely sparse. On December 8, 1941 they com-

prised troops totalling about a division – the 1st Burma Division, Burmese battalions stiffened by two British battalions and an Indian brigade. Towards the end of January 1942, the incomplete 17th Indian Division was shipped in. The whole was under Major-General T. J. Hutton. The R.A.F. was in an even worse position, with only four Bristol Blenheim light bombers and 32 superannuated Brewster Buffalo fighters, of which only 24 were airworthy.

Burma was as important to the Japanese as Malaya or India, not only for its oil and other natural resources, but because it contained the "Burma Road", which had only recently been completed and linked Lashio in Burma with Chungking in China. As President Roosevelt had just extended Lend-Lease to Nationalist China, the Japanese High Command considered it vital to sever this only artery supplying Generalissimo Chiang Kai-shek's forces with war supplies from the "arsenal of democracy". The task of destroying this link was entrusted to the 15th Army, under Lieutenant-General S. Iida.

The invaders also had aid in Burma in the form of a large number of agents, whom the Japanese had been enlisting for years. The British knew of this, and on January 18, 1942 arrested the Prime Minister, U Saw. On the same day the Japanese 15th Army took the port and airfield of Tavoy in the south and moved on Moulmein, at the mouth of the Salween. This river, which formed a considerable natural barrier, did not slow the Japanese for long. Moulmein fell on the 31st, and the Japanese pushed on towards the Sittang. The critical phase of the campaign was reached when the Japanese arrived at this river before the retreating 17th Indian Division, under the command of Major-General J. Smyth, V.C. The bridge the division was to have used was blown prematurely, resulting in the loss of two-thirds of the division's men, most of its transport, and all its artillery to the Japanese. This defeat, on February 22, decided the campaign.

Trouble with Australia again

After the fall of Singapore, it had been decided, with the agreement of the Dutch Government, that the 6th and 7th Australian Divisions, which had previously been allocated to the defence of Java and Sumatra, should return to their own country. As the convoy in which the two divisions was sailing was off Ceylon at the time of the attack on Burma, Churchill wished to divert one, if not both, of them to Rangoon. The only result was another rebuff from Mr. Curtin on February 23:

"4. With A.I.F. troops we sought to save Malaya and Singapore, falling back on Netherlands East Indies. All these northern defences are gone or going. Now you contemplate using the A.I.F. to save Burma. All this has been done, as in Greece, without adequate air support.

"5. We feel a primary obligation to save Australia not only for itself, but to preserve it as a base for the development of the war against Japan. In the circumstances it is quite impossible to reverse a decision which we made with the utmost care, and which we have affirmed and reaffirmed."

In this situation there can be no question but that the Australian Prime Minister was right. In so critical a situation, Churchill and the Combined Chiefs-of-Staff Committee would only have been writing off the division or divisions that ventured into this hopeless theatre of operations.

On March 5, 1942, General Sir Harold Alexander arrived from England to take over command in Burma from Hutton. The decision to send out a new commander was, to some extent, quite understandable.

Alexander was an optimistic and determined officer, but within a short time of his arrival realised that he was faced by problems very similar to those which he had met at Dunkirk.

Rangoon abandoned

The capital of Burma was defended by the remnants of the 17th Indian Division, while the 1st Burma Division, made up of native battalions with British and Indian strengthening, was operating against the invaders to the north. But the defenders were so short of men that a 125-mile gap had opened up between the two divisions, and through this the Japanese were infiltrating in considerable numbers. At first Alexander ordered that Rangoon must be held, but then came to Hutton's view that British forces were too weak for this task. He therefore decided to concentrate his troops for the defence

△ *Not British, but Americans (the British-style steel helmet was not replaced by the distinctive G.I. "battle bowler" until the late summer of 1942). These are men from the surrendered fortress of Corregidor Island in Manila Bay, whose fall effectively ended the Philippine campaign.*

f Upper Burma, and the retreat began. Rangoon was abandoned on March 7, the British retreating up the Irrawaddy valley to regroup their forces, now reinforced by the arrival of the British 7th Armoured Brigade, more infantry, and aerial reinforcements from Britain and China. Lieutenant-General William Slim was appointed to command these reorganised forces.

Alexander now decided that his primary strategic objective was the protection of the Yenangyaung oilfields, in which he was to be aided by the Chinese 5th and 6th Armies, under the command of Lieutenant-General "Vinegar Joe" Joseph Stilwell, the American officer who had been considered originally for the command of Operation "Super-Gymnast" but was now Chiang Kai-shek's military right hand. But co-operation with the Chinese proved difficult. A force equivalent in size to a British division was considered an army, and Chinese tactics bore very little resemblance either to Allied or Japanese ones. The following anecdote from Field-Marshal Lord Alexander's memoirs will serve to illustrate this:

"Before the battle of Mandalay I went round the front to inspect our defences and was much impressed to see how cleverly this Chinese Fifth Army had dug in its field guns, which were well sited and cleverly camouflaged. When contact had been gained with the advancing Japanese I again visited the front, and to my astonishment I found that the artillery had disappeared.

"When I asked the army commander what had happened to his guns he said that he had withdrawn them to safety.

" 'Then you mean,' I said, 'that they will take no part in the battle?'

" 'Exactly,' he replied.

" 'But then what use are they?'

"He said: 'General, the Fifth Chinese Army is our best army, because it is the only one which has any field guns, and I cannot afford to risk those guns. If I lose them the Fifth Army will no longer be our best.' "

Retreat to India

In the circumstances, upper Burma was no more defensible than lower Burma. The Japanese 15th Army had been reinforced by two more divisions and more

submarine *Platino* and at midnight on the 21st the battleship *Littorio*, flying the flag of Admiral Iachino, sailed from Taranto, whilst an hour later the cruisers *Gorizia*, *Trento*, and *Bande Nere* left Messina. Each of these two detachments was escorted by four destroyers. At 1427 hours Rear-Admiral Parona's three cruisers made contact with the enemy, whereupon Vian made his convoy turn south-west, covered by the guns of the anti-aircraft cruiser *Carlisle* and the *Hunts*, and engaged the Italians with the rest of his forces. The Italians would not join battle, but preferred to await the arrival of the battleship *Littorio*, which appeared on the scene towards 1640 hours.

Admiral Iachino's plan was to get between Malta and the convoy and then wipe out the ships, but the sirocco, blowing in gusts from the south-east, allowed Vian to take cover behind a smoke-screen, which the Italians, having no radar, could not penetrate. When one of the British cruisers did appear out of the smoke, the enemy could not engage it because of the spray and the smoke which obscured their range-finders. Thus the Italians' enormous superiority in firepower was of little avail to them. At nightfall Iachino made a last attempt to get near to the convoy but he had to withdraw, driven off by the volleys of torpedoes fired off at him by the British destroyers as they counter-attacked and, as none of his ships was equipped for night-fighting, he had to abandon the action a little before 1900 hours.

The result of this second battle of Sirte was not as disappointing for the Italians as it might at first have seemed. Admiral Cunningham had lost the destroyers *Havock* and *Kingston*, which had been heavily damaged and had had to make for Malta. The convoy, having had to sail south-west for hours, could not now reach Valletta before dawn on the 23rd. This caused the loss by bombing of the *Breconshire* and one merchant ship: the two survivors reached harbour but were sunk as they were unloading. And so, out of the 26,000 tons of supplies which had left Alexandria only 5,000 reached their destination. On the other hand two Italian destroyers, ploughing on through the storm, sank with most of their crews. The light cruiser *Bande Nere* was so severely damaged in the same storm that she had to be sent to La Spezia for repairs. On the way there she was sunk by the submarine *Urge* (Lieutenant-Commander E. P. Tomkinson). This was a compensation for the loss of the light cruiser *Naiad*, which had gone down under Rear-Admiral Vian on February 11 in the previous year, torpedoed off the coast of Egypt by *U-565*.

The tragic situation of Malta

The bombardment of Malta, which had been intensified from mid-December 1941 to the end of February, became in March a veritable ordeal by fire: in 31 days 4,927 bombing sorties were flown against the island, and in April no fewer than 9,599 dropped 6,700 tons of bombs. In the Grand Harbour three destroyers, including *Kingston* were sunk and the valiant *Penelope* was so riddled with shrapnel that her crew facetiously renamed her *Pepperpot*. To avoid destruction, the submarines of the 10th Flotilla had to submerge by day with reduced crews.

For its part, the island's air force was decimated in battles in the air or wiped out on the ground. On January 31 there were only 28 fighters left; a fortnight later, there were only 11. In this almost desperate situation help came from the west, that is from Force H, now commanded by Rear-Admiral E. N. Syfret who had taken over from Sir James Somerville. On March 6 the old *Argus*, the first "flat-top" of any navy in the world, and the *Eagle* sent 15 Spitfires, more capable than the Hurricanes of dealing with the Messerschmitt Bf 109F's of X *Fliegerkorps*. This operation was successfully repeated on March 21 and 29.

Generous gesture by America

To speed up the reinforcement of Malta's defence, Winston Churchill appealed to President Roosevelt. On April 1, after describing the tragic situation of Malta's defenders, who had only 20 to 30 fighters as against the 600 of the Axis, and the difficulties of sending them enough Spitfires on the carriers at his disposal, he added:

"Would you be willing to allow your carrier *Wasp* to do one of these trips provided details are satisfactorily agreed between the Naval Staffs? With her broad lifts, capacity and length, we

▽ *Rear-Admiral Sir Philip Vian, commanding the 15th Cruiser Squadron. He had first hit the headlines in the* Altmark *incident, and was now displaying the same panache and initiative in the Mediterranean.*

estimate that *Wasp* could take 50 or more Spitfires. Unless it were necessary for her to fuel, *Wasp* could proceed through the Straits at night without calling at Gibraltar until on the return journey, as the Spitfires would be embarked in the Clyde. Thus, instead of not being able to give Malta any further Spitfires during April, a powerful Spitfire force could be flown into Malta at a stroke and give us a chance of inflicting a very severe and possibly decisive check on the enemy. Operation might take place during third week of April."

President Roosevelt responded to his ally's request in a fine spirit of comradeship. Thus on April 20 *Wasp*, which had got within 620 miles of Malta, sent off 47 Spitfires; these were reduced to six four days later after redoubled attacks by the Luftwaffe. Churchill had therefore to ask for a second run by the American aircraft-carrier and he did this with an argument worth mentioning. He cabled the President on April 20:

"Without this aid I fear Malta will be pounded to bits. Meanwhile its defence is wearing out the enemy's Air Force and effectively aiding Russia."

Roosevelt responded again with help and *Wasp* went back into the Mediterranean on May 9. Together with *Eagle* she sent off 64 Spitfires to Malta; these were followed by a further 17 on May 18 from the British carrier alone. Churchill relates in his memoirs:

"It may be well here to complete the story of the *Wasp*. On May 9 she successfully delivered another important flight of Spitfires to struggling Malta. I made her a signal: 'Who said a wasp couldn't sting twice?' The *Wasp* thanked me for my 'gracious' message. Alas, poor *Wasp*! She left the dangerous Mediterranean for the Pacific and on September 15 was sunk by Japanese torpedoes. Happily her gallant crew were saved. They had been a link in our chain of causation."

The fact remains, however, that the population and the garrison of the island-fortress were put on short rations and that their supply of flour was due to run out on about June 15.

Axis plans against Malta

For a long time now Grand-Admiral Raeder had been maintaining to the Führer that the war would be won at Suez and Basra, but that the capture of these two objectives depended on the seizure of Malta. The day after Admiral Ciliax had forced a passage through the Straits of Dover, Hitler was somewhat more receptive to these ideas and, at the end of February, Field-Marshal Kesselring could write to Marshal Cavallero without fear of repudiation:

"The Führer is in complete agreement with the Italian Command for definite action against the island of Malta. He is following the development of this action with great interest; he will give it all possible support unless Britain attempts a landing on such a scale that it would require a maximum concentration of our forces."

And a few days later, Keitel, the Chief-of-Staff of O.K.W., wrote along the same lines to his Italian opposite number, who welcomed the news as he had long been in favour of this operation, which he considered risky but necessary. Hence on April 12 a Planning H.Q. was set up under General Fassi. The two dictators met on April 30 at Klessheim near Salzburg, and Cavallero, warmly supported by Kesselring, put forward his plan. This produced no practical or theoretical objections, Hitler merely remarking that "an operation like this must be planned down to the smallest detail for if it fails there can be no going back to the beginning." On this

agreement and the promise of substantial German support, the Chief-of-Staff of the *Comando Supremo* drew up his plan for a simultaneous attack on the islands of Malta and Gozo by:

1. Naval and air forces consisting of:
   a. 1,506 combat planes, including 666 from the Luftwaffe;
   b. Admiral Iachino's naval forces;
   c. Admiral Tur's 12th Naval Division (with all the means for landing); and
   d. 14 groups of submarines.
2. Land forces, under General Vecchiarelli, consisting of:
   a. the Luftwaffe's XI *Fliegerkorps* (General Student), a German parachute division, the "Folgore" parachute division, and the "Spezia" airborne division;
   b. XVI Corps (General Carlo Rossi), the "Assieta" Division and the "Napoli" Division; and
   c. XXX Corps (General Sogno), the "Superga", "Livorno", and "Friuli" Divisions.

△ *The American aircraft-carrier* Wasp (top), *and British* Argus. *Between them and the British* Eagle, *these two ships were largely instrumental in saving Malta by supplying her with fighter reinforcements.*

A heavily-laden Spitfire with a large "slipper"-type drop tank under its fuselage, roars down the flight deck of the carrier Eagle. On March 7, Eagle sent off 15 Spitfires, all flown by R.A.F. pilots having their first experience of carrier operations. All 15 aircraft reached Malta safely.

The operation was called "Herkules" by the Germans. They also contributed a number of heavy tanks and some 300 transport aircraft. The Axis powers would thus have eight divisions against the Allies' garrison on the two islands of 30,000–35,000 men under Lieutenant-General Sir William Dobbie.

It had been originally planned that the assault on Malta should precede Rommel's offensive. This was to start from the line Sollum–Halfaya–Sidi Omar. The need to train the "Folgore" Division paratroopers, however, compelled Cavallero to reverse this order of priority and the resultant delay was to have incalculable consequences.

General Carboni's opposition

Had Operation "Herkules", which the Italians called Esigenza "C3", any chance of success? The Duce's Chief-of-Staff did not doubt it, nor did Kesselring and Admiral Weichold, Raeder's liaison officer at Supermarina. On the other hand, at Leghorn, where he was conscientiously training the "Friuli" Division for its assault on the cliffs of Malta, General Giacomo Carboni considered that the enterprise was some new folly imposed on Italy by the Germans because of the servility of Cavallero. Nor did he keep this opinion to himself. In particular he spoke to Count Ciano of his pessimistic conclusions. Ciano often went to the great Tuscan port and Carboni had become friendly with him.

"I had a long and interesting conversation with Carboni," Ciano noted in his diary on May 31. "At the moment he is commanding one of the assault divisions which is to participate in the Malta operation. He is decidedly against it. He is convinced that we shall have heavy losses and that nothing will come of it. He takes it out on Cavallero, whom he considers to be an intriguer and a man of bad faith. He is also very pessimistic about the Russian Front. He doesn't think that the Germans can undertake any operations of far-reaching proportions during the summer. It is a war of position rather than anything else. From this he draws the most sinister conclusions about the German future. Carboni is a general of great ability. One must not forget, however, that he was dismissed by the Secret Military Intelligence for his anti-German attitude, and that he is the son of an American mother."

It was the same story again on June 20.

"General Carboni has come to Rome to talk over the Malta enterprise, which is set for the next new moon. He is convinced, technically convinced, that we are heading for an unheard-of disaster. Preparations have been childish, equipment is lacking and inadequate. The landing troops will never succeed in landing, or, if they land they are doomed to total destruction. All the commanders are convinced of this, but no one dares to speak for fear of reprisals by Cavallero."

But the commander of the "Friuli" Division went further than these talks with Ciano in what he calls his "preparatory fire against the General Staff". He did not hesitate, in fact, to inform the Prince of Piedmont of his misgivings. The Prince, as the relevant army group C.-in-C. had been called upon to supervise the operation. The memorandum sent to him by Carboni late in May 1942 covers two pages in the Prince's memoirs and we will give the reader only the introduction and the conclusion:

"The Malta operation, carried out with the inadequate means at our disposal, takes on the appearance of a new folly, the consequences of which will be not only a new loss of military and political prestige to us and an irreparable loss of men, ships, and planes but will also have another effect.

"There is reason to fear that the enemy might take advantage of a defeat on Malta by landing in Italy and that our ally might seize on this 'new confirmation of our strategic and tactical weakness' to take over command and ravage our country. And so the Malta expedition will be in every way profitable to the Germans. It has certain similarities with the operation at Sidi Barrani in the sense that it might have the same consequences for our country as Sidi Barrani had for Libya: it would bring the British or the Germans here, and perhaps both of them together."

Pessimist or realist?

After the heir to the throne, General Carboni approached the King himself during a royal inspection of his division, but apparently without any more success. The fact remains, however, that these complaints, which were not made through the proper channels, brought no sanctions on their author, though General Ambrosio, the Army Chief-of-Staff, was not unaware of them. Not only did General Carboni remain in command of the "Friuli" Division but in December 1942 he was appointed commander of the corps occupying Corsica. *Esigenza "C3"*

△ *Spitfire V's on a Malta airfield. All too soon, however, the overwhelming numerical superiority enjoyed by the Axis whittled away the reinforcements flown in from the carriers.*

▽ *April 24, 1942, and thick palls of dust from Malta's light soil drift over Floriana, south-west of Valletta, in the aftermath of a raid. The twin-spired church is St. Publius, badly damaged in the raids of April.*

▽ *The desperate condition of Malta meant that all useful hands were turned to the work in hand. Here soldiers make up ammunition belts for the 20-mm wing cannon of Spitfires.*
▽▽ *A pilot waits in his cockpit as soldiers and airmen refuel and rearm his Spitfire in its dispersal pen.*

was cancelled for reasons which we shall examine later. It is naturally difficult to decide who would have been right, Cavallero or Carboni, the optimist or the pessimist. There are, however, two observations to be made on this controversy:

1. That the Malta undertaking was not in any way imposed on the Chief-of-Staff of the *Comando Supremo* by the Germans, as the former commander of the "Friuli" Division states. From the beginning to the end of this affair, all the initiatives point to Cavallero rather than to O.K.W. It would seem that those concerned were only too glad to take advantage of Rommel's victories to climb down from the undertakings that had been made; and

2. It cannot be denied that the means at the disposal of General Vecchiarelli were "inadequate" for the execution of his mission, at least to some extent. But Carboni in his argument makes no allusion to the state in which a surprise

attack might have found the defenders. Neither General Dobbie on the spot nor the Chiefs-of-Staff Committee in London were very optimistic about holding Malta without a prompt and vigorous offensive by the 8th Army.

As we have quoted Count Ciano and General Carboni, witnesses for the prosecution in this historic dispute, it is only right that we should hear the witness for the defence, Admiral Vittorio Tur who, it will be remembered, had been put in charge of the landing operations proper. He wrote of Marshal Cavallero:

"I can state that the Marshal was a true leader for whom I had the highest esteem and devotion and whose end showed the firmness of his character and the uprightness of his conscience; a leader who always encouraged and appreciated the preparatory work which had been done, giving sound advice and intelligent orders, and who never had the slightest doubt about the outcome of the operation."

CHAPTER 33
DRIVE TO THE CAUCASUS

In his H.Q. at Poltava, Bock had chosen May 18 for Operation *"Fridericus I"*, a pincer movement intended to take the Izyum salient as ordered. But at dawn on May 12 he learned that his 6th Army (General Paulus) was itself being heavily attacked around Khar'kov. A few hours later it became clear that it was not simply a local attack but a major strategic offensive employing dozens of divisions and hundreds of tanks.

At the end of the winter, Stalin and his advisers in Moscow had refused to accept that they should remain on the defensive when spring came. On the contrary, they intended to attack. The *Great Patriotic War* includes this justifiable comment on their decision: "The Supreme Command G.H.Q. exaggerated the success of the counter-attack and ordered a general offensive in all important sectors, thus scattering their reserves."

Anyhow, at the end of March, *Stavka* rejected, because of lack of reserves, a plan put forward by Marshal Timoshenko which would have brought Russian forces back to the Dniepr between Gomel' and Cherkassy, and between Cherkassy and Nikolayev on the right bank of the river. Instead, they placed the South and South-West Fronts under his command, and gave him the much more modest objective of Khar'kov.

Khruschev is sent to Stalin

Timoshenko divided his forces into two. North, in the Volchansk area, the 28th Army (Lieutenant-General D. I. Ryabyshev) reinforced to 16 infantry and three cavalry divisions, and six armoured brigades, was to break through the German front and exploit its success towards the south-west. In the south, the 6th Army (Lieutenant-General A. M. Gorodnyansky: 11 infantry and six cavalry divisions, and 13 tank brigades) would break out of the Izyum salient, attack south of Khar'kov, and having broken through, then converge on the north-west, moving in front of Ryabyshev. Finally, cavalry and armoured forces would advance quickly on Dniepropetrovsk.

In the Volchansk sector, the 28th Army's attack, launched on May 9, was checked after having pushed out a salient of some 20 miles into the enemy lines. In the south, on the other hand, Gorodnyansky set General Paulus and Field-Marshal von Bock a very worrying problem. On May 14 VIII Corps was nearly in ruins; on May 16 the Russians arrived at Merefa and Karlovka on the heels of the 454th Security Division, which had given ground, and a Hungarian division which had done no better. Sixty-four guns had also been lost.

In these circumstances, could Operation *"Fridericus"* retrieve the situation? Paulus and Bock doubted it very much, and on May 14 the latter noted in his diary: "Although I am most unwilling to do this, I can only propose, as far as the Army Group is concerned, to grab from Kleist [right prong of the *"Fridericus"* pincer] everything we can get hold of, say three or four divisions, one of them armoured, and transport them to XI Panzer Corps' left flank. From there they will attack the southern flank of the enemy pocket."

In agreement for once, Hitler and Halder were intractable. Colonel-General von Kleist managed to save a day on his timetable and counter-attack at dawn on May 17. He fell on the Russian 9th and 57th Armies (South Front) under Major-General F. M. Kharitonov and Lieutenant-General K. P. Podlas, who had to protect the offensive by the South-West Front from surprise attacks. It is true that Kharitonov had only four divisions to hold a 65-mile front and that *Luftflotte* IV was applying its usual great pressure.

It took no miracle therefore for *Gruppe* von Kleist, with 15 divisions, including four Rumanian, to reach the Donets within 48 hours. Faced with this unex-

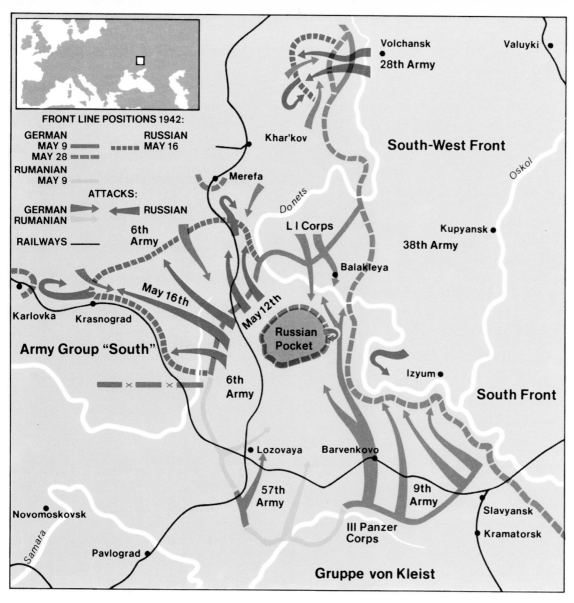

Map legend:

FRONT LINE POSITIONS 1942:
GERMAN RUSSIAN
MAY 9 ———— MAY 16 ▪▪▪▪▪
MAY 28 ▪▪▪▪▪
RUMANIAN
MAY 9 ————

ATTACKS:
GERMAN ⟶ ⟵ RUSSIAN
RUMANIAN

RAILWAYS ————

Volchansk
28th Army
Valuyki

Khar'kov
South-West Front
Merefa
Oskol
Donets
L I Corps
Kupyansk
38th Army
Balakleya
6th Army
May 16th
Karlovka
Krasnograd
Russian Pocket
May 12th
Army Group "South"
Izyum
South Front
6th Army
Lozovaya
Barvenkovo
9th Army
57th Army
Slavyansk
Novomoskovsk
III Panzer Corps
Kramatorsk
Samara
Pavlograd
Gruppe von Kleist

◁ *The Battle of Khar'kov. The German forces, while preparing their own major offensive, had been surprised by the Russian attack, but had responded with considerable speed and assurance to turn surprise into victory, with a total bag of 214,000 prisoners.*

pected reversal, Timoshenko asked the Supreme Command to authorise the abandonment of the Khar'kov attack. This was refused, so he appealed to Stalin through N. S. Khruschev, political member of the council of South-West Front. During the 20th Congress of the Communist Party of the Soviet Union in February 1956, Khruschev explained this fruitless attempt.

"Against all good sense Stalin rejected our proposal and ordered that the Khar'kov operation must continue; and yet several of our army units were already threatened with encirclement and extermination . . . I telephoned the Chief-of-Staff, Vasilevsky, and begged him to explain the situation to Comrade Stalin. But Vasilevsky replied that Comrade Stalin wanted to hear no more about it. So I telephoned Stalin at his villa. It was Malenkov who replied. I said I wanted to speak to Stalin personally. Stalin's answer was that I could speak to Malenkov. Again I asked for Stalin himself. But he

Tobruk Falls

On June 2, after a battle that looked as if it could go either way, the British 150th Brigade and 1st Army Tank Brigade capitulated at Got el Oualeb. Rommel then began to close the pincers on Bir Hakeim. The British counterattack was unco-ordinated and too widely dispersed to be effective and was defeated. At dawn on June 20 Rommel attacked Tobruk with his two Panzer divisions and the Italian XX Corps, supported by Stukas. On June 21, Major-General H.B. Klopper surrendered. The remains of the 8th Army took up position at El Alamein, where they were joined by the 9th Australian Division from Syria and the 4th Indian Division from Cyprus. By July 1, Rommel had only 6,400 men, 41 tanks and 71 guns under his command to face the British position. On July 17 his four armoured divisions only had 58 German and Italian tanks between them. The British attacked the Italian units and by July 22 had taken 7,000 prisoners.

continued to refuse, though he was only a few steps from the telephone. After having 'listened', so to speak, to our request Stalin ordered: 'Leave things as they are.' And what was the result? The worst one could expect – our armies were surrounded by the Germans and we lost hundreds of thousands of men."

Two armies destroyed

▽ *Advance to the Donets: German troops take a quick rest before the final drive to this major objective. Shortly after his armies had reached the river, however, Hitler altered his plans and diverted the advance from Stalingrad to the Caucasus. It was to prove a fatal change of plan.*

Khruschev's account may be somewhat embroidered but there is no doubt about Stalin's *"niet"*, and the results were disastrous. Unleashed at its appointed place, III Panzer Corps (General A. von Mackensen) moved up the right bank of the Donets, thrusting vigorously into the Russians' rear, and sealed off the Izyum bridgehead. On May 23 in the Balak-

leya area it joined up with LI Corps (General von Seydlitz-Kurzbach), thrown in by Paulus to meet it from the south-east of Khar'kov. Caught in the trap, the Russian 6th and 57th Armies counter-attacked furiously towards Izyum in the hope of breaking free. But in vain, for on May 28 the German 6th Army crushed the last centres of enemy resistance. Twenty infantry and seven cavalry divisions, and 13 armoured brigades had been wiped out, losing 214,000 prisoners, 1,246 tanks, and 2,026 guns. General Gorodnyansky was killed while fighting in the front line, and his colleague Podlas committed suicide with all his staff to escape captivity. Army Group "South" losses at this time were no more than 20,000, according to Field-Marshal von Bock.

While Stalin was still alive, Soviet historians did their best to conceal this major disaster. Since the sensational declarations by Khruschev at the Kiev Congress, there has been less reticence about its causes and consequences. In fact, on a throw of the dice, Stalin had wasted his strategic striking force, and before he could rebuild it Paulus reached the Volga and Kleist was threatening Grozny. The military historian V. P. Morosov, explaining Timoshenko's position just before Operation *"Blau"*, writes: "The reserves of the South-West Front were insignificant, since most of them had been used in previous battles in the Khar'kov sector."

The fall of Sevastopol'

The striking victory at Kerch' had freed the German 11th Army from any pressure on its rear, so Manstein was able to start the attack on Sevastopol' on June 7. He had received very strong reinforcements: three assault gun units, 24 *Nebelwerfer* rocket-launching batteries, and most of the siege artillery in general reserve. Amongst the last were two 60-cm *Karl* mortars and the 80-cm super-heavy *Gustav* railway gun, which fired seven-ton shells at the rate of three an hour. This monster's barrel was 100 feet long and weighed 130 tons. In addition, the Luftwaffe had provided 600 aircraft, including General von Richthofen's Stukas.

It was, nevertheless, a hard nut to crack. Commanded by General I. E. Petrov, the Sevastopol' garrison had seven divisions, plus one unmounted cavalry division and Vice-Admiral F. S. Oktyabrsky's three brigades of marines. It depended on 3,600 permanent or temporary fortified positions set up in depth over some 15 miles. Amongst these was the Maxim Gorky fort, with four 305-mm guns in two turrets. The Russians had no opposition for the enemy's overwhelming air power, however.

Manstein's attack involved three corps, including the Rumanian mountain corps, in all nine divisions, including two Rumanian. LIV Corps had the main task, to attack on the northern front, while XXX Corps with stronger forces took the southern front. It has been calculated that the German artillery fired about 46,700 tons of shells, and that the Luftwaffe dropped 125,000 bombs during 25,000 sorties in one month. But for all that, the defenders were not intimidated. Each attack had to be decided by close hand-to-hand combat. When German infantry and pioneers had overrun the portions of any particular fort above the ground, they had then to overcome resistance in the labyrinth of underground installations, with the risk of being blown up with the defenders. And with destroyers and submarines the Black Sea Fleet worked hard to reinforce and supply the garrison. But although the German 11th Army's progress was slow, it was still sure and relentless.

On June 27, LIV Corps reached the north side of North Bay, and during the night of June 28 and 29 got its 22nd Airborne Division across in motor assault craft. XXX Corps had taken the dominating heights of Sapun. Sevastopol' was lost, but the defenders still gave the 11th Army a hard task. On July 4 Hitler had made Colonel-General von Manstein a Field-Marshal, but he had to wait until July 9 before the last stubborn resistance in the Khersonesskiy peninsula was overcome, fighting to the last cartridge and the last drop of water.

The Germans lost 24,111 killed and wounded, but captured 95,000 prisoners and 467 guns. The Germans were now in possession of the whole Crimea except the southern mountains, where there were still partisans, and the 11th Army was now available for other tasks.

Meanwhile the German 6th Army, not satisfied with having overcome the Izyum and Volchansk bridgeheads, itself crossed the Donets to secure a good jumping off position on the Oskol, the left bank tributary of this important waterway. This part of *"Fridericus"* brought in 45,000 prisoners, 266 tanks, and 208 guns.

According to Halder's table, already referred to, Field-Marshal von Bock had on June 16, between the Kerch' Strait and the Kursk area, 73 divisions of all types, including nine Panzer, seven motorised (two of them *Waffen* S.S.), and 26 satellite divisions. If the *Great Patriotic War* is to be believed, Stalin drew no conclusions from this impressive concentration of forces. Thus we read: "The Soviet High Command of course thought it possible that the Wehrmacht might attack in the south. It considered however that the enemy would not make its main attack on Stalingrad and the Caucasus but, with its forces before Moscow, would try to outflank the centre groups of the Red Army and take Moscow and the central in-

dustrial area."

Hence, in this author's view, *Stavka*'s mistaken decisions during the first part of the summer campaign. Priority was given to reinforcements for the Bryansk Front which, if broken, would have let the enemy through to Tula and the capital. There is no doubt that this is what happened. But according to Accoce's *La guerre a été gagnée en Suisse*, the Soviet agent Rudolf Rössler had, from Lucerne, transmitted the text of Directive No. 41 to his superiors in Moscow. This was on April 14, ten days after Hitler had signed it. On May 3 Colonel-General Halder wrote this note: *"Exchange Telegraph* in Moscow is sending out surprising reports about our intentions."

Also, on June 20, eight days before the attack, a Fieseler *Storch* crashed behind the Russian lines while on its way back to the 23rd Panzer Division H.Q. In the aircraft, Major Reichel had apparently been carrying completely detailed operations orders for XL Corps. One can conclude that Stalin had therefore received more than enough information about enemy intentions from his Intelligence, but that he had ignored their reports.

Eastern Front, 1942

From 19 November, 1942, the *Wehrmacht* was outmanoeuvred by a Soviet counter-stroke. On November 23 five corps of the German forces were surrounded in the Stalingrad pocket. Air cover was reduced for the German forces on the Eastern Front as the Luftwaffe had increased commitments in Western Europe defending ports and other installations from British and American bombs, while the Russian air force continued to expand with the help of Lend-Lease.

Hitler had issued a directive for a summer offensive in which all the available German and Allied forces would be concentrated on the Don to conquer the Caucasian oil areas and to capture the passes giving access to the southern slopes of the Caucasus mountains. Stalingrad was to be taken, or eliminated, as an industrial and communications centre. After this the Caucasus would be invaded. If this plan was at all feasible, the likelihood of its success was reduced by the manner in which it was directed by Hitler, with frequent changes of plan depending on his mood at the time.

△ *The battle for Sevastopol'. A poster for occupied France extols the power of the German armed forces, and in this instance with reason. Aided by such powerful artillery, Manstein was able to progress slowly but surely to the overwhelming of the celebrated fortress of Sevastopol'.*

Why? Perhaps he thought he was being deliberately misled by the enemy, and clung more than ever to the belief that Moscow was to be the main objective of the coming German offensive.

Breakthrough on the Don

On June 28 *Gruppe* von Weichs attacked on a 90-mile front with its left south of Orel and its right at Oboyan. Colonel-General von Weichs sent in his own 2nd Army, the 4th *Panzerarmee* (Colonel-General Hoth), and the Hungarian 2nd Army (Colonel-General Jany), in all 23 divisions, including three Panzer and two motorised.

Two days later it was the turn of Paulus's 6th Army, which extended the attack another 50 miles, with 18 divisions, including two Panzer and one motorised. Paulus's XL Corps (3rd and 23rd Panzer Divisions and 29th Motorised Division) was to close the pincer with Hoth. It was a striking success. The left of the Bryansk Front (General Golikov) and the right of the South-West Front were broken. On July 1 the Panzers were at Stary-Oskol and reached Valuyki on July 3, while one of General Hoth's divisions stormed a bridge over the Don and pushed into Voronezh. This created a pocket in which 30,000 Russians were taken prisoner.

The Don-Donets corridor was therefore opened up according to the plan adopted on April 5. The Germans were to exploit this opening with Hoth and Paulus rolling through it to meet the 1st *Panzerarmee* (Colonel-General von Kleist), preparing to attack north-east across the Donets. Though fearing a counter-attack on his flank, Bock nevertheless kept his 4th *Panzerarmee* around Voronezh. This act of timidity cost him his command; on July 15 Colonel-General von Weichs took over Army Group "B", leaving his own 2nd Army, already in defensive positions on the Orel-Voronezh front, to General H. von Salmuth.

In spite of this error the 6th Army still moved on towards the great curve of the Don and threatened to overrun the South-West Front. This brought an order from Timoshenko on July 7 for a retreat. It meant that Army Group "A", attacking two days later, met only rearguards when crossing the Don. Field-Marshal List's forces, from left to right, were the 1st *Panzerarmee* (Kleist) and *Gruppe* Ruoff

(17th Army and the Italian 8th Army) that is another 24 German, five Rumanian, three Italian, and one Slovak (including four Panzer and four motorised) divisions.

At the same time, Paulus was arriving at Rossosh' and a gigantic pincer movement was taking shape between Voronezh and Rostov, involving 52 divisions, including 18 armoured and motorised (about 2,300 tanks). On July 12 List extended his operation to the Sea of Azov, broke through the enemy lines at Krasnyy Luch, and five days later took Voroshilovgrad. This new setback, to say the least, forced Stalin to order Lieutenant-General R. Ya. Malinovsky, commander of South Front, to fall back in his turn. He perhaps intended to bar the enemy's way to the bend of the Don along a line from Voronezh to Rostov, but in this case he had not appreciated the weakened state of his own forces and the offensive momentum of the Panzers.

So on July 15 Hoth and his *Panzerarmee* took Millerovo, having covered half the distance to Stalingrad in three weeks. In view of this situation, the next day Halder called together the heads of his Intelligence and Operations sections to discuss the possibility of lunging for Stalingrad without waiting for the fall of Rostov. He was thus remaining faithful to the spirit of the April 5 directive, while Hitler was moving further away from it.

Fearing that the 1st Army might run into difficulties at Rostov, the Führer, from July 13, had placed Hoth, now reinforced by XL Corps, under Army Group "A"; then he had ordered it to swing from east to south-east. This brought it on July 17 to Tsimlyansk, upstream from the junction of the Donets and the Don, while Kleist himself had forced the Donets at Kamensk-Shakhtinskiy. Hitler remained deaf to the warnings from Halder and thought he was going to be able to pull off a massive encircling movement as successful as those at Kiev and Bryansk-Vyaz'ma in 1941, thus opening up the way to the Caucasus and pulling off the great strategic coup of which he dreamed.

An enormous bottleneck and major supply difficulties then built up. But above all, without XL Corps' armoured and motorised strength, the 6th Army remained the only force still making for Stalingrad, instead of the two army groups as originally planned. Hoth's transfer prevented him from exploiting his newly-won bridgeheads on the southern Don and striking to the Volga. Paulus, having to depend on his own resources, was forced to mark time while the enemy were using every means in their power to organise quickly a new Stalingrad Front.

Moreover, Paulus himself was far from overjoyed with the situation. Talking after the battle with his son Ernest Alexander, who had been wounded in a tank, he told him: "You can see the damage your tanks inflicted on the Russians. There are heaps of their tanks destroyed on the battlefield. We were told this story by a captured Russian officer – Timoshenko had been watching a tank battle from an observation post, and when he saw the rate at which his tanks were literally shot to pieces by their opponents he went pale and left, muttering 'It's frightful, frightful'." However, the wounded son sensed concern rather than satisfaction behind his father's spirited account of events. Paulus was certainly wondering what new reserves might be produced by the enemy who seemed, like Lerna's hydra, to sprout new heads as soon as the old ones were cut off.

On July 23 Rostov fell to Colonel-General von Kleist, but did not yield the expected amount of prisoners and booty. Hitherto in a state of depression, Hitler, again for no good reason, became once more optimistic. Hence his Directive No. 45, to carry out Operation "Braunschweig". It was signed on July 23 at his new H.Q., set up at Vinnitsa in the western Ukraine to enable him to keep a closer watch on the current offensive. In his preamble he proclaimed: "In a three-week campaign the main objectives I had indicated behind the southern wing of the Eastern Front have been achieved. Only remnants of Timoshenko's armies have managed to escape encirclement and reach the south bank of the Don. It must be admitted that they will be reinforced from the Caucasus. The concentration of another group of armies is taking place near Stalingrad, where the enemy is likely to make a stubborn defence."

It was on these ill-conceived premises that he based the following orders for his army groups:

"A" was to:
1. occupy the east coast of the Black Sea from the Taman' peninsula, opposite Kerch', to Batumi, inclusively;
2. take the Maykop and Armavir heights, and by successive wheeling movements through the west Caucasian passes overcome enemy resistance in the coastal area; and

3. simultaneously launch a fast mobile force (1st and 4th *Panzerarmee*) towards Grozny and then Baku. The Italian Alpine Corps would be used in this operation, blocking the central Caucasian passes.

"B" was to:
1. defend the Don between Voronezh and the great river bend at Kalach;
2. destroy the enemy forces concentrating at Stalingrad and take the town;
3. extend the line of defence between the bend of the Don and the Volga, upstream from Stalingrad; and
4. launch a fast mobile force towards Astrakhan' and block the Volga, downstream from Stalingrad.

The July 23 directive has since the war found no defenders on the German side. All the West German military historians' accounts consulted agree that the disaster which followed was the direct result of the decision imposed on the High Command by Hitler. To quote just one writer, the former chief-of-staff of LII Corps, Major-General Hans Doerr, who took part in the campaign with Army Group "A": "This July 23 must be considered as the day it became clear that the German Supreme Command abandoned standard principles of warfare to adopt peculiar new approaches stemming rather from Adolf Hitler's irrational and diabolical power than from methodical and realistic military practice. Once again history proved that Faith and the Devil triumphed over Reason. The trained soldiers around

△ *July 4, 1942, and the German Army moves in to occupy its well-earned prize of Sevastopol'.*

△ Men of the Rumanian
Mountain Corps. While they held
the centre of the Axis front, the
German LIV and XXX Corps to
the north and south of them
closed in remorselessly on the
Sevastopol' garrison commanded
by General Petrov.

thus assumed that victory at Stalingrad and in the Caucasus would force Turkey, in the south, and Japan, in the Far East, to declare war on the U.S.S.R.)."

Hitler's blunder

Eremenko's argument is not convincing. The "important issue" was quite simply that in ignoring the aim set down in Directive No. 41–first Stalingrad, then the Caucasus–Hitler ordered simultaneous and, what is worse, divergent attacks on the two objectives.

But this is not all, for the Führer made ruinous reductions in the army groups intended to complete Operation "Braunschweig". In particular, the 9th and 11th Panzer Divisions were removed from the 2nd Army's inactive front and assigned to Field-Marshal von Kluge. An O.K.W. decision, dated July 9, ordered the S.S. Leibstandarte Motorised Division, which Hitler had not wanted to transfer, to France to repel any possible invasion landing. The excellent Grossdeutschland Division, held up at Rostov, would have joined them if it had not been sent on a futile errand to reinforce Army Group "Centre". Finally, though it had been planned that the whole 11th Army should cross the Kerch' Strait, it was decided that only XLII Corps and the 46th Division would take part in this movement, while six other divisions were dispersed to the four winds.

Eventually Army Groups "A" and "B", which had had 68 divisions on June 28, had no more than 57 on August 1. It is true that List and Weichs then had 36 satellite divisions instead of the initial 26, but it must be re-emphasised that these were not capable of taking the offensive. With reduced forces–besides the usual wastage from battle casualties–List and Weichs saw their two fronts lengthening inordinately before them:

500 miles on June 28;
750 miles on July 25, after reaching the Voronezh – Tsimlyansk – Rostov line;
Over 2,500 miles, after reaching their final objectives, along the line Voronezh – Stalingrad – Astrakhan' – Baku – Tbilisi – Batumi – Kerch' Strait.

Even subtracting 1,100 miles of coast from the last figure, the remaining 1,400 miles suffice to show that the July 23 directive was the product of megalomania, of a sick mind.

Hitler were virtually impotent, under the spell of the Devil."

Of course Russian historians do not agree with Major-General Doerr's view. One can only quote here the opinion of Marshal A. I. Eremenko, former commander of the Stalingrad Front. He writes: "German generals will not succeed in proving that if Hitler had not forced them to get bogged down in the battle for Stalingrad they would have achieved victory and in any case would have taken the Caucasus in the autumn of 1942. The most important issue was not that Hitler was thrusting simultaneously towards both Stalingrad and the Caucasus, but that he had insufficient forces to fight both battles successfully. He had imposed this impossible task on his army to prove to satellites and potential allies the strength of the Wehrmacht (it was

Stalin's analysis

What would have happened if the Führer had stuck to the April 5 plans? Without going as far as saying that he would have taken Stalingrad in his stride, one can draw up the list of the opposing forces that clashed on July 22 at the great bend of the Don, between Kletskaya in the north and Verkhne-Kumskiy in the south, over a 130-mile front:

1. On the German side, six Panzer and three motorised divisions from the 4th *Panzerarmee* and the 6th Army, followed by the best German infantry divisions.
2. On the Russian side, the 61st and 62nd Armies of the Stalingrad Front, which,

on July 12, came under Marshal Timoshenko on the South-West Front.

According to the *Great Patriotic War*, on July 22 the 62nd Army had six divisions in the line and the 64th only two; three more were moving up quickly by forced marches. But in the open plains 11 divisions extended over 130 miles could provide no more than an unsubstantial piecemeal defence. Also, the successive defeats sustained by the Red Army from the fall of Kerch' to the capture of Rostov had been a severe blow to morale, and a certain defeatism seemed to be gaining ground in its ranks. Soviet historians have been very discreet about this crisis, which reached its height about July 25. But it was serious enough for Stalin to issue his order of the day of July 28, of which the most important passages are

△ *German engineers take a breather as the first columns of infantry cross their partially completed bridge over one of the major river barriers so abundant in Russia.*

△ *An abandoned Russian A.A. gun, its barrel destroyed by the crew before they pulled back. Despite the number of excellent A.A. weapons available to it, the Red Army was still overwhelmed by the localised concentration of forces achieved by such formations as VIII Fliegerkorps.*

be left with no grain, fuel, metal, raw materials, workshops, factories, or railways. Therefore the moment has come to stop the retreat: not another step back! This must be our watchword. Every position and every yard of Soviet territory must be defended tenaciously and to the last drop of our blood. We must hang on to every piece of Soviet land, and defend it at all costs."

Stalin spoke of the satisfactory progress of Soviet war production and Hitler's mounting difficulties as he tried to achieve his objectives. He continued: "What do we need? Order and discipline in our companies, battalions, regiments, divisions, armoured units, and air force squadrons. This is our greatest weakness. If we want to defend and save our country we must impose much stricter discipline and order in the army. Cowards and panic-mongers will be executed on the spot. Henceforth every commander, soldier, and political officer must be subject to iron discipline. Not a step back unless ordered by the supreme commander!"

Perhaps Stalin wanted his subordinates to be blamed for the grim consequences of his own mistaken conduct of the operations. In any case, at the same time there was a whole series of changes and reshuffles of commands, both at front and at army level, which could indicate only a certain disarray amongst the generals.

reproduced below, as published in A. M. Samsonov's work on the Stalingrad campaign. Summing up 13 months of war, Stalin wrote:

"Since the loss of the Ukraine, White Russia, the Baltic States, the Donets basin and other areas, our territory is decidedly smaller at present, and any reserves of men, grain, metal, and factories are much weaker. We have lost 70 million inhabitants and an annual production of 13 million tons of grain and 10 million tons of metal. We have now lost our superiority in reserves of manpower and cereals. To continue to retreat is to give up ourselves and our country for lost.

"Every inch of territory we concede strengthens the enemy and weakens the defence of our country. We must oppose pitilessly the view that we can retreat indefinitely because our country is rich and large, our population immense, and our grain always abundant. Such statements are untrue and harmful; they weaken us and strengthen the enemy, since if we do not stop the retreat we shall

The Germans approach Stalingrad

Whatever the weakness of the Soviet forces barring his way to Stalingrad, Field-Marshal von Weichs, as a result of the July 23 directive, had only the 6th Army to break through them. But even this was not complete since Paulus was waiting for the Italian 8th Army (General Gariboldi) to extend the line from the Hungarian 2nd Army (General Jany) on the Don, and meanwhile had to cover his flank with his own forces. Again, fuel was in short supply and he could not use all his armour at once. This explains his slow progress from the bridgehead he had taken on July 20 at Bokovskaya on the Chir. On July 30 Hitler returned the 4th *Panzerarmee* to Army Group "B", but Hoth, on receiving his new orders, was over 90 miles to the south-west of Tsimlyansk, and his orders were to move towards Stalingrad by the left bank of the Don.

On August 4 the 6th Army was nevertheless at Kalach at the top of the river bend, but the Russian 1st Tank Army (Major-General K. S. Moskalenko) got across the river and put up a stubborn resistance which lasted a week. Paulus finally overcame it with a pincer movement. His XIV Panzer Corps (General G. von Wietersheim) pushed from north to south to meet the XXIV Panzer Corps (General W. von Langermann und Erlenkamp) in the enemy's rear. A brilliant success, but the 6th Army was not able to exploit it until August 21.

On that day LI Corps, magnificently supported by *Luftflotte* IV and with insignificant casualties, established two bridgeheads on the eastern bank of the Don, upstream of Kalach. On the evening of August 23 the 16th Panzer Division, leading the XIV Panzer Corps, arrived at Rynok on the west bank of the Volga after a thrust of over 30 miles. Wietersheim was counter-attacked furiously from north and south and wanted to retreat. Consequently he received the order to hand over his corps to Lieutenant-General Hube, commander of the 16th Panzer Division. A well-timed action by VIII Corps (General W. Heitz) relieved XIV Panzer Corps and made a defensive front possible between the Don and the Volga upstream from Stalingrad. LI Corps followed up its success towards the southeast, which allowed Paulus to combine his operations with Hoth's.

Making for the bend in the Volga by way of the left bank of the Don, Hoth had been reduced to six divisions, of which one was armoured and one motorised. It is not surprising therefore that with such slender resources he was stopped at the exit from Abganerovo on August 10. As Army Group "B" had no reserves it was up to Paulus to help them out, and he transferred his 297th Division and 24th Panzer Division. This was made possible by his success at Kalach. This reinforcement meant that the 4th *Panzerarmee* could renew the attack on Tinguta, but it was not enough for them to reach the heights overlooking the Volga downstream from Stalingrad. Failing further reinforcements, Hoth switched XLVIII Panzer Corps from his right to his left and pushed it due north. On September 2 he made contact with the 6th Army's right at Voroponvo.

In his attack orders on August 19, Colonel-General Paulus assigned the objective of the south and centre of Stalingrad to LI Corps, and the northern districts to XIV Panzer Corps. The latter could spare only a fraction of its forces for this task because, with VIII Corps, it had to cover the 6th Army in the Volga-Don isthmus. It was not appreciated that this town, which then had 445,000 inhabitants, extended over 20 miles along the Volga and that, in places, there were five miles between the river banks and the western edge of the town.

The assault on Stalingrad

This makeshift attack could only succeed if it met an enemy which was not only beaten but whose morale was extremely low. From the very first engagements in the streets of Stalingrad it was clear to the Germans that the Russians had recovered beyond anyone's expectations, and that the Russians' slogan "The Volga has only

▽ *A Russian infantryman waits in the ruins of a house for the Germans. Vicious street-fighting from such positions was becoming a vitally important part of the Russian campaign as the defence strove not to yield another inch of territory to the invader.*

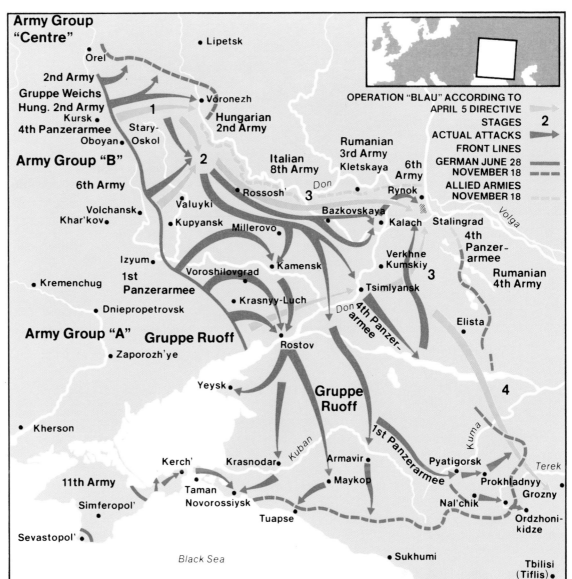

Army Group "Centre"

Lipetsk

Orel

2nd Army
Gruppe Weichs
Hung. 2nd Army
Kursk
4th Panzerarmee
Oboyan

Voronezh
Hungarian
2nd Army

Stary-Oskol

Army Group "B"

6th Army

Volchansk
Khar'kov
Kupyansk
Valuyki
Millerovo

Rossosh'

Italian
8th Army

Rumanian
3rd Army
Kletskaya

6th Army

Don

Bazkovskaya

Rynok

Kalach

Stalingrad

4th Panzer-armee

Volga

Izyum
Kremenchug

1st Panzerarmee

Voroshilovgrad

Kamensk

Verkhne Kumskiy

Rumanian 4th Army

Dniepropetrovsk

Krasnyy-Luch

Tsimlyansk

Don

4th Panzer-armee

Elista

Army Group "A" Gruppe Ruoff

Zaporozh'ye

Rostov

Yeysk

Gruppe Ruoff

Kherson

Kuban

1st Panzerarmee

Kuma

Terek

Kerch'

Krasnodar

Armavir

Pyatigorsk

Prokhladnyy

11th Army

Taman
Novorossiysk

Maykop

Nal'chik

Grozny

Simferopol'

Tuapse

Ordzhoni-kidze

Sevastopol'

Black Sea

Sukhumi

Tbilisi (Tiflis)

OPERATION "BLAU" ACCORDING TO
APRIL 5 DIRECTIVE
STAGES   2
ACTUAL ATTACKS
FRONT LINES
GERMAN JUNE 28
NOVEMBER 18
ALLIED ARMIES
NOVEMBER 18

▷ *The advance towards Stalingrad and the fatal wheel towards the Caucasus. Whatever he did after this, Hitler was doomed – he had lost the only chance he had ever had, that of knocking out his giant adversary in one or two swift blows.*

▽ *Recruiting poster for the Red Navy. Deprived of a more active rôle at sea, the Red Navy units in the Baltic and Black Sea Fleets provided useful and able reinforcements for the orthodox land forces of the Red Army.*

▽ ▷ *The desperate struggle for Sevastopol', as seen by the Soviet artist Krivonogov.*

ВПЕРЕД! НА ЗАПАД!

one bank" was no empty boast. On September 16 Colonel-General von Richthofen, now commander of *Luftflotte* IV, complaining of the lack of spirit in the 6th Army, wrote in his diary: "With a little enthusiastic effort, the town should fall in two days." Less than a week later, he noted, more justly: "September 22. In the town itself progress is desperately slow. The 6th Army will never finish the job at this rate. Above all because it is threatened from the north by the Russians and because reinforcements arrive only in dribs and drabs. We have to fight endless engagements, taking one cellar after another in order to gain any ground at all."

At the same time, in the Caucasus, Army Group "A"'s offensive reached what Clausewitz called a falling-off point, beyond which wear and tear take over from the initial drive and energy.

The day after the fall of Rostov, Field-Marshal List's only worries were about supplies. It was impossible to satisfy the needs of 26 advancing divisions, some moving south-west, some south, and some south-east—so much so that Colonel-General von Kleist jested: "No Russians in front of us; no supplies behind us!" Jerricans of petrol dropped from Junkers Ju 52 transports had to be brought to the Panzers by camel transport.

In spite of these logistic difficulties *Gruppe* Ruoff (German 17th Army and Rumanian 3rd Army) occupied simultaneously on August 9 the port of Yeysk on the south bank of the Sea of Azov, Krasnodar on the Kuban', and Maykop (whose oil wells had been so thoroughly sabotaged that they were not in operation again until four years after the war). On the same day the 1st *Panzerarmee* took Pyatigorsk at the bottom of the first foothills of the Caucasus; on its left, the 16th Motorised Division positioned itself at Elista in the centre of the Kalmuk Steppe and sent out patrols towards Astrakhan'. On August 21 a combined detachment (to avoid jealousies) of the 1st and 4th *Gebirgsjäger* Divisions scaled Mount El'brus (over 17,000 feet), while at the end of the month Kleist crossed the Terek not far from Prokhladnyy, some 80 miles from the Grozny oil wells.

It is true that the nearer they got to their respective objectives (Batumi and Baku), the more List's two groups became separated, and thus found themselves unable to co-ordinate their operations. In addition, Ruoff's outflanking movements over the mountains, intended to overcome resistance on the coast, became increasingly difficult as he moved southeast. On September 6 he succeeded in taking Novorossiysk, but he then had to reorganise his forces before tackling Tuapse.

Hitler reshuffles his commanders

Irritated by this lack of progress, Hitler blamed the local commanders. He therefore sent Colonel-General Jodl to Field-Marshal List to put matters right. But however loyal he was to his leader, Jodl knew his job, and when he was fully in the picture he approved the decisions taken by the Army Group "A"'s commander. On his return to Vinnitsa he made his report accordingly, but could not prevent the dismissal of List, who left his Krasnodar H.Q. on September 9. Moreover,

▽ *The foothills of the Caucasus almost within reach for the crew of this German 3.7-cm A.A. gun on a 5-ton ¾-tracked chassis. Hitler's premature diversion of troops to this southern lunge was to prove the undoing both of the attempt to take Stalingrad swiftly and of the drive to the oilfields of the Caucasus. From this time onwards, Germany lost the strategic initiative on the Eastern Front.*

△ *A shell bursts in front of a Pzkw IV advancing through a maize field in the approaches to the Caucasus* (top) *and the tank's accompanying infantry dive for cover* (bottom).

Hitler was so furious with the report that Jodl himself came very close to being ignominiously dismissed and replaced by Paulus. On September 24 Colonel-General Franz Halder had to hand over to General of Armoured Troops Kurt Zeitzler.

The new Chief-of-Staff of O.K.H. was said to be a National Socialist. Whether or not this was the case, it should be noted that, formerly chief-of-staff of the *Panzergruppe* von Kleist in 1940 and 1941, and then of the 1st *Panzerarmee*, he had only been appointed to this second post on March 15, 1942. On the same day he had moved to France with Field-Marshal von Rundstedt to become chief-of-staff of the latter's Army Group "D" at its headquarters in Saint Germain-en-Laye. He had thus been able to follow only from afar the disappointing progress of the second German summer offensive, and was not in a position to appraise the causes of its undeniable breakdown. Hitler was therefore able to do just as he pleased with him, whereas Halder had for a long time kept out of his reach.

The Führer not only removed his Chief of General Staff; he also did not appoint a successor to List but proposed himself to direct operations on the Caucasus front. But all the genius and dynamism he credited himself with were unable to improve their progress. This was hardly surprising. Army Group "A" had had to reassign 4th *Panzerarmee* to Army Group "B" and had not received the promised 11th Army, and so was reduced to 20 divisions. Fifteen of these were exhausted German troops, there were only 300 tanks, and the campaigning season was rapidly drawing to an end on the slopes of the Caucasus . . .

CHAPTER 34

THE RUSSIAN CONVOYS

According to Soviet historians, their country's Anglo-Saxon allies were feckless in the pursuit of victory. The second front was slow in coming and they did no better when it came to furnishing the arms, equipment, petrol and raw materials which shortly after Hitler's invasion the Soviet Union had been assured of receiving.

But it is only proper to note that this accusation can only be made to stand up by comparing the number of tanks, planes etc. that Churchill and Roosevelt had promised to Stalin with those that actually arrived in Russia, while, in justice the comparison ought to be made between the quantities promised and those which were embarked in American and British ports. For what was lost en route can scarcely be attributed to bad faith on the part of London or Washington. To get such supplies to the Soviet Union, Britain and America had the choice of three routes:

1. They could go via Vladivostok, through which Britain, could send sizable quantities of tin and rubber from Malaya to Siberia. After the opening of hostilities in the Far East, as we have noted, the Japanese did not stop Russian vessels plying between Vladivostok and America's Pacific ports. However, the Trans-Siberian Railway was capable at this time of carrying little more than it had been able to do at the beginning of the century.

2. There was the Persian Gulf route, which had become available on the occupation of Persia by Anglo-Soviet forces at the end of August 1941. But supplies flowed along these two lines very feebly and thought was now given to making significant improvements in them by sending out a large contingent of American engineers and technicians. Nevertheless, the Allied merchantmen taking this route and sailing from New York or Liverpool still had to round the Cape of Good Hope, which put the American Atlantic ports at 73 days sailing from Bandar-e-Shahpur on the Persian Gulf.

3. Lastly, there was the Arctic route to Archangel and Murmansk. The first of these two ports is inaccessible in winter and, anyway, was badly equipped in 1942. The other, thanks to the Gulf Stream, is open all the year round and, given the circumstances, was somewhat better fitted out.

During the winter, Allied Arctic convoys benefited form the cover of the long Arctic night. On the other hand, the advance of pack ice towards the south forced them to round North Cape at a distance which laid them open to short-range German attacks. In summer, the, retreat of the ice allowed the convoys to stand further off from the Norwegian coast, but for 24 hours out of 24 they were, if discovered, an easy prey to dive-bomber, torpedo aircraft, and submarine attacks.

On the outward journey these convoys were distinguished by the letter P.Q. followed by their sequence number. The ships, which were unloaded at Murmansk and Archangel, waited there until they were numerous enough to be regrouped as a Q.P. convoy, and raised anchor when the escort ships of an incoming convoy could accompany them on the voyage home.

The first Arctic convoys

Convoys P.Q.1 set sail from Scottish waters on September 29, 1941, and before the end of the year five others had followed it, landing in all 120,000 tons of supplies at Murmansk, including 600 tanks, 800 aircraft, and 1,400 motor vehicles. Opponents of Winston Churchill's war strategy claim that these supplies would have sufficed to check the Japanese at Singapore and to defeat Rommel at Tobruk. Whatever the truth of this assertion, it has to be admitted that the Germans found themselves considerably embarrassed by these first convoys, which they had not foreseen. It is also noteworthy that between September 29 and December 31, 1941, all 55 vessels of the first six convoys reached their destination safely.

During the first half of 1942 no less than ten convoys made the Arctic run, and of their 146 cargo vessels, 128 reached port despite the increasing opposition of the German Navy. As we have already seen, Hitler had feared an Anglo-American landing in Norway and in consequence had stationed the 43,000-ton battleship *Tirpitz*, the pocket battleships *Lutzow* and *Admiral Scheer*, the heavy cruiser *Admiral Hipper*, and a dozen U-boats between Trondheim and Narvik. And, at the return of spring, *Luftflotte* V had at its bases around the North Cape more than

△ *Colonel-General Hans Jürgen Stumpff, whose* Luftflotte V, *from its bases in Norway, had the task of spotting and then attacking the Allied convoys making for the Russian ports of Murmansk and Archangel.*

250 machines, including 130 Junkers Ju 87 and 88 bombers and 60 land and sea-plane torpedo aircraft.

Faced by this concentration of forces, the Admiralty was forced to provide the same protection for the Arctic convoys as for the Mediterranean ones. Yet at the same time it was the Admiralty which had to bear the brunt of the battle of the Atlantic – and after having just improvised another fleet for the Far East.

In consequence, the situation was very precarious, especially since Roosevelt continued to urge Churchill to intensify and speed up the provisioning of the Soviet Union. And to this end he attached Task Force 99 (Rear-Admiral R. C. Giffen) to the Home Fleet, with two 35,000-ton battleships, the aircraft-carrier *Wasp*, two heavy cruisers, and a flotilla of destroyers.

At the beginning of March *Tirpitz* came out to intercept and destroy the convoys P.Q. 12 and Q.P. 8, a total of 31 cargo vessels, but because of inadequate aerial reconnaissance the powerful battleship failed to locate her prey. The hunter now became the hunted, since the Home Fleet, which had been detailed to provide strategic cover for the operation, had not failed to notice *Tirpitz*'s movements; and on the morning of March 9 she was attacked by 12 torpedo-planes from *Victorious*. However, the undeniable bravery of the Fleet Air Arm pilots did not make up for their lack of training. None of the torpedoes hit its target.

Success for the Luftwaffe

The next convoy to arrive at Murmansk, between March 30 and April 1, lost five ships on the way. The U-boats and the Luftwaffe claimed two each, and the fifth went to a division of destroyers which had put out from the port of Kirkenes. But the Germans paid for this success with the loss of the destroyer *Z-26* and the U-boats *U-585* and *U-655*. In the course of the encounter that led to the sinking of *Z-26* the British cruiser *Trinidad* was damaged by one of her own torpedoes and had to put into Murmansk.

At the end of April the protection of P.Q. 15, with its 15 merchant vessels, occasioned the loss of the cruiser *Edinburgh*, torpedoed by *U-450* and finished off two days later by destroyer attack. For its part, *Trinidad* left Murmansk again only

▽ *A British destroyer picks up survivors of an Arctic convoy from the light cruiser* Scylla *late in 1942.*

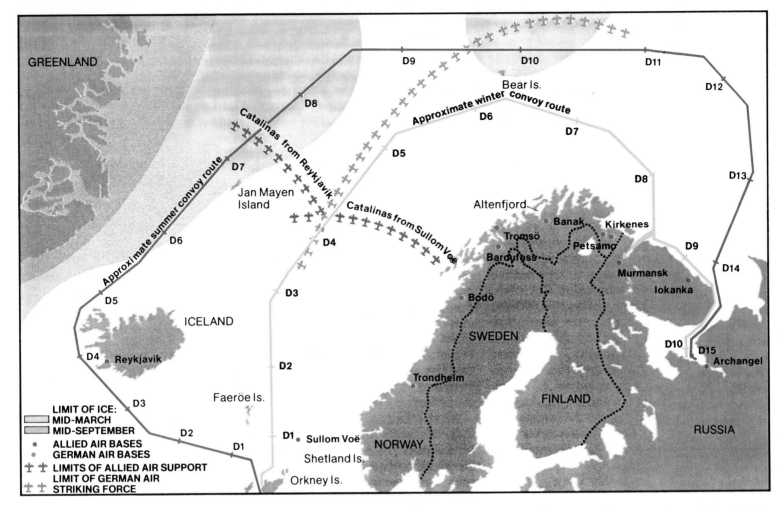

GREENLAND

Catalinas from Reykjavik

Approximate summer convoy route

Approximate winter convoy route

Bear Is.

Catalinas from Sullom Voë

Jan Mayen
Island

ICELAND

Altenfjord

Banak   Kirkenes
Tromsö   Petsamo
Bardufoss
Murmansk
Iokanka
Bodö

Reykjavik

SWEDEN

Archangel

FINLAND

Faeröe Is.

Trondheim

RUSSIA

Sullom Voë

NORWAY

Shetland Is.

Orkney Is.

LIMIT OF ICE:
MID-MARCH
MID-SEPTEMBER
•   ALLIED AIR BASES
•   GERMAN AIR BASES
✝ ✝ LIMITS OF ALLIED AIR SUPPORT
✝ ✝ LIMIT OF GERMAN AIR
✝ ✝ STRIKING FORCE

△ *The Russian convoy route.
Unlike the Atlantic convoy
routes, this was circumscribed
by the ice to the north and the
range of land-based aircraft to
the south.*

▽ *A victim, in the form of a
Focke-Wulf Fw 200 Condor. It
was these aircraft, with their
considerable range, that were one
of the main bugbears of the
Arctic convoys. Only rarely did
they venture within the range of
Allied anti-aircraft fire, preferring
to stay out of range and report
from there.*

to be sunk by a Junkers Ju 88, and to crown
misfortunes, in the fog, the battleship
King George V rammed the destroyer
Punjabi, which sank within a few minutes,
though not before her exploding depth-
charges had damaged *King George V*
severely.

As the days lengthened the losses of the
convoys mounted, despite the reinforcement of their escorts with anti-aircraft
vessels bristling with A.A. guns, and
C.A.M. ships, merchantmen from which a
Hurricane fighter could be catapulted into
the air. Of the 35 vessels that made up P.Q.
16, which set sail from the base at Hvalfjord, north of Reykjavik, seven fell into
the ambushes prepared for them by the
Luftwaffe and U-boats, with losses that
have been tabulated by Captain S. W.
Roskill as follows:

	Loaded	Lost
Tons	125,000	32,400
Tanks	468	147
Aircraft	201	77
Vehicles	3,277	770

However disappointing they may have
been, these losses were slight when
compared with the catastrophe which
overtook P.Q. 17, a disaster not only on
account of the strength of the attack to
which it succumbed, but also because of

the unfortunate intervention of the First
Lord of the Admiralty, Admiral of the
Fleet Sir Dudley Pound.

Convoy P.Q. 17 was composed of 35
vessels, 22 of which were American, eight
British, two Russian, two Panamanian,
and one Dutch. It set sail from the Bay of
Reykjavik on June 27, 1942, with an escort
of six destroyers, four corvettes, four
armed trawlers, three mine-sweepers, two
submarines and two auxiliary anti-aircraft
vessels. Further support was given by
Rear-Admiral L. H. K. Hamilton's squadron, which comprised four heavy cruisers,
two of which were American, and three
destroyers. Finally, Admiral Sir John
Tovey had ordered the Home Fleet to sea,
bringing together under his command the
battleships *Duke of York* and *Washington*
(U.S.N.), the aircraft-carrier *Victorious*,
the cruisers *Nigeria* and *Cumberland*, and
14 destroyers. The Admiralty had done
things in style.

Discovered on July 1, the convoy lost
three merchant vessels on July 4, all to
torpedoes dropped by German Heinkel
111's. By the evening of that same day the
convoy was still about 280 miles away
from Archangel by way of the North Cape
— for Murmansk had been almost completely destroyed by repeated bomber

attacks by *Luftflotte* V.

The Admiralty was now informed that *Tirpitz* had joined *Scheer* and *Hipper* in Altenfjord, which led to the inference that a powerful enemy formation would attack the convoy and Rear-Admiral Hamilton's supporting escort around dawn next day and would swiftly destroy them. Upon which, after brief deliberation, Sir Dudley Pound sent out these three messages, which sealed the convoy's fate.

"2111 Hours: Most immediate. Cruiser force withdraw to westward at high speed."

"2123 Hours: Immediate. Owing to the threat of surface ships convoy is to disperse and proceed to Russian ports."

"2136 Hours: Most Immediate. My 2123 of the 4th. Convoy is to scatter."

On receiving these orders Rear-Admiral Hamilton retired at the indicated speed, taking with him the six escort destroyers. The convoy dispersed as ordered. But of the 30 merchantmen which were left to make Archangel by themselves only 11 arrived at their destination between July 11 and July 25, some of them having made off eastwards towards Novaya Zemlya to escape their pursuers. Nine cargo ships fell prey to air attack from *Luftflotte* V and ten to the 82 torpedoes fired by the U-boats involved. The Germans lost only two bombers, three torpedo planes, and two reconnaissance aircraft.

Tirpitz and her companions, escorted by six destroyers, left Altenfjord at 1100 hours on July 5, more than 12 hours after Hitler had given his permission. But they did not get far, for the same day, at 2200 hours, they were ordered to return to base immediately.

As may be expected, this tragic episode gave rise to passionate dispute in Great Britain, and, as Captain Roskill judiciously points out, it is undeniable that in thinking it possible to exercise direct operational control from London over distant naval forces, the First Sea Lord was inviting just such a nemesis. Roskill concludes: "it is hard to justify such an intervention made in such a way."

The table of losses occasioned by the P.Q. 17 disaster is as follows:

	Loaded	Lost
Tons	156,492	99,316
Tanks	594	430
Aircraft	297	210
Vehicles	4,246	3,350

We may easily understand now that despite Stalin's exhortations, when faced with these figures, Winston Churchill should have waited until September before permitting P.Q. 18 to set out. And even though it was provided with a powerful escort – including the escort carrier *Avenger* – 13 of the 40 vessels that then sailed from Hvalfjord were lost. But on the German side losses were not light: four submarines and 41 aircraft. The struggle in the Arctic waters was now draining the strength of both sides.

ARMS FOR RUSSIA . . . A great convoy of British ships escorted by Soviet fighter planes sails into Murmansk harbour with vital supplies for the Red Army.

△ △ *The Russian port of Murmansk under German bombing attack. This primary port for Allied Arctic convoys was unfortunately only a few miles up the Kola Inlet on Russia's Barents Sea coast, and well within the range of bombers from the German airfields at Petsamo and Kirkenes.*

△ *A British poster extols the co-operation of British and Soviet forces in getting a convoy through to Russia.*

CHAPTER 35
PEDESTAL: THE WORST MALTA CONVOY

It was on the afternoon of June 21, in the elegant White House study of President Roosevelt, that Winston Churchill first learnt of the fall of Tobruk. According to Churchill's memoirs, on learning of the catastrophe, the President dropped everything and immediately summoned General Marshall. Lord Alanbrooke, on the other hand, in the 1946 additions to his war diaries, would have us believe that it was General Marshall himself who delivered the bad news to the two statesmen, as they conferred in the Oval Room of the White House.

"I can remember this incident as if it had occurred yesterday. Churchill and I were standing beside the President's desk talking to him, when Marshall walked in with a pink piece of paper containing a message of the fall of Tobruk. Neither Winston nor I had contemplated such an eventuality and it was a staggering blow. I cannot remember what the actual words were that the President used to convey his sympathy, but I remember vividly being impressed by the tact and real heartfelt sympathy which lay behind these words. There was not one word too much nor one word too little."

But Roosevelt did not stop at mere eloquent expressions of sympathy; quite spontaneously, he immediately asked what he could do to temper the effects of the disaster inflicted upon the British Army. His first idea was to send out the American 1st Armoured Division to the Middle East, but the carrying out of such a project would have created enormous difficulties; he and General Marshall, therefore, in a spirit of comradeship rarely known in coalitions, offered to refit the 8th Army, by giving it the 300 Sherman tanks that had just been distributed to the American armoured units. To complete this most generous gift, 100 self-propelled 105-mm guns were also offered. But even that was not all, for when the cargo vessel carrying the 300 tank engines was torpedoed and sunk off Bermuda, "without a single word from us the President and Marshall put a further supply of engines into another fast ship and dispatched it to overtake the convoy. 'A friend in need is a friend indeed.'"

The entry into active service of the 31-ton M4 Sherman tank upgraded the hitting power of the 8th Army in the Battle of El Alamein. Its long-barrelled (37.5 cali-

△ ▷ *Auchinleck meets Churchill on the latter's arrival in Cairo.*
▽ ▷ *An American M4 Sherman tank. Although a considerable improvement on the Grant and contemporary British tanks, the Sherman still left much to be desired in comparison with the latest German armoured fighting vehicles, especially in gun power.*

"Second Front Now"

Eisenhower believed that there would need to be definite signs of cracking German morale before an attack on the fortified coast of Western Europe could be attempted. "This was a very definite conviction, held by some of our experienced soldiers, sailors, and airmen, that the fortified coast of western Europe could not be successfully attacked. Already much was known of the tremendous effort the German was making to insure the integrity of his Atlantic Wall." Although American military opinion favoured a landing in 1942, the British, partly influenced by their experiences against Turkish batteries in the Dardanelles, were convinced this would not be practicable before 1943.

Hitler was nevertheless worried about the possibility of a cross-channel attack. His directive of July 9 to Army, Navy and Air Force included the following assessment: "Our swift and massive victories may force Great Britain to choose between launching a large-scale invasion, with a view to opening a second front, or seeing Russia eliminated as a military and political factor. Hence it is highly probable that we shall soon face an enemy landing within the O.K.H. command area."

Operation "Gymnast", a landing in French North Africa under American command, was, despite initial American scepticism, seen as the only viable alternative to an attack on the French coast, and it was re-christened Operation "Torch".

bre) 75-mm gun was almost as good as the shorter (24 calibre) 7.5-cm gun generally fitted to the heaviest tanks (the Pzkw IV) of the *Panzerarmee Afrika*; secondly it had a less obtrusive shape than its predecessor, the M3 Grant; finally, the latter's awkward sponson was replaced in the Sherman tank by a turret capable of traversing through 360 degrees.

For diplomatic reasons it was not revealed at the time that the Sherman was what General Sir Brian Horrocks, commander of XIII Corps at El Alamein, later in his memoirs called "a brilliant example of Anglo-American co-operation". American engineers were in charge of the tank's mechanical features (engine, transmission, and tracks), whilst the armament derived from researches carried out by a British team. It was, apparently, because he wanted the aid the Americans were so generously giving to receive full public recognition, that Churchill suppressed the extent of British participation.

R.A.F. reinforcements

At the same time (summer 1942), the Italo-German air forces fighting in North Africa finally lost their last remnants of superiority over the R.A.F., now being regularly reinforced by deliveries of American and British aircraft, which, technically and tactically, were of the highest quality: there was, for example, the Supermarine Spitfire Mark V interceptor and the Hawker Hurricane IID fighter-bomber, nicknamed the "tin-opener", because its 40-mm armour-piercing shells tore through the thickest Panzer armour with considerable ease. Later came the excellent North American P-51 Mustang fighter capable of 390 mph, and with a ceiling of 31,000 feet. Roosevelt's sympathetic understanding of Britain's needs also made it possible to increase to 117 the number of strategic bombers posted to this theatre, when the four-engined American Consolidated B-24 Liberator bomber joined the British-built Handley-Page Halifax.

It therefore follows that the R.A.F. not only recovered, conclusively and permanently, mastery of the air, but also that it was able to give the 8th Army, in both its defensive and offensive rôles, support that daily became more powerful and better organised. In his book on the war in the air, Air Vice-Marshal J. E. Johnson has

traced this development very precisely:

"Slowly, by trial, error, and the foresight of gifted men, not only airmen, the pattern of air support for the soldiers again took shape. Fighters to grind down the enemy bomber and fighter forces; fighters which could then be armed with bombs to attack the enemy ground forces; fighters which, armed or not with bombs, were always capable of protecting themselves and providing protection for the bombers. A bomber force which was as capable of bombing enemy airfields and installations as of attacking troops on the ground. A reconnaissance force to be the eyes of both Army and Air Force Commanders."

Among the "gifted men" whom the author mentions, pride of place must go to General Bernard Law Montgomery, who on taking over command of the 8th Army, set up his H.Q. next to that of Air Vice-Marshal Coningham, commanding the Desert Air Force, as the Middle East's tactical air force was called.

Churchill decides that Auchinleck must go

We have already seen that, since June 25, General Sir Claude Auchinleck had been

△ Churchill addresses some of the ever growing number of British troops in the Middle East. He told such men of how the Shermans they were about to receive "had been longed and thirsted for by the 1st United States Armoured Division, and how they had been taken from them . . . in order to give us the chance–or perhaps I said the certainty–of saving Alexandria, Cairo, and Egypt from conquest."
◁ The meeting of "All The Talents" in Cairo. Left to right, standing: Tedder, Brooke, Harwood, and R. G. Casey; sitting: Smuts, Churchill, Auchinleck, and Wavell.

at the head of both the 8th Army and the Middle East Land Forces, a situation of which Churchill fully approved, as is shown by his message of June 28; and on July 4, when he learnt that the 8th Army was not only standing its ground, but even counter-attacking, he again showed his satisfaction: "I must tell you how pleased I am with the way things are shaping," he wrote that day. "If fortune turns I am sure you will press your advantage, as you say, 'relentlessly'."

Auchinleck's strategy correct . . .

And yet, three weeks later, Churchill had decided, if not actually to dismiss him, at least to deprive him of his command in Egypt, Palestine, and Syria, thus limiting him to Iraq and Persia. Quite clearly, Churchill was once more itching to attack, whereas lack of resources, and the need to wait for the reinforcements which were coming around the Cape of Good Hope, made G.H.Q. Cairo wish to refrain from any large-scale offensive initiative until mid-September. And when it is realised that co-operation between armour and infantry was still very poor in the 8th Army, and that the new command team of Alexander and Montgomery waited until October 23 before attacking, it is difficult not to accept the view of Cairo command.

. . . but his psychology erroneous?

On the other hand General Brooke, whose sturdy independence vis-à-vis Churchill is well known, never stopped saying, in his war diaries, that "It was quite clear that something was radically wrong but not easy at a distance to judge what this something was, nor how far wrong it was . . . The crisis had now come and it was essential that I should go out to see what was wrong. But for this I wanted to be alone."

To help us interpret these somewhat veiled remarks, we have available the testimony of two very different personalities: Field-Marshal Smuts, the Prime Minister of South Africa, and Field-Marshal Montgomery. They criticised Sir Claude Auchinleck for an inability to choose his subordinate officers. Montgomery expressed himself on this subject with his usual directness.

"A good judge of men would never have selected General Corbett to be his Chief of Staff in the Middle East. And to suggest that Corbett should take command of the Eighth Army, as Auchinleck did, passed all comprehension.

"Again, nobody in his senses would have sent Ritchie to succeed Cunningham in command of the Eighth Army; Ritchie had not the experience or qualifications for the job and in the end he had to be removed too." A brutal judgement, certainly, but on August 4, 1942, Smuts had spoken in a similar vein to General Brooke during the latter's visit to Cairo.

Alexander takes over from Auchinleck

At all events, the C.I.G.S., General Brooke, went to Cairo, inspecting Gibraltar and Malta on the way–but not alone, as he would have liked; Churchill had also decided to go out and see for himself what

the situation was like, and had summoned General Wavell, C.-in-C. India, and Field-Marshal Smuts, both men whose opinion he valued, to meet him in Cairo.

"Had General Auchinleck or his staff lost the confidence of the Desert Army? If so, should he be relieved, and who could succeed him?" According to his memoirs, these were the two big questions that brought Churchill to Cairo, where he landed on the morning of August 4, only a few minutes before the C.I.G.S. In reality his mind was already made up, as is proved by the fact that on August 6, at dawn, he went to see Brooke, just as the latter was getting up ("practically naked"), and told him that he had decided to split the Middle East theatre into two. Relegated to Basra or Baghdad, Auchinleck would be given the new Persia and Iraq Command, separated from the rest of Middle East Command, which Churchill now offered to Brooke. The latter asked not to be appointed on the grounds that this was no time to disorganise the Imperial General Staff, and that in any case he had no knowledge of desert warfare. But that evening he confided to his diary:

"Another point which I did not mention was that, after working with the P.M. for close on nine months, I do feel at last that I can exercise a limited amount of control on some of his activities and that at last he is beginning to take my advice. I feel, therefore, that, tempting as the offer is, by

(page 329) Reinforcements for Coningham's Western Desert Air Force were now beginning to arrive in considerable quantities, and the R.A.F. was able to wrest command of the skies from the Luftwaffe and Regia Aeronautica.
△ ◁ *A Spitfire VB interceptor and fighter-bomber. Though its speed was reduced when the Vokes air filter necessary for operations in the Middle East was fitted, it was still capable of besting the Italian and German fighters operating over the Western Desert.*
△ ◁ *An American Maryland Bomber of the South African Air Force, drawing away after dropping a stick of bombs on Axis transport. Smoke is billowing from two large vehicles which have suffered direct hits.*
▽ *R.A.F. armourers bomb up a flight of Baltimores.*

been appointed to command the 8th Army, but the aircraft in which he was travelling was forced down by two German fighters; whilst he was helping other passengers caught in the wreckage, a second attack caused the plane to explode, leaving no survivors, and his successor, Brooke's candidate, took over and was told to get out to Cairo immediately. This was Lieutenant-General Bernard L. Montgomery – who had just introduced himself to Eisenhower as Alexander's successor as commander of the 1st Army. Small wonder that on being deprived of his second deputy in 48 hours, Eisenhower cynically asked, "Are the British taking 'Torch' seriously?"

To replace General Corbett, Alexander chose as his chief-of-staff Lieutenant-General R. McCreery; he was very popular, and Alexander wrote of him that "he was one of those officers who is as successful at H.Q. as at the head of his troops" and "faithful friend and companion" to him personally. Thus was formed the brilliant team which, with Air Chief Marshal Sir Arthur Tedder and Admiral Sir Henry Harwood, led the 8th Army from El Alamein to Tripoli in less than nine months.

General Auchinleck, relieved of his command because he had refused to attack before mid-September, accepted his disgrace with dignity, but refused the consolation prize that Churchill offered.

Churchill's instructions

On August 10 the British Prime Minister, accompanied by Generals Wavell and Brooke, flew to Moscow to inform the Russians of the Anglo-American decision to abandon Operation "Sledgehammer" in favour of Operation "Torch". But before leaving Cairo, Churchill had sent Alexander hand-written instructions, fixing his tasks in the following manner:

"1. Your prime and main duty will be to take or destroy at the earliest opportunity the German-Italian Army commanded by Field-Marshal Rommel together with all its supplies and establishments in Egypt and Libya.

2. You will discharge or cause to be discharged such other duties as pertain to your command without prejudice to the task described in paragraph 1, which must be considered paramount in His Majesty's interests."

General Sir Harold Alexander was born in 1891 and entered the British Army by means of Sandhurst. He served with great distinction with the Irish Guards in World War I and after the war in the Baltic States and in India. Alexander commanded the British rearguard at Dunkirk very ably, and further enhanced his reputation as G.O.C. Southern Command in 1940 and by his masterly retreat through Burma in 1942. He was then appointed Eisenhower's deputy for Operation "Torch", but was almost immediately asked to take over from Auchinleck in the Western Desert. With Montgomery commanding in the field, and Alexander in overall command, Rommel was pushed steadily back out of Egypt and Libya into Tunisia. February 1942 saw Alexander's appointment as Deputy Supreme Commander in North Africa and commander of the 18th Army Group. By May the Axis forces in Africa had been destroyed, and Alexander started planning the invasion of Italy.

accepting it I should definitely be taking a course which would on the whole help the war least. Finally, I could not bear the thought that Auchinleck might think that I had come out here on purpose to work myself into his shoes."

The new team

Brooke having thus refused, for the most honourable of reasons, Sir Harold Alexander was asked that very evening, on Brooke's recommendation, to take over the Middle East Command. A happy choice, for the new commander had shown the same imperturbability and resourcefulness at Dunkirk as later in the Burma jungle, and, in addition, wore his authority easily. "Calm, confident and charming – as always" was the impression the difficult Montgomery received on their first meeting at G.H.Q. Cairo. Alexander had just been appointed deputy to General Eisenhower, as commander of the British 1st Army taking part in "Torch", and Eisenhower now had to be asked to release him for this new post.

Originally, and in spite of Brooke's opposition, General W. H. E. Gott had

Operation "Pedestal"

Whilst Churchill and his advisers were setting off for Moscow via Teheran, 14 merchant ships slipped through the Straits of Gibraltar under cover of dense fog. The interruption of convoys to Archangel had allowed the Admiralty to devote considerable resources to this new operation of supplying Malta: three aircraft-carriers, *Eagle*, *Victorious*, and *Indomitable* with their 72 fighters; the two battleships *Nelson* and *Rodney*; seven cruisers, one of which was an anti-aircraft vessel; 24 destroyers; two tankers; four corvettes; and eight submarines. In addition, the old aircraft carrier *Furious*, with an escort of eight destroyers, was able to fly off 38 Spitfires to Malta. The convoy had 14 merchantmen.

This considerable naval force was under the overall command of Vice-Admiral Sir Neville Syfret, commanding Force H. Rear-Admiral H. M. Burrough, with four cruisers and 12 destroyers, was the convoy's immediate escort; bearing in mind what had happened the previous June, he was to escort the convoy as far as Malta. Such were the outlines of "Pedestal".

However, it was all the more difficult to keep such a large-scale undertaking secret as the Italian secret service had paid informers in the Bay of Algeciras, and the Germans and Italians were able to prepare, right down to the smallest details, a plan to intercept and destroy the "Pedestal" convoy. This shows the close co-operation which now existed between *Supermarina*, under Admiral Arturo Riccardi, *Superaero* (General Rino Corso Fougier), and the Germans, Field-Marshal Kesselring and Admiral Weichold. However, they had to recognise that they would not be able to use the four battleships available to them, so great had the fuel crisis become since June 15. The attack would therefore be carried out by the following aerial and naval forces:

1. sixteen Italian and five German submarines, which would share the task of attacking the enemy between the Straits of Algiers and the Sicilian Channel with 784 aircraft (447 bombers, 90 torpedo aircraft, and 247 fighters);

2. eighteen motor torpedo boats, which would be lurking between Cap Bon and the island of Pantelleria; and

3. six cruisers and 11 destroyers which, in combination with the aerial forces, would finish off the convoy.

▷ △ *The Dorset ploughs on through a storm of bomb bursts.*

▷ ▽ *Operation "Pedestal". Although escorted by very powerful British naval forces, the convoy of 14 merchantmen was harried almost to total loss by Axis aircraft and light naval forces. It was a story of skill and devotion on both sides, the Italians pressing home their torpedo attacks with great ability and courage, and the British forging on despite their losses in their effort to aid the island of Malta. Though British losses in this convoy could be likened to those of the ill-starred P.Q. 17, just enough supplies got through to tide the island over this last Axis effort.*

▽ *From top left to bottom right, the British carriers* Victorious, Indomitable, *and* Eagle, *whose fighters were to be the main defence against the heavy and determined Axis air attacks on the convoy and escort in the "Pedestal" operation. It was also to be the valiant* Eagle's *last mission.*

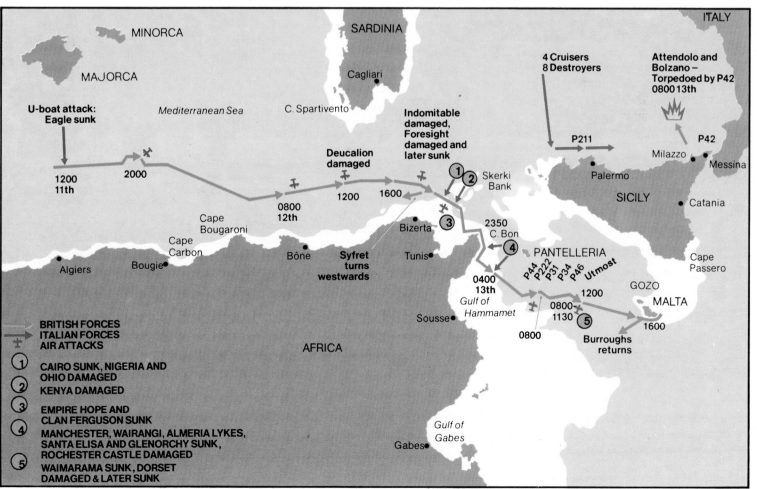

ITALY

MINORCA

SARDINIA

MAJORCA

Cagliari

Mediterranean Sea

C. Spartivento

4 Cruisers
8 Destroyers

Attendolo and
Bolzano –
Torpedoed by P42
0800 13th

**U-boat attack:
Eagle sunk**

**Indomitable
damaged,
Foresight
damaged and
later sunk**

**Deucalion
damaged**

P211

P42

1200
11th

2000

0800
12th

1200

1600

① Skerki
② Bank

Milazzo

Messina

Palermo

SICILY

Catania

Cape
Bougaroni

2350
C. Bon

③

④ PANTELLERIA

Cape
Carbon

Bizerta

P44
P222
P31
P34
P46 *Utmost*

GOZO

Algiers

Bougie

Bône

**Syfret
turns
westwards**

Tunis

1200

MALTA

0400
13th

*Gulf of
Hammamet*

0800-
1130

1600

Cape
Passero

**BRITISH FORCES
ITALIAN FORCES
AIR ATTACKS**

Sousse

0800

⑤

Burroughs
returns

① **CAIRO SUNK, NIGERIA AND
OHIO DAMAGED**

② **KENYA DAMAGED**

AFRICA

③ **EMPIRE HOPE AND
CLAN FERGUSON SUNK**

④ **MANCHESTER, WAIRANGI, ALMERIA LYKES,
SANTA ELISA AND GLENORCHY SUNK,
ROCHESTER CASTLE DAMAGED**

⑤ **WAIMARAMA SUNK, DORSET
DAMAGED & LATER SUNK**

*Gulf of
Gabes*

Gabes

The Allies suffer

It was Lieutenant Rosenbaum (*U-73*) who opened the Axis score when, early on the afternoon of August 11, a salvo of four torpedoes struck the aircraft-carrier *Eagle*, and sank her in eight minutes, thus ending the career of this fine old ship, which had played so vital a part in the supplying of Malta. On the Allies side, a few hours later the destroyer *Wolverine* rammed and sank the Italian submarine *Dagabur* as it was trying to torpedo *Furious*, which, having accomplished her mission, was returning to Gibraltar.

Throughout August 12, the Hurricanes of the three aircraft-carriers repulsed successive attacks from some 200 dive-bombers and torpedo-carrying planes, which had taken off from the Sardinian bases of Elmas and Decimomannu; in conjunction with the anti-aircraft fire of the convoy, the Hurricanes destroyed 28 aircraft, so that during this second phase of the battle, the successes of the Axis air forces were meagre indeed: one cargo ship, damaged by a bomb, lagged behind the convoy and was finished off during the night by a motor torpedo boat, while three German Ju 87's scored hits on the flight deck of *Indomitable*, whose planes were then taken on board *Victorious*. The destroyer *Foresight*, which had received a torpedo hit, was scuttled by her own crew, while the destroyer *Ithuriel* sank the Italian submarine *Cobalto*.

At 1900 hours, having reached a point north of Bizerta, Syfret, in accordance with instructions, headed for Gibraltar with his support force, wishing Burrough and his convoy a safe journey, a wish which was never granted, for the third and fourth acts of this aero-naval tragedy firmly established the victory of the Axis forces, and especially the Italian Navy.

The last acts of the tragedy started just after 2000 hours, when, near Cape Bon, the two submarines *Axum* and *Dessié* (commanded by Lieutenants Ferrini and Scandola) fired eight torpedoes, five of which struck home, sinking the anti-aircraft cruiser *Cairo*, and causing serious damage to one of the convoy's cargo ships (the tanker *Ohio*) and the cruiser *Nigeria*, Admiral Burrough's flagship. In the ensuing confusion a further air attack damaged two more merchant ships, which were sunk in the night by Italian naval forces. In addition, at about 2200 hours, the sub-marine *Alagi* (Lieutenant Puccini) damaged the cruiser *Kenya* and sank yet another cargo ship. In the early hours of the 13th the Italian motor torpedo boats, prowling between Cap Bon and Pantelleria, fell upon the remnants of the convoy and attacked continuously until sunrise, sinking four more merchantmen and the cruiser *Manchester*.

△ *Incredibly, the American tanker* Ohio *survived this torpedo hit and managed to get 10,000 tons of desperately needed fuel through to Malta.*

Italy's last victory

But at the same time an equally fierce battle was being waged within the Axis Supreme Command, between Admirals Riccardi and Weichold on the one hand, and Field-Marshal Kesselring and General Fougier on the other; the question at issue was the following: on August 13, should the fighter cover be given to the two squadrons of cruisers charged with finishing off the convoy south of Pantelleria, or should they protect the bomber squadrons, since they would not be able to protect both at the same time?

Unable to decide between the two rival claims, Marshal Cavallero put the question to Mussolini, who decided that the

The end of Ohio's *great ordeal.* △ Ohio *approaches Grand Harbour with two British destroyers tied alongside to help keep her afloat.*

▽ *The end in sight—tugs ease the crippled tanker, her decks almost awash, into Valletta's Grand Harbour.*

was intercepted on the way back to base by the submarine *Unbroken*, commanded by Lieutenant Alastair Mars, who scored two direct hits on the *Bolzano* and the *Attendolo*, damaging them so badly that they remained out of action till September 1943.

Bragadin's conclusion on this episode is that "the battle of mid-August 1942 marked the swan-song of the Italian Navy, and the last important victory of the Axis in the Mediterranean conflict". How right he was is seen from the fact that of the 85,000 tons of supplies loaded in the Clyde, 53,000 tons went to the bottom but the 32,000 tons that got through to Valletta were sufficient to see the island fortress through till November; and thanks to the admirable devotion to duty of Captain Dudley W. Mason and the crew of *Ohio*, which in impossible conditions managed to get through 10,000 tons of fuel, the torpedo planes and submarines stationed at Malta were able to engage their offensive against the Italian Navy with renewed vigour, until Rommel was finally and comprehensively defeated.

fighters should protect the bombers: a bad decision as the Stuka bombers and torpedo planes sank only one ship, whereas the six cruisers and 11 motor torpedo boats originally due to go into action would almost certainly have finished off the five ships still left of the convoy. To make matters worse, the Italian naval squadron

CHAPTER 36

ALAM HALFA: ROMMEL'S LAST THROW

The last Panzer offensive towards Cairo, Alexandria, and the Suez Canal gave rise to two battles. The first was lost by Rommel between August 31 and September 5, 1942; the second, less conclusive, was the verbal battle fought after the war by Churchill and Montgomery on the one hand, and Auchinleck and his chief-of-staff (Major-General Dorman-Smith, who shared his chief's fall from grace in August 1942), on the other. This quarrel has been revived by Correlli Barnett who, in his book *The Desert Generals*, has passed harsh judgement on both the British Prime Minister and Field-Marshal Montgomery. According to the latter, when he was received at Mena House on August 12, Auchinleck was anything but determined to defend the El Alamein position at all costs if there were an Italo-German offensive. Montgomery writes in his memoirs:

"He asked me if I knew he was to go. I said that I did. He explained to me his plan of operations; this was based on the fact that at all costs the Eighth Army was to be preserved 'in being' and must not be destroyed in battle. If Rommel attacked in strength, as was expected soon, the Eighth Army would fall back on the Delta; if Cairo and the Delta could not be held, the army would retreat southwards up the Nile, and another possibility was a withdrawal to Palestine. Plans were being made to move the Eighth Army H.Q. back up the Nile."

Auchinleck has categorically denied ever having uttered such words to Montgomery, and Montgomery's own publishers later made a disclaimer. Naturally, Auchinleck had considered the possibility of withdrawal. This did not mean, however, that Auchinleck would have deliberately retreated as soon as Rommel had begun his first large-scale manoeuvre, as Montgomery implies. On the contrary, everything seems to indicate that he fully intended to face up to an attack at El Alamein, in accordance with the plans drawn up by Major-General Dorman-Smith. Furthermore, it is fair to ask whether or not the new team at the head of the 8th Army, however determined it might be to fight, would have condemned it to destruction in the event of one of Rommel's typical outflanking movements. In fact, both under Auchinleck and later under Montgomery and Alexander, contingency plans were made to meet the "worst possible case" of a German breakthrough past the Alamein position. The problem of how to cope with such a breakthrough was naturally discussed by the successive sets of command.

Was Dorman-Smith's plan, adopted by Auchinleck, taken over without reference or acknowledgement by Montgomery? This is the claim put forward by Correlli Barnett. In reality, such a plan was forced upon both generals by Rommel's probable tactics, and also by the nature of the terrain, which dominated the surrounding countryside by nearly 200 feet and did not lend itself to the German general's usual outflanking tactics. To this plan, however, Montgomery added personal qualities of dynamism and cunning, which justify him calling the battle his own.

▽ *General Montgomery surveys his dispositions from on top of a Crusader tank's turret. As soon as he had taken over from Auchinleck, Montgomery had altered the style of command of the 8th Army, using his own brand of rhetoric and his flair for public relations. After the battle, Montgomery wrote: "My first encounter with Rommel was of great interest. Luckily I had time to tidy up the mess and to get my plans laid, so there was no difficulty in seeing him off. I feel that I have won the first game, when it was his service. Next time it will be my service, the score being one-love."*

Rommel forced to act precipitately

Faced with an opponent whom he knew to be getting stronger day by day, Rommel realised he had to attack, and quickly, otherwise he would soon be overrun by an opponent superior in numbers and equipment. He had been able to motorise his 90th Light Division, and had been reinforced by the 164th Division flown in from the Balkans–but without its vehicles; this was also the case with the parachute troops of the German Ramcke Brigade, and the Italian "Folgore" Division.

In the notes which he has left us, Rommel lays the blame for the failure of his last offensive on the way he was let down by the *Comando Supremo*, whose head, Marshal Cavallero, never stopped making him the most alluring promises. But it is difficult to accept this criticism, since it was no fault of Cavallero's that Malta was not neutralised and then besieged, instead of the boats of the

British 10th Submarine Flotilla being once more able to use Malta's large harbour from the beginning of July. As a result, Italian supplies lost in transit, about six per cent in July, shot up to 25 per cent of equipment and 41 per cent of fuel in August; indeed, Cavallero's diary for the period reads like an obituary:
"August 25. The *Pozarica* is torpedoed.
August 27. The *Camperio* is set on fire.
August 28. The *Dielpi* and the *Istria* are
     both sunk, the latter with all her crew.
August 30. The *Sant'Andrea* is sunk with
     1,300 tons of fuel for the D.A.K."

Another point is that Rommel's criticisms take no account of the fact that his supply lines had become far too long. To get from the front to Benghazi took a week, with a further five days to get to Tripoli for supplies. It is true that Tobruk was better placed, but it could only take small ships of up to 600 tons, and in any case had suffered very heavy attacks at the hands of the R.A.F. The responsibility for this state of affairs was Rommel's alone since, despite the doubts of Bastico, Cavallero, and Kesselring himself, he had insisted on exploiting his victories by going headlong after the enemy.

△ One of Rommel's dual purpose 4-cm anti-aircraft guns. But as Montgomery had ordered his armour to fight purely defensively, as dug-in artillery, Rommel's highly effective 4- and 8.8-cm guns had to restrict themselves to A.A. fire.

The German plan

Rommel's plan of attack included some decoy movements by the Italian X and XXI Corps, reinforced by German elements. These would engage the enemy head-on and prevent him getting wind too soon of the plan of attack. These dummy attacks were to begin at 0200 hours, giving Rommel the whole night to take his armoured forces (consisting of the Italian XX Corps and the *Deutsches Afrika Korps*) through the left wing of the enemy's lines, and up to 30 miles past their starting point. After this he would regroup his armour and wheel to the north, with the intention of reaching the Alexandria road behind the 8th Army, which would thus be cut off from its communications, caught on the retreat, and annihilated. There would then be a threefold pursuit of the enemy:

1. the Bismarck group (the 21st Panzer Division and the 164th Division) would make for Alexandria;
2. the *Afrika Korps* (the 15th Panzer Division and the 90th Light Division) would cross the Nile at Cairo and immediately head for the Suez Canal; and
3. the Italian XX Corps (the "Ariete" and "Littorio" Armoured Divisions) and the "Trieste" Motorised Division would clean up any resistance in the Wadi Natrun area.

As Paul Carell has said, this plan had Rommel written all over it. And Colonel Bayerlein, chief-of-staff of the *Panzerarmee* at this time, has confirmed that it was a tried and tested Rommel tactic, which he had used at Tobruk, Gazala, and Marsa Matrûh. All very true–but the point was that it had been used so often that it was now worn out, and was too typical not to be seen through quite easily. In fact, both the Auchinleck/ Dorman-Smith team and General Montgomery made their plans on the assumption that Rommel would do something like this: a deep eastward push into the southern sector of the El Alamein position, followed by a rapid turn up towards the Mediterranean.

When Montgomery assumed command (48 hours earlier than he was supposed to), the 8th Army was deployed as follows:

1. on the right, blocking the way to Alexandria, was Lieutenant-General William H. C. Ramsden's XXX Corps, made up of the 9th Australian, 1st South African,

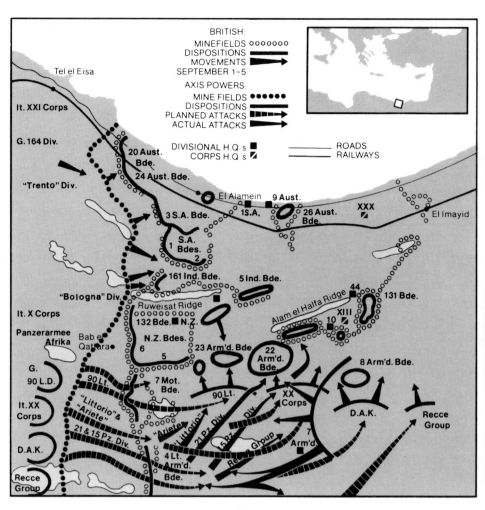

and 5th Indian Divisions; and

2. on the left, Lieutenant-General Brian Horrocks' XIII Corps had the New Zealand Division in the line with the 7th Armoured Division further south, for the purpose of slowing up Rommel's initial push and then making a flank attack as soon as he turned north.

These dispositions did not altogether please Montgomery; he thought in particular that Alam el Halfa ridge was too lightly defended, so he brought in the 44th Division, under Major-General I. T. P. Hughes, and also two armoured brigades of the 10th Armoured Division (a perfect example of the Montgomery "dynamism" mentioned earlier on). All in all, on August 31, the 8th Army had available 712 serviceable tanks, though this figure includes 164 Grants.

In spite of these reinforcements, Montgomery imposed an essentially defensive strategy upon his army. He thought that too often in the past the British tanks had been launched into attacks or counterattacks that Rommel had cunningly channelled so as to bring them up against his redoubtable anti-tank guns. This battle would therefore be essentially an artillery duel, with tank movements restricted to

△ *The Battle of Alam el Halfa, Rommel's last attempt to push through to the Suez Canal. Montgomery had deployed his troops in masterly fashion, with the tanks at his disposal dug in as extra artillery. Rommel, his initial advance not being as fast as usual, found himself at dawn in a position where his forces could be decimated by the heavy concentrations of artillery on the Alam el Halfa and Ruweisat Ridges. He therefore decided not to risk heavy casualties and pulled back. The last threat to Egypt was over.*

Breakthrough at Gazala

Operation "Venezia" was begun by Rommel on the evening of May 26, 1942. The plan was to annihilate British forces in the area of Bir el Gubi-Tobruk–Aïne el-Gazala–Bir Hakeim, following which the garrison of Tobruk would be taken.

Churchill was impatient for the British to undertake a large-scale offensive, but this was resisted by Sir Claude Auchinleck, who was supported by Air Chief Marshal Tedder.

On May 26 Rommel set out at dusk on the flanking attack which was to pass north and south of Bir Hakeim and take his tanks into the rear of the 8th Army. On his right the 90th Light Division was to make a feint towards El Adem, then turn back to Acroma and cut the Via Ballia, the enemy's last line of communication.

exceptional cases; so his tanks dug in. "Don't let yourself get bitten!" he never tired of repeating to Horrocks, upon whose corps the brunt of the Axis offensive was soon to fall.

A British trap

An element of cunning was brought into the operation by Montgomery's chief-of-staff, Brigadier Francis de Guingand, who made up a false map seeming to show the condition of the tracks, the positions of the areas of soft sand unusable by vehicles, and the minefield positions for XIII Corps' sector – all put in with more than a dash of fantasy. The next step was to fake in no-man's land an incident which would lead to the capture of this spurious document in such a way as not to arouse suspicion about its authenticity. This was brought about at the instigation of General Horrocks who, on being told that the precious map had disappeared from the wreck of the armoured car in which it had been left, telephoned Guingand thus: "Is that you Freddy? They've taken your egg away. Please God that they hatch out something from it." And, according to Colonel Fritz Bayerlein, they tended it with loving care until it did indeed hatch out on the night of August 30.

Rommel's lack of certainty

To launch his attack Rommel would have liked to take advantage of the full moon of August 26, but the supply difficulties mentioned above led to its postponement until August 30. That evening, just before H-hour, which had been fixed for 2200 hours, a stirring order of the day was read out to the troops, reminding them of their glorious past exploits, and exhorting them to the decisive effort:

"Our army, reinforced by new divisions, is moving in to annihilate the enemy.

"In the course of these decisive days, I expect every man to give of his best.

"Long live Fascist Italy! Long live Germany! Long live our glorious leaders!"

But Rommel was less certain of a successful outcome to the operation than his own proclamation indicated. Writing to his wife a few hours earlier, he had told her, after pointing out the deficiencies that still remained in his army:

"I've taken the risk, for it will be a long time before we get such favourable conditions of moonlight, relative strengths, etc., again. I, for my part, will do my utmost to contribute to success.

"As for my health, I'm feeling quite on top of my form. There are such big things at stake. If our blow succeeds, it might go some way towards deciding the whole course of the war. If it fails, at least I hope to give the enemy a pretty thorough beating. Neurath has seen the Führer, who sent me his best wishes. He is fully aware of my anxieties."

At 0200 hours on the 31st, the Italo-German motorised column reached the first British minefield. The D.A.K., consisting of the tough 15th and 21st Panzer Divisions, was in the lead, followed by the Italian XX Corps, now commanded by General de Stefanis. Bringing up the rear was the 90th Light Division, which remained in close contact with the Italian X Corps, holding a pivotal position in the Axis line. All in all there were 515 tanks, of which 234 were German machines, including 26 of the new mark of Pzkw IV's mounting a 7.5-cm 43-calibre gun. The D.A.K. also had available 72 mobile 8.8-cm guns, but these were hardly used in an anti-tank role, because the 8th Army had learnt its lesson, and tanks were dug in as supplementary artillery.

Axis withdrawal

By 0300 hours on the 31st, it had dawned on Rommel that things were not going with their usual smoothness. Fired on by the guns of the 7th Armoured Division, and bombed by the Desert Air Force, some German tanks were coming up against unmarked minefields, whilst others were getting bogged down in bad going to the south of the Allied position. So that instead of making a push of 30-odd miles into the enemy's lines, the Axis mechanised forces had only covered about ten. Rommel would consequently have to give up the wheel he had intended to make after an initial deep push; but if he turned north now, he would come under fire from the crest of Alam el Halfa ridge, where XIII Corps, with 64 artillery batteries, 300 anti-tank guns, and the same number of tanks, was waiting.

Shortly afterwards, even worse news reached Rommel: Major-General Georg von Bismarck, commanding the 21st Panzer Division, had been killed by a mine, and Lieutenant-General Walther Nehring, commanding the *Afrika Korps*, had been badly wounded in an air attack and replaced in the field by Colonel Bayerlein.

It was therefore no surprise that the D.A.K. attack on Hill 132, the highest point of the Alam el Halfa ridge, was repulsed; on its left, the Italian XX Corps fared no better–inevitably–in view of its light equipment; and the 90th Light Division, in the pivotal position, opposite the New Zealand Division, had its commander, Major-General Kleeman, seriously wounded in an air attack. The R.A.F., in fact, was everywhere, and on September 1 Rommel himself nearly met with the same fate as Nehring and Kleeman. Furthermore, despite the assurances showered on him by Cavallero and Kesselring, fuel supplies for the *Panzerarmee* were coming up more and more slowly. Accordingly, on the morning of September 3, Rommel took the decision to withdraw his troops.

First round to Montgomery

Preoccupied with his plans for a general offensive, Montgomery decided not to exploit this defensive success. It had cost the 8th Army 1,750 men and 67 tanks,

whilst Axis losses were 536 dead, 1,760 wounded, and 569 missing, together with 49 tanks, 55 guns, and 395 trucks captured or destroyed. These are the figures for the battle of Alam el Halfa, which General Mellenthin has described as follows:

"8th Army had every reason to be satisfied with this victory, which destroyed our last hope of reaching the Nile, and revealed a great improvement in British tactical methods. Montgomery's conduct of the battle can be assessed as a very able if cautious performance, in the best traditions of some of Wellington's victories."

The day after his victory, Montgomery wrote to a friend:

"My first encounter with Rommel was of great interest. Luckily I had time to tidy up the mess and to get my plans laid, so there was no difficulty in seeing him off. I feel that I have won the first game, when it was his service. Next time it will be my service, the score being one-love."

△ △ *A motor-drawn 40-mm Bofors anti-aircraft gun moves up towards the front.*
△ *One of Rommel's 536 dead, an Italian soldier.*

△ *Douglas Bostons of the Desert Air Force head out to harry the defeated Rommel's communications.*

Hitler promises Rommel reinforcements

At about this time, Rommel, whose health was poor, went on sick leave. The Goebbels propaganda machine greeted him rapturously, and put all sorts of optimistic forecasts into his mouth; and on visiting Hitler he received the most alluring promises: the *Afrika Korps* would soon be strengthened by the 10th Panzer Division, by the S.S. *Leibstandarte Adolf Hitler* Motorised Division, then stationed in France and also by the 22nd Airborne Division which had just left the Crimea for Crete. He could also have a brigade of *Nebelwerfer* rocket-launchers, and 40 56-ton Pzkw VI Tiger tanks, which in firepower and protective armour far outclassed even the newest of Allied tanks. It is a sad fact, however, that by the fateful day of October 23, none of these reinforcements had reached him, whilst fresh troops and equipment were reaching the Allies at an ever-increasing rate.

Early September saw the arrival in Egyptian ports of the 300 Sherman tanks and 100 self-propelled 105-mm guns that a generous President Roosevelt had provided; of course, this equipment could not be used immediately as sand filters had to be fitted to the tanks, and the British crews had to be trained to get the best out of these American tanks which they had never seen before. Almost simultaneously, two new divisions fresh from Great Britain disembarked at Suez: the 51st Highland Division, soon to add El Alamein to its battle honours, and the 8th Armoured Division, which had only a short existence.

Middle East aerial forces were also being built up: four squadrons of two-engined North American B-25 Mitchell bombers, with a range of more than 1,200 miles, were delivered to Egyptian bases, and the Vickers Wellington bombers of Sir Arthur Tedder – and even the Fleet Air Arm's Fairey Albacores – underwent training to enable them to take part in the 8th Army's operations. The advantage in "flying artillery" thus passed over to the Allies, and played the same vital rôle in the offensive as it had done at the time of the Blitzkrieg.

These then, are the preliminaries of the 2nd Battle of El Alamein, which as we shall see later, was to complement Operation "Torch".

CHAPTER 37
THE LONG AGONY

At the headquarters of the Soviet 62nd Army (Lieutenant-General V. I. Chuikov), defending Stalingrad, the officer who kept the army's war diary made the following entries on September 14, 1942:

"0730: the enemy has reached Academy Street.

  0740: 1st Battalion 38th Mechanised Brigade is cut off from our main forces.

  0750: fighting has flared up in the sector of Matveyev-Kurgan hill and in the streets leading to the station.

  0800: the station is in enemy hands.

  0840: the station is in our hands.

  0940: the station has been retaken by the enemy.

  1040: the enemy has reached Pushkin Street, 500 yards from the Army's Battle Headquarters.

  1100: two regiments of infantry supported by 30 tanks are moving towards the Technical Institution."

These brief notes, taken from the *Great Patriotic War*, are sufficient without further comment to show how bitter was the struggle between the Russians and the Germans, first in the streets, then in the ruins of Stalingrad. This struggle was now a grim conflict indeed.

On September 14, weakened by the battles in the great curve of the Don, the 62nd Army had only 50,000 fighting men left. On the following night, however, a Regiment of the 13th Guards Division was sent hurriedly across the Volga in reinforcement and this enabled Lieutenant-General Chuikov to retake Matveyev-Kurgan hill. On September 17 more men, an infantry brigade and an armoured brigade, also crossed the river on ferries to take part in the defence of Stalingrad.

These reinforcements did not, however, prevent the German 6th Army, powerfully supported by *Luftflotte* IV, from scoring victories. By September 20 they had

▽ *A soldier takes a final pull on his cigarette as German infantry wait the order to advance from their start line. In the workers' suburbs, the fighting was comparatively easy as most of the buildings were wood and could be burned or blasted by tanks or aircraft.*

reached the banks of the Volga, slightly downstream of the station which they had finally occupied. This cut off the 62nd Army on its left from the 64th (Major-General M. S. Shumilov), and trapped it against the river for some 15 miles.

Russian street fighting tactics

There is no doubt that in the battle for Stalingrad, Paulus had numerical and *matériel* superiority, but if he could not take advantage of it as he did on the Don, it was because the nature of the street fighting deprived him of most of the advantages of his tanks and planes. In his memoirs, Chuikov, later a Marshal, gives a clear indication of this: success "did not depend on strength, but on ability, skill, daring, guile. Buildings split up enemy formations like breakwaters, forcing them to follow the line of the streets. That is why we clung to the most solid ones, with small units capable of all-round defence. These buildings allowed us to set up centres of resistance from which the defenders mowed down the Nazis with their automatic weapons."

In this connection it must be recalled that the Russians had followed more closely than the Germans the fighting between the Spanish Nationalists and Republicans in December 1936 in the outer suburbs and, especially, the University City in Madrid. Experience had shown that large, modern concrete buildings were all but proof against medium artillery fire. And there were many such buildings in Stalingrad, especially large factory buildings, of which Marshal Chuikov said that their "solid construction in metal and concrete and the development of their underground installations allowed prolonged and bitter resistance".

At the request of Paulus, Colonel-General von Richthofen, the commander of *Luftflotte* IV, strove to make up for the lack of artillery by heavy bombing. But the only effect of this was to create enormous amounts of rubble in the streets, which prevented the use of armour, and the German engineers of the time had no bulldozers to clear such rubble away

△ *General Chuikov with some staff officers in one of his command posts. He was forced to move his headquarters, but he tried to keep to the west bank of the Volga since he felt that this would help to sustain his men's morale. It also added conviction to his slogan "For us there is no land across the Volga."*
▷ *General Paulus with his staff on the outskirts of the city. The 6th Army, which had driven so swiftly across the steppes of southern Russia, would bog down in the streets of Stalingrad.*

the marksmen who, with their semi-automatic rifles fitted with telescopic sights, decimated German detachments.

Hitler's directive of April 5, 1942 had left open the question as to whether Stalingrad should be taken or whether Germany should be content with wiping it out as a centre of war production and of communications. Did Hitler see in Stalingrad a symbol? Or did the elimination of this Soviet bridgehead on the west bank of the Volga seem to him necessary for the successful outcome of the operations then taking place in the Caucasus? We do not know. What is certain, however, is that Paulus received an unequivocal order to complete the conquest of the city at whatever cost. To help him, five battalions of sappers were dispatched to him by air.

Factory to factory combat

This gave new impetus to the attack, whilst increased support was given by the Stukas of the Luftflotte's VIII *Fliegerkorps*. The Orlovka salient was reduced and then, on a front of only two and a half miles, the 94th and 389th infantry, the 100th Jäger and the 14th and 24th Panzer Divisions hurled themselves on to the great industrial complexes known as the "Dzerzinsky" and the "Barricades" on October 14. For the 62nd Army this was a day of severe tests, as its war diary shows.

"0800: enemy attack with tanks and infantry. Battle raging over whole front.

0930: enemy attack on Tractor Factory repulsed. Ten tanks on fire in factory yard.

1000: tanks and infantry crush the 109th Regiment of the 37th Division (Major-General Zheludov).

1130: left flank of 524th Infantry Regiment of the 95th Division smashed in. Some 50 tanks are rolling up the Regiment's positions.

1150: enemy has occupied stadium at Tractor Factory. Our units cut off inside and fighting their way out.

1200: commander of 117th Regiment, Guards Major Andreyev, killed.

1220: radio message from unit of 416th Regiment from hexagonal block of flats: 'Surrounded; have water and cartridges; will die rather than surrender.'

1230: Stukas attack General Zheludov's H.Q. General in his collapsed shelt-

△ A Stuka pulls out over a burning fuel dump. When Chuikov discovered that the Luftwaffe would only bomb forward positions when there was a clear gap of no-man's land, he urged his troops to reduce this distance to hand grenade range. This meant that it was difficult for the Germans to neutralise buildings in the town which had been turned into strongpoints, for fear of hitting their own men.

under enemy fire. This was the lesson of experience, but let us note in passing that the Western Allies made the same mistakes both at Cassino and in Normandy.

The German tanks themselves were split up into units of some 15 to 20, but these were prevented from using the range of their guns in the streets, whereas the Russians, in attic windows, cellars, and manholes were able to attack them at a range of a few yards with Molotov cocktails, anti-tank grenades, and 14.5-mm anti-tank rifles, which would have been no good in open country.

The German infantry, moreover, was no better off than its comrades in the Panzers for, Chuikov writes, "the defenders of Stalingrad let the tanks come within range of their guns and anti-tank rifles, and this, at the same time, kept the infantry away from the tanks so that the enemy's normal order of battle was upset. The infantry were wiped out separately as the tanks went ahead of them. And without infantry the tanks were not much good on their own: they were stopped and suffered heavy losses when they pulled back."

In street fighting, rifles, machine guns, and sub-machine guns came into their own, but mention must also be made of er without communications. We are liaising with elements of his Division.

1310: two shelters collapse at Army H.Q. An officer trapped by legs in rubble. Can't free him.

1525: Army H.Q. guard now fighting in battle.

1635: Lieutenant-Colonel Ustinov, commanding infantry regiment, asks for artillery fire on his H.Q. He is surrounded by enemy with sub-machine guns."

From the opposing side, Major Grams offers us confirmation of the terrible battles of October, in which he took part as commander of a motorised battalion in the 14th Panzer Division. In his history of this famous unit he writes: "It was an appalling and exhausting battle at both ground level and underground in the ruins, the cellars, the drains of this large city. Man to man, hero to hero. Our tanks clambered over great mountains of rubble and plaster, their tracks screeching as they drove their way through ruined workshops, opening fire at point-blank range in narrow streets blocked by fallen masonry or in the narrow factory yards. Several of our armoured colossi shook visibly or blew up as they ran over mines."

The worst thing for the Germans to bear, according to Grams, was the fact that every night hundreds of ferries brought in reinforcements across the Volga and there was no way of stopping them. In fact, during the night of October 16–17, the Soviet 138th Division (Colonel I. I. Lyudnikov) arrived at a very opportune moment to bolster up the defence of the "Barricades" factory sector. LI Corps under General von Seydlitz had occupied the Tractor Factory itself, and had even reached the river bank but, faced with the Russians' continuous and insurmountable resistance, their attacks petered out, as previous ones had done.

Meanwhile Hitler, who was in Munich to celebrate the eighteenth anniversary of the abortive 1923 *Putsch* among the faithful, considered the battle for Stalingrad, and with it the war in Russia, as won. "I wished," he shouted in his raucous voice, "to get to the Volga and at a certain time and a certain place. It happens to be named after Stalin himself. But do not think that that is why I directed our efforts against it; it could have had quite a different name. No. It is because this is a particularly important place. This is where 30 million tons of traffic comes to

be sorted out, including some nine million tons of petrol. This is where all the cereals from the huge regions of the Ukraine and the Kuban' pass through on their way to the north. This is where manganese ore is sent. This is where there are huge trans-shipment facilities. I wanted to take it and let me tell you, for we are modest, we have it!" This message had more effect on the party members crowded into the Munich Beer Cellar than on the fighters on the Stalingrad front. They knew what the real truth was, and it was them Hitler now told to "finish it off". It also shows

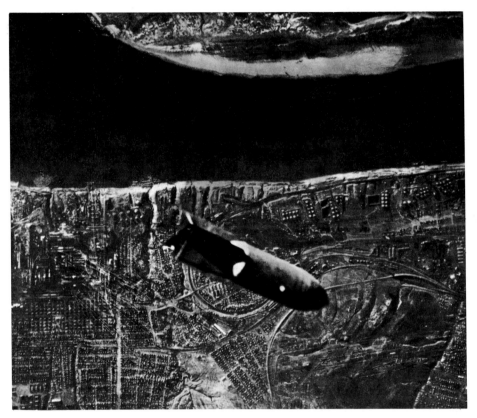

△ A heavy bomb descends on the "tennis racquet", a Russian bridgehead six miles square held by Chuikov's 62nd Army. The nickname for the area was derived from the circular shape of the railway marshalling yards.

that the Führer did not know–or pretended not to know–about the railway linking Astrakhan' and Saratov, bypassing Stalingrad and the Volga's great western bend.

More German advances

Yet on November 11, the German LI Corps, still fighting in the breach, renewed its assaults with armour and sappers; at the cost of incredible effort it succeeded in isolating from the rest of the Russian 62nd Army the defenders of the "Barricades", whose courage still remained steadfast, and in overrunning the workers' quarters attached to the "Red October" factory. They got inside the factory

The fighting in Stalingrad put great pressure on the junior N.C.O.s and sub-sections of both armies. A determined leader could turn a solid building into a fortress, or lead a patrol through the sewers and gullies that led from the river into the centre of the city.

△ A Russian patrol clambers through a maze of shattered buildings.

▽ A Soviet 76-mm gun fires through the dust and smoke of a street battle. Each side used artillery in direct support to batter down the factories and department stores that had been fortified.

itself, but then the attack ground to a halt. The 6th Army had worn itself out: its infantry companies were down to 80 or even 60 men, and the three divisions of its XIV Panzer Corps had only 199 tanks left of which many were inferior Czech types. The situation on the other side had also worsened considerably. On the west bank of the Volga the Russian 62nd Army only had 300 to 1,000 yards behind it. The river was beginning to bring down ice-floes large enough to prevent supplies or reinforcements from crossing. The fact still remains, however, that by now Chuikov knew secretly that he had won a sufficient margin of time, albeit a small one, for Russia, and that within ten days or so the enemy would have something else to think about.

Some of the famous units of the Red Army which distinguished themselves in the defence of Stalingrad have already been mentioned. To these must also be added the 112th and the 308th Divisions, commanded respectively by Colonels I. Zh. Ermolkin and L. N. Gurtiev. Mindful of the soldier in the front line, we quote the tribute to this gigantic struggle by Marshal Eremenko, then in command of the Stalingrad Front.

"The epic of Stalingrad brought out particularly the high and noble qualities of the Soviet people and their heroic army: fervent patriotism, devotion to the Communist cause, fighting comradeship between soldiers of all nationalities, inflexible courage and self-sacrifice, unshakable firmness in defence, forceful bravery in attack, constant liaison and unfailing help between the front and rear areas, brotherhood between soldiers and workers in the factories and the fields. The heroic spirit which has breathed over Stalingrad has borne illustrious testimony to the power of the great Communist Party to guide and inspire our lives and to adapt itself to every circumstance, trustee as it is of the eternal ideas of Lenin."

It will be recalled that Hitler had assumed direct command of Army Group "A" in the Caucasus on September 10. Reduced to some 20 divisions since the transfer of the 4th *Panzerarmee* to Army Group "B", the Germans ended up in late autumn by failing at their last objectives also, just as Stalin had forecast to Winston Churchill. In the Black Sea area, autumn was drawing in and *Gruppe* Ruoff had not got beyond the foothills of the Caucasus. It was thus unable to complete that encircling movement which the Führer had calculated would have given him at best the ports of Tuapse and Sukhumi. The defenders were helped by the forests, the altitude, the rain, and then the snow, all of which showed up the lack of training of the German mountain troops who, however, had been driven very hard. Colonel-General von Kleist had reached Prokhladny on the River Terek, which flows out into the Caspian, on August 27. He was no luckier than the others. Held some 50 miles from the Grozny oilfields, he rallied his III Panzer Corps (General von Mack-

ensen) and swung his attack upstream. This seems to have caught the defence by surprise and he took Nal'chik on October 25 and Alagir on November 5 but failed at Orzhonikidze as he was crossing the Terek. Worse still, this finger that he had rashly thrust into the enemy's positions was all but cut off in counter-attacks, and he nearly lost his 13th Panzer Division. Though it escaped, its near loss put an end to the 1st *Panzerarmee*'s offensive for good and all.

The North Caucasus and the Trans-Caucasus Fronts were now being reinforced week by week, so that on about November 15 the 22 Axis divisions (15 German, 6 Rumanian, and one Slovak) were opposed by almost 90 major formations, including 37 infantry and eight or nine cavalry divisions, and eight armoured brigades. The tide was about to turn on Germany's effort to secure Caucasian oil.

The Soviet comeback

During their conversations in August, Stalin had told Winston Churchill that he intended to launch a great offensive as winter approached. So during the first fortnight in September Colonel-General A. M. Vasilevskii, replacing the sick Marshal Shaposhnikov as Chief-of-Staff, and his colleague General N. N. Voronov, head of the Red Army's artillery, were sent to the banks of the Volga to deal with the situation. When they returned to *Stavka* it was decided that the forthcoming operation should be in the hands of General G. K. Zhukov. It was expected to engage several Fronts or army groups. Colonel-General Eremenko then had to be relieved of some of his large command, on the South-East and Stalingrad Fronts. The former was renamed the Stalingrad

△ *While the man on the right prepares to give covering fire, a section leader helps one of his men out of a communication trench. All the men are armed with PPSh M 41 sub-machine guns. Though some specialised weapons like flame-throwers were used effectively, the fighting called for mobility and here the sub-machine gun and hand grenade were invaluable.*

A rifleman breaks cover in the snow covered ruins of the city. The Germans never managed to master the art of these small unit tactics, and were even out-classed by the Russian snipers. General Chuikov said that "Every German soldier must be made to feel that he is living under the muzzle of a Russian gun, always ready to treat him to a fatal dose of lead."

Front and remained under his control; the second became the Don Front, under the command of Lieutenant-General K. K. Rokossovsky.

By the beginning of September 1942 the Soviet Supreme Command saw that the German reserves were becoming exhausted. They knew that the time had come when they could launch a major counter-attack against their opponents.

Zhukov and Vasilevsky discussed these questions with *Stavka*, and they went to the Volga Front to judge the situation for themselves before drawing up a plan for a counter-offensive against the Axis forces. They were told to keep the purpose of their visit secret. At Stalingrad Zhukov ascertained the 6th Army's strength and calculated the numbers of men, tanks and guns the Russians would require for a successful offensive. He also reconnoitred the bridgeheads held by the Russian forces to the south of the River Don at Kletskaya and Serafimovich. Vasilevsky went to the south of Stalingrad to see sectors of the front held by the Russian

51st and 57th Armies between Krasnoarmeysk and Lake Barmantsak. On their return to Moscow *Stavka* invited the General Staff's Operations Directorate to help them to work out the details of a practical plan. *Stavka* took a direct control of the two new fronts (Stalingrad and Don) which were to conduct the counter-attack. By the end of the month they approved the plan and the General Staff were engaged in working out the operational details. Vasilevsky commanded the Stalingrad Front and Zhukov was given charge of the Don Front and the newly created South-West Front. The attack was to consist of a concentric movement north and south of Stalingrad against the thinly held flanks of the 6th Army, the Rumanian 3rd and 4th Armies and the underequipped 4th Panzer Army. The attack would then link up to the west of Stalingrad, thus trapping the 6th Army and destroying it. By the second half of October these plans were complete. The attack would take place on a front of 250 miles.

The Russian forces move up

When these decisions had been taken, the next step was to transport men and *matériel* to their concentration areas. The 5th Tank Army (Lieutenant-General P. L. Romanenko) was recalled from the Bryansk Front to become the spearhead of Vatutin's attack. IV Mechanised Corps (Major-General A. G. Kravchenko) and XIII Mechanised Corps (Major-General Tanichikhin) occupied the lake area south of Stalingrad under strict camouflage precautions as part of Eremenko's front.

In view of the decisive result expected from the campaign, *Stavka* did not hesitate to call upon half its reserve of artillery. Vatutin, Rokossovsky, and Eremenko thus got an additional 75 artillery regiments, bringing their total up to 230, or 13,540 guns and mortars. They were also sent 115 *Katyusha* batteries, with a total of 10,000 launchers. Two air armies were sent to the South-West Front and one each to the Don and Stalingrad Fronts, so that the three fronts had a total of 1,000 planes, including 600 fighters, to call on. This weight of equipment was to batter a hole in the thinly-held German fronts.

These troop and equipment movements were usually carried out at night and the strictest orders were given to preserve secrecy. This was also secured by manoeuvres designed to deceive the enemy. Radio operators on the Bryansk Front, for instance, continued to transmit messages for the benefit of enemy listening-posts long after the troops had left the area, and did not rejoin their units on the Don Front until the very last moment.

Can we conclude with Marshal Eremenko that if the German Supreme Command admitted the likelihood of a Russian counter-attack, "it still did not know precisely where or when it would take place"? Eremenko was no doubt basing his opinion on the authority of Colonel-General Jodl, who is said to have declared after the capitulation of the Third Reich: "We had no idea of the gigantic concentrations of Russian forces on the flank of the 6th Army. We did not know in what strength the Soviet troops were massing in this sector. Shortly before the attacks, there was nothing there and suddenly we were struck a massive blow, a blow which was to have far-reaching, even fatal, consequences."

We should remember, however, that at O.K.W. Jodl enjoyed only a partial view of the Eastern Front. From mid-October, both in the German 6th Army and the Rumanian 3rd Army, there was constant concern about enemy activity in the

△ A Russian sailor in a heroic pose in one of Stalingrad's factory fortresses. Chuikov paid tribute to the Volga flotilla whose guns and ships supported and supplied the troops in the city.

▽ Soldiers in the ruined Tractor Factory. This was a focal point for defence in the north of the city, but it fell during the savage assaults late in October.

△ "Hitler and his War Machine" a Russian poster which has the slogan: "Do not waste useless words. The moral is clear to every onlooker: The machine has begun to give out, time for the 'leader' to give in as well."

bridgeheads he controlled and on the right bank of the Don in the areas of Kletskaya and Serafimovich. Similar signs of movement had been noticed in the sector of the 4th *Panzerarmee*, which extended the right flank of the 6th Army, and Colonel-General Paulus deduced that the enemy was preparing some pincer movement which would be all the more dangerous for the Germans as the Rumanians on the flank were very poorly equipped with anti-tank weapons. He therefore strengthened his left flank by bringing over the Don the armoured units of his 14th Panzer Division into General Strecker's XI Corps, but he could do no more as he had the strictest orders from Hitler to hold Stalingrad at all costs.

Zeitzler proposes a withdrawal

Paulus naturally informed Colonel-General von Weichs, commanding Army Group "B", of the way he thought things were going and Weichs passed this on, together with his own appreciation of the

situation, to O.K.H. Here General Zeitzler was sufficiently impressed to propose to Hitler that the attack on Stalingrad should be abandoned and the German 6th Army brought back into the great loop of the Don, whilst the 4th *Panzerarmee* blocked the Stalingrad–Novorossiysk railway opposite Kotel'nikovo.

Hitler's arbitrary solution

Hitler, however, came up with another solution. This was recorded in the O.K.W. diary, then being kept by the historian Helmuth Creiner. The entry for October 26 reads: "The Führer again expresses his concern over a large Soviet attack, perhaps a winter offensive starting in the sector held by our allied armies on the Don and aimed at Rostov. This concern is based on strong troop movements observed in the area and on the number of bridges the Russians have thrown over the river. The Führer orders each of the three allied armies to be stiffened with fighting divisions from the Luftwaffe. This will allow a number of divisions to be withdrawn from the front and, together with other units to be sent to the area, these will build up a reserve behind our allied armies."

This text, the authenticity of which is beyond doubt, is interesting from more than one point of view. First of all it shows that, contrary to what Marshal Eremenko says in his pamphlet against the German generals, O.K.H.'s new Chief-of-Staff had adopted the conclusions reached by Paulus and Weichs and had brought them to the knowledge of the Führer. Especially, however, it shows Hitler's favoured form of reasoning: he discards the approved method which, piecing together information received, consists in asking: "what are the possibilities for the enemy?" to ask the questions such as one might hear at a café-table discussion: "wherein lies the enemy's greatest advantage?" or again: "what would I have done if I had been Stalin?" Now an attack towards Rostov was markedly more advantageous to the Russians than the pincer movement adopted by *Stavka* since, when it had reached its objective, it would have meant the destruction not only of five of Weichs' seven armies, but also of the whole of Army Group "A" right down in the Caucasus. If Stalin had been Hitler he might have adopted this risky solution, but he was not and went for prudence.

Belated decision

The Rostov hypothesis, however, meant that the Italian 8th Army had to be strengthened. This would take the first brunt of any attack in this direction. It was reinforced by the XLVIII Panzer Corps under its recently-appointed commander, Lieutenant-General F. Heim. A few days later Hitler, no doubt on the receipt of further information, seems to have been converted as a very last extreme to Zeitzler's view. It is a fact that on November 16, that is on D-day minus three, XLVIII Panzer Corps received the order to move from Boguchar to Pèrelazovskiy in the area behind the Rumanian 3rd Army. These two places are 110 miles apart. Too late! We must therefore conclude that, if we accept Marshal Eremenko's view that "Hitler's command" was caught out by the event, this really meant only the Hitler-Keitel-Jodl trinity.

"How many divisions has the Pope?" Everyone knows this question, put by Stalin to one of his western visitors. But if, 30 years after the event, we ask the authors of Volume III of the *Great Patriotic War* how many divisions Stalin threw into the Stalingrad counter-offensive on the dates indicated, we have to state that no precise reply is obtainable, whereas we know down to regimental level the order of battle of Army Group "B" for November 15, 1942. On that day,

in his headquarters at Star'obel'sk Colonel-General von Weichs held a front from Elista in the Kalmuk Steppe to Kursk, a distance of 710 miles, with 80 divisions, four of which were for the protection of his rear areas, the other 76 being fighting units. The latter were divided into types and nationalities as follows:

	Infantry	Cavalry	Motorised	Armoured	Total
German	31	–	4	5	40
Italian	6*	1	2	–	9
Rumanian	13	4	–	1	18
Hungarian	8	–	–	1	9
Total	58	5	6	7	76

*including 3 Alpine divisions

The fact remains, it is true, that on November 19 and 20 the Soviet pincers bit into only seven German and 15 Rumanian divisions from the 4th *Panzerarmee*, XI Corps (6th Army), XLVIII Panzer Corps, and the Rumanian 3rd and 4th Armies. On the same dates Generals Vatutin, Rokossovsky, and Eremenko were able to deploy over a million men, divided into nine armies, which had 66 rifle divisions, five tank corps, and a mechanised corps: a comfortable superiority.

The same superiority was apparent in *matériel*. According to the *Great Patriotic*

◁ *"33 anti-tank riflemen", a Russian painting by I. E. Yevstigneyev. It is typical of the style of official painting showing the grim heroism of the Russian defenders.*

△ *An assault group moves in with grenades and sub-machine guns. In October and November Paulus was losing the equivalent of a division every five days, but Hitler had said in a meeting of the Party old guard at the Bürgerbräu House on November 9: "I wanted to take the place and we've pulled it off, we've got it really; except for a few enemy positions." And so the fighting had to go on.*

War the following was the picture on the Don battlefield and on the Steppe:

	Russians	Axis	Ratio
Armoured vehicles	894	675	1.3:1
Guns and mortars	13,540	10,300	1.3:1
Aircraft	1,115	1,216	1:1

These figures cannot be accepted, however. According to an entry in the O.K.W. war diary dated November 6, 1942, out of 1,134 Luftwaffe aircraft available over the whole front, *Luftflotte* IV disposed of only 600 which, moreover, had to meet the demands of both Army Group "A" and Army Group "B". As for tanks, the 6th Army's XIV Panzer Corps was reduced to 199 on the day the battle started, as we have seen, and on the day it arrived on the scene XLVIII Panzer Corps only had 84. When we add to these a handful of tanks the 27th Panzer Division and the Hungarian 1st Armoured Division, both of them units in the course of formation, we have scarcely reached the half of the Soviet historian's figure. Moreover, this figure cannot have taken into account the fact that the Panzers included a high proportion of Czech Pzkw 38(t)'s, whose obsolete 37-mm guns had no effect on the thick plating of the T-34's and KV-1's now making up the major part of the Red Army's armoured formations.

Fighting in the skeleton of a city. The Russians had received orders which left no room for misunderstanding: "There is only one road, the road that leads forward. Stalingrad will be saved by you, or be wiped out with you."
△ While a Degtyarev DP light machine gun covers their moves, a squad of soldiers doubles across a dangerous patch of open ground.
◁ Two German soldiers walk through the shattered remains of a factory. Even if they had captured the city there would have been nothing of value for the Germans.

The satellites' part

Even before the start of the battle which was to bring about the final destruction of his army group, Colonel-General von Weichs was not optimistic about the outcome after the adverse reports of his Intelligence units. On the preceding October 10, the Rumanian 3rd Army (General Dumitrescu) had taken up positions between the left flank of the German 6th Army and the right flank of the Italian 8th Army (General Gariboldi). This was in execution of the directive of April 5, which laid down that the Don front should be defended by the satellite powers.

But between the right flank of the Rumanian 3rd Army, which adjoined the left flank of the German 6th Army, and the left flank of the Hungarian 2nd Army (Colonel-General Jany) which adjoined the German 2nd Army, the Don front was some 310 miles long. The three satellite armies which were being asked to defend it had between them some 30 divisions. All of them were somewhat weak in infantry, lacking in mobility and, especially, very badly equipped both qualitatively and quantitatively to meet armour-

ed attack. The Rumanian 3rd Army was particularly badly situated as it faced the two bridgeheads at Kletskaya and Serafimovich, where the Russians had held out in the previous summer against all attacks and, without being able to take advantage of the river obstacle, the Rumanian battalions each had an average front of over three miles.

Marshal Antonescu, the Rumanian dictator, had not failed to draw Hitler's attention to the extreme danger of the situation. In particular he had asked Hitler for 5-cm anti-tank guns to replace the earlier 3.7-cm weapons with which the Rumanians were equipped and which were recognised as completely obsolete. The Führer had promised to supply these without delay, but his promise remained empty words and a catastrophe became inevitable. Army Group "B" was thus in a position of "pre-rupture".

The position was further blackened by the fact that the strategic reserves available to Weichs consisted of only four divisions, two German infantry divisions, and the two armoured divisions of the XLVIII Panzer Corps. One of these two, however, the Rumanian 1st Armoured Division (Radu) had never been in action, and both were under strength.

▽ *One German soldier who did reach the Volga. It was the German's failure to squeeze out the Russian salients over the river to the north of the city that left them as jumping-off points for a Soviet counter-offensive. Stalingrad had acted as a magnet drawing in the best of the German forces and the attention of the staff and officers of the 6th Army.*

CHAPTER 38
STALINGRAD: THE TRAP CLOSES

The operation, under Zhukov's overall command, had been baptised "Uranus" in Moscow and was launched in two phases.

At 0730 hours on November 19, after a general rocket barrage the artillery of the South-West and the Don Fronts opened up on the German-Rumanian positions north-west of Stalingrad with about 90 guns per mile of Front. According to the Russians, the density of this concentration was made less effective because of thick fog. Be that as it may, the entire telephone network of the Rumanian 3rd Army was put out of action as the wires were cut by the shelling. The fog also helped the surprise effect. At 0848 the Soviet barrage moved forward, and infantry and tanks flung themselves into the assault.

On the South-West Front, the 5th Tank Army (Lieutenant-General P. L. Romanenko) had as its task the annihilation of the Rumanian defence facing the Serafimovich bridgehead, but it met such resistance that its commander had to use up in the breakthrough some of the tanks he had planned to hold back for exploitation of the breach. But then the defence

collapsed. At nightfall, two Soviet tank corps, protected on their flanks by corps of cavalry, broke through the breach and poured into the enemy's rear, causing fearful panic.

Further to the east, the Soviet 21st Army broke out of the Kletskaya bridgehead on a front of nearly nine miles. Under the command of Major-General I. M. Chistyakov, it also had to use its armoured forces to overcome the resistance of the Rumanians. By the end of the day it had had the same success as the 5th Tank Army. The Rumanian V Armoured Corps (General M. Lascar), which was holding out between Kletskaya and Serafimovich, saw that it was doomed to encirclement.

On the Don Front, the Soviet 65th Army (Lieutenant-General P. I. Batov), attacking from the Kletskaya bridgehead towards Vertyachiy, where the Germans had bridged the Don, was caught at a disadvantage in deep ravines. It also ran up against the XI Corps, which formed the left flank of the 6th Army, and was counterattacked furiously by the 14th Panzer Division. It was therefore able to make only modest advances. The 24th Army

△ *A knocked-out Soviet medium anti-aircraft gun and tractor in the autumn mist. At the beginning of the attack on the city the Luftwaffe had total air superiority, and even added scrap iron to more lethal payloads dropped on Chuikov's men. But with the onset of autumn their temporary airfields became mud-bound, and maintenance and loading a gruelling task for the ground crews.*

△ *General Rokossovsky, commander of the Don Front, whose troops struck on November 19. A day later the Stalingrad Front under General Eremenko struck from the south of the city. The preparations for the counter-offensive had been a feat of outstanding organisation and secrecy. With the South-West Front under Vatutin, the Russians had about parity of men, and a slight superiority of weapons–but their men were fresh and their weapons were new, and their morale was very high.*

(Major-General I. Galanin), which had been ordered to advance along the left bank of the Don, was similarly held up. The 66th Army (Lieutenant-General A. S. Zhadov) was to make a diversion in the Don-Volga isthmus, stubbornly defended by the VIII Corps (General W. Heitz).

On the Axis side, the XLVIII Panzer Corps, on stand-by since dawn, rumbled off at 0930 hours towards Kletskaya, where it was thought that the main Russian effort was being made, with orders to engage it without worrying about the flanks. Towards 1100 hours, in the light of new information, General Heim was ordered to drive towards Sera-fimovich–a switch from north-east to north-west. In the fog this counter-order produced confusion, contact was lost, and both the 22nd Panzer Division (Major-General Rodt) and the Rumanian 1st Armoured Division ran blindly into the Soviet 5th Tank Army. In the evening Heim was surrounded and his troops were in a very bad way.

On November 20, to the south-west of Stalingrad, the second phase of the Soviet offensive opened under Colonel-General Eremenko, from a line Lake Tastsa–Lake Sarpa–Krasnoarmeysk, with the 64th, 57th, and 51st Armies under the command respectively of Major-Generals M. S. Shumilov, F. I. Tolbukhin and N. I. Trufanov. To exploit the expected break-through, Eremenko had put the XIII Mechanised Corps (Major-General T. I. Tanichikhin) under 57th Army, whilst the 51st Army had been given the IV Mecha-nised Corps and the IV Cavalry Corps (Major-Generals V. T. Volsky and T. T. Shapkin). On the other side, all Colonel-General Hoth had left of his former *Panzerarmee* was IV Corps (General E. Jaenecke), but he did have the Rumanian 4th Army, of which General C. A. Con-stantinescu was about to take over the command. He thus had seven infantry divisions (two of which were German), and two Rumanian cavalry divisions. He held in reserve the excellent 29th Motorised Division.

Delayed by fog, the attack started at 1000 hours, but by early afternoon the breakthrough had come in the sector of the Rumanian VI Corps whose 1st, 2nd, and 18th Divisions were virtually wiped out. The 29th Motorised Division tried to restore the situation and scored some early victories. But as the only unit capable of counter-attacking amidst the general rout, it soon had to abandon the positions it had won for fear of being surrounded. Eremenko was not long in letting loose his cavalry and mechanised units, and on the following day, at 1030 hours, IV Cavalry Corps galloped into the village of Abganerovo, a station on the Stalingrad–Novorossiysk railway line. A few minutes later Nikita Khrus-chev was on the scene, bringing con-gratulations and encouragement.

In the great sweep of the Don on this same November 20, Vatutin and Rokos-sovsky energetically exploited their suc-cesses of the day before. The former used his 5th Tank Army and the latter his IV Tank Corps (Major-General G. P. Krav-chenko) and his III Guards Corps (Major-General I. A. Pliev). Meanwhile the 21st Army completed the encirclement of the Rumanian V Corps, which then turned south and fought with some tenacity.

But how could it face an attack by some 900 tanks and two cavalry corps? At dawn on November 20, at Perelazovskiy, the staff of the Rumanian II Corps was so taken by surprise that when the patrols of the XXVI Tank Corps (Major-General A. G. Rodin) reached their headquarters they found tables laden with maps and docu-ments, cupboards open, keys in the locks of

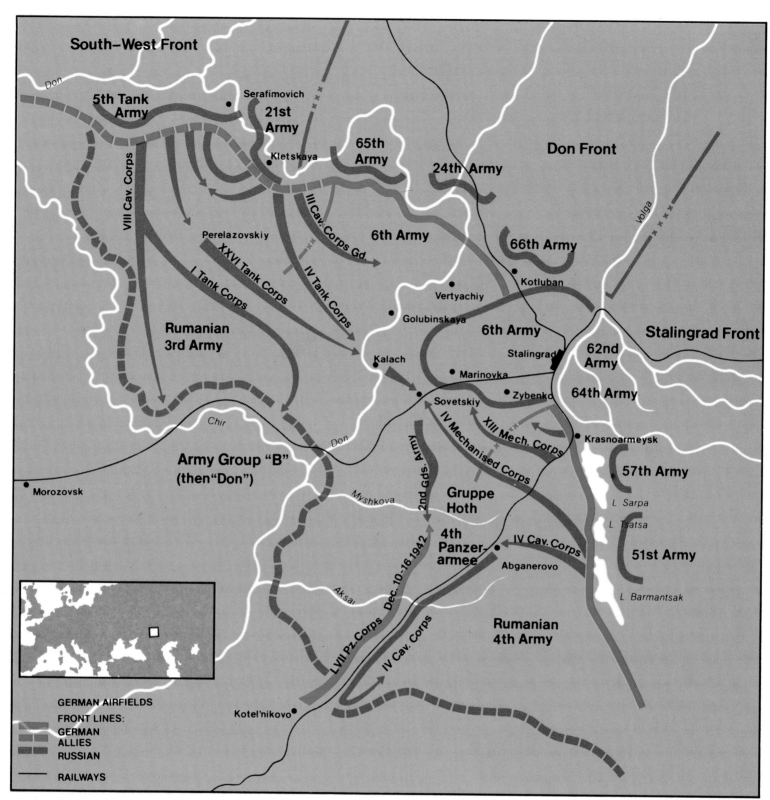

South–West Front

Don

5th Tank Army

Serafimovich

21st Army

Kletskaya

65th Army

24th Army

Don Front

VIII Cav. Corps

III Cav. Corps Gd.

6th Army

66th Army

Volga

Perelazovskiy

XXVI Tank Corps

I Tank Corps

IV Tank Corps

Kotluban

Vertyachiy

Rumanian 3rd Army

Golubinskaya

6th Army

Stalingrad Front

Kalach

Marinovka

Stalingrad

62nd Army

64th Army

Sovetskiy

Zybenko

Chir

Don

XIII Mech. Corps

Krasnoarmeysk

Army Group "B" (then "Don")

Myshkova

IV Mechanised Corps

57th Army

Morozovsk

2nd Gds. Army

Gruppe Hoth

L. Sarpa

L. Tsatsa

Aksai

4th Panzer-armee

IV Cav. Corps

51st Army

LVII Pz. Corps Dec. 10–16 1942

Abganerovo

L. Barmantsak

IV Cav. Corps

Rumanian 4th Army

GERMAN AIRFIELDS

FRONT LINES:
GERMAN
ALLIES
RUSSIAN
RAILWAYS

Kotel'nikovo

△ The pincers close. The attacks had been directed at the weak links in the Axis forces and preceded by a massive artillery and mortar barrage which cut communications and stunned the defenders. Then out of the mist came the tanks and infantry.

chests, teleprinters still connected, and officers' caps still hanging on their pegs. XLVIII Panzer Corps, as a result of a breakdown in radio communications, was out of touch with the Rumanian 1st Armoured Division, but managed to break out of the encirclement. In the evening of November 20 it would have obeyed Weichs' order to retreat had it not had, through a *Führerbefehl*, the overriding order to extricate the Rumanian V Corps. This was an impossible task, and

once again XLVIII Corps was surrounded. Yet it finally managed to reach the German lines, though at the cost of its 22nd Panzer Division, which was reduced virtually to scrap.

The day of November 22 had not yet dawned before destiny had given her verdict. The night before, the Soviet XXVI Tank Corps, forming General Romanenko's left-hand column, was within striking distance of Kalach after covering over 62 miles in three days. The disorder had to be exploited at once and so General Rodin decided to take the bridge over the Don by surprise. He put under the command of Colonel Philippov of the 14th Motorised Brigade a detachment of two infantry companies. They were to advance behind five captured and restored German tanks each carrying 12 men armed with sub-machine guns. Rumbling forward with all their lights on, as the Germans did, Philippov's detachment overwhelmed the bridge guard then drove off the German counter-attacks. The defence was further confused by the shooting-match going on at the same time between the tanks of the 6th Army and those of the Soviets.

Meanwhile Eremenko had eagerly exploited his victory of November 20. Driving his IV Cavalry Corps along the railway from Kuban', he moved his IV Mechanised Corps north-west until at 1030 hours on November 23 it linked up with the IV Tank Corps from the Don Front in the village of Sovetskiy some 18–19 miles south east of Kalach. This completed the encirclement of the Axis troops in the Stalingrad area. The following day Khruschev came in person to congratulate Generals Volsky and Kravchenko and to enquire about the needs of the troops. This same day (November 24) saw the end of all Rumanian resistance in the Don pockets. The previous evening General Lascar, who had just been awarded the Iron Cross with Oak Leaves by Hitler, had had to surrender through lack of ammunition. On the 24th General Stenesco did the same and 33,000 Rumanians took the road to captivity.

Hitler determines 6th Army's fate

Events of November 19 found Hitler at Berchtesgaden, whereas O.K.W. was in Salzburg and O.K.H. had for some weeks now been in East Prussia. The Führer's only contacts for three days were by telephone with Zeitzler, and his first reaction was to give command of Army Group "A" to Colonel-General von Kleist, which brought in its train the nomination to the command of the 1st *Panzerarmee* to General von Mackensen, the son of the famous Field-Marshal of World War I. On November 22, however, Hitler decided to go back to Rastenburg. He had already decided the fate of the 6th Army. When

the news reached him that afternoon that it was encircled between the Don and the Volga he ordered, over the heads of Colonel-General von Weichs and General Zeitzler: "The 6th Army will take up a hedgehog position and await help from outside."

A Soviet rocket exploding in Colonel-General Paulus's headquarters could not have had a more staggering effect on the mind of the commander of the 6th Army than this *Führerbefehl*, revealing as it did its author's complete misunderstanding of the tragedy which he was at that moment living. He had just had to evacuate in haste his headquarters at Golubinskaya in the loop of the Don. After consulting four of his five corps commanders he appealed to the Führer in the evening of November 23 on the grounds that he was "better informed".

"Since receipt of your telegram of evening of November 22 events have developed very quickly here. Enemy has not yet succeeded in closing the gap to west and south-west. But his preparations for attack are becoming evident.

△ *A Russian infantryman with pack and rifle advances under shell fire on the Eastern Front. The shell burst may have been caused by a Russian gun. Russian infantry often advanced close behind their own barrage so that they could attack the Germans before they could recover from the shelling.*

Soldiers in the snow. In the second year of the war in the East the Germans had special winter clothing, but as a result of transport and administrative problems it had not reached the 6th Army.
△ *Two ski troops in snow suits on the Terek front in the Caucasus.*
△ ▷ *An officer briefs his N.C.O. Both men have only greatcoats and gloves as extra clothing.*

"Our ammunition and petrol supplies are running out. Several batteries and anti-tank units have none left. Supplies not expected to reach them in time.

"Army heading for disaster if it does not succeed, within very short time, in pulling together all its strength to deal knockout blow against enemy now assailing it in south and west.

"For this it is essential to withdraw all our divisions from Stalingrad and northern front. Inevitable consequence will be that army must be able to drive through in south-west, neither north nor east fronts being tenable after this withdrawal . . ."

At Star'obel'sk Colonel-General von Weichs was still linked to the 6th Army by a telephone line which had escaped the attention of the Russians. When he was told of Paulus's intentions, he vigorously supported them in a message to O.K.H.

"Fully conscious of the unusual seriousness and implication of the decision to be taken," he sent over the teleprinter,

"it is my duty to advise you that I consider that the withdrawal of the 6th Army as suggested by General Paulus is necessary." He based his opinion both on the impossibility of supplying by air an army of 22 divisions and on the fact that the offensive needed to liberate the 6th Army could not possibly start before December 10 at the earliest. On the other hand, the fighting strength of the 6th Army seemed indispensable to him when it came to rebuilding a front and organising a counter-offensive. This strength had to be regained at all cost. With the help of this brief, which he energetically defended, Zeitzler did so well that at 0200 hours on November 24 he was able to assure the chief-of-staff of Army Group "B" that as soon as he awoke Hitler would sign the withdrawal order asked for by Paulus and recommended by Weichs.

The hours passed. But, instead of the expected confirmation, the radio at Star'obel'sk received a new *Führerbefehl* aimed directly at the 6th Army: "The 6th Army is temporarily surrounded by Russian forces. My intention is to concentrate it in the area north of Stalingrad – Kotluban – Hill 137 – Hill 135 – Marinovka – Zylenko – south of Stalingrad. The Army must be persuaded that I shall do all in my power to supply it adequately and to disengage it when the time is convenient. I know the valiant 6th Army and its Commander-in-Chief and that every man will do his duty.

Signed: Adolf Hitler."

Göring's responsibility

Shaken by the forceful argument of General Zeitzler, Hitler had been restored to vigour by the assurances of Reichsmarschall Göring. These were received in silence by Colonel-General Jeschonnek but had the support of Field-Marshal Keitel and Colonel-General Jodl. The 6th Army reckoned that it needed 700 tons of supplies a day. This meant the necessary food, animal fodder, petrol, and ammunition to keep going, albeit at a reduced rate, 250,000 men, 8,000 horses, 1,800 guns, and 10,000 vehicles. With a carelessness that can only be called criminal, Göring undertook to assure them of 500 tons a day. He based this on the successful supply of the far smaller pockets at Kholm and Demyansk where, for five months from January 1942, 100,000 Germans had held out thanks to supplies from the air. But he was forgetting that:

1. the transport squadrons of the Luftwaffe were no better equipped in November 1942 than they had been the preceding winter;
2. the pocket whose maintenance he was guaranteeing would be 125–250 miles away, or three times the distance of Kholm and Demyansk from their supply airfields;
3. the Soviet Air Force, almost nonexistent in the first quarter of 1942, had been considerably reinforced since then, particularly in fighters;
4. it would take time to assemble personnel and *matériel* on the bases to be used for this operation; and

5. with the onset of winter, the weather would deteriorate very rapidly.

Indeed, as Colonel-General von Richthofen, the man on the spot, had predicted from the outset, the supplying of the 6th Army by air was a complete and disastrous failure. In actual fact, from December 1 to 12 deliveries to the Stalingrad pocket amounted to an average of 97.3 tons of petrol and ammunition a day. From December 13 to 31 this increased by some 40 tons, then fell again as a consequence of the progressive deterioration of the strategic position and the weather. The average over the whole 70 days of the airlift was 91.16 tons a day, so that Göring's shortfall may be reckoned at 81 per cent. The loss of 488 planes, including 266 Junkers Ju 52's and 1,000 aircrew must also be included on the debit side. On the credit side, 25,000 sick and wounded were evacuated.

In the Stalingrad pocket, to which Paulus had transferred his headquarters, the *Führerbefehl* of November 23 had been the object of bitter argument at the highest level. General von Seydlitz (LI Corps) held that it should be ignored as Hitler did not know the realities of the situation, and that a breakout should be attempted along the line of the railway to Kuban'. Major-General Arthur Schmidt, chief-of-staff of the 6th Army, held the opposite view, both out of respect for orders and because he reckoned that the movement advised by the commander of LI Corps would end in catastrophe compounded by a complete breakdown of discipline. Paulus, though feeling little conviction, decided that his chief-of-staff was right. The German 6th Army thus dug itself into

▽ *Soviet soldiers clown with a pair of German felt boots. Like those made from plaited straw they were intended to be worn by sentries, but were very impractical compared with those seen on the Russian soldiers.*
▽▽ *Sub-machine gunners in position by ruined industrial plant. The weapons which won the battle of Stalingrad were made in the factories that had been so ruthlessly evacuated beyond the Urals at the beginning of the war. It was only later that the Russians would benefit from Lend-Lease trucks and rations in their pursuit of the Germans.*

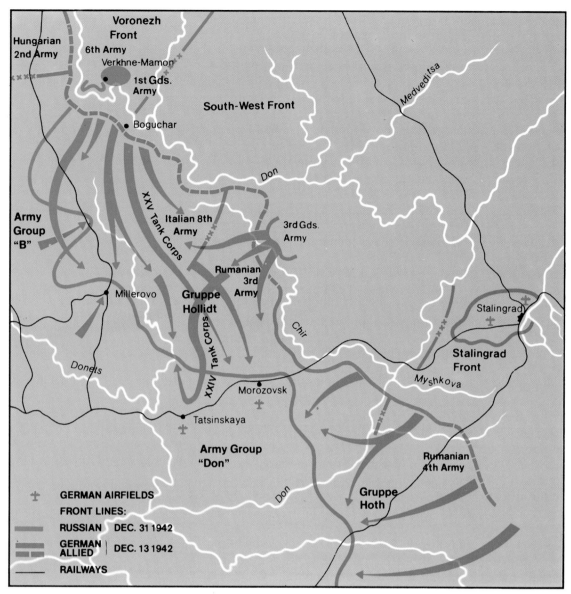

△ An agonised Hitler, in his hand a paper bearing war bulletins, begs for a re-examination of the toothache of the Eastern Front in this Russian cartoon.
◁ No less important than the breakthrough at Stalingrad was the follow-up. The Russians had to put as much territory between the 6th Army and the main German forces as possible. Even so, had the 6th Army attempted a break out during the relief operations mounted in December, there is a chance that a large number of fit men could have escaped.

a pocket measuring some 37 miles between Stalingrad and its western perimeter and 25 miles from north to south. The day after the breakthrough at Lake Tsatsa, IV Corps had come under 6th Army command, though XI Corps, as it retreated across the Don after the surprise attack at Kalach, had taken with it the Rumanian 1st Cavalry Division. Paulus thus commanded five corps, in all 15 infantry divisions, three motorised divisions, three Panzer divisions, and one division of cavalry. These totalled some 278,000 men including the units left outside the pocket.

Manstein's new task

Hitler entrusted the mission of freeing the beleaguered troops in Stalingrad to Field-Marshal Erich von Manstein.

A few days after his victory at Sevasto-pol', the new Field-Marshal, with four divisions of his 11th Army and the great guns which had demolished the Soviets' emplacements, was transferred to Army Group "North" for, in spite of Halder's objections, Hitler had decided to seize Leningrad without waiting for a solution on the Stalingrad front. This offensive, called "Nordlicht", never got started, as the Russians moved first and the 11th Army found itself from August 27 to October 2 using up its strength to bolster up a weakened 18th Army, which had given way, and then having to iron out the salients knocked into the front.

On November 21, when he was in Vitebsk, Manstein received the order to take over forthwith the command of a new army group, Army Group "Don", which would contain the 6th Army, Gruppen Hoth and Hollidt, and the Rumanian 3rd Army. Its task was defined as follows: "To arrest the enemy's attacks and to regain the ground lost since the beginning of his offensive."

On the 24th he was at the headquarters of Army Group "B", now reduced to the Italian 8th Army, the Hungarian 2nd Army, and the German 2nd Army. Colonel-General von Weichs informed him of the state in which he would find the units allotted to him. Now cut off, the German 6th Army had lost all freedom of movement. Along the line Stalingrad – Novorossiysk, *Gruppe* Hoth was, if the phrase may be permitted, no more than a strategic expression. Having lost its IV Corps and its 16th Motorised Division, immobilised on the Kalmuk Steppe by the express order of Hitler, the 4th *Panzerarmee* was reduced to a handful of Rumanian divisions which had escaped the *débâcle* of November 20. In the great loop of the Don, General Hollidt somehow improvised a defensive line behind the Chir so as to deny to the enemy the defence of the main river.

On November 26 Field-Marshal von Manstein set up his headquarters at Novocherkassk. On the 27th, 78 trains from France arrived in Kotel'nikovo station, 100 miles south-west of Stalingrad, bringing in the first units of the 6th Panzer Division (Major-General E. Raus). These were greeted by artillery fire and began their career on the Eastern Front by driving off the Soviet IV Cavalry Corps. This included a brigade of troops mounted on camels and recruited in Central Asia. Naturally enough, it was virtually wiped out.

Yet it was not before December 10 that the 4th *Panzerarmee*, part of *Gruppe* Hoth, was able to go over to the offensive. It was in fact reduced to nothing more than LVII Panzer Corps (General F. Kirchner), as the Rumanian VI and VII Corps could not be relied on. The 6th Panzer Division was soon up to its full strength with 160 tanks, a battalion of half-tracks, and 42 self-propelled guns. Not so the 23rd Panzer Division (Lieutenant-General von Boineburg-Lengsfeld) hurriedly brought up from the Caucasus, which went into action with only 20 tanks. These figures are important in view of the claims of Soviet historians that Manstein went into action in what they pompously call his "counter-offensive" with 460 armoured vehicles.

On December 12–13, LVII Panzer Corps nevertheless forced a crossing of the Aksay in spite of resistance from the Russian 51st Army of the Stalingrad Front. The valiant Eremenko thought this serious enough to appeal to Supreme Headquarters. "I reported it to J. V. Stalin," he wrote. "Alarmed by this information he sent a message 'Hold out. We will send you reserves immediately.' And he added 'Supreme Headquarters has finally realised what danger you were in.' The situation was becoming very serious: the reserves might be too late." This was why he threw in his XIII and IV Mechanised Corps, in spite of their being worn out. They counter-attacked furiously whilst the Germans put in their 17th Panzer Division, which had only 30 tanks, from the Orel front. The Panzer division's commander, Major-General F. von Senger und Etterlin signalled Hoth: "Situation regarding *matériel* very bad." Hoth replied: "Some divisions up front are even worse off. Yours has an excellent reputation. I am counting on you." The attacks started again and on December 15 Eremenko had to sound the alarm a second time. *Stavka* promised him the prompt aid of the 2nd Guards Army (Lieutenant-General R. Ya. Malinovsky). This army did, in fact, succeed in preventing Kirchner from breaking out of the bridgehead he had won on the north bank of the Myshkova. Hoth had thus won 50 miles in eight days and was within 30 miles of his objective. But he had worn out his men. Conscious of his subordinate's difficulties, Manstein planned to bring over the XLVIII Panzer Corps from the north to the south bank of the Don, which would allow him to take up again the

▽ *A spotter plane circles over a park of abandoned Marder III* Panzerjägers.

advance towards Stalingrad, from which Paulus now said he could not break out through lack of fuel. But things turned out very differently.

Operation "Saturn"

On December 16, the Soviet High Command set in motion Operation "Saturn", intended as a pincer movement by the South-West and Voronezh Front (Lieutenant-General F. I. Golikov) which was intended to destroy the Italian 8th Army and the Rumanian 3rd Army and open the way to Rostov. Co-ordination of the attack was entrusted to General Zhukov. The artillery preparation at dawn on D-day required the concentration of 5,000 guns and mortars. On the South-West Front the Russian 3rd Guards Army (Lieutenant-General D. D. Lelyushenko) soon overcame the resistance of the Rumanian 7th and 11th Divisions and forced the XVII Corps to abandon its positions. This done, it exploited its success in the rear areas of the Italian 8th Army (General Gariboldi), whose 230,000 men in nine divisions were deployed on a front of 170 miles. And the Don was now frozen hard enough for tanks to cross. Not only that, but the catastrophe of November 19 had forced Hitler to withdraw its "stays" (the 62nd and 294th Divisions). It had only 380 47-mm guns to defend itself against the enemy tanks, but even twice this number would still have been unable to pierce the Russian armour. Finally, the Italians had only 55 tanks, and these were obsolete. So the army which the boastful Mussolini had flung defiantly at the Russians was now the mere shadow of a real force.

General Golikov had massed in the Verkhne Mamon bridgehead the 1st Guards Army (Lieutenant-General V. I. Kuznetsov) and the 6th Army (Lieutenant-General F. M. Kharitonov). Between them they had 15 infantry divisions supported by many tanks, which operated at battalion strength. Opposite them was the Italian II Corps, with the "Cossiera" and the "Ravenna" Divisions. In such conditions of inequality, the breakthrough took only 48 hours and on December 18 no fewer than five armoured corps poured through the breach which Colonel-General von Weichs was striving in vain to close. How could he have done this when his 27th Panzer Division had only 50 tanks?

△ The civilians, the real victims of the war. After the fall of Stalingrad, the columns of German prisoners were marched off under only light guard. Frequently bands of armed civilians raided the columns, and exhausted Germans who dropped out were never seen again.

◁ △ A Heinkel He 111 is readied for a supply trip to Stalingrad. The Luftwaffe normally managed to get winter uniforms, but these men are as inadequately dressed as their comrades below.

◁ ▽ A party of soldiers surrenders in a shell-blasted wood. Their captors are well armed and well dressed.

At Novocherkassk the defeat of Army Group "B" forced Manstein not only to countermand the order to XLVIII Panzer Corps to go to the rescue of the LVII, but on December 23 to order Kirchner to pull the valiant 6th Panzer Division back across the Don. This latter was the only complete formation in the forces designated to free Paulus. It therefore meant that the whole enterprise had been abandoned; This was on a day when the temperature was 30 degrees centigrade below zero and the men's menu was:

Midday: rice and horsemeat.

Evening: 7 ounces of bread, two meatballs (horse) à la Stalingrad, $\frac{3}{4}$ ounce of butter and real coffee.

Extras: 4 ounces of bread, an ounce of boiled sweets, and 4 ounces of chocolate.

Tobacco: one cigar and two cigarettes.

The significance of this was conveyed by Paulus to a young major from *Luftflotte* IV attached to his staff. His words betray his emotion and despair: "We couldn't even pull in our outposts, as the men were falling down from exhaustion. They have had nothing to eat for four days. What can I reply, I an Army Commander, if a soldier comes up to me and says, 'Please, Colonel-General sir, a little bit of bread'? We have eaten the last horses. Could you ever imagine soldiers falling on a dead horse, cutting off its head, and devouring its brains raw? How can we go on fighting when the men haven't even got winter clothing? Who is

the man who said we would be supplied by air?"

Kirchner was now down to his 17th and 23rd Panzer Divisions with less than 60 tanks between them. Could he hold the Myshkova line? It was unlikely now that the enemy had thrown in the 2nd Guards Army with its numerous powerful armoured formations. The order of December 23 was therefore a sentence of death on the German 6th Army. Also the loss of the aerodromes at Tatsinskaya and Morozovsk meant that their supplies had to travel an extra 125 miles.

Manstein could not avoid involvement in this disastrous state of affairs. If Vatutin and Golikov got to Rostov, it would not be only the 6th Army which would be wiped out, but the catastrophe would spread to what was left of Army Groups "Don" and "A". We can only conclude that a system of operations is doomed to destruction when it subjects the commanders to such a dilemma.

"In war, a great disaster always pins great guilt on one man" said Napoleon. In obedience to this dictum Hitler had the commander of the XLVIII Panzer Corps, Lieutenant-General Heim, dragged before a court-martial presided over by Göring. He was condemned to death. Secretly imprisoned in the Moabit Gaol in Berlin, he was released without a word of explanation in May 1943 then, the next year, although banished from the army, nominated commander of the fortress at Boulogne.

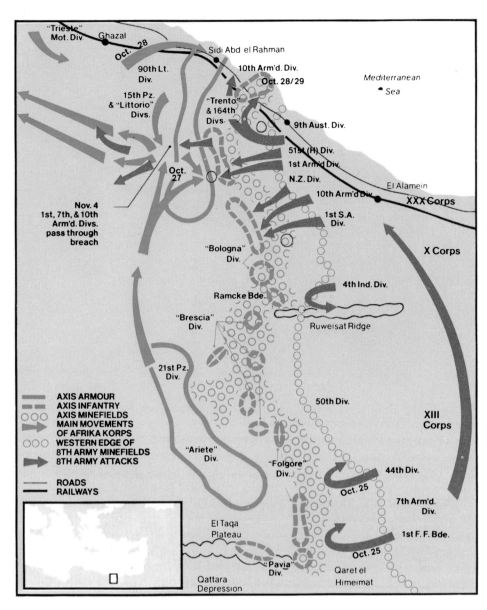

The Battle of El Alamein. The following labels appear on the map:

"Trieste" Mot. Div. — Ghazal — Oct. 28 — Sidi Abd el Rahman — 90th Lt. Div. — 10th Arm'd. Div. — Oct. 28/29 — Mediterranean Sea — 15th Pz. & "Littorio" Divs. — "Trento" & 164th Divs. — 9th Aust. Div. — Oct. 27 — 51st (H) Div. — 1st Arm'd Div. — N.Z. Div. — El Alamein — 10th Arm'd Div. — XXX Corps — Nov. 4 1st, 7th, & 10th Arm'd. Divs. pass through breach — 1st S.A. Div. — "Bologna" Div. — X Corps — Ramcke Bde. — 4th Ind. Div. — "Brescia" Div. — Ruweisat Ridge — 21st Pz. Div. — 50th Div. — XIII Corps — "Ariete" Div. — "Folgore" Div. — Oct. 25 — 44th Div. — 7th Arm'd. Div. — El Taqa Plateau — 1st F. F. Bde. — Oct. 25 — "Pavia" Div. — Qaret el Himeimat — Qattara Depression

AXIS ARMOUR
AXIS INFANTRY
AXIS MINEFIELDS
MAIN MOVEMENTS OF AFRIKA KORPS
WESTERN EDGE OF 8TH ARMY MINEFIELDS
8TH ARMY ATTACKS
ROADS
RAILWAYS

△ *The Battle of El Alamein. By careful planning and training, Montgomery was able to outwit Rommel and then crush him with forces superior in numbers, equipment, and preparation.*
△▷ *A moral whose dividends paid off handsomely at Alamein, where Montgomery was able to switch the main weight of his forces from the desert left flank to the coastal right flank unbeknown to Rommel, thanks to meticulous camouflage precautions.*

CAMOUFLAGE NETS
Baffle the Hun

CHAPTER 39
ALAMEIN

In his headquarters at Burg el Arab, Lieutenant-General Montgomery was carrying on with his preparations for Operation "Lightfoot", as G.H.Q. Cairo called the third British offensive in North Africa. First of all, in the light of experience gained at Alam el Halfa, Montgomery demanded new leaders for XXX Corps and the 7th Armoured Division. For the former he got Lieutenant-General Sir Oliver Leese, formerly commander of the Guards Armoured Division in Britain, and for the latter Major-General A. F. Harding. These were excellent choices, as can be seen from the later careers of these officers: Leese went on to command an

army group in Burma and Harding became a Field-Marshal after the war.

One of Montgomery's early decisions was where to make his first attack. So far, Wavell, Rommel, and Auchinleck had all manoeuvred over the desert in order to drive the enemy into the Mediterranean. But by launching his attack in the northern sector, that is between Ruweisat Ridge and the sea, Montgomery thought that there was a good chance that Rommel would be surprised – provided, of course, that he still believed that Montgomery himself would stick to the tried and tested tactics used by his predecessors and the Germans. Also, if he moved in from the north, the desert in the south would play the same part as the sea in offering a complete obstacle in the event of a breakthrough. Originally Montgomery had stuck to the tactics laid down by the British and German military doctrine of the period: if the enemy's tanks could be knocked out at the beginning, his infantry was at your mercy. He was courageous enough to state that in open ground, given the training of their crews, the Panzers were more manoeuvrable than the British tanks and had a good chance of tearing them to pieces. Montgomery was also determined, if at all possible, to adhere to one of the most basic rules of desert warfare. He had no intention of allowing his own tanks to attack Rommel's anti-tank guns, unless they were supported by Allied infantry.

So a change of method was needed and Montgomery has explained this perfectly clearly in his memoirs: "My modified plan now was to hold off, or contain, the enemy armour while we carried out a methodical destruction of the infantry divisions holding the defensive system. These un-armoured divisions would be destroyed by means of a 'crumbling' process, the enemy being attacked from the flank and the rear and cut off from their supplies. These operations would be carefully organised from a series of firm bases and would be within the capabilities of my troops."

Thus Rommel was due for a second surprise. Already deceived about the sector where the 8th Army would make its main thrust, he would also be caught out by his enemy's sudden change of tactics. It could be assumed that he would not remain inactive in face of the danger of seeing his divisions fall apart and then disintegrate. He could be expected to launch counter-attack after counter-attack, but it would only be to find his Panzers deprived of all freedom of movement in the middle of the innumerable minefields protecting the British infantry positions and being fired on by the British armour, waiting steadfastly for them as they had done at Alam el Halfa.

The successful execution of this plan in which nothing was left to chance, required the organisation of a third corps, in addition to XIII and XXX Corps. This was to be X Corps, under the command of Lieutenant-General Herbert Lumsden. It consisted of armoured divisions and its job was to be the immediate exploitation of the infantry's advance along the line of the main thrust, then, once a breach was made, to pursue and destroy the enemy. Originally it was to have had the 1st, 8th, and 10th Armoured Divisions, but, to the great chagrin of its commander, Major-General C. H. Gairdner, the 8th had to be disbanded to make up the tank strength of the other two.

The headquarters and communications units played an equally important part in the execution and success of Operation "Bertram". This was the name given by the 8th Army to the deceptions carried out under Major Charles Richardson to convince the enemy that the threat of attack was increasing in the south. To this end

the 8th Army used a large number of dummy vehicles, made of rubber and inflated by compressed air. No vehicle left the south for the northern sector without being replaced by a dummy. In the same sector Axis reconnaissance aircraft could watch the laying of a pipe-line, also a dummy, and calculate from the progress of the work that the expected attack would not start before November 1. Finally radio messages from the pseudo-8th Armoured Division made *Panzer-armee* H.Q. think that there was another armoured division between the Qattara Depression and the Ruweisat Ridge.

All this ingenuity would have been of little avail, however, if in the northern sector, where Montgomery was preparing to attack with seven divisions, the 8th Army's camouflage units had not successfully hidden from prying enemy aircraft the thousands of vehicles and enormous storage depôts, and if the secret of Oper-

△ *A Marmon-Herrington armoured car probes into the Axis rear areas at El Alamein as Rommel's forces begin to crumble.*

ation "Lightfoot" had not been jealously guarded. In fact, lower-ranking officers, N.C.O.s, and men were not informed of the date of the offensive until two days before the attack.

Parallel with this enormous effort of organisation, there was an intensive training programme for the troops by Montgomery, a first-class instructor. All this activity explains why, in spite of the Prime Minister's impatience, it was out of the question for the 8th Army to attack before the October full moon which was on the 23rd. We may therefore conclude that in once more tempering the ardour of Winston Churchill, General Sir Alan Brooke showed himself to be a truly great servant of his country and a major architect of her final victory.

German and Italian deployment

On the other side, Rommel had left Africa and handed over command of the *Panzerarmee* to General Georg Stumme, who had played an important part at the head of the XL Motorised Corps in Greece and then maintained his high reputation in Russia. This new posting relieved him of the disgrace into which he had fallen with the Führer as a consequence of his corps' operations orders falling into the hands of the Russians on the eve of Operation *"Blau"*, Germany's 1942 Russian offensive. He had merely a holding role, however, and was not allowed to take much initiative, having to content himself with the programme left him by Rommel.

The armoured elements of the *Panzerarmee* had been withdrawn from the front as the force went over to the defensive. This left the Ramcke Brigade and five infantry divisions, including the German 164th Division and the Italian "Folgore" Airborne Division, in fixed defences. To the rear, in the northern sector, were the tough and mobile "Ariete" Armoured Division and 21st Panzer while in the southern sector were the 15th Panzer Division and the "Littorio" tank Division. In army reserve, the 90th Light Division and the "Trieste" Motorised Division were deployed in depth along the coastal road. Thus the 164th Division and two battalions of the Ramcke Brigade together with the Italian XXI Corps held the position

◁ *Classic infantry scene – an Australian officer, armed with a revolver, leads his men forward to the attack, covered by a smoke screen.*
◁▽ *British infantrymen, bayonets fixed, move forward to the attack. Montgomery intended to give his infantry a more prominent rôle in the battle than had been usual in the desert. In counter-attacks to try to relieve the Axis infantry, Rommel's tanks were destroyed piecemeal by British anti-tank guns, tanks and aircraft.*

September 40,465 tons of war *matériel* and 31,061 tons of petrol reached North Africa, 80 per cent of the supplies loaded in Italy. But in October losses rose to 44 per cent and the Axis forces opposing Montgomery got only 12,308 tons of liquid fuel. Cavallero asked Kesselring to put pressure on Malta; he replied by recalling some bomber squadrons from Libya. Although 300 twin-engined German bombers took part in this renewed offensive, it was a total failure and the losses were so heavy that Göring, going over the head of *Comando Supremo* on October 20, ordered it to stop.

"Lightfoot" is launched

At 2140 hours on October 23, 1942, the El Alamein front lit up with a blaze of gunfire over its whole length. Between the sea and Ruweisat Ridge 456 guns opened fire to blast the way open for XXX Corps. In the south XIII Corps had 136 guns.

The attack was a complete surprise: at the time the battle started the commanders of the Italian XXI and X Corps (Generals Navarrini and Nebbia respectively) were on leave in Italy and only got back to their H.Q.s at the same time as Rommel. This was the curtain-raiser for 12 days of battle fought out between 12 Axis and 10 Allied divisions, though these numbers are misleading: Montgomery had the advantage in both men and *matériel*. In round numbers Montgomery deployed 195,000 men against some 50,000 Germans and 54,000 Italians. The following table, taken from the British Official History, gives the comparative figures for the two sides:

Strengths of the forces engaged on the El Alamein front on October 23, 1942
(Italian figures in brackets)

	Panzer-armee	8th Army
Infantry battalions	71 (40)	85
Field and medium guns	460 (260)	908
Anti-tank guns	850 (300)	1,451
Tanks	496	1,029
Armoured cars	192	435

This table does not show that the defenders were short of ammunition and fuel, whereas Montgomery was more than abundantly supplied. Also, the Axis had nothing to compare with Sir Arthur Tedder's 1,200 planes, in particular Air

△ Ready to go. The commander of a British Crusader tank, perched on the turret roof of his vehicle, waits for the command to move off at dawn on October 26. Note the identification marks deleted from the print by the wartime censor. Though the tank was in this, like most North African battles, the final arbiter, it was the infantry and artillery that had paved the way for it.

where the enemy attack was expected, while two battalions of paratroopers were stationed with X Corps south of the Ruweisat Ridge.

The time taken to mount Operation "Lightfoot" was naturally not wasted by the Axis forces, which were deployed in depth and considerably strengthened. The units were contained within closed strongpoints protected by more than 445,000 mines, of which 14,000 were anti-personnel ones intended to discourage the enemy's engineers. Under the direction of Colonel Hecker, Rommel's chief of engineering, Italian and German engineers had also contrived booby traps of truly diabolical imagination, using even aeroplane bombs. These defences were naturally covered by machine guns and anti-tank guns. As regards the latter, on October 23, 1942 the D.A.K. had 86 8.8-cm weapons and 95 Russian 7.62-cm guns, of which 30 had been mounted on Czech tank chassis. The British considered these almost as deadly as the famous "88".

It was a hard nut to crack. But between the opposing shores of the Mediterranean, traffic conditions had not improved. Far from it, though Cavallero had thrown in everything he could get hold of. In

Vice-Marshal Coningham's 550 light bombers and fighter-bombers.

The 8th Army's artillery barrage lasted 15 minutes. It effectively silenced the enemy's batteries and damaged his telephone communications and minefields, where many of the aircraft bombs were blown up. At 2200 hours the sappers advanced into no-man's-land, using the first mine-detectors to reach North Africa. Behind the sappers there were a small number of "Scorpion" tanks, special adaptations of ordinary tanks, designed to set off mines with whirling flails attached to a drum in front of the tank.

Behind these followed the infantry, with fixed bayonets.

In the southern sector, XIII Corps (Sir Brian Horrocks), whose rôle was to put on a diversionary attack, had been ordered to hold back its 7th Armoured Division. The advance of its major infantry formations, 44th Division (Major-General I. T. P. Hughes) and 50th Division (Major-General J. S. Nichols) was consequently limited and secured at heavy cost against the determined resistance of the "Pavia" and "Brescia" Divisions and the paratroops of the "Folgore", commanded respectively by Generals Scattaglia, Brunetti, and Frattini. On the left flank, the 1st Fighting French Brigade confirmed its fighting spirit on the Qaret el Himeimat, but had to yield some of the ground it had won. Horrocks' objective had been achieved: to prevent the enemy from deploying the "Ariete" Armoured Division (General F. Arena) and the 21st Panzer Division (Major-General von Randow) in support of the rest of the Axis forces in the northern sector.

The Axis infantry crumbles away

In the northern sector, XXX Corps' job was to make an inroad along two "corridors" in the minefields. The right-hand corridor was given to the 9th Australian

△ *A shell detonates beside a truck carrying motorised infantry up towards the British front. It was essential that such infantry assault as soon as the sappers had cleared a corridor through the minefields and so Montgomery's foresight in concentrating most of his transport in the crucial sectors was of prime importance in the successful outcome of the battle.*

△ *Not even the mighty "88"
could halt the remorseless
advance of Montgomery's troops.
The doubts of the above gun's
crew as to the successful outcome
of the action in which they are
engaged seems to be indicated by
the fact that they have brought
their gun into action on its
carriage rather than on its fixed
mounting.*

Division and the 51st (Highland) Division, newly arrived in North Africa and commanded by Major-General D. N. Wimberley; the left-hand corridor went to the New Zealand Division. None of these divisions reached the objectives marked for them on the map, but their action began the destruction of the enemy infantry, as foreseen by Montgomery. The "Trento" Division (General Masina) was very badly mauled and the 164th Division (Major-General Lungershausen) had two of its battalions virtually wiped out. But since the British infantry had failed to clear corridors right through the enemy minefields, the tanks of X Corps were jammed up in the enemy's defences. Montgomery ordered Lumsden to punch a way through but the attempt failed with considerable losses in men and machines. On the other side, General Stumme, who was roaming the battlefield alone, had a heart attack and fell from his vehicle without his driver noticing it. His death was a considerable blow to the Axis forces and his command was taken over in the evening of the 24th by the commander of the D.A.K., Lieutenant-General Ritter von Thoma.

On October 25 Montgomery ordered XIII and XXX Corps to press home their attacks. But they both failed to reach their objectives and so, with great coolness and resolution, Montgomery began to organise a fresh onslaught.

Rommel sees his danger

When he got back to his H.Q. in the evening of October 26, Rommel realised exactly how serious the situation was. It had been saved only by the engagement of the 90th Light Division and the armoured group in the northern sector. Major-General von Vaerst's 15th Panzer Division had only 39 tanks left and General Bitossi's "Littorio" Armoured Division only 69. He therefore ordered the 21st Panzer Division with its 106 tanks to move north of Ruweisat Ridge. Once he had concentrated his remaining armour Rommel tried to regain the initiative. He led the Axis tanks in a counter-stroke against the British penetrations. However, Montgomery's forces were ready to meet him. A heavy toll was taken of the Axis troops by bombers of the Desert Air Force and an anti-tank screen which contained many of the new 6-pounder anti-tank guns. Rommel was repulsed and this was a major success for Montgomery and the 8th Army. In XXX Corps, the 9th Australian

Division struck north-west and trapped the 164th Division against the sea. The 1st South African Division (Major-General D. H. Pienaar) and the 4th Indian Division (Major-General F. I. S. Tuker), which formed Sir Oliver Leese's left flank, made a deep penetration into the positions of the "Bologna" Division (General Gloria). The struggle had now become a battle of attrition. And since the 8th Army had a massive numerical superiority, it had all the advantages in this type of struggle. On October 29 Rommel wrote to his wife: "The situation continues very grave. By the time this letter arrives, it will no doubt have been decided whether we can hold on or not. I haven't much hope. At night I lie with my eyes wide open, unable to sleep for the load that is on my shoulders. In the day I am dead tired. What will happen if things go wrong here? That is the thought that torments me day and night. I can see no way out if that happens."

However, Churchill could not contain his impatience at Montgomery's failure to break-through to win a swift success and summoned General Brooke to his office the same day. "What," he asked, "was *my*

Monty doing now, allowing the battle to peter out? (Monty was always *my* Monty when he was out of favour.) He had done nothing now for the last three days and now he was withdrawing troops from the front. Why had he told us that he would be through in seven days if all he intended to do was to fight a half-hearted battle?"

Montgomery redoubles his efforts

As usual the Chief of the Imperial General Staff was able to placate Churchill and was well seconded in this by Field Marshal Smuts, who enjoyed the Prime Minister's special confidence. Montgomery had, in fact, withdrawn one brigade each from the 44th, 50th (XIII Corps), and 51st (XXX Corps) Divisions and given them to the New Zealand Division which, under Major-General Freyberg, was to be the spearhead of Operation "Supercharge" for the decisive breakthrough. Meanwhile XXX Corps had continued to hammer the enemy and forced Rommel to engage the "Ariete" Armoured Division and the "Trieste" Motorised Division, his last reserves.

"Supercharge" was being followed in London with some anxiety: "During the morning," Montgomery records, "I was visited at my Tactical H.Q. by Alexander and by Casey who was Minister of State in the Middle East. It was fairly clear to me that there had been consternation in Whitehall when I began to draw divisions into reserve on the 27th and 28th October, when I was getting ready for the final blow. Casey had been sent up to find out what was going on; Whitehall thought I was giving up, when in point of fact I was just about to win. I told him all about my plans and that I was certain of success; and de Guingand spoke to him very bluntly and told him to tell Whitehall not to bellyache."

"Supercharge", unleashed on November 2, gave rise to battles of a ferocity unheard of in this theatre. Italian anti-tank guns fired on British tanks at a range of 20 yards and General Freyberg's 9th Armoured Brigade was reported to have lost 70 out of the 94 tanks it had started with. At the end of the day, and in spite of repeated attacks by the Desert Air Force, what remained of the Axis army had managed to form the semblance of a front,

▽ *British soldiers examine part of the spoils of their victory.*
▷ *A German corpse, covered with flies, lies slumped over the edge of the trench where it fell.*
▷ ▷ *British troops experiment with clothing abandoned by a makeshift Italian front line quartermaster's stores.*
▷ ▽ *Prisoners from Rommel's* Panzerarmee Afrika, *some of the 30,000 prisoners taken by the British. The total bag included nine generals and 7,802 Germans.*

but this was the end. Rommel was now aware that his forces had reached the limits of effective resistance. The *Afrika Korps* had only 35 tanks left. These were far too few to stop the 8th Army's advance.

Hitler orders the *Afrika Korps* to its destruction . . .

Rommel drew his conclusions from the situation and ordered his troops to withdraw. The movement had just begun when, on November 3 at 1330 hours a message from Hitler, a *Führerbefehl*, reached him. It was drawn up in the following terms:

"To Field-Marshal Rommel,

"In the situation in which you find yourself there can be no other thought but to stand fast and throw every gun and every man into the battle. The utmost efforts are being made to help you. Your enemy, despite his superiority, must also be at the end of his strength. It would not be the first time in history that a strong will has triumphed over the bigger battalions. As to your troops, you can show them no other road than that to victory or death."

△ *A Hawker Hurricane IID tankbuster swoops over the desert in pursuit of its prey. The 40-mm cannon of such Hurricanes could rip open German tanks as though with a tin opener.*

. . . and precipitates the British victory at Alamein

As the disciplined soldier that he was Rommel cancelled his order and instructed his troops to hold their positions. Fortunately for Rommel, Montgomery failed to exploit the opportunity given to him by the *Führerbefehl* by driving swiftly on and surrounding the Axis troops. In the afternoon of November 4 the 8th Army made a breach 15 miles wide in the thread-like front of the enemy in the area of Tell el Aqqaqir. The tanks of X Corps broke through, demolished the "Ariete" Armoured Division in spite of heroic resistance and captured the commander of the D.A.K., General von Thoma, as he leapt out of his blazing vehicle. The mechanised units of Rommel's *Panzerarmee* managed to escape to the west, just as a fresh order arrived from Berlin sanctioning a withdrawal westwards after all. The whole of the Italian infantry, however, (the "Trento", "Bologna", "Brescia", and "Pavia" Divisions) were left stranded, as

were the "Folgore" Airborne Division and the headquarters of X Corps. 104,000 troops took part in this battle: the Axis powers lost 25,000 killed and wounded and 30,000 prisoners, including nine generals and 7,802 Germans. A thousand guns and 320 tanks were destroyed or captured by the victors. The Allies lost 13,560 men, of whom 4,610 were killed or missing; most of the missing turned out to be dead. 500 Axis tanks were put out of action and many of them were irreparable. At Alamein not only had Axis strength in North Africa been broken for ever but so was Rommel's morale, so that not for a moment did he consider making another stand at Halfaya and El Agheila, as *Comando Supremo* ordered. This gave rise to new friction between the Axis partners which was to bear fruit in 1943.

The long retreat starts

El Alamein was over. Rommel now started on his long retreat to Tunis, followed steadily by Montgomery's 8th Army, that was to see the end of Axis power in Africa.

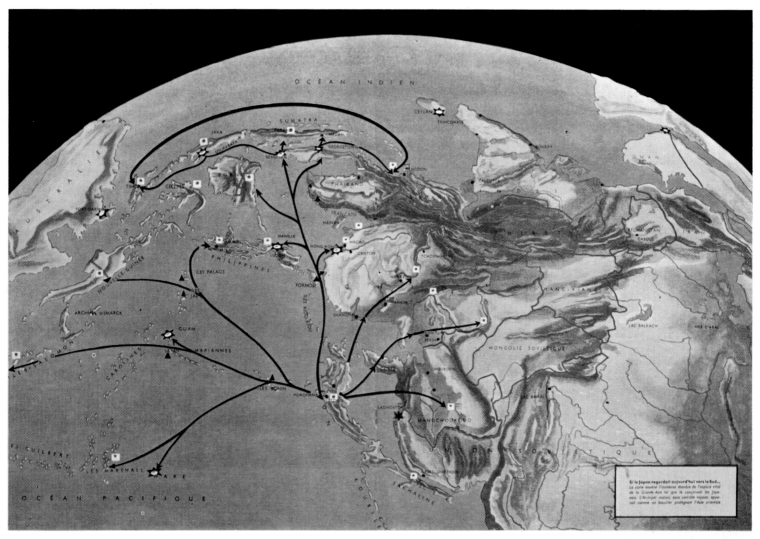

CHAPTER 40
CORAL SEA: THE CURTAIN RAISER

The question of whether the neutralisation of the American aero-naval forces based on Pearl Harbor should be exploited by a landing on the island of Oahu was discussed in Tokyo during the detailed planning for the December 7 attack. The answer had been "no". Those responsible for Japanese strategy were content with knocking out the main U.S. fleet, thus gaining the time necessary for their forces to overrun South-East Asia. After that they would consider the matter again.

And so, after the capture of Guam and Wake, in the south-eastern Pacific theatre, the Japanese contented themselves with the occupation of the Gilbert Islands, on which they based their major defensive hopes.

Pearl Harbor was a fatal blow to Operation "Rainbow", the American conquest of the Marshall and the Caroline Islands and

the organisation of an American base at Truk. The Pacific Fleet had had an offensive mission; now it was on the defensive, but this was only for the time being and there was no danger that it would become a passive force. This was the idea which Rear-Admiral Husband E. Kimmel expressed in a note to Navy Secretary Knox on December 11, 1941 when the latter arrived in Pearl Harbor:

"With the losses we have sustained, it is necessary to revise completely our strategy of a Pacific war. The loss of battleships commits us to the strategic defensive until our forces can again be built up. However, a very powerful striking force of carriers, cruisers and destroyers survives. These forces must be operated boldly and vigorously on the tactical offensive in order to retrieve our initial disaster."

In support of this opinion it should be

Admiral Chester Nimitz was born in Texas in 1885. He served in World War I as Chief-of-Staff to the Commander of the U.S. Atlantic Submarine Force, and after Pearl Harbor he was made Commander-in-Chief of the Pacific Fleet. His victories at the battles of Coral Sea and Midway crippled the Japanese fleet and assured the safety of the United States from direct naval attack.

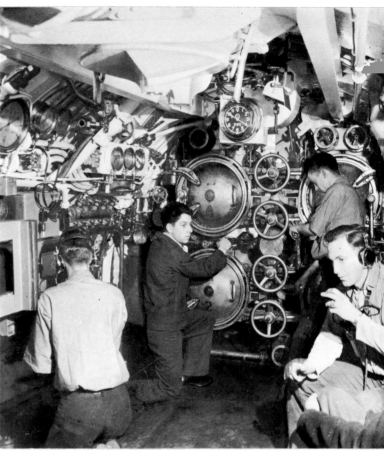

Previous page: *"When Japan looks south today" – a drum-beating piece of propaganda from Germany's* Signal *magazine, boasting of the impregnability of Japan's newly-won "southern barrier". But the main weight of the Allied counter-offensive would come not from the south but from the east . . .*

said that on that same day the Pacific Fleet still had in fighting trim the aircraft-carriers *Lexington*, *Saratoga*, and *Enterprise*, 16 cruisers, 44 destroyers, and 16 submarines, some at sea, others in bases at Pearl Harbor and Bremerton (Washington State). Also, when he heard of the Japanese attack, Vice-Admiral Stark, Chief of Naval Operations, ordered the Atlantic Fleet to send *Yorktown*, a carrier of the same class as *Enterprise*, through the Panama Canal to the Pacific – a vital reinforcement.

Nimitz takes over the Pacific Fleet

Scarcely had Kimmel formulated his rather optimistic plan than he was relieved of his command and replaced, on Roosevelt's personal choice, by Rear-Admiral Chester W. Nimitz: "a tow-haired, blue-eyed Texan, of the Naval Academy class of 1905. Tactful and modest, sound in his judgement of men and events, he was to prove a thoroughly fortunate choice." Such is the opinion of E. B.

Potter, a professor at the Annapolis Naval Academy, with whom Nimitz later wrote books on naval warfare in World War II.

On December 27 Nimitz took over as Commander-in-Chief Pacific Fleet, or Cincpac, with promotion to Admiral, whilst in Washington Admiral Ernest J. King was appointed head of the U.S. Navy, replacing Vice-Admiral Stark. King thus became Cincus, Commander-in-Chief United States Fleet, and addressed his first order to Cincpac, defining his mission in these terms:

"1) Covering and holding the Hawaii–Midway line and maintaining communications with the west coast.

2) Maintaining communications between the west coast and Australia, chiefly by covering, securing, and holding the Hawaii–Samoa line which should be extended to include Fiji at the earliest practical date."

The execution of this order postulated the setting up of an air-sea front running from Dutch Harbor (Alaska) to Midway, including New Caledonia and hinging on Port Moresby in New Guinea. Nimitz could, of course, call upon all possible facilities in the British and Australian possessions in the Pacific. The French

Memories of the U-boat war and the battle of the Atlantic have always eclipsed the equally vital submarine war fought out in the Pacific. There the outermost parts of Japan's over-extended empire depended solely upon supply by sea – and the American submarine force took the offensive right from the start. From a slow beginning during the dramatic events of 1941-42, American submarines wreaked havoc on Japan's Pacific sealanes, sinking well over half of her mercantile tonnage. Tactics varied from the "up the kilt shot" (surfacing astern of the victim and torpedoing from there) to the "down the throat shot" (surfacing directly ahead of the victim and torpedoing him head-on).
◁ ◁ In the control room, scanning the surface through the periscope.
◁ The torpedo-room, showing the crew in position for a shoot. The man on the right with the head-set is taking the orders from the control-room.
▷ △ and ▷ Two "kills" – Japanese merchantmen, sunk by prowling American submarines.

territories had gone over to de Gaulle in the summer of 1940 and in the following year an agreement reached between the Free French leader and the American Government gave the same facilities to the Americans in the case of aggression by the Japanese. The Pacific Fleet's task, therefore, was to engage and repel all enemy forces which attempted to force the front described above. But it was not to be restricted within this perimeter. On the contrary it was, as Admiral King is said to have put it, "to hold what you've got and hit them when you can".

American skirmishes

Admiral Nimitz set about his task as best he could, in spite of the temporary loss of *Saratoga*, damaged by a torpedo on January 11, 1942 and out of service for five months thereafter. On February 1, groups commanded by Rear-Admiral F. J. Fletcher and Vice-Admiral W. F. Halsey, each built round one carrier, "struck", the one in the Gilbert archipelago and the other in the Marshall Islands, to such effect that the Japanese High Command thought it necessary to withdraw the aircraft-carriers *Zuikaku* and *Shokaku* from the fleet then preparing to operate in the Indian Ocean. During another undertaking by Halsey, planes from *Enterprise* bombed Wake Island on February 24, then Marcus Island. The latter was only about 1,100 miles from the Japanese capital.

Cryptographers triumph

Annoying though they were, these were only pinpricks, and during this phase of the campaign they were less important than another victory which the Americans won over their enemy. This came about in the shade of an office in Pearl Harbor and was never the subject of any special communiqué. By dint of much patience and perspicacity, the code-breaking unit attached to the Pacific Fleet succeeded in deciphering the Japanese naval code. From then onwards, now that it was known what the enemy was going to do, the enemy was going to be undone, to paraphrase an old proverb. This proved to be a most tremendous advantage to the Americans in the future.

Japanese plans

Aboard the battleship *Nagato*, flying the flag of Admiral Yamamoto in Hiroshima Bay, the Combined Fleet's Chief-of-Staff, Rear-Admiral Ugaki, had been concerned since late January about what the next Japanese naval operations should be. In his opinion, it was important to take advantage immediately of the superiority of the naval and naval air forces enjoyed by Japan to crush the American fleet and seize Hawaii. Among the arguments which seemed to him to point to this conclusion we mention one:

"Time would work against Japan because of the vastly superior natural resources of the United States. Consequently, unless Japan quickly resumed the offensive–the sooner the better–she eventually would become incapable of doing anything more than sitting down and waiting for the American forces to counter-attack. Furthermore, although Japan had steeled herself to endure a prolonged struggle, it would be obviously to her advantage to shorten it if at all possible, and the only hope of so doing lay in offensive action."

But Rear-Admiral Ugaki was unable to convince his Chief of Operations, Captain Kuroshima, who considered that a new attack on Hawaii would no longer have the benefit of surprise. Quite to the contrary, and a Japanese fleet operating in these waters would now have to deal not only with the enemy's naval forces but also with his air force and coastal batteries. In the face of these difficulties Kuroshima opted for an offensive westwards: the destruction of the British fleet in the Indian Ocean, the conquest of Ceylon, and the establishment of contact with the Axis powers. These were the objectives he recommended to the Japanese High Command.

Ceylon is reprieved

Direct co-operation between Japan, Germany, and Italy soon had to be abandoned as the links between the three totalitarian allies were very tenuous. Kuroshima's proposal was nevertheless examined very carefully both by Admiral Yamamoto and at the highest level of the Naval General Staff by Admiral Nagano. This was the state of things in late February when the Army, under the pretext of the Soviet pressure on Manchukuo, refused their co-operation in any attack on Ceylon.

Meanwhile the headquarters of the Combined Fleet had been set up on board the giant battleship *Yamato*. Here Ugaki's arguments against any expectations of assistance seemed still to prevail. So, turned away from Ceylon by the Army's unwillingness, no time was lost in turning the offensive eastwards. Account was taken of the objections against a direct attack on Hawaii and it was therefore

△ ◁*The Battleship* Haruna, *which formed part of Yamamoto's "Sunday Punch" in the Midway plan: the concentrated fire-power of the most powerful battleships in the Combined Fleet.*
△ △ *Bomb damage in Tokyo. The picture shows Ginza, the city's main thoroughfare.*
△ *Four of the 62 crewmen who reached China. Their planes were the spearhead of raids that would devastate the Japanese cities.*

Section, where Admiral Fukudome was insisting on an attack against Australia. According to Commander Fuchida, whose account of the matter we have drawn on, the "Australian School", as the supporters of an offensive in this area were called, put forward the following arguments:

"Australia, because of its size and strategic location on the Japanese defensive perimeter, would almost certainly become the springboard for an eventual Allied counter-offensive. This counter-offensive, they reasoned, would be spearheaded by air power in order to take full advantage of American industrial capacity to produce planes by mass-production methods, and the effective utilisation of this massive air strength would require the use of land bases in Australia. Consequently, there would be a weak spot in Japan's defensive armour unless Australia were either placed under Japanese control or effectively cut off from the United States."

It is true that the Army had refused the Navy the one division thought necessary to overrun Ceylon, and it had all the more reason to refuse to put ten into an operation such as this. They would content themselves, therefore, with isolating Australia and this would be done by the progressive occupation of New Guinea, the Solomon Islands, New Caledonia, New Hebrides, Fiji, and Samoa.

The "Doolittle Raid"

Admiral Yamamoto did not agree with this line of reasoning. In his opinion the G.H.Q. plan would not give him the great naval battle which he thought so necessary for swift victory. Admiral Nagano supported him, though very much against his better judgement. These differences of opinion continued up to the day of the operation, but on April 18 an event occurred which cut short all discussion: the bombing of Tokyo by a handful of North American B-25 Mitchell twin-engined bombers under the command of Lieutenant-Colonel James H. Doolittle.

These planes weighed 13 tons fully loaded and nothing so heavy had ever taken off from an aircraft-carrier before. Lengthy preparations were therefore necessary. On April 13 the aircraft-carrier *Hornet*, with 16 of these B-25's on board, rendezvoused with Task Force 16, under Halsey, which was to escort her. The plan

△ *Lieutenant-Colonel James H. Doolittle. His 16 B-25 Mitchells were to cause little damage, but served to bring notice that the war could come to the heart of Japan. Besides boosting morale at home, the raid led the Japanese to adopt a strategy of further expansion to provide advanced warning of any further raids on the mainland. Overleaf: A flight of Douglas Dauntless dive-bombers, the best American carrier strike planes at the time of the battles of the Coral Sea and Midway.*

Admiral William F. Halsey, born in 1882, was the most colourful American admiral of World War II. A thrusting, ebullient personality, he was instrumental in restoring the fleet's morale in the months after Pearl Harbor. A gifted carrier commander, he nevertheless took no part in the Coral Sea fight and he went down with a skin disease shortly afterwards, being forced to hand over his Task Force 16 (*Enterprise* and *Hornet*) to Spruance for the Midway battle.

decided to mount an operation for the capture of Midway. This objective was far enough away from Oahu to prevent interference by land-based American aircraft; it was also important enough to compel the enemy fleet to fight, and without land-based support this would allow the Japanese battleships and aircraft-carriers to use their as yet undoubted superiority.

Admiral Yamamoto approved the plan submitted to him for the attack on Midway and sent it forward on April 2 for approval by the Naval High Command. But in Tokyo, among Nagano's colleagues, it ran into opposition from the Operations

was that Doolittle and his companions were to take off some 500 miles from Japan, carry out their mission, and land in Nationalist China, deck landings by B-25's being impossible. Some 200 miles east of the area from which the planes were to take off, Halsey's force fell in with an enemy patrol and the American admiral had to order Doolittle to take off at once as the necessary secrecy could no longer be guaranteed.

A few tons of bombs were shared out between the Japanese capital and the large cities of Nagoya and Kobe from 1300 hours on April 13, and no appreciable damage was done. But nonetheless the psychological impact of Doolittle's raiders on the Japanese people and on the Japanese armed forces was immense. The Emperor's own palace had been exposed to the danger of a direct attack. The Imperial Armed Forces' loss of face had to be made good.

Of the 16 twin-engined B-25s which took part in the raid, one landed on the aerodrome at Vladivostok and was seized by the Soviet authorities. The pilots of the remaining 15, running out of fuel, either crash landed or ordered their crews to bale out. Of the 80 crew, five were interned by the Russians, 62 were picked up by the Chinese, one was killed while descending by parachute, four drowned, and eight were taken prisoner by the Japanese. Three of these last were executed as "war criminals".

In the face of this air-raid, which was the bitterest humiliation for the whole Navy, there was no further disagreement over Yamamoto's plan. He offered his personal excuses to the Emperor. The Admiral was incensed by the American raid and he was bent on destroying the U.S. Pacific fleet by advancing to Hawaii. So on May 5 the Chief of Naval Operations issued "Naval Order No. 18 of the Grand Imperial Headquarters" requiring that before June 20 the Commander of the Combined Fleet should "proceed to the occupation of Midway Island and key positions in the Western Aleutians in collaboration with the army".

Meanwhile the 4th Fleet (Vice-Admiral Inouye), suitably reinforced, was to occupy Port Moresby on the south coast of eastern New Guinea and the little island of Tulagi in the Solomon archipelago opposite Guadalcanal. At the beginning of July they were expected to seize strategic points in New Caledonia and Fiji. As we shall see, the "Australian School"

had not given up its preferences, but Yamamoto took no notice, as meanwhile the conquest of Midway would give him the chance to wipe out the American fleet.

In April, at its base in Truk in the Caroline Islands, the Japanese 4th Fleet had been reinforced by two heavy cruisers and three aircraft-carriers, two fleet ones (*Zuikaku* and *Shokaku*, 25,700 tons each) and one small (*Shoho*, 11,300 tons). Acting on orders received, Vice-Admiral Shigeyoshi Inouye divided his Task Force "MO", based on the 4th Fleet, into a Carrier Striking Force, two Invasion Groups, a Support Group, and a Covering Group. The Tulagi Invasion Group occupied its objective without opposition on May 3. On the following day 14 transports of the Port Moresby Invasion Group set sail.

Moresby reinforced

Under an agreement of March 17 between London and Washington, the United States had agreed to take charge of the defence of the whole of the Pacific, including Australia and New Zealand. Alerted in time by his code-breakers,

Admiral Nimitz sent Task Force 17 (Rear-Admiral Fletcher) towards Port Moresby. The force was centred on two aircraft-carriers, *Yorktown* (Rear-Admiral Fletcher) and *Lexington* (Rear-Admiral A. W. Fitch) and was joined south of the Solomon Islands by an Australian task force of cruisers under Rear-Admiral J. C. Crace. The fact remains, however, that for the accomplishment of his mission Cincpac had no authority over the 300 American planes based in northern Australia and Port Moresby. These were under the Supreme Commander South-West Asia, General MacArthur, and hence there was a certain lack of co-ordination.

The ensuing actions between the opposing forces on May 6–8 came to be called the Battle of the Coral Sea. We have already remarked that the engagement marks a date in naval warfare as it was the first time that two fleets fought from over the horizon without ever being in sight of each other, and attempted to destroy each other by bombs and aerial torpedoes.

The eminent naval historian Professor Morison has called this action the "Battle of Naval Errors". He cannot be gainsaid, in view of the many mistakes committed

◁ *"Dixon to Carrier, Scratch one flattop!" was the exultant message radioed back to Fletcher during the massive American air strikes which overwhelmed the diminutive Japanese carrier* Shoho *during the battle of the Coral Sea.* Shoho *never had a chance, and the American planes swarming round her are clearly shown in the identifying rings.*
△ *Perhaps more important than* Shoho's *destruction was the serious damage done to the big Japanese fleet carrier* Shokaku *in the Coral Sea fight. She would not be ready for the deciding battle at Midway; nor would her sister ship* Zuikaku, *whose air group suffered crippling losses.*

by the airmen on both sides, errors both in navigation and in the identification of the enemy's ships, as well as in the assessment of aerial bombing and torpedoing. In their defence, however, it must be pointed out that rapidly alternating sunshine and heavy squalls over the Coral Sea could not have made their task easy. Tactically, success went to the Japanese, since against the loss of the light carrier *Shoho*, one destroyer, one minelayer, and three minesweepers, they sank the American *Lexington* (36,000 tons), the oiler *Neosho*, which they took for another aircraft-carrier, and the destroyer *Sims*.

"The *Yorktown*, which came first under attack, successfully evaded the torpedoes launched at her and took only a single bomb hit, which did not significantly impair her fighting effectiveness. But the *Lexington*, larger and less manoeuvrable, fell victim to an 'anvil' attack on both bows simultaneously and took two torpedoes on the port side, which flooded three boiler rooms. Two bomb hits, received at almost the same time, inflicted only minor damage. The list caused by the torpedo hits was quickly corrected by shifting oil. Her engines were unharmed, and her speed did not fall below 24 knots.

"But at 1445 there was a severe explosion. Fires passed rapidly out of control and the carrier was forced to call for assistance. The *Yorktown* took aboard the *Lexington*'s planes that were airborne, but there was no opportunity to transfer those already on the *Lexington*. With the ship burning furiously and shaken by frequent explosions there was no choice but to 'get the men off'."

Strategically, however, the advantage was on the Allies' side, as the serious damage done to *Shokaku* and the losses of the aircraft from *Zuikaku* forced Inouye to give up the idea of landing at Port Moresby.

Worse still, the several Task Forces of the Combined Fleet had to set off for Midway and the Aleutians by May 26 and it was not possible, in the short time available, either to repair *Shokaku* or to replace the aircraft lost by *Zuikaku*. On the other hand, the Japanese grossly exaggerated their successes. They claimed that *Yorktown* had met the same fate as *Lexington*, whereas she had been hit by only one 800-lb bomb. Hence the "spirit of imprudence and error" which seized Yamamoto. This is shown by the war game, or map exercise, carried out to check on Operation "Midway". The director of the exercise,

Rear-Admiral Ugaki, did not hesitate to cancel such decisions by the referee as seemed to him unfavourable to the Japanese side.

However, until the ships yet to be built under the American budgets of 1939 to 1941 came into service, the Japanese fleet enjoyed considerable superiority over its enemy. This is shown in the table at right, in which we give only the ships which took part in the actions of June 3–6 between Midway Atoll and Dutch Harbor in the Aleutians.

The Japanese aircraft-carriers had between them 410 planes, those of Admiral Nimitz 233. But Nimitz could also call upon the 115 concentrated on the airstrips at Midway in case of enemy attack. Yet these figures must not make us lose sight of the fact that the American inferiority in ships and planes was not only quantitative but qualitative as well. The Grumann F4F Wildcat fighters were less manoeuvrable and had a slower rate of climb than the Japanese Mitsubishi A6M Zeros. The torpedo bomber then in service with the U.S. Navy, the Douglas TBD-1 Devastator, with a top speed of only 206 mph, was entirely at the mercy of the Zero, Japan's standard carrier-borne fighter, which could reach some 340 mph. Also, the American air-dropped 21-inch torpedo was so slow to reach its target that the victim had a good chance of taking avoiding action. It is nevertheless true that the Japanese Commander-in-Chief threw away recklessly the enormous chances which, for the last time, his numerical and *matériel* superiority gave him.

△ Crewmen from the "Lady Lex" are hauled aboard a rescue ship. Many of Lexington's *crew members were in tears as she went down, being "plank owners"—men who had served with the ship since she had been commissioned.*

▽ The Japanese and American Fleets at the Battle of Midway.

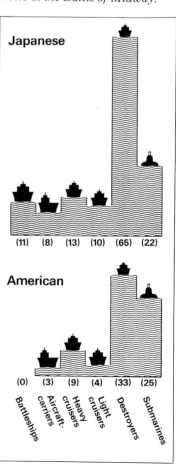

Japanese

(11) (8) (13) (10) (65) (22)

American

(0) (3) (9) (4) (33) (25)

Battleships Aircraft-carriers Heavy cruisers Light cruisers Destroyers Submarines

CHAPTER 41
MIDWAY: THE SHOWDOWN

For the operation designed to seize the islands of Attu and Kiska in the Aleutians, Yamamoto assembled a task force whose lavish size was out of all proportion to the strategic value of the objective: three heavy cruisers, three light cruisers, 13 destroyers, and the aircraft-carriers *Ryujo* and *Junyo* with between them 82 planes on board. In view of the impending threat to this theatre, however, the Americans sent out five cruisers and 13 destroyers (Task Force 8) under Rear-Admiral R. A. Theobald.

But there was a very serious and fundamental defect in the Japanese plan for the Midway operation. The Combined Fleet was split up into a number of separate task forces. They were deployed at considerable distances from each other, but the plan called on them to operate according to a rigid and complex timetable and yet to co-operate with each other in overcoming the Americans. The Japanese failed to concentrate their forces.

Admiral Yamamoto was convinced that his planned bombardment of Midway Island on June 4 and the assault on the atoll next day would provoke Nimitz into bringing out his fleet so that the engagement at sea, all being well, would take place on June 7 or 8. This would give Nagumo time to recover his liberty of action and the Japanese Commander-in-Chief to draw in his scattered forces. To leave nothing to chance, on June 2 two squadrons of submarines were to station themselves along all the routes the Americans might take on their way to assist Midway. Logical this might have been, but there was a basic error in its reasoning, as Professor Morison has pointed out:

"The vital defect in this sort of plan is that it depends on the enemy's doing exactly what is expected. If he is smart enough to do something different—in this case to have fast carriers on the spot—the operation is thrown into confusion."

But Yamamoto, of course, had no idea that the Americans knew his movements, and could act accordingly.

Rochefort's ruse

There was a somewhat tense atmosphere in Pearl Harbor in spite of the breaking of the Japanese codes. Men began to wonder if in fact they were not getting involved in some diabolical deception about the objective of the next Japanese move. Their last doubts were dispelled by a ruse thought up by Commander J. Rochefort, head of the Combat Intelligence Unit at Pearl Harbor: the commander in each of the areas where a Japanese attack might be expected was required to signal some deficiency in his equipment. The Midway commander chose his seawater distillation plant, and a few days later the Americans intercepted a report from a Japanese listening post announcing that it had heard "AF" report such a deficiency. "AF" had been mentioned as the objective of Japan's present move, and Rochefort now knew for certain that Midway was the target about to be attacked.

The whole archipelago of Hawaii had been in a state of alert against a landing ever since May 14. The little Sand and Eastern Islands, the only land surfaces of any size in Midway Atoll, were rightly the object of particular care and attention and were so well reinforced with A.A. guns, reconnaissance planes, and fighter planes that the commanders on Midway, Commander Cyril T. Simard and Marine Lieutenant-Colonel Harold Shannon (soon promoted to Captain and Colonel respectively) had just over 3,000 men and 115 planes under them.

Nimitz's ambush

Not counting Rear-Admiral Theobald's squadron, Admiral Nimitz's forces were divided into two groups:
1. Task Force 16, based on the aircraft-carriers *Enterprise* and *Hornet,* together with six cruisers and nine destroyers. Vice-Admiral Halsey was now in hospital and so command of this force was given to Rear-Admiral Raymond A. Spruance, whose intellectual powers were so formidable as to earn him the nickname of "electric brain".
2. Task Force 17, still under the command of Rear-Admiral F. J. Fletcher, based on the aircraft-carrier *Yorktown,* together with two cruisers and five destroyers. The damage sustained by *Yorktown* on the previous May 8 would have taken two months to repair in peacetime. The 1,400 men of the Pearl Harbor dockyard did it in less than 48 hours. This allowed Fletcher to set sail on the morning of May 30, behind Task Force 16 which had left on May 28.
And so when the Japanese submarines,

which were behind schedule anyway, reached the watching stations assigned to them, Admiral Nimitz's ships had already gone, and they were thus unable to report the enemy's dispositions or strength. On June 3 at 0900 hours, when the first enemy sighting reports reached them, Fletcher and Spruance were north-east of Midway and they were in a good position to attack from the flank of the Japanese force. Leaving Pearl Harbor they had received the following warning from Cincpac in anticipation of the enemy's superior strength:

"You will be governed by the principle of calculated risk, which you shall interpret to mean the avoidance of exposure of your force to attack by superior enemy forces without good prospect of inflicting,

(page 381) An American carrier task force steaming ahead in the Pacific.

▽ *Patching up the "Old Lady" at Pearl Harbor. It should have taken months to repair the damage suffered by* Yorktown *at the Coral Sea–but under Nimitz's goading she was made seaworthy again in an incredibly short time–well under 48 hours.*

as a result of such exposure, greater damage on the enemy."

But as Professor Potter and Admiral Nimitz point out, "to fight cautiously, to meet a superior enemy force without unduly exposing one's own is difficult in the highest degree. That Fletcher and Spruance were able to carry out these orders successfully was due primarily to their skilful exploitation of intelligence, which enabled them to turn the element of surprise against the Japanese."

Even before the Japanese fleet left its bases, Rear-Admiral Ryunosuke Kusaka, Nagumo's chief-of-staff, made the following observation to Yamamoto: so as not to hinder take-off and landing on the flight decks, the aircraft-carriers had had their masts shortened to such an extent that their radio aerials were incapable of intercepting any enemy wireless traffic. Thus the carrier forces which would be the first to make contact would be deprived of an

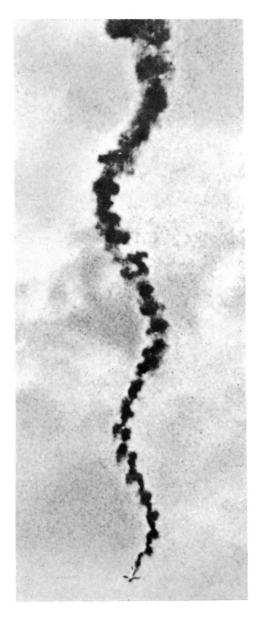

▷ *The death-plunge of a Japanese plane. The superb Zero, although far and away the best fighter in the Pacific theatre at the time of Midway, was nevertheless a comparatively easy victim–if it could be held in the gun sights at the right moment. It lacked armour plate protection, and tended to explode readily when hit in the fuel tanks.*

Battle in the sky

It was shortly after 0900 on June 3 when the first contact with the enemy was reported. A Catalina searching 470 miles to the south-west of Midway had been fired on by two Japanese patrol craft. Further confirmation that the Japanese were moving on Midway came when another Catalina spotted the convoy and escorts of the Midway Occupation Force.

In Walter Lord's words:

"Farther to the west, Ensign Jack Reid piloted another PBY across an empty ocean. He had started earlier than the rest, was now 700 miles from Midway, nearing the end of his outward leg. So far, nothing worth reporting. With the PBY on automatic pilot, Reid again studied the sea with his binoculars. Still nothing– occasional cloud puffs and a light haze hung over the Pacific, but not enough to bother him. It was shortly before 9:25 A.M., and Ensign Reid was a man with no problems at all.

"Suddenly he looked, then looked again. Thirty miles dead ahead he could make out dark objects along the horizon. Ships, lots of them, all heading toward him. Handing the glasses to his co-pilot Ensign Hardeman, he calmly asked, 'Do you see what I see?'

"Hardeman took one look: 'You are damned right I do.'

"Commander Yasumi Toyama looked up from his charts on the bridge of the light cruiser *Jintsu*. For once all the transports were keeping in column, but the destroyer on the port side forward was raising a fuss. She hoisted a signal, then fired a smoke shell. Toyama rushed out on the bridge wing, and there was no need to ask what had happened. Everyone was looking and pointing. There, low and well out of range on the horizon, hovered a PBY."

That afternoon the convoy was attacked from high altitude by a formation of Flying Fortresses.

At dawn Nagumo had reached a position 280 miles north-west of Midway Island. He turned his force into the wind. Then the carriers *Akagi*, *Kaga*, *Hiryu*, and *Soryu* unleashed 36 level bombers, 36 dive-bombers, and 36 fighters. At the same time six seaplanes took off to reconnoitre for American warships, followed half an hour later by a seventh, delayed by a breakdown in the catapult gear on the cruiser *Tone*.

essential source of information. It was therefore suggested that the battleship *Yamato* should accompany the aircraft-carriers, but this was rejected by the Commander-in-Chief.

Even so, the Japanese admiral's flagship intercepted in the single day of June 1 180 messages from Hawaii, 72 of which were classified "urgent". This sudden intensification of radio traffic, as well as the great increase in aerial reconnaissance, could mean that the enemy forces were now at sea or about to set sail. Should Nagumo, sailing on more than 600 miles ahead of *Yamato*, be alerted? This would mean breaking the sacrosanct radio silence and Yamamoto could not bring himself to do it, although the Americans already seemed to have penetrated the secret of Operation Midway. In such a situation the Germans would have said "*Wirkung geht vor Tarnung*", or "effectiveness comes before camouflage".

On Midway Captain Simard was alerted in time and put up all his planes, but his 26 fighters were no match for the Japanese Zeros, which knocked out 17 of them and crippled seven others to such an extent that they had to be written off. The Japanese lost only six. The Midway air force was not silenced for all that. Lieutenant Joichi Tomonaga, who led the first wave, signalled back to Nagumo that in his opinion a second attack was necessary.

The Japanese Admiral acted on Tomonaga's report and ordered that the torpedo-carrying bombers of the second wave (108 planes), armed to attack any U.S. ships that might appear, should have their torpedoes replaced by bombs, and the dive-bombers their armour-piercing bombs by high-explosive ones. This decision seemed justified by the ferocity of the Midway air force's counter-attack. It is true that Captain Simard's pilots pressed their charges home, as the saying was in the days of cavalry; it is also true that the training of the men on the one side and the efficiency of the machines on the other were unequal to the courage displayed. Thirty-nine torpedo-carrying aircraft and dive-bombers had attacked the Japanese without causing any damage to their ships; 17 of these planes had been shot down and seven were declared beyond repair on their return. A squadron of Flying Fortresses then bombed the enemy convoy from a height of 21,000 feet, also without success. Though these attacks had been fruitless, Admiral Nagumo nevertheless threw in his second wave of fighters.

Bombs or torpedoes?

Meanwhile, at 0728 hours, *Tone*'s seaplane signalled that it had spotted ten enemy ships 240 miles away, steaming south-south-east. Not until 0820 hours did the pilot see, and then only vaguely, that there was an aircraft-carrier with them. Though this report was far from clear, it put Nagumo in a very embarrassing position. If he sent up his second wave dive-bombers (36 planes) to attack this formation, they would be without fighter escort and would take a heavy beating. The same danger faced *Akagi*'s and *Kaga*'s torpedo-bombers, which were now loaded with bombs instead of torpedoes. These were less likely to be successful against warships. If he

waited for the first wave to land on his carriers when they returned from Midway he would then be able to attack with all his forces. And so at 0855 hours Nagumo signalled his squadron: "After landing, formation will proceed north provisionally. We expect to make contact with the enemy and destroy him."

Whereupon the armourers of the aircraft-carriers again threw themselves into the task of changing the weapons on the aircraft, replacing H.E. bombs with torpedoes and armour-piercing bombs. As time was short, they piled up the bombs alongside the aircraft in the hangars.

A change of fortune

At 0552 hours on June 4 a message to Admirals Fletcher and Spruance announced that the enemy forces with four aircraft-carriers were 230 miles to their south-west. Fletcher, the senior of the two officers and therefore in command of the whole force, gave the order to attack. From 0702 hours Task Force 16, now sailing towards the enemy, sent up 116 planes. *Yorktown*, in Task Force 17, waited until 0838 hours before launching her 35.

It has been said that Rear-Admiral Spruance had calculated the time so as to surprise the enemy aircraft-carriers just when their flight-decks would be cluttered up with planes returning from Midway. With admirable, almost unprecedented modesty he himself has denied the flattering legend in his preface to Commanders Fuchida's and Okumiya's book, *Midway*.

"When I read the account of the events of June 4, 1942 I am struck once more by the part played by chance in warfare. The authors congratulate us on having chosen the moment of our attack on the Japanese aircraft-carriers when they were at their most vulnerable, that is with their flight-decks encumbered with planes ready to take off. We did not choose this moment deliberately. For my part I had only the feeling that we had to achieve surprise and strike the enemy planes with all the strength at our command as soon as we met them."

The first U.S. Navy squadron to attack, 15 TBD Devastator torpedo-bombers under Lieutenant-Commander John Waldron, from *Hornet*, appeared at about 0930, skimming over the tops of the waves. A few minutes later they had all been shot

down and only one out of their total crew of 30 survived. They were slow and vulnerable to enemy fire. Fuchida and Okumiya described this unsuccessful but heroic attack in the following words:

"The first enemy carrier planes to attack were 15 torpedo bombers. When first spotted by our screening ships and combat air patrol, they were still not visible from the carriers, but they soon appeared as tiny dark specks in the sky, a little above the horizon, on *Akagi*'s starboard bow. The distant wings flashed in the sun. Occasionally one of the specks burst into a spark of flame and trailed black smoke as it fell into the water. Our fighters were on the job, and the enemy again seemed to be without fighter protection.

"Presently a report came in from a Zero group leader: 'All 15 enemy torpedo bombers shot down.' Nearly 50 Zeros had gone to intercept the unprotected enemy formation! Small wonder that it did not get through."

The squadrons of Devastator torpedo-bombers from *Enterprise* and *Yorktown* were almost as unfortunate: they lost 20 out of 26 planes to the Japanese fighters and A.A. guns. Worse still, not a single

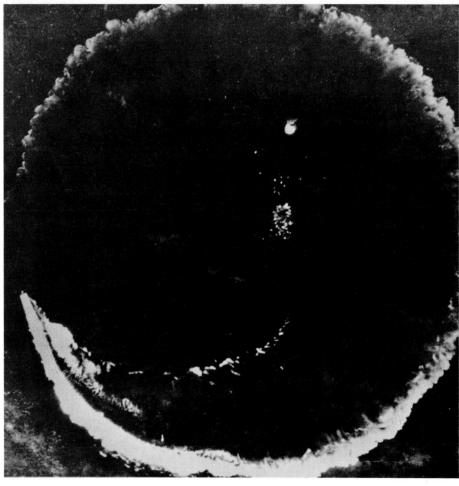

Hiryu *escaped the first shattering dive-bomber attack which knocked out Kaga, Akagi, and Soryu—but not for long. Here her blazing and abandoned hulk wallows sluggishly in a calm sea. She finally sank around 0915 on June 5.*

carriers themselves, the Japanese were too busy warding off torpedoes to see the second attack.

The scene has been described by an eye-witness on the flight-deck of the ill-fated *Akagi:*

"I looked up to see three black enemy planes plummeting towards our ship. Some of our machine guns managed to fire a few frantic bursts at them, but it was too late. The plump silhouettes of the American 'Dauntless' dive-bombers grew larger, and then a number of black objects suddenly floated eerily from their wings. Bombs! Down they came straight towards me! I fell intuitively to the deck and crawled behind a command post mantlet.

"The terrifying scream of the dive bombers reached me first, followed by the crashing explosion of a direct hit. There was a blinding flash and then a second explosion, much louder than the first. I was shaken by a weird blast of warm air. There was still another shock, but less severe, apparently a near-miss. Then followed a startling quiet as the barking of guns suddenly ceased. I got up and looked at the sky. The enemy planes were already gone from sight ...

"Looking about, I was horrified at the destruction that had been wrought in a matter of seconds. There was a huge hole in the flight deck just behind the amidships elevator. The elevator itself, twisted like molten glass, was drooping into the hangar. Deck plates reeled upwards in grotesque configurations. Planes stood tail up, belching livid flame and jet black smoke. Reluctant tears streamed down my cheeks as I watched the fires spread."

one of their torpedoes reached its target.

So by 1015 hours Nagumo was winning. At the cost of six of his own planes he had destroyed 83 of his enemy's and at 1030 hours he would unleash on the American squadron a wave of 102 planes, including 54 torpedo-bombers and 36 dive-bombers. He was confident that they would destroy the Americans.

By 1028 hours, however, the Rising Sun had been decisively defeated.

The American planes had encountered difficulties during their approach, as the position they had been given was erroneous, the Japanese ships having changed direction. This caused an unwelcome detour. Some Wildcat fighter squadrons lost the torpedo-carrying aircraft they were supposed to be escorting. The massacre described above was the result. But the heroic sacrifice of Waldron and his men payed off a few minutes later. The Zero fighters were so busy tracking down Waldron's planes at low level that they were too late to prevent an attack by Douglas SBD Dauntlesses, which dive-bombed the Japanese aircraft-carriers from a height of nearly 20,000 feet. On the

Japan checked

So everything was decided on June 4 between Vice-Admiral Nagumo's four air-craft-carriers (272 planes) and Rear-Admirals Fletcher and Spruance's three (233 planes) supported by 115 planes from Midway. The 64,200 ton *Yamato*, 9 other battleships, 11 cruisers and 32 destroyers never fired a shot, and the 41 planes on board the light aircraft-carriers *Zuiho* and *Hosho* took no part in the action.

Taken together, the battles of the Coral Sea and Midway represented a decisive check on the Japanese navy, and signalled the turn of the tide in the war in the Pacific. From now on, Japan was to be on the defensive.

Nagumo's force destroyed

The end of the battle of Midway was swift. The *Akagi* was racked by explosions as her petrol and piles of bombs went up, causing widespread fires and destruction. *Akagi*'s radio was out of action, and Vice-Admiral Nagumo and his staff left the ship at 1046 hours.

"As the number of dead and wounded increased and the fires got further out of control, Captain Aoki finally decided at 1800 that the ship must be abandoned. The injured were lowered into boats and cutters sent alongside by the screening destroyers. Many uninjured men leapt into the sea and swam away from the stricken ship. Destroyers *Arashi* and *Nowaki* picked up all survivors. When the rescue work was complete, Captain Aoki radioed to Admiral Nagumo at 1920 from one of the destroyers, asking permission to sink the crippled carrier. This inquiry was monitored by the combined fleet flagship, whence Admiral Yamamoto dispatched an order at 2225 to delay the carrier's disposition. Upon receipt of this instruction, the captain returned to his carrier alone. He reached the anchor deck, which was still free from fire, and there lashed himself to an anchor . . ."

A few miles away, *Kaga*, hit by four bombs, had also become a raging inferno and her crew were attempting to control the flames amidst explosions which were causing widespread death and destruction. The ship had been attacked by *Enterprise*'s and *Hornet*'s dive-bombers which were under the command of Lieutenant-Commander Clarence W. McClusky. *Soryu* was bombed by planes led by Lieutenant-Commander Maxwell Leslie and by formations from *Yorktown*. By 1040 hours *Soryu*'s rudder and engines were out of action and her crew was surrounded by fires and explosions.

The only unit of the Japanese Carrier Striking Force now fit to fight was *Hiryu*. In accordance with Nagumo's order she sent off some 40 planes in two waves to attack Task Force 17. At mid-day, 18 dive-bombers appeared above *Yorktown*. The Americans had been warned in time by radar, and the A.A. wiped out 12 planes, but two bombs reached their target and the powerful vessel was brought to a standstill at 1220 hours. She had got under way but *Hiryu*'s aircraft attacked again

△ *The shattered wreck of the Japanese cruiser* Mikuma. *She had been retiring from Midway when she collided with* Mogami, *and as the two cruisers limped on in the wake of Kurita's other cruisers they were set upon by an American air strike. On the wrecked rear turret can be seen the remains of Captain Fleming's Vindicator bomber, which he deliberately crashed on the target when he was fatally hit during his bombing run. Further attacks late on June 5 finished off* Mikuma.

△ Japanese painting of an air-sea battle in the Pacific. The planes in the foreground are from a strike wave of "Val" dive-bombers; their Zero escorts have just shot down a gaggle of Wildcat fighters.

▷ Men of Patton's Western Task Force clamber down boarding nets from a cruiser to their landing craft.

through a seemingly impenetrable barrage of fire and scored hits with two torpedoes. Seeing his ship in danger of capsizing, her commander ordered her to be abandoned and taken in tow. This was to be *Hiryu*'s last action. Only 15 of her planes, including six fighters, returned. At 1630 hours, Spruance sighted her and sent in 24 Dauntlesses under McClusky. The Japanese vessel whipped her speed up to 33 knots, but she was hit by four bombs at 1700 hours. All the planes on the flight deck were set on fire and all means of escape from the ship were cut off. At dusk Task Force 16 set course eastwards as Spruance did not care to risk a night battle with an enemy force containing the battleships *Haruna* and *Kirishima,* against which he was clearly at a disadvantage.

Between 1900 and 1930 hours, *Soryu* and *Kaga* both disappeared beneath the waters of the Pacific. In the morning of the following day Nagumo, with the authority of Admiral Yamamoto, finished off the wrecks of *Akagi* and *Hiryu* with torpedoes. The commander of the second, Rear-Admiral Tamon Yamaguchi, obstinately refused to leave his ship and, to ensure that he went down with her, tied himself to the bridge.

Yamamoto gives up

On board *Yamato,* the Commander-in-Chief of the Combined Fleet could do no more than admit his powerlessness to redeem the situation now that his various detachments were so widely scattered. After a series of orders and counter-orders, on June 5 he finally confirmed the aban-

donment of operations against Midway and the return to their bases of his several detachments.

This was not to be done without further loss, however. In the 7th Cruiser Division, *Mogami* was in collision during the night with *Mikuma.* Hounded by enemy planes in the daylight, the former was further damaged and put out of action for a year. The latter went down at about noon on June 6. A few hours later the Japanese submarine *I-168* (Lieutenant-Commander Yahachi Tanabe), which had shelled Midway on the night of June 4–5, surprised *Yorktown* as she was being towed slowly back to Pearl Harbor. Manoeuvring swiftly and decisively it sank her with two torpedoes and cut the destroyer *Hammann* in half with a third.

This was the end of one of the most decisive battles of World War II, the effects of which were felt far beyond the waters of the Pacific. It deprived Japan of her freedom of action and it allowed the two Anglo-Saxon powers to go ahead with their policy of "Germany first", as agreed between Churchill and Roosevelt.

The Americans had lost 307 dead and 147 planes. The Japanese lost 4 fleet carriers, 332 planes and 3,500 dead, and these heavy losses included the cream of her naval air forces. The results show that, though they had been dealt a worse hand than the enemy, Nimitz, Fletcher, and Spruance had played their cards better than Yamamoto and Nagumo. Chance had played her part too, though. What would have happened if *Tone*'s seaplane had not been half an hour late in taking off? We shall never know.

On June 6–7 the Japanese occupied the undefended islands of Kiska and Attu in the Aleutians.

CHAPTER 42

TORCH: A TWO-FRONT WAR FOR ROMMEL

The whole preliminary period came to an end late in October, as the official historian has written, "in an atmosphere of unrelieved improvisation and haste, an unavoidable consequence of the determination to undertake an operation which stretched resources to the limit".

More than 100 ships transported Patton's men, and this was too large a convoy to go from a single port without attracting attention. They left in small packets at various times from various places, ostensibly bound for different destinations, and then assembled at sea. They were discovered by a U-boat during the crossing, but they managed to get off the shore of Morocco at the designated time. There a high surf, a more or less normal condition in those waters, threatened to end the invasion before it started.

In the United Kingdom, the units comprising the Centre and Eastern Task Forces prepared for "Torch" in similarly exasperating circumstances. The 1st Armoured Division, commanded by Major-General Orlando Ward, the 1st Infantry Division, headed by Major-General Terry Allen, and the 34th Infantry Division were the major American components, and they had skimpy amphibious training because time was lacking. Nor were there enough ships and boats, or even suitable training sites, to provide thorough rehearsals for the forthcoming combat. Armoured formations trained in Northern Ireland while some elements worked in Scotland and much of the staff was involved in planning in London. The infantry had equally frustrating experiences.

It could well be said, as the official historian remarks, that what the Allies were attempting to do was "the best thing possible within the limitations imposed by inexperience, uncertainty, and the shortness of time, rather than trying to turn out a force completely ready".

The assault ships of the Centre and Eastern Task Forces loaded in Liverpool and Glasgow late in September. In

accordance with a complex schedule, the ships proceeded to the Firth of Clyde. By October 17, the entire expedition was assembled there. Five days later, the force moved out in a series of small convoys, which proceeded toward Gibraltar. It moved safely through the straits during the night of November 5–6.

Would the French co-operate?

Deep within the Rock of Gibraltar, in damp and restricted quarters, Eisenhower, Clark, and the principal staff members of Allied Force Headquarters—who had flown there from the United Kingdom—listened for news of the impending contest. Eisenhower and Clark also awaited the arrival on November 7 of General Henri Giraud, who was brought secretly by submarine from southern France to discuss whether, and how, he could contribute to the operation.

"Tension at the Top"

When presented with the Allied plan for Operation "Torch", Stalin was impressed by its strategic advantages, including hitting Rommel in the back and exposing Italy to the brunt of the war. It would also re-open the Mediterranean to Allied shipping and avoid the long detour via the Cape.

Message du Président des Etats Unis

Le Président des Etats Unis m'a chargé comme Général Commandant en Chef des Forces Expéditionnaires Américaines de faire parvenir aux peuples de l'Afrique française du Nord le message suivant:

Aucune nation n'est plus intimement liée, tant par l'histoire que par l'amitié profonde, au peuple de France et à ses amis que ne le sont les Etats Unis d'Amérique.

Les Américains luttent actuellement, non seulement pour assurer leur avenir, mais pour restituer les libertés et les principes démocratiques de tous ceux qui ont vécu sous le drapeau tricolore.

Nous venons chez vous pour vous libérer des conquérants qui ne désirent que vous priver à tout jamais de vos droits souverains, de votre droit à la liberté du culte, de votre droit de mener votre train de vie en paix.

Nous venons chez vous uniquement pour anéantir vos ennemis — nous ne voulons pas vous faire de mal.

Nous venons chez vous en vous assurant que nous partirons dès que la menace de l'Allemagne et de l'Italie aura été dissipée.

Je fais appel à votre sens des réalités ainsi qu'à votre idéalisme.

Ne faites rien pour entraver l'accomplissement de ce grand dessein.

Aidez-nous, et l'avènement du jour de la paix universelle sera hâté.

Dwight D. Eisenhower (signature)

DWIGHT D. EISENHOWER
Lieutenant Général, Commandant en Chef
des Forces Expéditionnaires Américaines.

▽ *As the invasion got under way, thousands of leaflets like this, claiming that the Americans came as the friends of France, to fight against Germany and Italy, were dropped. Vichy reacted as might have been expected – the landings were to be treated as nothing less than an overt act of war and were to be resisted.*

In what seemed like interminable conversations, Eisenhower was unable to persuade Giraud to go to North Africa and try to rally the French authorities, who were loyal to the government of Marshal Pétain, over to the Allied side. Giraud would do so only if he received supreme command of the Allied expedition then under way and if he could divert part of it directly to a landing in southern France. This was, of course, hardly practical.

After the invasion Giraud agreed to help. By this time, the Allies were negotiating with Admiral Darlan, Pétain's second in command, who by chance had happened to be in Algiers visiting his sick son in hospital there. Darlan was the highest governmental official on the scene, and he represented the legal authority of France. The Darlan deal, as the arrangements were later called, would prevent a protracted Allied struggle with the French in North Africa. But this could hardly be envisaged as the Allies made ready to assault the coast.

All three task forces were to land simultaneously in order to make the maximum impression on the French. Although the military were sure to offer at least token resistance, some French officers had promised to help the Americans come ashore. These had learned vaguely of the planned invasion from Robert Murphy, an American diplomat stationed in Algiers, and from General Clark who, two weeks before the landings, made a secret and hazardous trip by submarine to a clandestine meeting with sympathisers at Cherchell in Algeria. Unfortunately, security considerations made it impossible to inform the French of the exact time and places of the landings. As a consequence, the assistance that was given so forthrightly was poorly co-ordinated and of small concrete value.

The amphibious forces were to hit the beaches before dawn November 8. Yet each task force commander had discretion to set his exact time because of differing conditions of tide, moonlight, wind, and sunrise at the various sites. The Eastern and Centre Task Forces adopted an H-hour of 0100 hours, Greenwich time; the Western 0400.

The Western Task Force planned to anchor its troop transports several miles offshore, there to release the landing craft already swinging from davits. These boats would assemble alongside the transports to take aboard the troops. Thus loaded, the landing craft would circle nearby until a signal was given for them to form into waves at a line of departure marked by two control vessels. Escorted by guiding vessels equipped with radar and other navigational aids, the landing craft would then proceed on a predetermined schedule toward the shore. There was to be no preliminary shelling, but fire support ships were to take stations from which to shell shore targets if necessary. The waves of landing craft would go in at intervals to allow each wave to unload and pull back from the

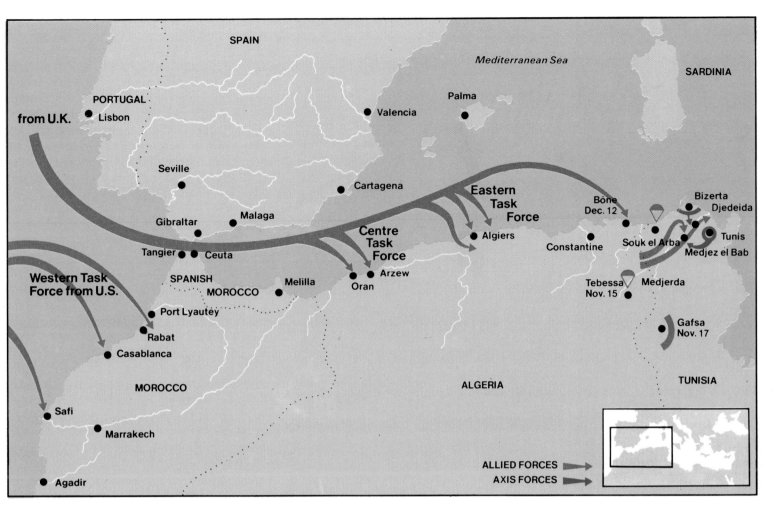

Map labels:

SPAIN
Mediterranean Sea
SARDINIA
PORTUGAL
from U.K.
Lisbon
Palma
Valencia
Seville
Cartagena
Eastern Task Force
Bône Dec. 12
Bizerta
Djedeida
Gibraltar
Malaga
Centre Task Force
Algiers
Constantine
Souk el Arba
Tunis
Tangier
Ceuta
Medjez el Bab
Western Task Force from U.S.
SPANISH MOROCCO
Melilla
Arzew
Oran
Tebessa Nov. 15
Medjerda
Port Lyautey
Rabat
Casablanca
Gafsa Nov. 17
MOROCCO
ALGERIA
TUNISIA
Safi
Marrakech
Agadir

ALLIED FORCES →
AXIS FORCES →

Torch: the American Viewpoint

One of the most important factors behind Operation Torch was the wish of the U.S. President to indicate to the Russians, who were under extreme duress in 1942, that the Anglo-American members of the Grand Alliance fighting the Axis nations were making an active contribution to the war effort. In all the discussions revolving around strategic decisions, the Western Allies consistently sought to assist the Russians by taking action that would draw German forces away from the Eastern Front. Roosevelt, moreover, wished to demonstrate that feasibility of combined Anglo-American operations.

General Eisenhower was Commander-in-Chief for Operation "Torch". Eisenhower's H.Q. was run by Major-General Walter Bedell Smith on the basis of allied unity. Major-General George Patton was to lead the American ground forces and General Kenneth Anderson the British forces. Torch was to consist of three major landings: the Western Task Force, to land near Casablanca, was wholly American, sailing from Virginia. The Centre Task Force, to land at Oran, was American but transported from Britain in British ships. The Eastern Task Force, to land near Algiers, would have a token American advance guard to soothe French sensibilities, but was to be predominantly British.

△ *The "Torch" landings, bringing together the invasion fleets from the United States and Great Britain for America's first commitment to the European Theatre of Operations and the "Germany first" principle.*

▽ *The Allied hand stretches out greedily to take North Africa's wine, grain, dried vegetables, potatoes, and oil in this somewhat fanciful Vichy poster aimed at the metropolitan French housewife.*

△ *Major-General Ernest N. Harmon, who commanded the American forces that landed at Safi, some 6,500 in number.*
△ *Vice-Admiral Henry Kent Hewitt commanded the American naval element in the Western Task Force.*

△ ▷ *An American White half-track patrols the streets of Casablanca.*

▽ *Major-General Charles W. Ryder* (left) *led the Eastern Task Force and Major-General Lloyd R. Fredendall the Centre Task Force.*

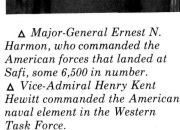

beach in time to make room for the wave following behind. The first troops to land were to capture the beach and prepare to receive succeeding waves. Later arrivals would reconnoitre inland, expand the beach-head, and penetrate the interior to reach special objectives.

Patton, who had read the Koran during the voyage, issued a circular to his men. "The local population," he said, "will respect strong, quiet men who live up to their promises. Do not boast nor brag, and keep any agreement you make." To his officers he said, "There is not the least doubt but that we are better in all respects than our enemies, but to win, the men must KNOW this. It must be their absolute belief. WE MUST HAVE A SUPERIORITY COMPLEX!"

The Casablanca landings

During the night of November 7, the Western Task Force split into three attack groups and took sub-task forces to positions off the beaches of Safi, Fedala, and Mehdia. Although Patton's objective was Casablanca, the city was too strongly fortified and defended to be taken by frontal assault from the sea. He had therefore divided his troops into three landing forces. Those going ashore at Mehdia were to capture the airport at Salé; the other two forces, after establishing beach-heads, were to converge on Casablanca from the landward side.

Up to virtually the last minute, the surf conditions made landings dubious. But when final readings indicated that the weather might moderate, Hewitt decided to gamble and go. Instead of finding a heavy swell, the troops sailed the last few miles to their beaches in almost a flat calm. In a letter to Marshall about a week later, Patton explained why this had happened. "In spite of my unfortunate proficiency in profanity," he wrote, "I have at bottom a strongly religious nature. It is my considered opinion that the success of the operation was largely dependent on what people generally call 'luck', but what I believe to be Divine help."

Major-General Lucian Truscott was in charge at Mehdia, with about 9,000 men from the 2nd Armoured and 9th Divisions. A cavalryman who had accompanied the Canadian troops in the ill-fated Dieppe raid, he showed the competence and dash that would lead him eventually to division, corps, and army command. With his usual proficiency, he took in hand the members of his force, which had become somewhat disorganised in the initial landings at five different points along the shore. French resistance was immediate and strong, and an air bombardment of the ships offshore at dawn of November 8 delayed and reduced the prompt reinforcement and support that had been planned.

At nightfall of D-day, the Americans were in precarious positions. Hard fighting carried them through the second day. Not until the late afternoon of November 10 was the airfield objective taken and secured. As the battle was about to start again on November 11, word came that a cease-fire had been arranged in Algiers.

To obtain the airfield and seaplane base judged to be required for control of the area, Truscott's men had sustained considerable casualties, including 79 killed. The outcome of the operation would have been extremely uncertain but for the cease-fire.

Resistance and armistice

The Safi landings were under Major-General Ernest N. Harmon, a cavalry and tank officer who commanded the 2nd Armoured Division. A bluff and rather rough fellow who was a fighter through and through and who would eventually command a corps, Harmon had a force of about 6,500 men from the 2nd Armoured and 9th Divisions. Their limited training and experience showed at once as they left their transports and moved ashore. There was considerable disorganisation.

On the beaches the Americans met strong opposition from the French. But they fought inland and established a beach-head. On the following day, at Bou Guedra, they met a French force marching from Marrakech to engage them, and a serious battle ensued. Not until November 10, after blocking the French troops, could Harmon start north toward Casablanca. He took Mazagan on the coast on the morning of November 11 and was starting for Casablanca, 50 miles away, when he learned of the

cease-fire.

At Fedala, Major-General Jonathan Anderson, the 3rd Division's commander, headed a force of 16,000 men built around his division. The same difficulties of getting ashore were encountered, and the same strong French opposition from naval batteries and ground forces was met. The Americans established a beach-head and extended it by heavy fighting, then started toward Casablanca. On the morning of November 11, as they were about to open

△ *A French merchantman capsized at Casablanca.*

◁ A contrast in attitudes: U.S. infantry mop up a damaged battery blockhouse at Fedala while its erstwhile owners display an apparent indifference.

a bombardment of the city as a preliminary for assault, news came of the armistice.

There had been serious fighting at all three landings of the Western Task Force, the assumption or the hope that the French were anxiously awaiting their liberation by the Allies proving completely wrong. Patton, a long-time friend of the French, had attempted to negotiate a local armistice throughout the fighting, but his efforts had failed until a general settlement was arranged. After three days of combat in Morocco, American casualties totalled about 550, including 150 killed.

Success at Oran

At Oran, the Centre Task Force, numbering about 22,000 men, was to come ashore in three major operations involving seven different amphibious groups. In general, the 1st Armoured Division, only about half of which was present, was to thrust inland before daylight and close on the city from the south. The 1st Infantry Division was to encircle the city from the west and east and block the arrival of possible French reinforcements.

The assault convoys found their beacon submarines around 2130 hours on November 7, and sent motor launches to pick up pilot officers. Then the transport groups, preceded by minesweepers, headed for their assembly positions. Landing craft organised themselves into waves and carried men to the beaches of Marsa bou Zedjar, les Andalouses, and the Gulf of Arzew.

The landings were uniformly successful, although the number of troops ashore at the end of the first day was somewhat less than expected. Arzew was captured intact, as was an airfield. The French naval installations and ships at Oran and Mers-el-Kébir offered weak opposition, and French air efforts were negligible. Only a frontal assault on the Oran harbour, a suicide mission, and an airborne attack on Tafaraoui airfield miscarried.

French forces counter-attacked on the second day, and there was serious fighting. On the third day, an attack on Oran resulted in a sudden armoured penetration into the city. The French authorities surrendered at noon.

▽ The reconciliation starts: a G.I. lights up a cigarette for a French sailor.

△ *Some of the first Americans to land move up through Oran.*

▽ *Admiral Darlan (in civilian clothes) talks to Allied war correspondents after the armistice had come into force.*

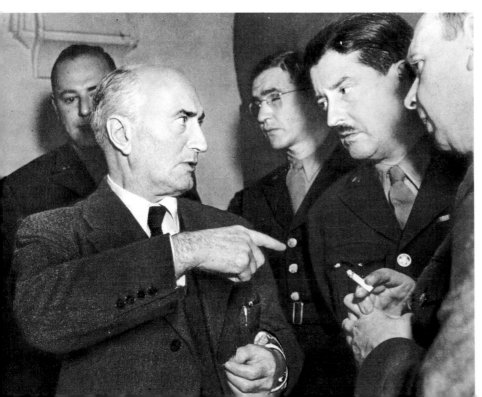

The seizure of Oran had been accomplished in less than three days by military means alone. This was the only action wholly won by force of arms. Surprise had taken the men ashore without significant French opposition. Sheer determination had carried them inland and to their main objectives rapidly. American casualties totalled about 275 killed, 325 wounded, and 15 missing.

Algiers, the key

Algiers was the most important objective of "Torch" because it was closest to Tunis, the ultimate goal. In addition, the port, railway terminal, two airfields, space for a supply base, city facilities for headquarters, and the fact that Algiers was the seat of government for all of French North Africa made it a great prize.

The Eastern Naval Task Force divided into three columns, one heading for Cape Matifou, two toward Cape Sidi Ferruch. Because there were insufficient Americans for the landings, 7,200 British troops of the 11th Infantry Brigade Group came ashore west of Algiers near Castiglione. The operations went smoothly. French units in the area said they had been instructed not to resist.

Part of the U.S. 34th Division landed closer to the city on its western side. Components were scattered by landing craft along 15 miles of the coast, and all met some French resistance. But the force of 4,350 American and 1,000 British troops took Blida airfield and a small

The French Army started to serve with the Allies.
△ General Noguès, latterly the Vichy régime's Resident-General in Morocco, takes the salute at a parade of French troops.
▽ French prisoners await their release after the armistice.
▷ △ The advance into Tunisia: American paratroopers regroup after dropping on an airfield well in advance of the conventional ground forces.
▷ ▽ Watched by a group of British soldiers, Americans heave part of their equipment, a gun, up a beach.

group entered the city.

The 39th Regimental Combat Team, of about 5,700 Americans reinforced by 200 British Commandos, landed successfully east of Algiers and moved to their assigned positions.

A suicide group of 650 Americans and several British officers in American uniforms made a direct assault on the harbour. By 0800 hours on November 8, they had taken their objectives, an electric power station, a petroleum storage depôt, a seaplane base, port offices, docks, and moles. They were then surrounded by

French military units, and had to surrender.

Meanwhile, Algiers had come briefly under the control of pro-American irregulars of the French Resistance, who held the important centres of communication. They were dispossessed, however, and French Army units took over.

The presence of Darlan in the city was fortuitous. Having to decide whether French North Africa would pass to the Allies with or without bloodshed, he radioed Pétain for instructions and received authority to act freely. Around 1600 hours, with Allied troops closing in on the city, Darlan authorised General Alphonse Juin to negotiate for an armistice in Algiers, but not for all of French North Africa. Two and a half hours later, agreement was reached to halt the fighting.

On the following day, Clark arrived in Algiers to negotiate with Darlan a settlement for the rest of North Africa. They reached agreement late on November 10, and hostilities between the French and the Allies ended.

By then, General Anderson had arrived in Algiers on November 9, and was getting his 1st Army's movement eastward organised and started. Tunis, along with Bizerta, was 380 miles away, and the Axis nations had already started to pour troops into the north-eastern corner of Tunisia by sea and air. French forces offered no resistance, for officers and men were anguished by the conflict between their strong sense of duty to Pétain and Darlan and by their strong desire to join the Allies and fight the Axis. While negotiations took place in Algiers, French officers waited for instructions on whether to collaborate with the Axis or with the Allies. Meanwhile, considerable numbers of German and Italian troops arrived through the ports and airfields of Bizerta and Tunis and established a strong beach-head. Not until mid-November could French ground troops form a thin defensive line to keep the Axis units somewhat bottled up while Anderson's forces rushed to their aid.

Given the distances, the poor roads, and the rough terrain, the Eastern Task Force, predominantly British, made excellent progress. By November 20, Anderson's formations were in contact with Axis units. Five days later, the British, reinforced by a relatively few American units known as Blade Force and by French forces, attacked. But

combat strengths on both sides of the front were equal, and Anderson was at a disadvantage. His line of communications was weak, a depôt system was lacking, and air support was difficult to obtain.

Anderson was not to blame. Allied planners had long been aware that the precipitous advance to Tunis on a shoestring would be a gamble. Although Anderson tried for another month to crack the enemy defences, increasingly bad weather, including heavy rains, made it obvious that the Allies could not force a favourable decision before the end of the year.

Eisenhower had done all he could to help. He had sent U.S. units from Algiers and Oran, indeed as far away as Morocco, to reinforce Anderson. He had put pressure on the airmen and logistics experts to give Anderson as much support as possible. But on December 24, after visiting Anderson, Eisenhower had to agree that an immediate attempt to capture Bizerta and Tunis would have to be abandoned. A stalemate disappointing to the Allies now set in.

This brought "Torch", the landings and the sweep to the east, to an end. The

△ *American paratroopers. Though they managed to capture some strategic points in Tunisia, it took the conventional ground forces some time to move up, and this gave the Axis sufficient time to secure a large bridgehead. To overrun this proved impossible with the limited resources available to the Allies late in 1942.*

assassination of Admiral Darlan on the same day, December 24, underscored the conclusion of the operation. A new political situation now had to be dealt with. There were also new military conditions. Rommel's forces had been driven from Egypt and across Libya and were about to enter southern Tunisia.

"Torch" represented the first successful major Anglo-American combined offensive, and it set the pattern for Allied unity and cohesion in subsequent coalition ventures. Largely improvised, "Torch" was a triumph of planning and execution, for it required an unprecedented effort to build up an American task force in the United States, separated by 3,000 miles from the other two task forces and from Eisenhower's headquarters, then to arrange for the entire force to converge simultaneously on the North African coast.

If "Torch" did not immediately bring American troops into contact with the armed forces of Germany, the last two months of 1942 placed them in proximity to Germans and Italians on the field of battle. That confrontation would take place in 1943, probably earlier than could have been expected if the initial operation had been launched elsewhere. But the quick success that the Americans had enjoyed over the French was unfortunate, for as a result an overconfidence, even an arrogance, arose in the ranks. Many American soldiers came to believe that they were invincible. They had but to appear before the Germans, they thought, to win. The battle of Kasserine Pass in the following year would expose how terribly inexperienced they really were.

The hope of securing a quick cessation of French resistance, not only to facilitate the landings but also to enhance the subsequent operations into Tunisia, had worked. The French had fought bravely despite their outmoded weapons and equipment. Many were wounded, and more than 650 were killed in the fighting. They could with honour enter into the Allied camp and join in the continuing struggle to liberate Europe from the power of Nazi Germany.

Finally, "Torch" was the first of a series of large-scale coalition amphibious landings–Sicily, southern Italy, southern France, Normandy–that would lead the Allies to the final battle with the enemy.

CHAPTER 43
VICHY FRANCE FALLS

△ *General Henri Giraud. He had escaped from a German prisoner-of-war camp in April 1942, and shortly before the "Torch" landings was ferried by British submarine from France to North Africa.*

△ △ *Pierre Laval at the ceremony in April 1942 when he once more became Prime Minister of Vichy France. His active collaboration with the Germans did much to engender the feeling amongst the military that the only hopes of salvation lay with the Allies.*

Echoes of the gunfire in North Africa had already reached Vichy when the U.S. *chargé d'affaires* presented himself before Marshal Pétain to read a message from President Roosevelt, announcing the preventive occupation of French North Africa and asking him not to oppose it. Pétain's reply was:

"It is with stupor and sadness that I learned tonight of the aggression of your troops against North Africa.

"I have read your message. You invoke pretexts which nothing justifies . . . France and her honour are at stake. We are attacked; we shall defend ourselves; this is the order I am giving."

In Algiers, however, General Juin cancelled the orders for a counter-attack and proclaimed a cease-fire. This had been agreed with Major-General Charles W. Ryder in the evening of November 8 and he had no difficulty in getting it confirmed by Admiral Darlan, who had come to North Africa to visit his son, who was seriously ill.

On November 9, Generals Clark and Giraud arrived in Algiers, but the latter found that his comrades cold-shouldered him because of his "rebellion". On the following day Darlan nevertheless agreed to a general armistice throughout North Africa and, as requested by General Clark, did so without reference to Vichy. At the same time General Juin notified the troops in Tunisia that the orders to resist "other foreign troops" still stood. This was the end of the fighting between

Frenchmen and Americans, which had lasted since the night of November 7–8. According to such statistics as we have been able to find, the French lost a little under 700 killed, about 1,400 wounded, and 400 missing. The 2nd Light Squadron (Rear-Admiral Gervais de Lafond) lost the cruiser *Primauguet* and six destroyers sunk or completely wrecked. Off Oran two other destroyers were lost, one sunk and one driven ashore. Four submarines were also lost, which explains the large number of men missing. The first contacts between General Juin and General Clark were not without their difficulties.

"I confess," Marshal Juin wrote later in his memoirs, "that General Clark, with whom I was subsequently to have such close and friendly relations, especially during the Italian campaign, made a very bad impression on me at this first meeting. This American giant, in his untidy battle-dress, had a hard, secretive look on his face, which was drawn and weary as he had clearly not had any sleep for 48 hours. He always spoke curtly. His badly written note had its own quality of brutal offensiveness. No doubt he was deeply disturbed by the situation he found in Algiers and by the news of the fighting going on in Morocco and around Oran, where the plot to come over to the Allies had not succeeded, and also he probably couldn't make out the respective positions of Darlan and Giraud. He was, in fact, to cable Eisenhower in Gibraltar that night to say that he now had two men on his hands, whereas he had only expected one, and that he didn't know which one he had to deal with."

The Axis riposte

We will not linger over the comedy of errors which followed Marshal Pétain's playing to the gallery as he disavowed Darlan's cease-fire.

On November 11, however, in violation of the Rethondes armistice, the Germans and Italians invaded the unoccupied zone of France. The French Head of State's protests at this act had no practical effect within the country itself, but when broadcast, freed some consciences on the other side of the Mediterranean.

In all this confusion a very important rôle was played by Rear-Admiral Auphan, Minister of Marine at Vichy, and this should be recorded. Through secret channels he managed to let the commander-in-chief of the French forces know that even if Pétain disavowed him with his words he nevertheless approved of his action with his heart. To this effect he had a code which, in defiance of the armistice, had been kept secret from the Germans on June 25, 1940. Thus he cabled Darlan on November 13: "Reference telegram 50803. Complete agreement by Marshal and President Laval but official decision submitted to occupying authorities."

Reorganisation in North Africa

Thereupon agreement was reached in Algiers not only between the Allied command and Admiral Darlan, but between Admiral Darlan and General Giraud, the first assuming the post of High Commissioner in North Africa and the second that of Commander-in-Chief of the French Armed Forces. When he heard this news, the Governor-General, Pierre Boisson, after verifying the authenticity of the telegram quoted above, rallied French West Africa to the Government of Algeria. "This arrangement," wrote Juin, "was communicated to General Clark and Mr. Murphy and was sealed in the afternoon (of November 13, 1942) during the course of a solemn interview with General Eisenhower, the Allied Commander-in-Chief, and Admiral Sir Andrew Cunningham, the only British admiral since Mers-el-Kébir to find favour with Admiral Darlan for the high qualities of a sailor which he had shown in the Mediterranean and for the way in which he had treated the fleet of Admiral Godfroy when it had taken refuge in Alexandria." As this arrangement could have provoked some astonishment both in London and Washington, General Eisenhower explained it on November 14 to General Marshall in a long telegram, of which we quote only some essentials:

"November 14.

Completely understand the bewilderment in London and Washington because of the turn that negotiations with French North Africans have taken. Existing French sentiment here does not remotely agree with prior calculations. The following facts are pertinent and it is important that no precipitate action at home upset the equilibrium we have been able to establish.

"The name of Marshal Pétain is something to conjure with here. Everyone attempts to create the impression that he lives and acts under the shadow of the Marshal's figure. Civil governors, military leaders, and naval commanders agree that only one man has an obvious right to assume the Marshal's mantle in North Africa. He is Darlan. Even Giraud, who has been our trusted adviser and staunch friend since early conferences succeeded in bringing him down to earth, recognizes this overriding consideration and has modified his own intentions accordingly.

"The resistance we first met was offered because all ranks believed this to be the Marshal's wish. For this reason Giraud is deemed to have been guilty of at least a touch of insubordination in urging non-resistance to our landing. General Giraud understands and appears to have some sympathy for this universal attitude. All

▽ A German soldier on guard duty in Marseilles after the occupation of Vichy France. In the background is Marseilles Cathedral.

concerned say they are ready to help us provided Darlan tells them to do so, but they are not willing to follow anyone else. Admiral Estéva in Tunis says he will take orders from Darlan. Noguès stopped fighting in Morocco by Darlan's order. Recognition of Darlan's position in this regard cannot be escaped.

"The gist of the agreement is that the French will do what they can to assist us in taking Tunisia. The group will organize for effective co-operation and will begin, under Giraud, reorganization of selected military forces for participation in the war."

On November 12 a British detachment was welcomed with open arms. On the 15th a battalion of American parachutists landed in the region of Tébessa and, on the following day (also dropped by parachute) the vanguard of the 78th Division (Major-General Eveleigh) occupied Souk el Arba in Tunisia, some 90 miles from the capital.

Confused situation in Tunisia

In Tunis Admiral Estéva, the Resident-General, and in Bizerta Rear-Admiral Derrien were both caught between contradictory orders. They had anxiously awaited an Anglo-American landing, but the first troops to arrive on the airport at El Aouïna were German paratroopers in the afternoon of November 9. The situation was all the more delicate in that General Barré, the Supreme Commander in Tunisia, had only 12,000 men under him and that, in accordance with orders dating back to 1941, but still in force, he had to cover the concentration of the Algerian army on the line Béja–Téboursouk–Le Kef in case of invasion by the Axis powers. This line would have afforded him the necessary hilly features to make a stand. In Tunis, however, the Germans and Italians were being reinforced at the rate of 1,000 men a day.

On November 17 Lieutenant-General Walther Nehring, recovered from his wounds sustained at Alam el Halfa, took over command of XC Corps, containing the Axis forces which had landed in Tunisia. At 1100 hours on the 19th he summoned General Barré to clear the way for him into Algeria, and when this was refused he tried in vain to cross the Medjerda at Medjez el Bab. General Anderson advanced with part of his 78th

△ *French sailors march off under the eyes of their American captors to a P.O.W. camp.*
▽ *A review of French and U.S. troops in Casablanca late in December 1942. It was the swift transition from the above stage to co-belligerency that prompted the Germans to take over Vichy France to prevent her going over to the Allies.*

Division, reinforced by a detachment of the British 6th Armoured Division and a group from the 1st American Armoured Division. On November 30 the Allies had established contact with Barré and had advanced to within 12 miles of Tunis.

The end of victory hopes for 1942

Under these circumstances it is easy to see how Eisenhower optimistically came to announce to Washington the imminent fall of Bizerta. But Nehring was reinforced daily and fighting from his bases, whereas the understrength British V Corps under Lieutenant-General C. W. Allfrey had its communications very stretched. The long guns of the German Pzkw IV and VI Tiger tanks were also making their presence felt. Finally, heavy rains turned the makeshift airfields into lakes and grounded the Anglo-American planes, whereas the Luftwaffe was taking off without difficulty from the tarmac strips at Tunis-El Aouïna and Bizerta. On December 10 the British 1st Army had lost Djedeïda, Mateur, and Tebourba again and with them 1,100 prisoners, 41 guns, and 72 tanks. With these losses went all their hopes of victory before 1943.

The French fleet is scuttled

In France, on November 27, by a fresh violation of undertakings already given, Hitler proceeded to dismember the armistice forces and attempted to seize the fleet which Admiral Laborde had not wished to send out to sea from Toulon when he heard of the German invasion of the occupied zone. The French sailors, carrying out Admiral Darlan's word given to Sir Dudley Pound at the time of the armistice, thereupon scuttled:

    one battleship
    two battle-cruisers
    four heavy cruisers
    three light cruisers
    24 destroyers
    ten submarines
    19 other miscellaneous vessels.

In spite of the surprise, the submarines *Marsouin, Glorieux,* and *Casabianca* succeeded in reaching Algiers, though the *Iris* got herself interned at Carthage. Admiral Darlan did not long survive the fleet which he had done so much to create and train. On December 24, in circumstances which have never been made clear, he was shot by a young fanatic. It can be said of him in justification that he had taken on his new duties with utter dedication and with his usual energy.

△ △ *The end of the splendid French fleet in Toulon: the destroyers* Kersaint *and* Vauquelin, *2,400 tons and five 5.5-inch guns, lie on the bottom in Toulon harbour.*
△ *A detachment of German soldiers watches with stupefaction as major units of the French fleet go up in flames.*

CHAPTER 44
CASABLANCA CONFERENCE

In his speech at the Lord Mayor's Banquet at the Mansion House on November 10, 1942, Winston Churchill commented on the recent successes of Anglo-American strategy from Montgomery's victory at Alamein to the successful Operation "Torch" landings in French North Africa. At the close of his address, which Sir Alan Brooke described as "very good", the War Premier said cautiously and with some reserve:

"This must not be taken as the end; it may possibly be the beginning of the end, but it certainly is the end of the beginning."

But the British and American governments still had to discuss and decide how best to exploit these considerable achievements; to hammer out finally the strategic shape of their joint effort in 1943. Such was the purpose of the Casablanca Conference (codenamed "Symbol"), which was attended by Churchill, Roosevelt and their chiefs-of-staff from January 14 to 23, 1943.

The two principals were luxuriously housed in adjoining villas in sub-tropical gardens; their staffs in a nearby hotel; the entire site being isolated and easily guarded. Full communications facilities were afforded by the British headquarters ship HMS *Bulolo*. Alan Brooke has left a colourful picture of Churchill at his ease amid the splendours of his borrowed villa:

"I had frequently seen him in bed, but never anything to touch the present setting. It was all I could do to remain serious. The room must have been Mrs Taylor's bedroom and was done up in

American Build up

On September 2, 1945, the United States had put into service four army groups, nine armies, 23 corps, 89 divisions. These were supported, covered and moved by 12 air forces totalling 273 air combat groups which on the day of the surrender of the Japanese Empire, were divided into five very heavy bomber, 96 heavy bomber, 26 medium bomber, eight light bomber, 87 fighter, 24 reconnaissance, and 27 transport groups. A total of 14 million young Americans were, in one respect or another, affected by the general mobilisation order which was the response to the attack on Pearl Harbor. This seems low compared with 17 million Germans who donned one of the several uniforms of the Wehrmacht or Waffen S.S. or the 22 million men and women whom the Soviet Union hurled into the heat of conflict between June 22, 1941 and September 15, 1945, but it should be remembered that all American personnel and equipment had to be built up from a minute nucleus.

The American infantry division was in no essential way different from its European and Japanese counterparts. The armoured division was different, however, with a reconnaissance battalion, four battalions of medium tanks, three battalions of infantry in half-tracks, three battalions of self-propelled 105mm howitzers, an engineer battalion, a separate engineer company, a medical battalion, a repair and maintenance battalion and other rear formations. The American armoured division had 227 tanks against the Panzer division's 160. The American armoured divisions were flexibly assembled in tactical groups known as Combat Commands. Each division had at first two Combat Commands, later increased to three.

Mussolini in Danger

Hitler's determination to continue with a war on two fronts and Mussolini's determination to continue to support his ally created discontent among the Italian leader's ministers. Mussolini instituted a reshuffle to rid himself of those like Count Ciano who saw the defeat of the Axis as inevitable and who promoted an understanding with Great Britain. The King, Victor Emmanuel III, however, wished to overthrow Mussolini's totalitarian regime and his confidante, Count Dino Grandi, President of the Fascist Chamber, continued to undermine Mussolini.

△ *Pious American expectations for moves against Hitler in 1943.*

Moorish style, the ceiling was a marvellous fresco of green, blue and gold. The head of the bed rested in an alcove of Moorish design with a religious light shining on either side; the bed was covered with a light blue silk covering with a 6-in wide *entre-deux* and the rest of the room in harmony with the Arabic ceiling. And there in the bed was Winston in his green, red and gold dragon dressing-gown, his hair, or what there was of it, standing on end, the religious lights shining on his cheeks, and a large cigar in his face!"

The choice of Casablanca

Churchill and Roosevelt had chosen Casablanca in preference to the mooted alternatives for various reasons. Iceland, though geographically convenient, did not attract for a midwinter meeting. As Roosevelt wrote to Churchill, "I prefer an oasis to the raft at Tilsit" (a reference to Napoleon's meeting with the Tsar Alexander in 1807). Constitutional considerations made it impossible for the President to travel as far as Cairo or Khartoum. On the other hand he could justify a visit to French North Africa on the score of inspecting the American forces there in his rôle as Commander-in-Chief.

Soviet Russia absent

It had been Roosevelt's original idea that the conference should be limited to the heads of the armed services and that Soviet Russia should participate. Churchill, however, pointed out that only Stalin counted in Russian circles, and that, therefore, mere service leaders could not deal with him, nor fend off the kind of searching questions he would pose concerning the relative Anglo-American contribution to the struggle against Nazi Germany. Likewise, Churchill wanted there to be a preliminary meeting between British and Americans so that the Western Allies could present an agreed strategic package to the Russians. The President was against such a meeting, "because I do not want to give Stalin the impression that we are settling everything between ourselves before we meet him." In fact on December 6, 1942 Stalin courteously declined the invitation to take part in the summit on the grounds that the war situation (the battle against the trapped German 6th Army at Stalingrad was then at its height) made it impossible for him to leave the Soviet Union. He made it clear at the same time, however, that for him the salient question for the British and Americans to decide was the opening of a Second Front in Europe by the spring of 1943.

Thus it came about that the Casablanca Conference was a purely Anglo-American affair in which heads of governments as well as service chiefs took part.

In Britain and the United States alike there had already been long and wearisome argument as to the shape of future strategy. Thanks to the close-knit planning organisation forged in Britain by the pressures of war and the personal involvement of Churchill as Minister of Defence, all this hard discussion of projects and available resources had finally resulted in an agreed strategy buttressed by facts, figures and a closely argued case. But the American side came to Casablanca with no similar agreed strategy of its own. Since in certain fundamental respects the conference finally came round to agree with the British analysis, a legend arose in America after the war that the cunning British had "conned" the innocent Americans. The record belies this: the arguments turned in the end on the realities of available logistical resources and fighting strength, not on a simple British-versus-American line-up. This is not to say that there were not underlying differences of national temperament and approach, or lurking suspicions as to the sincerity behind an apparent commitment.

Allocation of resources

At the heart of the conference discussions on grand strategy lay two inter-related questions: the proportion of resources to be allotted respectively to the war against Germany and the war against Japan, and the rival merits of making the main Allied effort against Germany in 1943 in the Mediterranean or across the Channel (Operation "Round-up"). The war against Japan–except for the Burma front–had become an exclusively American preserve controlled by Admiral Ernest J. King, the U.S. Chief of Naval Operations, a man blunt of speech and powerful of will. Grappling as he was with the problems of "Triphibious" warfare at the end of 3,000 miles of sea communications against a formidable enemy, King believed that the Pacific theatre was being dangerously starved of resources in favour of the German war with the consequent risk that the Japanese could dig themselves into a perimeter defence so strong that the allies might have great difficulties later in overcoming it. King, therefore, demanded a higher proportion of resources, even mentioning a percentage of 30 per cent as against the present 15 per cent. This would permit him to proceed with a series of step-by-step offensives aimed at retaining the initiative over the Japanese.

The British, being understandably preoccupied with Germany and enjoying little or no say over operations in the Pacific, suspected King of seeking to overturn the order of strategic priority decided at the Washington Conference in December 1941, whereby Germany was to be beaten first, and then Allied resources switched to Japan. They wanted to see this priority clearly re-affirmed, with only minimum force going to the Pacific theatre until Germany had been defeated. None the less, there was a certain refusal to face facts in so believing that the Japanese war could be virtually kept on ice in the meantime.

Brooke's argument

With regard to strategy against Germany, the British had come to the conclusion–Churchill had taken a lot of convincing–that the Allied plan agreed in the summer of 1942 (to follow the conquest of North Africa with a cross-Channel invasion in 1943) was not a practicable operation of war. Instead they wished the principal Allied effort for 1943 to take place in the Mediterranean, exploiting the victories already being won in that theatre.

Sir Alan Brooke presented the British case at the opening session of the Combined Chiefs-of-Staff Committee on the morning of January 14. He pointed out that victory over the U-boat was essential to the war against Germany: "The shortage of shipping was a stranglehold on all offensive operations, and unless we could effectively combat the U-boat menace we might not be able to win the war." On land, he went on, Germany now lay on the defensive both in Russia and North Africa, while her allies were losing heart. It was not impossible that she could be brought down in 1943. The best means of achieving this lay in affording all possible aid to Soviet Russia, stepping up strategic bombing of the German homeland, and in launching amphibious operations. The latter, in the British analysis, should take place where poor communications made it most difficult for the Germans to concentrate and maintain large forces. Whereas excellent rail communications enabled the Germans to switch seven divisions at a time from Russia to Western Europe in 12–14 days, the Alps bottleneck meant that they could only move one division at a time into Italy. In the Balkans too, communications were scanty and exposed. With such scattered territories to defend along the northern shores of the Mediterranean, the Germans would be forced to disperse their strength. An offensive in the Mediterranean would thus maintain unremitting pressure, bring more effective support to Russia than a risky cross-Channel attack, and

Air Chief Marshal Sir Arthur Tedder was born in 1890. He joined the Army in 1913, and after serving in Fiji and in France transferred to the Royal Flying Corps in 1915. After the war Tedder served in Turkey and then attended a course at the Naval War College before holding posts in the Air Ministry. Between 1936 and 1939 he was A.O.C. Far East, and in 1939 was Director of Research and Development at the Air Ministry. After transfer to the Middle East, Tedder was appointed A.O.C. Middle East in May 1941, as which he carefully built up and trained his command into a superb tactical air force, which won final mastery of the North African skies in time for the Battle of El Alamein. As a result of the Casablanca Conference, Tedder became Allied Air Commander in the Mediterranean. Eisenhower, impressed by Tedder's strategic abilities, made him Deputy Supreme Commander for the invasion of North-West Europe.

△ *The Presidential party en route to Casablanca. From left to right are Admiral William Leahy, Roosevelt, Harry Hopkins and Lieutenant Howard M. Cone.*

open up possibilities of forcing Italy out of the war and bringing Turkey in. Brooke nevertheless conceded–partly in deference to Churchill's fiercely held wishes– that the Allies should stand ready in England later in the summer to land in Europe if Germany should show signs of cracking up.

In the afternoon Admiral King argued his case for strengthening the Allied effort against Japan. The offensive in the Solomons had been undertaken in order to clear the Japanese threat away from the main line of communications between Australia and the United States, but due to shortage of reserves, it could not be pressed beyond Guadalcanal and Tulagi. A further advance, however, opened up the possibility of advancing deep into the Japanese perimeter either via the Netherlands East Indies, or via Truk and the Marianas. King contended that it was essential to maintain constant pressure in order to prevent the Japanese consolidating their defences at leisure, but that his present forces were quite inadequate to achieve this.

Thus King opened up the debate on basic strategic priorities that lay at the heart of the conference. Probing questions by Brooke and Air Chief Marshal Portal, the Chief of Air Staff, as to exactly what would be entailed by maintaining pressure on Japan revealed British uneasiness lest King's requests led to an open-ended commitment that would decisively weaken the Allied effort against Germany. King, with characteristic directness, voiced a counter-suspicion that, once Germany was defeated, Britain would leave America to finish off Japan

alone. On a suggestion by Portal, it was agreed to direct the Combined Staff Planners to examine and report on "what it was we had to prevent the Japanese from doing, and what forces we should require for the purpose".

Deadlock in planning

But after four days of work the Combined Planners remained deadlocked and, therefore, wrote separate national papers instead of a joint one. Even though the British saw the force of the American argument that the Japanese must be pushed further north away from the Australia–America line of communications, they still wished to allot the minimum resources to the Japanese conflict necessary to achieve certain tightly defined and limited objectives. The American paper argued for a much more flexible attitude by which "Germany is recognised as the primary, or most powerful and pressing enemy, and that the major part of the forces of the United Nations are to be directed against Germany in so far as is consistent with the overall objective of bringing the war to an early conclusion . . ." It was necessary, contended the American planners, to keep the initiative over Japan by forcing battles on her and so denying her the opportunity of launching offensives at times and places of her own choosing. They therefore considered that in 1943 the Allies could and should carry out offensives from their present positions in the Solomons and New Guinea aimed at reaching New Britain and the Japanese advanced base at Rabaul on New Ireland and the Lae-Salamau Peninsula on New Guinea. In the Central Pacific area, the American planners proposed a thrust through the Gilbert, the Marshall and the Caroline Islands aimed at the Japanese main fleet base of Truk. A subsidiary offensive in the Aleutians should yield Kiska and Agattu. At the same time there should be an offensive in Burma to re-open the lower Burma road in order to bring succour to Chiang Kai-shek's China, which American opinion (and in particular Roosevelt) persisted in regarding as a powerful and effective ally. The American planners also wanted a seaborne invasion of Burma (codenamed Operation "Anakim"). To carry out this strategy would, the American planners reckoned, demand an extra

210,000 men, 500 aircraft and a million and a quarter tons of shipping.

Their British colleagues, inured to waging war with scant resources, felt that this American strategy–born of a buoyant sense of America's immense industrial and human resources–was over-ambitious. They argued that only the offensives in the Solomons towards Rabaul and on New Guinea towards Lae, together with limited operations in Burma against the port of Akyab and to open a road route to China were really necessary in 1943; and that although planning for the further offensives should be put in hand, a decision as to their launching should be delayed until late in the year. In particular the British planners contended that simultaneous operations against Truk and Burma ("Anakim") "cannot but react adversely on the early defeat of Germany".

Here the British put their fingers on the basic factor in a global amphibious war such as Britain and America had to wage–the availability of assault and supply shipping and the naval forces to cover them, and above all the availability of landing craft. Since the United States were overwhelmingly the principal producer of landing craft, and since the disposition of American landing craft lay entirely with Admiral King, the British did not enjoy the strongest bargaining position.

On January 18, the Combined Chiefs-of-Staff met to grapple with the problem of composing the differences between the two papers. In the meantime, however, they themselves had been arguing about the rival merits of an offensive in the Mediterranean or across the Channel as the more effective means of relieving pressure on the Russians and weakening Nazi Germany. In these discussions, differing national traditions and attitudes to strategy again manifested themselves. Since the fall of France and the end of the Western Front in 1940, the British had had to contend with the conundrum of how to wage war with heavily outnumbered land forces against a great Continental power; a conundrum they had encountered many times before in their history. The traditional British answer lay in maritime landings in peripheral areas where the enemy could not deploy his full strength because of poor land communications. Only in the Great War had the British fielded a mass army and engaged the main body of the enemy army in protracted battles; an experience which had made a lasting and profoundly discouraging impression on British soldiers and statesmen alike. Therefore, although Sir Alan Brooke offered a convincing (and in retrospect, entirely justified) case for postponing a major cross-Channel landing until 1944 in favour of an offensive in the Mediterranean in 1943, there underlay the British position a deep unwillingness to risk directly taking on the German army until operations elsewhere (above all on the Russian Front) had decisively weakened it.

The American tradition of warfare, on

▽ *And even from occupied Europe more reinforcements arrived to swell the armed forces of the United Nations. Here the French submarine* Casabianca, *which had managed to slip out of Toulon as the rest of the French fleet was being scuttled, is seen arriving in the port of Algiers.*

△ *Vichy French reaction to the loss of North Africa was both swift and predictable—as usual it was the Jew who was behind the Allied "theft" of France's North Africa.*

△△ *President Roosevelt (in jeep) and Major-General Mark Clark (at left in windcheater) at one of the ceremonies of the Casablanca Conference. One of the questions much discussed at the conference, the invasion of Italy, was to give Clark command of an army then an army group.*

the other hand, derived from Continental European models, together with an awareness of America's huge resources. The American mind was less pragmatic than the British; it preferred a clear-cut "overall strategic concept" into which everything fitted neatly. General Marshall, therefore, thought in almost opposite terms from Brooke; his instinct was to engage the main body of the German army in the West at the earliest possible moment and by the most direct route—across the Channel. He was highly suspicious of the British preference for an "indirect approach" of strategic bombing and attacking via the Mediterranean. He had unwillingly accepted the necessity for the "Torch" landings in 1942 in place of "Round-up" (crossing the Channel), fearing nevertheless that "Torch" could lead on to further commitments that would continued to prejudice "Round-up". Now at Casablanca he saw the British arguing for exactly such a further involvement in the Mediterranean. Just as the British themselves feared that Admiral King's strategy for the Pacific could become an open-ended commitment prejudicing the war against Germany, so Marshall feared that the British Mediterranean strategy would prove equally open-ended, delaying and perhaps even preventing an eventual invasion of France. While conceding that

one of the strongest arguments in favour of the Mediterranean was that "there will be an excess of troops in North Africa once Tunisia has been cleared of Axis forces", he wanted to know whether a Mediterranean offensive would be an end in itself or a means to an end.

Brooke had already spent wearisome weeks convincing his Prime Minister that a cross-Channel landing in 1943 was simply beyond Allied resources, and he was, therefore, prepared to argue with Marshall. He pointed out in detail that the Allies would lack the land forces in the United Kingdom and the landing-craft lift to have a chance of defeating the 44 divisions the Germans could concentrate for the defence of the West without even weakening the Russian Front. Better, therefore, in his analysis, to invade Sicily from North Africa and force Italy out of the war, so compelling the Germans to find troops for the occupation of Italy and in replacement of the Italian forces garrisoning the Balkans. Brooke was not, however, looking beyond the conquest of Sicily at this time. Far from advocating a campaign on the Italian mainland, he specifically warned the Combined Chiefs-of-Staff against "accepting any invitation to support an anti-Fascist insurrection. To do so might only immobilise a considerable force to no useful purpose".

△ *German comment on the Allied discussions in North Africa had an element of truth about it, but not to the extent claimed here, with peevish Allied leaders not wishing to sit at the same table.*
◁ *The "big two" meet on the lawn of Roosevelt's villa at Casablanca.*

The Mediterranean strategy accepted

In his discussion with Marshall, Brooke was acting as spokesman for a carefully planned set of policy decisions, whereas General Marshall's arguments were merely expressing a personal view. His own air colleague, General Arnold, agreed with Air Chief Marshal Portal that operations in the Mediterranean would better force the Germans to disperse their air power than "Round-up", and that the collapse of Italy would open the way for the destruction of German oil resources and other key targets from the air. Admiral King, himself a maritime war expert, likewise saw the force of the British case in favour of the Mediterranean especially on the grounds that since the Allies had the troops in the theatre they might as well make use of them. He favoured Sicily rather than Sardinia as an objective, and promised the necessary naval support. President Roosevelt, worked on in private by Churchill, also came to favour the Sicily operation. Even some members of Marshall's own staff recognised that hard

facts told against "Round-up" in 1943. Marshall, therefore, yielded to the consensus. It was decided that there would be no "Round-up" that year except in the event of a sudden German disintegration, and the principal Allied effort would be made against Sicily. The Cross-Channel attack had to wait until 1944.

Nevertheless this Mediterranean strategy did come under further discussion at the Combined Chiefs-of-Staff meeting on January 18, when it had to be married to a final agreement on the balance of priority between the German war and the Japanese war. Brooke, deploying yet again the British arguments in favour of a fixed minimum allotment of resources to fighting Japan until after Germany had been beaten, emphasised the need for constant pressure on Germany to prevent her from recovering from her present setbacks; that was, by operations in the Mediterranean. Marshall now voiced an anxiety lest this should mean that large forces would sit around in the United Kingdom throughout the year waiting for some problematical German collapse, for such forces could be better employed in the Pacific. He was, he said, "anxious to get a secure position in the Pacific so that we knew where we were".

△ *Roosevelt meets General Henri Giraud (seated at left) on January 17, 1943. It was through Giraud that the Allies had hoped to start a rapprochement with France and so they smuggled him to North Africa by submarine.*

A compromise formula

It was Air Vice Marshal Slessor who helped break the deadlock by drafting a compromise formula which, put forward by Brooke that afternoon, was accepted by the American side, and made possible the drawing up of the final Memorandum on the Conduct of the War in 1943, formally agreed by the Combined Chiefs-of-Staff next day and later approved by the President and Prime Minister.

This memorandum constituted the strategic fruit of the Casablanca Conference, the basis of all subsequent detailed planning. "Operations in the European Theatre," it stated, "will be conducted with the object of defeating Germany in 1943 with the maximum forces which can be brought to bear on her by the United Nations." Then came the balancing clause: "In order to ensure that these operations and preparations are not prejudiced by the necessity to retrieve an adverse situation elsewhere, adequate

forces shall be allocated to the Pacific and Far Eastern Theatres." In those theatres operations were to continue with the forces allocated, with the object of maintaining pressure on Japan, retaining the initiative and attaining a position of readiness for the "full scale offensive against Japan by the United Nations as soon as Germany is defeated". The memorandum laid down that such interim operations "must be kept within such limits as will not, in the opinion of the Combined Chiefs-of-Staff, jeopardise the capacity of the United Nations to take advantage of any favourable opportunity that may present itself for the decisive defeat of Germany in 1943". Within the broad Far Eastern and Pacific strategy the memorandum gave priority to the "Anakim" operation (the seaborne invasion of southern Burma) in 1943 over the drive through the Marshall and Caroline islands on Truk, unless, in the event, time and resources permitted both.

So far as strategy against Germany was concerned, the memorandum laid down, as agreed, that the Mediterranean was to be the scene of the principal effort and Sicily the first objective; the general object being to divert German pressure from the Russian front, increase the pressure on Italy and if possible draw Turkey into the war. However, such forces as could be built up in the United Kingdom after satisfying the needs of the Mediterranean operations and the Japanese war were to stand ready to re-enter the Continent "as soon as German resistance is weakened to the required extent". Otherwise offensive action from the United Kingdom was to take the form of an intensified strategic air offensive against the German economy.

On two fundamental grand-strategic questions there had been no argument among the Combined Chiefs-of-Staff. As the opening two paragraphs of the final memorandum put it, "defeat of U-boat remains first charge on resources", and "Russia must be sustained by greatest volume of supplies transportable to Russia without prohibitive cost in shipping".

The Mediterranean and not the Channel

Hindsight casts its own light on the basic strategic decision taken at Casablanca to make the main Allied effort against Germany in 1943 in the Mediterranean rather than across the Channel. Marshall's misgivings, shared by some members of his own staff like General Wedemeyer (who bitterly claim-ed after the war that, "We even lost our shirts" to the British), that the Mediterranean option could lead to an ever deeper involvement was to be fully borne out when the Allies embarked on the long slog up the mountainous spine of Italy. Yet the British calculation that the Allies would not be strong enough to launch a victorious cross-Channel in-vasion in 1943 was shown to be correct by the relatively narrow margin by which the Normandy invasion succeeded even a year later. With regard to the British fear that the Japanese war could suck in an ever greater quantity of Allied resources, the course of events was to demonstrate just such a tendency to slippage, and despite the firm statement agreed at Casablanca whereby clear priority was accorded to beating Germany.

It remained to put the operational flesh on the strategic bones; a task which occupied the last five days of the Casablanca Conference, as the Joint Planners worked out a series of detailed planning papers to be amended and agreed by the Combined Chiefs-of-Staff. As the Memorandum on the Conduct of the War in 1943 has stated, defeat of the U-boat was crucial—and at that moment the U-boat was winning. During 1942 a total of 7,790,697 tons of Allied shipping had been sunk, the bulk of it by submarine, while only 7 million tons had been turned out by Allied shipyards, so that year by year Allied shipping resources were being progressively whittled down. Moreover Germany was producing U-boats faster than the Allies were destroying them, so that the number of operational boats had risen during the last year from 91 to 212. The key to defeating the U-boat, as the Conference agreed on the basis of the Joint Planners' paper, lay in convoy escort ships and Atlantic air cover. However the shortfall in escort ships, in view of the competition for such craft offered by amphibious operations in the Mediterranean and Pacific, meant that it would be late summer before the Atlantic convoys could be given the protection they needed. At Admiral Sir Dudley Pound's suggestion, the Combined Chiefs-of-Staff added a rider to their Memorandum on the Conduct of the War to the effect that they recognised this danger. In its resolution on the Battle of the Atlantic the Conference agreed that the U-boat must be beaten firstly by attacking its building yards and bases

▽ *General Henry Arnold and Air Chief Marshal Sir Charles Portal (right), the Chief of the Air Staff, in conversation at Casablanca. Portal was strongly in favour of more Mediterranean enterprises, as they would prevent the Germans from moving forces to Russia or the Channel coast.*

with heavy bombers; secondly by Britain and America combing their existing allocations of escort vessels for other purposes in order to meet without delay half the present shortfall on the Atlantic; thirdly by providing light escort carriers to afford convoys air cover in the mid-Atlantic "air-gap" as quickly as possible, and lastly supplying very-long-range aircraft for the same purpose.

Bombers and Convoys

The global shortage of escort vessels also affected the question of the number of Arctic convoys that could be run to Russia. The Combined Chiefs-of-Staff were determined that "supplies to Russia shall not be continued at prohibitive cost to the United Nations effort", but Churchill, mindful of Stalin's likely disappointment at there being no Second Front in 1943, argued that "no investment could pay a better military dividend" than aid to Russia, and so secured an assurance from the Chiefs-of-Staff that everything possible would be done to keep the convoys flowing even while the invasion of Sicily was under way.

Discussion of the paper on the Allied strategic air offensive against Germany brought fresh problems of clashing demands on limited available resources. Air Chief Marshal Portal, supported by General Brooke, argued that if too literal an interpretation were made of the priority accorded in the Memorandum on the Conduct of the War to bombing U-boat yards and bases, it would seriously reduce the general bombing of the German war economy. British and American airmen stood united in a faith that the bomber could play a key role in bringing Germany to her knees, even though the British air marshals were sceptical about the American belief in daylight precision bombing by unescorted bomber fleets—rightly, as it turned out. Admirals King and Pound retorted that in view of the shortage of surface escorts it was more than ever necessary to concentrate air strength against the U-boat. The final Conference Directive for the Bomber Offensive attempted to compromise between the sailors and the airmen by reaffirming the bomber-offensive's objective as "the progressive destruction and dislocation of the German military, industrial and economic system, and the undermin-

ing of the morale of the German people, to a point where their capacity for armed resistance is fatally weakened", while at the same laying down that U-boat building yards must be the priority target, followed by the German aircraft industry, transportation network and oil resources.

The way was clear for the combined British and American bomber offensive which in 1943 was to inflict grievous but never decisive damage on the German economy and end in the clear, if short-lived, defeat of both Bomber Command and the U.S. Eighth Air Force at the hands of the enemy air defence. However, despite the Chiefs-of-Staff's statement that the U-boat must be the priority target, the airmen were to prove profoundly reluctant to release aircraft from the general bombing of Germany, and the battle of the Atlantic was for some months to be starved of very-long range aircraft equipped with the new 20-cm radar—another case where conference decisions failed to be fulfilled completely.

The timing of Operation "Husky"

During the general strategic debate earlier in the Conference, it had been decided to invade Sicily (Operation "Husky") rather than Sardinia (Operation "Brimstone"), which had been the preference of the British Joint Planners and the Chief of Combined Operations, Lord Louis Mountbatten. Both Churchill and Roosevelt as well as the Combined Chiefs-of-Staff themselves favoured Sicily. The argument now turned on the planners' draft operational plan for "Husky" and its timing. Given that Tunisia would be finally captured by April, the Joint Planners reckoned that the necessary air, sea and land forces for "Husky" could not be assembled and trained before August 30. They envisaged a British invasion force based solely on Middle East ports landing on the south-east corner of Sicily while the American force, based on French North African ports, landed on the south-western coast and at Palermo. Churchill was outraged by the proposed D-Day, which meant that the Allied forces would be standing idle for four months after the conquest of Tunisia. As a result of his urging, the Combined Chiefs-of-Staff hammered out a

fresh schedule by which the Allies would seek to launch "Husky" during the July moon period. General Eisenhower, the Supreme Commander Designate, was to report back not later than March 1 as to whether this would be possible or whether "Husky" would have to be delayed into August. But Churchill was still not satisfied. With the skill born of years of cross-examining generals and admirals, he demanded convincing reasons why the operation could not be launched still sooner. Nevertheless, the Combined Chiefs-of-Staff remained adamant that if the Allies were not to risk a disastrous repulse adequate forces could not be concentrated and trained in a shorter time. Churchill would not have it. At his and Roosevelt's insistence the directive to

Eisenhower carried the rider that "an intense effort" was to be made during the next three weeks to study whether "by contrivance and ingenuity" the invasion could not be launched during the June moon period; and they returned to the charge at the end of the Conference in a note to their advisers stressing the importance of not leaving Allied forces idle beyond June. In the event the invasion of Sicily began on July 10, some six weeks earlier than the date first suggested; an instance where, as Michael Howard points out in *Grand Strategy*, Vol IV (HMSO 1972), Churchill's impatient prodding proved of great benefit to the Allied war effort.

The remaining strategic question discussed at the Casablanca Conference was

△ *Churchill and Roosevelt with some of their senior strategic advisors at Casablanca. Seated (from left to right): Admiral E. J. King, Mr. Churchill, President Roosevelt. Standing: Major General Sir Hastings Ismay (second from left), Lord Louis Mountbatten (third from left) and Field Marshal Sir John Dill (right).*

that of the rate of build-up of U.S. land forces in the United Kingdom ("Bolero") for a possible limited cross-Channel operation late in 1943 ("Sledgehammer"). On January 20 Churchill, in reporting conference decisions to the War Cabinet, wrote: "At home 'Bolero' is to go ahead as fast as our commitments allow, with a view to a 'Sledgehammer' of some sort this year or a return to the Continent with all available forces if Germany shows definite signs of collapse." Thus, just as General Marshall had always feared, the original decision for "Torch" and the fresh decision at Casablanca for "Husky" were at the expense of the creation of a mighty invasion from the UK. In July 1942 it had been expected that there would be over half a million American troops in Britain by the end of the year; in fact there were fewer than a hundred thousand, excluding

troops earmarked for "Torch". As with all aspects of Allied strategy the key factor in "Bolero" lay in shipping space. Nevertheless, on January 21 the Casablanca Conference began to tackle the problem of how to maintain the momentum of "Bolero" during 1943 despite all other commitments. General Marshall expressed the hope that American forces in Britain might be increased to some 400,000 by the beginning of July, giving five to six divisions for a "Sledgehammer" landing in France by the beginning of August; four extra divisions could be supplied in time for a mid-September attack. However, a detailed study of shipping space by Lord Leathers and General Somerwell proved much less sanguine: four American divisions in Britain by mid-August, seven by mid-September, 15 by the end of the

calculated flow of German reserves was put at five brigade groups supported by ten parachute battalions and an airborne division, with reinforcements of eight more divisions in the first forty-eight hours. But the expected total of available landing craft would only be sufficient to lift a fraction of this force. The Joint Planners, therefore, concluded that "Sledgehammer" would not be feasible in 1943 unless the German reserves had first been greatly worn down. The Conference, therefore, decided merely that planning should continue for a contingency operation by August 1 to exploit some sudden German weakness. Far more important, it was decided to accept the recommendations of the Joint Planners in their paper ponderously entitled "Proposed Organisation of Command, Control, Planning and Training for Operations for a Re-entry to the Continent across the Channel beginning in 1943" that the Allies should plan for a full-scale invasion in 1944, and that either a Supreme Commander or a Chief-of-Staff, with a nucleus staff, should be appointed without delay. The British Lieutenant-General F. E. Morgan was, therefore, appointed COSSAC, Chief-of-Staff to the (as yet undesignated) Supreme Allied Commander, with the task of planning the invasion. Here was the first step along the path of complex preparation that eventually was to lead to D-Day on June 6, 1944.

General Sir Alan Brooke was born in 1883 and entered the Army via Woolwich Academy. As commander of II Corps in 1940, Brooke fought a masterly rearguard action covering the retreat to Dunkirk, and was later that year appointed C.-in-C. Home Forces, with the immensely difficult task of organising the defences against the expected German invasion. Brooke succeeded Sir John Dill as Chief of the Imperial General Staff late in 1941, and became Chairman of the Chiefs-of-Staff Committee in June 1942. In this capacity he was at the head of the military establishment in Great Britain, with the difficult problem of translating the ideas dreamed up by Churchill into realistic terms, and dissuading their author from those that were impossible.

year. And although Churchill in his eagerness to launch some kind of "Sledgehammer" late in the summer criticised these estimates as too pessimistic, the event was in fact to prove them too optimistic.

Sledgehammer postponed

In any case, staff studies of possible "Sledgehammer" operations gave little scope for optimism. The Cotentin Peninsula, the planners thought, was "the only area with a short and easily defensible line within a reasonable distance of the beaches, and one which, at the same time, permits reasonable air support". The minimum strength needed to seize a bridgehead and defend it against the

Problems with the French

Grand strategy and operational planning were not, however, the only matters to be tackled by the President and the Prime Minister and their advisers at Casablanca; there were political questions too, the thorniest being that of the future government of French Africa, spiky as this was with the susceptibilities of Generals de Gaulle and Giraud (High Commissioner in North Africa in succession to the assassinated Admiral Darlan). The British and American governments wished to create gradually a single administration for the former Vichy colonies in Africa and those which had rallied to de Gaulle's Free French Movement; and eventually a single French national organisation, or shadow French government. This entailed in the first place getting agreement between

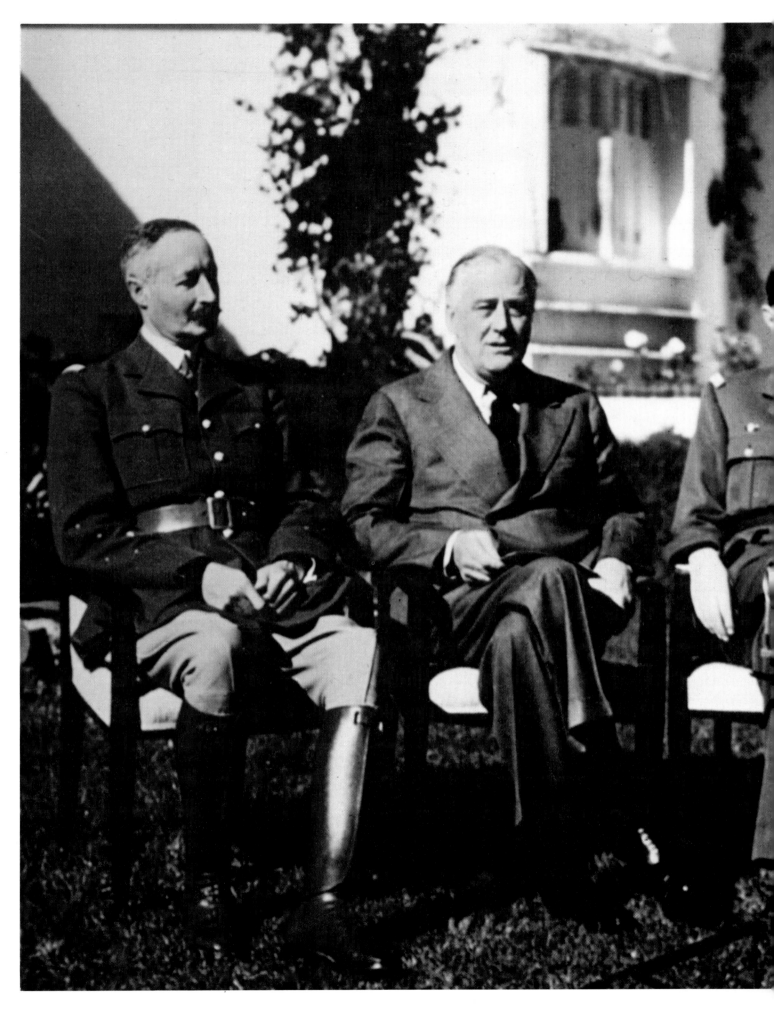

General Giraud and de Gaulle, the head of the French National Committee in London, and both leaders were, therefore, invited to Casablanca. While Giraud readily agreed to come, de Gaulle refused. He felt slighted at not having been privy to the "Torch" landings, and was highly suspicious of any deal with former Vichy elements wished on him by the Anglo-Saxons. As Churchill wrote later: "I understood and admired, while I resented his arrogant behaviour. Here he was–a refugee, an exile from his country under sentence of death, in a position entirely dependent on the goodwill of the British Government, and now also of the United States . . . He had no real foothold anywhere. Never mind; he defied all. Always, even when he was behaving worst, he seemed to express the personality of France–a great nation, with all its pride, authority, and ambition."

De Gaulle and Giraud

In order to get de Gaulle to Casablanca Churchill finally instructed Eden, the British Foreign Secretary, to warn him that if he failed to come, "The position of His Majesty's Government towards your Movement while you remain at its head will also require to be reviewed. If with your eyes open you reject this unique opportunity we shall endeavour to get on as well as we can without you". And Churchill advised Eden: "For his own sake, you ought to knock him about pretty hard."

So on January 22 de Gaulle duly arrived in Casablanca. A three-hour conversation with Giraud produced no acceptance of the Anglo-American plan for a combined French leadership and administration, but instead a characteristic Gaullist public statement by the two generals:

"We have met. We have talked. We have registered our entire agreement.

"The end to be achieved is the liberation of France and the triumph of human liberties by the total defeat of the enemy.

"This end will be attained by the union in war of all Frenchmen fighting side by side with all their allies."

So, resolutely and skilfully, de Gaulle went his own way; a way that was to end in the 1960s with himself as leader of a resurgent France dominating western Europe, from which high position he was

The controversy over this "unconditional surrender" policy has turned on the strategic wisdom of leaving the enemy nation no recourse but resistance to the bitter end, so, it is argued, binding them indissolubly to the fortunes of their fascist régimes, and hence prolonging the war. Certainly, as the Casablanca Conference records make clear, the possible strategic consequences of such a policy were never analysed and discussed. Nevertheless it remains impossible to establish how much, if at all, the demand for unconditional surrender in fact lengthened the resistance of the three enemy states, especially in view of the tight grip in which the German and Japanese régimes in particular held their peoples. It must also remain a matter of historical doubt whether it would have been of greater benefit to future peace and stability if the Allies had negotiated an armistice with some alternative German or Japanese government. The 1918 Armistice with Germany does not offer a favourable precedent.

But in any event "unconditional surrender" no more than expressed the will and wish of the British and American, as well as the Russian, peoples that this time German military power should be demonstrably and unambiguously crushed into the dust and the whole of Germany occupied. Hindsight must also take account of the deep anger felt at the time of peoples who had been wantonly attacked, bombed and occupied.

Did Churchill give his consent?

However, controversy also centres on the actual timing of the President's announcement of the policy of "unconditional surrender", and on the degree of prior consultation with his British colleague. Roosevelt himself said later that the thought came to him impromptu in the very course of the press conference:

"We had had so much trouble getting those two French generals together that I thought to myself that this was as difficult as arranging the meeting between Grant and Lee (at the end of the American Civil War in 1865, so that Lee might surrender his army)—and then suddenly this press conference was on, and Winston and I had no time to prepare for it, and the thought

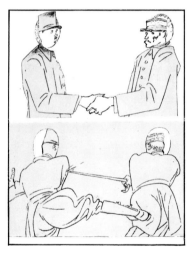

△ △ *Seeing themselves as rivals for the leadership of the French serving with the Allies, Giraud and de Gaulle did not at first see eye to eye—de Gaulle even refused to go to Casablanca at first, only arriving on January 22.*
△ *An all-too-accurate German assessment of the* rapprochement *between Giraud and de Gaulle. Previous Page: A study in contrasts at Casablanca. From left to right an indifferent Giraud, neutral Roosevelt, bored de Gaulle, and happy Churchill.*

to pay Britain and America back in full for such wartime humiliations as the peremptory summons to Casablanca.

The last formal proceedings of the Casablanca Conference took place on Sunday, January 24, 1943—a press conference given by Roosevelt and Churchill, to the astonishment of journalists who until then had had no inkling that they were absent from Washington and London. Yet it was this final press conference which of all the transactions at Casablanca led to perhaps the most lasting controversy. The American President added at the end of his address: ". . . I think we had all had it in our hearts and heads before, but I don't think that it has ever been put down on paper by the Prime Minister and myself, and that is the determination that peace can come to the world only by the total elimination of German and Japanese war power.

"Some of you Britishers know the old story—we had a General called U.S. Grant. His name was Ulysses Simpson Grant, but in my, and the Prime Minister's early days he was called 'Unconditional Surrender Grant'. The elimination of German, Japanese and Italian war power means the unconditional surrender by Germany, Japan and Italy. . . This meeting may be called 'the unconditional surrender meeting'."

popped into my mind that they called Grant 'Old Unconditional Surrender' and the next thing I knew, I had said it."

But this could not have been so, because Roosevelt spoke from notes in which the famous words appear several times.

Churchill's own later recollections of the matter seem equally at fault. In his war memoirs he wrote that although he loyally spoke up in the press conference in support of Roosevelt's announcement of "unconditional surrender", he had himself heard the President's words "with some feeling of surprise". In point of fact, it was Churchill who, at a meeting with the President and the Combined Chiefs-of-Staff on January 18, had suggested that a public statement be issued after the conference "to the effect that the United Nations are resolved to pursue the war to the bitter end, neither party relaxing its efforts until the unconditional surrender of Germany and Japan has been achieved." This was, according to Michael Howard the British official historian, the first time the phrase occurs in the official record. Furthermore Churchill referred the proposal to the War Cabinet in London, which not merely fully concurred but recommended the inclusion of Italy as well. Thus the British War Premier and War Cabinet fully and freely supported the "unconditional surrender" policy and its announcement at Casablanca.

Political considerations

The truth is that "unconditional surrender" had as much to do with appeasing mutual suspicions among the Allies as with impressing enemies. In the first place, the British and Americans recognised that Stalin could only regard Sicily as a poor substitute for a Second Front in 1943, and might well doubt the Western Allies' commitment to Nazi Germany's defeat. "Unconditional surrender" served publicly to re-assure Stalin on this point. Secondly, Admiral King had voiced during the Conference a lurking American suspicion that once Germany had been beaten the British would not prove very keen on fully participating in the war against Japan. Churchill's suggestion at the meeting of January 18 of a public statement about "unconditional surrender" was intended to allay this American mistrust; in fact, he had even offered to enter into a solemn public treaty if that should be desired by American opinion.

△ *Roosevelt addresses the press conference of January 24 in which the Allies' demand for the unconditional surrender of all their enemies was made. On January 20, in a report to the British War Cabinet, Churchill had said "I should be glad to know what the War Cabinet would think of our including in [the communiqué] a declaration of the firm intention of the United States and the British Empire to continue the war relentlessly until we have brought about the 'unconditional surrender' of Germany and Japan. The omission of Italy would be to encourage a break-up there. The President liked the idea, it would stimulate our friends in every country." In his memoirs, Churchill then states that it "was with a feeling of surprise that I heard the President say . . . that we would force 'unconditional surrender' upon all our enemies . . . In my speech . . . I of course supported him and concurred in what he had said. Any divergence between us, even by omission, would . . . have been damaging or even dangerous to our war effort."*

△ *Roosevelt's reception for the Sultan Mohammed V of Morocco (on Roosevelt's right). Behind the Sultan is Crown Prince Hassan, with General Noguès, the Resident-General of Morocco, on his left.*

Franco's opinion

Perhaps the real danger of the "unconditional surrender policy" lay in that it crystallised a British, and even more an American, concentration on winning the war, to the detriment of far-sighted consideration of the shape of post-war Europe and the post-war world. Stalin, for his part, had been looking ahead to an eastern Europe under the Soviet thumb since the autumn of 1941, a time when the German panzers were approaching Moscow. The Spanish dictator Franco, a no less shrewd and subtle politician, wrote to Sir Samuel Hoare, the British Ambassador in Madrid, a month after the Casablanca Conference about the dangers of a Russian takeover of Germany:

"If Germany had not existed Europeans would have invented her and it would be ridiculous to think that her place could be taken by a confederation of Lithuanians, Poles, Czechs and Rumanians which would rapidly be converted into so many more states of the Soviet confederation."

Sir Samuel Hoare replied in confident terms that Soviet power would be balanced after the war by the economic strength and the resources of fresh troops enjoyed by Britain and America. "We shall not shirk our responsibilities to European civilisation", he wrote, "or throw away our great strength by premature unilateral disarmament. Having, with our Allies, won the war, we intend to maintain our full influence in Europe, and to take our full share in its reconstruction." Events were to belie this assurance: not until 1944 did Churchill really awaken to the menace of Soviet expansionism in eastern Europe, while it was not until 1945, after Roosevelt's death, that American policy ceased to look on Soviet Russia as a friendly ally with whom it would be easy to get along. The years 1945–48 were to witness just that consolidation of Soviet empire in eastern and central Europe against which Franco had warned Hoare in February 1943, and just that unilateral disarmament by the Western Allies which Hoare assured Franco would not take place. The "unconditional surrender" policy announced at Casablanca encouraged the Western Allies to see victory as an end in itself.

CHAPTER 45
AFRICA: THE END

On February 20, 1943 General Alexander, whose new command had got off to such a bad start, called upon Montgomery to lend a hand in easing the enemy pressure on the British 1st Army. Eager to help, Montgomery, whose 51st Division and 7th Armoured Division had just taken the Tunisian townships of Ben Gardane, Foum Tatahouine, and Medenine, pushed his advanced forces almost as far as the Mareth Line, which General Messe was holding with six Italian and two German divisions. But on February 22, Rommel, leaving the "Centauro" Armoured Division to cope with the American II Corps, had left Thala and dashed southeast with the 10th and 21st Panzer Divisions.

The final plan was not Rommel's but Messe's and Ziegler's. The Italian 1st Army would engage the British head on, whilst an armoured force consisting of the 10th, 15th, and 21st Panzer Divisions, plus the 164th Light Division, would strike from the Matmata mountains and head for Métameur and Medenine, attacking the enemy from the rear, and driving to the Gulf of Gabès. In other words, a repeat performance of Gazala and Alam el Halfa. But this time the three Panzer divisions, with only 141 tanks, were two-thirds below strength, and air support, provided by 160 planes (of which 60 were Bf 109 fighters and 20 Stukas), was very meagre. Neither Messe nor Rommel had any great illusions about the eventual success of their attack, which was due to be launched on March 5.

Montgomery halts Rommel

Did the Allies get wind of this Operation "Capri"? Kesselring implies this, and Paul Carell, in his *Foxes of the Desert,* puts forward the same theory. But there is no need to fall back upon such a hypothesis to explain the defeat of the Axis forces in this, their last attempt to secure a change of fortune.

Montgomery knew his Rommel well, and at the first hint of an attack, he regrouped his 2nd New Zealand Division, two other infantry brigades, and two armoured brigades, and positioned them on a front all of 43,000 yards long, at right angles to Rommel's expected line of attack. 810 medium, field and anti-tank guns, including many of the brand new 17-pounder anti-tank guns being used in

Rommel Retreats

After the defeat at El Alamein, Rommel planned to reach Tunisia as quickly as possible so as to be able to surprise the Anglo-American army which had just arrived in Algeria, and inflict a severe defeat on it. His view was that if the German Army remained in Africa it would be destroyed, since it had been starved of reinforcements and supplies. While Montgomery cautiously moved up to engage German forces at Mareth, Rommel decided to deliver a heavy blow on the American 2nd Corps before the 8th Army could come to their aid. Rommel launched his offensive on February 14. The American 1st Armoured Division was forced out from the Faid Pass and defeated. Gafsa was evacuated without a shot. The Axis forces then attempted to capture the Grande Dorsale. Although Rommel wanted to thrust beyond Tébessa, forcing the Allies to pull back into Algeria, the Commando Supremo ordered an attack towards the line Thala and le Kef. Rommel regarded this order as the beginning of the end for the Axis forces in Africa and his attack on Thala failed.

battle for the very first time, lay waiting for the moment to open fire.

Firing a series of concentrated and accurate salvoes at the slightest sign of enemy movement within range, the British artillery forced Rommel to break off contact, with the loss of 52 tanks and 640 men killed, wounded, or missing. The British lost one Sherman tank and 130 men. Montgomery expressly forbade his men to pursue the enemy, who retreated behind the Matmata mountains.

Tanks against artillery

Paul Carell has described this battle of March 6 grippingly. "The grenadiers, laden with ammunition boxes, had pushed their steel helmets on to the back of their heads. Many of them had cigarettes in the corners of their mouths. They had looked exactly the same in front of the Maginot Line, on the Bug, on the Dniepr, and before Stalingrad.

"When General Cramer visited the tactical headquarters of the 21st Panzer Division, its commander, Major-General Hildebrandt, stood under shell fire with his armoured reserve looking very grave. 'We're making no progress,' he said. But Cramer could see for himself that ahead lay a heavy barrage of fire. British batteries kept up an infernal bombardment against the attacking armour. The stony ground produced a rain of shrapnel with deadly effect on grenadiers and gunners. Major Schlickes' men of the 326th Observer Detachment lay ahead with their sound-rangers and range-finders, trying to pinpoint the artillery positions. The question posed by all the commanders was 'where's all this awful artillery come from?'"

Arnim takes over

Two days later Rommel left Africa for good, but his departure was kept secret, so as not to jeopardise German morale and encourage the enemy. Colonel-General von Arnim succeeded him as C.-in-C. of Army Group "Africa", and tank specialist General Gustav von Vaerst took command of Pz. A.O.K. 5, Major-General Fritz Bayerlein going to General Messe's Italian 1st Army as chief-of-staff.

Meanwhile, O.K.W. had transferred to North Africa the "Hermann Göring" Panzer Division, the "Manteuffel" Division, and the 999th Division, recruited from among military prisoners, who were thus offered the chance of rehabilitating themselves.

But these reinforcements, which raised the number of divisions under Arnim's command to 16, should not deceive us. A number of the divisions were worn out, and the stubbornness of the two dictators forced them to defend a front nearly 400 miles long. Furthermore, it was becoming more and more difficult to supply them from Europe. The Italian merchant navy was, in fact, at its last gasp, as can be seen from the figures which the Communications Minister, Vittorio Cini, laid before Mussolini on March 3, 1943, and which can be summed up as follows:

Situation	Ships	Tons
On June 10, 1940	772	3,292,584
Additions up to March 1943	129	563,068
Total	901	3,855,652
Losses as of March 1943	568	2,134,786
Remaining	333	1,720,866

Deducting further the number of ships

▽ *The senior Allied field commander operating against the northern part of the Axis bridgehead, Lieutenant-General K. A. N. Anderson (left), commander of the British 1st Army.*

absent from the Mediterranean, liners and ships used for civil and military transport in the Tyrrhenian, Adriatic, and Aegean Seas, and those ships which were being repaired, less than 300,000 tons were available for the army. And, Cini added, despite the Tripoli evacuation, merchant navy losses through Allied action were continuing at an alarming rate: 87,818 tons in January, 69,438 tons in February.

In March and April the Sicilian Channel lived up to the reputation of the "route of Death" which the Italians had given it. During these two months, out of 132,986 tons of supplies and *matériel* which sailed from Italy, only 77,984 tons got to Bizerta and Tunis, just over a quarter of what Rommel considered necessary to allow the Axis troops to resist a major Allied offensive. This being so, the order given by Hitler and Mussolini to Arnim, after their Klessheim meeting of April 8, 1943, to hold Tunisia at all costs, was pure wishful thinking. However, the view held by Rommel, and later by Arnim, that some of the Axis forces engaged between Mareth and Cape Serrat could be evacuated from Tunisia to Italy, was also rather unrealistic.

On February 21, as the battle for Thala was at its height, General Alexander was briefing his commanders on his strategic

▽ Grants forge ahead along a half-submerged road.
▷ Sherman tanks (their unit identification markings scratched off the negative by the war-time censor) on the move. With Axis tank strength now at a low ebb, and even the Tigers neutralised by the latest British anti-tank gun, the 17-pdr, Allied armour met little opposition during this last campaign in North Africa. And while the Allies received constant reinforcements, a considerable portion of that which reached the Germans was made up of assault guns, rather than the tanks that were so desperately needed.

aims. To destroy the enemy forces engaged in Tunisia, he planned that the necessary operations should be subdivided into two phases: firstly the 8th Army would break through at Gabès and join up with the British 1st Army; then together they would crush the enemy by a careful and overwhelming concentration of land, sea, and air power.

The problem was not so much the size of the forces available, which were increasing week by week, but the time limit it imposed on Alexander. If, as the

Casablanca Conference had laid down, the Allies were to land in Sicily during the July full moon, the North African campaign would have to be decided by May 15 at the very latest.

On March 14 Alexander completed his briefing with a general directive whose chief quality was its great good sense. It ordered the regrouping of the American, British and French in separate sectors, the withdrawal of the tanks from their advanced positions, the creating of reserves, and the training of troops. The second part of the directive was devoted to a discussion by Air Marshal Coningham of air questions, and the co-operation of the air and land forces.

The Mareth Line

On March 20 Montgomery addressed a rousing order of the day to his 8th Army, now up to complete strength. Two of its points are quoted below:

"3. In the battle that is now to start, the Eighth Army:
(a) Will destroy the enemy now facing us in the Mareth position.
(b) Will burst through the Gabès Gap.
(c) Will then drive northwards on Sfax, Sousse, and finally Tunis.

4. We will not stop, or let up, till Tunis has been captured, and the enemy has either given up the struggle or has been pushed into the sea."

At 2230 hours on the same day, the 8th Army's artillery opened fire on General Messe's forces: from right to left, i.e. from the Matmata mountains up to the Gulf of Gabès, these comprised the XXI and XX Corps commanded by Generals Berardi and Orlando. Thirty minutes later, the British XXX Corps (Lieutenant-General Oliver Leese) attacked the enemy along its coastal sector.

This frontal attack was to be accompanied by a flanking attack carried out by Lieutenant-General Freyberg's New Zealand Corps which, advancing along the corridor bounded on the left by the Grand Erg and on the right by the Matmata mountains, would take the El Hamma pass, held by General Mannerini's Sahara group, and dash for Gabès, where it could cut the Italian 1st Army's lines of communication; since El Hamma was 120 miles away from Foum-Tatahouine, Freyberg had begun to advance on March 18. His 2nd New Zealand Division was reinforced by the 8th Armoured Brigade and Leclerc's column. Such was the general aim of Operation "Pugilist".

The results, however, fell far short of the aims proclaimed in Montgomery's order of the day. On the afternoon of the first day, heavy rain had made a quagmire

△ *Allied troops in the ruins of Gafsa in March 1943.*

▷ △ *The final stages of the war in North Africa.*
▷ ▽ *The wreckage of an American Lockheed P-38 Lightning, being examined by three Axis soldiers.*

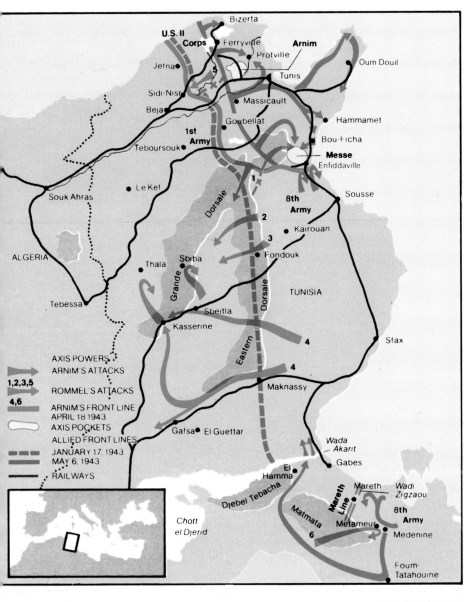

of the Wadi Zigzaou, which flowed in front of the Mareth positions and formed an anti-tank ditch 40 yards wide and 4 yards deep, so that by dawn on March 21, only six of the 50th Royal Tank Regiment's tanks had managed to get through to the opposite side and support Major-General J. S. Nichols's 50th Division, which was having a very bad time under the concentrated fire of the "Giovani Fascisti" Division under General Sozzani. An attempt by the Royal Engineers' bulldozers to breach the bank of the Wadi Zigzaou fared no better. Then the 15th Panzer Division (Major-General Willibald Borowietz), which was being held in reserve, counter-attacked with great vigour: by March 23 the attackers had only one foothold on the left bank.

Faced with this heavy setback, Montgomery became convinced that he would have to change his plan.

Instead of using the New Zealand Division in a subsidiary operation he decided that Freyberg's men would make his main thrust. Whilst the 4th Indian Division under Major-General F.I.S. Tuker was attacking the Matmata range on Messe's flank, X Corps and the 1st Armoured Division (Major-General R. Briggs) had been released in the wake of the 2nd New Zealand Division, and in order to deceive the enemy still further, Major-General G. W. E. J. Erskine's 7th Armoured Division had been brought into the front line. Truth to tell, this ruse did not have as much success as had been hoped for it, for by March 21 General Messe had already got wind of Freyberg's move, and had sent the 164th Light Division and the 21st Panzer Division towards El Hamma.

At 1600 hours on March 26, only 20 minutes after the 1st Armoured Division's last tank had entered the line, Lieutenant-General Horrocks gave the signal for the attack, greatly helped by the sun and a violent sandstorm, which blinded the enemy. The trump card, however, was probably the Desert Air Force, which hurled itself at the defence with devastating effect, making use of 22 squadrons of Spitfires, Kittyhawks, and Hurricane anti-tank fighters, and operating in an area beyond the range of the artillery. "In that area every vehicle", writes Montgomery, "and anything that appeared or moved, was shot to pieces. Brilliant and brave work by the pilots completely stunned the enemy; our attack burst through the resistance and the battle was won."

Messe pulls back

The Allied breakthrough at El Hamma took place too late to enable X Corps to reach Gabès before the bulk of the Italian army could be withdrawn. Whilst the loss of 16 infantry battalions, 31 guns, and 60 tanks was a heavy blow, Messe was nevertheless able to regroup his forces in a very strong position along the Wadi Akarit. Here he had only to defend the narrow eight-mile front that lay between the Gulf of Gabès and the lake of Chott el Djerid, and included three hills standing nearly 1,000 feet above the deep furrow that the wadi's high waters had cut into the plain.

Quite rightly, Messe discounted the possibility of a daylight attack on such a strong position; wrongly, however, he supposed that Montgomery would wait for the next full moon, April 19–20, before attacking.

Arnim decides on retreat

Since, as we have seen, time was of the essence, XXX Corps attacked at midnight on April 5, taking advantage of the darkness of the new moon. To avoid any errors they pushed forward in a single line. There was a moment of panic and confusion before the defence steadied itself and inflicted heavy losses on Major-General D. N. Wimberley's 51st (Highland) Division, going over itself to the counter-attack as dawn came up. The following day, at about midday, X Corps' tanks entered the fray, and a few hours later Arnim decided to retreat, a decision he stuck to in spite of Messe's opinion that they were not yet beaten. The battle of Mareth–El Hamma had given the Allies 10,000 prisoners, and Wadi Akarit brought in 7,000 more.

Arnim's decision was probably justified, as a result of the threat that was looming up on the Italian 1st Army's right flank. Here the dynamic General Patton had not taken long to instil a new spirit into both officers and men of his new command. On March 17 he captured Gafsa, and straightway pushed forward toward El Guettar, Maknassy, and Sbeïtla. On April 8, on the Gabès–El Guettar road, he joined up with the 8th Army, whilst on his left, the French XIX Corps moved towards the Eastern Dorsale. But neither of them was able to intercept the Italian army as it retreated north towards Enfidaville via Sfax and Sousse. This was because of the vast numbers of land-mines that Italian and German sappers had laid, one of which, on April 6, killed the bold aggressive Major-General Edouard Welvert, commanding the "Constantine" Motorised Division, as they were entering Kairouan.

On April 15, Army Group "Africa" was established along a 135-mile front marked by Cape Serrat, Jefina, Sidi Nsir, Medjez el Bab, Bou Arada, the Djebel Garci mountains, Takrouna, and Enfidaville on the Gulf of Hammamet. To defend this line

△ General the Hon. Sir Harold Alexander, commander of the 18th Army Group and Deputy Allied Commander-in-Chief, North African Theatre.

△ British infantry, supported by a Honey tank, continue their advance.

Arnim had 16 divisions. But what kind of divisions? The Italian Army's historical department, in its work on the Tunisia campaign, gives us the answer.

The "Spezia" Infantry Division and the "Centauro" Armoured Division had been all but destroyed; the "Giovani Fascisti" and the "Pistoia" Infantry Divisions, and the "Trieste" Motorised Division, could muster only 11 battalions and 84 guns between them. The army's total artillery strength consisted of 17 105-mm and 149-mm guns. Nor were the German units under Messe's command any better off: four battalions and a few guns for the 90th Light Division, two battalions and no artillery for the 164th, a dozen or so tanks and three decimated battalions for the 15th Panzer Division. The nine German divisions comprised only some 60,000 men and 100 tanks. Furthermore, petrol was in such short supply that radio communication was cut down for lack of fuel to drive the generators.

American infantry move cautiously into the suburbs of Bizerta, the main port on the north coast of Tunisia.

▽ Alexander's order of the day on April 21. The second paragraph of point 3 was all too true for the Axis – their backs were to the wall, or rather the sea, and only a tiny fraction of their number was to escape to fight again.

A different story for the Allies

And what of the Allies? During the winter, the British 1st Army had been increased by one corps (IX Corps, under Lieutenant-General J. T. Crocker), and two infantry divisions (the 1st and the 4th). The 8th Army had lost XIII Corps, the 44th Division, the 1st South African Division, and the 9th Australian Division, but had gained the two French divisions, commanded by Major-Generals de Larminat and Leclerc respectively. So including the American II Corps and the French XIX Corps, General Alexander could count on 20 divisions, all equipped (except for the French) with new *matériel* and abundant supplies. This was also the period when the British Churchill Mk. IV tank made its first appearance with the British 6th Armoured Division; it weighed 39 tons, and had a 57-mm gun, whilst its heavy armour allowed it to be used to support the infantry.

The American II Corps' advance had

not yet taken it beyond the Gafsa – Fondouk – Maknassy region, whereas ahead of it the French XIX Corps had made contact with the left wing of the 8th Army. Under Alexander's plan for eliminating the Axis Tunis–Bizerta bridgehead the main thrust was to be made by the 1st Army and the U.S. II Corps. The latter was transferred from the right to the left flank of General Anderson's forces – a delicate operation involving as it did the movement of 110,000 men and 30,000 vehicles over a distance of between 150 and 250 miles, through the 1st Army's rear. Begun on April 10, it was concluded without any serious difficulties by April 19, which speaks volumes for the administrative efficiency of General Patton's H.Q.

Omar Bradley takes command

However, on April 15, Patton took leave of II Corps, being ordered to Rabat, where Eisenhower had entrusted him with the organisation of America's share in Operation "Husky". It was therefore his second-in-command, Major-General Omar Bradley, who was given the glittering prize of Bizerta to aim for; besides his four American divisions, he also commanded a French unit consisting of the African Rifle Brigade and the Moroccan mountain troops of Colonel de Monsabert.

Dominant rôle for the 1st Army

The lie of the land had led Alexander to entrust the starring rôle in this final operation to the British 1st Army. He decided to make it the 8th Army's task to engage the enemy and immobilise its remaining slender reserves by making a strong attack on the southern half of the bridgehead extending from Bizerta to Tunis. April 21 marked a definite setback for the 8th Army which, it is true, captured Enfidaville and Takrouna, but could not break out, being beaten back on the slopes of Djebel Garci, which rise to a height of about 1,600 feet. But the slopes were not the only reason for the

defeat. The Axis forces hung on grimly, fighting desperately to maintain their positions. Alexander later wrote of the episode:

"The enemy counter-attacked continuously and, at the cost of very heavy casualties, succeeded in holding the attack. It was noticed that the Italians fought particularly well, outdoing the Germans in line with them . . . In spite of severe losses from our massed artillery fire the enemy kept up his policy of continuous counter-attacks and it became clear that it would cost us heavily to advance further into this tangled mass of mountains. General Montgomery therefore decided late on the 21st to abandon the thrust in the centre and concentrate on forcing the coastal defile."

Final decision in the balance

On the other hand, the French XIX Corps, of three divisions, had succeeded in overcoming enemy resistance in the Djebel Fifrine massif (3,000 feet), and on the morning of May 5, approached the western outskirts of Pont du Fahs. At the centre of the British 1st Army, the IX and V Corps had been attacking both banks of the Medjerda river since April 23, and although they had not defeated the enemy, they had at least beaten the Axis forces from the most favourable defensive positions; but each British attack provoked a German counter-attack, such as the "Hermann Göring" Panzer Division's thrust during the night of April 21–22, which cost it 34 out of the 70 tanks it had thrown into the action near Goubellat.

At the head of his II Corps, Major-General Bradley showed himself to be as good a tactician in practice as he had been in theory when an instructor at Fort Benning. By manoeuvring on the heights, he got the better of resistance in the Tine Valley and thus, at just the right moment, was able to release his 1st Armoured Division to cut the Tunis–Bizerta railway line at Mateur, on May 5. And on that same day, on his left, the 9th Division (Major-General Manton Eddy) and the African Rifle Brigade reached the north shore of Lake Achktel, less than ten miles from Bizerta.

On May 6 General Alexander was to deliver the final blow.

Operation "Strike"

On April 30, Alexander had detached the 4th Indian Division, the 7th Armoured Division, and the 201st Guards Brigade from the 8th Army, and allocated them to IX Corps, which had taken up a position between Lake Kourzia and the south bank of the Medjerda; with the wounding of Lieutenant-General Crocker at this time, Lieutenant-General Brian Horrocks, who has given us a colourful description of the episode, took over from him at a moment's notice. To disguise the direction of the attack still more from the enemy, the 1st Armoured Division, operating in the Goubellat area, was reinforced by a large number of dummy tanks. At 0300 hours on the first day of this attack, christened Operation "Strike", IX Corps began to advance on a very narrow front, less than two miles wide; the initial attack would be carried out by the 4th Indian Division and the 4th Division (Major-General J.L.T. Hawksworth); 6th and 7th Armoured Divisions were to form the second wave. Artillery preparation consisted of the concentrated fire of 100 batteries, whose psychological effect on the enemy was increased by the massive intervention of the whole of the Desert Air Force. Under such a battering, the resistance of the 334th Division and the "Hermann Göring" Panzer Division – or rather what was left of them – soon disintegrated. At 0730 hours, General Horrocks told his armoured divisions to head the advance; that evening there was one last skirmish when 20 tanks of the 15th Panzer Division tried to counter-attack in the Massicault area.

Tunis and Bizerta fall to the Allies

In the early afternoon of May 7, the 11th Hussars, forming the advance guard of the 7th Armoured Division, entered Tunis. At the same time, the American 9th Division liberated Bizerta, and the 1st Armoured Division bypassed Ferryville and headed for Protville to meet up with the 7th Armoured Division. This link-up, carried out on May 8, led General von Vaerst, the commander of the Axis 5th Army, to ask Bradley for an armistice. And

◁△ *The shrinking bridgehead: an Italian armoured car patrol, less than 25 miles from Tunis.*
◁◁ *Elements of the British 1st Army penetrate into the outskirts of Tunis.*
◁▽ *Victorious British infantry arrive on board a Valentine tank.*
◁ *Major-General von Sponeck, commander of the 90th Light Division (in the front of the car) arrives to surrender to Lieutenant-General Freyberg.*
▽ *The French high command in North Africa. From left to right: Juin, Catroux, and Giraud.*
▽▽ *Smiles of victory.*

on the next day, Vaerst surrendered unconditionally. "The fall of Tunis and Bizerta
clearly came to the German Command
both in Africa and Berlin, as a most severe
shock," Alexander wrote. "It was not
until the evening of the 8th May that
the High Command issued a statement
that Africa would now be abandoned and
the 'thirty-one thousand Germans and
thirty thousand Italians remaining'
would be withdrawn by sea. I commented
in a report to General Eisenhower that
night that the Navy and Air Forces would
interfere with this programme, which in
any event depended on the enemy holding
a firm bridgehead in Cape Bon, and
reminded him of Mr Churchill's words
in August 1940: 'We are waiting, so are
the fishes.'"

Thus fell the Axis' northern stronghold,
which according to Arnim's order should
have prolonged Axis resistance in Africa.
The southern stronghold, which included
the Cape Bon peninsula and the Zaghouan
mountains, was cut in two by a raid
carried out by the 6th Armoured Division,
which found the Hamman-Lif pass
undefended and on May 10 reached the

Gulf of Hammamet in the rear of the Italian
army. That same day the British V and
the French XIX Corps surrounded the
Zaghouan mountains and mopped up the
remnants of the *Afrika Korps*. Having
exhausted its ammunition, the "Superga"
Division surrendered to the "Oran" Motorised Division (Major-General Boissau) at
Sainte Marie du Zit, and in the Zaghouan
mountains the "Morocco" Motorised
Division finished off the 21st Panzer
Division, and forced the Italian XXI Corps
to surrender to General Koeltz. However,
XX Corps continued to offer valiant
resistance to the British 8th Army. When,
on the evening of May 12, the 90th Light
Division was crushed at Bou Ficha and
forced to surrender, the knell of the
Axis 1st Army sounded. In the circumstances, at 1935 hours, Mussolini sent a
telegram to General Messe: "Cease fire!
You are appointed a Marshal of Italy!
You and your men have fought the good
fight." Arnim was captured by troops of
the 4th Indian Division under the command of Major-General "Gertie" Tuker
after very heavy fighting.

"Masters of the North African shores"

The exact number of prisoners taken by
the Allies is not known. But on May 25
they held 238,243 unwounded prisoners,
including 101,784 Germans, 89,442 Italians
and 47,017 of unspecified nationality. Of
the once-mighty Axis forces, only 638
soldiers succeeded in reaching Italy,
among them Lieutenant-General Alfred
Gause, Rommel's former chief-of-staff,
Bayerlein, Major-General Josef Schmid,
commander of the "Hermann Göring"
Panzer Division, and General Sogno,
commander of the Italian XXX Corps.
The Allies, during this seven months'
campaign, had suffered 42,924 killed and
wounded. 11,104 lost their lives: 2,156
Frenchmen, 6,233 British and Empire
troops and 2,715 Americans.

On May 13, two days earlier than
planned at the Casablanca Conference,
General Alexander could send the
following restrained but joyful telegram
to London:

"Sir, It is my duty to report that the
Tunisian Campaign is over. All enemy
resistance has ceased. We are masters
of the North African shores."

△ *The war in North Africa is
finished.*
▽ *The next step – Sicily. This
pre-war Italian poster asserts
that Bizerta in French hands
was a pistol aimed at Sicily.
So it was, though the French had
no intention of using it. But
now it was not just the French.
It was the British and
Americans, with all their other
allies, and they had every
intention of firing the pistol.*

CHAPTER 46
STALINGRAD AND AFTER

On December 24, 1942, the South-West Front's offensive against Rostov forced the Luftwaffe formations which were supplying the Stalingrad pocket to make a hurried departure from their bases at Morozovsk and Tatsinskaya and establish a new base at Sal'sk, and obliged them to fly over 200, instead of 120, miles to carry out their missions. The retreat of the 4th *Panzerarmee* along the Stalingrad–Novo-rossiysk railway forced them to withdraw further on January 4, 1943. Now they had to take off from Shakhty and Novocherkassk, some 275 miles from the 6th Army's aerodromes. In this way the development of the strategic situation aggravated the consequences of the criminal irresponsibility with which Göring had boasted of being able to supply the so-called "fortress" at a rate of 500 tons a day. In fact there were only six days between January 4 and 21 during which the unfortunate forces of the besieged army received more than 100 tons of supplies.

The supplying of Stalingrad by air was therefore a failure and one of the most important causes of the surrender. This theme recurs constantly in Field-Marshal Paulus's notes: "You are in fact addressing yourself to men who are already dead", he wrote in answer to a suggestion that he make sorties. "We have stayed here on the orders of the Führer. The Air Force has left us in the lurch and has never kept its promises."

A decision was reached on three drop zones for parachuting supplies behind the divisional sectors, but Paulus objected: "If you insist on parachuting supplies, this army is finished. You must land because our most absolute need is for fuel."

Later, there is a diatribe against Göring: "At the same time I learn from Manstein and Zeitzler that, during a vital meeting, the *Reichsmarschall* said that re-supplying was not going so badly out there! . . . He has big boots so it wouldn't do him any harm to come here himself and see the situation! Clearly my reports have not been passed on to him or he has not taken them seriously. In the old days I should have made my decision at once but now they treat you like a naughty child and what else can you do but grin and bear it?"

The New Panzers

Guderian advised Hitler to hold back newly developed tanks like the Pzkw V Panther in reserve until enough had been moved up to achieve the advantage of mass and surprise. Hitler, however, was impatient to avenge Stalingrad by launching an operation in the spring with the aim of destroying the Soviet forces in the Kursk salient.

On January 1, 1943, the land forces of the *Wehrmacht*, including the Waffen S.S. had 286 divisions at the front. By the following October, there were 328, 197 of which were on the Eastern Front. Of the 41 armoured and motorised divisions, six were destroyed at Stalingrad and four in Tunisia. It was impossible to make up the losses, amounting to some 500 tanks a month, that were being sustained by the armoured divisions fighting on the Eastern Front.

Balance of Strength

Between November 19, 1942 and April 24, 1944 the Russians were on the attack for more than 11 months. On June 22, 1941 the Red Army had 4,700,000 men. By December 1944 this figure had risen to 5,100,000. In June 1941 the Red Army had 78 armoured and mechanised brigades; by the end of 1943 the figure was 290. Among other supplies the Soviet Union received, the following amount of equipment under Lend-Lease:

	Tanks	Aircraft	A.A. Guns
Great Britain	4,292	5,800	4,111
United States	3,734	6,430	
Canada	1,188		
Totals	**9,214**	**12,230**	**4,111**

Cold and starvation

The situation was serious, as is shown by a note in the O.K.W. war diary, written by its editor at the time, Helmut Greiner. The daily ration of the troops which Paulus, it must be stressed, also lived on, was by January 10, 1943, as little as $2\frac{1}{2}$ ounces of bread, 7 ounces of horsemeat (bones included), $\frac{2}{5}$ of an ounce of fats, $\frac{2}{5}$ of an ounce of sugar, and 1 cigarette.

The ordeal of hunger was increased by that of the cold because, for reasons which have not been elucidated, the winter kit of the 6th Army had not got further than the railway stations of Khar'kov and Kiev. But for weeks, under a bitter north-east wind, the thermometer read between 25 and 35 degrees Centigrade below zero. Artillery, ammunition and fuel were in very short supply, which excluded all but very localised counter-attacks.

At the turn of the year, *Stavka* revised its order of battle between the Don and the Volga. Colonel-General Eremenko was required to give up his 57th, 62nd, and 64th Armies to the Don Front which, now consisting of seven armies in all, would take on the task of liquidating the German forces besieged in the Stalingrad pocket. The Russian commander, Lieutenant-General K. K. Rokossovsky, therefore had under his command about 90 brigades and divisions against the 22 decimated and starved divisions of the German 6th Army. Attached to his staff, as representative of *Stavka*, was Colonel-General N. N. Voronov, for whom the destruction of the Germans would mean the baton of a Marshal of Artillery. The 16th Air Army (Major-General S. I. Rudenko) gave the Don Front efficient support and challenged

the aircraft of the Luftwaffe which attempted to supply the 6th Army in ever more difficult conditions.

The Russians call for surrender

Preparations for the attack had been completed when on January 8, two Soviet officers, carrying a flag of truce, crossed the siege lines, not without some difficulty, and submitted conditions for surrender to Paulus. These had been drawn up and dictated by Voronov and Rokossovsky in the most formal and proper terms.

"In view," they wrote to him, "of the hopeless situation of the German forces, and to avoid unnecessary loss of life, we suggest the following terms of surrender:
1. All German troops who are besieged, including yourself and your staff, will cease all resistance.
2. All members of the Wehrmacht will surrender by units. All arms, equipment and other property of the Army are to be handed over in good condition.

"We guarantee the lives and safety of all officers, non-commissioned officers and other ranks who cease fire, and, after the war, their free return to Germany or the country of their choice, according to the wishes of the prisoners.

"Wehrmacht troops who surrender will retain their uniforms, rank insignia, decorations, and objects of value. Senior officers will be permitted to retain their swords or daggers. Officers, non-commissioned officers, and other ranks who surrender will receive normal rations at

△ *Russian tank riders roar into action on the back of T34/76Bs. Armed with PPSh sub-machine guns, they provided the tanks with instant infantry support. When their tank was knocked out, these troops would simply board another. Their life expectancy was short, but while they lasted they brought the war to the Axis in a terrifying and novel way.*

Δ , ▷ and ▽ *Russian defenders in the pulverised remains of Stalingrad's city centre. Fighting floor by floor and even room by room they had trapped and exhausted the 6th Army, and now finally they turned to crush it. The Russians too suffered severely during the battle but whereas the Red Army could make up its losses, the Germans never recovered.*

once. Medical care will be given to the wounded, sick, and victims of frostbite."

Previously, Eremenko had tried to use captured German pilots for this purpose. He describes their reaction in these words:

"I brought them together in my headquarters and suggested that they should be sent back to Paulus. 'Make your report and say that you have been shot down and made prisoners, that you have had an interview with the Russian commander of the Stalingrad Front and that Eremenko has promised to guarantee the lives of the whole garrison of Stalingrad, if they surrender.' The pilots asked for a few minutes to consider my proposal. A lively argument arose among them. Some of them were inclined to accept my suggestion but the majority were opposed to it and soon the former came around to their point of view. Finally, one of the prisoners asked permission to ask a question. I gave it. He said. 'Sir, what would be your reaction if a Russian officer came to you and suggested that your troops should surrender?' 'I should have sent him for court martial,' I replied. 'Well,' he said, 'if we do so, one single mention of surrender and we should be shot out of hand. With your permission we shall not go back to Paulus but shall stay as prisoners, however unpleasant conditions may be.'"

No reply was made to the Russian proposals. But should one accuse Paulus of inhumanity, following the line of historians behind the Iron Curtain, because of his silence and because by that date there was no further point in the 6th Army resisting? This question may be answered perfectly well by another: what would have happened to the German forces on the Eastern Front as a whole if the defenders of the Stalingrad pocket had laid down their arms on January 9? And the answer given by Field-Marshal von Manstein in his memoirs should be recorded:

"The army had to go on fighting, even if it had no future itself. Every day it gained was of decisive importance for the rest of the German front. It would be quite incorrect to say that the war was finally lost and it would have been better to bring it to a swift end so as to spare suffering. Such a statement would simply be being wise after the event. At that time, it was not at all certain that Germany would lose the war by force of arms. A negotiated peace remained within the realm of possibility, but, in order to achieve this, we had to stabilise the situation on this part of the front, which we did in the end. To achieve this, the 6th Army had to hold down enemy forces locked in battle with it for as long as it could. Cruel necessity forced the High Command to demand this last sacrifice on the part of the valiant troops."

"Die, but save your brother," proclaimed General Dragonmirov, one of the leading lights of the Tsarist Army in the 1880's. Nevertheless, there is no doubt that this pitiless command was imposed on Paulus because of the unbelievable errors committed in the conduct of operations by Hitler and Göring. The *Great Patriotic War* records the reception encountered by the Communist refugees Walter Ulbricht, Erich Weinert, and Willi Bredel in their attempts to suborn the besieged troops with leaflets and radio appeals. It writes: "The men continued to obey Fascist discipline unquestioningly. They did not have the strength to make up their own minds to surrender over the heads of their officers and General."

The only question that arises after reading this is what would the writer of this passage have recorded about the Russian garrison of Brest-Litovsk if it had behaved any differently in July 1941 than did the 6th Army in Stalingrad.

The fate of Stalingrad sealed

On January 10, 1943, at 0805 hours, the entire artillery of the Don Front, grouped under the command of Lieutenant-General M. I. Kazakov, with more than 7,000 guns and mortars, opened a torrential fire on the positions of the 6th Army. At 0900 hours, the barrage started to creep forward, thus giving the Soviet 65th and 21st Armies (Lieutenant-General P. I. Batov and Major-General I. M. Chistyakov) the signal to attack. Within three days they had wiped out the Marinovka salient in concentric assaults. By January 17, unleashing his 24th and 57th Armies (Generals I. V. Galinin and F. I. Tolbukhin) on the left and the right, Rokossovsky, who had arrived at Voroponvo, had reconquered two-thirds of the pocket and, most importantly, had taken the aerodrome at Gumrak, the last one still left in German hands, thus preventing German aircraft from landing.

From then on, the remains of the 6th Army were supplied as far as possible by

△ Evacuating Russian wounded. German losses through the cold or wounds were so severe that only 5,000 out of the original 91,000 prisoners survived. About 150,000 Germans and about 50,000 Russians were killed.
▽ A Russian assault group in action in a ruined factory.

△ *The triumph of the Red Army.*
▽ *Medals for the defence of Stalingrad (above) and the Caucasus (below).*

dropping containers. But the end was close, for the physical and moral resistance of the defenders was becoming rapidly exhausted and, at 1600 hours on January 22, Paulus transmitted the following message to Hitler:

"After having repelled at the outset massive enemy attacks, wide and deep gaps torn in the lines of the XIV Panzer Corps and the IV Corps noon on 22. All ammunition has been exhausted. Russians advancing on both sides of Voroponvo on a 6-kilometre front. Flags waving here and there. No longer any chance of stemming the flood. Neighbouring fronts, also without any ammunition, contracting. Sharing ammunition with other fronts no longer feasible either. Food running out. More than 12,000 wounded in the pocket untended. What orders should I issue to troops who have no more ammunition and are under continuous attack from masses of artillery, tanks, and infantry? Immediate reply essential as signs of collapse already evident in places. Yet confidence still maintained in the command."

Manstein pressed Hitler to answer this telegram, which hinted at surrender, by giving his permission to Paulus to lay down his arms. But three-quarters of an hour of telephoned appeals did not succeed in weakening the Führer's savage obstinacy. And so, on January 26, as the 21st Army exploited its success of January 22 by pushing eastward, it linked up on Mamaev-Kurgan hill with the Soviet 62nd Army (Lieutenant-General V. I. Chuikov) which had so bravely defended the ruins of Stalingrad. And thus the German pocket was split in two.

In the southern pocket, General von Hartmann, commander of the 71st Division, rashly exposed himself to fire and was killed rifle in hand, while General Stempel of the 113th committed suicide. Their fellow commanders Drebber and Dimitriu surrendered the 297th Division and the Rumanian 20th Division; General von Seydlitz-Kurzbach, commander of the LI Corps, followed their example.

Paulus surrenders

Paulus, on whom, as the end approached, the Führer had conferred the supreme distinction of promotion to Field-Marshal, was by dawn on January 30 trapped in the basement of the large department store in

Stalingrad where he had set up his final headquarters. Together with his staff he accepted the inevitable. General M. S. Shumilov, commanding the Soviet 64th Army, gives the following account of his surrender:

"As our officers entered the room, Paulus was sitting on his bed. According to the accounts given by members of the Russian group, he gave the impression of a man in the last stages of exhaustion. The staff of the 6th Army was given one hour to move out. At that moment Major-General Laskin, Chief-of-Staff of the 64th Army, arrived, with my order to bring Paulus and Schmidt, his chief-of-staff, to 64th Army headquarters at Beketovka.

"A tall, wasted, greying man, in the uniform of a Colonel-General, entered the room. It was Paulus.

"Following the custom under the Hitler régime, he raised his arm as if he were about to give the regulation 'Heil Hitler' cry. But he stopped himself in time, lowered his arm, and wished us the usual German 'Guten Tag'.

"General Shumilov requested the prisoner to show his identity documents. Paulus took a wallet out of his pocket and handed the Soviet army commander his military paybook, the usual document carried by German officers. Mikhail Stepanovich looked at it and then asked for other identification confirming that Paulus was in fact the commander of the German 6th Army. Holding these documents, he then asked if it was true that Paulus had been promoted *Generalfeldmarschall*. General Schmidt declared:

"'By order of the Führer, the Colonel-

△ *The newly appointed Field-Marshal Friedrich Paulus arrives at the Soviet 64th Army headquarters to sign the surrender documents.*
◁ *A Red Army officer observes the military custom of saluting the senior officer of the German party. When Paulus discovered that he could expect civilised treatment from his captors, he relaxed and at lunch proposed a toast for his staff officers, "To those who defeated us, the Russian Army and its leaders."*

▽ *From* Simplicissimus: *the spirit of Stalingrad claims "You think you have beaten me, Stalin. But in the end I will defeat you."*

General was promoted yesterday to the highest rank in the Reich, *Generalfeldmarschall*.'

"'Then can I tell our Supreme Command Headquarters that *Generalfeldmarschall* Paulus has been taken prisoner by troops of my army?' insisted Shumilov, addressing himself to Paulus.

"'*Jawohl*,' came the reply, which needs no translation."

All the same, the northern pocket continued to hold out until February 2, and General Strecker, commanding the XI Corps, was the last to surrender.

Hitler's fury

When he heard the news, Hitler flew into an indescribable rage, the effects of which fill no less than eight pages of the stenographic record that was taken of his statements from 1942 onwards. In Hitler's words, Paulus and his staff had dishonoured themselves by preferring surrender to suicide: "When you have a revolver," he exclaimed to Zeitzler, "it's quite easy. How cowardly you must be to flinch before such a deed! It would be better to allow yourself to be buried alive! It's even worse. Paulus was in a position where he knew that his death would make the other pocket resist even more fiercely. After all, when you give the sort of example he has given, you can't expect men to go on fighting." Zeitzler replied: "There's no excuse. When you feel that you're losing your nerve, then you ought to blow your brains out first." Hitler agreed. "When your nerves give way, there's nothing else for it but [to say] 'I'm at the end of my tether' and kill yourself. One could also say: 'That man must kill himself just as in the old times [leaders] used to rush on their swords when they saw that their cause was irretrievably lost. It's self-evident. Even Varus ordered his slave to kill him.'"

It would not be out of place to reply to this tirade by pointing out that the reincarnation of the foolhardy Varus should be sought not in the cellar of the Stalingrad department store, but in the temporary headquarters at Rastenburg.

In spite of the violent anger which he showed when he heard of the German capitulation at Stalingrad, Hitler for once assumed entire responsibility, as Manstein recalls:

"On February 6 I was summoned to the

Führer's headquarters, although previously I had had no reply to all my requests for Hitler to observe what was going on in our front with his own eyes, or to send for that purpose at least the Chief of the General Staff or General Jodl.

"Hitler began the meeting by saying: 'As for Stalingrad, I alone bear the responsibility. I might perhaps say that Göring gave me an inaccurate picture of the Luftwaffe's capabilities of supplying the Army from the air and so I could possibly make him take some of the blame. But I myself have appointed him to succeed me and so I must accept the responsibility entirely myself.'"

The toll

The cold facts of the matter were that the Russians buried 147,200 German and Rumanian dead in the Stalingrad pocket, while they themselves suffered 46,700 dead, according to Marshal Eremenko. These figures illustrate the savagery of that final battle. The five corps and the 22 divisions (two Rumanian) which perished left in Russian hands slightly more than 91,000 prisoners, including 24 generals and 2,500 officers, as well as more than 6,000 guns and 60,000 motor vehicles. The only troops to escape the trap by being flown out were 24,000 sick and wounded and 18,000 specialists or high-ranking officers marked down for promotion. Of the 91,000 prisoners, very few were still alive in 1950.

After the surrender, the Russians cele-

△ *Paulus, his face drawn with strain, sits twitching as he is interrogated at the Russian H.Q. After a successful career as a member of the General Staff under General Halder he was given command of the 6th Army. He was a man of ability, having taken part in the campaigns in Poland, Belgium, and France. He saw the need for more supplies, but when there was a chance of breaking out of the Stalingrad pocket, he remained stubbornly loyal to Hitler's command not to retreat.*

▽ *Colonel-General Andrei Ivanovich Eremenko, aged 39, aggressive optimist and a favourite of Stalin. He commanded the troops of the Stalingrad Front.*

brated their victory. Recalling the moment, Marshal Eremenko recounts the following story:

"During the evening, at the very modest dinner to which the city council entertained us, General Shumilov, commander of the 64th Army, whose units had taken Field-Marshal Paulus prisoner together with his Staff, handed the German's personal weapon over to Nikita Sergeivich [Khruschev], saying: 'The weapon of the defeated Field-Marshal belongs by right to the commander of the Stalingrad Front, which has taken all the weight of the Nazi attack and also an important part in our counter-offensive.'

"Nikita Sergeivich came to see me on his way back to the front headquarters. I was in bed, with constant and cramping leg pains. Comrade Khruschev gave me an account of his day and then handed me a small burnished metal revolver: 'It's Field-Marshal Paulus's personal weapon. The Commander of the 64th Army hands it over to the commander of the Stalingrad Front, now happily no longer in existence. I consider that it is yours by right, Andrei Ivanovich.'

"So I took the pistol gratefully, as a symbol of the unforgettable days of the great battle."

The Russians move on

As described above, the defeat of the Rumanian 3rd Army and the Italian 8th Army in the great bend of the Don had forced *Gruppe* "Hoth", which was moving towards the pocket, to suspend its offensive on the evening of December 23, 1942. Already extremely weakened, it was thrown back by Colonel-General Eremenko, who had just been opportunely reinforced by the 2nd Guards Tank Army (Lieutenant-General R. Ya. Malinovsky.) On December 29, Hoth lost Kotel'nikovo, two days later Elista, on the Kalmuk Steppe, and, on January 2, moved back behind the Tsimlyansk–Remontnoye line. Of course, in the battles themselves Hoth had not lost the 571 tanks that the special Moscow communiqué claimed he had, for he had never more than 200 under his command. All the same, the troops of the Russian South Front now saw the road to Rostov open to them. The South Front had replaced the Stalingrad Front on January 2, under the same commander, Eremenko.

△ *With tank support, a group of German soldiers moves off into the winter fog. They are dressed in greatcoats, for despite the pleas of Paulus, the special winter uniforms for the 6th Army remained stacked in railway wagons far behind the lines.*

△ *American comment: the last kick of the Cossack dance.*

The Caucasus abandoned

Conditions were worsening day by day. After a long struggle, on the night of December 27–28, Colonel-General Zeitzler had managed to get Hitler to sign an order to Army Group "A", fighting in the Caucasus between Tuapse, Nal'chik, and Mozdok, to begin a full-scale retreat. On January 5 Eremenko was holding Tsimlyansk on the left bank of the Don and was thus 165 miles from Rostov, while Colonel-General von Mackensen's 1st *Panzerarmee* had only just recrossed the Terek, at Prokhladnyy, 365 miles from the same point. In this situation the commander of Army Group "Don", Manstein, would have preferred his fellow-general Kleist to speed up, whereas the latter was retreating slowly and methodically in order to keep his *matériel* and evacuate his depôts properly.

Two circumstances, however, spared Army Group "A" and Colonel-General von Kleist the fate of Paulus and his 6th Army. In the first place, there was no real aggressive pursuit by the Transcaucasus Front's troops, fighting under the command of General I. V. Tyulenev. His Northern Group (Lieutenant-General I. I. Maslennikov), consisting of four armies and two corps of Cossack cavalry, did not succeed in troubling the 1st *Panzerarmee's* retreat to any serious degree, and the Black Sea Group, (Lieutenant-General I. E. Petrov) with its three armies, in spite of a few local successes, was not able to interfere with the withdrawal of the German 17th Army.

But the most important point was that Manstein's able manoeuvring, on the left bank of the Don and along the Stalingrad–Novorossiysk axis, had put a very successful brake on the advance of Colonel-General Eremenko, which had been very serious for a short time. On January 21, the 2nd Guards Tank Army forced the Manych at Proletarskaya only to be thrown back on the 25th by the 11th Panzer Division, sent in at the right moment by the army group commander under Lieutenant-General H. Balck's excellent leadership. A few days later the German 1st and 4th *Panzerarmee* moved back over the bridges at Rostov together and without too much of a delay. On Hitler's orders the 17th Army, with eight German and three Rumanian divisions, established itself on the Taman' peninsula with its right at Novorossiysk, vainly attacked by Petrov in an amphibious operation, and its left backed up against the Sea of Azov.

In fact, Hitler had not given up his Caucasian dream; sooner or later, he thought, the chance would come for him to break out of the bridgehead and seize the Kuban' oil-wells. In vain did Manstein try to put him on his guard against detaching these troops. Since the Hungarian 2nd Army had collapsed completely, broken on the Voronezh Front, the last days of January were ominous with the threat of a second Stalingrad, menacing not only Army Group "A" but also Army Group

▽ *The remains of the 6th Army shuffles through the ruins of Stalingrad. After the men had been moved to a temporary camp, a typhus epidemic broke out, killing about 50,000 of the exhausted survivors. Many more were to die while being marched to camps in the hinterland of Russia. Here they were put to forced labour and the last of them only returned in 1955. Nearly all the 24 generals who were captured survived their imprisonment, and indeed Paulus became a member of the anti-Nazi "Free Officers' Committee" and made broadcasts over Moscow radio.*

△ △ *German tanks move towards a burning village in a counter-attack. If troops could be forced into the open their chances of surviving a night were slim, and each side fought to win cover or deprive its enemies of it.*

△ *Soldiers of the German 208th Infantry Division in a quiet sector of the Russian front.*

"Don" and Army Group "B"–in other words all those German and satellite forces fighting between Novorossiysk and Kursk.

German disorder

Manstein had his work cut out trying to prevent the armies of the South-West Front (Lieutenant-General N. F. Vatutin) from engulfing *Gruppe* "Hollidt" and crossing the Donets near Kamensk-Shakhtinskiy and Voroshilovgrad, which would have opened the way dangerously towards Taganrog. So the defeat of Army Group "B" burst upon him like a thunderbolt in his headquarters at Stalino.

Overall command of this third act of the Soviet winter offensive had been entrusted to Lieutenant-General F. I. Golikov, commanding the Voronezh Front. His left wing, positioned in the region of Kantemirovka, faced the Italian Alpine Corps, and his right, to the north-west of Voronezh, was in contact with the German 2nd Army (Colonel-General von Salmuth.) On December 20, 1942 Golikov received orders from *Stavka* to crush the enemy forces between Kantemirovka and Voronezh, principally the Hungarian 2nd Army under Colonel-General Jany.

For this purpose, Golikov divided his forces into three main attack groups. On his left, the 3rd Tank Army (Lieutenant-General P. S. Rybalko) would move out from a line stretching from Kantemirovka

to Novaya Kalitva and push in a north-westerly direction towards Alekseyevka; there it would make contact with the 40th Army of Major-General K. S. Moskalenko, which in its turn would move off from the bridgehead that the Russians had kept at Storogevoye on the right bank of the Don, 100 miles south of Voronezh. In that way the Hungarian 2nd Army would be caught in a pincer while, by using the bridgehead at Bobrov, the XVIII Corps (Major-General Sykov) would attack in the centre and try to cut through the enemy's rear and meet Rybalko's right wing. Although it is true, as the *Great Patriotic War* states, that the attacking forces had superiority only in artillery and armour, their superiority in these two arms must have been considerable.

With two armoured corps and eight armoured brigades, Golikov must have had about 900 tanks to face the 19th and 27th Panzer Divisions and the Hungarian 1st Armoured Division (15 tanks). As for the artillery, it should be noted that when the Russian 40th Army moved out of the Storogevoye bridgehead, its advance was heralded by a barrage laid down by 750 guns and howitzers and 672 mortars, in other words by 179 guns per mile. Furthermore, one-fifth of the Russian artillery, including medium calibre 122-mm and 152-mm guns, fired directly at enemy positions which had been pinpointed for a long time. On January 13, after a ferocious two-hour bombardment, the armour of the Soviet 3rd Tank Army was seen to move forward, 48 vehicles to each mile of front. Success was total. Not only did the Hun-

garian 2nd Army disintegrate under the powerful thrust, but the XXIV Panzer Corps and the Italian Alpine Corps, on the right, were also swept away in the defeat. As a result, by January 19 Rybalko's tanks were already close to Valuyki on the Oskol, 75 miles from their jumping-off point. In addition, the Hungarian rout endangered the German 2nd Army, which was positioned between the Don above Voronezh and the region north of Kursk, linking Army Group "B" with Army Group "Centre" (Field-Marshal von Kluge). To sum up, the break-up of the German front had taken place in a few days over a front of more than 215 miles from Livny to Kantemirovka, while Manstein had no firm positions left on the Donets above Voroshilovgrad.

△ One of the orderly cemeteries which the Germans left from Moscow to the borders of the Reich. After Stalingrad the soldier who was sent East was a hero or martyr whose chances of survival were low compared to his comrade in the West.

▽ A Sturmgeschütz *III with infantry in their reversible winter uniforms. These suits had a white or grey or camouflaged face, and were fitted with hoods and draw cords.*

△ Field-Marshal von Manstein in a briefing with his staff on the Donets front. After a series of victories in the early years of the war, he was to show great versatility in grim defensive battles in the East. His success in the field was of assistance when he came to deal with Hitler, from whom he was able to win concessions.

▽ German machine gunners cover an exposed road junction on the outskirts of Khar'kov.

Russian exploitation

At that moment, Colonel-General A. M. Vasilevsky, who had overall command of the Voronezh and South-West Fronts, slipped the leash on his two subordinate commanders. Golikov crashed through the remains of Army Group "B" while Vatutin, on his left, received orders to attack Army Group "Don" across the Donets. Golikov moved swiftly west and south-west and, on February 8, his 60th Army (Major-General I. D. Chernyakhovsky) took Kursk, which had been held against all attacks the previous winter, while his 40th Army moved through Belgorod and Volchansk, and his 3rd Tank Army, further to the south, described a pincer movement which would give it Khar'kov. Vatutin, passing through Kupyansk, reached the Donets on February 7, crossed it the following day at Izyum and Balakleya, and fanned out south of the river. All in all, the style of campaign of May 12, 1942 was being repeated, but with better chances of success than the previous year for, on one hand, the German armies had been bled white and on the other, the Russian forces of the South-West Front had Manstein in a trap, both on the Mius front and on the Donets at Voroshilovgrad. In those circumstances, Stalin thought that, on February 6, he could safely order the South-West Front to "Seize Sinel'nikovo with the 6th Army and then, with all speed, Zaporozh'ye, so as to cut the enemy off from all possibility of retreat on the west bank of the Dniepr over the bridges at Dniepropetrovsk and Zaporozh'ye."

In the same tone an order was dispatched to the Voronezh Front to press energetically on to Poltava so as to reach the Dniepr near Kremenchug. But, as the *Great Patriotic War* correctly points out, this *ukase* took no account of the losses suffered by Golikov and Vatutin during six weeks of attacks which had taken them 200 and 240 miles respectively from their supply bases. Some armoured brigades, for example, had been reduced to six tanks and some infantry battalions to 20-odd men. Even the better off units were absolutely exhausted.

△ *Panzers in the Caucasus. The troops who had thrust south in July and August 1942 had now to be extracted before they were trapped by the Russian winter offensive. Once more Hitler's reluctance to give up ground made this operation more hazardous than it would have been in normal conditions.*

Hitler confers with Kluge and Manstein

To consider Stalin's order feasible would also imply a complete lack of respect for the readiness, determination, and boldness of Field-Marshal von Manstein. In circumstances which were close to tragic, Manstein showed himself to be one of the most outstanding tacticians of his time, more than anything because to extract his armies from the serious situation in which they were trapped, he had to fight on two fronts; against the Russians and, moreover, against Hitler. The obstinacy of the latter was no less difficult to combat than the determination of the former.

We have already seen how the wills of Hitler and Manstein had clashed concerning the mission to be entrusted to the 1st *Panzerarmee* as it retreated from the Caucasus. It was, of course, true that the commander of Army Group "Don" had obtained permission from the Führer to engage it on the Donets after *Gruppe* "Hollidt" had been withdrawn; but it had been obliged to leave behind some of its forces, including the 13th Panzer Division, on the Taman' peninsula. This allowed Vatutin to pursue his outflanking manoeuvre towards Mariupol' on the Sea of Azov.

On February 6, following the defeat of Army Group "B", Hitler summoned Field-Marshals von Kluge and von Manstein to his headquarters at Rastenburg to study the situation. Without making too many difficulties, he authorised Kluge to carry on with Operation *"Buffle"*, which he had been refusing for months. This operation consisted of methodically evacuating the Rzhev salient. With the troops recuperated in this way, he could extend the 2nd *Panzerarmee* southward. It would link up again with the 2nd Army and prevent all enemy attempts to exploit the victories on the Voronezh Front and the Bryansk Front (Lieutenant-General M. A. Reiter) by taking Orel in an outflanking move.

Hitler's discussion with Manstein was more heated. In the latter's opinion, the situation demanded the urgent evacuation of the Don–Donets salient between Rostov and Voroshilovgrad, except that Hollidt would defend the original Mius position and the 4th *Panzerarmee*, once reformed after being evacuated from the salient, would move swiftly behind the 1st *Panzerarmee* and take up position on its left. In that way there would be a link-up with the *Waffen* S.S. I Panzer Corps, which was arriving at Khar'kov precisely at that moment. The enemy would be prevented from penetrating in the direction of Dniepropetrovsk. However, the decision had to be taken there and then for, given the state of communications, Colonel-General Hoth would need a fortnight to get his forces into place. To all this Hitler replied with involved arguments that the shortening of the front would also benefit the enemy, which was untrue, for the Germans had the advantage of interior lines of communications. Hitler also added that the thaw would once more make the Don and the Dniepr natural obstacles, and so on. In the end, Manstein got his way, but only just.

On February 12, O.K.H. announced that Army Group "B" had been dissolved. This decision placed the 2nd Army, retreating west of Kursk, under Kluge's orders and gave Manstein authority over the Khar'kov sector, where the *Waffen* S.S. Panzer Corps was in great danger of being encircled by the armies of General Golikov. Should the capital of the Ukraine be evacuated or not? This question gave rise to another tense situation between Army Group "South", which had replaced Army Group "Don", and the Führer's headquarters at Rastenburg. In this case, however, it was settled over the heads of the parties on the initiative of General Hausser, commander of this armoured force, who abandoned the city during the course of February 15 and fell back on the Krasnograd–Karlovka region.

Manstein's view prevails

Two days later, accompanied by Field-Marshal Keitel and Generals Jodl and Zeitzler, Hitler arrived at Zaporozh'ye, to which Manstein had transferred his headquarters. There was a large map of the campaign marked as follows:
1. in the new 6th Army (ex-*Gruppe* "Hollidt") zone, the enemy had crossed the Mius at Matveyev-Kurgan; and
2. in the 1st *Panzerarmee* zone, a cavalry corps had reached the railway junction at Debal'tsevo while at Grishino an enemy armoured column had cut the Voroshilovgrad – Dniepropetrovsk railway line. However, the Soviet drives had been contained in the end and were even being pushed back. By contrast there was a gap of more than 60 miles between Pavlograd and Krasnograd, through which Russian armour was advancing, clearly directed against the elbow of the Dniepr. It was true that with the 4th *Panzerarmee* in line or almost, this corner could be nipped off by pushing the I *Waffen* S.S. Panzer Corps to join Colonel-General Hoth as he moved in.

Hitler was slow to admit this reasoning as, for reasons of prestige, he would have preferred the *Waffen* S.S. to begin its campaign by recapturing Khar'kov. Manstein, however, answered Hitler's points by indicating that the thaw was moving from south to north and a counter-attack in a southerly direction was urgent, leaving aside the question of retaking Khar'kov. Without a southward attack, even if the city was retaken, the Germans

risked being hemmed in by mud. For the third time, Manstein won the battle of words. But even so, in the meantime, General Vatutin's flying columns had reached Novomoskovsk, only 20 miles from Dniepropetrovsk, and also Sinel'-nikovo, 40 miles from Zaporozh'ye. Therefore Manstein sighed with relief when the Führer and his retinue returned to Rastenburg by air on the afternoon of the 19.

Manstein's successes

Army Group "South" unleashed a counter-offensive on February 21. In this it broke the rule which seemed, in the judgement of the most prudent, to sum up the experience of 1918: contain, and only then counter-attack. It is true that there were insufficient numbers of infantry available for containment and that Manstein had command of 13 divisions of armour or of *Panzergrenadiers*, in all about 800 tanks, including a considerable number of Pzkw VI Tigers. But the Russians misunderstood the reshuffling of Manstein's forces. This is how the *Great Patriotic War* describes the situation:

"Both the South-West Front command and Soviet Supreme Command were led to believe from the enemy's retreat from the lower Donets to the Mius and the transfer of his armoured and motorised divisions from around Rostov to near Konstanti-novka, that the Germans intended to evacuate the Donets basin and retire behind the Dniepr. That is why Supreme Headquarters kept to its decision to develop its attack as soon as possible."

The result of this error of judgement and of the German initiative was a series of battles and clashes in which the clumsier Russians did not come off best.

On February 22, attacking due south from Krasnograd, the S.S. I Panzer Corps (1st *"Leibstandarte" Panzergrenadier* Division and 2nd *"Das Reich" Panzergrenadier* Division) crushed the Russian forces attacking Novomoskovsk as they advanced; then, reinforced by the 3rd *"Totenkopf" Panzergrenadier* Division of the *Waffen* S.S., the corps pushed on hard towards Pavlograd where it came under the 4th *Panzerarmee*, which Manstein was pushing towards Lozovaya at the same speed. During these strategic moves, Lieutenant-General M. M. Popov's armoured force was utterly destroyed and, with its defeat, the entire South-

The conquerors who stayed behind.
△ *A German soldier, frozen where he fell among the litter of war, bears witness by his inadequate clothing to Germany's unpreparedness for the severity of the Russian winter.*

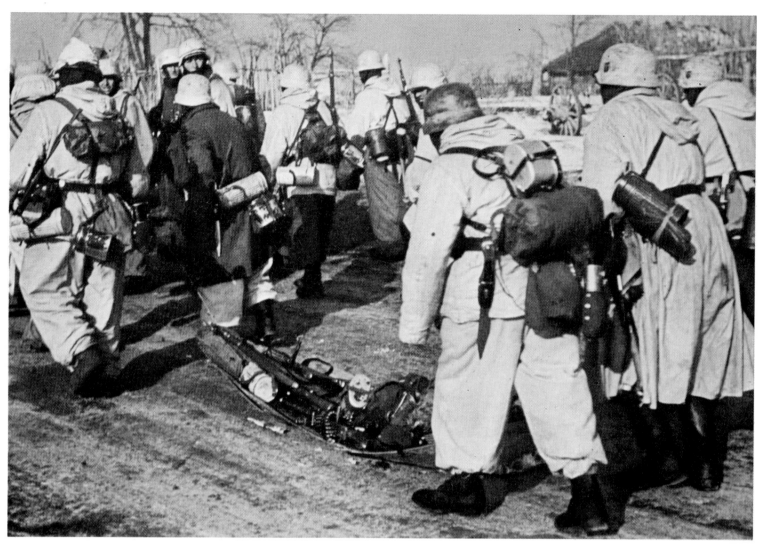

West Front behind the Donets was forced into flight.

Khar'kov retaken

Though this retreat was justified in the circumstances (General Vatutin had lost 32,000 killed and captured, 615 tanks, and 423 guns), it nevertheless exposed the left wing of the Voronezh Front, which was now threatened halfway between Khar' kov and Poltava. On March 5, the 4th *Panzerarmee* hit the Soviet 3rd Tank Army hard near Krasnograd. Then a pincer attack enabled the S.S. I Panzer Corps to "lay Khar'kov at the feet of the Führer" on March 14, 1943. *Gruppe* "Kempf", fighting to the north of the city, drove forward at the same time and, on March 18, its *Panzergrenadier* division, the *"Gross- deutschland"*, reoccupied Belgorod.

The III and XL Panzer Corps of the 1st *Panzerarmee* mopped up the Debal'tsevo, Makeyevka, and Kramatorskaya pockets. The result of this drive was that the VII

Guards Cavalry Corps (Major-General Borisov), the IV Guards Mechanised Corps (Major-General Tanichikhin), and the XXV Tank Corps (Major-General Pavlov) found themselves trapped and then surrounded. The bridgehead at Matveyev-Kurgan, on the west bank of the Mius, was retaken by the 6th Army.

The spring thaw

About March 18, the thaw and the resultant mud caused operations to come to a halt between Kursk and the Sea of Azov. On that day, an O.K.W. communiqué proclaimed that Manstein's counter-attack had cost the enemy more than 50,000 killed, 19,594 prisoners, 3,000 guns, and 1,410 tanks. Without even questioning the figures, it is easy to put them into proportion by revealing that, in contrast, the Red Army had destroyed between 40 and 45 German and satellite divisions – a quarter of the forces the Russians had before them – in four months.

CHAPTER 47
CRISIS IN NEW GUINEA

At the beginning of March 1942 Japanese bombs were falling on the eastern half of New Guinea, the great jungle-covered island off the northern coast of Australia. The bombers came from Rabaul on the island of New Britain, to the east.

Rabaul, the capital of territory mandated to Australia at the end of World War I, which included the Bismarcks and a strip along the northern coast of New Guinea, had been captured on January 23 by the Japanese Army's 5,000-man South Seas Detachment (Major-General Tomitaro Horii) supported by the Navy's 4th Fleet (Vice-Admiral Shigeyoshi Inouye). Sailing into its spacious harbour, ringed by smoking volcanoes, the invaders in a few hours forced the small Australian garrison to scatter into the hills.

The Japanese found Rabaul "a nice little town", with wide-eaved bungalows surrounded by red hibiscus. General Horii, the conqueror of Guam, rounded up the white civilians and sent them off to Japan in the transport *Montevideo Maru* (they were all lost *en route* when the ship was sunk by an American submarine). Then he began building an air base. Admiral Inouye helped to make the

△ *They saved Port Moresby and turned the tide in the Owen Stanleys: Australian troops, fording a river in New Guinea.*
◁ *Native stretcher-bearers in New Guinea resting in a coconut grove, while carrying American front-line wounded to hospitals.*

base secure by occupying Kavieng on New Ireland to the north. To the south-east, bombing took care of Bougainville, northernmost of the long string of Solomon Islands.

The towns of Lae and Salamaua, in the Huon Gulf in the east of New Guinea, had been heavily bombed in the preliminary attack on Rabaul on January 21. The civilians fled, some on foot to the wild interior, some in native canoes down the Solomon Sea, hugging the New Guinea coast. One party, after a voyage of about two weeks, put in at Gona, an Anglican mission on the coast in Australia's own Territory of Papua, in the south-east of New Guinea.

The arrival of the refugees from the Mandated Territory was long remembered by Father James Benson, the priest at Gona. The big sailing canoes against a flaming sunset sky brought through the surf "thirty-two woefully weatherbeaten refugees whose poor sun- and salt-cracked lips and bearded faces bore evidence of a fortnight's constant exposure." With only the clothes they fled in, "they looked indeed a sorry lot of ragamuffins". Next morning they began the five-day walk to Kokoda, a government station about 50 miles inland. From there planes could take them to Port Moresby, the territorial capital on the Coral Sea, facing Australia.

Planes flying from Kokoda to Port Moresby had to skim the green peaks of the Owen Stanley Range, the towering,

jungle-covered mountain chain that runs the length of the Papuan peninsula. After a flight of about 45 minutes they put down at a dusty airstrip in bare brown foothills. From the foothills a road descended to Port Moresby, in peacetime a sleepy copra port with tin-roofed warehouses baking in the tropical sun along the waterfront. A single jetty extended into a big harbour; beyond, a channel led to a second harbour large enough to have sheltered the Australian fleet in World War I.

Because of its fine harbour and its position dominating the populous east coast of Australia, Port Moresby was heavily ringed on military maps in Tokyo. On orders from Imperial General Headquarters the first air raid was launched from Rabaul on February 3. The bombers did a thorough job and returned unscathed. Port Moresby's handful of obsolete planes and small anti-aircraft guns was no match for modern Japanese aircraft.

Star of the Japanese air fleet was the Mitsubishi A6M Zero fighter-bomber, one of the best planes of the war. Armed with two 20-mm cannon and two 7.7-mm machine guns, it could carry 264 pounds of bombs and was fast and agile. Its range of 1,150 miles and ceiling of 32,800 feet also made it invaluable for reconnaissance.

To facilitate the bombing of Port Moresby, some 550 miles from Rabaul,

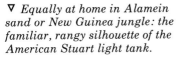

▽ *Equally at home in Alamein sand or New Guinea jungle: the familiar, rangy silhouette of the American Stuart light tank.*

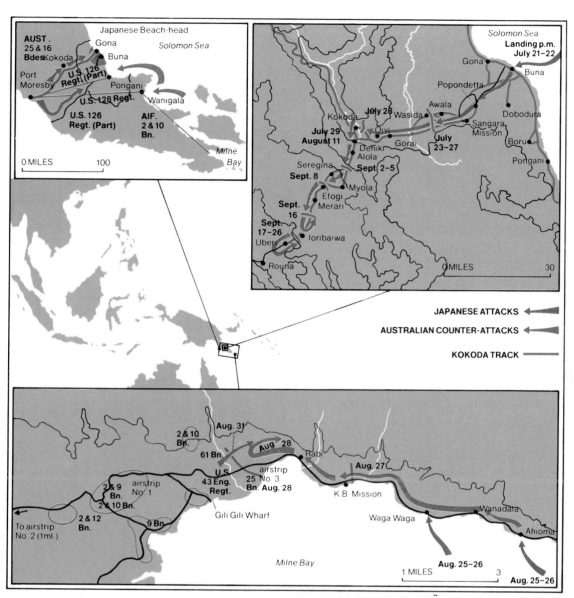

JAPANESE ATTACKS

AUSTRALIAN COUNTER-ATTACKS

KOKODA TRACK

△ A dense column of smoke marks the grave of an Allied plane, destroyed in a surprise Japanese raid on the air base at Port Moresby.
◁ The Japanese attacks and Australian counter-attacks on New Guinea.
▽ Australian soldiers survey the bodies of four dead Japanese, killed in the destruction of their jungle pillbox.

Tokyo ordered General Horii to occupy Lae and Salamaua, Lae to be used as an advanced air base, Salamaua to secure Lae. At 0100 hours on the morning of March 8 a battalion of Horii's 144th Regiment made an unopposed landing at Salamaua–the first Japanese landing on New Guinea. An hour later Inouye's Maizuru 2nd Special Naval Landing Force (S.N.L.F.) marines occupied Lae. The naval force, which included engineers and a base unit, then took over at Salamaua. Horii's infantrymen returned to Rabaul to await orders for the next move in the south-west Pacific.

The offensive planned

When Lae and Salamaua were captured, the next move was being hotly debated at Imperial General Headquarters in Tokyo. The Navy, flushed with its easy victories

△ *How to cross rivers in New Guinea without getting wet: an Australian demonstrates a "Flying Fox" ropeway platform.*

▽ *American sappers hack a road through the dense jungle of New Guinea.*

in south-east Asia, wanted to invade Australia. During operations against the Dutch/Portuguese island of Timor, from February 19 carrier aircraft had repeatedly bombed Australia's north-western coast, with little opposition. The east coast was lightly defended, since the bulk of the Australian Army was still in the Middle East. Naval officers believed that the invasion would need only five divisions.

Army officers objected, arguing that to conquer and hold the vast continental area would require 12 divisions and a million tons of shipping–far more than the Army could afford. The Navy warned that the Allies would use bases in Australia for counter-attacks on Japanese bases. This point was reinforced by the news in late March that General Douglas Mac-Arthur had arrived in Australia from the Philippines.

The argument went on for two weeks, at times coming close to blows at the Army and Navy Club. At the end of March a compromise was reached. Australia would not be invaded, but Port Moresby would be captured. This move, with the conquest of Samoa, Fiji, and New Caledonia out in the South Pacific, would isolate Australia by cutting her supply line from the United States.

On April 20 the south Pacific operations were postponed in favour of an ambitious Navy-sponsored plan to take Midway and the Aleutians; but preparations went forward for an amphibious assault on Port Moresby, codenamed Operation "MO". General Horii issued the orders on April 29, an auspicious date, for it was the Emperor's birthday. The landing was to take place on May 10.

Operation "MO"

On May 2, while the South Seas Detachment was boarding its transports, a force left Rabaul harbour for the small island of Tagula in the southern Solomons to establish a seaplane base in support of Operation "MO". It landed without opposition the following day, and a few days later put a construction unit ashore on the large island of Guadalcanal to build an airfield.

The Port Moresby invasion force steamed south from Rabaul on May 4 in five transports, well escorted. Off Bou-

gainville the convoy was joined by the light carrier *Shoho*, with six cruisers. Two fleet carriers, *Shokaku* and *Zuikaku*, stood by south of the Solomons. As the invasion convoy was nearing the eastern point of New Guinea on May 7, the carrier *Shoho*, in the lead, was attacked by U.S. carrier planes and sunk, along with a cruiser. Admiral Inouye then ordered the transports back to Rabaul.

The following day the Battle of the Coral Sea was fought between the U.S. carriers *Lexington* and *Yorktown* and the Japanese *Shokaku* and *Zuikaku*–the first carrier battle in history. One Japanese carrier was damaged, the other lost most of her planes. The *Lexington* was sunk. The battle was therefore not a clear-cut victory for either side; but the invasion of Port Moresby had been blocked. For this, credit was due to the U.S. Navy

cryptanalysts in Hawaii who had cracked the Japanese fleet code and thus enabled the Allies to intercept the convoy.

Operation "MO" was not abandoned, only postponed; and the release of Japanese forces from the Philippines after the surrender of Bataan and Corregidor on May 6 made an expanded operation possible, with the Yazawa and Aoba Detachments at Davao and the Kawaguchi Detachment at Palau added to the South Seas Detachment, all to come under the 17th Army (Lieutenant-General Haruki-chi Hyakutake), which was established on May 18.

In Tokyo, euphoria was at its height. At Army headquarters in late May, Seizo Okada, a war correspondent assigned to the South Seas Detachment, had to fight his way through a crowd of "provincials" (Japanese Army slang for

▽ *Pushing the jungle road across a gulch over a log bridge.*

△ This detail from a Japanese painting vividly expresses the desperate fight put up by the Japanese in their do-or-die attempt to take Port Moresby.

Plans for operations in the southern Pacific had to be revised. Assaults against New Caledonia, Fiji, and Samoa were postponed indefinitely; and, for lack of carriers, Operation "MO" was changed from an amphibious assault to a land attack on Port Moresby over the·Owen Stanley mountains, to be made by the South Seas Detachment with the help of the 15th Independent Engineer Regiment (Colonel Yosuke Yokoyama).

An advance echelon under Colonel Yokoyama, consisting of the engineers, a battalion of Horii's 144th Infantry Regiment, a company of marines of the Sasebo 5th S.N.L.F., and some artillery, anti-aircraft, and service units, in all about 1,800 men, was to land between Gona and Buna, an Australian government station about ten miles down the coast, advance inland to capture Kokoda, and prepare they way for Horii's main force to cross the Owen Stanley Range. Reconnaissance Zeros had spotted a red ribbon of earth winding over the mountains and assumed it to be a road. The engineers were to put it into shape to take trucks, if possible, or at least pack horses.

While the Yokoyama Force was embarking in Rabaul harbour, General Hyakutake on July 18 prepared a plan to assist Horii with a flanking seaplane attack based on Samarai at the entrance to Milne Bay, the 20-mile long, 7-mile wide bay at the eastern end of New Guinea. The Navy was to seize Samarai on August 25 with the help of a battalion of the Kawaguchi Detachment. In this latest version of Operation "MO", the Yazawa Detachment, consisting mainly of the 41st Infantry Regiment (Colonel Kiyomi Yazawa), was allocated to Horii.

civilians) clamouring for permission to go abroad with the Army. After receiving his credentials from a major, Okada asked for a pair of army boots. "Behind a screen that stood by the Major some staff officers were talking and puffing at cigarettes. One of them, as plump as a pig, broke in, 'Hey, what are you talking about? Boots? Don't worry about your boots. You'll get lots of beautiful ones out there–damned beautiful enemy boots'.

"The mocking words drove the other officers into a fit of boisterous laughter. They too, like myself or any other Japanese, were puffed up like toy balloons by the 'brilliant initial success' of the Pacific War."

A week later came news of the first crushing setback. At Midway on June 7 the Japanese Navy was decisively defeated by the U.S. fleet, with a heavy loss of carriers.

Advance to Kokoda

Late on the afternoon of July 21, the Yokoyama Force, in three heavily-escorted transports, began landing on the New Guinea coast just east of Gona. Allied planes arrived and damaged two transports, but only 40 men were lost, and there was no other opposition. At Gona the missionaries had fled, and Buna was found to be deserted when the marines arrived next day to start building an airfield. Colonel Yokoyama concentrated his army troops at a point about half-way between Gona and Buna, where a corduroy road led inland for about 15 miles.

On the evening of the landing the infantry battalion (Lieutenant-Colonel Hatsuo Tsukamoto) and a company of engineers began the march inland, about 900 men with torches, some on bicycles, with orders to "push on night and day to the line of the mountain range".

Half-way to Kokoda they were fired upon by a few Australian and native soldiers, but these were easily dispersed. The natives melted away into the jungle. The Australians, part of a company of raw militiamen, tried to stop the invaders by destroying the bridge that carried the road over the Kumusi river, but when the Japanese threw up a bridge and pressed on, they retreated. On the night of July 28, in a thick mist, Tsukamoto bombarded Kokoda with mortars and a mountain gun and drove the defenders out.

The Japanese were puzzled by the weakness of the opposition. They did not know that the Allies, after recovering from the surprise of the landing, had persuaded themselves that the object of the landing was only to establish airfields in the Buna area. The Australians found it impossible to believe that the Japanese would attempt an overland attack on Port Moresby. The "road" over the mountains was only a native footpath, two or three feet wide.

Known as the Kokoda Track, the path crossed a range of mountains described graphically by an Australian who had made the crossing on foot: "Imagine an area of approximately one hundred miles long. Crumple and fold this into a series of ridges, each rising higher and higher until 7,000 feet is reached, then declining in ridges of 3,000 feet. Cover this thickly with jungle, short trees and tall trees, tangled with great, entwining savage vines." The days were hot and humid, the nights cold; frequent afternoon rains made the track "a treacherous mass of moving mud".

By August 21, when the main Japanese force got ashore under cover of a storm, Horii had landed on the New Guinea coast a total of 8,000 Army troops, 3,000 naval construction troops, and some 450 marines of the Sasebo 5th S.N.L.F. At the head of a formidable body of fighting troops he rode into Kokoda astride his white horse on August 24.

He found that Colonel Tsukamoto's infantry had already pushed up the Kokoda Track for several miles and taken the next village, Deniki, from which the Australian militiamen, evidently reinforced, had been trying to retake Kokoda. Defeated at Deniki, they had withdrawn up a steep slope to Isurava. This was to be Horii's first objective. He began shelling it on August 26.

△ G.Is tackle heavy jungle.
▽ Australians peer cautiously at some Japanese killed beside the track. Japanese sick and wounded, left behind by the retreating Japanese, frequently proved a great menace to the advancing Allies by lying in wait and firing at the first sight of an Australian or American soldier.

The Japanese fighting man

Horii's men had two 70-mm howitzers, outranging any Australian weapon on the Kokoda Track, and light enough to be manhandled over the mountains. They

△△ *Douglas A-26 Invader bombers head out for an air strike.*
△ *American airmen line the bar at "Sloopy Joe's", a popular canteen on the Port Moresby airfield for a quick cup of tea and a snack.*
▷▷ △ *One for the record: a Combat Photography Unit takes pictures on the scene of another jungle battle.*
▷▷ ▽ *Australians at rest in a native village. In the background can be seen a line of native recruits, dubbed "Fuzzy-Wuzzy Angels" for their magnificent work in carrying supplies and bringing out the wounded.*

the rain or mist or in the dark. They cannot conceive night to be a proper time for battle–though it is excellent for dancing. In these weaknesses lie our great opportunity." In night attacks the Japanese smeared their faces with mud; officers wore strips of white cloth crisscrossed on their backs so their men could follow them in the dark, or doused themselves with perfume and issued orders to "follow your noses".

The Japanese soldier was admirably equipped for jungle warfare. He was camouflaged by a green uniform and green leaves stuck in a net on his helmet; under his helmet he wore a cloth to keep sweat from running into his eyes. He had been instructed to add salt to his tea and salt plums to his rice. He was used to carrying heavy loads–the infantryman about 100 pounds–consisting of rice, powdered bean paste, powdered soy, hand grenades, rifle ammunition, a shovel, a pickaxe, and tenting; the artilleryman and engineer carried some 16 additional pounds.

Seizo Okada, arriving at Kokoda with Horii's headquarters, observed that the soldiers had made "a kind of woodman's carrying rack" for their load and "like pilgrims with portable shrines, carried it on their backs. Now they plodded on, step by step, supported by a stick, through those mountains of New Guinea".

Progress over the mountains

At Isurava, Horii met unexpected resistance. From ground so high that the Japanese referred to it as "Mt. Isurava", the Australians poured down a heavy fire that stopped him for three days. On August 28 his casualties were so heavy that a Japanese officer wrote in his diary, "The outcome of the battle is very difficult to foresee."

That evening, at his command post on a neighbouring hill lit by fires in which his men were cremating their dead, Horii learned the reason for the repulse: the untrained Australian militiamen of the 39th Battalion had been reinforced by experienced regulars of the 21st Brigade, brought home from the Middle East. Horii ordered his reserve forward from Kokoda and on the afternoon of August 29 launched an onslaught that drove the

had an efficient machine gun, the *Juki*, with a rapid rate of fire. They knew how to use their weapons to best advantage, outflanking and encircling prepared positions. They had been taught that they must not be captured, even if wounded. Their manual read, "Bear in mind the fact that to be captured means not only disgracing the Army but that your parents and family will never be able to hold up their heads again. Always save the last round for yourself." They would fight to the death.

They were adept at night operations and preferred to attack in the rain. The manual told them that "Westerners– being very haughty, effeminate, and cowardly–intensely dislike fighting in defenders out of Isurava. By the evening of August 30 the Australian forces were in full retreat up the Kokoda Track.

General Horii subjected them to constant pressure, using alternately his 144th (Colonel Masao Kusunose) and his 41st (Colonel Yazawa) Infantry Regiments. Following closely to keep the Australians off balance he gave them no time to prepare counter-attacks, outflanking them from high ground, and bombarding them with his mountain guns at ranges they could not match. His troops crossed mountain after mountain, "an endless serpentine movement of infantry, artillery, transport unit, infantry again, first-aid station, field hospital, signal unit, and engineers".

Between the mountains, swift torrents roared through deep ravines. Beyond Eora Creek the track ascended to the crest of the range, covered with moss forest. "The jungle became thicker and thicker, and even at mid-day we walked in the half-light of dusk." The ground was covered with thick, velvety green moss. "We felt as if we were treading on some living animal." Rain fell almost all day and all night. "The soldiers got wet to the skin through their boots and the undercloth round their bellies."

Coming down from the crest on the morning of September 7, slipping and sliding on the muddy downward track, the Japanese vanguard found the Australians preparing to make a stand on the ridge behind a ravine at Efogi. During the morning Allied planes came over, strafing and bombing, but in the thick jungle did little damage. The following day before dawn the Japanese attacked, and by noon, in bitter hand-to-hand fighting that left about 200 Japanese and Australian bodies scattered in the ravine, they pushed the defenders off the ridge.

In mid-September the Australians, reinforced by a fresh brigade of regulars, the 25th, tried to hold on a ridge at Ioribaiwa, only 30 miles from Port Moresby, so near that when the wind was right the drone of motors from the airfield could be heard. But on September 17 the Japanese, who still outnumbered them, forced them to withdraw across a deep ravine to the last mountain above the port, Imita Ridge.

At Ioribaiwa, Horii halted, his forces weakened by a breakdown in supply and by Allied air attacks. In any case, he had orders not to move on Port Moresby until an advance could be made by sea from Milne Bay.

Disaster in Milne Bay

Bad luck dogged the Milne Bay operation from the start. The second week in August, the battalion of the Kawaguchi Detachment assigned to the 8th Fleet (Vice-Admiral Gunichi Mikawa) for the operation was sent instead to help clear Guadalcanal in the Solomons, where U.S. Marines had landed on August 7. A replacement battalion could not arrive in time. Admiral Mikawa, who had won a brilliant naval victory at Guadalcanal on August 9, would have no help from the Army at Milne Bay.

At the last minute the target was changed. Reports from reconnaissance planes in mid-August that the Allies were building an airfield at the head of Milne Bay near Gili Gili led planners to change the landing from Samarai, at the mouth of the bay, to Gili Gili.

The Japanese knew little about the Gili Gili area, in peace-time the site of a coconut plantation. Low-lying rain clouds usually protected it from reconnaissance. Estimating that it was held by not more than three infantry companies and 30 aircraft, Mikawa allotted only about 1,500 men to the invasion. Most of them were to come from Kavieng: 612 marines of the Kure 5th S.N.L.F. (Commander Shojiro Hayashi), 362 16th Naval Pioneer Unit troops, and 197 marines of the Sasebo 5th S.N.L.F. The Kavieng convoys were to sail up Milne Bay and land at Rabi, about three miles east of the Gili Gili jetty. At the same time, 353 marines of the Sasebo 5th S.N.L.F. at Buna, carried in seven big, wooden, motor-driven barges, were to land at Taupota on the Solomon Sea side and march over the mountains to Gili Gili.

The overland force was the first casualty of the operation. As it chugged down the coast under cloud cover on August 24 it was sighted and reported by a "coastwatcher"–one of the Australian organisation of planters and officials who had taken to the hills with wireless sets. The following day the marines beached the barges on Goodenough Island and went ashore to eat lunch. At that moment the clouds parted and 12 Australian P-40 fighter planes swooped low and destroyed the barges. The Buna marines were left stranded.

Two cruiser-escorted transports with Commander Hayashi and the first echelon of the Kavieng marines arrived safely at the head of Milne Bay in a downpour on the night of August 25. Shortly before midnight Hayashi began the landings at a point he believed to be Rabi. But he had no reliable map, and in the darkness and rain he landed about seven miles to the east on a swampy coastal shelf where the mountains came down almost to the water. His only means of advance westward toward Gili Gili was a muddy 12-foot track.

Hayashi was a stickler for night operations. He waited until darkness fell on August 26 to attack his first objective, a plantation astride the track at K. B. Mission, lightly held by Australian militia. Preceded by a flame-thrower, his troops tried to outflank the defenders by wading into the bay on one side and the swamp on the other. By dawn they had almost succeeded; but at first light they retired into the jungle.

The following night the attack was resumed in greater force, the second echelon from Kavieng having arrived. This time the Japanese used two small tanks–the first tanks to be landed on the New Guinea coast. They each had a strong headlight which, shining through the rain, enabled them to illuminate the Australian positions while the attackers remained in darkness. With the help of the tanks, Hayashi's men cleared K. B. Mission, crossed the Gama river beyond, and before dawn on August 28 were attacking an airstrip that U.S. engineers were building between Rabi and Gili Gili. There, lacking the tanks, which had bogged down in mud and had had to be abandoned, they were stopped by heavy fire. At daylight they withdrew into the jungle.

Commander Hayashi had already asked Admiral Mikawa to send him reinforcements. He had been deprived of his overland force and had lost a considerable part of his food and ammunition when Allied aircraft sank the steel barges ferrying it ashore. He had met ground opposition greater than he expected and found the terrain worse than anything he could have imagined. Reinforcements landed on the night of August 29 under cover of a heavy mist. They were 568 marines of the Kure 3rd S.N.L.F. and 200 of the Yokosuka 5th S.N.L.F., all under Commander Minoro Yano who, being senior to Hayashi, took command of operations.

Before one o'clock on the morning of August 31 the combined Japanese forces launched a furious assault on the airstrip. They were beaten back by intense fire from anti-tank guns, heavy machine guns, and mortars, expertly sited with a clear field of fire and backed by heavy artillery positioned in the rear. Before day broke, three Japanese bugle calls rang out, the signal for retreat.

The Australians pursued. By nightfall on September 1 they had retaken K. B. Mission. Commander Yano, setting up defences on the track to block the pursuit, cabled Admiral Mikawa on September 3 for permission to withdraw from Milne Bay. He himself had been wounded; Hayashi had been killed; he had lost 600 men and had more than 300 wounded on his hands. The rest of the men, most of

them suffering from trench foot, jungle rot, and tropical fevers, could not hold out.

Mikawa sanctioned the evacuation. By dawn of September 6, Japanese ships, carrying the 1,300 men remaining of the 1,900-man invasion force, were on their way to Rabaul.

The crowning misfortune of the Milne Bay invasion was the miscalculation of the strength of the defenders. Unknown to the Japanese, the Allies had landed at the head of Milne Bay between June 25 and August 20 some 4,500 Australian infantrymen, supported by about 3,000 Australian and 1,300 American engineer, artillery, and service units.

Japanese fanaticism had met its match; but it had been a close run thing.

◁ ◁ A smashed Japanese transport. Allied air supremacy made it impossible for the Japanese to send sufficient seaborne reinforcements either to New Guinea or to the Solomons.
◁ ◁ ▽ The advance continues, past the wreckage caused by a recent bombardment.

△ Japanese dead, huddled in the trench where they fell.
◁ ◁ A keen look at a knocked-out Japanese light tank.

△ *Moving out a stretcher case from an advanced dressing station. Without facilities such as this, the Japanese losses rose even higher than the figure of those killed or wounded in combat.*

▽ *The luckier ones: Australian "walking wounded".*

The Japanese retreat

On September 20 General Horii called together his commanders and praised them for their success in crossing "the so-called impregnable Stanley Range". At the proper time they were "to strike a crushing blow at the enemy's positions at Port Moresby". The halt at Ioribaiwa would give the tired troops, many of them wounded and ill, a chance to regain their fighting strength. Most were hungry; little or no rice remained in the dumps. Horii had already ordered detachments to dig up native gardens in the area and sent parties over the mountains to bring up provisions from the rear. To block an Australian attack, he ordered his engineers to build a stockade of tree trunks.

The Australians did not attack; but no supplies came from the rear, no Zeros flew over. "An atmosphere of uneasiness," noted Okada, "stole over the mountain, a feeling that things were not going well at Guadalcanal. On September 24 in a night of drizzling rain the blow fell. A signal commander came into Horii's tent with a message from Imperial General Headquarters ordering Horii to withdraw his force from the Owen Stanleys to the coast at Buna."

The reason for the order was a major defeat at Guadalcanal on September 15, in which the Kawaguchi Detachment had been virtually wiped out. Imperial General Headquarters decided to subordinate everything to the retaking of Guadalcanal. Once that had been accomplished, it would be possible to resume Operation "MO". In the meantime, Horii's mission was to defend the Buna beach-head.

For Horii, the order "to abandon this position after all the blood the soldiers have shed and the hardships they have endured" was agonising. He sent his chief-of-staff, Lieutenant-Colonel Toyanari Tanaka, to break the news to the battalion commanders. Some of them almost rebelled, urging a desperate, single-handed thrust into Port Moresby.

On September 25 the movement back over the mountains began. The order to withdraw had crushed the spirit of the soldiers, which, Okada reported, "had been kept up through sheer pride". For a time they remained stupefied. "Then they began to move, and once in retreat they fled for dear life. None of them had ever thought that a Japanese soldier would turn his back on the enemy. But they were actually beating a retreat!"

As soon as they accepted this bitter fact, "they were seized by an instinctive desire to live". Each tried to flee faster than his comrades. Passing by bodies of men killed in the fighting of early September, already rotting and covered with maggots, the soldiers stopped only to dig for taroes or yams. They found little; the fields had been dug up almost inch by inch. By the time they reached the crest of the Range, they were fleeing from starvation, a greater menace than the Allied planes roaring overhead or enemy guns rumbling in the rear.

To delay the Australian pursuit, which began on September 27, Horii ordered a rearguard battalion to make a stand on the heights above Eora Creek. There it was attacked by troops of the Australian 16th Brigade on October 21. Reinforced from Kokoda and Buna, it held out for seven days, long enough for Horii to evacuate Kokoda and set up his last defences, at Oivi and Gorari in the foothills between Kokoda and the Kumusi river.

At Oivi, strongly fortified by Colonel Yazawa, the Australians attacking on November 5 could make no headway; but at Gorari, where Colonel Tsukamoto was in command (Colonel Kusunose having been evacuated because of sickness and wounds), an Australian assault on November 10 succeeded, after heavy fighting. Yazawa's position was now untenable. He withdrew his 900-man force after dark that evening over a little-known track leading north-east to the mouth of the Kumusi. With him was General Horii, who had been on an inspection trip to Oivi.

The rest of the South Seas Detachment, about 1,200 men, began crossing the Kumusi river on the night of November 12, guided by the light of a bonfire. They had no bridge. Incendiary bombs dropped from Allied planes had burned the wooden bridge built in August by the Yokoyama Force and defeated all attempts to replace it. The soldiers crossed in six-man folding boats, then pushed on in the darkness toward Buna.

Seizo Okada crossed with the vanguard. Stopping at a newsmen's hut about half-way to Buna, he watched the "men of the mountains" as they moved along the road, day and night, toward the coast. "They had shaggy hair and beards. Their uniforms were soiled with blood and mud and sweat, and torn to pieces. There were infantrymen without rifles, men walking on bare feet, men wearing blankets or straw rice-bags instead of uniforms, men reduced to skin and bone plodding along with the help of a stick, men gasping and crawling on the ground."

The stretcher-bearers, themselves too weak to carry stretchers, dragged the sick and wounded to the overcrowded field hospital near Buna and laid them on straw mats in the jungle. "The soldiers had eaten anything to appease hunger—young shoots of trees, roots of grass, even cakes of earth. These things had injured their stomachs so badly that when they were brought back to the field hospital they could no longer digest any food. Many of them vomited blood and died."

Later, Okada learned that General Horii had drowned while on the march northwards with Yazawa. Horii, anxious to rejoin his men at Buna, tried to cross the lower Kumusi river on a log raft. In the swift current the raft carrying him and Colonel Tanaka overturned.

So ended, in tragedy, the overland march on Port Moresby. Misgivings about it had been felt by at least one officer at Imperial General Headquarters, Colonel Masanobu Tsuji, who warned, "Cross the mountains and you will get the worst of it." At the end his verdict was, "a blunder".

Though the Buna beach-head was reinforced from Rabaul and held out for several months, Operation "MO" was never resumed. Beginning early in October, the attention of Imperial General Headquarters was diverted from New Guinea and focused on Guadalcanal.

◁ ◁ ▽ *The confidence of victory. An Australian platoon advances.*
△ *Fitting out a paratrooper.*
▽ *The first hot soup after eleven days of combat for the victors of Buna.*

CHAPTER 48
GUADALCANAL: ORDEAL

Allied resources in the Pacific were stretched to the limit in the summer of 1942, and the greater part of the American war effort was directed toward the European theatre and the defeat of Germany. The Japanese, checked only by the crucial naval Battle of Midway in June 1942, were riding a tide of victory and easy conquests. Tulagi Island, site of the headquarters of the British Solomon Islands Protectorate, was not on the original schedule of targets the Japanese had projected for the South Pacific, but it too was taken as the victory tide swept onward. The seaplane base and radio station that the Japanese had established on Tulagi did not particularly worry the Allies, but reports in June 1942 that Japanese troops had begun levelling an aircraft runway on the kunai grass plains of the Lunga river on the large island of Guadalcanal, 20 miles south across Sealark Channel from Tulagi, were a different story. Here was a clear threat to the shipping lifeline stretched across the South Pacific from the U.S. to New Zealand and Australia.

At the time the Japanese moved to Tagula, the nearest American troops were on the outposts of Espiritu Santo in the New Hebrides, 550 miles away. An airfield was rushed to completion there, to be ready by the end of July to support operations against the Japanese. The American Joint Chiefs-of-Staff, urged on by the Navy's leader, Admiral Ernest

▽ *America hits back: in the landing-craft, heading for the beaches.*
▽▽ *Moment of truth: the Marines storm ashore on Guadalcanal.*

J. King, had decided to mount a ground offensive to halt the enemy drive to the south and to provide a base for offensive operations against Rabaul, the Japanese area headquarters and nerve centre on New Britain in the Bismarcks.

Guadalcanal and Tulagi were the objectives, and the assault force was the only amphibious trained division readily available, the 1st Marine Division. It was, in fact, the only unit of its size that was available. Commanded by Major-General Alexander A. Vandegrift, a veteran of the jungle fighting of the Banana Wars in the Caribbean, the 1st Division had been formed in 1940 and included many veteran Marines in its ranks as well as a number of men without combat or expeditionary experience. Its forward echelon had just arrived in Wellington, New Zealand, for six months of intensive combat training when the word was passed that it would go into battle instead. Some troops were still at sea; one of its regiments, the 7th Marines, was committed to the defence of Samoa and the 2nd Marines of the 2nd Marine Division had to be sent out from San Diego to replace it. Other major elements to be attached to the 1st Division were located on New Caledonia and in the Hawaiian Islands. All had to be alerted, equipped, and assembled in less than a month's time to meet a D-day of August 7, 1942.

Working around the clock and pushing aside New Zealand dock workers who wanted to invoke union labour rules, the Marines in Wellington unloaded transports as fast as they arrived, sorted and repacked equipment and supplies for combat, and loaded ship again. There was not enough room for all the division's motor transport and most of the heavier trucks had to be left behind. Only 60 days of supplies and rations, ammunition for 10 days' heavy fighting (units of fire), and the bare minimum of individual equipment were taken.

The expedition sails

The amphibious task force which would transport, land, and support the Marines was commanded by Rear-Admiral Richmond K. Turner; overall commander of the naval expeditionary force, including carriers and their escorts, was Rear-Admiral Frank J. Fletcher. Since this

was to be a naval campaign and the landing force was to be of Marines, Admiral King had insisted that it be conducted under naval leadership. Accordingly, the Joint Chiefs-of-Staff shifted the boundary of Vice-Admiral Richard H. Ghormley's South Pacific Theatre northward to include all of the 90-mile-long island of Guadalcanal, which precluded the possibility that General Douglas MacArthur, the South-West Pacific Area commander, would control operations.

The plan for the seizure of the objective, codenamed "Watchtower", called for two separate landings, one by the division's main body near Lunga Point on Guadalcanal and the other at Tulagi by an assault force made up of the 2nd Battalion, 5th Marines and the 1st Raider and 1st Parachute Battalions. In all, General Vandegrift had about 19,000 men under his command when the transports and escorts moved into position on D-day. They had come from a rehearsal at Koro, in the Fiji Islands, where the inexperienced ships'

△ *A Marine patrol probes the jungle on the outskirts of the American beach-head on Guadalcanal.*

▽ *Shattered and half buried by American bombardment: Japanese bodies on the beach at Guadalcanal, killed before they even had the chance to close with the Marines.*

△ *A dusk patrol sent out by Vandegrift's Marines sets out, tramping through the Matanikau river.*

crews and the polyglot Marine units reinforcing the 1st Division had combined to take part in a run-through that General Vandegrift called a "complete bust".

Behind a thunderous preparation by cruisers and destroyers and under an overhead cover of Admiral Fletcher's carrier aircraft, the landing craft streaked ashore at both targets. Surprise had been achieved; there was no opposition on the beaches at either objective. True to preliminary Intelligence estimates, however, the Japanese soon fought back savagely from prepared positions on Tagula.

It took three days of heavy fighting to wrest the headquarters island and two small neighbouring islets, Gavutu and Tanambogo, from the Japanese naval troops who defended them. All three battalions of the 2nd Marines were needed to lend their weight to the American attacks against Japanese hidden in pillboxes and caves and ready to fight to the death. The garrison commander had radioed to Rabaul on the morning of August 7: "Enemy troop strength is overwhelming. We will defend to the last man." There were 27 prisoners, mostly labourers. A few men escaped by swimming to nearby Florida Island, but the rest of the 750 to 800-man garrison went down fighting.

On Guadalcanal, the labour troops working on the airfield fled when naval gunfire crashed into their bivouac areas. Consequently, there was no opposition as the lead regiment, the 1st Marines, overran the partially completed field on August 8. Japanese engineering equipment, six workable road rollers, some 50 handcarts, about 75 shovels, and two tiny petrol locomotives with hopper cars, were left behind. It was a good thing that this gear was abandoned, for the American engineering equipment that came to Guadalcanal on Turner's ships also left on Turner's ships, which departed from the area on August 9. Unwilling to risk his precious carriers any longer against the superior Japanese air power which threatened from Rabaul, Admiral Fletcher was withdrawing. Without air cover, Turner's force was naked. Japanese cruisers and destroyers and flights of medium bombers from Rabaul had made the amphibious task force commander's position untenable.

Constant air attack

Almost constant Japanese air attacks, which began on the afternoon of August 7, thoroughly disrupted unloading as the transports and escorts manoeuvred to escape the rain of bombs. The Marines

△ *For the honour of the Emperor.*

did not have enough shore party troops to handle the supplies that did reach the beach. Ships' captains in a hurry to empty their holds and inexperienced coxswains combined forces to dump an unprogrammed jumble of ammunition, rations, tentage, vehicles, and assorted supplies on the shoreline, offering another tempting target for the Japanese planes. When Turner reluctantly sailed south to Espiritu Santo and New Caledonia, only 37 days' supply of rations and four units of fire had been landed. Vandegrift had 16,000 men ashore, 6,000 on Tulagi, with the rest still on board ship when the task force departed.

After this event, the commanding general of Army forces in the South Pacific, Major-General Millard F. Harmon, was far from optimistic about the chances of success for the Guadalcanal venture. On August 11 he wrote to the Army's Chief-of-Staff in Washington, General George C. Marshall:

"The thing that impresses me more than anything else in connection with the Solomon action is that we are not prepared to follow up . . . We have seized a strategic position from which future operations in the Bismarcks can be strongly supported. Can the Marines hold it? There is considerable room for doubt."

Cast loose, or at least promised only a

tenuous lifeline to Allied support bases, the 1st Marine Division made do with what it had. The completion of the airfield that the Japanese had begun was crucial; without it there was little ground for hope that the Marines could stay on Guadalcanal. Japanese engineering equipment was used to the fullest extent; captured Japanese weapons were included in defensive positions; Japanese rations were added to the Marines' meagre stocks; and Japanese trucks were used to supplement the small American motor pool. The airfield was ready for use on August 18; it was named Henderson Field after a Marine pilot killed in the Battle of Midway. On the day that the runway was finished, the Japanese took their first step toward wresting control of the island back from the Americans, landing a battalion of the 28th Regiment to the east of Vandegrift's perimeter. This was to be the first of many runs by the "Tokyo Express," a cruiser–destroyer transport force commanded by Rear-Admiral Raizo Tanaka, which was largely responsible for the reinforcement and resupply of the Japanese on Guadalcanal.

The red letter day for the Marines was August 20. Two squadrons flew in to Henderson Field from the escort carrier *Long Island,* 19 Grumman F4F Wildcat fighters from Marine Fighting Squadron 223 and 12 Douglas SBD-3 Dauntless dive-bombers from Marine Scout-Bomber Squadron 232. The planes came just

▽ *Two Marines discover for themselves what they are up against: resistance to the death.*

in time to help with the destruction of the Japanese battalion that had landed two days before. Making a night attack headlong against the positions of the 1st Marines' battalion holding the west bank of the Ilu River, which marked the eastern edge of Vandegrift's perimeter, the Japanese were ground up in a fury of artillery, machine gun, and 37-mm canister fire. When daylight came, a Marine battalion mopped up the remnants of the attacking force, helped by strafing attacks by the newly arrived Wildcats. The Japanese commander, Colonel Kiyono Ichiki, disheartened by his failure, committed suicide; 800 of his men had died in the fighting.

Colonel Ichiki, like his superior in Rabaul, Lieutenant-General Harukichi Hyakutake, commanding the 17th Army, had underestimated both the strength and the determination of the Marines to hold out. Time and again, the Japanese were to repeat Ichiki's error, sending thousands of men from Rabaul but never enough at one time so that Vandegrift could not handle them. The troops available to Hyakutake in August and September was more than enough to overwhelm the Marine defences, but these troops were never committed in sufficient force to sustain a determined attack.

△ As in New Guinea, the Allies battling their way down the chain of the Solomons found that the natives were eager to join up and fight against the hated "Japani".
▷ The ordeal of Vandegrift's Marines, penned for months in the narrow beach-head near the original landing-ground on Guadalcanal.

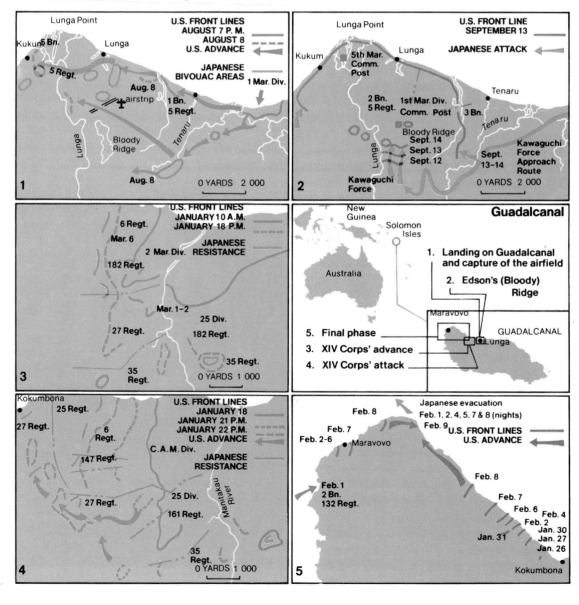

CHAPTER 49
GUADALCANAL: TRIUMPH

General Vandegrift never lost sight of his primary mission of defending Henderson Field. He was aggressive and mounted a number of limited objective offensives; he kept strong combat and reconnaissance patrols forward of his lines constantly. But he always kept his perimeter intact, always maintained a reserve, and showed a marvellous ability for meeting strength with strength. The Japanese pattern of reinforcing Guadalcanal, and the impetuosity of Japanese leaders once they reached the island, played right into the American general's hands. Typically, a few thousand Japanese troops would be landed at night by Tanaka's Tokyo Express a few miles to either side of the Marine perimeter and they would attack almost without delay. The action would be furious at the point of contact, sometimes the Marine lines would be penetrated, but then the fire-brigade would arrive – a fresh infantry battalion, a platoon of tanks, the fire of an additional reinforcing artillery battalion, a flight of dive-bombers, perhaps all of these at once, and the Japanese would be thrown back, decimated by their own relentless courage in the face of killing fire.

The same fate that befell the Ichiki battalion was met by a 6,000-man brigade under Major-General Kiyotaki Kawaguchi, which landed on both sides of the 9,000-yard-wide perimeter in early September. The main body, about 4,000 men, mostly of the 124th Infantry, pressed inland under cover of the jungle to attack from the south against the inland perimeter toward the airfield. That portion of the Marine line was thinly held, as the greatest danger was expected from attacks along the coast or from the sea.

Fortunately, Vandegrift had moved the original assault force at Tulagi across Sealark Channel to bolster the Marine defences. Combining the raider and parachute battalions under one commander, Colonel Merritt A. Edson, he placed this unit astride an open, grassy ridge that led directly to the division command post and the airfield. The 2nd Battalion, 5th Marines was one mile away in reserve and a battalion of 105-mm howitzers from the division's artillery regiment, the 11th Marines, was in direct support. The Kawaguchi Force lightly probed Edson's position on September 12, while a Japanese cruiser and several destroyers shelled Henderson Field, a frequent accompaniment to Japanese ground attacks. On the 13th, Edson tried a counterattack but was forced back to his original positions; the Japanese were too strong. That night, in a driving rain that severely limited visibility, the Japanese poured out of the jungle, smashing into the ridge position and forcing the American flanking companies back on the centre of the ridge. There the Marines held, the artillery smothered the attacking columns and troop assembly areas, and reinforcements from the 5th Marines joined the raiders and paratroopers in their fox-

▽ *A Marine struggles with the murderous jungle on Guadalcanal. The battle lasted six months. Not once did the intensity of the combat slacken. It was, quite literally, "the Stalingrad of the Pacific".*

holes. In the morning there was little left to do but mop up. Only about 500 of Kawaguchi's men struggled back alive through the jungle. A pair of diversionary attacks, mounted against the coastal perimeters while Kawaguchi struck, died in the face of stubborn Marine fire.

Japanese misinterpretation

Another much needed respite had been gained by the Japanese failure to appreciate the Marines' strength. The 1st Marine Division had received no reinforcements or ammunition since the landing in August, the troops were eating only two meals a day and part of those were Japanese rations, and tropical diseases, particularly malaria, were beginning to fell large numbers of men. The "Cactus Air Force", so named by its pilots after the island's codename, was now a battered collection of Army P-40's, Navy fighters and dive-bombers from damaged carriers, and Marine Corps aircraft. Plane availability was often less than 50 and all types were woefully short of fuel and parts. The forward echelon of the 1st Marine Aircraft Wing under Brigadier-General Roy S. Geiger controlled the motley air force, but its attrition rate was heavy from its constant clashes with the Japanese and operational accidents caused by the primitive condition of the runways, and Geiger was hard put to it to provide replacement aircraft.

For both the ground and air elements of Vandegrift's force, then, September 18 was a day for celebration. The 7th Marines arrived from Samoa to rejoin the division; with its reinforcing artillery battalion of 75-mm pack howitzers, the regiment stood at 4,262 very welcome men.

The newly arrived regiment soon got a chance to test its mettle in combat. The Japanese were building up their forces west of the Marine perimeter and on the 23rd Vandegrift sent the 1st Battalion, 7th Marines inland toward Mt. Austen, which overlooks the Lunga plain, with the mission of crossing the jungle-covered foothills and turning north to patrol to the mouth of the Matanikau River. It was a hotly contested advance and the 2nd Battalion, 5th Marines came up to reinforce and help evacuate casualties. The Raider battalion moved along the coast to probe across the Matanikau. The Japanese made a stand at the river mouth

and the action escalated. Colonel Edson, who now commanded the combined force, decided on a landing behind the Japanese position and chose the 7th Marines battalion for the job. Using the landing craft that had been left at Guadalcanal by damaged and sunken transports, the Marines made a shore-to-shore movement and drove inland to a ridge about 500 yards from the beach. The Japanese closed in behind them and cut them off from their boats. The battalion's radio was inoperative, but an SBD pilot overhead saw its predicament and repeatedly attacked the encroaching Japanese troops. Offshore, the destroyer *Ballard* used her 5-inch guns to blast a path to the beach and cover the landing craft. The battalion fought its way out of the trap, taking 47 Marine casualties with it.

This fight was just the first of a series of violent clashes, as Vandegrift sought to drive the Japanese away from the perimeter. Heavy artillery, 150-mm howitzers, had been landed near Kokumbona, the Japanese headquarters, and these guns could now shell Henderson Field and a fighter strip which had been completed nearby. If the Cactus Air Force could be kept from flying, the Japanese transports and bombardment ships could have an unmolested run-in with reinforcements. As long as the mixed bag of American fighters and bombers could fly, Sealark Channel was virtually shut off to the Japanese during daylight hours.

The Marines advance

On October 7, the Marines set out again in force with two battalions of the 5th Marines to engage the Japanese at the mouth of the Matanikau. Inland, two battalions of the 7th Marines, the 3rd Battalion, 2nd Marines, and the division's scout-sniper detachment were to drive west and then south after crossing the Matanikau upstream to pin the Japanese against the coast. Three battalions of artillery were in direct support of the attack. The advancing Marines ran into the Japanese 4th Infantry Regiment, which was also moving forward to the attack. The resulting action spread over two days in the rain-swept jungle. The Americans trapped one sizable pocket of Japanese near the coast; only a few escaped death. Another force of 1,500 men was isolated in a deep ravine inland.

△ *Major-General Alexander A. Vandegrift, commander of the Marine forces on Guadalcanal.*

△ *A rapid cash-in on the souvenir market; the "novelty shop" set up by Corporal Robert E. Weeks of Illinois. His stock-in-trade consisted of painted-up Japanese trophies.*

△ *Unglamorous war trophy: a Japanese steamroller, used to level the airstrip at "Henderson Field" before falling into American hands.*

There, while Marine riflemen on the high ground picked off the hapless enemy soldiers as they struggled up the steep slopes, artillery shells methodically blasted the floor of the ravine. Vandegrift broke off the action on October 9 when Intelligence indicated that a strong Japanese attack would be mounted from the Kokumbona area. When the Marine battalions retired to the perimeter, they took with them 65 dead and 125 wounded, but they left behind 700 Japanese dead.

The Intelligence was correct. General Hyakutake himself had landed on Guadal-

△ *A dramatic piece of propaganda by the American war artist Lea. A dogged U.S. pilot on a mission over the Solomons heads back into combat, with a suitably-punctured aircraft, victory tallies marking past kills, and a Japanese plane plunging into the sea behind him.*

canal on October 9 to take personal charge of the Japanese effort. He brought with him heavy reinforcements, the rest of the 2nd Division to join those elements already on the island, two battalions of the 38th Division, and more artillery. By mid-October, Hyakutake's strength was about 20,000 men, but Vandegrift had 23,000, for on October 13, the first American Army troops arrived on Guadalcanal, the 164th Infantry of the Americal Division from New Caledonia. The night after the 164th arrived, Japanese battleships fired a 90-minute bombardment against Henderson Field, partly to cover a daylight run of Tanaka's transports carrying Hyakutake's reinforcements. Although only 42 of Geiger's 90 planes were operational when the bombardment ended and Henderson Field was a shambles, the pilots used the fighter strip as soon as the sun rose and made the muddy runway firm enough to take off from.

Any plane that could carry a bomb or torpedo, including General Vandegrift's lumbering PBY flying boat, attacked the transports. Three were left burning and beached and the other two fled, but some 4,000 men of the 2nd Division were able to get ashore.

The jungle spoils Japanese plans

Hyakutake's plan was to attack the inland perimeter as Kawaguchi had done with some 6,000 men of Lieutenant-General Masao Maruyama's 2nd Division, while another 3,000 men simultaneously struck along the Matanikau, where the Marines now maintained a strong forward position. On October 16, Maruyama's column began cutting its way through the jungle, using the impenetrable cover of the giant trees to escape American observation planes. The march inland was a nightmare for the Japanese: all heavy equipment, including artillery, had to be abandoned and the time schedule kept slipping backwards. On the 19th, when the two-pronged attack was to have been launched, the serpentine column had not even reached the upper reaches of the Lunga river. Hyakutake set the date back to October 22, but even that was not enough, and further days were added.

But the Japanese commander at the Matanikau got his signals crossed and attacked one day early, launching a tank-led thrust across the mouth of the Matanikau on the 23rd. Marine 37-mm guns stopped the tanks dead in their tracks and artillery massacred the following infantry. One result of this abortive attack, however, was that a battalion of the 7th Marines was pulled out of the inland defensive perimeter to reinforce along the Matanikau.

The battle for Bloody Ridge

On October 24, therefore, the 1st Battalion, 7th Marines held 2,500 yards of jungle front anchored on the ridge, now generally known as Edson's Ridge or Bloody Ridge, which the raiders and parachute troops had defended so gallantly in September. To the Marine battalion's left, the 2nd Battalion of the

164th Infantry held the portion of the line that curved back toward the coast. The two American battalions held the area that was to be the focal point of Japanese attacks. When Maruyama's soldiers surged forward from the jungle after nightfall on the 24th, they were met by a solid wall of Marine and Army small arms fire, canister shells from 37's, and a deadly rain of artillery and mortar fire. As soon as it became apparent that the main thrust of the attack was aimed at Edson's Ridge, the 3rd Battalion, 164th Infantry, in reserve, was started forward to reinforce the Marines. Slipping and stumbling through the rainy darkness, the soldiers were fed into the Marine positions as they arrived and wherever they were needed. The lines held and they held again the next night as Maruyama made another attempt with his dwindling forces. Then it was over, and all Japanese attempts to penetrate the 1st Division's lines had failed; 3,500 of the enemy lay dead in, around, and in front of the American

▽ "One of ours"–an American plane swoops over a Marine post at "Hell's Corner" on the Matanikau river.

positions, including the 2nd Division's infantry group commander and two regimental commanders. One of these, Colonel Sejiro Furumiya of the 29th Infantry, had made a pledge to his men when they landed on Guadalcanal, that if they were unsuccessful in capturing the island "not even one man should expect to return alive".

Things were looking up for Vandegrift's troops. Despite the horrendous losses that the Allies had suffered in sea battles in the waters off Guadalcanal, a steady stream of supplies and men continued to be landed on the island under the protective cover of the "Cactus" pilots. And on October 18, the vibrant and aggressive Vice-Admiral William F. Halsey relieved Admiral Ghormley as Commander, South Pacific Area and brought with him a resolve that Guadalcanal would be held and the Japanese driven off. In that determination he was supported by President Roosevelt, who personally ordered the tempo of aid to the defenders to be stepped up. The 25th Infantry Division in Hawaii was alerted for a move to Guadalcanal, and the rest of the 2nd Marine Division and the Americal Division were also ordered forward.

Heartened by the promise of reinforcements, Vandegrift continued to keep the Japanese off balance with the troops he had. On November 3, six battalions under Colonel Edson probed forward and trapped a Japanese force near Point Cruz and eliminated another 300 men of Hyakutake's army. At the same time, on the eastern side of the perimeter, a reconnaissance in force by the 7th Marines, backed up by two battalions of the 164th Infantry, punished a 1,500-man Japanese reinforcement group from the 38th Division which landed near Koli Point, driving the enemy soldiers into the jungle. Partly as a result of this action, Hyakutake decided to abandon the concept of the two-sided attack on the American position and ordered the 38th Division's troops to move overland to Kokumbona. Five hundred of the retreating Japanese failed to complete the trip. They were hunted down and killed by the Marines of the 2nd Raider Battalion who landed at Aola Bay 40 miles west of the Lunga on November 4. These men were part of a project dear to Admiral Turner's heart, an attempt to set up another airfield on Guadalcanal. Vandegrift wanted nothing to do with any scheme that dispersed American ground forces on

Guadalcanal, but lost the argument to his naval superior. He did, however, get permission for the raiders to patrol overland to the Henderson Field perimeter and they accounted for the Japanese straggling through the jungle.

Reinforcements pour in

The further landing of 38th Division troops on Guadalcanal was part of a massive reinforcement effort which included the daylight landing of Japanese forces on November 14. While shore-based aircraft and planes from the carrier *Enterprise* sank seven of 11 transports carrying the Japanese soldiers, Tanaka's destroyers were able to rescue many of the men and Hyakutake had 10,000 fresh troops. But Vandegrift had two new reinforced regiments too, the 8th Marines from Samoa and the 182nd Infantry from New Caledonia, and he retained his

numerical advantage. He continued to pressure the Japanese, repeatedly probing and jabbing toward Kokumbona in November, using many of his newly arrived Army and Marine battalions.

The Marine general needed the fresh men. His own division, after four months of fighting in the jungle heat and humidity, was worn out; over half the men had contracted malaria or other tropical diseases. His original Marine units had suffered nearly 2,000 casualties, 681 of them killed in action or dead of wounds. The decision was made to withdraw the 1st Marine Division to Australia for rest and rehabilitation. On December 9, 1942, General Vandegrift turned over command of the troops on Guadalcanal to Major-General Alexander M. Patch of the Americal Division, and the 5th Marines boarded ship to leave the island, leading the exodus of the 1st Division.

Patch's mission was to drive the Japanese off Guadalcanal, and his forces were increased substantially to give him

▽ *Mute witness to the start of the campaign: the smashed Japanese base on Tanambogo Island.*

the means to carry out this task. Major-General J. Lawton Collins' 25th Infantry Division began landing on Guadalcanal on December 17 and the last elements of the 2nd Marine Division came in on January 4 under command of Brigadier-General Alphonse de Carre. New Army and Marine squadrons swelled the ranks of the Cactus Air Force and the situation was grim indeed for the Japanese.

By the beginning of January, General Patch had 50,000 men of all services under his command. Hyakutake's 17th Army troops amounted to about 25,000 men, but they were now cut off from effective reinforcement or resupply by Allied air power and a resurgent naval effort. His men were on short rations and low on ammunition; many were sick with the same tropical diseases that had ravaged the

▽ *Marines advance over a pontoon bridge across the Matanikau.*

Marines of Vandegrift's division, but there were not enough medical supplies to aid them back to health. While the Japanese were still capable of hard fighting, they could not sustain a serious offensive effort. The decision was made in Rabaul about mid-December to abandon the ill-fated attempt to recapture Guadalcanal and to rescue as many of Hyakutake's men as possible.

General Patch unwittingly reinforced the Japanese decision to get out. Commander since January 2 of a newly organised XIV Corps run by a skeletal staff from the Americal Division, he used his three divisions to drive unrelentingly west from the Lunga perimeter. Using Collins' 25th Division inland and de Carre's 2nd Division along the coast, he hammered steadily at the Japanese. The defenders fell back slowly, fighting hard but unable to hold any position long before the American troops, who used massive

artillery, air, and naval gunfire support, drove them out. Kokumbona, so long the objective of Vandegrift's attacks, was occupied by the 25th Division on January 23. Here Patch held up the attack, anxious because reports of a Japanese shipping build-up at Rabaul and in the Shortland Islands presaged another attempt to take Guadalcanal. Actually, this was the Japanese destroyer force that was intended to evacuate Hyakutake's men.

Patch cautiously resumed his advance on January 30. He had a small blocking force in the mountain passes inland to prevent the Japanese crossing to the other side of the island, and he sent an Army battalion around Cape Esperance to the western coast to block that route of escape also. By February 5, when the advance was held up again by reports of a large Japanese flotilla lurking in the northern Solomons, the lead Army regiment, the 161st Infantry, had reached positions 3,500 yards west of Tassafaronga and only about 12 miles from Cape Esperance.

On the night of February 7-8, Japanese destroyers under the command of Rear-Admiral Koniji Koyonagi executed a masterly evacuation of 13,000 Japanese troops from Guadalcanal. Many of these men would fight the Americans again on other battlefields in the Solomons and on New Britain. But there were many others who would fight no more. Casualties had been high on both sides in this bitterly fought contest in the jungles and malaria infested swamps of Guadalcanal. However, thanks to their superior medical facilities and greater regard for human life, American casualties were correspondingly lower.

On January 8, 1943, the official ending of the Guadalcanal land campaign, General Patch could report "the complete and total defeat of Japanese forces on Guadalcanal." After the struggle for control of the island was decided, the Japanese never again advanced in the Pacific. The staggering Japanese losses of ships, planes, and pilots that were equally a feature of the Guadalcanal campaign with the bitter ground fighting were not replaceable in kind. Admiral Tanaka, whose Tokyo Express had done so much to sustain the Japanese on the island, considered that "Japan's doom was sealed with the closing of the struggle for Guadalcanal". The strategic initiative in the southwest Pacific now passed to the Allies, for good.

CHAPTER 50
DÖNITZ TAKES OVER

On the morning of December 31, 1942 an engagement took place in the Barents Sea which had no important strategic consequences, but should be mentioned as it provoked a crisis in the German high command. The occasion was the passage off the North Cape in Norway of convoy J.W. 51B; its 14 merchant ships and tankers were taking 2,040 trucks, 202 tanks, 87 fighters, 43 bombers, 20,120 tons of oil fuel, 12,650 tons of petrol, and 54,321 tons of various products to Murmansk.

This large convoy was escorted by a minesweeper, two trawlers, two corvettes, and six destroyers (shortly reduced to five, as one had to give up after its gyroscopic compass had broken down). The small escort was commanded by Captain Robert St. V. Sherbrooke, a direct descendant of the famous Admiral Jervis who became Lord St. Vincent after his victory in 1797 over the Spanish fleet. Under the command of Rear-Admiral R. L. Burnett, a veteran of the Arctic run, the cruisers *Sheffield* and *Jamaica*,

from Kolos were also sent in to help. Lastly, nine submarines (including the Polish *Sokol* and the Dutch *O 14*) provided a protective screen for the convoy as it passed the Norwegian coast. However, because of the winter ice floes the convoy J.W. 51B was sailing in single file about 240 miles from the German base at Altenfjord and its position had been signalled to Grand-Admiral Raeder by the *U-354* (Lieutenant Herschleb). Raeder acted very quickly on receiving this signal, as Hitler had recently made some extremely unflattering remarks about the Kriegsmarine. Therefore on that same evening of December 30, the pocket battleship *Lützow*, the heavy cruiser *Admiral Hipper*, and six destroyers put out to sea to intercept and destroy the convoy the following dawn. For this purpose, Vice-Admiral Kummetz, who was in command at sea, sent off his two major units in a pincer movement. But as he weighed anchor, he received a message from Admiral Kübler, the commander of the northern sector, which was clearly not

△ The occasional failure to heed such warnings sometimes cost the Allies very dear: Convoy S.C. 118 suffered heavily at the beginning of February because a captive talked.
▽ The unmistakable sign of a blazing tanker – a thick, black column of smoke, drawing U-boats to the convoy like ants to honey.

△ *The British destroyer* Orwell, *sister ship of Sherbrooke's* Onslow *and one of the four "O"-class destroyers involved in the Battle of the Barents Sea. The ships of this class were all launched in 1941 and 1942, and had a displacement of 1,540 tons, an armament of four 4.7-inch guns and eight 21-inch torpedo tubes, and a speed of 36.75 knots. The class was designed with quick conversion into minelayers in mind, and four of the eight eventually underwent the conversion.*

calculated to spur him on:

"Contrary to the operational order regarding contact against the enemy [you are] to use caution even against enemy of equal strength because it is undesirable for the cruisers to take any great risks."

Here Kübler was merely repeating the instructions sent to him by the chief of the *Oberkommando der Kriegsmarine* through Kiel and Admiral Carls. But Raeder was following a standing order promulgated by the Führer after the sinking of the *Bismarck,* and that evening Vice-Admiral Krancke, who had informed Hitler that the two ships and their escort vessels had sailed, wrote:

"The Führer emphasised that he wished to have all reports immediately since, as I well knew, he could not sleep a wink when ships were operating.

"I passed this message subsequently to the Operations Division of the Naval Staff, requesting that any information be telephoned immediately."

Hitler's anxiety was certainly peculiar, since he did not lose any sleep over the terrible fate of the 230,000 Germans encircled in the Stalingrad pocket.

On the next day, at about 0915, Kummetz, who had chosen *Hipper* as his

flagship, came into contact with the rear of the convoy. But *Onslow* (Captain Sherbrooke) fearlessly attacked the Germans, followed by three other destroyers. Meanwhile a fifth destroyer, which was under enemy fire, covered the merchant ships withdrawing towards the south-east under a smokescreen. In spite of his impressive superiority in guns, the German admiral did not dare to launch a full-scale attack, as he was afraid that in the prevailing half-light he would not be able to defend himself against the torpedoes which the British would certainly use against him if he came within range. At 1019 the first 8-inch shell hit *Onslow;* three more hits followed, killing 14 men and wounding 33, including Captain Sherbrooke, who lost an eye and had his nose fractured, but continued leading his division.

Lützow appeared a little later and tried to attack the convoy from the rear whilst *Hipper* engaged the escort vessels; however, as visibility was poor and her commander too unenterprising, her six 11- and eight 6-inch guns were hardly fired once. At 1130, the balance of the engagement changed; Rear-Admiral Burnett, who had been alerted by Sherbrooke, appeared on the scene just at the right time; as he was north of *Hipper*, he was able to take advantage of the light to the south while remaining in the darkness himself. Moreover *Sheffield* and *Jamaica,* which both remained unscathed, scored three hits on the German flagship, which retreated with a boiler room flooded with a mixture of sea water and oil fuel.

We shall not describe the game of blind man's buff that followed; during the engagement, the destroyer *Friedrich Eckholdt* was sunk by the British cruisers, which she took for *Lützow* and *Hipper*. *Lützow* fired 86 11-inch and 76 6-inch shells, but none of them scored a direct hit. When the darkness increased, Kummetz broke off contact and the convoy set off again, reaching Murmansk without further mishap. Apart from the damage done to *Onslow,* the convoy had also lost the minesweeper *Bramble* and the destroyer *Achates,* which had heroically sacrificed herself in protecting the front of the convoy.

Hitler's adverse opinion

At Rastenburg, Hitler was awaiting news of the engagement with feverish impatience. At 1145 a message from *U-354* was intercepted and this appeared to indicate a major success; then, a few minutes later, came Kummetz's order to abandon the operation. But on his return journey Kummetz quite properly observed radio silence, and when he had anchored in the Altenfjord a whole series of fortuitous incidents combined to delay the transmission of his report, with the result that at 1700 on January 1 the Führer had nothing but the British communiqué to hand concerning the previous day's engagement. He violently upbraided Admiral Krancke:

"He said that it was an unheard of impudence not to inform him; and that such behaviour and the entire action showed that the ships were utterly useless; that they were nothing but a breeding ground for revolution, idly lying about and lacking any desire to get into action.

"This meant the passing of the High Seas Fleet, he said, adding that it was now his irrevocable decision to do away with these useless ships. He would put the good personnel, the good weapons, and the armour plating to better use."

He received Kummetz's report a few hours later, but it failed to placate him. Far from it, for according to Krancke:

"There was another outburst of anger with special reference to the fact that the action had not been fought to the finish. This, said the Führer, was typical of German ships, just the opposite of the British, who, true to their tradition, fought to the bitter end.

"If an English commander behaved like that he would immediately be relieved of his command. The whole thing spelled the end of the German High Seas Fleet, he declared. I was to inform the Grand-Admiral immediately that he was to come to the Führer at once, so that he could be informed personally of this irrevocable decision."

He added: "I am not an obliging civilian, but the commander-in-chief of all the armed forces."

In this long diatribe, the argument that Vice-Admiral Kummetz had not pursued the engagement to its conclusion was perfectly correct. But it was hardly seemly for Krancke to call Hitler to account for the paralysing effect that his orders had had on the movements of the

▽ Onslow *arrives home after her ordeal. She had been hit by four 8-inch shells from* Hipper, *and these had knocked out her two forward guns, killed 14 of her crew, and severely wounded her commander, Captain Sherbrooke.*

fleet on that occasion. Grand-Admiral Raeder arrived at Rastenburg on January 6, 1943 and was immediately faced with an indictment which began with the part played by the Royal Prussian Navy in the war over the Duchies of Schleswig and Holstein (1864) and went on for over 90 minutes; Hitler's tone was bitterly hostile throughout and he used arguments which, according to Raeder, were so incompetent that they seemed to show the influence of *Reichsmarschall* Hermann Göring.

"Battleships," raged Hitler, "to which he had always devoted his full attention and which had filled him with so much pride were no longer of the slightest use. They required the permanent protection of planes and small ships. In the event of an Allied attack on Norway, these planes would be more usefully employed against the invasion fleet than protecting our own fleet. Large battleships no longer served any purpose and therefore must be taken out of commission, after their guns had been removed. There was an urgent need for their guns on land."

Raeder was, however, authorised to submit to Hitler a memo expressing his objections. Feeling himself offended and discredited by Hitler's manner of address-

ing him, Raeder, who was over 66 years old, asked for and obtained his retirement. On January 30, 1943 he therefore gave up the high command he had held for 15 years and took over an honorary inspectorate-general. But before handing over the command of the German Navy to Admiral Dönitz, he regarded it as his duty to inform the Führer of the disagreeable but inevitable consequences of discarding the Grand Fleet.

The Royal Navy would obtain at no cost to themselves the equivalent of a great naval victory. But even more important, Hitler had overlooked the fact that the application of his "irrevocable decision" would perceptibly affect the balance of forces in the Mediterranean, the Indian Ocean, and the Pacific. In fact, as soon as the potential threat of the German major warships in the North Atlantic disappeared, the Admiralty, recovering full freedom of action, would profit by it and crush Japan.

Events showed that Raeder saw clearly. It is now known that Churchill was impatiently waiting for the time when the elimination of German surface warships would allow the Navy to appear in the Far East again; he was determined to

Captain F. Walker, Britain's most prolific U-boat killer. He was born in 1896, and at the beginning of the war was head of the experimental department at the Navy's anti-submarine school. Late in 1941 he was given command of the sloop *Stork* and the 36th Group, with which he sank seven U-boats between December 1941 and June 1942. After a spell on shore, he returned to sea in the sloop *Starling* as commander of the famous 2nd Escort Group. He died on board his ship on July 9, 1944, and was buried at sea.

Fleet, thus giving it a wide margin of superiority in any circumstance. Thus when the powerful *Richelieu* had been refitted and sailed from Brooklyn dockyard, the Admiralty ensured that in November 1943 she joined the other ships at Scapa Flow.

Although he was a U-boat officer, the new Grand-Admiral deferred to the arguments of his predecessor, and Hitler was hardly in a position to thwart him immediately after his appointment.

In these circumstances, by a decision taken on February 18, 1943, the old battleships *Schlesien* and *Schleswig-Holstein,* which had been launched in 1906, the heavy cruiser *Admiral Hipper,* and the light cruisers *Köln* and *Leipzig* were merely declared obsolete, and the radical measures advocated by Hitler were not carried out. In fact, even this decision was only partially carried out; in autumn 1944 some of these units were to appear again in the Baltic to give gunfire support to Army Group "North" in its defence of the Kurland bridgehead.

Captain Sherbrooke had the exceptional distinction of winning the Victoria Cross for his exploit in the Barents Sea.

△ *The ex-Admiralty yacht* Enchantress *takes on supplies at sea. Note the lattice-work H/F D/F mast on the quarterdeck, which allowed German U-boat radio transmissions to be picked up and plotted.*
▽ *The depth charge crew of an armed trawler in action. The desperate shortage of inshore escort craft meant that many hundreds of trawlers would be converted to undertake this vital war work.*

restore British prestige there, impaired as it had been by the loss of Singapore; and Churchill doubtless had no wish to concede the monopoly of victory over Japan to the Americans, as he was well aware of the fanatical anti-colonialism displayed by Roosevelt. Hitler's whim, if it had been acted upon, would therefore have benefited only the Allies. This is shown by the fact that the Admiralty had to attach a force of battleships and aircraft-carriers to the Home

The *guerre de course*

"The balance sheet of profit and loss in mercantile tonnage was one of the most disturbing issues which confronted the Casablanca Conference when it opened on the 14th of January 1943. Until the U-boats were defeated the offensive strategy to which the Allies were committed could not succeed. Europe could never be invaded until the battle of the Atlantic had been won, and the latter purpose had therefore to be made a first charge on all Allied resources."

Thus Stephen Roskill, the Royal Navy's official historian, begins his chapter describing the decisive phase of this merciless struggle, and one can only confirm his judgement. There is no doubt that even after this battle had been won, the Western Allies would still have gained nothing until the European continent had been invaded, but if this first battle had been lost, all would have been lost with it.

When he took over the command of the German Navy, Karl Dönitz probably made no attempt to disown responsibility for the battle of the Atlantic; he knew what was at stake better than anyone else on the German side. Therefore the new commander-in-chief of U-boats, Rear-Admiral Godt, whom Dönitz himself selected, became even more closely subordinate to the latter's authority than the latter himself had previously been to Raeder. Consequently Dönitz was responsible for all the successes and defeats in this campaign, both before and after his promotion to the command of the Kriegsmarine, though one must make allowances for the fact that he was never free of Hitler's interference.

On January 1, 1943, the German Navy had 212 operational submarines, more than double its strength compared with the same date in 1942, when it had 91. In addition it had another 181 in the Baltic, either training or on trials. Moreover, the Third Reich's shipyards produced 23 or 24 submarines a month in 1943, in spite of Anglo-American bombing. However, as they lacked crews, the U-boats stayed longer and longer in the dockyards when they returned from their cruises; at the end of 1942 they averaged two months in dock to 40 days at sea.

At the beginning of 1943, in this decisive year, the 212 operational submarines

were distributed as follows:

Atlantic: 164
Mediterranean: 24
North Sea: 21
Black Sea: 3, moving down the Danube from Regensburg.

In the main theatre of operations, 98 units were at sea at this time. However, 59 of them were in transit. These were forbidden to attack when they left harbour, unless in exceptional circumstances, and they very often had no torpedoes on the way back. They still used pack tactics, and the strength of their packs had doubled and even tripled since the beginning of 1942. In February and March 1943 there were sometimes 10, 12, or even 16 submarines attacking the same convoy for days on end. Their effectiveness was much strengthened by the fact that German Naval Counter-Intelligence managed continually to decipher Allied communications. "Thus we obtained," Admiral Dönitz wrote at this time, "not only information about the convoys but also, in January and February 1943, the 'U-boat positions', communicated from time to time by the British Admiralty to the commanders of convoys at sea to show them the confirmed or conjectured positions of our warships

△ △ *Impromptu conference in the North Atlantic between two U-boats. With the gradual closing of the "Atlantic gap" and the strengthening of Allied escorts for convoys, it was now becoming very dangerous for U-boats to stay on the surface in daylight and also to communicate with each other or with headquarters by radio.*
△ *The U-boat pens at Lorient. Quite wrongly the R.A.F. had decided to attack these only when they were finished – which proved to be a fruitless task as their concrete construction made them impregnable.*

▲ ▲ *The U-boat pens at Trondheim in Norway, main base for the packs operating against the Arctic convoys. The boat on the left is a Type VIIC (769/871 tons, five 21-inch tubes, 17/7.5 knots) with a Type IXD2 (1,616/1,804, six 21-inch tubes, 19.25/7 knots) on the right.*

▲ *A U-boat returns after a successful cruise against Allied shipping.*

in their sector. This was extremely valuable, as we often asked ourselves what the enemy knew about us."

Even today, it is hard to explain the reasons why Dönitz was allowed to read, so to speak, over his enemy's shoulder; the British in fact knew nothing of this for three years and never took the appropriate counter-measures.

When they returned from their cruises,

the U-boats were sheltered in the concrete pens at Lorient and la Pallice from December 1941, and later at Brest, St. Nazaire, and Bordeaux; the pens' 22-foot thick roofs were capable of withstanding the heaviest bombs. As has been mentioned, the R.A.F. did not attack them while they were being built, and when it did so, in accordance with a decision taken at Casablanca, there was no military result. From January to May 1943 English and American bombers dropped about 9,000 tons of bombs and incendiaries on the German Atlantic bases, all to no effect; in vain they destroyed Brest, Lorient, and St. Nazaire without obtaining a single hit on their real targets. The only U-boat sunk at anchor was *U-622,* which was destroyed at Trondheim by a U.S. plane on July 24, 1943. And whilst the French population suffered very severely in these badly directed operations, they cost the Allies 98 planes. One final point: it appears that Raeder's successor was now reduced to using anything that came to hand for sustaining the enormous effort of the submarine war. Unquestionably, his fleets became more and more accident-prone. There were three in 1942 and nine in the following year, seven of them training in the Baltic.

Moreover, the new Grand Admiral had to withstand the weight of this campaign alone. He could not expect any assistance from the Luftwaffe. In fact, during 1943 R.A.F. patrols sank 41 U-boats in the Bay of Biscay without any serious interference from the Germans. It is not surprising that Dönitz, exasperated by the frequent criticisms of the German Navy continually made by Hermann Göring to Hitler, permitted himself a tart reply: "Herr *Reichsmarschall*, kindly spare me your criticisms of the Kriegsmarine. You have got quite enough to do looking after the Luftwaffe!"

Stepped-up production

We shall now consider the Allies' defence against the U-boats.

During 1943 the Western powers' anti-U-boat weapons production was sufficient to meet the extent and urgency of the threat, but the Allied effort was not as one-sided as the German as it placed more importance on the aerial side of naval warfare. However, one must have many reservations about the use the British and Americans made of their air forces in their campaign against the U-boats.

This effort was from now on mainly American. Admittedly, the tactics and technology were mostly British, but the mass production needed to get them into action was predominantly American. The difference in industrial power between the two countries was enormous; the United States, moreover, which had suffered neither Blitz nor black-out, made tremendous innovations in prefabrication.

Escort craft

Amongst escort ships, the British frigate corresponded in its general features to the escort destroyer of the U.S. Navy. But from 1943 till the end of hostilities, Great Britain, with the help of Canadian dockyards, produced 100 frigates, whilst the Americans in the same space of time built 565 escort destroyers; 78 of these were handed over to Britain under Lend-Lease, while eight went to Brazil and six

◁ *The raw stuff of Germany's naval struggle. Despite the increasingly heavy losses now suffered by the U-boat service, Dönitz was never short of volunteers for his submarine crews.*

It was as if some outside agency had suddenly decided to take a hand on the Allied side—all of a sudden U-boat losses started to climb considerably, while merchant shipping losses declined at an even faster rate. The crisis had been reached and passed, and although the Germans continued their offensive with all the means at their disposal, the Allies had weathered this critical point in their fortunes.

△ *A stricken U-boat begins to founder amid a welter of spray.*

to France. These ships were a little faster than the corvettes of 1940; they had considerable freedom of movement and were profusely armed and equipped for their specialised rôle.

Escort carriers

The story of escort carriers is similar. The British had commissioned their first such carrier, *Audacity,* in November 1941; she was sunk on December 21, 1941, but had performed such signal services that the Admiralty decided to build half a dozen similar ships. The British could not produce as many as the Americans, however, who built 115 between the summer of 1942 and the capitulation of Japan, on new hulls or by converting cargo ships or tankers. But again these 7,000 to 12,000 ton ships were produced quickly and promptly by the prefabrication methods previously referred to. One may take as examples the aircraft carriers *Bogue, Card,* and *Core:*

	Laid down	Launched	Commissioned
Bogue	October 1, 1941	January 15, 1942	September 26, 1942
Card	October 27, 1941	February 21, 1942	November 8, 1942
Core	January 2, 1942	May 15, 1942	December 10, 1942

Considering their escort rôle, a speed of not more than 20 knots was acceptable for carriers of this type. As a result of this feature and the restricted length of their flight decks, catapults had to be installed to launch the planes, of which there were about 20 (fighters and torpedo-bombers). In addition, escort carriers were employed in landing operations as aircraft transports, and as tankers; as they served so many purposes and in such large numbers, they were nicknamed "Woolworth carriers".

By July 1943, the American fleet already had 29 escort carriers in service. Their usefulness soon became evident: by December 31 in the same year they had already destroyed 26 U-boats, and the *Card* alone had accounted for eight of these. Thirty-eight of the 115 escort carriers built by the Americans fought under the British flag.

Operational research

Owing to the increase in the number of escort ships, the convoys were now reinforced; later, "support groups" were also formed as a strategic reserve. The work of the Department of Operational Studies facilitated this development; it was initiated by the Admiralty under the direction of P. M. S. Blackett, professor of physics at Manchester University and Nobel prizewinner in 1948. This organisation also made a most important deduction concerning merchant ship losses; as Captain Macintyre puts it:

"Whereas the number of ships lost in a convoy battle depended, as might be expected, upon the number of U-boats attacking and the size of the escort, it was quite independent of the size of the convoy."

When he demonstrated that the number of escort ships was being built up much more slowly than that of the ships to be escorted, Professor Blackett proved thereby, and in the face of most people's idea of common sense, that large convoys were proportionately less vulnerable than small ones. An important conclusion followed. Macintyre puts it thus:

"Then, as has been said, the economy of force, achieved by reducing the number of convoys to be defended, provided a surplus of warships which could be formed into Support Groups. These themselves resulted in a further economy. For, provided that the convoy escort could be reinforced during the passage of the most dangerous areas, a smaller escort could safely be given for the remainder of the convoy's voyage. Thus Operational Research, too often neglected or ignored, was responsible for a revolution in organisation, which came about in March 1943 with an adjustment of the North Atlantic convoy cycle, whereby fewer and larger convoys were sailed each way."

To the best of our knowledge, this was the first application of what is today called operational research, which is now essential, with the aid of computers, not only in military operations but also in sociology, economics, industry, and commerce.

As regards anti-submarine equipment, we may mention that centimetric wavelength radar equipment was installed on Allied ships and planes; its pulses could not be picked up by the detection apparatus installed by German engineers on all U-boats. In July, however, an R.A.F. bomber carrying this most modern radar equipment was brought down over Rotterdam. Grand-Admiral Dönitz thus learned the secret of the defeat he had suffered, but it was now too late.

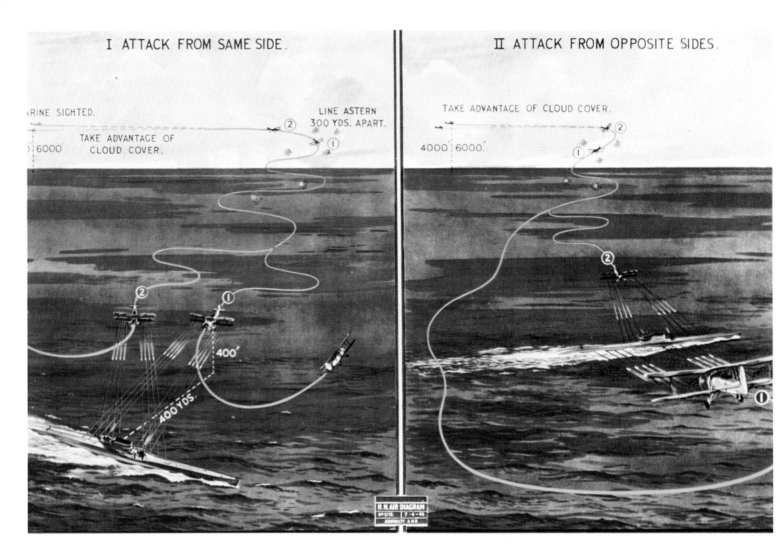

RINE SIGHTED.   LINE ASTERN   TAKE ADVANTAGE OF CLOUD COVER.
                                              300 YDS. APART.
6000   TAKE ADVANTAGE OF   4000' 6000'
        CLOUD COVER.

400'

400 YDS.

R.N. AIR DIAGRAM
No 1/16. 7-4-44
ADMIRALTY A.N.R.

△ *Yet another rôle for the obsolescent but still versatile Fairey Swordfish: anti-submarine rocket operations. With their docile handling characteristics and low landing speed, these aircraft were ideal for operation from the new escort carriers. From now to the end of the war, large numbers of U-boats were fated to fall to the aircraft of these carriers.*

"Huff Duff" . . .

H/F D/F (High Frequency Direction Finder), goniometric radio equipment, nicknamed "Huff Duff", was undoubtedly another factor in the Allies' success in the Battle of the Atlantic. This had the capacity to detect U-boats whenever they were compelled to transmit. Thus the convoy could be directed away from the area where a pack of submarines was gathering, and a support group of "Hunter-Killers", as the Americans called them, could be launched against them. The U.S. Navy and Army Air Force ordered no less than 3,200 sets of this equipment.

. . . and "Hedgehog"

At the beginning of 1943, the "Hedgehog" was put into general use. This was a projector, fitted in the bows of an escort vessel, which fired a pattern of 24 contact-fused bombs to a range of 250 yards. Thus the pursuer did not have to pass vertically over the top of the submerged target before firing its depth charges.

Finally the rockets which were successfully used by Montgomery's fighter-bombers against the Panzers were also used with the same redoubtable efficiency against the U-boats by the R.A.F.'s, U.S.A.A.F.'s, and U.S.N.'s anti-submarine patrol aircraft.

On May 23, 1943 the new weapon was first used with success by a Swordfish from the British escort carrier *Archer.* In his excellent book on fleet air arm warfare Admiral Barjot gives the following description:

"On the morning of May 23, the convoy was in sight off Newfoundland and the first wave started to attack. The Swordfish B 819 then took off and almost immediately had the good fortune to surprise *U-572,* which had surfaced to keep up with the convoy. The eight rockets lanced off towards the U-boat, holing it so that it had to surface again quickly, as its batteries were flooded. It tried to use its guns, but the fight only lasted a few minutes. A Martlet fighter arrived and machine gunned the U-boat, killing its captain and several men. The rest of the crew lost hope and abandoned ship, the U-boat sinking almost immediately. A few Germans were picked up later by the destroyer *Escapade*."

Bomber Command's part

Following a decision at the Casablanca Conference, the R.A.F.'s Bomber Command and the bomber groups of the American 8th Air Force in England redoubled their attacks against the German shipyards where submarines were under construction. Thus it was hoped to eliminate the danger at its source. In fact, according to Roskill, between May 1 and June 1 the British and American heavy squadrons carried out 3,414 sorties and dropped 5,572 tons of bombs and 4,173 of incendiaries on these targets, now recognised as of prime importance.

But in spite of the loss of 168 planes, the efforts were virtually fruitless. Even worse, this air offensive, which had been so warmly recommended by Churchill and Roosevelt, frustrated the British and American effort in the Atlantic; Bomber Command's requests for reinforcements and replacements could in fact only be satisfied if a parsimonious policy was maintained towards Coastal Command, at least as regards long-range four-engined aircraft for convoy protection.

Professor Blackett realised this perfectly clearly. In 1943 he extended his criticism to all R.A.F. Bomber Command operations:

"From the figures on the effectiveness of air cover, it could be calculated that a long-range Liberator operating from Iceland and escorting the convoys in the middle of the Atlantic *saved* at least half a dozen merchant ships in its service lifetime of some thirty flying sorties. If used for bombing Berlin, the same aircraft in its service life would drop less than 100 tons of bombs and kill not more than a couple of dozen enemy men, women and children and destroy a number of houses.

"No one would dispute that the saving of six merchant ships and their crews and cargoes was of incomparably more value to the Allied war effort than the killing of some two dozen enemy civilians, the destruction of a number of houses and a certain very small effect on production.

"The difficulty was to get the figures believed. But believed they eventually were and more long-range aircraft were made available to Coastal Command."

In fact in February 1943, Air-Marshal Sir John Slessor, who succeeded Sir Philip Joubert de la Ferté as head of Coastal Command, had only ten four-engined B-24 Liberators, whilst the American Navy had only 52. On July 1, however, the figures had risen to 37 and 209 respectively.

▽ *The commander of a German U-boat weighs up the situation before deciding whether or not to make an attack.*
▽ ▽ *While the captain makes his decision, the torpedo-room crew complete their final preparations on the weapons in the tubes and on the reloads.*

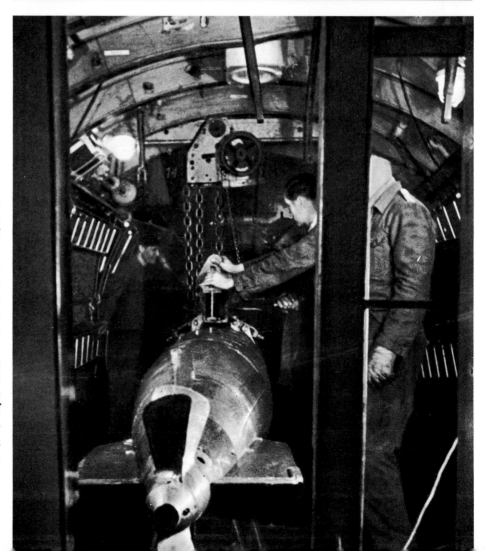

CHAPTER 51

DEFEAT OF THE U-BOATS

a careless word...

A NEEDLESS LOSS

△ *Another poster harping on one of the main themes of Allied propaganda: the need for secrecy where convoys and shipping movements were concerned.*

The graph below gives a precise account of the changing fortunes of the Battle of the Atlantic in 1943, and little more comment is needed. As can be seen, January was relatively favourable to the Allies, as winter storms raged over the North Atlantic; in fact they only lost 50 merchant vessels (261,359 tons) against 106 (419,907 tons) in the same month of the previous year.

West of the Canaries, however, a pack of eight submarines skilfully directed to its rendezvous by Dönitz attacked a convoy of nine tankers heading for North Africa; seven of these were sunk; this was a remarkable feat for which Dönitz duly received General von Arnim's congratulations. In February, Allied losses increased and were slightly over 400,000 tons (73 ships). Nonetheless, between the 4th and 9th of this month, the slow convoy S.C. 118 (63 merchantmen and ten escort vessels) fought off 20 U-boats for four successive nights. A survivor from a previous attack, picked up by *U-632*, had been criminally indiscreet and drawn the attention of his captors to the convoy: the survivor's remarks caused the loss of several hundreds of his comrades' lives. In fact 13 cargo-boats were sunk at dawn on February 9, but as Grand-Admiral

Dönitz stated, the defence was keen: "It was", he wrote, "perhaps the worst battle of the whole submarine war. Honour to the crews and commanders who waged it in the harsh winter conditions of the Atlantic! It went on for four successive nights, and the captains were unable to leave their bridges for the whole period. Their ships' safety often depended on the speed of their decisions. It is hard to imagine the self-discipline that is required after a terrible depth-charge attack, to give orders to surface, to approach the convoy, and to bear down on it through its protective screen, bristling with steel, with the alternative of success or destruction. The submarine commanders never performed such a colossal feat in the course of both world wars."

This opinion can be confirmed. The loss of the 13 cargo vessels previously mentioned was countered by that of three U-boats sunk by the escort vessels. They included *U-609* (Lieutenant Rudloff) which was sunk by a depth charge from the French corvette *Lobelia* (Lieutenant de Morsier). In other engagements, a further 16 U-boats were lost during February; on February 28, for the first time since hostilities began, the number of U-boats lost almost equalled the number

▽ *Evidence that the threat of the U-boat was finally beaten: merchant shipping losses falling, U-boat losses rising.*

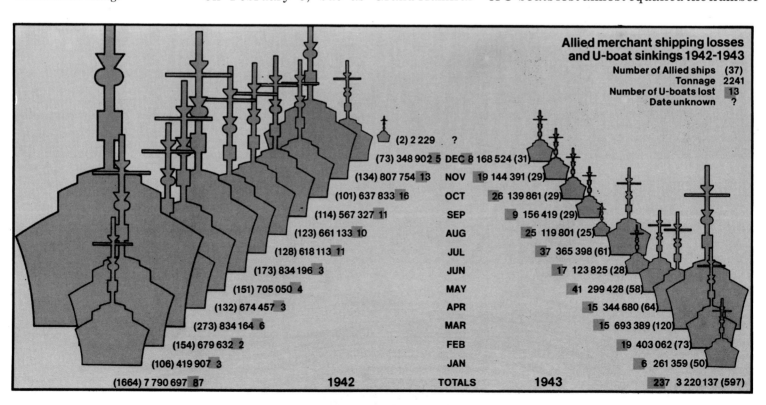

Allied merchant shipping losses and U-boat sinkings 1942-1943

	Number of Allied ships	(37)
	Tonnage	2241
	Number of U-boats lost	13
	Date unknown	?

1942 (Allied ships) tonnage U-boats	Month	1943 U-boats tonnage (Allied ships)
		(2) 2 229 ?
(73) 348 902 5	DEC	8 168 524 (31)
(134) 807 754 13	NOV	19 144 391 (29)
(101) 637 833 16	OCT	26 139 861 (29)
(114) 567 327 11	SEP	9 156 419 (29)
(123) 661 133 10	AUG	25 119 801 (25)
(128) 618 113 11	JUL	37 365 398 (61)
(173) 834 196 3	JUN	17 123 825 (28)
(151) 705 050 4	MAY	41 299 428 (58)
(132) 674 457 3	APR	15 344 680 (64)
(273) 834 164 6	MAR	15 693 389 (120)
(154) 679 632 2	FEB	19 403 062 (73)
(106) 419 907 3	JAN	6 261 359 (50)
(1664) 7 790 697 87	**1942** TOTALS 1943	237 3 220 137 (597)

completed by German yards.

In view of this slaughter and the escape, which was often noted, of the convoys from the U-boat onslaught, Dönitz thought for a time that a spy or even a traitor must have penetrated his own staff. The *Abwehr* conducted a search to locate him, but without success. This was not surprising, as, when they changed course to avoid packs, the British and the Americans relied on the contact signals transmitted by their opponents and picked up by their Huff Duff devices. Huff Duff operators had now had so much experience that they were no longer content only to spy out the enemy, but as they were personally involved in operating the device, they also often managed to identify him. In fact the Kriegsmarine only got to the bottom of the mystery in 1945.

In 1956 the official historian of the Royal Navy came to the following conclusion about the sea engagements of

March 1943:

"Nor can one yet look back on that month without feeling something approaching horror over the losses we suffered. In the first ten days, in all waters, we lost forty-one ships; in the second ten days fifty-six. More than half a million tons of shipping was sunk in those twenty days; and, what made the losses so much more serious than the bare figures can indicate, was that nearly two-thirds of the ships sunk during the month were in convoy."

Had the system of convoys, begun in September 1939, outlived its usefulness? This was the question which the Admiralty was now anxiously debating. Captain Roskill quotes the following comment from one of its reports, drawn up at the end of 1943:

"The Germans never came so near to disrupting communications between the New World and the Old as in the first

△ *Part of the team that beat Dönitz's U-boats. Seen at Coastal Command's headquarters at Northwood in Middlesex are Air-Marshal Sir John Slessor, Commander-in-Chief of Coastal Command (centre), Air Vice Marshal A. Durston, Slessor's Senior Air Staff Officer (left), and Captain D. V. Peyton-Ward, Slessor's Senior Naval Staff Officer (right). Behind them a W.A.A.F. is plotting movements on a large wall map. According to Slessor, the Bay of Biscay was "the trunk of the Atlantic U-boat menace", and in this area Coastal Command sank 25 U-boats between April and August 1943.*

△ *U-boat eye view of a sinking merchantman. Note the marks of the periscope graticule, which helped the commander gauge the range and speed of the target for incorporation into the calculations made on the plotting table. This gave the captain information as to when and where to fire his torpedoes, plus the best speed and depth to set them to run.*

twenty days of March 1943."

Between March 7 and 11, the slow convoy S.C. 121 lost 13 of its ships, and these losses remained unavenged. The submarines were not so lucky when they engaged the fast convoy H.X. 228; four merchant ships were destroyed at the cost of two U-boats. During this engagement, according to Captain Macintyre, the commander of the cargo vessel *Kingswood* almost rammed a German U-boat:

"In the darkness and the gale, as he peered anxiously out from his bridge, his eye was caught by what seemed to be a particularly heavy breaking sea on his port bow. Then he saw that the white flurry was travelling with some speed towards him. 'It's a torpedo,' he shouted to the mate standing beside him. But almost at once he realised that he was in fact looking at the wash of a submarine travelling at high speed on the surface. He ran to the telegraph and gave a double ring, calling for the utmost emergency speed and steered to ram. 'I really felt we could not miss,' he recorded.

"'Collision seemed inevitable. About this time I heard the U-boat's engine and a voice in the distance. I was sort of hanging on waiting for the crash when I saw the submarine's wake curling round – the voice I heard must have been the U-boat's commander shouting "Hard a Port" in German. The submarine's wake curled right under my stem – how its tail missed us I still do not know.'"

On March 11, the destroyer *Harvester*

(Commander A. Tait) rammed *U-444* (Sub-Lieutenant Langfeld) which was then sunk by the French corvette *Aconit* (Lieutenant Levasseur). *Harvester,* however, had her propellers badly damaged and became an easy target for *U-432* (Lieutenant Eckhardt). When he saw the column of smoke that indicated *Harvester*'s end, Levasseur returned to the fray and managed to avenge Tait, who had gone down with his ship. From March 16 to 19, the battle reached its high point, pitting 38 submarines against the two convoys H.X. 229 and S.C. 122: in the three nights 21 cargo vessels were sunk whilst the attackers lost only one U-boat.

In all, 120 merchant ships and tankers, a total of 693,389 tons, were sunk by German action during March: a serious situation for the Allies.

The U-boats had much less success during April, however. Half the number of merchant ships were destroyed (344,680 tons), for the same number of submarines sunk (15). Moreover, the support groups and escort-carriers began to pursue the enemy more and more closely. The results were clear in May. In that month, at least 47 U-boats were destroyed: 41 were sunk in the North Atlantic, whilst Allied losses fell to below 300,000 tons.

"The situation was changing," wrote Dönitz, acknowledging defeat. "Radar, particularly in aircraft, virtually cancelled out the ability of our submarines to attack on the surface. The previous tactics of our submarines could now no longer be employed in the North Atlantic, a theatre where air reconnaissance was too strong for us. Before using such tactics again, we had to restore our submarines' fighting abilities. I drew my own conclusion and we evacuated the North Atlantic. On May 24 I ordered the submarines to rendezvous in the area south-west of the Azores, taking all the necessary precautions. We had lost the Battle of the Atlantic."

Captain Roskill warmly praises the British captains and crews and summarises the episode as follows:

"In its intensity, and in the certainty that its outcome would decide the issue of the war, the battle may be compared to the Battle of Britain of 1940. Just as Göring then tried with all the forces of the Luftwaffe to gain command of the skies over Britain, so now did Dönitz seek to gain command of the Atlantic with his U-boats. And the men who defeated him—the crews of the little ships, of the air escorts and of our tiny force of long-range aircraft—may justly be immortalised alongside 'the few' who won the 1940 battle of the air."

Amongst these "few", Captain F. J. Walker's name should be mentioned; by March 14, 1944 his 2nd Escort Group had sunk 13 U-boats.

Dönitz shifts theatres

The first five months of 1943 had cost the Allies 365 ships (2,001,918 tons); in the following seven, the losses were reduced to 232 (1,218,219 tons). July was the only month in which the tonnage destroyed (365,398 tons) recalled the position in the first six months, but the Germans paid heavily for this.

Thirty-seven U-boats were lost, one per 10,000 tons sunk, whilst in March the proportion had been one to 46,200 tons.

As the British squadrons were reinforced by Coastal Command and supported by U.S. planes, they went over to the offensive in the Bay of Biscay. Dönitz thought he could ward off this threat by fitting quadruple 2-cm cannon on the conning towers of his U-boats. However, he was underestimating the danger of planes which were kept informed by radar and armed with heavy machine guns, rockets, bombs, and depth-charges. His failure to understand the situation cost him 22 U-boats between June 1 and September 1, 1943: he was therefore compelled to order his captains to submerge by day when they passed through these dangerous waters; thus their cruises took considerably longer. At night, when they recharged their batteries, his raiders still had to reckon with the enemy bombers, which were fitted with powerful radar-aimed Leigh searchlights.

In bringing the submarine war to the south-west of the Azores, the Grand-Admiral came up against the American defences.

At the Pentagon (which had just been built), Admiral Ernest J. King had appointed Rear-Admiral Francis Low as deputy chief-of-staff specially entrusted with anti-submarine problems. On receiving his report, King set up a 10th Fleet on the following May 20, which by his decision on that day "was to exercise (under the direct command of COMINCH [C.-in-C.

U.S. Fleet]) unity of control over U.S. antisubmarine operations in that part of the Atlantic under U.S. strategic control."

Low therefore only acted by King's delegation, whilst King retained command of the organisation. On the other hand, in contrast with what was happening on the other side of the Atlantic, where Sir Max Horton, C.-in-C. Western Approaches, had ships and marine aircraft, the 10th Fleet in Washington controlled neither boats nor planes. In the action it was directing, it therefore had to make use of the aircraft and formations of the Atlantic Fleet, to which it was not allowed to give any orders. This was the reason for what Ladislas Farago, the historian of the 10th Fleet, has called "an impressive flowering of periphrases" in its relations with Admiral Ingersoll, such as "suggest that you...", "it is recommended that you...", "would it be possible for you to...?"

In spite of its paradoxical situation this organisation worked extremely efficiently from the beginning. In July and August the loss of 35 out of the 60 German submarines sunk in all theatres of war was undoubtedly due to the Americans. In the South Atlantic, where the U.S. 4th Fleet was operating, the groups centred on the escort carriers *Core, Santee, Card,* and *Bogue* (under the command respectively of Captains Greer, Fisk, Isbell, and Short) took a prominent and praiseworthy part in this success. The result was that in his commentary on this period of the merchant navy war, Admiral Dönitz wrote: "Every zone in the South Atlantic was closely watched by long-range four-engined planes or by planes from American aircraft-carriers which were specially deployed to hunt submarines in the central and southern Atlantic. The same strict observation was practised even in the Indian Ocean, although not on such a wide scale. The planes of the two great naval powers therefore took a considerable part in the pursuit of our U-boats, and this continued till the end of hostilities.

"The situation was similar in more distant operational sectors.

"West of the Azores, our ships were still able in mid-June 1943 to refuel from a submarine tanker without interference, before operating in their sectors, which extended from the Straits of Florida to south of Rio de Janeiro and from Dakar to the interior of the Gulf of Guinea. Each

△ △ *A change at the head of the Home Fleet: Admiral Sir John Tovey (left) greets Vice-Admiral Sir Bruce Fraser on board his flagship as the latter takes over from him on May 8, 1943.*
△ *Rear-Admiral R. L. Burnett, who commanded the cruiser force in the action against* Hipper *and* Lützow *on December 31, 1942.*

commander had a vast area in which to operate as circumstances permitted. We systematically avoided any concentration in order not to provoke a parallel defence concentration. At first the results were favourable, as 16 enemy vessels were sunk initially. But air observation increased rapidly and the boats, particularly those off the American coast, had difficulty in maintaining themselves in their sectors. Similarly, naval refuelling became so dangerous that we had to give it up, thus considerably shortening the length of operations."

Amongst the U-boats destroyed in this sector we may mention some returning from Penang in Malaya, which had valuable cargoes of raw materials.

The episodes of the submarine war are often moving, irrespective of one's sympathies. Ladislas Farago tells one story which may be found amusing. Lieutenant Johannsen's *U-569* had been put out of action by a plane from *Bogue*:

"Johannsen ordered his men to hoist the time-honoured symbol of surrender but the hapless submariners could not find anything white on the boat whose curtains, tablecovers and sheets were all made of some oil resistant drab green cloth. They waved what they had, but those improvised green surrender flags, whose colour blended with that of an angry sea, could not have been made out by Roberts who kept up his fire. However, they were spotted by the Canadian destroyer *St. Laurent* and such evident eagerness to surrender induced her skipper to make preparations for boarding the sub to capture. Johannsen's engineer officer spoiled the scheme. In the last moment he slipped below, opened the flood-valves and went down with the boat, leaving but twenty-four U-boat men for the *St. Laurent* to capture.

"Citing the *U-Johannsen's* fate, we recommended that the U-boats carry something white on board because our pilots could not be expected to distinguish any green cloth waved at them from the level of the green sea. Our suggestion was promptly heeded. A few weeks later the *U-460* was in Johannsen's predicament. Its crew waved that 'something white' we had recommended to keep handy for such emergencies. The 'surrender flag' turned out to be the skipper's dress shirt."

On October 8, 1943 the agreement between the Portuguese and British Governments granting the British naval and air forces the right to establish a base in the Azores was a new blow for German naval strategy; a few months later, moreover, the Americans were granted the same concession. Thus the "Atlantic gap" was finally closed.

The balance of losses

On December 31, 1943, the German submarine flotillas consisted of only 168 operational units; there had been 212 on the preceding January 1. During the year they had lost 237 U-boats and their crews. Eight of these were the result of accident, 75 were sunk by the Americans, five by the French, one by the Russians, and the remainder (148) by the Royal Navy and Coastal Command squadrons. As against these losses, we must put the losses of all kinds of Allied merchant vessels in 1943: they amounted to 3,220,137 tons, made up of 597 ships. These figures may appear very large, but they are nevertheless 4,570,560 tons and 1,067 ships less than the figures in 1942. During the same period merchant ships and tankers of about 13 million tons were launched in British, Canadian, and American shipyards. Here again the predominance of the U.S.A. became apparent. Their Liberty ships, which

were succeeded by their Victory ships, were built with prefabricated parts by methods recommended by the industrialist Henry Kayser, an organiser of genius; they played a distinguished part in the Allied victory of 1945 and the reconstruction of Western Europe, including Germany and Italy, after the close of hostilities. But in spite of this Dönitz did not give up. He believed that new arms would bring victory in 1944, and in the meantime he counted on forcing the enemy to squander his effort within the bounds of the Atlantic; otherwise the Allies would concentrate their resources even more against the industrial might of the Third Reich.

From January 1 to December 31, 1943, more than 680,000 Allied combatants were disembarked in Great Britain and Northern Ireland by 66 convoys as a part of Operation "Bolero", whilst about 127,000 left the British Isles for Africa, Sicily, and Italy. As a general rule the troops crossed the Atlantic without a convoy on fast liners which managed to

△△ *Waist gunners of a Sunderland flying boat. Their duties when on patrol were as much to watch for U-boats as to guard against German air attacks.*
△ *A quadruple 2-pdr "pom-pom" A.A. mounting on board a British warship.*

△△ *Captain F. J. Walker,*
commander of the 2nd Escort
Group, comes ashore from his
sloop Starling.

△ *Lieutenant-Commander*
P. W. Gretton, who led the B7
Escort Group with Convoy S.C.
130. On the Atlantic crossing
from St. Johns to Londonderry
between May 14 and 20, five
U-boats were sunk.

▷△ Scharnhorst *at sea. Visible*
here is part of the turreted
secondary armament of 5.9-inch
guns, with four of the 4.1-inch
A.A. guns above them and a pair
of 3.7-cm A.A. guns in the
foreground.

▷▷ *The British light cruiser*
Sheffield.

▷▽ *The King George V-class*
battleship Duke of York.
Opening fire at long range by
radar, she soon slowed
Scharnhorst with a hit in a
boiler room. This long range fire
proved to be the decisive factor
in the battle–Duke of York's
14-inch shells, plunging steeply
down from the top of their high
trajectory, were too much for
Scharnhorst's deck armour.

elude U-boat ambushes. Using the "hot berth" system (two berths for three soldiers), the *Queen Elizabeth* and the *Queen Mary* transported 15,000 men per crossing, whilst the French ship *Pasteur* accommodated 4,500.

Nevertheless the rations, fighting equipment, vehicles, fuel, and ammunition for these 680,000 men went via the usual convoy route, and most of the bombers for the U.S. 8th Air Force and all the fighters reached Britain by sea. Even if they had crossed the Atlantic by air, or via Iceland, their fuel supply could only have been secured by the use of tankers. For this reason, we may conclude that if the German submarine raiders had not been defeated in 1943, there would have been no Second Front in Western Europe in 1944.

End of the *Scharnhorst*

At the end of March 1943, the battle-cruiser *Scharnhorst* joined the battleship *Tirpitz* and pocket battleship *Lützow* at Trondheim, and then together the three reached Kåfjord, a small section of the Altenfjord about halfway between Tromsö and the North Cape. From this position they could harass the Allied convoys in the Arctic or even resume the war against the merchant ships in the Atlantic. As the Sicilian operations and the Salerno landing required six British warships in the Mediterranean, the Home Fleet, as whose commander Admiral Tovey had been succeeded by Sir Bruce Fraser in June 1943, had some difficulty in intercepting the German ships.

In addition, the Admiralty in London organised Operation "Source" under the command of Rear-Admiral C. B. Barry, Flag Officer Submarines. The purpose of this operation was to destroy this dangerous German force at anchor by using six 30-ton midget submarines; their armament consisted of two 2-ton charges which could be released to sink under the hull of the target, exploding when set off by a clockwork mechanism. A squadron of reconnaissance planes made Murmansk their base and gave the attackers all possible Intelligence about the obstacles and defences around the anchored German ships.

On September 11, six midget submarines (each manned by four men and towed by conventional submarines), left

an unobtrusive harbour in the north of Scotland and sailed towards Altenfjord. One of them *(X-8)* was to attack *Lützow*, two *(X-9* and *X-10) Scharnhorst*, and the remaining three *(X-5, X-6,* and *X-7) Tirpitz*. But *X-9* was lost with all hands during the crossing, and *X-8* had to be scuttled because it was heavily damaged. The four remaining submarines suffered mishaps of all kinds; even if their compasses managed to work, their periscope tubes filled with water or the electrical engine used for raising them failed.

In spite of all this, at dawn on September 22 Lieutenants Cameron and Place managed to steer *X-6* and *X-7* below *Tirpitz* and release their charges. When *X-6* accidentally surfaced, the huge warship was alerted and had enough time to slew round at her anchorage, thereby managing to escape the worst. But two of her 15-inch gun turrets were immobilised and her engines were badly damaged, and she was out of action for several months. *X-5*, which followed *X-6* and 7, was shelled and sunk. Cameron with his crew of three and Place with only one other survivor were taken prisoner on the ship they had crippled; they were treated in a way that did credit to their heroism. *X-10* was scuttled on its return journey as it was found to have the same defects as its companion submarines. It had missed *Scharnhorst*, its intended victim, because the battle-cruiser was engaged in target practice off the Altenfjord, but it lost nothing by waiting.

On December 22 a Luftwaffe reconnaissance plane spotted an enemy convoy 465 miles west of Tromsö; in fact this was J.W. 55B, which consisted of 19 merchant ships and ten destroyers; it was due to pass R.A. 55A, bringing back 22 empty ships from Murmansk, in the neighbourhood of Bear Island. Vice-Admiral Burnett was responsible for protecting this two-way passage with the heavy cruiser *Norfolk* and the light cruisers *Sheffield* and *Belfast*. In order to provide distant cover, Sir Bruce Fraser, flying his flag on the battleship *Duke of York*, with the light cruiser *Jamaica* and four destroyers, sailed from the Akureyri, the Allied base on the north coast of Iceland, on December 23.

When it received the first signal of an enemy convoy, the German naval group at Kåfjord, as whose commander Rear-Admiral E. Bey had just succeeded Vice-Admiral O. Kummetz, had been put at the alert; on the evening of December 25 it was ordered to attack the convoy. A few hours later, a message from Dönitz arrived to confirm its mission:

"1. By sending the Russians a large consignment of food supplies and *matériel,* the enemy is trying to make our army's heroic struggles on the Eastern Front even more difficult. We must go to the help of our soldiers.

2. Attack the convoy with *Scharnhorst* and destroyers."

Though the mission was clear, the Grand-Admiral followed it with contradictory instructions. Bey should not be satisfied with a "half-success", but should seize the opportunity of "attacking in force". Nevertheless he was allowed the option of breaking off the engagement, and he was reminded that the "essential thing" was always to avoid any "engagement against superior forces".

While Bey was ploughing on and pursuing the enemy, in these bitterly cold northern waters, the Admiralty was able to send a signal to Fraser that *Scharnhorst* was probably at sea. At approximately 0400 on December 26 the Home Fleet commander ordered convoy J.W. 55B to withdraw to the north, with Vice-Admiral Burnett covering its withdrawal. Fraser himself increased to 24 knots to close *Scharnhorst,* which he placed about 250 to 275 miles from *Duke of York.*

At 0840 *Belfast*'s radar identified a large enemy warship about 20 miles to the north-west and at 0924, at a distance of eight miles, *Belfast* fired her first star-shell, illuminating *Scharnhorst.* During a brief engagement, *Norfolk,* without being hit, obtained two direct hits with 8-inch shells and destroyed the radar rangefinder in *Scharnhorst*'s bows. Bey withdrew, doubtless hoping to circle round the British detachment and attack the convoy which, it will be recalled, was his chief target. This manoeuvre was frustrated by Burnett, who in the meantime had requested the convoy to lend him four destroyers. These moves led to a second engagement at approximately 1230, and this time the light favoured the battle-cruiser; one of her 11-inch shells put *Norfolk*'s aft gun-turret out of action, whilst *Sheffield* was covered with shell splinters.

In spite of this success, the German admiral retreated for the second time at a speed of 28 knots. In his memoirs, Dönitz shows moderation in his comments on the movements of his unfortunate sub-

"The Sinking of the Scharnhorst" by C. E. Turner. The German pocket-battleship proved a resilient foe—13 14-inch shells and 11 torpedoes were needed to sink her.

ordinate, but clearly they do not meet with his approval. However, it is only fair to point out that Bey kept strictly to Dönitz's instruction not to endanger his ship; he would have disobeyed this order had he ventured further with his radar not functioning in the half-light of the Arctic day. On the other hand a message from a plane was signalled to him at 1100: "Five ships north-west of North Cape." As none of *Scharnhorst*'s 36 survivors had a hand in the decision which was to lead to its destruction, one must be careful in one's comments.

When he headed for his base at about 1430, the German admiral, who was pursued by Burnett at the limit of radar range, had no idea that he was about to meet the Home Fleet; moreover he did not know that the plane message received at 1100 had an important passage missing: "Including probably one heavy ship." In fact, at 1617 *Scharnhorst* appeared on *Duke of York*'s radar screen 25½ miles to the north-north-east, approaching rapidly. At 1650 the English warship, at a range of less than 6½ miles, opened fire on her adversary, who was lit up by *Belfast*'s star-shells. Total surprise was achieved. The German battle-cruiser tur-

ned north again, and then meeting Burnett, tried to escape in an easterly direction. During this engagement she had been hit by three 14-inch shells; one of them exploded in a boiler room, and another put the forward 11-inch turret out of action. Although disabled, *Scharnhorst* managed to break contact at 1820 when Bey signalled: "We shall fight to the last shell." By this time the battleship *Duke of York* had ceased fire, but Sir Bruce Fraser's four destroyers attacked *Scharnhorst* on both sides. Although she managed to avoid *Scorpion*'s and *Stord*'s torpedoes, she laid herself open to the wave of 12 torpedoes launched at her by *Savage* and *Saumarez* at point-blank range. Three hit their mark a little before 1850.

Crushed by *Duke of York*'s shells and all the light ships' torpedoes, *Scharnhorst* sank at 1945 on December 26. The victors picked up only 36 out of a crew of just under 1,900 men; both Rear-Admiral Bey and his flag captain, Captain Hintze, were lost. According to Stephen Roskill, 13 14-inch shells and 11 torpedoes were necessary to sink this heroic ship. "Once again the ability of the Germans to build tremendously stout ships had been demonstrated."

CHAPTER 52
DESCENT ON SICILY

If the catastrophe which befell the Axis forces in Tunisia was a defeat of some magnitude and of so far unforeseeable consequences for the Third Reich, for Fascist Italy it was nothing less than a death sentence, without appeal or reprieve.

The mobilisation decree of June 10, 1940 had given *Comando Supremo* an army of 75 divisions. Since that date 20 more had been raised, but these were not enough to make up for the losses sustained since June 10, 1940.

Two divisions had disappeared with the Italian East African empire and 25 more went in the Libyan, Egyptian, and Tunisian campaigns between December 8, 1940 and May 13, 1943. Of the divisions which had fought in the ranks of the Italian Expeditionary Force (later the Italian 8th Army) which Mussolini, over-riding all objections, had sent to join the "crusade against Bolshevism", only straggling remnants had returned. The table below bears eloquent witness to these losses. It was drawn up by the Historical Services of the Italian Army and relates to the state of the Italian armed forces at the time of the defensive battle of the Don.

Less than three years of hostilities had therefore cost Italy more than a third of her field army. Even so, on the date in question, no fewer than 36 divisions were immobilised outside Italy and her island dependencies, occupying France or re-pressing guerrillas in the Balkans.

The situation from Crete to the Italian–Yugoslav frontier as laid down on April 6, 1940 was clearly not improving. Far from it. A communiqué from Rome gave 10,570 killed, wounded, and missing among the Italian occupation troops in the first five months of 1943. The maquis were organising in Savoy and the Dauphiné, whilst in Corsica arms were reaching the resistance fighters via the underwater shuttle-service run by Lieutenant-Commander L'Herminier in the submarine *Casabianca*. No massive recoupment of losses could therefore be made from these 36 divisions.

The defence of the Italian peninsula, Sardinia, and Sicily was thus entrusted to some 30 divisions, but not all these

were immediately available. Two armoured divisions, including the Blackshirt "M" Armoured Division, equipped with German tanks, had not yet finished training. A great effort was therefore made to reconstitute the "Ariete" and the "Centauro" Armoured Divisions, which had escaped from Russia under conditions which we have already described. And so *Comando Supremo* had only about 20 divisions (with equipment no better than it had been in 1940) with which to face the threatened invasion. Its pessimism, in view of the Anglo-American preparations in North Africa, can well be imagined. No reliance could be placed on the so-called "coastal" defences (21 divisions and five brigades) which, as their name indicates, were to offer an initial defence against the enemy landing on the beaches. These units had only local recruits, all in the top age-groups, and they were very poorly officered. Mussolini quoted the case of Sicily, where two battalions were commanded by 2nd Lieutenants retired in 1918 and only recently recalled to the colours. The weapons and equipment of these formations were even more deficient than those of any other divisions. To ease the only too evident shortages, the Duce was counting on the *matériel* coming to him under the Villa Incisa agreement and on what could be pillaged from the now disbanded Vichy French army. But the weapons he did

△ *New York's* Bulldog *derides the ignominious dashing of Mussolini's dream of an African empire.*

▽ *The savage losses of the Italian 8th Army in Russia.*

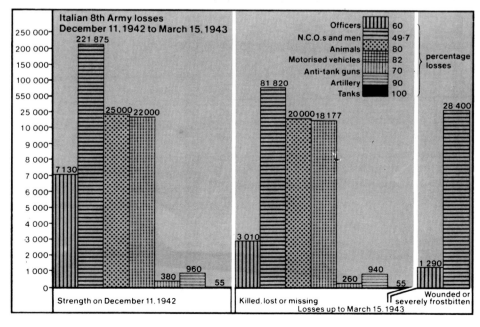

LA DOMENICA DEL CORRIERE

ITALIA ESTERO	Si pubblica a Milano ogni settimana	Uffici del giornale Via Solferino, 28 - Milano
Anno . . . . L. 28,— L. 34,— Semestre . . . . » 12,— » 19,— Per le inserzioni rivolgersi all'Amministrazione del Corriere della Sera - Via Solferino, 28 - Milano.	Supplemento illustrato del "Corriere della Sera" Spedizione in abbonamento postale - Gruppo 2	Per tutti gli articoli e illustrazioni e riservata la proprietà letteraria e artistica, secondo le leggi e i trattati internazionali.

| Anno 45 — N. 12 | 21 Marzo 1943 XXI | Centesimi 50 la copia |

△ *Italy's Domenica del Corriere attempts to inspire faith in the country's defences against Allied invasion: "the guns of a coastal battery point menacingly out to sea."*

get from these sources often reached him without ammunition or accessories: sometimes they had been astutely sabotaged. Finally, the units were strung out along the coast like a line of customs posts. In Sicily there were 41 men to the mile.

The Italian Air Force impotent

If we remember that the R.A.F.'s defeat of the Luftwaffe in 1940 caused the abandonment of Operation "Sea Lion", it is pertinent to ask what was the state of the Italian Air Force at this time. On June 14, 1943, in the presence of General Ambrosio, Chief of the Italian General Staff, and of the Commanders-in-Chief of the three armed forces, Mussolini had stated unequivocally: "We have neither a powerful bombing force nor the fighters to protect it."

No doubt things would tend to improve in the second half of 1944, but at first it would merely be a drop in the ocean. That is why, Mussolini went on, "it is *absolutely essential* for Germany to supply our needs for A.A. defence in our homeland, that is planes and guns." In calling blithely on the services of his Axis partner, Mussolini was relying on the good will of the Führer, and quite properly. But did he know that the Luftwaffe was then in very dire straits and likely to remain so? On the one hand the Germans had lost all air superiority in the East; on the other they were having to fight off increasing air attacks by Anglo-American bombers on their war industries. There was thus little that could be done to make good the deficiencies in the Italian air strength. Moreover, the aerodromes of Sicily, Sardinia, and southern Italy were regularly being hammered by the Allies.

The Navy hard pressed

By May 13, 1943, 35 months of war had caused the deaths, by killing or drowning, of 35,000 officers and men and the loss of the following ships: one battleship, five heavy cruisers, seven light cruisers, 74 destroyers, and 85 submarines.

It had, of course, proved impossible to build enough new ships to make up for all these losses. Admiral Riccardi, Chief-of-Staff at *Supermarina,* still had, it is true, six battleships, a dozen cruisers, some 60 destroyers and torpedo-boats and the same number of submarines. The smaller surface vessels, however, were worn out after three years' hard escort service. The day after the Battle of Matapan the Duce had decided that until the converted liners *Roma* and *Augustus* came into service as aircraft-carriers, the fleet would not venture outside the radius of action of land-based fighters. No-one had foreseen that the day would come when there was to be no fighter support at all. When the Anglo-Americans set up a powerful bombing force in North Africa, Admiral Riccardi had been compelled to move his squadrons away from their moorings at Taranto, Messina, and Naples. On April 12 the cruiser *Trieste* was sunk by air attack as she lay at anchor in the roads at La Maddalena off the north coast of Sardinia. On June 5 a raid by Flying Fortresses on La Spezia caused varying degrees of damage to the big battleships *Roma, Littorio,* and *Vittorio Veneto.* The fuel crisis had now become critical, and to economise on supplies the cruisers *Duilio, Doria,* and *Cesare* were laid up, the first two at Taranto and the third at Pola.

No way to counter-attack

Faced with this disastrous state of affairs, Mussolini came to the following conclusions on point 2 of the note on which he commented on June 14 to his Chiefs-of-Staff:

"In the present state of the war the Italian forces no longer hold any possibility of initiative. They are forced onto the defensive. The army no longer has any possibility of initiative. It lacks, amongst other things, room to manoeuvre. It can only counter-attack the enemy who lands at one point on our territory and drive him back into the sea." We shall comment no further on Mussolini's remarks on the possibilities open to the Italian Navy and Air Force, as these have been mentioned already. It should be noted, however, that in asking the Army to counter-attack the enemy as he landed and throw him back

△ △ *An Italian mortar crew. The basic equipment of the troops was no better than it had been in 1935.*
△ *Training with an anti-tank gun. Most of them had been lost in Africa.*
◁ *The crew of a coastal battery go through their gun drill.*

into the sea, Mussolini had overlooked the report made to him on May 8 by the Chief of the General Staff after an inspection in Sardinia.

After noting certain differences of conception in the organisation of defences against landings, General Ambrosio recommended the adoption of what he called the "modern technique". This was to break up the landing on the beaches or, even better, crush the opposing forces whilst they were still at sea. The advanced defensive position therefore had to have guns capable of dealing with ships, landing-craft, personnel, and tanks, not only to stop the mechanised columns which might break through the first defence line, but also to knock out approaching flotillas and all the troops who managed to set foot ashore. "It is all the more necessary to stop the attack on the beach before it can secure a foothold as, not having enough armour, we shall not be able to halt a well-equipped adversary once he has landed and started to make his way inland."

Thus Ambrosio did not believe, any more than Rommel was to in 1944, in a counter-attack from inland against an enemy who had secured an extensive beach-head. His scepticism was backed by a decisive argument: the Italians did not have in their army any powerfully-equipped shock force to carry it out. Had the Duce any more faith in it? Probably not. In his note to his four Chiefs-of-Staff he had sensibly written: "It has been said that the artillery wins the ground and the infantry occupies it." He did not hesitate to apply to Sicily the very recent precedent of Pantelleria. Against Ambrosio it must be remembered that nowhere did the coastal units have the weapons he was recommending and that he was well aware of this. Thus there was no way of driving any invasion force back into the sea or of counter-attacking it as it was striking inland. In other words they had reached the situation covered by the saying quoted by Mussolini on June 14: "He who defends himself dies!"

The peace faction

But was it necessary to die? As we have seen, Mussolini was counting on German aid to drive back the invaders. But even within his own party, a majority of its leaders thought that Hitler's intentions were less to defend Italy than to defend Germany in Italy, and that the final defeat of the Third Reich was written in the stars anyway. The peninsula must therefore not be allowed to become a battlefield. Italy must get out of the war one way or another–and immediately, as she had already lost the war irremediably. We have seen that Ciano, Grandi, and Bottaï, all three former ministers of the Duce, shared this opinion with Marshals Badoglio and Caviglia, with the "young" Generals Castellano and Carboni, with the former Prime Ministers of the liberal era Orlando and Bonomi, and with those close to the King. The Chief of the General Staff accepted the principle of a rupture of the Axis and a cessation of hostilities but, as he continually urged him, preferred Mussolini to take the initiative for this change of tack. Failing this he envisaged arresting the Duce. Finally, General Chierici, Chief of Police, and General Hazon, Commander of the Corps of Carabinieri, also declared themselves in favour of an eventual show of force.

The King, however, hesitated to give the signal. We would impute this not to lack of personal courage but to the fear of provoking indescribable chaos if the elimination of Mussolini, which he thought would be necessary, were to be carried out by other than legal means. In particular the presence in the Lake Bracciano area, some 25 miles from the capital, of the Blackshirt "M" Armoured Division, militated against any ill-considered gesture, and whilst Germany was reinforcing her strength in the peninsula, she could be counted upon to react with some force.

The King's reserve caused Count Grandi to lose patience. On June 3, recalling to Victor Emmanuel III the ups and downs of the House of Savoy, he said: "Your Majesty, there is no choice: either Novara, namely abdication, or a change of front in the style of Victor Amadeus II who, when he realised the mistake of the alliance with the King of France, saved Piedmont and the dynasty at the last moment, by going over to the Imperial camp."

Marshal Badoglio felt the same way on July 17, when he said to Senator Casati: "Either the King accepts the solution which, in agreement with us, he has already anticipated, or he resigns himself to waiting for another moment. In the second case each one of us can choose the way he wishes to follow."

△ Tough, well-armed, and with a superb combat tradition: German paratroopers, who formed the core of the Axis defence of Sicily and went on to add to their laurels on the defensive in Italy.

△ *An Italian marshalling-yard gets a dose of Allied bombs. All key strategic centres were thoroughly bombed before the invasion, as well as the defences along the coast.*

Sardinia or Sicily?

As we have seen in the preceding chapter, Hitler thought that the first objective of the Anglo-American invasion would be Sardinia. General Ambrosio's inspection of the island's defences in early May would seem to indicate that the *Comando Supremo* agreed with the Führer. After the event, Marshal Badoglio gave it as his opinion that the strategists in London and Washington had made a great mistake in preferring the easier way of a landing in Sicily.

This would be correct if the two Western powers had proposed an immediate conquest of Italy, for the occupation of Sardinia means that the peninsula south of a line La Spezia–Ancona cannot be defended and allows, through Corsica and after landings in Liguria, the turning of the Apennine bastion.

But when plans were being drawn up for Operation "Husky", the Anglo-Americans were proposing nothing of the sort. They anticipated, first of all, clearing the

Sicilian Channel, and then securing a bridgehead, including Naples and Foggia, whose great aerodromes would allow bombing raids on the Rumanian oil-fields. But at the "Trident" Conference on May 12-25 in Washington, attended by Roosevelt and Churchill, which was to decide on the follow-up to "Husky", the Americans expressed their conviction that the British had "led them down the garden path by taking them into North Africa". "They also think," continued Alanbrooke in his diary, "that at Casablanca we again misled them by inducing them to attack Sicily. And now they do not intend to be led astray again."

And the American President agreed, apart from a few minor reservations, with the thinking of the Pentagon. According to Alanbrooke, Roosevelt admitted, it is true, "the urgent need to consider where to go from Sicily and how to keep employed the score or more of battle-trained Anglo-American divisions in the Mediterranean. But the continuing drain involved in any attempt to occupy Italy might prejudice the build-up of forces for a cross-Channel invasion, and, though there now seemed no chance of the latter in 1943, it would have to be launched on the largest scale in the spring of 1944."

After long arguments between the British and the Americans, it was agreed that while an invasion of France in late spring 1944 remained the principal Allied operation against Germany, the Allied forces in the Mediterranean after "Husky" were to mount "such operations as are best calculated to eliminate Italy from the war and to contain the maximum number of German divisions".

For "Husky" General Eisenhower kept the same team which had brought him victory in Tunisia. Under his control General Alexander would direct the operations of the 15th Army Group, the number being the sum of its two constituent armies, the American 7th (Lieutenant-General Patton) and the British 8th (Montgomery): an experienced and able high command.

According to the original plan, the British 8th Army was to land between Syracuse and Gela and the American 7th Army on each side of Trapani at the other end of the island. Montgomery, however, objected because, as he wrote to Alexander on April 24: "Planning to date has been on the assumption that resistance will be slight and Sicily will be

captured easily . . . If we work on the assumption of little resistance, and disperse our effort as is being done in all planning to date, we will merely have a disaster. We must plan for fierce resistance, by the Germans at any rate, and for a real dog fight battle to follow the initial assault."

The original plan had therefore to be concentrated so that the two Allied armies could give each other mutual support if either ran into trouble. Credit is due to both Eisenhower and Alexander for having accepted without too much difficulty Montgomery's reasoning. The revised plan set Scoglitti, Gela, and Licata as Patton's first objectives, whilst Montgomery moved his left flank objective over from the Gela area to Cape Passero so as to be able to seize this important promontory at the south-eastern tip of Sicily in a pincer movement.

The British 8th Army comprised the following:

1. XIII Corps (Lieutenant-General Dempsey), made up of the 5th Division (Major-General Bucknall), the 50th Division (Major-General Kirkman), and the 231st Brigade (Brigadier-

General Urquhart); and

2. XXX Corps (Lieutenant-General Leese), made up of the 51st Division (Major-General Wimberley) and the 1st Canadian Division (Major-General Simmonds).

The American 7th Army comprised the II Corps (Lieutenant-General Bradley), made up of the 45th Division (Major-

△ △ *Loading up the landing-craft at Sousse in Tunisia before the descent on Sicily.*
△ *Supply from the air: Douglas C-47 transports are loaded.*

General Middleton), the 1st Division (Major-General Allen), and the 2nd Armoured Division (Major-General Grittenberger), plus also the 3rd Division (Major-General Truscott), unattached to a corps.

Each army had an airborne spearhead of brigade strength, and one division held provisionally in reserve in North Africa.

Admiral Cunningham's armada

An armada of 2,590 ships, large and small, took part in Operation "Husky" under the command of Admiral Cunningham. Under him Admiral Sir Bertram H. Ramsay was in command of the landings.

△ U.S. soldiers head into the beaches.
▽ Bombs and shells explode around ships of the invasion fleet as it nears the coast of Sicily.

Ramsay's experience went back to the Dunkirk evacuation, and this time he had 237 merchant vessels and troop transports and 1,742 motorised landing-craft to bring ashore the men, tanks, and supplies. The fighting units had two missions: to neutralise by gun fire all resistance on the shore and to deal with the Italian fleet. They had therefore been given generous support: six battle-ships, two fleet aircraft-carriers (both British), three monitors, 15 cruisers (five American), 128 destroyers (48 American, six Greek, and three Polish), and 26 sub-marines (one Dutch and two Polish).

An enormous concentration, but during the first phase of the operation 115,000 British and Canadians and more than 66,000 Americans had to be put ashore.

As for the Allied air forces, they had 4,000 planes under Air Chief-Marshal Tedder. By D-day they had virtually wiped out the enemy's defences. Over Sicily the opposition was a mere 200 Italian and 320 German planes.

Pantelleria capitulates

On June 12 the *matériel* and morale effect of the air bombardment of Pantelleria was such that Admiral Pavesi surrendered this island fortress of 12,000 men to the Allies after losing only 56 killed and 116 wounded. According to Mussolini, Pavesi had deceived him by giving the reason for his request to surrender as lack of water. According to Admiral Bernotti it was not so much the water which was short as the means of distributing it. There were only four tanker-lorries and three wells for 10,000 civilians and 12,000 troops. Add to this the physical shock of the explosion of 6,550 tons of bombs in six days and it will be seen that the capitulation of June 12 was understandable.

At the same time, the Allied air forces redoubled their attacks on Sicily, particu-larly on the aerodromes and the harbours. Messina alone received 5,000 tons of bombs. Communications with the main-land were severely affected and feeding the civilian population began to bring enormous problems to the administration. At the end of June there were only 30 days' supplies of flour left.

On June 8, Generals Eisenhower and Alexander and Admiral Cunningham went to Malta. All was going well apart from the deteriorating weather. The meteorological office reported Force 4 to 5 winds over the sea but there was no going back.

The strength of the Axis forces

Let us now go over to the other side.

On June 1 General Guzzoni succeeded General Roatta in command of the Italian 6th Army, with the task of defending Sicily to the last. According to Mussolini, the enemy was to be wiped out before breaking through inland or "as he took off his bath-robe and before he had had time to get dressed".

As soon as he was informed of the Anglo-American invasion preparations, the Duce, said Marshal Badoglio, "had rushed to make a speech to the nation; the stupidest he ever gave. Later it became known as the 'bath-robe' speech."

The plan adopted for the defence corresponded so closely to the invasion plan abandoned at the request of Montgomery that it can be asked if in fact the Anglo-Americans had not leaked it on purpose. Guzzoni established his headquarters at Enna in the centre of the island and divided his forces into two:

1. west of the line Licata (inclusive)– Cefalú: XII Corps (H.Q. at Corleone) to defend Marsala, Trapani, and Palermo. Commanded by General Arisio it comprised the "Aosta" Division (General Romano) and the "Assietta" Division (General Papini) with the 207th, 202nd, and 208th Coastal Divisions; and

2. east of this line: XVI Corps (H.Q. at Piazza Armerina) to defend Gela, Syracuse, Catania, and Messina. Commanded by General Rossi, it had the "Napoli" Division (General Gotti-Porcinari), the 206th and 213th Coastal Divisions, and the 18th and 19th Coastal Brigades.

The "Livorno" Division (General Chirieleison) was held in army reserve at Mazzarino.

Including the Fascist Militia there were thus 230,000 men and 1,500 guns in the Italian 6th Army which, however, was not very mobile as there were very few motorised units among its formations. The coastal units had tremendous stretches of land to defend: the 206th

Division (General d'Havet) had nearly 83 miles between Cassibile and Punte Braccetto, and the 18th Brigade (General Mariscalco) 36 miles between Punte Braccetto to east of Licata. These two units were to take the brunt of the six British and American divisions, while the American attack by 3rd Division was to face only two battalions of the 207th Division (General Schreiber).

The Italian 6th Army was supported by two German divisions, the 15th *Panzergrenadier* (Major-General Rodt) and the "Hermann Göring" Panzer Division (Lieutenant-General Conrath). The first of these was only partially motorised and the second had only two battalions of infantry and fewer than 100 tanks, though these included a company of Tigers. O.K.W. had appointed Major-General von Senger und Etterlin as liaison officer to General Guzzoni.

When Hitler received Senger und Etterlin on June 22 he did not disguise his mistrust of the Italian court, society, and

△ On the alert as the Allied armada surges onward. The total command of the air which the Allies enjoyed meant that the Axis powers could hardly impede this invasion force.

▽ Moment of truth. American tanks hit the beach at Licata.

△ Paratroopers struggle into their harness before a drop. Most of the airborne operations in Sicily went badly awry, and essential lessons were learned the hard way.

▽ German paratroopers on the look-out.

high command. In spite of this he was optimistic about the outcome of the operations as, he assured Senger und Etterlin, the Allies "by neglecting to attack Sicily immediately after their landings in North Africa had virtually thrown away the war in the Mediterranean!"

General Warlimont, Chief of the Operations Staff at O.K.W., did not share these illusions. "He laid the situation clearly before me" wrote Senger und Etterlin, adding: "the best solution to the mission entrusted to me was to be, in case of heavy enemy attacks, to bring back to the mainland the majority of the troops stationed in Sicily. He recognised that we could not expect to bring back the bulk of our war *matériel*. This appreciation of the situation and the definition of my mission was a corrective to Hitler's viewpoint."

At Enna, where he had gone together with Field-Marshal Kesselring, the question of the intervention of the German units in the battle, now expected any day, gave rise to somewhat confused discussions. In the end the 15th Panzer Division, less one detachment, was relegated to the western tip of the island whilst the "Hermann Göring" Panzer Division was divided between the plain of Catania and the Caltagirone area.

The landing on July 10 came as no surprise. The evening before, Axis aircraft had spotted six Allied convoys leaving Malta and, towards five o'clock in the morning, Enna H.Q. reported that several parachutists had landed. These landings were unfortunate, as the men were widely scattered by the wind; nevertheless they succeeded in harrassing the enemy's movements. Brigadier-General Lathbury, at the head of a hundred or so British troops, seized the bridge at Primosole south of Catania and held out there for five days, preventing its destruction until the arrival of the 8th Army.

Allied success

At dawn, naval guns and tactical aircraft pounded the Italian coastal defences whilst many landing-craft, loaded with men and tanks, advanced on to their objectives in spite of a choppy sea. D.U.K.W.s, American amphibious trucks, were the first vehicles to land. Franz Kurokowski's monograph on the Sicilian campaign tells of numerous acts of heroism by men of the 206th Division and the 18th Brigade, but faced with companies, battalions, and regiments supported by tanks they were overrun and virtually wiped out. In the evening General Guzzoni ordered the 15th Panzer Division to move towards Enna and the "Hermann Göring" Panzer Division, together with the "Livorno" Division, to mop up the American bridgehead at Gela. In the morning of July 11 the Panzers ran into the forward posts of the 1st American Division in the area of Niscemi but when they had got to within 2,000 yards of the beach they were caught by fire from the cruisers *Boise* and *Savannah* and six destroyers, which together loosed off no fewer than 3,194 6- and 5-inch shells at them and wiped out 30 tanks. The "Livorno" Division was also very badly knocked about. On the same day Montgomery occupied, without a shot being fired, the two harbours of Syracuse and Augusta, which had been abandoned by their garrisons in somewhat obscure circumstances.

On July 14 the American 7th Army and the British 8th Army met. This gave them the aerodromes at Ragusa and Comiso, which were put back into shape in record time. Was Montgomery going to race the enemy to Messina and force a surrender, as he had planned? No. Kesselring managed by a great feat to bring over to Sicily two paratroop regiments and the

29th *Panzergrenadier* Division (Major-General Fries). On July 17 General Hube and the staff of XIV Panzer Corps took command of all German fighting troops in Sicily and resistance stiffened on both sides of Mount Etna. The 8th Army was stopped at Catania and so attacked west of Etna, upsetting the advancing Americans.

Patton, by a miracle of improvisation, then threw his army against Palermo, which fell on July 22, having overcome on the way the "Assietta" Division. He then resumed his advance towards Messina, hoping, like Montgomery, to get there before the Germans. Once again, however, Hube parried and on July 23 the forward units of the American 7th Army were stopped in front of the little town of Santo Stefano on the coastal road. Meanwhile the 1st Canadian Division, which formed Montgomery's left flank, after bypassing the important crossroads at Enna, tried to turn the Etna massif from the north-west.

Masters of Sicily

Meanwhile the American 9th Division (Major-General Eddy), which had landed at Palermo, and the British 78th Division (Major-General Keightley), now ashore at Syracuse, brought the number of divisions in the 15th Army Group to 11 and gave the Allies an enormous superiority. Hube therefore began to withdraw, and did it so well that two-thirds of his forces got across to Italy.

Messina and the straits were bristling with A.A., which made life very difficult for Anglo-American aircraft. At 0530 hours on August 17 the commander of XIV Panzer Corps embarked on the last assault-boat leaving for Calabria. Three hours later the Americans and the British were congratulating each other in the ruined streets of Messina.

In his final communiqué, General Alexander announced the capture of 132,000 prisoners, 260 tanks, and 520 guns, and we know from General Faldella, former Chief-of-Staff of the 6th Army, that today there are 4,278 Italian and 4,325 German dead in the war cemeteries in Sicily. On the Allied side, out of 467,000 men in Operation "Husky" the losses were 5,532 killed, 2,869 missing and 14,410 wounded.

The Italian fleet

Though the battleships *Caio Duilio* and *Andrea Doria* had been brought back into service late in July, the Italian fleet, through lack of sufficient escort and air support, played only a passive rôle in the operation. Furthermore the bulk of the fleet, stationed as it was in La Spezia, was badly placed to intervene in the waters round Cape Passero. Admiral Riccardi thus limited his support to submarines, torpedo planes, and fast patrol boats. At the high cost of nine of their numbers sunk, the Italian submarines torpedoed and damaged the cruisers *Newfoundland* and *Cleopatra*, and sent to the bottom four merchant-vessels and a tanker. The American destroyer *Maddox* was sunk by aerial bombardment on July 10.

◁ *German soldiers watch a bombardment.*
▽ *The first supply-dumps begin to build up on the beaches. As Axis resistance to the landings increased, more and more* matériel *was needed to support the advance to Messina.*

CHAPTER 53
SALERNO: THE INVASION OF ITALY

As we have seen, in the case of defection by the Italians, Field-Marshal Kesselring was ordered to withdraw the 90th *Panzergrenadier* Division from Sardinia and send it across the Bonifacio channel to join the forces defending Corsica. To this effect, O.K.W. put the troops stationed on the two islands under the command of General von Senger und Etterlin, who arrived in Ajaccio on board a Dornier Do 17 on September 7.

On Sardinia General Basso, who was in command of the island, had under him XVI and XXX Corps (two infantry and three coastal defence divisions), plus the "Bari" Division and the "Nembo" Parachute Division. This would appear to have been more than enough to deal with the 90th *Panzergrenadier*. It should not be forgotten, however, that the German formation, being in reserve, was concentrated in the centre of the island, completely motorised and commanded by a man of high quality, Lieutenant-General Lungershausen. It also had the high morale of all former *Afrika Korps* units.

On the opposing side the Italians had half their forces scattered along the coastline, whilst their "mobile" reserves simply lacked mobility and their anti-tank guns were no use against the Panzers. Under these conditions all General Basso could do was to follow the 90th *Panzergrenadier* as it withdrew. At the end of the day on September 18, the German evacuation of Sardinia was complete. The Germans had left behind them 50 dead, 100 wounded, and 395 prisoners, against the Italians' 120.

The Fall of Mussolini

At a conference at Feltre on July 19, 1943 between the Duce, the Führer, Bastianini, the Under-Secretary of State for Foreign Affairs, Ambassadors Alfiere and Machensen, Field Marshal Keitel, and Generals Ambrosio, Warlimont and Rintelen the Führer exhorted his allies to stand firm. The Italians asked for more support, but Hitler would not commit himself. On Saturday July 24 there was a meeting of the Fascist Grand Council in the Palazzo Venezia at which the party's hierarchy, led by Grandi, formerly disavowed its leader by a majority of nearly eight to three. On July 26 Mussolini was informed by the king that it was his intention to relieve him of his powers and appoint Badoglio as head of the government. Rommel was given command of Operation "Alarich", which had been devised in case of an Italian defection. After preliminary discussions in Lisbon with the Allies, on September 3, 1943 Italy signed an armistice at Cassabile. Within minutes of the Italian announcement on September 8, Hitler put Operation "Achse", formerly "Alarich", into effect. On September 9, three battleships, six light cruisers and nine destroyers left La Spezia for Malta. They were intercepted by 15 Dornier DO 217s and the battleship *Roma* was sunk. The Italian Taranto squadron also escaped to Malta. The Italian "Acqui" Division was almost completely wiped out after capitulating to the Germans. A similar fate awaited the "Bergamo" Division defending Spalato against the Waffen S.S. On September 12 Mussolini was rescued by German commandos, and on September 18 he declared the Italian Social Republic.

On Corsica the Axis forces under General Magli comprised VII Corps ("Cremona" and "Friuli" Divisions), two coastal defence divisions, and an armoured brigade of the *Waffen S.S. Leibstandarte*. On the announcement of the Italian armistice the resistance forces which, since December 1942, had received by submarine or air-drop more than 10,000 automatic weapons, occupied Ajaccio, joined General Magli and appealed for help to Algiers. Meanwhile the Germans were able to drive their former allies out of Bonifacio and Bastia.

General Giraud in Algiers did not turn a deaf ear to the appeal from Corsica. With the help of Rear-Admiral Lemmonier, he improvised a small expeditionary force whose forward units reached Ajaccio on the night of September 12-13. These were 109 men of the famous Shock Battalion, who had crammed themselves aboard the submarine *Casabianca* which was still under the command of L'Herminier. On the following day the large destroyers *Fantasque* and *Terrible* landed over 500 men from the battalion and kept up the shuttle service together with the destroyers *Tempête* and *Alcyon;* then the cruisers *Montcalm* and *Jeanne d'Arc* joined in, despite the Luftwaffe's latest glide bomb.

Italy joins the Allies

But on September 12 O.K.W. had changed its mind and orders were sent to Senger und Etterlin to abandon Corsica and evacuate the 90th *Panzergrenadier* to Piombino. This move was completed by October 4. The 5,000 infantry and *goums* of the 4th Moroccan Mountain Division, with the help of their new Italian allies, had managed to repel the German rearguard but were quite unable to cut off the main force. The British and Americans, busy south of Naples, were too late to get to this miniature Dunkirk, which rescued some 28,000 men for the Wehrmacht.

Only a partial success, in spite of the sacrifice of 222 Frenchmen and 637 Italians, the occupation of Corsica nevertheless gave the Allies a strategic position of the first importance, with 17 aerodromes capable of taking and maintaining 2,000 planes which the American air force moved onto the island within a matter of months. As the armed forces of the Third Reich had by now spilt copious

amounts of Italian blood, Marshal Badoglio's government declared war on it on October 13 and received from the "United Nations", as Roosevelt called them, the status of "co-belligerent." This raised the hackles of Harry Hopkins but was fully approved by Stalin.

Near disaster at Salerno

"Salerno: A near disaster" was the title given by General Mark Wayne Clark, commander of the American 5th Army, to the chapter of his memoirs in which he described the landings at Salerno. The whole affair was indeed nearly a disaster and that the Allies did in fact win through

▽ *Bren-gun carriers head inland. Proof against small arms fire, these light carriers provided useful battlefield mobility for tactical infantry units.*

was the result not only of Clark's obstinacy and Montgomery's promptness but also, and perhaps more so, of the bad relationship between Rommel and Kesselring.

The plan drawn up by Generals Eisenhower and Alexander, Air Chief Marshal Tedder, and Admiral Cunningham involved a diversionary action by the 8th Army across the Strait of Messina to pin down the enemy's forces. When this had been done, the 5th Army was to land in the Gulf of Salerno.

On September 3, under cover of fire

from a naval force led by Vice-Admiral Willis, and from some 600 8th Army guns the British XIII Corps made a landing on the coast of Calabria north-west of Reggio di Calabria. It met no serious resistance as the 29th *Panzergrenadier* Division which, with the 26th Panzer Division and the 1st Parachute Division, formed the LXXVI Panzer Corps (General Dostler), had received orders not to get caught up in any engagement. General Dempsey thus had no difficulty in pushing his 5th Division up to Pizzo and his 1st Canadian Division to Crotone. This withdrawal by the enemy had not entered into the plans of the Allied 15th Army Group.

On September 8 Kesselring learned at his H.Q. in Frascati that a powerful Anglo-American fleet was now in the waters of the Tyrrhenian Sea and concluded that a landing must be imminent, though there was nothing to show whether it would be in the Gulf of Salerno, in the Bay of Naples, or on the beaches opposite Rome. To oppose it he had had under his command since August 8 the 10th Army (General von Vietinghoff), the units of which were deployed as follows:

1. XIV Panzer Corps, back from Sicily, had its 15th *Panzergrenadier* at Formia, its "Hermann Göring" Panzer Division in Naples, and its 16th Panzer Division (Major-General Sieckenius) in the Salerno area (by August 22, Hitler had told Vietinghoff to regard Salerno as "the centre of gravity", and this was why 16th Panzer had been moved there);

2. LXXVI Panzer Corps, as we have seen, was engaged in Calabria; and

3. Though earmarked for Operation "Achse", the 2nd Parachute Division and the 3rd *Panzergrenadier* Division were well placed to cover the Italian capital.

The curtain rose at dawn on September 9 when the first elements of the American VI Corps (Major-General Ernest W. Dawley) and the British X Corps (Lieutenant-General Richard L. Mc-Creery) landed between Paestum and Maiori, on either side of Salerno. The naval forces assigned to the operation (codename "Avalanche") were somewhat similar to those used against Sicily: they included seven aircraft-carriers for first-line support and were led by the American Vice-Admiral H. Kent Hewitt.

Attacked on a front of some 25 miles, the 16th Panzer Division had to give ground but did not disintegrate. By the end of the day the American 36th Division had got five miles inland, but

the British X Corps had not reached all its objectives and fighting continued in the streets of Salerno. Sieckenius still controlled the high ground which overlooked the coastal strip from a distance of 600 to 1000 yards. The American 45th Division was landed and this allowed Clark to extend and deepen his bridgehead, which on September 11 was 11 miles inland at its furthest point and stretched from Agropoli to Amalfi with a circumference of over 43 miles.

"Avalanche" was off to a good start. In Frascati, however, Kesselring had remained calm and XIV Panzer Corps was ordered to concentrate and counter-attack. LXXVI Corps also came to the rescue, leaving Montgomery facing only its 1st Parachute Division and part of the 26th Panzer Division. The capture of Rome enabled Kesselring to give the 3rd *Panzergrenadier* Division (Lieutenant-General Graeser) to the 10th Army, so that by September 12 Vietinghoff had five and a half divisions, admittedly understrength, against his enemy's four, scattered over a wide front. This led to a crisis that did not end until September 15.

Profiting from the fact that the British right flank (56th Division) had made slower progress than the American left (45th Division), the Germans attempted to get a pincer movement round the latter, cut the British off from the Americans, and destroy both piecemeal. The crux of this battle was at Ponte Bruciato, where Clark threw in everything he had, including two artillery battalions, a regimental band, and his H.Q. orderlies and cooks. The German advance was slowed down and eventually stopped some five miles from the beach, where it

▷ *Although uncertain where exactly the Allies intended to land in Italy, Kesselring had a shrewd idea that it was going to be Salerno, and had deployed his forces well. With the aid of large calibre guns he hoped to be able to deal heavy blows to the invasion forces as they approached the beaches, but the first class gunfire support from Allied warships lying off the shore was more than a match for the German artillery shelling the beach-head.*

was pinned down by the concentrated fire of the fleet which Admiral Hewitt had brought as close inshore as possible. Although the capture of Rome by the Germans had freed the 3rd *Panzergrenadier* Division for Kesselring, it also released the American 82nd Parachute Division (Major-General Ridgway) which was to have landed in support of the Italians; during the night of September 13–14 a first paratroop regiment reached the bridgehead.

Rommel's pessimism

What would have happened if, on the morning of the 9th, Rommel had put at Kesselring's disposal his 24th Panzer Division and the "*Leibstandarte Adolf Hitler*", and Kesselring had then used them at Salerno? The question cannot be answered as the Führer refused to reinforce the 10th Army, having been advised by Rommel that Italy could not be defended south of a line La Spezia–Rimini. In face of the threat to the American 5th Army, Alexander called on Montgomery to come up in haste and catch the forces attacking the bridgehead. Montgomery managed to do this, though in his memoirs he gallantly states that it was more or less all over on September 16 when his 5th Division got to Agropoli. On that day the 5th Army had five divisions or their equivalent engaged in the battle and had lost 5,674 officers, N.C.O.s, and men, including 756 killed and 2,150 missing. In addition, the British battleship *Warspite* and the cruiser *Uganda*, as well as the American cruiser *Savannah*, had been badly damaged by the Luftwaffe's new radio-controlled bombs. After this crisis, Clark got Eisenhower's permission to relieve VI Corps' commander and replaced him by Major-General John P. Lucas. The British Army was assigned the province of Apulia and the Cassibile armistice allowed the uneventful landing of its V Corps (Lieutenant-General Allfrey) in the well-equipped ports of Taranto and Brindisi.

The final defeat of the German 10th Army at Salerno and the threat to his rear forced Kesselring to disengage on September 16, but this brought a renewed conflict with Rommel, who wanted to abandon Rome, whereas Kesselring maintained that the Eternal City could be covered from a line running roughly Formia–Cassino–Pescara, using the Garigliano and the Rapido valleys and the Abruzzi mountains, which reached over 9,000 feet at La Malella. On November 21 Hitler recalled Rommel and moved Kesselring from his position as C.-in-C. South to head a new Army Group "C", thus leaving him in complete command in Italy.

Hitler transferred the 24th Panzer Division and the S.S. *"Leibstandarte"* Division to the Eastern Front. Kesselring allotted three divisions to the 10th Army and the balance of Army Group "B" in northern Italy went to form a new 14th Army under General von Mackensen.

Careful retreat

Meanwhile Vietinghoff, turning to great advantage the demolition and destruction which had been caused and the heavy autumn rains which, according to Montgomery, covered the roads in "chocolate sauce", did not allow his forces to get caught anywhere, either at Termoli on October 4, in spite of a commando landing behind his left flank, or on the Sangro on November 27 when the three divisions and an armoured brigade of V Corps broke out of the bridgehead and advanced along the line Sulmona–Avezzano to wipe out his 65th Division (Lieutenant-General von Ziehlberg). The rubble left after artillery shelling and aerial bombardment by the British, which their own tanks then had to get through (a sight which was to recur in the Caen campaign) made any exploitation impossible and in a couple of days Vietinghoff was making a stand again and stopping the Allied advance.

Enter the French

In spite of the evacuation of Naples on October 1, it was the same thing along the way to Rome through Cassino and through Formia. When it had got through Venafro and Sessa-Aurunca, the 5th Army came up against the mountains and the deep valley of the Garigliano. The reinforcements which the 5th Army had just received, II Corps and the 1st Armoured Division, were not the most likely formations to cross these obstacles. Invited by General Clark to give his opinion, General Juin stated on October 1

◁ *Italian children celebrate the arrival of the Allies, in the form of a Sherman tank and its British crew.*
▽ *Sherman tanks of a Canadian armoured regiment, attached to an Indian division. From this railway station they gave close support in the capture of the village of San Donato.*

△△ *German wounded await
evacuation to the north by Ju 52
transports.*
△ *An over-hasty assessment, for
Italy could never be crossed off
– the Germans resisted right up to
the end of the war.*

"The whole way along the road from Salerno to Naples we kept running into the British 7th Division in close formation and incapable of getting off the road and deploying in the completely mountainous terrain. I had immediately concluded, along with Carpentier [his chief-of-staff], that the mechanisation of the British and American armies could actually hinder our rapid progress up the Italian peninsula. There is no doubt that the North African divisions would be very welcome . . ."

And indeed from November 22 onwards the French Expeditionary Corps did begin to land in Italy. It consisted of the 2nd Moroccan Division and the 3rd Algerian Division, totalling 65,000 men, 2,500 horses and mules, and 12,000 vehicles. But the corps was not used as such. Its 2nd Moroccan Division (General Dody) was attached to VI Corps which was trying to break out of the Mignano area, and General Lucas used it on his right some seven miles north of Venafro. The fortified position at Pantano was his first

objective. This was defended by 305th Division (Lieutenant-General Hauck), a division which, wrote Marshal Juin "could never be caught napping". By December 18 the 2nd Moroccan Division, which had never before been under fire, had got the better of the difficult terrain and the strong enemy resistance. On the 26th it had a further success when it took Mount Mainarde and this enabled General Juin to claim a permanent position for his French Expeditionary Corps. He was successful, and the corps was allocated a position on the right of 5th Army's VI Corps.

All the same, Kesselring's strategy had to a large extent imposed itself on his enemy, so that unless a completely new offensive were to be mounted at once, the victory in Sicily, in spite of the Italian armistice, would now run out of steam. On December 24 Generals Eisenhower, Montgomery, and Spaatz flew to London and the Italian theatre of operations was relegated to the background.

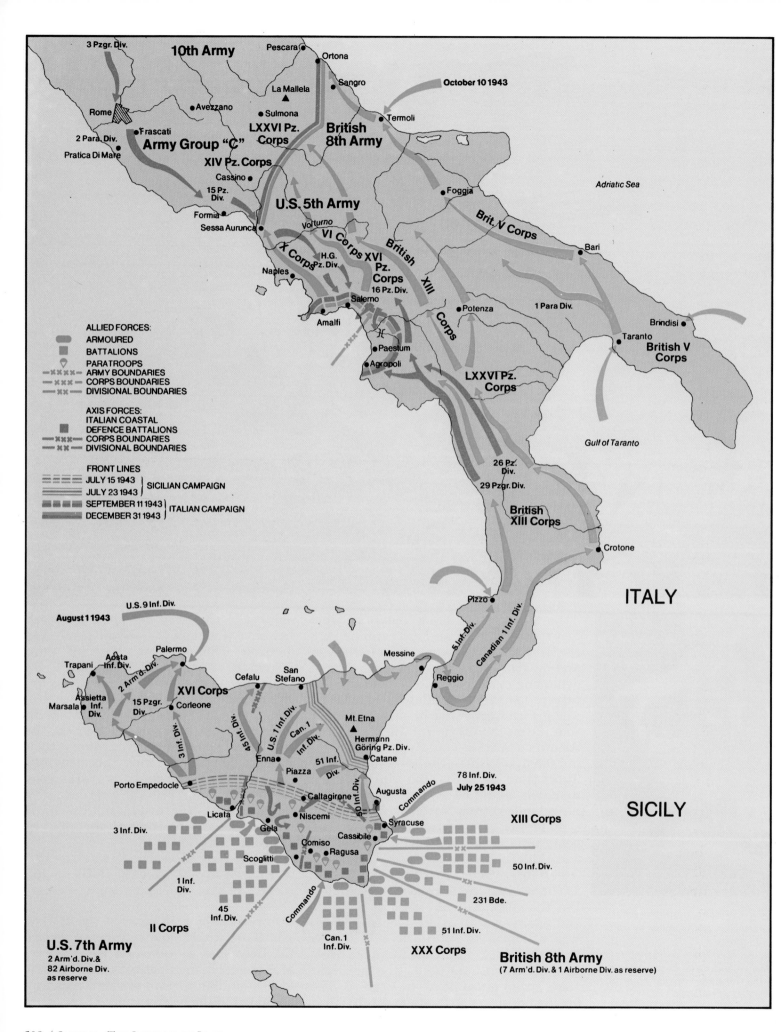

ALLIED FORCES:
ARMOURED
BATTALIONS
PARATROOPS
ARMY BOUNDARIES
CORPS BOUNDARIES
DIVISIONAL BOUNDARIES

AXIS FORCES:
ITALIAN COASTAL
DEFENCE BATTALIONS
CORPS BOUNDARIES
DIVISIONAL BOUNDARIES

FRONT LINES
JULY 15 1943 } SICILIAN CAMPAIGN
JULY 23 1943 }
SEPTEMBER 11 1943 } ITALIAN CAMPAIGN
DECEMBER 31 1943 }

3 Pzgr. Div.

10th Army

Pescara
Ortona
Sangro
La Mallela
Termoli
October 10 1943

Rome
Frascati
2 Para. Div.
Pratica Di Mare
Avezzano
Sulmona
LXXVI Pz. Corps
Army Group "C"
XIV Pz. Corps
Cassino
15 Pz. Div.
Formia
Sessa Aurunca
Volturno

British 8th Army

Adriatic Sea

Foggia

Brit. V Corps

Bari

U.S. 5th Army
X Corps
VI Corps
H.G. Pz. Div.
XVI Pz. Corps
Naples
16 Pz. Div.
Salerno
Amalfi
Paestum
Agropoli

British XIII Corps

Potenza

1 Para Div.

Brindisi
Taranto
British V Corps

LXXVI Pz. Corps

Gulf of Taranto

26 Pz. Div.
29 Pzgr. Div.

British XIII Corps

Crotone

ITALY

Pizzo

5 Inf. Div.
Canadian 1 Inf. Div.

August 1 1943
U.S. 9 Inf. Div.

Messine

Reggio

Palermo
Trapani
Aosta Inf. Div.
2 Arm'd. Div.
Cefalu
San Stefano
XVI Corps
Assietta Inf. Div.
Marsala
15 Pzgr. Div.
Corleone
3 Inf. Div.
45 Inf. Div.
U.S. 1 Inf. Div.
Enna
Can. 1 Inf. Div.
Piazza
Mt. Etna
Hermann Göring Pz. Div.
Catane
51 Inf. Div.
50 Inf. Div.
Augusta
Commando
78 Inf. Div.
July 25 1943
XIII Corps

SICILY

Porto Empedocle
Licata
3 Inf. Div.
Gela
Niscemi
Caltagirone
Comiso
Ragusa
Cassibile
Syracuse
50 Inf. Div.
231 Bde.
51 Inf. Div.

Scoglitti
1 Inf. Div.
45 Inf. Div.
II Corps
Commando
Can. 1 Inf. Div.
XXX Corps

U.S. 7th Army
2 Arm'd. Div. &
82 Airborne Div.
as reserve

British 8th Army
(7 Arm'd. Div. & 1 Airborne Div. as reserve)

CHAPTER 54
KURSK: GREATEST LAND BATTLE

Operation *"Zitadelle"* was launched on July 5 against the Kursk salient and constituted the final attempt by the German Army to recover the operational initiative on the Eastern Front. But before turning our attention to this, it is desirable to examine briefly the events that occurred during the first three months of 1943 along the somewhat circuitous front line running from north of Kursk to Lake Ladoga. These were deliberately omitted from Chapter 83 so as to give full effect to the account of the Battle of Stalingrad and its consequences.

On this front Army Groups "Centre" and "North", still commanded by Field-Marshals von Kluge and von Küchler respectively, were composed of seven armies (23 corps of 117 divisions or their equivalent on January 1, nine of them Panzer and eight motorised). The extremely winding course of the line on which the Germans had stabilised their positions at the end of March 1942 meant that it could not be held in any depth. To make matters worse, the lakes, rivers, and marshy tracts, so characteristic of the region, freeze hard and allow not only infantry and cavalry to pass over them but also lorries, artillery, and even tanks.

On January 4, the 3rd *Panzerarmee* on Kluge's left flank was broken through by troops of the 3rd Shock Army (Kalinin Front) on either side of Velikiye-Luki. A fortnight later, after every attempt to relieve the citadel of the town had failed, its defenders, reduced to 102 in number, managed to find their way back to the German lines, leaving 200 wounded behind them.

Of graver consequence was the defeat inflicted on the German 18th Army (Colonel-General G. Lindemann) to the south of Lake Ladoga. At O.K.H. this sector was known as the "bottleneck" on account of the pronounced salient formed by the front between Mga and the southern shore of the lake. But to evacuate it would have meant abandoning the siege of Leningrad; and for this reason Hitler had always opposed any suggestion that it should be done. XVI Corps (General Wodrig) held the salient and was hence liable to be cut off as soon as the Neva, which covered its left flank, no longer constituted an obstacle to the enemy.

▽ *A corporal moves up through a communications trench. He is carrying two Teller 43 anti-tank mines, possibly one of the most efficient mines of World War II.*

Back to the Dniepr

On July 12, Generals Sokolovsky and Popov started the Soviet summer offensive by attacking the Orel salient from the north and east along a front of some 190 miles.

After three days' heavy fighting, the Russians broke through the main lines of the German defences.

The Germans also suffered reverses north-west of Belgorod by the Sea of Azov, over a front of 650 miles defended by Manstein, who was outnumbered about seven to one. On August 3 Colonel Generals Vatutin and Kenev drove a wedge between the German Gruppe "Kempf" and the 4th Panzerarmee. The breakthrough posed a danger for the German forces between the Sea of Azov and Khar'kov. On August 22 Khar'kov fell. By September 7 Manstein's Panzer and Panzergrenadier forces had only 257 tanks and 220 assault guns left. Hitler eventually gave permission for the army group to withdraw behind the Dniepr. The Soviets crossed the Dniepr and on the night of November 5-6 they liberated Kiev.

Voroshilov relieves Leningrad

The task of co-ordinating the combined action of the Leningrad Front (Lieutenant-General M. A. Govorov) and the Volkhov Front (General K. A. Meretskov) was entrusted to Marshal K. Voroshilov. Govorov's 67th Army (Lieutenant-General V. P. Sviridov) was ordered to make contact with the 2nd Shock Army (Lieutenant-General I. I. Fedyuninsky) and the 8th Army (Lieutenant-General F. N. Starikov) both under the command of General Meretskov. According to a chart drawn up in Moscow, the operation involved 12 divisions and one infantry brigade taking on four German divisions. And whereas the Soviet divisions in all probability numbered some 10,000 men each, those of the Reich were severely reduced. In particular, the Russians could deploy almost 100 guns and mortars per mile, and each of the two fronts had its own air cover and support.

Hence the Russian attack on January 12, 1943 was backed by massive firepower and followed a sustained artillery bombardment lasting 90 minutes. Nevertheless, XVI Corps held the attack, with Lindemann, then Küchler, soon coming to its aid. Consequently it took a full week for the 2nd Shock Army advancing from the west and the 67th Army from the east to fight their way across the ten miles that divided them. On January 17, General Sviridov's troops entered Petrokrepost'; the following day, the entire population of Leningrad, delirious with joy, learnt that after 17 months' trials and privations borne with fortitude and stoicism, the siege had been broken. On February 6, railway communications between Peter the Great's capital city and the outside world were re-established. But the Russians were halted short of Mga, which meant that Leningrad's lifeline was restricted to a corridor six to seven miles wide. Stalin, however, was so pleased with the result that 19,000 decorations were awarded to the victorious troops who had raised the siege of Russia's second city.

This disaster, in which the 41st and 277th Infantry Divisions were almost entirely destroyed, and still more the rapid and tragic succession of defeats suffered south of Kursk, induced Hitler to

△△ A German machine-gunner in the frozen shell-torn soil of the Lake Ladoga sector. With winter the German lines came under greater pressure as the Russians were able to cross the frozen lakes and marshes.

△ A Russian officer mans a scissor binocular in an observation post in a ruined village. The assault in January 1943 was preceded by a 90-minute bombardment.

▷ A Soviet soldier carries a wounded comrade to the rear. Medical facilities were severely strained during the siege of Leningrad.

agree to certain adjustments to the front line which he had obstinately refused to allow his generals to make the previous year, on the grounds that enormous quantities of *matériel* might be lost in the course of withdrawal.

Strategic retreat by O.K.H.

With this authorisation, O.K.H., between the 19th and the end of February, effected the evacuation of the "fortress" of Demy'ansk, which was linked to the 16th Army's front line only by a narrow corridor under constant threat. The withdrawal was an orderly one and permitted a front line economy of seven divisions.

Next, starting on March 2, Operation *"Buffle"*, whereby 30 divisions of the German 4th and 9th Armies withdrew 100 miles, was set in motion. Once again, the actual manoeuvre failed to justify the Führer's apprehensions, feigned or real. Rzhev, Gzhatsk, then Vyaz'ma were one after the other evacuated in the course of a manoeuvre which lasted more than three weeks, without the Russians, who in the event were considerably delayed by numerous minefields, showing themselves particularly aggressive. The evacuation of the salient, which had a front of 410 miles, was completed on March 25. Field-Marshal von Kluge was thus able to deploy his armies along a front slightly less than half as long (230 miles), thus releasing 14 divisions.

Two comments seem appropriate here. Firstly, that the 21 divisions pulled back out of salients, in February and March 1943, were more or less equivalent in numbers to the Rumanian 3rd Army and the Italian 8th Army, whose destruction had sealed the fate of the German 6th Army in the Stalingrad pocket. What might the result have been if it had been they who were called on to reinforce Army Group "B" when Paulus reached the Volga? The question is one of pure speculation, however. Secondly, if the Rzhev salient was defended by one division for every 16 miles of front, Operation *"Buffle"*, which left Kluge with 16 divisions in order to hold 240 miles, made no appreciable difference to his own situation (15 miles per division). And proof of this would be given no later than July 13 following, on the occasion of the Soviet offensive directed against the Orel salient. But how could anything else have been done?

The orders go out for Operation *"Zitadelle"*

In any event, this agonising question did not preoccupy Hitler who, on April 15, put his signature to the 13 copies of Operational Order No. 16. The document is

△ *Encumbered by greatcoats, Russian infantrymen double through the misty woodland on the Leningrad Front.*

▽ *A Russian 152-mm howitzer pounds German positions in the Bryansk area.*

△ *With a flame-thrower at point, a column of S.S. troopers plod through the rolling steppe. After "Zitadelle" their losses were so severe that they made up with volunteers from occupied countries, though the original units attempted to maintain their Germanic character.*

▽ *Pzkw IVF2s move through the outskirts of a Russian town. Even with extra armour and a more powerful gun, the Pzkw IV was still a stop-gap weapon when used on the Eastern Front.*

a long one, as are all those which Hitler wrote, and the following extract will serve to illuminate the events that subsequently took place:

"I am resolved, as soon as the weather allows, to launch Operation 'Zitadelle', as the first offensive action of this year," were his opening words. "Hence the importance of this offensive. It must lead to a rapid and decisive success. It *must* give us the initiative for the coming spring and summer. In view of this, preparations must be conducted with the utmost precaution and the utmost energy. At the main points of attack the finest units, the finest weapons, the finest commanders will be committed, and plentiful supplies of munitions will be ensured. Every commander, every fighting man must be imbued with the capital significance of this offensive. The victory of Kursk must be as a beacon to the whole world.

"To this effect, I order:

1. Objective of the offensive: by means of a highly concentrated, and savage attack vigorously conducted by two armies, one from the area of Belgorod, the other from south of Orel, to encircle the enemy forces situated in the region of Kursk and annihilate them by concentric attacks.

"In the course of this offensive a new and shorter front line will be established,

permitting economies of means, along the line joining Nejega, Korocha, Skorodnoye, Tim, passing east of Shchigry, and Sosna."

Under Point 2, the Führer went on to define the conditions necessary for the success of the enterprise:

"(a) to ensure to the full the advantage of surprise, and principally to keep the enemy ignorant of the timing of attack;

(b) to concentrate to the utmost the attacking forces on narrow fronts so as to obtain an overwhelming local superiority in all arms (tanks, assault guns, artillery, and rocket launchers) grouped in a single echelon until junction between the two armies in the rear of the enemy is effected, thereby cutting him off from his rear areas;

(c) to bring up as fast as possible, from the rear, the forces necessary to cover the flanks of the offensive thrusts, thus enabling the attacking forces to concentrate solely on their advance;

(d) by driving into the pocket from all sides and with all possible speed, to give the enemy no respite, and to accelerate his destruction;

(e) to execute the attack at a speed so rapid that the enemy can neither prevent encirclement nor bring up reserves from his other fronts; and

(f) by the speedy establishment of the new front line, to allow the disengagement

of forces, especially the Panzer forces, with all possible despatch, so that they can be used for other purposes."

Then the Führer fixed the parts to be played by Army Groups "Centre" and "South" and the Luftwaffe, apportioned the means at their disposal, and laid down certain requirements for misleading the enemy as to the German intentions, and for the maintenance of secrecy. As from April 28, Kluge and Manstein were to be ready to launch the attack within six days of receiving the order from O.K.H., the earliest date suggested for the offensive being May 3.

Guderian's violent opposition

Hitler's initiative, which in fact stemmed from Colonel-General Kurt Zeitzler, Chief-of-Staff at O.K.H., nevertheless elicited varying reactions amongst the generals. Kluge gave determined support to Operation "Zitadelle", but many others raised objection to it, some categorically, others only provisionally.

On May 2, Hitler had summoned the top commanders concerned in the enterprise, plus Colonel-General Guderian, to Munich. In his capacity as Inspector-General of Armoured Troops, Guderian put forward a whole series of impressive arguments against the projected offensive, which he sums up as follows in his memoirs:

"I asked permission to express my views and declared that the attack was pointless; we had only just completed the reorganisation and re-equipment of our Eastern Front; if we attacked according to the plan of the Chief of the General Staff we were certain to suffer heavy tank casualties, which we would not be in a position to replace in 1943; on the contrary, we ought to be devoting our new tank production to the Western Front so as to have mobile reserves available for use against the Allied landing which could be expected with certainty to take place in 1944. Furthermore, I pointed out that the Panthers, on whose performance the Chief of the Army General Staff was relying so heavily, were still suffering from many teething troubles inherent in all new equipment and it seemed unlikely that these could be put right in time for the launching of the attack."

Manstein expresses his preferences

Manstein had during the previous February and March declared his preference for a plan of operations radically different to that outlined in the order of April 15. He had told Hitler of this on the occasion of the Führer's visit to his H.Q. in Zaporozh'ye. In substance, his idea was to await the offensive that the enemy was bound to launch in order to recover the Donets basin. Once this had got under way, the Germans would conduct an orderly retreat to the Melitopol'–Dniepropetrovsk line, while at the same time a powerful armoured force would be assembled in the Poltava–Khar'kov region. Once the Russians had been led into the trap, this force would counter-attack with lightning speed in the direction of the Sea of Azov, and the superiority which

△ △ A "Marder" self-propelled anti-tank gun passes a group of S.S. men who have occupied an abandoned Russian trench near Belgorod. Two captured Red soldiers can be seen in the middle of the group.
△ Hauptmann (Flight-Lieutenant) Hans-Ulrich Rudel after receiving the Oak Leaves to his Knight's Cross. Rudel destroyed 12 Russian tanks on the first day of "Zitadelle" and by the end of the war he had flown 2,530 operational sorties and destroyed 519 tanks.

△ "Marder" III tank destroyers, German PaK 40 7.5-cm guns mounted on Czech T-38 chassis, move up through a shell-ravaged Russian village. These Marders were useful, but no real substitute for tanks.

▽ A Pzkw VI Tiger. These heavy tanks first appeared on the Eastern Front in 1942 and in Tunisia in 1943. Their armour, up to 100-mm thick, proved invulnerable to the fire of Allied 75- and 76·2-mm anti-tank guns.

German commanders had always shown over their Russian counterparts in mobile warfare would bring them victory.

"The guiding principle of this operation was radically different from that of the German offensive in 1942. We would attack by a counter-stroke at the moment when the enemy had largely engaged and partially expended his assault forces. Our objective would no longer be the conquest of distant geographical points but the destruction of the Soviet southern wing by trapping it against the coast. To prevent his escape eastwards, as was the case in 1942, we would entice him to the lower Dniepr, as it would be impossible for him to resist this.

"If the operation succeeded, with the consequent heavy losses he would sustain, we could perhaps strike a second blow northwards, towards the centre of the front."

Certainly Manstein was under no illusion that the method he advocated could decide the war in favour of the Third Reich; but at least the situation would again be in Germany's favour and she would obtain what Manstein terms a "putting off" and Mellenthin a "stalemate", enabling her to bide her time. But Hitler did not agree with this line of argument, countering it with his usual economic arguments: Nikopol' manganese, for instance – "to lose Nikopol' would be to lose the war" was his last word, and at the meeting in Munich, Manstein did not raise his plan again.

Red espionage succeeds again

The Soviet authorities still deny the implication of Manstein's criticism of the Red Army high command, yet the counter-offensive which had recently given Khar'kov back to the Germans seems to furnish abundant proof of Manstein's point.

Nonetheless, there is no certainty that Manstein's plan would have been as successful as he claimed it would. Indeed, just as with the offensive directed against the Kursk salient, it had little chance of securing the advantage of surprise. Never before had the direct line linking O.K.W. and O.K.H. with the Soviet agent Rudolf Rössler functioned so surely and swiftly. And it is certain–

insofar as can be discovered – that Stalin had got wind of German intentions within 48 hours of Hitler's issuing an operational order classified "Top Secret" wherein, unknown to Manstein, he took up the suggestion of "attack by counter-strike" with which the commander of Army Group "South" had provided him.

Model and Mellenthin also against Hitler's plan

At all events, when he opened proceedings, Hitler had made reference to a report that had been sent him by Colonel-General Walther Model, whose 9th Army was to supply the north-to-south thrust of the operation. It is beyond question that a commander of Model's dynamic energy approved of the offensive in principle, but he registered concern at making an attempt in May that should have been made in March, for the enemy forces in the Kursk salient had not meanwhile been wasting their time. According to Guderian, "Model had produced information, based largely on air photography, which showed that the Russians were preparing deep and very strong defensive positions in exactly those areas where the attack by the two army groups were

to go in. The Russians had already withdrawn the mass of their mobile formations from the forward area of the salient; in anticipation of a pincer attack, as proposed in this plan of ours, they had strengthened the localities of our possible break-throughs with unusually strong artillery and anti-tank forces. Model drew the correct deduction from this, namely, that the enemy was counting on our launching this attack and that in order to achieve success we must adopt a fresh tactical approach; the alternative was to abandon the whole idea."

Some weeks earlier, Colonel von Mellenthin, in his capacity as chief-of-staff of XLVIII Panzer Corps, which had been given an important part to play in the plans, had voiced the same opinion to General Zeitzler. By holding up the offensive until a first brigade of Panther tanks had been formed, as Hitler intended, the Russians would be given time to recover from the losses inflicted on them. For this they only needed a month or two, and the operation would then be a far more difficult, and hence costly, one. Although Manstein had been lukewarm in his attitude towards the operation at the outset, once it had been decided he pronounced against any procrastination: "Any delay with *'Zitadelle'* would increase the risk to Army Group 'South's' defensive front considerably. The enemy

△ *While the fighting for the Kursk salient continued, the Russians completed the plans for their summer offensive. Here General Lyudnikov, commander of the 39th Army, studies a situation map.*

▽ *Soviet infantry counter-attack past a burning German armoured vehicle.*

of the offensive be decided by the state of preparedness of the Panthers. On information that 324 Panthers would be ready on May 31, he settled D-day for June 15, in spite of Manstein's advice. But there were further delays, and Operation "Zitadelle" was not begun until July 5, a delay of two months on the original timetable.

As had been pointed out above, the left flank of the offensive was drawn from Army Group "Centre" and the right from Army Group "South". Manstein had concentrated *Gruppe* Kempf, reinforced by one Panzer corps and two infantry corps in the Belgorod sector; its rôle as it moved northwards was to guard the eastward flank of the armoured units of the 4th *Panzerarmee* (Colonel-General Hoth) upon which the main task would devolve; he therefore transferred to it the II *Waffen* S.S. Panzer Corps (General Hausser) with its three *Panzergrenadier* divisions: *"Leibstandarte"*, *"Das Reich"*, and *"Totenkopf"*, as well as XLVIII Panzer Corps, which under the command of General O. von Knobelsdorff included an infantry division, the 3rd and 11th Panzer Divisions, and the *"Grossdeutschland" Panzergrenadier* Division, whose 190 tanks and self-propelled guns were supported by a brigade of 200 Panthers. XXIV Panzer Corps (17th Panzer Division and *"Wiking" Panzergrenadier* Division) were held in reserve.

In Army Group "Centre", the 9th Army, to the south of Orel, had organised itself as a wedge. In the centre, XLVII Panzer Corps (General Rauss), with five Panzer divisions, constituted its battering ram; it was flanked on the right by XLVI Panzer Corps and XX Corps, on the left by XLI Panzer Corps and XXIII Corps; this flank, which was exposed to counter-attacks from the east, had been reinforced by the 12th Panzer Division and the 10th *Panzergrenadier* Division, under the command of XLI Panzer Corps. General Model's reserve consisted of one Panzer and one *Panzergrenadier* division.

Taken together, *"Zitadelle"* involved 41 divisions, all of them German, including 18 Panzer and *Panzergrenadier* divisions. Manstein had at his own disposal 1,081 tanks and 376 assault guns; air support was given by *Luftflotte* IV, as whose commander Manstein would have liked to see Field-Marshal von Richthofen, who was kicking his heels in Italy. But Hitler was obstinate in his refusal to transfer him. Model, whose

was not yet in a position to launch an attack on the Mius and the Donets. But he certainly would be in June. 'Zitadelle' was certainly not going to be easy, but I concluded that we must stick by the decision to launch it at the earliest possible moment and, like a cavalryman, 'leaping before you look', a comparison which I quickly realised made no effect on Hitler, who had little appreciation either of cavalrymen or horses."

Model's line of reasoning made its due impression on Hitler, who had total confidence in him. On May 10, Hitler told Guderian: "Whenever I think of this attack my stomach turns over." And he was all the more disposed to let the date

eight Panzer divisions had been brought up to a strength of 100 tanks each, had as many vehicles as he could use. His air support was provided by *Luftflotte* VI.

Massive Russian defence lines

According to a perfectly correct comment in the *Great Patriotic War,* when spring came round again, Stalin had more than sufficient means at hand to take the initiative. But confronted by the German preparations against the Kursk salient reported to him by General N. F. Vatutin, new commander of the Voronezh Front, from April 21 onwards Stalin felt, the same work assures us, that it "was more expedient to oppose the enemy with a defensive system constructed in due time,

Dniepr, and Kerch' Strait, thus liberating the eastern parts of White Russia and the Ukraine, the Donets basin, and what the Germans still held in the Kuban'.

It is true that in adopting these tactics, Stalin had the advantage of detailed information as to the strength and intentions of the adversary and that he followed the *"Zitadelle"* preparations very closely: "Rössler," write Accoce and Quiet, "gave them full and detailed description in his despatches. Once again, *Werther,* his little team inside O.K.W., had achieved a miracle. Nothing was missing. The sectors to be attacked, the men and *matériel* to be used, the position of the supply columns, the chain of command, the positions of reinforcements, D-day, and zero hour. There was nothing more to be desired and the Russians desired nothing more. They simply waited, confident of victory."

And their confidence was all the greater

◁ *The Soviets did not have things all their own way, particularly at the beginning of the battle. Here a German soldier prepares to take the crew of a T-34 prisoner.*

◁▽ *German dispatch rider.*
▽ *The Russian counter-offensive gets under way–tanks and infantry of the Voronezh Front move south towards Belgorod.*
▽ ▽ *One of Russia's tank aces, Akim Lysenko. He destroyed seven German tanks in the great battle for the Kursk salient.*

echeloned in depth, and insuperable. On the basis of propositions made to it by the commanders at the front, Supreme Headquarters resolved to wear the enemy out decisively in the course of his assault, by defensive action, then to smash him by means of a counter-offensive."

Hence, by a curious coincidence, Stalin came round to the idea of "return attack" at the very time that Hitler refused to let Manstein attempt to apply it. With the Panzers smashed in the salient around Kursk, it would be a far easier task to defeat Army Groups "Centre" and "South" and attain the objectives that had been set for the end of autumn 1943: Smolensk, the Sozh, the middle and lower

because first-hand information and reports from partisans confirmed the radio messages of their conscientious informer in Lucerne. Accoce and Quiet make no exaggeration. From a memo of the period it appears that in July 1943 Stalin believed he had 210 enemy divisions, excluding Finns, facing him. The official O.K.W. record for July 7 of that year gives 210 exactly, plus five regiments.

Hitler's delays allowed the Russians to organise the battlefield on which the attack was anticipated and to do so to a depth of between 16 and 25 miles. A cunning combination of minefields was intended to channel the German armoured units onto what the Russians called "anti-

tank fronts", solid defence sectors particularly well provided with anti-tank guns.

The defence of the Kursk salient, which had a front of about 340 miles, was entrusted to the Central and Voronezh Fronts. The Central Front, under the command of General Rokossovsky, had five armies deployed forward, a tank army in second echelon, and two tank corps and a cavalry corps in reserve. The Voronezh Front

▽ *The standard pattern of Soviet attacks – an interwoven line of infantry and tanks.*

△ *Dismounted Russian cavalry put in an assault on a small village. By Western standards they are not only very exposed, but have a long distance to go before they reach the enemy positions. Though the picture may be posed, it still reflects the rudimentary tactics employed by the Red Army, even late in the war.*

(General Vatutin) had four armies forward, two more armies (one of them a tank army) in second echelon, and two tank and one rifle corps in reserve. The Steppe Front (Colonel-General I. S. Konev), positioned east of Kursk, constituted the *Stavka* reserve, and comprised five (including one tank) armies, plus one tank, one mechanised, and three cavalry corps in reserve.

Air support was provided by some 2,500 planes from the 2nd and 16th Air Armies.

Even now, Soviet historians, who are

so precise in the case of the German Army, decline to tell us the number of divisions and tanks involved in this battle; nevertheless, if we take a figure of roughly 75 infantry divisions and 3,600 tanks, this would appear to be about right. The *Great Patriotic War,* however, drops its reserve in speaking of the artillery. If we believe what we read, and there is no reason not to do so, Rokossovsky and Vatutin could count on no fewer than 20,000 guns, howitzers, and mortars, including 6,000 anti-tank guns, and 920 rocket launchers. For example, in order to bar the axis along which it was expected that Model's main thrust would be developed, Rokossovsky allocated to Pukhov's 13th Army a whole additional corps of artillery, totalling some 700 guns and mortars. The defensive potential of the Red Army thus surpassed the offensive potential of the Germans, and their complete knowledge of Field-Marshals von Kluge's and von Manstein's dispositions and proposed axes of advance enabled the Russians to concentrate their artillery and armoured units so as to prevent them moving in the direction intended. In the evening of July 4 a pioneer from a Sudeten division deserted to the Russians and revealed the zero hour for Operation *"Zitadelle".*

Failure all the way

Now that most of the pieces on the chessboard are in place we can deal quickly with the actual sequence of events in the Battle of Kursk which, on July 12, ended in an irreversible defeat for the Wehrmacht. Far from taking the enemy by surprise, the German 9th Army, following close on the desertion mentioned above, was itself surprised by a massive artillery counter-barrage, which struck its jump-off points in the final stages of preparation 20 minutes before zero hour. By evening, XLVII and XLI Panzer Corps, consisting of seven armoured divisions, had advanced only six miles across the defences of the Soviet 13th Army, and their 90 "Ferdinands" or *"Elefants",* being without machine guns, were unable to cope with the Russian infantry. More important, XXIII Corps, guarding the left flank, was stopped short of Malo-Arkhangelsk. On July 7, spurred on by the vigorous leadership of General Rauss, XLVII Panzer Corps reached the

outskirts of Olkhovatka, less than 12 miles from its start line. There the German 9th Army was finally halted.

Army Group "South's" part of "Zitadelle" got off to a better start, thanks largely to impeccable co-ordination between tanks and dive-bombers. In the course of engagements which Manstein in his memoirs describes as extremely tough, *Gruppe* Kempf succeeded in breaking through two defence lines and reaching a point where it could intercept Steppe Front reinforcements coming to the aid of Voronezh Front. On July 11 the situation might be thought to be promising.

For 48 hours the 4th *Panzerarmee* met a solid wall of resistance of which General F. W. von Mellenthin, at that time chief-of-staff to XLVIII Panzer Corps, provides the following description in his book *Panzer Battles:*

"During the second and third days of the offensive we met with our first reverses. In spite of our soldiers' courage and determination, we were unable to find a gap in the enemy's second defence line. The *Panzergrenadier* Division "Grossdeutschland" (Lieutenant-General Hoerlein) which had gone into battle in extremely tight formation and had come up against an extremely marshy tract of ground, was stopped by prepared fortifications defended with anti-tank guns, flame-throwers, and T-34 tanks, and was met by violent artillery fire. For some time it remained unable to move in the middle of the battlefield devised by the enemy. It was no easy task for our pioneers to find and fix a passable route through numerous minefields or across the tracts of marshland. A large number of tanks were blown up by mines or destroyed by aerial attacks: the Red Air Force showed little regard for the fact of the Luftwaffe's superiority and fought the battle with remarkable determination and spirit."

On July 7, however, XLVIII Panzer Corps and on its right II *Waffen* S.S. Panzer Corps found themselves unopposed, after repulsing heavy counterattacks by tanks which developed as pincer movements. Thus on July 11, after establishing a bridgehead on the Psel and getting close to Oboyan, the 4th *Panzerarmee* had advanced 18 to 20 miles through Vatutin's lines, while *Gruppe* Kempf, without having been able to land on the western bank of the Korocha had nevertheless managed to fulfil its primary task of protecting the 4th *Panzerarmee's* right flank. Two days

later, Manstein reported that since D-day he had taken 24,000 prisoners and destroyed or captured 100 tanks and 108 anti-tank guns, and intended to move up his reserve, XXIV Panzer Corps.

These, however, were limited successes and "Zitadelle" was a serious reverse for Hitler. Between the spearhead of the 4th *Panzerarmee,* on the edge of Oboyan, and the vanguard of the 9th Army, forced to halt before Olkhovatka, the gap between the two armies remained, and would remain, 75 miles.

Far from feeling discouragement, Vatutin made known to *Stavka* in the evening of July 10 his intention of counterattacking, and bringing up for this pur-

△ *Soviet infantry and tanks approaching the Kursk area. The Russians were able to keep their reserves undamaged until the Germans had driven themselves to breaking point on the fixed defences in the Kursk salient, and then the Red Army went on to the counter-attack.*

▽ *A Pzkw III emerges from the smoke of a grass fire during the opening stages of "Zitadelle". The operation was to squander the tanks and vehicles that Guderian had built up.*

△ *Lieutenant-General Rotmistrov and Major-General Rodimtsev. Rotmistrov commanded the 5th Guards Tank Army in the Battle of Kursk. He brought it by forced marches over 200 miles and then after a heavy bombardment sent in his force of 850 tanks and assault guns against Hausser's II S.S Panzer Corps, which was fighting in the Prokhorovka area.*

▽ *A Soviet 76-mm gun crew prepares to fire. Before the Germans moved off from their start lines on the first day of Kursk, they were subject to a morale-shattering bombardment.*

pose his 5th Guards Tank Army (Lieutenant-General P. A. Rotmistrov) with its 850 tanks and assault guns, as well as the 1st Tank Army (Lieutenant-General M. E. Katukov).

On the other side of the battlefield, Rokossovsky addressed the following rousing order of the day to his troops on July 12: "The soldiers of the Central Front who met the enemy with a rampart of murderous steel and truly Russian grit and tenacity have exhausted him after a week of unrelenting and unremitting fighting; they have contained the enemy's drive. The first phase of the battle is over."

And indeed, on that same July 12, the Soviet armies of the Bryansk and West Front, following a predetermined plan, proceeded to launch a major offensive against the German-held Orel salient.

Hitler's choice: Sicily or "Zitadelle"

With the unexpected development of the situation in the Kursk area, Hitler summoned Kluge and Manstein to his H.Q. at Rastenburg on July 13. Kluge left the Führer with no illusions: the 9th Army, which had lost 20,000 men in a single week, was both incapable of advancing further and at the same time

obliged to relinquish part of its remaining strength to bolster the defence of the Orel salient. Manstein was less pessimistic, yet in order for him to be able to compel the Russians to continue to fight, as he proposed, on this altered front in the Kursk region, Kluge had to pin down the maximum Soviet forces in his sector. The argument was thus circular.

Hitler decided matters by simply abandoning the operation. Yet—and this has been insufficiently remarked upon—his decision was motivated not so much by the local situation or by the Russian offensive in the Orel salient as by the fact of the Anglo-American landings in Sicily.

According to Manstein, the Führer took a particularly gloomy view of the immediate outlook in this new theatre of operations: "The situation in Sicily has become extremely serious," he informed the two field-marshals. "The Italians are not resisting and the island will probably be lost. As a result, the Western powers will be able to land in the Balkans or in southern Italy. Hence new armies must be formed in these areas, which means taking troops from the Eastern Front, and hence calling a halt to *'Zitadelle'*." And there is the proof that the second front in the Mediterranean, derided by President Roosevelt, by Harry Hopkins, and by General Marshall, achieved what none of them expected of it: relief for Russia.

The end of the greatest tank battle

Thus ended the Battle of Kursk which, involving as it did more than 5,400 armoured and tracked vehicles, must be counted the greatest tank battle of World War II.

Some commentators have compared it with the ill-starred offensive launched by General Nivelle which ground to a halt on April 16, 1917 on the steep slopes up to the Chemin des Dames. But it would seem to bear greater similarity to Ludendorff's final attempt to give victory to the German Army. On July 15, 1918, the Quartermaster-General of the Imperial German Army was brought to a standstill in Champagne by Pétain's system of defence in depth, and this failure allowed Foch to detach Mangin and Degoutte in a French offensive against

he Château-Thierry salient. Subsequently the new Marshal of France extended his battle-line to left and to right, and the German retreat lasted until the Armistice on November 11, 1918.

There is one difference between these two sets of circumstances. On August 10, 1918, on receiving the news that Sir Douglas Haig's tanks had scattered the German defence in Picardy, Wilhelm II declared to Hindenburg and to Ludendorff: "This to my mind is the final reckoning", and this flash of common sense spared Germany the horrors of invasion. In July 1943, Hitler, the head of state, was incapable of making a similar observation to Hitler, the war leader, still less of parting company with him as the Kaiser parted company with Ludendorff on October 26, 1918.

The Panzer defeat in the Kursk salient has had its historians in both camps, but it also had its prophet, who in the spring of 1939 mused on the question of what might be the result should an army of tanks collide with a similar army given a defensive function. And in the course of examining this hypothesis which he declared had been neglected, he arrived at the following conclusion and another question: "On land, there does exist a means of halting a tank offensive: a combination of mines and anti-tank guns. What would happen to an offensive by tank divisions which encountered a

defence composed of similar tank divisions, but ones which had been carefully deployed and had had time to work out a considered fire-plan on the chosen battlefield, on which anti-tank firepower was closely co-ordinated with natural obstacles reinforced by minefields?"

Thus, three or four months before the war broke out, Marshal Pétain expressed himself in a preface to General Chauvineau's book *Is an Invasion Still Possible?* that is often quoted and never read. And the event itself would prove him right – but on a scale beyond the wildest imaginings in 1939: to stop 1,800 German tanks it required 3,600 Soviet tanks, 6,000 anti-tank weapons, and 400,000 mines!

△ *A shattered Pzkw III, one of the hundreds of knocked out tanks that the Germans left on the battle field. After Stalingrad they began to fear they could not win the war, but Kursk confirmed that they would lose it.*

▽ *A group of prisoners. German losses during the Battle of Kursk were about 20,000, and by now it was becoming harder for these losses to be replaced. In addition, the Red Army was recovering lost territory and gaining new conscripts.*

CHAPTER 55
THE TEHERAN CONFERENCE

In Teheran, Stalin and Churchill took up residence in the adjacent Russian and British embassies, which were protected by a single perimeter under British and Russian guard. But Roosevelt, in the American embassy, lay a mile or so distant, entailing the inconvenience, if not the danger, of mutual journeyings to meet in session. Molotov, the Russian foreign minister, suggested that Roosevelt come to live in an annexe to the Russian embassy; Churchill backed the idea; and the President and his staff duly moved in. With hindsight and knowledge of Russian skills in "bugging", it may be surmised that Molotov was not only prompted by emotions of hospitality and concern for the President's safety; certainly the Russian delegation was to show itself acutely aware of the differences over strategy and policy between the British and Americans. Harry Hopkins wrote:

"The servants who made their beds and cleaned their rooms were all members of the highly efficient NKVD, the secret police, and expressive bulges were plainly discernible in the hip pockets under their white coats. It was a nervous time for Michael F. Reilly and his own White House secret service men, who were trained to suspect *everybody* and who did not like to admit into the President's presence anyone who was armed with as much as a gold toothpick."

On the afternoon of November 28 the first plenary session of the Teheran Conference ("Eureka") opened in the Russian embassy under, as with all the sessions, President Roosevelt's chairmanship. Flanked by Molotov and Marshal Voroshilov, Stalin was resplendent in a uniform, according to Lord Moran, "that looks as if it has not been worn before, and gives the impression that it has been specially designed for the occasion. It looks, too, as if the tailor has put on it a shelf on each shoulder, and on it dumped a lot of gold lace with white stars. And there is a broad red stripe down the trousers, which are immaculately creased. All this is crowned with a dreadful hat, smothered with gold braid." Gaudily uniformed or not, Stalin dominated the conference from the start. In his very opening statement he announced that after Germany's defeat

Russia would join in the war against Japan, a development that at once threw Anglo-American grand strategy in the Pacific and Far East into the melting-pot.

Churchill's ideas

Churchill followed by putting forward the British concept for the war against Germany: "Overlord" in the late spring or the summer of 1944, to be undertaken by 35 strong divisions, of which 16 would be British; the capture of Rome and an advance to the Pisa–Rimini line, with the option of advancing later either into southern France or north-eastward towards the Danube; an attempt to bring Turkey into the war, followed by the capture of the Dodecanese. Hereupon Stalin moved in masterfully by cross-examining Churchill not only about the details of these operations, but also about the depth of the British commitment to launch "Overlord". In the first place he wanted to know the proportion of Allied land forces to be allotted to "Overlord" and the Mediterranean. Churchill confirmed that "Overlord" would have 35 "very strong" divisions, leaving 22 in the Mediterranean region. After questioning the Prime Minister further about the present state of plans for invading southern France and the number of divisions thought necessary for the support of Turkey and the capture of the Dodecanese (should Turkey enter the war), Stalin proceeded to lay down unequivocally his own conception of the right strategy for the Western Allies. According to the conference record:

"Marshal Stalin thought it would be a mistake to disperse forces by sending part to Turkey and elsewhere, and part to southern France. The best course would be to make 'Overlord' the basic operation for 1944 and, once Rome had been captured, to send all available forces in Italy to southern France. These forces could then join hands with the 'Overlord' forces when the invasion was launched. France was the weakest spot on the German front. He himself did not expect Turkey to enter the war."

Allied Problems: 1944

The Anglo-American summit conference held in Quebec in 1943 barely hid the emergence of the new world order of two superpowers, the United States and the Soviet Union. There was also tension over what the Americans regarded as a weak British commitment to Overlord and too great an interest in the Mediterranean. At the conference the Americans succeeded in gaining a greater British commitment to Overlord, as well as the previously agreed return of seven divisions from the Mediterranean to the U.K. General Brooke thought that an important opportunity had been missed in Italy and that with greater commitment the Balkans might have been set ablaze.

With regard to Burma, Sir Claude Auchinleck told London that poor rail and road communications severely restricted strategic options while Orde Wingate suggested long-range penetration offensives. Churchill's sympathies lay with the latter. A south-east Asia Command was set up under Vice-Admiral Lord Louis Mountbatten, with "Vinegar Joe" Stilwell as his deputy.

A Quebec Agreement was signed over nuclear research, which once again, despite the fact that most initial research had been conducted in British universities, put Britain in second place to the U.S.A.

In a further exchange with Churchill, Stalin agreed that it was worthwhile taking the Dodecanese if this involved only three or four divisions, but "repeated that 'Overlord' was a very serious operation and that it was better to help it by invading the South of France . . ."

Stalin's influence

All this was congenial enough to Roosevelt, who now suggested that Stalin's suggestion of invading southern France two months before D-day should be examined by the military experts. Stalin added:

". . . the experience gained by the Soviets during the last two years of campaigning was that a big offensive, if undertaken from only one direction, rarely yielded results. The better course was to launch offensives from two or more directions simultaneously . . . He suggested that this principle might well be applied to the problem under discussion."

Thus, to the surprise of both Americans and British, Stalin had placed all the weight of the Soviet Union and his own formidable personality behind the American strategy of concentrating on "Overlord" and abjuring wider commitments in the Mediterranean and Aegean. Churchill, however, did not agree with them and he resorted to bluster about the size of British-Empire forces in the Mediterranean area:

". . . he did not disagree in principle with Marshal Stalin. The suggestions he [Churchill] had made for action in Yugoslavia and in respect of Turkey did not, in his view, conflict in any way with that general conception. At the same time, he wished it to be placed on record that he could not in any circumstances agree to sacrifice the activities of the armies in the Mediterranean, which included 20 British and British-controlled divisions, merely in order to keep the exact date of the 1st May for 'Overlord' . . ."

Brooke cross-examined

President Roosevelt now suggested that the question should be referred to the staffs for study and report. This vital session took place next day, when Marshal Voroshilov, following Stalin's line,

The presentation of the "Stalingrad Sword" to Stalin. It had been forged to commemorate the defence of Stalingrad, and its display in London had drawn large crowds. Writing of the presentation Churchill said, "When, after a few sentences of explanation, I handed the splendid weapon to Marshal Stalin he raised it in a most impressive gesture to his lips and kissed the scabbard. He then passed it to Voroshilov, who dropped it. It was carried from the room with great solemnity by a Russian guard of honour. As this procession moved away I saw the President sitting at the side of the room, obviously stirred by the ceremony."
▷ Stalin chuckles as Churchill takes out a cigar. Though the photographs seem to show the Allies in agreement, Brooke, commenting on Stalin's intransigence and the strain of working with interpreters, said "After listening to the arguments put forward during the last two days I felt like entering a lunatic asylum or a nursing-home!"

unmistakably sided with the Americans against the British. Sir Alan Brooke found himself the victim at Voroshilov's hands of the kind of suspicious cross-examination about the sincerity of the British commitment to "Overlord" that he had been forced to endure from his American colleagues at earlier summit conferences.

"Marshal Voroshilov said he understood from General Marshall that the United States High Command and United States Government considered 'Overlord' to be an operation of the first importance. He said he would like to know whether Sir Alan Brooke considered this to be an operation of the first importance; whether he both thought the operation was necessary and that it must be carried out, or whether, alternatively, it might be replaced by another operation if Turkey came into the war."

Voroshilov's arguments

When Brooke answered that Mediterranean operations were designed to ensure "Overlord's" success, Voroshilov did not disagree, but insisted that any such operations must be secondary to "Overlord" and not compete with it. He went on:

". . . the suggestion made yesterday by Marshal Stalin was that, at the same time as the operation in Northern France, operations should be undertaken in South-

ern France. Operations in Italy and elsewhere in the Mediterranean must be considered of secondary importance, because, from those areas, Germany could not be attacked directly with the Alps in the way. Italy . . . offered great possibilities for defence. Defences should be organised there with the minimum of troops. The remaining troops would be used for the South of France in order to attack the enemy from two sides."

Voroshilov added that "Marshal Stalin did not insist on an operation against the South of France, but that he did insist that the operation against the North of France should take place in the manner and on the date already agreed upon".

Stalin and Churchill

That afternoon the second plenary session of the conference saw Stalin press even more strongly the Russian case for total concentration on "Overlord". Firstly, he wanted to know the name of the Allied supreme commander for the operation; an embarrassing question since the American proposal at Cairo for a super supremo had put the former appointment in the melting-pot. Roosevelt answered that a staff officer with an Anglo-American staff had already brought plans and preparations for "Overlord" to an advanced stage. But Stalin, justifiably enough, observed that the commander might want to alter

such plans, and should therefore be appointed at once so he could become responsible for the planning and execution of the operation. It was agreed that this appointment should be made within two weeks and the Russians informed of the name of the new supreme commander. In this case too, therefore, Stalin's intervention proved decisive.

When in the same plenary session Churchill tried yet again to make a case for the British Mediterranean strategy, Stalin simply ploughed on remorselessly:

"In his view there were three main matters to be decided. First, the date of the operation ['Overlord'] should be determined. This should be some time in May and no later. Secondly, Operation 'Overlord' should be supported by a landing in the South of France . . . He regarded the assault on the South of France as a supporting operation which would be definitely helpful to 'Overlord'. The capture of Rome and other operations in the Mediterranean could only be regarded as diversions.

"The third matter to be decided was the appointment of a Commander-in-Chief for the 'Overlord' operation. He would like to see this appointment made before the conclusion of the present conference. If this was not possible, at least within a week."

Churchill, still game, brought up the question of available landing-craft in relation to the timings of "Overlord", the invasion of southern France and "Buc-

caneer", and put in a last plea for his favourite Aegean and Turkish strategy. On his suggestion, amended by Roosevelt, it was agreed to refer the subsidiary operations to an *ad hoc* military committee (in fact the Combined Chiefs-of-Staff) which was to submit detailed recommendations for approval. But Stalin, like the Americans before him, was now deeply suspicious of the sincerity of the British belief in "Overlord". At the close of the session, according to the British official record:

"Marshal Stalin said . . . he wished to pose a very direct question to the Prime Minister about 'Overlord'. Did the Prime Minister and the British Staffs really believe in 'Overlord'?

"The Prime Minister replied that, provided the conditions previously stated for 'Overlord' were to obtain when the time came, he firmly believed it would be our stern duty to hurl across the Channel against the Germans every sinew of our strength."

British isolation

The British sense of isolation was enhanced by President Roosevelt's own conduct since arriving in Teheran. Churchill relates in his memoirs how he, Churchill, was led at this juncture to seek a personal interview with Stalin on account of the fact that "the President was in private contact with Marshal Stalin and dwelling at the Soviet Embassy, and he had avoided ever seeing me alone since we left Cairo, in spite of our hitherto intimate relations and the way our vital affairs were interwoven." In this interview, which took place on Churchill's 69th birthday, the Prime Minister sought to destroy "the false idea" forming in Stalin's mind "that", to put it shortly, "Churchill and the British Staff mean to stop 'Overlord' if they can, because they want to invade the Balkans instead". Churchill argued that if Roosevelt could be persuaded to call off Operation "Buccaneer" in the Indian Ocean, there would be enough landing-craft both for the Mediterranean and a "punctual" (*sic*) "Overlord". And yet, given Churchill's predilections earlier in 1943 for a major Anglo-American effort to bring about a collapse of the German position in the Balkans, and given also the bitter regrets Sir Alan Brooke was confiding to his diary only a month before the Teheran Conference about the chances missed for achieving this, was Stalin's mistrust unjustified?

Agreement is reached on future strategy

At four o'clock that afternoon the final plenary session ratified the recommendations agreed after exhaustive argument by the military committee in the morning:

"(a) That we should continue to advance in Italy to the Pisa–Rimini line. (This means that the 68 LST's which are due to be sent from the Mediterranean to the United Kingdom for 'Overlord' must be kept in the Mediterranean until 15th January.)

"(b) That an operation shall be mounted against the South of France on as big a scale as landing-craft will permit. For planning purposes D-day to be the same as 'Overlord' D-day.

"(c) ... that we will launch 'Overlord' in May, in conjunction with a supporting operation against the South of France ..."

The military committee reported, however, that they were unable to reach agreement about operations in the Aegean until they received fresh instructions from the President and Prime Minister.

Thus, thanks to Stalin, the Western

Allies had finally agreed on their strategy against Germany in 1944. In military terms Teheran had been Stalin's conference all the way. Sir Alan Brooke, by now a connoisseur of politicians at war, later recorded his appreciation of Stalin's qualities:

"During this meeting and the subsequent ones we had with Stalin, I rapidly grew to appreciate the fact that he had a military brain of the highest calibre. Never once in any of his statements did he make any strategic error, nor did he ever fail to appreciate all the implications of a situation with a quick and unerring eye. In this respect he stood out compared with his two colleagues. Roosevelt never made any great pretence of being a strategist

△ *A German poster displayed in Poland: "The German soldier is the guarantor of victories." Here Russia becomes a ravening wolf, the American eagle a balding vulture, and Britain (perfidious Albion) a snake.*

and left either Marshall or Leahy to talk for him. Winston, on the other hand, was more erratic, brilliant at times, but too impulsive and inclined to favour unsuitable plans without giving them the preliminary deep thought they required."

It may be that Stalin so strongly urged concentration on "Overlord" at the expense of Italy and the eastern Mediterranean because Russia as a great land power had a natural affinity with America in preferring a massive offensive proceeding along one major axis, in contrast to the British preference for opportunistic, peripheral and relatively small-scale operations. Nevertheless, the decisions taken at Teheran at Stalin's instigation, by shepherding the Western Allies away from the Balkans and making it less likely than ever that the Anglo-American army in Italy would eventually advance northeastward towards the Danube, also paved the way for the unhindered extension of Russian dominion over Rumania, Hungary, Bulgaria and Yugoslavia.

Political considerations

Although no far-reaching political decisions were reached at Teheran, Stalin proved hardly less the master in this sphere than in the purely military. In particular, his ruthless and farsighted sense of Russia's postwar interests contrasted with Roosevelt's naïve idealism and goodwill. Much of the political talk took place informally at mealtimes, or in private à deux–Roosevelt courted Stalin behind Churchill's back, Churchill courted Stalin behind Roosevelt's back. After dinner on the opening night of the conference, Churchill led Stalin to a sofa and suggested that they should talk about the postwar world. Stalin agreed, and proceeded to outline a profound fear of Germany's capacity for recovery, citing her prewar resurgence despite the Versailles Treaty. When Churchill asked him how soon he expected such a recovery, Stalin answered: "Within fifteen to twenty years." The Prime Minister remarked:

". . . Our duty is to make the world safe for at least fifty years by German disarmament, by preventing rearmament, by supervision of German factories, by forbidding all aviation, and by territorial changes of a far-reaching character. It all comes back to the question whether Great Britain, the United States, and the USSR can keep a close friendship and supervise Germany in their mutual interest."

Postwar problems: the fate of Germany

When Stalin noted that control of this kind had failed after the last war, Churchill suggested that Prussia should be dealt with more harshly than the rest of Germany, and be isolated and reduced, while Bavaria might join Austria and Hungary in a broad, harmless Danubian confederation. But Stalin commented, "All very good, but insufficient."

The topic of postwar Germany came up for formal discussion at the very last plenary session of the Conference on December 1. Roosevelt put forward a plan to divide her into five self-governing parts, plus two areas–Kiel–Hamburg and the Ruhr/Saar industrial regions–under direct United Nations control. Churchill said again that the most important thing was to isolate and weaken Prussia; he believed Roosevelt's five independent German states would be too small to be viable, and that they should be attached to larger non-German groupings. In particular he put forward his idea of a Danubian confederation including southern Germany, whose population he reckoned to be less ferocious than the Prussians. However, in Stalin's estimation, north and south Germans, and Austrians, were equally ferocious. He expressed the fear that Germans would come to dominate Churchill's proposed Danubian confederation, and therefore he wanted there to be no more large combinations in Europe once Germany was broken up. The Germans themselves, even if split up, would always seek to re-unite themselves, a process Stalin thought must be neutralised by economic measures and if necessary by force. Churchill then asked Stalin if he contemplated a Europe of disjointed little states with no large units; a good question. According to Churchill's memoirs, Stalin replied that "he was speaking of Germany not Europe. Poland and France were large States, Rumania and Bulgaria were small States. But Germany should at all costs be broken up so that she could not reunite." Finally it was agreed to set up a special three-power committee under the European Advisory Commission to study the matter.

Poland

Tightly linked to these questions of the postwar anatomy of Germany and Stalin's anxiety over a revived German threat to Russia's western frontier was the question of Poland. Churchill brought the topic up unofficially during his conversation with the Soviet leader after dinner on the first night of the conference, proposing that the three powers should agree future Polish frontiers between themselves and put the result to the Poles. He suggested that Poland might sidestep westwards, giving up territory in the east to Russia in exchange for German territory; an idea which, in Churchill's words, "pleased Stalin". But postwar Poland, like postwar Germany, did not figure in official discussions until the final plenary session on December 1. Roosevelt opened the topic by expressing the hope that the Soviet and Polish governments would resume diplomatic relations (broken off by the Soviet Union because the Polish Government-in-exile in London had associated itself with the German claim that the Polish officers whose corpses had been found at Katyn had been murdered by the Russians). Churchill reminded his hearers of the importance to Britain of Poland's future, since Britain had originally gone to war on her behalf. He repeated his suggestion that Poland should be sidestepped westwards and reminded Stalin of his own remark earlier that he would not object if Poland reached the Oder. Stalin, however, now shrewdly drew a distinction between discussing the frontiers of a future Poland and discussing a future Polish government. According to Churchill's account, Stalin went on:

"Russia, even more than other States, was interested in good relations with Poland, because for her it was a question of the security of her frontiers. Russia was in favour of the reconstruction, development, and expansion of Poland mainly at the expense of Germany. But he separated Poland from the Polish Government-in-exile. He had broken off relations with the Polish Government-in-exile, not on account of caprice, but because it had joined with Hitler in slanderous propaganda against Russia. He would like to have a guarantee that the Polish Government in exile would not kill Partisans, but, on the contrary, would urge the Poles to fight the Germans . . . He would welcome any Polish Government which would take such active measures, and he would be glad to renew relations with them. But he was by no means sure that the Polish Government-in-exile was ever likely to become the sort of Government it ought to be."

New frontiers

In this statement were all the essential clues to the policy Stalin was to pursue towards Poland in the coming years, and which would reduce her to a Russian satellite. At Teheran, however, neither western leader challenged Stalin's comments about the Polish Government-in-exile or seemed to perceive their significance. Instead the discussion turned to Poland's future frontiers. After much consultation of maps and dispute as to the exact course of the Curzon Line of 1920, fixing the Russo-Polish frontier, the three leaders and their advisers agreed to a formula devised by Churchill that "it was thought in principle that the home of the Polish State and nation should be in between the so-called Curzon Line and the line of the Oder, including, for Poland, East Prussia and Oppeln, but the actual line required careful study . . ." Stalin's only caveat was to state that Russia also wanted Königsberg. All this was duly to come to pass.

Churchill's 69th birthday, which on November 30 came as finale to the Teheran conference. For Churchill it was "a memorable occasion in my life. On my right sat the President of the United States on my left the master of Russia. Together we controlled a large preponderance of the naval and three-quarters of all the air forces in the world, and could direct armies of nearly twenty millions of men."

Roosevelt's suggestions for world peace

At a private meeting on November 29 with Stalin and Molotov, Roosevelt had unveiled his ideas for a world peace-keeping organisation after the war which would avoid the built-in weaknesses of the League of Nations created by his predecessor President Woodrow Wilson. The preservation of peace would be entrusted to the "Four Policemen": the Soviet Union, the United States, Great Britain and China. But Stalin, more realistic than Roosevelt about the status of Chiang Kai-shek's China as a great power, did not respond to the President's visionary scheme. He doubted whether China would be very powerful after the war; he thought that European states would in any case resent being policed by China. Instead he suggested regional committees for Europe and the Far East, the Soviet Union, the United States and Britain being members of both. This, as Roosevelt acknowledged, tied in with a similar idea of Churchill's, although the Prime Minister wanted a supreme United Nations Council as well (an item which Roosevelt omitted to pass on to Stalin). But Roosevelt went on to tell the Soviet leader that the American Congress would be unwilling to sanction American participation in an exclusively European committee, which might demand the despatch of American troops to Europe. When Stalin pointed out that the same objection applied to the President's own concept of the "Four Policemen", Roosevelt, in an unguarded admission potentially dangerous for the future, answered that he had only considered committing American air and sea power; it would be up to Britain and the Soviet Union to find the land forces to deal with a future threat to peace in Europe. No doubt all this was carefully stored away in Stalin's memory and helped formulate his postwar policy.

The Teheran Conference concluded with a dinner at which friendly and flattering mutual toasts were exchanged by the three leaders, expressing the satisfaction felt by all of them at the results of their meetings; indeed expressing at that moment a true comradeship in the face of the enemy. But beyond the joint strategy and operations now agreed for the defeat of Germany and Japan lay the

undecided questions of postwar Europe and the postwar world. Churchill wrote later in his memoirs: "It would not have been right at Teheran for the Western democracies to found their plans upon suspicions of the Russian attitude in the hour of triumph and when all her dangers were removed." But with hindsight it might be argued that it would have been just as "right" for the Western democracies to look shrewdly to their own long-term interests as it was for Stalin to look to those of Soviet Russia.

Back to Cairo

On December 2, 1943, Roosevelt and Churchill arrived back in Cairo to thrash out with the Combined Chiefs-of-Staff the details of the operations agreed on at Teheran and to settle the question of the supreme command. Once again the military staffs and the plenary sessions

△ △ *General Wladyslaw Sikorski, Premier of the Polish Government-in-exile. He was killed in an air crash on July 4, 1943.*
△ *His successor Stanislas Mikolajczyk. Relations between the Poles and the Russians broke down after the Katyn disclosures.*

According to Robert Sherwood, this was the only time during the war that Roosevelt overruled his chiefs-of-staff.

Eisenhower or Marshall?

There remained the question of a supreme commander for "Overlord". In the face of the strong British objections, the Americans had quietly given up their idea of a super supremo responsible for all operations everywhere against Germany. Yet only such a post would have been important enough to warrant moving General Marshall from Washington, where he was a key figure, and without giving the impression of a demotion. Roosevelt therefore came to another hard decision, this time one taken against the advice of Hopkins and Stimson as well as the known preference of Churchill and Stalin. He told Marshall, "I feel I could not sleep at night with you out of the country." Next day Roosevelt informed Churchill that Eisenhower would command "Overlord". It had already been agreed to create a single Mediterranean theatre command under a British supreme commander, who was named on December 18 as General Sir Maitland Wilson.

Final agreement

Thus the "Sextant" and "Eureka" conferences, when taken together the longest, toughest inter-Allied meeting ever held, came to an end with all the great strategic issues at last resolved. For all the arguing and bargaining, the British and Americans parted in amity, as the concluding remarks of the final session record:

"Sir Alan Brooke said he would like to express on behalf of the British Chiefs of Staff their deep gratitude for the way in which the United States Chiefs had met their views . . .

"General Marshall said that he very much appreciated Sir Alan Brooke's gracious tributes . . ."

On his way home Roosevelt summoned Eisenhower to Tunis, and as soon as Eisenhower had joined him in his car, he said: "Well, Ike, you are going to command 'Overlord'!" Eisenhower replied:

"Mr. President, I realise that such an appointment involved difficult decisions. I hope you will not be disappointed."

△ *General Dwight D. Eisenhower. He was promoted to command the Allied invasion force for operation "Overlord", a move which was politically expedient, but which disappointed Brooke, who had been promised the command by Churchill.*
▽ *General Sir Henry Maitland Wilson, who succeeded Eisenhower as Supreme Allied Commander in the Mediterranean theatre of operations.*

grappled with the old question of available landing-craft in relation to "Buccaneer", "Overlord", the invasion of southern France and the residual operations in the eastern Mediterranean. Fresh examination of the "Overlord" plan in the light of the experience of the invasion of Sicily and Italy suggested that a larger initial assault force was desirable, and that meant yet more landing-craft. The British Chiefs-of-Staff therefore once more sought to get "Buccaneer" abandoned, and with it the planned concurrent land offensive in northern Burma; their American opposite numbers nevertheless still argued that these operations were politically and militarily essential. Three days of discussion led only to deadlock. But on the evening of December 5, after hard thinking in private, Roosevelt came to a difficult decision. He sent Churchill the terse message "Buccaneer is off" Next day he signalled Chiang that European commitments left no margin for the operation.

CHAPTER 56
SMASHING THE DNIEPR FRONT

The first five months of 1944 were marked by new Red Army offensives to the south of the Pripet Marshes. The offensives led to the liberation of the Ukraine and Crimea as well as to the conquest of the northern part of Rumanian Moldavia, while in the Leningrad region they succeeded in throwing the Germans back from a line linking Oranienbaum–Volkhov–Novgorod–Lake Ilmen onto one linking Narva–Lake Peipus and Pskov. At the same time, the Western Allies were also putting the pressure on Germany.

Further south, General Sir Henry Maitland Wilson, new Allied Commander-in-Chief in the Mediterranean, endeavoured to carry out the limited mission which had been entrusted to him in implementation of decisions recently taken at the Teheran Conference. Two days before the Normandy landings, the advance guard of his 15th Army Group under General Sir Harold Alexander had entered Rome hard on the enemy's heels. Thereby the allies had achieved their strictly geographical objective, but arguably at the price of sacrificing their strategic objective in Italy, namely the destruction of the enemy forces.

Parallel to this, in Great Britain the preparations for Operation "Overlord", with all their attendant difficulties, were rapidly approaching their climax. While the divisions taking part in the landings by sea and by air were undergoing intensive training, in London Generals Eisenhower and Montgomery were putting the final touches to the invasion plans drawn up by the American and British Combined Chiefs-of-Staff, C.O.S.S.A.C., and submitted for their approval by General Morgan.

Bombing stepped up

Anglo-American bomber formations intensified their missions by day and by night over the Third Reich as well as over occupied Europe. Most probably the results obtained over the first six months were no more significant in their impact on German war production than during the previous year. However, systematic pinpointing of synthetic oil plants from spring onwards, as well as of the Ploiesti oil-wells, enabled the Allied air forces for the first time to influence events on land directly by precipitating an extremely serious fuel crisis in the Wehrmacht. Furthermore, in the western and southern theatres British and American fighter-bombers and medium bombers constantly pounded the enemy's communications

▽ *"Crush the Fascist Reptile!" A typically virulent Russian poster. In the early days of the war, when they were exhibited near the front line, posters were used to demoralise the attacking Germans in addition to whipping the Russians into greater hatred of the invaders.*

▷ *U-boats of the excellent XXI type under construction in a Bremen yard at the time of Germany's capitulation.*

> ▷ *U-boats of the excellent XXI type under construction in a Bremen yard at the time of Germany's capitulation.*

Katyn: the Burden of Guilt

On April 13, 1943 the Germans found piled up 12 deep the mummified bodies of 4,143 Polish officers, all felled by pistol shots to the back of the neck. It was later revealed that they had been murdered by the Soviet N.K.V.D.

system. In France and Belgium their aim was to obstruct rapid reinforcement of the German 7th Army, which was in position on the coast between Cabourg and St. Nazaire; in Italy their main targets were the Po bridges and the course of the Adige, the route by which enemy supplies and reinforcements moved after crossing the Brenner Pass. Moreover, the Luftwaffe was being forced to sacrifice itself against the mass American daylight raids escorted by long-range fighters.

War in the Atlantic

On June 22, 1941, Hitler became involved unwisely in a "war on two fronts" such as had cost Wilhelm II his throne, in spite of the fact that the Emperor's ghost might have seemed to have been exorcised by the Soviet-German Pact of August 23, 1939. And now on January 1, 1944, the Third Reich and its Führer were in a position of having to conduct a "war on all fronts" (*Allfrontenkrieg*).

The only way in which Germany might have escaped the inevitable consequences of the powerful efforts of the Allies to surround and close in on her, would have

been to resume the U-boat offensive in the Atlantic with the same success as in 1942. But for all his energy, intelligence, and experience, Grand-Admiral Dönitz was unable to stem the swelling tide of troops, war *matériel,* and supplies converging on Europe from America.

The facts are made clear in the following table, based on figures supplied by Captain Roskill, of Allied mercantile losses in 1942 and 1944 in the North Atlantic:

	1942		1944	
	tonnage	ships	tonnage	ships
January	276,795	48	36,065	5
February	429,891	73	12,577	2
March	534,064	95	36,867	7
April	391,044	66	34,224	5
May	576,350	120	0	0
Totals	2,208,144	402	119,733	19

The figures show the extent to which Britain and America recovered complete supremacy in the North Atlantic, with consequent complete freedom of manoeuvre and strategy. Although Grand-Admiral Dönitz was keeping new and unpleasant secret weapons up his sleeve, they were not as yet ready, and until they were there was a great deal that could happen.

Hitler's predictions

The immediate consequences of this complete reversal of the situation were perfectly clear to Hitler. One only need refer to the arguments propounded on November 3, 1943 in support of measures prescribed by his Directive No. 51, as regards the conduct of the war; in his own words:

"The hard and costly struggle against Bolshevism during the last two-and-a-half years, which has involved the bulk of our military strength in the East, has demanded extreme exertions. The greatness of the danger and the general situation demanded it. But the situation has since changed. The danger in the East still remains, but a greater danger now appears in the West: an Anglo-Saxon landing! In the East, the vast extent of the territory makes it possible for us to lose ground, even on a large scale, without a fatal blow being dealt to the nervous system of Germany.

"It is very different in the West! Should the enemy succeed in breaching our defences on a wide front here, the immediate consequences would be unpredictable. Everything indicates that the enemy will launch an offensive against the Western front of Europe, at the latest in the spring, perhaps even earlier.

"I can therefore no longer take responsibility for further weakening the West, in favour of other theatres of war. I have therefore decided to reinforce its defences, particularly those places from which the long-range bombardment of England will begin. For it is here that the enemy must and will attack, and it is here – unless all indications are misleading – that the decisive battle against the landing forces will be fought."

On December 20 following, Hitler returned to the question in the presence of his generals. It appears from the shorthand account of his statement that, while he was convinced that the invasion would take place, he was less than convinced that the British would have their hearts in it:

"It stands to reason that the English have less confidence in this enterprise than has Eisenhower. Eisenhower has effected one [sic] successful invasion, but this was solely due to the work of traitors. Here with our soldiers he will find none to help him. Here, we mean business, make no mistake! It is a totally different matter to invade North Africa and be greeted by Monsieur Giraud or be confronted by the Italians who for the most part stay in their holes without firing a single shot, and to set foot in the West in the face of unrelenting fire. And so long as a battery is capable of firing, it will continue firing. That is a certainty."

German misconceptions

The above extract from Directive No. 51 is interesting from more than one aspect. Its third paragraph adds a further reason to those normally advanced by way of explaining why O.K.W. situated the centre of gravity of its western defensive system between Le Havre and the Pas-de-Calais. The argument at Rastenburg ran as follows: the fact that the launching sites for the V-1 and V-2, whose effect was directed against Britain, were in this area would in all probability lead the British to urge their allies that this was the best place to make the landings. This argument was plausible enough, but its effectiveness required one condition,

▽ *Evidence of the Red Air Force's growing power – German transport destroyed during the retreat in the Ukraine. From now on the Luftwaffe could only very rarely assure the ground forces of any useful air cover.*

△ *German and satellite infantry wait to board a train leaving for the Russian front.*

namely that the Germans should be the first to open fire. Yet Hitler knew perfectly well that the V-1 missiles (let alone V-2) would not be operational before the date when he expected his enemies to attempt invasion across the Channel.

Furthermore, insisting as he did on the peril that was looming in the West to the extent of giving it priority in the short run over the Soviet threat, Hitler's judgement was correct. On the basis of this eminently reasonable view of the situation, seen from the perspective of O.K.W., Hitler went on to deduce that the Anglo-American attempt at invasion would fail so long as he did not, as he had done during the winters of 1941–2 and 1942–3, prop up the now tottering Eastern Front with troops from among those guarding the Atlantic battlements.

Thence it follows that he to whom the directive of November 3, 1943 was principally addressed, that is Hitler himself, this time in his capacity as Commander-in-Chief of German land forces, would draw the logical conclusions from the premises he had just himself stated in his office at Rastenburg.

At O.K.H., Colonel-General Zeitzler perhaps flattered himself for several weeks that he would be given more freedom of action than hitherto in the conduct of operations. Was it not there in writing, in Hitler's own hand, that if it were a case of absolute necessity on the Eastern Front, withdrawals on a fairly considerable scale could be countenanced without necessarily putting the "nervous system" of the Third Reich in mortal danger?

The Führer and Russia

But when it came down to it, the Russians' third winter offensive, the Führer showed the same persistent and mistaken obstinacy as he had done in the previous years, bringing his familiar arguments of high politics and the war economy to bear against his army group commanders every time one of them sought to advise him of a suitable chance to disengage in the face of the sheer weight, regardless of cost, of the Soviet onslaught.

And evidence of this came with the fresh disasters that occurred, principally to the south of the Pripet Marshes, when towards the end of January 1944 Kanev and Korsun' and, on the following May 13, Sevastopol' found their doleful place in the annals of German military history. So it was again a case of immediately arresting the possible consequences of these new defeats sustained by the Third Reich and, since the few reinforcements still available on the Eastern Front were quite inadequate, Hitler the head of O.K.H. sought help from Hitler the head of O.K.W. in order to avert imminent catastrophe. In these circumstances, born of his quite inexcusable obstinacy, Hitler the supreme commander had no alternative but to depart from the principle he had laid down in his Directive of November 3, 1943. At the end of the winter of 1943, the *Waffen*-S.S. II Panzer Corps had to be transferred from the Alençon sector, and hence missed the rendezvous of June 6, 1944 in Normandy.

Manstein's impossible task

The Soviet winter offensive began on December 24, 1943 on either side of the Kiev-Zhitomir road and within a few weeks involved the whole of Army Group "South" which, at that time, stretching as it did between the estuary of the Dniepr and the Mozyr' region, comprised the 6th Army (General Hollidt), the 1st *Panzerarmee* (General Hube), the 8th Army (General Wöhler), and the 4th *Panzerarmee* (General Raus). The entire group, commanded as before by Field-Marshal Erich von Manstein, was made up of 73 of the 180 understrength divisions that were then engaged on the front between Kerch' Strait and the Oranienbaum bridgehead on the Baltic.

In particular, 22 of the 32 Panzer and *Panzergrenadier* divisions on the Eastern Front were allocated to Army Group "South".

The 18th Artillery Division had also been assigned there, with its eight tracked or motorised battalions, comprising nine 21-cm howitzers, plus 30 15-cm, 48 10.5-cm, and 12 10-cm guns. This was a new formation, based on similar ones in the Red Army, and much was expected of it. But it proved disappointing and was disbanded after a few months. A total of 73 divisions seems impressive, but the figure is mis-

leading. Between July 31, 1943 and July 31, 1944, Manstein lost 405,409 killed, wounded, and missing, yet in the same period his reinforcements in officers, N.C.O.s, and other ranks amounted to only 221,893. His divisions, particularly the infantry ones, were thin on the ground. It was the same story with the Panzer divisions, which in spite of increased production of tanks, were 50 to 60 per cent below complement. And the front to be defended, in the Führer's words "with no thought of retreat", measured a good 650 miles.

4th *Panzerarmee* defeated

As has been noted, the 1st Ukrainian Front (General N. F. Vatutin) inaugurated the Soviet winter offensive on December 24. With fire support from four artillery divisions and ten artillery regiments (936 guns and howitzers) assigned from general reserve, Vatutin launched an attack on an 18-mile front in the direction of Zhitomir, with 18 divisions (38th Army and 1st Guards Army) backed by six armoured or mechanised corps. The XXIV Panzer Corps (General Nehring: 8th and 19th Panzer

▽ *A German 15-cm gun battery on the move on one of Russia's better roads. With the already efficient Russian artillery growing ever stronger, German artillery now found itself in very dire straits.*

Divisions and *Waffen*-S.S. 2nd Panzer Division *"Das Reich"*) put up a stubborn resistance for 48 hours, then, in spite of being reinforced by XLVIII Panzer Corps (General Balck) broke under the impact. The 3rd Guards Tank Army (General Rybalko) stormed through the breach and on the last day of the year recaptured Zhitomir and by January 3 reached Novograd-Volinskiy, over 85 miles from its jumping-off point. Further to the right, the Soviet 60th and 13th Armies, comprising 14 infantry divisions, had retaken Korosten and were close to the Russo-Polish frontier of the pre-war period. On Rybalko's left, Vatutin's centre was overwhelming the defenders of Berdichev.

Hence the defeat of the 4th *Panzerarmee* took on a strategic dimension, and in the event of Vatutin exploiting his success to the south-west resolutely and with vigour, could have led to the total destruction of Army Groups "South" and "A". As early as December 25, Manstein had been aware of the possibility of such a danger and had alerted O.K.H. to this effect, confronting it with the following dilemma: "The 4th Army was no longer capable of defending the flank of Army Groups 'South' and 'A'; effective reinforcements were vital. If O.K.H. was unable to provide these, we would be obliged to take five or six divisions at least from our right wing, which clearly could not then maintain its positions inside the Dniepr loop. We sought our liberty of movement for that wing."

Hitler reminisces

During the period when he was writing his memoirs, Manstein had no knowledge of the disobliging, indeed absurd, comments that his report had drawn from the Führer: that Manstein had inflated the enemy numbers knowingly in the hope of imposing his personal decisions on O.K.H. Furthermore, the troops were bound to mirror their commander's attitude, and if some divisions failed to measure up to the standards needed, it was because Manstein, lacking in conviction, had failed to inspire his men.

Hitler went on, in the presence of Zeitzler, who must have been somewhat dumbfounded, about the heroic times when the party assumed power, capturing in turn Mecklenburg, East Prussia ("refractory and reactionary"), Cologne ("red

△ *A small party of Soviet troops advances past the wreckage of a shot-up motor convoy.*
◁ *Russian infantry move in to dislodge the Germans from a village they are holding.*

and black"), and–according to the stenographic account of the meeting– "Thuringia was dyed a deep red, but then I had a Koch at the time I wanted him, at another time a Ley or a Sauckel. There were men for you. When, by some mischance, I didn't have the right men at hand, there was trouble. I took it as axiomatic that good *Gaus* made good *Gauleiters*. And it's not a jot different today."

Manstein pleads for reinforcements . . .

In any case, whatever the parallel between the situation of the Nazi Party in its electoral campaigns and the Russian campaign, Manstein, who had been offered two or three divisions by Hitler with which to plug the two breaches, each 45 to 50 miles in width, to right and left of the

4th *Panzerarmee,* proceeded on December 29 to carry out the manoeuvre he had proposed in his report of December 25. The 1st *Panzerarmee* command was switched from right to left of the 8th Army, transferring III Panzer Corps (General Breith) with its four divisions from the Dniepr loop and completing the movement by shifting VII Corps and XXIV Panzer Corps, which formed Raus's right flank, to the south-east of Berdichev. This manoeuvre, which was approved by O.K.H., provided some relief for Army Group "South", added to the fact that Vatutin failed to exploit his opportunity to drive to the Dniestr from Kamenets-Podolskiy. Hitler, however, had not let pass without response Manstein's proposal to evacuate the Dniepr loop and the Nikopol' bridgehead. It so happened that on January 3, General Konev himself launched an attack in the Kirovograd sector, where the German 6th Army had just relieved the completely exhausted 1st *Panzerarmee.*

▷ *"Dniepropetrovsk is ours!" thunders this Kukryniksy cartoon of the "Bandit of Melitopol" being driven back out of Russia.*

△ *Colonel-General P. S. Rybalko, twice a "Hero of the Soviet Union", was one of Stalin's most able and respected tank generals.*

. . . and tries to convince Hitler

A clear decision was called for and with the object of obtaining one, Manstein went to Rastenburg in person, hoping that he would carry more weight with the Führer than his teletype messages. He put his case as follows:

"If the high command could not bring up strong reinforcements immediately, our Southern wing would have to fall back, abandoning Nikopol', and hence the Crimea, simply in order to make good the deficiency; and this in our opinion was only a first step. We had reconnoitred positions in the rear and given orders for their preparation. These positions more or less followed the course of the Bug, making use of any high ground that seemed advantageous, up to a point south of the sector where our Northern wing

ДНЕПРОПЕТРОВСК НАШ!

ПРОКЛЯТЫЙ ФАКЕЛЬЩИК, БАНДИТ,
ИЗ МЕЛИТОПОЛЯ ДАВ ТЯГУ,
ПОПАЛ В ДРУГУЮ ПЕРЕДРЯГУ.
—ДНЕПРОПЕТРОВСК,—ПОДЛЕЦ ТВЕРДИТ,
Я ВВЕРИЛ АРМИИ НЕРОБКОЙ!—
И ВОТ, ТЕРЯЯ ВЕСЬ КРЕДИТ,
УЖ ОН ЛЕТИТ ОТТУДА ПРОБКОЙ!

was at the moment engaged in fighting. Occupation of these new positions would reduce the 600 mile front by almost half, held too thinly by the 6th and 8th Armies. Such a drastic reduction, and the availability of the 17th Army once it was withdrawn from Crimea, would enable us to achieve the degree of consolidation required in the Northern wing."

And anticipating the likely objection of the Führer, he added: "Naturally the Russians would also benefit by the operation, but since our front would thereby achieve greater solidity, its defensive capacity would be enhanced–and this is the greatest asset in war–so as to be able to resist even massive assault. Furthermore, the destruction of the railway system would prevent the enemy moving the forces now available to him with sufficient speed to allow him to maintain his superiority to west of Kiev."

Hitler stubbornly opposed the propositions made to him in these terms. The need for Nikopol' manganese, whose mining had been suspended for several weeks, prohibited him from abandoning the Dniepr loop. And as for evacuating the Crimea, the idea should be totally excluded; it could well bring about the defection of Bulgaria and a declaration of war on Germany by Turkey. Nor was

there any question of finding reinforcements from Army Group "North": if Field-Marshal von Küchler was forced to abandon his positions dominating the Gulf of Finland, Russian submarines would operate freely in the Baltic and cut the supply lines for Swedish iron-ore between Luleå and factories in Germany.

Manstein returned, disabused and empty-handed, to his H.Q. at Vinnitsa. From one of his several meetings with Hitler, the Field-Marshal took away the following impression of the dictator's face gripped, as was then the case, with inner fury:

"I saw Hitler's features harden. He threw me a glance which signified 'there is no further argument'. I cannot remember ever in my life having seen anyone portray such force of character. One of the foreign ambassadors accredited to Berlin speaks in his memoirs of the effect produced on him by Hitler's eyes. Alone in a coarse and undistinguished face they constituted the single striking feature, certainly the only expressive one. Those eyes fixed me as if they would annihilate me. The comparison with a Hindu snake-charmer suddenly struck me. For the space of a few seconds a kind of mute struggle took place between us. That gaze told me how he had contrived

△ *Maintenance work in progress on a Büssing-NAG SWS heavy gun tractor fitted with a ten-barrel 15-cm* Nebelwerfer *battery.*

to dominate so many people."

The intervention of the 1st *Panzerarmee*, under the command of the gallant General Hube, may have allowed Manstein both to contain the centre of the 1st Ukrainian Front and even make it give ground a little after sustaining heavy casualties (during the second half of January on the furious Pogrebishche sector), but General Raus's northern wing, which presented a ragged line northwards to the Pripet Marshes, proved unable to resist the pressure applied on it by General Vatutin's right wing. On the previous January 4, in the course of his visit to O.K.H., Manstein had urged Hitler to build up a strong reserve in the Rovno region. His advice had not been followed, and this important fortress-town fell to the Russians on February 5, 1944. Since its breakthrough on December 24, the 1st Ukrainian Front had thus far advanced 170 miles westwards, with the result that the line Army Group "South" was required to hold was vastly lengthened from its furthest point at Nikopol', without receiving proportionate reinforcement. Also, lines of communication were increasingly under threat to the extent that the Russians exploited their gains in the direction of Tarnopol', only 90 miles to the south of Rovno.

Dangerous salient

In the immediate future, the situation was still more serious. On Hitler's express orders, the right of the 1st *Panzerarmee* and the left of the 8th Army were maintained on the banks of the Dniepr between Kanev and upstream of Cherkassy. With Vatutin's advance as far as Zhachkov and with Konev in possession of Kirovograd on January 10 a dangerous salient 100 miles wide and some 90 miles deep had formed in this sector, which gave the enemy the opportunity for a pincer movement. The reduction of the front (on the lines proposed to the Führer by Manstein at their meeting on January 4 at Rastenburg, a course which he continued to advocate in notes and personal letters) brooked no further argument; and subsequent events show that the whole manoeuvre, delicate though it was, might well have succeeded with the least cost; reckoning from January 4, there was an effective delay of three weeks, while the 1st and 2nd Ukrainian

Fronts together cut off the area between Kanev and Cherkassy; of almost four weeks before the 3rd Ukrainian Front (under General Malinovsky) attacked the Nikopol' bridgehead; and of nearly five weeks before General Vatutin's armoured and mechanised advanced units reached the Rovno–Shepetovka line.

The weather takes a hand

Soviet commentators attribute the relatively slow progress of the Russians to the constant changes in temperature and alternation of rain and snow recorded in the west of the Ukraine during the months of January and February 1944.

Writing in 1956, Colonel A. N. Grylev of the Soviet Army has this to say:

"Unfavourable weather conditions created more difficulties for our troops than did the crossing of rivers. An unusually early spring caused the snow to melt as early as the end of January. Rain and melting snow aggravated the difficulties. Rivers overflowed their banks.

▽ *Hungarian artillerymen move a somewhat antiquated piece of field artillery into position.*

Roads and tracks became as impracticable for vehicles as was the terrain for infantry. These various factors had a considerable effect on our military activities, limiting the possibility of manoeuvre and hampering supplies of food, fuel, and munitions."

Lest it should be felt that the writer is trying to excuse the purely relative failure of the Soviet armies to annihilate the German army groups facing the four Ukrainian Fronts, Colonel Grylev's testimony is borne out in detail by General

von Vormann, who was in the same area as commander of the hard-pressed XLVII Panzer Corps:

"The *rasputitsa* (thaw) had set in astonishingly early; everywhere it is spring mud ... Worked on by the sun, the rain, and the warm winds, the heavy, black Ukraine earth turns into thick sticky mud during the day. There is not one metalled road in the country. On foot you sink down to your shins and after a few steps lose shoes and socks there. Wheeled vehicles stall and get stuck. Suction by the mud tore away the too-narrow tracks of our all-purpose transports. The only machines capable of making any headway were the tractors and the tanks, which rolled their way forwards at a maximum speed of 3 miles an hour but at the cost of tremendous strain on the engine and huge petrol consumption."

At all events, it is clear that the mud worked more to the disadvantage of the Russians than of the Germans, since in their task of attack and pursuit they also had to cope with the battlefield debris left by the retreating enemy, who destroyed everything of any value behind him.

Manstein a defeatist?

In Manstein's dispute with Hitler, are there grounds for accusing the former—as has been alleged from time to time—of having been obsessed with withdrawal in the face of any build-up in enemy strength or else of having been unjustifiably alarmed by the spectre of encirclement?

It is clear that at this juncture Manstein no longer displayed the genius for bold moves that had characterised his performance between 1941 and 1943; yet it is also abundantly clear that he was no longer in a position where he could act boldly. Apart from XLVI Panzer Corps, which had recently been assigned to him, he knew that he could expect no further reinforcements from the west and that on the Eastern Front it was a case of robbing Peter to pay Paul. The liquidation of a pocket containing half a dozen divisions would mean not only the loss of some 60,000 men and most of their *matériel,* but, further, a breach of 75 to 90 miles in his now dangerously reduced defensive system. The battle of Korsun'-Shevchenkovskiy would show that his appreciation of the situation – and he had vainly tried to prevail on Hitler to accept it – was the correct one.

On January 25, Marshal Zhukov, who had been delegated by *Stavka* to co-ordinate operations, threw the troops of the 1st and 2nd Ukrainian Fronts into an assault on the Kanev salient. General Vatutin brought his 40th Army (Lieutenant-General E. F. Zhmachenko) and 27th Army (Lieutenant-General S. G. Trofimenko) to bear on the western front of the salient. They had a considerable job in overcoming German resistance so as to open a breach for brigades of the 6th Tank Army (Lieutenant-General A. G. Kravchenko) to move south-eastwards. The 2nd Ukrainian Front, under General Konev, seems to have had an easier task; delivering its attack at the point of junction of XLVII Panzer Corps and XI Corps, the 4th Guards Army (Major-General A. I. Ryzhov) and 53rd Army (Major-General I. V. Galanin) swiftly broke through the lines held by the 389th Infantry Division, thus enabling the 5th Guards Tank Army, under the command of General P. A. Rotmistrov, to be unleashed without further ado.

"There could be no other adequate analogy. The sea-dikes had given and the tide, interminable and vast, spread across the plain, passing either side of our tanks which, with packets of infantry round them, had the appearance of reefs rising from the swell. Our amazement was at its peak when in the afternoon cavalry units, galloping westwards, broke through our screen of fire in close formation. It was a sight long-forgotten, almost a mirage – V Guards Cavalry Corps, with the 11th, 12th, and 63rd Cavalry Divisions under the command of Selimanov." Thus, in a monograph dealing with this episode, the former commander of XLVII Panzer Corps describes the breakthrough at Krasnosilka (30 miles north-west of Kirovograd). In these conditions, it is not surprising that Vatutin's and Konev's tanks effected a meeting on January 28 in the region of Zvenigorodka. XI Corps, which formed the left of the German 8th Army, and XLII Corps, on the right of the 1st *Panzerarmee,* were caught in the trap along with four infantry divisions (the 57th, 72nd, 88th, and 389th), the 5th S.S. *Panzergrenadier* Division "Wiking" and the S.S. *Freiwilligen Sturmbrigade "Wallonie",* which Himmler had recruited in the French-speaking provinces of Belgium.

By virtue of seniority over his comrade Lieutenant-General T. Lieb, General W. Stemmermann, commander of XI Corps, assumed command of those encircled.

Hitler hangs on to Kanev

Hitler was determined to defend the Kanev salient at all costs, as he considered it the base for launching an offensive which would force the Russians to cross back over the Dniepr in the region of Kiev. Hence orders were given to Stemmermann to hold his positions and to establish himself so as to be able to repulse any attacks from the south; to General O. Wöhler, commanding the 8th Army, to hurl his XLVII Panzer Corps, reinforced to a strength of five Panzer divisions, at the eastern face of the pocket; and to General H. V. Hube, to drive his III Panzer Corps, comprising four Panzer divisions (among them the 1st S.S. Panzer Division *"Leibstandarte Adolf Hitler")* at the western face of the pocket.

Such a plan, involving the concentration of nine Panzer divisions against

the Kanev pocket, was nevertheless doomed to failure within the time limit imposed by the defenders' capacity to hold out, though an airlift was being organised to keep them in supplies. Moreover, most of the Panzer divisions designated by Hitler were already engaged elsewhere, and hence it was a case of relieving them, pulling them out of line, and moving them to their jump-off

△ *Russian peasant women greet the arrival of liberating Soviet armour, complete with tank-riders.*

points. Furthermore, they were far short of complement; in particular their grenadier regiments were reduced to only several hundred rifles, and there were grounds for feeling some apprehension that they lacked the resilience necessary for a rapid thrust. Yet in counter-attacks speed is all.

Indeed, on February 2, XLVII and III Panzer Corps still had only four Panzer divisions and, what is more, one of them was immediately withdrawn from General N. von Vormann's XLVII Panzer Corps by special order of the Führer, on receipt of the news that units of the 3rd Ukrainian Front were advancing on Apostolovo, which lies half-way between Nikopol' and Krivoy-Rog. The following night, the *rasputitsa* arrived, covering the western Ukraine with the sea of mud described above. Now the unseasonable weather worked to the advantage of the Russians, delaying their enemy's movements still further. When the earth grew hard again, around February 10, the Soviet encirclement of the Korsun' pocket was con-

solidated to such an extent that III Panzer Corps only managed to reach the area of Lysyanka, eight miles from the lines held by the besieged forces.

Break-out attempt

General Stemmermann, as one might expect, had not succeeded in forming a front to the south as he had been enjoined to do in his orders from Rastenburg, without at the same time abandoning Kanev and the banks of the Dniepr, which would have been in defiance of these orders. On February 8 he gave no reply to a summons to capitulate transmitted to him from General Konev, under orders to reduce the pocket. Both Stemmermann and his subordinates turned a deaf ear to the exhortations made to them by representatives of the "Committee for a Free Germany" who had been conveyed to the battlefield on Moscow's orders and were led by General von

Seydlitz-Kurzbach, former commander of LI Corps, who had been taken prisoner at Stalingrad. The tracts and individual free passes scattered among the soldiers with a view to encouraging surrender were equally ignored.

Notwithstanding, the airlift worked poorly in the face of an abundant and highly effective Soviet fighter force, and those encircled at Korsun' saw their strength diminish further each day. It was inevitable that the order should come to attempt to break out towards III Panzer Corps, which had been conclusively halted by the mud. It was the only chance left.

To this effect, General Stemmermann reassembled the remnants of his two corps round the village of Shanderovka and organised them in three echelons: at the head the grenadiers, bayonets fixed, next the heavy infantry units, and then finally the artillery and service troops. The 57th and 88th Infantry Divisions protected the rear and showed themselves equal to the sacrifice they

were called upon to give. The attempt took place on the night of February 16–17, but at first light Soviet artillery, tanks, and aircraft were able to react with vigour and immediate effect:

"Till now," writes General von Vormann, "our forces had dragged all their heavy equipment across gullies filled with thick, impacted snow. But then enemy shelling proved our undoing. Artillery and assault guns were abandoned after they had exhausted their ammunition. And then the wounded moving with the troops met their fate . . . Veritable hordes of hundreds of soldiers from every type of unit headed westwards under the nearest available officer. The enemy infantry were swept out of the way by our advancing bayonets; even the tanks turned in their tracks. But all the same Russian fire struck with impunity at the masses, moving forward with heads down, unevenly and unprotected. Our losses multiplied . . . "

This hopeless charge by 40,000 men foundered on the natural obstacle of the Gniloy-Tikich, a stream which had thawed only a few days previously, and was now 25 feet wide and just deep enough for a man to drown in. And it heralded a fresh disaster, which the Belgian Léon Degrelle, fighting in the ranks of the S.S. *Sturmbrigade "Wallonie"*, describes in unforgettable terms:

"The artillery teams which had escaped destruction plunged first into the waves and ice floes. The banks of the river were steep, the horses turned back and were drowned. Men then threw themselves in to cross the river by swimming. But hardly had they got to the other side than they were transformed into blocks of ice, and their clothes frozen to their bodies. They tried to throw their equipment over the river. But often their uniforms fell into the current. Soon hundreds of soldiers, completely naked and red as lobsters, were thronging the other bank. Many soldiers did not know how to swim. Maddened by the approach of the Russian armour which was coming down the slope and firing at them, they threw themselves pell-mell into the icy water. Some escaped death by clinging to trees which had been hastily felled . . . but hundreds were drowned. Under the fire of tanks thousands upon thousands of soldiers, half clothed, streaming with icy water or naked as the day they were born, ran through the snow towards the distant cottages of Lysyanka."

▽ *A German assessment of Russian thinking: "Be careful, comrades! The Germans are bandits, and the Americans gangsters. But worst of all are the British: they're our allies!"*

By the beginning of 1944 the "Nazi Victory Express" had not only been halted but pushed firmly into reverse by Stalin's "adjustments" to the line.

The hecatomb of Lysyanka

In short, between February 16 and 18, III Panzer Corps at Lysyanka retrieved only 30,000 survivors, unarmed for the most part; among them, General Lieb, commander of XLII Corps. The valiant Stemmermann had been killed by a piece of shrapnel. According to the Soviet historian B. S. Telpukhovsky, of the Moscow Academy of Sciences, on this one occasion the Russians accounted for more than 52,000 dead and 11,000 prisoners but his German colleagues Hillgruber and Jacobsen take issue with him: "Just before the investment occurred the two German corps numbered 54,000 all told, including rear area troops, some of whom escaped encirclement."

Allowing for the 30,000 or 32,000 survivors of this 21-day tragedy, German losses in the sector could barely have risen to more than one third of the total claimed by Moscow nearly 15 years after Germany's unconditional surrender. Hillgruber's and Jacobsen's figures are beyond question.

Alexander Werth quotes the account of a Soviet eye witness of these tragic events which confirms General von Vormann's account. On the day following, Major Kampov told Werth:

"I remember that last fateful night of the 17th of February. A terrible blizzard was blowing. Konev himself was travelling in a tank through the shell-shattered 'corridor'. I rode on horseback from one point in the corridor to another, with a dispatch from the General; it was so dark that I could not see the horse's ears. I mention this darkness and this blizzard because they are an important factor in what happened . . .

"It was during that night, or the evening before, that the encircled Germans, having abandoned all hope of ever being rescued by Hube, decided to make a last desperate effort to break out . . .

"Driven out of their warm huts they had to abandon Shanderovka. They flocked into the ravines near the village, and then took the desperate decision to break through early in the morning . . . So that morning they formed themselves into two marching columns of about 14,000 each . . .

"It was about six o'clock in the morning. Our tanks and our cavalry suddenly appeared and rushed straight into the thick of the two columns. What happened then is hard to describe. The Germans ran in all directions. And for the next four hours our tanks raced up and down the plain crushing them by the hundred. Our cavalry, competing with the tanks, chased them through the ravines where it was hard for the tanks to pursue them. Most of the time the tanks were not using their guns lest they hit their own cavalry. Hundreds and hundreds of cavalry were hacking at them with their sabres, and massacred the Fritzes as no one had ever been massacred by cavalry before. There was no time to take prisoners. It was the kind of carnage that nothing could stop till it was all over. In a small area over 20,000 Germans were killed."

In connection with this episode, General von Vormann, in the study mentioned above, raises an interesting question. Observing that the encirclement of XI and XLII Corps on January 28 had opened a 65-mile breach between the right of III Panzer Corps and the left of XLVII, he considers why the Soviet high command failed to exploit the opportunity of a breakthrough afforded. In his opinion, on that day there was nothing to prevent Stalin driving his armoured units towards Uman' and across the Bug, assigning to them distant objectives on the Dniestr, the Prut, and in the Rumanian Carpathians. This not impossible objective would have sealed the fate of Army Groups "A" and "South".

This question was raised in 1954, but it is still impossible to provide an answer which documents can verify. We must be content with the supposition that Stalin acted with extreme prudence, by annihilating the Korsun' pocket before embarking on more hazardous enterprises, and it should be noted that 12 months from then Chernyakhovsky, Rokossovsky, Zhukov, and Konev had far more freedom of action. But by then, from Tilsit to the Polish Carpathians, the German Army was little more than a ruin.

What is certain is that Stalin showed himself eminently satisfied by the way in which Zhukov and those under him had conducted the business; the proof of it being that on February 23, 1944 a decree of the Praesidium of the Supreme Council of the U.S.S.R. conferred upon General of the Army Konev the title of Marshal of the Soviet Union and upon General Rotmistrov that of Marshal of Tank Forces. Even if the generals had missed a golden opportunity, they had certainly won a great victory.

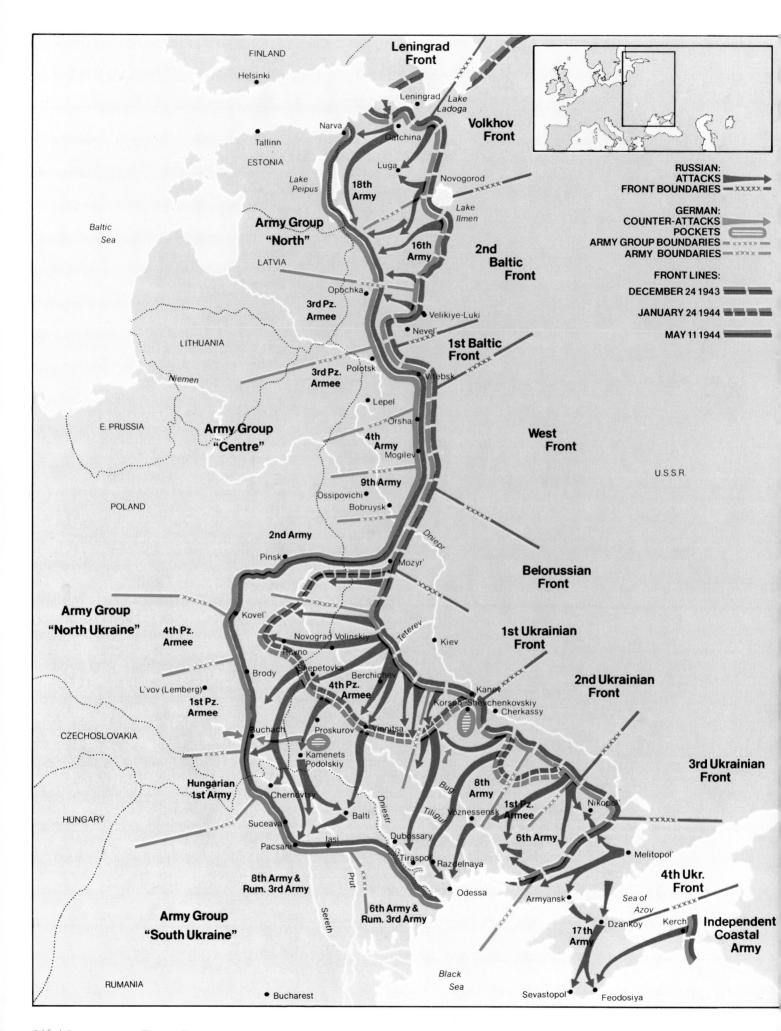

CHAPTER 57
ANZIO: FAILURE OR FOUNDATION ?

A map on the scale of 1:1,000,000 is sufficient to give us an immediate picture of the results of the Soviet winter offensive in the first quarter of 1944, but to follow the Allies' progress in Italy the scale would have to be at least 1:100,000. Even on this scale we would not find all the heights and place names we shall be mentioning in our narrative.

A cartoonist in the Third Reich showed a map of Italy at this time as a boot, up which a snail, wearing the Allied flags, is slowly climbing. At about Easter, Allied public opinion did not attempt to conceal its disappointment, not to say impatience, at the results of Anglo-American strategy in the Mediterranean. As can well be imagined, political and military leaders in London and Washington were hardly able to pacify these frustrations by making

public the vast organisation, training, and preparation then going on towards an operation which was to bear its first fruits at dawn on June 6. Certainly after five months of marking time the Allies scored a decisive victory over their enemy in Italy, but only less than 30 days before the Normandy landings and thus a little late in the day. The normal course of development of Allied strategy was hindered by a chain of unfortunate circumstances which, it must be said, had nothing to do with politics.

On January 16, 1944 the American 5th Army, still under the command of Lieutenant-General Mark Clark, renewed its attack on the Cassino redoubt, which was defended by XIV Panzer Corps from the 10th Army (General von Vietinghoff-Scheel). The main objective of this under-

▽ American soldiers splash ashore at Anzio on January 22. The Allies gained complete strategic surprise by the landing, which went in against negligible opposition. It took the Germans some six hours to realise that an invasion was in progress behind the Cassino front.

taking in such difficult terrain was to force Kesselring to move up the reinforcements at present around Rome to strengthen his front. When this had been achieved, the American VI Corps (Major-General John P. Lucas), which was to effect a surprise landing on the beaches at Anzio and Nettuno, would find the way open to drive inland and attack the enemy's communications. This was the fundamental idea of Operation "Shingle", a pet scheme of Churchill, who had succeeded in winning over both Roosevelt and Stalin. He had even agreed to sacrifice to it the amphibious forces collected together for a landing on Rhodes. Did Churchill see further than his Allies? It seems likely that had the German 10th Army been annihilated during the first two weeks of February, nothing would have prevented Churchill from renewing his demands on his Allies and perhaps demanding an exploitation of this victory in the direction of Ljubljana and the abandonment of a landing in Provence, as planned at Teheran.

But everything was to go against him. First of all, General Clark considerably toned down the instructions given to him on January 12 by Sir Harold Alexander, commanding the 15th Army Group. Alexander saw the mission of the American VI Corps as follows: "to cut the enemy's main communications in the Colli Laziali (Alban Hills) area southeast of Rome, and threaten the rear of the XIV German Corps". Clark's directive of the same date to General Lucas merely required him "to seize and secure a beachhead in the vicinity of Anzio" and thence "to advance on the Colli Laziali".

This threefold manoeuvre (seize, secure, and advance) clearly did not reflect Alexander's original intention, but Alexander did not order Clark to change his directive so as to bring it into line with his own. As we shall see him giving in to his subordinate again on the following May 26, we can take it that it was not merely an oversight. We must believe that in acting as he did, General Clark was still under the strain of the Salerno landings, though he says nothing of this in his memoirs. John Lucas, entrusted with carrying out Operation "Shingle", noted in his diary: "It will be worse than the Dardanelles". His friend George S. Patton, spitting fire and smelling a fight in the offing, had said to him:

"'John, there is no one in the Army I

△ For the benefit of the Allies in Italy: a cynical German comment on the slow pace of the march on Rome.
◁ A landing ship heads inshore, packed with motor transport.

▷ △ On the quayside.
▷ ▽ Down the ramp and into Anzio town.

would hate to see killed as much as you, but you can't get out of this alive. Of course, you might be badly wounded. No one ever blames a *wounded* general!' He advised Lucas to read the Bible when the going got tough, and then turned to one of the VI Corps commander's aides and said, 'Look here; if things get too bad, shoot the old man in the backside; but don't you dare kill the man!'"

About a week before D-day, an ill-fated landing exercise hastily carried out in the Gulf of Salerno only served to confirm Major-General Lucas's pessimistic forecast.

The wrong analysis

The 5th Army plan to take the Cassino defile placed the main burden on the American II Corps (Major-General Geoffrey Keyes). Forcing the Rapido at San Angelo, five miles south of Cassino, it would drive up the Liri valley and its tanks would exploit the success towards Frosinone then Anzio. This action was to be supported on the right by the French Expeditionary Corps (General Juin) and on the left by the British X Corps (Lieutenant-General Sir Richard McCreery).

"It was a somewhat simple concept," wrote Marshal Juin, "revealing a bold temperament which everyone recognised in the 5th Army commander, but at the same time it was at fault in that it ignored certain strategic principles and betrayed a false notion of distances and especially of the terrain in this peninsula of Italy where mountains – and what mountains! – dominate the landscape."

Sure enough the British X Corps, though it established a bridgehead on the right bank of the Garigliano (resulting from the confluence of the Liri and the Rapido), came to grief on the slopes of Monte Maio. The American 36th Division (Major-General F. L. Walker) of II Corps was even less fortunate, losing the strip of land it had won two days before on the right bank of the Rapido with casualties of 143 dead, 663 wounded, and 875 missing. On the right the 3rd Algerian Division (General de Monsabert) and the 2nd Moroccan Division (General Dody), attacking in line abreast, captured the heights of Monna Casale and Costa San Pietro (4,920 ft). But the French Expeditionary Corps did not have the reserves to exploit this success in the direction of

Atina, from where it might have been possible to get down into the Liri valley behind the defence line along the Rapido.

General Clark had six divisions (54 battalions) and his opponent, General von Senger und Etterlin (XIV Panzer Corps), had four with only six battalions apiece. This indicates how the terrain favoured the defenders, who were also valiant, well-trained, and better led. They were, however, stretched to the limit and Vietinghoff had to ask Kesselring for reinforcements. Kesselring took it upon himself to send him the 29th and the 90th *Panzergrenadier* Divisions from Rome, where they had been stationed in reserve.

"Considering what happened," General Westphal, at the time chief-of-staff of Army Group "C", wrote in 1953, "it was a mistake. The attack and the crossing at the mouth of the Garigliano were only a diversion intended to pin down our forces and to get us to drain our resources away from Rome as far as possible. The Allied commander's aim was fully achieved." Three years later Kesselring answered this charge, though without naming Westphal, to some point:

"I was well aware of the enemy's possible moves. One of these possibilities always stood out more clearly than the others. The attack by the American II Corps and the French Expeditionary Corps on positions north of Monte Cassino was clearly linked to the fighting on the Garigliano and increased its chances of success.

"Another possibility, that is the landing, was still only a faint one. We did not know yet when or where this would be. If I had refused the request of the 10th Army's commander, his right flank could have been dented and there seemed to be no way of knowing how it could have been restored." The German field-marshal seems to have been right in his judgement

▷ *Extending the limited accommodation of Anzio harbour: a floating causeway from ship to shore.*

▽ *Kesselring's gunners wake up: a German shell scores a near hit on D.U.K.W.s heading in towards the beaches.*

because on the eve of the event Admiral Canaris, head of the *Abwehr,* had told him that in his opinion no Allied landing was to be expected in Italy in the near future.

The Anzio landings

No other landing in Europe or the Pacific was initially as successful, and at such little cost, as that at Anzio-Nettuno in Operation "Shingle". By midnight on January 22, that is after 22 hours of operations, Rear-Admirals Frank J. Lowry of the U.S. Navy and Thomas H. Troubridge of the Royal Navy had landed 36,034 men, 3,069 vehicles, and 90 per cent of the assault equipment of the U.S. VI Corps. This comprised the British 1st Division (Major-General W. Penney), the American 3rd Division (Major-General L. K. Truscott), a regiment and a battalion of paratroops, three battalions of Rangers, and a brigade of Commandos. Losses amounted to 13 killed, 44 missing, and 97 wounded. The supporting naval forces, four light cruisers and 24 destroyers, had neutralised the fire of the shore batteries and two German battalions had been overrun on the beaches. "And that was all," wrote General Westphal as he reckoned up his weak forces. "There was nothing else in the area we could have thrown against the enemy on that same day. The road to Rome (37 miles) was now open. No-one could have prevented a force which drove on hard from entering the Eternal City. For two days after the landing we were in a breath-taking situation. Our counter-measures could only take effect after 48 hours."

Kesselring musters his strength

The General Staff of Army Group "C" had made several studies of a possible Allied landing of some strategic importance. For each hypothesis envisaged (Istria, Ravenna, Civitavecchia, Leghorn, Viareggio), the formations which would fight it had been detailed off, the routes they would have to take marked out, and their tasks laid down. Each hypothetical situation had been given a keyword. Kesselring only had to signal *"Fall*

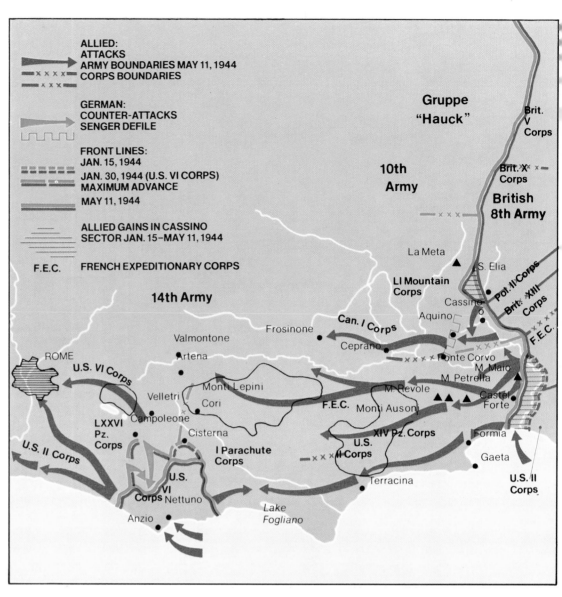

▷ *The Anzio landings and the break-through at Cassino.*

ALLIED:
ATTACKS
ARMY BOUNDARIES MAY 11, 1944
CORPS BOUNDARIES

GERMAN:
COUNTER-ATTACKS
SENGER DEFILE

FRONT LINES:
JAN. 15, 1944
JAN. 30, 1944 (U.S. VI CORPS)
MAXIMUM ADVANCE
MAY 11, 1944

ALLIED GAINS IN CASSINO
SECTOR JAN. 15–MAY 11, 1944

F.E.C. FRENCH EXPEDITIONARY CORPS

Gruppe "Hauck"

Brit. V Corps

10th Army

Brit. X Corps

British 8th Army

La Meta

S. Elia

LI Mountain Corps

Pol. II Corps

14th Army

Cassino

Aquino

Brit. XIII Corps

Can. I Corps

Frosinone

Ceprano

F.E.C.

Valmontone

Artena

Ponte Corvo

M. Maio

M. Petrella

ROME

U.S. VI Corps

Monti Lepini

Cori

M. Revole

F.E.C.

Monti Ausoni

Castel Forte

Velletri

LXXVI Pz. Corps

Campoleone

Cisterna

XIV Pz. Corps

U.S. II Corps

Formia

U.S. II Corps

Gaeta

U.S. VI Corps

Nettuno

I Parachute Corps

Terracina

U.S. II Corps

Anzio

Lake Fogliano

▽ *A Sherman tank heads inland from the beach-head. With the forces, both infantry and tank, available to him soon after the initial landings, could Lucas have pressed on inland and cut the Germans' communications between Rome and Cassino?*

Richard" for the following to converge on the Anzio bridgehead:

1. the "Hermann Göring" Panzer Division from the area of Frosinone and the 4th Parachute Division from Terni, both in I Parachute Corps (General Schlemm)
2. from the Sangro front LXXVI Panzer Corps (General Herr: 26th Panzer and 3rd *Panzergrenadier* Divisions); from the Gariationgliano front the 29th *Panzergrenadier* Division, newly arrived in the sector; and
3. from northern Italy the staff of the 14th Army and the 65th and 362nd Divisions which had crossed the Apennines as quickly as the frost and snow would allow them.

But O.K.W. intervened and ordered Field-Marshal von Rundstedt to hand over to Kesselring the 715th Division, then stationed in the Marseilles area, and Colonel-General Löhr, commanding in the Balkans, to send him his 114th *Jäger* Division.

On January 23, when Colonel-General von Mackensen arrived to take charge of operations against the Allied forces, all that lay between Anzio and Rome was a detachment of the "Hermann Göring" Panzer Division and a hotchpotch of artillery ranging from the odd 8.8-cm A.A. to Italian, French, and Yugoslav field guns. Despite the talents of Kesselring as an improviser and the capabilities of his general staff, a week was to pass before the German 14th Army could offer any consistent opposition to the Allied offensive.

On the Allied side, however, Major-General John P. Lucas thought only of consolidating his bridgehead and getting ashore the balance of his corps, the 45th Division (Major-General W. Eagles) and the 1st Armoured Division (Major-General E. N. Harmon). It will be recognised that in so doing he was only carrying out the task allotted to the 5th Army. On January 28 his 1st Armoured Division had indeed captured Aprilia, over ten miles north of Anzio, but on his right the American 3rd Division had been driven back opposite Cisterna. On the same day Mackensen had three divisions in the line and enough units to make up a fourth; by the last day of the month he was to have eight.

Was a great strategic opportunity lost between dawn on January 22 and twilight on the 28th? In London Churchill was champing with impatience and wrote to Sir Harold Alexander: "I expected to see a wild cat roaring into the mountains—

and what do I find? A whale wallowing on the beaches!"

Returning to the subject in his memoirs, Churchill wrote: "The spectacle of 18,000 vehicles accumulated ashore by the fourteenth day for only 70,000 men, or less than four men to a vehicle, including drivers and attendants . . . was astonishing."

Churchill might perhaps be accused of yielding too easily to the spite he felt at the setbacks of Operation "Shingle", for which he had pleaded so eagerly to Stalin and Roosevelt. These were, however, not the feelings of the official historian of the U.S. Navy who wrote ten years after the event:

"It was the only amphibious operation in that theater where the Army was unable promptly to exploit a successful landing, or where the enemy contained Allied forces on a beachhead for a prolonged period. Indeed, in the entire war there is none to compare with it; even the Okinawa campaign in the Pacific was shorter."

We would go along with this statement, implying as it does that the blame lay here, were it not for General Truscott's opinion, which is entirely opposed to Morison's quoted above. Truscott lived through every detail of the Anzio landings as commander of the 3rd Division, then as second-in-command to General Lucas, whom he eventually replaced. He was recognised by his fellow-officers as a first-class leader, resolute, aggressive,

△ *Part of 5th Army's complement (over-extravagant according to Churchill) of soft skinned and armoured vehicles.*

and very competent. His evidence is therefore to be reckoned with:

"I suppose that armchair strategists will always labour under the delusion that there was a 'fleeting opportunity' at Anzio during which some Napoleonic figure would have charged over the Colli Laziali (Alban Hills), played havoc with the German line of communications, and galloped on into Rome. Any such concept betrays lack of comprehension of the military problem involved. It was necessary to occupy the Corps Beachhead Line to prevent the enemy from interfering with the beaches, otherwise enemy artillery and armoured detachments operating against the flanks could have cut us off from the beach and prevented the unloading of troops, supplies, and equipment. As it was, the Corps Beachhead Line was barely distant enough to prevent direct artillery fire on the beaches.

"On January 24th (i.e. on D+2) my division, with three Ranger battalions and the 504th Parachute Regiment attached, was extended on the Corps Beachhead Line, over a front of twenty miles... Two brigade groups of the British 1st Division held a front of more than seven miles."

In his opinion again the Allied high command overestimated the psychological effect on the enemy's morale of the simple news of an Anglo-American landing behind the 10th Army. This is shown by the text of a leaflet dropped to German troops, pointing out the apparently impossible strategic situation in which they were now caught, pinned down at Cassino and outflanked at Anzio, and urging them to surrender.

Kesselring beats Alexander to the punch

But far from allowing himself to be intimidated, Kesselring assembled his forces with a promptness underestimated by Alexander and Clark. Another reason why he was able to race them to it was because the latter were somewhat short of *matériel* for amphibious operations. The figures speak for themselves: on June 6, 1944 for a first wave of 12 divisions Eisenhower had 3,065 landing craft, whereas Anzio had 237 for four divisions.

Under these conditions, even if Lucas had had the temperament of a Patton, one could hardly have expected him to throw his forces into an attack on the Colli Laziali, over 20 miles from Anzio, with the two divisions of his first echelon and not worry also about his flanks and communications. Finally, Lucas did not have this cavalier temperament, and the day after the landings he noted in his diary: "The tension in a battle like this is terrible. Who the hell would be a general?"

Enter Hitler

The chances lost here, however, were to give rise during the months of February and March to two of the most furious battles of the war. They both ended in defeat for the attacker. On February 29 Mackensen had to abandon his attempt to crush the Anzio beach-head and Clark reported that his repeated attempts to force the Cassino defile had failed.

The battle for the beach-head arose from Hitler's initiative. On January 28 he sent Kesselring the following directive, which is worth quoting in full, so well does it reveal the Führer's state of mind on the day after the disasters suffered by Army Group "South" on the Dniepr at Kanev, and at a time when everyone was expecting an Anglo-American attack across the Channel.

◁ ▵ *D.U.K.W.s on the beach at Anzio.*
◁ ▽ *A U.S. 155-mm "Long Tom" in action at Anzio.*
◁ *Almost like World War I all over again: a communication trench linking pillboxes in the British sector of the Anzio line.*
▽ *A British patrol pushes forward from the main Allied beach-head on a reconnaissance mission.*
▽ ▽ *War photographers receive their briefing in a wine cellar in Nettuno before moving to their assigned areas.*

"In a few days from now," he wrote, "the 'Battle for Rome' will start: this will decide the defence of Central Italy and the fate of the 10th Army. But it has an even greater significance, for the Nettuno landing is the first step of the invasion of Europe planned for 1944.

"The enemy's aim is to pin down and to wear out major German forces as far as possible from the English base in which the main body of the invasion force is being held in a constant state of readiness, and to gain experience for their future operations.

"The significance of the battle to be fought by the 14th Army must be made clear to each one of its soldiers.

"It will not be enough to give clear and correct tactical orders. The army, the air force, and the navy must be imbued with a fanatical determination to come

out victorious from this battle and to hang on until the last enemy soldier has been exterminated or driven back into the sea. The men will fight with a solemn hatred against an enemy who is waging a relentless war of extermination against the German people, an enemy to whom everything seems a legitimate means to this end, an enemy who, in the absence of any high ethical intention, is plotting the destruction of Germany and, along with her, that of European civilisation. The battle must be hard and without pity, and not only against the enemy but also against any leader of men who, in this decisive hour, shows any sign of weakness.

"As in Sicily, on the Rapido, and at Ortona, the enemy must be shown that the fighting strength of the German Army is still intact and that the great invasion of 1944 will be an invasion which will drown in the blood of the Anglo-Saxon soldiers."

That is why the German 14th Army, whilst it drove off the repeated attempts of the U.S. VI Corps to break out from Aprilia and to cut off the Rome–Gaeta railway at Campoleone, actively prepared to go over to the counter-attack as ordered. On February 10 a counter-attack led by the 3rd *Panzergrenadier* Division (Lieutenant-General Gräser) retook the station at Carroceto. That day the German communiqué announced 4,000 prisoners taken since January 22, whereas the Allies' figure was only 2,800. Rightly alarmed by these setbacks, General Clark sent the British 56th Division (Major-General Templer) into the bridgehead; also, at Alexander's suggestion, he appointed Truscott second-in-command of VI Corps. Meanwhile Colonel-General von Mackensen had been called to O.K.W. to put his plan for a counter-offensive before the Führer. The latter offered no objection when Mackensen explained his idea of driving his attack along the Albano–Anzio line, with diversionary attacks on either side. Hitler did not stop there, however, but took it upon himself to interfere in every detail of the plan, from which he expected wonders. Mackensen thus saw the front on which he was to attack, the troops he was to use, and even the deployment these forces were to adopt, all altered by Hitler.

The operation was entrusted to LXXVI Panzer Corps. It was to attack on a front of less than four miles with two divisions up and the 26th *Panzergrenadier* Division (Lieutenant-General von Lüttwitz) and the 20th *Panzergrenadier* Division (Lieutenant-General Fries) in army reserve. Hitler ordered this so the infantry could be given supporting fire that would pulverise the enemy's defences. Mackensen tried in vain to point out that such a massive concentration would present a sitting target to the Anglo-American air forces and that *Luftflotte* II, under the command of Field-Marshal von Richthofen, did not have the means to fight them off. It was no good. Hitler also refused to listen to the argument that it was useless lining up the guns wheel to wheel with insufficient ammunition for them to fire at the required rate.

The attack started on February 16 as ordered by Hitler. There was a preliminary softening up by 300 guns, but the 114th and 715th Divisions, which were to advance side by side, were to be denied the support of a creeping barrage. The spongy ground of the Pontine marshes prevented the tanks and the assault guns, which were to support the waves of infantry, from getting off the roads. The 14th Army's offensive might have had the intermittent support of 20 to 30 Luftwaffe fighter-bombers, but the German troops on the ground had to withstand the assault of no less than 1,100 tons of bombs. The Anglo-American tactical air forces boxed in the battlefield and considerably hindered the movement of supplies up towards the 14th Army's front line units.

By nightfall LXXVI Panzer Corps had

◁ ◁ *General Alexander (left) and Lieutenant-General Clark (centre), commander of the U.S. 5th Army, with Lieutenant-General McCreery (right), commander of the British X Corps. Much of the Anzio landings' ill fortune stemmed from the differing views on exploitation held by Alexander and Clark.*
▽ ◁ *German prisoners, under U.S. guard, await transport out of the Anzio area.*
▽ ▽ ◁ *Improvised entertainment at Anzio: "horse" racing on the throw of a dice.*
▽ *A wounded British soldier.*
▽ ▽ *A German "Goliath" wire-controlled tank. Ingeniously contrived to deliver an explosive charge by remote control, the "Goliath" suffered the major disadvantage of being slow and thus easily shot up.*

▷ *The ruins of Anzio town.*

▽ *An American armoured car moves up towards the line through Anzio.*

advanced some three to four miles into the Allied lines and was about seven to eight miles from its objective of Anzio-Nettuno. Its guns had fired 6,500 shells, but had received ten times as many. For three days Mackensen attempted to regain the upper hand, but in vain: Truscott, who had just relieved Lucas, was too vigilant for him. On February 29, I Parachute Corps took up the attack again in the Cisterna area, but this came to a halt a few hundred yards from its point of departure. The battle around the bridgehead died down and General Clark reinforced the position with the British 5th and the American 34th Divisions. The beaches and the Allies' rear positions continued to be harassed by German heavy artillery with its observation posts up in the Colli Laziali. A huge 11-inch railway gun in particular played havoc among the defenders. The air force was unable to silence it since, as soon as it had fired, "Leopold", as its crew, or "Anzio Annie", as the Allies called it, withdrew into a tunnel near Castel Gandolfo.

At sea, Operation "Shingle" cost Admiral Sir John Cunningham, C.-in-C. Mediterranean, the light cruisers *Spartan* and *Penelope* and three destroyers, all of the Royal Navy. Amongst the weapons used by the Germans were glide bombs and human torpedoes, the latter making their first appearance with the Kriegsmarine.

CHAPTER 58

BURMA: THE ARAKAN CAMPAIGNS

By May 1942, the Japanese had reached the limits they had set themselves in South-East Asia. They had driven the British from Burma and now prepared to go over to the defensive. The British forces under General Wavell, the Commander-in-Chief in India, took this opportunity to attack, and a series of campaigns began which eventually brought about the final Japanese surrender. The fighting in Burma often seemed isolated from the rest of the war, for it had its own momentum, set by the monsoon rains and enormous supply problems.

It was on September 17, 1942, that Wavell despatched from India an operation instruction to the G.O.C.-in-C. Eastern Army, Lieutenant-General N. M. S. Irwin, which gave the objects for the army in the 1942–1943 dry season (October–May): first to develop communications for the purpose of reconquering Burma and opening the Burma Road; and second to bring the Japanese to battle in order to use up their strength, especially in the air.

▽ *Men of the Tripura Rifles cross a stream in the Arakan. This regiment had just completed six months of guerrilla warfare in the Kaladan valley.*

Wavell gave four objectives as his immediate intention in order to attain these ends:

1. to capture Akyab and reoccupy the upper Arakan;
2. to strengthen British positions in the Chin hills;
3. to occupy Kalewa and Sittaung on the Chindwin; and thence to raid Japanese lines of communication (Wavell had already given Brigadier Orde Wingate orders to raise and train a Long Range Penetration Brigade for this purpose); and
4. to make necessary administrative arrangements to allow for a rapid advance into upper or lower Burma should opportunity offer.

We are here immediately concerned with the first objective, the British attempt to capture Akyab in the dry season 1942–43. Throughout this narrative it is important to remember that the Japanese forces in the Arakan were seasoned victorious soldiers, whereas their British and Indian opponents were raw, inexperienced troops, often new recruits.

The Japanese 213th Regiment in the Arakan, under the command of Colonel K. Miyawaki and consisting of two battalions (II/213th and III/213th), had moved into Akyab during the summer of 1942 after chasing the British/Indian forces from Yenangyaung, Myingan, Monywa, Shwegyin, and finally Kalewa, which it had captured on May 11. The 33rd Division, of which it formed a part, had advanced from Siam for the initial invasion of Burma, but the 213th Regiment had been left in Siam and had not rejoined its division until after the fall of Rangoon. It was, therefore, the freshest regiment and had had the fewest casualties in the conquest of Burma and was full of fight.

As the British/Indian 14th Division started its southward advance from Chittagong to Cox's Bazar and beyond, Miyawaki in mid-October sent his II/213th battalion up the Mayu river by launch to occupy the line Buthidaung–"Tunnels" Road–Maungdaw, where first contact was made with the 1/15th Punjab battalion on October 23. The "Tunnels" Road was the only all-weather road in the area in 1942.

On September 21 Lieutenant-General Irwin had ordered the 14th Indian Divi-

△ *Lieutenant-General Tadashi Hanaya.*

▽ *The disastrous first campaign in the Arakan.*

sion, commanded by Major-General W. L. Lloyd, to move towards Akyab to forestall the Japanese arrival on the Buthidaung–Maungdaw line.

Earlier in the year the 14th Division had been earmarked for operations in Burma, but the fall of Rangoon had prevented its arrival. After the British defeat in Burma a special committee had reported that one of the reasons for this defeat was the over-modernisation of Indian divisions. Certain divisions were, therefore, reorganised to become "light divisions" with their transport mainly on a jeep and animal basis. The 14th Division, which had recently been responsible for the defence of Bengal, Bihar, and Orissa, was not so reorganised.

This division consisted of four brigades (47th, 55th, 88th, and 123rd), with two British and ten Indian battalions plus one British field regiment and one Indian mountain regiment of artillery. The Indian battalions came mainly from the dry areas of the Punjab, Baluchistan, and Rajputana and were unused to the hot, steamy, malarial swamps of the Arakan. Later another brigade joined the division. For this rôle the 14th Division was supported by a special reconnaissance force ("V" Force) hidden, with its wireless sets, in the hills, and No. 2000 Flotilla, a scratch collection of steamboats, launches, and sampans, to help the units across and down the rivers and to supply them.

The Arakan, on Burma's north-west coast, is a country of steep, densely-forested hill ranges up to 2,000 feet high, running parallel from north to south, separated by narrow cultivated valleys filled with rice fields, mangroves, and tidal creeks. The coastal strip from Maungdaw to the tip of the Mayu peninsula, Foul Point, opposite Akyab Island, is 45 miles long and ten miles wide in the north but tapers down to a few hundred yards wide at Foul Point.

To the east winds the Mayu river (called the Kalapanzin in its upper reaches), flanked by swamps of elephant grass and bamboo, and divided by knife-edged limestone ridges, 150 feet high.

East of the Mayu valley rises the great jumbled mass of the Arakan Tracts, reaching as far as the Kaladan river valley, and 2,500 feet high. Further east again are the Arakan Yomas.

In the dry season, fair-weather tracks for wheeled vehicles can be made over the dry paddy fields and along the coastal strip at low tide. From mid-May to October the annual 200-inch rainfall is almost unceasing, with malaria and other tropical diseases hyperendemic. In the dry season from November to March the weather is delightful.

As it advanced, the 14th Division's line of communication from railhead was by sea from Chittagong to Cox's Bazar, motor transport to Tumbru, sampans on the Naf river to Bawli Bazar, and pack transport onwards.

In spite of reinforcements of motor launches, landing craft, and three paddle-steamers given to him, Major-General Lloyd by November 17 could still guarantee the maintenance of only four battalions to attack the Japanese. Being able to apply superior strength was always a problem for the British in the Arakan.

The Japanese, although outnumbered, were much better trained in watermanship and were thus able to take full

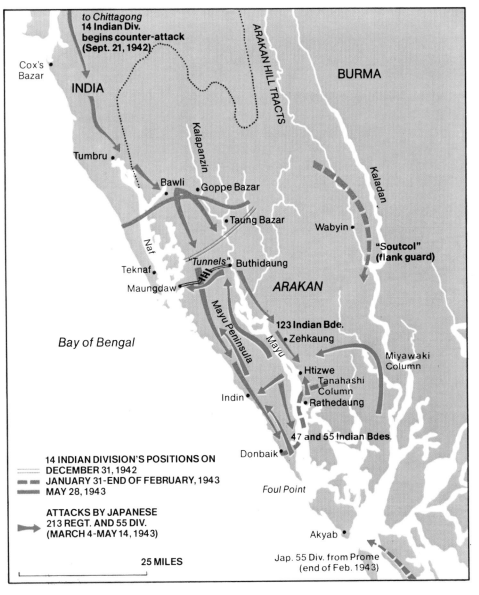

to Chittagong
14 Indian Div. begins counter-attack (Sept. 21, 1942)

Cox's Bazar

INDIA

BURMA

ARAKAN HILL TRACTS

Tumbru

Kalapanzin

Bawli • Goppe Bazar

• Taung Bazar

Kaladan

Wabyin •

"Soutcol" (flank guard)

Naf

"Tunnels" Buthidaung

Teknaf.

Maungdaw

ARAKAN

123 Indian Bde.
• Zehkaung

Mayu Peninsula

Mayu

Miyawaki Column

Bay of Bengal

• Htizwe
Tanahashi Column
• Rathedaung

Indin •

47 and 55 Indian Bdes.

Donbaik •

14 INDIAN DIVISION'S POSITIONS ON
⋯⋯⋯ DECEMBER 31, 1942
▬ ▬ JANUARY 31-END OF FEBRUARY, 1943
▬▬ MAY 28, 1943

ATTACKS BY JAPANESE
213 REGT. AND 55 DIV.
(MARCH 4-MAY 14, 1943)

Foul Point

Akyab •

Jap. 55 Div. from Prome
(end of Feb. 1943)

25 MILES

advantage of all types of river transport, especially as Akyab Island was at the hub of the river system running north. Thus their water communication could easily be switched from one valley to another, whereas the British lines of approach were divided by virtually inaccessible ridges.

In December 1942, the Japanese air situation in the south-west Pacific had become so grave that two Japanese air brigades were despatched from Burma, leaving the 5th Air Division with only about 50 fighters and 90 medium bombers available for the whole of the Burma front – to meet a growing Allied air strength.

No. 224 Group, R.A.F., consisting of six Hawker Hurricane squadrons, two light bomber squadrons of Bristol Blenheims and Bisleys, and one Beaufighter squadron (totalling about 120 aircraft), was ordered to support the 14th Division's advance. But at that time these squadrons had not been trained in close air support, the Hurricanes were not fitted with bomb racks, and there were no ground controllers with the brigades, so the group's efforts were initially of little value to the infantry (especially in comparison with

later operations). Thus the group's aircraft were used chiefly for interdiction along the sparse Japanese supply routes, including the sea-lanes to Akyab. In fact, during the first year the R.A.F. had very little effect on the ground campaign apart from moral support by the sound of the engines. Except at high altitude the Hurricane was no match for the Mitsubishi A6M Zero, and the R.A.F. had no long-range fighters available to sustain an offensive against the Japanese air bases. In spite of this the R.A.F. did slowly begin to win air superiority, which made efficient close air support, as well as vital air supply, possible later.

All these administrative and training shortcomings of the British forces must be remembered, as otherwise it is difficult to understand how Colonel Miyawaki, with a maximum of only two battalions on the mainland, could hold up 12 battalions of infantry supported by six batteries of artillery for a period of 13 weeks from first contact on October 23 to January 22 1943, when the first detachments of the 55th Division started to arrive in the Akyab area. The difficulty Lloyd had was to apply his strength.

Irwin's original plan was for a sea-

△ *During the tense days of February 1944, when the British front-line divisions were isolated from each other by the Japanese counter-attack: two men of the 1st Punjab Regiment – a Sepoy behind the Bren gun and Lance-Naik Ghulam Ali – lie up in a forward position overlooking the 7th Indian Division's "Admin. Box".*

△ *Major-General F. W. Messervy, commander of the 7th Indian Division.*
▽ *As they pierced the Japanese lines deeper and deeper, sniper patrols were used on all sides to cover the main body of troops.*
▷▷ *The road to Buthidaung. By December 1944 British patrols were active south of the road, probing the strength of Japanese forward positions.*

borne landing on Akyab accompanied by a land advance down the Mayu peninsula to Foul Point. But by the end of October Wavell came to the conclusion that a direct seaborne attack in which transport and warships would be exposed to heavy air attack for a minimum of three days was no longer practicable.

Irwin therefore decided to use the 6th Infantry Brigade Group from the British 2nd Division to land on Akyab Island with the help of five motor launches, 72 landing craft, and three paddle-steamers which Admiral Sir James Somerville had placed at his disposal, as soon as Lloyd had advanced to Foul Point. The speed of the overland advance was therefore vital.

However, Irwin postponed Lloyd's advance to the attack in order to give him time to improve his communications, so that he could bring an extra brigade to bear. This delayed Lloyd by three weeks so that just when he was about to attack, Miyawaki withdrew his II/213th battalion facing Lloyd to a general line Gwedauk–Kondon, thus drawing Lloyd further away from his base.

Lloyd finally made contact again on December 22, when he attacked on either side of the Mayu range and also detached one battalion to the Kaladan river. The Japanese repulsed all attacks but the wide front forced Miyiwaki to commit his only other battalion, the III/213th, on December 29. Further British attacks were repulsed. The confident Japanese, having now got a measure of their enemy, started to harass Lloyd's two forward brigades by small patrol attacks at night and sudden bombardments from mortars, which startled these inexperienced troops and led them to believe that there were many more Japanese opposing them than just two battalions. Miyawaki, however, during this period took the risk of leaving the defence of Akyab Island to his anti-aircraft gunners, supported by administrative personnel.

During a visit with Wavell to the Donbaik front on December 10, Irwin criticised Lloyd for dispersing his force so widely that he had insufficient strength on the coast. He ordered Lloyd to concentrate and break through at Donbaik.

However, two more attacks by the 14th Division on their two objectives, Rathedaung and Donbaik, during the first two weeks in January, again failed. Repeated attacks by fresh troops on January 18 and 19 also failed with comparatively heavy losses.

But early in January, Lieutenant-General Shojiro Iida, commanding the 15th Army, realising the importance of, and threat to, Akyab ordered Lieutenant-General Takishi Koga to move his 55th Division to hold Akyab. The 55th Division was a battle-trained formation which had fought in China and then advanced from Siam to Burma in 1942. During the previous year, it had fought through from Moulmein in the south via Pegu, Toungoo, and Mandalay to Bhamo and the Chinese frontier.

Koga ordered a rapid overland advance via Pakokku to the Kaladan valley on the one hand, whilst at the same time opening up an administrative sea route from Toungup to Akyab. He ordered Miyawaki's 213th Regiment to hold the Rathedaung–Laungchaung–Donbaik line at all costs. On January 22 No. 224 Group R.A.F. attacked the Japanese columns on the Pakokku trail.

Irwin reinforced Lloyd with two fresh brigades, artillery, and eight Valentine tanks. On February 1, after a heavy but badly co-ordinated R.A.F. bombardment, these fresh troops with the Valentines attacked the Japanese dug-in position at Donbaik, but after repeated assaults and heavy casualties over two days, were thrown back. Two days later similar frontal attacks on Rathedaung also failed.

The Japanese had won the race to Akyab, for by the end of February Koga

had assembled the whole of the 55th Division, less one battalion, in that area.

Iida expected Koga to consolidate, but the latter saw the six British/Indian brigades under Lloyd split up by rivers and ranges into three quite separate identities, with his own forces holding a central position at the confluence of the Arakan rivers. Koga saw an excellent opportunity to counter-attack these tired brigades and destroy them piecemeal.

Koga laid a three-phase plan. First, the enemy forces in the Kaladan valley were to be overwhelmed by the "Miyawaki" Column (one infantry battalion and one mountain artillery battalion). Then the brigade east of the Mayu river was to be encircled by the "Tanahashi" Column (two infantry battalions and one mountain regiment) operating from Rathedaung and supported by a flank advance by Miyawaki from the Kaladan. Finally, the combined forces of this right hook, resupplied by launches moving up the Mayu, would cross the river and the Mayu range to seize Indin. This would cut off the British/Indian brigades threatening the Donbaik–Laungchaung line. Koga left one battalion to hold Akyab and three battalions ("Uno" Column) to hold the Mayu peninsula.

Meanwhile, Lloyd was reorganising for another attack on Donbaik, but Irwin, aware of supply difficulties and danger from the east flank, ordered him to withdraw, intending to replace his division with the 26th. However, Wavell, egged on by Churchill, felt that it was essential for the morale of the whole Indian Army to score some sort of victory, rather than ignominiously retreat after suffering, by European standards, quite minor casualties. On February 26 Wavell directed Irwin to order Lloyd to attack Donbaik again with two brigades and to destroy "the numerically insignificant opposition". Irwin delayed the attack but also the withdrawal. At this time Irwin sent Slim, then commanding XV Corps in India, to visit the front and report on the situation. He later told Irwin that Lloyd's command was now far too large for a single divisional headquarters, and that Lloyd's tactics were too obviously frontal (a reflection on Irwin's own instructions). But Irwin did not place Slim in command of operations, nor heed his advice.

By February 21 the first phase of Koga's plan started.

By March 7 the "Miyawaki" Column had cleared the Kaladan valley as far as

Kyauktaw, and "Tanahashi" Column had captured Rathedaung. The British/Indian 6th Brigade, with six battalions, obeyed Wavell's orders and carried out a deliberate attack on March 18 on the "Uno" Column dug in at Donbaik, but fell back after receiving only 300 casualties out of the 6,000-strong attacking force. With the "Miyawaki" and "Tanahashi" Columns now poised on the east bank of the Mayu river, and the "Uno" Column as the anvil, having withstood the British attack at Donbaik, Koga launched the third phase of his attack, starting on the night March 24–25. He called for and was given all available air support from the 5th Air Division.

Tanahashi sent one battalion northwest, which cut the coastal road at Gyindaw, whilst he, with the remaining two battalions of his force, advanced on Indin. In spite of a strenuous counter-attack and exhortations from their commanders, the brigades of the 14th Division on the coastal plain were unable to stop Tanahashi, who occupied Indin on April 6, thus cutting off 11 British/Indian battalions and attached troops south of that point. After an attack by a third brigade from the north had failed to remove this block, the 6th Brigade managed to escape with its transport along the beach at low tide, but the 47th Brigade had to leave all its transport and guns and retreat in small dispersal groups through the jungle.

Lieutenant-General Koga had completed his three-phase encirclement of the British/Indian brigades in one calendar month, exactly according to plan, and had inflicted severe casualties on a much larger force. With seven battalions and one pack regiment of artillery he had temporarily destroyed the 47th Brigade and defeated the 4th, 6th, and 71st Brigades with their three regiments of artillery (totalling seven British and ten Indian battalions).

With the arrival of his fresh II/214th battalion, which completed the strength of his division, Koga, who saw his enemy reeling, asked Iida if he could continue to attack until the monsoon. Iida, who trusted Koga, gave him *carte blanche*.

Meanwhile, Lloyd had been replaced by Major-General C. E. N. Lomax and his 26th Division headquarters. Lieutenant-General Slim, commander of XV Indian Corps, whose duties during the past seven months had been to suppress the vicious insurgency campaign in Bengal led by the Indian Congress Party, which had stated categorically that they would prefer Japanese to British rule, was placed in overall command of the Arakan front on April 5.

Slim had been in active command of the British/Indian forces in their 1,000-mile retreat from Burma the previous year and, as was his wont, had learnt much from his victorious, pugnacious enemy, who was trained to expect to fight against all odds. Slim found a most unsatisfactory state of affairs. Most of the units now under command of the 26th Division had had their morale lowered by abortive attacks on Rathedaung and Donbaik, and then had been eased out of their own defensive positions by the Japanese capacity for manoeuvres, flank attacks, and ability to bring all their weapons and troops, however inferior in numbers, to bear at a decisive point. All units, especially the Indian ones, were frustrated and bewildered and, as the British official history states, "the morale of the troops was generally poor and in some units very low".

Slim ordered Lomax to hold the Maungdaw–"Tunnels"–Buthidaung line. He re-

inforced Lomax's four brigades (4th, 6th, 55th, and 71st) with the 36th Brigade, bringing the force to a total of 19 battalions including seven British, 11 Indian, and one Gurkha.

Meanwhile, General Koga had eight battalions available for attack. He left one battalion to contain the British forces on the coastal strip, and one battalion with a mountain artillery regiment ("Miyawaki" Column) to hold his enemy east of the Mayu river. He divided his remaining six battalions, each supported by pack artillery, into "Uno" and "Tanahashi" Columns, and gave them the task of seizing Buthidaung and the Tunnels line and then wheeling left to capture Maungdaw. At this juncture the "Miyawaki" Column, east of the Mayu, would advance due north and capture Taung Bazar. The Japanese started their advance on April 23.

The "Uno" Column met with stubborn resistance at Kanthe, so the "Tanahashi"

△ ◁ *The effect of a smoke grenade thrown by Garhwali troops against a Japanese bunker in Maungdaw.*
◁ ◁ *Major-General H. C. Stockwell, commander of the 82nd West African Division, keeps his feet dry. With an offshore H.Q. on* Stella, *such trips to and from a waiting dinghy were frequent.*
△ *Brigadier Cotterill-Hill, 71st Indian Brigade, wades ashore during the invasion of Ramree Island.*
◁ *The second Arakan campaign.*

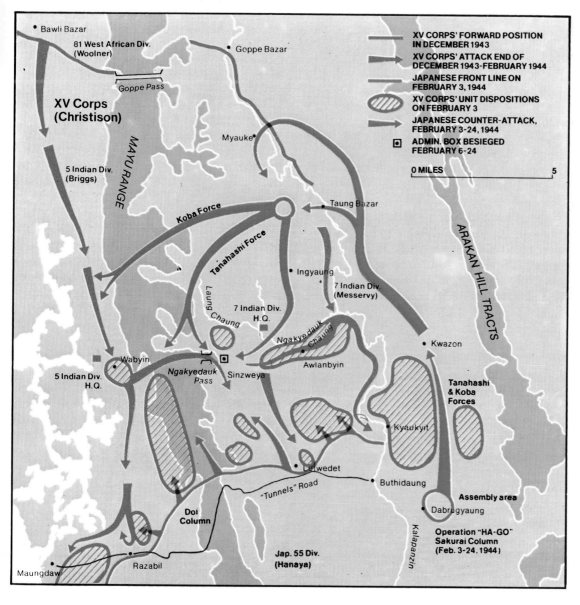

△ *Typical of Arakan country – a heavily-wooded steep hill that made the going really tough for the troops.*
▷△ *Men of the 81st West African Division watch their supplies being dropped. They hold a captured position west of Paletiva in the Kaladan valley, taken as they moved to outflank the Japanese.*
▷▷ *Wounded.*

Column by-passed Kanthe by advancing along the razor beak Mayu range and seized Point 551 overlooking the Tunnels area of the Maungdaw–Buthidaung Road. Lomax cleverly formed an open box to trap the advancing Japanese between his 4th and 6th Brigades to the west, 55th Brigade to the east, and 71st Brigade to the north, forming the lid. The Japanese, however, launched their northward drive in earnest on May 2 and, by May 3, the sides of the box had crumbled and the lid had opened "without adequate reason". The plan was a good one, but the training and morale of the British/Indian troops inevitably led to its failure.

As Buthidaung and the Tunnels area fell to the Japanese, Slim, realising how badly his superior forces had once again been defeated in the jungle, wanted to retreat 60 miles back to Cox's Bazar, with the intention of luring the Japanese forces into open country where his troops could oppose them on ground more suitable to their training and armament, and at the same time stretch and expose the enemy's communications.

Irwin, however, opposed this plan and ordered Slim to hold the line Bawli Bazar–Goppe Bazar–Taung Bazar, only 20 miles north of the line Maungdaw–Buthidaung, and gave Lomax a sixth brigade, with orders to prepare a counter-attack to retake Maungdaw by surprise.

British operations in the Arakan ended in May 1943 with their forces back on their start-line and the stubborn and mistaken Irwin, who had wished to sack Slim, being sacked himself.

By May 11 General Koga had again won a striking victory over superior forces. The partial failure of the British demolition plan, and the disappearance in panic of all the civilian labour on which the British/Indian forces relied overmuch, resulted in very large quantities of booty falling into his hands. In view of the depth of the British retreat and the arrival of the monsoon, Koga decided to take up a defensive position on the general line Buthidaung–Maungdaw with five battalions and a regiment of artillery and withdraw the remainder of his division to Akyab for rest and recuperation. In 16 weeks he had caused his enemy to suffer over 5,000 battle casualties.

The news of the British failure in the Arakan, resulting in the loss of Buthidaung and Maungdaw, reached Washington just when the "Trident" Conference, which had been called to decide on future Allied policy in South-East Asia, was taking place. General Wavell, the Indian Army commander, and the commanders in the Arakan all came under most severe criticism. Churchill ordered that new commanders must be found and battalions whose morale had broken should be severely disciplined. If, he said, Indian Army troops were incapable of fighting in the jungle, commando formations should be formed as a prototype and an example to show them how to fight. Answers from India were that the Indian Army had been grossly over-expanded since Pearl Harbor and the best Indian units were in the Middle East, leaving a "second class army" to oppose the Japanese. Jungle fighting required, above all, good infantry but the infantry had also been milked of its best and most intelligent men to form technical corps like the expanded Indian artillery, previously manned wholly by the British. Indian troops had had their loyalty undermined by subversion from the newly formed Indian Independence League with its Indian National Army fighting alongside the Japanese. British officers drafted into the Indian Army had not had time to learn the language and get to know their men. Reinforcements to replace battle and malarial casualties had arrived piecemeal and many of them half-trained. Some units had been left in the front line for many months without relief. Congress-sponsored riots in August and September 1942, accompanied by mal-distribution of food as a result of their depredations and destruction of communications, resulted in widespread famine in which 4 million had died, and this led to a disaffection amongst reinforcements moving through these areas to the battle line, so that they spread subversion amongst the forward troops.

Wavell was only too well aware that the failure in the Arakan, following as it did the disastrous campaigns in Malaya and Burma, had dealt the army in India a severe shock. Yet he knew that the Japanese were not "invincible" and had shown grave weaknesses of which advantage could be taken by a better trained army reinforced with self-confidence and self-respect. One undoubted advantage gained by the British was that during the year the R.A.F. had begun to attain air superiority throughout the whole front. This in itself could be made into a battle-winning factor. The success of the first Chindit operation, with its total reliance on air supply, offset the failures in the Arakan and pointed the way to victory in the future.

Wavell appointed a special committee to report on the readiness for war of British and Indian infantry battalions in India, and to make recommendations for improvement.

A new command set-up was created. Wavell was promoted Viceroy of India to look after the civil side and to see that the population would support its armed forces.

General Sir Claude Auchinleck was recalled from the Middle East to be C.-in-C. India and to make the Indian sub-continent into an efficient administrative and training base from which the fighting forces could draw their strength. He eventually created a self-confident new model Indian Army which had become one of the best fighting machines in the world by 1945.

Lord Louis Mountbatten, who had previously been head of Combined Operations in Britain, was now appointed Allied Supreme Commander, South-East Asia Command, with his headquarters in Ceylon. Under him was a new 11th Army Group (General Sir George Giffard), and under Giffard a new 14th Army (Lieutenant-General Slim) responsible for operations in Burma. Additionally XV Corps, under Lieutenant-General A. F. P. Christison, operating in the Arakan, came under Slim's command.

Brigades were to be formed of one British, one Indian, and one Gurkha battalion. Much more reliance was to be placed on the redoubtable Gurkhas, who had been represented by only one battalion in the Arakan débâcle.

After the first Chindit operation had proved the reliability of air supply, this form of support would be developed and taught to all units so that they need never retreat or disintegrate if the Japanese got behind them.

The R.A.F. was persuaded to co-operate more fully in developing more reliable and accurate close air support for the army involving more intimate mutual signal arrangements and co-operation so that aircraft could take the place of artillery where necessary in the deep jungle.

All ranks were given more jungle, river, and night training in order that these seemingly hostile circumstances could be used to the men's positive advantage rather than handicapping them as in the past.

Rations and methods of cooking in the forward areas were improved so that detachments could fend for themselves for many weeks, and special rations were issued during training to build up men before operations so that they were capable of enduring long periods of duress.

Malaria, which was causing a hundred times more casualties than bullets or shells, was tackled by mepacrine, strict anti-malarial measures, and forward malarial treatment centres so that men needing treatment were not evacuated to base areas but remained in the line as a reserve to protect communications. This reform was one of the most effective means of ensuring that battalions in the line maintained their strength.

An illustration of the disproportionate losses from diseases is the British XXXIII Corps' casualty figures for June to November 1944, which were typical of all formations in this theatre:
Battle casualties   3,289
Sickness   47,098 (including 20,430 malaria cases).

These remedial actions have been emphasised because they were to turn the scales in the Arakan in 1944 when the Japanese for a third time launched their short range penetration forces with again, it must be added, numerically very much inferior forces. Also it must be remembered that if the Japanese had had air superiority and as good air support, air supply, and intercommunication as the British were to enjoy, the outcome might have been very different.

The third Arakan campaign.

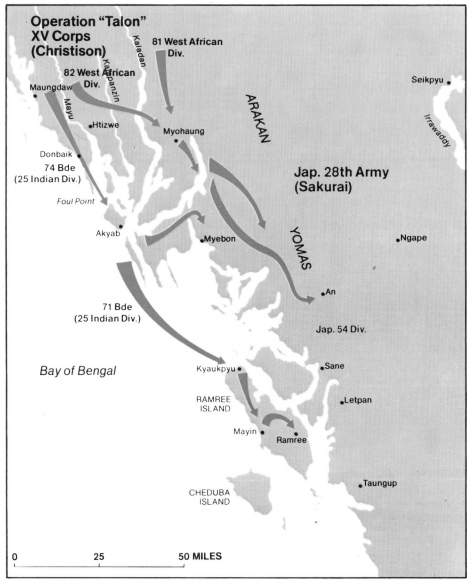

Operation "Talon"
XV Corps
(Christison)

81 West African Div.

82 West African Div.

Kaladan

Kalapanzin

Maungdaw

Mayu

Htizwe

Myohaung

ARAKAN

Seikpyu

Irrawaddy

Donbaik
74 Bde
(25 Indian Div.)

Foul Point

Akyab

Myebon

Jap. 28th Army
(Sakurai)

YOMAS

Ngape

An

71 Bde
(25 Indian Div.)

Jap. 54 Div.

Bay of Bengal

Kyaukpyu

Sane

RAMREE ISLAND

Letpan

Mayin

Ramree

CHEDUBA ISLAND

Taungup

0   25   50 MILES

New advance

During the summer of 1943, British and Commonwealth forces in the Arakan were built up and re-organised. The material superiority of the Allies was reflected in this theatre as in others.

XV Corps in November 1943 consisted of the 5th and 7th Indian Divisions with 81st West African Division (less one brigade) in the Kaladan. No. 224 Group, with headquarters at Chittagong, consisted of 14 fighter and fighter-bomber squadrons made up of Hurricanes, Spitfires, Beaufighters, and Vengeances, totalling 200 aircraft. At call were the U.S.A.A.F. and R.A.F. Strategic Air Force and Brigadier-General W. D. Old's U.S.A.A.F. and R.A.F. Troop Carrier Command. During this phase of the Arakan fighting, XV Corps was reinforced by No. 3 Special Service Brigade (two, later four, commandos), 25th and 26th Indian, and British 36th Divisions, making a total of 6½ divisions.

A large engineer contingent was employed in improving communications and building airfields, whilst flotillas of small boats from the Royal Navy, the Royal Engineers, and the Service Corps supplemented the supply lines.

Opposing this formidable force was the Japanese 55th Division (Lieutenant-General T. Hanaya) and a depleted 5th Air Division (maximum 80 aircraft) which was responsible for the defence of all Burma. The 54th Division was moving to protect the coast-line south of Akyab but took no part in the Arakan operation. Hanaya's fragile communications were by track across the Arakan Yomas to Pakokku on the Irrawaddy; from Prome to Taungup and thence by launch to Akyab.

During the post-monsoon months of 1943 Christison had advanced his forces methodically down the Mayu peninsula so that by mid-January 1944 he was poised to attack the heavily-fortified Japanese Maungdaw–Buthidaung line.

Meanwhile the Japanese high command, realising from the exploits of the Chindits in the previous year that neither the jungles nor the hills of Burma were impassable to determined troops, and seeing the British forces in Assam hanging down on a 300-mile-long stalk from the

▽ *Keeping a look-out on a 40-mm Bofors anti-aircraft gun on a self-propelled mounting.*

main stem on the Brahmaputra like a bunch of grapes ripe for plucking, had decided that the best means for the defence of Burma was attack. Their main plan for 1944 was to attack west over the Chindwin hills, to cut the lines of communication of IV Corps at Imphal and destroy the Allied forces in that area. As a diversion to draw away as many divisions as possible over the other side of the Arakan Yomas they would first use penetration tactics to attack and destroy the Allied forces in the Arakan. This was named the *"HA-GO"* offensive and was planned to start on February 3.

By that date the 5th Division, supported by tanks, was attacking the Japanese in the Tunnels area with three brigades up; the 7th Division in the Mayu valley was attacking Buthidaung, and the 81st West African Division was far away on the Kaladan river, where it achieved very little effect on the campaign apart from being a drain on the Allied air supply resources. Also behind these forward divisions were the 26th and 36th Divisions.

Hanaya divided his division into four. Two battalions would hold Akyab. One battalion could guard the coast of the Mayu peninsula. Two battalions ("Doi" Column) could hold the redoubts between the Mayu river and the sea which was being attacked by the six brigades (with tanks) of the 5th and 7th Divisions. He entrusted his reconnaissance regiment to screen off the West Africans in the Kaladan valley. This left Hanaya five battalions and an engineer regiment (about 5,000 strong) for his penetration force under Major-General T. Sakurai. The rôle of the "Sakurai" Column was to pass straight through the 7th Indian Division on the night of February 3–4, seize Taung Bazar, turn left, cross the Mayu river, and cut the communications of both the 5th and 7th Divisions. Meanwhile, the "Doi" Column, manning the redoubts, would attack from the south.

All at first went well for the "Sakurai" Column. Sixteen abreast they strode along the flat paddy fields, through the heart of the 7th Division at midnight and occupied Taung Bazar 12 miles away by

morning. Within an hour one battalion had crossed the Mayu river in captured boats. By noon on February 5 the whole force was behind the 5th Division and one detachment had seized Briasco Bridge on the coast road whilst the remainder overran the 5th Division's headquarters and started attacking the Administrative Area, at Sinzweya.

Here Slim's new training instructions and orders started to take effect. The Administrative Area, the capture of which the Japanese depended on for their supplies, closed up like a box. All brigades stood firm. Air supply was made available to the two forward divisions. They fought on, improvising where necessary. Giffard ordered the 36th Division to move south from Chittagong. Hanaya reinforced "Doi" Column and urged it to attack north all the harder to help Sakurai. The 7th Division cut Sakurai's tenuous lines of communication running through the area. Sakurai's code book with wireless frequencies was captured and with it his signals communication list of call signs with the result that his powers of command and control of the battles started to fail. The Administrative Box held out, all ranks of whatever arm taking part in its defence.

Christison at one point wavered, believing his 7th Division overrun, and ordered the 5th Division to move back across the Mayu range. But the more experienced Slim countermanded this order and exhorted the 26th and 36th Divisions to hasten forward to destroy the Japanese penetration forces. As long as the "Admin. Box" at Sinzweya held out, the Japanese could get no supplies and their offensive was doomed. It held from February 6 to 24, when the Ngakyedauk Pass was reopened.

The Japanese put their whole air strength into the battle and flew 350 bomber sorties. But the R.A.F. counterattacked and, although losing some transport aircraft shot down, Troop Carrier Command succeeded in delivering 2,710 tons of supplies to the Sinzweya box and the two forward divisions.

On February 24, with the approval of

his army headquarters, Hanaya abandoned the "*HA-GO*" offensive. This was the end. The Japanese withdrew uneventfully. XV Corps had suffered 3,506 casualties but had held its ground, thus giving a tremendous fillip to morale throughout the army in India, an event of which the political, psychological, and propaganda sections made the maximum use.

But the Japanese in the Arakan had achieved the object given to them. One Japanese division had thrown two divisions into temporary disarray, and tied down a total of six and a half divisions. The actual "*HA-GO*" offensive was carried out by about eight battalions totalling not more than 8,000 troops. Twenty-seven Indian, 18 British, seven West African, and five Gurkha battalions, accompanied by a total of 26 regiments of artillery, were brought against them. It was no fault of the Japanese soldiers that, owing to Allied technical superiority, many of these battalions and regiments could be and were quickly switched by air to the Imphal front to restore the situation there.

Meanwhile, during the "*HA-GO*" offensive, the Japanese 28th Army had relieved Hanaya of responsibility for the Kaladan front and had on February 18 formed the "Koba" Force, under Colonel T. Koba, which consisted of a regimental headquarters, the 55th Reconnaissance Regiment, plus the equivalent of three infantry battalions, to face Major-General C. G. Woolner's 81st West African Division. Woolner underestimated the Japanese strength. Koba, by manoeuvre, ambush, and outflanking movement, but never by frontal attack, drove the West Africans 40 miles back from Kyauktaw and started to ooze them out of the Kaladan valley.

The attack on Imphal had now started, and Giffard wanted to transfer the 5th and 7th Divisions by air to that front ad soon as possible. He allowed Christison time for the 7th Division to capture Buthidaung and 5th Division Razabil, before they were relieved by the 26th Indian and British 36th Divisions on March 22. The 25th Indian Division was also moved forward and relieved the 36th Division, which was to come under General Stilwell's command in north Burma to relieve the Chindits. Hanaya ordered all his forward units to attack and harass the British forces from all directions and to give an impression of strength during the next four weeks, so as to hold the British in the area before he withdrew to monsoon positions. By using false identity badges and other deception methods, he made British Intelligence believe that the 54th Division had moved into the area. Koga, in the Kaladan, followed suit so successfully that the West Africans were thrown right out of the Kaladan valley and ceased to be a threat to the Japanese flank. Christison's forces, however, obtained possession of Maungdaw and the much fought over Point 551, which he thought would be a good starting line for the post-monsoon offensive.

But Giffard realised that the Arakan was a bad area in which to fight the Japanese. Having inflicted over 3,500 casualties on the British in the "*HA-GO*" offensive, the Japanese had caused a further 3,360 casualties in the period before the monsoon, and this excludes casualties from sickness, which were always high. So Giffard, on July 14, 1944, recommended that any idea of an offensive in Arakan in the dry season of 1944-45 should be abandoned. In fact, however, this had been, in its own way, a true British victory—a moral turning point which destroyed the myth of Japanese invincibility and gave the Commonwealth and Indian forces new confidence.

The last Arakan campaign will be dealt with in a later chapter.

△ *A group of Chindits, sporting the beards they were permitted to grow in the jungle. Their operations were a source of good propaganda for the British forces and the home front, who had seen the Japanese drive through the British Asian Empire in a series of apparently effortless victories.*

△ ▷ *A radio operator with his bulky and heavy equipment, which had to be carried on mules. The jungle-covered hills, with deep valleys and fierce electric storms, made signalling a difficult and exhausting job, to which was added the problem of encoding messages for security.*

▷ ▷ *Armed with the two essentials of his trade, a rifle and a spade, a Chindit soldier strides through the jungle. His battered bush hat betrays the multitude of uses to which it has been put, keeping off sun and rain, and acting as a pillow at night.*

CHAPTER 59

WINGATE'S DREAM: THE 1ST CHINDIT OPERATION

by Brigadier Michael Calvert

In January 1942, when the Japanese invaded Burma, the British War Office offered General Wavell, Commander-in-Chief India, the services of Lieutenant-Colonel Orde Wingate, D.S.O. and bar, who had previously carried out guerrilla operations in Palestine and Abyssinia with conspicuous success. Wavell, under whom Wingate had served, recognised his excellent if unorthodox qualities, saw a role for him in Burma, and accepted this offer.

On Wingate's arrival in India after the fall of Rangoon, Wavell sent him to carry out a reconnaissance in north Burma,

which he thought might be suitable terrain for guerrillas. Wingate flew in and was conducted around north Burma by the commandant of the Bush Warfare School at Maymyo, Major J. M. Calvert, who was later to join him. Calvert also motored Wingate south some hundreds of miles to Prome to meet Lieutenant-General Slim, commander of I Burma Corps. This corps had only just been formed, after the fall of Rangoon.

After a detailed reconnaissance and after discussing the matter with many people, including Chiang Kai-shek in Chungking, Wingate returned to India.

He reported to Wavell that at that juncture there were neither time nor troops available to form a pattern of guerrilla warfare in north Burma, but he did recommend forming and training a special force of brigade strength, which could penetrate behind the Japanese forces and destroy their communications and perhaps manoeuvre them out of the area.

The first Chindits

This experimental force became the 77th Indian Infantry Brigade, made up of the 13th King's (Liverpool) Regiment; 3rd/2nd Gurkha Rifles; British 142nd Commando Company; a Burma Rifle battalion, which was split into detachments amongst each column; as well as skilled signal and R.A.F. sections attached to each column. In addition there was a small tactical Brigade Headquarters which General Wingate took into the field. Behind this, in the rear areas, was a supply organisation which remained at base and which looked after all the administrative and supply arrangements of the columns in the field. This rear headquarters looked large to those who saw it in India. But it must be remembered that all those who would normally be attached to a battalion to look after its administration and would normally accompany it into battle, were extracted from the columns in the field and carried out their supply and administrative duties from a distance through the medium of aircraft and radio.

Rigorous training

This force was trained most rigorously by Wingate in the sparse jungles of the Central Provinces. The men forming the force had nothing very special about them. There was a small nucleus of officers and men from the Bush Warfare School in Maymyo, which in itself was a cover name for a special mission to China. But apart from these men and a draft from the Commandos in the Middle East, which helped form No. 142 Commando (which never numbered more than 100 men), the remainder of the infantry forming this brigade came from second or third line troops who had not had much training. The Burma Rifles turned out to be very good in reconnaissance and in their

knowledge of the country, which helped the column forward. Their officers, largely ex-forestry officers, were excellent. Most of the officers and other ranks of the battalion were not picked men and it is all to their credit that they did so well. The fact that they were not picked men made all other units in the Burma Army realise after the operation that if these men could do it, they too could do it.

Wingate himself trained cadres of officers and N.C.O.s in every little detail of column and bivouac life, including quick reaction to alarm and taking offensive action. He taught men how to cook in the jungle, the use of machine guns, mortars, camouflage, navigation through the jungle, how to look after mules, how to cross rivers, and so on. He himself was tireless in his attention to detail. He then expected his officers to follow his example and teach their men.

He stressed that total reliance was to be placed on mulepack transport for all weapons, ammunition, signals, and medical supplies, supplemented by direct air supply to each column in the field at the request of the R.A.F. officers accompanying the column. Mules would feed on bamboo shoots collected by the mule leaders and augmented by grain, free dropped from the air. Wingate made up a ration of nuts, raisins, biscuits, tea, salt, and sugar, which was to be augmented by the purchase of rice and buffalo meat whenever possible.

Calvert's adjutant at the Bush Warfare School, Major Peter Lord, who had once been secretary of the International Club at Tientsin, set up and organised the

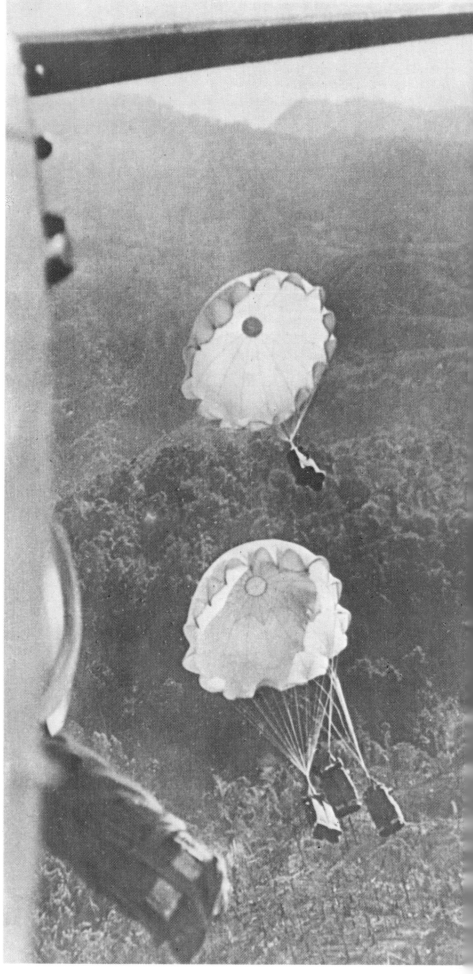

whole air supply system, assisted and advised by Squadron-Leader Longmore and Squadron-Leader R. Thompson.

This force was named the "Chindits", which was an anglicised version of the name of the mythical griffon, the "Chinthe", the protector of the Burma pagodas.

Wavell's dilemma, and his final decision

Originally the raid planned for the seven Chindit columns, each of about 400 men and 100 mules with two 3-inch mortars and two medium machine guns, was to be supported by a general offensive by IV Corps from Imphal. But IV Corps' (Scoones) communications were not ready, and so it was reluctant to advance across the Chindwin in any strength. Wavell, however, was determined that this experimental brigade should test out not only the Japanese but these new means of operating in the deep jungle. Wavell came forward to Imphal, inspected the

77th Brigade and, after deep thought, directed it into the attack alone. Wavell had had to consider whether the risk of losing all or part of this brigade on a mission of little strategic value, in order to attempt to burst the bubble of Japanese invincibility, would be balanced by the experience gained and the loss of technical surprise when such tactics had to be used later to support a general offensive. He finally decided that it was worth the risk, because the operation would help raise morale in the army in India, by showing that Allied forces could operate in jungle terrain and need not feel inferior to the Japanese in fighting along unconventional lines.

Gurkhas move into action

On February 14 the headquarters and three British and four Gurkha columns of the 77th Brigade successfully crossed the Chindwin and advanced secretly on a broad front through the jungle-covered

△ ◁ *A supply drop in progress. The lessons learned about re-supply from the air were acted upon during the second Chindit expedition in 1944.*

◁ ◁ *A dispatcher's view of a supply drop. Some unbreakable stores were dropped without parachutes, and while this saved silk and parachute cord, it could be dangerous for the collecting party. Some men suffered serious injuries when they were hit by free-falling panniers, and in one disastrous drop the bottom came out of a bag of 5,000 rupees.*

△ *Chindits move off the track for a break during the march. Japanese search parties worked up the waterways when they were looking for Chindit bivouacs, so the latter took care not to camp close to streams.*

△ *Lance-Corporal James Rogerson, a Gurkha private, and Private Jack Wilson after their tour behind the enemy lines. The men carried a 72-pound pack, which included seven days' rations, a rifle and bayonet, a* dah *or* kukri *(machete or Gurkha knife), three grenades, ground-sheet, spare shirt and trousers, four spare pairs of socks, balaclava helmet, jack-knife, rubber shoes, housewife, toggle-rope, canvas life-jacket, mess tin, ration-bags, water bottle, and a* chagal *(canvas water bottle), besides other items of personal kit. Blankets and Bren guns were carried by mules.*

hills into central Burma. Their objective was the main north-south Burma railway between Mandalay and Mogaung. The distance from their starting point to the railway direct was about 140 miles. Major Dunlop's No. 1 (Gurkha) Column was the first to reach the railway on March 3 when it destroyed railway bridges near Kyaikthin. No. 3 (Gurkha) Column (Calvert) did the same 40 miles north at Nankan on the night March 5-6. No. 5 (King's) Column (Fergusson) on the same night brought down an avalanche of rock onto the railway in the Bongyaung (Bonchaung) Gorge. The forces taking part in this operation totalled about 3,000 men and 800 mules.

The Japanese 18th and 33rd divisions of the 15th Army, under Lieutenant-General Iida, were the formations most affected by this raid, and for a while they were bewildered by it. They did not take the situation seriously until Dunlop (Royal Scots) blew the railway on March 3. Then Iida ordered three regiments, each of three battalions, to round up the raiders.

Wingate, however, exalted by this first success, ordered his columns to cross the 1,000-yard wide Irrawaddy. He envisaged

forming a base in the friendly Kachin Hills to the north-east, from where he could operate with his back to the Chinese during the next few months. But he also ordered Calvert and Fergusson to attack the Burma Road in the Maymyo area, where the Japanese headquarters were situated and therefore where the maximum reaction to the raid would result.

First defeat

But one of the Gurkha columns had already met with disaster when approaching the railway, and had been dispersed. The news of this spread to the other Gurkha columns and it became more difficult to keep up their morale. It should be explained that whilst the Gurkhas, when properly trained and with officers who speak their language, are magnificent troops, they naturally cannot so easily change the tactics and methods taught them at their depots at short notice as can, for example, British troops, who understood the language in which the new concepts of such tactics are taught. The Gurkha battalion given to Wingate for this operation was woefully short of experienced officers and men, and only about one officer in each column spoke Gurkhali well. In Calvert's column, for instance, only one British officer with the Gurkha company was over the age of 19. It is all the more remarkable that these young officers led their fine young men, assisted by excellent Gurkhali warrant officers and N.C.O.s, through nearly three months of operations in the jungle without cracking.

The crossing of the Irrawaddy was not easy and more than one column was attacked whilst carrying out this difficult manoeuvre. Perhaps the crossing was a mistake. After their initial rapid march and successful demolitions, the Chindits found themselves hemmed in between the Irrawaddy and the Shweli rivers in a dry inhospitable area with no nearby targets to attack and at the extreme range of their wireless sets and air supply communications. The Japanese used regiments from three (18th, 33rd, 56th) of their four divisions in Burma at that time to try to surround and destroy the Chindits.

Many small actions were fought until the time came when Wingate, after radio consultation with IV Corps, decided to withdraw his force. He ordered his column commanders to try to bring back their columns complete into India or to take them on to China. He gave them the alternative option of splitting into dispersal groups as taught in training, so that they might infiltrate between the strands of the Japanese net which was now surrounding them. One King's column (Gilkes) chose the longer, more arduous, but safer route to China. Another King's column, under Scott, who had been a Royal Engineer, chose to make an airstrip in an open space in the jungle and be flown out from the other side of the Irrawaddy. The remainder recrossed the Irrawaddy either in dispersal groups or columns and made their way back to the Chindwin. Unfortunately many of them thought they were safe on reaching the Chindwin, but IV Corps had withdrawn from it and the Japanese were now using it as a stop line to catch the Chindit columns in that area. The result was that many prisoners were taken on the Chindwin itself, when the dispersal group thought that it had reached safe harbour and had relaxed.

Of the 3,000 men and 800 mules which

△ *Major Bernard Fergusson, Black Watch, who led Number 5 Column. In 1944 Stilwell described him in a letter of introduction, "Help this man, he looks like a dude, but I think he's a soldier." "On the whole I liked it," commented Fergusson.*
▽ *The first Chindit expedition.*

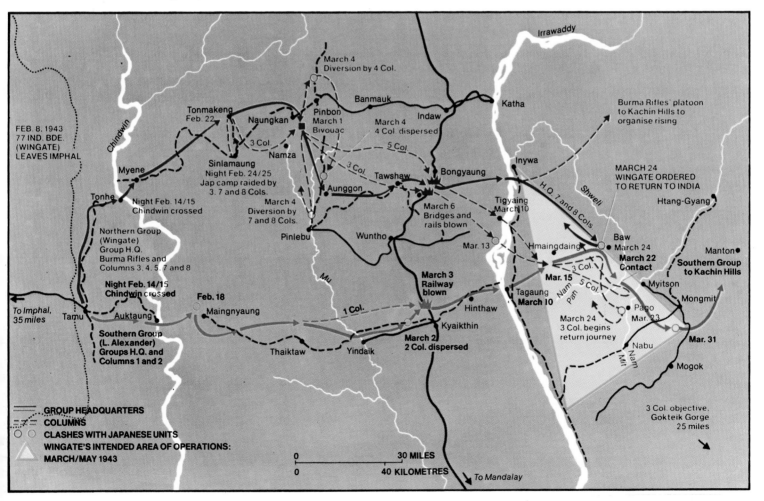

had crossed the Chindwin, about 2,182 men and two mules returned, having covered between 1,000 and 1,500 miles in enemy-dominated territory. The remainder had been killed, captured, or if mules, eaten. But those who returned, although suffering from malaria, dysentery, jungle sores, and malnutrition, were in high spirits and proud of their achievement. Sent on leave and supported by a well-directed public relations campaign in the press, they had a startling effect on the raising of morale of all ranks throughout India, especially at that time when the defeats in the Arakan had further depressed men's minds. There they were,

ordinary second line battalions and anything but picked troops, but they had gone through Burma and "singed Tojo's moustache". So their comrades in units throughout India and Assam said "if that lot can run rings round the Japanese we can do better".

Japanese conclusions

However, there was another unexpected reaction. General Mutaguchi, a man of strong personality who had been uniformly successful in battle since 1937, and who was acknowledged "victor of Singapore", was commanding the 18th

Division during the Chindit operation. He had studies Wingate's tactics and use of ground closely and came to admire his methods. So when he was promoted to command of the 15th Army he wanted to emulate Wingate's methods and to improve on them. Initially, he arranged a discussion group on the results of the first Wingate operation. He then ordered a reconnaissance to be made over the Chindwin and proposed a Chindit-type operation for the 1944 season against Imphal and Kohima, but on a much greater scale, with a force totalling three divisions relying mainly on pack transport. War games were held to test out his

ideas and, with some misgivings, especially from the Japanese Army Air Force, Imperial General Headquarters in Tokyo agreed with Mutaguchi's plan – with the proviso that it should be linked with a campaign by the newly formed Indian National Army to instigate an insurrection in India, coupled with other subversive activities.

Imphal idea born

This the first Chindit operation was the direct begetter of Mutaguchi's *"U-Go"* offensive against the 14th Army at Imphal in March 1944. This operation, after

▽ ◁ ◁ *A party of Chindits carrying wounded on an extemporised stretcher.*
▽ ◁ *A rigger and radio operator greeted by Major Walter P. Scott at an airfield in Burma.*
▽ *Rubber assault boats used during the march in Burma. The Chindwin, and other rivers which flow from northern Burma to the sea and divide the country in half, were a major natural obstacle. For the Japanese they also served as a stop line on to which they could drive some of the small parties of Chindits when the columns had broken up.*

△ *One of six officers and men of the King's Regiment on the first expedition in 1943 is decorated by Lord Wavell, Viceroy of India. Fergusson admitted that the Chindits had not achieved a great deal, though they had distracted the Japanese from some operations. However, they had "amassed experience on which a future has already begun to be built". Wingate went home and captured the imagination of both Churchill and Roosevelt.*

achieving initial success, failed because Mutaguchi had apparently not understood that the vital necessity for such an operation was dominance of the air, and consequent reliable air supply and close air support in lieu of artillery.

Much has been made of the divergencies of opinion amongst the Allies on how they should conduct the war against Japan, but one decision made in 1943 stands out plainly. At the Combined Chiefs-of-Staff "Quadrant" Conference in Quebec in August 1943, which Brigadier Wingate attended at Churchill's request, it was decided "To carry out operations for the capture of upper Burma in order to improve the air route and establish overland communications with China. Our main

effort should be put into offensive operations to achieve this object."

In order to achieve this result the British Chiefs-of-Staff decided to form six Long Range Penetration Groups (L.R.P.G.), which would conduct operations as outlined by Brigadier Wingate and enable the Allies to seize sufficient of north Burma to open a road to China.

These six L.R.P. brigades would each consist of four battalions and attached troops. The force, which was known variously as the Special Force, the 3rd Indian Infantry Division (as a cover name), or the Chindits, would consist of two Indian infantry brigades (77th and 111th) already in being; three brigades formed from the battle-experienced British 70th Division; and one brigade formed from the 81st West African Division. The three battalions of this African brigade would be available to this force to act as garrisons for the air bases formed in the jungle to support each brigade.

These bases, which Wingate called "strongholds", were what the modern tactician tends to call "pivots of manoeuvre".

To support China

At the "Sextant" Conference held in Cairo in November 1943, which Chiang Kai-shek attended, the Combined Chiefs-of-Staff ordered "the occupation of Upper Burma by the Allies to start in February 1944 in order to improve (a) the air and (b) the land routes to China. What was attempted elsewhere in Asia would be in support of this main effort."

The main reason for the Allies giving this plan of operations top priority was the real fear that, unless the British and Americans opened up even such tenuous communications to China in the manner projected, China would drop out of the war and thus allow the 26 Japanese divisions operating in China to be used elsewhere against the Allies. It is important that this agreed plan of action by the Allies should be borne in mind throughout all discussions on this campaign, because future operations by either side as the battlefield spread, tended to blur the horizon and deflect certain commanders' minds away from the maintenance of this objective which had been laid down by the inter-Allied high command.

CHAPTER 60
ALLIED AIR OFFENSIVE

By 1943 ruins were piling up from one end of the Third Reich to the other, the effect of night raids by R.A.F. Bomber 8th Air Force. The 15th Air Force joined them after October 9 from its air base Force from October 9 from their air base at Foggia, hastily brought back into action after its capture by the British 8th Army on September 27. These round-the-clock attacks were the result of a plan adopted at Casablanca late in January 1943 at a meeting of the British and American Combined Chiefs-of-Staff Committee. A list of proposed objectives was drawn up in order of priority:

"(a) German submarine construction yards.
(b) The German aircraft industry.
(c) Transportation.
(d) Oil plants.
(e) Other targets in enemy war industry."

However, this order did not reflect the realities of strategic bombing. In fact the agreed directive specified the general objective of the strategic air offensive as the destruction of the German industrial system and the undermining of the German home morale.

After the complete failure of a series of American bombing raids on German submarine construction yards, followed by a similar British lack of success, it became clear that bombing techniques would need drastic improvement or, at least, that less demanding targets should be selected. Fortunately for the Allies, by the end of 1943 the U-boat menace was no longer pressing. It should be recalled that in order to keep up his U-boat campaign against all opposition Dönitz was at this time claiming that to abandon it would subject Germany's cities to even greater ordeals as enemy bombing raids grew in ferocity. In this he was not mistaken.

Difficulties in co-ordination

It had not been easy for the British and the Americans to come to an agreement over the best use of the U.S. 8th Air Force. The first unit of this force had arrived in Great Britain on July 1, 1942 when the Flying Fortress "Jarring Jenny" had touched down at Prestwick airport in Scotland.

It was the opinion of Air Chief Marshal Sir Charles Portal, Chief of the Air Staff, that the squadrons of Flying Fortresses

△ General Carl A. Spaatz, head of the 8th Air Force in 1942 and of the U.S. Strategic Air Forces, comprising the 8th and 15th Air Forces, from January 1944.
▽ A damaged Flying Fortress under repair at a Mobile Machine Shop.

should take part in the night bombing raids of Bomber Command, whose C.-in-C. naturally welcomed the idea of having eventually twice or three times as many planes at his disposal. Both men thought that day bombing against A.A. and Göring's fighters would suffer unbearable losses for a very mediocre profit. But in Washington, General H. H. Arnold, U.S.A.A.F. Chief-of-Staff, and at H.Q. 8th Air Force, Lieutenant-General Ira C. Eaker both disagreed with British optimism about night operations. If the Anglo-American strategic force was to carry out its mission successfully it would, in their opinion, have to attack by day and nothing would make them change their minds. But if, under certain conditions, which were not all fulfilled late in 1942, the Flying Fortresses and the Liberators were to take on the considerable risks of day bombing, this was not to be so for the R.A.F., whatever the courage or the state of training of its crews.

R.A.F. by night, U.S.A.A.F. by day

And so that task was divided round the clock equally between the British and the Americans, the former taking off at nightfall and the latter by day, each sticking to his task with ruthless obstinacy and without complaining of his losses. This was the system adopted after heated discussions. For Generals Arnold and Eaker there was the additional advantage (though perhaps not admitted) that the Americans would still retain their autonomy though working under a joint command. This division of labour meant that the two air forces came to use totally different methods of action.

By day the 8th Air Force performed what it called precision bombing. Well-defined objectives were thus allotted: a particular factory, construction-yard, assembly-shop in Germany or in an occupied country, in the latter of which only where civilian casualties could be spared as far as was compatible with the successful completion of the mission. The American crews nevertheless greatly exaggerated the degree of precision they could obtain with their Norden bomb-sights.

As it operated by night, Bomber Command could not expect results like these, and so performed area bombing, applying to Germany what nuclear arms specialists today have come to call "anti-city" strategy. In addition to H.E. bombs, they used a great variety of incendiary devices, some packed with jellied products of horrifying efficiency. Air Chief Marshal Sir Arthur Harris, A.O.C. Bomber Command, did not limit his task to the simple destruction of the Third Reich's war potential, but aimed also at destroying the morale of the German people. In

in spite of the loss during the year of 1,261 four-engined planes and most of their crews, the growing strength of the 8th Air Force is shown in the following table:

	Groups	
	B-17 Flying Fortresses	B-24 Liberators
January 1	5	2
April 1	5	2
July 1	11	–
October 1	17	4
December 1	19	7

This shows that the number of four-engined bombers at the disposal of Major-General James H. Doolittle, who succeeded Eaker as 8th Air Force commander at the end of the year, increased over three and a half times in 12 months. The number of sorties made by these planes rose at an even faster, one could say spectacular, rate:

January	279
April	379
July	2,334
October	2,159
December	5,618

Flying Fortresses in action

Compared with the Consolidated B-24 Liberator, the American crews operating over Germany preferred the Boeing B-17 Flying Fortress, of which over 12,000 were finally made by a consortium of the original builders with Douglas and Lockheed-Vega. Weighing 24 tons loaded, this four-engined plane could reach a top speed of 325 mph and had a range of 2,000 miles. The B-17E had eleven .3- and .5-inch machine guns which the Americans believed gave it all-round fire-power. This optimism was proved false by experience. For example, on August 17, 1943 the 8th Air Force lost 60 out of the 376 Flying Fortresses sent on raids on the Schweinfurt ball-bearing factory and the Messerschmitt assembly plant at Regensburg. On October 14 a new attack on the first of these objectives cost another 60 planes out of the 291 which had taken off, and altogether the loss of aircraft on these raids over the month was running at the intolerably high level of 9.1 per cent. Under these conditions it can be imagined that questions were raised as to whether or not the methods advocated by General Arnold were failing for, if it was relatively easy to replace the planes, it was not the

this he was free to act. Returning to the matter after the event, he wrote that the Casablanca Conference released him from his last moral scruples. His hands from that time forward were free as far as the bombing war was concerned.

After this account of the basic methods used by the Anglo-American forces in their air offensive against Germany we must now consider briefly the material means which they used with varying success.

From January 1 to December 31, 1943,

△ △ *Bombing up a Handley-Page Hampden, Britain's best bomber, together with the Vickers Wellington, during the first two years of the war. The Hampden could carry a worthwhile load a considerable range, but had a completely inadequate defensive armament. The type was phased out of service with Bomber Command by September 1942, but continued as a minelayer and torpedo bomber with Coastal Command until 1944.*

△ *In the cockpit of an R.A.F. bomber.*

▷ *The bomb-aimer's position in the nose of a Short Stirling. (page 584) Armstrong-Whitworth Whitley, another of Britain's standard bombers early in the war.*

▷ ▷ *Two Stirling bombers. Britain's first war-time four-engined heavy bomber, the type entered service in 1940. Note the long under-carriage legs, to give the wings the right angle of attack at take-off.*

▷ ▽ *Avro Manchester (right), the unsuccessful two-engined precursor of the Lancaster. Note the Wellington in the background.*

same thing for the crews and, after the second attack on Schweinfurt some loss of morale was noticeable among their ranks. This can be illustrated by one anecdote quoted by Werner Girbig in his *1000 Tage über Deutschland*. There was a manufacturer's advertisement in a magazine which, occupying a complete page, showed an Army Air Force machine gunner, his eye staring fiercely through the back-sight of his .5-inch gun, which he was aiming at a swarm of Focke-Wulf 190's. The caption read: "Who's afraid of the Big Bad Wolf?"

"An 8th Air Force pilot tore the page out, pinned it up on the blackboard in the Orderly Room and stuck on it a long strip of paper on which he wrote in red ink 'WE ARE'. Every officer, including the Station Commander, added his signature. Then the whole lot was sent back, without comment, to the manufacturer."

By the autumn of 1943 the Luftwaffe had won a major victory over the 8th Air Force. On deep penetration raids the German day fighters were shooting the U.S.A.A.F. out of the sky. It was during the period leading up to the bombing run that the Luftwaffe struck hardest. The German fighter commanders had discovered the American practice of formation bombing by order of the bombardier in the lead

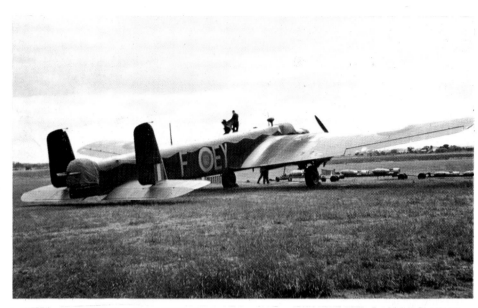

plane. Thus the lead groups in large formations suffered mercilessly from fighter attacks, as was the case on the "second" Schweinfurt raid when the lead formation was virtually wiped-out. On one notorious raid against the Ploeşti oil refineries in Rumania, the casualty rate was nearly a third of all planes involved.

Deep penetration raids had to be abandoned, with the clear result that the 8th Air Force's losses fell by more than half: in November they were 3.9 per cent, in December 3.4 per cent.

But in the early months of 1944 increasing numbers of long range Mustang P-51 fighters enabled the U.S. Air Force to renew its deep penetration bombing—and decimate the German fighter force.

The British offensive

Bomber Command continued its area-bombing offensive against Germany's cities during 1943. Improved equipment was now making possible greatly improved standards of navigational and bombing accuracy.

But Kesselring, throwing in everything he could lay hands on, sent units of the 90th *Panzergrenadier,* the 305th, and the 26th Panzer Divisions to stop them. He also sent the 29th *Panzergrenadier* Division against the American II Corps, which had advanced through Formia and Itri and by May 22 was threatening Terracina. This was trying to pay Paul by robbing Peter, that is to say Colonel-General von Mackensen. Reinforced to the equivalent of eight divisions by the transfer of the American 36th Division to the Anzio bridgehead, the American VI Corps had no particular difficulty in breaking the resistance of the German 14th Army during the day of May 23. Forty-eight hours later II and VI Corps met on the shores of Lake Fogliano. On the same May 23 the French Expeditionary Corps was spreading out over the Monti Ausoni whilst the Canadian I Corps (Lieutenant-General E. L. M. Burns: 1st Infantry and 5th Armoured Divisions), which had just relieved the British XIII Corps, was forcing its way through the Pontecorvo defile.

Kesselring attempts to cover Rome

Kesselring tried once more to protect Rome by establishing a new position on the line Colli Laziali–Monti Lepini to secure Vietinghoff's right, and to achieve this he withdrew from the Leghorn area his last reserve motorised division, the "Hermann Göring" Panzer Division, and sent it immediately to Valmontone. The bombing by the Anglo-American air force, which on one single day (May 26) destroyed 665 vehicles of the 14th Army alone, considerably held up these troop movements. Now Valmontone was, in accordance with General Alexander's instructions, precisely the objective of the American VI Corps. If Truscott, now in Cisterna, therefore advanced with the main body of his forces along the Corti–Artena axis, he had every chance of cutting off the 10th Army's move to cover Rome. The latter's rearguard was still at Ceprano, some 40 miles or more from Valmontone, and the Germans would thus be driven back against the Abruzzi mountains, which were virtually impassable, and entirely cut off.

But, for reasons which Alexander said were inexplicable, Clark ordered VI Corps to attack with its 34th, 45th Infantry, and 1st Armoured Divisions north west to the line Velletri–Colli Laziali, sending only a slightly reinforced 3rd Division along the Valmontone axis (northwards). This decision, taken in the afternoon of May 25, brought only a slight reaction from Alexander, who remarked to General Gruenther, the American 5th Army chief-of-staff, when the latter brought him the news: "I am sure that the army commander will continue to push toward Valmontone, won't he?"

"Rome the great prize" was the title General Mark Clark gave to the 15th chapter of his memoirs. We are thus forced to conclude that this able but impetuous man had lost sight of the fact that a commander's supreme reward is to receive in his tent those who have been sent on behalf of the enemy commander to sue for conditions of surrender. But Alexander was also taken in by the Roman mirage at this time: did he not forbid the French Expeditionary Corps, then coming down from the Monti Lepini,

◁ △ *Homeless Italians, victims of the war, abandon their home in the battlezone.*
◁ ▽ *Italian refugees pass through the Allied lines on their way to the safety of the rear areas.*
◁ *A village destroyed in the Allied advance from Cassino.*
▽ *Mark Clark (left) enters the suburbs of Rome.*

to use the Frosinone–Rome highway, which he intended to restrict to the British 8th Army?

Oddly enough, back in London, Churchill tried to put Alexander on his guard against the attractions of this prestige objective. On May 28 he wrote to him: "at this distance it seems much more important to cut their line of retreat than anything else. I am sure you will have carefully considered moving more armour by the Appian Way up to the northernmost spearhead directed against the Valmontone-Frosinone road. A cop is much more important than Rome which would anyhow come as its consequence. The cop is the one thing that matters." Two days later he came back to the point: "But I should feel myself wanting in comradeship if I did not let you know that the glory of this battle, already great, will be measured, not by the capture of Rome or the juncture with the bridgehead, but by the number of German divisions cut off. I am sure you will have revolved all this in your mind, and perhaps you have already acted in this way. Nevertheless I feel I ought to tell you that it is the cop that counts."

Rome declared an "open city"

▷▷ *American troops in the Piazza Venezia.*
▷▷▽ *A 5th Army patrol in Rome.*
▷ *A happy group of Italians watches flour supplies for the bakeries of Rome being unloaded. Within a few days of Rome's capture, the Allies were feeding about 500,000 of the city's population.*
▽ *Men of the Italian Co-Belligerent Forces, newly supplied with British equipment, parade through Rome.*

These were words of wisdom indeed, but in Italy the die was cast in the shape of the objective given to the American VI Corps. On May 31 its 36th Division found a gap in the German 14th Army defences, turned the Velletri position and scaled the Colli Laziali. Furious at this setback, Kesselring recalled Mackensen and replaced him with General Lemelsen. He now had to order the evacuation of Rome, which he proclaimed an "open city". On June 4 the American 88th Division (Major-General J. E. Sloan) was the first unit to enter the Eternal City.

General Clark tells a story worthy of inclusion in any history of the campaign. Writing of his first visit to Rome he says:

"Many Romans seemed to be on the

verge of hysteria in their enthusiasm for the American troops. The Americans were enthusiastic too, and kept looking for ancient landmarks that they had read about in their history books. It was on that day that a doughboy made the classic remark of the Italian campaign when he took a long look at the ruins of the old Colosseum, whistled softly, and said, 'Geez, I didn't know our bombers had done *that* much damage in Rome!'"

German and Allied losses

On May 11 Kesselring had 23 divisions. These had been reduced to remnants. The 44th, 71st, 94th, 362nd, and 715th had been virtually wiped out. His Panzer and *Panzergrenadier* divisions had lost most of their equipment. Amongst the reinforcements which Hitler had sent

through the Brenner there were badly trained divisions such as the 162nd, recruited from Turkman contingents, the Luftwaffe 20th Infantry Division, and the 16th *Panzergrenadier* Division of the *Waffen* S.S. These went to pieces at the first onslaught.

During the same period the Americans lost 18,000 killed, missing, and wounded, the British 10,500, the French 7,260, the Canadians 3,742, and the Poles 3,700. Some 25,000 Allied prisoners were taken.

Churchill's hopes of a new offensive

These losses were not enough to hold up the 15th Army Group's advance. Also, in North Africa the 9th Colonial Infantry Division and the 1st and 5th French Armoured Divisions were now ready for combat. It is clear that a bold

▽ *Mark Clark talks to a priest outside St. Peter's on his arrival in the city on June 4.*

action along the Rome–Terni–Ancona axis could have brought to an end all enemy resistance south of the Apennines.

Churchill wrote to Alexander on May 31: "I will support you in obtaining the first priority in everything you need to achieve this glorious victory. I am sure the American Chiefs-of-Staff would now feel this was a bad moment to pull out of the battle or in any way weaken its force for the sake of other operations of an amphibious character, which may very soon take their place in the van of our ideas."

In other words the Prime Minister was flattering himself that he could get General Marshall to abandon Operation "Anvil" and exploit the victories of the 15th Army Group across the Apennines.

On June 7, three days after the fall of Rome, Alexander reported that not even the Alps could daunt his army. He struck a chord in Churchill's mind for the Prime Minister now saw a chance of reaching Yugoslavia or even Vienna (across the

▽ *A tank brigade of the U.S. 5th Army lined up and ready to strike.*

△ *Lieutenant Rex Metcalfe of Flint, Michigan, inspects his men before setting off to do guard duty.*

iterranean theatre now that "Overlord" had taken place, and all effort had to be concentrated.

Marshall, it would appear, was merely obeying the dictates of high strategy. It was clear to him, in effect, that an Anglo-American drive towards Vienna, and out of line with the main thrust, would contribute less to the success of Operation "Overlord" than would a landing in Provence, which would open up the ports of Marseilles and Toulon to Allied men and *matériel,* whilst a strong Franco-American force, operating first up the Rhône, then the Saône, would give a right wing to Eisenhower when he broke out into Champagne. To him this reasoning respected the principle of the convergence of effort, so dear to American military doctrine. It can easily be seen how Marshall froze at Churchill's passionate arguments.

In any case, it is highly doubtful on military grounds whether an advance to the Alps or into Yugoslavia in 1944 was practicable, even if Alexander's armies had not been weakened for the sake of "Dragoon". The German commanders had proved themselves masters of defensive warfare in mountain regions, and they were to continue giving the Allies immense problems even when operating with minimal resources and under pressure from all sides.

Kesselring re-establishes himself in the Apennines

Although Roosevelt could not accept his colleague's views, he was nevertheless unable to bring nearer by even a single day because of questions of transport, men, and *matériel,* the start of Operation "Anvil" scheduled for August 15. Between June 11 and July 22, three American and five French divisions successively dropped out and became inactive, though the 9th Colonial Division did take Elba between July 17 and 19 in Operation "Brassard", led by General de Lattre de Tassigny. This Allied inactivity allowed Kesselring, who lost no chances, to re-establish himself in the Apennines and especially to give Field-Marshal von Rundstedt his 3rd and 15th *Panzergrenadier* Divisions, whilst the "Hermann Göring" Panzer Division was sent off to the Eastern Front.

so-called Ljubljana gap) before the Russians, whose political ambitions he was beginning to fear. Additionally Churchill had always favoured an invasion of German-occupied Europe from the Mediterranean.

The agreed strategy is confirmed

However, not even the British Chiefs-of-Staff believed that an advance to the Alps and beyond that year was practical, while President Roosevelt and the American Chiefs-of-Staff remained adamant that Operation "Dragoon" (formerly "Anvil"), the landing in the south of France, must, as formally agreed, now take precedence over any other operations in the Med-

CHAPTER 62

ROMMEL'S ACHIEVEMENT

On D-Day, Rundstedt, as Commander-in-Chief in the West, had the following under his command: two army groups ("B" and "G"), comprising four armies (7th, 15th, 1st, and 19th). These in turn had 15 corps between them, totalling 40 infantry, four parachute, four Luftwaffe field, nine Panzer, and one *Panzergrenadier* divisions.

However, for all this it is by no means true that Rundstedt exercised over this force the authority normally given to a commander-in-chief. In the first place, the Luftwaffe units (one corps, eight divisions) were only under his tactical command; the same was true of his four *Waffen*-S.S. divisions and the I S.S. Panzer Corps. He had no authority over these units in the questions of training, promotions, the appointment of commanders or in the field of discipline. That is what Hitler cruelly reminded Rommel, who had requested that action be taken against the 2nd *"Das Reich"* Panzer Division of the *Waffen*-S.S., after the appalling massacre at Oradour-sur-Glâne.

Even more, O.B.W. had had it made quite clear that it could not, without the Führer's permission, move two of its best armoured divisions, the 12th *"Hitler-jugend"* *Waffen*-S.S. Panzer Division, stationed near Lisieux, and the 130th Panzer-*"Lehr"* Division, formed the previous winter from Panzer instructors and now stationed around Châteaudun. Moreover, O.K.W. did not cease interfering in Rundstedt's sphere of command, as the latter explained bitterly to the British officers who questioned him after his capture:

"I did not have my way. As Commander-in-Chief in the West my only authority was to change the guards in front of my gate."

Hitler incapable of rapid decisions

As will be seen later, everything confirms the truth of this account. Therefore it appears that Hitler did not appreciate the complete incompatibility between despotic, arrogant, and meddling authority, and the need to make rapid decisions, the vital importance of which he soon came to recognise.

A major part of the success of the landings can be explained by the inefficiency of the German Intelligence services. Here the Nazis Kaltenbrunner and Schellenberg, who had ousted the professionals Canaris and Oster, could neither get a clear idea of the British and American plans nor escape being deceived by the Allies' diversionary manoeuvres. Therefore hypotheses were the order of the day

△ *Rommel* (left) *confers on the siting of a new battery with German Navy officers. Army/Navy co-operation on such matters was less than smooth.*

▽ *A German flak crew goes through its gun drill during preparations for the Anglo-American invasion.*

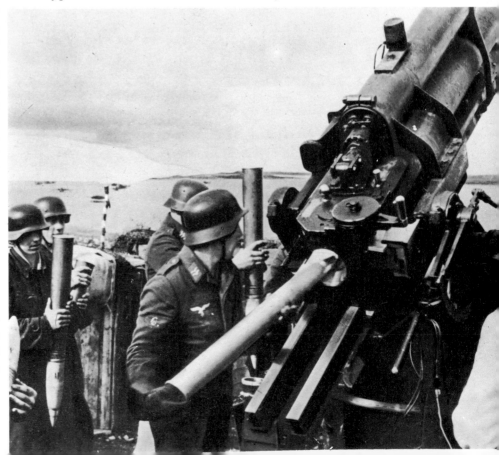

▽ *Wheeling a "Belgian Gate" into position on the foreshore – a massive construction of angle-iron designed to disembowel landing-craft. There were other unpleasant surprises, too – but never enough of them to satisfy Rommel.*
▷▽ *Like an outsize concrete bolster – a tank trap doubling as a parapet for the infantry behind.*

at O.K.W. as well as Saint-Germain-en-Laye, headquarters of Western Command (O.B.W.) and la Roche-Guyon, headquarters of Army Group "B".

Hitler had given a long analysis on the situation on March 20. Though he recognised that there was no way of being sure in which area the Allies would land, over the whole coastline from Norway to Greece, he nevertheless made his point:

"At no place along our long front is a landing impossible, except perhaps where the coast is broken by cliffs. The most suitable and hence the most threatened areas are the two west coast peninsulas, Cherbourg and Brest, which are very tempting and offer the best possibilities for the formation of a bridgehead, which would then be enlarged systematically by the use of air forces and heavy weapons of all kinds."

This hypothesis was perfectly logical and the order of battle of the German 7th Army (Colonel-General Dollmann), was correctly arranged to face this possibility. Of its 14 divisions, 12 were deployed between the Rivers Vire and Loire.

Rundstedt did not share Hitler's opinion, and considered that there were a great many more advantages from the Allied point of view for them to cross the Channel and land in the Pas-de-Calais. Later, in 1945, he supported his views by using these arguments, according to Milton Shulman:

"In the first place an attack from Dover against Calais would be using the shortest sea route to the Continent. Secondly, the V-1 and V-2 sites were located in this area. Thirdly this was the shortest route to the Ruhr and the heart of industrial Germany, and once a successful landing had been made it would take only four days to reach the Rhine. Fourthly, such an operation would sever the forces in Northern France from those along the Mediterranean coast. Against the Pas-de-Calais being chosen was the fact that this area had the strongest coastal defences, and was the only part of the Atlantic Wall that even remotely lived up to its reputation. I always used to tell my staff that if I was Montgomery I would attack the Pas-de-Calais."

But this would have meant coming up against the strongest part of the Atlantic Wall, whose concrete-housed batteries on either side of Cape Gris-Nez kept the English coast between Ramsgate and Dungeness under the fire of their 14 11-, 12-, 15-, and 16-inch guns; also Colonel-General von Salmuth's 15th Army was well deployed in the area, with 18 divisions between Antwerp and Cabourg. These troops were of good quality, and so it would seem that at O.K.W. Field-Marshal Keitel and Generals Jodl and Warlimont expected a landing between the mouths of the Rivers Somme and Seine, outside the range of the heavy artillery mentioned above but still within the 15th Army's sector, under the overall command of Field-Marshal Rommel.

Problems for Coastal Defence

Rommel commanded Army Group "B", which included the 7th and 15th Armies and LXXXVIII Corps, with three divisions for the defence of Holland. His main worry was the weakness of the defences on the beaches of the bay of the Seine, where three divisions were thinly stretched between Cabourg (exclusive) and the port of Cherbourg. More important, this weakness was not compensated for by the density or heavy calibre of the coastal artillery. Actually, on the 125-mile front between Le Havre and Cape Barfleur, the Swedish coastal artillery expert Colonel Stjernfelt has identified only 18 batteries, 12 of which could not reach the Calvados beaches or did not fire at all on D-Day.

Another concern of Rommel's was what form he should give to this defensive battle for which he was responsible and which might begin any day. But on this question, his point of view was almost exactly the same as the Führer's, detailed previously.

In his opinion, a sea-borne landing differs from a ground attack essentially in that the latter has its maximum force on the first day of the offensive. It then decreases in momentum because of the losses that are suffered and logistic difficulties. This allows the defending army to put off its counter-attack. On the other hand, the enemy who comes from the sea will be weak at the moment of landing, but will become steadily stronger within his bridgehead, so that any delay at all in the counter-attack will reduce in like proportion its chance of success.

The Panzers were indubitably the best means of counter-attack, and so the sensible thing was to deploy them in such a manner that they could be hurled against the enemy wherever he might appear (Low Countries, Pas-de-Calais, Normandy, or Brittany) on the actual day of the landing. This is what Rommel explained in a letter to Jodl on April 23, 1944:

"If, in spite of the enemy's air superiority, we succeed in getting a large part of our mobile force into action in the threatened coast defence sectors in the first few hours, I am convinced that the enemy attack on the coast will collapse completely on its first day."

But he added: "My only real anxiety concerns the mobile forces. Contrary to what was decided at the conference on the 21st March, they have so far not been placed under my command. Some of them are dispersed over a large area inland, which means they will arrive too late to play any part in the battle for the coast. With the heavy enemy air superiority we can expect, any large-scale movement of motorised forces to the coast will be exposed to air attacks of tremendous weight and long duration.

△ *Japan's military attaché, General Komatsu, chats with a Todt Organisation official on the Channel coast.*

But without rapid assistance from the armoured divisions and mobile units, our coast divisions will be hard put to it to counter attacks coming simultaneously from the sea and from airborne troops inland. Their land front is too thinly held for that. The dispositions of both combat and reserve forces should be such as to ensure that the minimum possible movement will be required to counter an attack at any of most likely points . . . and to ensure that the greater part of the enemy troops, sea and airborne, will be destroyed by our fire during their approach."

This led him to conclude: "The most decisive battle of the war, and the fate of the German people itself, is at stake. Failing a tight command in one single hand of all the forces available for defence, failing the early engagement of all our mobile forces in the battle for the coast, victory will be in grave doubt. If I am to wait until the enemy landing has actually taken place, before I can demand, through normal channels, the command and dispatch of the mobile forces, delays will be inevitable. This will mean that they will probably arrive too late to

▽ Simplicissimus *comments on Churchill and Roosevelt hesitating before taking the plunge in the "bath of blood".*

△ △ *Dollmann, commander of 7th Army in Normandy.*
△ *Geyr von Schweppenburg, of Panzergruppe "West".*
▽ *Bayerlein, commander of the Panzer-"Lehr" Division.*
▷ *Overleaf: Wehrmacht deployment in the West.*

intervene successfully in the battle for the coast and prevent the enemy landing. A second Nettuno, a highly undesirable situation for us, could result . . ."

The Generals in disagreement

And, in fact, after the conference of March 20, Rommel had received from the Führer the right to have *Panzergruppe* "West" put immediately under his direct command. This force, under General Geyr von Schweppenburg, constituted Rundstedt's armoured reserve and, on D-Day, consisted of:

1. I *Waffen* S.S. Panzer Corps;
2. 1st *"Leibstandarte Adolf Hitler"* S.S. Panzer Division (at Beverloo, 45 miles east of Antwerp);
3. 2nd Panzer Division (at Amiens);
4. 116th Panzer Division (in the Gisors–Beauvais region);
5. 12th *"Hitlerjugend"* S.S. Panzer Division (in the Evreux–Lisieux region);
6. 130th Panzer-*"Lehr"* Division (near Châteaudun); and
7. 21st Panzer Division (at Saint-Pierre-sur-Dives, 20 miles south-east of Caen).

But no order had come from O.K.W. to give executive force to Hitler's concession. And so Schweppenburg refused the rôle which Rommel allotted to him. His view was that the Western Front's armoured reserve should be concentrated in a central position downstream from Paris, so that it could intervene with all its strength in that sector where it looked as if the enemy was about to make his main push, after all tricks and feinting movements had been discounted. From this point of view, the way that Army Group "B" at la Roche-Guyon wanted to distribute the Panzers seemed to fit the verdict that Frederick the Great had proclaimed against all systems of wide-stretched defence: *"Wer alles defendieren will, defendiert gar nichts"* (He who tries to defend everything, defends nothing).

Rundstedt, and also Colonel-General Guderian, agreed with this point of view, which could clearly be defended on the principles of war. But were they applicable in those circumstances? Rommel denied that they were and cited as an example, as has been seen, his North African experience. His opponents had

not had this experience as they had all come from the Eastern Front, where the enemy's tactical air force was only just beginning to show its power to paralyse ground movement. Events showed that his reasoning was without doubt the more pertinent. However that may be and in spite of his attempt on April 23, Rommel received no satisfaction on this vital point. Better–or worse still–depending on one's point of view, the Führer was equally negative when Rommel suggested that he should advance the Panzer-*"Lehr"* Division to between the Orne and the Vire, deploy the *"Hitlerjugend"* Division in the region of Saint-Lô, and reinforce this sector, which seemed dangerously weak to Rommel, by a brigade of *Nebelwerfers* (976 15-, 21-, and 30-cm barrels) and a large number of heavy (8.8-cm) anti-aircraft batteries. Faced with silence from Hitler, Rommel left la Roche-Guyon at dawn on June 4 for Berchtesgaden, not without having consulted his barometer and obtained Rundstedt's leave.

Hitler's personality ensures failure

In spite of the documents published since 1945, Hitler's attitude when faced with the problems of the German high command remains incomprehensible, for it abounds in contradictions. The facts speak for themselves.

Though he did not believe the forecasts of his subordinates at O.K.W. and of Rundstedt, all of whom envisaged the British and the Americans approaching the French coast between Le Havre and the Pas-de-Calais, he accepted their forecast the day after the Allies landed in the bay of the Seine and stuck to it obstinately until a decisive hole was punched in the German line on the left bank of the Vire by the 1st American Army. In fact he was convinced, up to July 24, that the only purpose of the Battle of Normandy was to trick him into lowering his guard in the Pas-de-Calais. Here he too was deceived by the Allied cover plan, which continued to give the impression that there were powerful forces in south-east England about to attack directly across the Channel in the Pas-de-Calais.

However, though his hypothesis of March 20, concerning the first objec-

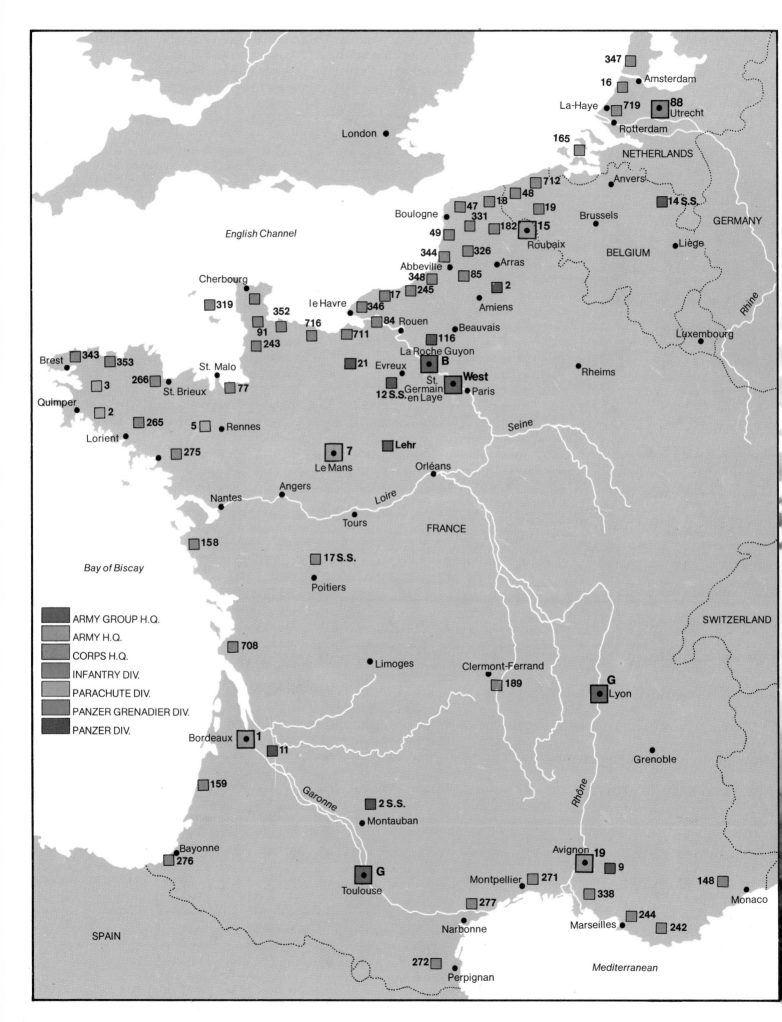

ARMY GROUP H.Q.
ARMY H.Q.
CORPS H.Q.
INFANTRY DIV.
PARACHUTE DIV.
PANZER GRENADIER DIV.
PANZER DIV.

tives of the Allied attack, only partially coincided with Rommel's views, in other respects there was perfect agreement between the two men concerning the way to repel it: an immediate counterattack on the beaches so as to avoid a long battle of attrition, like the one the armies had fought at Anzio–Nettuno.

But here there came a further contradiction. If, for perfectly valid reasons, the Führer rejected the plans of deployment put forward by Geyr von Schweppenburg, he nevertheless refused Rommel the means to fight the battle according to the plans on which he had been in entire agreement with him. Though it is a risky business to try to rewrite history, it will be noted that if Hitler had drawn all the conclusions from the principles he had enunciated, and had agreed with the suggestions of his distinguished general, the following would have happened:

1. Rommel would have been at his headquarters at la Roche-Guyon on June 6, and would have been alerted by British and American parachute drops, slightly after 0130 hours, while in the event he only knew of them five hours later while still at his private house in Herrlingen on the outskirts of Ulm.

2. The counter-attack launched in the afternoon of June 6 by just the 21st Panzer Division in only the British sector, could have been executed by the Panzer-"Lehr" Division and the 12th

The men of the Atlantic Wall:
△ Workers pressing on with the
uncompleted defences . . .
▷ . . . the soldier who would
have to defend them.

"Hitlerjugend" S.S. Panzer Division.
From the positions which Rommel
wanted them to occupy, they could
have simultaneously attacked the
bridgeheads that the Americans were
establishing. By reinforcing these two
with 400 or 450 tanks and assault
guns, the first would almost certainly
have wiped out "Omaha" Beach before
nightfall and the second was well-
placed to attack the poorly placed
parachute units around Saint-Mère-
Eglise.

True enough, if this had in fact
happened, the Panzer-"Lehr" would have
found itself under the fire of the Allied
naval forces, and the precedents of Gela
and Salerno showed how redoubtable and
efficient their heavy shells were against
tanks. This argument had been used by
Geyr von Schweppenburg during the
stormy arguments he had had with Rommel about the distribution of armoured
divisions. But though this was a real
danger, does it follow that they should
have abstained from any attack at all on
D-Day and that they should not have
taken advantage of the fleeting moment
when the enemy had not yet consolidated
his bridgeheads?

CHAPTER 63
ON THE BRINK

In the space available it is not possible to present a complete picture of the operations carried out by the British and American strategic air forces against the German industrial machine. The following is a summing-up of these operations and an analysis of the results achieved by June 1944.

On January 11, some 720 four-engined bombers of the 8th Air Force, forming a column of more than 200 miles long, shared between them the targets of Halberstadt, Brunswick, Magdeburg, and Aschersleben. During the battles in the Westphalian sky, no less than 59 American bombers were shot down. It would still have been a great success if 152 German aircraft had shared the same fate, as was announced by General Doolittle's headquarters. However, it was learnt after the war that the Luftwaffe's losses that day were no more than 40 aircraft.

United States airmen refer to the week of February 20 to February 26 as the "Big Week". For seven days the 8th and 15th Air Forces, relieved at night by R.A.F. Bomber Command, concentrated on the German aircraft industry. In a report to Stimson on February 27, 1945, General Arnold declared:

"The week of February 20-26, 1944 may well be classed by future historians as marking a decisive battle of history, one as decisive and of greater world importance than Gettysburg."

After calm appraisal, though, the historian cannot ratify this opinion, which puts the "Big Week" on the same level as July 3 and 4, 1863, days that saw Robert E. Lee and the cause of the Confederacy falling back finally before the superiority of the Union. Flying 3,000 sorties, the Americans suffered the loss of 244 bombers and 33 fighters while the R.A.F. lost 157 four-engined aircraft. The communiqué from London which announced, when the operations had finished, that 692 enemy aircraft had been shot down or destroyed on the ground, was very much mistaken in its figures. Nevertheless, thanks to the new Mustang long-range fighter escorts, American bomber losses were only 3·5% of aircraft despatched, while the rate of German fighter losses began to rise steeply. The heart of the Luftwaffe was

▽ *Destroying key German centres of communication behind the invasion sector was a vital part of the build-up phase. This is how Orléans marshalling-yard looked after massive Allied air attacks.*

being gradually torn out–inside the Reich itself.

However, in spite of the carpet of bombs which fell on the factories of Brunswick, Aschersleben, Bernburg, Leipzig, Augsburg, Regensburg, Stuttgart, Fürth, Gotha, Schweinfurt, Tutow, and Posen, German industry continued to build aircraft, by an elaborate process of decentralising production away from major cities. By August 1, 1944, the average monthly figure for the first seven months of the year had reached 3,650, of which 2,500 were day fighters, 250 night fighters, and 250 bombers. All the same, Göring had to defend the vital targets, and to do this he was forced to make painful decisions and to take aircraft away from the fighter squadrons behind the Atlantic Wall. Here it is true to say that the American attack on the German aircraft industry helped the Allied landings in France.

For 36 days and 55 nights, from January 1 to June 5, 1944, the great cities of the Reich suffered 102 serious attacks which devastated Berlin (17 raids), Brunswick (13 raids), Frankfurt (eight raids), Hanover (five raids), Magdeburg, Leipzig, Duisburg, and many others. In January, the 15th Air Force bombed Klagenfurt; on March 17, Vienna was raided for the first time. May 18 saw the port of Gdynia and the East Prussian city of Marienburg under attack. As can be seen, the whole of Germany was now vulnerable.

The right targets

Though General Spaatz's success in the battle against Germany's aircraft industry had only been partial, he unquestionably won a great victory in the attack he launched at the beginning of April 1944 against the Reich's sources of liquid, natural, and synthetic fuel.

On August 1, 1943, 179 B-24 Liberators of the American 9th Air Force had taken off from Benghazi and bombed the oil-wells and installations at Ploieşti. But the success of the raid had not been equal to its boldness, for the Americans had lost 53 aircraft, eight of which were interned in Turkey. On April 4, 1944, the 15th Air Force, based around Foggia, made a fresh start with 230 four-engined bombers and produced far better results. The bombers extended their raids to refineries in Bucharest, Giurgiu, Budapest, and

Eisenhower's Build up

General Eisenhower wrote to General Marshall on December 23, 1943: "In the early stages of Overlord I see no necessity for British and American Army Group Commanders. In fact, any such setup would be destructive of the essential co-ordination between Ground and Air Forces." Consequently, he entrusted Montgomery with the command of British and American land forces taking part in the landing itself and in later operations designed to consolidate and then extend the bridgeheads.

The initial C.O.S.S.A.C. project, which envisaged a relatively narrow front for landing, was changed after reservations expressed by Eisenhower and Montgomery so as to take in a wider front, including "Utah" Beach on the right and "Sword" Beach on the left. Montgomery's plan was to secure a good footing in Normandy and then to threaten a break out on the eastern flank, in the Caen sector, so as to attract enemy reserves to that area. The real break out would then occur on the Western flank.

Vienna, to the Danube ports and the convoys of barges going up the river, and this managed to reduce the amount of oil that Germany was drawing from Rumania by 80 per cent. From 200,000 tons in February 1944, the amount had fallen to 40,000 in June.

But the most important aspect was the plan approved on April 19 by General Eisenhower, by which the 8th Air Force and Bomber Command began a systematic attack on the German synthetic fuel industry. On May 12, 935 American bombers dropped a hail of high-explosive and incendiary bombs on plant at Leuna,

△ *B-24 Liberators unload.*
▷ *A direct hit on the viaduct at Poix. A train can be seen steaming on to the viaduct at the bottom of the picture, but subsequent air reconnaissance did not establish whether its brakes were good enough.*
▽ *Another smashed station.*

Böhlen, Zeitz, Lützkendorf, and Brüx. On May 28 and May 29, the well-defended American four-engined bombers returned to the targets and completely laid waste the great coal hydrogenation plants of Politz in Pomerania. In their struggle against the German war sinews, the 8th Army Air Force had found the right target. This was seen clearly by General Spaatz, though perhaps not by others, when on June 8 he sent a directive to the 8th and 15th Air Forces ordering them to concentrate on Germany's fuel production centres. Bomber Command also joined this offensive.

In a memorandum to the Führer on June 30, Speer, the German Minister of War Production, wrote:

"If we cannot manage to protect our hydrogenation factories and our refineries by all possible means, it will be impossible to get them back into working order from the state they are in now. If that happens, then by September we shall no longer be capable of covering the Wehrmacht's most urgent needs. In other words, from then on there will be a gap which will be impossible to fill and which will bring in its train inevitable tragic consequences."

Albert Speer, whose organisational gifts are recognised by all, did not exaggerate matters in Hitler's style. This is clearly evident from the following table, the figures for which are taken from the book which Wolfgang Birkenfeld wrote in 1964 on the history of the manufacture of synthetic fuel during the Third Reich.

Aviation fuel (in thousands of tons)			
	Pro-grammed	Produced	Con-sumed
January	165	159	122
February	165	164	135
March	169	181	156
April	172	175	164
May	184	156	195
June	198	52	182
July	207	35	136
August	213	17	115
September	221	10	60
October	228	20	53
November	230	49	53
December	223	26	44

Similar conclusions could be reached from the figures for ordinary petrol and diesel fuel. It is calculated that a Panzer division, according to its 1944 establishment, consumed in battle some 55,000 gallons of fuel a day. Towards the end of summer 1944, the aircraft and tanks of the Third Reich were running on almost empty fuel tanks.

Occupied areas to be bombed?

Sir Trafford Leigh-Mallory's air forces had the mission of preparing for the landings and creating conditions which would permit the British and American armies fighting in Normandy to win the great air and ground battle over the Reich which, it was expected, would lead to final victory.

Even so, all General Eisenhower's energy and power of argument was required to get the green light from Churchill for the bombing planned, for the Prime Minister hated the idea of bombing the peoples whom Operation "Overlord" was to free from the German yoke.

German communications

While attacks on the V-1 launching sites and on German industry continued, the bulk of the Allied effort, including Bomber Command whose aircraft could now bomb more accurately, and with heavier loads than American bombers, was to be devoted to destroying enemy communications in France, to inhibit the free movement of German troops after the landings.

Bombing objectives in Western Europe

1. To halt the movement of reserves

The systematic attack on communications was aimed at preventing O.K.W. and Army Group "B" reserves from reaching the battlefields. But at the same time it was at all costs essential to avoid revealing, by the choice of targets, the primary objectives of Operation "Overlord".

Bearing in mind these two contradictory requirements, which had to be satisfied at the same time, the Allied squadrons began by dropping two curtains of bombs, one along the Seine between Rouen and Paris and the other following the line of the Albert Canal from Antwerp to Liège, finishing at Namur. Within these lines, about 20 principal railway junctions were completely wiped out. As the Allies did not wish to inflict this treatment on Paris, they restricted themselves to destroying the marshalling yards of its outer suburban area: Trappes, Juvisy, and Villeneuve Saint Georges. In this way the Allies counted on preventing the German 15th Army from intervening on the left bank of the Seine and at the same time convincing German high command that the probable landing-zone was the Pas-de-Calais far from the planned attack on Normandy.

2. To cut lines of communication

Even so, Rundstedt had to be prevented from reinforcing the Normandy battlefields with the eight divisions he had in Brittany, or from Army Group "G" (Colonel-General Blaskowitz), which had 15, including three Panzer, divisions between Nantes and Hendaye and between Perpignan and Menton. This was the reason for the hail of bombs which fell at intervals on Rennes, Nantes, Le Mans, Angers, and the most important towns of the Loire valley, while the bombing of Lyons, Saint Etienne, Avignon, Marseilles, and Toulon made Hitler think an attack on the Côte d'Azur was being prepared. Finally, in Lorraine, Alsace, and Champagne, the lines along which O.K.W. might route its reserves to reinforce the Western Front were also cut.

On May 4, the bridge at Gaillon collapsed under the very eyes of Rommel, who had just completed an inspection at Riva Bella. Mantes bridge had also been

△ A stick of "heavies" makes for its target.

▽ A German housewife, clutching hastily-snatched belongings, runs from her burning home.

△ *The spectre that hung over "Fortress Europe" – Boeing B-17's in mass formation.*
▷ *Bitter German propaganda stressing the inevitable by-product of strategic bombing: civilian deaths and maimings.*

destroyed on the same day, leaving no other passable bridges over the Seine below Paris. On the same day the Loire bridges downstream from Blois had met the same fate.

This campaign against the railway communications of Western Europe met with absolute success, particularly because from May 1 onward the British and American tactical air forces harried locomotives, both on the track and in the repair sheds. So intense and accurate was this offensive that by June 6, railway traffic had fallen to half its January 1943 level in the rest of France and to only 13 per cent in the area north of the Loire. Catastrophic consequences for German strategy followed. Here the example often given is that of the *Waffen*-S.S. II Panzer Corps, which had been lent to Model to re-establish the line in Eastern Galicia. When the invasion was reported, the corps was entrained at L'vov and took five days to reach Nancy. After here, the railways were in such a state that the corps had to be detrained and sent to the Normandy front by road. At a time when every hour was vital, this brought it into battle four days later than calculated.

Another result of the bombing had not been foreseen by S.H.A.E.F. Because of the destruction and the absolute priority given to military transport, iron ore ceased to flow into the Saar factories, while the coal stocks at the pit-heads mounted up.

3. To destroy coastal radar and guns
Another success for British and American air forces was the action they took against the radar network set up by the Germans between Cape Gris-Nez and Cape Barfleur. Also the attack on the coastal batteries placed or in course of emplacement between Le Havre and Cherbourg brought about the destruction of a certain number of large-calibre guns or caused the Germans to move them back inland, with the result that they took no part in repelling the landings. In any case, there had been so much delay in building the concrete shelters intended to house them that they were not usable.

Sperrle's air force in France had been defeated in the air or wiped out on the ground and was almost destroyed. And so, as they instructed raw recruits moving up to the front, the old soldiers of the Wehrmacht would say: "If you see a white plane, it's an American; if it's black, it's the R.A.F. If you don't see any planes, it's the Luftwaffe."

CHAPTER 64
ASSAULT AND LODGEMENT

△ *The Allied press celebrates the long-awaited event.*

Cornelius Ryan, in his book *The Longest Day,* emphasises the importance of the H-hour decision when he described the historic scene:

"Eisenhower now polled his commanders one by one. General Smith thought that the attack should go in on the sixth – it was a gamble, but one that should be taken. Tedder and Leigh-Mallory were both fearful that even the predicted cloud cover would prove too much for the air forces to operate effectively . . . Montgomery stuck to the decision that he had made the night before when the June 5 D-Day had been postponed. 'I would say Go,' he said.

"It was now up to Ike. The moment had come when only he could make the decision. There was a long silence as Eisenhower weighed all the possibilities. General Smith, watching, was struck by the 'isolation and loneliness' of the Supreme Commander as he sat, hands clasped before him, looking down at the table. The minutes ticked by; some say two minutes passed, others as many as five. Then Eisenhower, his face strained,

looked up and announced his decision. Slowly he said, 'I am quite positive we must give the order . . . I don't like it, but there it is . . . I don't see how we can do anything else,' Eisenhower stood up. He looked tired, but some of the tension had left his face."

When one reviews the first 24 hours of Operation "Overlord", the rôle of the Resistance must first be mentioned. It was in fact vital. This opinion is based on the evidence of the Allied and German combatants, and the works on the Resistance by Colonel Rémy, Pierre Nord, and George Martelli should also be carefully considered. No military operation was ever based on such comprehensive Intelligence as "Overlord". Evidence for this is offered by the remarks of the operations officer of the 12th *"Hitlerjugend"* S.S. Panzer Division when he examined a map which had been found on June 8 in the wreck of a Canadian tank. "We were astounded at the accuracy with which all the German fortifications were marked in; even the weapons, right down to the light machine guns and mortars, were listed. And we were disgusted that our own Intelligence had not been able to stop this sort of spying. We found out, later on, that a Frenchman had been arrested who admitted that he had spied for years in the Orne sector, appearing every day in his greengrocer's van on the coastal road. We could clearly see on this map the result of his activities, and that of other spies also."

These were the results obtained by the networks organised by Colonel Rémy from 1942 onwards. Admittedly there were some slight errors and omissions in their summaries: these were inevitable. The English would probably not have embarked on the dangerous airborne attack on the Merville battery if they had known that instead of the 4-inch guns it was thought to have had, it had four 3-inch guns which were not powerful enough to affect the landing of the British 3rd Division at Riva-Bella. Similarly, the Rangers would not have scaled Pointe de Hoe had they known that its casemates were without the six long range guns they were reported to have.

General Bradley moreover did not know that Rommel had advanced five battalions from the 352nd Division to support the regiment on the left wing of the 716th Division. The two carrier-pigeons bringing news of this considerable reinforcement of the enemy's defences had been shot down in flight. However, the Allies' otherwise excellent information concerning the German army's plans was gained at the expense of considerable personal sacrifice and much loss of life.

Weather conditions against the Allies

It is well known that weather conditions played an important part in the way that the Germans were taken by surprise at dawn on June 6. They had a paralysing effect. Rommel's opinion, that the landing would only take place when dawn and high tide coincided, was also mistaken. His naval commander, Vice-Admiral Ruge, noted in his diary on June 4: "Rain and a very strong west wind". Moreover, before leaving la Roche-Guyon via Herrlingen for Berchtesgaden, Rommel noted in the Army Group "B" diary at 0600 hours on the same day that "he had no doubts about leaving as the tides would be very unfavourable for a landing in his absence,

and air reconnaissance gave no reason to think that a landing could possibly be imminent." At the same time, on the other side of the Channel, Eisenhower had just postponed "Overlord". On the next day, owing to the temporary spell of good weather forecast by Group-Captain Stagg, Eisenhower decided to cross on June 6, while the German weathermen at O.B.W. still maintained that a landing was out of the question.

Up to now the weather conditions had favoured the Allies. After midnight on June 5, the weather turned against them;

Growth of the French Resistance

De Gaulle became the figurehead and inspiration of the French Resistance. Until the end of 1941 the main contribution of the French Resistance was not acts of sabotage but the steady flow of sketched intelligence matter. After the outbreak of the Russo-German war on June 22, 1941, the Resistance movement in Occupied France burgeoned. By October 1940 the Belgian resistance had been organised into three zones and nine provinces, grouped in regions and sub-regions. Escape routes, or "chains" were set up by the Resistance movements, with links extending to the Pyrenees, so that British servicemen could be passed through to safety. The "Comet" Chain, set up by Andree de Jongh, alone helped thousands of British and American airmen to safety.

although the wind had fallen a little, as Group-Captain Stagg had predicted, it was blowing strongly enough to scatter widely the paratroopers of the 82nd and 101st American Airborne Divisions, who had dropped over the Cotentin peninsula, and the British 6th Airborne Division which had dropped between the Orne and the Dives.

A few hours later, the bomber attack failed for the same reason to neutralise the "Omaha" Beach defences. In the same sector, disaster met the amphibious tank formation which was to support the left wing of the American 1st Division: of the 32 tanks which were launched into the water 6,000 yards from the shore, 27 sank like stones with most of their crews; the canvas flotation skirt supported by a tubular framework gave the tanks only about 3 feet free-board – but the sea was running with a swell of more than 3 feet. The Americans who landed between Vierville and Saint Laurent were therefore put to a gruelling test.

One other apparently accidental factor this time favoured the attackers. On the evening of June 5 Lieutenant-Colonel Hellmuth Meyer, chief Intelligence officer of the German 15th Army, interrupted Colonel-General von Salmuth's game of bridge and told him that the B.B.C. had just broadcast a special message for the French resistance networks:

"Blessent mon coeur
D'une langueur
Monotone"

(a quotation from Verlaine's poem *Chanson d'automne*).

The *Abwehr* had found out, though it is not yet known how, that the code message meant that the landing would take place within 48 hours after midnight of the day of the message.

When he received this news, the commander of the 15th Army not only alerted his staff without delay, but also transmitted this vital information to his superiors at Army Group "B", O.B.W., and O.K.W. At la Roche-Guyon Lieutenant-General Speidel, who was deputising in Rommel's absence, did not think of urging the 7th Army at Le Mans to prepare for action, and at St. Germain-en-Laye no one checked that he had done so.

In his book, *Invasion – They're Coming*, Paul Carell comments:

"Here is the well-nigh incredible story of why, nevertheless, they were caught unawares." Can we do better than the author of *Invasion – They're Coming*? Field-Marshal von Rundstedt can be exonerated, since he had just signed an Intelligence report for the German High Command. The following excerpts are taken from Cornelius Ryan's book:

"The systematic and distinct increase

△ Men and vehicles of the U.S. 1st Army land on the coast of Normandy. The Americans, putting their amphibious tanks into the water further out than the British, suffered fairly heavy losses when the swell proved too much for the D.D. tanks and sank all but five at Omaha.

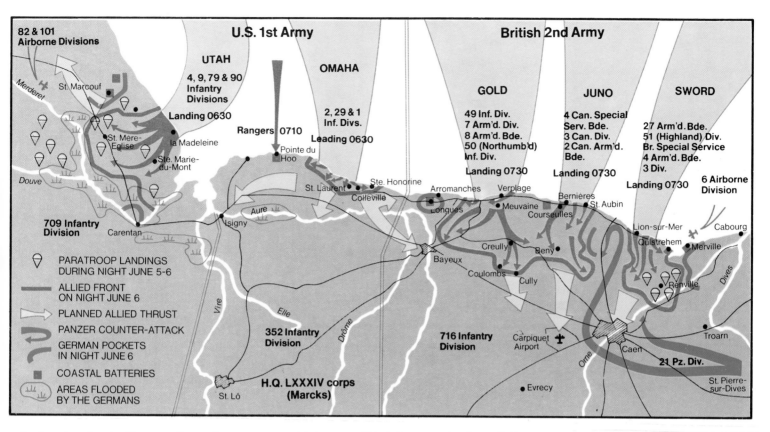

82 & 101 Airborne Divisions

U.S. 1st Army

British 2nd Army

UTAH
4, 9, 79 & 90 Infantry Divisions
Landing 0630

OMAHA
2, 29 & 1 Inf. Divs.
Leading 0630

Rangers 0710

GOLD
49 Inf. Div.
7 Arm'd. Div.
8 Arm'd. Bde.
50 (Northumb'd)
Inf. Div.
Landing 0730

JUNO
4 Can. Special
Serv. Bde.
3 Can. Div.
2 Can. Arm'd.
Bde.
Landing 0730

SWORD
27 Arm'd. Bde.
51 (Highland) Div.
Br. Special Service
4 Arm'd. Bde.
3 Div.
Landing 0730

6 Airborne Division

709 Infantry Division

PARATROOP LANDINGS
DURING NIGHT JUNE 5-6

ALLIED FRONT
ON NIGHT JUNE 6

PLANNED ALLIED THRUST

PANZER COUNTER-ATTACK

GERMAN POCKETS
IN NIGHT JUNE 6

COASTAL BATTERIES

AREAS FLOODED
BY THE GERMANS

352 Infantry Division

716 Infantry Division

H.Q. LXXXIV corps (Marcks)

21 Pz. Div.

Carpiquet Airport

(Map labels: Merderet, St. Marcouf, St. Mère-Eglise, la Madeleine, Ste. Marie-du-Mont, Douve, Carentan, Isigny, Aure, Vire, Elle, Drôme, St. Lô, Pointe du Hoo, St. Laurent, Colleville, Ste. Honorine, Arromanches, Verplage, Longues, Bayeux, Creully, Coulombs, Cully, Beny, Meuvaine, Courseulles, Bernières, St. Aubin, Lion-sur-Mer, Ouistrehem, Merville, Renville, Caen, Orne, Evrecy, Troarn, Dives, St. Pierre-sur-Dives, Cabourg)

of air attacks indicates that the enemy has reached a high degree of readiness. The probable invasion front remains the sector from the Scheldt (in Holland) to Normandy . . . and it is not impossible that the north front of Brittany might be included . . . it is still not clear where the enemy will invade within this total area. Concentrated air attacks on the coast defences between Dunkirk and Dieppe may mean that the main Allied invasion effort will be made there . . . (but) imminence of invasion is not recognisable.''

After accepting the report's rather vague conclusions (it was called *The Allies' Probable Intentions),* Rundstedt, it can be assumed, considered that the 15th Army's alert position, with its right on the Escaut and its left at Cabourg, was ready for any emergency.

One may also assume that Speidel, the chief-of-staff of Army Group ''B'', was still influenced by Rommel, who had said definitely the day before that the Allies could not possibly make the big attempt in his absence. Moreover, there is no doubt that too frequent alerts would have harmed the troops' morale and prejudiced their training, as well as interrupting the fortification work in which they were engaged.

Admittedly, if the 7th Army and LXXXIV Corps had been alerted at about 2300 hours on July 5, the *coup* attempted by a glider detachment of the British 6th Airborne Division and the U.S. 82nd Airborne Division's attack on Sainte Mère-Eglise would almost certainly have failed.

Allied air supremacy all important

Admiral Sir Bertram Ramsay, the commander of the naval Operation ''Fortune'' supporting ''Overlord'', is said to have likened the invasion army to a shell fired by the navy, but Montgomery asserted that only air supremacy would ensure naval supremacy.

On June 6, 1944, the Anglo-American forces conformed to the two conditions laid down by the two British war leaders. In the air General Eisenhower, faced with 419 Luftwaffe planes, had more than 10,500 fighting planes at his disposal:

    3,467 four-engined bombers
    1,645 twin-engined bombers
    5,409 fighter bombers and interceptor fighters

Therefore he was in a position to use 2,355 transport planes and 867 gliders carrying about 27,000 troops and their *matériel* including light tanks, with no risk of attack by German fighters, though there was still the threat of anti-aircraft defences.

△ In this German poster, issued for the benefit of occupied France, Death smokes a pipe while calmly awaiting the Allied invasion. In the event, it was the German armies that were to suffer crippling losses as a result of D-Day.
△△ Operation ''Overlord'' June 6, 1944. The map shows details of the long-awaited Allied landings.

△ Part of the vast Allied invasion force wallows in the Channel off Normandy, unhindered by the weather and virtually undisturbed by the Luftwaffe.

▽ Men of the 3rd Canadian Division disembark at Courselles, on "Juno" Beach.

The Allied invasion fleet

At sea, the embarkation fleet from British ports consisted of 4,126 transport vessels, including converted liners acting as floating headquarters to the major units being landed, and the LCT(R) support craft firing salvoes of 792 5-inch rockets which saturated an area of 750 by 160 yards. This fleet included 1,173 large and small ships transporting armoured vehicles, which shows how important it was for the infantry attacking the Atlantic Wall to have support from tanks and their guns. The fleet for the initial assault consisted (it is reliably reported) of 1,213 ships of all sizes flying seven different flags; three-quarters of them flew the Royal Navy's White Ensign. They included:

- 7 battleships (3 American)
- 2 monitors
- 23 cruisers (3 American, 2 French, 1 Polish)
- 80 destroyers (34 American, 2 Polish, 2 Norwegian)
- 25 torpedo-boats (1 French, 2 Polish, 1 Norwegian)
- 63 corvettes (3 French, 2 Norwegian, 2 Greek)
- 2 Dutch gunboats
- 98 minesweepers (9 American)

Of this fleet, all the warships, monitors and gunboats, 18 cruisers and about 50 destroyers had been assigned fire targets of the German batteries between Villerville (opposite Le Havre) and the Barfleur cape: these batteries were therefore engaged by 52 12-inch, 14-inch, and 15-

inch guns and more than 500 medium calibre guns whose fire was all the more effective as it was controlled from the air by Spitfire fighters especially detailed for this purpose.

This huge fleet of 5,339 ships was in the Channel on Sunday June 4 when it received the signal that the assault was deferred from the following day to June 6; a part of the fleet spent the day cruising in the area. But the bad weather which caused the postponement also kept the Luftwaffe patrols grounded; otherwise they would have spotted and reported this unusual concentration of ships. On the evening of June 5 the fleet assembled south of the Isle of Wight and made for its objectives in ten columns.

Admiral Lemonnier, who was on the bridge of the *Montcalm*, described the night crossing: "Spotted the buoy at the entrance to the channel which we must follow for four hours behind a flotilla of minesweepers.

"Now we are only doing 6 knots. The sweepers aren't moving. Possibly they've found some mines and the rough sea is hampering them in their work.

"We have to stop continually. We can only move forward in fits, as we have to take care to stay in our narrow channel. This isn't the time to be put stupidly out of action by a mine.

"We feel as though we are in one of those endless rows of cars blocked outside a big city on a Sunday evening, moving forward by pressing the accelerator slightly, then putting the brake on, touching the rear light of the car ahead – with one difference, that here there is not the slightest light to mark the stern of the ship ahead. Luckily there is just enough light to make out the outlines of the *Georges Leygues* and to keep a look-out."

Ramsay's objectives

Admiral Ramsay had divided his forces into two:
1. Under the American Rear-Admiral A. G. Kirk, the Western Naval Task Force was to land and support the American V and VII Corps on the "Utah" and "Omaha" Beaches on both sides of the Vire estuary. All ships flying the Stars and Stripes, including the *Nevada*, a survivor from Pearl Harbor, had appropriately been assigned to him.
2. Under Rear-Admiral Sir Philip Vian,

Threadbare Fortress

While General Eisenhower had absolute control over land and sea forces in his theatre of operations, the O.B.W., Field-Marshal von Rundstedt, was not entitled to give orders to Admiral Krancke, who commanded German naval forces in the West, or to Field-Marshal Sperrle, head of Luftflotte III, or to General Pickert, who commanded III Anti-Aircraft Corps. The subsequent lack of coordination in the German forces was to have serious consequences during the Normandy invasion.

◁ First to land were the airborne troops. Seen here are men of the British 6th Airborne Division, which was to land on and hold the left flank of the 2nd Army's sector until the conventional ground forces reached them.

the Eastern Naval Task Force was to perform identical services for the British I and XXX Corps which were to come ashore between Ver-Plage and Ouistreham on the beaches called (from west to east), "Gold", "Juno", and "Sword".

When reviewing the Allied air and naval forces, the power and quality of the support they gave the land forces in the hard fighting against the defenders of the Atlantic Wall must be emphasised. For example, two of the three Czechoslovak 8-inch guns comprising the Saint Marcouf battery had been destroyed; similarly the four 6-inch guns of the Longues battery, near Port-en-Bessin, were silenced by the fire of the cruisers *Ajax, Montcalm,* and *Georges Leygues*. In addition, Allied air forces over the battle sector had been increased and they responded rapidly, accurately and efficiently to all requests from the ground forces. From dawn to dusk they had made over 4,600 sorties, while only about 50 planes reminded both sides of the Luftwaffe's existence.

The Germans guarding the coast on the night of June 5-6 were frequently caught off their guard, and several comic incidents were reported. Paul Carell gives an example:

"Hoffman stepped outside the bunker. He gave a start. Six giant birds were making straight for his battle head-quarters. They were clearly visible, for

△ Safe landing for a British Horsa glider beside a tree-lined road.

the moon had just broken through the clouds. 'They're bailing out.' For an instant Hoffman thought the aircraft had been damaged and its crew was going to jump. But then he understood. This was an airborne landing by para-troops. The white mushrooms were floating down–straight at his bunker.

"'Alarm! Enemy parachutists!' The men at 3rd Battalion head-quarters had never pulled on their trousers so fast before.

"Besides reports of parachute landings, radar stations began to signal huge concentrations of aircraft.

"But both in Paris and in Rastenburg the news was received sceptically. 'What, in this weather?' Even the chief-of-staff C.-in-C. West scoffed: 'Maybe a flock of seagulls?'"

At the end of the first day, Eisenhower and Montgomery were in a position to make the following estimate of their gains and losses:

On the whole, the landing had been successful, but the Americans and the British had nowhere gained their prescribed objectives for the evening of D-Day. North of the Vire the American 82nd and 101st Airborne Divisions, under Major-Generals M. B. Ridgway and M. D. Taylor respectively, which were due to protect VII Corps' right (Lieutenant-General J. L. Collins) and give it access to the right bank of the Merderet, had scattered in small pockets in the night; in addition they lost many men and much

had been completely and devastatingly effective.

"In Ste. Mère-Eglise, as the stunned townspeople watched from behind their shuttered windows, paratroops of the 82nd's 505th Regiment slipped cautiously through the empty streets. The church bell was silent now. On the steeple Private John Steele's empty parachute hung limp . . .

"Passing round the back of the church, P. F. C. William Tucker reached the square and set up his machine-gun behind a tree. Then as he looked out on the moonlit square he saw a parachute and, lying next to him, a dead German. On the far side were the crumpled, sprawled shapes of other bodies. As Tucker sat there in the semi-darkness trying to figure out what happened, he began to feel that

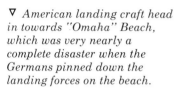

▽ *American landing craft head in towards "Omaha" Beach, which was very nearly a complete disaster when the Germans pinned down the landing forces on the beach.*

matériel in the shallow floods and mine-fields laid by the Germans. In short, of the 17,262 fighting men of the two divisions who jumped or landed on "the longest day", 2,499, or nearly 15 per cent, were missing.

Nevertheless a regiment from the 82nd Airborne Division had occupied the small town of Sainte Mère-Eglise (because of the panic flight of a service unit of German A.A. defences), maintained its ground, and in the evening had made contact with the American 4th Division which had landed on "Utah" Beach. This unit under Major-General Barton had had a relatively easy task, as the air and naval bombardment on the support points of the German 709th Division (Lieutenant-General von Schlieben) barring its way

he was not alone—that somebody was standing behind him. Grabbing the cumbersome machine-gun, he whirled around. His eyes came level with a pair of boots slowly swaying back and forth. Tucker hastily stepped back. A dead paratrooper was hanging in the tree looking down at him.

"Then (Lt.-Colonel) Krause pulled an American flag from his pocket. It was old and worn—the same flag that the 505th had raised over Naples . . . He walked to the townhall, and on the flagpole by the side of the door, ran up the colours. There was no ceremony. In the square of the dead paratroopers the fighting was over. The Stars and Stripes flew over the first town to be liberated by the Americans in France."

Power of the Allied offensive

Paul Carell, who conducted a careful survey among the German survivors of this campaign, describes the destruction of the defence-works W.5 surrounding the beach near the small village of la Madeleine.

"All the fortifications they had laboriously dug and built through the weeks had been churned up like a children's sand-pit. The 75-millimetre anti-tank gun was a heap of twisted metal. The 88-millimetre gun had taken some bad knocks. Two ammunition bunkers had blown up. The machine-gun nests had

been buried by avalanches of sand.

"Immediately the infernal concert started – rockets. They were firing only at the two corner bunkers with their 50-millimetre armoured carrier-cannon. The rockets slammed against the bunkers. They smacked through the apertures. The left bunker blew up at once, evidently a direct hit, through the aperture, among the stored shells. The bunker on the right was enveloped in smoke and flames. When the attack was over both bunkers and guns were only rubble and scrap metal. The crews had been killed or severely wounded."

A plane appeared and disappeared. "But evidently it delivered its message. The heavy naval bombardment began. Continuous, uninterrupted hell. Blow upon

blow the huge shells crashed into the strongpoint. Trenches were levelled. Barbed wire was torn to shreds. Minefields were blown up. Bunkers were drowned in the loose sand of the dunes. The stone building with the telephone exchange crumbled. The fire-control posts of the flame-throwers received a direct hit."

It is not therefore surprising that the losses of the American 4th Division amounted only to 197 killed, wounded, and missing on June 6. At midnight the whole division had landed (with the exception of one battery), a total of 21,328 men, 1,742 vehicles, and 1,950 tons of *matériel*, munitions, and fuel.

When it landed at "Omaha", the American 1st Division (Major-General C. R. Huebner) had been given the main road N.

△ △ *Commandos press inland from the beach area. Note the bridging tank in the background.*
△ *The beach area. Only by the most careful planning and training were the schedules so vital for success ensured, and the chaos that could so easily have jeopardised the whole operation avoided.*

13, which runs from Caen to Cherbourg, as its objective for the day. This required an advance of three miles from the Vierville beach. It was also to extend its right as far as Isigny and its left as far as the western approach to Bayeux, where it was to make contact with the inner flank of the British 2nd Army. For this purpose Major-General L. T. Gerow, commander of V Corps, had reinforced his corps with a combined regiment drawn from the 29th Division. At nightfall the 1st Division had not got beyond the small villages of Saint Laurent and Colleville.

In addition the air bombardment had missed its target, the majority of the D.D. tanks had sunk before they reached the beaches, and the 1st Division had come up against the newly-arrived, elite 352nd Division. Although U.S. Command knew of this development they had failed to inform their combat troops. At about 1000 hours General Bradley, the commander of the American 1st Army, had sent ashore his chief-of-staff and received a discouraging report from him:

"The 1st Division lay pinned down behind the sea wall while the enemy swept the beaches with small-arms fire. Artillery chased the landing craft where they milled offshore. Much of the difficulty had been caused by the underwater obstructions. Not only had the demolition teams suffered paralysing casualties, but much of their equipment had been swept away. Only six paths had been blown in that barricade before the tide halted their operations. Unable to break through the obstacles that blocked their assigned beaches, craft turned toward Easy Red where the gaps had been blown. Then as successive waves ran in toward the cluttered beach-head they soon found themselves snarled in a jam off-shore."

The crisis passes on Omaha beach

Admiral Kirk, however, had no intention of letting his colleagues on land bleed to death; he bunched together his destroyers on the coast, and they fired at the maximum rate on all the German fire-points that showed themselves. At the same time, the German 352nd Division battery positions began running out of shells, and as the Allies' cruisers and their tactical air forces attacked all the crossroads, the Germans were not able to supply their artillery with fresh ammunition. At about 1300 hours, the crisis was over and the infantrymen, after the sappers had blown up the anti-tank dike surrounding the beach, infiltrated the German position through the narrow gullies running up the cliff.

During the night of June 6-7, the remainder of the 29th Division (Major-General C. H. Gerhardt) was landed. But V Corps' losses had been heavy: 3,881 killed, wounded, and missing.

▽ *The invasion fleet, as seen from one of the most powerful of the escorts and support ships, the battleship* Warspite.
▽ ▽ *American troops inspect the results of gunfire support: an 11-inch gun casemate comprehensively destroyed by heavy shells.*

New breaches in Atlantic Wall

The British 2nd Army (General Miles C. Dempsey) had been assigned Bayeux, Caen, and Troarn (9 miles east of Caen) as its D-Day objectives. It was also ordered to extend its reconnaissance to Villers-Bocage and Evrecy, that is along approximately 18 miles of the Calvados coast. This ambitious programme was not fulfilled.

The British 6th Airborne Division (Major-General Richard N. Gale) was to protect the flanks of the operation. It was ordered:

1. To capture intact the bridges across the Orne and its canal between Bénouville and Ranville;
2. To destroy the Merville battery;
3. To destroy the Dives bridges between Troarn and the coast.

Although the wind prevented the paratroopers from landing accurately on their targets, the division completed these three missions brilliantly. At 0030 hours the British sappers and infantry had jumped from five gliders and captured the Bénouville bridges, clearing them of mines. At about 0400 hours Lieutenant-Colonel Otway had only collected 150 paratroopers from his battalion which was practically without *matériel*, and

the gliders which were due to land on the superstructure of the defence works had failed to appear. Nevertheless, he had captured the Merville battery in a fierce fight in which he lost 70 dead and wounded, whilst the garrison of 130 men was left with only 22 survivors. The Dives mission was also completely successful. "All around the battery", according to Georges Blond, "the grass was strewn with corpses, British and German mixed together. Several attackers who had already gone into the defence works ran back:

" 'The guns aren't 6-inch, sir, they're 3-inch.'

" 'Fine,' said Otway, 'Blow them up.'

"The British had lost 5 officers and 65 N.C.O.'s and men, killed and wounded in the attack. It was now nearly dawn. Otway saw one of his officers apparently searching for something in his battle-dress blouse:

" 'What are you doing?'

" 'I'm sending a message to England, sir.'

"The communications officer pulled a pigeon with closed wings from his breast, turning its little head from side to side. It had taken part in the attack too. When it was released, it rose unhesitatingly into the whitening sky."

At dawn, Rear-Admiral Vian's naval forces opened fire on the German defences, and up to nightfall discharged 500 15-inch shells, 3,500 6-inch shells, and 1,380 small calibre missiles. They made

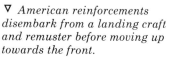

▽ *American reinforcements disembark from a landing craft and remuster before moving up towards the front.*

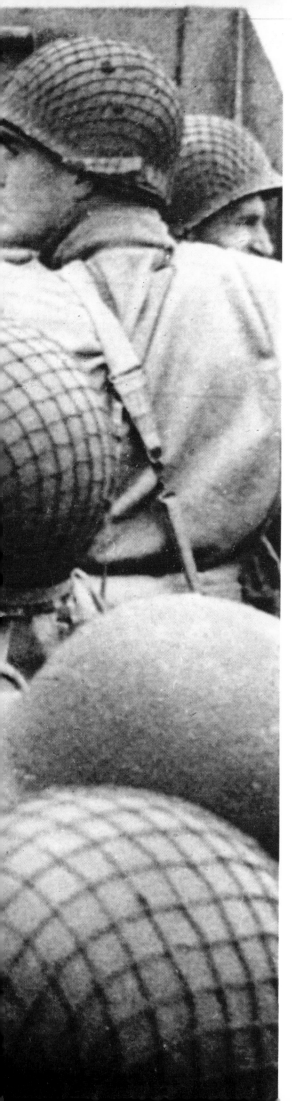

wide breaches in the Atlantic Wall. Two further circumstances favoured the British landing. First, the amphibious tanks were lowered into the water much closer to the shore than at "Omaha", and were sometimes landed directly on the beaches. Secondly, large numbers of the special vehicles designed by Major-General Sir Percy Hobart, commander of the 79th Armoured Division, were used in the first waves of the infantry attack.

In addition to the Crabs, or flail tanks, which cleared the ground of the mines obstructing their tracks and had been used since El Alamein, the British 2nd Army also brought its Crocodiles and its A.V.R.E.s into the line: the Crocodiles were flame-thrower tanks which cast a 360-foot jet of burning oil beyond the range of the enemy's rocket-launchers; these tanks had trailers filled with about 400 gallons of fuel and could sustain prolonged actions; the A.V.R.E.s were mortar tanks carrying a 9-inch mortar on a Churchill tank chassis, and intended for work against armoured strongpoints.

On the other hand, against the British I and XXX Corps (commanded respectively by Lieutenant-Generals J. T. Crocker and G. T. Bucknall) the German 716th Division (Lieutenant-General W. Richter) only had four battalions and their quality

◁ U.S. infantry await the moment of truth.
△ Rudimentary mechanisation: British infantry bring their bicycles ashore.

was inferior to that of the Allies.

In these conditions, the 50th Division (Major-General D. A. H. Graham), the advance-guard of XXX Corps, proceeded from "Gold" Beach without much difficulty. By the end of the day it had some armour at the approaches of Bayeux and had moved forward about six miles.

In I Corps, the 3rd Canadian Division (Major-General R. F. L. Keller) had a more difficult landing because the Calvados reefs presented a natural obstacle; nevertheless it had advanced eight miles from Bernières ("Juno" Beach) and was near its objective, the Carpiquet airfield. On the other hand the armoured column which it had launched towards Evrecy was driven back with losses above Bretteville-l'Orgueilleuse. The result was that between its left at Saint Aubin-sur-Mer

The Germans resisted the invasion with great tenacity, but the sheer size of the landing forces alone was almost too much for them. Except where terrain made the Allies' task particularly difficult, all that the Germans could do was to try to contain the invasion. It was a hard, an impossible task.

▽ *Outside Sainte Mère-Eglise.*

and the right of the 50th Division, towards Arromanches, the Atlantic Wall had been breached over a front of 12 miles.

Landing at "Sword" Beach in the Riva-Bella area, the British 3rd Division (Major-General G. T. Rennie) had managed to join with the 6th Airborne Division over the Bénouville bridge. In the evening it had advanced to Biéville three miles north of Caen and repelled a counter-attack from the 21st Panzer Division. With its right close up against Lion-sur-Mer it was four or five miles from the Canadian 3rd Division.

D-Day casualties

The British 2nd Army had a total of less than 3,000 killed, wounded, and missing on D-Day.

Allied naval and air losses were insignificant: 114 planes, mainly brought down by A.A. fire; some landing craft and two destroyers—one of these, the *Corry* (U.S. Navy) blew up on a mine in the "Utah" Beach waters; the other, the Norwegian *Svenner*, succumbed to an attack on the Eastern Naval Task Force by three German destroyers from Le Havre commanded by Lieutenant-Commander Hoffmann.

Hitler holds back reinforcements

At 0111 hours (German time) General Erich Marcks, commander of LXXXIV Corps, was at his H.Q. in Saint Lô celebrating his 53rd birthday when he heard from the 716th Division that the paratroopers were coming down between the Orne and the Dives and that the bridges of these two rivers were apparently their objectives. Twenty minutes later the 709th Division signalled the landing of American paratroopers on both sides of the Merderet in the Sainte Mère-Eglise area. Quite correctly, Marcks decided that this was the invasion. He therefore alerted the troops on the coast and informed the 7th Army H.Q. at Le Mans.

The 7th Army quickly transmitted the information to la Roche-Guyon and Saint Germain. Although he hesitated when he received LXXXIV Corps' appreciation, supported by the 7th Army,

Rundstedt alerted the Panzer-*"Lehr"* Division and the 12th *"Hitlerjugend"* Panzer Division and contacted O.K.W., but Hitler forbade him to move them till further orders, which would be given him as soon as the situation was clear.

There was no further news till 0630 hours, when information was received that the Calvados coast defences were being subjected to intensive naval bombardment. At that time, however, the Führer, who had gone to bed as usual two

hours earlier, was fast asleep, thanks to Dr. Morell's pills, and no one dared to have him woken. When they finally plucked up the courage, Hitler's reaction was fairly dramatic:

"He was in a dressing-gown when he came out of his bedroom. He listened calmly to the report of his aides and then sent for O.K.W.'s chief, Field-Marshal Wilhelm Keitel, and Jodl. By the time they arrived Hitler was dressed and waiting – and excited.

△ *A Sherman Crab anti-mine flail tank moves up. The correct and widespread use of such specialised armour played a very significant part in the Allies' success.*

▽ *A British Sherman Duplex Drive tank advances towards a Horsa glider. Note the folded flotation screen on top of the hull.*

"The conference that followed was, as Pultkamer recalls, 'extremely agitated'. Information was scanty, but on the basis of what was known Hitler was convinced that this was not the main invasion, and he kept repeating that over and over again. The conference lasted only a few minutes and ended abruptly, as Jodl was later to remember, when Hitler suddenly thundered at him and Keitel, 'Well, is it or isn't it the invasion?'"

Therefore it was only at 1432 that Army Group "B" received the authority, which it had sought for 12 hours, to order the 12th S.S. Panzer Division to support the 7th Army, and at 1507 hours to move the *Waffen*-S.S. I Panzer Corps and the Panzer-*"Lehr"* Division.

But after so much delay, Colonel-General Dollmann now showed excessive haste. Lieutenant-General Bayerlein, commander of the Panzer-*"Lehr"* Division, after leaving his unit to obtain instructions from 7th Army H.Q., was ordered to move towards Caen at 1700 hours. Without success the former chief-of-staff of the *Afrika Korps* (who had had much experience of British air tactics) attempted to persuade Dollmann how foolish it was to set out on the French roads before nightfall. Nevertheless Dollmann kept to his decision, thinking he would thus be able to bring the Panzer-*"Lehr"* Division into action south of Caen at dawn on the following day, June 7. But the first bombs began falling before Bayerlein and his staff had passed Beaumont-sur-Sarthe, south of Alençon.

"For once we were lucky. But the columns were getting farther and farther apart all the time. Since the Army had ordered a radio silence we had to maintain contact by dispatch riders. As if radio silence could have stopped the fighter-bombers and reconnaissance planes from spotting us! All it did was prevent the divisional staff from forming a picture of the state of the advance—if it was moving smoothly or whether there were hold-ups and losses. I was for ever sending off officers or else seeking out units myself.

"We were moving along all five routes of advance. Naturally our move had been spotted by enemy air-reconnaissance. And before long the bombers were hovering above the roads, smashing crossroads, villages, and towns along our line of advance, and pouncing on the long columns of vehicles. At 2300 we drove through Sées. The place was lit up by

△ A Panther tank. Despite the Allies' considerable numerical superiority in matériel, *the Panther was a tank still very much to be feared.*
◁ Another of Germany's best weapons, the dreaded Nebelwerfer.
▽ One of Britain's specialised armoured vehicles, the Churchill Assault Vehicle Royal Engineers (A.V.R.E.), fitted with a spigot mortar to fire a 40-lb "dustbin" demolition charge up to 230 yards.

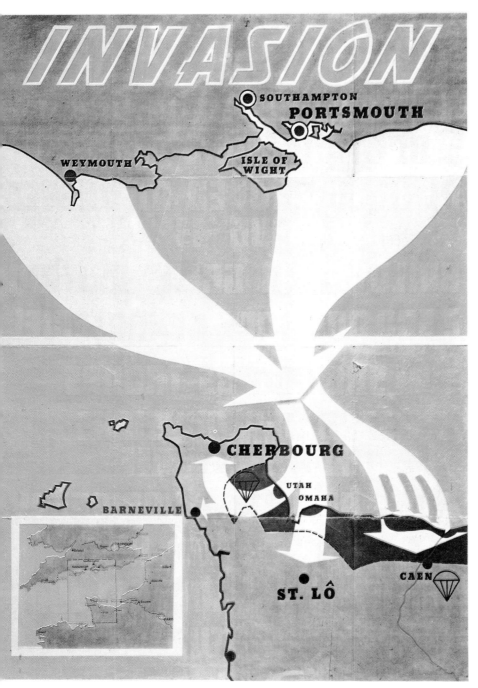

INVASION

SOUTHAMPTON
PORTSMOUTH

WEYMOUTH

ISLE OF
WIGHT

CHERBOURG

UTAH
OMAHA

BARNEVILLE

CAEN

ST. LÔ

△ *A simplified view of the mounting and primary objectives of Operation "Overlord".*

flares hanging above it like candles on a Christmas-tree, and heavy bombs were crashing down on the houses which were already burning. But we managed to get through."

In the Saint Pierre-sur-Dives region, the 21st Panzer Division (Major-General Feuchtinger) was in a rather different situation: it was Army Group "B"'s reserve, but its commander was authorised to put his infantry into action to support the 716th Division if there was a landing; however, he was not allowed to engage his armour. In accordance with these orders Feuchtinger launched one of his grenadier regiments on the right bank of the Orne to engage the British paratroopers and as he received no orders

from la Roche-Guyon, he sent his armoured regiment to follow them. At 0700 hours, he was informed that he was subordinate to the 7th Army; two hours later that he would now take his orders from LXXXIV Corps.

But now General Marcks was becoming more aware of the danger from the sea; for this reason, at 1000 hours, he ordered his new subordinate to abandon the action his armoured regiment was about to take against the enemy paratroopers, and to send it over the Orne to give support to the 716th Division units barring the approach to Caen from the British. This move was completed at 1430 hours and the Germans counter-attacked at 1700 hours. At nightfall the 21st Panzer Division had managed to reach Luc-sur-Mer with its infantry, but its armoured regiment had been engaged by the British 3rd Division and had suffered heavy losses. Moreover it had nearly run out of petrol. Therefore Feuchtinger, who had 146 tanks and 51 assault guns when the engagement commenced, retreated on orders, abandoning the wrecks of 40 tracked vehicles.

The German position

At 1300 hours, a report from LXXXIV Corps to the 7th Army gave an accurate description of the fluctuations of this merciless struggle: "In the Caen area, in the British sector, the enemy is successful. East of the American sector, the landing is more or less repulsed at Vierville. Our counter-attack is in progress in the Sainte Mère-Eglise district; the 8th Regiment of the American 4th Division (Colonel van Fleet) is pinned down there. Where is our air support? Enemy aircraft prevent us from moving or supplying our troops by day."

At midnight, an entry in the 7th Army's signals diary showed the worsening situation in the afternoon in the Caen sector:

"2400 hours. 716 Infantry Division is still defending itself at strongpoints. Communications between division, regimental and battalion headquarters, however, no longer exist, so that nothing is known as to the number of strong-points still holding out or of those liquidated . . . The Chief-of-Staff of Seventh Army gives the order that the counter attack of June 7 must reach the coast without fail, since the strong-point defenders expect it of us."

CHAPTER 65
THE PANZERS ATTACK

The Battle of Normandy started very unpromisingly for the Wehrmacht. Nevertheless the Allies took a little more than six weeks to break out of the Avranches bottleneck, although according to plans they should have done so on D+20, June 27; they required another three weeks to complete the defeat of Army Group "B". This delay was due to two different factors:

1. The Normandy *bocage* (mixed woodland and pastureland), where the defenders were undoubtedly favoured by their natural surroundings. The countryside between Troarn and Bayeux, the British 2nd Army sector, was certainly suitable for use by armoured formations, but it assisted the German tanks and anti-tank devices even more; the range of their guns was greater than the Allies'. Moreover in the Norman *bocage* between Bayeux and the western Cotentin coast, the U.S. 1st Army sector, there were fields surrounded by tall, thick hedges with sunken roads between them, very suitable for ambushes, whether by the *Chouans* at the time of the French Revolution, or by the German grenadiers, who spotted enemy tanks and discharged the almost invariably lethal shots from *Panzerfaust* or *Panzerschreck* launchers at very short range. The attackers' task was also complicated by the rivers Vire, Taute, Douve, and Merderet, marshy tracts, and the 7th Army's flooding operations. General Bradley wrote: "Not even

in Tunisia had we found more exasperating defensive terrain. Collins called it no less formidable than the jungles of Guadalcanal."

2. The inferior quality of their armour compared with the Germans' was another very serious handicap for the Allies. The journalist Alan Moorehead, who was a war correspondent at Montgomery's G.H.Q., stated quite frankly after the end of the war: "Our tanks were Shermans, Churchills and Cromwells. None of them was the equal of the German Mark V (the Panther), or the Mark VI (the Tiger) . . .

"The Germans had much thicker armour than we had. Their tanks were effective at a thousand yards or more: ours at ranges around five hundred yards . . . Our tanks were unequal to the job because they were not good enough. There may be various ways of dodging this plain truth, but anyone who wishes to do so will find himself arguing with the crews of more than three British armoured divisions which fought in France."

Admittedly Moorehead was a journalist, but General Bradley is recognised as one of the best brains in the American army. "Originally", he wrote, "the Sherman had come equipped with a 75-mm gun, an almost totally ineffective weapon against the heavy frontal plate of these German tanks. Only by swarming around the panzers to hit them on the flank,

▽ *The first German prisoners taken in Normandy wait in a P.O.W. cage on the beach for transportation to England.*

could our Shermans knock the enemy out. But too often the American tankers complained it cost them a tank or two, with crews, to get the enemy's panzers but only by expending more tanks than we cared to lose. Ordnance thereafter replaced the antedated 75 with a new 76-mm high-velocity gun. But even this new weapon often scuffed rather than penetrated the enemy's armour.

"Eisenhower was angry when he heard of these limitations of the new 76."

We shall not repeat him, as we know that the Pzkw V Panther had an armour thickness of $4\frac{1}{2}$ inches and the Pzkw VI Tiger $5\frac{1}{2}$ inches. The British got their best results when they re-armed their Shermans with the 17-pounder anti-tank guns which they had had since 1943. Firing an armour-piercing shell at an initial velocity of about 2,900 feet per second, it was certainly superior to the American version, but nevertheless it was markedly inferior to the Panther's 7.5-cm, which fired at 3,068 feet per second, and even more to the 8.8-cm of the Tiger II or the *Königstiger* with shells of 20- and 22-lb with a higher velocity, which at 500 yards could penetrate 112 and 182-mm of armour respectively. Even worse, the British and the Americans found that their Shermans were inclined to catch fire suddenly like bowls of flaming punch.

However, the Panzers' undeniable tech-

nical superiority was of little help to Rommel, as he was unable to supply them with the required fuel or to defend them against the continuous attacks of the Allied tactical air force, of which they were rightly a priority target.

The word *Jabo* (*Jagdbomber*: fighter-bomber) recurs in all the accounts left by the German combatants after the Normandy battle. In their attacks against enemy armour, the Allies preferred rockets, which were more accurate than bombs and more effective than the 20-mm or 40-mm shell. The R.A.F.'s Hawker Typhoon fighter carried eight 60-pounder rockets, whilst the Republic P-47 Thunderbolt had ten 5-inch anti-tank rockets.

In this ground-air battle, the rôle of the Allied engineers has perhaps not been sufficiently appreciated. They quickly cleared the rubble left in the Normandy towns and villages by the bombardments and restored communications as the troops moved forward. They also had better equipment, notably in machines of American manufacture, and in the Bailey bridge, which had prefabricated components and could be assembled in a great variety of combinations. By May 8 1945, 7,500 Bailey bridges had been built in the Western and Italian war theatres; they certainly contributed not only to the defeat of the Third Reich, but also to the

reconstruction of this part of the continent.

On June 7 and 8 successively the 12th *"Hitlerjugend"* S.S. Panzer Division and the Panzer-*"Lehr"* Division failed to drive the British back to the Channel. On June 7 the first of these major units (which under Major-General Witt included 177 tanks and 28 assault guns) should have counter-attacked in the direction of the Douvres operational base (six miles north

△ *Another weapon used in Normandy: a remote-controlled tank, about the size of a Bren gun carrier, designed to deliver a heavy explosive charge into the Allied lines.*

of Caen) with the 21st Panzer Division, which was immediately to its left. It managed to maul a Canadian armoured brigade in the Carpiquet region but when it reached its goal it was halted by massive artillery fire and turned to the left.

The following day the Panzer-*"Lehr"* Division came into the line on the left of the 12th S.S. Panzer Division, but between Sées and Tilly-sur-Seulles it had lost five tanks, 84 all-purpose transport vehicles, 90 cars and lorries, and 40 petrol tankers; these considerable losses caused no less concern to Lieutenant-General Bayerlein than the 12th S.S. Panzer Division's had to his colleague Witt. Moreover Vice-

▽ *Canadian troops move up in the Caen sector.*

Admiral Ruge noted in his personal diary at the la Roche-Guyon H.Q., to which Rommel had returned late in the afternoon on June 6: "The enemy's air superiority is having the effect the Field-Marshal had foreseen: our movements are extremely slow, supplies don't get through, any deployment is becoming impossible, the artillery can't move to its firing positions any more. Precisely the same thing is happening on land here as happened at sea in the Tunisian campaign."

On June 8, when the U.S. 1st Army and the British 2nd Army joined up at Bayeux, Rundstedt put Rommel in charge of *Panzergruppe* "West", which became responsible for the conduct of operations in the sector between the mouth of the Dives and the Tilly-sur-Seulles area, while the 7th Army from now on faced the Americans alone. General Geyr von Schweppenburg, when he assumed this heavy task, was assigned the mission of retaking Bayeux and he proposed that he should break through to the Channel with his three Panzer divisions. But as soon as he set up his headquarters in the Thury–Harcourt region, he was seriously wounded in an air attack which killed many of his staff. Sepp Dietrich took over and ordered his troops to stay on the defensive while they waited for better opportunities to attack.

Intervention of the heavy Panzers

In fact on June 12, with the intervention of the 2nd Panzer Division (Lieutenant-General von Lüttwitz) which had been brought up from the Amiens region, Dietrich managed to halt an assault by the British XXX Corps which had launched the 7th Armoured Division (Major-General G. W. Erskine) against its left wing and its rear. The celebrated Desert Rats got the worst of this chance encounter, which was fought for Villers-Bocage, not for lack of energy and courage but because they were let down by their *matériel*. Chester Wilmot proves this in his description of the episode:

"The troops had dismounted to stretch their legs while the tanks reconnoitred the way ahead, when the crack of a gun split the crisp morning air and the leading half-track burst into flames. Out of the woods to the north lumbered a Tiger tank, which drove on to the road and proceeded right down the line of half-tracks 'brewing up' one vehicle after another. Behind these there was some incidental armour – a dozen tanks belonging to Regimental H.Q., the artillery observers and a reconnaissance troop. The Tiger destroyed them in quick succession, scorning the fire of one Cromwell, which saw its 75-mm shells bounce off the sides of the German tank even at the range of a few yards! Within a matter of minutes the road was an inferno with 25 armoured vehicles blazing – all the victims of this one lone Tiger."

While we do not want to undervalue Captain Wittmann's exploit (he was the tank's commander) we must point out that the Cromwell was very inadequately armed with a 75-mm gun and also had totally inadequate armour protection; for this reason the Desert Rats' morale suffered seriously for several weeks.

The British 2nd Army's defeat was fully compensated for on the same day by the fall of Carentan, whose defenders succumbed to the concentric thrust of the American 29th Division and 101st Airborne Division. The 17th S.S. *Panzergrenadier* Division *"Götz von Berlichingen"* (Lieutenant-General Ostermann) was alerted on June 7 at its stations at Thouars but arrived too late to prevent General Bradley's V and VII Corps from joining up. When it crossed the Loire it received the same treatment from the fighter-bombers as the Panzer-*"Lehr"* Division. The Anglo-Americans now had a continuous front between the Dives and Saint Marcouf.

Allied reinforcements

During the first days of battle the Germans had already lost 10,000 prisoners and 150 tanks. Even more important, Montgomery and Eisenhower were as aware as Rommel and Rundstedt that, contrary to expectations, the defenders were not getting reinforcements as quickly as the attackers at this stage.

From June 7 to 12 the British and Americans put in their floating reserves, which had sailed on the same day as the first echelon; these consisted of five infantry and three airborne divisions. The American V Corps was joined by the 9th and 20th Divisions; the British XXX

△ Six days after D-Day and Churchill crosses the Channel to see for himself.

▽ Montgomery shows Churchill a map of the beach-head while General Dempsey of 2nd Army looks on.

Americans in Carentan, the first major town captured in their sector.

Corps by the 7th Armoured and the 49th Divisions; and the British I Corps by the 51st Highland Division, giving 15 divisions (eight American) out of a total of 37 stationed in the U.K.: 362,547 men, 54,186 vehicles, and about 102,000 tons of supplies landed in a week.

According to S.H.A.E.F.'s estimates, Montgomery was faced by 21 divisions on June 12. In fact, the defence was reinforced at the following rate:

June 6 21st Panzer Division
June 7 12th Panzer Division
June 8 Panzer-*"Lehr"* Division
June 9 353rd Panzer Division
June 11 17th S.S. *Panzergrenadier*
        Division
June 12 2nd Panzer and 3rd
        Parachute Divisions

Including the five divisions guarding the area between Cabourg and Mont Saint Michel on D-Day, *Panzergruppe* "West" and the German 7th Army had 12 divisions (including five armoured divisions) in the line; however, the 716th Division was only a cypher and the 352nd and 709th Divisions had been badly mauled. The Panzers went into the attack at random, always behind schedule, and under strength.

German communications disorganised

The air offensive against the French and Belgian railway networks broadly paid the dividends expected of it. This action continued, but from the night of June 5-6 it was made doubly successful by the intervention of the Resistance against the German communications in accordance with the "Green Plan" compiled by French Railways, while the "Tortoise Plan" drawn up by the French Post Office was carried out just as successfully against the occupying forces' telephone communications.

Pierre de Préval has listed 278 acts of sabotage carried out by the French Resistance from June 6 to September 15, 1944 in the department of Meurthe-et-Moselle, and the position was similar in the other departments. On the route from Montauban to the Normandy front, the *Waffen*-S.S. 2nd Panzer Division *"Das Reich"* (Lieutenant-General Lammerding) was harried by the Corrèze *maquis;* the terrible reprisals taken on the inhabitants of Tulle and Oradour by this division to avenge these ambushes remain unforgotten.

From now on the delay in building up the German defence on the invasion front is perfectly understandable, as the combined action of the Anglo-American forces and the French Resistance networks was effectively assisted by Hitler's personal interference in war operations.

Hitler's error

We have mentioned that when he was expecting the landing, the Führer had an intuition that Normandy might well be the invasion's objective. But he revised his view as soon as Eisenhower had launched Operation "Overlord". Plainly, he thought, he was faced with a diversionary manoeuvre aimed at making him lower his guard in the Pas-de-Calais. If he were to fall into the trap laid for him, the final thrust would be aimed at him in the sector he had unwisely uncovered... but he was not so stupid! Nevertheless on June 8 Major Hayn, LXXXIV Corps' chief Intelligence officer, was brought

△ On June 14 Charles de Gaulle crossed the Channel to tour the narrow strip of liberated France inside the beach-head. Here he gets an enthusiastic welcome from the people of Bayeux.
◁ A smile and a handshake from Montgomery.

◁◁ Two soldiers taking the opportunity of a much needed break.

△ *American Firefly tanks roll through a Normandy town.*
▷ *Looking south towards St. Lô –a deceptive vision of the Promised Land. Every hedgerow and ridge crossing the path of the Allied advance was a wasp's nest of German defences.*

a copy of U.S. VII Corps' battle orders which had been discovered on board a barge that had grounded near Isigny after its crew had been killed. This document, which was quite unnecessarily verbose, not only revealed General Collins's intentions, but also listed V Corps' and the British XXX Corps' objectives. The Americans' mission was to reach the Cotentin western coast as soon as possible, and then to change direction to the north and capture Cherbourg. Without delay this battle order was passed through the correct channels; 7th Army, Army Group "B", Supreme Command West, and O.K.W. Hitler, however, obstinately stuck to his opinion that this was a deceptive manoeuvre, and in support of his view he quoted the *Abwehr*'s summaries stating that just before the landing there were 60 or even 67 British and American divisions stationed in Britain. He never asked himself whether the real deception lay in simulating the existence of 30 divisions concentrated in Kent and ready to cross the English Channel at its narrowest point. At the front, on the other hand, where the Germans saw most of the Allied units they had previously met in Africa and Sicily (U.S. 1st and 9th Divisions, British 7th Armoured Division and 50th and 51st Divisions), they dismissed the idea of a second landing in the north of France. But nothing was done and Rommel was forbidden to use the 18 divisions of the 15th Army which, with the exception of the 346th and 711th Divisions, which were engaged on the right bank of the Orne, remained in reserve until after the breakthrough.

Rommel's plan abandoned

After a week's fighting, Rommel transmitted his appreciation and his intentions to Keitel: "The Army Group is endeavouring to replace the Panzer formations by infantry formations as soon as possible, and re-form mobile reserves with them. The Army Group intends to switch its *Schwerpunkt* in the next few days to the area Carentan–Montebourg to annihilate the enemy there and avert the danger to Cherbourg. Only when this has been done can the enemy between the Orne and the Vire be attacked."

The following conclusions can be drawn from this telephone message:

1. Rommel stated he was compelled to give up his first plan to push the enemy back into the sea immediately. Hitler therefore was not able to recover on the Western Front the forces which he hoped to collect for the Eastern Front.
2. In order to release his armoured formations from the front, he would have had to have the same number of infantry formations at his disposal at the appropriate time. For this purpose the veto imposed on him by Hitler on taking troops from the 15th Army did not simplify matters.
3. Even if he had obtained these infantry formations, what he stated in any case shows that Montgomery's idea of free manoeuvre, which he put into practice in Normandy, was soundly and judiciously conceived.
4. Without these formations he could not displace Army Group "B"'s point of main effort from the Caen–Tilly-sur-Seulles area to the Carentan–Montebourg area, and therefore the "strong point" of Cherbourg was from now on virtually written off.

Churchill visits the Normandy front

Georges Blond has written:

"On Monday June 12 shortly after midday a D.U.K.W. landed at Courseulles and drove over the sand. A group of officers who had been looking at the D.U.K.W. through their field glasses for a few moments came forward quickly. A corpulent gentleman was sitting behind the driver, wearing a blue cap and smoking a cigar. As soon as the vehicle had stopped he asked the officers in a loud voice: 'How do I get down?' Just then a soldier hurried up carrying a small ladder. Churchill walked down it with all possible dignity. He shook hands with Montgomery who was standing in front of him in a leather jacket and a black beret, and then with the other officers, Field-Marshal Smuts, Field-Marshal Alan Brooke, and Rear-Admiral Sir Philip Vian, commander of the British Eastern Naval Task Force.

"He then went to his waiting jeep. The jeep started off."

On the following morning, June 13 the first V-1 rockets were fired in the direction of London.

▽ *An American M7 trundles past a knocked-out* Pzkw *IV.*

CHAPTER 66
THE TENSION GROWS

△ The British advance–past the grave of a German soldier.

The unsavoury gossip about Bradley was nothing to the criticisms made of Montgomery regarding the mediocre victories which the British 2nd Army could claim at that time. It had in fact to attack three times, and it was not until July 9, 1944 that it was able to announce the capture of Caen, its D-Day objective.

Of course, Montgomery could hardly reveal to the journalists whom he gathered round him for periodical press conferences that he had no intention of opening up the route to Paris. Still less could he tell them that his plan aimed first and foremost at forcing Rommel to concentrate his Panzers against the British 2nd Army, and wearing them down on this front by a series of purely local actions. Having said this, however, it may be said that in this battle of equipment, Montgomery the master-tactician did not sufficiently bear in mind the

enormous technical superiority that German armour enjoyed over the British and American tanks. If we look again at accounts of the furious battles fought out in the Caen sector in June and July, 1944, all we seem to read about is Sherman tanks burning like torches, Cromwell tanks riddled like sieves, and Churchill tanks, whose armour was considered sufficiently thick, never surviving a direct hit. Here, for example, is part of Major-General Roberts's description of Operation "Goodwood" on July 19 and 20.

"But 3 R.T.R. were through. They had started with 52 tanks, been given 11 replacements, making 63 tanks in all. With Bras now in their hands, they had nine tanks left. Major Close's A Squadron had lost 17 tanks in two days, seven being completely destroyed, the others recoverable; all Troop officers had been killed or wounded, and only one troop Sergeant was

left. The Fife and Forfar had fared rather worse."

In the circumstances it is not surprising that the famous units that had formed part of the 8th Army in North Africa (the 50th and 51st Infantry Divisions, and the 7th Armoured Division) did not have the success expected of them in this new theatre of operations. Writing of these veterans of Bir Hakeim, Tobruk, and El Alamein, Belfield and Essame remind us of the old saying current in the British Army—"An old soldier is a cautious soldier, that is why he is an old soldier." Quite probably. But perhaps the hiding the Desert Rats received at Villers-Bocage on June 12, when they first came into contact with the 2nd Panzer Division, was such as to make even the most reckless prudent.

As for the 12 British divisions which came under fire for the very first time in Normandy, however realistic their training may have been, however keen they may have been to fight, the real thing was very different, and the conditions they were called upon to face in real combat sometimes took away some of their aggressiveness.

It is also possible to criticise the British High Command for the tendency in its instructions to try to foresee everything, even the unforeseeable. Having seen orders issued by the main American commanders, we know that they subscribed to the same theory as the Germans, that the order should contain all that the lesser commander needs to know to carry out his task but nothing more; whereas British orders tended to go into further detail, limiting the initiative of the tactical commanders, because of theoretical situations that did not always arise. For in war, it is said, it is the unexpected that happens.

In this list of Montgomery's resources, an honourable mention must be made of the artillery, for which Rommel's grenadiers had a special dislike, for it fired quickly and accurately. In particular, the 25-pounder "gun-howitzer" fired so rapidly that the Germans thought it must have been fitted with a system of automatic loading. And this fact goes a long way to explain the form which the fighting took in the Caen sector, for if the British tanks

▷ *A British patrol pushes into the ruins of Caen.*
▽ *The Cassino of France. What was left of Caen.*

failed in all their attempts at breakthrough whenever they came up against the German Panthers, Tigers, and the 8.8-cm anti-tank guns of *Panzergruppe* "West", the German counter-attacks collapsed under the murderous fire of the British artillery concentrations whenever they went beyond purely local engagements. All the more so since at that distance from the coast the big guns of the Royal Navy were able to take a hand. So it was that on June 16 in the region of Thury-Harcourt, about 20 miles from Riva-Bella, a 16-inch shell from the *Rodney* or the *Nelson* killed Lieutenant-General Witt, commanding the 12th S.S. Panzer Division *"Hitlerjugend"*.

The failure of British XXX Armoured Corps and the 7th Armoured Division to turn the front of *Panzergruppe* "West" at Villers-Bocage seems to have caused Montgomery to shift the centre of gravity of his attack to the countryside around Caen, where his armour would find a more suitable terrain.

Operation "Epsom", begun on June 25, brought into action VIII Corps, just landed in Normandy and commanded by Sir Richard O'Connor, released from captivity by the signing of the Italian armistice. Covered on his right by XXX Corps' 49th Division, O'Connor was to cross the Caen–Bayeux road to the west of the Carpiquet aerodrome, push on past the Fossé de l' Odon, then switching the direction of his attack from south to south-west, he would finally reach Brette-ville-sur-Laize, ten miles south of Caen, near the Caen–Falaise road. This would give the British 2nd Army not only the capital of Normandy, but also the Carpiquet air base, upon which Air-Marshals Coningham and Leigh-Mallory had long been casting envious eyes.

VIII Corps had 60,000 men, 600 tanks, and 700 guns. The 15th and 43rd Divisions, each reinforced by a brigade of Churchill tanks, provided O'Connor with his shock troops, whilst the 11th Armoured Division would then exploit the situation. For all three divisions it was their first taste of combat.

Whilst the left wing of XXX Corps attacked the Panzer-"Lehr" Division, VIII Corps' attack brought it into contact with the 12th S.S. Panzer Division "Hitlerjugend", commanded, since the death of General Witt, by General Kurt Meyer, a leader of extreme resolution, of rapid and correct decisions, whom his men had nicknamed "Panzer-Meyer". By nightfall, at the price of fierce combat and despite incessant counter-attacks, the British infantry was able to bed down near the Caen–Villers-Bocage road, three miles from their starting point. On June 27, the 15th Division managed to capture a sound bridge over the Odon, and the 11th Armoured Division advanced and began the switching movement mentioned earlier: the first objective was Hill 112, the summit of the ridge which separates the Odon and Orne Valleys.

German counter-attack fails

The VIII Corps, however, was now behind schedule, and some very troublesome bottlenecks were building up at its rear. These difficulties enabled Sepp Dietrich, commanding I S.S. Panzer Corps, to avoid the worst by bringing in General Paul Hausser's II S.S. Panzer Corps, which had just come back from the Galician front. He even tried to take the 11th Armoured Division in a pincer movement between the 9th S.S. Panzer Division "Hohenstaufen" and the 10th S.S. Panzer Division "Frundsberg" and only failed because O'Connor evacuated his troops from a salient that had become too exposed.

On the other hand the Panzergruppe "West" failed in its efforts to turn this defensive success into a general offensive, for II S.S. Panzer Corps was literally pinned down by artillery fire and tactical air bombardment whenever it made the slightest move. In this connection General Harzer, Chief Operations Staff Officer of the 9th S.S. Panzergrenadier Division said later: "Now, if the Luftwaffe had been able to deal with the Allied navies and also stop the accurate bombing of certain targets, I think that the British-Canadian landings would once again have 'fallen in the ditch', as they say. As it was, our counter-offensive broke down under air attack and artillery fire, particularly the heavy guns of the battleships. They were devastating. When one of these shells dropped near a Panther, the 56-ton (sic) tank was blown over on its side, just from the blast. It was these broadsides

△ *When a ditch becomes an improvised trench. An American section prepares to break cover.*

from the warships, more than the defensive fighting of the enemy's troops, which halted our division's Panzer Regiment." At all events, after this sharp lesson, the Germans gave up any further idea of throwing the enemy back into the sea. Instead, they had been forced to feed into a defensive battle the reserves they needed for a major counter-strike.

Montgomery, in his June 30 directive to Generals Bradley and Dempsey, declared himself to be quite satisfied with the results obtained, although Operation "Epsom" had only dented the enemy line.

"All this is good ... by forcing the enemy to place the bulk of his strength in front of the Second Army, we have made easier the acquisition of territory on the western flank.

"Our policy has been so successful that the Second Army is now opposed by a formidable array of German Panzer Divisions – eight definitely identified, and possibly more to come ...

"To hold the maximum number of enemy divisions on our eastern flank between Caen and Villers Bocage, and to swing the western or right flank of the Army Group southwards and eastwards in a wide sweep so as to threaten the line of withdrawal of such enemy divisions to the south of Paris."

The carrying out of this plan meant continuing to place the main weight of this battle of attrition on the shoulders of General Dempsey, for the slightest slackening of pressure would mean that Rommel would be able to reorganise and re-form.

Caen occupied

On July 9, Caen and Carpiquet aerodrome fell to Lieutenant-General J. T. Crocker's British I Corps. The old Norman town, already badly bombed by the R.A.F. on the night of June 5-6, was now reduced to rubble by the dropping of 2,500 tons of bombs. The only part more or less spared was the area around the majestic Abbaye-aux-Hommes, which was protected by the Geneva Convention and was a refuge for many thousands of homeless. Although this pitiless bombing forced the *"Hitlerjugend"* Division to retreat, it also created such ruin, and slowed down the advance of the Canadian 3rd Division so much, that when it arrived at the Orne it found all the bridges blown.

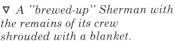

▽ *A "brewed-up" Sherman with the remains of its crew shrouded with a blanket.*

The British attack again: Operation "Goodwood"

Because of a delay by the U.S. 1st Army out on the Allied right flank, in preparing Operation "Cobra", the attack which was to crush German resistance, Montgomery asked Dempsey for one more effort to engage and tie down the Panzers on his front, and, if possible, to advance the armoured units of his 2nd Army into the region around Falaise. To this end, Operation "Goodwood" had moved the centre of gravity of the attack back to the right bank of the Orne, where the British 1st and 8th Armies were massed, whilst the Canadian II Corps, two divisions strong, was concentrated within the ruins of Caen. To it fell the task of capturing the suburbs of the town to the south of the river, and of developing an attack towards Falaise. The enemy's front, tied down in the centre, would be by-passed and rolled back from left to right by the three armoured divisions (the 7th and 11th, and the Guards Armoured Divisions), breaking out from the narrow bridgehead between the Orne and the Dives, which General Gale's parachute troops had captured on the night of June 5-6. VIII Corps possessed 1,100 tanks, 720 guns and a stockpile of 250,000 shells. But above all, the Allied air forces would support and prepare the attack on a scale hitherto undreamed of: 1,600 four-engined planes, and 600 two-engined planes and fighter-bombers would drop more than 7,000 tons of explosives on enemy positions, and then support VIII Corps' armour as it advanced.

However, the Germans had seen through the Allies' intentions, and had organised themselves to a depth of ten miles; it is true that they only had in the line one division, the 16th Luftwaffe Field Division, and what was left of the 21st Panzer Division, but they still possessed considerable fire-power, in the shape of 272 6-tube rocket launchers and a hundred or so 8.8-cm anti-aircraft guns operating as anti-tank guns. So the Allies were to find difficulty in making their overall superiority tell.

On July 18, at 0530 hours, the thunder of 720 guns signalled the beginning of Operation "Goodwood". Then, as one member of VIII Corps put it, the aircraft "came lounging across the sky,

△ *American combat team: rifles, sub-machine gun, and a mortar.*

▽ *British tanks and armour passing through the ruins of Falaise to forward positions.*

scattered, leisurely, indifferent. The first ones crossed our lines, and the earth began to shake to a continuous rumble which lasted for three-quarters of an hour; and at no time during that period were fewer than fifty 'planes visible. The din was tremendous. We could see the bombs leaving the 'planes and drifting down almost gently, like milt from a salmon, and as they disappeared behind the trees the rumble rose a little and then sunk to its old level again. The Jocks were all standing grinning at the sky. After weeks of skulking in trenches, here was action; action on a bigger scale than any of them had dreamed was possible."

At 0745 hours the 11th Armoured Division, preceded by a continuous barrage of an intensity never before experienced, began to advance, and quickly got through the first position, defended by troops still groggy from the pounding

△ *British Bren-gunner on the Caen–Falaise front, where every ruined house was a nest of resistance by the hard-pressed German forces.*
▷ *An American paratroop patrol encounters German corpses.*

inflicted by Bomber Command. But towards mid-day the attack came up against the railway line running from Caen to Paris, where it stopped.

Meagre success for the British

This was due, first, to the fact that the British artillery, which had stayed on the left bank of the Orne, no longer had the enemy within range; and second, that on the bridges which the Guards and the 7th Armoured Division had to take to get across to the right bank and link up with the 11th Division, there were tremendous bottlenecks. Above all, however, was the fact that 8.8-cm guns and *Nebelwerfers* were firing from the many villages on the outskirts of the town. At nightfall the 1st S.S. Panzer Division *"Leibstandarte"*, which formed Sepp Dietrich's reserve, surprised the 11th Armoured Division, just when it was about to bed down, and according to its commander, Major-General Wisch, destroyed about 40 tanks.

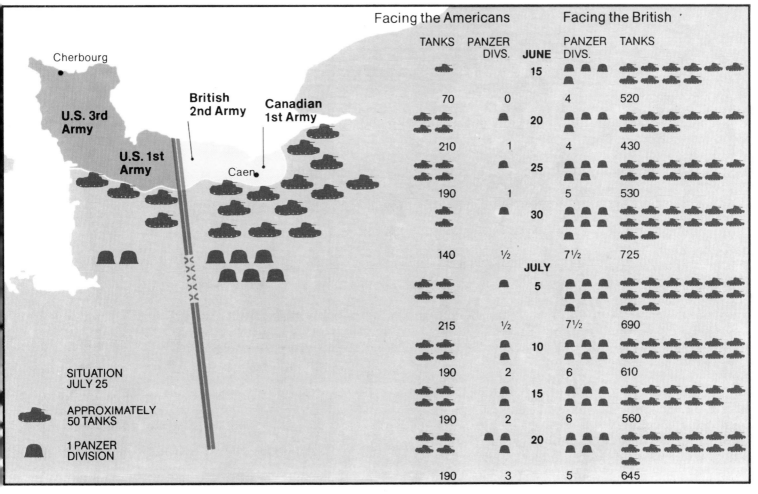

Cherbourg

U.S. 3rd Army

U.S. 1st Army

British 2nd Army

Canadian 1st Army

Caen

SITUATION JULY 25

APPROXIMATELY 50 TANKS

1 PANZER DIVISION

	Facing the Americans			Facing the British	
	TANKS	PANZER DIVS.	JUNE	PANZER DIVS.	TANKS
			15		
	70	0	20	4	520
	210	1	25	4	430
	190	1	30	5	530
	140	1/2	**JULY**	7 1/2	725
			5		
	215	1/2	10	7 1/2	690
	190	2	15	6	610
	190	2	20	6	560
	190	3		5	645

△ *The answer to the many complaints that Montgomery was being too cautious. By July 15 there were over three times as many German tanks facing the British and Canadians than were deployed on Bradley's front. The decisive breakout was approaching fast.*
◁△ *Tired German prisoners limp through the British lines to the rear.*
◁▷ *A U.S. artillery team digs in its "Long Tom" 155-mm gun.*

On July 19, with the rain taking a hand, the terrain got into such a state owing to the bombing the day before, that operations had to stop. South and south-west of Caen, the British and Canadians had advanced about five miles into the enemy's defensive positions, but had not succeeded in overrunning them. All in all it was rather a meagre success, especially as it had been paid for at the enormous price of 413 tanks, but there was a certain strategic compensation, as the 116th Panzer Division of the German 15th Army, stationed up till then near Amiens, was ordered to move towards Caen; and then Kluge, Rundstedt's successor at the head of Army Group "B", afraid of a British breakthrough in the direction of Falaise, thought it advisable to move his 2nd Panzer Division from Saint Lô to Caen, less than a week before the beginning of Operation "Cobra".

By this same day of July 19, the losses of the British 2nd Army since June 6 had amounted to 34,700 officers and men, of whom 6,010 were killed, and 28,690 were missing. They were therefore far less severe than those suffered during the same period by the American 1st Army (62,028 men). Of course, on D-Day the American 1st Division, on "Omaha" Beach, and the 82nd and 101st Airborne Divisions, around Sainte Mère-Eglise, had had a harder time of it. But in the Normandy woodlands the infantry-based American attacks had also been more expensive, in terms of men, than the British tank-based attacks in the Caen area – which seemed to prove once more Guderian's theory that tanks are a weapon that saves lives.

Montgomery's tactics

Basing his calculations on the figures supplied by Brigadier Williams, head of his Intelligence staff, Montgomery saw a situation arising in which, in spite of the apparent failures of the British 2nd Army, he would in a few days be able to send in the American 1st Army. Between June 6 and July 25, German strength had shifted away from the American front to that of their Allies, the British, as can be seen from the chart above, based on figures culled from Montgomery's *Memoirs*. The moment for the final break-through was approaching.

CHAPTER 67
MONTGOMERY'S NEW PLAN

Although, of course, Montgomery's superiors, General Eisenhower and the Combined Chiefs-of-Staff Committee, as well as his most important subordinates, were aware of the strategic objective hidden by his apparently slow manoeuvres, S.H.A.E.F. was beginning to show some signs of impatience. Writing ten years after the event, Montgomery thought he saw personal reasons, unconnected with the military situation, behind many of the criticisms made of his methods within the Allied High Command.

"One of the reasons for this in my belief was that the original COSSAC plan had been, in fact, to break out from the Caen–Falaise area, on our eastern flank. I had refused to accept this plan and had changed it. General Morgan who had made the COSSAC plan was now at Supreme Headquarters as Deputy Chief of Staff. He considered Eisenhower was a god; since I had discarded many of his plans, he placed me at the other end of the celestial ladder. So here were the seeds of discord. Morgan and those around him (the displaced strategists) lost no opportunity of trying to persuade Eisenhower that I was defensively minded and that we were unlikely to break out anywhere!"

As far as Sir Frederick Morgan is concerned, Montgomery may have been right, but he is surely on more dangerous ground when he goes on to assert that Air-Marshal Coningham, commander of the Tactical Air Force, associated himself with these criticisms for similar reasons. Coningham, he wrote, "was particularly interested in getting his airfields south-west of Caen. They were mentioned in the plan and to him they were all-important. I don't blame him. But they were not all-important to me. If we won the battle of Normandy, everything else would follow, airfields and all. I wasn't fighting to capture airfields; I was fighting to defeat Rommel in Normandy. This Coningham could scarcely appreciate: and for two reasons. First, we were not seeing each

▷ *Montgomery and Bradley confer with Paton, whose 3rd Army would spearhead the break-out operation.*
▷▽ *"Better roll up your map, Herr General–I don't think your counter-attack's going to come off"–a sardonic comment by Giles of the* Daily Express.
▽ *American sappers probe for mines on one of the approach-roads to St. Lô. The wreckage of a jeep trailer, recent victim of a mine, litters the ditch to the left.*

other daily as in the desert days, for at this stage I was working direct to Leigh-Mallory. Secondly, Coningham wanted the airfields in order to defeat Rommel, whereas I wanted to defeat Rommel in order, only incidentally, to capture the airfields."

And events were to show that in order to defeat Army Group "B", it was not necessary to be in possession of the airfields that Coningham would have liked. It is still true, however, that by remaining in the Caen area, instead of wearing the enemy down in the Falaise area, 15 miles further south, as the original project had planned, the British 2nd Army asked its air force for a great deal of support, and yet placed it in a difficult position.

In the Normandy beach-head airfields were scarce, and their runways were so short that for the pilots getting fighter-bombers loaded with a ton of bombs or rockets into the air was a real problem. And landing posed similar problems; as Belfield and Essame have noted, "anyone who flew over the bridgehead in Normandy must have retained vivid memories of fighter aircraft, twin engined Dakotas (used as ambulances) and the small Austers all milling about in a horribly confined airspace. The perpetual risk of collisions greatly increased the strain on the pilots who had to fly from the bridgehead".

It may be that the commander of the 2nd Tactical Air Force did not like being treated as a subordinate by the man with whom he had been on equal terms in North Africa, but his criticisms did not all spring from personal ill-feeling. And it should be noted that at S.H.A.E.F. Air-Marshals Leigh-Mallory and Tedder both approved Coningham's attitude.

As for Eisenhower, it may fairly be said that his memoirs are marked with a calm philosophy that he was far from feeling when Operation "Goodwood" was breaking down on the Bourguébus ridge. For after all, according to the plan worked out by Montgomery, Bradley's enveloping movement ought to have begun on D-Day plus seventeen, June 23, when the Allies would be firmly established on a front extending from Granville to Caen, passing through Vire, Argentan, and Falaise. "This meant", he wrote, "that Falaise would be in our possession before the great wheel began. The line that we actually held when the breakout began on D plus 50 was approximately that planned for D plus 5.

"This was a far different story, but one which had to be accepted. Battle is not a one-sided affair. It is a case of action and reciprocal action repeated over and over again as contestants seek to gain position and other advantage by which they may inflict the greatest possible damage upon their respective opponents."

Be that as it may, in his opinion Montgomery needed a touch not of the brake, but of the accelerator, and Eisenhower's repeated efforts to get Montgomery to show more aggression could not have failed to annoy his troublesome subordinate.

In this argument, which went as far as Winston Churchill, Montgomery had a faithful defender in Brooke, who did all he could to prevent this potential conflict from becoming too bitter. At the time Montgomery was also on the best of terms with Bradley, who wrote that "Montgomery exercised his Allied authority with wisdom, forbearance, and restraint. While coordinating our movements with those of Dempsey's Monty carefully avoided getting mixed up in U.S. command decisions, but instead granted us the latitude to operate as freely and as independently as we chose. At no time did he probe into First Army with the indulgent manner he sometimes displayed among those subordinates who were also his countrymen. I could not have wanted a more tolerant or judicious commander. Not once did he confront us with an arbitrary directive and not once did he reject any plan that we had devised."

There is no doubt therefore that Bradley, who enjoyed Eisenhower's full confidence, tried to influence him the same way as Brooke. The differences over strategy that arose between Bradley and Montgomery from the autumn of 1944, and the coolness that affected their relations afterwards, right up to the end of the war, are very well known, which makes Bradley's comments on Montgomery's handling of this initial phase of the Battle of Normandy all the more valuable. "Whilst Collins was hoisting the flag of VII Corps above Cherbourg, Montgomery was losing his reputation in the long and arduous siege of the old university town of Caen. For three weeks he had been engaging his troops against those armoured divisions that he had deliberately lured towards Caen, in accordance with our diversionary strategy. The town was an important communications centre which he would eventually

need, but for the moment the taking of the town was an end in itself, for his task, first and foremost, was to commit German troops against the British front, so that we could capture Cherbourg that much easier, and prepare a further attack.

"In this diversionary mission Monty was more than successful, for the harder he hammered toward Caen, the more German troops he drew into that sector. Too many correspondents, however, had overrated the importance of Caen itself, and when Monty failed to take it, they

△ *Eisenhower takes a snack lunch while visiting the U.S. 79th Division.*

▽ *De Gaulle makes a point to Eisenhower.*

△ *A picture vividly expressive of the strain of the fighting for St. Lô.*

blamed him for the delay. But had we attempted to exonerate Montgomery by explaining how successfully he had hoodwinked the German by diverting him toward Caen from Cotentin, we would have also given our strategy away. We desperately wanted the Germans to believe this attack on Caen was the main Allied effort." It seems pretty clear that Montgomery was right. During World War I, Joffre had been severely criticised for his phrase "I'm nibbling away at them". Thirty years later, it must be admitted that Montgomery, though paying a heavy price, "nibbled" his opponent's armoured units, which were technically superior and on the whole very well trained, to excellent effect.

Caen may also be compared with Verdun, in World War I, where Colonel-General Falkenhayn intended to bleed the French Army white. But where

the head of the Kaiser's General Staff failed against Joffre, Montgomery succeeded against Rommel, and with the American 1st Army and Patton behind Bradley, he had at his disposal a force ready to exploit the situation such as Falkenhayn never had.

At all events, the accredited pressmen at S.H.A.E.F. did not spare Montgomery, and above him Eisenhower, whom they criticised for tolerating the inefficiency of his second-in-command. It was even insinuated in the American press that with typical British cunning, Montgomery was trying to save his troops at the expense of the Americans, and that, most careful of English lives, he preferred to expend American soldiers, without the naïve Eisenhower realising what was happening.

However far-fetched such quarrels may seem, they continued long after the war, but under a different guise. For after the brilliant success of Operation "Cobra", which took Bradley almost in one fell swoop from Avranches, in Normandy, to Commercy and Maastricht on the Meuse, it would have been both indecent and ridiculous to accuse Montgomery of having kept the best things for the Anglo-Canadian troops, and given the Americans nothing but the scraps. Critics now tried to show that his attempts to tie down the enemy's mobile reserves with General Dempsey's troops failed. Thus, in 1946, Ralph Ingersoll, a war correspondent with Bradley's forces, portrayed the "Master" as being impatient to fight it out with Rommel: "The blow . . . could be struck with British forces under a British headquarters, for British credit and prestige". This would have confirmed Montgomery's domination of the American armies. "The result of Montgomery's decision was the battle of Caen–which was really two battles, two successive all-out attacks, continuing after Caen itself had fallen. Beginning in mid-June and ending nearly a month later, it was a defeat from which British arms on the continent never recovered. It was the first and last all-British battle fought in Europe. As he had feared, Montgomery was never again able to fight alone but thereafter had always to borrow troops and supplies to gain the superiority without which he would not even plan an attack."

What does this mean? That the 2nd British Army's attacks did not reach their geographical objectives is beyond question, but when one realises the tactical and material advantages gained over the enemy, it is impossible to join with Ingersoll and talk of "defeat". This can be seen in the cries of alarm, and later of despair, which German O.B. West sent to O.K.W. Of course, Ingersoll wrote his book in 1946, and was not in a position to appreciate all this.

Mistakes of the German strategists

Colonel-General Count von Schlieffen, the old Chief-of-Staff of the Imperial German Army, used to say to his students at the Military Academy, that when analysing a campaign, due allowance was never given to the way in which the vanquished

◁ Once the Germans built dummy tanks to conceal their strength; now the dummies were desperately offered to the swarming Allied fighter-bombers.
▽ A typical scene from the tank battle of July.

positively helped the victor. It will therefore be instructive to see how Rommel, Rundstedt, and Hitler smoothed the path of Montgomery and Eisenhower.

Hitler's blindness

In all this Rundstedt played a very secondary rôle. The great strategist whose Army Group "A" had conquered Poland, and who had played such a big part in the defeat of France, no longer dominated, nor did he seem to want to do so; Lieutenant-General Speidel, Chief-of-Staff of Army Group "B", paints him as having adopted an attitude of "sarcastic resignation", considering the "representations" and "despatches full of gravity" sent to Hitler as being the height of wisdom. He did, however, loyally support Rommel

△ *Two nuns and a housewife give directions to a party of G.I.s.*

▽ *Alfresco meal for American paratroops in a Normandy farmyard.*

they had reached by June 12, it would have been necessary to disengage the armoured units that Rommel had thrown in against Montgomery in the Caen sector, but this would only have been possible by drawing upon the 15th Army, stationed between the Seine and the Escaut, and the best placed to intervene. But Hitler expressly forbade Army Group "B" to do this. The Germans were therefore obliged, after scouring Brittany, to seek reinforcements at the very opposite end of France, and on June 12, the 276th Division received orders to leave Bayonne and get to the front: "The broken railways, the destroyed bridges and the French Maquis so delayed them that the last elements of the division finally arrived at Hottot in Normandy on July 4. In other words, to make a journey of some 400 miles, which could normally be completed by rail in seventy-two hours, required no less than twenty-two days. The main body of the division had to march at least one-third of the distance on foot, averaging approximately twenty miles each night."

Similar misfortunes befell the 272nd Division, drawn from Perpignan, and the 274th Division, hastily organised in the Narbonne area; whilst, in order to reach the Caen sector, the 16th L.F.D., on watch over the coast at IJmuiden, had first to follow the Rhine as far as Koblenz. All this makes it easy to understand why Army Group "B" was confined to a series of piecemeal tactical operations, devoid of any overall strategy.

in his discussions with Hitler—nothing more, nothing less.

Responsibility for the German defeat in the West therefore has to be shared between Rommel and Hitler. On D-Day, both wondered if this attack was not rather a diversion, covering a second landing aimed at the Pas-de-Calais. And due to the successful Allied deception measures, Hitler remained true to this idea until the end of July, whilst Rommel abandoned it when the American VII Corps' orders fell into his hands. The results of such blindness were catastrophic. To stop the Allies on the front

Hitler meets his Field-Marshals

At Rundstedt's urgent request Hitler agreed to meet him and Rommel together at the command post he had installed in 1940, at Margival, near Soissons, when Operation *"Seelöwe"* had been planned to conquer Great Britain. According to Lieutenant-General Speidel's account: "Hitler had arrived with Colonel-General Jodl and staff on the morning of June 17. He had travelled in an armoured car from Metz, where he had flown from Berchtesgaden. He looked pale and worn for lack of sleep. His fingers played nervously with his spectacles and the pencils before him. Hunched on a stool, with his marshals standing before him,

△ *Captured while he slept, a German soldier hurriedly hauls on his boots under the gaze of his captor.*

▽ *Objective Falaise – a Canadian column on the move.*

his former magnetism seemed to have vanished.

"After a few cold words of greeting, Hitler, in a high, bitter voice, railed on about the success of the Allied landing, and tried to blame the local commanders. He ordered that Cherbourg be held at all costs."

Rommel, who also spoke for Rundstedt, defended his officers from these attacks. When they began to discuss future action, the gulf between the two commanders and their garrulous leader became even more pronounced.

In Hitler's view, the use of flying bombs would soon bring the Third Reich victory, provided that they were concentrated against London; whereas, logically, it was suggested that he ought to use them against the embarkation ports which were sending over reinforcements to Normandy. Hitler did not deny the short-comings of the Luftwaffe, but asserted that within a short time the coming into service of jet fighters would wrest from the Allies their present supremacy, and thus allow the Wehrmacht's land forces to resume the initiative. But without Hitler's earlier obstruction, the jets would have already entered service . . .

Hitler intervenes . . .

Above all, however, was the fact that Rommel, backed by Rundstedt, categorically rejected the possibility of a second Allied landing north of the Seine, and demanded complete freedom of action, for it was now to be expected that the enemy would "break out of the Caen and Bayeux areas, and also from the Cotentin, towards the south, aiming for Paris, with a secondary attack upon Avranches to isolate Brittany". To cancel out this threat, they would have to bring into action the infantry divisions stationed in the Orne sector, then carry out "a limited withdrawal to be made southwards, with the object of launching an armoured thrust into the flank of the enemy and fighting the battle outside the range of the enemy's naval artillery . . ."

Hitler vetoed this plan absolutely: it was to be total resistance, no retreat, as at the time of the Battle of Moscow. Events have shown that this policy condemned the German forces in Normandy to disaster. But whether Rommel's plan would have been possible, given the

enormous Allied superiority and the dilapidated state of his troops, is doubtful, to say the least.

... and changes the High Command

As was to be expected, the fall of Cherbourg and the Cotentin operations increased even further the tension between those at the front and Hitler.

Furious at the way things were going, the Führer, despite Rommel's and Rundstedt's objections, ordered Colonel-General Dollman to be the subject of a judicial enquiry. On hearing this news, Dollman suffered a heart attack at Le Mans on June 29, and was replaced at the head of the 7th Army by General Hausser, who handed over command of II Waffen-S.S. Panzer Corps to his colleague Bittrich. On the same day Panzergruppe "West" was re-christened the 5th Panzerarmee, but General Geyr von Schweppenburg, only just recovered from the wounds he had sustained on June 12, having resumed command, had been dismissed and

replaced by General Eberbach, because he had had the temerity to point out the strategic patching-up of the Supreme Command.

The same day also, Rommel and Rundstedt were called to the Berghof by Hitler, who, however, refused to speak to them in private, and added nothing new to the rantings with which he had assailed their ears at Margival, about the decisive effect which the new weapons would have upon the course of the war. As for the two marshals, they emphasised the urgent necessity of ending the war on the west, so as to enable the Reich to fight on in the east. On seeing the indignant way in which their suggestion was greeted, they both thought they were going to be sacked on the spot. In fact the Führer's wrath fell only on Rundstedt, and even then it was somewhat mitigated by the award of the Oak Leaves to his Knight's Cross. He was replaced by Kluge, who had now recovered from the winter car accident which had obliged him to give up his command on the Eastern Front. At the Berghof, the new Supreme Commander in the West was duly spoken to by Hitler, Keitel, and Jodl, who impressed upon him the necessity of making his subordinate, Rommel, see reason. Hence the violent incident which took place at la Roche-Guyon, when the hero of Tobruk was told in no uncertain terms by his new chief that "he would now have to get accustomed to carrying out orders".

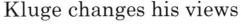

Kluge changes his views

Rommel reacted to these remarks with a written protest on July 3, to which he added a long aide-mémoire in justification, whose reasoning, both honest and full of good sense, led Kluge, an intelligent man, completely to revise his opinion.

In any case, the developing situation in Normandy allowed no other conclusion than Rommel's. The 5th Panzerarmee and the 7th Army were still containing the Allied advance, but with more and more difficulty. Despite their losses, Allied numbers and supplies were increasing daily, whereas the German forces' losses could not be made up. Between June 6 and July 15 it had only received 6,000 men to replace 97,000 killed, missing, and wounded, amongst whom there were 2,360 officers, including 28 generals and 354 lieutenant-generals. Its supply position

△ Moment of humour during Churchill's visit to the beach-head: a Cherbourg worker offers the Prime Minister a light.

△ A drink of water and a cigarette for a wounded German.

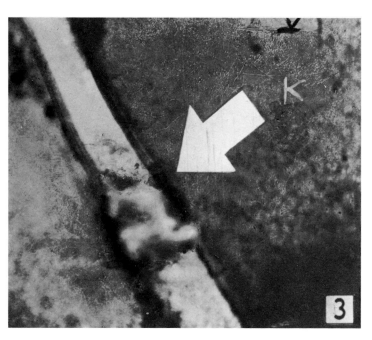

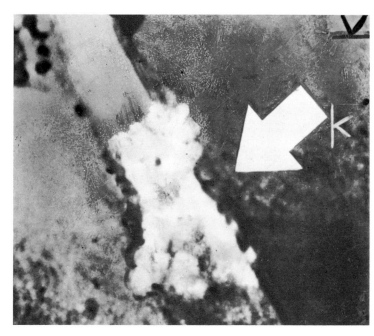

△ *Was this the attack that knocked Rommel out of the battle for Normandy? These pictures are "stills" from the camera-gun film exposed during a strafing run by Lieutenant Harold O. Miller of the U.S. 8th Air Force. For a while it was believed that Rommel had been killed in the attack – but he survived. There was a grimmer fate in store for him . . .*

had become so precarious because of enemy bombing that the most drastic economies were imposed.

Such were the facts that Rommel, with the approval of Kluge, pointed out in his last report to Hitler on July 15 1944 – a sad catalogue leading to the following conclusions:

"It must therefore be expected that within the next two to three weeks, the enemy will break through our weakened front, and advance in depth through France, an action which will have the gravest consequences.

"Everywhere our troops are fighting heroically, but this unequal struggle is inevitably drawing to a close. I am forced to ask you to draw the necessary conclusions from this situation, without delay. As leader of your Western forces,

I felt it my duty to explain it to you as clearly as possible."

What would have happened if Rommel had not been badly wounded on the Livarot–Vimoutiers road, the very day after dispatching this strong message? Hitler would almost certainly have refused, told him that he must not surrender, and would probably even have dismissed him. In that event, would Rommel have sent officers to parley with Montgomery? He would have been able to count on all his general staff, and certain field-commanders, such as Lüttwitz and Schwerin, at the head of the 2nd and 116th Panzer Divisions respectively. But would he have taken this enormous step after the shattering news came through of the bomb attempt on Hitler's life and the collapse of the "July Plot"?

CHAPTER 68
ASSAULT FROM THE EAST

In 1944 the Soviet summer offensive was to move forward successively over all sectors of the front from the Arctic tundra to the mouth of the Dniestr on the Black Sea. It can thus be compared in extent to Hitler's Operation "Barbarossa" begun three years before. Now the situation was reversed.

In addition to the will to destroy the armed forces of Germany and her satellites, the U.S.S.R. also had territorial and political ambitions: to impose a dictated peace on Finland; to bring Estonia, Latvia, and Lithuania back under Soviet rule; to install a puppet government in Poland; and to prepare to take over Rumania, Bulgaria, Hungary, and Yugoslavia.

Stalin, the head of the Soviet Government and Secretary General of the Soviet Communist Party, was not only taking as axiomatic, Clausewitz's view of war as subordinate to politics; but he was also going further, along the principles laid down by Lenin: "War is essentially a political fact . . . war is one part of a whole: that whole is politics", and by Frunze, the Soviet military theorist:

Exit Manstein

By the end of February the German 6th Army, in considerable disarray, had taken up positions behind the Ingulets, a tributary of the Dniepr. There were heavy losses in the fighting at Korsun', Nikopl', and Krivoy-Rog, with the Panzer divisions being reduced to an average of about 30 tanks, 20 per cent of their normal strength.

Although Russian losses had been heavy in January and February, they still had about 1,500 tanks against less than 400 for the Germans.

Marshal Zhukov in command of the armies of the 1st Belorussian Front, launched an offensive on March 4, 1944 with three tank and six rifle armies. By March 6 his 3rd Guards Tank Army was approaching the L'vov-Odessa railway line at Volchisk and the German 8th Army was forced to withdraw towards Uman'. General Manstein ordered XLVIII Panzer Corps to go to the defence of Tarnopol. The Soviets first crossed the river Bug, putting pressure on the 1st *Panzerarmee*, then also the Dniestr. On March 30 Manstein and Kleist were sacked by Hitler, to be replaced by Model and Schörner.

The 2nd S.S. Panzer Corps arrived in the L'vov region and contact was reestablished with the 1st *Panzerarmee*, which had retreated 120 miles through enemy territory, crossing four rivers.

△ *Soviet soldiers inspect a ruined Finnish emplacement on the road to Viipuri, or Vyborg as it was known to the Russians. As in the Winter War of 1939-40, the Russians attacked across the Karelian isthmus in overwhelming numerical and matériel superiority, but this time the advantage of strength was matched by the skill with which it was used.*

"Questions of military strategy and political and economic strategy are closely inter-related and form a coherent whole."

This is clearly opposed to the American military doctrine which Eisenhower obeyed in early April 1945 when he stopped his 12th Army Group on the Elbe at Magdeburg, since Berlin no longer had any importance militarily. There have, it is true, been many cases in which military operations have been gravely compromised by political interference.

Stavka's resources

In view of the failing strength of the Wehrmacht, Stalin could well afford to plan boldly, using the Red Army's material superiority in pursuit of long-term goals. Early in the summer of 1944 *Stavka* had 500 infantry and 40 artillery divisions, and 300 armoured or mechanised brigades with over 9,000 tanks, supported by 16,600 fighters, fighter-bombers, and twin-engined bombers, whilst behind the front the effort put into training, organisation, and industrial production in 1943 was kept up at the same rate in 1944. It should also be emphasised that the Red

Army's conduct of operations was now more relaxed. A judicious series of promotions had brought to the top of the major units many exceptionally able commanders. Stalin and *Stavka* allowed them an easier rein than in the past, whereas their enemy was being deprived of all initiative by the despot of Berchtesgaden.

First offensive: Finland

The first blows of the Soviet summer offensive fell on Finland. As we have seen, thanks to the Swedish Government's action as an intermediary, negotiations were on the point of being concluded between Helsinki and Moscow in the late winter, and the Finns were no longer insisting on the return to the *status quo* of March 1940. The talks fell through, however, because Moscow demanded from this small unhappy country an indemnity of 600 million dollars' worth of raw materials and goods, spread over the next five years.

When spring came, the situation of Finland and her valiant army could hardly give rise to optimism. The defeat

Back to the Crimea

The German 6th Army evacuated Odessa on April 6th. Hitler was determined to hold on to the Crimea but the Soviets were equally determined to re-take it and for this purpose built up a superiority in men and material. On April 8, General Tolbukhin unleashed the offensive under a large and powerful air umbrella. Schörner and Jaenecke argued in vain with Hitler for the evacuation of the 17th Army. On May 7 the Soviet 2nd Guards Army attacked the German northern flank and on May 8 the Soviets entered Sevastopol. The German evacuation had been left too late and the Soviets were determined not to allow their enemy to escape.

Similarly, the request of the commander of Army Group "North" to withdraw his 16th and 18th Armies to a a prepared position ("Panther" line) was also rejected by Hitler. The 18th Army under Colonel-General von Lindemann was duly caught in a pincer movement. The Soviets were also successful on the Leningrad and Volkhov fronts and on 17 February the 18th Army, now under Field-Marshal Model, began its withdrawal to the "Panther" line.

On March 27, 11 German divisions began Operation "Margarethe", the occupation of Hungary. Admiral Horthy accepted the "fait accompli", taking the view that he would be better placed to protect Hungarian patriots and Jews by retaining some vestiges of power as regent.

---

of Field-Marshal von Küchler and the German Army Group "North", driven from the banks of the Neva to those of the Narva, deprived Marshal Mannerheim of any hope of German help in the event of a Soviet offensive.

Mannerheim had therefore divided the bulk of his forces in two: in the isthmus between the Gulf of Finland and Lake Ladoga he had put six divisions, including his 1st Armoured Division, and two brigades, all under III and IV Corps; on the front of the river Svir', which runs from Lake Onega to Lake Ladoga, he had nine divisions and three brigades. This was a lot, to be sure but, Mannerheim wrote:

"A reduction of the troops in East Karelia would, however, constitute a surrender of this strategically valuable area and be a good bargaining-point for the attainment of peace. The disposition of the troops was also based on the not unreasonable hope that the fortifications of the Isthmus would compensate for the weakness of man-power."

The Finnish III and IV Corps could in fact count on three successive lines of fortifications, the first two from 44 to 50 miles long and the third 75 miles.

This was small stuff against the powerful forces massed by the Russians, especially in artillery, for the Leningrad Front, still under the command of General L. A. Govorov. Finnish Intelligence sources revealed that the Russians put some 20 infantry divisions on the Finnish front, together with four armoured brigades, five or six tank regiments, and four regiments of assault guns, that is some 450 armoured vehicles in all, and about 1,000 aircraft. For their part the official Soviet sources give no figures, so that we are inclined to believe the Finns. Silence implies consent.

Karelia overrun

On June 9 the Leningrad Front went over to the attack, with an artillery barrage of up to 250 guns per mile. Lieutenant-General D. N. Gussev and his 21st Army had been given the main task and this developed over a ten-mile front along the coastal sector, which allowed the Red Navy's Baltic Fleet to take part under the command of Admiral V. F. Tributs.

Mannerheim wrote: "June 10th may

▷ *Safe from the prying eyes of Axis aircraft: a Russian tank turret dug in as a strongpoint on the Karelian front.*

△ *Women of Petrosavodsk on the Karelian front greet Major-General Kupryanon with light refreshments.*

with reason be described as the black day of our war history. The infantry assault, carried out by three divisions of the Guards against a single Finnish regiment, broke the defence and forced the front in the coastal sector back about six miles. Furious fighting raged at a number of holding lines, but the on-storming massed armour broke their resistance.

"Because of the enemy's rapid advance, the 10th Division fighting on the coast sector lost most of its artillery. On June 11th, its cut-up units were withdrawn behind the V.T. (Vammelsuu-Taipale) position to be brought up to strength."

But hardly had the defenders of the isthmus taken up their positions than they were driven back by an attack which broke through north of the Leningrad–Viipuri (Vyborg) railway. The 1st Armoured Division counter-attacked, but

to no avail. Faced with this rapidly deteriorating situation, Mannerheim left the defence of the isthmus to General Oesch and ordered the evacuation of Karelia. This enabled him to pull out four divisions. Before there could be any reployment in force in the threatened sector, the Russian 21st Army made a fresh breakthrough and seized Viipuri on June 20.

What would have happened to the defence if the armies of the Karelian Front (General K. A. Meretskov) had come into battle on the same day as the Leningrad Front and had trapped the Finnish V and VI Corps between Lakes Ladoga and Onega? For unknown reasons the Russians only started their attack five or six days after Mannerheim had ordered the defenders to break off contact.

The Russian offensive in eastern Karelia took the form of a pincer movement. One army crossed the Svir' and pushed northwards to meet the other which, having forced the Masselskaya defile, exploited this success southwards. But the pincers closed on a vacuum and at the beginning of July the Finns, though reduced to four divisions, had nevertheless succeeded in re-establishing their positions on a pre-arranged line from Lake Ladoga on their right to Lake Loymola on their left, some 45 miles from the present Soviet-Finnish frontier.

Between Lake Ladoga and the Gulf of Finland, Govorov had a few more successes, in particular establishing a bridgehead on the north bank of the Vuoksa, along which ran the third defen-

Aftermath

The plot against Hitler had its roots in the German aristocracy, especially in the Prussian nobility, in the upper middle classes, and in certain intellectual, university, and religious circles which had little to do with the ordinary people, and the savage repression of the uprising aroused no feeling of reprobration or even of sympathy in the majority of the nation.

The assassination attempt was made at the Rastenburg headquarters on July 20, 1944, when a time-bomb in a briefcase left by Lieutenant-Colonel Claus Schenk von Stauffenberg exploded at Hitler's feet. As a result of the plot, 17 generals were executed. A wave of terror swept through the Army and the National Socialists took control in a way that would ensure not just military defeat for Germany but national catastrophe.

sive position between Viipuri and Taipale. But finally everything quietened down and about July 15 General Oesch was able to state that the enemy forces opposite him were considerably thinner on the ground.

It would certainly be absurd to deny that the Red Army had won. The Finns had been driven back to their last line of defence and had lost the Karelia area, which they had intended to use as a counter in the forthcoming peace negotiations. The Soviet Union had also got the use of the Leningrad–Murmansk railway and canal which the Finns had begun in 1941.

In spite of the defeat, however, the fighting spirit of the Finnish Army lived on. It counter-attacked incessantly and in the whole campaign very few Finns were taken prisoners. On balance Moscow seems to have realised that to wipe out the Finnish Army would have cost more than the literal submission of Helsinki to the March 1940 conditions was worth.

Time to get out

As we can see, Mannerheim had played the cards of dissuasion well. But, like his government, he agreed that the time had come for Finland to get out of the war. During the battle, instead of the six divisions for which he had asked O.K.H., he had got only one, the 129th, and a brigade of 80 assault guns. All the assurances, intermingled with threats,

proffered by Ribbentrop to President Ryti could not make up the difference. The day after Viipuri fell, and with it Finland's hopes, the Wehrmacht was suffering in Russia one of the heaviest defeats in the history of the German Army, including Jena and Stalingrad.

On June 28, when he rejoined the German 20th Army fighting north of the Arctic Circle, Colonel-General Rendulic wrote of the impression Mannerheim made on him at their first meeting: "In spite of the prudence which he continually showed in official declarations, his words had an unmistakably pessimistic ring." This goes to show that the 76-year old Marshal saw further than Rendulic.

▽ *Soviet troops move up towards the front through Viipuri. Note the large number of anti-tank rifles in evidence.*

△ *A formation of Petlyakov Pe-2 light bomber and general purpose aircraft. One of the best machines of the war, the Pe-2 was pressed into service in a multitude of rôles.*

Second offensive: Polotsk and the Pripet

On June 22, 1944, as if to celebrate the third anniversary of the German aggression, Stalin opened his last great summer offensive between the Polotsk area and the north bank of the Pripet. This brought into action Bagramyan's 1st Baltic Front, Chernyakhovsky's 3rd Belorussian Front, Zakharov's 2nd Belorussian Front, and Rokossovsky's 1st Belorussian Front.

According to the *Great Patriotic War,* which we quote in Alexander Werth's version, the following were engaged in this offensive, including reserves: 166 infantry divisions, 31,000 guns and mortars, 5,200 tanks and self-propelled guns, and 6,000 aircraft. The Red Army had never before achieved such a concentration of force or had such huge quantities of supporting *matériel,* which included 25,000 two-ton lorries.

Michel Garder gives a lively account of the atmosphere of the Soviet summer offensive in his book *A War Unlike The Others.* He says:

"The patient work of the Red Army's general staff, which had prepared in great detail the grand plan of *Stavka,* resulted in this fantastic cavalcade. This was the true revenge for the summer of 1941! In the burning-hot July sky the Red Air Force was unopposed. White with dust the T-34's drove on westwards, breaking through the hedges, crushing down thickets, spitting out flame . . . with clusters of infantry clinging on to their rear platforms, adventure-bound. Swarms of men on motor-cycles . . . shouting cavalry . . . infantry in lorries . . . rocket-artillery cluttering up the road . . . the tracks . . . the paths . . . mowing down everything in their way.

"This was a long way from the stereotyped image of 'dejected troops herded to slaughter by Jewish political commissars'."

Marshal Vasilevsky had been sent to

Bagramyan and Chernyakhovsky as *Stavka*'s representative to co-ordinate their operations. Zhukov performed the same function with Zakharov and Rokossovsky.

The objective of the Soviet offensive was the destruction of Army Group "Centre", then commanded by Field-Marshal Busch, who in the early days of 1944 had taken over from Kluge at the latter's H.Q. at Minsk. Busch had four armies deployed from north to south as follows:

1. 3rd *Panzerarmee* (Colonel-General Reinhardt)
2. 4th Army (General von Tippelskirch)
3. 9th Army (General Jordan)
4. 2nd Army (Colonel-General Weiss)

By the end of the winter the withdrawals forced upon Army Groups "North" and "South" by the Soviet winter offensives had left Army Group "Centre" in a salient: the fortified area of Vitebsk on the Dvina was two-thirds encircled, whereas south of the Pripet Marshes Rokossovsky had got as far as the approaches to Kovel'. To counteract the threat to Field-Marshal Model's left at the end of March, Busch had been asked to send him eight divisions, including two Panzer.

Russian superiority in tanks and aircraft

When the Soviet summer offensive started, Army Group "Centre" was thus reduced to 37 divisions. On June 22 the 2nd Army was not attacked, and so the initial clash in the battle for Belorussia was between 166 Soviet and 28 German divisions, on a front extending over 435 miles. The Russian divisions each had 10,000 men. Those of Generals Jordan, Tippelskirch, and Reinhardt were very much understrength, as can be seen in the account given by Major-General Heidkämper, chief-of-staff of the 3rd *Panzerarmee*. He showed that the Vitebsk salient was being held by LIII Corps along a front of 55 miles with the 206th, 4th and 6th Luftwaffe, and 246th Divisions, with 8,123 rifles (about 150 rifles per mile). Reserves consisted of a battalion of heavy artillery, two heavy anti-tank companies, and one Luftwaffe special service battalion.

Colonel-General Reinhardt's VI and IX Corps were no better off, nor were the

4th and 9th Armies. German dispositions between the Pripet and the Dvina were thus as thin as a spider's web.

The mobile reserves which were to slow down then stop the onslaught of 4,500 Soviet tanks consisted of only the 20th Panzer and the 18th, 25th, and 60th *Panzergrenadier* Divisions with 400 tracked vehicles between them. For good measure add the same number of assault guns, and it will be seen that in armour the Germans were outnumbered by 5.6 to 1.

It was the same in the air: *Luftflotte* VI could get only an insignificant number of planes off the ground.

"Fortified areas"

The situation of Army Group "Centre" was such that if the enemy unleashed against it an attack of any strength it

△ *The proof: German dead in the wake of the 2nd Belorussian Front's triumphant progress.*

△ *Scorched earth policy, 1944 German variety.*

could not expect to hold it. Again Hitler was to intervene and make Stalin's task easier. Firstly he laid down, in an order dated March 8, 1944, the building on the Eastern Front of a number of "fortified areas" to take over the rôles of the former fortresses. "Their task," his *Führerbefehl* of that day ordered, "is to prevent the enemy from seizing centres of decisive strategic importance. They are to allow themselves to be encircled so as to engage as many of the enemy as possible. They are to create opportunities for fruitful counter-attacks."

Controlled by an army group or army, the strongpoint garrison had instructions to hold out to the last man and no one except the Führer, acting on information from the army group commander, had the right to order withdrawal.

In the Army Group "Centre" sector nine towns were to be made fortified areas. These included Bobruysk on the Berezina, Mogilev and Orsha on the Dniepr, and Vitebsk on the Dvina. The troops manning these new areas were to be taken from the armies in the field, which their commanders regarded as a heresy.

Reinhardt made repeated objections to Hitler's orders, transmitted to him through Field-Marshal Busch, to shut away LIII

Corps (General Gollwitzer) and three divisions in the so-called "fortified area" of Vitebsk. In the event of an attack in this sector the absence of these units would open up a breach which could not possibly be stopped, and enemy armour would thus pour through. Reinhardt even went to Minsk to state his case and was told sharply on April 21:

"Vitebsk's value is as a fortified area and the Führer will not change this point of view at any price. His opinion is that Vitebsk can engage between 30 and 40 enemy divisions which would otherwise be free to attack west and south west," then: "It is also a matter of prestige. Vitebsk is the only place on the Eastern Front whose loss would resound throughout the world."

Reinhardt was dismissed in these terms; neither Tippelskirch nor Jordan were any better received by Busch. Jordan, who on the following May 20 proposed to Hitler that if it were to appear likely that the Soviets would launch an offensive in Belorussia, the Germans should withdraw to the Dniepr and the Berezina, thus shortening their line from 435 to 280 miles, was summarily dismissed with: "Another of those generals perpetually looking backwards".

△ *The promise that was wearing thin: the German Army staving off the Red flood from Poland's agricultural areas.*
◁ *Albert Speer, wearing an Organisation "Todt" brassard, in conversation with Major Dr. Kupfer. Upon Speer's department fell most of the work involved in throwing up Germany's eastern ramparts.*

Hitler misunderstands Soviet intentions

It is true that the Führer did not consider that Army Group "Centre" would be the immediate objective of the offensive which, he admitted, the enemy would launch as soon as the ground was sufficiently hard again. In all evidence it was Army Groups "North Ukraine" and "South Ukraine" which were threatened, as Stalin clearly had his eyes fixed on the Rumanian capital and the Ploieşti oil-fields, then the Balkan peninsula and the Turkish narrows, the age-old goal of Imperial Russia, not to mention Budapest and the rich Hungarian plains.

From early June onwards reports from the front, based on direct information, on aerial reconnaissance by the Luft-waffe, on the interception and analysis of radio messages, and on the interrogation of prisoners and deserters, all seemed to indicate the progressive build-up of a powerful assault force between the Pripet and the Dvina. In particular the Red Air Force was growing steadily in numbers every day. When Major-General Gehlen, head of Section East of O.K.H. Intelligence, told Hitler about all this, the Führer retorted that it was merely a clumsy decoy movement. Stalin wanted the Germans to bring over from Moldavia to Belorussia the forces they were holding opposite the true centre of gravity of Russian strategy, but Hitler was not going to fall into that trap.

This opinion was so fixed in his mind that during the night of June 24–25 he obstinately refused to yield to the despair of his closest collaborators, who entreated him to agree to the measures which had become necessary consequent upon the collapse of the 3rd *Panzerarmee* in the Vitebsk sector, whilst at the confluence

of the Dniepr and the Berezina the 9th Army had reached the limits of endurance under ever increasing attacks. There was an eye-witness to these events.

Colonel-General Dr. Lothar Rendulic was at the Berghof that evening, having been summoned there urgently to be given command of the German 20th Army (Lappland) after the accidental death of Colonel-General Dietl. In his memoirs Rendulic says:

"Hitler thought that the main Soviet effort was developing in the south and considered that these Russian attacks east of Warsaw were mere demonstrations. It was a notable miscalculation, as events were to show. He forbade any reserves to be taken from the south and moved to Warsaw. I can say here that when I came out of the conference I asked Colonel-General Jodl how he could let this appreciation of the situation go unchallenged. He replied: 'We fought the Führer for two whole days, then when he ran out of arguments he said: "Leave me. I am relying on my intuition." What can you do in a situation like that?'"

The offensive begins

During the night of June 19–20 the 240,000 partisans who controlled the forests in Belorussia cut the lines of communication of Army Group "Centre" in more than 10,000 places as far west as

◁ top: Russian infantry double over a pontoon bridge across the River Bug, another major river barrier overcome.
centre: Germans struggle to extricate a sidecar combination during the retreat from Vitebsk.
bottom: The same problem for horsed transport.
▷ The inhabitants of the Minsk area left behind by the Germans greet the liberating Russian forces.
▷ ▽ Ground crew at work on Lavochkin fighters on a forward airfield. Note the Russian-built "Dakota" landing. By 1944 the Red Air Force's disasters of 1941 and 1942 were no more than evil memories. Its squadrons now had good equipment and enjoyed total superiority over the Luftwaffe.

Minsk. At dawn on the 22nd the forces of the 1st Baltic and the 3rd Belorussian Fronts went over to the attack on both sides of Vitebsk. The 1st Belorussian Front went into action on the following day. Generals Bagramyan and Chernyakhovsky had been given as their first objective the capture of Vitebsk by a pincer movement, which would give their comrade Rokossovsky the time to pierce the German 9th Army's positions in the area of Bobruysk. When both these results had been achieved the two Belorussian Fronts would let loose their armoured formations, which would converge in the direction of Minsk. A second pincer would thus be formed and this would crush Army Group "Centre". Bagramyan and Chernyakhovsky took just 48 hours to overpower the resistance of the 3rd *Panzerarmee* north-west and south-east of Vitebsk. During this brief spell the German commander also used up his meagre reserves as well as the 14th Division, sent to him by Busch as a reinforcement. Busch could ill afford the loss. In particular the German right wing, which consisted of VI Corps (General Pfeiffer, killed in this action), collapsed completely under the impact of the Soviet 5th Army and four armoured brigades, whose attack was preceded and supported by V Artillery Corps (520 heavy guns) and tactical air formations acting with a strength, a spirit, and an accuracy hitherto unknown on the Eastern Front.

No retreat from Vitebsk

At 1520 hours on June 24 Zeitzler called Reinhardt from the Berghof to ask if he considered the mission assigned to him at the fortified area of Vitebsk to be vital. The army commander, according to his chief-of-staff, replied candidly that "LIII Corps was surrounded, though still only

△ *Houses are fired by retreating German troops. The level of destruction on the Eastern Front was unparalleled elsewhere.*
△▷ *Russian infantry pour over a partially demolished bridge. The infantry could then secure a bridgehead and allow the engineers to throw up a bridge for the tanks to cross.*
▽▷ *German demolition in Vitebsk.*

▽ *A Russian poster warns of the reception German aircraft will receive. But by the middle of 1944 the few aircraft that the Luftwaffe could still muster were wholly on the defensive.*

ВСТРЕЧАЙ
самолеты врага
ЛИВНЕМ ОГНЯ С ЗЕМЛИ !

weakly; that this was the moment to order him to try to break out; that every quarter of an hour the Russian ring to the west of Vitebsk was thickening."

When Zeitzler remarked that the Führer feared heavy losses in supplies of all kinds if the fortified area were to be abandoned hastily, Reinhardt burst out: "If the ring closes we shall lose not only supplies and ammunition, but the whole of LIII Corps with its five divisions." As usual nothing came of these remonstrations, for at 1528 hours Zeitzler came back from seeing Hitler and informed Reinhardt: "The Führer has decided that Vitebsk will be held." According to Major-General Heidkämper, Reinhardt stood "petrified" at the news.

At 1830 hours, however, the incompetent despot agreed to some relaxation of this grotesque order and signalled 3rd *Panzerarmee*: "LIII Corps will leave one division to garrison Vitebsk and break out westwards to rejoin our lines. Report name of commander of this division. Swear him in by radio as new commander of 'Vitebsk fortified area'. Make him confirm his oath."

This order was no less absurd than the one which went before it. The 206th Division (Lieutenant-General Hitter) was nominated. To this unit alone was entrusted the defence of positions prepared for four divisions. And it was too late. LIII Corps was intercepted and crushed during its retreat and when its commander, General Gollwitzer, surrendered to the

Russians on June 27 he had only 200 of his men with him and of these 180 were wounded. The worst had happened: the destruction of Vitebsk opened a breach in the German line more than 28 miles wide. Reinhardt was now reduced to three worn-out divisions and 70 guns. Nothing and nobody could now stop the thrustful Chernyakhovsky from driving on along the Lepel'–Minsk axis with the 5th Guards Army under Marshal of Armoured Forces Pavel A. Rotmistrov.

Rokossovsky takes Bobruysk

Further south on the Belorussian front, the same causes could only produce the same effects and General Jordan, C.-in-C. 9th Army, was no luckier than Reinhardt; XXXV Corps, defending the fortified area of Bobruysk with four divisions, suffered the same fate as LIII Corps. When he opened his offensive on June 24, General Rokossovsky had taken good care not to launch his 1st Belorussian Front forces against the German fortified areas, but to push them into gaps north and south of the River Berezina. Three days of hard fighting brought him victory. South of Bobruysk he overcame XLI Panzer Corps (Lieutenant-General Hoffmeister) and cut off the retreating XXXV Corps (Lieutenant-General von Lützow), leaving

it trapped in the fortified area.

On June 29 16,000 Germans emerged from the pocket and gave themselves up, leaving behind them the bodies of 18,000 of their comrades. By now the mounted, motorised, mechanised, and armoured forces of General Pliev, one of the most brilliant cavalry commanders of the war, had reached Ossipovichi, some eight miles south-east of Minsk, and were rumbling forward to meet the 5th Guards Tank Army, which had passed Lepel' and was now in Borisov.

The situation of the German 4th Army, now at grips with greatly superior forces on the 2nd Belorussian Front, was scarcely any better. Faced with disasters on his right and left, General von Tippelskirch, now in command *vice* Colonel-General Heinrici, had to use all his initiative to get his army out of its positions along the River Proina and back to the Dniepr. The fortified areas of Mogilev and Orsha on the Dniepr, however, were soon overcome by Zakharov and Chernyakhovsky, and became the graveyards respectively of the 6th (Lieutenant-General Henie) and the 12th (Lieutenant-General Wagner) Divisions.

Tippelskirch thus had to continue his retreat westwards across rough forest land infested with marches and, particularly, thick with partisans. It is no wonder that, as planned by *Stavka,* Rotmistrov and Pliev got to Minsk before him on July 3, joining forces behind his back and condemning his XII and XXVII

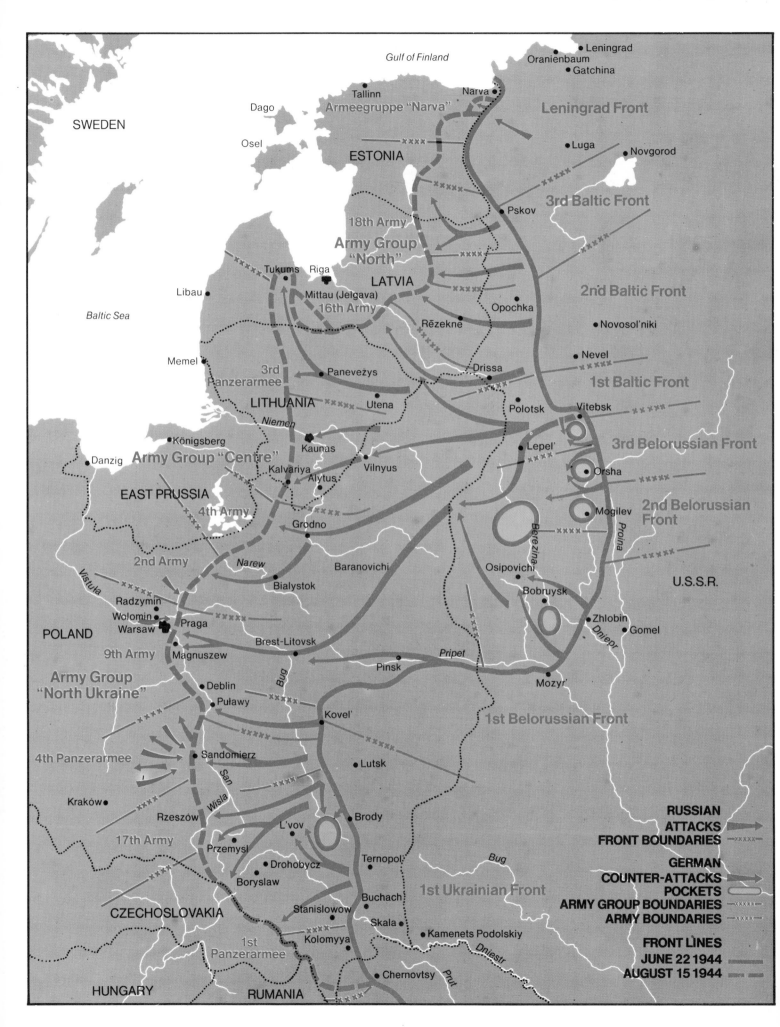

SWEDEN

Baltic Sea

Gulf of Finland

Leningrad
Oranienbaum
Gatchina

Tallinn
Narva
Armeegruppe "Narva"

Leningrad Front

Dago

Osel

ESTONIA

Luga
Novgorod

3rd Baltic Front

Pskov

18th Army
Army Group "North"

LATVIA

Tukums
Riga

Libau

Mittau (Jelgava)
16th Army

Opochka

2nd Baltic Front

Rēzekne

Novosol'niki

Memel

3rd Panzerarmee

Panevežys

Drissa

Nevel

1st Baltic Front

LITHUANIA
Utena

Polotsk

Vitebsk

Königsberg

Kaunas

Lepel'

3rd Belorussian Front

Danzig

Army Group "Centre"

Kalvariya
Alytus

Vilnyus

Orsha

2nd Belorussian Front

EAST PRUSSIA
4th Army

Mogilev

Niemen

Grodno

Berezina

Proina

2nd Army

Narew

Baranovichi

Osipovichi

U.S.S.R.

Bialystok

Bobruysk

Visula

Radzymin
Wolomin
Warsaw
Praga

Zhlobin
Gomel

Dniepr

POLAND

9th Army
Magnuszew

Brest-Litovsk

Pripet

Pinsk

Mozyr'

Army Group "North Ukraine"

Deblin

Puławy

Kovel'

1st Belorussian Front

4th Panzerarmee

Bug

Lutsk

Sandomierz

San

Kraków

Wisla

Rzeszów

L'vov

Brody

17th Army

Przemysl

Ternopol

Bug

Drohobycz

Boryslaw

Buchach

1st Ukrainian Front

CZECHOSLOVAKIA

Stanislowow

Skala

Kamenets Podolskiy

1st Panzerarmee

Kolomyya

Dniestr

Chernovtsy

Prut

HUNGARY   RUMANIA

RUSSIAN ATTACKS

FRONT BOUNDARIES

GERMAN COUNTER-ATTACKS

POCKETS

ARMY GROUP BOUNDARIES

ARMY BOUNDARIES

FRONT LINES

JUNE 22 1944

AUGUST 15 1944

Corps and XXXIX Panzer Corps (respectively under Generals Vincenz Müller, Voelkers, Martinek) to the sad fate of "moving pockets".

A defeat worse than Stalingrad

▽ The Russian assault moves into a German-held village.

It was June 28 before Hitler finally admitted that the Belorussian offensive was something more than a diversion. On that day he sacked General Busch, who had obeyed his directives unquestioningly, and replaced him by Field-

Marshal Model, who strove to limit the extent of the disaster. Army Group "North", though now uncovered on its right flank by the defeat of the 3rd *Panzerarmee,* was required to give up three divisions. Ten more, including four Panzer, were taken from Army Group "North Ukraine". These units were sent to the Belorussian front in the hope of an attack on the flank of Rokossovsky, who was now exploiting his victory along the line Minsk – Baranovichi – Brest-Litovsk. The breach now open between the Pripet and the Dvina was some 185 miles wide and, according to the O.K.H., this was swallowing up 126 infantry divisions and no fewer than 62 armoured or

mechanised brigades with at least 2,500 tanks. On July 8 the last "moving pocket" surrendered behind the Russian lines with 17,000 men, having run out of ammunition. Out of 37 divisions in Army Group "Centre" on the previous June 22, 28 had been badly mauled, if not actually cut to pieces, and an enormous mass of *matériel,* including 215 tanks and more than 1,300 guns, had been captured.

According to statistics from Moscow, which appear reliable, the Germans lost between these two dates some 285,000 dead and prisoners, including 19 corps and divisional commanders. The Belorussian disaster was thus worse than Stalingrad and all the more so since, when Paulus resigned himself to the inevitable, the "Second Front" was still only a distant threat to the Third Reich.

Stalin celebrated in true Roman style by marching seemingly endless columns of 57,600 prisoners-of-war through the streets of Moscow with their generals at the head. Alexander Werth, the *Sunday Times* correspondent, was there and he described the behaviour of the Russian crowd as the men passed by:

"Youngsters booed and whistled, and even threw things at the Germans, only to be immediately restrained by the adults; men looked on grimly and in silence; but many women, especially elderly women, were full of commiseration (some even had tears in their eyes) as they looked at these bedraggled 'Fritzes'. I remember one old woman murmuring 'just like our poor boys . . . tozhe pognali ne voinu (also driven into war)'."

CHAPTER 69

"THE GREAT MARIANAS TURKEY SHOOT"

To start his New Guinea campaign, Mac-Arthur put on a cunning diversionary operation to make the Japanese believe they were going to be attacked frontally in the area of Wewak. Lieutenant-General Hatazo Adachi, C.-in-C. Japanese 18th Army in New Guinea, fell into the trap. April 22 was thus a day of easy triumph for the U.S. I Corps (Lieutenant-General Robert L. Eichelberger) which landed, without much difficulty, its 24th Division (Major-General F. A. Irving) at Tanah-merah Bay and its 41st (Major-General H. H. Fuller) at Hollandia and Aitape. When he had got over his surprise, Adachi tried to turn his forces round and re-establish his communications. During July the Aitape sector was the scene of furious fighting, throughout which Adachi urged on the Japanese 18th Army in terms of mingled despair and determination:

"I cannot find any means or method which will solve this situation strategical-ly or tactically. Therefore, I intend to overcome this by relying on our Japanese *Bushido*. I am determined to destroy the enemy in Aitape by attacking him ruth-lessly with the concentration of our entire force in that area. This will be our final opportunity to employ our entire strength to annihilate the enemy. Make the supreme sacrifice, display the spirit of the Imperial Army."

This appeal was understood and followed, but the time and trouble it cost Adachi to turn round gave the Allies an advantage which they did not let slip, especially as they were also able to decode the Japanese radio messages. And so, during the night of July 11-12, the 18th Army's counter-attack found the Allies alert and reinforced by Major-Generals Charles P. Hall's XI Corps and William

◁ ◁top: *Civilians freed from a Nazi labour camp near Minsk begin their journey home.* bottom: *Some of the 57,600 prisoners taken by the Belorussian Fronts waiting to be paraded through the streets of Moscow: a symbol of Soviet triumph over the Nazi aggressor.*

Build-up in the Pacific

The Americans carried out a huge logistical organisation to refit and bring into service new ships and to provide supply vessels for a Maintenance Fleet. In 1943 ships brought into service were:

2 fast battleships of 45,000 tons
6 fleet carriers of 27,000 tons
9 light aircraft carriers of 11,000 tons
24 escort carriers
4 heavy-cruisers (8-inch guns)
7 light-cruisers (6-inch guns)
128 destroyers
200 submarines

On the day after Pearl Harbor the American Navy had 337,274 officers, petty officers, and other ranks. Twelve months later there were more than a million, reaching three million in December 1944. These men were well trained and well disciplined.

For his attack on the objectives in the Gilbert group, the American 5th Fleet (Vice-Admiral Raymond A. Spruance) had six 27,000-ton aircraft-carriers, five 11,000 ton light carriers and eight escort carriers with between them some 700 fighters and bombers. The Americans also had the advantage of having broken the Japanese naval communications code.

H. Gill's 32nd Division. The Japanese were held.

MacArthur strikes along the coast

MacArthur was already hopping from one island to the next along the coast of New Guinea. On May 17, his 41st Division landed at Wakde, 125 miles west of Hollandia. On the 27th, a further hop of 200 miles brought him to Biak, where the Japanese put up fierce resistance. Virtually ignoring this as a local incident, he pushed on to the island of Numfoor on July 2 and on the 30th he reached the beak of the Vogelkop. This was at Sansapor, over 600 miles from Hollandia. By now some 120,000 Japanese were cut off,

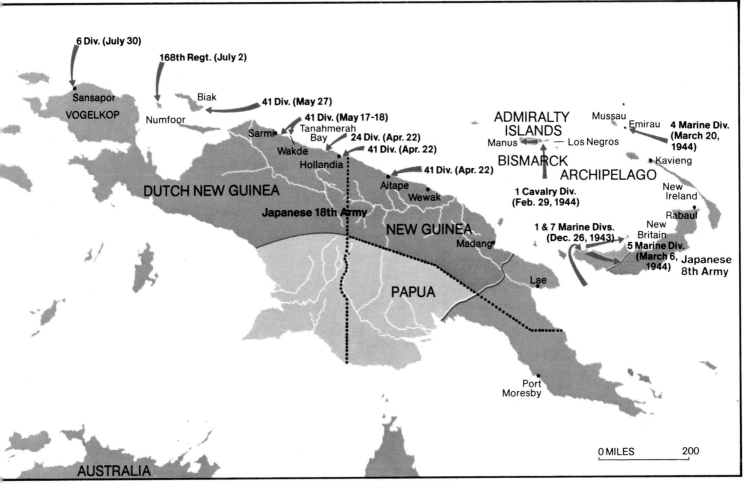

trapped in the "green hell" of the jungle in one of the worst climates in the world, and defenceless against malaria. It is understandable that, in face of this great success, MacArthur telegraphed to Eichelberger:

"The succession of surprises effected and the small losses suffered, the great extent of territory conquered and the casualties inflicted on the enemy, together with the large Japanese forces which have been isolated, all combine to make your operations of the past one and a half months models of strategical and tactical manoeuvres."

In fact, according to a table drawn up by General Willoughby, chief of Intelligence, Allied Forces in the South-West Pacific, in dead alone the losses on both sides were:

Battle areas	American	Japanese	Ratio
Arawe-Gloucester	472	4,914	1:10
Saidor	55	1,275	1:23
Admiralty Islands	155	4,143	1:27
Hollandia	87	4,441	1:51
Aitape	440	8,370	1:19
Wakde	646	3,899	1:6
Biak	524	5,093	1:10
Numfoor	63	2,328	1:37
Sansapor	2	374	1:187

It should also be remembered that the death-rate in American hospitals was three per cent, whereas it was very much higher amongst the Japanese because of the appallingly unsanitary conditions under which they had to fight. MacArthur received Marshall's congratulations with justifiable satisfaction, but was even more pleased when the Pentagon announced that he was to get another corps, of five divisions, an extra air force, and 60 extra ships. What he had called the "stony-broke" war was a thing of the past.

The attack on Biak made the first dent in the Japanese defensive perimeter as described by the Imperial H.Q. directive commented on above. So Admiral Toyoda, who like the Americans had just formed a 1st Mobile Fleet (C.-in-C. Vice-Admiral Jisaburo Ozawa), resolved to attack MacArthur's flank. He despatched to the Moluccas an Attack Division (Vice-Admiral Matome Ugaki) consisting mainly of the giant battleships *Yamato* and *Musashi*, but on June 11, when it had scarcely reached its departure-point, it was suddenly ordered to abandon the

△ *MacArthur's conquest of the New Guinea coastline and the islands to the north, which now opened the way for his next move to Morotai and thence the Philippines.*

◁△ *Australian and American troops take a look at two Japanese tanks knocked out in the coastal fighting in New Guinea.*

◁◁ *Escorted by a destroyer, an L.S.T. taking part in the Hollandia operation noses into Tanahmerah Bay.*

Struggle for the Solomons

The battle for Guadalcanal was over by February 1943. It had cost some 24,000 Japanese lives while the Americans had about 1,600 men killed and over 4,000 wounded. Japanese aircraft losses, still difficult to assess precisely, were probably well over 800, far outnumbering American planes destroyed. Both sides suffered heavily in numbers of ships sunk, but the Americans could build new ones more readily. The American victory at Guadalcanal was matched by similar gains in eastern New Guinea by General MacArthur's forces.

On the night of June 29-30, some 6,000 U.S. troops went ashore on Rendova Island. On July 2 they landed on New Georgia. Fierce resistance from the more experienced Japanese jungle fighters resulted in deadlock. The tide gradually began to turn under the new command of General John H. Hodge and by the end of August the entire island of New Georgia had been cleared of Japanese. When faced with another jungle battle to gain the airstrip on Kolanbangara, the Americans decided to bypass it and build their own on the more lightly defended island of Vella Lavella. The Americans won the battle for Bougainville which began on November 1 and also neutralised the Japanese base at Rabaul. In the Solomons campaign the Japanese suffered dearly in losses of men, warships, transports, and aircraft. Japanese naval air power was almost wiped out, making it impossible for them to oppose the U.S. Central Pacific offensive or the projected attack on the Philippines. This made the American victory in the Solomons a decisive factor in the ultimate defeat of Japan.

operation and to rejoin Ozawa east of the Philippines. The reason was the air attacks on Saipan, Tinian, and Guam in the Marianas.

The double offensive which had paid off for Nimitz at Tarawa was now working for MacArthur. Mitscher's bombers had an easy job of it over their objectives because the Biak affair had drawn off many fighters from the defence of the Marianas. Washington's misgivings were thus allayed by events.

The Marianas

As the Joint Chiefs-of-Staff directive of March 12 pointed out, the capture of the three islands mentioned above gave them a base for an attack on Mindanao in the Philippines. At Saipan, Army Air Force engineers would lay down the runways needed for the B-29 Superfortresses of the 20th Air Force to take off on their missions of destruction over the great industrial centres of the Japanese mainland. Operation "Forager", started on July 6, involved 535 warships and 127,571 men of the Marine Corps and the Army. Task Force 58 was followed by the Joint Expeditionary Force, Task Force 51, whose job it was to put ashore two corps of four divisions and one brigade:

1. V Amphibious Corps (Lieutenant-General Holland M. Smith: 2nd and 4th Marine Divisions);
2. III Amphibious Corps (Major-General Roy S. Geiger: 3rd Infantry Division and 1st Provisional Marine Brigade); and
3. floating reserve: 27th Division (Major-General Ralph Smith).

Admiral Spruance was C.-in-C., and Vice-Admiral Turner commanded the sea, air, and land forces involved in the

△ *A paratrooper taking part in the conquest of Numfoor Island swings from a tree in which his parachute has become entangled.*

Spruance was much stronger in Operation "Forager" than he had been in "Galvanic". This is shown by the number of fast carriers available to the 5th Fleet: 11 at the Gilberts, 12 at the Marshalls, and 15 at the Marianas.

The same was true for other types of ship. When the clash came, the opposing forces had the following:

	Spruance	Ozawa
Carriers	15	9
Battleships	7	5
Cruisers	21	13
Destroyers	69	28
Totals	112	55

Spruance thwarts Ozawa's plans . . .

American superiority in naval aircraft was over two to one. Spruance had 891, his adversary 430. The Japanese pilots, after their idleness at anchor in Tawitawi, had lost what little efficiency they had had. The Japanese carrier-force had two problems: it did not dare put out to sea because of the submarine threat; and there were no aerodromes near its base where its pilots could be trained. Ozawa's carriers did, it is true, have a greater range of action, but this had been achieved by the sacrifice of a certain amount of armour protection and a reduction in water-tight integrity, which rendered them very vulnerable.

Ozawa, in whom the historian Samuel Eliot Morison recognises "a scientific brain and a flair for trying new expedients, as well as a seaman's innate sense of what can be accomplished with ships", overlooked all these weaknesses in the hope of overcoming them by close collaboration with land-based aircraft from the Marianas and the organisation of a shuttle-service between his own and the "unsinkable carriers" of Guam and Rota. But this plan was thwarted by Spruance.

Moreover, Japanese strategy could no longer choose between offensive and defensive operations for, unless the Mobile Fleet were engaged, they would lose the Marianas, and the Philippines soon afterwards. In which case, Admiral Toyoda declared later:

"Even though the fleet should be left, the shipping lane to the south would be completely cut off so that the fleet, if it

landing. Both had recently been promoted.

This powerful combination of forces spelled the end of Japanese strategy as it had been conceived since the Washington Naval Conference of 1922. Then, when they had conceded a numerical superiority to the U.S. of five to three in battleships, the Japanese could still persuade themselves that their security was not at risk. In their opinion the bulk of the enemy's forces would be trapped and destroyed piecemeal in ambushes laid for them in the Marshall and Caroline Islands. The balance of strength would thus be in their favour in the Marianas. This turned out to be incorrect. In fact, far from losing strength as he advanced,

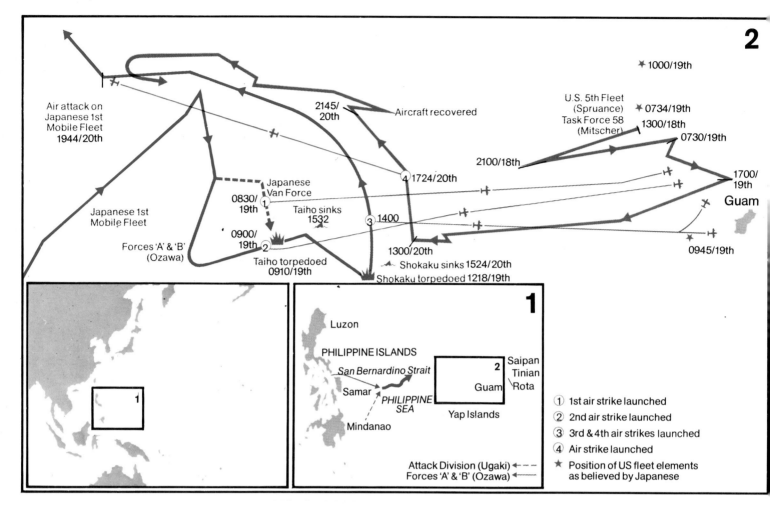

Labels within the map image (part of figure):

2

1000/19th

U.S. 5th Fleet
(Spruance)
Task Force 58
(Mitscher)

0734/19th

1300/18th

0730/19th

Air attack on
Japanese 1st
Mobile Fleet
1944/20th

2145/
20th

Aircraft recovered

2100/18th

1700/
19th

Guam

4 1724/20th

Japanese
Van Force

0830/
19th 1

Taiho sinks
1532

3 1400

Japanese 1st
Mobile Fleet

0900/
19th 2

Forces 'A' & 'B'
(Ozawa)

Taiho torpedoed
0910/19th

1300/20th

0945/19th

Shokaku sinks 1524/20th
Shokaku torpedoed 1218/19th

1

Luzon

PHILIPPINE ISLANDS

San Bernardino Strait

Samar

Mindanao

PHILIPPINE
SEA

2

Guam

Saipan
Tinian
Rota

Yap Islands

Attack Division (Ugaki)
Forces 'A' & 'B' (Ozawa)

① 1st air strike launched
② 2nd air strike launched
③ 3rd & 4th air strikes launched
④ Air strike launched
✱ Position of US fleet elements
as believed by Japanese

---

should come back to Japanese waters, could not obtain its fuel supply. If it should remain in southern waters, it could not receive supplies of ammunition and arms. There would be no sense in saving the fleet at the expense of the loss of the Philippines.''

It is hoped that the forces will exert their utmost and achieve as magnificent results as in the Battle of Tsushima.' ''

There was, however, nothing in common between the American 5th Fleet and the Russian 2nd Pacific Squadron destroyed by Admiral Togo on May 27 and 28, 1905.

△ *The Battle of the Philippine Sea, which marked the end of the Imperial Japanese Navy's air arm.*

. . . and Ozawa reaches the Philippine Sea

This was why, when he heard about the bombing of the Marianas, Toyoda ordered Ozawa to put in action the plan for a counter-offensive which had been drawn up for this purpose. During the evening of June 15, Ozawa sailed into the Philippine Sea through the San Bernardino Strait and 24 hours later joined up with Ugaki's Attack Division. At 0008 hours on the 18th, he sent the following message to the Mobile Fleet:

"I humbly transmit to you the message I have just received from the Emperor via the Chief-of-Staff, Naval Section, Imperial G.H.Q.: 'This operation has immense bearing on the fate of the Empire.

Spruance moves out

Patrolling off Tawitawi and at the exit of the San Bernardino Strait, Vice-Admiral Lockwood's submarines had signalled the approach of the Japanese Mobile Fleet and, with some uncertainty, its composition. In view of the coming battle, Spruance called back his forces which had just been bombing the Bonin and Volcano Islands north of the Marianas, and redeployed his units. On the flanks of his four carrier task groups, still under Vice-Admiral Mitscher, he drew up a Battle Line under Vice-Admiral W. A. Lee: his seven fast battleships, four cruisers, and 13 destroyers. At 1415 hours on June 17 he defined his intentions to his immediate subordinates:

△ A column of L.V.T.s or "Water Buffaloes" awaits the order to embark on the L.S.T. that will move them up for the final part of the New Guinea campaign—the landings at Sansapor on the "Vogelkop".

"Our air will first knock out enemy carriers, then will attack enemy battleships and cruisers to slow down or disable them. Battle line will destroy enemy fleet either by fleet action if the enemy elects to fight or by sinking slowed or crippled ships if enemy retreats. Action against the enemy must be pushed vigorously by all hands to ensure complete destruction of his fleet."

Spruance's intentions were thus purely offensive. He could not, however, go outside the parameters of his mission, which was to take, occupy, and defend Saipan, Tinian, and Guam. By giving chase to the enemy he would have left V Amphibious Corps' bridgehead unprotected and risked exposing it to attack from any Japanese force moving in from north or south. He therefore decided to sit back and wait a while.

The Japanese fleet advances

At dawn on June 19, the Japanese Mobile Fleet consisted of two detachments: a Van Force (Vice-Admiral Takeo Kurita) with three divisions, two of battleships and one of heavy cruisers, each protecting a light carrier, and 120 miles behind it a Main Body (Ozawa) composed of Forces "A" and "B", with six carriers, five of them fleet carriers. The Japanese sailed in against the wind: their planes were thus able to take off straight towards the enemy, with the return flight shorter than the outward one.

Between daybreak and 1445 hours, Ozawa made four raids on the 5th Fleet. These were all disastrous because of American superiority in training and in the quality of their aircraft. 373 of the 473 Japanese planes available (including floatplanes) took off and met 450 U.S. fighters, which massacred them. Those which escaped got caught in the massive A.A. fire of the Task Groups and the Battle Line. Those of the fourth wave which attempted to land at the airfield on Guam were destroyed in the air or so badly damaged on landing (the runways being pitted with bomb craters) that none of them ever took off again. Only 130 Japanese planes returned to their ships. There was no compensation for the Japanese as the U.S. forces lost only 18 fighters and 12 bombers and suffered only slight damage

◁ *The American carrier* Intrepid *under way with her planes ready on the flight deck.* ▽ *A Japanese aircraft plummets down towards the sea in flames.*

to the carrier *Bunker Hill* and the battleship *South Dakota*. The 5th Fleet lost altogether 58 men killed, including 27 pilots. Worse still for Ozawa, at 0910 hours the submarine *Albacore* (Commander J. W. Blanchard) put a torpedo into the fleet carrier *Taiho* (29,300 tons), Vice-Admiral Ozawa's flagship. Then at 1220 hours the submarine *Cavalla* (Lieutenant-Commander H. J. Kossler) scored three hits on the carrier *Shokaku;* she sank towards 1730 in the afternoon with 22 of her planes, which had just returned, on board. Both the *Shokaku* and the *Taiho* were lost because of explosions of the fumes from the fuel taken on at Tarakan. Damage to the *Taiho* was negligible, but a damage-control officer unfortunately gave the order to ventilate the ship and the petroleum fumes swept through from stem to stern. This led to a colossal explosion, as a result of which the ship sank immediately.

Twilight pursuit

Ozawa transferred his flag to the heavy cruiser *Haguro* and, misinformed about Japanese losses and misled by exaggerated reports by his own pilots of U.S. casualties, pressed on with his attack regardless. There is no doubt that the remainder of the Japanese fleet would have been wiped out in the course of June 20 if Spruance's aerial reconnaissance had spotted it in time, but it failed to do so, despite the beautiful weather. It was 1600 hours before a plane sighted the Japanese "250 miles" (it was in fact over 300) north-north-west of Task Force 58. Despite the distance and the lateness of the hour, Spruance turned his carriers into the wind and sent up 85 fighters, 77 dive-bombers, and 54 torpedo-bombers inside ten minutes.

The sun was sinking below the horizon when the Americans saw the fighter screen protecting the Mobile Fleet. Each Japanese ship then took a separate zig-zag course and opened up with all its guns. Forty Japanese planes were shot down for a loss to the Americans of 20, but only a small carrier, the *Hiyo,* was sunk. Meanwhile Mitscher was sailing full steam ahead to save his planes as much milage as possible. To get them back on board at 2000 hours, Task Force 58 turned up-wind and, in spite of the submarine danger, turned on all their land-

Jap plane also tried to land on one of our carriers. Our planes continued to land as we continued on our way after the Jap fleet. It was quite a sight to see all the ships lit up, flares and rafts in the water and some planes crashing into the water, and pilots and crews also in the water. You could see the planes circle and then land on the carriers. A great job was done by everyone to save our pilots' lives. The Japs would never do anything like this."

Even so, out of 176 planes which got back to Task Force 58, 80 ran out of fuel and fell into the sea or crash-landed. Thanks to Mitscher's initiative, 101 crew were picked up. Another 59 were saved on the following day, making the losses for the 20th 49. Ozawa was informed that only 35 out of his 473 planes were left, and so he broke off contact.

A catastrophe for the Japanese

The Philippine Sea was thus the grave-yard of the Japanese naval air arm. The Japanese carriers, bereft of planes and pilots, were like rifles without cartridges. At the cost of 130 of the 956 planes his task force had at dawn on June 19, and of 138 sailors and airmen killed or missing, Spruance had thus scored a victory the consequences of which were to last until the Japanese capitulation of September 2, 1945.

The fact remains that a number of Spruance's subordinate officers and fellow-commanders, who did not know of the loss of the *Taiho*, however, expressed their disappointment that the Mobile Fleet had not been destroyed, a result of what they considered excessive caution on Spruance's part. Nimitz and King backed him up, however. Perhaps by so doing they were merely vindicating themselves in that this incomplete victory could have been the result of their somewhat restrictive instruction to take, occupy, and defend Saipan, Tinian, and Guam. Be that as it may, some months later Admiral W. F. Halsey found that the order sending him to Leyte contained the following paragraph:

"In case opportunity for destruction of major portion of the enemy fleet offers or can be created, such destruction becomes the primary task."

△ ◁ *Flight deck crew throw themselves flat as a Japanese torpedo bomber thunders in at low altitude towards their carrier.*

△ ▷ *The plane is hit under its port wing. The men at the bottom are the crew of an A.A. gun.*

△ *The twilight sky over an American task force is pitted with the black bursts of A.A. fire.*

ing lights. A few hours later, on board the cruiser *Montpelier,* Leading Seaman James J. Fahey noted in his invaluable diary:

"It was a great decision to make and everyone thought the world of Admiral Marc Mitscher for doing this. This would make it easier for our pilots to land, and if they did hit the water they could be saved. The big carriers were all lighted so the pilots could see where to land, a lot of our destroyers were left behind to pick the men out of the water. I saw one pilot on the wing of his plane waving his shirt. There were so many lights it must have been hard to land on the carriers. A

The disaster of the Philippine Sea was soon to be followed by the loss of the Marianas Islands: Tinian, Saipan and Guam. A consequence of these defeats was the forced resignation of General Tojo as Prime Minister.

On July 18, 1944, Hirohito appointed General Kuniaki Koiso as Tojo's successor. The new Prime Minister had been Governor of Korea, had left the Army in 1938, and had the reputation of being a moderate. The War Ministry went to Field-Marshal Sugiyama, the Navy to Admiral Yonai. Shigemitsu, who had taken part in the conspiracy within the Tojo cabinet, remained Foreign Minister.

The search for peace

The Emperor ended his audience with the new Prime Minister with the following words: "You will need to collaborate to put an end to the war in Asia and I recommend you not to upset Russia."

In guarded terms the Emperor was therefore ordering Koiso and Yonai to attempt a negotiated settlement with the United States and Great Britain. The new Navy Minister saw the situation in the same light. When he had asked Admiral Toyoda: "Can we hold out until the end of the year?" the reply was: "It will in all probability be very difficult."

When we realise that the Japanese language is full of circumlocutions and delicate shades of meaning we see what that meant. The army chiefs had still to be reckoned with, however, and they refused to admit that any negotiated settlement could be compatible with the Emperor's honour, of which they considered themselves the absolute and final judges, regardless of their devotion to his person. "Divine Presence" was one of the Emperor's attributes, but for the military man this was only on condition that he took no part in major policy decisions. Even if the army leaders had been more foreseeing than this, General Koiso would still have found it just as difficult to overcome this obstacle. Potter and Nimitz note this clearly:

"On the Allied side, the goal of unconditional surrender set by Roosevelt and Churchill at Casablanca forbade the proffering of terms which might have served as bases for negotiation."

And so the road led inevitably to Hiroshima and Nagasaki.

CHAPTER 70
ON TO THE VISTULA

Stalin gave Bagramyan, Chernyakhovsky, Zakharov, and Rokossovsky the job of exploiting as deeply and as fast as possible the victory at Minsk, the extent of which, thanks to Hitler, seems to have exceeded even *Stavka*'s highest hopes.

Under the terms of the new directives, the forces of the 1st Baltic Front were given as their objective the Gulf of Riga, whilst the three Belorussian Fronts would move first on to the line Kaunas–Grodno–Brest-Litovsk, then force their way across the Niemen and the Bug, as they had done over the Dniepr and the Berezina. Colonel-General Chernyakhovsky would then take on the defences of eastern Prussia, whilst Zakharov and Rokossovsky (the latter just having been promoted Marshal of the U.S.S.R.) would invade Poland.

For three weeks the victors of Minsk covered their ten to fifteen miles a day, by-passing without much difficulty at first the units which Field-Marshal Model, like General Weygand after June 11, 1940, threw in piecemeal to stop the gaps. Model, the new C.-in-C. Army Group "Centre", now had the job of holding back the enemy long enough for O.K.H. to regroup its forces and to reform the

indispensable continuous front. He was more highly regarded by Hitler than his unfortunate predecessor, and was thus able to obtain in time permission to evacuate a whole series of so-called "fortified areas" which otherwise would have become so many death-traps for the army's divisions. This meant, of course, considerable sacrifices of territory:

July 13: Chernyakhovsky takes Vilnyus;
July 14: Rokossovsky envelops Pinsk, on the Pripet;
July 15: Chernyakhovsky forces the Niemen at Alytus, while Zakharov takes Grodno;
July 18: Rokossovsky crosses the Russo-Polish frontier fixed at Teheran;
July 23: Rokossovsky's advance guard enters Lublin;
July 27: Zakharov breaks through the defences of Białystok;
July 28: Rokossovsky takes Brest-Litovsk;
July 31: Rokossovsky enters Praga, across the Vistula from Warsaw;
August 1: Chernyakhovsky reaches Kalvariya, 15 miles from the Prussian frontier; and
August 2: Chernyakhovsky takes Kaunas.

On Chernyakhovsky's right, General Bagramyan and the armies of the 1st

◁ *American heavy units loose off at targets on shore during a pre-landing bombardment. Note the fire-control radar behind the mast.*

▽ *A wounded German officer awaits transport at a dressing station on the Eastern Front. The label gives details of the wound and treatment he has received. The war in Russia had drained Germany of many of its older experienced soldiers, and they were now being replaced by new recruits unversed in battle craft and the skills of survival.*

△ *Soviet troops in position with a 45-mm anti-tank gun.*
▷ *In liberated Vilnyus Russian officers pass a rather more potent tank killer: an 8.8-cm Flak gun and a Volkswagen* Kübelwagen *captured from the Germans.*

▽ *A Russian junior lieutenant with his sergeant check their map during a reconnaissance in a forward position.*

Baltic Front poured through the breaches in the inner flanks of Army Groups "North" and "Centre" caused by the Vitebsk catastrophe. Whilst the means were lacking to stop the enemy's advance towards Riga, was it advisable to keep the German 16th and 18th Armies on the Polotsk–Pskov–Lake Peipus line, which they had been holding since their painful retreat of the preceding winter? Colonel-General Lindemann, C.-in-C. Army Group "North", concluded that it was not and advised the withdrawal of his forces on the left bank of the Dvina. He was also being asked to transfer certain of his units to Army Group "Centre", which strengthened his point of view.

But to abandon Estonia might risk the "defection" of Finland, as O.K.W. put it. And so on July 2 Hitler relieved Lindemann of his command and handed it over to General Friessner, who in February 1944 had distinguished himself as commander of *Armeegruppe* "Narva". This change of personnel did nothing to improve the strategic situation.

On July 11 Bagramyan crossed the Dvina at Drissa and further to the left his advance guard reached Utena in Lithuania. On the following day the 2nd Baltic Front (General A. I. Eremenko) came into the battle and, breaking out from the area of Novosol'niki, drove deep into the positions of the German 16th Army (General Loch).

Caught up in front by Eremenko and behind by Bagramyan, the latter threatening his communications, Friessner, who had had to give up 12 divisions to Model, could only come to the same conclusions on July 12 as his predecessor had done. But, faced with the same refusal from Hitler to meet the situation with common sense, he did not hesitate, at the end of his letter dated that day, to stake his command:

"If, *mein Führer*," he wrote, "you are not prepared to accept my idea and give me the liberty of action necessary to carry out the measures proposed above, I shall be compelled to ask you to relieve me of the responsibilities I have assumed so far." Summoned by return of post to Rastenburg, Friessner upheld his view in the presence of the Führer, who reproached him for having used threats and for having shown an unmilitary attitude throughout. Reminding Hitler that he was responsible for some 700,000 men, and that he was fighting at the relative strength of one to eight, according to the account he has left of this interview he went so far as to say:

"I am not trying to hang on to my job. You can relieve me of it. You can even have me shot if you want to. But to ask me, *in full knowledge of the facts and against the dictates of my conscience,* to lead the men entrusted to me *to certain destruction* – that you can never do."

Hitler, with tears in his eyes, is thereupon supposed to have seized General Friessner's hand and promised him every support. But the facts are that each one stuck to his own position. And so Colonel-General Schörner, C.-in-C. Army Group "South Ukraine", was ordered on July 23 to change places immediately with Friessner, C.-in-C. Army Group "North", who was himself promoted to Colonel-General.

Army Group "North" cut off

Amongst the general officers of the Wehrmacht, Schörner was one of the few who was unswerving in his loyalty to the Führer. However great his National Socialist zeal, however, it was not in his power to satisfy Hitler, for the 3rd Baltic Front (General Maslennikov) now went over to the offensive and extended the battle further northwards. This was followed on July 25 by an attack by the Leningrad Front (Marshal of the U.S.S.R. L. A. Govorov). In all a dozen armies totalling at least 80 divisions took part in this concentric offensive.

▽ *Soviet 76-mm guns on the 2nd Belorussian Front. With a range of over 12,000 yards these guns were the backbone of Soviet field artillery. The heavy losses suffered at the beginning of "Barbarossa" allowed the Russians to start from scratch with the reorganisation and standardisation of their artillery, some of which dated back to before World War I.*

Whilst Govorov was breaking through the Narva defile and Maslennikov, after liberating Pskov on July 21, was also driving on into Estonia, on July 26 Eremenko, anchoring his left flank on the Dvina, captured the towns of Rēzekne (Rositten) and Dvinsk (Daugav'pils) in Latvia. Bagramyan, who was using what Hitler called the "hole in the Wehrmacht", or the still gaping breach between the right and left of Army Groups "North" and "Centre", changed direction from west to northwest and, driving through Panevežys, Jelgava (Mittau), and Tukums, reached the Gulf of Riga to the west of the great Latvian port in the evening of August 1. As Generals Lindemann and Friessner had never ceased to predict, Army Group "North", with some 30 divisions, was cut off in Estonia and northern Latvia. More fortunate than Paulus at Stalingrad, however, Schörner could confidently rely on the Baltic for supplies and evacuation, since the Gulf of Finland was blocked right across so that Soviet submarines could not operate in the open sea. In the Gulf of Riga his right flank was efficiently supported by the guns of the German fleet – by the very warships which Hitler had wanted to scrap in 1943.

Konev attacks

On the German side of the immense front line stretching from the Baltic to the Carpathians, the second fortnight in July brought defeat to Army Group "North Ukraine". This added further disaster to the crushing of Army Group "Centre", the last consequences of which were still far from being played out. The tension was such that, taking also into account the American breakthrough in Normandy, it might have been thought that the last hour had struck for the Wehrmacht and for Greater Germany's Third Reich. This was how Marshal Rokossovsky saw events when he stated to a correspondent of the British *Exchange Telegraph* on July 26:

"It is no longer important to capture such and such a position. The essential thing is to give the enemy no respite. The Germans are running to their deaths . . . Their troops have lost all contact with their command."

On the following day a spokesman of *Stavka* spoke in the same terms at a press conference: "The Führer's G.H.Q. will

no more be able to hold the line of the Vistula than it did those of the Bug and the San. The German Army is irremediably beaten and breaking up."

Also on July 13 Marshal Konev and the forces of the 1st Ukrainian Front had come into the battle, extending the action of the three Belorussian Fronts from the area of Kovel' to the left bank of the Dniestr. According to the Soviet military historian Boris S. Telpukhovsky, whose account we have no reason to doubt, Konev had been given by *Stavka* all the necessary men and *matériel* to secure an easy victory over Army Group "North Ukraine", which was still, together with Army Group "Centre", under the command of Model. For this assault Konev had 16,213 guns and rocket-launchers, 1,573 tanks, 463 assault guns, 3,240 aircraft, and no fewer than seven armies, including the 1st and 3rd Guards Tank Armies and the 4th Tank Army, commanded respectively by Generals M. E. Katukov, P. S. Rybalko, and D. D. Lelyushenko, all three very experienced tank commanders.

On the German side, Army Group "North Ukraine" had had to give up to Army Group "Centre" four Panzer and three infantry divisions since June 22 and was reduced to 43 divisions (of which five were Panzer and one *Panzergrenadier*) and two mountain brigades. Assuming that between April and June the German armoured divisions had been brought up to their normal strength of 160 fighting and command tanks which, knowing the aberrations of Adolf Hitler, seems highly unlikely, the Russians outnumbered them by two to one. In the air Russian superiority was of the order of five to one. Hence the disaster which befell 8th Panzer Division on July 14. Disregarding orders, it took the main road to Brody to speed up its counter-attack. Major-General von Mellenthin writes:

"Eighth Panzer was caught on the move by Russian aircraft and suffered devastating losses. Long columns of tanks and lorries went up in flames, and all hope of counterattack disappeared."

Marshal Konev had forces so powerful and so numerous at his command that he could give his offensive two centres of gravity. On the right, in the area southwest of Lutsk, a first group containing notably the 1st Guards Tank Army, was to break up the 4th *Panzerarmee* (General Harpe) then exploit its victory in a general south-west direction. On the

△ *Rokossovsky: "It is no longer important to capture such and such a position. The essential thing is to give the enemy no respite. The Germans are running to their deaths . . ."*

△ *Schörner, one of Hitler's most fanatically loyal generals – he, too, was given the impossible task of plugging the vast breaches torn open in the German front.*

△ *Illusion. "The Führer is saved!" "Then the secret weapon's failed." (From Götenborg Hand Tidning).*

△ *Detroit Star's cartoonist Burch neatly sums up Hitler's unenviable position: "Between two fires".*

▽ *From Moscow's Krokodil. The "Hitlerite hordes" dash themselves to ruin against the rock of the Red Army.*

left a second group, containing the 3rd Guards Tank Army and the 4th Tank Army, had concentrated in the area of Ternopol': attacking due west it was to engage the 1st *Panzerarmee* (Colonel-General Raus) and form a pincer with the first group.

Model retreats

By evening on D-day the German defences in the two sectors were already seriously damaged. On the following day Colonel-General Raus put the 1st and 8th Panzer Divisions under XLVIII Panzer Corps for an eventual counter-attack, but this failed as a result of the circumstances described above by Mellenthin. Twenty-four hours later not only had the Russians broken through at the points previously designated by Konev, but the pincers had closed on General Hauffe's XIII Corps between L'vov and Brody.

And so a new "moving pocket" was formed, from which several thousand men managed to escape during a night-attack of hand-to-hand fighting. On July 23, however, General Hauffe had been taken prisoner together with 17,000 men of his corps and the victors counted 30,000 German corpses on the battlefield.

In the German sectors facing Rokossovsky and Konev, it was Model's intention to re-establish his line along the Bug. This evidently over-optimistic plan came to nothing in view of the weakness of Army Group "Centre" and the recent defeat of Army Group "North Ukraine". Worse still, the breach between the right flank of the 4th *Panzerarmee* and the left flank of the 1st was now wide open and there was the great danger that the latter's communications with Kraków would be cut and that the army would be driven back against the Carpathians. Hence, in full agreement with Colonel-General Guderian, who had succeeded Zeitzler as Chief-of-Staff at O.K.H. after the attempt on Hitler's life on July 20, Model drew back to the line of the Vistula and its extension the San above Deblin.

Even if the Germans, after their defeats of June 22 and July 13, had managed to establish a front line behind these ditches, this last-minute attempt could not have saved the Polish oilwells at Drogobycz and Boryslaw which became a heavy and irreparable loss to the military economy of the Third Reich. The situation between the Narew and the Carpathians was now deteriorating so rapidly that O.K.H. had to draw on the strength of Army Group "South Ukraine" and send four Panzer and seven infantry divisions from Moldavia to Galicia.

The Russians reach the Vistula

Before these reinforcements could be put to use, Marshals Rokossovsky and Konev had reached the Vistula and the San at Blitzkrieg speed, mopping up German columns retreating on foot or in horse-drawn vehicles. Between July 28 and 31, tanks of the 1st Belorussian Front covered the 120 miles between Brest-Litovsk and the suburbs of Warsaw. They also crossed the Vistula at Magnuszew and Pulawy, upstream from the capital. Rokossovsky's optimistic view of events quoted above seems to have been justified. The 1st Ukrainian Front had similar quick successes, covering 125 miles on a front some 250 miles wide on July 27. On that same day its formations on the right got beyond Przemysl on the west bank of the San and cleaned up L'vov on the way, whilst on the left, having crossed the Dniestr, it captured Stanislawow and threw back to the Carpathians the Hungarian 1st and 2nd Armies, which had formed the right flank of Army Group "North Ukraine" since the end of the winter. The situation now looked very dangerous.

A few days later Konev got a bridge-head over 30 miles deep over the Vistula in the area of Sandomierz, drove on beyond the San as far as Rzeszów, more than 90 miles beyond L'vov, and on August 7 occupied the oil wells at Drogobycz and Boryslaw.

Massive losses

A Moscow communiqué dated July 25 put the German losses since the start of the summer offensive at some 60 divisions, or 380,000 killed and more than 150,000 prisoners. The figures seem acceptable. On the other hand, the figure of 2,700 tanks destroyed or captured, as the complement of 17 fully-equipped Panzer divisions, seems unlikely.

The retreat halts

From the Dvina at Vitebsk to the Niemen at Kaunas is 250 miles as the crow flies and from the Dniepr at Orsha to the Vistula at Warsaw 400; the bridgehead at Sandomierz reached by Konev's advance guard was over 180 miles from the area of Lutsk. The 1944 Russian summer offensive, carried out on the old cavalry principle of "to the last breath of the last horse and the last horseman" had therefore reached its strategic limit.

Between the Carpathians and the Narew, O.K.H.'s reinforcements, though desperate and improvised, were beginning to take effect. The 17th Army (General Schulz) filled the gap between the 1st and 4th *Panzerarmee* and the 9th Army (General von Vormann) occupied the left flank of the 4th *Panzerarmee* between the Sandomierz bridgehead and a point downstream of Warsaw. There also came into the battle from the interior or from Moldavia a good half-dozen armoured divisions, including the "Hermann Göring", the S.S. 3rd *"Totenkopf"* and 5th *"Wiking"* Panzer, and the excellent *"Grossdeutschland" Panzergrenadier*. Volume IV of the *Great Patriotic War* gives a good account of this change in the situation of the two sides:

"At the end of July . . . the tempo of the

offensive had greatly slowed down. The German High Command had by this time thrown very strong reserves against the main sectors of our advance. German resistance was strong and stubborn. It should also be considered that our rifle divisions and tank corps had suffered heavy losses in previous battles; and the artillery and the supply bases were lagging behind, and that the troops were short of both petrol and munitions.

"Infantry and tanks were not receiving nearly enough artillery support. During the delays in re-basing our air force on new airfields, this was much less active than before. At the beginning of the Belorussian Campaign, we had complete control of the air. At the beginning of

△ △ *A 76-mm gun of the 1st Ukrainian Front in action as an anti-tank weapon.*
△ *A Panther tank and a column of trucks overtake bicycle riding infantrymen during the German retreat through Galicia. The bicycle featured throughout the war as a cheap and efficient mode of transport which did not need convoys of petrol tankers. Even towards the end of the war, British airborne troops used a handy collapsible version.*

August our superiority was temporarily lost. In the 1st Belorussian sector between August 1 and 13 our planes carried out 3,170 sorties and the enemy planes 3,316."

The situation reviewed

Doubtless, and for reasons which we shall see shortly, these statements by the Soviet writers are not completely impartial. Nevertheless by August 16, soon after Model had been given the job of repairing the situation, the position on the Eastern Front can be said to have stabilised temporarily between Kalvariya and the Carpathians. In particular the 4th *Panzerarmee* and the 9th Army had managed to reduce the bridgeheads at Sandomierz (Baranow), Pulawy, and Magnuszew, but not to eliminate them completely. On the right bank of the Vistula the Soviet 2nd Tank Army suffered a defeat at Wolomin and Radzymin, a few

▷▽ *A Wespe self-propelled howitzer. Armed with the standard 10.5-cm gun of the German artillery, the Wespe was one of the best known self-propelled guns of the war.*
▽ *Russian gunners using captured German 105-mm guns to supplement the fire of their 76-mm guns in a shoot in the Carpathians. Both sides used captured equipment, from tanks and artillery to boots and small arms.*

miles from Warsaw, which cost 3,000 killed and 6,000 prisoners together with a considerable amount of *matériel*.

This pause gives us an opportunity to put forward some conclusions on these six weeks of operations on the Eastern Front:

1. Warsaw may be 400 miles from Orsha, but it is only 350 from Berlin. So a repetition of the German mistakes which led to this victory by the Red Army would land the Russians in the heart of the Third Reich.

2. Between June 1 and August 30, 1944, Germany's land forces lost on the Eastern Front alone 916,860 in killed, wounded, and prisoners. The human resources of the Third Reich were therefore rapidly running out and would not be made up by the expedient of "people's grenadier" (*Volksgrenadier*) divisions.

3. French émigrés returning to their country after the fall of Napoleon were said to have learned nothing and forgotten nothing. Hitler's example shows that one can do worse: he learned nothing and forgot everything. The failure of the attempt on his life on July 20 would therefore allow him to indulge his despotism and incompetence to the full.

4. The fourth and last conclusion comes in the form of a question. The *Great Patriotic War* says that the forces of

the 1st Belorussian Front arrived exhausted on the banks of the Vistula, which explains the halt in their advance: but could not *Stavka* have made up its strength with units and *matériel* already earmarked for campaigns in Rumania and Hungary so as to maintain the drive westwards?

As we are aware that a theatre of operations can only absorb as many men and as much *matériel* as can be supplied by its means of communication, we leave the last question unanswered.

Warsaw – betrayed?

We are thus brought to the controversy which arose between the West and the Soviets over the behaviour of Stalin, *Stavka,* and the Red Army towards the Warsaw rising started at 1700 hours on August 1 by General Bor-Komorowski, C.-in-C. of the Polish Home Army. We cannot imitate Telpukhovsky, who maintains a prudent silence on this subject but nevertheless devotes a page and a half of his extensive work to the liberation of the little Polish village of Guerasimowichy on July 26, 1944. In his memoirs, Winston Churchill, reporting the return to Praga of Rokossovsky about September 15, made no bones about the reasons for the tragic episode as he saw them:

"The Russians occupied the Praga suburb, but went no further. They wished to have the non-Communist Poles destroyed to the full, but also to keep alive the idea that they were going to their rescue.

"Such was their liberation of Poland, where they now rule. But this cannot be the end of the story."

Churchill was doubtless writing under the influence of the exchange of telegraph messages he had had with Stalin on the subject of Warsaw, and was remembering the help he had wanted to give by air to the stricken city and its heroic defenders. He did not know then as well as we do now about the operations in the suburbs of the Polish capital between August 1 and 4. Michel Garder, writing in 1961 after carefully researching Soviet material published after 1953, agrees in broad essentials with Churchill. "With Rokossovsky within 32 miles of Warsaw," he writes, "it seemed to General Bor-Komorowski that the arrival of the Russian troops could only be a matter of

a few days. It was the duty of the Poles to welcome the Soviets as allies and not as 'liberator-occupiers'. This was just what Stalin did not want.

"In the eyes of the Kremlin, the Polish Home Army was merely a tool of the 'reactionary Polish clique' in London whose leaders, in addition to their 'enslavement to capitalism' and their 'bourgeois chauvinism' had had the effrontery to state that the Katyn massacres were the work of the N.K.V.D.

"Having suddenly run out of steam, the irresistible 1st Belorussian Front offensive had found itself facing the German bridgehead in front of Warsaw. To get so far had, it is true, cost Rokossovsky's armies a great effort. Their lines of communication were stretched. They needed a few days' respite and probably considerable reinforcements in men and *matériel* to bring them back up to strength. But nothing, other than political considerations by the Kremlin, could justify the semi-inertia of the Soviet troops in September when they reached the suburbs of Praga."

Werth is less certain than Churchill or Garder. He seems to give credence to the pessimistic figures for the 1st Belo-

△ *German prisoners in Maidanek concentration camp march past stacks of unrecognisable human remains. The Russians showed the camp to their own soldiers and to Western journalists. Alexander Werth reported that "the Germans went through the camp, at first at an ordinary pace, and then faster and faster, till they ran in a frantic panicky stampede, and they were green with terror, and their hands shook and their teeth chattered."*

△ Soviet sub-machine gunners ford the west Bug river in the Ukraine.

▽ A KV-85 roars past the shattered remains of a 37-mm anti-tank gun during the fighting before Warsaw.

russian Front on August 1 quoted above from the *Great Patriotic War*. On the other hand, he does not omit the passage which refers to the defeat of the Soviet 2nd Tank Army before Praga, where it was attacked on its left flank by five German divisions, including four Panzer. It is interesting to see that he was personally involved on one occasion. Received in Lublin by Rokossovsky he recorded the following on the spot:

"'I can't go into any details. But I'll tell you just this. After several weeks' heavy fighting in Belorussia and eastern Poland we finally reached the outskirts of Praga about the 1st of August. The Germans, at this point, threw in four armoured divisions, and we were driven back.'

'How far back?'

'I can't tell you exactly, but let's say nearly 100 kilometres (sixty-five miles).'

'Are you still retreating?'

'No—we are now advancing–but slowly.'

'Did you think on August 1 (as was suggested by the *Pravda* correspondent that day) that you could take Warsaw within a very few days?'

'If the Germans had not thrown in all that armour, we could have taken Warsaw, though not in a frontal attack; but it was never more than a 50-50 chance. A German counter-attack at Praga was not to be excluded, though we now know that before these armoured divisions arrived, the Germans inside Warsaw were in a panic, and were packing up in a great hurry.'

'Wasn't the Warsaw Rising justified in the circumstances?'

'No it was a bad mistake. The insurgents started it off their own bat, without consulting us.'

'There was a broadcast from Moscow calling on them to rise.'

'That was routine stuff *(sic)*. There were similar calls to rise from *Swit* radio [Home Army], and also from the Polish service of the BBC–so I'm told, though I didn't hear it myself. Let's be serious. An armed insurrection in a place like Warsaw could only have succeeded if it had been carefully co-ordinated with the Red Army. The question of timing was of the utmost importance. The Warsaw insurgents were badly armed, and the rising would have made sense only if we were already on the point of *entering Warsaw. That point had not been reached*

△ Russian prisoners digging an anti-tank trench near Warsaw. Aware of the threat that the large numbers of people in Warsaw posed to their rear areas, the Germans had plans to evacuate the population of the city.

at any stage, and I'll admit that some Soviet correspondents were much too optimistic on the 1st of August. We were pushed back. We couldn't have got Warsaw before the middle of August, even in the best of circumstances. But circumstances were not good, but bad. Such things do happen in war. It happened at Kharkov in March 1943 and at Zhitomir last winter.'

'What prospect is there of your getting back to Praga within the next few weeks?'

'I can't go into that. All I can say is that we shall try to capture both Praga and Warsaw, but it won't be easy.'

'But you have bridgeheads south of Warsaw.'

'Yes, but the Germans are doing their damnedest to reduce them. We're having much difficulty in holding them, and we are losing a lot of men. Mind you, we have fought non-stop for over two months now.''

Whilst accepting the good faith and accuracy of Werth's report, it would seem that it should be interpreted as follows: Rokossovsky and, behind him, the Soviet high command, had well and

truly got over their elation of July 26, and at a distance now of 30 days were claiming never to have felt it. However, at 2015 hours on July 15 Radio Moscow broadcast a stirring appeal to the population of Warsaw and a few hours later the Union of Polish Patriots station, which followed the Soviet line, took up the call:

"The Polish Army now entering Polish territory had been trained in the U.S.S.R. It unites with the People's Army to form the body of the Polish Armed Forces, the backbone of our nation in her struggle for independence. The sons of Warsaw will rally to its ranks tomorrow. Together with the allied army they will drive out the enemy to the west, expel Hitler's vermin from Poland and deal a mortal blow to the remains of Prussian imperialism. For Warsaw which did not yield, but fought on, the hour has struck."

And, as it was to be expected that the enemy, now cornered, would retreat into the capital, the appeal for an uprising continued: "This is why . . . by energetic hand-to-hand fighting in the streets of Warsaw, in the houses, the factories, the warehouses, not only shall we hasten the coming of our final liberation, but we shall safeguard our national heritage and the lives of our brothers."

Stalin stands aloof

On August 5 Churchill sent Stalin a request to intervene on behalf of the insurrectionists, but he was answered by scepticism: Stalin doubted, if not the reality, at least the importance of the uprising.

On August 16, when Churchill repeated his demands, Stalin expressed his conviction that "the Warsaw operation is a horrible and senseless venture which is costing the lives of a great many of the population. This would not have arisen if the Soviet Command had been informed beforehand and if the Poles had kept in constant touch with us."

However, it was not Mikołajczyk's Polish Government-in-Exile which had broken off relations with the Kremlin. Must one therefore assume that Stalin supposed that the Home Army would be deaf to the call to arms given on July 29? Surely not. Be that as it may, this led Stalin to the following conclusion: "From the situation thus created, the Soviet Command deduces that it must dissociate itself from the Warsaw adventure, as it has no responsibility, either direct or indirect, in the operation."

Stalin was not content, however, merely with dissociating himself from the insurrectionists (whom he called on August 22 a "handful of criminals who, in order to seize power, have unleashed the Warsaw venture") but also obstinately refused to allow Anglo-American aircraft to land on Soviet territory in order to refuel from their operations over Warsaw. He knew that this would severely restrict the Allies, who were attempting to fly in supplies to the defenders of the unhappy city.

No help from Roosevelt

Would Stalin eventually have given in to Churchill if Roosevelt had thrown in the weight of his authority? We do not know. What we do know, however, is that on August 26, taking into account the "general perspectives of the war", the American President refused to join

forces with the British Prime Minister in a new approach to Stalin. He was doubtless influenced by Hopkins and Morgenthau. On September 2, James V. Forrestal, who had succeeded Frank Knox (who died on April 28, 1944) as Secretary of the Navy, noted in his diary:

"I find that whenever any American suggests that we act in accordance with the needs of our own security he is apt to be called a god-damned fascist or imperialist, while if Uncle Joe suggests that he needs the Baltic Provinces, half Poland, all Bessarabia and access to the Mediterranean, all hands agree that he is a fine frank, candid and generally delightful fellow who is very easy to deal with because he is so explicit in what he wants."

Warsaw's epic fight

The rest is history. The defenders of Warsaw met their fate with the most sublime heroism. Having driven the Russians back over 30 miles from the right bank of the Vistula, the Germans calmly set about the reconquest of the Polish capital with large numbers of Tiger tanks, assault guns, and little

△ Soviet soldiers move cautiously through a state room of Razdravanu Castle, during the fighting for Iaşi.

▽ Know your enemy: German soldiers examine a captured T-34, taken during the fighting near the Warsaw suburb of Praga.

△ *A section of Russian riflemen moves forward during the fighting in Praga. The right flank of the 1st Belorussian Front reached the suburb on July 31, and the Warsaw Rising began a day later.*

Goliath tanks, a kind of remote-controlled bomb on tracks. The heaviest weapons the defenders had were of 20-mm calibre.

They fought from barricade to barricade, from house to house, from storey to storey and even in the sewers. The area occupied by the defenders gradually shrank, so that the meagre supplies dropped by Anglo-American aircraft fell increasingly into enemy hands. The repression of the uprising was entrusted to Himmler. He appointed *Waffen*-S.S. General von dem Bach-Zalewski and gave him, amongst others, S.S. police units, a brigade of Russian ex-prisoners, and a brigade of ex-convicts, all of whom had committed such excesses that Guderian had persuaded Hitler to remove them from the front.

In the second fortnight of September the Russians reoccupied Praga but remained virtually passive opposite the capital. Under these conditions Bor-Komorowski, who had had 22,000 killed, missing, or seriously wounded out of his 40,000 fighters, resigned himself to surrender on October 2, obtaining from von dem Bach-Zalewski an assurance that his men would without exception be treated under the Geneva Convention of August 27, 1929 governing prisoners-of-war.

Stalin's responsibility

From this brief summary of the essential facts it is possible to conclude:

1. The Warsaw "venture", which aroused the ire and indignation of Stalin, was sparked off by a radio broadcast from Moscow, but without criminal intent.
2. Since the Russians played down as much as possible the defeat of Rokossovsky at Praga, the will to let the Polish Home Army be massacred was imputed to an inertia which arose to a great extent from impotence.
3. Under these conditions it cannot be proved that Anglo-American aircraft taking off from Foggia could have saved the Home Army if Stalin had allowed them to land on Soviet territory.
4. But it can be stated that, by refusing them this permission, Stalin left no alternative to the insurrectionists of August 1 but death or captivity and that he did so knowingly and willingly.

The Poles will never forget.

CHAPTER 71
IMPHAL AND KOHIMA

The so-called "March on Delhi", the Japanese offensive against the British IV Corps on the Tiddim-Imphal-Kohima front which started rolling when Lieutenant-General G. Yanagida's 33rd Division crossed the Chindwin in force on the night of March 7-8, was the brainchild of Lieutenant-General Renya Mutaguchi, aged 55.

To the Japanese it was known as the "U-GO" offensive and its limited object-ive was to forestall a British offensive by attacking and destroying the British base at Imphal, thus strengthening the Japan-ese defence of Burma.

A subsidiary objective was, with the use of the Indian National Army division raised and commanded by the plausible and resourceful Subhas Chandra Bhose, to "exercise political control over India". This was to be achieved by encouraging and supporting dissident anti-British ele-ments, who had in the previous year created a most serious situation in Bengal and Bihar by their widespread sabotage of bridges, communications, and airfields. As it happened Chandra Bhose stayed comfortably in Rangoon and the I.N.A. division, which had the strength of only a brigade (totalling about 7,000 men), had

little effect on either the battle or the political situation.

The date of the "U-GO" offensive was timed to phase in with the successful outcome of Major-General T. Sakurai's "HA-GO" offensive in the Arakan. The latter's purpose was to draw off the Allied reserve divisions to the Arakan prior to Mutaguchi's attack on Imphal. This task Sakurai's 55th Division had successfully achieved for, by the end of February 1944, six divisions (5th, 7th, 25th, 26th, 36th, and 81st West African), a parachute brigade, and a special service (commando) brigade, had been drawn into that theatre. This concentration, coupled with the extensive use of air supply, had certainly foiled Sakurai's raid after three weeks of hard fighting. But Mutaguchi should have crossed the Chindwin in mid-February as planned in order to take the maximum advantage of Sakurai's feint.

Unfortunately Lieutenant-General M. Yamauchi's 15th Division, which Muta-guchi intended to use for the direct assault on Imphal, had become stuck in Siam. It was not until February 11, after Mutaguchi himself had signalled Field-Marshal Count Terauchi, command-

△ *Naga tribesmen at work road clearing in the Imphal-Kohima area.*

er of the Southern Army at Singapore, that the 15th Division started to concentrate in Burma, arriving ill-equipped, ill-fed, and ill-tempered.

This division had been training in northern Siam and some of its units had been improving the Chiengmai–Toungoo road as an alternative route to the much bombed Burma–Siam railway. Assisted by ten motor transport companies, it had marched the 700-mile long road from Chiengmai to Shwebo via Kentung and Mandalay in order to toughen itself up and prepare itself for its task ahead.

D-day for the "U-GO" offensive was fixed for March 15, by which time the 15th Division must not only be re-equipped but have moved to its start line between Paungbyin and Sittaung on the Chindwin, as well as organising its communications forward from Indaw and Wuntho on the railway via Pinlebu.

The other two divisions in Mutaguchi's 15th Army were in a much better state.

The 33rd Division had operated for many years in China and had taken part from the start in the conquest of Burma as well as combatting the first Chindit operation in 1943. This division, advancing initially along comparatively good roads, would carry with it all the armour and heavy artillery (4th Tank Regiment, 1st Anti-Tank Battalion, 3rd and 18th Heavy Field Artillery Regiments) that the Japanese could muster for this attack.

The 31st Division (Lieutenant-General K. Sato), whose task was the unenviable one of advancing from Homalin and Tamanthi on the upper reaches of the Chindwin river, and then over a series of parallel ridges (reaching a height of over 7,000 feet) to Jessami and Kohima, had previously operated only in China, although some of its units had been stationed on islands in the Pacific. It had arrived in Burma between June and September 1943 and had immediately been sent to the Chindwin front, where it had crossed swords with the battle-experienced 20th Indian Division (Major-General D.D. Gracey). The 31st Division had had, therefore, plenty of time to get inured to the conditions in that area. It would operate on a mule and horse transport basis, trusting on a tenuous 100-mile long line of communications from Mawlu and Indaw on the railway to Tamanthi and Homalin, supported by a three-week reserve of food, ammunition, and fodder built up on the line of the Chindwin.

Mutaguchi, "the victor of Singapore", had previously commanded the 18th Division in north Burma and had been most impressed by the activities of the Chindits and their leader, Brigadier Wingate, whom he held in high regard. Mutaguchi had, with some difficulty, sold his plan to knock out IV Corps by a three-pronged, three-divisional thrust against the 200-mile road leading down from the Brahmaputra valley parallel to the Chindwin. Prime Minister Tojo and Count Terauchi agreed to this gamble only because they needed some offensive success to offset the disasters which had been occurring in the Pacific. They then agreed only with the proviso that it should be combined with an attempt to start widespread insurrection in East India with the co-operation of Subhas Chandra Bhose's Indian National Army, on which they placed great hopes of success.

Lieutenant-General M. Kawabe, commanding the Burma Area Army, was sceptical of the whole plan and had

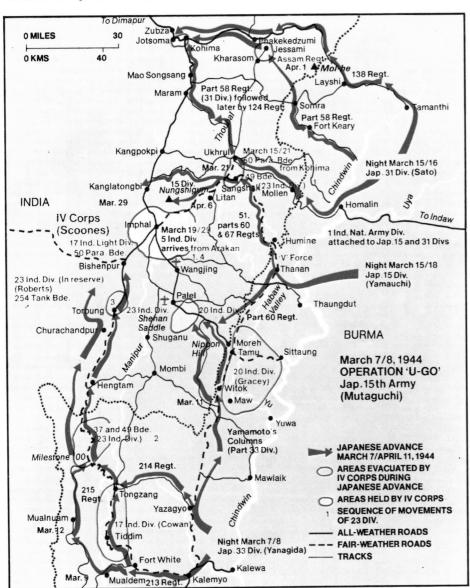

OPERATION 'U-GO'
Jap. 15th Army
(Mutaguchi)

March 7/8, 1944
BURMA

orders to prevent Mutaguchi from over-reaching himself. Lieutenant-General Tazoe, commanding the 5th Air Division, had no faith in Mutaguchi's plan whatsoever. He was apprehensive of what the Allied airborne forces (the Chindits) would do, for his reconnaissance aircraft had shown they were ready to be sent in again. He pointed out to Mutaguchi that he would be totally incapable of helping him with air supply once he had crossed the Chindwin.

Mutaguchi's plan was for the 33rd Division, with the bulk of his armour and artillery, to advance from its bridgehead at Kalewa and to attack and surround the 17th Indian Division (Major-General D.T. Cowan) at Tiddim and Tongzang. Leaving a small containing force, the 33rd Division would push forward with all speed northwards to the Imphal plain, where it would also cut the Bishenpur Track running west to Silchar. One regiment,

under Major-General T. Yamamoto, would meanwhile advance north from Kalemyo up the Kabaw valley and open a road through to support the 15th Division, bringing most of the wheeled and track vehicles with it.

The 33rd Division would start its advance one week before D-day, when the 15th and 31st Divisions would cross the Chindwin.

The 15th Division's task was to cross the Chindwin near Thaungdut and advance on tracks via Ukhrul to cut the Dimapur road north of Imphal near Kanglatongbi. It would also detail one column to contain the 20th Division (Gracey) east of Palel. With the 33rd Division, its final objective was to overrun the rich Imphal plain, destroy IV Corps, and capture the airfields and a vast quantity of supplies.

The 31st Division had the more arduous task of advancing 70 to 100 miles along

△ *A Bren gun team of the R.A.F. Regiment in position above an airfield in the Imphal valley. Airfield defence was of primary importance in the Imphal campaign, for without it the besieged defenders could not have received the supplies needed for their 88-day defence.*

footpaths from the riverine villages of Tamanthi and Homalin, through the Naga Hills, and over a series of bare mountain ranges to capture Kohima, a small, obscure village and staging post on a 4,000-foot pass on the Dimapur–Imphal road. Whether it would exploit its success from there by attacking the undefended railhead at Dimapur depended on circumstances.

Mutaguchi hoped that the whole operation would be resolved within three weeks, by which time he also hoped to have road communications functioning from Kalewa via Palel to Imphal and north to Kohima.

The command set-up in Burma as far as 14th Army was concerned was rather top heavy. The Supreme Commander, Lord Louis Mountbatten, gave his orders to General Giffard, commanding 11th Army Group, who commanded only one army, Lieutenant-General Slim's 14th Army. 14th Army initially had under command XV Corps (Lieutenant-General A.F.P. Christison) in the Arakan, IV Corps (Lieutenant-General G.A.P. Scoones), the Northern Combat Area Command (Lieutenant-General J.W. Stilwell), and Special Force (Major-General O.C. Wingate). Later XXXIII Corps (Lieutenant-General M.G.N. Stopford) was formed in the Brahmaputra valley to counter the Japanese advance, and XV Corps came under the direct command of General Sir George Giffard's 11th Army Group.

Slim had not been deceived by the violence of Sakurai's Arakan attack and his countering the threat by the fly-in of

overwhelming numbers, coupled with his strict orders that all units should stand firm if their communications were cut and await supply by air, had converted what might have been a disaster in the Arakan to a morale-raising victory.

Slim realised from Intelligence reports that IV Corps might suffer similar long-range penetration attacks, but he thought that these could not be in a strength greater than two regiments. He made his plans accordingly. On the night of March 5-6 he allowed the Chindit airborne operation to start its fly-in across the Chindwin to block the Japanese communications facing General Stilwell's forces (N.C.A.C.), in accordance with the orders of the Combined Chiefs-of-Staff.

IV Corps consisted of three divisions (17th, 20th, and 23rd) and the 254th Indian Tank Brigade (with Shermans and Grants). The 17th Division, after its retreat from Burma in 1942, had stayed for two years patrolling in the 7,000-foot Tiddim Hills, 100 miles south of Imphal. This light division consisted of two, mainly Gurkha, brigades on a mule/jeep transport basis.

The 20th Division was based on Palel and Tamu south-east of Imphal and patrolled towards the Chindwin.

The 23rd Division (Major-General O.L. Roberts) was in reserve at Imphal.

Lieutenant-General Scoones, who had commanded IV Corps since its formation, was a clever, quiet, forceful personality who achieved results through efficiency and attention to detail rather than by flamboyant leadership. With him his subordinates would know that everything would be in its place and up to strength.

Scoones' plan, which had been approved by Slim, was, on being attacked, to withdraw his two forward divisions back to the wide open Imphal plain, where he would be able to bring to bear his superiority in tanks heavy artillery, and close air support, which could outgun and destroy anything that the Japanese could bring over the hills and across the Chindwin against them. He would then have three divisions, with a promise of a fourth to be flown in, to combat the Japanese raid. The vital factor in his plan was when to give the order for the 17th Division to start its 100-mile retirement back from Tiddim to Imphal.

Slim planned to fly in the 5th Indian Division (Major-General H.R. Briggs) from the Arakan as soon as news of an

attack in strength was confirmed. The 50th Parachute Brigade (Brigadier M.R.J. Hope-Thompson) was due to be flown into Imphal and directed towards Ukhrul. Scoones planned to fly out all unnecessary administrative personnel and the very large number of engineers and their civilian working force who were engaged on improving communications and airfields within the Imphal area. In fact over 40,000 "unwanted mouths" were flown out as the battle progressed.

IV Corps consisted eventually of the 5th, 17th, 20th, and 23rd Indian Divisions, the 50th Indian Parachute Brigade, and the 254th Indian Tank Brigade (Shermans and Grants), comprising 49 infantry battalions (nine British, 24 Indian, and 16 Gurkha), and 120 tanks. Besides this, IV Corps had the 8th Medium Regiment, Royal Artillery, with 5.5-inch guns, as well as the usual complement of divisional artillery and engineers. In all there were about 120,000 men, excluding constructional engineers and Royal Air Force.

The strength of the Japanese 15th Army which crossed the Chindwin was 84,280 Japanese and 7,000 Indians. A further 4,000 reinforcements arrived during operations. The Japanese divided each division into three columns of varying size and composition, according to their tasks, but the total number of units which can be compared with those of IV Corps were as follows: nine infantry regiments, totalling 26 battalions (one battalion of the 15th Division had been sent back to deal with the landing of the airborne forces, but was later returned to the 15th Division during its attack on Imphal); two heavy artillery regiments; and one tank regiment.

Besides these there were divisional artillery, with much of it on a light mountain pack basis, and three engineer regiments, which were often used as infantry.

The British XXXIII Corps at its maximum strength consisted of two divisions (British 2nd and 7th Indian, under Major-Generals J.M.L. Grover and F.W. Messervy respectively), the 149th Regiment, Royal Armoured Corps, the 23rd (L.R.P.) Brigade (Brigadier L.E.C.M. Perowne), the 3rd Special Service (Commando) Brigade (Brigadier W.I. Nonweiler), and the Lushai Brigade (Brigadier P.C. Marindin), totalling about 75,000 troops, including 34 infantry battalions (20 British, 11 Indian, and three Gurkha).

Yanagida started his advance to attack

△ *The District Commissioner's Bungalow, destroyed in the heavy fighting for Kohima.*

on the night of March 7-8. The 215th Regiment went up the high mountains to Fort White and crossed the Manipur river to get into a position west of the 17th Indian Division's position at Tiddim and Tongzang.

The 214th Regiment marched northwest and advanced directly on Tongzang. Both regiments formed blocks across the Tiddim–Imphal road. Cowan, commanding the 17th Indian Division, had not told his brigadiers that there were plans for withdrawal, so on March 13, when he got Scoones's order to withdraw, his brigades had to have time to see that the orders reached every man. This meant a 24-hour delay. This particular division, consisting of a preponderance of Gurkhas, was well trained and had great confidence in itself and its quiet commander. Withdrawal continued according to plan and at each road-block the Gurkhas put into operation plans they had rehearsed and the Japanese blocks were removed without great difficulty, but with considerable loss to the Japanese.

However, Scoones was apprehensive of how successfully the 17th Division would be able to carry out this 100-mile long withdrawal on a road through high hills and where there were ambush positions every few hundred yards. So he committed some of his reserve division, the 23rd, which he had moved to Torbung. The 37th and 49th Brigades, with a squadron of tanks, were moved forward to Milestone 100.

Yanagida pressed on, but his troops were losing their momentum and after the fourth block across the road had been successfully removed by the British forces, Yanagida became depressed. On the night of March 23, after receiving many casualties, Yanagida sent a rather panicky signal to Mutaguchi implying that his position was hopeless. Yanagida had been appalled at the success of the Sherman and Grant medium tanks, against which neither his artillery nor his anti-tank guns seemed to have any affect.

After an exchange of furious signals Mutaguchi decided to remove Yanagida

Moving further north, Yamauchi's 15th Division crossed the Chindwin on the night of March 15-16 and moved quickly up the hills towards Ukhrul. According to plan he also sent a detachment to make contact with Yamamoto's column on the Palel Road. By March 21 Yamamoto was in contact with the 50th Parachute Brigade at Ukhrul, where it had taken over from the 23rd Division's 49th Brigade, which in turn had been moved to assist the 17th Division. All this time it must be remembered that Mutaguchi was in Maymyo, 200 miles to the east, the pleasant

▽ *The Tennis Court area just west of the District Commissioner's Bungalow, also destroyed in the short, savage fight for Kohima.*

and sent for a successor. It must be emphasised that this took place at the beginning of the campaign and affected the command and consequently the morale of the division on which the success of the whole operation depended.

Major-General Yamamoto's column which, it will be remembered, had the preponderance of Japanese armour, advanced quickly and surely up the Kabaw valley until by March 11 it had reached a position at Maw on the right flank of Gracey's 20th Indian Division. Gracey had taken his brigade commanders into his confidence about what action the division would take when Scoones gave the order to withdraw. So his brigades knew exactly what to do when he ordered them to destroy unnecessary stores, disengage, move back, and reform on the Shenam Heights just east of Palel. This withdrawal took place in good order and without a hitch, but was followed up by Yamamoto. Heavy fighting soon took place on the Palel road at a point that became known as Nippon Hill.

hill station in which he had set up his headquarters. It was from this viewpoint that he sent signals exhorting his three divisional commanders to greater effort.

The 15th Division's orders were to bypass Ukhrul and move towards the hills north of the Imphal plain to seize Kanglatongbi.

Further north still, Sato's 31st Division which, having been in the area for many months, had had time to reconnoitre the routes over the hills, and done remarkably well. Crossing the Chindwin between Homalin and Tamanthi on the night of March 15-16, his left-hand column reached Ukhrul, where it made contact with Yamauchi's forces. Whilst Yamauchi pushed on, Sato's left-hand column, under the command of Major-General Shigesburo Miyazaki, made contact with the Indian Parachute Brigade at Sangshak near Ukhrul. After pushing out the paratroops, Miyazaki advanced northwest and set up a road block at Maram on March 27, a few miles south of Kohima.

Meanwhile Sato's 58th and 124th Regiments advanced on Jessami. Jessami was weakly held by the Assam Regiment and was captured on April 1.

Kohima itself had originally been defended by Brigadier D.F.W. Warren's 161st Brigade of the 5th Division, which had been flown up from the Arakan to Dimapur. When Lieutenant-General Stopford took command of the area with his XXXIII Corps, he unfortunately withdrew Brigadier Warren from Kohima to protect Dimapur itself, where there were 60,000 unarmed rear echelon troops looking after the stores and administration. This move left Kohima virtually unprotected. Sato continued his advance and by April 15 Kohima itself was invested.

Slim's calculations had been that not more than one Japanese regiment could be maintained at Kohima. This was, in fact, the case and Sato's men were to suffer for it later. But in the meantime this attack by a whole division threw the British defence plans out of gear.

The battles which followed centred around the sieges of Imphal and Kohima, but for the British, success depended also upon the co-ordination of forces in the whole of Burma, a formidable logistical problem.

Scoones had mapped out a very sensible defence of the Imphal plain. He formed fortresses or "boxes" around each area where there were stores or airfields, and had detailed a commander with staff in charge of that area with a force to defend it. This worked well, but when pressure from the Japanese intensified he had to reduce the size of these areas and give up some of the stores, which then fell into Japanese hands. By this time he had four divisions and the parachute brigade with the formidable 254th Medium Tank Brigade to fight his battle. He also had

△ *Garrison Hill, near the Tennis Court area in Kohima. After heavy fighting between May 4 and 7, the 6th and 33rd Brigades failed in their efforts to break past this point, and it was not until another major attack between the 11th and the 13th that the line of hills from the District Commissioner's Bungalow to Jail Hill was taken from the Japanese.*

27 squadrons of fighters and fighter-bombers at short call to harass and destroy the Japanese, who were better targets now that they were emerging into the open plain. It must also be remembered that on the high ground the hills were bare and Sato's 31st Division suffered heavily from air attack when caught out in the open at Litan during its advance on Kohima.

Into the trap

In the Brahmaputra valley XXXIII Corps, whose nucleus was the 2nd British Division (which had originally been the theatre reserve and had been training for operations in Sumatra or Malaya), was now forming fast. The 2nd Division had too many vehicles for the type of country, but as it advanced it soon learnt how to fight with only one road as its main axis. Stopford, realising his mistake in withdrawing Warren's 161st Brigade, sent them back to the Kohima area, where a tiny garrison of the Royal West Kents and Assam Rifles was holding out gallantly.

It was now five weeks since Sato had crossed the Chindwin, and his supplies were beginning to dry up. He was faced by a series of problems: exceptionally difficult terrain, poor communications and the activities of the Chindits who had destroyed the Japanese railway supply lines and cut off 300 trucks from Sato.

Sato signalled Mutaguchi that he was running out of supplies and was having to eat his mules. He suggested that he should start retiring whilst he still had some pack animals left. Mutaguchi was appalled by this message and sent some extremely rude signals to the conscientious Sato.

Meanwhile, the Chindit 23rd (L.R.P.) Brigade had been put under Stopford's command. He gave it the task of making a wide sweep to the east to get behind the Japanese 31st Division and to advance all the way to Ukhrul. The eight columns of the brigade pushed on along the footpaths over the high ridge with their mule transport and with supply by air. Many small actions were fought and although it was not possible in this country with its many paths to "cut" communications, the force threatened Sato's communications to such an extent that he told Mutaguchi that he must withdraw.

Mutaguchi was going through a bad time. He had replaced Yanagida with Major-General N. Tanaka, who was a tough, resilient, earthy soldier who had fought in north China. Mutaguchi had no luck with the 15th Division either, as the divisional commander, Yamauchi, died of malaria. He was replaced by Lieutenant-General U. Shibata, a man, it was said, "with an ox-like presence".

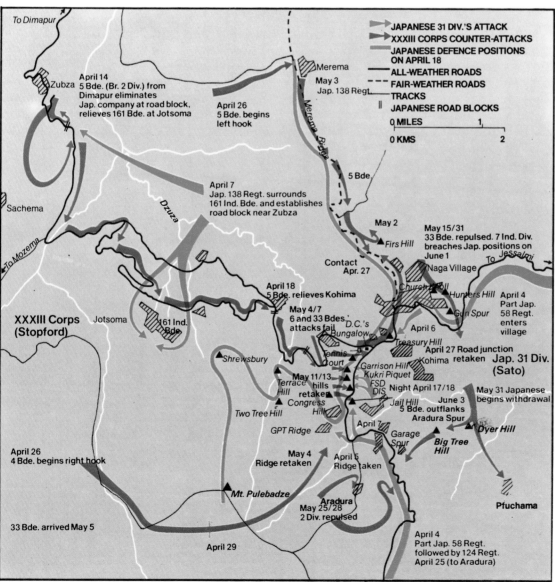

JAPANESE 31 DIV.'S ATTACK
XXXIII CORPS COUNTER-ATTACKS
**JAPANESE DEFENCE POSITIONS
ON APRIL 18**
ALL-WEATHER ROADS
FAIR-WEATHER ROADS
TRACKS
JAPANESE ROAD BLOCKS

0 MILES 1
0 KMS 2

To Dimapur

Zubza
April 14
5 Bde. (Br. 2 Div.) from
Dimapur eliminates
Jap. company at road block,
relieves 161 Bde. at Jotsoma

Merema
May 3
Jap. 138 Regt.

April 26
5 Bde. begins
left hook

5 Bde.

Sachema

Dzuza

April 7
Jap. 138 Regt. surrounds
161 Ind. Bde. and establishes
road block near Zubza

May 2

May 15/31
33 Bde. repulsed. 7 Ind. Div.
breaches Jap. positions on
June 1

Firs Hill

To Mozema

Contact
Apr. 27

Naga Village

To Jessami

**XXXIII Corps
(Stopford)**

Jotsoma

161 Ind.
Bde.

April 18
5 Bde. relieves Kohima

May 4/7
6 and 33 Bdes.
attacks fail

D.C.'s
Bungalow

Church Knoll

Hunters Hill

Gun Spur

April 4
Part Jap.
58 Regt.
enters
village

April 6

Treasury Hill

April 27 Road junction

Shrewsbury

Tennis
Court

Kohima retaken

**Jap. 31 Div.
(Sato)**

Garrison Hill
Kukri Piquet

May 11/13
Terrace
Hill

hills
retaken

FSD
DIS

Night April 17/18

May 31 Japanese
begins withdrawal

Congress
Hill

Jail Hill

June 3
5 Bde. outflanks
Aradura Spur

Two Tree Hill

April 7

Dyer Hill

GPT Ridge

Garage
Spur

Big Tree
Hill

April 26
4 Bde. begins right hook

May 4
Ridge retaken

April 5
Ridge taken

Pfuchama

33 Bde. arrived May 5

Mt. Pulebadze

Aradura
May 25/28
2 Div. repulsed

April 29

April 4
Part Jap. 58 Regt.
followed by 124 Regt.
April 25 (to Aradura)

△ *Men of the 3/10th Gurkha
Rifles (23rd Indian Division) on
Scraggy Hill, a point dominating
the Palel–Tamu road south-east
of Imphal. The hill was taken
on July 24 at the cost of 112
Gurkha casualties.*
◁ *The desperate battle for the
little town of Kohima.*

△ *Troops wait on a forward airfield in the Imphal hills before going into action. One of the most noteworthy features of the campaign was the way in which Allied air superiority allowed supplies and reinforcements to be flown in.*

The Japanese collapse

As the fighting for Kohima went on, Mutaguchi was issuing orders of the day appealing to all ranks, saying that the throne of the Emperor depended on them and so on. But this did not move the intelligent and worldly-wise Sato. Mutaguchi sent staff officers to see him, but Sato took no notice of them. On April 30 Sato signalled again, pointing out the hopelessness of his position. These signals continued until on June 1 Sato signalled "Propose retreating from Kohima with rearguard." Mutaguchi replied "Retreat and I will court-marshal you." Sato replied "Do as you please I will bring you down with me." This gives some idea of the division and state of mind of the Japanese force commanders, who were fighting against odds at Kohima and Imphal. Sato was quite adamant as he saw his men staggering back half naked, without ammunition and weapons, and relying on bamboo shoots and roots for their sustenance. He was determined that Mutaguchi should be brought back to

Tokyo for court-marshal for basic neglect of administration.

Sato left Miyazaki with 750 of his best and fittest men to form a rearguard south of Kohima, which had now been cleared by the 2nd Division, and retreated. The rest of his division, all supplies having been stopped by the Chindits, ceased to exist and melted away.

Around Imphal, however, very heavy fighting continued. With their two new divisional commanders, the 15th Division and 33rd Divisions were attacking Scoones from all directions, and it was only as a result of the skill and high morale of his divisions, coupled with the technical superiority of his tanks, the R.A.F., and the 8th Medium Artillery Regiment, that he could keep at bay the fanatical assaults of these Japanese.

It is worth digressing here to point out that defence against well-trained soldiers who are quite prepared to take part in suicidal attacks is quite different from defence against reasonable men who, when they see a situation is hopeless, will withdraw or surrender. This was one reason why commanders who came from the European theatre took some time to settle down to the new type of tactics. Their enemy in this theatre had not only to be outmanoeuvred, beaten, and have their weapons overcome, but they themselves had to be destroyed one by one.

From a distance, in London and Washington, it appeared that IV Corps was not making sufficient effort to fight its way out, and some criticism was received on this count, but IV Corps had also to expend and disperse men to protect airfields and stores against suicide attacks and so was not quite free to launch the strong offensive towards Ukhrul which it had been ordered to make. Both the 20th and 23rd Divisions had been ordered to capture Ukhrul, but both had made little progress.

The 2nd Division continued its advance down the road and on June 22 contact was made between the two corps at Milestone 109, just north of the Imphal plain. Stopford had advanced 70 miles

from Kohima but Scoones had fought less than ten miles uphill out of the plain. The monsoon was now in full spate, but Slim ordered the two corps to pursue. This was easier said than done. The Japanese 15th Division, suffering severely from disease and lack of supplies, as the Chindits had cut their communications east to the railway, was in a very bad way. But it managed to hold out at Ukhrul and had prevented the pincer movement which Slim had designed to cut it off.

The 33rd Division, with its new commander, was in better shape and was fighting well on the roads running south to Kalemyo and Kalewa.

The 19th Indian Division had joined the British 2nd Division in its advance south so that the Allied forces had managed to collect the equivalent of nine divisions with overwhelming air superiority against the Japanese three divisions and the I.N.A. brigade. As the monsoon wore on, the Japanese defeat became more com-

△ Lieutenant-General G.A.P. Scoones, commander of IV Corps in the Imphal–Kohima area.
◁▽ The battle of Imphal plain where, unlike the Japanese, the Allies had the benefit of efficient air support and supply drops.

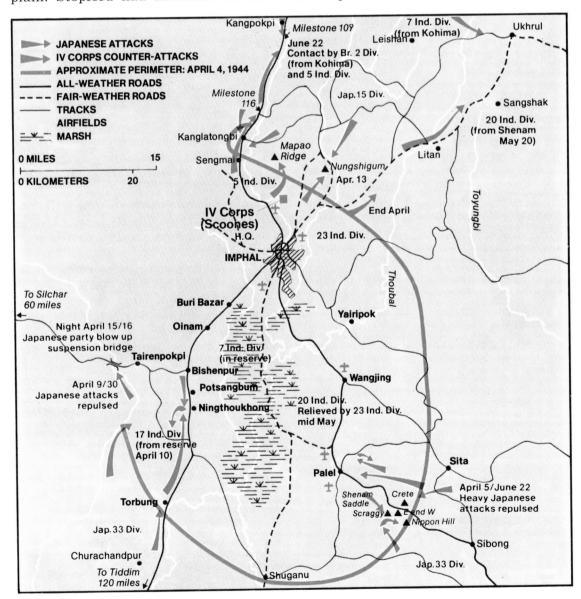

△ *Private Reg Maycox* (left), *a member of a small patrol being briefed by its company commander* (with pipe).

plete as a result of disease and lack of supplies. The British have the reputation of not being good in pursuit, and there was undoubtedly a slackening in follow-up, but the British commanders felt that the monsoon was completing their victory. Chandra Bhose's I.N.A. melted away, whilst Sato returned accusing Mutaguchi of negligence and incompetance, stating that his division had received no ammunition or supplies for six weeks. Mutaguchi had on May 15 moved his headquarters to Tamu, and it was only then when he saw the condition of his men and experienced the absolute dominance of the air by the R.A.F. that he realised the extent to which he was being defeated. Of the 88,000 Japanese (including reinforcements) who had crossed the Irrawaddy, 53,505 became casualties, including 30,502 killed, missing, or dead of disease.

Victory at Kohima/Imphal would probably not have been possible without absolute air superiority, air supply, and close air support.

Deliveries to IV Corps on the Imphal plain between April 18 and June 30 totalled 18,824 tons of stores of all sorts and at least 12,561 personnel. On their return flights the transport aircraft (R.A.F. and U.S.A.A.F.) evacuated 13,000 casualties and 43,000 non-combatants. The total number of reinforcements carried is difficult to calculate, as space was always made available to take in extra men. But 1,540 sorties were flown to move the 5th Division, the 7th Division (33rd and 89th Brigades), and the 4th Brigade of the 2nd Division to the Central Front. The Lushai Brigade and the 23rd Brigade were wholly, and XXXIII Corps was partially, supplied by air during their advance.

Between March 10 and July 30, R.A.F. fighters of the 3rd T.A.F. flew 18,860 sorties and those of the U.S.A.A.F. 10,800 sorties, losing 130 R.A.F. and 40 U.S. A.A.F. aircraft. The majority of these 29,660 sorties flown was for close air support of troops on the ground. During the same period the J.A.A.F. flew 1,750 sorties.

This gives some idea of the Allied dominance of the air and the importance of the construction of all-weather airfields on the ground in this campaign.

In spite of their evident superiority in numbers, all ranks of the British and Indian units had fought hard and very well, and had learnt to trust each other.

▽ *Kohima after the battle.*
▽ ▽ *Naga Hill people inspect equipment abandoned by the Japanese as they were forced off Garrison Hill.*
▽ ▷ *Mules are ferried across the swift Manipur river on special rafts, which prevent the mules seeing the water and panicking.*

British and Indian casualties during the battles of Imphal and Kohima were just under 16,700, of which approximately a quarter were incurred at Kohima in spite of strict medical and anti-malarial precautions, sickness caused more than 12 times the number of battle casualties, although many of those who went sick could return to their units.

After Imphal was relieved on June 22, Slim reformed his forces on that front. IV Corps, with the 17th and 20th Divisions who had been holding the line for two years, was withdrawn to India for a refit. The 50th Parachute Brigade was also withdrawn. Slim moved his own headquarters into Imphal and ordered Stopford's XXXIII Corps to continue the pursuit of the Japanese 33rd Division southwards, XXXIII Corps now consisted of the British 2nd, 5th and 20th Indian, and 11th East African Divisions. Movement through the mountains in the monsoon, coupled with extensive demolitions by the Japanese 33rd Division, slowed the British advance to a snail's pace, so that the Chindwin was not reached or crossed until early December, by which time Northern Combat Area Command's British 86th Division (Festing) had advanced down the railway from Mogaung to within 100 miles north of Mandalay. This "turned" the front of the Japanese facing XXXIII Corps so that the former swung back facing north, with their axis on Kalewa.

The Japanese 15th Army had been beaten. The Allies were now on the dry plains of Burma where tanks, artillery, and aircraft could be used to the maximum effect. The time was ripe for the ejection of the Japanese from Burma. The orders given to the Supreme Commander, Lord Louis Mountbatten, by the Chiefs-of-Staff had been fulfilled. He now received new orders to drive the Japanese out of Burma completely, by advancing on Mandalay and then on Rangoon.

CHAPTER 72
BREAKOUT

◁ *American motorised forces head for Coutances in the summer heat.*

Major-General Joseph "Lightning Joe" Collins was born in 1896 and graduated from West Point Military Academy in 1917. He was a battalion commander of the 18th Infantry Regiment in Koblenz after World War I. Between the wars he served both as an infantry and artillery instructor. In 1941 Collins was chief-of-staff of VII Corps and then of the Hawaii Department. Early in 1943 he commanded the 25th Division in the last stages of the campaign that drove the Japanese off the island of Guadalcanal. Collins was then transferred to Europe to command VII Corps in the battle for Normandy. Here he captured Cherbourg 20 days after D-Day and then spear-headed the break out at the western side of the Cotentin peninsula. Later his corps broke through the *Westwall*, took Cologne and Aix-la-Chapelle, closed the pincer round the Ruhr from the south, and then pushed on to meet the Russians at Dessau on the Elbe. He had an enviable reputation as a hard, yet flexible, infantry commander.

It is now time to return to the Western Front, where on July 25 General Bradley began Operation "Cobra".

On that day the German forces defending Normandy consisted of:

1. from the coastal battery at Merville to the area of Caumont-l'Eventé: 5th *Panzerarmee* (General Eberbach) comprising LXXXVI Corps, I and II *Waffen*-S.S. Panzer Corps, LXXIV Corps, with between them 11 divisions, including two Panzer and two *Panzergrenadier*, with about 645 tanks (these faced the British and Canadian forces); and

2. from Caumont-l'Eventé to the western coast of the Cotentin peninsula: 7th Army (General Hausser) astride the Vire with three corps of 13 divisions: on the right bank of the river XLVII Panzer Corps and II Parachute Corps with between them six infantry divisions and on the left bank LXXXIV Corps with one *Panzergrenadier* and two Panzer divisions with about 190 tanks (these faced the Americans).

But, we would repeat, there are divi-

sions and divisions. Let us take the case of LXXXIV Corps, which was going to bear the brunt of the attack. Its 91st, 243rd, and 352nd Divisions had only 2,500 rifles between them, after the fierce fighting in the *bocage,* and its three armoured divisions *("Lehr"* and 2nd S.S. *"Das Reich"* Panzer, and 17th S.S. *"Götz von Berlichingen" Panzergrenadier)* were down to something like half their establishment. The German front twisted and turned along the stretch Bradley was to attack, and the German 7th Army was very weak because Montgomery had drawn the weight of the German forces into the Caen sector. Bradley brought up no less than 12 divisions, including four armoured:

1. on the left the American VII Corps (Major-General J. L. Collins), with its left flank along the Vire, was given the job of making the breakthrough. The 30th, 4th, and 9th Divisions were engaged in first echelon along a four mile front. The breach came in the Marigny area and the 1st Infantry and the 2nd and 3rd Armoured Divisions

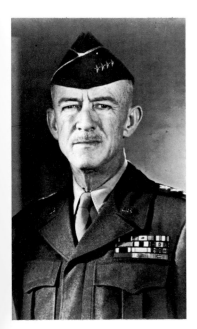

△ △ *American personnel carriers await the order to move up.*
△ *General Courtney H. Hodges, Bradley's able successor as head of the American 1st Army.*

poured through south and south-west, not, however, going beyond Coutances on their right, so as to leave the way open for VIII Corps; and

2. VIII Corps (Major-General T. H. Middleton) had the 8th, 79th, 83rd, and 90th Infantry and the 4th and 6th Armoured Divisions and, by a frontal attack, seized Coutances and pressed on to Avranches. When it reached Pontaubault on the Brittany border, it was to come under General George S. Patton's 3rd Army, which was to exploit this success towards the Loire and the Seine.

The 1st Army attacks

The attack of July 25 had the benefit of exceptionally powerful air preparation, the details of which were drawn up by General Bradley and Air Chief Marshal Leigh-Mallory. On July 24 4,000 tons of bombs fell on LXXXIV Corps' positions. During the morning of the following day no fewer than 1,880 four-engined and twin-engined bombers, and 550 fighter-bombers dropped 4,150 tons of bombs opposite the American VII Corps front to a depth of a mile and a half and on the bridges upstream of the Vire from Saint Lô. By special orders from Bradley, who did not want the terrain to be pitted with deep craters, only light bombs and napalm were used.

In spite of precautions, bombing errors caused casualties to the tune of 111 dead and 490 wounded in VII Corps. Amongst the dead was Lieutenant-General McNair, C.-in-C. of the "shadow" army group ostensibly stationed in south-east England to deceive the enemy into expecting a landing across the Straits of Dover. These were tragic losses: on the enemy side the bombing cut a swathe of death through the defences. "Nothing could withstand it," wrote the German historian Paul Carell. "Trenches, gun-emplacements: ploughed up. Petrol-, ammunition- and supply-dumps: set on fire." The Panzer-*"Lehr"* Division, in particular, down to 5,000 men, was heavily knocked about: "at least half its personnel was put out of action: killed, wounded, buried alive or driven out of their minds.

All the tanks and guns in the forward positions were wiped out. Every road in the area was made useless."

Neither Colonel-General Hausser nor Field-Marshal von Kluge expected an attack of such violence from the American 1st Army between the Vire and the Channel. General von Choltitz, commanding LXXXIV Corps, who had seen it coming and whose warning had not been heeded by his superiors, now had to rely on his own resources to plug the gap created by the annihilation of the Panzer-"Lehr" Division. On July 26 Collins was able to pass his 2nd and 3rd Armoured Divisions (respectively Major Generals Edward H. Brooks and Leroy H. Watson) through his infantry lines. By evening the 3rd had passed through Marigny and was on its way to Coutances and the 2nd was patrolling through Saint Gilles and Canisy, some seven to eight miles from its point of departure.

The 2nd and 116th Panzer Divisions were hastily withdrawn from the 5th *Panzerarmee* in the Caen area but did not get to the breach until July 29, by which time it was widening every hour. There was therefore no alternative for LXXXIV

Corps but to retreat, and do so quickly, as its left flank had been pierced in the area of Périers by the American VIII Corps. The direction this retreat was to take gave rise to a conflict between the LXXXIV Corps and 7th Army commanders. The latter, anxious to retain some coherence in his dispositions, wanted Choltitz to withdraw south-east-wards, whereupon the latter protested vehemently that if he were to do this he would be opening the way for the enemy to get into Brittany. This is what happened, in fact; Kluge wrongly attributed the blame to Choltitz and replaced him by Lieutenant-General Elfeldt. Choltitz had no difficulty in clearing himself and was rewarded with the command of *Gross Paris*.

Coutances and Avranches captured

On July 28 the U.S. 4th Armoured Division (Major-General John S. Wood) took Coutances and that same night got across

△ ◁ *American armour crashes forward along the road and through fields in the lightning advance after the breakthrough at Saint Lô.*
△ *Technician 5th Grade Floyd L. Meyer of Potter Valley, California, examines the aftermath of a strafing run by Allied fighter-bombers: a knocked-out SdKfz 4/1 Opel Type S/SSM "Maultier" (Mule) carrier fitted with a ten-tube 15-cm Panzerwerfer 42. Note the dead crewman's maps strewn across the ground.*

he Sienne at Cérences. Twenty-four hours later 6th Armoured Division (Major-General Robert W. Grow), moving on the right flank of the 4th, crossed the See and took Avranches. Facing them there was absolute confusion: continually compelled to move their headquarters by the advancing Americans, the German leaders lost all contact with their men, units got mixed up together and many of them, overtaken by Allied tanks, became moving pockets. At 0100 hours on July 31 Lieutenant-General Speidel telephoned Kluge: "The left flank has collapsed."

Kluge calls for reinforcements . . .

A few minutes later the C.-in-C. West was again called: this time by General Farmbacher, commanding XXV Corps, to say that, responsible now for organising the defence of Brittany, he found that the Kriegsmarine and the Luftwaffe, sheltering respectively behind Dönitz and Göring, were being removed from his authority. At 1045 hours the wretched Field-Marshal got in touch with O.K.W. and gave General Warlimont, Chief of Operations, a realistic picture of the situation:

"C.-in-C. West . . . informs that enemy is in Avranches and possibly also in Villedieu . . . These key positions for future operations must be held at all costs . . . All available strength from Saint Malo has been brought up. Spare naval and air force units, absolutely necessary for decisive struggle which will determine future of bridgehead, . . . impossible to get. General Warlimont agrees to put matter before the Führer.

"C.-in-C. West describes the situation with impressive eloquence. It might even be asked if the enemy can in fact be stopped at this point. His air superiority is terrifying and stifles our every move. On the other hand all his movements are prepared and protected by air strength. Our losses of men and *matériel* are extraordinary. Morale of troops has suffered greatly from the enemy's constant withering fire, especially as all infantry units are now only hastily-assembled groups and can no longer offer solid and co-ordinated resistance. Behind the front lines the terrorists [resistance] feel the

end is at hand and are becoming ever bolder. This, and the destruction of many communication installations, makes an ordered command very difficult."

Kluge therefore demanded reinforcements, and urgently, reminding O.K.W. of the example of the taxis of the Marne.

Faced with the development of Operation "Cobra", Hitler at O.K.W. finally gave up the obsession with a second landing north of the Somme which had dominated all his strategy since dawn on June 6.

. . . and gets them, but too late

Responding to Kluge's call for help, Hitler ordered Salmuth to withdraw LXXXI Corps and 85th and 89th Divisions from the 15th Army and send them at once to 5th *Panzerarmee*. Meanwhile Army Group "G", responsible for the defence of "Fortress Europe" between the Loire estuary and the Franco-Italian frontier, was ordered to send its LVIII Panzer Corps, 708th Infantry, and 9th Panzer Divisions to the 7th Army. The 9th Panzer was stationed in the Avignon area and the army group's commander, Colonel-General Blaskowitz, would have liked to see it replaced by the 11th Panzer, stationed in Montauban, as an Allied landing in Provence was expected. The Führer, as was to be expected, failed to see that this was common sense.

Patton's new objectives

Hitler's decisions, however, came too late. On July 31, General Patton, who now controlled VIII Corps (and was soon to become commander of a new Third Army) was given the welcome information from the corps H.Q. that the 4th Armoured Division had reached its objective at Sélune and that the bridge at Pontaubault was still in good order. He made up his mind at once: "All through military history", he cried, "wars have been lost because rivers weren't crossed." He sent off the 6th Armoured and 79th Infantry Divisions (Major-General Ira T. Wyche) towards Brest and the 4th Armoured and 8th Infantry (Major-General Donald Stroh) towards Rennes. The breach was complete, the German 7th Army was beaten

General George S. Patton Jr. was born in 1885 and served with the American armoured forces in France during 1918. This experience led him to become a fanatical tank enthusiast, an interest he developed and expanded between the wars. In 1942 he was the commander of the American forces in the "Torch" landings, and at beginning of the next year he led U.S. II Corps for a short time. Patton headed the U.S. 7th Army during the invasion of Sicily, during which he led a wide sweeping movement to the west, capturing Palermo, and then drove through to Messina. Early in 1944 he was the commander of the "shadow" Allied army group in southeast England intended to deceive the Germans into thinking that a landing in the Pas-de-Calais was imminent. After the Normandy landings, Patton was given the command of the U.S. 3rd Army, which he led in its superb dash from the breakout at Avranches to Metz. The campaign was notable for Patton's almost total disregard of orders and of orthodox military methods. He raised the siege of Bastogne in the "Battle of the Bulge" and then continued his advance into Germany and Czechoslovakia. Patton, one of the most controversial generals of the last war, was without doubt one of the ablest "cavalry" generals ever. He died after an accident in Germany in 1945.

and LXXXIV Corps, from which most of the 20,000 prisoners taken by the Americans since July 25 had come, was virtually wiped out. On August 1 General Bradley, now commanding 21 divisions, including six armoured, took over the American 12th Army Group in accordance with decisions taken in London on the eve of "Overlord". He handed over his 1st Army to General Courtney H. Hodges, having no qualms about his successor:

"A quiet and methodical commander, he knew his profession well and was recognised in the army as one of our most able trainers of troops. Whereas Patton could seldom be bothered with details, Hodges studied his problems with infinite care and was thus better qualified to execute the more intricate operations. A steady, undramatic, and dependable man with great tenacity and persistence, Hodges became the almost anonymous inside man who smashed the German Seventh Army while Patton skirted the end."

Changes in the Allied command structure

The 1st Army at this time included V, VII, and XIX Corps. It had transferred VIII Corps to the 3rd Army, fighting alongside it, and Bradley had also moved over to 3rd Army XII, XV, and XX Corps (respectively Major-Generals R. Cook, Wade H. Haislip, and Walton H. Walker). The new C.-in-C. 12th Army Group, promoted over the head of the impetuous Patton, six years his senior, did not much relish the idea of having to send him directives but acknowledged that "George" was a great-hearted and highly intelligent soldier who, in spite of his celebrated outbursts of temper, served him with "unbounded loyalty and eagerness".

The same occasion brought the formation of the British 21st Army Group, under General Montgomery, with the British 2nd Army, still under Sir Miles Dempsey, and the Canadian 1st Army (Lieutenant-General H. D. G. Crerar). On August 15, 21st Army Group was to have five corps of 16 divisions, including six armoured, and several brigades. This reorganisation of the land forces ought to have brought General Eisenhower to their head as previously agreed. Thinking

that his presence was more necessary in England, he postponed taking over command until September 1. Montgomery, therefore, continued to act as Eisenhower's representative, sending orders to Bradley under his authority, whilst at the same time retaining the command of his own army group.

Hitler envisages withdrawal

In the afternoon of July 31 Colonel-General Jodl, having informed Hitler of his concern at the capture of Avranches, noted in his diary: "The Führer reacted favourably to the idea of an order for eventual withdrawal in France. This confirms that he thinks such an order is necessary at the present time.

"1615 hours: called Blumentritt (chief-of-staff to C.-in-C. West). Advised him in guarded terms to be ready for such an order, adding that certain actions had to be taken straight away within G.H.Q. and that he should put a small working party on to it from among the general staff."

The matter of withdrawal seemed virtually settled and Lieutenant-General Warlimont was designated as liaison officer with C.-in-C. West. But on the following morning, when the O.K.W. delegate was leaving, the Führer said: "Tell Field-Marshal von Kluge that his job is to look forwards to the enemy, not backwards!"

Warlimont was thus in an embarrassing situation, caught between the "yes" of July 31 and the "no" of August 1. On August 3, the expected order from O.K.W. reached Kluge in the morning, but instead of confirming the withdrawal intimated by Jodl, it ordered a counter-attack. By driving towards Avranches Hitler hoped the 7th Army would trap those American forces which had ventured into Brittany. And, doing half Kluge's job for him, O.K.W. issued an order giving details for the operation. According to General Blumentritt:

"O.K.W. settled the precise divisions which were to be used and which were therefore to be taken out of the line as soon as possible. The exact limits of the sector in which the attack was to take place were laid down, as well as the routes to be taken and even the villages the troops

△ *A French resistance fighter poses in front of some of the evidence of the late German occupation of Rennes.*

△△ *The American advance under a smoke-blackened sky.*
△ *American troops round up a motley assortment of German prisoners-of-war.*

were to pass through. These plans were all made in Berlin on large-scale maps and the opinions of the commanding generals in France were neither asked for nor encouraged."

The plan was to assemble an armoured mass on the left flank of the 7th Army under General von Funck, C.-in-C. XLVII Panzer Corps, attack towards Avranches through Mortain, and cut the communications of the American 3rd Army. But Hitler would not stop there. Funck was then to press on to Saint Lô and overwhelm the American 1st Army by an outflanking attack. This would give Germany an eleventh-hour game and match in the West.

More time needed

Kluge was dumbfounded when he read Hitler's directive. He wrote to Hitler on August 18, before he took poison, to say that, except for the one single division, the 2nd Panzer, "the armoured units, after all the fighting they had done, were so weakened that they were incapable of any shock tactics . . . Your order was based on a completely erroneous supposition. When I first learned of it I immediately had the impression that I was being asked to do something which would go down in history as a grandiose and supremely daring operation but which, unfortunately, it was virtually impossible to carry out so that, logically, the blame would fall on the military commander responsible . . .

"On the basis of these facts I am still convinced that there was no possible chance of success. On the contrary: the attacks laid down for me could only make the situation of the Army Group decidedly worse. And that is what happened."

Kluge was in no position to claim freedom of action in face of this order, as stupid as it was absolute. He was aware that Hitler knew of the part he had played in the July 20 plot and that the slightest disobedience would cost him his life. The discussion therefore centred less on the principles involved than on the date of the operation, which was to be called "Lüttich" (Liège). Hitler wanted to hold back until as many American divisions as possible had been drawn into the net; Kluge urged the threat to the left flank and even to the rear of the 7th Army and asked for a start on August 7, to which Hitler agreed.

Allied aircraft beat the Panzers

At dawn on D-day, helped by fog, XLVII Corps (116th and 2nd Panzer Divisions, 1st *"Leibstandarte"* and 2nd *"Das Reich"* S.S. Panzer Divisions) attacked between the See and the Sélune towards Avranches. Mortain fell fairly easily. But neither the American 30th Division (Major-General Leland S. Hobbs), though it had one battalion surrounded, nor the American VII Corps (Major-General J. L. Collins)

Mixed British and American forces in the Caen area. While the American forces to the west were fanning out to the south, through Brittany, and also towards Paris, the British and Canadian troops in the Caen area were fighting a slow and remorseless battle on the northern edge of what was to become the "Falaise pocket". Overleaf: By the date of this poster, 1943, the days of the "Blitzkrieg" were over and the German army had been forced on to the defensive. But the Panzer forces proved as effective as ever. In one engagement, during the battle for Normandy, for instance, a single Tiger tank, commanded by Hauptsturmführer Wittmann, destroyed 25 Allied vehicles.

were thrown off their stride, and towards mid-day *"Das Reich"* was stopped less than two miles from Saint Hilaire-du-Harcouët, over 14 miles from its objective of Pontaubault.

The fog had lifted by now, and the Panzers were caught by British Typhoon fighter-bombers, whose armour-piercing rockets again proved their deadly efficiency. The previous day General Bülowius thought he could guarantee the C.-in-C. 7th Army that 300 Luftwaffe fighters would be continuously sweeping the skies above the battlefield. These had been intercepted by Anglo-American fighters as soon as they took off from the Paris area.

Faced with this lack of success, Kluge gave it as his opinion that the German forces should hold on to what they had got, or even let go. The answer was an order to throw in II S.S. Panzer Corps (General Bittrich: 9th *"Hohenstaufen"* and 10th *"Frundsberg"* Panzer Divisions), to be withdrawn from the already depleted 5th *Panzerarmee*. Once more C.-in-C. West had to give in, in spite of vehement protests from General Eberbach, who was expecting a strong Anglo-Canadian attack southwards along the Caen–Falaise axis.

The Americans hesitate in Brittany

In spite of appearances, the first engagements of the American 3rd Army in Brittany betrayed a certain lack of initiative. This is not attributable in any way to lack of enthusiasm on Patton's part, but seems rather to have sprung from the inadequacy of his means of communication, which prevented his driving spirit from reaching down to his men. At the speed with which the armoured formations advanced, the supply of telephone cable within VIII Corps turned out to be insufficient, with a consequential overloading of the radio network and the use of squadrons of message-carrying jeeps to make up for it.

There were also interferences in the chain of command. The 4th Armoured Division received the order from VIII Corps, confirmed by General Bradley, not to go beyond Dinan until Saint Malo was cleared, whereas Patton had ordered it to drive on towards Brest (150 miles west of Rennes) with no intermediate objective. This left a gap in the enemy lines once Rennes had been passed, which 6th Armoured Division exploited along the axis Chartres–Paris, turning then towards Chateaubriant instead of Lorient. It was recalled to its original objective and found, when it got to Lorient, the German 265th Division in a defensive position around this large base. The 4th Armoured Division did manage to destroy the 266th Division, which had tried to take refuge inside Brest, but the German 2nd Parachute Division got there first and its commander, Lieutenant-General Ramcke, was not the sort of man to be impressed by cavalier raids, even ones made in considerable force.

The responsibility for this Allied mix-up must belong to the Anglo-American high command, which had given two objectives to the forces breaking out of the Avranches bottleneck: the Breton ports and the rear areas of Army Group "B". This was how Eisenhower saw it when on August 5 he ordered only the minimum indispensable forces to be engaged in Brittany.

Patton sweeps on through the breach

This directive from Eisenhower gave Patton the chance to streak out through the enormous gap (65 miles) between Rennes and Nantes, which he did with XV Corps on the left, XX Corps in the centre, and XII Corps on the right with its right flank along the Loire. By August 7, XV Corps was in Laval and Château-Gontier whilst XII Corps liberated Nantes and Angers, ignoring enemy resistance in Saint Nazaire.

Thus Operation *"Lüttich"* did not deflect Montgomery and Bradley from their initial plan. On D-day the German XLVII Corps lost some 50 tanks out of the 120 with which it had started out at dawn. The American VII Corps, strengthened to five divisions, including one armoured, immediately went over to the counter-attack. This was the last chance for Army Group "B" to break out of the ring now beginning to take shape as Patton pushed ahead towards Le Mans. But Hitler obstinately refused to consider any withdrawal.

CHAPTER 73
SLAUGHTER AT FALAISE

Operation "Totalize" which was to capture Falaise, began at 2330 hours on 7 August. The Canadian 1st Army attacked south of Caen with its II Corps of four divisions, including two armoured. Montgomery now had a chance to start a pincer movement which was to bring about the defeat of Army Group "B" between the Orne and the Dives on August 18 and the disgrace and suicide of the wretched Kluge.

At zero hour four mechanised columns, consisting of one armoured brigade on each flank and two motorised infantry brigades in the centre, crossed the first German line. When they had covered

△ *British armour on t the Falaise area. Note the result of Allied bon*

between two and three miles in the dark, the Canadian and Scottish infantry, from the 2nd Canadian and 51st (Highland) Divisions, left their vehicles to attack the strongpoints of the German line, illuminated for them by green tracer shells. At dawn it was clear that the H.Q. of I S.S. Panzer Corps had been overrun, the 89th Division, recently arrived on the scene, had collapsed, and the 272nd looked like giving way.

Once more the famous Panzer-Meyer (Brigadier Kurt Meyer) and his 12th *"Hitlerjugend"* Panzer Division saved the situation with the help of 80 assault guns and the 8.8-cm guns sent to them as

A British column pushes south from Caen. With the aid of the Americans, sweeping up north towards Argentan, Montgomery hoped to trap the 5th Panzerarmee at Falaise and wipe it out.

reinforcement. These young veterans, who had been in the line since June 8, were pitted against the Canadian 4th Armoured Division (Major-General G. Kitching) and the Polish 1st Armoured Division (Major-General S. Maczek), both of which were in action for the first time. The military cemeteries in the area bear witness to the valiant fighting of the Allied forces, but they did not succeed in breaking through and "Totalize" ground to a halt some ten miles short of Falaise on August 9.

General Leclerc's charge

On the same day the American XV Corps, having captured Le Mans, turned north. On its left the French 2nd Armoured Division (General Leclerc) was moving down to Alençon with the 79th Division in its wake. On the right the American 5th Armoured Division (Major-General Lundsford E. Oliver) was on the road to Argentan, followed by the 90th Division which, newly commanded by Major-General Raymond S. MacLain, was to recover from the unfortunate reputation it had acquired in the bocage. Conscious of the threat to his rear areas, Kluge attempted to ward it off by improvising a Panzergruppe "Eberbach" consisting of LXXXI Corps (General Kuntzen), 708th Division (Lieutenant-General Wilck), and 9th Panzer Division (Lieutenant-General Jolasse) brought up from the south.

The French 2nd Armoured Division, vigorously led by General Leclerc, ran into the 9th Panzer Division on August 11, just as the Germans were moving into their positions. As night fell the French took the bridges at Alençon whilst they were still intact. On their right, the American 5th Armoured Division had crossed the Sarthe and captured Sées, having overcome the feeble resistance of the German 708th Division. On the following day Leclerc had to fight

it out with the 2nd *"Das Reich"* S.S. Panzer Division's forward units and the 116th Panzer Division, both of which Kluge had thrown into XV Corps' sector without any further regard for O.K.W.'s orders. The French nevertheless pushed their left flank as far as Carrouges and their right to the outskirts of Argentan.

At dawn on August 13 the American XV Corps was within 16 miles of Falaise, whilst the German 7th Army, caught up in the Condé-sur-Noireau–Tinchebray–Domfront area, had between 34 and 37 miles to go under enemy-controlled skies before it broke out of the pocket. In the afternoon, however, Haislip was ordered by Patton to stop and even to pull back the units "in the neighbourhood of Falaise or north of Argentan".

Why Bradley, via Patton, should have forbidden XV Corps to close the ring round Army Group "B" in the Falaise area has often been discussed, and the reasons given by the two generals in their memoirs do not carry conviction. No more do the arguments of General Eisen-

hower, who takes up Bradley's argument in his *Crusade in Europe*, saying:

"Mix-ups on the front occurred, and there was no way to halt them except by stopping troops in place, even at the cost of allowing some Germans to escape. In the aggregate considerable numbers of Germans succeeded in getting away. Their escape, however, meant an almost complete abandonment of their heavy equipment and was accomplished only by terrific sacrifices.

"I was in Bradley's headquarters when messages began to arrive from commanders of the advancing American columns, complaining that the limits placed upon them by their orders were allowing Germans to escape. I completely supported Bradley in his decision that it was necessary to obey the orders, prescribing the boundary between the army groups, exactly as written; otherwise a calamitous battle between friends could have resulted."

Certainly by exploiting his success on August 12 north of Argentan Haislip had

△ *A Sherman tank stands guard at the cross-roads in St. Martin-des-Besares as a carrier, towing a 57-mm anti-tank gun, and infantry pass through the village.*

△ *R.A.F. pilots burst from the "ready" tent after a call for fighter support from an R.A.F. Visual Control Point in the front line.*

overstepped the boundary between 12th and 21st Army Groups and risked running into the bombing destined for the Germans opposite the Canadian 1st Army. Was this boundary so vague, though, that the Anglo-American strategic air force, which was admittedly sometimes not very accurate, could not have been given clear orders? And the juncture between the Polish 1st Armoured Division and the American 90th did in fact take place without incident in the area of Chambois-sur-Dives on August 19.

This is why one is inclined to believe, like Jacques Mordal, that Eisenhower and Bradley, under the influence of Montgomery, were unwilling to content themselves with a "little" pincer around Falaise, as they were sure that they could bring about a much bigger one on the left bank of the Seine. They ignored the proverb of the bird in hand and when they said "stop" to Haislip they were intend-

ing to give him a new and bigger task.

Kluge orders retreat

From August 15, Army Group "B" was on the retreat. Kluge did not wait for O.K.W. to confirm, but went ahead, setting in motion an operation involving two armies, seven corps, and no fewer than 23 divisions of all types. On August 17 General Dietrich, who had succeeded Eberbach as C.-in-C. 5th *Panzerarmee*, got I S.S. Panzer Corps out of the net and re-assembled the bits at Vimoutiers. But the Canadians took Falaise and the Polish 1st Armoured Division, advancing up the right bank of the Dives, established contact with the American V Corps (1st Army) which at that moment formed the southern arm of the pincer which was remorselessly closing in.

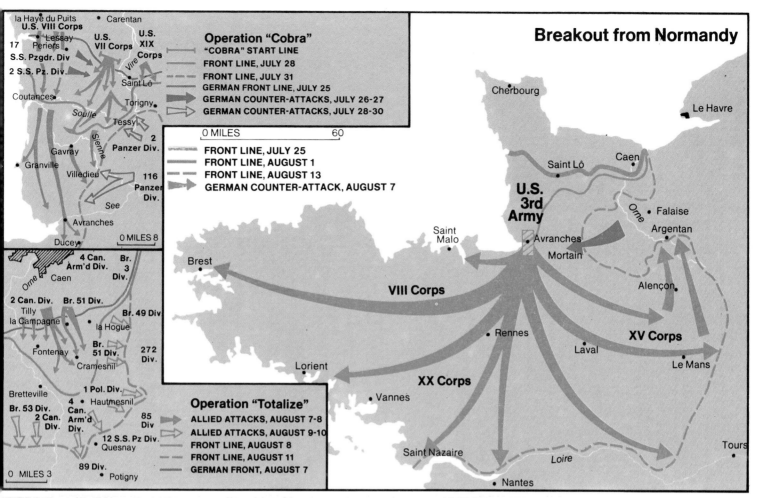

Breakout from Normandy

Operation "Cobra"
┬ "COBRA" START LINE
── FRONT LINE, JULY 28
--- FRONT LINE, JULY 31
── GERMAN FRONT LINE, JULY 25
➡ GERMAN COUNTER-ATTACKS, JULY 26-27
⇨ GERMAN COUNTER-ATTACKS, JULY 28-30

0 MILES 60

── FRONT LINE, JULY 25
── FRONT LINE, AUGUST 1
--- FRONT LINE, AUGUST 13
➡ GERMAN COUNTER-ATTACK, AUGUST 7

Operation "Totalize"
➡ ALLIED ATTACKS, AUGUST 7-8
⇨ ALLIED ATTACKS, AUGUST 9-10
── FRONT LINE, AUGUST 8
--- FRONT LINE, AUGUST 11
── GERMAN FRONT, AUGUST 7

0 MILES 8

0 MILES 3

la Haye du Puits • Carentan
U.S. VIII Corps
17 • Lessay
• Periers
S.S. Pzgdr. Div.
2 S.S. Pz. Div.
Coutances •
Soulle
Gavray •
• Granville
Villedieu •
See
• Avranches
Ducey
U.S. VII Corps
U.S. XIX Corps
Saint Lô
Torigny •
Tessy
2 Panzer Div.
Sienne
116 Panzer Div.

4 Can. Arm'd Div.
Br. 3 Div.
Orne Caen •
2 Can. Div.
Tilly •
la Campagne •
Br. 51 Div.
• la Hogue
Br. 49 Div.
Fontenay •
Br. 51 Div.
Cramesnil •
272 Div.
Bretteville •
Br. 53 Div.
2 Can. Div.
4 Can. Arm'd Div.
1 Pol. Div.
• Hautmesnil
85 Div.
12 S.S. Pz Div.
• Quesnay
89 Div.
• Potigny

Cherbourg
Le Havre
Saint Lô
Caen
U.S. 3rd Army
Saint Malo
Avranches
Mortain
Orne
• Falaise
Argentan
Brest
VIII Corps
Alençon •
• Rennes
Laval •
XV Corps
Le Mans
Lorient
XX Corps
• Vannes
Saint Nazaire
Loire
• Nantes
Tours

△ The Allied breakout from Normandy and the beginning of the Falaise pocket.
◁ British infantry prepare for an assault near Cagny.

▷△ *Happy soldiers of the French Forces of the Interior escort a German officer prisoner captured near Chartres.* ▽ *The British advance continues towards the east.*

A German disaster

On August 20, according to Martin Blumenson, the author of the volume devoted to this episode in the official history of the U.S. Army, there occurred the "artillery-man's dream":

"Five battalions pulverized columns driving towards the Dives. American soldiers cheered when German horses, carts, trucks, volkswagens, tanks, vehicles, and weapons went flying into the air, disintegrating in flashes of fire and puffs of smoke."

Nevertheless I S.S. Panzer Corps, which had got out of this attack, collected together some 20,000 Germans from all units and, refusing to be dismayed, managed to find a crack in the Allied lines, through which they got 25 tanks and 60 guns. Included in these forces was General Hausser, C.-in-C. 7th Army, who was seriously wounded in the face. On the following day, however, all firing ceased in the Argentan–Nécy–Brieux–Chambois area. Here the Allies took 50,000 prisoners; there were 10,000 dead. The unhappy decision of August 13 thus left the Germans now with only 40,000 men. Fifteen divisions of Army Group "B" were wiped out in the course of this pitiless battle. According to Blumenson, one American officer, a veteran of the 1918 battles in the area of Soissons, Saint Mihiel, and the Argonne in 1918 and the terrible bombing of London in 1940, said:

"None of these compared in the effect upon the imagination with what I saw yesterday south west of Trun . . . The grass and trees were vividly green as in all Normandy and a surprising number of houses (were) . . . untouched. That rather peaceful setting framed a picture of destruction so great that it cannot be described. It was as if an avenging angel had swept the area bent on destroying all things German.

"I stood on a lane, surrounded by 20 or 30 dead horses or parts of horses, most of them still hitched to their wagons and carts . . . As far as my eye could reach (about 200 yards) on every line of sight there were . . . vehicles, wagons, tanks, guns, prime movers, sedans, rolling kitchens, etc., in various stages of destruction.

"I stepped over hundreds of rifles in the mud and saw hundreds more stacked along sheds . . . I walked through a mile or more of lanes where the vehicles had been caught closely packed . . . I saw probably 300 field pieces and tanks, mounting large caliber guns, that were apparently undamaged.

"I saw no foxholes or any other type of shelter or field fortifications. The Germans were trying to run and had no place to run. They were probably too

French civilians welcome their liberators. Note the Panther on the right.

tired even to surrender.

"I left this area rather regretting I'd seen it . . . Under such conditions there are no supermen – all men become rabbits looking for a hole."

Most of the German *matériel* was lost. The French 2nd Armoured Division alone took 100 guns and 700 vehicles and the 90th Division 380 armoured vehicles, 700 guns, and more than 5,000 lorries.

Model succeeds Kluge

This was the situation which Field-Marshal Model inherited when he took over from Kluge at his H.Q. at Saint Germain-en-Laye on August 17. Two days previously a fortuitous incident had, if not provoked, at least hastened, the disgrace of Kluge. Whilst he was up at the front an aircraft bomb had demolished the radio truck which gave him permanent contact with O.K.W., and the ensuing prolonged silence caused Hitler to conclude that C.-in-C. West had finally betrayed him and gone to see Montgomery about surrender terms.

Kluge's farewell to Hitler

When he said goodbye to his successor, Kluge assured him that he would speak to Hitler with all the clarity which the situation demanded. But in the car taking him back to Germany he rightly persuaded himself that the dictator would give him, not an audience at O.K.W., but a criminal trial and an ignominious death. Potassium cyanide removed him from the Führer's vengeance, but before he committed suicide on August 18, 1944 he sent a letter to Hitler, the conclusion of which is worth recalling:

"I do not know if Field-Marshal Model, who has proved himself in all respects, will be capable of mastering the situation. I hope so with all my heart. If that is not to be the case and if the new· weapons –

especially air weapons, which you are so eagerly awaiting, are not to bring you success, then *mein Führer,* make up your mind to finish the war. The German people have endured such unspeakable sufferings that the time has come to put an end to their terrors. There must be ways to arrive at this conclusion and, above all, to prevent the Reich from being condemned to the hell of Bolshevism ... *Mein Führer,* I have always admired your greatness and your iron will to assert your authority and uphold National Socialism. If your destiny overcomes your will and your genius, it will be because Providence has willed it so. You have fought a good and honourable fight. History will bear witness to this. If it ever becomes necessary, show yourself great enough to put an end to a struggle which has become hopeless."

We know what became of this advice from a man about to die: if it had been accepted Germany would have been spared, not the rigours of occupation (this had been decided at Teheran), but at least the appalling horrors of invasion.

Churchill again opposes a landing in Provence ...

On the same August 15 when Army Group "B" was trying to escape from the Normandy net, the landing of an Allied force in Provence compelled O.K.W. for the first time to impose on the C.-in-C. West a withdrawal of considerable strategic importance. Right up to the last minute Churchill had tried to urge his American allies to abandon this operation, which was called first "Anvil" then "Dragoon", in favour of his projected offensive towards Vienna and the Danube across the Apennines, the Giulian Alps, and the Ljubljana gap.

In a letter dated August 6 to his friend Harry Hopkins, Churchill expressed his conviction that as the ports of Brest, Lorient, Saint Nazaire, and Nantes might fall into Allied hands "at any time", there was no logistic value left in Toulon or Marseilles. On the other hand, why not take the bull by the horns? "Dragoon", he wrote, would have to be carried out against an enemy who "at the outset [would] be much stronger than we are, and where our advance runs cross-grained

△ △ *General Leclerc, holding the map board, follows the progress of his armoured division.*
△ *Lieutenant-General Omar N. Bradley, commander of the U.S. 12th Army Group.*

to the country, which abounds in most formidable rocky positions, ridges, and gullies."

"But", he noted in particular, "after taking the two fortresses of Toulon and Marseilles we have before us the lengthy advance up the Rhône valley before we even get to Lyons. None of this operation can influence Eisenhower's battle for probably ninety days after the landings."

... in favour of a campaign in the Balkans

On the next day he went to Portsmouth and saw Eisenhower about it, speaking his mind more openly than he had done to Hopkins, and not concealing his interest in a campaign in the Balkans, a subject which he had not broached in his letter. Eisenhower soon realised that the Prime Minister, in his opposition to "Dragoon", was putting forward reasons of strategy so as not to have to declare the political reasons which had made him take up this attitude.

Eisenhower's reserve

As a good American soldier General Eisenhower reckoned that he should not interfere in matters which were the responsibility of the White House and the State Department. He was to react the same way over Berlin later. He makes this perfectly clear in his memoirs when he says:

"Although I never heard him say so, I felt that the Prime Minister's real concern was possibly of a political rather than a military nature. He may have thought that a post-war situation which would see the western Allies posted in great strength in the Balkans would be far more effective in producing a stable post-hostilities world than if the Russian armies should be the ones to occupy that region. I told him that if this were his reason for advocating the campaign into the Balkans he should go instantly to the President and lay the facts, as well as his own conclusions on the table. I well understood that strategy can be affected by political considerations, and if the President and the Prime Minister should decide that it was worth while to prolong

the war, thereby increasing its cost in men and money, in order to secure the political objectives they deemed necessary, then I would instantly and loyally adjust my plans accordingly. But I did insist that as long as he argued the matter on military grounds alone I could not concede validity to his arguments."

And he was clearly right. The supreme commander may lay down strategic objectives, but it is the political leaders who set the aims of warfare. Moreover Churchill was too late. The drive for Vienna may have been conceivable on June 5 so long as everything was done to annihilate Kesselring south of the line Rimini–La Spezia, but it was not now, on August 7, by which time the enemy, whose

losses in retreat had not been overwhelming, was re-establishing his line along the ridges of the Apennines. At best the Allies would have been caught in late autumn on the narrow hemmed-in roads in the area of Klagenfurt or Ljubljana and have had to fight for peaks between 3,000 and 4,000 feet high. The mountainous terrain and the weather, to say nothing of enemy action, would have severely restricted all movement. As Michael Howard has explained in *The Mediterranean Strategy in the Second World War*: "a pursuit to Vienna through terrain where even comparatively small units could have imposed repeated delays would have been a very difficult matter indeed." Churchill's plans were hopelessly unrealistic.

△ *The scene that was to greet the Allies when they reached the Seine: wholesale destruction, plus great dumps of ruined* matériel *such as this one at Rouen.*

CHAPTER 74

DRAGOON: THE DRIVE THROUGH SOUTHERN FRANCE

Operation "Dragoon", supervised by General Maitland Wilson, C.-in-C. Mediterranean, was to be the landing between Saint Raphael and le Lavandou of the American 7th Army under Lieutenant-General A. M. Patch, who the previous year had been so successful in cleaning up Guadalcanal. The landing operation was to be carried out by the American VI Corps with its 3rd, 36th, and 45th Divisions, well experienced in amphibious operations. It was to be supported by an Anglo-American parachute division under Major-General Robert T. Frederick landing in the area of le Muy with the object of opening up the Argens valley. A position nearer Toulon was not chosen because of the danger of the two twin turrets at Cap Cépet whose guns could hurl a 119-pound shell a distance of nearly 22 miles.

A thousand ships were required: warships, troop transports, and supply vessels. These included five battleships, nine escort carriers (216 aircraft), 24 cruisers, 122 destroyers and escort vessels, and 466 landing craft, all from five navies: American, British, Australian, French, and Greek. The fleet, named the Western Task Force, was commanded by Vice-Admiral H. Kent Hewitt. On board his flagship was James Forrestal, the new U.S. Navy Secretary.

Air support came from the U.S. 12th Air Force, under Brigadier-General Gordon P. Saville, with 2,100 aircraft. Its heavy bombers operated from the area of Rome, its medium bombers, fighter-bombers, and fighters from 14 airstrips which had been built in the Bastia area. Any objectives out of range of the latter would be dealt with by carrier-based aircraft under Rear-Admiral T. H. Troubridge, R.N. On August 13 and 14, the four-engined bombers prepared the way for the landings by attacking gun-emplacements, communication centres, bridges, and viaducts. These attacks were spread over an area from Port-Vendres to Genoa to deceive the enemy.

The German defences

The defence of the 400 miles of coastline between Menton and Cerbère was the responsibility of the German 19th Army.

▽ American transport speeds the advance to the north.

△ *Build-up. Massed vehicles in Italy, earmarked for "Dragoon".*

On D-day it had six divisions, deployed with three on each side of the Rhône. Between June 6 and August 4 it had had to give up its 217th, 272nd, and 277th Divisions, receiving in exchange only the 198th and the remnants of the 716th, which had been thrashed at Caen. Colonel-General Blaskowitz, C.-in-C. Army Group "G", wrote to C.-in-C. West on that day:

"The Army Group does not in the least deny the necessity of weakening the 19th Army to this extent, having regard to the situation of Army Group "B". It nevertheless feels obliged to point out that the consequences of these losses of men and *matériel* will be such that the Army's defences will be so diminished that it cannot guarantee to hold the coastline."

On August 10, however, the 19th Army had to lose its 338th Division. 11th Panzer Division was ordered to Avignon from Montauban by Hitler, but not until August 13, so that by the following day the whole of this division was still over on the right bank of the Rhône. This was the situation facing General Wiese, C.-in-C. 19th Army.

The German naval forces in the south of France consisted of only a limited number of small units and a few U-boats. The American air forces increased their attacks on Toulon, however, and four U-boats were sunk on August 6. The Luftwaffe had only 70 fighters and 130 bombers, a total of only one-tenth of the Allied aircraft used in Operation "Dragoon".

The first landings

On the single day of August 15, Allied aircraft flew 4,250 sorties and only 60 German planes managed to get off the ground. Admiral Hewitt's fleet fired 50,000 shells, including 3,000 12-inch or heavier, either during the preparations or at the request of the troops landing. The American VI Corps' attack, supported by the "Sudre" Combat Command of the French 1st Armoured Division, was against the German 148th Division (Lieutenant-General Otto Fretter-Pico) on the right and the 242nd Division (Lieutenant-

General Bässler) on the left, the latter being responsible for the defence of Toulon. Both German units were part of LXII Corps (General Neuling) but corps H.Q. at Draguignan was cut off from its troops by the landing of the "Frederick" Division, supported by the Var *maquis*. The only Allied unit to run into difficulties was the U.S. 36th Division (Major-General John E. Dahlquist) in the area of Agay. Everywhere else the operation went like clockwork. By evening the Allies had landed 60,000 men, 6,000 vehicles, and 50,000 tons of *matériel,* all at the cost of 320 killed who, for the most part, had stumbled onto mines.

Amongst the day's exploits those of Colonel Bouvet's commando are worth recording. It landed in the middle of the night between Cavalaire and Cavalière and captured the fortifications on Cap Nègre. By the evening of the 15th it had advanced over nine miles and taken 1,000 prisoners.

Twenty-four hours later the 7th Army beach-head extended from Anthéor on the right through Draguignan, where General Neuling and his staff were taken prisoner, to le Luc on the road to Aix and over 24 miles from Fréjus, then back to the Mediterranean between Cavalière and le Lavandou. On the beaches Patch's second echelon arrived ahead of time and landed with the 1st Moroccan (General Brosset), the 3rd Algerian (General de Monsabert), and the 9th Colonial (General Magnan) Divisions, the remainder of the French 1st Armoured Division (General Touzet du Vigier) and General Guillaume's Moroccan *goumiers,* North African mountain troops.

De Lattre

On the following day this vanguard of the French 1st Army went into battle under General de Lattre de Tassigny. In the exercise of his command de Lattre seemed to be everywhere and to appear as if by miracle in places where his decision was needed. He cared deeply for the fate of his men and was often rude to staff and services on their behalf if the occasion warranted it.

Two men from very different backgrounds have borne witness to his character. On September 30, 1935, as he left manoeuvres at Mailly, Captain Hans Speidel, assistant military attaché at the German Embassy in Paris, made the following comment on the officer commanding the 151st Regiment: "De Lattre makes an exceptional impression: he is a man of great vitality and fine intelligence and his bearing and discernment are quite out of the ordinary. His fellow-officers predict a great future for him in the French Army." This judgement by Rommel's future chief-of-staff is echoed by General de Gaulle in his memoirs:

"De Lattre was emotional, flexible, far-sighted and a man of wide interests, influencing the minds around him by the ardour of his personality, heading towards his goal by sudden and unexpected leaps, although often well thought out ones.

"De Lattre, on each occasion, courted opportunity above all. Until he found it he endured the ordeal of his tentative efforts, devoured by an impatience that often provoked scenes among his contacts. Suddenly seeing where, when and

▽ *From the beaches of Provence to the Vosges. When the "Dragoon" force joined hands with the right-wing armies advancing from Normandy, the Allied front was extended from the Channel to the Swiss frontier.*

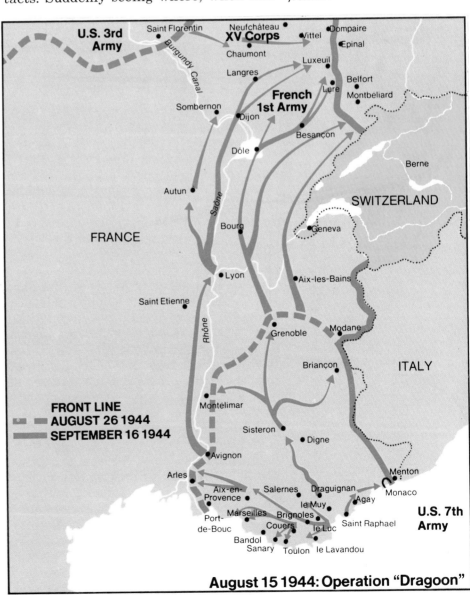

August 15 1944: Operation "Dragoon"

△ *Keeping up the pressure: a tank pushes north. Despite the pace of their advance the French and Americans failed to cut off and annihilate the Germans in the south.*

how the issue could be determined, he then set about the task of building it up and exploiting it. All the resources of a rich personality and extraordinary energy were put to work, demanding a limitless effort of those he engaged in it, but certain that he was preparing them for success."

It is no disrespect to this strategist and leader of men to say that the weapon Weygand and Giraud had forged for him, and which General Juin had tempered in the recent Italian campaign, had a keen edge. The Frenchmen from North Africa were enthusiastic at the idea that they were going to liberate their brothers in the home country, and were encouraged by the presence amongst them of 18,000 escapees from the unhappy armistice army. Considering the 9th Colonial Division's attack on the German positions in the area of Villars-les-Blamont on November 14 and 22, when the division's artillery crushed the 198th Division in the area of le Puix-Suarce, we can say with some justice that the 1st Army, by its bravery and its accomplishments, was the equal of any other Allied force.

A better judge was Major-General von Mellenthin, then chief-of-staff of Army Group "G". In *Panzer Battles* he writes: "The French tanks, reflecting the tempera-

ment of their army commander, General de Lattre de Tassigny, attacked with extraordinary spirit and *élan*." A worthy tribute from an enemy who knew what he was talking about, to General du Vigier and his colleague Vernejoul, commander of the French 5th Armoured Division. The French opened their score with the capture of Salernes, Brignoles, and Cuers, the latter some nine miles north-east of Toulon.

The American VI Corps, acting on local information, sent a motorised column along the axis Digne–Sisteron with orders to intercept the German 19th Army at Montélimar. Close on its heels was the 36th Division. The 45th Division (Major-General William W. Eagles) had taken the road to Aix-en-Provence.

Hitler orders retreat

In view of the reports he had received, and réalising that there was no longer any hope of throwing the enemy back into the sea, on August 16 Hitler ordered Colonel-General Blaskowitz to begin at once the evacuation of south and south-west France. Army Group "G" would

△ *Arrival at the Swiss frontier.*
▷ ▷ △ *Battle-stained G.I.s throng a field kitchen.*
▷ ▷ *The new occupants take over–Americans in a former German headquarters.*

link up in the region of Sens with Model's left as the latter fell back to the Seine, whilst the 19th Army would proceed up the Rhône valley and hold as long as possible the line Côte d'Or–Lyon–Aix-les-Bains so as to keep Switzerland encircled. The 242nd Division at Toulon and the 244th at Marseilles (Major-General Schaeffer) would defend the ports to the last and raze their installations to the ground. The 148th Division, fighting in the Estérel massif, and the 157th in the Dauphiné, would come under Field-Marshal Kesselring's command and hold the French side of the Alps.

General von der Chevallerie, C.-in-C. of the German 1st Army, had transferred his H.Q. from Bordeaux to Fontainebleau on August 10 and so the conduct of the German retreat in the south-west fell to General Sachs, commander of LXIV Corps (158th and 159th Divisions). He left strong garrisons in the "fortresses" of la Pointe-de-Grave, Royan, and la Rochelle. General Wiese's task was to co-ordinate the movements of the Luftwaffe IV Corps (General Petersen: 189th, 198th, and 716th Divisions) and LXXXV Corps (338th Division). The 11th Panzer Division, under a particularly distin-guished commander, Lieutenant-General Gustav von Wietersheim, was ordered to cover the retreat.

Hitler's new directive

On August 20, as a consequence of this order to Army Group "G" and the increasingly serious situation of Army Group "B", whose left flank was being rolled up by Patton and the American 3rd Army, the Führer issued a new directive. This has been summarised by Professor Percy Ernst Schramm, then editor and now publisher of the O.K.W. war diaries for 1944 and 1945:

"C.-in-C. West was ordered to hold the bridgehead west of Paris and prevent the enemy drive towards Dijon. First of all what remained of the 5th *Panzerarmee* and the 7th Army had to be withdrawn behind the River Touques and reorganised so that their armoured formations could be brought back into the left flank. If it turned out to be impossible to hold out in front of the Seine, the Paris bridgehead had to be held and also the line Seine–Yonne – Burgundy Canal – Dijon – Dôle –

Swiss frontier. The withdrawal of the 7th Army behind the Seine was to be prepared at once. The 5th *Panzerarmee* would protect its crossing over to the right bank so as to prevent the enemy engaged in the Seine valley from driving north and then eastwards after crossing the river."

Downstream from Paris the 1st Army, now under Army Group "B", would block off the narrow valleys on either side of Montargis to allow the occupation of the Burgundy Canal and the area north-west of Dijon.

300,000 Germans cut off

This directive calls for two remarks. Firstly, it took no account of the 230,000 men from the army (86,337), navy and air force trapped in the "fortresses" in the West.

Amongst these, Saint Malo had fallen on August 17 after epic resistance. It

△ An American M3 half-track is
utilised in an anti-aircraft role.

took the 8-inch and 240-mm howitzers of
the U.S. artillery, the 15-inch guns of
the battleship *Warspite,* and the use of
napalm to force Colonel von Aulock
to hoist the white flag on the little island
of Cézembre, the last centre of resistance,
on September 2. The Brest garrison was
attacked by the U.S. 2nd, 8th, and 29th
Divisions and defended with equal
tenacity by Lieutenant-General Ramcke
and the 2nd Parachute Division. On
September 17 fighting ceased in this
unhappy town, which had been very
heavily shelled. A further 48 hours were
to elapse before Ramcke gave up the
struggle in the Crozon peninsula.

Neither of the "fortresses" of Lorient
or Saint Nazaire on opposite banks of
the Loire was attacked; nor were the
Channel Islands, where the 319th Division (Lieutenant-General von Schmet-
tow) had some 30,000 men. The latter
were sufficiently aware of the futility of
their mission to call themselves the
"Guernsey P.O.W.s" or the "non-stop
card-players". But on the other hand, the

shortage of usable ports was to prove a
considerable handicap to the Allied
supply network, and hence to the whole
advance to Germany.

German divisions
bled white

Our second remark is that this directive
certainly came too late. It might have
been possible to carry it out on August 1,
when the vanguard of the 4th Panzer
Division was forcing a crossing of the
Sélune at Pontaubault. But it was no
longer possible on the 20th, when Patton
was driving his XII and XX Corps towards
Sens and Montereau and ordering XV
Corps to cross the Seine at Mantes without a moment's delay.

Hitler's directive, overtaken by events,
was also at fault because it was issued
without regard to the means left at Field-
Marshal Model's disposal. In effect,

according to H. M. Cole of the historical service of the U.S. Army, who bases his figures on minute research of German military archives, on August 31 the 60-odd divisions of the Wehrmacht and the *Waffen*-S.S. then engaged on the Western Front had lost 293,802 officers, N.C.O.s, and men killed, wounded, and missing since June 6. This was an average of about 5,000 men per division, a loss which must have sapped the strength of every formation.

Losses in *matériel*

In July Guderian, the Inspector General of the *Panzerwaffe*, recorded the destruction of 282 Pzkw IV, 375 Panther, and 140 Tiger tanks; in August these figures were respectively 279, 358, and 97, giving an overall total of 1,529 in 62 days of fighting. It was the same for the rest of the equipment: by August 25, 1,500 guns, (field, A.A., and anti-tank) and 500 assault guns had been destroyed. The Führer's order to the C.-in-C. West might have been impossible to carry out, but there was also little chance of the latter's beaten armies establishing themselves in the position just reconnoitred by General Kitzinger of the Luftwaffe behind the Seine and the Burgundy Canal.

This line ran along the Somme, the Crozat Canal, the Aisne at Soissons, the Marne from Epernay to Chaumont, the Langres plateau, and ended up at the Swiss frontier in the region of Pontarlier.

A new defence line

On August 24 Hitler dictated to Seyss-Inquart, the Nazi High Commissioner in Holland, *Gauleiters* Simon, Bürkel, and Wagner (his representatives in Luxembourg, Lorraine, and Alsace), and the military authorities concerned an order to develop a "German position in the West" for which they would have recourse to a mass levy.

There would be a continuous anti-tank obstacle, behind which the land would be laid waste and positions in depth organised. It would straddle the Scheldt estuary, use the line of the Albert Canal, cover Aix-la-Chapelle and Trier, the fortified complex of Thionville–Metz, turn up the Moselle as far as Saint Maurice and finally block the gap at Belfort.

Did Hitler realise that, from Model's reports, his directive of August 20 was out of date by the 24th? The fact remains that twice in four days he had recognised that he was beaten in the West.

CHAPTER 75
"Paris Libéré!"

On August 16, the very day when the American XX Corps reached Chartres, the Paris police went on strike. This was the start of the uprising in the city. S.H.A.E.F.'s plan was not to mount a frontal attack on an urban area of this importance, but to outflank it on both sides so that it would fall of its own accord, thus sparing the city the fighting and all the destruction this would entail. According to calculations made in London, this operation was to take place between 120 and 150 days after D-Day. On August 16 at Chartres General Patton was about 20 days ahead of schedule.

"What to do about Paris?" Eisenhower asked himself. A critical problem indeed, as he has pointed out in his memoirs, since the liberation of Paris would bring the need for supplying food to the capital at a rate calculated by S.H.A.E.F. experts

at 4,000 tons a day. This figure caused the C.-in-C. 12th Army Group to refuse.

"However, in spite of this danger of famine in Paris, I was determined that we would not be dissuaded from our plan to by-pass the city. If we could rush on to the Siegfried Line with tonnage that might otherwise be diverted to Paris, the city would be compensated for its additional week of occupation with an earlier end to the war. But we had not reckoned with the impatience of those Parisians who had waited four years for the armies that now approached their gates. My plan to pinch out Paris was exploded on an airstrip near Laval the morning of August 23."

General de Gaulle, in his rôle of head of the provisional government, had also addressed himself to the Allied C.-in-C. On August 21, newly arrived at Rennes

▽ The ecstasy of liberation. A convoy of civilian cars follows Allied vehicles in a spontaneous demonstration during the liberation of Paris. It was some days before the city was completely free of snipers, though the bulk of German forces had surrendered by August 25.

△ Shooting continued after the surrender. Here members of the "F.F.I." return fire during General de Gaulle's visit to Notre-Dame.
page 746 above: A German officer stands perilously outside the Chamber of Deputies, during the negotiations for the surrender of the 400 Germans who had held out inside.
below: Two soldiers of the U.S. 4th Infantry Division shelter behind a truck as they watch for snipers.
page 747 above: A children's magazine with a rather imaginative picture of the liberation.
below: General Koenig and staff. Cdt. Duperior, Col. de Chevigné, Capt. Lucas, Koenig, Col. de Wavrin, Comm. Raulin.

from Algiers, he had said:

"Information reaching me from Paris leads me to believe that as the police and the German armed forces have almost disappeared from the city, and as there is an extreme shortage of food, serious trouble may be expected within a very short time. I think it is vital to occupy Paris as soon as possible with French and Allied troops, even if some fighting results and there is some damage in the city.

"If a disorderly situation arises now in Paris, it will be difficult later on to get control of the city without serious incidents and this could even affect later operations.

"I am sending you General Koenig, who has been nominated Military Governor of Paris and C.-in-C. of the Paris Region, to study the occupation question with you in case, as I request of you, you decide to proceed without delay."

In his war memoirs de Gaulle tells us

why he intervened. It was a matter of preventing the formation, under cover of an uprising, of a predominantly Communist government. If this were to happen, he said, "on my arrival I should find this 'popular' government functioning: it would crown me with a laurel wreath, invite me to take my place within its organisation, and then pull all the strings. For those in control the rest would then be alternate boldness and prudence, the spread of state interference everywhere under cover of purges, suppression of public opinion by control of information and a militia, the progressive elimination of their earlier associates until the dictatorship of the proletariat was established."

Eisenhower agreed to the request, and Leclerc's division was sent off to Paris. This was what they had been waiting for, stamping with impatience until they were given free rein, ever since they had been transferred from North Africa to Great

Britain. Meanwhile this French 2nd Armoured Division had been moved from the U.S. 3rd to the U.S. 1st Army and put under V Corps. The least that can be said about this new arrangement is that Generals Gerow and Leclerc just were not on the same wavelength.

Choltitz and Hitler

On the German side the principal actors in the drama were General Dietrich von Choltitz, the Swedish Consul-General Raoul Nordling, and the leaders of the Paris insurrection.

Choltitz's behaviour is to be explained thus: since the previous autumn, when he had commanded XLVIII Panzer Corps on the Dniepr, he had maintained, in the presence of his chief-of-staff, Major-General von Mellenthin, that the tide of the Soviet advance would sooner or later burst over the dykes the Germans were erecting to hold it, and flood out all over Germany. Events since 1943 had only served to confirm his pessimism. When he left the O.K.W. meeting on August 7 after being invested by Hitler with the command of *Gross Paris* he had the impression that he had been dealing with a madman:

"Finally Hitler came to July 20 and I witnessed the explosion of a man filled to bursting with hatred. He yelled at me that he was glad to have bagged the whole opposition at one go and that he would crush it. He was in a state of feverish excitement. Saliva was literally running from his mouth. He was trembling all over and the desk on which he was leaning shook with him. He was bathed in perspiration and became more agitated still as he shouted that his generals would be 'strung up'. I was convinced there and then: the man opposite me was mad!"

If the means at Choltitz's disposal were enough to contain an uprising within the capital, the situation became completely different on August 21 as soon as O.K.W. ordered that the "Paris bridgehead" was to be held against the Americans. Hitler himself wrote to him, in order to underline the "supreme importance of the defence of Paris from the military and political points of view" and declared that "its fall would cause the breakdown of the whole coastal front north of the Seine and compel us to abandon bases used by

18 au 25 Août 1944

Colonel Roll-Tanguy

Colonel Fabien

PARIS SE LIBÈRE

our V-weapons against England". And Choltitz could also be reminded that "in the course of history the loss of Paris has also meant the loss of France". This did not, however, alter in any way the situation of the 22,000 men from two or three different divisions with whom he was being asked to hold a bridgehead from the Seine at Poissy to the Marne at Creteil (about 32 miles). The end of the order: "The Seine bridges will be prepared for destruction. Paris must only fall into enemy hands as a heap of rubble", revealed more a state of terrorism than sound strategic thinking. As an experienced soldier Choltitz was well aware that neither the heap of rubble nor the destruction of the bridges (if they were all blown) would slow down the Allied advance. There would have to be more than 60 demolition charges laid, two or three at least would fail to go off and all the experience of the Blitzkrieg had shown that destroyed bridges are no good unless protected by covering fire. For all these reasons the C.-in-C. *Gross Paris* lent a willing ear to Raoul Nordling, not however forgetting that in Germany the freedom and perhaps the lives of his wife and children might depend on the way his behaviour was judged by the Führer. In this double life he was compelled to live he was ably seconded by Lieutenant-General Speidel, chief-of-staff of Army Group "B", though they both had to converse in guarded terms because their telephones were liable to be tapped.

Paris liberated

On August 23 the French 2nd Armoured Division bore down on Paris, the "Langlade" and "Dio" Combat Commands along the axis Sées–Rambouillet–Pont de Sèvres, and the "Billotte" Combat Command via Alençon–Chartres–Arpajon–Porte d'Italie, causing an overlap along the sector given by U.S. V Corps to its 4th Division and a new disagreement between Generals Gerow and Leclerc. During the advance German 8.8-cm guns in ambush along the roads caused the loss of 317 men and 41 tanks and self-propelled guns. In the night of August 24-25 Captain Dronne and the tanks *Romilly, Champaubert,* and *Montmirail* passed through the Porte de Gentilly and reached the square in front of the Hôtel de Ville.

On the following day, with the aid of the *Forces Françaises de l'Intérieur* under Colonel Rol-Tanguy, the 2nd Armoured Division liberated Paris, and Choltitz, who had not left his headquarters in the Hôtel Meurice, surrendered.

"Destroy Paris!"

As soon as he heard that Paris had fallen, Hitler flew into a rage and ordered it to be wiped out. With this end in view he had the great siege mortar *Karl* readied. This huge gun had a calibre of 60 cms (23.6 inches), fired 2.2-ton shells, and had not been in action since Sevastopol'. The V-weapons and all available aircraft were now also to be brought into action.

Speidel forbade the transmission of this order. It had not the least strategic value and it would have caused thousands of civilian victims, and the destruction of buildings of inestimable artistic value. Speidel was later arrested on suspicion of being implicated in the July Plot and was lucky to escape the horrible torture which befell Witzleben and Hoeppner. If any conclusion is to be drawn from this episode it must come in the form of a question: what stage would the intellectual and moral reconstruction of Western Europe have reached today if Generals von Choltitz and Speidel had not, at the risk of their lives, thwarted the bloodthirsty plans of Adolf Hitler?

De Lattre presses on . . .

In Provence, General de Lattre de Tassigny had meanwhile managed to wriggle out of the plan by which he was intended to concentrate all his efforts on Toulon, and only move on to Marseilles when the large military port had been mopped up. This plan was calculated to lead to the hoisting of the tricolour on Notre Dame de la Garde on D-day plus 45, that is on September 28, if all went well.

On August 18 two solutions seemed possible to this ardent, yet calculating leader, as he says in his memoirs: "Given our recent successes, ought I to stick to the original plan? Or should I try to extend its scope? These were the alternatives that faced me on that day. It was very difficult, for the consequences of an error of judgement could only be very serious. If I opted for prudence, I could attack in strength, but all the benefits of surprise, and the chaos this would have caused in the enemy's ranks, would be lost. The Germans would have time to redeploy, move up reserves, and make full use of the enormous capabilities of the Toulon defence system. Thus caution would mean a siege, with all its consequent delays and suffering.

"If, on the other hand, I opted for boldness, 1 could expect to profit from the confusion caused by the strength of Truscott's attack, but my men would have to attack with one man against two, in the open and against reinforced concrete and protected gun emplacements. Boldness could break the French Army before it was even brought together.

"These were dramatic moments for the soul of a commander, but they could not be prolonged. After all, if the surprise attack failed, I could halt it and allow another commander to try again with more reinforcements. The risk was small compared with the enormous gains that might result from a swift success."

De Lattre went for boldness and got the

Two scenes typical of the liberation.
△ *A Parisienne gives a G.I. a victor's greeting, watched by a smiling gendarme.*

▽ *Police and members of the "F.F.I." escort away a suspected collaborator. The round-up of suspects after the liberation was haphazard and at times unjust.*

approval of General Patch, who overcame the misgivings of his staff. The French commander was, we would suggest, bolstering up a right decision with wrong premises, because on the same day, far from thinking of reinforcing the defence of Marseilles and Toulon, his adversary, acting under a directive from O.K.W., was actually putting into effect an order for withdrawal which was to take his 19th Army back to the area Lyons–Aix-les-Bains. De Lattre did not know, and could not have known, that Wiese was getting ready to retreat. The risk he mentioned was a real one to him and had to be faced.

This points to the difference between the military historian and the war-time commander: the one draws upon documents calmly collated in the peace of a library; the other makes his decisions from information which is never complete and "works on human skin", as Catherine the Great remarked forcibly to the intellectual Diderot, who carried no responsibility.

Now left to its fate, 242nd Division defended Toulon to the last ounce of its

△ *Sheltering behind an American tank, civilians shoot at a building still held by German troops.*
◁ *Parisians take cover behind parked M7 "Priest" self-propelled guns, during a battle with a sniper. These fire fights were often one-sided, for no snipers were ever captured, and Frenchmen found on the roof tops claimed that they too were hunting snipers or German stragglers.*

strength. On August 21 the 1st Free French Division had got as far as Hyères, in spite of stiff resistance, and Colonel Bouvet's commandos, working under the 9th Colonial Division, had scaled the walls of Fort Coudon on ropes and hunted down the 120 men of the garrison in the galleries: "At 1530 hours," General de Lattre reported, "when the Kriegsmarine decided to give in, it had only six unwounded men. But at the moment of surrender, their commander signalled: 'Fire on us.' Violent shelling then began on the fort and lasted for several minutes. Germans and Frenchmen alike were hit, and amongst the latter was Lieutenant Girardon, one of the heroes of the assault."

Defended to the last man

The same thing happened the next day in the ammunition magazine at Toulon, where the galleries had to be taken one by one by Lieutenant-Colonel Gambiez's battalion of shock troops, supported by two tank-destroyers firing point-blank and a battalion of artillery, which reduced the works above the ground.

"Only the dead stopped fighting," de Lattre wrote when describing this action. At nightfall, when the flame-throwers had overcome the last of the resistance, he went on, "the inside of the fortress was no more than a huge open charnel-

house over which hung a frightful stench of death. It was being devoured by flames which caused boxes of ammunition to explode at every moment. There were 250 corpses strewn on the ground and only 180 men had been taken prisoner. Of these 60 were seriously wounded. This macabre spectacle suddenly reminded me of the most tragic sights at Douaumont and Thiaumont in 1916. It is a fine thing that our lads, many of whom are in battle for the first time, have equalled the exploits of the hardened *poilus* of Verdun. Their enemy was in no way inferior to the one their fathers faced. One of the defenders was asked to give the reason for this heroic and desperate resistance. 'We defended ourselves, that's all. I am an officer, a lieutenant. It's war for me as well as for you, gentlemen,' he replied.''

The victorious advance of the 9th Colonial Division through the defences of Toulon relieved the 3rd Algerian Division of its first mission, during which

◁ *Behind his own barricade, a French soldier covers a road with a .50 calibre machine gun.*
▽ ◁ *An M8 light armoured car of the 4th U.S. Infantry Division drives down the Champs Elysées. Four years earlier the soldiers and horses of the Wehrmacht had clattered down the same wide avenues.*
▽ *Two German officers and a medical orderly are escorted away by a mixed group of "F.F.I." and regular French soldiers. With the large numbers of small arms in circulation in August 1944, these Germans were still targets for revenge by individual Frenchmen even when they had become prisoners.*

it had reached Sanary and Bandol, thus ensuring the investment of the western side of the fortress.

Reinforced in due time by General Guillaume's *goums,* General de Monsabert rapidly turned towards Marseilles, where the firemen, the sailors, and the F.F.I. had taken up arms on August 21. The French forces took the mountain route and outflanked 244th Division's defence points along the main axes. On the 23rd General de Monsabert presented himself at 15th Military District H.Q. He sent for Lieutenant-General Schäffer, who then refused to surrender.

Toulon liberated

The liberation of Toulon was completed on August 27 by the capitulation of Rear-Admiral Ruhfus, who had found a last refuge from the shells of the navy and the bombs of the air force in the Saint Mandrier peninsula. The assault on Toulon had cost the French 2,700 men killed and wounded, but they had taken over 17,000 prisoners and several hundred guns. The Cape Cépet battery, which had been such a thorn in the flesh of the attackers, was pounded by 1,400 shells of 12-inch calibre or higher and 809 1,000- and 2,000-lb bombs. There were four direct hits on its turrets. One jammed, the other had one gun put out of action. The only gun undamaged fired 250 shells, but without appreciable effect.

Marseilles falls

On August 23 de Lattre sent the 1st Armoured Division into Marseilles, and together with the 3rd Algerian Division and the Moroccan *goums* it overcame the resistance within the city. As in Toulon, the Germans defended themselves bitterly, using rocket launchers, mines, and flame-throwers. The loss successively of Notre Dame de la Garde and Fort Saint Nicolas, however, ended Schäffer's resistance and in the evening of the 27th he wrote to Monsabert:

"Prolonged resistance seems pointless in view of your superior strength. I ask you to cease firing from 2100 to 0800 hours so that surrender terms may be finalised for mid-day on the 28th and that I may have a decision from you which will

allow me either to surrender with honour or to fight to the finish."

Neither General de Monsabert nor his commander were men to overlook the valour of the 244th Division. And so the armistice was signed on August 28 shortly before 0800 hours.

Allied victory in Provence

The Allies were now a month ahead of schedule. The fury of their attacks had cost them 4,000 killed and wounded, but they had wiped out two enemy divisions and captured 37,000 prisoners.

Before ceasing all resistance the Germans blew up the port installations in Marseilles and Toulon. Until these were restored, the Provence beaches had landed 380,000 men, 69,312 vehicles, 306,000 tons of supplies and *matériel,* and 17,848 tons of fuel. By May 8, 1945, 905,512 men and 4,123,794 tons of *matériel* had passed through the hastily-reconstructed ports of Marseilles, Toulon, and Port de Bouc. These figures are taken from Morison, who claims, and we would agree with him, that for this alone Operation "Dragoon" was justified.

△ *General Dwight D. Eisenhower, Supreme Commander Allied Expeditionary Forces, at the Arc de Triomphe, when he visited Paris on September 1, 1944. With him are (left) Lieutenant-General Omar N. Bradley and (right) General Joseph Koenig, military commander of Paris, and Air Chief-Marshal Arthur Tedder (extreme right). Koenig, the hero of Bir Hakeim, was to comment a few days after the liberation "The worst danger in Paris at the moment are the F.F.I."*

CHAPTER 76
ARNHEM: MONTY'S GAMBLE FAILS

General Bradley was to describe his stupefaction on learning of Operation "Market Garden" which Montgomery had got Eisenhower to approve and with which Bradley did not agree:

"Had the pious teetotaling Montgomery wobbled into S.H.A.E.F. with a hangover, I could not have been more astonished than I was by the daring adventure he proposed. For in contrast to the conservative tactics Montgomery ordinarily chose, the Arnhem attack was to be made over a 60-mile carpet of airborne troops. Although I never reconciled myself to the venture, I nevertheless freely concede that Monty's plan for Arnhem was one of the most imaginative of the war."

In effect the "carpet" over which XXX Corps was to advance towards the northern outskirts of Arnhem was 60 miles long and criss-crossed six times by canals and watercourses. Eisenhower had put at Montgomery's disposal the 1st Airborne Army. Commanded by U.S. Lieutenant-General L. H. Brereton, it engaged its I Airborne Corps (Lieutenant-General F. A. M. Browning) as follows:

1. U.S. 101st Airborne Division (Major-General Maxwell D. Taylor) would take Eindhoven by surprise and seize the bridges on the Wilhelmina Canal, the Dommel, and the Willems Canal;

2. U.S. 82nd Airborne Division (Major-General James M. Gavin) would take the Grave bridge over the Maas and the Nijmegen bridge over the Waal (the southern arm of the Rhine); and

3. British 1st Airborne Division (Major-General R. E. Urquhart) would take the bridges over the Neder Rijn (the

Across the Seine

On August 26, the 21st Army Group had the left flank of its Canadian 1st Army in the area of Honfleur and linked up with the British 2nd Army around Louviers. The right of the British 2nd Army was in Vernon, where it had a bridgehead on the north bank of the Seine. Between Nantes and Saint Nazaire, the American 12th Army Group formed a hairpin including the Seine crossings at Nantes, Paris, Melun, and Troyes, then through Saint Florentin and Joigny, back to the Loire at Gien. In the south, while the 7th Army Group was mopping up in Toulon and Marseilles, the American VI Corps had liberated Grenoble and was trying to cut off the retreat of the German 19th Army in the area of Montelimar. By September 10 the Germans had only three fortresses in the north of France: Boulogne, Calais and Dunkirk. Montgomery occupied Bruges, Ghent and Antwerp while his 2nd Army was on the north bank of the Albert Canal. The American 12th Army Group was in Liege, Bastogne and Luxembourg, and on the outskirts of Thionville, Metz and Nancy.

Eisenhower preferred a broad-front pursuit of the Germans, aimed at both the Ruhr and Saar, to the concentrated effort proposed by Montgomery, which would have moved north of the Ardennes and put a pincer round the Ruhr.

On August 28, XII Corps crossed the Marne at Chalons. On August 29, XX Corps passed through Epernay and Chateau-Thierny before occupying Rheims. Patton then pushed on for the Meuse, but by the time the Meuse River bridgeheads had been established between Verdun and Commercy, his supply lines were at breaking point.

On September 9 the U.S. 5th Armoured Division liberated Luxembourg and crossed the Sure at Wallendorf, making a breach in the Siegfried Line. During the night of August 30-31 the British XXX Corps took Amiens and then pushed on to Lens. The Guards reached Brussels on September 3. On September 4 Antwerp fell into the hands of the 11th Armoured Division, aided by the Belgian resistance. On September 5 Lieutenant-General Ritchie's XII Corps liberated Ghent.

△ △ *Two film cameramen, part of the team that gave extensive press coverage to the operation. They were to record the struggle in some of the most vivid film and photographs of the war.*

△ *Two paratroopers of the 82nd Airborne Division check their kit before emplaning. The 82nd Airborne jumped at Nijmegen and captured bridges over the Maas and Maas-Waal canal, but failed to reach the Nijmegen bridges. These were later taken in a joint assault with XXX Corps.*

▷ *The interior of a Dakota; the soldiers carry their weapons, with their kit packed in leg bags, or worn under their smocks to prevent it catching in the parachute harness.*

northern arm of the Rhine) at Arnhem. It would then establish a bridgehead around the town and be reinforced by the Polish 1st Parachute Brigade, then by the British 52nd (Airportable) Division.

It was along the corridor opened up by these forces that the three divisions of the British XXX Corps (the Guards Armoured, the 43rd, and the 50th Divisions) under Horrocks were to advance towards Arnhem and, breaking out of the bridgehead, drive on at full speed to the Zuiderzee, a final run of about 37 miles.

Allied Intelligence misses II Panzer Corps

All things considered, it does seem that Operation "Market Garden" relied heavily on what Frederick the Great called "Her Sacred Majesty Chance" and the expectation that she would favour Generals Browning and Horrocks for several days and under all circumstances. Even had she favoured them throughout, however, it is unlikely that XXX Corps could have made the run to Berlin all alone, as Eisenhower had no strategic reserves or logistic resources to exploit fully any initial success of this risky enterprise.

Yet XXX Corps' advance had to take place up a single road flanked by low-lying country, covered with a network of drainage ditches. This was to provide ideal terrain for the Germans to slow down or even halt the advance with a tenacious anti-tank defence, while launching flank attacks against XXX Corps' own communications. And this, in fact, was what was to happen.

Although Montgomery knew from intelligence reports that two Panzer divisions (part of the II S.S. Panzer Corps)

◁ *The fatal delay. Between four and six hours elapsed before the troops could arrive at the bridge. Some were slowed down by enthusiastic Dutch civilians, who greeted them as liberators.*
◁ ▽ *Landing Zone "Z" covered with gliders, some of which have been broken in half for unloading.*
▽ *Parachutes litter the ground on a dropping zone outside Arnhem.*

were refitting just north of Arnhem, he believed them incapable of effective action and Horrocks, the commander of XXX Corps, was not even informed that these German forces lay so close to the battle area.

In fact, these forces also included the 1st Parachute Army which was being built up in the region of 's Hertogenbosch under the command of Colonel-General Kurt Student, the victor of Crete. The Allied forces, with their limited resources, had little chance of success. Additionally, it is arguable that the objectives of "Market Garden" were beyond the Allies' capabilities. The plan would clearly involve a great deal of risk; and it seemed a highly dangerous operation to informed critics such as Bradley, who wrote later:

". . . as soon as I learned of Monty's plan, I telephoned Ike and objected strenuously to it. For in abandoning the joint offensive, Monty would slip off on a tangent and leave us holding the bag. But Ike silenced my objections; he thought the plan a fair gamble. It might enable us to outflank the Siegfried Line, perhaps even snatch a Rhine bridgehead."

Events were to prove Bradley all too right.

Operation "Market Garden"

On Sunday September 17, 1944, zero hour struck at 1430. Under the near or distant cover of 1,200 fighters the first elements of Lieutenant-General Browning's three airborne divisions, which had been packed into 2,800 aircraft and 1,600 gliders, jumped or landed as close as possible to their objectives without undue losses.

For the 101st Airborne Division all went well, except for the Son bridge over the Wilhelmina Canal which it could not save from destruction. The 82nd managed to surprise the Grave bridge, but in the evening, when the Germans had got over the shock, it failed in its first attempt on Nijmegen. By this time General Student had got the plans for "Market Garden" which had been found on board an American glider shot down behind the German lines. Because of heavy A.A. fire round Arnhem it had been decided that the first echelon of the British 1st Airborne Division would drop in heath-land seven miles from the Neder Rijn bridges. Moreover there were not enough aircraft to carry the whole division in one lift, so that three successive drops were necessary.

Field-Marshal Model, commander of Army Group "B" at Oosterbeek, alerted General Bittrich, commanding II S.S. Panzer Corps, and counter-attacked with the 9th *Hohenstaufen* Panzer Division through

▽ *A German soldier surrenders to the Guards Armoured Division during the vain dash towards Arnhem.*

Arnhem and the 10th *"Frundsberg"* along the left bank of the Neder Rijn.

The British outpaced

The British no longer had surprise, and now problems mounted as for technical and topographical reasons, their radio communications broke down. The divisional commander, Urquhart, decided to go up to the front himself, and within minutes he had lost all means of co-ordinating the movements of his division. Towards 2000 hours Lieutenant-Colonel Frost's battalion, whose commander had led the raid on Bruneval in 1942, had reached a point opposite the road bridge at Arnhem, but was almost surrounded.

Supported on the left by XII Corps and on the right by VIII Corps (Lieutenant-General Evelyn H. Baring), XXX Corps got off to a good start. Admirably supported, as its commander said, by No. 83 Group, Tactical Air Force (Air Vice-Marshal H. Broadhurst), it reached Valkenswaard at the end of the day. A day later its Guards Armoured Division was at Son, where the bridge over the canal was repaired by dawn on the 19th. There was good contact with the 82nd Airborne Division, which had resumed its attack on Nijmegen, but without much success.

By now it had begun to rain. "Market Garden", in fact, enjoyed only one day of blue skies out of ten. Were the weather forecasts ignored? There were consequential delays in the reinforcement of the airborne divisions and a notable drop in efficiency of the ground support. XXX Corps had only one axis along which to advance its 23,000 vehicles. During the 19th, Horrocks was able to get his tanks from Son to Nijmegen (36 miles), but it was not until the evening of the following day that the British and the Americans, fighting side by side, succeeded in crossing the Waal and seizing the road and rail bridges which Model had ordered to be left intact for a counter-attack.

When he had been given his orders the day before "Market Garden" was launched, Browning asked Montgomery how long he would have to hold the Arnhem bridge.

"Two days" said Monty briskly. "They'll be up with you by then."

"We can hold it for four." Browning replied. "But I think we might be going a bridge too far."

The British driven back

The operation was now in its fifth day, and during the night of September 19-20 Urquhart had had to resign himself to abandoning Frost to his fate and to pulling his unit into the district of Oosterbeek with its back to the Neder Rijn. The bad weather continued, air supplies were

◁ △ *A 6-pdr anti-tank gun in ambush. The crew are about to fire on an assault gun which is only 80 yards away.*
△ *A 75-mm pack howitzer of the 1st Airlanding Light Regiment in action. They were used as anti-tank weapons to supplement the 1st and 2nd Anti-Tank Batteries, but were a poor substitute with their low muzzle velocity and slow cross-axle traverse.*

reduced to practically nothing, and what was dropped fell equally amongst the Germans and the Allies. In the evening of the 21st, Lieutenant-Colonel Frost was seriously wounded and his battalion, now reduced to about 100 men, was captured by the Germans. On the 21st and 22nd the Polish 1st Parachute Brigade (Major-General Sosabowski) landed almost opposite Oosterbeek, whilst the Guards (Major-General Allan Adair) and the 43rd Division (Major-General Ivor Thomas) were caught in flank by the 10th *"Frundsberg"* S.S. Panzer Division as they tried to cover the ten miles between the Waal and the Neder Rijn. XXX Corps' forward positions, now sticking out like a finger in the German lines, risked being cut off at any moment from either east or west.

The survivors of the British 1st Airborne Division now received the order to pull back to the left bank of the Neder Rijn. 2,163 of them got across during the night of September 25-26 out of a total of 8,905 officers, N.C.O.s, and men and the 1,100 glider-pilots who had held off the attacks of II S.S. Panzer Corps for the last ten days. The Poles left behind 1,000 of their men and the U.S. 82nd and 101st Airborne Divisions lost respectively 1,669 and 2,074 killed, wounded, and missing. Between September 17 and 30, then, about one-third of the 34,876 men who fought between Eindhoven and Arnhem were lost. The people of Arnhem showed admirable devotion and courage in hiding 250 British paratroopers and helping them to escape: among these were Brigadiers J. W. Hackett and G. W. Lathbury.

Major-General Urquhart's epic at Arnhem

In a letter dated September 28 and written in his own hand, Field-Marshal Montgomery expressed the admiration he felt at the bearing of Major-General Urquhart's division. Recalling the centuries-old roll-call of famous deeds by British arms, he wrote to him:

"There can be few episodes more glorious than the epic of Arnhem, and those that follow after will find it hard to live up to the high standards that you have set.

"So long as we have in the armies of the British Empire officers and men who will do as you have done, then we can indeed look forward with complete confidence to the future. In years to come it will be a great thing for a man to be able to say 'I fought at Arnhem!'"

"Market Garden" a failure

History will bear out this judgement. It is not certain, however, that it will also ratify Montgomery's conclusions on the glorious and tragic episode. In his opinion, if the success of the undertaking was not as great as had been expected, this was because the supply services, contrary to Eisenhower's orders, refused to cut down on rations for the American 3rd Army. General Bradley thought otherwise and wrote to the C.-in-C. on September 21: ". . . all plans for the future operations always lead back to the fact that in order to supply an operation of any size beyond the Rhine, the port of Antwerp is essential."

On September 4 the Scheldt estuary could have been cleared within a few days, and the rapidity of this success would have been a real shot in the arm to the Allied supply problem. Instead, the operation started on September 29 by the 21st Army Group dragged on for a whole month. By November 3 it was all over, but the Germans had profited from the delay by mining the canal, and clearing operations took another three weeks of dangerous and intensive work. Antwerp's major port facilities thus went unused from September 4 to November 23, whilst less than 90 miles away to the south-west the U.S. 1st Army was reduced to cutting down on petrol and ammunition. There were, of course, the "Red Ball Highways". The American historian Robert W. Merrian, writing of these roads, organised from August 25 onwards by Lieutenant-General J. C. H. Lee, says of the service:

"The Red Ball supply high road grew and grew, like Topsy, until it stretched over 700 well-marked miles, thoroughly equipped with fast wreckage and servicing stations manned twenty-four hours a day. The Red Ball began operating on August 25 with 5,400 vehicles, hauled a daily average of about 5,000 tons of supplies for the eighty-one days of its operation. On its peak day of operation, over 12,000 tons of supplies were hauled to the front, more than enough for twelve fighting divisions. Operating on a circle route,

▽ *Field-Marshal Walther Model. His aggressive reaction, and the presence of the 9th and 10th Divisions of II S.S. Panzer Corps north of Arnhem, were to unhinge "Market Garden" before it could begin.*

it was a vast one-way traffic circle, along which raced the life blood of the advancing troops. The driving was hard, the roads merciless on the vehicles, the turnover of equipment staggering, but the supplies were pushed through.''

If Operation "Market Garden" proved Allied logistics to have been at fault, it also prejudiced the build-up of a 100-mile salient which was necessary to support Bradley's offensive towards Bonn and Cologne. As Bradley had feared, the British 2nd Army's northwards push ended up between Maastricht, Nijmegen, and Breda. When Antwerp finally got priority Bradley had had to lend two divisions temporarily to 21st Army Group to help in its capture.

Meanwhile the Canadian 1st Army had seized Le Havre (September 12), Boulogne (September 22), and Calais (October 1), capturing more than 28,000 prisoners. The combined effects of Allied bombardment and German destruction meant that it took longer than expected to get the ports working again. Le Havre in particular had had nearly 10,000 tons of bombs dropped on it and by late October was down to 15 per cent of its capacity. The day after the capture of Boulogne, however, the Allies were able to lay between this port and Dungeness a second 16-tube pipeline, which greatly alleviated the Allied petrol problem.

△ △ *Survivors from the Border Regiment raise a smile for the camera.*
△ *An S.S. officer interrogates two captured soldiers. On the night of September 25/26 the survivors of the Arnhem "Cauldron" had been ordered to withdraw across the Rhine.*
▷ △ *Walking wounded. Over 300 wounded were taken prisoner in the perimeter. Almost ten times that number had already been captured, and were in Dutch hospitals and German dressing stations. Over 1,200 British soldiers were dead, and 3,400 Germans were dead or wounded.*

CHAPTER 77
CONFUSION IN THE BALKANS

As the Red Army moved deeper into the Balkans, the uneasy anti-Axis truce between the Royalists and the Communists in Greece broke down completely. The latter, in the hope of securing Russian intervention in Greece, started an insurrection in Athens. But Greece fell within the British sphere of influence, and Churchill reacted swiftly. Comprising airborne landings and subsequent amphibious reinforcement, Operation "Manna" was intended to nip the Communist flower in the bud. But soon General Scobie's III Corps found itself embroiled in a full scale civil war.

On August 23, the German forces occupying Albania, mainland Greece, and the Aegean Islands came under Colonel-General Löhr, commanding Army Group "E" with headquarters at Salonika. These forces were subdivided into four corps (Tiranë, Yanina, Athens, and Salonika) totalling ten divisions (seven of which were on the mainland) and six fortress brigades: in all, about 300,000 men, to whom must be added 33,000 sailors (most of whom were attached to the coastal artillery) and 12,000 airmen and anti-aircraft gunners.

The day following the Rumanian cease-fire, Löhr was confronted by an order from O.K.W. ordering him to begin evacuation of the Aegean and Ionian islands and mainland Greece, south of a line running from Corfu to Métsovon and Mt. Olympus. But a few days later Sofia's declaration of war on Berlin forced Hitler to annul this order and to instruct Army Group "E" to retreat to a line running along the line Scutari–Skopje–Bulgarian/Yugoslav frontier of 1939–Iron Gate Pass on the Danube. On the other side of the river he would be in contact with the 2nd *Panzerarmee* (General de Angelis). The latter would relieve Field-Marshal von

Weichs's Army Group "F". In this way a continuous front between the Carpathians and the Adriatic would be formed to bar the enemy from the Danube plain.

Time was pressing, and it was not possible to recover all the 60,000 men who garrisoned the Aegean. Using the very few transport aircraft available and a large number of powered *caiques*, two-thirds of the men were brought back to mainland Greece. The remainder continued to hold Rhodes, Léros, Kos, and Tílos under the command of Major-General Wagner, as well as Crete and the island of Mílos under General Benthak. They remained there until after the end of the war on May 9, 1945.

The evacuation of the Peloponnese gave rise to some clashes between the 41st Division (Lieutenant-General Hauser) and the royalist guerrillas of Napoleon Zervas, opportunely reinforced by the British 2nd Airborne Brigade, which liberated Patras on October 4. All the same, the Germans reached Corinth, then Athens which General Felmy, commanding LXVIII Corps, handed over to the control of its mayor that same day. In Epiros, the troops of XXII Mountain Corps (General Lanz) fought bitter battles

The Allies Confer

The Anglo-American conference at Quebec took place in September, 1944. Issues raised included participation of the British against Japan, the British aim to reach Vienna before the Russians and the division of occupation zones in Germany. The Morgenthau Plan, which would have stripped Germany of any industrial power, was eventually rejected after opposition in both London and Washington.

During October 9 to 16, 1944, Churchill visited Moscow, his main concern being spheres of influence in the Balkans and particularly the liberty of Greece and Poland. He renounced Western interest in either Rumania or Bulgaria.

The Polish delegation of the government in exile was aghast to discover that the Big Three at Teheran had allotted 48 per cent of Polish territory to the Soviet Union. The Polish Prime Minister Stanislas Mikolcjczyk was given short shrift by Churchill when he protested.

At the Yalta Conference 4-11 February 1945 the British felt they were at disadvantage in the face of skilful Russian diplomacy and American vacillation. Yalta consummated Churchill's failure to preserve Polish independence.

with partisans. But, all in all, the evacuation of Greece took place with very few losses and serious delays to the retreating Germans.

Mention should be made here that in 1947, the Greek Government revealed to the United Nations the text of an agreement made between a representative of the 11th Luftwaffe Division and a delegate of the "E.L.A.S." partisans, according to whose terms the men of the "Peoples' Army" agreed not to hinder the German retreat on the condition that they were given a certain quantity of heavy arms and other military equipment for their forthcoming war with the loyalists.

◁ *Male and female soldiers of E.L.A.S. With the Germans pulling back towards Yugoslavia, E.L.A.S. now saw its task as leading Greece into the Communist bloc.*

Finland Drops Out

Between the 2nd and 3rd Belorussian Fronts, the outline of the pincer movement which would lead to the encirclement and then the conquest of East Prussia was forming. A "Polish Committee of National Liberation" was set up in Lublin under the Communist E.B. Osobka-Morawski, who was totally submissive to the Kremlin.

Guderian wanted to evacuate Estonia and the eastern part of Lithuania in order to give more strength to Army Group "North", but his request was refused by Hitler who feared the defection of Finland. On September 3, 1944 Hitler was informed of the Finno-Soviet armistice. By now Army Group "North" had only 32 divisions against 130 Russian ones. By September 24, Marshal Goverov had almost completely occupied Estonia. On October 13, the Russians entered Riga. On October 5 the Russians breached Schörner's defensive screen in the Siauliai region and five days later reached the Baltic at Palanga, cutting off Army Group "North". On the 220-mile front between the Niemen and the Narew at Nowogrod, the Russians were checked by the German 4th Army. On October 21 and 22 the 11th Guards Army was thrown back by General F. Hossbach when it tried to cross the River Angerrapp.

On August 1, Marshal Mannerheim was appointed head of state in Finland. Aware of the implications, the Germans put into effect Operation "Birke" (Birch Tree), whereby the German 20th Army would retreat on the Finno-Norwegian frontier. On September 2 the Finnish parliament authorised the government to re-open discussions with the Soviet Union. On September 5 there was a ceasefire between the Finns and Russians. The date of evacuation of German forces was set for September 14. Under Hitler's orders, the Germans attacked the island of Sur Sari, but were defeated by the Finns. On October 15 the Russians occupied Petsamo, and then pushed on as far as Kirkenes in Norway. On September 19, 1944 an armistice treaty was signed between Finland and the Soviet Union in which, in addition to the losses sustained in the treaty of March 7, 1940, Finland now suffered the amputation of the Petsamo region and lease of the Pork-kala promontory on the Gulf of Finland.

Trouble in Yugoslavia

It was in Yugoslavia that things became difficult for Army Group "E". On October 14, the Bulgarian 5th Army took Niš, on the most practical route for the Germans to reach the Danube. In addition, on October 1, Tolbukhin had crossed the Danube near Turnu Severin and then forced his way over the Morava against the resistance of XXXIV Corps' (General F. W. Müller) two divisions. Then the Russians marched on Belgrade. On October 20, working with Marshal Tito's troops, they overcame the final resistance in the streets of the Yugoslav capital, undertaken by *Armeegruppe* "Felber" (Army Group "F").

The fall of Niš had forced Löhr to think of a way to escape the noose and he decided to follow a route through Skopje, Mitrovica, Novi Pazar, and Višegrad. The Belgrade road would have enabled Tolbukhin to cut Army Group "E"'s last line of retreat if his enemy had not opportunely guarded his flanks around Kraljevo and Užice. In short, Colonel-General Löhr established his headquarters at Sarajevo on November 15, having managed to bring his four corps through

▽ *Loyalists demonstrate in favour of Papandreou and the Western Allies.*

without being encircled. Marshal Tito's Yugoslav partisans had failed in their attempts to hinder the retreat of Army Group "E" for long enough to allow Tolbukhin to develop his manoeuvre. All the same the partisans sowed hostility behind the Germans' backs in Bosnia and Hercegovina and increased their activities in Croatia and Slovenia. On the Adriatic Coast they liberated Cattaro (Kotor), Ragusa (Dubrovnik), and Spalato (Split) and, on November 8, occupied the Italian town of Zara (Zadar), which would be "slavicised" by means which Hitler would not have disdained.

Churchill pressures Bulgaria

As has been mentioned, on October 4 a British airborne force had helped to liberate Patras. A few days later, other parachute forces dropped on the aerodromes at Elevsís and Mégara. On October 14, a mixed Greek and British squadron under Rear-Admiral Troubridge dropped anchor in the Piraeus and disembarked most of the British III Corps under the command of Lieutenant-General R. M. Scobie.

This operation, code-named "Manna", had two aims. Following the terms of the armistice, the Bulgarian Government had agreed to return to the borders of April 6, 1941. But although Tito and Gheorghiev reached immediate understanding, the Bulgarian leader cherished the hope of being able to keep the Greek provinces of Western Thrace and Eastern Macedonia within Communist Bulgaria. These provinces had been granted to King Boris by Hitler. Here he thought he could count on the aid of E.L.A.S. (Greek Peoples' Liberation Army).

Communist *coup* prevented

Furthermore, General Scobie was ordered to prevent, by force if need be, the Peoples' Liberation Army from overturning the established system in Greece by absolutely unconstitutional means. The personality of the prime minister, George Papandreou, gave this regime a liberal and democratic aspect, which was quite acceptable to the Western Allies. However, it was clear that the danger of

Defeat in the Balkans

Soviet troops attacked Iasi, capital of Moldavia on August 20, 1944 and on Christmas Eve laid siege to Budapest.

Three days later King Michael summoned Antonescu and his Minister of Foreign Affairs to the palace and ordered them to conclude an immediate armistice with the Allies. Receiving no assurance, the king had them both arrested. At 2200 hours, Radio Bucharest broadcast the cease-fire order to all Rumanian forces. Hitler ordered Luftwaffe formations based on Ploiesti to bomb Bucharest, concentrating on the Royal Palace and the Prime Minister's residence. On August 25 Rumania declared war on the Third Reich and opened the Danube, Prut and Siretul crossings to the Russians. Consequently, fourteen divisions of the German 6th Army were annihilated in a pincer movement. The German 8th Army was also trapped and the remains of its 79th and 376th Divisions were forced to lay down their arms. Of 24 German divisions which he had under his command on August 20, the Colonel-General Friessner had lost 16 in the space of a fortnight.

subversion was growing day by day and, summoned by a Liberation Committee of Communist inspiration (E.A.M.), units of E.L.A.S. converged on Athens, passing the retreating Germans without clashing.

In spite of the reservations of the White House and the State Department, and the furious onslaughts of the Labour M.P.s Emmanuel Shinwell and Aneurin Bevan, the cold disapproval of *The Times* and the *Manchester Guardian,* everybody knows that Churchill did not hesitate to oppose E.L.A.S. with force, such was his fear of Communism. Nevertheless, it was the beginning of a civil war. It would be waged savagely until the day in June 1948 when the quarrel broke between Tito and Moscow. Deprived of the important aid that Tito provided, the insurrection wavered and then collapsed under the blows struck at it in the following year by Marshal Papagos.

Malinovsky slows down

Marshal Malinovsky was last seen crossing the Wallachian Carpathians and establishing his front along the Braşov–Sibiu–Alba Iulia line. Doubtless his intention was to push straight on north and to strike the German 8th Army in the rear. This German army had established itself along the Moldavian Carpathians. But Colonel-General Friessner foresaw Malinovsky's plan, and counter-attacked from near Cluj (known then as Koloszvar) in a southerly direction, with the Hungarian 2nd Army (General Veress) and III Panzer Corps (General Breith), which had just been attached to his command. He was able to pull his 8th Army out of the Szecklers salient. In spite of this, a breach was opened between the right of the Army Group "South" (ex-"South Ukraine") and the left of Army Group "F". This breach was weakly held by the Hungarian IV and VII Corps. The 6th Guards Army plunged into it and though Friessner had received five divisions as reinforcements, two from Field-Marshal von Weichs and three from O.K.H., he could not stop Malinovsky establishing himself along a line from Oradea (Nagyvárad) through Arad to Timişoara. And so, on Rumanian soil, was fought the prologue to the battle of Hungary.

The fact that, in this duel between the 2nd Ukrainian Front and the German Army Group "South", Malinovsky needed

△ *Marshall Rodion Malinovsky.*
◁ *A Soviet Frontier Post re-erected on the Rumanian border.*

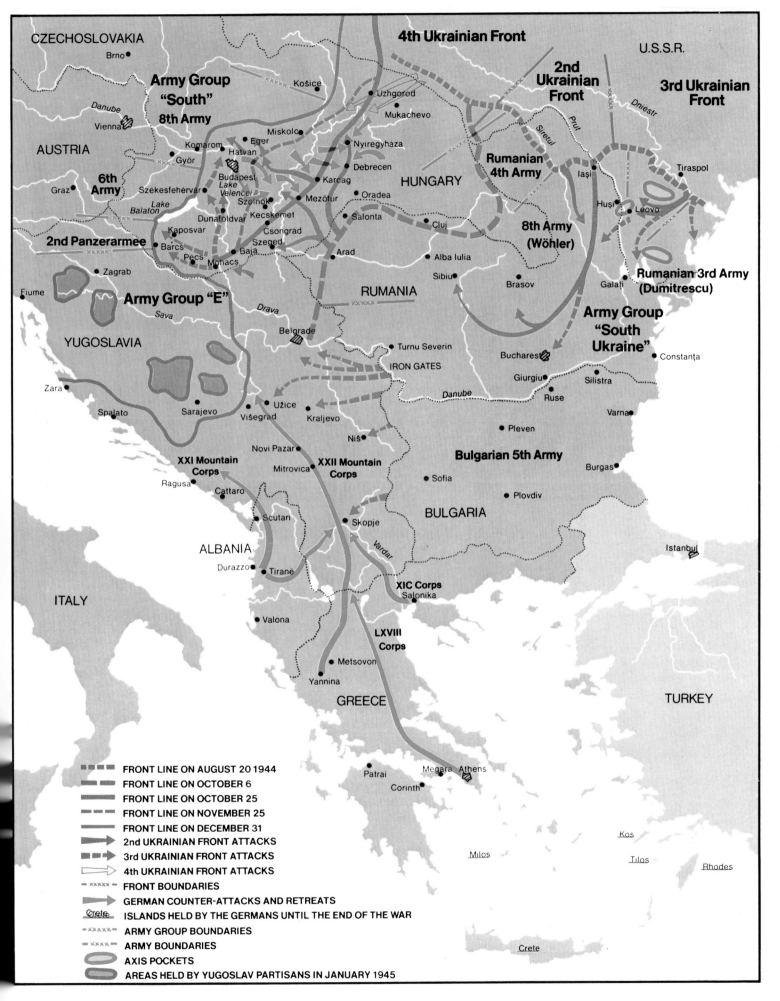

CZECHOSLOVAKIA
Brno•

4th Ukrainian Front

U.S.S.R.

Army Group "South" 8th Army

Danube
Vienna•

Košice•

Uzhgorod•
Mukachevo•

2nd Ukrainian Front

3rd Ukrainian Front

AUSTRIA

Miskolc•

Nyiregyhaza•

Komarom• Eger•

Dniestr

Tiraspol•

Győr• Hatvan•

Debrecen•

HUNGARY

Iaşi•

6th Army

Budapest *Lake Velencei*

Karcag•

Rumanian 4th Army

Prut

Huşi•

Graz•

Szekesfehervar•

Oradea•

Leovo•

Szolnok•

Mezotur•

Lake Balaton

Dunafoldvar•

Kecskemet•

Salonta•

Cluj•

8th Army (Wöhler)

2nd Panzerarmee

Csongrad•

Barcs•

Szeged•

Arad•

Pecs•

Baja•

Alba Iulia•

Rumanian 3rd Army (Dumitrescu)

Zagrab•

Mohacs•

Sibiu•

Galaţi•

Brasov•

Army Group "E"

RUMANIA

Fiume•

Sava

Drava

Army Group "South Ukraine"

YUGOSLAVIA

Belgrade•

Bucharest•

Constanţa•

Zara•

Turnu Severin•

IRON GATES

Giurgiu•

Silistra•

Ruse•

Spalato•

Sarajevo•

Užice•

Danube

Varna•

Visegrad•

Kraljevo•

Pleven•

XXI Mountain Corps

Novi Pazar•

Niš•

XXII Mountain Corps

Bulgarian 5th Army

Burgas•

Ragusa•

Mitrovica•

Sofia•

Cattaro•

Plovdiv•

Scutari•

Skopje•

BULGARIA

ALBANIA

Vardar

Istanbul•

Durazzo•

Tirane•

XIC Corps
Salonika•

ITALY

Valona•

LXVIII Corps

Metsovon•

TURKEY

Yannina•

GREECE

Kos

Megara Athens•

Patrai•

Milos

Corinth•

Tilos

Rhodes

Crete

░░░░ FRONT LINE ON AUGUST 20 1944
▬▬▬ FRONT LINE ON OCTOBER 6
▬▬▬ FRONT LINE ON OCTOBER 25
▬ ▬ ▬ FRONT LINE ON NOVEMBER 25
▬▬▬ FRONT LINE ON DECEMBER 31
➤ 2nd UKRAINIAN FRONT ATTACKS
➤ 3rd UKRAINIAN FRONT ATTACKS
➤ 4th UKRAINIAN FRONT ATTACKS
- ×××× - FRONT BOUNDARIES
➤ GERMAN COUNTER-ATTACKS AND RETREATS
Crete ISLANDS HELD BY THE GERMANS UNTIL THE END OF THE WAR
- ×××× - ARMY GROUP BOUNDARIES
- ×××× - ARMY BOUNDARIES
⬭ AXIS POCKETS
⬭ AREAS HELD BY YUGOSLAV PARTISANS IN JANUARY 1945

△△ "One of my Tiger tanks in the square in front of the castle in Budapest. The troops on the tank and all troops with arms were troops under my command" – S.S. Hauptsturmführer Otto Skorzeny describing this photograph. Skorzeny led the raid of October 1944 that nullified the armistice that Hungary had agreed with the Soviet Union.

between plains and mountains composed of the following:

1. Hungarian 3rd Army (General Heszlenyi);
2. German 6th Army (General Fretter-Pico); and
3. *Armeegruppe* "Wöhler", with the Hungarian 2nd Army and the German 8th Army.

In all there were nine corps and 26 divisions or their equivalent. True, they were at half their establishment strength. But IV Panzer Corps and the 24th Panzer Division would join the force shortly.

Tank clashes

One important point was that in this force there were 14 Hungarian divisions, whose combat performance caused the commander of Army Group "South" some anxiety.

On October 6, the 2nd Ukrainian Front went over to the offensive towards the north-west and the west, and attacked Salonta and south of Arad with the 6th Guards Tank Army and the 53rd and 46th Armies, whose seven tank and mechanised corps gave considerable impetus to the attack. Under the impact, the Hungarian 3rd Army broke, confirming the most pessimistic estimates of Colonel-General Friessner. Even before night had fallen, the Russians were fanning out over the Hungarian plain, some towards Debrecen, some towards Szolnok or Szeged across the Tisza.

Yet the Soviet tanks hurled themselves ahead to exploit their success at a speed that the infantry could not match. Furthermore, the mostly treeless Hungarian plain allowed the Panzers, as in North Africa, to adopt "warship" tactics and seek out the flanks and rear of enemy columns which kept to the roads. On the outskirts of Debrecen on October 10 the 6th Guards Tank Army was trapped in such a manoeuvre by III Panzer Corps while, on its left, the Soviet 27th Army was itself violently halted in front of Mezőtúr and Karcag.

This was further proof of the qualitative superiority of Germany's armoured forces, which were now called upon to perform an essentially defensive role. Despite heavy losses, and the growing realisation that the war was inevitably lost, the morale of the German Army was still holding up remarkably well.

four attempts and the aid of Tolbukhin to overcome the Axis forces, when the superiority of forces was entirely to his advantage, speaks highly for the tactical ability of the German command and the standard of training of its officers and men. At the beginning of October, with his right to the south of Timişoara and his left on the Carpathians, Colonel-General Friessner could present a line

8th Army escapes

The Soviet commander, Marshal Malinovsky took Debrecen on October 20 and thus, on the 22nd, the armoured group under General Pliev managed to thrust 47 miles into the Tokay vineyards on the left bank of the Tisza. He profited little by it, for he was caught in a pincer from the east and west near Nyiregyháza.

On October 30, an O.K.W. communiqué claimed that Malinovsky had lost close on 12,000 killed and 6,662 prisoners, and suffered the destruction or capture of about 1,000 tanks and more than 900 guns. But the losses of the German 6th Army, the temporary victors, were not small. Its six Panzer divisions now had only 67 tanks and 57 assault guns.

This hard fought success was to be among the last for the German armies. Inevitably, the sheer weight of Russian numbers was to prove too much for the hard pressed Wehrmacht. Scarcity of manpower and *matériel* was an insuperable problem for the German commanders, who found that even the most limited plans were severely circumscribed by shortages of essential material, especially of engine fuel, the life-line of the Panzers.

Colonel-General Friessner, an experienced and able commander, now faced the task of re-organising the tank forces he had sacrificed, in preparation for the next Soviet assault.

It was by paying this price that Friessner had checked Malinovsky for the second time in his attempt to cut off the retreat of the German 8th Army and to drive it into a corner in the Carpathians. Now it could align itself on the west bank of the Tisza, with the 6th Army. Following hard behind it, Colonel-General Petrov's 4th Ukrainian Front penetrated the ancient Czech province of Ruthenia. On October 26, it occupied Mukachevo and the day after, Uzhgorod.

Hungarian armistice

In spite of the occupation of Hungary, Admiral Horthy had managed to maintain his secret contacts with the British and Americans. As the situation grew worse he was obliged to give way to the demands of London and Washington, who directed him towards the Soviet Union. And so,

at the end of September, Lieutenant-Marshal Farago, once a military attaché in Moscow, slipped away from the watching eye of the Gestapo and arrived in the Russian capital. He was, Horthy tells us, authorised to conclude an armistice, if possible under the following conditions:

"Immediate cessation of hostilities. The British and Americans to share in the occupation of Hungary. Unhindered re-

"С НОВЫМ ГОДОМ!"

△ A Russian poster bids the "Fascist rabble" a Happy New Year with the cheering thought that this last year of the war would see the Germans so hard pressed that they would not even be able to bury their dead.
◁◁ German troops armed with an MP-40 (left) and an MG-42 in Hungary, 1944.

treat of German troops."

And so, on October 11, a preliminary armistice agreement received the signature of both parties. Did Stalin mean to press matters so as to place a *fait accompli* before the Western powers while Washington, through Churchill and Eden (then on a visit to Moscow), protested against being left out of the negotiations?

This is the version that Horthy gives in his memoirs. Eden's contain no suggestion of any such procedure. And Churchill, on October 12, 1944, telegraphed to his colleagues:

"As it is the Soviet armies which are obtaining control of Hungary, it would be natural that a major share of influence should rest with them, subject of course to an agreement with Great Britain and probably the United States, who, though not actually operating in Hungary, must view it as a Central European and not a Balkan State."

From this it is clear that Great Britain, and more so the United States, took little interest in the negotiations in course between Budapest and Moscow.

Meanwhile Admiral Horthy reached full agreement with the Prime Minister, Lakatos, and, at one in the afternoon of October 15, proclaimed an armistice in a broadcast over Budapest radio.

This broadcast was a complete condemnation of Hitler and his policies, and concluded:

"Today for everyone who can see plainly, Germany has lost the war. All governments responsible for the fate of their countries must draw their conclusions from this fact, for, as was said once by the great German statesman Bismarck: 'No nation is forced by its obligations to sacrifice itself on the altar of an alliance.'"

▽ *Russian armour races across the Hungarian* puszta. *Outnumbered and pressed steadily backwards, all that the German armoured divisions could do was to inflict the occasional heavy tactical reverses on the Russians.*
▷ *Otto Skorzeny, in the uniform of an S.S.* Hauptsturmführer *or Captain. It was this daring and resourceful man who had led the raid to rescue Mussolini, and he was now called upon to abduct the wavering Horthy.*

Skorzeny's raid

But the secret of the Hungarian-Soviet negotiations had leaked out and Hitler could count on the complicity of the Hungarian Nazis. Everything was ready for a strike. Led by the Ministers Rahn and Weesenmayer, the *Waffen*-S.S. General von dem Bach-Zalewski, and Colonel Skorzeny, it took place with lightning speed. Admiral Horthy was kidnapped in his mansion in Buda and taken under escort to the castle of Weilheim, close to Munich.

Major Szálasi, leader of the "Arrow Cross", was summoned to replace him, but in spite of his fanaticism and his ferocity, it was beyond his powers to breathe new life into the Hungarian Army. General Vörös, the chief-of-staff,

△ Two Soviet infantrymen, armed with PPS M1943 sub-machine guns, cover three of their comrades during the street fighting for Budapest.

surrendered at Malinovsky's headquarters. So did General Miklos, commander of the 1st Army and Louis Veress, the latter in the motor car which Guderian had just given him. The coup, however, could do nothing to halt the slide of German fortunes in the East, and was a forlorn gesture in the face of the mounting Soviet pressure.

Malinovsky rolls on

The fall of Szeged around October 10 had forced Friessner to organise a defence line between the Tisza at Csongrád and the Danube at Baja, where he was in contact with Army Group "F". This sector was evidently the weakest, and thus it was here that Malinovsky transferred his 6th Guards Tank Army. On October 29, the 6th reopened the offensive. Its attack was directed on the Hungarian 3rd Army, which broke like a reed and opened the road to Budapest to three Soviet tank corps. In one single movement, they reached Kecskemét, only 40 miles from the capital.

But Friessner and Fretter-Pico did not lose a moment in preparing their defence.

In the Budapest bridgeheads III Panzer Corps repelled the attackers and, at the same time, the *"Feldherrnhalle" Panzergrenadier* Division (Colonel Pape) with the four Panzer divisions of LVII Panzer Corps (General Kirchner) caught the enemy columns in the flank as they moved out of Cegléd. The Russians were better organised than before, and held their ground everywhere except between Debrecen and Nyiregyháza. Moreover, the defection of the Hungarian troops in the centre and on the left of the German 6th Army allowed them to obtain several bridgeheads on the west bank of the Tisza. Even so, Malinovsky had to regroup his forces for the drive which, he hoped, would finish the business.

Germans exhausted

The Germans were nearing the end of their tether. There were very few infantry battalions which could muster 200 men. The Panzer divisions, so essential for counter-attack, were no longer more than a shadow of what they had been. The consequences of an insufficient inspection and test programme at the end of the factory assembly-lines were mechanical defects which became more and more frequent in the new machines reaching the front. So the number of tanks available to each division daily was no more than five or six.

Even though it is true that the losses of the 2nd Ukrainian Front since October 6 had not been light, it still maintained an enormous numerical and *matériel* advantage over its adversary.

Faced with this situation, Hitler agreed to send three new Panzer divisions into Hungary. These were the 3rd, 6th, and 8th Panzer Divisions. He also sent three battalions of Panther tanks. But while waiting for these reinforcements to be put into line, Army Group "South" had to fall back from the Tisza above Tokay and dig in on the heights of the Mátra mountains, overlooking Hatvan, Eger, and Miskolc. It had to limit its counter-attacks to local actions only, as a result of the previously mentioned exhaustion of its men and equipment. And so the curtain fell on the third act of this tragedy, the overall direction of which was assumed by Marshal Timoshenko in the name of the *Stavka*.

6th Army forced back by Tolbukhin

The curtain rose again on November 27 with the appearance on the stage of the forces of the 3rd Ukrainian Front, available now that Belgrade had surrendered. On that day, Marshal Tolbukhin unexpectedly forced the Danube at Mohacs. This was 125 miles up river from Belgrade past the confluence of the Drava and the Danube. Brushing aside the weak defences of the 2nd *Panzerarmee,* his 57th Army swept along a line from Pécs to Kaposvár and, by December 5, called a halt after an advance of 75 miles between the south-west tip of Lake Balaton and the River Drava at Barcs.

On December 3, on Tolbukhin's right, the 3rd Guards Army arrived at Duna-földvár, 60 miles north of Mohacs. As a result, in order to avoid its right being rolled up, the German 6th Army could only pull back along a line Lake Balaton–Lake Velencei–Budapest.

Tolbukhin's advance northward allowed his partner Malinovsky to re-arrange his deployment yet again. At the foot of the Mátra mountains, he built up a strategic battering-ram, with the Pliev Group and the 6th Guards Tank Army. Near Hatvan on December 7, the exhausted German 6th Army broke under the force of the attack launched by the Russians and, several days later, Pliev reached the elbow formed by the Danube above the Hungarian capital and could now bring the strings of barges which supplied it under the fire of his artillery. Furthermore, between the Danube and the Mátra mountains, on December 14, Soviet armour captured Ypolisag. And so the Russians had almost completely out-flanked the right of the 8th Army, and were once more threatening to hem it in against the Carpathians.

Last desperate effort

However the 8th Panzer Division, newly arrived, was immediately put under the command of LVII Panzer Corps, and this formation kept disaster at bay. Friessner would have liked to reinforce Kirchner with the 3rd and the 6th Panzer Divisions, which had just been stationed on the isthmus which separates Lakes Balaton and Velencei. If they hurried, he maintained, there was a great opportunity to crush the 6th Guards Tank Army, which was in a salient around Ypolisag. When Hitler received this proposal, he ordered Friessner to attack from the isthmus between the two lakes and to throw Tolbukhin back to the Danube. To which the commander of Army Group "South" retorted that the state of the ground between Lake Balaton and the Danube, after long weeks of sleet and rain, was absolutely impassable.

Wrong compromise

Guderian forced a very poor compromise in this dispute on December 18: the *Führerbefehl* would be carried out when frost had hardened the ground. Meanwhile, the 3rd and 6th Panzer Divisions would cross the Danube at Komarom, carry out Friessner's proposed counter-attack, but leave their tank battalions behind. In vain did Friessner protest that this plan would deprive them of their entire striking power. He was told that he should either obey or resign.

▵ ▵ ▵ *The pale light of dawn: the Hun surveys the empty seats of the Axis defaulters.*
▵ ▵ *Stalin's lengthening shadow in the south, from the* London *Punch.*
▵ *A "family scene in Central Europe", from the* London Star. *"It's nothing, mother," says Hungary. "I'm opening a second front with Rumania."*

△ *A scene typical of the street fighting in which the Russians took Budapest street by street, house by house, reducing it virtually to rubble in the process. Note the "dragon's teeth" anti-tank obstacles in the background.*

This is the version that Friessner gives of this episode, and Guderian's silence on it seems to indicate that he agrees.

Tolbukhin's advantage

Forty-eight hours later, Tolbukhin was attacking the sector between the Danube and Lake Balaton defended by III Panzer and LXXII Corps (General August Schmidt) of the 6th Army. In front of him roved a first echelon of about ten divisions which, very cleverly, moved along the roads impassable to tanks because of the soft terrain. Between the river and Lake Velencei, the 217th *Volksgrenadier* Division was crushed on the first day. Between Lake Velencei and Lake Balaton, the 153rd Infantry Division and the 1st and 23rd Panzer Divisions defended the little mediaeval town of Székesfehérvár to the end, without the tanks held in reserve by Guderian's express order being of any help to them. By December 24, all was over and the Kremlin communiqué claimed that the Germans had lost 12,000 dead, 5,468 prisoners, 311 tanks, and 248 guns destroyed or captured.

On the same day Tolbukhin launched his armoured formations through this gap, now over 40 miles wide. On December 27, after an excursion of 55 miles through the rearguard of the Army Group "South", they occupied Esztergom on the right bank of the Danube and, from the other side of the river, recognised the 6th Guards Tank Army that LVII Panzer Corps had been quite unable to dislodge.

"Fortress" Budapest under siege

On December 1, the Führer had proclaimed that the Hungarian capital was a "fortress". This took it out of the authority of Army Group "South". The garrison consisted of the S.S. IX Mountain Corps (General Pfeffer-Wildenbruch). When Friessner realised that the 3rd Ukrainian Front was attacking, he wanted to take it in flank by a counter-attack with this corps, but the manoeuvre would involve the evacuation of Budapest. So, on the night of December 22/23, Friessner was relieved and ordered to hand over to General Wöhler. Fretter-Pico shared his disgrace.

Two S.S. cavalry divisions, the 13th Panzer Division, and the *"Feldherrnhalle" Panzergrenadier* Division were thus caught in the trap. Having got them cut off, Hitler now had to get them out, so without consulting O.K.H., he robbed Army Group "Centre", which was responsible for the defence of East Prussia. He took IV S.S. Panzer Corps (General Gille: 3rd *"Totenkopf"* Panzer Division and 5th *"Wiking"* Panzer Division) and sent them over the Carpathians. This order was made on Christmas Day, and, though Guderian tried to have the units recalled, he wrote:

"All my protests were useless. Hitler thought it was more important to free the city of Budapest than to defend Eastern Germany."

All the same, Hitler was acting more logically than Guderian gives him credit for. The day before, while Guderian tried to draw Hitler's attention to the increasing number of signs pointing to a coming Soviet offensive between the Carpathians and the Niemen, the Führer had riposted:

"Now, my dear General, I do not believe in this Russian attack. It is all a gigantic bluff. The figures produced by your 'Foreign Armies: East' section are far too exaggerated. You worry too much. I am firmly convinced that nothing will happen in the East."

Obsession with the Soviet threat could deceive Major-General Gehlen, head of "Foreign Armies: East" of O.K.H.; it could even impress Colonel-General Guderian. But it had no effect on the far-sightedness and *sang froid* of the Führer!

CHAPTER 78
OBJECTIVE TOKYO

The return of General Douglas MacArthur to the Philippines was assured. As his aircraft climbed above Oahu in the afternoon sunlight he turned to an aide and said, "We've sold it!"

He had sold his plan for an invasion of the Philippines to President Roosevelt and Admiral Nimitz. On board the *Baltimore* and at a private house near Pearl Harbor they had spent the afternoon of July 26, 1944 and the morning of the following day in discussion. Finally they agreed that both sound strategy and national honour required the liberation of the Philippines.

It was further agreed that "the Philippines should be recovered with ground and air power then available in the Western Pacific" as they were not going to wait until the defeat of Germany.

Nimitz was to add that "from hindsight I think that decision was correct". But at the time there were two strongly-held strategic concepts of the war in the Pacific.

In the autumn of 1943, MacArthur had submitted his views for the future to the Joint Chiefs-of-Staff. After neutralising the Japanese air base in Rabaul by capturing the neighbouring base of Kavieng, and establishing himself further up the New Guinea coast at Hollandia and Aitape, he wished to strike north at Mindanao in the southern Philippines, and thence if possible at Luzon. These operations depended on a clear superiority of air and sea power over the Japanese in the area. They would probably require the presence of the main American fleet, as well as the other naval forces in the south Pacific.

With these forces MacArthur felt that he could be in Mindanao in December 1944, and Luzon the following spring. With his existing forces he was committed to a subsidiary rôle.

But in addition to these strategic considerations there was an emotional tie with the Philippines for MacArthur.

As military adviser to the Philippine Army he had created and trained it on the model of the Swiss Army.

When the Japanese landed 200,000 men in December 1941, MacArthur led a mixed American and Filipino army of about half that number. Fighting a defensive battle, he retreated to the Bataan peninsula and the island of Corregidor.

In the spring of 1942 Roosevelt ordered MacArthur to Canberra as C.-in-C. of the newly-formed S.W. Pacific Area. He was reluctant to go, but obeyed the order, and when he arrived in Australia promised "I came through and I shall return." He had thought that the Allies could mount an attack to relieve the Bataan garrison before it was overwhelmed by the Japanese, but now he felt that this promise was true for the whole of the Philippines.

Now MacArthur held an unusual position in the American military hierarchy. Unlike other senior commanders, he had not for some time had any direct connection with the War Department, yet he was considerably senior to any other serving officer, having retired as a Chief-of-Staff of the U.S. Army in 1935, when Marshall held the rank of Colonel. His background and his own self-confidence did not incline him to act as a subordinate in the manner of the other commanders.

A pronounced consciousness of his position, and the political importance which it fostered, gave to his relations

By the beginning of 1944, U.S. industry was working in top gear to produce the necessary matériel for the final effort against Japan.
◁ *A bulkhead is lifted into a Liberty Ship in one piece. Such methods meant the ship would leave the yard within 60 days.*

with Washington something of the flavour of an independent power. But in service circles Admiral Leahy commented that "the mention of the name of Mac-Arthur seemed to generate more heat than light".

He had not been to America since 1935, did not meet any of the American chiefs-of-staff until December 1943, had not received a direct communication from the President since assuming command of the South-West Pacific Area, and at the end of 1943 had never met Admiral Nimitz, his colleague in the Central Pacific.

Added to this difference of personalities there was the natural rivalry of the Army and Navy which was brought out by the two proposed plans.

The Navy's plan: Formosa the goal

Admiral King, supported by Admiral Nimitz, based his planning on the experience of the fighting in New Guinea and the Solomon Islands. He definitely considered it "essential to avoid as long as possible fighting the Japanese army in any land area where they could delay . . . operations". American strength lay at sea and in the air, and not in slow and expensive fighting in jungle and urban areas.

The Navy submitted that the most

FREE LABOR WILL WIN

△ *The Labor Day slogan of the U.S. labour movement on a poster distributed by the Office of War Information. The purpose of these slogans was two-fold: they urged workers to greater efforts and also made them feel as important to the war effort as men in the forces.*

◁ *The shipyards at Beaumont, Texas.*

Will you give at least 10% of your pay in War Bonds?

◄ A direct appeal to the emotions in this War Bonds poster.
▼ Precision work on a grand scale. This turbine spindle, soon to power the propeller shaft of a tanker, is just one of more than a hundred in production at a Westinghouse works.

fruitful line of advance therefore lay through the Carolines and the Marianas, with Formosa as the eventual goal. Given the necessary priority, it was confident that it could capture the eastern Carolines by the end of July 1944, and Guam and the Marianas in September or October. By the end of the year, it could begin to bomb Japan from the latter base.

The Joint Chiefs-of-Staff were in favour of the plan, for as King had put it, it would "put the cork in the bottle" of the enemy communications when the Americans captured Formosa. From bases in China, Formosa, and the Bonin islands they could strangle the Japanese mainland islands by submarine and air attack on the traffic through the South China Sea. MacArthur would liberate Mindanao and set up bases for the Far Eastern Air Forces to pound down Japanese air power on Luzon, after which he would help the Pacific Fleet to capture Formosa.

The Navy felt that this plan would bring about the defeat of Japan more quickly than the rather more systematic approach advocated by MacArthur. By-passing the Philippines would be no real hardship for its inhabitants, and might even liberate them more quickly than by landing on the islands themselves.

It was as protagonists for these two conflicting doctrines that MacArthur and Nimitz met with President Roosevelt at Oahu.

Admiral Leahy, who was one of those present at the meetings, remembers: "It was both pleasant and very informative to have these two men who had been pictured as antagonists calmly present their differing views to the Commander-in-Chief." Rear-Admiral Wilson Brown stated that in no conference attended by him did the speakers stick so closely to the subject or make such clear, concise, and candid expressions of opinion.

Undoubtedly the conference was also a triumph for Roosevelt who "was at his best as he tactfully steered the discussion from one point to another and narrowed down the area of disagreement between MacArthur and Nimitz". At the meetings the speakers were dealing with facts, and not second-hand reports handled by politicians.

When MacArthur took his leave on July 27, he assured the President that despite the differences between himself and Nimitz there was no cause for concern; agreement was near.

CHAPTER 79
LEYTE: THE PLANNING

△ MacArthur (left) and Nimitz: often at odds with each other they were dominant figures in the Pacific.

There were still differences between General MacArthur and Admiral Nimitz as to the best strategy for winning the war but the two sides had reached agreement. Leahy was later to assert that "the agreement...and the President's familiarity with the situation at this conference were to be of great value in preventing an unnecessary invasion of Japan which the planning staffs of the Joint Chiefs and the War Department were advocating, regardless of the loss of life that would result from an attack on Japan's forces in their own country."

Despite this top-level agreement, the J.C.S. continued to discuss the Pacific strategy. It was a short while later, on September 1, 1944, that Rear-Admiral Forrest Sherman, Admiral Nimitz's chief planner, confronted them. He said that it was high time a decision was reached, and that even a bad one would be better than none. Central Pacific armed forces had no directive for anything beyond the Palaus objective, which was due in two weeks. Admiral King still opposed Luzon, which he said would slow up the war for mere sentimental reasons (earlier he had dismissed MacArthur's plans as "desires and visions").

The plans, however, had won a powerful ally in General Marshall, who appreciated the argument about national honour and also that Luzon would be easier to capture than Formosa. MacArthur had warned the J.C.S. that if they left the 16 million population of the Philippines to "wither on the vine" until the end of the war with Japan, they would not only inflict unpredictable hardships on the loyal Filipinos, but also cause all Asia to lose faith in American honour.

The J.C.S. planners worked out a timetable to be presented to the "Octagon" Combined Chiefs-of-Staff conference at Quebec on September 11, 1944:

1. September 15, South-West Pacific Forces occupy Morotai; Central Pacific forces occupy Peleliu October 5; occupy Yap, with Ulithi to follow.

2. October 15, South-West Pacific Forces occupy Salebaboe Island; November 15, land at Sarangani Bay, Mindanao; December 20, at Leyte.

3. South-West Pacific and Central Pacific forces then combine to occupy either (1) Luzon, to secure Manila by February 20, or (2) Formosa and Amoy on the China coast by March 1, 1945.

But as with many of the best laid plans,

this timetable was scrambled within a week.

Task Force 38, under Admiral Halsey, left Eniwetok on August 28, 1944, to bomb Yap, the Palaus, and Mindanao, and make a one-group diversionary strike on the Bonin Islands. The aim was to destroy Japanese air forces which might challenge the forthcoming landings on Morotai and Peleliu, and to deceive the enemy as to the next target. The Palaus were bombed on September 6-8, Mindanao airstrips near Sarangani Bay on September 9-10. These attacks were unopposed, and this caused Halsey to cancel later strikes for Mindanao and move to the Visayas on the 12th. The task force moved in close and flew 2,400 sorties in two days; about 200 enemy planes were shot down or destroyed on the ground. Several ships were sunk and many installations destroyed.

It seemed to Halsey and his staff that the Japanese air forces were practically finished, and at noon on September 13, he sent a very important signal to Nimitz. He recommended that the Palau, Yap, Morotai, and Mindanao landings be cancelled as unnecessary, and that Task Force 38 and the men earmarked for these operations be diverted to MacArthur for an immediate seizure of Leyte. This signal was passed on to King and MacArthur.

With a force of fast carriers available MacArthur no longer needed to develop airfields in the southern Philippines before invading Leyte or Luzon; the Navy could furnish the air support the Army needed until it had captured or developed airfields on the target island.

If the 30,000 troops who were to land on Mindanao on November 15, and XXIV Corps (intended for Yap) could be diverted to Leyte, MacArthur would have an effective invasion force.

In MacArthur's name General Sutherland informed the J.C.S. and Nimitz on September 14 that if Halsey's recom-

▽ *A Boeing B-29 Superfortress under construction. Production of these bombers was based at four main plants. Between June 1943 and the Japanese surrender in August 1945, more than 4,200 of these aircraft were built.*

mendations were adopted, MacArthur would invade Leyte on October 20, that is two months ahead of the target date. Nimitz agreed, but said that the Palaus operation should not be cancelled because it would be needed as an anchorage and air base.

After their earlier performance, the J.C.S. acted with commendable alacrity. The Combined Chiefs-of-Staff conference, with Roosevelt, Churchill, and Mackenzie King, was still in session at Quebec when the new proposals came through. Breaking off from a dinner, the J.C.S. held a brief consultation. "Having the utmost confidence in General MacArthur, Admiral Nimitz and Admiral Halsey," wrote General Marshall, "It was not a difficult decision to make. Within 90 minutes after the signal had been received in Quebec, General MacArthur and Admiral Nimitz had received their instructions to execute the Leyte operation."

The target date was fixed for October 20,

and this avoided the three intermediate landings at Yap, the Talauds, and Mindanao. MacArthur's acknowledgment reached Marshall as he was leaving the dinner to return to his rooms.

The instructions were formalised soon after in the following message:

"1. Admiral Wilkinson's YAP ATTACK FORCE, the XXIV Army Corps, then loaded or at sea, will be assigned to General MacArthur to land LEYTE 20 October.

"2. All shipping used in the Palaus operation, after unloading, to be sent to Southwest Pacific ports to help VII 'Phib lift General Krueger's Sixth Army to LEYTE.

"3. ALL FIRE SUPPORT SHIPS and ESCORT CARRIERS used in the Palaus operation to be assigned temporarily to Admiral Kinkaid, Commander Seventh Fleet, to help cover LEYTE.

"4. ULITHI to be seized promptly, as an advanced fleet base".

▷ ▷ △ *The assembly line at the Boeing works in Seattle.*
▷ ▷ ▽ *Women at work inside the fuselage of a B-24 Liberator at Fort Worth, Texas.*

▽ *A Helldiver peels off before coming in to land on its base carrier. Below, the crew prepare the flight deck for a landing.*

There followed a series of planning conferences by the commanders of the forces involved. The operation would employ all the American military forces not engaged in Europe or on garrison duties in places like the Aleutian and Marshall Islands. Though no Australian troops were to be used, ships of the Royal Australian Navy would participate, and one ship of the Royal Navy, the fast minelayer *Ariadne*.

While the ships were assembled, and planning continued at all levels of command, the J.C.S. discussed the next move after Leyte. Was it to be Luzon, or Formosa?

After pressure against the Formosa operation by General Millard Harmon, commanding the Army Air Forces in the Central Pacific, and by General Simon Bolivar Buckner, commanding the 10th Army, it was shelved in favour of Luzon.

It was a logical and strategically sound move, for if Leyte could be captured in reasonable time, III and VII Amphibious Forces would be capable of putting in a second major landing before the end of 1944. Formosa would require an assault force of at least nine divisions, which would not be available until about the middle of 1945.

Japanese air strength was still too great to allow the invasion of Okinawa, so after clearing Luzon, the Americans could take Iwo Jima, as a rung in the "ladder up the Bonins", and Okinawa, as a base for air attacks and the final invasions of the Japanese home islands.

On October 3, 1944 the Joint Chiefs-of-Staff issued a directive to Nimitz and MacArthur, which seemed to be the final tribute to the general's skills as a salesman.

"General MacArthur will liberate Luzon, starting 20 December, and establish bases there to support later operations. Admiral Nimitz will provide fleet cover and support, occupy one or more positions in the Bonin-Volcano Island group 20 January 1945, and invade the Ryukyus, target date 1 March 1945."

Yet the liberation of the Philippines had been decided by many events beyond his control. Landings on the China coast in support of the Formosa operation were ruled out because of the strength of the Japanese in both areas. Chinese Nationalist forces would be of little help, partly because of their lack of equipment and training, but also because of the enmity between Stilwell and Chiang

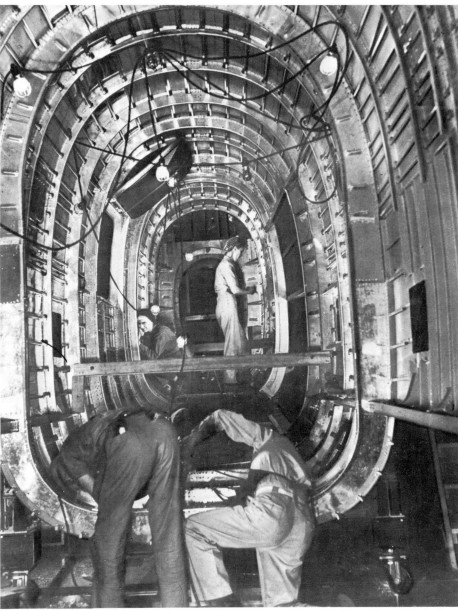

UNITED WE WIN

"My girl's a WOW"

WOMAN ORDNANCE WORKER

Kai-shek.

The naval forces assigned to him from Halsey's Task Force 38, had been released through a misconception. Halsey believed that Japanese air-power in the Palaus, Mindanao, and Visayas was finished; in fact the Imperial General Headquarters had ordered that it be held back in readiness for the major landings which were expected in that area.

Yet despite this, the landings on Leyte and Luzon vindicated MacArthur's promise to return, and set the American forces in the Pacific on a return journey which would end less than 11 months after "Octagon", with the surrender of Japan.

Two amphibious operations brought the converging forces of MacArthur and Nimitz to within striking range of Leyte.

On September 15, 1944, the 31st Division under MacArthur began landing on Morotai island. He planned to expand its partially-completed airfield to cover operations to the south of the Philippine islands.

There was no opposition, but the airfield was unusable; another (ready for fighter operations on October 4 and bombers on the 15th) was quickly built.

On September 15 Halsey assaulted the Palau Islands. Fringed by coral reefs, this island group is 470 miles east of Mindanao. Halsey planned to use it as a seaplane base and anchorage for the attack on the Philippines.

The landing on Peleliu was strongly opposed. On the first day the 1st Marine Division had secured a beach-head; on the second it had occupied, but not secured, the airfield. The tough, well-sited bunkers which covered the airfield were eventually cleared, and by October 1 the field was taking fighters and a week later medium bombers. The Japanese, however, hung on in the island for another six weeks.

On September 17, the 81st Division landed on Angaur island, six miles south of Peleliu, and by noon had practically secured it. By the 21st an airstrip had been built and was taking Liberators. On the 23rd the 81st was landed on Ulithi atoll, which proved to be abandoned. It was quickly developed and became the main fleet base in October.

MacArthur, by way of the south-west, and Nimitz, through the central Pacific, had now reached their forming-up points for Leyte.

CHAPTER 80

"I HAVE RETURNED": THE LANDINGS ON LEYTE

On the U.S. side, although everyone stuck to the item of the March 12 directive which laid down that the major objective of the coming offensive was to be Mindanao, opinion varied as to the direction the offensive was to take after this objective had been secured.

In the Pentagon Admiral King, supported, albeit with slight differences of opinion, by Nimitz, reckoned that there would be no harm in neglecting the rest of the Philippines and taking a leap forward to Formosa and Amoy on the south coast of China. This would cut communications between the Japanese homeland and its sources of raw materials and fuel, and would thus force a capitulation. But in his command post at Hollandia, General MacArthur was sickened by the idea of leaving Luzon and more than seven million Filipinos exposed to the rigours of a Japanese military occupation any longer. When he left Corregidor in March 1942, he had given his solemn promise to the Filipinos that he would return, and he did not intend that anyone should make him break his word. Roosevelt summoned MacArthur to Pearl Harbor and there MacArthur laid before him arguments not only of sentiment and prestige but also of sound military strategy:

"I argued against the naval concept of frontal assault against the strongly held island positions of Iwo Jima or Okinawa. In my argument, I stressed that our losses would be far too heavy to justify the benefits to be gained by seizing these outposts. They were not essential to the enemy's defeat, and by cutting them off from supplies, they could be easily reduced and their effectiveness completely neutralized with negligible loss to ourselves. They were not in themselves possessed of sufficient resources to act as main bases in our advance.

"In addition, I felt that Formosa, with a hostile population, might prove doubt-

General MacArthur, accompanied by Lieutenant-General George C. Kenney, Lieutenant-General Richard K. Sutherland, his chief-of-staff, and Major-General Mudge, commander of the 1st Cavalry Division, inspects the beach-head at Leyte, October 20, 1944.

ful to serve as a base of attack against Japan itself."

This was how MacArthur, according to his memoirs, spoke to Roosevelt, who had Admiral Leahy with him. And, as it later turned out, MacArthur was to a certain extent right. He captured Luzon, at the cost of some 8,300 dead between January 9 and June 25, 1945. The seven and a half square miles of the little island of Iwo Jima cost Nimitz 7,000 more, and Okinawa was captured by the U.S. 10th Army with the loss of 8,000 dead. As was his wont, the President took no part in this strategic debate, and Leahy and Nimitz were not insensitive to MacArthur's argument. The "Octagon" Conference, which opened at Quebec on September 11, 1944, envisaged after preliminary operations and the

capture of Mindanao, that there would be a landing at Leyte in the central Philippines on December 20, after which the two Allied forces in the Pacific would unite to occupy "either (1) Luzon to secure Manila by 2nd February, or (2) Formosa and Amoy on the China coast by 1st May 1945."

By now Nimitz's fleet was so large that it was decided to appoint two flag officers under him to command alternately. While one was at sea, the other would be at Pearl Harbor planning the next major operation. When commanded by Admiral Spruance it would be known as the 5th Fleet; while under Halsey, the 3rd Fleet. Sub-units would similarly exchange commanders and designations.

In August 1944 Spruance was relieved by Halsey, and Vice-Admiral Theodore Wilkinson relieved Richmond Turner in command of the 5th (now the 3rd) Amphibious Force. However, Mitscher remained in command of the Fast Carrier Force of 17 fast carriers, six new battleships, 13 cruisers, 58 destroyers, and 1,100 fighters, and dive- and torpedo-bombers, now Task Force 38 instead of 58.

On August 28, Halsey set out from Eniwetok to bombard Yap Island, the Palau Islands, and Mindanao, paving the way for the landings Nimitz and MacArthur were preparing at Peleliu and Morotai. The results exceeded all expectations: in 2,400 sorties Mitscher's squadrons shot down 200 enemy aircraft at a cost of only eight of their own and dealt a very hard blow to the Japanese bases in this sector, giving MacArthur the necessary air superiority.

◁ △ *The landings on Leyte were preceded by a massive shore bombardment. American troops watch columns of smoke rising from the island as they approach the beach.*
◁ *A wave of L.C.V.(P.)s heads for the beach-head . . .*
△ *. . . and the troops wade ashore after disembarking.*

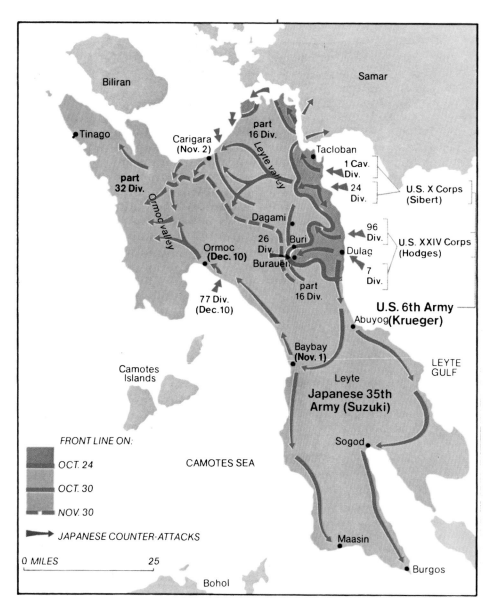

Leyte

Japanese 35th
Army (Suzuki)

FRONT LINE ON:

OCT. 24

OCT. 30

NOV. 30

JAPANESE COUNTER-ATTACKS

0 MILES   25

△ Operation "King II" – the
assault on Leyte.
△▷ An L.V.T. rolls ashore at
Leyte.
▷ On the beach, U.S. troops
"hit the dirt" as they come
under fire from Japanese
snipers and machine gunners.

Leyte plans approved

Interpreting the weakness shown by the enemy somewhat optimistically, the impetuous Halsey submitted the following suggestion to Nimitz on September 13: cut out the intermediate objectives and make straight for Leyte. MacArthur seized upon this idea, remarking that this would save two months on the schedule and, as Nimitz agreed, the Chiefs-of-Staff, still in session at Quebec, took only an hour and a half to concur, such was the confidence of General Marshall and Admiral King in their subordinates. Yap and Mindanao were thus set aside and a landing on Leyte was fixed for October 20. On October 3, Allied commanders in the Central and South-West Pacific received the following directive for the next stage in the operations:

"General MacArthur will liberate

Luzon, starting 20 December, and establish bases there to support later operations. Admiral Nimitz will provide fleet cover and support, occupy one or more positions in the Bonin-Volcano Island group 20 January 1945, and invade the Ryukyus, target date March 1945."

Formosa and Amoy were thus to be taken off the Pentagon's calendar of events. MacArthur and Nimitz, the one leaving from Australia and the other from Hawaii, were to meet in Leyte Gulf. Their commands remained contiguous, and the only transfer of units was that of 3rd Amphibious Force and XXIV Corps (Major-General J. R. Hodge) from Nimitz to MacArthur.

MacArthur takes Morotai . . .

Whilst waiting for the start of this new offensive operation, to be called "King II", MacArthur seized the island of Morotai north of Halmahera. His losses were insignificant as the Japanese were not expecting to be attacked. Yet its fall meant that the Moluccas were now useless to them.

. . . and Nimitz Peleliu

Meanwhile, Halsey's 3rd Fleet attacked Peleliu in strength. The island was defended by the excellent Japanese 14th Division, whose commander (Lieutenant-General Inouye) had intelligently applied the new instructions from Tokyo. Instead of the usual cordon of men defending the beach, he had deployed his forces in depth, taking advantage of the caves to provide cover from aerial and naval bombardment. And so, although the first wave of the U.S. 1st Marine Division (Major-General W. H. Rupertus) landed on September 15, it was not until November 25 that the last enemy surrendered, and meanwhile the Americans had had to bring in their 85th Division (Major-General P. J. Mueller) as reinforcement. The U.S. forces suffered considerable losses: 2,000 killed and over 8,500 wounded, or approximately the same as the garrison which they completely wiped out. On the other hand, in the same group of the Palau Islands, III Amphibious

Force occupied the large atoll of Ulithi without loss, giving the U.S. 3rd Fleet a very safe, well-sited base 1,000 miles from Manila and 1,400 from Okinawa. This action ended on September 23.

So, ten months after the assault on Tarawa, Nimitz had reached a point 4,250 miles from Pearl Harbor.

"I have returned"

Between October 10 and 15, and using the method which had been so successful against the Gilberts, the Marshalls, and the Marianas, Task Force 38 ensured the success of Operation "King II" by plastering the bases on the Ryūkyū Islands, Formosa, and Luzon, from which the Japanese might have attacked the Leyte landings. A thousand Japanese planes took off, but Mitscher scored a clear victory, knocking out over 500 of them at a cost of 110 of his own. It is true that two cruisers were torpedoed during this action, which took Task Force 38 to within 60 miles of Formosa, but the U.S. Navy's rescue services were so efficient that the damaged ships were able to be towed to Ulithi. The Japanese airmen greatly exaggerated this little success, which was no compensation for the loss of their planes and some 40 merchant ships. They claimed to have sunk 11 aircraft-carriers, two battleships, and four

cruisers and to have damaged or set on fire 28 other vessels. It would appear that the threat to the Japanese Empire had miraculously melted away.

This was what Tokyo was beginning to believe when, at dawn on October 17, a huge U.S. armada sailed into Leyte Gulf. It was the 7th Fleet under Vice-Admiral Thomas C. Kinkaid, 700 ships strong, which was also carrying 174,000 men of the U.S. 6th Army. On the same day, detachments seized the island commanding the entrance to Leyte Gulf then, for two whole days, the guns of the old battleships, cruisers, and destroyers of 3rd and 7th Amphibious Forces, or Task Forces 79 and 78, (Admirals T. S. Wilkinson and D. E. Barbey) roared out and the aircraft of 18 escort carriers joined in.

The defence of the Philippines had been entrusted to the victor of Singapore, General Tomoyoki Yamashita, under Field-Marshal Count Hisaichi Terauchi, C.-in-C. Southern Army. Yamashita's 14th Area Army had seven divisions, with a total of 265,000 men, but on Leyte there was only one division, the 16th (Lieutenant-General Makino). However,

the Japanese High Command had now decided to fight for Leyte rather than concentrate for the defence of Luzon, although the American attack had pre-empted their planned reinforcement.

The landing achieved local tactical surprise. In the evening of October 20 the U.S. 6th Army (General Krueger) had established a front of over 17 miles. On the right, X Corps (Major-General F. C. Sibert: 1st Cavalry and 24th Divisions) had occupied Tacloban and its aerodrome; on the left, XXIV Corps (Major-General J. R. Hodge: 96th and 7th Divisions) had got as far as Dulag, where 100,000 tons of *matériel* and stores had been landed on the beach. The cruiser *Honolulu* had been hit by an aerial torpedo, but this was the only noteworthy incident of the day. General MacArthur landed with the third wave: his promise to return had at last been kept. His implacable will and dynamic personality had ensured that the Philippines would have priority, but one major obstacle stood before his return to Manila: the remains of the Imperial Japanese fleet.

CHAPTER 81
LEYTE GULF: THE GREATEST SEA BATTLE OF ALL

In expectation of the U.S. offensive, Admiral Toyoda, C.-in-C. Combined Fleet, had drawn up Plan "*SHO GO*" (Operation "Victory"), one variant of which was to cover the event which actually took place. And so at 0809 hours on October 17, he had merely to signal "*SHO GO 1*" from the Tokyo area for his subordinates to set the plan in motion. This alert order found the Japanese fleet disposed as follows:

1. in Japan, under Vice-Admiral Ozawa, a carrier force (of which only four carriers were operational through lack of trained aircrew), the battleship-carriers *Ise* and *Hyuga*, three light cruisers, and eight destroyers;
2. in the Ryūkyūs, under Vice-Admiral K. Shima, a force of two heavy cruisers, one light cruiser, and nine destroyers; and
3. in Lingga roads, off a group of islands half way between Singapore and Sumatra, Vice-Admiral Kurita's force of seven battleships, 11 heavy cruisers, two light cruisers, and 19 destroyers.

The plan was as follows:
The carrier force with its 116 aircraft, including 80 fighters, would act as bait, advancing without too much precaution into the Philippine Sea east of Luzon; it would thus draw out Mitscher's carrier force towards the north and, by sacrificing itself, would enable Kurita and Shima

to carry out the tasks allotted to them: to destroy the U.S. landing forces and their escort ships of the 7th Fleet.

Kurita would form two sub-forces:
1. Force "A", under Kurita himself, and composed of five battleships, 12 cruisers, and 15 destroyers, would advance through the San Bernardino Strait between Samar and Luzon to meet Force "C" in Leyte Gulf, and
2. Force "C", of two battleships, one cruiser, and four destroyers under Vice-Admiral S. Nishimura would sail through the Surigao Strait between Leyte and Mindanao.

Shima finally received the order to follow Nishimura and, when the time came, to co-operate with him. After the destruction of the U.S. transports and the 7th Fleet in Leyte Gulf, MacArthur would have to surrender to Yamashita, who was already counting on greeting him with the trenchant words he had used to Percival at Singapore: "All I want to know is: Do you surrender unconditionally or not?"

Cunning though the plan was, it nevertheless meant 68 Japanese ships against 275 American, and a one to four inferiority in aircraft for the Japanese. Even including the planes they had in the Philippines, the Japanese were a long way from matching Halsey's and Kinkaid's 1,500. Also, it would take greater

△ *The* Princeton *on fire after sustaining a hit from a "Judy" dive-bomber. At right is the U.S. heavy cruiser* Reno.

co-ordination than could be expected between Kurita and Nishimura to close their pincer in Leyte Gulf. Again, and this was the most important point, "SHO GO" envisaged nothing beyond October 25 and ignored what the 3rd Fleet was likely to do after Ozawa's diversion had fizzled out and Halsey set off full-steam ahead southwards with his 17 carriers and six fast battleships. If he did nothing, Toyoda would be left in Japan with Ozawa and no fuel oil, and Kurita would be left at Lingga with no ammunition or spare parts. Like Hitler on the Western Front, he was thus forced to go over to the offensive. He gave his order at 1100 hours on October 18.

Kurita mauled off Palawan . . .

On October 22, having refuelled at Brunei, Kurita separated from Nishimura. At dawn on the 23rd he was heading north-east of the island of Palawan, a stepping-stone between Borneo and Mindanao, when he was attacked by the submarines *Dace* and *Darter* (Commanders Claggett and McClintock). *Dace* scored a bulls-eye on the heavy cruiser *Maya,* which blew up. *Darter* scored a double, damaging the *Takao* so badly that she had to be sent back under escort, and sinking Kurita's flagship, the heavy cruiser *Atago.* The admiral was saved but he lost part of his signals and coding staff, which was to hamper his control of operations.

. . . and loses the giant battleship *Musashi*

Despite the loss of these three cruisers, Kurita was off Mindoro 24 hours later, and at the same time Nishimura was between Mindanao and Negros Islands. Shima, coming down from the north, was following Nishimura at a great distance and remained out of contact with him for fear of interception by U.S. tracking devices.

Ozawa finally set out from Kure on October 20 and progressed without incident along the path of sacrifice. In the evening of the 23rd the carrier *Zuikaku,* his flagship, sent out a long message designed to draw to herself the attentions of the enemy.

As expected, the *Darter* sent out a signal to report contact. This reached Halsey at 0620 hours on the 23rd. Nishimura and Shima were spotted in the early morning of the 24th. When he got McClintock's message from the *Darter,* the C.-in-C. of the 3rd Fleet, now reduced to Task Force 38, closed in to within 150 miles of the Philippines with his total force except for Vice-Admiral J. S. McCain's Task Group 38.1, which was re-forming at Ulithi. So Halsey had Rear-Admiral F. C. Sherman's Task Group 38.3 off Luzon, Rear-Admiral G. F. Bogan's Task Group 38.2 off San Bernardino Strait, and Rear-Admiral R. E. Davison's Task Group 38.4 off Leyte. This gave Mitscher a total of 835 aircraft.

▽ *The giant battleship* Yamato *under attack from American Liberator bombers on October 26, 1944. Sister ship to the 64,200-ton* Musashi, *sunk in the Battle of Leyte Gulf, she finally went down off Okinawa.*

△ Smoke rises from burning docks and shore installations of the former American naval base of Cavite City in Manila Bay– hit by carrier-based planes of the U.S. Navy.
Overleaf: Operation "Sho Go 1" (Victory) gets under way. Vice-Admiral Ozawa's carrier force acting as bait off the Philippines lured Halsey's 3rd Fleet away whilst Vice-Admirals Kurita and Nishimura closed in a pincer move on the unsuspecting 7th Fleet in Leyte Gulf. Nishimura's arm of the pincer was destroyed in the battle of Surigao Strait (see inset 1) but Kurita, undeterred by heavy losses in initial engagements in the Sibuyan Sea, went ahead and almost succeeded in destroying Task Group 77.4 in the battle off Samar Island (see inset 2). This latter battle also saw the first widespread use of Japan's new weapon – the kamikaze. The Battle of Cape Engano (see inset 3) where Halsey's 3rd Fleet sank four Japanese aircraft carriers.

From the information given by tactical reconnaissance in the early morning of the 24th, Admiral Halsey deduced that he could leave all enemy forces observed in the south-east to be dealt with by Kinkaid and that he himself should concentrate his attention on the larger enemy force apparently intending to pass through the San Bernardino Strait. As one can never be too strong in attack, he ordered Vice-Admiral McCain to join him. Between 1026 and 1350 hours, Task Force 38 flew 259 sorties against Kurita's force, concentrating most of its attacks on the giant (64,200-ton) battleship *Musashi*. In spite of protective A.A. fire from nearly 130 guns, the *Musashi* was hit by 19 torpedoes and 17 bombs and went down during the evening with half her crew. The heavy cruiser *Myoko* had to be sent back to Brunei; three other cruisers suffered minor damage. These attacks forced the Japanese admiral to turn about and caused him to be late on the schedule agreed with Nishimura. No Japanese planes were used in this first engagement. Admiral Fukudome, C.-in-C. of the 2nd Air Fleet in the Philippines, considered

that his pilots were incapable of measuring up to the U.S. airmen and sent them instead against 3rd Fleet. At the cost of heavy losses one of them scored a direct hit on the light carrier *Princeton*. Explosions and fires rent the unhappy vessel and caused heavy losses amongst the ships which went to her rescue. So Rear-Admiral Sherman ordered her to be finished off with a torpedo.

Halsey's controversial decision

Halsey now assumed that Kurita's force no longer offered a threat. He therefore took his entire fleet north to attack Ozawa's carriers, so completely taking the Japanese bait. His reaction has since been the subject of lively discussion in the U.S. Navy and Army. The day after his victory he explained his decision as follows:

"As it seemed childish to me to guard statically San Bernardino Strait, I concentrated TF 38 during the night and steamed north to attack the Northern Force at dawn. I believed that the Center Force had been so heavily damaged in the Sibuyan Sea that it could no longer be considered a serious menace to Seventh Fleet."

Nimitz's instructions

As we can see, Halsey greatly exaggerated the effects of his aircraft on Kurita's force, but he could not know that the hangars of the four enemy carriers, of whose approach he had just been informed, were half empty. He had to ask himself if his reconnaissance had given him the full tally of this new force. Moreover, by sailing northwards, Halsey was conscious of obeying the instructions of Nimitz who, as we have seen, required him to consider as his main mission the destruction of an important part of the Japanese fleet if the opportunity arose. This reveals the serious snags in the organisation of command as conceived by the Pentagon, for if the 3rd Fleet had been under Mac-Arthur, there is no doubt that he would have forbidden it to leave the San Bernardino Strait uncovered.

Though he was told just before night-

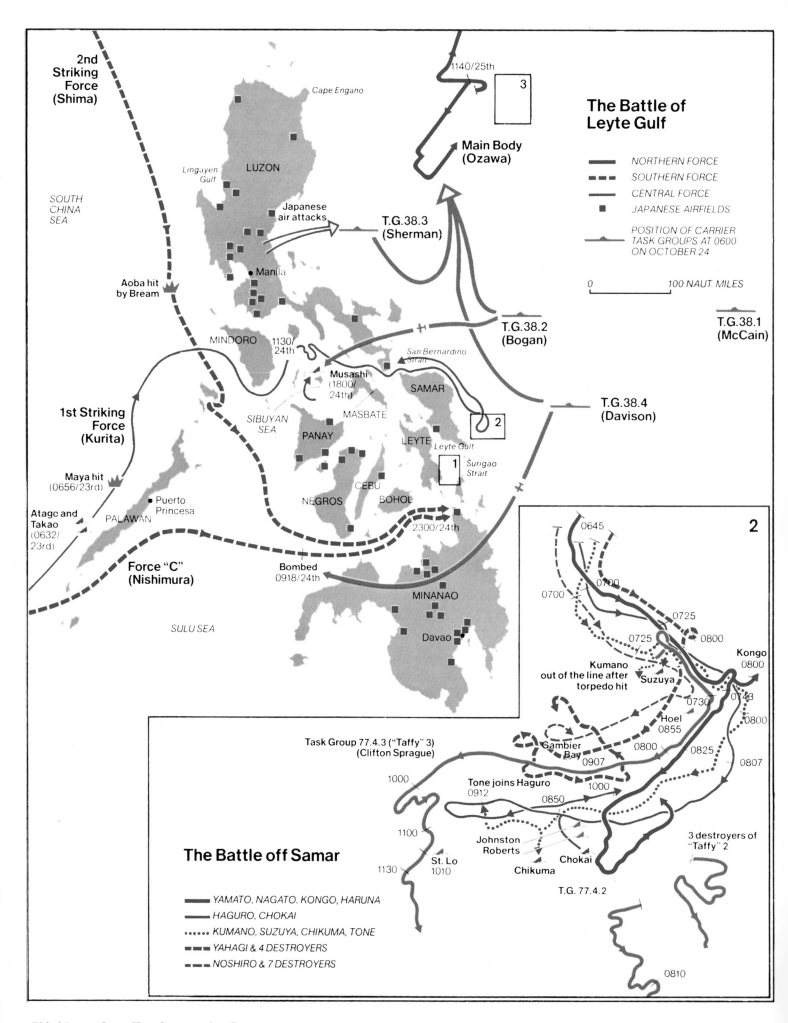

The Battle of Leyte Gulf

2nd Striking Force (Shima)

Cape Engano

Lingayen Gulf
LUZON

SOUTH CHINA SEA

Japanese air attacks

Aoba hit by Bream

Manila

MINDORO

1130/24th

1st Striking Force (Kurita)

Maya hit (0656/23rd)

Atago and Takao (0632/23rd)

PALAWAN
Puerto Princesa

Force "C" (Nishimura)

SIBUYAN SEA

Musashi (1800/24th)

PANAY
MASBATE

SAMAR

LEYTE

Leyte Gulf

Surigao Strait

CEBU
NEGROS
BOHOL

Bombed 0918/24th

2300/24th

MINANAO

Davao

SULU SEA

1140/25th

Main Body (Ozawa)

T.G.38.3 (Sherman)

T.G.38.2 (Bogan)

San Bernardino Strait

T.G.38.4 (Davison)

T.G.38.1 (McCain)

NORTHERN FORCE
SOUTHERN FORCE
CENTRAL FORCE
■ JAPANESE AIRFIELDS
POSITION OF CARRIER TASK GROUPS AT 0600 ON OCTOBER 24

0 ———— 100 NAUT. MILES

The Battle off Samar

Task Group 77.4.3 ("Taffy" 3) (Clifton Sprague)

0645
0700
0700
0725
0725
0800
Kongo 0800
Kumano out of the line after torpedo hit
Suzuya
0730
0743
0800
Hoel 0855
Gambier Bay
0907
0800
0825
0807
Tone joins Haguro 0912
0850
1000
1000
Johnston Roberts
Chokai
Chikuma
3 destroyers of "Taffy" 2
St. Lo 1010
T.G. 77.4.2
1100
1130
0810

YAMATO, NAGATO. KONGO, HARUNA
HAGURO, CHOKAI
KUMANO, SUZUYA, CHIKUMA, TONE
YAHAGI & 4 DESTROYERS
NOSHIRO & 7 DESTROYERS

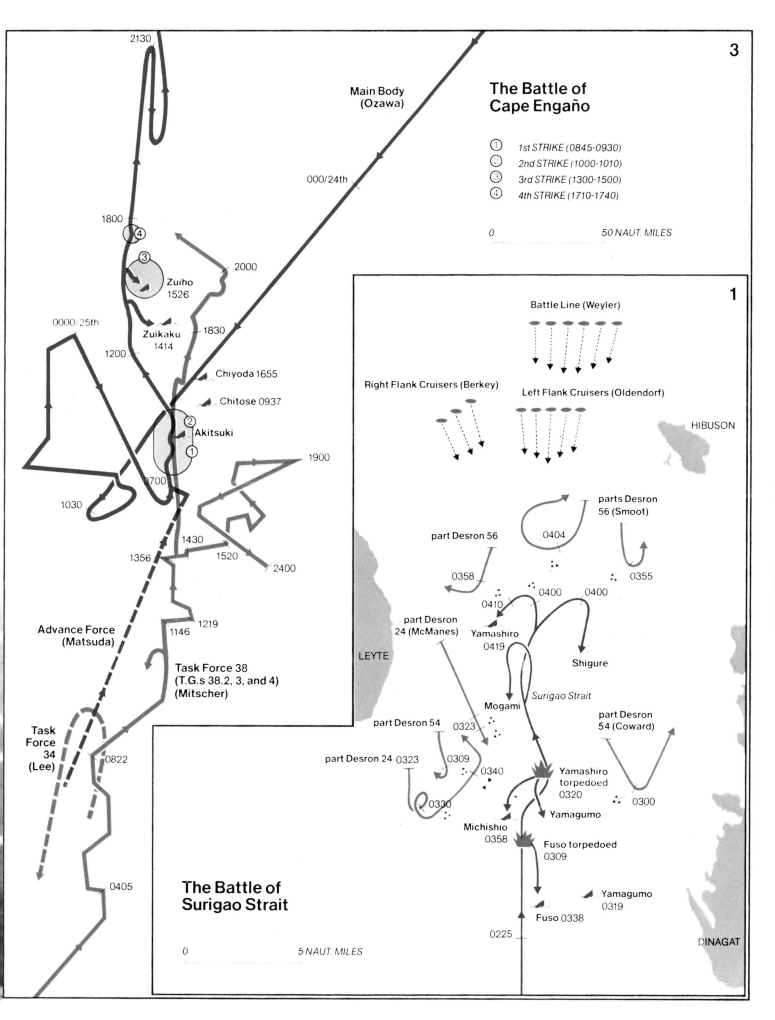

3

The Battle of Cape Engaño

Main Body (Ozawa)

000/24th

① 1st STRIKE (0845-0930)
② 2nd STRIKE (1000-1010)
③ 3rd STRIKE (1300-1500)
④ 4th STRIKE (1710-1740)

0   50 NAUT. MILES

2130

1800

④
③ Zuiho 1526
2000

0000/25th
1200
Zuikaku 1414
1830

Chiyoda 1655

Chitose 0937

② Akitsuki
①
1900
0700
1030
1430
1520
1356   2400

Advance Force (Matsuda)
1219
1146

Task Force 38
(T.G.s 38.2, 3, and 4)
(Mitscher)

Task Force 34 (Lee)
0822

0405

1

Battle Line (Weyler)

Right Flank Cruisers (Berkey)   Left Flank Cruisers (Oldendorf)

HIBUSON

parts Desron 56 (Smoot)

part Desron 56
0404

0358   0355

0410   0400   0400

part Desron 24 (McManes)
Yamashiro 0419

Shigure

Mogami

Surigao Strait

LEYTE

part Desron 54
0323

part Desron 54 (Coward)

part Desron 24   0323   0309
0340
0330   0300

Yamashiro torpedoed 0320

Yamagumo

Michishio 0358

Fuso torpedoed 0309

Yamagumo 0319

The Battle of Surigao Strait

0   5 NAUT. MILES

Fuso 0338

0225

DINAGAT

fall that Kurita had turned eastwards again, Halsey refused to part with his battleships, not wishing to leave them without air protection and wanting to give his carriers the cover of their guns. Mitscher, Bogan, and Vice-Admiral W. A. Lee, the last of whom commanded Task Force 34, all disapproved of their commander's initiative, but Halsey was in no mood to extemporise and they gave in.

Kinkaid destroys Nishimura and Shima

In Leyte Gulf, Vice-Admiral Kinkaid was hourly following the movements of Nishimura and Shima. He spent the afternoon setting a series of ambushes for them in Surigao Strait. He had six old

battleships, eight cruisers, and 28 destroyers, whereas his adversary had only 19 warships altogether.

As Vice-Admiral Kinkaid sailed up the Surigao Strait between 2300 hours on October 24 and 0300 hours on the 25th, Nishimura was attacked by 30 P.T. boats, which fired torpedoes; all of them missed. A few minutes later his force, steaming in line ahead, was caught in a crossfire from the destroyers of the Eastern and Western Attack Groups under Captain Coward and Commander Phillips. The battleship *Fuso* was hit, and 30 minutes later broke in two; three destroyers were wrecked. Though hit, Nishimura's flagship, the battleship *Yamashiro*, maintained her course and, followed by the cruiser *Mogami*, sailed into Leyte Gulf. At 0353 hours Rear-Admiral G. L. Weyler's six battleships "crossed the T" and opened fire on the Japanese, loosing off 285 14-

▽ *The* Lexington *at sea, with Hellcats parked forward. Together with the* Essex, *she formed the heart of Task Force 38, the Fast Carrier Task Force of the U.S. Pacific Fleet, commanded by Vice-Admiral Marc A. Mitscher. During the Battle of Cape Engaño the Task Force accounted for four carriers and two destroyers of Admiral Ozawa's 3rd Fleet.*

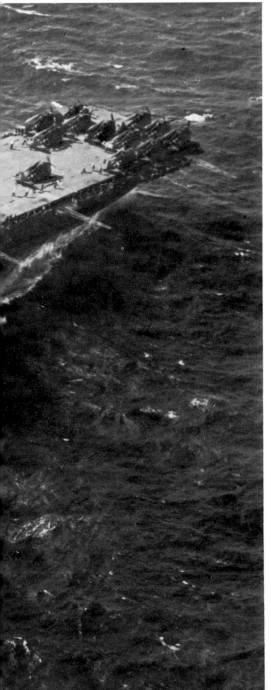

and 16-inch shells. *Mogami* succeeded in turning about, but *Yamashiro* capsized and sank at 0419 hours, taking down with her her obstinate admiral and almost all her crew. At this moment Shima appeared, having followed Nishimura some 30 miles behind. It did not take him long to sum up the situation, and at 0425 hours he decided on a "temporary withdrawal". In doing so he came under attack from the P.T. boats then, when dawn came, from the 7th Fleet's aircraft. All told, out of 19 Japanese ships which ventured into this trap, only two survived, including the old destroyer *Shigure* which had so often flirted with death in the Solomon Islands. Rear-Admiral J. B. Oldendorf lost 39 men killed and 114 wounded.

△ *The deck of the escort carrier Kitkun Bay shrouded in smoke from bursting Japanese shells. She was one of six escort carriers in the "Taffy 3" (TG 77.4.3) group commanded by Rear-Admiral Clifton Sprague, which fought a desperate action in the Battle off Samar against the numerically superior Force "A" commanded by Admiral Kurita.*

Kurita attacks again

On board their floating H.Q., the amphibious force flagship *Wasatch,* Kinkaid and his staff hardly had time to congratulate themselves on their night victory at Surigao before the astounding news reached them that off Samar Island Task Group 77.4, consisting of 6 escort carriers and 20 destroyers under Rear-Admiral Thomas L. Sprague, was engaging a heavy Japanese force.

When asked by Kinkaid at 0412 hours "Is Task Force 34 guarding San Bernardino Strait?" Halsey had replied: "Negative. TF 34 is with carrier groups now engaging enemy carrier force."

△ *The American destroyer Hoel, under Commander L. S. Kintberger, took part in the gallant delaying action fought by Task Group 77.4.3 on October 25. Despite the disparity in armament and speed, the Hoel selected the battleship Kongo as her target and succeeded in launching half her torpedoes, in spite of sustaining heavy damage to her bridge and superstructure. With only two guns still operative, the Hoel launched her remaining torpedoes at the heavy cruiser Haguro. By now Hoel was too seriously damaged to maintain speed and she came under a murderous fire from the Japanese fleet, sustaining more than 40 shell hits. The order to abandon ship was given only after a shell in the engine room brought her to a standstill: she was already listing to port and on fire. She sank at 0855.*

Kinkaid had misinterpreted ambiguous instructions from Halsey which said that Task Force 34 "will be formed" to block the San Bernadino Strait–a statement of future intention, not of fact. Kinkaid was now exposed to attack by vastly more powerful forces.

Kurita's force, much less heavily damaged than Halsey had supposed, had returned to the attack at the steady speed of 20 knots. Nishimura's catastrophe had in no way put Kurita off his intention of making for Leyte Gulf and destroying everything he found there.

At 0658 hours on October 25, the first shells fell on the American ships nearest the Japanese, Task Group 77.4.3 (Rear-Admiral Clifton A. F. Sprague).

If victory had depended on *matériel* superiority, the Americans would have suffered total defeat. No U.S. ship had a gun over 5-inch in calibre and the escort carriers' top speed was 20 knots. Kurita,

on the other hand, had the 33 14-, 16-, and 18-inch guns of his four battleships, the 8- and 6.1-inch guns of his eight cruisers, and the torpedoes of his 15 destroyers. And the slowest of his ships could do five knots more than the fastest of the Americans'. But his first order was "General chase". This was a blunder, as it prevented any concerted action.

Gallant resistance

The Americans, in spite of what could only seem a desperate situation from the point of view of *matériel*, conducted themselves with gallantry and a spirit of both sacrifice and initiative. Whilst the escort carriers commanded by Admiral Sprague protected themselves behind a smoke screen or took refuge in the rainstorms, the U.S. destroyers fired off their torpe-

does and then opened up with their guns. In the air, Task Group 77.4's planes flew back empty over their targets in increasing numbers, after dropping their last bombs, to draw the Japanese fire.

The Japanese fleet retires

This confusion allowed the Japanese no time to take advantage of their enormous numerical and *matériel* superiority. The carrier *Gambier Bay* was sunk by the 8-inch shells of the cruiser *Chikuma* which, together with her sister-ship *Chokai,* was then sunk by Commander R. L. Fowler's torpedo-bombers. The destroyer *Johnston* torpedoed the *Kumano* then, though hit by three 14-inch shells, went on fighting until the last of her guns

was destroyed. The *Hoel* and the escort destroyer *Samuel B. Roberts* met with an equally heroic end. These sacrifices were not in vain, as the heavy cruiser *Suzuya* was sunk in its turn. So E. B. Potter and Admiral Nimitz are right when they say of the battle off Samar:

"The history of the United States Navy records no more glorious two hours of resolution, sacrifice, and success."

Rear-Admiral C. A. Sprague writes:

"At 0925 my mind was occupied with dodging torpedoes when near the bridge I heard one of the signalmen yell, 'Goddammit, boys, they're getting away!' I could not believe my eyes, but it looked as if the whole Japanese Fleet was indeed retiring. However, it took a whole series of reports from circling planes to convince me. And still I could not get the fact to soak into my battle-numbed brain. At best, I had expected to be swimming by this time."

▽ *The American escort carrier Gambier Bay was also a member of Task Group 77.4.3. She was launched on November 22, 1943 as a "Christmas gift" to the Navy from the Kaiser Vancouver shipyard—one over the year's allotment of 18. Armed with a single 5-inch gun, the Gambier Bay, and her sister ship Kalinin Bay, were no match for the four Japanese cruisers that stood to port and astern at ranges of less than 18,000 yards. Although badly hit, Kalinin Bay was kept afloat. Gambier Bay, however, after escaping damage for some time was severely damaged and set on fire by hits from the Chikuma. The remaining cruisers—Haguro, Chokai, and Tone—closed in for the kill and the order to abandon ship was given just 15 minutes before Gambier Bay turned turtle and sank at 0907.*

All Kurita had to do at that moment was to draw in his forces so as to start again in better conditions, but on reflection he decided to pull out and before nightfall he had returned to the San Bernardino Strait. From the somewhat confused explanations of his decision he has given since the war, it turns out that he thought he was up against Task Force 38, and that he reckoned he had carried out his mission when his ships reported the destruction of three or four light carriers and several cruisers. The least that can be said is that he missed the chance of a great victory for which he would most likely have had to pay within the following 48 hours with an equally crushing defeat.

Kamikaze

Kurita's withdrawal did not put an end to the troubles of Task Group 77.4. Some hours later Vice-Admiral T. Ohnishi sent out his new weapon, the *kamikazes*. One of them sank the escort carrier *Saint Lo*, and five others caused losses and damage to five more. By the end of the day the battle off Samar had cost Thomas Kinkaid five ships, 23 planes, 1,130 men killed and 913 wounded.

Ozawa caught

At midnight on October 25, Admiral Ozawa had only 29 fighters and bombers left, whereas Halsey was bearing down on him with ten fast carriers, whose planes were to carry out 527 sorties in six waves from dawn to dusk. The first wave took off at 0540 hours. It caught the Japanese forces sailing north toward Halsey off Cape Engaño, sank the light carrier *Chitose* and left the fleet carrier *Zuikaku* so badly damaged that Ozawa had to transfer his flag to a cruiser. The second wave set fire to the light carrier *Chiyoda*, which was then left limping behind. Towards mid-day Mitscher sent up his third wave of 200 planes. This settled its account with the *Zuikaku*,

▽ *A barrage of anti-aircraft shells bursts in the sky and a plume of black smoke rises from a burning ship as Japanese bombers attack the American fleet.*

the last survivor of the six carriers which had bombed Pearl Harbor. She succumbed under the blows of three torpedoes at 1414 hours. About an hour later, the fourth wave sank the light carrier *Zuiho*.

Halsey and the pursuit

This success was only partial, however, as Halsey could not turn a deaf ear to Kinkaid's S.O.S., which came first in code then in clear. At 0848 he ordered McCain's task group to hasten to the rescue then, shortly before 1100 hours, on an order from Nimitz, he sent Task Force 34 and Bogan's task group southwards. The Japanese withdrawal was greatly helped by these detachments, though Rear-Admiral Du Bose's cruisers did finish off the *Chiyoda* with gunfire and sink two of Ozawa's destroyers. The latter also lost the light cruiser *Tama*, shattered by a clutch of torpedoes from the submarine *Jallao*.

Leyte Gulf, the greatest naval battle of all time, had involved 244 ships totalling 2,014,890 tons. By comparison, Jutland brought together under Scheer and Jellicoe some 254 ships totalling 1,616,836 tons. Thirty-two ships were lost:

	Japanese	U.S.
Battleships	3	0
Aircraft-carriers	4	1
Escort carriers	0	2
Cruisers	10	0
Destroyers	9	3
Totals	26	6
Tonnage	306,000	37,000

These figures reveal the crushing defeat inflicted on the Japanese Navy, although Ozawa had carried out his decoy mission brilliantly.

Japan's impossible task

When questioned after the capitulation by an American commission of enquiry about the consequences of this battle, Admiral Yonai, Navy Minister in General Koiso's cabinet, replied:

"Our defeat at Leyte was tantamount to the loss of the Philippines. When you took the Philippines, that was the end of our resources."

△ *Admiral William F. Halsey, pugnacious Commander-in-Chief of the U.S. Navy's 3rd Fleet at the Battle of Leyte Gulf.*

Yamashita trapped in the Philippines

Indeed Yamashita was virtually cut off in the archipelago and, what is more, could only move his troops from one island to another with the greatest of difficulty, whereas his adversary had complete liberty of movement and almost unlimited supplies. In spite of a superiority of men and *matériel,* which increased in proportion to the Japanese losses, MacArthur never used overwhelming strength in hammer-blow attacks, but showed the same qualities as a tactician as he had done in the Papua

△ *The escort carrier* St Lo, *last victim of the Battle off Samar. Hit by one of the earliest* kamikaze *attacks, she sank in less than 30 minutes.*

divisions, lost 3,508 killed and 12,076 wounded, two-thirds of these only lightly. On the same day it was relieved by the U.S. 8th Army.

MacArthur moves on

Without waiting to clear up on Leyte, MacArthur pressed on to Panay and Negros; then, when Yamashita had dropped his guard, Brigadier-General W. C. Dunckel's Western Visayan Task Force landed on Mindoro on December 15. This was 310 miles north of Leyte and it was taken without the loss of a single man. It brought U.S. aircraft to within striking distance of Luzon, the bay of Manila and Lingayen Gulf. The Philippines were now cut in two and Japanese communications with the Dutch East Indies were almost severed. Lingayen Gulf, from where the Japanese first landed on Luzon on December 22, 1941, was MacArthur's next objective. For this he gave I and XIV Corps (Major-Generals Innis W. Swift and Oscar W. Griswold respectively) to the 6th Army. The divisions involved were the 6th and 43rd (I Corps) and 37th and 41st (XIV Corps). Transport and supplies were to be the job of III and VII Amphibious Forces.

After a decoy action to make Yamashita think that the invasion of Luzon would come from Mindoro, the Americans landed on January 9, 1945, and met no stronger opposition than some sporadic mortar fire. A week later they were 30 miles along the road to Manila for the loss of 900 men, including 250 killed.

In the restricted waters off-shore the *kamikaze* corps, under Vice-Admiral Takijiro Ohnishi, had some success against the U.S. 7th Fleet. In the Mindoro operation on December 15 one of them damaged the cruiser *Nashville*, causing her to turn back with 131 dead and 158 wounded on board, including Vice-Admiral A. D. Struble. During the Lingayen landings between January 1 and 31, 54 U.S. and Australian ships were attacked by these suicide planes but, apart from the escort carrier *Ommaney Bay* and two small ships, they all survived. On January 6, however, on the bridge of the battleship *New Mexico*, Lieutenant-General Sir Herbert Lumsden, British liaison officer with MacArthur, was killed, giving the Anglo-Saxons a foretaste of what they were to get off Okinawa.

days of stringency.

If we realise that the reconquest of the Philippines required no fewer than 38 amphibious operations, we can see that no further comment is necessary unless it be to add to the praise of MacArthur a tribute to his airmen, Generals G. C. Kenney and E. C. Whitehead, and his sailors, Admirals T. C. Kinkaid and D. E. Barbey.

In the days following the landing on Leyte, nearly 50,000 Japanese still managed to get across to the island. The "no withdrawal" defence of Leyte fell to the Japanese 35th Army (Lieutenant-General Sasaku Suzuki). But its adversary, the U.S. 6th Army, increased from 101,000 men on November 12 to over 183,000 on December 2. MacArthur was cooking up one of his specials for Yamashita: on December 7 his 77th Division made a surprise landing in the Gulf of Ormoc on the west side of Leyte. Stabbed in the back, the 35th Army crumpled, then collapsed.

"I am exhausted. We have no food. The enemy are now within 500 meters from us. Mother, my dear wife and son, I am writing this letter to you by dim candle light. Our end is near. What will be the future of Japan if this island should fall into enemy hands? Our air force has not arrived. General Yamashita has not arrived. Hundreds of pale soldiers of Japan are awaiting our glorious end and nothing else. This is a repetition of what occurred in the Solomons, New Georgia, and other islands. How well are the people of Japan prepared to fight the decisive battle with the will to win . . .?"

This was a last letter from a soldier of the Japanese 1st Division a few days before December 26, the end of the battle, when the Japanese had run out of men. 80,577 of them died, and 878 were taken prisoner. The U.S. 6th Army, with seven

CHAPTER 82
THE STRUGGLE FOR LEYTE

by Richard Humble

The first Americans to return to the Philippines were a small Ranger task force with their destroyer transports and escort.

The Dinagat Attack Group, under Rear-Admiral Arthur D. Struble, transported the 500 men of Company D, 6th Ranger Battalion, U.S. Army, commanded by Lieutenant-Colonel H. A. Mucci. In the darkness of October 17 and 18, 1944 they were to demolish the Japanese radio location equipment on four islands at the two entrances to Leyte Gulf. If these electronic feelers were not ripped out, it was feared that they would signal the arrival of the invasion fleet on the 20th.

The main landings were planned for mid-day to allow a daylight run into the gulf, in which floating mines and obstacles had been reported. Throughout the morning the warships moved into position, and the transports halted about eight miles off the beach. The landing craft were hoisted out, and began circling round their larger parent ships. The noise and apparent confusion of a major amphibious operation had begun to build up.

From 0700, fire support units had been in action in the pre-landing shoot. First to arrive were the battleships *Mississippi*, *Maryland*, and *West Virginia*. At 0900

△ *Improvised supply dump on the beach at Leyte. Soon after the landings, supplies were arriving so quickly and in such disarray that the dumps began to spill over onto the airfields, with a consequent threat to air operations.*

they were relieved by the Close Covering Group, after they had sent 30 shells per main battery gun rumbling over the fleet into the jungle coast line.

Throughout these manoeuvres, fighters, torpedo-bombers, and reconnaissance aircraft from the 3rd and 7th Fleets made attacks on the airfields in northern Mindanao, Cebu, Negros, Panay, and Leyte, and conducted sweeps over the surrounding areas.

Rear-Admiral D. E. Barbey, whose air plan was administered by Captain Whitehead, had ordered a break in the bombing and strafing of the beach 45 minutes before H-hour. This was a departure from the standard operating procedure of that time. The gap was covered by high-angled naval gunfire and rocket barrages from 0915 to 1000.

By 0930 the bombardment was reaching its cacophonous climax and the landing craft had formed up for the 5,000 yard dash for the beach. At 0943 the signal flag was run up on the control vessel *PC-623,* and preceded by 11 L.C.I. rocket craft, the boats went in.

In a couple of minutes the L.C.I.s had fired 10,000 4.5-inch rockets in a close pattern over the northern and southern landing areas.

Behind the L.C.I.s came the first wave of amphtrack tanks, followed by L.V.T.s and then the amphtrack personnel carriers.

By the time the fourth wave had hit "Red" Beach in the northern landing area, the enemy had begun to hit back with mortars sited in the neighbouring hills. With the correct range and deflection they dropped bombs on the L.C.V.(P.)s from the *Elmore* and sank a boat from *Aquarius,* killing 3 men and injuring 15.

On the southern beaches a 75-mm battery near Catmon Hill took on the destroyer *Bennion,* straddling her repeatedly and wounding five men with a near miss. Artillery and mortar fire fell on "Blue" Beach as the 96th Division was landing.

Both the Japanese and the Americans realised that they had begun a battle that was of considerable strategic importance. If the Japanese lost the Philippines they would no longer control the sea-lanes to the oil of the Netherlands East Indies, tin and rubber from Malaya, and rice from Indo-China, nor have access to the varied mineral resources of the islands themselves.

The American leaders Roosevelt, Nimitz, and the Joint Chiefs-of-Staff had been persuaded by General MacArthur, and also by the course of the war, that the capture of the Philippines would be easier than that of Formosa, and would liberate a large and loyal population.

It would also cut off supplies to Japan and give the Americans a base for operations leading to the invasion of the Japanese home islands.

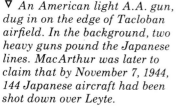

▽ *An American light A.A. gun, dug in on the edge of Tacloban airfield. In the background, two heavy guns pound the Japanese lines. MacArthur was later to claim that by November 7, 1944, 144 Japanese aircraft had been shot down over Leyte.*

Yamashita's threadbare forces

With this in mind, each adversary approached the battle with as much determination and as many resources as he could muster.

Field-Marshal Terauchi (Southern Army) whose area included the Philippines, had made the 14th Area Army and the 4th Air Army responsible for their defence. The 14th Army was so under strength that he had ordered it to concentrate on the defence of Luzon and regard the southern islands as of secondary importance.

The 14th Army consisted of eight infantry divisions and three independent mixed brigades. On October 6, Lieutenant-General T. Yamashita, the "Tiger of Malaya", had assumed command. He made Lieutenant-General S. Suzuki, with three infantry divisions and two mixed brigades, responsible for the defence of the central and southern islands. Suzuki in turn gave the 16th Division, under Lieutenant-General S. Makino, the task of defending Leyte.

The island which Makino had to defend is about 115 miles long north to south, and between 15 and 45 miles wide east to west. It is rugged and mountainous, except for a strip of flat land running north from Ormoc in the west, and a broad fertile valley in the north-east which narrows and fades out halfway down the east coast. The main Japanese airstrips were one each at Tacloban near the entrance to the San Juanico Strait and at Dulag 11 miles to the south, with three at Burauen further inland. It was on two beaches near Tacloban and Dulag that MacArthur planned to land.

He was assembling his invasion forces at Hollandia, which had become the main base in New Guinea, and at Manus in the Admiralty Islands. Naval forces consisted of the U.S. 7th Fleet (Vice-Admiral T. C. Kinkaid), which included two cruisers and two destroyers from the Royal Australian Navy, and the *Ariadne*, a fast minelayer of the Royal Navy. The U.S. 3rd Amphibious Force had joined it from the central Pacific. The U.S. 3rd Fleet, under Halsey, which included four fast carrier groups, was to cover and support MacArthur, but would remain under Nimitz's orders. The U.S. 6th

Army (X and XXIV Corps), under Lieutenant-General W. Krueger, provided the land forces and the 5th U.S.A.A.F. the supporting air force.

Carrier strikes

In preparation for the landings, the 15 fast carriers of the 3rd Fleet made a series of heavy raids on Japanese bases in Okinawa, Luzon, and Formosa. They came under very heavy aerial attack during these operations and between October 10 and 17 lost 26 aircraft and had two cruisers put out of action.

The Japanese, however, claimed that they had sunk two battleships and 11 carriers, and damaged many others, for the loss of 320 aircraft. Basing their moves on these spurious successes they altered their plans for the defence of Leyte and the Philippines.

Admiral S. Toyoda, Commander-in-Chief of the Japanese Combined Fleet, ordered the land-based aircraft to undertake the decisive battle for the Philippines under the operational title "SHO-1". The 2nd Air Fleet (350 operational aircraft) together with 150 carrier aircraft of Vice-Admiral J. Ozawa's 3rd and 4th Carrier Divisions, moved to Formosa. The 5th Fleet (Vice-Admiral K. Shima),

△ *American troops move up through Tacloban. In this area the 1st Cavalry Division swung up to the north to mop up part of the Japanese 16th Division, cross over to Samar, and then launch a series of amphibious landings along the north coast. Slightly to the south, the 24th Division cleared the Leyte valley and drove on round to the north of the Ormoc valley. As it was driving south along the valley, it met elements of the 77th Division, which had landed just south of Ormoc on December 7.*

△ *An American jeep column moves through Tacloban.*

▷ △ *Filipinos welcome American troops ashore.*

▷ ▽ *An American soldier helps his wounded comrade.*

consisting of the 16th and 21st Cruiser Squadrons, was ordered to sail from the Inland Sea to seek out and destroy any American ships damaged in the action.

5th fleet moves on

Concurrently with these moves the Imperial General Headquarters instructed Southern Army to fight the decisive battle on Leyte instead of Luzon. Terauchi ordered the 14th Area Army to

deploy its maximum strength to hold the island. Yamashita protested, but the order was repeated on the 22nd, two days after the American landings, and so he ordered the 35th Army to concentrate for the defence of Leyte.

The naval section of Imperial General Headquarters subsequently discovered that the reports of U.S. naval losses were inaccurate, and ordered the 5th Fleet to make for the Ryūkyū islands. This information, however, was not passed on to Yamashita. The land forces were now committed to Leyte without naval support.

MacArthur's powerful forces

For the Leyte invasion MacArthur had 200,000 men of General Walter Krueger's 6th Army, Lieutenant-General C. Kenney's 2,500 combat aircraft, and the 7th Fleet–often called "MacArthur's Navy" which had an additional 500 aircraft. The

3rd Fleet had 1,000 aircraft as well as nearly 100 of the most modern warships in the world.

He would need these resources because the invasion would be conducted out of range of land-based aircraft. However, MacArthur did not exercise direct command over Halsey and the 3rd Fleet, who were under Nimitz and so could be ordered away to attack the Japanese fleet if it approached.

Airstrips: the vital factor

The 7th Fleet had some small escort carriers, but they would be inadequate to defend the fleet and transports, and cover the beach-head if major units of the Japanese Navy or Air Forces succeeded in evading the 3rd Fleet. Consequently it was essential that Kenney's Far East Air Forces should start operating from local airstrips as soon as the invasion forces had captured them.

With this in mind the invasion beaches chosen were close to, or opposite, the coastal airstrips near Tacloban and Dulag.

As soon as he heard of the landings, Suzuki (35th Army) instructed the 16th Division to keep control of the airfields at all costs, and ordered Leyte to be reinforced by four battalions. On the October 22 Yamashita told him that he was to fight a decisive battle on Leyte and that he would be getting two divisions and an independent mixed brigade from Luzon. With further reinforcements from Davao and Cebu, Suzuki had the equivalent of four strong divisions on the island.

If the decisive naval and air battles were successful, the Japanese land forces could be sent against the estimated two divisions which the Americans had put ashore. The 16th Division was ordered to hold a line Burauen–Dagami, whilst the bulk of the Japanese forces concentrated in the Carigara plain.

These deployments assisted the Americans, who advanced rapidly against light opposition, and by November 2 the 6th Army had reached a line Carigara–

△ A Japanese Type 95 light tank, knocked out during the American advance, comes under inspection. Designed in 1935, the Type 95 remained in production until 1943, but was totally obsolete by Allied standards when Japan entered the war.

Jaro – Dagami – Abuyog. They had an advanced detachment at Baybay and had captured all five airstrips.

"I have returned"

Before examining the American plans for the break-out from their beach-head, let us recall an incident which took place on the first day.

General George MacArthur had last visited Leyte Gulf in 1903 as a 2nd Lieutenant of Army Engineers. Forty-one years later he boarded a landing craft with President Osmeña, Resident Commissioner Romulo, Chief-of-Staff Sutherland, and Air Commander Kenney.

After the craft had grounded, MacArthur waded through the knee-deep surf, inspected the beach, and walked inland about 200 yards to examine the effects of the bombardment.

It may not have looked like the return of a conquering hero, but MacArthur made up for this in his broadcast on the "Voice of Freedom" network.

Standing on the beach in front of the microphone, his hands shook and his voice betrayed his deep emotion:

"People of the Philippines, I have returned. By the grace of Almighty God our forces stand again on Philippine soil."

He urged the population to rally to him, and also introduced the new president Sergio Osmeña. A passionate yet restrained speech, it was an outlet for powerful emotions held in check and only betrayed earlier when, with a smile, he had remarked "Well, believe it or not, we're here."

After the war General Yamashita said that he had imagined that the film of MacArthur's return had been mocked up in New Guinea. Had he known that the general was at the front he would have launched the whole strength of the Japanese forces in a suicide raid on MacArthur's headquarters to avenge the death of Admiral Yamamoto.

Meanwhile unloading was proceeding at a fast and sometimes chaotic rate. L.S.T.s originally intended for "Red" Beach were diverted to Tacloban air-

strip, and here the rapidly-growing supply dump began to restrict the work of the airfield engineers. On October 24, Kenney made the drastic threat that everything not removed from the airstrip by dawn on the 25th would be bulldozed.

Engineers' nightmare

The airstrips proved to be almost unusable, despite the hard work and constant attention of the Army Engineers and Filipino labourers. The Dulag strip was still soft, with many rough spots, on October 25, but served as an emergency landing ground during the Leyte sea battle. Tacloban was a little better, despite the fact that the water table was only 18 inches below the surface. One engineer reported that "an airstrip there could at best be a thin slice of coral or metal laid upon a jelly mold".

Krueger visited this airstrip and told the engineers that unless they started laying gravel, they would be digging foxholes for their lives in 24 hours. The

work was done, and again this strip saved about 100 pilots, though the surface was so bad that about a quarter of the aircraft were destroyed when they crash-landed or nosed over on soft spots.

Three of the fast carrier groups remained in the area to provide air cover and attack the Japanese airfields which were beginning to receive reinforcements from Formosa.

Japanese troop reinforcements began to arrive via Ormoc, but the shipping and naval escorts suffered heavy losses. Four battalions from Davao and Cebu arrived between the 26th and 28th. The main body of the 1st Division and some 2,000 men of the 26th Division from Luzon were landed between November 1 and 2. The convoy carrying the remainder of the 1st Division and some 10,000 of the 26th Division left Manila on November 8th. It came under low level attack by the 5th U.S.A.A.F. and sustained considerable superficial damage. The men were landed without their equipment. A day later the empty convoy was caught again by the 5th U.S.A.A.F. and all but one ship were sunk. A day later, aircraft from Halsey's carriers attacked a convoy carrying the remainder of the 26th Division, and for the loss of nine aircraft, sank all the transports and four of the escorting destroyers.

Japanese reinforcements

Between October 22 and December 11, the Japanese succeeded in reinforcing the original garrison of 15,000 men with some 45,000 men and 10,000 tons of stores. Their operations cost them one light cruiser, eight destroyers, six escort craft, and 17 transports – shipping they could ill afford to lose. Despite this, the 35th Army was outnumbered by the 6th Army, whose strength stood at 183,000 by December 2.

By November 1, Suzuki realised that he was up against two American corps, each of two divisions, and that he lacked the strength to carry out his original plan. He ordered the 1st Division and the truncated 26th, when they arrived at Carigara and Jaro respectively, to hold the U.S. X Corps in the north. The remaining reinforcements were sent to assist the 16th Division under attack by

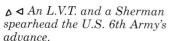

△ ◁ An L.V.T. and a Sherman spearhead the U.S. 6th Army's advance.
◁ The prompt treatment of battle casualties plays an important part in the morale of fighting troops.
▽ Heavy going in a swamp. Note the man (centre right) being pulled out of a particularly soft piece of ground by his comrades, the soldier with the Browning Automatic Rifle (foreground), and the mortar bomb containers being carried by the man second from right.

the U.S. XXIV Corps in the south. In the ensuing heavy fighting the Americans were halted near Limon and to the west of Jaro.

At a conference with Terauchi, on November 9 and 10, Yamashita urged that the reinforcement of Leyte was weakening the defences of Luzon, and proving too costly in transports and naval vessels. Terauchi agreed that there was little hope of holding the island and that supply operations should cease.

Yamashita plans . . .

Despite this, Yamashita ordered the 35th Army to use the 26th Division on the Burauen front with a view to launching an attack with the 16th Division to recapture some of the airfields. Suzuki, who had hoped to concentrate his forces in the north, was now forced to send the 26th Division along the Albuera–Burauen track and the 102nd Division to the Mount Pina area to protect the right of the 1st Division, holding out at Limon.

The 4th Air Army proposed an air-borne counter-attack with the 40 aircraft and 250 paratroops of the 2nd Raiding Group, which had flown in from Japan. Yamashita decided that a joint air and ground attack should be launched near the end of the month, preceded by an air attack between the 23rd and 27th.

. . . the counter-attack

In a spectacular, but fumbled, attack on November 27, three transport aircraft carrying demolition troops were sent to crash-land on the strips at Dulag and Tacloban.

One aircraft crashed on Buri airstrip killing all its occupants, the second hit the beach and most of the men escaped, and the third landed in the surf near the H.Q. of the U.S. 728th Amphibious Battalion, between Rizal and Tarragona. A brisk hand-to-hand fight ensued, in which some Japanese were killed and others escaped to the jungle.

A second and more serious attempt was made on the Buri strip on the night of December 5-6. About 150 infantrymen

▽ American "Long Tom" 155-mm guns directed at Japanese positions further inland. The Long Tom was probably the best gun used by the Americans in the war, having a first class performance, as well as ruggedness and good cross-country movement capabilities.

had worked down through the mountains and attacked American troops bivouacking near the strip. The Japanese were driven off at dawn.

Paratroop landings fail

Through a piece of bad co-ordination, the paratroop attack came 20 hours later. Between 39 and 40 aircraft, carrying about 15 to 20 men apiece, roared over Tacloban and Dulag. At the former they were destroyed or driven off by the A.A. fire, while the Dulag section crash-landed killing crew and paratroopers.

However, a drop from 35 different aircraft on the Burauen strips met with greater success. The Japanese set fire to stores, fuel, ammunition, and some small liaison aircraft. For two days and nights ground crews and other air force personnel stalked one another and the Japanese, before the paratroopers were eliminated.

Ironically, the weather had proved more effective than these airborne sorties, for the U.S.A.A.F. had abandoned the Burauen strips, which had become waterlogged, leaving only rear echelon units behind.

With his X Corps held up near Limon, and XXIV Corps delayed in its advance north from Baybay, Krueger decided to make a fresh landing south of Ormoc, to drive a wedge between the two wings of his opponents.

On the morning of the 7th, the U.S. 77th Division landed four miles south of Ormoc and met no resistance. The convoy and escorts, however, came under attack after the landing and during the return, and lost two destroyers sunk and two damaged to *kamikaze* attacks.

Suzuki was forced to switch his 16th and 26th Divisions from the front to oppose this landing. On December 10, however, the 77th beat him in the race for Ormoc.

With the main Japanese base in American hands, Yamashita told Suzuki that he was on his own. Japanese resistance began to crumble fast. On December 20, X Corps and the 77th Division met at Cananga, and part of this force turned west. On Christmas Day, with the help of a force moved by sea from Ormoc, it captured Palompon, the only port of any significance left to the Japanese.

Though organised resistance ceased,

△ *The Japanese heavy cruiser* Nachi *under air attack in Manila Bay on November 5, 1944. She was sunk in this attack.*

▽ *U.S. Amphibious force off Leyte, on first day of the invasion.*

there were still groups of Japanese obeying Yamashita's order to live off the country and keep up the struggle with the Americans. As the official naval history comments "Japanese unorganised resistance can be very tough." Following his instructions to keep up the struggle, Yamashita added a message explaining that the high command had decided to concentrate on the defence of Luzon, and that he was shedding "tears of remorse" for the tens of thousands of his countrymen who must fight to the death on Leyte.

Mopping up continued until March 17, 1945. There was still over a full division of Japanese troops on the island. Some used the rugged and badly-mapped terrain for guerrilla tactics, whilst small units tried to escape to Cebu across the 25 miles of the Camotes Sea.

By March 1945, despite sweeps by the U.S. 77th Division, there were still several thousand Japanese at large. On March 17, two ships appeared off the coast and embarked Suzuki and part of his staff. For a month they sailed in search of a Japanese-held port until on April 16 they were caught by U.S. aircraft off Negros, and General Suzuki was killed.

Small groups of Japanese continued to be hunted and killed by Filipino guerrillas until the end of the war.

The Leyte campaign was a costly operation. The U.S. Navy and Marine Corps lost several hundred men on and around the island, in addition to the heavy losses sustained in the battle off Samar.

The Army, not including the A.A.F., had 15,584 battle casualties, of which the 3,508 killed were about equally distributed between X and XXIV Corps. In January their full strength stood at 257,766 officers and men.

Understandably, estimates of Japanese casualties vary greatly. The 6th and 8th Armies reported 80,557 confirmed dead, almost one-third of which had occurred during the mopping up operations. The American forces took only 828 Japanese prisoners.

▽ *A Japanese destroyer manoeuvres at high speed in an effort to avoid the bombs of four B-25 Mitchells of the 30th Bombardment Group, attacking her in Ormoc Bay. During this action, 16 of the 20 Japanese fighters sent up to intercept the bombers were shot down by American escort fighters.*

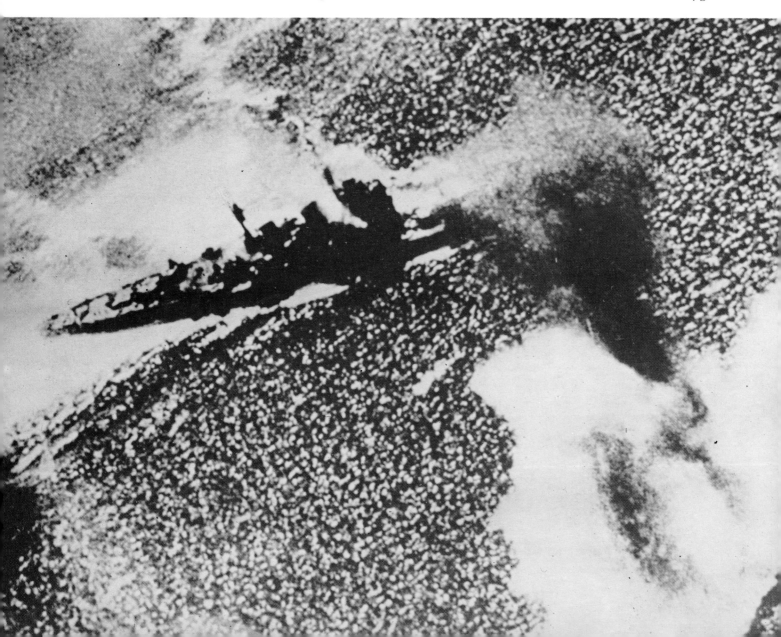

CHAPTER 83

THE ARDENNES GAMBLE

It is now well known that the "Battle of the Bulge", the offensive often known as Rundstedt's, was in reality forced upon him, and that the rôle played by O.B. West in the attack begun on December 16 was limited to that of passing on to Army Group "B" the instructions of Hitler, Keitel, and Jodl at O.K.W.

It was quite clear to Rundstedt, Model, and even to Sepp Dietrich, that the objectives assigned to Operation *"Herbstnebel"* ("Autumn Fog") were far too ambitious for the Wehrmacht's limited capabilities, and they tried to convince the Führer of this. On the other hand they agreed with him–and history bears out their judgement–that if the Third Reich was not to be annihilated in less than six months, they would have to go over to the offensive, the Western Front being the only theatre where this might be possible. Italy was not vital to the Western Allies, even if the terrain and the season had made such an operation there successful; and in the East, it was generally agreed that they would not be able to force a decisive result. According to Major-General Gehlen's calculations, Stalin had something like 520 infantry divisions and more than 300 armoured and mechanised brigades at his command, and so could lose up to 30 divisions, or retreat up to 150 miles, without suffering a decisive defeat. In any case, what could be the advantage to the Germans of advancing once more to the Dniepr or the Dvina, if in the meantime the Western Allies broke through the *Westwall* and occupied the Ruhr and Saar basins?

The German chiefs thus agreed unanimously on a counter-offensive in the West, being fully aware of the logistical difficulties and man-power shortage by which Eisenhower was being plagued. However, there was deep disagreement between the Führer and his front-line generals on how far to carry the offensive. Hitler maintained that they ought to go all out, and inflict on Eisenhower a defeat as crushing as that suffered by Gamelin when the Panzer divisions had pushed through to the Somme estuary in 1940. And the fact that the Ardennes mountains were so lightly held seemed to provide him with an opportunity identical to the one he had exploited in May 1940– we now know that he did in fact send to

German soldier flattens elf against the ground as ll explodes up ahead.

Eisenhower Slows Down

Short of men and supplies, the Allied armies were further slowed down by torrential rain in the autumn of 1944. A new American 9th Army was created which, after taking Brest, was shifted to the Ardennes front, then to the left of the 1st Army. A new Allied 6th Army Group was created for operations between Epinal and the Swiss frontier. Field Marshal von Rundstedt had 30 divisions, five of which were Panzer, to be joined by a further 11. These would in turn be reinforced by 28 inferior "people's grenadier divisions". Rundstedt would also get three more Panzer brigades.

On October 1 the British I Corps moved north from Antwerp and closed the Woensdrecht Isthmus to the island of Zuid-Beveland. On October 22 Breshens, opposite Flushing, fell. On November 3 German resistance on the island of Walcheren was broken. On October 8 the attack on the Westwall was begun by the American XIX Corps. On October 18 a double thrust strategy promoted by General Bradley was agreed on in Montgomery's headquarters.

Liegnitz for the documents pertaining to *"Fall Gelb"*. The plan was being prepared at H.Q. in absolute secrecy–and neither Rundstedt nor Model knew of it. Three armies were to take part: the newly formed 6th S.S. *Panzerarmee,* commanded by Colonel-General Dietrich; the 5th *Panzerarmee* under General Hasso von Manteuffel, which was withdrawn from the Aachen front (neither Model nor Rundstedt was informed of the rôle it was going to play); and the 7th Army, under General Brandenberger, which was then in the Eifel sector.

According to O.K.W.'s plan, the 5th and 6th *Panzerarmee* were to get to the Meuse in 48 hours; after this Sepp Dietrich, crossing the river north of Liège, would aim for Antwerp, via Saint Truiden and Aarschot, whilst Manteuffel, crossing the river on both sides of Namur, would aim for Brussels. The 7th Army would pivot round at Echternach and thus cover the operation against any Allied counter-attack coming from the south. With Manteuffel and Dietrich intercepting their communications at Namur and Antwerp, the whole of the Allied 21st Army Group, and most of the 12th Army Group, would be attacked on two fronts and annihilated, with the destruction of 37 of the 64 divisions that Eisenhower deployed at that time.

On October 24, Lieutenant-Generals Krebs and Westphal, chiefs-of-staff of Army Group "B" and of O.B. West respectively, had an interview with the Führer, who informed them of the plan which he had conceived, and whose execution was provisionally fixed for November 25. Both at Koblenz and at Field-Marshal Model's H.Q., the *Führer-befehl* had been severely criticised by those who would have to carry it out, as– and Krebs and Westphal had already hinted as much on a previous visit to O.K.W.–the plan bore no relationship to the resources being made available to them. Since, however, they were both in favour of a strategic counter-attack, on November 3 they submitted a counter-proposition to Hitler, better suited to the capabilities of Army Group "B", and called the "little solution" *(kleine Lösung)*.

Instead of embarking on the very risky task of recapturing Antwerp, they suggested that it would be better to take advantage of the salient that the American 1st and 9th Armies had created in the *Westwall,* east and north-east of Aachen, and then envelop it in a pincer movement, enabling Dietrich to break out of the Roermond region and Manteuffel out of the Eifel region. If such an attack were completely successful, 20 Allied divisions would be destroyed and Model could then perhaps exploit Bradley's defeat and strike out for Antwerp.

As can be seen, Model, who had conceived this plan, and Rundstedt, who had forwarded it to O.K.W. with his approval, looked upon the operation as a mere sortie, just as the commander of a besieged 18th century fortress would suddenly make a night attack on the besieging forces, forcing them to start their siege preparations anew. But such an operation gained only a few weeks' respite and, sooner or later, unless help was forthcoming from elsewhere, surrender would be inevitable. Understandably then, Hitler angrily rejected such a solution, for what he needed was not a short respite,

Into the Siegfried Line

On November 8 the American 3rd Army under Patton attacked the Westwall, which was defended by the German 1st Army. The U.S. 5th Infantry Division set about outflanking Metz and the 95th Infantry Division crossed the Moselle above Thierville during the night of November 8-9. The 90th Infantry Division reached the Franco-German frontier on November 20. The U.S. 6th Army won a convincing victory in the Saverne Gap.

but a decisive military victory in the West. So, as early as November 1, he had written at the head of his orders to O.B. West, that "the intention, the organisation, and the objective of this offensive are irrevocable". On receiving the counter-proposition of Model and Rundstedt, he got Jodl to reply within 24 hours that "the Führer has decided that the operation is irrevocably decided, down to its last details".

However, none of the H.Q. staff had solved any of the difficulties which the men in field command of the operation had felt obliged to point out. As Rundstedt explained on October 25, 1945, whilst being interrogated by Major Shulman of Canadian 1st Army Intelligence:

"When I was first told about the proposed offensive in the Ardennes, I protested against it as vigorously as I could. The forces at our disposal were much, much too weak for such far-reaching objectives. It was only up to one to obey. It was a nonsensical operation, and the most stupid part of it was the setting of Antwerp as the target. If

▽ *American vehicles captured by the Germans in Belgium. By the skilful and daring use of such captured equipment, the Germans hoped to sow distrust and worry in the Allied rear areas.*

The Fight for Alsace

On November 14 the units of the French 1st Army under General de Lattre de Tassigny attacked near the Swiss border and by the evening of November 17th de Lattre was able to order his I Corps to head for the Rhine, to reduce the fortress of Belfort and reincorporate the 5th Armoured Division with a view to attacking Cernay. II Corps would thrust its right forward via Giromagny on Colmar and its left would storm the Col de la Schlucht.

On November 19, 1944, the French 1st Army reached the Rhine–the first Allied army to do so. On the 20th the French completely invested the fortress town of Belfort. By November 25 the German 19th Army was caught in a pincer movement. The French went on to capture Saverne, opening the Saverne gap, re-opening liaison with American units and opening the way to Strasbourg.

we reached the Meuse we should have got down on our knees and thanked God – let alone try to reach Antwerp."

Hitler paid no more heed to Sepp Dietrich than he had to Model and Rundstedt, his only concession being to put back the date of the offensive from November 25, first to December 10, then to December 16. He also agreed to Manteuffel's suggestion to replace the three-hour artillery barrage that he had ordered by an artillery attack of only 45 minutes.

The forces assemble

The operation forced O.K.W. to redeploy its western forces. To free Model of any worries concerning his right wing, an Army Group "H" was organised, responsible for operations between the North Sea and Roermond, and commanded by Colonel-General Student, who relinquished his 1st Parachute Army to General Schlemm.

The 15th Army relieved the 5th *Panzerarmee* on the Roer, being relieved in turn between the North Sea and Nijmegen by a 25th Army under the command of General Christiansen.

According to General von Manteuffel,

at 0530 hours on December 16, 21 German divisions of all types launched their attack on the American line between Monschau and Echternach, on a 90-mile front. From north to south, the forces involved were:

1. 6th S.S. *Panzerarmee:* LXVII Corps (General Hitzfeld), with the 272nd and 326th *Volksgrenadier* Divisions; I S.S. Panzer Corps (General Priess), with the 277th and 12th *Volksgrenadier,* 3rd Parachute, and 1st and 12th S.S. Panzer Divisions; and II S.S. Panzer Corps (General Bittrich), with the 2nd and 9th S.S. Panzer Divisions.
2. 5th *Panzerarmee:* LXVI Corps (General Lucht), with the 18th and 62nd *Volksgrenadier* Divisions; LVIII Panzer Corps (General Krüger), with the 116th Panzer and 560th *Volksgrenadier* Divisions; and XLVII Panzer Corps (General von Lüttwitz), with the 2nd Panzer, Panzer-*"Lehr",* and 26th *Volksgrenadier* Divisions.
3. 7th Army: LXXXV Corps (General Kniess), with the 5th Parachute and 352nd *Volksgrenadier* Divisions; and LXXX Corps (General Beyer), with the 276th and 212th *Volksgrenadier* Divisions.

It should be noted that although the four *Waffen*-S.S. Panzer divisions had been brought up to full strength, with a total of

Colmar Pocket

The manoeuvre to take Strasbourg began on November 23 at 0645 hours and at 1800 the French flag was flying atop the cathedral spire. Hitler set about reconstituting the Colmar bridgehead, with the German 19th Army under General Wiese. General de Lattre's II Corps was ordered to attack the north-west front of the pocket while I Corps attacked from a line between Mulhouse and Thann.

640 Panther and Pzkw IV tanks available to Dietrich, Manteuffel's three Panzer divisions had only been restored to about two-thirds of their full strength, about 320 tanks in all. And in fact, if they had been at full strength, the fuel problem would have been even more acute than it was. According to the plan, the Panzers should have attacked with sufficient petrol for five refuellings, which would have given them a range of up to 170 miles; on the day of the attack, they had only enough for two refills, as for camouflage reasons Hitler had forbidden the creation of fuel dumps close to the line. More important, he had made no allowances either for the difficult terrain or for the very bad weather. On December 28, describing the failure of the Ardennes offensive to his generals, Hitler described as follows the misfortunes that befell the 12th *"Hitlerjugend"* Panzer Division on the roads of the Ardennes:

"Only the first wave of the 12th S.S. Panzer Division's tanks was in action, whilst behind them there was an enormous convoy jammed solid, so that they could go neither forward nor back. Finally, not even the petrol could get through. Everything was stationary, and the tanks' engines were merely idling. To avoid frost damage, etc., the engines had to be run all night, which also had the advantage of keeping the men warm. This created enormous petrol requirements. The roads were bad. They could only use first gear . . . there was no end to it."

Skorzeny's special forces

Among the special forces used during this operation, mention should be made of the so-called 150th Panzer Brigade, made up of about 2,000 men conversant with American army slang, using jeeps and even old Sherman tanks rescued from the battlefield. The brigade had a double purpose: firstly, small patrols were to infiltrate the enemy lines and cause panic by spreading alarmist rumours and sabotaging telephone communications and signposts; then, when the break-through was being exploited, small motorised columns would be sent out to capture the Meuse bridges and hold them until the rest of the armour arrived.

This "Trojan horse" invented by Hitler was placed under the command of Otto Skorzeny, who had been promoted to colonel after capturing Admiral Horthy. The stratagem, which was quite contrary to the Geneva Convention, had some initial success because of its surprise element, but the counter-measures immediately devised by the Americans were most effective. Germans captured in American uniforms were immediately tried and shot, although some of them had only taken part in the operation when threatened with a German firing-squad.

The paratroops who spread confusion deep behind the American front line, even as far as France, never numbered more than 1,200, discounting the dummies used, and were commanded by Lieutenant-Colonel Heydte; but the pilots of the Junkers Ju 52s from which they were to jump were so badly trained that three-quarters of them jumped behind the German lines. The Allies thought they had been entrusted with the task of killing Eisenhower, but post-war research has revealed how groundless these suppositions were, although they did interfere with the normal functions of the Allied high command.

Inadequate reserves

Behind the first wave of troops, there were eight reserve divisions, seven of which were subject to O.K.W. orders. Model thus found himself with very little chance of exploiting any slight advantages he might gain without referring to Hitler. In addition there were two newly formed Panzer brigades, but that was all.

Theoretically, the attack was to be supported by 3,000 bombers and fighter-bombers, but on the first day a mere 325 planes took off, of which 80 were jets. Hitler could not bring himself to expose German towns to Allied air attacks by depriving them of fighter cover.

On December 10, O.K.W. left Berlin for Ziegenberg near Giessen, where, in preparation for the 1940 Blitzkrieg against France, a command post—never used—had been set up. It was here that two days later, having first made them hand in their pistols and brief-cases, Hitler harangued the commanders of the units engaged in this action. "There were about 30 generals including divisional commanders," writes Jacques Nobécourt. "They had been brought from Koblenz during the night by bus, twisting, turning, and going back on its tracks to deceive them regarding the

route being followed. All along the wall of the lecture hall stood S.S. men keeping an eagle eye on all present."

"No one in the audience dared move, or even take out a handkerchief," wrote Bayerlein, commander of the Panzer-*"Lehr"*, who thought Hitler looked ill and depressed.

"For two solid hours Hitler spoke, using no notes." Although we do not have the authentic verbatim account of his speech, the French version presented by Raymond Henry takes up 11 pages of his book. In it, Hitler once more reminded his listeners of the steadfastness of Frederick the Great refusing to surrender in 1761, in spite of the heavy pressure exerted on him by his brother, his ministers, and his generals; and Hitler spoke of the weakness of the coalition opposing Germany:

"On the one hand the ultra-capitalist states, on the other ultra-marxist states; on the one hand a great empire, the British Empire, slowly dying; on the other a colony just waiting to take over. Countries whose aims are becoming more and more different day by day. And if you watch closely, you can see differences arising hour by hour. A few well-struck blows and this artificial common front could come crashing down at any moment."

When Hitler had finished, Rundstedt assured him of the devoted loyalty of all his generals.

In the Allied camp

Amongst the Allies, the battle of the Ardennes was and has been the subject of considerable argument. It allowed Montgomery once more to lay claim to the title of head of Allied land forces, and even today the discussion rages between supporters of the American supreme commander and of his brilliant but independent second-in-command; just as for 20 years after the disappointing Battle of Jutland, there were divisions between supporters of Admiral Beatty, and those of Admiral Jellicoe. In his *Memoirs,* published in 1958, Montgomery expresses himself with his usual freedom, whereas Eisenhower, both during his tenure of the White House and during his later retirement, maintained a discreet silence.

We are here simply concerned with two questions: the first concerns the Allied forces holding the Ardennes, the second concerns the surprise offensive of December 16, 1944.

It must first be noted that with his right wing north of Trier and his left in the Losheim gap, south of Monschau, Major-General Middleton, commanding the American VIII Corps, held an 80-mile front with only four divisions. The 4th and 28th Divisions had been badly mauled in the unsuccessful attack on the

△ *Patton on a inspection tour. Unlike most of his compatriots, Patton realised that a major offensive through the Ardennes might be coming, and had already started laying contingency plans for switching his 3rd Army's axis of advance from east to north. This would take the German offensive in the flank and crush it.*

Roer dams; the 9th Armoured Division (Major-General John W. Leonard) had never been under fire, nor had the 106th Division (Major-General Alan W. Jones) which had only taken over the Schnee Eifel sector of the front on December 11, after trailing all through France and southern Belgium in freezing rain and open lorries.

Bradley's dilemma

But did the Americans have any choice? In his *A Soldier's Story,* General Bradley explains the situation in a perfectly convincing way: to give Middleton more troops would have meant taking troops away from the two groups due to attack, to the north and south, in November. Even as it was, Hodges and Simpson had only 14 divisions between them for their 60-mile front north of the Ardennes, whilst to the south, Patton had only nine divisions, stretched over a 90-mile front. The Americans were so short of troops that the offensive was put back a week so that they could get back from Montgomery just one division they had lent him to mop up the Scheldt estuary. And to concentrate the 3rd Army's attack on a narrow front, the Americans had to transfer part of Patton's sector to Devers's 6th Army Group. If they had

wanted to reduce the risks of a German attack against Middleton's thinly held Ardennes positions, the Americans could have cancelled Patton's offensive, as Montgomery had suggested, and even dug in along the front for the winter. Both these alternatives were, to Bradley, out of the question. Middleton's forces would be stretched as thinly as possible, risking the chance of an enemy attack, and the Americans would throw all available divisions into the November offensive. Thus troops were taken away from the Ardennes to reinforce the winter offensive. It was a calculated risk which Bradley had decided to take, and one to which he stuck both then and afterwards.

Eisenhower, whilst claiming his due share of responsibility, justifies Bradley:

"The responsibility for maintaining only four divisions on the Ardennes front and for running the risk of a large German penetration in that area was mine. At any moment from November 1 onward I could have passed to the defensive along the whole front and made our lines absolutely secure from attack while we awaited reinforcements. My basic decision was to continue the offensive to the extreme limit of our ability, and it was this decision that was responsible for the startling successes of the first week of the German December attack."

It seems quite clear, after this, that the calculated risk about which Eisenhower

▽ *Lieutenant-General Leonard T. Gerow. As a major-general, Gerow commanded the American V Corps, which was holding the sector of the Ardennes front attacked by the right wing of Dietrich's 6th Panzerarmee.*

and Bradley talk was not something dreamed up after the event to excuse the weaknesses of their actions.

Hitler underestimated

It must be admitted, however, that Eisenhower and Bradley calculated things very tightly, as neither imagined for one minute that Hitler would fix Antwerp as the objective for his Panzers. And, of course, their reasoning followed the same lines as that of Model, Rundstedt, and Manteuffel, who all declared that the plan was impracticable and would have the most catastrophic consequences.

When he became aware of enemy troop concentrations, Colonel Dickson, head of General Hodges's Intelligence staff, said on December 10 that the defence of the Reich was based on the following strategy: the halting of the Allied offensive, followed by a counter-attack, with all forces concentrated between the Roer and the Erft.

In other words, Dickson assumed that if there was a counter-attack, it would follow the lines of the "little solution" that Rundstedt and Model had unsuccessfully suggested to Hitler, since more ambitious plans were far beyond the Wehrmacht's capabilities.

The Allies were thus quite aware that

German troops had been brought into position in readiness for a counter-attack, but they thought that these concentrations would form a flank attack on Hodges's troops preparing to attack Cologne, and that it would be combined with the breaching of the Roer dams. Later, Dickson's assumption was taken as being the correct one, and it was only on the day before the attack took place that Allied Intelligence found out that rubber boats and other craft had been assembled on the German side of the River Our.

Oddly enough, Colonel Koch, head of the American 3rd Army's Intelligence staff, was more worried than Dickson about the American situation; he even managed to get General Patton to share his apprehension, since on December 12 the latter ordered his chief-of-staff to work out "a study of what the Third Army would do if called upon to counter-attack such a break-through". And on the night of December 15-16, when he knew that the enemy was observing radio silence, he said "I want you, gentlemen, to start making plans for pulling the Third Army out of its eastward attack, change the direction ninety degrees, moving to Luxemburg and attacking north."

With all the information before us, Bradley was probably right when he said that although the Allies may have been wrong about the enemy's intentions, their estimate of his capabilities at that time was on the whole correct. For – and events were to bear this out in the following weeks – against forces as large as the Allies', Rundstedt did not have the resources necessary to ensure the success of an offensive strategy.

Thus, because they had failed to reckon with Adolf Hitler's megalomania, the Allied chiefs were caught badly napping on December 16 – not least Field-Marshal Montgomery, who on the very morning of the German offensive had summed up the enemy's possibilities of action in the following words:

"The enemy is at present fighting a defensive campaign on all fronts, his situation is such that he cannot stage major offensive operations. Furthermore, at all costs he has to prevent the war from entering on a mobile phase; he has not the transport or the petrol that would be necessary for mobile operations, nor could his tanks compete with ours in the mobile battle."

CHAPTER 84
BATTLE OF THE BULGE

German infantryman, laden down with ammunition, weapons, and entrenching equipment. In this last major offensive on the Western Front, the Germans used up the few remaining first-class fighting troops they still had, and from now on the burden was to fall on secondrate troops and even on the Volkssturm.
(page 820) The German offensive in the Ardennes, better known as the "Battle of the Bulge".

On the first day of the offensive, the 6th S.S. *Panzerarmee* attacked with its infantry divisions, keeping its Panzers in reserve to exploit the initial success. On the right it came up against the American 2nd and 99th Divisions, of V Corps, still commanded by Major-General Leonard Gerow; the 2nd Division was an experienced, battle-hardened unit which overcame its surprise very quickly, whereas the 99th Division, which had never before seen major action, had more difficulty in recovering its composure. In the end, V Corps managed to hold on to the Elsenborn ridge in spite of all enemy attacks. But Dietrich easily broke through the Losheim gap, lightly held by the 14th Armoured Division, which opened up the road to Stavelot, and in addition enabled him to turn the left flank of the 106th Division.

On the very same day this division was pierced on its left by the 5th *Panzerarmee*'s attack, which also threw back the 28th Division towards Clervaux (Clerf). The two regiments of the 106th Division holding the Schnee Eifel plateau were in imminent danger of being surrounded.

The 7th Army, reduced to four divisions, had to be satisfied with pivoting around Echternach, instead of including Luxembourg in its plan of attack, as originally planned. Although it had to yield some ground, the American 4th Division, which made up Middleton's right flank, was less severely tested than the 28th.

The Allied response

When the first news of the German attack reached S.H.A.E.F., Bradley was in Versailles, conferring with General Bedell Smith, Eisenhower's chief-of-staff. A few hours later, a further report indicated that the American 1st Army had identified eight German divisions.

Eisenhower and Bradley immediately realised the implications of this offensive, but the reserves available to them on December 16 were even less than those available to General Gamelin on May 13, 1940. They were in fact limited to XVIII Airborne Corps (Major-General Ridgeway), two of whose divisions, the 82nd and the 101st, were being reformed near Rheims, after two months' action in the Nijmegen salient. This corps was immediately alerted, and the 9th and 3rd Armies received orders to make their 7th and 10th Armoured Divisions respectively available to the 1st Army.

In a few days' time Eisenhower would also be able to call upon the 2nd Armoured Division, which had just landed in France, as well as the 87th Division and the 17th Airborne Division, which

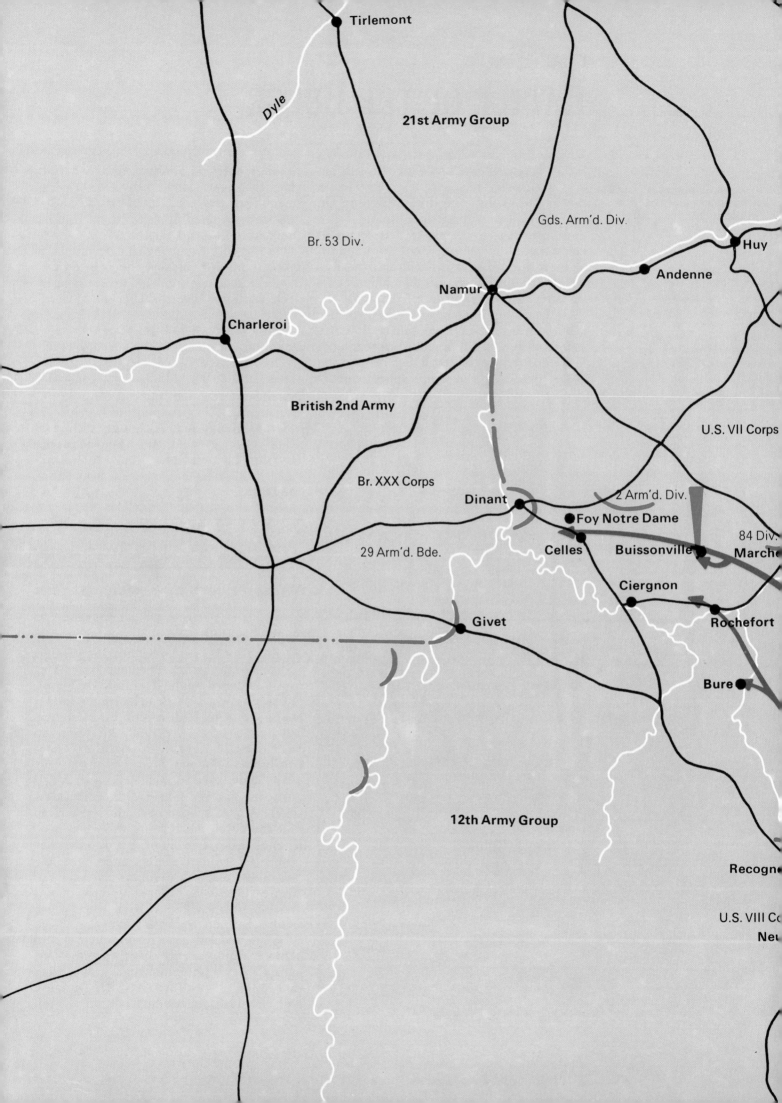

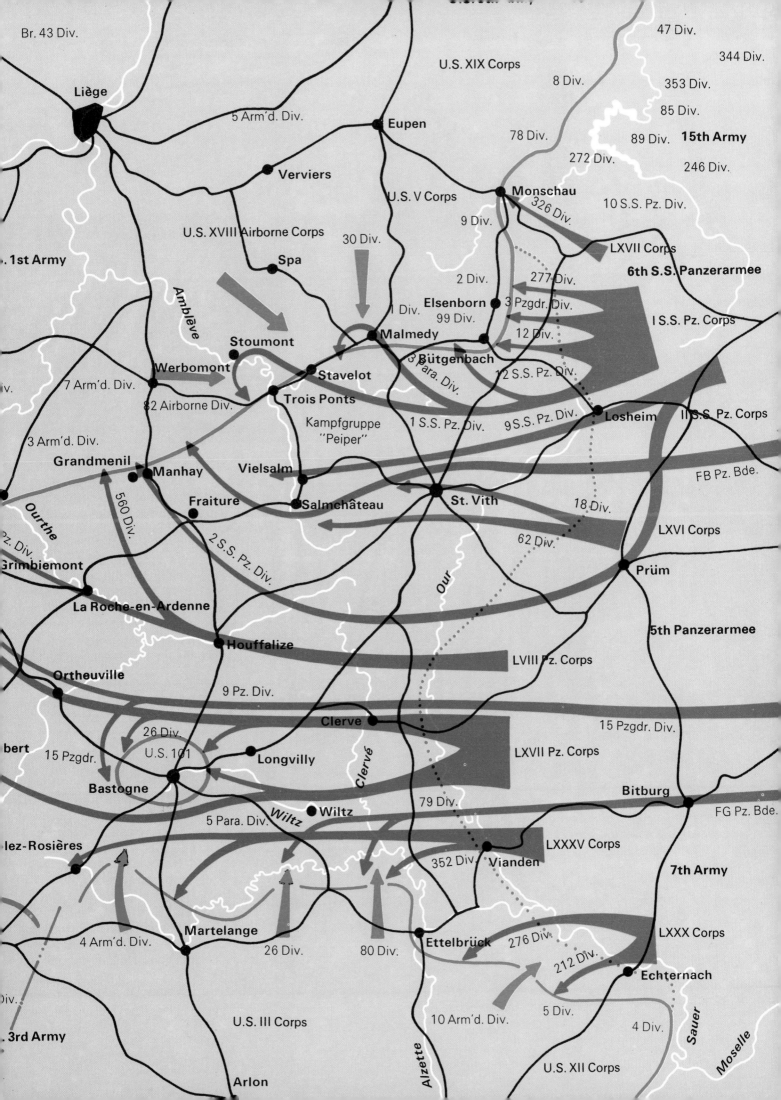

were still in England, but about to embark for France. Even then it would take time for them to come into the line, In addition, although the successes of Skorzeny's commandos and von der Heydte's paratroopers were very slight, rumour greatly magnified them. Above all, the bad weather of that week reduced Allied air strikes almost to nothing. But "low cloud" and "thick fog" were phrases that the weather forecasters repeated with monotonous regularity throughout the week December 16-23.

The Germans waver

In the public mind the Ardennes campaign is summed up in the one word: Bastogne, and rightly so, since Brigadier-General A. C. McAuliffe and his 101st Airborne Division fought heroically around the little town, although the behaviour under fire of the 7th Armoured Division and its commander, Brigadier-General Robert Hasbrook, was also worthy of the highest praise. Between December 18 and 22, the defensive position of Saint Vith compelled the 5th *Panzer-armee* to disperse its energies, and the town was only evacuated after an express order.

It is true that on December 19, in the Schnee Eifel plateau region, two regi-

ments of the 106th Division were trapped, and 6,000 men had to surrender, but everywhere else the Americans stood up gallantly under all the attacks. As Jacques Mordal very rightly says:

"The great merit of the American troops was that despite the surprise and initial disorder, a few commanders and a few handfuls of troops were found who saved the situation by holding on grimly to certain vital positions; and it may be said that rarely has the fate of so many divisions depended on a few isolated engagements. A mere handful of artillerymen firing their few guns saved Bütgenbach on December 16, and prevented the complete isolation of the 2nd and 99th Divisions. A battalion of sappers was to save Malmédy; and a company of the 51st Engineer Combat Battalion stopped the advance of the leading elements of *Kampfgruppe* 'Peiper'. They blew up the Trois-Ponts bridge across the Salm, and forced Peiper to go back via Amblève, and find a further bridge at Werbomont,

Overleaf, top: *Members of Otto Skorzeny's special commando, caught in American uniforms, are brought before a firing squad.* Bottom: *American prisoners are marched off to the rear past a column of advancing German armour. Their faces have been deliberately rendered unrecognisable by a censor.*
◁ *German troops pass a knocked-out American motor transport column.*
▽ ◁ *German soldiers help themselves to clothing and equipment from American dead. Note the bare feet of the corpse on the left.*
▽ *A* Königstiger *or* Tiger II *heavy tank advances through the heavily-forested Ardennes hills.*

where the pioneers of the 291st Battalion fought heroically to prevent his crossing; for the second time the German troops saw a bridge blown up in front of them, and they also suffered losses from air attacks launched in spite of the weather.

"Stavelot, lost on December 17, was recaptured two days later. The battle went on in the sunken valley of the Amblève, where after five days of hard combat, Peiper, out of fuel, was forced to leave behind all his equipment and withdraw the few hundred men remaining on foot, in the snow, and following impossible tracks."

On the German side, Dietrich made the big mistake of stubbornly trying to take the Elsenborn ridge, whose defences had been greatly strengthened by the transfer to General Gerow of that first-class fighting unit, the American 1st Division; thus the 12th *"Hitlerjugend"* S.S. Panzer Division was halted around Bütgenbach. As for the celebrated *"Leibstandarte"*, it became separated from its advanced elements, which had pushed forward into the Amblève valley, on Colonel Peiper's orders. In short, four days after the initial attack, the 6th *Panzerarmee* was still far from the Meuse bridges—which it should have reached within 72 hours.

Bastogne reached

While Dietrich wasted time in attempts to secure the Elsenborn Ridge, Manteuffel displayed more tactical flair. The latter received further help from the fact that General Hodges found it more difficult to reinforce his VIII Corps' elements in Luxembourg than those between Elsenborn and Trois-Points: Clervaux and Wiltz fell easily, and the way to Bastogne was opened up. Faced with this most unexpected development–for after all, it had been thought that Dietrich's forces would have the starring rôle in this offensive–Model and Rundstedt recommended the immediate transfer of II S.S. Panzer Corps from the 5th to the 6th *Panzerarmee,* following the principle that successful operations ought to be exploited in preference to the less successful.

But Hitler refused categorically to allow this transfer; no doubt because he dreaded admitting, even implicitly, the failure of Dietrich and the *Waffen*-S.S., and did not want to place one of the Nazi Party's armed units under the command of the Wehrmacht generals for whom for a long time he felt nothing but mistrust, and even hate.

Had Eisenhower known that his adversary was making this tactical mistake, he would probably have refrained from taking some of the measures which marked his intervention on December 19. But with all his reports from the front indicating that Bastogne and the 101st Airborne Division were practically surrounded, he decided that the time had come to throw all his authority into the struggle. So, at 1100 hours on December 19, he convened a meeting with Bradley and Devers, together with Patton.

Eisenhower decides on his counter-offensive

According to his memoirs, Eisenhower opened the meeting by declaring that "the present situation is to be regarded as one of opportunity for us and not disaster. There will be only cheerful faces at this conference table."

And in fact these confident phrases represented exactly the calm coolness that Eisenhower really felt on that important day. Thus the American historian Ladislas Farago, in his biography of General Patton, which he bases upon numerous unpublished documents and eye-witness accounts, has written:

"The historic Verdun conference of 19th December 1944 was, I submit, one of the high points of Dwight D. Eisenhower's generalship in the war. He was variously described as having been pale and nervous, showing not only signs of the strain but also an intimate kind of concern, as if he worried about his personal future in the aftermath of this crisis. Actually, Ike was in top form, concise and lucid, holding the conference with iron hands to its key issue–the Allied counter-attack. It was obvious to all that he knew what he wanted and was the full master of the situation. He had in full measure that special inner strength which always filled him when he was called upon to make *absolute* decisions."

The main decision taken was to move the six divisions of General Patton's III and XII Corps from the Saar front to the Echternach–Diekirch–Bastogne front, at the same time subordinating VIII Corps to the 3rd Army. This meant that

▽ *The tide begins to turn: a Tiger II tank knocked out during the bitter fighting for the small town of Stavelot.*

the right flank of General Devers's army group would be extended from Bitche to Saarbrücken. Such a manoeuvre had already been discussed at 3rd Army H.Q., so that a single telephone call made from Verdun by its commander was enough to get it started. According to Farago, this order, which meant the moving of 133,178 vehicles over a total of some 1,500,000 miles, was carried out in five days. During this time, the 3rd Army's rear echelons transported 62,000 tons of supplies, the Intelligence staff distributed thousands of maps of the new sector, and the communications section put down 40,000 yards of telephone cable. And all this was achieved in snow and on roads covered with black ice. This proves that Patton may have been a swashbuckler (that very day he said to Bradley: "' Brad, this time the Kraut's stuck his head in the meatgrinder.' With a turn of his fist he added, 'And this time I've got hold of the handle.'"), but he was also a thinker, and an organiser of the highest class. This combination of intellect and dash made Patton unique.

"Act aggressively with our full capabilities"

On December 20, Eisenhower placed Montgomery in charge of the northern flank of the German penetration (with the U.S. 1st and 9th armies under his command), and gave Bradley the southern flank. As he reported to the Combined Chiefs-of-Staff: with the enemy thrusting towards Namur, "our front is divided into two main parts on each of which we must act aggressively and with our full capabilities."

▽ *An American mortar crew in action. With its lightweight and simple construction, the mortar was an ideal infantry weapon.*

Bastogne hangs on

On the morning of December 19, the 101st Division entered Bastogne, joining up with those elements of the 9th and 10th Armoured Divisions defending the town. The next day, XLVII Panzer Corps, following its instructions, by-passed the town to north and south, leaving the 26th *Volksgrenadier* Division the job of laying siege to it. When the commander of this formation, Lieutenant-General Heinz Kokott, called upon General McAuliffe to surrender, he received the rudest of replies: "Nuts". The garrison's high morale was kept up, firstly, by the wholehearted support of the town population under their mayor, Monsieur Jacmin, and secondly by the sound of III Corps' guns announcing the beginning of the counter-attack in the south.

On the northern half of the bulge, an attack by the 30th Division, called by the Germans "Roosevelt's S.S.", enabled Hodges to close up the Amblève valley sector by lengthening the position held by V Corps. However, by sending in II S.S. Panzer Corps to the left of I S.S. Panzer Corps, Dietrich succeeded in re-vitalising the offensive, forcing Hasbrook to evacuate Saint Vith on December 21. The intervention, firstly of XVIII Airborne Corps (although reduced to the 82nd Airborne Division), and secondly, of General Collins's VII Corps, comprising the 75th, 83rd, and 84th Divisions, and the 3rd Armoured Division, enabled a continuous front to be re-established on a line Manhay – Grandmenil – Hotton – Marche.

Montgomery steps in

In carrying out his tasks as commander of the 21st Army Group, Montgomery had a few difficulties with his American subordinates. His main aim was to prevent the Germans from crossing the Meuse, and provided this was done he was not very worried by the loss of a small Ardennes village here or there. He conducted the campaign according to the methods of 1918: plug the gap then, when quite ready, counter-attack. Hodges, Collins, and Ridgeway, on the other hand, hated giving up ground, and wanted to make the enemy feel the weight of their strength. To guard against every eventuality, the meticulous Montgomery established General Horrocks's British XXX Corps, comprising the 43rd, 51st, and 53rd Divisions, and the Guards Armoured Division half-way between Namur and Brussels, thereby greatly facilitating the American 1st Army's movements, which up to December 24, had involved 248,000 men and 48,000 vehicles.

By December 22, at Koblenz, Rundstedt had decided upon immediate withdrawal from the engagement, already running into trouble. Of course, Hitler, at

△ △ *3rd Army infantry advance to the relief of beleaguered Bastogne.*
△ *A soldier of the 3rd Army works his way forward under a barbed wire fence about five miles from Bastogne.*

(page 828) △ *The ruins of St. Vith after its recapture by the U.S. 7th Armoured Division.*
▽ *En route from Hunnange to S. Vith: men of Company C, 23rd Armoured Battalion, 7th Armoured Division.*

Ziegenberg, refused to ratify this suggestion; he thought that if they threw in the O.K.W. reserves, especially the 9th Panzer and 3rd and 15th *Panzergrenadier* Divisions, they would be able to resume the offensive, or at least capture Bastogne, the main thorn in their side.

Allied air power to the fore

On December 23, an anti-cyclone brought with it a week of brilliant sunshine over the whole of the Ardennes front. The Allied air forces were immediately unleashed, flying 2,000 missions on the first day, and 15,000 in the next three days. On Christmas Eve, at a cost of 39 planes lost, 2,000 American bombers, escorted by 900 fighters, attacked the airfields near Frankfurt and the communications networks of Kaiserslautern, Bad Munster, Koblenz, Neuwied, and Euskirchen. At the same time, other air attacks were successfully launched on the enemy's

rear and on certain battlefield objectives. Last, but not least, 961 Dakotas and 61 gliders were able to drop 850 tons of supplies and ammunition to beleaguered Bastogne.

On the darker side, the small town of Malmédy, already in American hands, was twice bombed in error. Whilst the 6th *Panzerarmee* was now exhausted, the 5th managed to advance yet again some 25 miles on a line Saint Hubert–Rochefort–Dinant, moving north-west.

This movement laid bare Patton's left flank, and Eisenhower transferred to the 3rd Army the 87th Division, the 11th Armoured Division, and the 17th Airborne Division. Thus, by December 24, 32 Allied divisions were in action or in reserve on the Ardennes front, against 29 German divisions calculated by S.H.A.E.F. to be involved.

△ *As the weather improved, Allied air power began to play a decisive part in the battle, not only offensively with strikes against German armour, but also defensively with supply drops. Here part of the massive Dakota fleet passes over a Sherman on its way to drop food and ammunition into Bastogne.*
▷ *Men of the U.S. 1st Army dig in on the northern side of the salient driven into the Allied front by the German attack.*
▽ *British troops, who were met by the Germans at the furthest extent of their penetration to the west. The leading Sherman is fitted with a 17-pounder gun, far superior to the more usual 75- and 76-mm guns.*

2nd Panzer Division wiped out

Faced with this further deterioration of the situation, Rundstedt renewed his plea that the offensive be abandoned. He was very strongly supported this time by General Guderian, who knew that in the East, Soviet forces were massing on the Vistula bridge-heads. Once again the Führer refused categorically, in spite of the arguments of his H.Q., only too aware of the disasters that his obstinacy would inevitably bring. In the meantime Lieutenant-General von Lauchert's 2nd Panzer Division had reached Ciney, Beauraing, and Celles, in contact with the British 29th Armoured Brigade, and only six miles from the Meuse at Dinant. On Christmas Day, it suffered a flank attack at the hands of the American 2nd Armoured Division (Major-General Harmon), which had just been transferred to VII Corps. The effect was one of total surprise, and the disaster was no less complete. By the end of the day, Lauchert's losses were as follows: 1,050 prisoners, 2,500 killed, 81 tanks (out of a total of 88), seven assault guns, all his artillery (74 pieces), and 405 vehicles. That day the American 2nd Armoured Division certainly lived up to its nickname of "Hell on Wheels". Confronted with this crushing blow, Manteuffel could only withdraw his XLVII Panzer Corps to Rochefort.

Patton relieves Bastogne

Patton's 3rd Army had a little more difficulty in relieving Bastogne, as the German 5th Parachute Division under Lieutenant-General Hellmann, on the right of the German 7th Army, put up a very spirited resistance. It was not until December 26 that the American 4th Armoured Division under Major-General Gaffey managed to link up with the beleaguered garrison, and even then it was only by means of a narrow corridor a few hundred yards wide.

Half-success into defeat

Faced with these defeats, Hitler disengaged. But was he deceiving himself, or trying to deceive others? On December 28, haranguing his generals who were about to take part in Operation *"Nordwind"*, against the American 7th Army, he pretended to be satisfied with the results of *"Herbstnebel"*:

"There is no doubt that our short offensive has had the initial result of greatly easing the situation along the whole front, although unfortunately it has not had quite the great success we expected. The enemy has been forced to abandon all idea of attack; he has been compelled to regroup his forces completely, and put back into action troops completely worn out by previous engage-

ments. His strategic intentions have been completely thwarted. The psychological factor is against him, for public opinion is bitterly critical. He now has to assert that an end to the fighting cannot be envisaged before August, perhaps before the end of the year. We have therefore a complete reversal of the situation, which was certainly not considered possible a fortnight ago."

What does all this mean? Probably that Hitler would have been far better advised to have taken his head out of the "meatgrinder", when the results were in his favour. However, instead of rapidly withdrawing his 5th and 6th *Panzerarmee* behind the *Westwall,* he insisted

△ *Private Frank Vukasin of Great Falls, Montana, reloads his Garand M1 beside the corpses of two Germans during the 83rd Division's attack towards Houffalize.*

▽ *The bitterness of the fighting for Bastogne can be gauged from this photograph of German dead caught by American machine gun fire after their protecting tanks had been knocked out.*

on their trying to hold the Ardennes salient in impossible conditions, so turning his half-success of December 16 into a clear failure. That this is so is clear from the losses of the two sides: in manpower the Americans had suffered 76,890 casualties to the Germans' 81,834; in tanks 733 to 324; and aircraft 592 to 320. Whereas the Americans could replace their *matériel* losses with little difficulty, the Germans could not.

When one realises that German possibilities of rebuilding the Wehrmacht's strength were slowly diminishing, and that on January 12, 1945 Stalin unleashed his fifth and last winter offensive, there is no doubt that

these figures confirm the German defeat, not only in the Ardennes, but on the whole of the Western Front.

To the despair of Guderian the abandonment of Operation *"Herbstnebel"* did not mean a reinforcement of the Eastern Front forces, for Hitler saw *"Herbstnebel"* as only the first of a set of offensives in the West. The first, aimed at the recovery of Alsace and Lorraine, was propounded by Hitler to his generals on December 18. "Our first objective", he said, "must be to clean up the situation in the West by offensive action."

In this mood of total fantasy, Germany's Supreme Commander brought in the New Year, 1945.

CHAPTER 85

HIMMLER'S OFFENSIVE

Before he could accept the German surrender, the offer of which was to be brought to him at Rheims by a delegation headed by Colonel-General Jodl, General Eisenhower still had to repel two attacks, one directed against his own authority, and the other against the 6th Army Group in lower Alsace.

On December 28, 1944, Eisenhower went to Hasselt, where Montgomery had set up his headquarters. He wanted to go over the plans for future operations with him, to begin as soon as the Ardennes pocket had been nipped off. Eisenhower and Montgomery had no difficulty in reaching agreement on the objective to be set for the offensive they were about

to launch. Both favoured the Ruhr. But Montgomery thought that the "major crisis" that had just been resolved authorised him to adopt the claim he had pressed at the beginning of the preceding August. He wanted control of operations, and he thought himself the more qualified to bear the responsibility since Eisenhower had put the American 1st and 9th Armies under his command. Hence his letter to "Ike", dated December 29. Point 6 of this read:

"I suggest that your directive should finish with this sentence:

"'12 and 21 Army Groups will develop operations in accordance with the above instructions.

△ *General Leclerc (wearing the* képi) *inspects the men and the machines of his French 2nd Armoured Division. After helping in the defence of Strasbourg during Operation* "Nordwind", *the division was moved south as part of the French II Corps for the crushing of the Colmar pocket.*

"'From now onwards full operational direction, control, and co-ordination of these operations is vested in the C.-in-C. 21 Army Group, subject to such instructions as may be issued by the Supreme Commander from time to time.'"

In writing this, Montgomery was disregarding the prudent advice contained in Brooke's letter of December 24 to him:

"I would like to give you a word of warning. Events and enemy action have forced on Eisenhower the setting up of a more satisfactory system of command. I feel it is most important that you should not even in the slightest degree appear to rub this undoubted fact in to anyone at S.H.A.E.F. or elsewhere."

Eisenhower rejected his subordinate's suggestion by return of post. But, even had he not done this on his own initiative, he would have been ordered to do so by General Marshall, who cabled him from Washington on December 30:

"They may or may not have brought to your attention articles in certain London papers proposing a British deputy commander for all your ground forces and implying that you have undertaken too much of a task yourself. My feeling is this: under no circumstances make any concessions of any kind whatsoever. I am not assuming that you had in mind such a concession I just wish you to be certain of our attitude. You are doing a grand job, and go on and give them hell."

The matter would have stopped there if, on January 5, 1945, Montgomery had not given a press conference on the Battle of the Ardennes, which drove the American generals to the limit of exasperation. The text of the conference was published by General Bradley and it can be said that although Montgomery polished his own image and took some pleasure in exaggerating the part played by British forces in the Ardennes, he did not criticise his allies or their leaders in any way.

The crisis reached flashpoint when Bradley informed his old friend Eisenhower that he would ask to be recalled to the United States rather than serve under Montgomery's command. In view of the rumours spread by Goebbels's propaganda services, Churchill thought he ought to step in, which he did in the House of Commons on January 18. His excellent speech made special mention of the all-important part that the U.S. Army had played in the battle and placated everyone.

Besides this, another move of the Prime Minister's contributed to relieving the tension between S.H.A.E.F. and the 21st Army Group. As operations in Italy had slowed down considerably, it was suggested that Alexander was being wasted there. So Eisenhower's deputy, Tedder, was to be recalled to ordinary R.A.F. service, his place being taken by Alexander. Though this compromise did not win Eisenhower's approval, it also came up against Montgomery's decided opposition. If he could not control operations himself, he did not want to see anybody else get the job.

Nevertheless, Montgomery's importunity had brought him within an ace of losing his own job. Only an emollient letter of apology personally from him to Eisenhower, written at the insistence of his Chief-of-Staff "Freddie" de Guingand, prevented a final showdown.

Himmler's offensive

During the night of December 31/January

The German Pzkw VI Tiger II heavy tank

Weight: 68.65 tons.
Crew: 5.
Armament: one 8.8-cm KwK 43 gun with 80 rounds, plus one 7.92-mm MG 42 and two 7.92-mm MG 34 machine guns with 5,850 rounds.
Engine: one Maybach HL 230 P30 inline, 600-hp.
Speed: 25.7 mph on roads and 12 mph cross-country.
Range: 106 miles on roads and 75 miles cross-country.
Length: 33 feet 8 inches.

1, Himmler, as commander of Army Group *"Oberrhein"*, unleashed Operation *"Nordwind"*, giving his troops as objective the Saverne gap. In this way the American 7th Army would be cut in two and its fighting troops in the Bitche–Lauterbourg–Strasbourg salient annihilated. After the fast advance that Patton had been ordered to make on December 19, General Patch had had to extend his left flank as far as Saint Avold and, in the threatened sector, could only field VI Corps against eight German divisions, including the 21st Panzer and the 17th *"Götz von Berlichingen"* S.S. *Panzergrenadier* Divisions.

When he had redeployed as ordered (which stretched the seven divisions of the 7th Army over a front of 90 miles), the commander of the 6th Army Group, General Devers, had naturally been concerned about what to do in the event of a German offensive. In agreement with S.H.A.E.F., he had provided in such an event for his forces to fall back on the eastern slopes of the Vosges and the

Belfort gap. This implied abandoning the plain of Alsace. In the afternoon of January 1, after a telephone call from Eisenhower, he issued the order to begin the movements planned for this eventuality.

de Gaulle disapproves

As Chief-of-Staff to the French Ministry of National Defence, General Juin had been advised since December 28 of the intentions of the 6th Army Group, confirmed by S.H.A.E.F. He had immediately informed General de Gaulle. The latter, seeing the possibility approach, wrote to General Eisenhower on January 1:

"For its part, the French Government cannot allow Strasbourg to fall into enemy hands again without doing everything in its power to defend it."

At the same time, he gave General de Lattre the following order:

"In the event of Allied forces falling

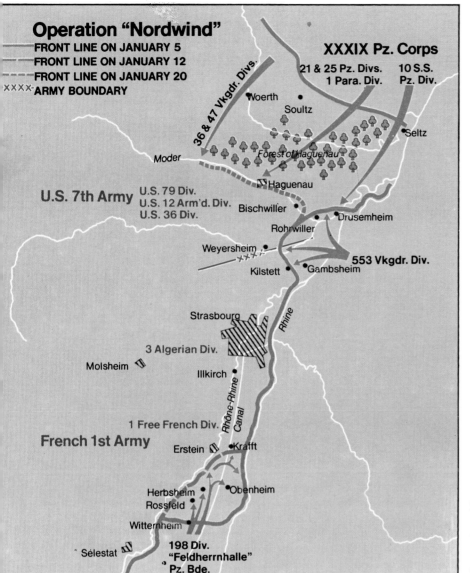

Operation "Nordwind"

FRONT LINE ON JANUARY 5
FRONT LINE ON JANUARY 12
FRONT LINE ON JANUARY 20
XXXX ARMY BOUNDARY

XXXIX Pz. Corps
21 & 25 Pz. Divs.   10 S.S.
1 Para. Div.   Pz. Div.

36 & 47 Vkgdr. Divs.

Woerth
Soultz
Seltz
Moder
Forest of Haguenau
Haguenau

U.S. 7th Army   U.S. 79 Div.
U.S. 12 Arm'd. Div.
U.S. 36 Div.   Bischwiller
Drusemheim
Rohrwiller
Weyersheim
553 Vkgdr. Div.
Kilstett   Gambsheim

Strasbourg   Rhine

3 Algerian Div.
Molsheim
Illkirch

Rhône-Rhine Canal

1 Free French Div.
French 1st Army   Erstein   Krafft

Herbsheim   Obenheim
Rossfeld
Witternheim

Sélestat   198 Div.
"Feldherrnhalle"
Pz. Bde.

△ Operation "Nordwind", Reichsführer-S.S. Heinrich Himmler's ill-advised offensive against Strasbourg.

▷ General de Lattre de Tassigny's proclamation to the citizens of Strasbourg on January 6, 1945. It called for calm and confidence, and pledged the French 1st Army to the successful defence of the city.

◁ Armoured vehicles (in the foreground Stuart light tanks) of the French Foreign Legion parade through the streets of Strasbourg.

◁ △ Strasbourg Cathedral on the day of the city's liberation.

back from their present positions to the north of the French 1st Army, I instruct you to act on your own and take over the defence of Strasbourg."

These letters had gone when General de Gaulle was advised of the order to withdraw that had been circulated by General Devers. On receiving the news, he cabled President Roosevelt and the Prime Minister to make clear that he was opposed to evacuating Strasbourg and he instructed General Juin to express the same opinion at S.H.A.E.F.

The interview between Juin and General Bedell Smith, who met him the next day at S.H.A.E.F., was stormy, as was to be expected from two such plain-spoken men. There were even threats about what would happen if the French 1st Army removed itself from the authority of General Devers. All the same, noted Juin:

"Bedell Smith, who had blanched, nevertheless seemed to want to help and assured me before I left that he would try once more to convince his superior and I secured an interview for General de Gaulle with General Eisenhower the next day."

On receiving the report prepared for him by Juin, de Gaulle once more appealed against the S.H.A.E.F. decision which, he had just learned, affected not only Strasbourg but the entire plain of Alsace. In particular, he wrote to Eisenhower on January 3:

"In any case, I must confirm that the French Government cannot accept that Alsace and a part of Lorraine should be intentionally evacuated without fighting, so to speak, especially since the French Army occupies most of the area. To agree to such an evacuation and in such conditions would be an error from the point of view of the general conduct of the war, which stems not only from the military command, but also from the Allied governments. It would also be a serious error from the French national point of view, to which the government is answerable.

"Therefore I have once more to instruct General de Lattre to use the French forces he has to defend the positions he now occupies and also to defend Strasbourg, even if the American forces on his left withdraw.

"From my point of view, I am extremely sorry that this disagreement has occurred at a serious moment and I should like to hope that we can resolve our differences."

In *Crusade in Europe,* General Eisenhower mentions this incident and writes that:

"At first glance de Gaulle's argument seemed to be based upon political considerations founded more on emotion than on logic and consideration."

This represents the typical reasoning of the American strategist of the time, according to whom a military leader should not consider any objective but the destruction of the enemy's organised forces, without regard for political, geographical, sentimental, or prestige aims. In short, his thought regarding Strasbourg was the same as it had been before Paris the previous summer, and as it would be before Berlin three months later. Nevertheless, against this same point of view, he had to think of the consequences that a Franco-American crisis could have on Allied relations.

Churchill sides with de Gaulle

Churchill had been alerted by de Gaulle and, accompanied by Brooke, travelled to Paris. According to Brooke, they found Eisenhower "most depressed looking" when they walked down the steps from the plane, and it is certain that, at the lunch that followed, the Prime Minister was preaching to one already half-converted. A few hours later, Generals de Gaulle and Juin met Eisenhower, in the presence of Bedell Smith, Churchill, and Brooke, who noted that very evening:

"De Gaulle painted a gloomy picture of the massacres that would ensue if the Germans returned to portions of Alsace-Lorraine. However, Ike had already decided to alter his dispositions so as to leave the divisions practically where they were and not to withdraw the two divisions that were to have been moved up into Patton's reserve."

Juin confirms this: "When General de Gaulle and I arrived at Eisenhower's headquarters at Versailles . . . Churchill was already there. As soon as we came in

he informed us that it was all settled and that Strasbourg would not be abandoned. There was not even any discussion, and the only thing that was decided was that I should go with General Bedell Smith the next day to Vittel to inform General Devers, commanding the 6th Army Group."

Moreover, the tension between Eisenhower and de Gaulle eased so much as soon as this incident was settled that Eisenhower could not restrain himself from confiding to de Gaulle the difficulties he was having with Montgomery.

The battle for Strasbourg

Both on his own initiative and in virtue of the orders he received from Paris, General de Lattre was absolutely determined to hold Strasbourg. And so, on the night of January 2-3, he promptly sent in the solid 3rd Algerian Division, under the command of General du Vigier, recently appointed governor of the city. But, in spite of this, de Lattre intended to remain as long as he could under the control of General Devers and not make difficulties

△ *G.I.s catch up with their mail and with the news while waiting for the German offensive to break on them. Although he at first advocated the abandonment of the plain of Alsace, Eisenhower was at last persuaded by General de Gaulle's political objections to change his mind and order the American 7th Army to hold the Moder line.*

△ *"For whom tolls the bell?"*
"It tolls death for Hitler." And
with the Allies on the Rhine and
Oder, the defeat of the Third
Reich and Hitler's suicide were
only weeks away.

for inter-Allied strategy. That is why, at 2200 hours on January 3, he was very happy to receive the signal announcing that the 6th Army Group had received new orders.

As a result, the American VI Corps, between the Rhine and the Sarre, received orders to continue its retreat only as far as the Moder. But, on January 5, while VI Corps was digging in at this position and the 3rd Algerian Division completed its positions in Strasbourg, the 553rd *Volksgrenadier* Division crossed the Rhine at Gambsheim, between Strasbourg and the confluence of the Moder and Rhine. The next day, it was the turn of the German 19th Army to go over to the offensive, from the Colmar bridgehead. Pressing between the Ill and the Rhône-Rhine Canal, the *"Feldherrnhalle"* Panzer Brigade and the 198th Division managed to get as far as the Erstein heights, less than 13 miles from Strasbourg and 20 from the Gambsheim bridgehead that the 553rd Division had extended as far as the village of Killstett.

Around Strasbourg, attack and counter-attack followed ceaselessly. The Germans had forced the Moder a little above Haguenau and for a short time managed to establish a link with their 553rd Division. However, on January 26, they had definitely lost it again and the battlefield fell silent. O.B. West was very unhappy with the tactics Himmler had used in this offensive, for, instead of wearing down the enemy, he had wasted 11 divisions, four of them of the *Waffen*-S.S., frittering them away in piecemeal actions, ignoring the fact that the barrier of the Rhine prevented him from co-ordinating their movements. All the same, it was General Wiese who paid for the failure of *"Nordwind"*. He received the order to hand over command of the 19th Army to his comrade Rasp. As for Himmler, his flattering promotion to the command of Army Group "Vistula" led, on January 28, to the appointment of Colonel-General Hausser, still recuperating from the wounds he had received during the bloody fighting in the Falaise pocket, to command of Army Group *"Oberrhein"*.

In spite of Operation *"Nordwind"*, on January 15 de Lattre signed his "Personal and Secret Instruction Number 7":

"Leave the Germans no chance of escape. Free Colmar undamaged. The task consists of strangling the pocket alongside the Rhine where it receives its supplies, that is around Brisach.

"Two convergent wedges will be driven in this direction. The first will go northward and will be made by Béthouart's I Corps, which will throw the enemy off balance and suck in his reserves. Then, two days later, II Corps will go into action. This staggering is required by the time it will take to get the expected reserves into place. Its effect will be to increase the surprise of the enemy. Between the two offensive blocs, in the high Vosges, the front will remain inactive at the beginning. It will begin to move when our net along the Rhine is so tightly stretched that the fish is ready to be pulled in."

At this time, Devers and Eisenhower were so concerned about cutting off the Colmar pocket quickly that they did not hesitate to provide substantial reinforcements for the French 1st Army: the U.S. 3rd Division remained under its command, and it also received, though with certain limitations, the 28th Division and the 12th Armoured Division (Major-Generals Norman D. Cota and Roderik R. Allen), as well as the French 2nd Armoured Division under Leclerc, transferred from the Strasbourg area specifically for this purpose.

So, by January 20, 1945, the forces available to de Lattre amounted to 12 divisions, four of which were armoured. However, it should be pointed out that the 3rd Algerian Division was still engaged in and around Killstett and did not take part in the battle of Colmar and that, in the high Vosges, the newly-created 10th Division (General Billotte) was restricted to the modest rôle described above.

The German defence

Facing these forces along the 100-mile long Alsace bridgehead, the German 19th Army deployed its LXIV and LXIII Corps north and south under the command, respectively, of General Thumm and Lieutenant-General Abraham. The two corps had seven infantry or mountain divisions and the 106th *"Feldherrnhalle"* Panzer Brigade. But these forces were threadbare. Including the reinforcements attached to them, the best-equipped (the 198th Division: Colonel Barde) had exactly 6,891 men in the line, and the 716th *Volksgrenadier* Division (Colonel Hafner) had only 4,546. Furthermore, although de Lattre complained about not receiving all the supplies he thought he needed, by the eighth day of battle General Rasp was reduced to ordering strict economy to his gunners: 12 15-cm and 15 10.5-cm shells per day per gun, compared with 90 155-mm and 120 105-mm shells in the French 1st Army.

Terrain, weather, tanks

Three circumstances, however, compensated a little for the numerical and *matériel* inferiority of the defenders:

1. the terrain, which was no more than "a network of streams and rivers" according to de Lattre. Within it are many woods and even more villages, among which should be mentioned the manufacturing and industrial towns of the Mulhouse region;

2. the weather. On the first day, I Corps attacked LXIII Corps in the face of a snowstorm blowing from the northeast. At night, the temperature fell to 20 and even 25 degrees Centigrade below zero. Finally, just when German resistance was softening, an unexpected rise in the temperature swelled the rivers and made the roads into sloughs of mud; and

3. though far less numerous, the Panther tanks and *"Jagdpanther"* and *"Nashorn"* tank destroyers, with their very high velocity 8.8-cm guns, were far superior to the French 1st Army's Sherman tanks and M10 tank destroyers. This superiority was emphasised by the German vehicles' wide tracks, which allowed them to manoeuvre on the snow in weather conditions with which their opponents were not able to cope.

At 0700 hours on January 20, H-hour sounded for the reinforced I Corps. Its task was to break the enemy line between Thann and the Forest of Nünenbruck, to capture Cernay, and then to push on without stopping towards Ensisheim and Réguisheim on the Ill. For this purpose, over a 14-mile front, Béthouart had the 9th Colonial Division (General Morlière) around Mulhouse, the 2nd Moroccan Division (General Carpentier) in the centre, and the 4th Moroccan Mountain Division (General de Hesdin) around Thann. In spite of the support of the tanks of the 1st Armoured Division (General Sudre), the attempt to break the enemy lines towards Cernay was not very successful, both because of the tough resistance

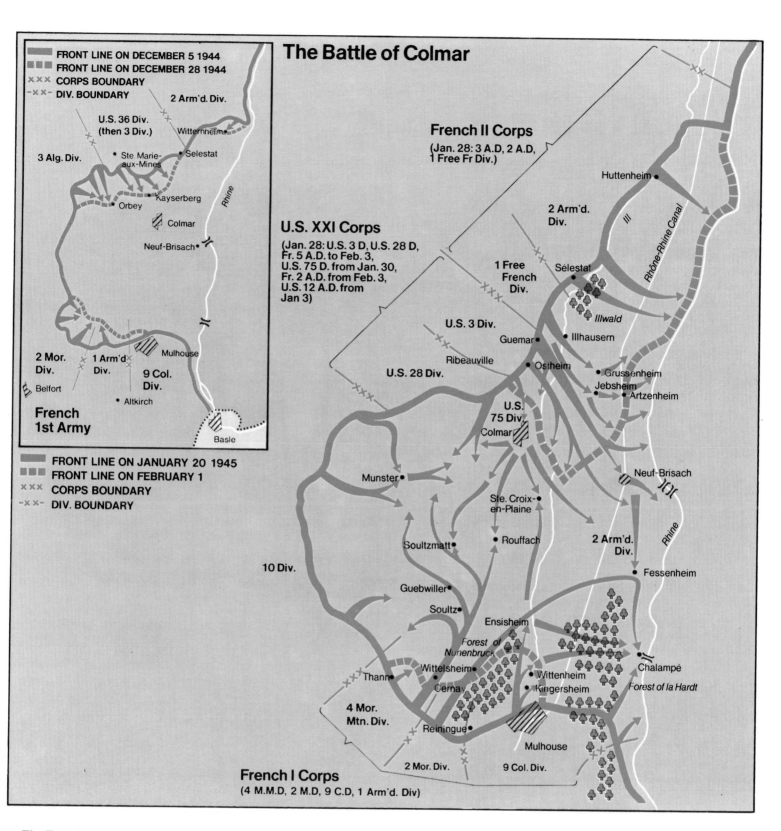

The Battle of Colmar

Inset map legend:

━━━ FRONT LINE ON DECEMBER 5 1944
▪▪▪ FRONT LINE ON DECEMBER 28 1944
××× CORPS BOUNDARY
-×× - DIV. BOUNDARY

2 Arm'd. Div.

U.S. 36 Div. (then 3 Div.)

Witternheim

3 Alg. Div.

Ste. Marie-aux-Mines

Sélestat

Rhine

Kayserberg

Orbey

Colmar

Neuf-Brisach

2 Mor. Div.

1 Arm'd. Div.

Mulhouse

Belfort

9 Col. Div.

Altkirch

French 1st Army

Basle

━━━ FRONT LINE ON JANUARY 20 1945
▪▪▪ FRONT LINE ON FEBRUARY 1
××× CORPS BOUNDARY
-×× - DIV. BOUNDARY

French II Corps
(Jan. 28: 3 A.D, 2 A.D, 1 Free Fr Div.)

Huttenheim

2 Arm'd. Div.

U.S. XXI Corps
(Jan. 28: U.S. 3 D, U.S. 28 D,
Fr. 5 A.D. to Feb. 3,
U.S. 75 D. from Jan. 30,
Fr. 2 A.D. from Feb. 3,
U.S. 12 A.D. from
Jan 3)

1 Free French Div.

Sélestat

Illwald

Rhône-Rhine Canal

Ill

U.S. 3 Div.

Guemar

Illhausern

Ribeauville

Ostheim

Grussenheim

Jebsheim

Artzenheim

U.S. 28 Div.

U.S. 75 Div.

Colmar

Neuf-Brisach

Munster

Ste. Croix-en-Plaine

2 Arm'd. Div.

Rhine

Rouffach

Fessenheim

Soultzmatt

10 Div.

Guebwiller

Soultz

Ensisheim

Forest of Nünenbruck

Chalampé

Forest of la Hardt

Wittelsheim

Thann

Wittenheim

Kingersheim

Cernay

4 Mor. Mtn. Div.

Reiningue

Mulhouse

2 Mor. Div.

9 Col. Div.

French I Corps
(4 M.M.D, 2 M.D, 9 C.D, 1 Arm'd. Div)

△ *The French 1st Army's battle to eliminate the German 19th Army's pocket around Colmar.*

◁ *A mine explodes in the path of an M10 tank destroyer of a French armoured division. These French formations had been equipped with the latest American equipment.*

met, aided by well-sited minefields, and because of the snowstorms which made artillery observation impossible.

On the other hand, the secondary attack, which had been entrusted to the 9th Colonial Division, took the villages of Burtzwiller, Illzach, Kingersheim, Pfastadt, and Lutterbach, a remarkable success due to the dash with which General Salan had led the infantry.

On the following day, LXIII Corps counter-attacked and, on January 22, with the storm blowing worse than ever, General Béthouart expressed the opinion that they should wait for it to blow itself out. But any let-up on the part of I Corps would have prejudiced the attack of II Corps, which was just finishing its preparations. So Béthouart was ordered to press on with his attack, and a fierce, bitter struggle was waged close to Wittelsheim, in the Forest of Nünenbruck, and for the factory towns with their potassium deposits. These towns had to be cleared one by one.

The Colmar pocket wiped out

On January 23, II Corps, still under the command of General G. de Monsabert, forced a second wedge into the German line. This was achieved with more ease than the first, even though General Rasp had got wind of the French plans.

On the right, the American 3rd Division had taken Ostheïm. On the left, the 1st Free French Division had fought bitterly to capture the village of Illhausern and had formed a bridgehead on the right bank of the Ill, thus preparing to outflank Colmar to the north. But LXIV Corps stiffened its resistance and counterattacked, preventing Monsabert from any swift exploitation of his success towards Neuf-Brisach. LXIII Corps was likewise preventing Béthouart from moving on. Hidden in the woods, or even inside houses, the Panzers exacted a heavy toll from the men of the 2nd and 5th Armoured Divisions, supporting the infantry. However, on January 27, the U.S. 3rd Division reached the Colmar Canal, while General Garbay's 1st Free French Division, reinforced by Colonel Faure's paratroops, took the villages of Jebsheim and Grussenheim. Seeing how serious the situation had become, O.K.W. authorised Rasp to pull the 198th Division back over the Rhine, i.e. to give up all the ground won between Rhinau and Erstein by the attack of January 7.

Wishing to press on and complete the attack, General Devers, at the request of the commander of the French 1st Army, put XXI Corps (Major-General Frank W. Milburn) under his command, as well as the U.S. 75th Division (Major-General Porter). Milburn, who from this time on commanded all the American forces involved in the offensive, and the French 5th Armoured Division, was ordered to position his forces between Monsabert's II Corps and Billotte's 10th Division, and then push on towards Neuf-Brisach and also south towards Ensisheim to meet Béthouart. The offensive began again. In the evening of January 30, after a terrifying artillery bombardment of 16,438 105-mm and 155-mm shells,

the United States 3rd Division (Major-General O'Daniel) succeeded in crossing the Colmar Canal, and this allowed the United States 28th Division to advance as far as the suburbs of Colmar. The division did not enter Colmar itself, for at the gates of the city, which had been left intact, General Norman D. Cota was courteous enough to give that honour to his comrade-in-arms Schlesser, commanding the 4th Combat Command (5th Armoured Division).

Medieval assault

The United States 12th Armoured Division sped south to exploit its victory, with the intention of linking up with I Corps, which had taken Ensisheim, Soultz, and Guebwiller on February 4 and then pushed both the 1st Armoured Division and 4th Moroccan Mountain Division forward.

The next day, French and American forces linked up at Rouffach and Sainte Croix-en-Plaine. Twenty-four hours later, in the light of searchlights shining towards the night sky, General O'Daniel's infantry "scaled" the ramparts of Neuf-Brisach in the best mediaeval style. Lastly, at 0800 hours on February 9, a deafening explosion told the men of the French 1st and 2nd Armoured Divisions, who were mopping-up the Forest of la Hardt, together with the 2nd Moroccan Division, that the Germans had just blown the Chalampé bridge, on the Mulhouse–Freiburg road, behind them as they pulled back over the Rhine.

△ *An M3 half-track of the French 1st Army moves into Colmar on February 2, 1945.*

▽ *General Emile Béthouart, commander of the French I Corps. Operating on the south side of the Colmar pocket, his troops initially had a very hard time of it, and Béthouart wished to call off his attack. But de Lattre ordered him to press on regardless so that German forces would not be able to switch to the northern sector, where General de Monsabert's II Corps was about to launch its offensive.*

Despite the fact that Luzon, the "capital island" of the Philippines, was the largest Japanese-held island between New Guinea and Tokyo, the American planners had by no means been unanimous in the opinion that it should be recaptured. Admirals King and Nimitz had argued that it would be better, once a foothold had been established in the Philippines with the capture of Leyte and Mindanao, to by-pass Luzon and go straight for Formosa. General MacArthur was the passionate champion of the liberation of all the Philippine islands before making the next advance towards Japan. When it was decided to invade Leyte in October 1944 – two months ahead of the original schedule – MacArthur announced that he would be ready to invade Luzon by the end of December, giving the 20th as a provisional date. This was so much in advance of the earliest possible date by which an invasion force could be deployed for an assault on Formosa that it was decided – a fortnight before the troops went in on Leyte – to invade Luzon.

MacArthur was forced to postpone the date for the Luzon landing by the slow progress of the battle for Leyte. Here the American forces were bedevilled by sluicing autumnal rains, which converted the island battlefield into a quagmire. By the end of November the Luzon attack had been put back to the second week of January: the 9th. In addition, it was decided to capture the island of Mindoro as a curtain-raiser to the main landing on Luzon. This would mean that the Luzon force would not have to rely on the flooded airfields on Leyte – apart from the fleet aircraft-carriers – to provide air cover for the landings. Mindoro, right on Luzon's doorstep, would provide excellent "front-line" airstrips for round-the-clock operations; and its capture was entrusted to a specially-formed unit known as the Western Visayan Task Force. Consisting of two reinforced regiments under the command of Brigadier-General William C. Dunckel, it was to attack on December 15, while the struggle for Leyte was still moving to its close.

During the three-day voyage from Leyte to Mindoro the ships of the Task Force had to endure heavy *kamikaze* attacks; the flagship *Nashville* was badly damaged by a *kamikaze*, and Dunckel himself was wounded (though he was able to stay in command). But the Mindoro landing went in according to plan on the morning of the 15th. It was unopposed; Dunckel's men

CHAPTER 86

LUZON

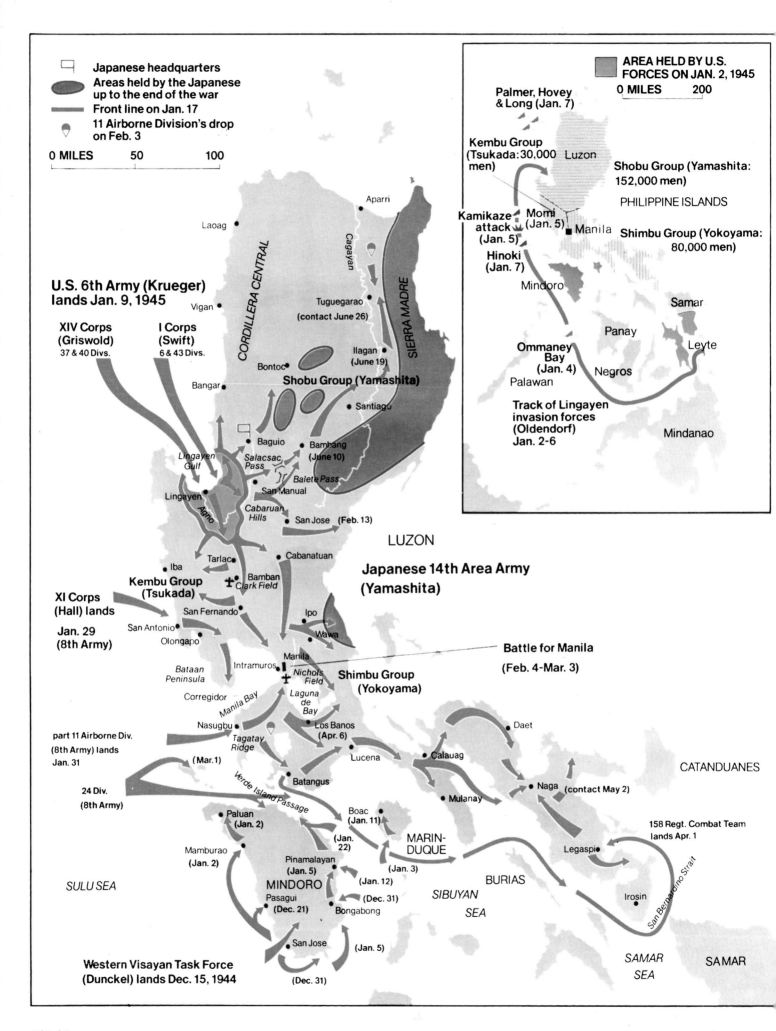

Legend

⌐	Japanese headquarters
⬭	Areas held by the Japanese up to the end of the war
—	Front line on Jan. 17
⬩	11 Airborne Division's drop on Feb. 3

0 MILES 50 100

AREA HELD BY U.S. FORCES ON JAN. 2, 1945

0 MILES 200

Palmer, Hovey & Long (Jan. 7)

Kembu Group (Tsukada: 30,000 men)

Luzon

Shobu Group (Yamashita: 152,000 men)

PHILIPPINE ISLANDS

Kamikaze attack (Jan. 5)

Momi (Jan. 5)

Manila

Hinoki (Jan. 7)

Shimbu Group (Yokoyama: 80,000 men)

Mindoro

Ommaney Bay (Jan. 4)

Palawan

Samar

Panay

Leyte

Negros

Track of Lingayen invasion forces (Oldendorf) Jan. 2-6

Mindanao

Aparri

Laoag

U.S. 6th Army (Krueger) lands Jan. 9, 1945

Vigan

CORDILLERA CENTRAL

Cagayan

SIERRA MADRE

XIV Corps (Griswold) 37 & 40 Divs.

I Corps (Swift) 6 & 43 Divs.

Tuguegarao (contact June 26)

Ilagan (June 19)

Bontoc

Shobu Group (Yamashita)

Bangar

Santiago

Lingayen Gulf

Baguio

Bambang (June 10)

Salacsac Pass

Balete Pass

Lingayen

San Manual

Agno

Cabaruan Hills

San Jose (Feb. 13)

Iba

Tarlac

Cabanatuan

LUZON

Japanese 14th Area Army (Yamashita)

Kembu Group (Tsukada)

Bamban
Clark Field

XI Corps (Hall) lands

Jan. 29 (8th Army)

San Fernando

San Antonio

Olongapo

Ipo

Wawa

Bataan Peninsula

Intramuros

Manila

Nichols Field

Battle for Manila

(Feb. 4-Mar. 3)

Corregidor

Shimbu Group (Yokoyama)

Manila Bay

Laguna de Bay

part 11 Airborne Div. (8th Army) lands Jan. 31

Nasugbu

Los Banos (Apr. 6)

Daet

Tagatay Ridge

(Mar. 1)

Lucena

Calauag

CATANDUANES

24 Div. (8th Army)

Batangus

Verde Island Passage

Naga (contact May 2)

Mulanay

Paluan (Jan. 2)

Boac (Jan. 11)

MARIN-DUQUE

158 Regt. Combat Team lands Apr. 1

Mamburao (Jan. 2)

(Jan. 22)

Pinamalayan (Jan. 5)

(Jan. 3)

Legaspi

SULU SEA

MINDORO

(Jan. 12)

BURIAS

Pasagui (Dec. 21)

(Dec. 31)

Bongabong

SIBUYAN SEA

Irosin

San Bernardino Strait

San Jose

(Jan. 5)

SAMAR SEA

SAMAR

Western Visayan Task Force (Dunckel) lands Dec. 15, 1944

(Dec. 31)

pegged out a large beach-head with no difficulty and work on the airstrips began at once, while the interior was still being mopped up. By December 23 two new airstrips were already in use on Mindoro and the build-up of aircraft for the Luzon attack could begin. To use MacArthur's own words, "Mindoro was the gate": the turn of Luzon had come.

Yamashita's problems

On paper, the Japanese force which would defend Luzon looked a formidable one: over 250,000 men of the 14th Area Army, commanded by General Tomoyuki Yamashita. But in fact Yamashita's prospects were not bright, and he knew it very well. Most of his units were under-strength and short of supplies. The virtual elimination of the Japanese Combined Fleet at Leyte Gulf meant that he would be getting no more supplies by sea. And the air battles during the prolonged fight for Leyte had whittled down the number of operational aircraft on Luzon to around 150. These would have no chance of halting the

American invasion force as it approached Luzon, let alone of commanding the skies over the land battlefield. Yamashita knew that his troops would not be able to stop the invaders getting ashore, and that he did not have sufficient men to defend the whole of Luzon.

In total contrast was the strength of the American forces. They were organised in the fashion which had launched the attack on Leyte. The land fighting was entrusted to General Walter Krueger's 6th Army – over 200,000 men, exclusive of reinforcements – which would be conveyed to its destination and shielded on landing by Vice-Admiral Thomas C. Kinkaid's 7th Fleet. The 7th Fleet – over 850 vessels strong – included the battle fleet, under Vice-Admiral Jessie B. Oldendorf, which had smashed Nishimura's battle squadron in the Surigao Strait during the battle of Leyte Gulf, and which was now to spearhead the invasion of Luzon by bombarding the landing beaches. Admiral William F. Halsey's 3rd Fleet would provide strategic air cover by launching carrier strikes on northern Luzon and Formosa, and land-based air cover would be the contribution of General George F.

◁ *American operations to clear Luzon.*
△ *A column of American amphibian tanks pauses along a road on Luzon. Despite the glum expression on the face of the Filipino at left, the original war-time caption enthuses "... natives greet the tanks and assure them that although their village was destroyed, they would much rather have the Americans than the plundering Japs".*

Kenney's Far East Air Forces, which would begin the battle from their bases on Leyte and Mindoro.

Bombardment and assault

It was obvious to both sides where the invasion must be directed: across the superb beaches of Lingayen Gulf, which was where the Japanese had landed their main forces in December 1941. Lingayen Gulf leads directly into the central plain of Luzon, to Manila and the magnificent anchorage of Manila Bay.

Yamashita was not going to attempt to meet the invaders on the beaches, nor offer them a set-piece battle once ashore. He grouped his forces in three major concentrations which, he hoped, would confine the Americans to the central plain. Yamashita's strategy, in short, was very like Rommel's attempts to "rope off" the Allies in the Normandy *bocage* after D-Day. But—as events in Normandy had already proved conclusively—the most

dogged defence was not likely to hold out for long against an invader with control of the air and uninterrupted supplies and reinforcements from the sea.

On January 2, 1945, the first ships of Oldendorf's bombardment force headed out of Leyte Gulf, their destination Lingayen. A punishing ordeal lay ahead of them, for they became the prime targets for Luzon-based *kamikaze* attacks which began on the 4th, while Oldendorf's force was still threading its way through the Sulu Sea. On that day a twin-engined *kamikaze* crashed into the escort carrier *Ommaney Bay*, damaging her so badly that she was beyond salvation and had to be sunk. On the 5th the American force was well within reach of the Japanese airfields on Luzon—under 150 miles—and the *kamikaze* attacks rose in pitch. In the afternoon, while the Americans were passing the mouth of Manila Bay, 16 *kamikazes* broke through the American air screen and attacked, inflicting damage on nearly a dozen American and Australian ships, including two escort carriers, two heavy cruisers, and two destroyers. Nor were

the Japanese attacks confined to aircraft alone; two Japanese destroyers appeared, but were seen off in short order. Air strikes from the escort carriers sank one, *Momi,* and damaged the other.

On January 6 Oldendorf's ships entered Lingayen Gulf and began to move into position for the bombardment – and the *kamikaze* attacks reached their climax. The weather was working for the Japanese. A low, dense overcast blanketed the airfields on northern Luzon, preventing Halsey's pilots from masking them with continuous patrols. Bad weather meant nothing to the Japanese pilots – except that their chances of immolating themselves on their targets were enhanced. By nightfall on the 7th two American battleships – *New Mexico* and *California* – three cruisers, three destroyers, and several other vessels had been more or less badly damaged, and three of them, fast minesweepers (*Palmer, Long,* and *Hovey*), sunk. But this was the last great effort of the *kamikazes* of Luzon. On the 7th, Halsey's planes battered the Luzon airfields so heavily that the last operational Japanese aircraft were withdrawn from the Philippines.

Oldendorf's ships had played an invaluable rôle in soaking up the punishment which might otherwise have savaged the troop transports and landing-craft bringing the invasion force. Now they went ahead with their bombardment programme, which raged for the next three days. Early on the morning of January 9 the troop convoys moved into Lingayen Gulf. At 0700 hours the final stage of the pre-landing barrage was opened and at 0900 the first wave of landing-craft headed in to the beaches. Shortly after 0930 the spearhead troops were ashore – but there were no Japanese troops to meet them. Yamashita had pulled back all his forces not only from the beaches but from the immediate hinterland, with the result that by nightfall on the 9th Krueger's army had established for itself a beach-head 17 miles wide, which reached four miles inland at its deepest extremities. And, true to form, MacArthur himself had landed in triumph, duly captured for

▽ *The build-up of equipment on Luzon continues – bulldozers and cranes roll ashore over a pontoon quay. Clearing obstacles from the main routes across the island and rubble from city streets was as important a task for these back-up forces as repairing and extending runways for aircraft.*
Overleaf:
Above: *Troops from Blue Beach Lingayen Gulf, fan out into the interior of Luzon island. Early resistance was light, thanks to the massive bombardment mounted by sea and air.*
Below: *The still-smouldering bodies of Japanese soldiers killed by a flame-thrower. They were among 23 flushed out of their foxhole by men of the 25th Infantry Division.*

posterity by the camera.

The 6th Army punch was a two-corps affair. On the right flank was Major-General Oscar W. Griswold with XIV Corps, consisting of the 37th and 40th Infantry Divisions. Griswold's corps had the task of breaking through to Manila and liberating the capital, a task obviously dear to MacArthur's heart. But before this could be done the left flank of the lodgment area had to be made secure from any heavy counter-attacks from the north, and this was the job of Major-General Innis P. Swift's I Corps (the 6th and 43rd Infantry Divisions). Until Swift had made the left flank secure, Krueger was going to take his time about pushing on to Manila—and he was wise to do so. For Swift's corps was faced by the "Shobu" Group, the largest of Yamashita's three concentrations, 152,000-men strong and well dug in along a chain of strongpoints 25 miles long, from Lingayen Gulf to the Cabaruan Hills. Foul weather on the 10th, ramming home the vulnerability of the landing beaches by causing considerable disruption, made it clear that Swift's task was of vital importance. But his progress against the tough Japanese defences remained slow, much to MacArthur's chagrin. Not until the end of the month did I Corps, reinforced with the 25th and 32nd Divisions, push the Japanese back into the mountains after a tank battle at San Manuel on the 28th. They reached the approaches to Yamashita's H.Q. at Baguio and drove east through San Jose to reach the eastern shore of Luzon, pushing a corridor across the island. This now cut off Yamashita from his troops in the island's centre and south.

Griswold and XIV Corps met with scanty opposition as they began their advance to the south. By the 16th they were across the Agno river, still with little or no opposition—but Krueger was yet unwilling to push too far ahead in the south until he was convinced that the northern flank was secure. But on January 17 MacArthur intervened, stressing the need for an immediate drive on Manila. There were plenty of good reasons. The Americans needed the port; they needed the airfield complex at Clark Field for Kenney's planes; and they were anxious to liberate the inmates of military and civilian prison camps before the Japanese had time to harm them further. But now Griswold's corps in its turn came up against the second of Yamashita's defensive concentrations.

Battle for Manila

The second part of Yamashita's forces that the American troops encountered on Luzon was the "*Kembu*" Group, 30,000 men under Major-General Rikichi Tsukada, stationed in the mountains west of the central plain of Luzon to defend the Clark Field sector. Griswold's corps first encountered heavy opposition from the "*Kembu*" Group at the town of Bamban on January 23. It took over a week of extremely heavy fighting before XIV Corps forced the Japanese back from Clark Field. By January 31 the "*Kembu*" Group had lost over 2,500 men and had been forced to retreat into the mountains; the Clark Field complex was in American hands and Griswold was able to resume his drive on Manila.

In the last days of January, two more American units landed on Luzon. The first was XI Corps, commanded by Major-General Charles P. Hall, consisting of the 38th Infantry Division and a regiment of the 24th Division. It landed on the west coast of the island to the north of the Bataan Peninsula, and its mission was to capture the Olongapo naval base and drive across the root of the Bataan Peninsula to Manila Bay. Unlike MacArthur in 1942, Yamashita refused to run the risk of getting any of his troops trapped on Bataan, but Hall's corps had two weeks of tough fighting before it reached Manila Bay. The second landing went in south of the bay at Nasugbu, 50 miles south-west of Manila. It was made by the bulk of the 11th Airborne Division; the plan was to tie down Japanese troops in southern Luzon and open up a second approach route to the capital. On February 3 the rest of the division dropped inland, on Tagaytay Ridge; the division concentrated and moved north-east towards Manila, but was stopped on the outskirts.

It was clear that if Manila was to be taken it would have to be from the north. Once again the impetus came from MacArthur. "Go to Manila!" he urged on January 30. "Go around the Nips, bounce off the Nips, but go to Manila!" His exhortations went right down the line of Griswold's corps to the two divisions which would do the job: the 37th Infantry and the newly-arrived 1st Cavalry.

Their main concern and objective was the big civilian internment camp at Santo Tomas, which was liberated on February 3 by a "flying column" of tanks from the 1st Cavalry. The prisoners in Santo Tomas were in an unenviable position, hearing the sounds of a tough battle outside the walls and fearing the worst until an unmistakable American bellow of "Where the hell's the front gate?" was followed by 1st Cavalry tanks smashing through the entrance. Hard on the heels of 1st Cavalry came the 37th Infantry, which pushed through to Old Bilibid Prison and liberated 1,300 civilian internees and P.O.W.s. The northern suburbs of Manila were in American hands. But the battle for the city was only beginning.

In 1942 MacArthur had declared Manila an open city rather than turn it into a battlefield, and Yamashita had no intention of fighting for the city in 1945. But there were 17,000 fighting men in Manila over whom he had no control—they were not Army troops. They were naval forces under the command of Rear-Admiral Sanji Iwabachi, who was determined to hold Manila to the last. He split his men into separate battle groups, gave each of them a section of the city to defend, and prepared for an all-out battle. A unique episode was about to be added to the history of the Pacific war: its only urban battle.

The Americans took some time to realise what lay before them, but a week of vicious fighting and rapidly-mounting casualties forced them to accept that there could be no question of taking Manila without cracking the Japanese out of their positions at the expense of the city's buildings. By the 12th, XIV Corps had forced the Japanese in front of them back into Intramuros, the old walled inner city of Manila. South of the city the paratroopers of the 11th Airborne Division had run up against tough defensive positions built by the Japanese sailors on Nichols Field. Here, too, an inch-by-inch struggle developed, with the paratroopers getting artillery support from the guns of XIV Corps to the north. It was an unrelieved killing-match, eliciting a grim signal from one of 11th Airborne's company commanders: "Tell Halsey to stop looking for the Jap Fleet; it's dying on Nichols Field."

Even after the 11th Airborne joined hands with 1st Cavalry on February 12,

the battle for Manila was far from over. Iwabachi's sailors held on grimly both in Intramuros and the rest of the city and over a fortnight of murderous fighting lay ahead. It was given a fresh element of horror by the fact that the Japanese refused to evacuate non-combatants, and it went on until the very last flickers of Japanese resistance were stamped out on March 3. MacArthur's obsession with the recapture of Manila had exacted a terrible price. The Filipino capital lay in ruins. Civilian casualties have been set as high as 100,000. American losses topped 1,000 killed and 5,500 wounded. As for the Japanese defenders of Manila, they had upheld the fighting traditions of the Imperial Japanese Navy by dying virtually to a man.

While the slaughter in Manila was still running its course, the clearing of the island forts in Manila Bay had begun. First came the overrunning of the Bataan Peninsula by XI Corps, begun on the 14th and aided by a landing at Mariveles, at

the tip of the peninsula, on the following day. It only took a week to flush the scanty Japanese forces out of their positions on Bataan; compared with the carnage in Manila it was an easy task.

Corregidor, the strongest fortress in Manila Bay, was a different story. In May 1942 the American garrison had capitulated within 48 hours of the first Japanese landings on the island. In 1945 it took over ten days of bitter fighting before the Americans got the island back. Their assault went in on February 16, a combined parachute drop and amphibious landing which rapidly gained control of the surface defences. But the Japanese still had to be flushed from their positions underground, and the island was not declared secure until the 28th. MacArthur himself visited Corregidor on March 2. Ready as always with a memorable *bon mot*, he announced: "I see that the old flagpole still stands. Have your troops hoist the colours to its peak and let no enemy ever haul them down."

The three smaller forts in the Bay remained. On Caballo and El Fraile, horrible measures were taken to break the resistance of the Japanese when they refused to surrender. Diesel oil was pumped into their positions and ignited with phosphorus shells and fused T.N.T.; Caballo was cleared on April 13, El Fraile on the 18th. The Japanese evacuated the third island, Canabao, and the Americans encountered no resistance when they landed there on April 16.

Three months after the first American landings in Lingayen Gulf the Japanese had been forced out of central Luzon, the capital had been liberated, and Manila Bay was clear to Allied shipping. But still the battle for Luzon was far from over. Yamashita still had 172,000 Japanese troops under arms. They held the north and south-east of the island; Manila itself was still within range of Japanese guns, and the dams and reservoirs containing the bulk of the capital's water supplies were still in Japanese hands.

Pilots of the 201st Mexican Fighter Squadron line up in front of their P-47's on Clark Field, Luzon, in July 1945.

△ *The only street fighting of the Pacific war took place in Manila, capital of the Philippines. G.I.s pass through still smoking ruins in the city's suburbs.*

▷△ *and* ▷▷ *Bombing Japanese air power into oblivion. Clark Field was under almost constant attack by both bombers and fighters. In both pictures "parafrag" bombs–fragmentation bombs released by parachute–can be seen hitting the airfield.*

Moreover, the Japanese still controlled the most direct sea route through the central Philippines, forcing any Allied shipping heading west for Manila to take an expensive 500-mile detour. Until these problems had been solved and Yamashita's forces had been ground down to total impotence, there could be no question of taking the next step towards Tokyo. The last stage of the battle for Luzon began.

The most urgent problem facing the 6th Army was the big Japanese concentration east of Manila. This was the *"Shimbu"* Group, under the command of Lieutenant-General Shizuo Yokoyama: 80,000-odd troops, based on the 8th and 105th Divisions. The bulk of the *"Shimbu"* Group, 30,000 strong, was dug in along the southern end of the Sierra Madre range along the line Ipo Dam–Wawa Dam–Antipolo, extending south to the great lake of Laguna de Bay. Griswold and XIV Corps launched the first determined narrow-front attack against this strong position on March 8, following two days of intense softening-up by Kenney's bombers. By the 12th, the 1st Cavalry Division had battered its way through the maze of fiercely-defended Japanese cave defences and was

relieved on the 13th by the 43rd Division, which kept up the pressure and, in conjunction with 6th Division, punched deep into the centre of the *"Shimbu"* Group's line. On the 14th, General Hall's XI Corps relieved Griswold on this front and continued the offensive. By the end of March, the 43rd Division had struggled through to the east side of Laguna de Bay and had completely unhinged Yokoyama's left.

Further to the north, however, the 6th Division failed in its drive to capture Wawa and Ipo Dams. It took the whole of April, in the face of implacable Japanese resistance, for the 6th Division to struggle forward into position for a final assault. By this time the successes in the south enabled the 43rd Division to be switched north to add more weight to the next attack.

This was heralded by three days of saturation bombing which dumped 250,000 gallons of napalm on the Japanese positions. The attack proper was launched on the night of May 6 by the 43rd Division. In this battle the American forces were aided to the north by 3,000 Filipino guerrillas, who kept Yokoyama's left flank fully engaged. At last, on May 17, joint Ameri-

can and Filipino attacks seized Ipo Dam intact. Further south, the 6th Division was relieved by the 38th Division, which ground away at the exhausted Japanese. Finally American persistance told, and the "Shimbu" Group's survivors began to melt away. Wawa Dam fell—also intact—on May 28, by which time the "Shimbu" Group had been destroyed.

By this time, too, the lesser problem of the "Kembu" Group, west of Clark Field, had also been solved. While the bulk of Griswold's corps prepared for the final advance on Manila at the end of January, the 40th Division had been left to mask the "Kembu" force of 25,000 in the heights to which it had retreated after the loss of Clark Field. Here, too, the Japanese made the fullest use of their advantage in terrain and it took over two months of concentrated pressure by three American divisions—first the 40th, then the 43rd and finally the 38th—before Tsukada accepted the inevitable. On April 6 he ordered his surviving forces to go over to independent guerrilla warfare.

Two more Japanese concentrations south of Manila were also successfully broken up in these gruelling weeks. These were the "Fuji" Force commanded by Colonel Fujishige—an Army/Navy agglo-

meration of about 13,000 men, originally part of "*Shimbu*" Group–and 3,000 Army and Navy troops down on the Bicol Peninsula, the south-eastern "tail" of Luzon. Again, it was a story of repeated battles throughout February and March, with Filipino guerrillas working in co-ordination with the regular American forces. By the end of April "*Fuji*" Force had gone the same way as the "*Kembu*" Group, while an amphibious landing at Legaspi on the Bicol Peninsula by the 158th Regimental Combat Team had battered west and joined up with 1st Cavalry Division. Southern Luzon was free.

But the greatest obstacle of all remained: Yamashita and the 110,000 troops of the "*Shobu*" Group in the north. While the battles in the centre and south of Luzon continued, it was impossible for Krueger to send more than three divisions against Yamashita: the 33rd, 32nd, and 25th. Aided by the 37th Division, the 33rd pushed forward to take Baguio, Yamashita's former H.Q., on April 26; but it took the whole of May and June for Swift's I Corps to break across the Balete Pass, take Bambang, and push on into the Cagayan valley. Airborne forces were dropped at

△ *To be captured by the enemy was a worse fate than death, according to the Japanese military code of honour. When men of the 37th Infantry Division entered the town of Bayombong on Luzon, they found this hospital ward–with all the patients dead. Before evacuating the town, the Japanese had killed their own wounded rather than let them suffer the humiliation of falling into the hands of the enemy.*

◁ *American troops examine a Type 95 light tank, knocked out by tank destroyers.*

▷ △ *Sherman tanks rumble past the Far Eastern University–one of the few buildings still relatively undamaged left standing in the city.*
▷ ▽ *The result of the tenacious defence put up by the Japanese in the streets of Manila–collapsing buildings and bodies hinder the work of American medical units.*

the northern end of the Cagayan valley towards the end of June; they drove south and joined up with 37th Division at Tuguegarao on June 26.

By the end of June Yamashita had 65,000 men still under arms. They had been forced back into the mountains to the south of Bontoc and although it was now quite impossible for them to make any effective challenge to the American hold on Luzon, they nevertheless held out until the end of the war and kept four divisions tied down in consequence. Of all the Japanese forces told to hold the Philippines for the Emperor, Yamashita's men were the ones who came closest to fulfilling their mission.

Thus by the end of June 1945 the battle of Luzon was over. It had been a unique struggle, the most "European" battle of the entire Pacific war. Fought out on an island the size of Britain, it had seen tank battles, amphibious landings, paratroop drops and guerrilla warfare, with a bloody street battle as well. Japanese losses were immense, totalling around 190,000. Ameri-

The debris of war – three children huddle for shelter in the ruins of Manila. At least they survived to be cared for by the Americans – some 100,000 civilian residents of the city died.

can losses were 8,000 killed and 30,000 wounded. Further hard fighting lay ahead before the Pacific war would be brought to its close. But there would never be another conflict like the fight for Luzon.

MacArthur had never been ordered to liberate the entire Philippine archipelago. In fact, the British had been told by General Marshall that once the vital objectives had been secured in the Philippines, the liberation of the smaller islands would be left to the Filipinos themselves, with no major American forces taking part. But MacArthur had other ideas; and as long as it was clear that there were no other major objectives for the considerable American land, sea, and air forces in the Philippine area, he was allowed to have his way.

The clearing of the central and southern Philippines was entrusted to the U.S. 8th Army, under Lieutenant-General Robert L. Eichelberger, whose first task was to clear the short-cut sea route through the Visayan Passages. This began with a landing on the north-west coast of Samar on February 19 to clear the San Bernardino Strait and it continued through the month of March, with the occupation of small islands such as Burias, Siniara, Romblon, and Tablas. The last in the sequence was Masbate, and on April 5 Eichelberger reported to MacArthur that the Visayan Passages had been cleared.

In the meantime, the liberation of the key islands in the central and southern Philippines had already begun.

Eichelberger's opponent in the area was the commander of the Japanese 35th Army: Lieutenant-General Sosaku Suzuki. His forces numbered 100,000, dotted over scores of islands, unable to concentrate or assist each other, but prepared to put up as tenacious a fight as their colleagues on Luzon. And fight they did. By the middle of April Eichelberger's forces

THE FIGHTING FILIPINOS
E WILL ALWAYS FIGHT FOR *FREEDOM!*

had made a grand total of 38 amphibious landings in the central and southern Philippines. None was on the same scale as Leyte or Luzon–but each met with resistance that was no less determined.

Palawan was the first major target: 270 miles long, the westernmost outrider of the Philippine archipelago. The American 186th Regimental Combat Team from the 41st Division landed on Palawan on February 28, but it took it over a week to break the resistance of the 1,750 Army and Navy troops on the island. On March 20 an airstrip at Puerto Princesa began to function.

Ten days before this, however, the rest of the 41st Division had descended on the westernmost tip of Mindanao, second largest and most southerly of the Philippine group. The long, thin Zamboanga Peninsula was their objective, but again it took over two weeks of fighting before their foothold was secure. In the meantime, 41st Division units had been detached to clean out the Sulu Archipelago, the string of diminutive islands stretched between Mindanao and Borneo. This

◁ *An American poster designed to boost Filipino morale.*
▽ *Clearing the Philippines and the recapture of the key areas in northern Borneo. This latter task was entrusted to the Australian I Corps under Lieutenant-General Sir Leslie Morshead. The Japanese had some 16 Army battalions and two Navy detachments of the 37th Army in the island. I Corps' naval support was furnished by the U.S. 7th Fleet. Although it had been planned to retake the whole of Borneo as a stepping stone towards Java, it was finally decided only to capture the oil producing areas and Brunei.*

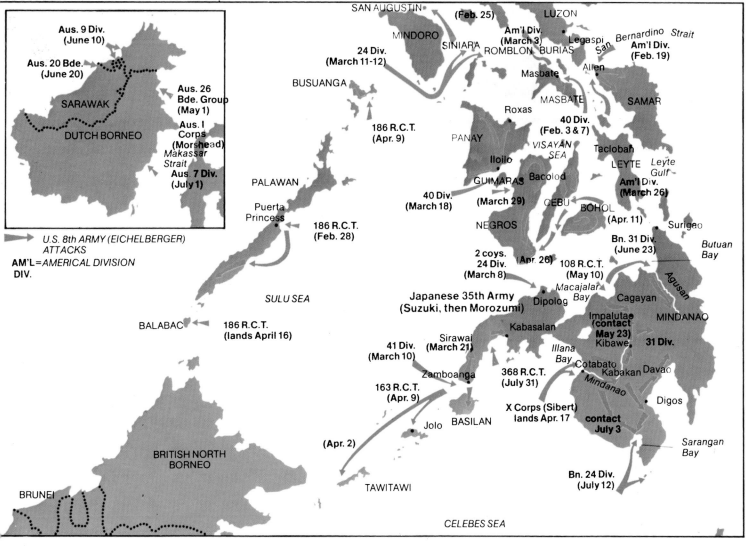

started easily – Basilan, nearest island in the Sulu group to Zamboanga, was unoccupied – but Jolo, in the centre of the chain, was another matter. It was held by 4,000 Japanese troops who fought hard for three weeks after the landing went in on April 9. Even after the main resistance was broken mopping-up continued in the interior of Jolo until July.

Next came the turn of the southern Visayas, four medium-sized islands on roughly the same latitude: from east to west, Bohol, Cebu, Negros, and Panay. Eichelberger divided this group into two, aided by the mountain spine of Negros which partitions the island into Negros Occidental and Negros Oriental. Panay and western Negros were given to the 40th Division; eastern Negros, Cebu, and Bohol to the Americal Division, originally raised in New Caledonia from non-divisional units in the Pacific theatre, and veterans of Guadalcanal, Bougainville, and Leyte.

The 40th Division landed on Panay on March 18 and wasted no time in completing its assignment. It was considerably helped by strong guerrilla forces; they took Panay's largest port, Iloilo, on the 20th, crossed straight to the island of Guimaras, and landed on the western coast of Negros on March 29. Surprise had been their biggest ally to date, but awaiting them was the biggest Japanese force in the Visayas: 13,500 Army and air force troops commanded by Lieutenant-General Takeshi Kono. A prolonged battle lasted through April and May before Kono made the inevitable decision to take to the mountains. Over 6,000 of his men were still alive when the war ended.

By far the biggest fight in the Visayas fell to the Americal Division, which landed near Cebu City on March 26. There it found formidable defences, including mined beaches – an obstacle which 8th Army forces had not had to tackle before. A fortnight's hard fighting was needed to prise the Japanese out of their defences and start the mopping-up – but, once again, the Japanese were still holding out in June. In the meantime, Americal troops had subdued Bohol in a mere two weeks after their landing on April 11, and had crossed to eastern Negros, where they joined 40th Division in hunting down the last 1,300 Japanese troops still on the run.

After the clearing of the Visayas and the Sulu Archipelago, only Mindanao remained: Mindanao, second largest island in the Philippines, and the island which MacArthur had originally planned to liberate first. It was a formidable obstacle. Suzuki had placed over half the 35th Army on Mindanao, intending to make the island the last bastion of Japanese resistance in the Philippines. He did not live to fight this last-ditch battle himself, as he was killed by American aircraft in April. His successor was Lieutenant-General Gyosaku Morozumi, who took over the 43,000 men of the garrison.

Despite the imposing size of their forces on Mindanao, the Japanese only controlled about five per cent of the island. The remainder was under the virtual control of the best equipped, organised, and led guerrilla forces in the Philippines, under the command of Colonel Wendell W. Fertig. The fact remained, however, that the Japanese held all the populated areas of Mindanao – hence MacArthur's determination to oust them.

The battle for Mindanao began on April 17, 1945, when General Sibert's X Corps landed at Illana Bay. Driving rapidly inland, Sibert's forces covered 115 miles in 15 days and pounced on Davao, depriving the Japanese of their last major town in the Philippines. Davao fell on May 3, but over a month of hard fighting in the hills of the interior lay ahead. Subsequent landings on the north coast of Mindanao, at Macalajar Bay and Butuan Bay, sent further American columns inland to split up the Japanese mass, which was not disrupted and forced into the jungle until the last week of June.

There remained some 2,000 Japanese in the extreme south of the island, who had been cut off there ever since Sibert's pounce on Davao in April-May. These fugitives were the objective of the last seaborne landing of the long struggle for the Philippines which had begun in Leyte Gulf in October 1944. On July 12 a battalion of the 24th Division went ashore to work with the local Filipino guerrillas in rounding up the Japanese. And they landed in Sarangani Bay, the southernmost inlet on Mindanao's coast. Once MacArthur had planned to launch the reconquest of the Philippines at this point. Instead it was the scene of the very last action in the campaign.

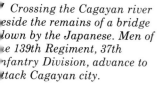

Crossing the Cagayan river beside the remains of a bridge down by the Japanese. Men of the 139th Regiment, 37th Infantry Division, advance to attack Cagayan city.

CHAPTER 87

REMAGEN BRIDGE

It should be noted that there had been much inter-Allied squabbling about the length of time that the battle for Colmar was taking: the Allied high command wanted this irritating pocket cleared out of the way as quickly as possible, so that all available Allied forces might be readied for the last devastating blow against Germany that would win the war in the West. The irritation caused by the Colmar delay was perhaps exacerbated by another clash between Eisenhower and Montgomery. But what increased the trouble even more was the fact that Brooke backed Montgomery with all the weight of his authority. Once more S.H.A.E.F. and the 21st Army Group were divided on the alternatives of the "concentrated push" or the "wide front".

Eisenhower rejected Montgomery's intention of supervising Bradley's operations, but nevertheless, on December 31, 1944, informed Montgomery of his plan of operations:

"Basic plan—to destroy enemy forces west of Rhine, north of the Moselle, and to prepare for crossing the Rhine in force with the *main effort north of the Ruhr.*"

Once the Ardennes salient had been pinched out (Point *a*), Eisenhower envisaged the following general offensive:

"*b.* Thereafter First and Third Armies to drive to north-east on general line Prum-Bonn, eventually to Rhine.

"*c.* When *a* is accomplished, 21st Army Group, with Ninth U.S. Army under operational command, to resume preparations for 'Veritable'."

In practical terms, this plan required Montgomery to force the Reichswald forest position, which bars the corridor between the Maas and the Rhine on the Dutch-German frontier, to secure the left bank of the Rhine between Emmerich and Düsseldorf, and to prepare to force a passage of the river north of its junction with the Ruhr. This sketch of a plan pleased Montgomery, who wrote:

"It did all I wanted except in the realm of operational control, and because of Marshall's telegram that subject was

▽ *Shermans of the French 1st Army push on towards the Rhine after the liberation of Colmar.*

closed. It put the weight in the north and gave the Ninth American Army to 21 Army Group. It gave me power of decision in the event of disagreement with Bradley on the boundary between 12 and 21 Army Groups. In fact, I had been given very nearly all that I had been asking for since August. Better late than never. I obviously could not ask for more."

Nevertheless, when one considers the allotment of forces and in particular the fixing of objectives, there is no avoiding the fact that the two sides did not speak a common language any more.

Actually, Montgomery estimated that if "Veritable" was to be successful, American reinforcements should consist of five corps, (16 divisions), of which four corps (13 divisions) should be placed under the command of the American 9th Army, and the rest under the British 2nd Army. In these estimates, he seems to

have been completely unaware of the principles established by his superior at the beginning of his outline dated December 31: "to destroy enemy forces west of Rhine". According to Eisenhower's clearly-expressed opinion, this required a second push from around Prüm towards the Rhine at Bonn approaching the Ruhr from the south, which would reduce the United States' forces which could be detached for "Veritable" to only three corps and 12 divisions.

Montgomery was obliged to give in, but he resumed the argument on January 20 when he heard the news that Bradley, far from limiting himself to reducing the Ardennes salient, intended to follow up his attack for another fortnight. Montgomery wrote to Brooke:

"Both Ike and Bradley are emphatic that we should not–not–cross the Rhine in strength anywhere until we are lined

▷ *German prisoners from a* Volksgrenadier *regiment await removal to a P.O.W. camp.*
▽ *General Marshall, head of the U.S. Army, arrives in Malta en route to Yalta. Marshall sided firmly with Eisenhower in the dispute the latter was having with Montgomery.*

up along its entire length from Nijmegen to Switzerland."

Two days later, in a second letter which, like the first, he has not quoted in his memoirs, he harped on the same question: "My latest information is that S.H.A.E.F. are very worried about situation in South about Colmar and Strasbourg..."

As the commander-in-chief seemed ready to reinforce this sector, it followed that "Veritable" would be postponed indefinitely. This led him to conclude bitterly:

"I fear that the old snags of indecision and vacillation and refusal to consider the military problem fairly and squarely are coming to the front again ... The real trouble is that there is no control and the three Army Groups are each intent on their own affairs. Patton to-day issued a stirring order to Third Army, saying the next step would be Cologne ... one has to preserve a sense of humour these days, otherwise one would go mad."

Support for Eisenhower

Brooke was appreciative of this argument and "cordially, but very gravely", as General Eisenhower writes, expressed the view to him that putting his plan into effect would have the result of producing an "organised dispersion" of Allied forces. Eisenhower opposed this view, and events proved him right. First of all, the Germans had to be deprived of the advantage of permanent fortifications which allowed them to economise their means and then build up massive forces in the sector where the main attack would be launched:

"If, however, we should first, in a series of concentrated and powerful attacks, destroy the German forces west of the Rhine, the effect would be to give us all along the great front a defensive line of equal strength to the enemy's. We calculated that with the western bank of the Rhine in our possession we could hurl some seventy-five reinforced divisions against the Germans in great converging attacks. If we allowed the enemy south of the Ruhr to remain in the Siegfried, we would be limited to a single offensive by some thirty-five divisions.

"A second advantage of our plan would be the deflection of the enemy forces later to be met at the crossings of the Rhine obstacle. Moreover, the effect of the converging attack is multiplied when it is accompanied by such air power as we had in Europe in the early months of 1945. Through its use we could prevent the enemy from switching forces back and forth at will against either of the attacking columns and we could likewise employ our entire air power at any moment to further the advance in any area desired."

But although Eisenhower had refuted Brooke's point, he was unable to convert the latter to his way of thinking. That is why he travelled to Marseilles on January 25 to explain to Marshall, who was on his way to Yalta via Malta, his plan of operations and the objections it was coming up against among the British. He had no difficulty in obtaining Marshall's complete agreement, and the latter said to him at the end of the interview:

"I can, of course, uphold your position merely on the principle that these decisions fall within your sphere of responsibility. But your plan is so sound that I think it better for you to send General Smith to Malta so that he may explain

△ American infantry move up through a snowstorm, typical of the weather that helped the Germans considerably at the beginning of 1945.

△ *Evidence of American artillery superiority: a destroyed German triple 2-cm self-propelled mounting.*

these matters in detail. Their logic will be convincing."

This was done and, after some explanations by Bedell Smith and some amendments on the part of the Combined Chiefs-of-Staff Committee, Eisenhower's plan, comprising of a double push towards the Rhine and a double encirclement of the Ruhr, was adopted and Montgomery would spare nothing to make it a success.

Ardennes cleared

On January 16, the American 3rd and 1st Armies crushed the tip of the Ardennes salient and linked up in the ruins of Houffalize. The following day, as agreed, the 1st Army was returned to the command of Bradley, to his great satisfaction. But he was far less pleased with the task

now given him, that of engaging the Germans in the wooded and hilly region of Schleiden and Schmidt, which had cost him so dear the previous autumn, and of capturing the hydro-electric system of the Raer, the Erft, and the Olef. On February 8, V Corps (under Major-General L. T. Gerow), of the 1st Army had reached its objective. That was that. At dawn, on the next day, the Germans blew up the reservoir gates; and the water rose rapidly in front of the 9th Army.

Meanwhile, the left of this army, still under the command of Lieutenant-General William H. Simpson, and the right of the British 2nd Army, under General Miles C. Dempsey, were taking out the salient which the enemy was holding between the Maas and the Raer, now an enclave between the Allied flanks. The little Dutch village of Roermond was still held by the German 15th Army, which formed the right of Army Group "B". On January 28, this rectifying operation, a prelude to the pincer attack called "Veritable/Grenade", was brought to a successful conclusion.

Rundstedt powerless

In this duel between Field-Marshal von Rundstedt and General Eisenhower, the former had at his disposal at the beginning of February (after he had lost the 6th *Panzerarmee,* taken away to help the Hungarian front), 73 divisions, including eight Panzer or *Panzergrenadier.* But the infantry divisions had fallen to an average of about 7,000 men each. As for the armoured formations, whatever may have been the excellent quality of their *matériel,* they suffered a continual shortage of petrol because of the Allied air offensive against the German synthetic petrol plants. In other words, as had started to become evident in the battle of Colmar, the crisis in munitions was getting ever more desperate at the front. The land forces of the Third Reich, moreover, could not rely on any support from the Luftwaffe, whose jet fighters were fully engaged attempting to defend what

◁ *Field Marshal Gerd Von Rundstedt shown with his son Lt. Hans G Von Rundstedt.*

△ *Montgomery* (standing, right) *confers with Horrocks* (standing, left). *Note the insignia on the jeep: four stars, signifying that the owner was a general.*

was left of Germany's cities against the redoubled attacks of the British and American Strategic Air Forces.

The last straw was that Rundstedt, in his office at Koblenz, was faced by a hopeless situation, and had been stripped of all initiative in the direction of operations. On January 21, he received the following incredible *Führerbefehl*, with orders to distribute it down to divisional level:

"Commanders-in-chief, army, corps, and divisional commanders are personally responsible to me for reporting in good time:

"*(a)* Every decision to execute an operational movement.

"*(b)* Every offensive plan from divisional level upwards that does not fit exactly with the directives of the higher command.

"*(c)* Every attack in a quiet sector intended to draw the enemy's attention to that sector, with the exception of normal shock troop actions.

"*(d)* Every plan for withdrawal or retreat.

"*(e)* Every intention of surrendering a position, a strongpoint, or a fortress.

"Commanders must make sure that I have time to intervene as I see fit, and that my orders can reach the front line troops in good time."

And the *Führer* further announced that any commander or staff officer who by "deliberate intent, carelessness, or oversight" hindered the execution of this order, would be punished with "draconian severity".

Allied superiority

From the Swiss frontier to the North Sea, Eisenhower had 70 divisions under his command on January 1, 1945:

	Infantry	Armoured	Airborne	Total
U.S.	31	11	3	45
British	7	4	1	12
Canadian	2	1	–	3
French	6	3	–	9
Polish	–	1	–	1
Totals	46	20	4	70

By May 8 this number would have been increased by another 15 American divisions (including four armoured), six French divisions, and two Canadian divisions (including one armoured).

Deducting six divisions fighting in the Alps or besieging German fortresses, this would give S.H.A.E.F. 87 divisions at the end of the war.

Despite the losses they had to bear, the

Allied divisions at this time were far less restricted than their German counterparts. The supply crisis, so acute in September, was now no more than an unpleasant memory. Petrol was in good supply and there was no shortage of shells at the front. The proximity fuses with which they were fitted allowed the gunners to fire shells which burst in the air, wreaking havoc among exposed troops. With reference to armour, the introduction into the United States Army of the heavy (41-ton) M26 General Pershing tank was significant. It was well-armoured, and had a 90-mm gun and good cross-country performance, the result of its Christie-type suspension and wide tracks. The Americans had rediscovered this suspension after seeing the results it gave in the service of the Germans, who had borrowed the idea from the Russians. The latter had acquired a licence to build the Christie suspension from the United States, after 1919, when the American military authorities had refused, in spite of the urging of the young Major George S. Patton, to take any firm interest in Christie and his advanced designs.

Thus the Allies' land forces were far more numerous than the Germans'. They also enjoyed powerful air support from a force which was both numerous and well-trained. Here General Devers had the Franco-American 1st Tactical Air Force (Major-General R. M. Webster), in which the French I Air Corps (Brigadier-General P. Gerardot) was itself attached to the French 1st Army. The United States 9th Air Force (Lieutenant-General Hoyt S. Vandenberg,) came under the overall command of General Bradley, and the British 2nd Tactical Air Force (Air-Marshal Sir Arthur Coningham) efficiently seconded Field-Marshal Montgomery's operations. On the German side there was nothing which could resist this formidable mass of flying artillery.

On November 12, 1944, 28 R.A.F. Lancasters attacked the great battleship *Tirpitz* in Tromsö with 12,000-lb "Tallboy" bombs and sank her at her anchorage. What was now left of the surface forces of the Kriegsmarine was being expended in the Baltic in attempts to help the army. As for the U-boats, which had lost 242 of their number during 1944, their successes in the North Atlantic between June 6, 1944 and May 8, 1945, were limited to the sinking of 31 merchant ships, displacing

altogether only 178,000 tons. This was virtually nothing at all.

△ *Introduced in 1945 the Pershing saw only limited service, although in one instance a single M.26 destroyed a Tiger and two Pzkw Mk IV tanks in rapid succession.*

Complete surprise

At 0500 hours on February 8, 1,400 guns of the Canadian 1st Army blasted the German 84th Division, which had dug itself in along a seven-mile front between the Maas and the Waal close to the Dutch-German frontier. At 1030 hours, the British XXX Corps, which Montgomery had put under the command of General Crerar, moved in to the attack with five divisions (the British 51st, 53rd, and 15th and the Canadian 2nd and 3rd) in the first wave and the 43rd Division and the Guards Armoured Division in reserve. In all, according to the commander of the corps, Lieutenant-General Horrocks, there were 200,000 men and 35,000 vehicles.

The German position was heavily mined, and included a flooded area on the right and the thick Reichswald forest on the left. Moreover, the day before the attack, a thaw had softened the ground. Neither Hitler, at O.K.W., nor Colonel-General Blaskowitz, commanding Army Group "H", had been willing to accept the idea that Montgomery would choose such a sector in which to attack. Yet

General Schlemm, commanding the 1st Parachute Army, had warned them of this possibility. At the end of the day the 84th Division had lost 1,300 prisoners and was close to breaking-point.

Meanwhile the American 9th Army had been ordered to unleash Operation "Grenade" on February 10. This would cross the Roer and advance to the Rhine at Düsseldorf. Now came the flooding caused by the destruction of the Eifel dams, which held up the American 9th Army completely for 12 days and slowed down the British XXX Corps. The latter's units were also hopelessly mixed up. These delays allowed Schlemm to send his 7th and 6th Parachute, 15th *Panzergrenadier*, and then 116th Panzer Divisions to the rescue one after the other. And as Colonel C. P. Stacey, the official Canadian Army historian, notes, the Germans, at the edge of the abyss, had lost none of their morale:

"In this, the twilight of their gods, the defenders of the Reich displayed the recklessness of fanaticism and the courage of despair. In the contests west of the Rhine, in particular, they fought with special ferocity and resolution, rendering the battles in the Reichswald and Hochwald forests grimly memorable in the annals of this war."

On February 13, the Canadian 1st Army had mopped up the Reichswald and the little town of Kleve, and had reached Gennep, where it was reinforced across the Maas by the British 52nd Division and 11th Armoured Division. Schlemm threw two divisions of infantry into the battle as well as the famous Panzer-*"Lehr"* Division, and so the intervention of Lieutenant-General G. G. Simonds's Canadian II Corps at the side of the British XXX Corps did not have the decisive effect that Crerar expected. The 11th day of the offensive saw the attackers marking time on the Goch–Kalkar line about 15 miles from their jumping-off point.

But, just like the British 2nd Army in Normandy, the Canadian 1st Army had

The end of the Tirpitz, *Germany's second and last battleship. Lying capsized in Tromsö fjord, with small vessels moored by her keel, she looks more like an island than a once-proud capital ship.*

attracted the larger part of the enemy's forces, while the flood water in the Roer valley was going down. The weather also turned finer, and Montgomery fixed February 23 for the launching of Operation "Grenade". In his order of the day to the men of the 21st Army Group, Montgomery assured them that this was to be the beginning of the last round against Germany. The Third Reich was ready for the knock-out blow, which would be delivered from several directions.

Then, as an opening move, the Anglo-American Strategic Air Force launched 10,000 bombers and fighter escorts and made the heaviest attack of the war on the Third Reich's communications network.

More than 200 targets featured on the programme of this attack, which went under the name of Operation "Clarion". Some of these objectives were bombed from only 4,500 feet because enemy anti-aircraft action was almost totally ineffective since Hitler had stripped it

to supply the Eastern Front. The results of this bombing on February 22 were still noticeable when Colonel-General Jodl came to bring General Eisenhower the surrender of the Third Reich.

The following day, at 0245 hours, the artillery of the United States 9th Army opened fire on German positions on the Roer. The 15th Army (General von Zangen) which defended them, formed the right of Army Group "B" (Field-Marshal Model). Though it defended itself well, his 353rd Division was still thrown out of the ruins of Julich by the American XIX Corps (Major-General Raymond S. Maclain). Meanwhile, in the Linnich sector, XIII Corps (Major-General Alvan C. Gillem) had established a bridgehead a mile and a half deep. VII Corps (Lieutenant-General John L. Collins) of the American 1st Army, had also taken part in the attack and, by the end of the day, had mopped up Duren.

Hitler, Rundstedt, and Model used every last resource to tackle this new crisis looming on the horizon. Schlemm was stripped of the reinforcements which had just been despatched to him, and to these were added the 9th and 11th Panzer Divisions and the 3rd *Panzergrenadier* Division. These forces were instructed to hit the enemy's north-easterly push in its flank.

All the same, by February 27, the Allied breakthrough was complete near Erkelenz, and two days later, XIII Corps swept through the conurbation of Rheydt –Mönchengladbach. At the same time, to the right of the 9th Army, XVI Corps (Major-General J. B. Anderson) hurtled towards Roermond and Venlo behind the 1st Parachute Army, while on the right, XIX Corps was approaching Neuss.

In these circumstances Schlemm was ordered to retreat to the right bank of the Rhine, and he must be given all credit for carrying out this delicate and dangerous mission with remarkable skill. Rearguard skirmishes at Rheinberg, Sonsbeck, and Xanten gave him the time to get the bulk of his forces across and to complete the planned demolitions without fault. On March 6, the United States 9th Army and the Canadian 1st Army linked up opposite Wesel.

This joint Operation "Veritable/ Grenade" cost the 18 German divisions engaged 53,000 prisoners. But Crerar alone had suffered 15,634 dead, wounded, and missing, of whom 5,304 were Canadian troops.

△ *The "Masters of the World" return home.*

◁ *First use of the C-46s was on the mission near Wesel.*

Crossing the Rhine

On March 6, 1945, the leading division of the American VII Corps reached the city of Cologne. Now the Allies were lining the Rhine between Cologne and Nijmegen, more than 100 miles downstream, where the river, if the stream slows down, widens to reach a breadth as great as 250 or 300 yards, and all the bridges had been destroyed. Forcing the Rhine north of the Ruhr, according to Montgomery's formula, would result in a delay of two weeks and necessitate considerable reinforcements for the 21st Army Group. And here can be seen Eisenhower's farsightedness in keeping to his plan of operations of December 31, 1944: to defeat the enemy west of the Rhine. For, if he had kept Bradley marking time then, Hitler could have detached the forces necessary to check Montgomery on the Rhine below Cologne.

This did not happen, for, on March 6, Army Group "B" was fighting the American 1st Army on its right and the 3rd on its centre. Its 5th *Panzerarmee* (Colonel-General Harpe) was now well and truly outflanked and overrun on both wings. According to the original plan, the American 1st Army was to provide the left flank of Operation "Grenade". With this in view, General Bradley had increased its size to three corps (14 divisions). But it was not foreseen that the 3rd Army would take part in the attack and it was only by a rather surreptitious move that, during the second week of January, Patton had pushed his forces as far as the Moselle in Luxembourg, the Sûre, and the Our near the *Westwall,* covering himself at S.H.A.E.F. by claiming that his moves were "offensive defence", when his aggression had no other aim but that of reaching the Rhine at Koblenz.

The defeat of the German 15th Army opened a breach in Field-Marshal Model's line which General Hodges and his 1st Army did not delay in exploiting. Having occupied Cologne, VII Corps set off for Bonn on March 7. III Corps (Major-General J. Millikin), which was advancing on the right of VII Corps, had orders to take the crossings over the Ahr. This task was entrusted to the 9th Armoured Division (Major-General John W. Leonard).

Towards the end of the morning of March 7, Brigadier-General William M. Hoge, leading Combat Command "B" of the 9th Armoured Division, was informed that the Ludendorff Bridge near Remagen was still intact. He decided not to follow his orders (which had specified Sinzig as his target) to the letter and resolved there and then to chance his luck and seize the bridge. A little before 1600 hours, 2nd Lieutenant Karl Timmermann ventured on to the bridge, followed by the Burrows section. Seeing them, the German guard tried to set off the demolition charges, but in vain. Under American fire, Sergeant Faust, another hero of this episode, then lit the fuse. But the effect of the explosion was insignificant, and, a few minutes later, Sergeant Alex Drabik was the first American fighting man to step on the right bank of the Rhine. Behind him, Lieutenant Hugh B. Mott, a combat engineer, and three sappers tore the charges from the girders and threw the explosives into the river.

"The enemy had reached Kreuzberg and as far as a bridge near Remagen which, it appears, was encumbered with fugitives. They crossed the bridge and succeeded in forming a bridgehead on the eastern bank of the river. Counterattack early this morning. The 11th Panzer Division will be brought from Bonn. But petrol is in short supply."

The O.K.W. war diary records this national catastrophe in these unemotional words. Therefore it gives no account of Hitler's rage, which was terrible. Major Scheler and three others were declared responsible, on Hitler's orders, for the success of the Allied surprise attack, court-martialled, and shot.

Twenty-four hours after this surprise, there were already 8,000 Americans in the bridgehead. By March 17, four divisions (9th, 78th, 99th, and 9th Armoured) were dug in. On the same day the bridge collapsed. Hitler had concentrated the fire of a battery of 17-cm guns on it, as well as ordering aircraft and V-2 attacks, and even attempts by Kriegsmarine human torpedoes and frogmen. But, protected by booms and nets, 1st Army engineers had already built another bridge and both banks of the Rhine were bristling with anti-aircraft guns.

Having transferred III Corps (three divisions) to the 1st Army, Patton remained in command of VIII, XII, and XX Corps, which had 12 divisions, three of which were armoured. The crossing of the Our and the Sûre, on the Saint Vith – Echternach line, was no little matter because

△ *The nemesis of Germany's civilian bombing campaigns early in the war: the avenging angel of the British and American strategic bombing forces.*

the rivers were in flood. The forcing of *Westwall* was also very tough. In XII Corps there was one division which had to reduce 120 concrete casemates. This it did with self-propelled 155-mm guns, pounding the embrasures from a range of only 300 yards.

In spite of everything, by the end of February VIII and XII Corps were on the Kyll, having advanced about 20 miles into German territory. XX Corps had taken Saarburg and advanced as far as the apex of the triangle formed by the Mosel and the Saar at their confluence a little above Trier. Up till then the German 7th Army (General Brandenberger), which faced Patton, had defended itself tenaciously, but this very tenacity explains why, on March 1, having exhausted its supplies, it literally collapsed. On that day, wrote Patton:

"At 14.15, Walker [commander of XX Corps] called up to say the 10th Armoured Division was in Trier and had captured a bridge over the Moselle intact. The capture of this bridge was due to the heroic act of Lieutenant Colonel J. J. Richardson, deceased. He was riding in the leading vehicle of his battalion of armoured infantry when he saw the wires leading to the demolition charges at the far end of the bridge. Jumping out of the vehicle, he raced across the bridge under heavy fire and cut the wires. The acid test of battle brings out the pure metal."

On March 3, the forcing of the Kyll at Kyllburg by the 5th Division, under Major-General S. LeRoy Irwin, enabled Major-General Manton Eddy, commanding XII Corps, to detach his 4th Division. Under the command of Major-General Hugh J. Gaffey, this division made a raid of mad audacity, covering 26 miles on March 4 alone and reaching Daun in the evening. Two days later, it reached the Rhine above Koblenz. On its left, the 11th Armoured Division (Major-General Holmes E. Dager), advancing ahead of VII Corps, established first contact with the American 1st Army on March 11, near Brohl.

On March 8, the O.K.W. war diary noted that LIII Corps had been steamrollered and that any co-ordinated conduct of operations was henceforth impossible. The truth of this is illustrated by the capture of General von Rothkirch und Panthen, in command of LIII Corps. Bradley recounts the story thus:

"So rapid was the dissolution that even the senior German commanders lost

△ △ *The last stand . . .*
△ *. . . and the last* Heil.

touch with their crumbling front. One day a German corps commander drove into a field of listless soldiers and asked why they were not fighting the Allies. Not until an American MP clasped him on the shoulder and invited him to join the throng, did the general learn that he had stumbled into a PW concentration."

Altogether, the second phase of the battle for the Rhineland, called Operation "Lumberjack", had brought the 12th Army Group 51,000 prisoners. It had also given it the priceless bridgehead at Remagen, which the German 15th Army was unable to destroy, since the four Panzer divisions which Model had given

△ *A German soldier lies dead on the bank of the Rhine, the Third Reich's "uncrossable" natural defence in the West.*

the energetic Lieutenant-General Bayerlein for this purpose did not total more than 5,000 men, 60 tanks, and 30 guns. On the other side of the battlefield, the Americans spread out in all directions. So great and thorough was their push that, on March 22, they were on the right bank of the Rhine in a bridgehead 25 miles long and ten miles deep.

No retreat

As explained earlier, because of the forces and *matériel* requested by Montgomery in order to lead his army group across the Rhine to the north of the Ruhr, Eisenhower had at first limited his operation to the left bank of the Mosel. However, Hitler's obstinate decision to keep his Army Group "G" inside the salient limited by Haguenau, Saarbrücken, Cochem (north of the Mosel), and Koblenz, would convince him that the best thing to do was to strike a third blow at the enemy on the west of the Rhine, which meant that the 3rd Army and the 6th Army Group would be able to take part.

Colonel-General Hausser, commanding Army Group "G", had just been given

△ *An American artillery column streams past the wreckage of a German convoy blasted by the Allies' heavy guns.*

the 7th Army, recently taken over by General Obstfelder, and which was at present heavily engaged against Patton.

Hausser still had the 1st Army (General Foertsch), which was occupying the Moder front and the Siegfried Line or *Westwall* as far as the approaches to Forbach. The 19th Army, having evacuated the Colmar pocket, now came directly under the command of O.K.W. But at this time all these units totalled only 13 divisions, most of them badly worn, though some of them still gave a good account of themselves, for example the 2nd Mountain Division (Lieutenant-General Degen), and the 6th S.S. Mountain Division (Lieutenant-General Brenner).

Under these conditions, Hausser and his army commanders were of the opinion that they ought to put the Rhine, between the junctures of the Mosel and the Lauter,

behind them as soon as possible and be ready to abandon the Siegfried Line after having destroyed all its installations. But Hitler reacted indignantly to this suggestion of destroying a masterpiece of German military engineering to which he had contributed so much.

The Führer was mistaken about the value of this construction, however. Patton, who visited one of the fortresses taken by the 76th Division, points out its weak point with his usual perspicacity:

"It consisted of a three storey submerged barracks with toilets, shower baths, a hospital, laundry, kitchen, store rooms and every conceivable convenience plus an enormous telephone installation. Electricity and heat were produced by a pair of identical diesel engines with generators. Yet the whole offensive capacity of this installation consisted of two machine guns and a 60-mm mortar operating from steel cupolas which worked up and down by means of hydraulic lifts. The 60-mm mortar was peculiar in that it was operated by remote control. As in all cases, this particular pill box was taken by a dynamite charge against the back door. We found marks on the cupolas, which were ten inches thick, where our 90-mm shells fired at a range of two hundred yards, had simply bounced."

But neither Hitler nor his subordinates imagined that Patton would need only four or five days to shift the centre of gravity of his 3rd Army from Brohl and Koblenz on the Rhine to Mayen on the Nette and Cochem on the Mosel. On the left, VIII Corps, now reduced to two divisions, would keep watch on Koblenz. In the centre, XII Corps, increased to six divisions (5th, 76th, 89th, and 90th Infantry, and 4th and 11th Armoured), was given Bingen on the Rhine and Bad-Kreuznach on the Nahe as its first targets. On the right, XX Corps with four divisions (26th, 80th, and 94th Infantry and 10th Armoured) had orders to press on to Kaiserslautern behind the backs of the defenders of the *Westwall,* which would be attacked frontally by the American 7th Army. The latter, commanded by Lieutenant-General Alexander M. Patch, had 12 divisions, including the 3rd Algerian Division. As can be seen, the third act of the Battle of the Rhine, named "Undertone" was about to match 22 more or less intact Allied divisions against 13 worn-out German ones. Actually, since the end of January, the 7th Army had been waiting poised between Haguenau and Forbach.

As for the 3rd Army, its losses, between January 29 and March 12, amounted to only 21,581 officers, N.C.O.s, and men, of which 3,650 had been killed and 1,374 were missing, which gives a daily divisional average of eight killed or missing and 32 wounded. These figures would suggest that despite his nickname of "Blood and Guts", Patton was not at all prodigal with the lives of his men.

Triumphant advance

On the evening of March 14, XII Corps had already got most of its 5th and 90th Divisions over on the right bank of the Mosel at Treis, eight miles below Cochem. Eddy then wasted no time in unleashing his 4th and 11th Armoured Divisions.

To his right, XX Corps was attacking towards Saint Wendel, in the rear of the *Westwall.* At last, at dawn on March 15, H-hour came for the 7th Army. Its VI Corps (3rd Algerian, 36th, 42nd, and 103rd Divisions and 14th Armoured Division), went into the attack on the Moder front. Its 15th Division attacked the *Westwall,* its left towards Saarlautern, the French Sarrelouis, in contact with XX Corps.

By March 16, the 4th Armoured Division had advanced 32 miles in 48 hours. As it crossed the Nahe, near Bad-Kreuznach, it clashed violently with the 2nd Panzer Division (Major-General von Lauchert). But Patton was aware of the audacity of Gaffey, his ex-chief-of-staff, and had not let him fight it out alone. Opportunely reinforced, the 4th Armoured Division defeated the desperate counter-attack and moved forward again. By March 19, it had arrived seven miles west of Worms and 12 miles south-west of Mainz. On the same day, XX Corps, to which the 7th Army had given the 12th Armoured Division, under Major-General R. R. Allen, pushed its armoured spearheads as far as 15 miles from Kaiserslautern. Since the crossing of the Mosel, the 3rd Army had lost, including accidents, only 800 men, while it had taken 12,000 prisoners.

Forty-eight hours later, in XII Corps, the 90th Division, which had lost two commanders in Normandy, was busy mopping up Mainz, the 4th Armoured Division was occupying Worms, and the 11th was pushing on to the south of the city.

In XX Corps, Major-General Walton H. Walker had thrown his 12th Armoured Division into Ludwigshafen and was pushing his 10th towards Landau. Just as the difficult terrain of the Eifel had been no impediment, that of the Hunsruck, which is just as bad, had not been able to hold back the *élan* of the 3rd Army, supported flexibly and efficiently by Major-General Otto P. Weyland's XIX Tactical Air Command of the 9th Air Force.

Facing the German 1st Army, the American 7th Army had had a considerably more difficult task. There is some evidence of this in a note made by Pierre Lyautey who, as liaison officer, was with the 3rd Algerian Division (General

△ *General Sir Miles Dempsey, commander of the British 2nd Army, on an inspection tour of his front line units.*

△ *An American quadruple .5-inch A.A. mounting on a half-track chassis on watch against German aircraft near the Chateau de Vianden in Luxembourg.*

Guillaume), when it attacked across the Moder.

"March 15: Artillery preparation. The planned 2,000 shells light up the scene. Attack by the 4th Tunisians. Skirmishes. The leading company runs, at seven in the morning, from ruin to ruin, lonely wall to lonely wall, reaches the railway, dives into the underground passage and jumps up into the mangled and dismantled gasworks. Violent reaction from German artillery, mortar, and machine guns. Impossible to move out. The whole sector is alive with fire. The company shelters in the gas-works. First one tank explodes, then another. Beyond the church, the scene is one of a major offensive: stretcher-bearers, stretchers, limping men walking around with white cards, a smell of blood, stifling heat. The last cows of Oberhoffen-Bénarès are in their death agony among the rubble."

It took four days for Major-General Edward H. Brooks, commanding VI Corps, to take back from the Germans the ground lost in lower Alsace as a result of Operation *"Nordwind"*. Then he closed in on the *Westwall* between the Rhine and the Vosges.

Both General de Gaulle and General de Lattre had no intention, however, of allowing the French Army to be restricted to a purely defensive function on the left bank of the Rhine. They wanted to see it play a part in the invasion of the Third Reich. While awaiting a definite decision

from S.H.A.E.F., General de Gaulle writes, "General Devers, a good ally and a good friend, sympathised with de Lattre's wishes".

That is why, on March 18, General de Monsabert received command of a task force comprising the 3rd Algerian Division and two-thirds of the 5th Armoured Division; aiming for Speyer, it would give the French 1st Army a front over the Rhine in Germany.

The three infantry divisions of the United States VI Corps took three days and lost 2,200 men to overcome that part of the *Westwall* allotted to them as objective, but using its infantry and engineers

in turn, Brooks finally pierced the defences between Wissembourg and Pirmasens. As for Monsabert, he had difficulty in front of the Bienwald. Nevertheless, his tanks were around Maximiliansau opposite Karlsruhe by the evening of March 24.

Patch had taken Landau the day before, so the Battle of the Palatinate, the third act of the Battle of the Rhine, was drawing to its end.

The battle had been conducted to Eisenhower's complete satisfaction. Between February 8 and March 24, the enemy had lost 280,000 prisoners, the remains of five German armies which had crossed back over the Rhine between the German-Dutch and Franco-German frontiers. Army Group "B" had suffered most. Patton alone could claim 140,112 prisoners, against the 53,000 taken by the 21st Army Group in Operation "Veritable/ Grenade". Therefore Eisenhower had proved his superiority not only over Hitler's arms but also over Montgomery's arguments.

Furthermore, on the night of March 22/23, Patton also succeeded in crossing the Rhine as Bradley had recommended, profiting from the Germans' disorder. The banks there being suitable, Patton chose the stretch near Oppenheim, which

△ *The great prize. Men and vehicles of the American 1st Army pour across the Ludendorff railway bridge over the Rhine at Remagen to establish an invincible bridgehead on the right bank.*

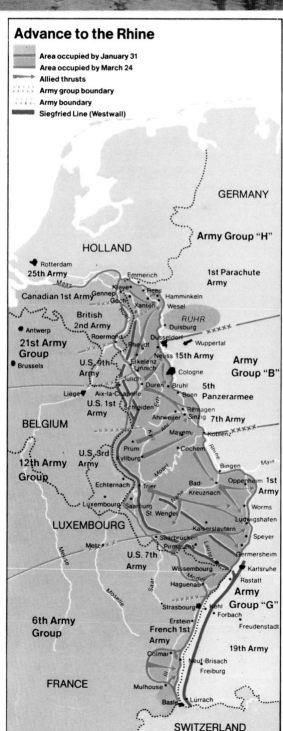

△ *A Sherman of the U.S. Army is ferried across a river on a section of pontoon bridge pushed by motor-boats.*
▷ *The Allied advance to the Rhine, and the establishment of the first bridgeheads at Remagen and Oppenheim.*

Advance to the Rhine

- Area occupied by January 31
- Area occupied by March 24
- Allied thrusts
- Army group boundary
- Army boundary
- Siegfried Line (Westwall)

was occupied by the 5th Division (Major-General S. LeRoy Irwin), half-way between Worms and Mainz.

Surprise crossing

At 2230 hours, 200 Piper L-4 Grasshoppers began to shuttle from one bank to the other. These small observation and artillery-spotting aircraft carried an armed infantryman instead of an observer. Once the first bridgehead had thus been formed, the 12 L.C.V.P.s (Landing Craft Vehicle/Personnel) of the "naval detachment" which Patton had trained to a high pitch of efficiency on the Moselle at Toul, entered the river while his bridging crews, from which he had refused to be separated (lest he not get them back) when he had driven hard from the Sarre to the Ardennes, began to work at once under the command of Brigadier-General Conklin, the 3rd Army's chief engineer.

At dawn on March 23, the 5th Division had already placed six infantry battalions, about 4,000 or 5,000 men, on the right bank of the Rhine, at the cost of only eight killed and 20 wounded. The Germans were so surprised that when Patton made his report to Bradley, he asked him not to publicise the news, so as to keep the Germans in the dark while they expected him at the approaches to Mainz. As an all-American soldier, he was happy to have stolen a march over "Monty" by forcing the Rhine before him and without making any demands on anybody.

As a result, 48 hours later, five divisions of the 3rd Army had crossed the Rhine at Oppenheim, stretched along the valley of the Main: XII Corps towards Aschaffenburg, and XX Corps towards Hanau.

CHAPTER 88
IWO JIMA

As a piece of real estate, Iwo Jima has little to offer anyone: it is an island 4⅔ miles long and 2½ miles wide at its southern end, dominated by the 550-foot high Mount Suribachi, an extinct volcano. There are some sulphur deposits, a plain of black volcanic sand, and in the north a plateau of ridges and gorges between 340 and 368 feet high. In 1944 there were five villages on the island, in the centre and to the north of the plateau.

The importance of the island to both the Japanese and the Americans lay in the two airfields that had been built, and the third under construction, by the Japanese. From these bases Japanese aircraft could intercept the B-29's bombing Japan, and operate against the bomber bases in the Marianas. The island, if captured, would provide the U.S. with a fighter base and emergency landing strips for crippled bombers.

The island's commander, Lieutenant-General Tadamichi Kuribayashi, was fully aware of the island's importance, and set out a series of "Courageous Battle Vows" for the defenders. One of these was "Above all, we shall dedicate ourselves and our entire strength to the defence of the islands."

Kuribayashi's men worked hard, and by the summer of 1944 had driven tunnels through the plateau, laid minefields, and built gun and machine gun emplacements.

U.S. reconnaissance aircraft and submarines located 642 blockhouses before the landings.

Never loath to expend vast amounts of material in an effort to spare the lives of their men, the Americans began early with the bombardment of Iwo Jima. On June 15, 1944, carrier planes struck at the island. The attacks continued during the rest of the year, reaching a climax with continuous strikes for 74 days by Saipan-based bombers. The final three-day naval bombardment was carried out by six battleships and their support elements.

The leading wave of L.V.T.s hit the beach at 0902 hours on February 19, 1945 to the north-east of Mt. Suribachi and began immediately to claw its way up the black sand.

The assault troops were men of the 4th Marine (Major-General Clifton B. Cates) and 5th Marine (Major-General Keller E. Rockey) Divisions, both part of Major-General Harry Schmidt's V 'Phib. Corps. The 3rd Marine Division (Major-General Graves B. Erskine) was in corps reserve. In overall command was Lieutenant-General Holland M. Smith.

The troops had practised landings on a similar stretch of beach, and had "stormed" a hill resembling Mount Suribachi. Reconnaissance had also given them some idea of the strength of the

△ The first two assault waves close the beach shortly before 0900 hours on February 19. The first wave hit the beaches at 0902, with elements of the 4th and 5th Marine Divisions soon moving inland to consolidate the beach-head.
(page 876) △ Iwo Jima in February 1945: a small, black volcanic island, dominated from its southern end by Mount Suribachi.
▽ The assault on Iwo Jima by the U.S. V Amphibious Corps.

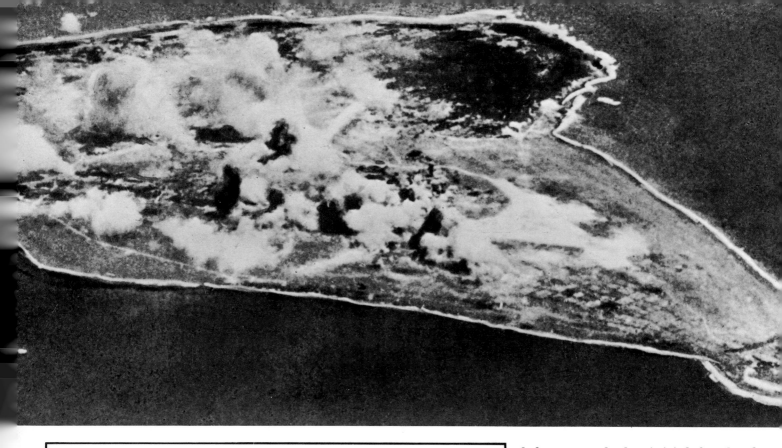

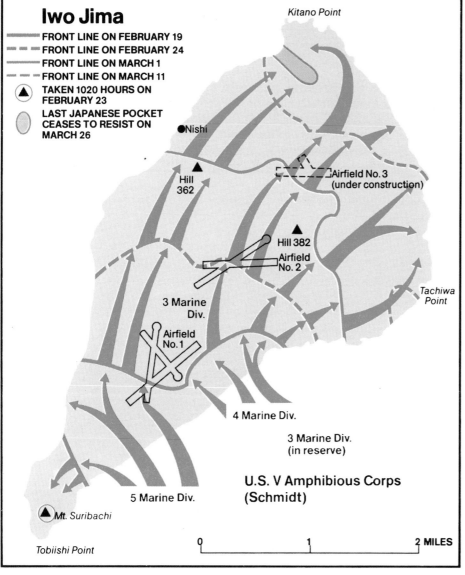

Iwo Jima

- ▦▦▦▦ FRONT LINE ON FEBRUARY 19
- ▬ ▬ ▬ FRONT LINE ON FEBRUARY 24
- ▬▬▬▬ FRONT LINE ON MARCH 1
- ▬ ▬ ▬ FRONT LINE ON MARCH 11
- ▲ TAKEN 1020 HOURS ON FEBRUARY 23
- ⬭ LAST JAPANESE POCKET CEASES TO RESIST ON MARCH 26

Kitano Point

●Nishi

Hill 362 ▲

Airfield No. 3 (under construction)

Hill 382 ▲

Airfield No. 2

Tachiwa Point

3 Marine Div.

Airfield No.1

4 Marine Div.

3 Marine Div. (in reserve)

U.S. V Amphibious Corps (Schmidt)

5 Marine Div.

▲ Mt. Suribachi

Tobiishi Point

0   1   2 MILES

defences and the initial bombardment had blown away some of the camouflage and exposed further emplacements. But what they did not know was that the adversaries had built what was probably the most complex defence system in the Pacific. Although only eight square miles in area, Iwo had 800 pillboxes and three miles of tunnels (Kuribayashi had planned 18). Guns were carefully sited to cover the beaches and a series of inland defence lines. The formation entrusted with the defence, the 109th Division, had 13,586 men by February 1, and there were also some 7,347 Navy troops on the island. There were 361 guns of over 75-mm calibre (with 100,000 rounds of ammunition), 300 A.A. guns (150,000 rounds), 20,000 light guns and machine guns (22 million rounds), 130 howitzers (11,700 rounds), 12 heavy mortars (800 rounds), 70 rocket launchers (3,500 rounds), 40 47-mm anti-tank guns (600 rounds), 20 37-mm anti-tank guns (500 rounds), and 22 tanks.

Kuribayashi had elected to fight a static battle inshore from the beaches, but the Navy had insisted that possible landing beaches should be covered by bunkers. The Japanese tanks were no match for the American Shermans, and so were positioned hull down in the gullies that scored the island. The gun sites were dug so that the weapon slits were just visible at ground level, and the positions were linked with tunnels. An awesome struggle awaited the Americans.

The Japanese hit back

Massive air and naval bombardment before the landings on Iwo Jima drove the Japanese into their bunkers, and when the Marines landed, optimists suggested that it might be an easy operation. Indeed, it is hard to imagine that any of the defenders could have survived the bombardment, whose finale had included 1,950 rounds of 16-inch shell, 1,500 of 14-inch, 400 of 12-inch, 1,700 of 8-inch, 2,000 of 6-inch, and 31,000 of 5-inch. It was the heaviest pre-landing bombardment of the war. In addition to shellfire, the Navy had also used aircraft to drop bombs and napalm, and fire a multitude of rockets. But although some of their weapons were destroyed, "the Japanese garrison cozily sat it out in their deep underground shelters".

The first wave of Marines had crossed just 200 yards of the beach when they were caught in a savage cross-fire from hidden machine guns. Simultaneously, mortars firing from pits only a few feet wide began to drop bombs on the men and vessels along the shore. The U.S. Marine Corps had embarked on the most costly operation of its history.

Despite the fire from these positions that needed explosives, flame-throwers

or tanks to overcome, elements of the 5th Marine Division managed to drive across the island on the morning of D-day. When the advance halted for the night at 1800 the Americans were far short of their objectives, but had managed to isolate Mount Suribachi.

Such was the strength of the Japanese positions, however, that it was not until D + 3 that the extinct volcano was firmly surrounded. The following morning, the 28th Marines (with the 2nd and 3rd Battalions forward and the 1st in reserve) gained 200 yards of the mountain's lower slopes. The next day an air strike by 40 planes preceded an attack that reached the foot of the mountain. On the 23rd a patrol of the 2nd Battalion's Company F reported that the Japanese had gone to ground. A larger patrol reached the rim of the crater and was involved in a brisk fire fight.

This patrol, under Lieutenant Harold G. Shrier, hoisted a small (54 × 28 inch) Stars and Stripes flag. Shortly afterwards a larger flag was obtained from an L.S.T., and Schrier decided that this should be raised instead of the first flag. This was photographed by Joe Rosenthal, an Associated Press photographer. The picture of the six men struggling to drive the pole into the volcanic soil has become a classic of the last war.

On March 1, the 28th Marines were moved to the northern sector, to join battalions of the 23rd, 24th, and 25th Marines (4th Division) and the 26th and 27th Marines (5th Division), which had been entrusted with the task of clearing Airfield No. 1 and driving northwards.

It was a battle in which daily gains were measured in hundreds of yards. On February 21 the 21st Marines (3rd Division) were ordered ashore to help.

On the morning of the 24th, after a 76-minute naval bombardment, an air strike, and fire from Marine artillery, the tanks of the 4th and 5th Divisions moved off. One thrust was directed along the western side, and the other along the eastern side, of the airfield. Mines and anti-tank guns stopped the first, but the second pushed on and began to take Japanese emplacements under close range fire. The 5th Division had gained some 500 yards by the end of the day.

On the same day, the 3rd Marine Division landed. and was allotted the task of driving along the centre of Iwo's northern plateau. Once this was taken, the Marines would be able to push down the spurs leading to the sea. The plateau was an extraordinary feature, eroded into fantastic shapes by wind, rain, and volcanic activity.

The division launched its attack at 0930 on the 25th. It was a slow and costly operation, as the attack met the main Japanese line of defences. Three days of attacks, in which the Marines brought up flame-throwing tanks to incinerate the Japanese in their shell-proof bunkers, finally broke through the line. On the 28th the Marines secured the ruins of Motoyama village and the hills overlooking Airfield No. 3. The Americans now held all three airfields, the objectives of the landings, but the fighting was by no means over.

On the last day of the month, the Marines attacked the two small features of Hills 382 and 362A. Their size was misleading, for each contained a warren of tunnels and bunkers. The crest of Hill 382 had been hollowed out and turned

Previous page, ▵ A Marine helps a wounded comrade to the beach from which he could be transported to a hospital ship.
▿ left to right: Men of the 28th Marines, 5th Marine Division, capture the first prisoner to be taken on Iwo Jima. For one and a half days he had feigned death in a shell crater until a Marine saw him breathing faintly. He was given a cigarette and then pulled out.
▿ A captain of the 21st Marine Regiment, 3rd Marine Division, inspects a Japanese dug-out after it has been hit by a bomb.

◁ Marines shelter by the remnants of a Japanese sulphur mine and refinery.
▽ A 155-mm howitzer blasts away at one of the last Japanese positions in the north of the island.

into a huge bunker housing anti-tank guns and other artillery. Tanks were sited in the gullies. To the south of the hill there was a massive rock which became known as Turkey Knob, with a natural bowl christened the Amphitheater. The fighting for both features became so intense that they became known as the Meatgrinder. A series of savage local battles was fought on March 1. And although Hill 382 fell that day, it was not until the 10th that the Japanese defending Turkey Knob and the Amphitheater were destroyed.

The attack on the Hill 362A complex on March 2 was a marked departure from normal Marine practice–they attacked at night. Although movement through the rugged terrain was slow and tiring, the tactics surprised the enemy. After a fierce fight on the 8th, the Marines were in possession of the whole area.

Despite the loss of these key points, the Japanese continued to fight with their customary aggressiveness. On the 8th

they launched an attack on the junction between the 23rd and 24th Marines. Caught in the open without artillery support, the attack failed with 650 dead. With this defeat the Japanese defence began to crumble, and the battle moved into the mopping up stage. Individual strongpoints were in no mood to surrender, however, and as they had ample stocks of food, water, and ammunition, they could hold out for some time. Indeed, on March 15, many of the last defenders attempted to infiltrate the American lines.

The last pocket to be destroyed was that at Kitano Point, which was declared officially secure on March 25. But that night over 200 Japanese emerged from the flame-blackened and shell-scarred rocks. Led in person by Kuribayashi, some say, they tore into the bivouac area occupied by the sleeping men of the 5th Pioneer Battalion. A defensive line was set up by the Army's VII Fighter Command and the Marines' 8th Field Depot and by dawn at least 223 Japanese, including their leader, lay dead.

The conquest of Iwo Jima had cost the Marines 5,931 dead and 17,372 wounded. But by the end of the war the island's airfields had saved the lives of 24,761 American pilots and aircrew. Of the 21,000 Japanese defending the island, only 216 were taken prisoner. If this was the cost of taking an island of only eight square miles and which had been Japanese only since 1891, what would be the cost of the conquest of Japan?

▽ *The Americans consolidate: telephone lines fan out from a headquarters north of Mount Suribachi to improve communications between commanders and front line forces mopping up Japanese resistance.*

CHAPTER 89
THE BATTLE OF LAKE BALATON

By May 1945, the German resistance had collapsed before the Red Army. The ring was closing round the New Chancellery in Berlin, and Vienna, the second capital of the Nazi Greater Germany, had been under Marshal Tolbukhin's control since April 13.

Between the Drava and the Carpathians, General Wöhler, commanding Army Group "South", had tried to break the Budapest blockade during the first fortnight of January. Although he had been reinforced by IV S.S. Panzer Corps, which had been withdrawn from East Prussia just before the Soviet attack on the Vistula, he failed in this attempt. The German 6th Army, which had just been transferred to General Balck's command, nevertheless managed to regain possession of the important military position of Székesfehérvár, but the effort exhausted its strength.

This setback sealed the fate of IX S.S. Mountain Corps, which, under the command of General Pfeffer-Wildenbruch, made up the Hungarian capital's garrison. On February 13, Buda castle, the defenders' last stronghold, fell to Marshal Malinovsky's troops (2nd Ukrainian Front), whilst the 3rd Ukrainian Front under Marshal Tolbukhin cleared Pest. The Russians claimed the Germans had lost 41,000 killed and 110,000 prisoners. The figures are certainly exaggerated, but nevertheless the 13th Panzer Division, the *"Feldherrnhalle"* Panzergrenadier Division, and the 33rd Hungarian S.S. Cavalry Division had been wiped out.

On March 6, the 6th *Panzerarmee*

The Gilberts and Marshalls

The continuing reinforcement of American power in the Pacific allowed Admirals E.J. King in the Pentagon, C.W. Nimitz at Pearl Harbor, and Vice-Admirals W.F. Halsey, R.A. Spruance, and T.C. Kincaid at sea to take risks which would have been unthought of at Guadalcanal. The increase in the numbers of fast aircraft-carriers available would, however, not have been as effective had not the U.S. at the same time rebuilt its naval air force. This involved the replacement of the 325 mph Grumman F4F Wildcat fighter by the 375 mph Grumman F6F Hellcat, the supplementing of the Douglas SBD Dauntless by the Curtiss SB2C Helldiver and the all-round use of the Vought F4U Corsair.

It was evident by November 20, 1943 that the war was lost for Japan and Tojo. The American plan was to cut Japan's industries off from their source of supply. Nimitz would drive through the central Pacific along the axis Pearl Harbor-Marshall Islands-Caroline Islands-Marianas while MacArthur attacked along the line New Guinea-Mindanao.

Nimitz changed his first objective to the Gilbert Islands, which would be taken under Operation "Galvanic". After the Gilbert Islands had been captured, the U.S. 5th Fleet captured the Majuro, Kwajalein and Eniwetok atolls in the Marshall Islands.

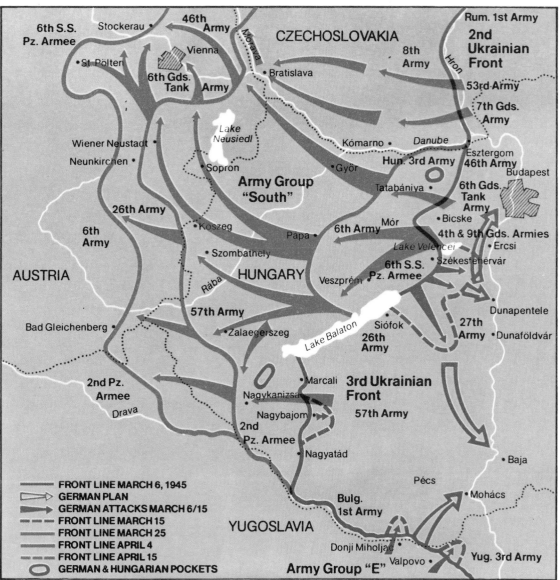

FRONT LINE MARCH 6, 1945
GERMAN PLAN
GERMAN ATTACKS MARCH 6/15
FRONT LINE MARCH 15
FRONT LINE MARCH 25
FRONT LINE APRIL 4
FRONT LINE APRIL 15
GERMAN & HUNGARIAN POCKETS

(Colonel-General Sepp Dietrich) went
over to the offensive from the bastion of
Székesfehérvár. Dietrich had left the
Ardennes front on about January 25; it
had taken six weeks for him to travel and
take up his position. He might, on the other
hand have reached the Oder front between
February 5 and 10 if the plan that Guderian
had vainly recommended to the Führer
had been followed. The Führer in fact
expected a miracle from this new offensive, indeed even the recapture of the
Ploieşti oilfields.

The 3rd Ukrainian Front was to be
smashed under the impact of a triple
attack:

1. the left, the 6th *Panzerarmee*, consisting of eight Panzer (including the
"Leibstandarte Adolf Hitler", *"Das
Reich"*, *"Hohenstaufen"*, and *"Hitlerjugend"*), three infantry, and two
cavalry divisions, was to deliver the
main blow; it was to reach the Danube
at Dunaföldvar and exploit its victory

towards the south, with its left close
to the Danube, its right on Lake Balaton;
2. between Lake Balaton and the Drava,
the 2nd *Panzerarmee* (General de Angelis: six divisions) would immobilise
Tolbukhin by attacking towards
Kaposzvár; and
3. on the right, Army Group "E" (Colonel-
General Löhr), in Yugoslavia, would
send a corps of three divisions across
the Drava, and from Mohacs move to
the Danube.

The offensive of March 6 therefore committed 22 German divisions, including 19
from Army Group "South", out of the 39
that General Wöhler had under his
command at the time. But this tremendous effort was of no avail. On the Drava
and south of Lake Balaton, the German
attack collapsed after 48 hours. The outlook for the 6th *Panzerarmee* seemed
better on the day the engagement started,
as the Panzers, massed on a narrow front,

succeeded in breaking through, but the poorly-trained infantry proved incapable of exploiting this brief success. Tolbukhin, on the other hand, had organised his forces in depth and countered with his self-propelled guns. In fact, on March 12, Dietrich was halted about 19 miles from his starting point, but about 16 miles from his Danube objective.

The Russian riposte

On March 16, Marshals Malinovsky and Tolbukhin in their turn went over to the attack from the junction point of their two Fronts. Malinovsky planned to drive the German 6th Army back to the Danube between Esztergom and Komárom, whilst Tolbukhin, driving north-west of Lakes Velencei and Balaton, intended to split at its base the salient made in the Soviet lines by the 6th *Panzerarmee*.

The 2nd Ukrainian Front's troops had the easier task and reached their first objective by March 21, cutting off four of the 6th Army's divisions.

Tolbukhin, on the other hand, met such firm resistance on March 16 and 17 from IV S.S. Panzer Corps, forming Balck's right, that the *Stavka* put the 6th Guards Tank Army at his disposal. However, because of Malinovsky's success, Wöhler took two Panzer divisions from the 6th *Panzerarmee* and set them against Malinovsky's forces. As the inequality between attack and defence became increasingly marked, Dietrich managed to evacuate the salient he had captured between March 6 and 12, and then on March 24 he brought his troops back through the bottleneck at Székesfehérvár. But what he saved from the trap was merely a hotchpotch of worn-out men with neither supplies nor equipment.

On March 27, the 6th Guards Tank Army was at Veszprém and Devecser, 35 and 48 miles from its starting point. On March 29, Tolbukhin crossed the Rába at Sárvár, and Malinovsky crossed it at Györ, where it meets the Danube. The Hungarian front had therefore collapsed; this was not surprising as Wöhler, who had no reserves, had had 11 Panzer divisions more or less destroyed between March 16 and 27.

On April 6 Hitler, consistent in his misjudgement, stripped Wöhler of command of Army Group "South" and gave it to Colonel-General Rendulic, whom he

recalled from the Kurland pocket for the task.

Vienna falls

But Malinovsky had already driven between Lake Neusiedl and the Danube on April 2, and had forced the Leitha at Bruck, whilst Tolbukhin, who had captured the large industrial centre of Wiener Neustadt, launched one column along the Semmering road towards Graz and another towards Mödling and Vienna. The day he took over his command, Rendulic was informed that the advance guard of the 3rd Ukrainian Front was already in Klosterneuburg north of Vienna, and that the 2nd Ukrainian Front was already approaching it from the south. A week later, a cease-fire was signed in the famous Prater Park, but in addition to the ordeal of a week's street fighting, the wretched Viennese still had to suffer much brutality and shameless looting from their "liberators".

Tolbukhin, who boasted of the capture of 130,000 prisoners, 1,350 tanks, and 2,250 guns, went up the right bank of the Danube, but his main forces did not go further than Amstetten, a small town 75 miles west of Vienna. On May 4, his patrols in the outskirts of Linz met a reconnaissance unit of the U.S. 3rd Army, and on the same day made contact with the advance guard of the British 8th Army on the Graz road. After helping to clear Vienna, Malinovsky sent his armies on the left across the Danube in the direction of Moravia. At Mikulov they crossed the pre-Munich (1938) Austro-Czechoslovak frontier. On the left bank of the Danube, the right wing of the 2nd Ukrainian Front, including the Rumanian 1st and 4th Armies (Generals Atanasiu and Dascalesco), liberated Slovakia and then, converging towards the north-west, occupied Brno on April 24 and were close to Olomouc when hostilities ceased. Slovakia's administration was handed over to the representatives of the Czechoslovak government-in-exile under Eduard Beneš as the occupation proceeded.

◁ *The Nazi party attacked from within: an army officer hanged for having negotiated with the Russians in Vienna.*
▽ *Russian T-34/85 medium tanks move through an Austrian village in the closing days of the war.*

CHAPTER 90
ACROSS THE RHINE

On March 8, 1945, Field-Marshal Kesselring was ordered to leave the Italian theatre of operations immediately and go to an audience with the *Führer*. The following afternoon, Hitler told him that as a result of the unfortunate situation at Remagen, he had decided to make him Commander-in-Chief in the West. In his account of the meeting, Kesselring writes:

"Without attaching any blame to Rundstedt, Hitler justified his action with the argument that a younger and more flexible leader, with greater experience of fighting the Western powers, and still possessing the troops' full confidence, could perhaps make himself master of the situation in the West. He was aware of the inherent difficulties of assuming command at such a juncture, but there

▽ *British forces cross the great natural obstacle. Men of the Dorsetshire Regiment get under way in their Buffalo.*

△ Trucks fitted with special jigs move pontoons up towards the west bank of the Rhine in preparation for the American 9th Army's crossing.

was no alternative but for me to make this sacrifice in spite of the poor state of my health. He had full confidence in me and expected me to do all that was humanly possible."

Such was the conclusion of the general review of the situation that Hitler had spent several hours discussing with Kesselring, first alone, later in the company of Keitel and Jodl. On the whole, Hitler was optimistic about the future. One might have suspected him of trying to mislead Kesselring as to the true situation were it not for his own unique capacity for self-deception. In any event, he appeared satisfied with the course of events on the Eastern Front.

Hitler certainly thought that a collapse in the East would be the end of the war, but he had provided for this eventuality and added, according to Kesselring's notes taken immediately after the audience: "our main military effort is

directed to the East. He [Hitler] envisages the decisive battle there, with complete confidence. And he expects the enemy's main attack to be launched at Berlin."

For this reason the 9th Army, which was charged with the defence of the city, had been given priority consideration. Under the command of General T. Busse, it had:

1. adequate infantry strength, together with Panzer and anti-tank forces;
2. standard artillery strength and more than adequate anti-aircraft defences, deployed in considerable depth under the best artillery commanders available;
3. excellent positions, with the best of defences, especially water barriers, on both sides of the main battle line; and
4. in its rear the strongest position of all, Berlin, with its fortified perimeter and whole defensive organisation.

So there were grounds for assurance that the Berlin front would not be broken; similarly with Army Group "Centre", on the borders of Silesia and Czechoslovakia, which had gained notable successes. Its commander, Schörner, assured Hitler that "with reinforcements and sufficient supplies, he would repel all enemy attacks launched at him".

As regards the situation on the Western Front, the heavy losses sustained by the British, Americans, and French over months of heavy fighting were a factor that should be taken into account. Furthermore, in Hitler's opinion, "the Allies could not dismiss the natural obstacles covering the German Army's positions. The Allied bridgehead at Remagen was the danger point and it was urgent it should be mopped up; but there too Hitler was confident."

In these conditions, Kesselring's task was to hold on long enough for the Eastern Front armies to be brought up to strength, so that O.K.W. could then despatch the necessary reinforcements to the armies in the West. Within a short while, the deficiencies of the Luftwaffe, held to blame for the failures of recent months, would be forgotten and Grand-Admiral Dönitz's new submarines would have turned the tables in the Battle of the Atlantic, bringing much needed relief to the defence of the Third Reich.

Kesselring caught off balance

Thus armed with encouragement, Kesselring received his chief-of-staff's report in the night of March 9-10 at the H.Q. at Ziegenberg just vacated by Rundstedt. General Westphal had been his chief-of-staff during his time as supreme commander in Italy, and Kesselring had complete confidence in him.

The new commander must have been considerably shocked by the un-embroidered account of the situation that he received. With 55 battle-worn divisions giving him, on average, a coverage of 63 fighting men for each mile of the front, it was his task to hold 85 full strength Allied divisions, which also enjoyed all the benefits of undisputed air superiority.

On March 11, at the H.Q. of LIII Corps, Kesselring met Field-Marshal Model and General von Zangen, commanding the 15th Army, which had been given the job of wiping out the Remagen bridgehead. All were agreed that this objective could not be attained unless there was considerable speeding up in the supply of substantial reinforcements, and above all of ammunition, and this filled Kesselring with apprehension. The morale of Army Group "H" gave him some comfort, however, especially since the enemy attack across the lower Rhine was taking time in getting under way. On the other hand, the position of Army Group "G", without any mobile reserves worthy of the name, seemed fraught with risk.

Hence Kesselring was not so much caught unawares as off guard by Operation "Undertone", the American offensive south of the Moselle, which he learnt had been launched when he returned from this rapid tour of inspection. The series of attacks by the American generals came as a disagreeable revelation to the Germans; Kesselring wrote:

"What clearly emerged was the rapid succession of operations (showing that the Allies had abandoned their Italian campaign strategy) as well as the competency of command and the almost reckless engagement of armoured units in terrain that was quite unsuited for the use of heavy tanks. On the basis of my experience in Italy in similar terrain, I was not expecting the American armoured forces to achieve rapid success, in spite of the fact that the reduced strength of tired German troops gave undoubted advantage to the enemy operation."

In the face of this violent American thrust, O.B. West appealed to O.K.W. for authorisation to withdraw the German 1st and 7th Armies to the right bank of the Rhine; typically, Hitler procrastinated until it was too late to accept this eminently reasonable course. And the only reinforcement destined for the Western Front was a single division, which was not even combat-worthy as it had spent some considerable time in Denmark on garrison duties. To cap this, Kesselring was informed of the surprise attack at Oppenheim, while the 1st Parachute Army brought news that north of the Ruhr, smokescreens maintained over several hours showed that Montgomery was putting the final touches to his careful preparations.

To surrender or not?

It was in these circumstances that Kesselring was contacted by *Obergruppenführer* Karl Wolff of the *Waffen*-S.S., whom he had known in the capacity of "Plenipotentiary for the Wehrmacht in the rear of the Italian Front". For the past few weeks, this officer had been engaged, via Major Waibel of Swiss Army Intelligence, in negotiation with Allen Dulles, head of the American Secret Services in Berne, about terms for the capitulation of the German forces fighting in Italy. On March 23, Kesselring, who knew what Wolff was up to, saw him in his office in Ziegenberg, where Wolff suggested directly that the German armies in the West should be associated with this bid for surrender.

Kesselring refused, in spite of the succession of telephone calls informing him of the rapid progress made by the Americans, who had broken out of the Oppenheim bridgehead. According to Wolff's report to Dulles, Kesselring's opposition was based on both moral and practical arguments:

"He was defending soil and he was bound to continue even if he died himself in the fighting. He said he personally owed everything to the Führer, his rank, his appointment, his decorations. To this he added that he hardly knew the generals commanding the corps and divisions under him. Moreover, he had a couple of well-armed S.S. divisions behind him which he was certain would take action against him if he undertook anything

Field-Marshal Albrecht von Kesselring was born in Bavaria in 1885. He served as a staff officer in the artillery throughout World War I and the 1920's, and in 1933 he was transferred to the air force. He commanded the Luftwaffe in the German invasion of Poland and Belgium, and ordered the bombing of the B.E.F. as it evacuated Dunkirk. He conducted the extremely successful bombing raids on R.A.F. bases in southern England in 1940 and in July of that year he was made a Field-Marshal. In 1941 he was appointed C.-in-C., South, sharing with Rommel the command of the North African campaign and taking over during Rommel's absence and later during the retreat from Tunisia. In 1943 he was C.-in-C. in Italy, conducting a brilliant campaign despite the indifference of his superiors to his constant pleas for air reinforcements. For over a year he held out against the Allied advance, with a superbly conceived line of defences behind Cassino. In 1945 he succeeded the cream of Hitler's generals on the Western Front in a desperate attempt to check the Allied advance, but in March he had to surrender the southern half of the German forces to the Allies. He was sentenced to death by a British military court for executing Italian hostages, but in 1947 his sentence was commuted to life imprisonment and in 1952 he was released on the grounds of ill health. He died in 1960.

△ *A German N.C.O. illustrates how to fire a* Panzerfaust 30m *anti-tank rocket projector. There were four* Panzerfaust *models, all working the same way: the rocket was contained in a tube held under the arm or over the shoulder. When fired, the rocket motor drove the weapon out of the tube and on towards the target. Just as the weapon left the tube, a cap at the latter's rear was pushed off, allowing the exhaust to fan out to the rear. The warhead of the rocket was a hollow-charge device containing 3 pounds 7½ ounces of explosive, capable of penetrating 200 mm of armour sloped at 30 degrees. It was an extremely efficient weapon, with a punch equal to that of the dual-purpose 8.8-cm gun.*

△▷ *German prisoners are escorted through the town of Hamminkeln by their captors, men of the British 6th Airborne Division.*

▽▷ *German civilians and prisoners hug the ground in the courtyard of a captured farmhouse in an effort to protect themselves from retaliatory German artillery fire.*

against the Führer's orders."

Nevertheless Kesselring had no objection to a German capitulation in Italy, and the *Obergruppenführer* was quite free to convey to the former's successor, Colonel-General von Vietinghoff, that O.B. West entirely approved the project as outlined to him.

Scorched earth policy

Whatever one may think of the ethical considerations behind Kesselring's refusal, he understandably felt no scruples in giving his support to Albert Speer, Reich Minister for Armaments and War Production, who was doing all he could to sabotage the execution of the "scorched earth" order promulgated by Hitler on March 19, 1945.

In setting out its motives, the monstrous *Führerbefehl* used the following line of argument:

"The fight for the existence of our people obliges us to make total use, even within the Reich, of whatever means may weaken the fighting power of the enemy and prevent him from pursuing his advance. Any means capable, directly or indirectly, of inflicting lasting damage on the offensive strength of the enemy must be resorted to. It is erroneous to think that by leaving them intact or with only superficial damage, we may more profitably resume exploitation of our communication and transport systems and our industrial or productive installations when we reconquer our invaded territory. When the enemy comes to retreat, he will have no consideration for the population, and will leave only scorched earth behind him.

"For this reason I command:

1. that within the Reich the communications and military transport systems, and the industrial and productive installations, which the enemy may use immediately or within a limited period for the prosecution of the war, be destroyed."

Article 2 of the same decree divided powers for this purpose between the military chiefs and the civil administrators; and Article 3, ordering the immediate transmission of the order to army commanders, declared invalid any directive which sought to nullify it.

So Hitler joined Morgenthau, whereas even Churchill and Roosevelt had re-

jected the inhuman and demented notion of "pastoralising" the German people. Albert Speer, however, devoted his entire energies to opposing the implementation of this insane order: verbally on March 18; and in writing in two letters, the second of which, dated March 29, is preserved among the appendices that Percy Ernst Schramm adds as a supplement to his masterly edition of the O.K.W. war diary.

"From what you have told me this evening [March 18] the following emerges clearly and unequivocally, unless I have misunderstood you: if we are to lose the war, the German people are to be lost as well. This destiny is unavoidable. This being so, it is not necessary to secure the basic conditions to enable our people to ensure their own survival even in the most primitive form. Rather, on the contrary, we should ourselves destroy them. For they will have proved themselves the weaker, and the future will belong exclusively to the people of the east, who will have shown themselves the stronger. Furthermore, only the unworthy will survive since the best and bravest will have fallen." Here revealed was the ugly bedrock of Hitler's totally nihilistic nature.

Speer's opposition

Speer did not limit his opposition merely to pious utterances. He put the enormous weight of influence he had as dictator of industrial production to the task of avoiding implementation of the "scorched earth" order.

In this covert activity he received positive support from Kesselring; as a result, in its retreat from the Rhine to the Elbe and beyond, the German Army restricted itself to forms of destruction which are common in such cases to all the armies in the world. Two circumstances favoured Speer in carrying out his policy: the headlong nature of the Allied advance after March 31 and, in the German camp, the explosives crisis, further exacerbated by the disorganisation of transport.

At the end of 1966, on his release from Spandau prison, to which he had been sent by the Nuremberg trial, Albert Speer was greeted by manifestations of sympathy. This was interpreted by some as the sign they had been seeking since

1945 of a recrudescence of Nazism in the Federal Republic. Such an interpretation seems quite unwarranted. Rather, it would seem that Speer's sympathisers wanted to show public recognition of the man who, in spite of Hitler and at the risk of his life, had chosen to safeguard the means of survival and recovery so that one day another Germany might live.

Montgomery prepares to cross the Rhine

On March 23, at 1530 hours, under a clear sky and with a favourable weather forecast, Montgomery launched Operation "Plunder/Varsity" and addressed the American, British, and Canadian troops under his command with an order of the day which concluded with these words: "6. 21 ARMY GROUP WILL NOW

Advance into Germany

NORTH SEA

Eckernförde
Kiel
Neumünster
Cuxhaven
Rostock
Wismar
Lübeck
Hamburg
1
U.S. XVIII
Airborne Corps
GERMANY
Wilhelmshaven
Bremerhaven
Br. XXX Corps
Stettin
Groningen
Lüneburg
Assen
Ems
Can. II Corps
21st
Army
Group
Br
VIII Corps
Wittenberge
Oder
Meppel
Can. I Corps
Almelo
Lingen
Berlin
Amsterdam
Deventer
Br. XII Corps
Minden
Hannover
Aller
Magdeburg
HOLLAND
Zutphen
Brunswick
Elba
Dessau
2
Wittenberg
Emmerich
Münster
12th Army
Group
Weser
U.S. VIII Corps
Torgau
Can. 1st Army
Kleve
Eisleben
Halle
Br. 2nd Army
Wesel
Lippe
Mündem
Nordhausen
U.S. VII Corps
Leipzig
Mulde
21st
U.S. 9th Army
Duisburg
Kassel
Mühlhausen
Elba
Army Group
Rhine
Wuppertal
Erfurt
Naumberg
U.S. 15th Army
Cologne
Sieg
Marburg
Fulda
Werra
Jena
U.S. XX Corps
Chemnitz
BELGIUM
Bonn
Giessen
Thüringerwald
Saafeld
U.S. VIII Corps
12th Army
Group
U.S. 1st Army
Remagen
Fulda
Saale
Plauen
Koblenz
Karlovy Vary
Ascheffenburg
Schweinfurt
CZECHOSLOVAKIA
U.S. 3rd Army
Oppenheim
Würzburg
Bamberg
Bayreuth
LUXEMBOURG
Worms
Michelstadt
Main
Plzeň
Ludwigshafen
U.S. 7th Army
Nuremberg
Fr. 1st Army
Neckar
Heilbronn
Ceské
Budějovice
Lauter
Karlsruhe
Altmühl
U.S. V Corps
Rastatt
6th Army
Group
Regensburg
U.S. XII Corps
Herrenalb
Stuttgart
Danube
Linz
6th Army Group
Kehl
Tübingen
Murg
Freudenstadt
Horb
Ulm
BAVARIA
Braunau
FRANCE
Black
Forest
Biberach
Inn
U.S. III Corps
Freiburg
Munich
Salzburg
Rosenheim
Berchtesgaden
Basle
Dornbirn
Innsbruck
AUSTRIA
SWITZERLAND
St. Anton
3
Vipiteno
Bolzano
YUGOSLAVIA

	AREA OCCUPIED BY MARCH 27 1945
	AREA OCCUPIED BY APRIL 9
	AREA OCCUPIED BY APRIL 19
	AREA OCCUPIED BY MAY 7
	ALLIED ATTACKS
	GERMAN POCKETS
1	FIRST RUSSO-BRITISH CONTACT MAY 2
2	FIRST RUSSO-AMERICAN CONTACT APRIL 25
3	CONTACT WITH U.S. 5TH ARMY MAY 4
	RUSSIAN ATTACK APRIL 16
-x-x-x-x-	ARMY GROUP BOUNDARIES

ITALY

CROSS THE RHINE

The enemy possibly thinks he is safe behind this great river obstacle. We all agree that it is a great obstacle; but we will show the enemy that he is far from safe behind it. This great Allied fighting machine, composed of integrated land and air forces, will deal with the problem in no uncertain manner.

7. And having crossed the Rhine, we will crack about in the plains of Northern Germany, chasing the enemy from pillar to post. The swifter and the more energetic our action, the sooner the war will be over, and that is what we all desire; to get on with the job and finish off the German war as soon as possible.

8. Over the Rhine, then, let us go. And good hunting to you all on the other side.

9. May 'The Lord mighty in battle' give us the victory in this our latest undertaking, as He has done in all our battles since we landed in Normandy on D-Day."

The Rhine, which in 21st Army Group's sector is about 400 yards wide and has a current of about six feet per second, was the "great obstacle" of which Montgomery spoke. But the means given him to cross it were also great.

Under his command he had two armies, eight corps, and 27 divisions (17 infantry, eight armoured, and two airborne; or, in national terms, 13 American, 12 British, and two Canadian). To these should be added the equivalent of three divisions represented by five armoured brigades, a British commando brigade, and the Canadian 9th Infantry Brigade.

The British 2nd Army's attack, supplemented by the Canadian II Corps, was prepared for and supported by 1,300 pieces of artillery, with 600 guns fulfilling the same function for XVI Corps, which was to open the right bank of the Rhine for the American 9th Army. Such concentration of firepower necessitated the transport and dumping of 60,000 tons of ammunition. Massive area bombing by the Allied air forces extended the artillery action to German rail and road communications, isolating the battlefield. Between March 20 and 22, R.A.F. Bomber Command and the U.S. 8th and 9th Air Forces made 16,000 sorties over the area in question and dropped 49,500 tons of bombs (including 22,000-lb "Grand Slams").

△ *A battery of British 40-mm Bofors guns in action in the direct support rôle.*
◁ *Operation "Plunder" takes the western Allies across the Rhine into the heartlands of Germany to meet up with the Red Army closing in from the east.*

Special attacks were launched on airfields where the Luftwaffe's new jet aircraft were stationed.

To build bridges across the Rhine, 30,000 tons of engineering equipment and 59,000 engineers had to be transported to the area. But before the construction required by Operation "Plunder" could be used, divisions in the first line of attack had to be conveyed from one bank to the other by other means. This task was carried out by a detachment of the Royal Navy, which left Antwerp to reach its departure point by a series of Belgian, Dutch, and German canals. With Vice-Admiral Sir Harold M. Burrough in overall command, it comprised 45 landing craft (L.C.M.), plus a formation of the 12-ton amphibious tanks known by the British as Buffaloes and as Alligators by the Americans. Prepara-

tions on this scale were obviously observable by the enemy, but the final deployment of the Allied forces was concealed by the smokescreen which hid the left bank of the Rhine over a distance of 75 miles between dawn on March 21 and 1700 hours on March 23.

As is apparent, Montgomery had once more showed his immense capacity for organisation. In the course of the battle which followed, he would confirm his reputation as an exceptional tactician, by winning back for himself the advantage of surprise which he had lost as a result of such tremendous concentration of forces. And, it should be noted, there are few men who, like him, combine such attention to detail in preparation with such vigour of execution.

On the right bank of the Rhine, the 1st Parachute Army was deployed with its

right slightly upstream of Emmerich and its left in the region of Duisburg. It was thus defending a front of 45 miles with seven weak and, by now, worn-out divisions, but nonetheless, an adequate concentration for defence bearing in mind the natural obstacle of the broad river, had the divisions been at full complement. During the relative lull following March 11, they had dug themselves in well and the rapid construction of their defensive positions was entirely satisfactory to Kesselring. General Schlemm had played a considerable rôle here; Major Milton Shulman, of the Canadian 1st Army, had the opportunity of interrogating him later, and writes:

"His record, coupled with an orderly mind and a keen grasp of tactical problems, placed him amongst the more able generals available in the Wehrmacht."

Schlemm's only mobile reserves were the 116th Panzer and 15th *Panzergrenadier* Divisions, of XLVII Panzer Corps, which he had put in reserve behind his centre. At a higher command level, in Army Group "H", Colonel-General Blaskowitz was similarly short of men, and the meagre reserves found by Kesselring were spent in containing the twin thrust of the American 1st Army bursting out of the Remagen bridgehead, and the 3rd Army exploiting at record speed the bridgeheads it had won at Hanau and Aschaffenburg on the Main.

O.K.W. and O.B. West confidently expected an airborne landing. Accordingly, an entire anti-aircraft corps was put at the disposal of Blaskowitz, who deployed batteries all over the area between Munster and the right bank of the Rhine. But apparently to little effect:

▽ *An American Landing Vehicle Tracked (L.V.T.) splashes into the Rhine under cover of a thick smokescreen.*

△ *The disillusionment of defeat on the face of a 16-year old captured by the Americans.*
▷ *U.S. troops move off towards the front after crossing the Rhine.*

as on previous occasions the German soldier had to put up with implacable and practically unchallenged machine gun and cannon fire and bombing from Allied aircraft without seeing any fighters of his own in the sky.

The battle begins

At 1700 hours on March 23, the smoke-screen vanished and the entire artillery of the British 2nd Army and the American 9th Army opened fire on the enemy positions, maintaining their barrage of shells of all calibres until 0945 hours the following morning. This was, however, interspersed with pauses at times varying from sector to sector to allow the divisions launching the attack to feel out the enemy strength.

The main action devolved upon the British 2nd Army, in position north of the Lippe. On its left, XXX Corps had during the night got four battalions of the 51st Division (Major-General Thomas Rennie) across the Rhine; on its right, XII Corps had established its 15th Division (Major-General Colin Muir Barber) on the right bank of the river, opposite Xanten, while the 1st Commando Brigade went into action against the 180th Division in the ruins of Wesel. Further south, the American 9th Army, whose task was to cover the flank of the British attack, engaged its XVI Corps, whose 30th and 79th Divisions crossed the Rhine to either side of Rheinberg. According to Montgomery, German resistance was only sporadic, and certainly the two American divisions mentioned above suffered only 31 killed in the enterprise.

The offensive undertaken by the 21st Army Group was no surprise for Blaskowitz, who had even correctly estimated its main point of impact and line of advance. Accordingly–and with a degree of haste for which Kesselring reproached him–he judged it opportune to throw in his armoured reserves. The dawn saw furious counter-attacks which drew the following observation from Sir Brian Horrocks, then in command of XXX Corps:

"Reports were coming in of Germans surrendering in large numbers to the British and American forces on our flanks but there was no sign of any collapse on our front. In fact the 51st Highland Division reported that the enemy was fighting harder than at any time since Normandy. It says a lot for the morale of those German parachute and panzer troops that with chaos, disorganisation and disillusionment all around them they should still be resisting so stubbornly."

In the course of the fighting between XXX Corps and the 15th *Panzergrenadier* Division, which brought into the line the paratroops from the German 6th and 7th Parachute Divisions, Major-General Rennie was killed, evidence enough of the enemy's determination.

Airborne landings

However, at 1000 hours the "event", in the Napoleonic sense of the word, took place. In the German camp, remembering the precedent of Arnhem, the Allies' airborne troops were expected to attack at the time that Montgomery's infantry was attempting to cross the Rhine, and to drop to the rear of the battlefield to effect a vertical encirclement of the 1st Parachute Army. But their attack came three hours after it had been anticipated, and the drop took place in the region of Hamminkeln, barely five miles from the right bank of the river. Under the command of Lieutenant-General Matthew B. Ridgway, XVIII Airborne Corps comprised the British 6th Airborne (Major-General E. Bols) and the American 17th Airborne (Major-General William E. Miley) Divisions, their transport being undertaken by 1,572 planes and 1,326 gliders, under close escort from 889 fighters. The 6th Airborne Division took off from 11 airfields in the south-east of England, the American 17th from 17 that had just been built in the area bounded by Rheims, Orléans, Evreux, and Amiens. The effect of surprise was so great and the German *flak* so well neutralised by Allied artillery pounding from the left bank that losses on landing amounted to no more than 46 transport planes and three per cent of the glider force employed in this operation, known as "Varsity".

The British and Americans fell on the enemy battery positions and reduced a good many of them to silence, then thrust on across the Diersforterwald to meet XII Corps, whose advance was strongly supported by 580 heavy guns of the 2nd Army, responding to calls for fire cover with most admirable speed and precision.

At the end of the day, XVIII Airborne Corps made contact with the British XII Corps. Furthermore, thanks to units flown in by glider, XVIII Airborne Corps had taken intact a number of bridges over the IJssel which, flowing as it does parallel to the Rhine between Wesel and Emmerich, could have constituted an obstacle to the rapid exploitation of the day's successes. Moreover, the 84th Division was taken in rear and as good as annihilated, with the loss of most of the 3,789 prisoners counted by General Ridgway's Intelligence services.

Large bridgehead

As night fell, in the zone between Dinslaken and Rees, where resistance from German parachute troops had lost none of its spirit, the 21st Army Group had taken a bridgehead 30 miles wide on the right bank of the Rhine, running, in the British XII Corps' (Lieutenant-General Sir Neil Methuen Ritchie) sector to a depth of nearly eight miles; the Allied bridge builders were free to get to work without any threat of retaliation on the part of enemy artillery. Montgomery could feel all the more satisfaction with the way things had gone on March 24 as he had committed only four of his eight corps.

Eisenhower's excellent plan

From an observation post situated a mile or so south of Xanten, which commanded a good view over the vast Westphalian plain, Churchill, together with Brooke and Eisenhower, saw the British and American XVIII Airborne Corps' transport planes cross overhead and return, but missed the drop itself because of the mist. As the success of the operation became apparent, General Eisenhower reports that Field-Marshal Brooke turned to him and said:

"Thank God, Ike, you stuck by your plan. You were completely right, and I am sorry if my fear of dispersed effort added to your burdens. The German is now licked. It is merely a question of when he chooses to quit. Thank God, you stuck by your guns."

△ *Supplies for the 9th Army arrive by D.U.K.W. and jeep on the east bank of the Rhine.*

been rendered mobile, as well as all the units brought up from the rear to fill the gaps."

Collapse of the German 15th Army

On March 25 and 28, two further events of comparable scale and importance took place on the 12th Army Group's front: firstly, the collapse of the German 15th Army, whose task it was to contain the enemy within the Remagen bridgehead; and secondly, adding its effect to the clean breakthrough by the American 1st Army, the crossing of the Main at the Aschaffenburg and Hanau bridges by the American 3rd Army. This manoeuvre followed from a carefully prepared plan of General Bradley's after the launching of Operation "Lumberjack", which was given its final touches following the surprise assault on Remagen. He describes it as follows in *A Soldier's Story:*

"Now that Hodges had established the Remagen bridgehead to the south of Bonn, he was to trace that original pattern. First he would speed his tanks down the autobahn where it ran through Limburg on the road to Frankfurt. At Limburg he was to turn east up the Lahn Valley to Giessen. There he would join Patton's pincer coming up from the Main.

"The First and Third Armies would then advance abreast of one another in a parallel column with Hodges on the inside, Patton on his flank, up the broad Wetteran corridor toward a union with Simpson. Then while Hodges and Simpson locked themselves around the Ruhr preparatory to cleaning it out, Patton would face his Army to the east and be prepared to advance toward the oncoming Russians."

So it was, but according to Kesselring, the execution of Bradley's plan was considerably eased by Model's preconceived ideas of the enemy's intentions. The commander of Army Group "B" was obsessed with his right flank, fearing an attack down the eastern bank of the Rhine aimed at an assault on the Ruhr industrial complex from the south; and he was deaf to all telephone calls from his superior, remonstrating with him for leaving his centre thinly protected. This was a serious mistake.

Coming across this passage in *Crusade in Europe*, Lord Alanbrooke refers to an entry in his diary made at the close of that same March 24, claiming that Eisenhower's remarks resulted from a misunderstanding, and that he had not in fact "seen the light" that day near Xanten. He wrote in 1949:

"To the best of my memory I congratulated him heartily on his success and said that, as matters had turned out, his policy was now the correct one; that, with the German in his defeated condition, no dangers now existed in a dispersal of effort."

Thus Brooke corrects the remark attributed to him (on this occasion) by Eisenhower. Obviously there is a difference between the two versions. Nevertheless, it does not necessarily follow that Eisenhower was mistaken in defending his strategic plans, unless it can be shown that the German armies would have fallen into the state of ruin and confusion noted by Brooke that March 25 evening had not Operations "Lumberjack" and "Undertone" taken place.

Kesselring settles that question with greater authority than we can possibly lay claim to when he writes:

"Just as Remagen became the tomb of Army Group 'B', the Oppenheim bridgehead seemed destined to become that of Army Group 'G'. There too, the initial pocket became a deep chasm, and devoured all the strength of the other parts of the front, that somehow or other had

The Ruhr pocket

On March 25, the American 1st Army began its fresh offensive by smashing LXXIV Corps in the region of Breitscheid. Hodges immediately unleashed his 3rd, 7th, and 9th Armoured Divisions, which reached Giessen and Marburg on the 28th, 53 and 66 miles respectively from the Rhine at Neuwied. On the same day, in the 3rd Army, VIII Corps completed the mopping up of Frankfurt and made contact with Hodges's right in the region of Wiesbaden, thus trapping the enemy elements left on the right bank of the Rhine between the Lahn and the Main. But most strikingly, Patton's 4th, 6th, and 11th Armoured Divisions, in formation ahead of XII and XX Corps, had moved from the Main valley into that of the Fulda, making in the direction of Kassel. Thus Hodges, whose task was to reach the eastern outlets of the Ruhr

basin, found himself provided with cover, just as Bradley intended, against a counter-attack striking from the Harz mountains.

On the day after the surprise breakthrough at Oppenheim, Kesselring, according to his own account, had wondered "whether it was not best to accept the army groups' proposals and withdraw the entire front from the Rhine. I finally refrained from doing so, because the only result would have been to retreat in disorder. Our troops were heavily laden, barely mobile, in large part battle-weary, and encumbered by units in the rear which were still in a state of disorder. The enemy had all-round superiority, especially in mobility and in the air. If nothing occurred to check or slow his advance, our retreating columns would be overtaken and smashed. This type of combat would have become an end in itself – no longer a means employed to an end – the end being to gain time. Every day on the Rhine, on the contrary, was a day

△ *American armour rumbles through the streets of Mönchengladbach in the Ruhr industrial area.*

△ *Sherman tanks roll into the ruins of Munster on April 3.*

gained, signifying a strengthening of the front, even if it were only to enable points in the rear to be mopped up or stray troops to be rounded up."

Quite clearly, at the point reached in the German camp on March 28, Kesselring's conclusions were still more justified.

This was all the more true as the sappers of the 21st Army Group had by March 26 opened seven 40-ton bridges to traffic, and the American 9th Army and British 2nd Army came down both banks of the Lippe to overwhelm the 1st Parachute Army. Two days later, on the left bank of this river, Lieutenant-General Simpson had his 8th Armoured Division (Major-General J. M. Devine) in the region of

Haltern, more than 25 miles east of the Rhine. At the same time, Sir Miles Dempsey pushed the Guards Armoured Division (Major-General Allan Adair) down the Münster road, while his XXX and Canadian II Corps, on a line linking Borken – Bocholt – Isselburg – Emmerich, reached the Dutch frontier. The 1st Parachute Army was helplessly cut off, and its LXIII Corps and XLVII Panzer Corps (five divisions) were thrown back onto Army Group "B". And Montgomery poured his armoured units resolutely into the breach.

On April 2, 1945, as the day closed, the inevitable happened. The American 3rd Armoured Division, driving ahead of

region of the Ruhr". To reduce it, General Bradley formed a new 15th Army, under the command of Lieutenant-General Leonard T. Gerow, with a strength of five corps, including the newly-formed XXII and XXIII Corps, in all 18 divisions taken from the 1st and 9th Armies.

The encirclement of the Ruhr meant not only the rapid destruction of Army Group "B", but more importantly, the end of all organised resistance on the part of the Wehrmacht between Würzburg on the Main and Minden on the Weser. Between the inside of the wings of Army Groups "G" and "H", a breach of more than 180 miles was opened. It was too late for the unfortunate Kesselring to cherish the notion of repositioning his armies on a line along the courses of the Weser, Werra, Main, Altmuhl, and Lech, as favoured by 18th Century strategists.

Eisenhower gives up the idea of Berlin . . .

To stop this breach, O.K.W. still had, in the Harz mountains, the 11th Army, comprising five divisions under the command of General Wenck, and a 12th Army being formed on the right bank of the Elbe. But clearly the way to Berlin lay open to the 12th Army Group and on April 4 S.H.A.E.F. transferred it to the American 9th Army, to the great satisfaction of General Simpson, its commander, and even more so of General Bradley, who saw the forces under his command now rise to four armies (11 corps of 48 divisions, 14 of them armoured, with some 3,600 tanks). But Eisenhower had no intention of giving Bradley the German capital as an objective. The question had already been considered by him among other options open to him after the encirclement of the Ruhr, and he had decided against going for Berlin for strategic and logistic reasons—in particular the lengthening of his lines of communication that this would entail, and the obstacle of the Elbe, something short of 200 miles from the Rhine and 125 from Berlin.

As a result of this decision, Eisenhower set himself the following objectives:
1. to make contact without delay with the Soviet forces moving west, and thus make it impossible for the enemy to try to regroup;

△ *Ulm Cathedral, surprisingly undamaged amidst the debris of the rest of the city.*

VII Corps (1st Army), met up at Lippstatt with the 8th Armoured Division coming from Haltern. In the course of this fighting, Major-General Rose, commanding the 3rd Armoured Division in its finest foray, was killed. Now Army Group "B" was encircled, with the exception of LXVII Corps, which had been attached to Army Group "B" following the breakthrough at Breitscheid.

Including the ruins of the 1st Parachute Army mentioned above, there were the 5th *Panzerarmee* and the 15th Army, of seven corps or 19 divisions (three of them Panzer, and the 3rd *Panzergrenadier* Division) caught in a trap that Hitler was quick to qualify as "the fortified

2. to hurl the 21st Army Group to the north-east, its right wing keeping its objective steadily fixed on Lübeck, to cut off the Wehrmacht forces occupying Norway and Denmark; and
3. for the 12th and 6th Army Groups, Eisenhower writes:

"Equally important was the desirability of penetrating and destroying the so-called 'National Redoubt'. For many weeks we had been receiving reports that the Nazi intention, in extremity, was to withdraw the cream of the S.S., Gestapo, and other organisations fanatically devoted to Hitler, into the mountains of southern Bavaria, western Austria, and northern Italy. There they expected to block the tortuous mountain passes and to hold out indefinitely against the Allies. Such a stronghold could always be reduced by eventual starvation if in no other way. But if the German was permitted to establish the redoubt he might possibly force us to engage in a long-drawn-out guerrilla type of warfare, or a costly siege. Thus he could keep alive his desperate hope that through disagreement among the Allies he might yet be able to secure terms more favourable than those of unconditional surrender. The evidence was clear that the Nazi intended to make the attempt and I decided to give him no opportunity to carry it out."

So, with the Elbe reached in the vicinity of Magdeburg, it was understood that Bradley would make his main line of advance along a line Erfurt–Leipzig–Dresden, with a secondary thrust on Regensburg and Linz. Contact would be made with the Russians in Saxony, and at the same time a march would be stolen on Army Group "G" in its task of occupying the redoubt. However logical this line of argument was from a strategic point of view, it rested on a hypothesis which was shown to be false after Germany's capitulation: the "national redoubt" concept was no more than a figment of the imagination of those who fed it to S.H.A.E.F.'s Intelligence services.

Stalin approves warmly . . .

In any event, on March 24, in accordance with a decision taken at the Yalta Conference, Eisenhower communicated his plan, summarised above, to Stalin who approved it most warmly. In the terms of a telegram cited in Churchill's memoirs but absent from *Crusade in Europe,* Stalin assured Eisenhower that his plan "entirely coincides with the plan of the Soviet High Command . . . Berlin has lost its former strategic importance. The Soviet High Command therefore plans to allot secondary forces in the direction of Berlin." Knowing as we do that at the very moment these lines were dictated, Stalin was concentrating five tank armies and 25,000 guns (expending 25,600 tons of shell) on an allegedly secondary objective, one sees what was in the wind.

. . . but Churchill objects violently

The plan elaborated by S.H.A.E.F. found its strongest opponent in Churchill. Embodying as he did the ancient traditions which had inspired British diplomacy since the reign of Henry VIII, he held as a maxim that "as a war waged by a coalition draws to its end political aspects have a mounting importance."

So it seemed obvious to him that since the military collapse of the Third Reich was a matter of only a few weeks, the time had come for the two great Anglo-Saxon powers quietly to dismiss purely strategic considerations and consider political issues while there was still time. And in this field he was forced to admit that Stalin and Molotov viewed the Yalta agreement about Poland as no more than a scrap of paper.

Likewise, on March 2, Vishinsky, Soviet Deputy Minister of Foreign Affairs, in the course of a scene of abominable violence, had imposed a government chosen by the Kremlin on King Michael of Rumania. The ten per cent minority voice that Churchill had reserved in that country had fallen to all but nothing, and things were worse still in Bulgaria.

Hence Churchill thought that future operations conducted by S.H.A.E.F. should take account of political as well as military considerations, and these he enumerated and summarised as follows:

"*First,* that Soviet Russia had become a mortal danger to the free world.
Secondly, that a new front must be immediately created against her onward sweep.
Thirdly, that this front in Europe should

▷ *M26 Pershing tanks of the American 9th Army's 2nd Armoured Division pass the wrecked town hall of Magdeburg.*
▽ *A huge column of German prisoners wends its way back towards the American rear along one of the* Autobahns *constructed by the Nazis to move troops and equipment swiftly – but with a different aim in mind.*

be as far east as possible.

Fourthly, that Berlin was the prime and true objective of the Anglo-American armies.

Fifthly, that the liberation of Czechoslovakia and the entry into Prague of American troops was of high consequence.

Sixthly, that Vienna, and indeed Austria, must be regulated by the Western Powers, at least upon an equality with the Russian Soviets.

Seventhly, that Marshal Tito's aggressive pretensions against Italy must be curbed.

Finally, and above all, that a settlement must be reached on all major issues between the West and the East *before the armies of democracy melted,* or the Western Allies yielded any part of the German territories they had conquered, or, as it could soon be written, liberated from totalitarian tyranny.''

Eisenhower's plan therefore displeased him all the more because in communicating his intentions to Stalin, the Supreme Allied Commander appeared to have exceeded the commonly accepted limits of competence of a military chief; a somewhat dubious argument since Stalin had concentrated in himself the functions of head of government and generalissimo of the Soviet armed forces, in which capacity the communication had been addressed to him. With the approval of the British Chief-of-Staffs Committee and of Montgomery, the Prime Minister endeavoured to persuade Eisenhower to go back on his decision, and on April 1 an appeal was made to President Roosevelt, Field-Marshal Brooke making a similar appeal to General Marshall.

Eisenhower cabled Marshall:

"I am the first to admit that a war is waged in pursuance of political aims, and if the Combined Chiefs-of-Staff should decide that the Allied effort to take Berlin outweighs purely military considerations in this theatre, I should cheerfully readjust my plans and my thinking so as to carry out such an operation."

However, the future zonal boundaries had already been formally agreed between Russia, Britain and America, and there was little political point in occupying territory which would have to be evacuated.

In his appeal to the American President, Churchill based his case for the occupation of Berlin on the following hypothesis:

"The Russian armies will no doubt overrun all Austria and enter Vienna.

If they also take Berlin will not their impression that they have been the overwhelming contributor to our common victory be unduly imprinted in their minds, and may this not lead them into a mood which will raise grave and formidable difficulties in the future?''

Eisenhower refuses to countermand his orders

On the next day Eisenhower received a telegram from the American Joint Chiefs-of-Staff, telling him that despite the objections of the British chiefs, they supported him entirely, and that, in particular, the communication of his future plans to Stalin seemed to them "to be a necessity dictated by operations". Marshall concluded with the following point to his allies:

"To deliberately turn away from the exploitation of the enemy's weakness does not appear sound. The single objective should be quick and complete victory. While recognising there are factors not of direct concern to S.C.A.E.F., the U.S. chiefs consider his strategic concept is sound and should receive full support. He should continue to communicate freely with the Commander-in-Chief of the Soviet Army."

Lt.-Gen. Sir Miles Dempsey was born in 1896 and first came to prominence at the head of XIII Corps in the Sicilian and Italian campaigns. Before the Normandy landings he was promoted to command the 2nd Army, which he then led up to the end of the war, winning a considerable reputation for committing his men to major actions only when he was convinced that success was almost certain.

Lt.-Gen. Henry Crerar was born in 1888 and served with the Canadian artillery in World War I. From 1935 to 1938 he was Director of Military Operations and Intelligence. He was Chief-of-Staff of the Canadian Army in 1940. He commanded the Canadian I Corps and later the 1st Army in Europe.

CHAPTER 91

THE END IN ITALY

Originally known as the Apennine Position, the Gothic Line ran across the mountains, coast to coast, for 200 miles, from near La Spezia on the Gulf of Genoa to Pesaro on the Adriatic. It was longer than the line through Cassino, and the mountain barrier reached across the peninsula to within a short distance of Route 16, which followed the coast-line through the narrow plain to Rimini. Orders for the line to be reconnoitred and fortified had in fact been given by Jodl almost a month before the evacuation of Sicily, but more recently the work had been interrupted by the pressing demands for *matériel* and labour for building the defences of the Gustav and Hitler Lines.

At the time of the capture of Rome, Alexander estimated that Kesselring would have only the equivalent of ten divisions to man the Apennine positions, but Hitler's immediate reaction to the threat of an Allied advance into northern Italy had completely changed the situation. Kesselring was now able to gain much-needed time for the Organisation Todt to complete most of the defences that had been so carefully planned.

At the very height of the fighting in Normandy, Hitler dispatched no fewer than seven divisions, withdrawn from Denmark, Holland, Hungary, and even the Russian front, to reinforce Army Group "C" in Italy. Finally O.K.W. sent a battalion of Tiger tanks from

△ *Sherman tank of the U.S. 1st Armoured Division moves up towards Lucca before the campaign to break the Gothic Line.*
▷ *The final moves in the Italian campaign.*

The End in Italy

A: CORIANO AND GEMMANO RIDGE OFFENSIVE, SEPTEMBER 1944
B: 5th ARMY ATTACK, SEPTEMBER 1944
C: ADVANCE TO BOLOGNA, OCTOBER 1944

GOTHIC LINE
ALLIED ADVANCE

Inset A (top left): 5th Army attack

German 14th Army
GOTHIC LINE
XIV Pz. Corps

16 S.S Pzgdr. Div.
Serchio
Bagni di Lucca
Borgo a Mozzano

362 Div.
334 Div.
Vernio
Futa Pass
4 Para. Div.
Firenzuola
Giogo Pass
715 Div.
1 Para Div.
▲ Mt. Pratone
▲ Mt. Prefetto
305 Div.
Casaglia

U.S. 34 Div.
U.S. 91 Div.
U.S. 88 Div.
Prato
U.S. 85 Div.

8 Ind. Div.
Br. 6 Arm'd. Div.
Br. 1 Div.

Pisa
Arno
Empoli
Florence
Bagno
Pontassieve

U.S. II Corps
Br. XIII Corps

Task Force 45
Leghorn
U.S. IV Corps
U.S. 1 Arm'd. Div.

U.S. 5th Army

Inset C (top right): Advance to Bologna

C
Bologna

Reno
65 Div.
29 Pzgdr. Div.
362 Div.
305 Div.
90 Pzgdr. Div.
1 Para Div.
4 Para. Div.
▲ Mt. Grande
16 S.S. Pzgdr. Div.
Livergnano
334 Div.
▲ Mt. Sole

U.S. 91 Div.
U.S. 34 Div.
U.S. 85 Div.
U.S. 88 Div.
U.S. 78 Div.

U.S. 1 Arm'd. Div.
6 S.A. Arm'd. Div.
1 Gds. Bde.

Inset (left): Coriano and Gemmano Ridge offensive

GOTHIC LINE
RIMINI LINE
RIDGES

German 10th Army

Cesena
Marecchia
Rimini
San Fortunato
Can. 1 Div.
U.S. 1 Arm'd. Div.
4 Ind. Div.
Coriano
46 Div.
Riccione
56 Div.
Gemmano
46 Div.
Cattolica
I Mtn. Corps
56 Div.
LXXVI Pz.Corps
Montegridolfo
Foglia
Ind. Div.
2 Arm'd. Div.
46 Div.
Pesaro
Can. 5 Arm'd. Div.
Can. 1 Div.

British 8th Army
Br. V Corps
Can. I Corps
Pol. II Corps

Main map:

GERMANY
AUSTRIA
SWITZERLAND
YUGOSLAVIA

Brenner Pass

Trento

Udine
Trieste

Brescia
Verona
Venice

Milan
Pavia
Turin
Po
Route 9

Genoa

ITALY
German 10th Army
German 14th Army

Finale Emilia
Ferrara
The Wedge
Po

La Spezia

Argenta
Bastia
Lake Comacchio
The Spit
Bologna
Massa Lombarda
Lugo
Ravenna
ROMAGNA
Imola
Fiumi Uniti
Reno
Faenza
Forlì
Santerno
▲ Mt. Battaglia
Modigliana
Cesena
Rimini
San Fortunato
Coriano Ridge
Pesaro
Route 65
Route 67
Montone
Ronco
Route 71
Savio
B
C
A
Serchio
Pisa
Arno
Pontassieve
Florence
Fiumi
Foglia
Metauro
Route 16
Ancona
Leghorn
Arezzo

U.S. 5th Army
British 8th Army

France and the whole of three divisions, forming in Germany, to fill up the ranks of the infantry divisions that had been virtually annihilated in the Liri valley.

Although Alexander had been warned as early as May 22, 1944, that he must be prepared to provide seven divisions for a landing in the south of France, it was not until July 5, when the battle for Arezzo was in the balance and the Polish II Corps was still short of Ancona, that he was told that his pleas to be allowed to keep his force intact, for a thrust into northern Italy and beyond, had finally been turned down.

The task that Alexander was now given was:

1. to cross the Apennines to the line of the River Po; and
2. to cross the river and seize the line Venice – Padua – Verona – Brescia

After this he would receive further instructions.

In spite of the loss of so many divisions including the French Expeditionary Corps with all its mountain troops, the Allied offensive must continue.

The long summer days were running out and the chance of any large scale penetration into the Po valley before winter set in now appeared most unlikely. But in Normandy the Battle of Caen was

▽ German reinforcements en route to the Italian front. The two vehicles in the foreground are ex-Austrian Army "Mulus" wheeled/tracked carriers, and the conventional vehicles appear to be civilian vehicles taken over by the military.

about to start–it was imperative that the pressure by the Allies in Italy should be maintained, even increased.

So long as there had been hopes of a rapid advance, the bridges over the Po had been spared by the Allied bombers. On July 12 the Tactical Air Force went to work and in three days cut all 23 of the rail and road bridges over the river. The battle for the Gothic Line had begun.

Superb defences

In the mountains the German engineers had already constructed a series of strong-points astride the routes leading to the Po valley at Borgo a Mozzano, Porretta, the Vernio pass north of Prato, and the Futa and Il Giogo passes north of Florence. From here the line ran south-east, again with every route blocked, from Casaglia to below Bagno and the Mandrioli pass, before turning eastwards to drop down to the valley of the Foglia and Pesaro on the Adriatic. Here, in the narrow coastal plain, was Route 16, the only road that the Allies could take which did not mean a climb across the great mountain barrier. This corridor, however, between the foot-hills and the sea, was cut across by numerous rivers; and the succession of ridges, which similarly were at right angles to the line of advance, was admirably suited for defence. Moreover, the rivers were liable to sudden flooding and rain quickly turned the heavy soil into a sea

Deutsche Soldaten im Reich der Dolomiten
P-K-Aufnahme: Kriegsberichter Riedel

△ *German infantry move down through the Dolomites from Austria towards the front.*

▽ *American motor transport in typical Italian terrain. The problems faced by the attackers in such country were particularly difficult: firstly the logistic difficulties of moving up men and supplies, and then the tactical disadvantage of having to attack uphill.*

of mud. The fortifications in this sector had been skilfully prepared, with anti-tank ditches, extensive minefields, and the usual deep bunkers. In June and July, while Kesselring's rearguards were slowly falling back through Tuscany, Todt engineers, with thousands of conscripted Italian labourers, were frantically engaged in constructing a ten mile deep belt of obstacles along the whole line, and in the mountains a series of positions to link up with the main strongholds, so as to form a continuous front. A report on the defences that had been

completed when the battle started listed 2,376 machine gun nests, 479 anti-tank gun, mortar, and assault gun positions, 120,000 yards of wire entanglement, and many miles of anti-tank ditches. Only four out of the 30 7.5-cm Panther gun turrets ordered by O.K.W., however, were in position.

The balance of forces in the opening stages of the forthcoming battle pitted 26 German divisions, including six Panzer and *Panzergrenadier* divisions, and some six Italian divisions, against 20 Allied divisions, which included four armoured divisions. For the Germans the battle would be fought solely on the ground, as the Luftwaffe in Italy was reduced to 170 aircraft, the majority of which were obsolete. The Allies, with some 75 complete squadrons in the Tactical Air Force alone, enjoyed complete air superiority. This advantage, however, would soon be reduced as the weather deteriorated. Meanwhile Kesselring could neither "see over the hill", nor strike out at his enemy's rear communications. In spite of this and a weakness in both artillery and armour, he viewed his task of beating off the coming offensive with growing confidence, especially after an inspection of the defences on his eastern flank.

Throughout the whole campaign the Germans had overestimated the Allied capability to carry out amphibious operations against their rear and Kesselring, sensitive to the preparations for "Dragoon" (as "Anvil" was now named), feared a landing on the Ligurian coast or even in the Gulf of Venice. Consequently he allocated no fewer than six divisions to coastal defence. A further weakening of his forces resulted from the active resistance, backed by the Communists, of Italian workers in the industrial areas to Mussolini's puppet government. In effect civil war had broken out, and in spite of the arrival of two German-trained Italian divisions the partisans were also beginning to show their true strength in attacks on military depots and lines of communication. Thus there remained only 19 divisions to hold the Gothic Line itself. On the right was the 14th Army, with XIV Panzer Corps allocated to the long mountain stretch from the coast to Empoli, and I Parachute Corps to hold the shorter and more critical central section facing Florence, both with three divisions. In reserve were the inexperienced 20th Luftwaffe Field Division and the 29th *Panzergrenadier* Division, north of Florence. East of Pontassieve was the 10th Army, with LI Mountain Corps (five divisions) holding the spine of the Apennine range as far as Sansepolcro and LXXVI Panzer Corps in the foothills and coastal plain, again with five divisions, of which two were echeloned back watching the coast. The newly arrived 98th Division was in army reserve around Bologna. This again emphasised Kesselring's preoccupation with the central section of the mountain barrier, which was only 50 miles deep at this point, in spite of his prediction that the attack would be made on the Adriatic flank. Meanwhile the front line remained on the line of the Arno.

Revised plans

Alexander's initial plan was to press an early attack, with both armies side by side, into the mountains on the axis Florence–Bologna. Indeed the cover plan, with fake wireless traffic and soldiers arriving in the Adriatic sector wearing Canadian I Corps flashes, had already started. But this was before Clark's 5th Army was reduced to a single corps and the total strength of both armies to 20 divisions. Moreover there was no chance of any reinforcements other than the U.S. 92nd Division in September and a Brazilian division by the end of October. So there could be no diversionary operations and no reserve to maintain the impetus of the advance. In spite of this, General Harding, Alexander's chief-of-staff, recommended the plan should stand. Lieutenant-General Sir Oliver Leese, the 8th Army commander, whose troops would have to bear the brunt of the fighting, felt there was a far better chance of breaking through on the Adriatic sector, where his superiority in tanks and guns could be employed to greater effect.

Furthermore General Clark would have greater freedom to make his own dis-

△ *Lieutenant-Colonel J. Sokol, of the Polish 3rd Carpathian Infantry Division, inspects U.S. artillery positions. The division formed part of the Polish II Corps that took Pesaro.*

▽ *Canadian armour crosses the Sieve, which flows into the Arno at Pontassieve, ten miles east of Florence.*

A 2½-ton truck of the Quartermaster's Corps of the U.S. 88th Division surges across a flooded road in the Bologna area, towing another vehicle.
▷ △ U.S. infantry south of Bologna.
▷ ▽ American forces in the Piazza del Campo in Siena.

positions. This plan suited one of Alexander's favourite strategies, the "two-handed punch", in that by striking at both Ravenna and Bologna the enemy's reserves would be split. At a secret meeting in Orvieto on August 4, 1944 between the two commanders, with only Harding present, the matter was decided by Alexander in favour of Leese's alternative proposal. As practically the whole of the 8th Army had to be moved across the mountains to the east coast, D-day was put back to August 25. The cover plan was put into reverse, with 5th Army being told to make "ostentatious preparations" for an attack against the centre of the mountain positions. In the greatest secrecy the regrouping of both armies was started immediately.

Roadworks delay

The transfer to north of Ancona of the bulk of the 8th Army–two complete corps headquarters, some eight divisions, and a mass of corps troops, with over 80,000 vehicles–was achieved in 15 days. This was a remarkable feat as there were only two roads over the mountains, and both had been systematically demolished by the Germans during their retreat. In many places the roads had to be entirely rebuilt and no fewer than 40 Bailey bridges were constructed by the Royal Engineers before the roads could be reopened. Even so the roads were largely one-way, and the movement tables were further complicated by the need to operate the tank transporters on a con-

short time available for the concentration of the tank brigades.

Meanwhile the British XIII Corps, of three divisions under Lieutenant-General Sidney Kirkman, joined the U.S. 5th Army, so as to be ready alongside U.S. II Corps to deliver the second blow of "the two-handed punch" towards Bologna. The remaining two U.S. divisions, joined by the 6th South African Armoured Division and a mixed force of American and British anti-aircraft and other support units, hastily trained as infantry, formed Major-General Crittenberger's U.S. IV Corps. This had the task of holding the remainder of the 5th Army front. On the inner flank, acting as a link between the two armies, was X Corps, with the 10th Indian Division, a tank brigade, and several "dismounted" armoured car regiments. Every other available man of the 8th Army was committed to the main assault on the right flank.

Leese's plan was to break into the Gothic Line defences on a narrow front, with the Polish II Corps directed on Pesaro (before going into reserve), and the Canadians making straight for Rimini. The main attack would be through the hills further inland towards Route 9 by Lieutenant-General Sir Charles Keightley's V Corps, with the British 4th, 46th, and 56th, and 1st Armoured Divisions, and 4th Indian Division. The latter was briefed for the pursuit, and would attack alongside the Canadian 5th Armoured Division as soon as the breakthrough was achieved.

Initially all went well. When the Allied advance started the Germans were engaged in carrying out a series of reliefs in tinuous shuttle service as a result of the the coastal area, which involved the pulling back of a division from forward positions on the Metauro. Kesselring indeed assumed that the attack on August 25 was no more than a follow-up of this withdrawal. Vietinghoff himself was on leave and only got back late on August 28. The next day the Allied infantry reached the Foglia and Kesselring, who had been taken completely by surprise, at last ordered up reinforcements. But it was too late to stop the penetration of the carefully prepared Gothic Line positions. On August 31 the 46th Division held the formidable bastion of Montegridolfo and the following night Gurkhas of the 4th Indian Division, using only grenades and kukris, captured the strongly fortified town of Tavoleto. In the plain, the Canadians had suffered heavily crossing the river but by dawn on September 3 had a bridgehead across the Conca alongside Route 16. Meanwhile both the 26th Panzer and 98th Divisions had reached the battle area and already suffered heavily.

The way to a breakthrough by V Corps lay in the capture of two hill features, the Coriano and Gemmano Ridges, situated just where the plain begins to widen out. These afforded the Germans excellent observation and fine positions. The task of breaking through was given to the 46th and 56th Divisions. Meanwhile, the British 1st Armoured Division, with some 300 tanks, had already started (on August 31) to move forward in accordance with the original plan. The approach march over narrow and often precipitous tracks, which got progressively worse, proved a nightmare. On one stage "along razor-edged mountain ridges" to reach the Foglia, which was crossed on September 3, drivers of the heavier vehicles had to reverse to get round every corner and some spent 50 hours at the wheel. The tank route proved even more hazardous, and 20 tanks were lost before reaching the assembly area. The driving conditions were extremely exhausting and as the column ground its way forward in low gear many tanks ran out of petrol, while those at the rear of the column were engulfed in dense clouds of choking white dust.

At this critical moment the German 162nd Division and Kesselring's last mobile reserve, the experienced 29th *Panzergrenadier* Division (from Bologna) began to arrive. The renewed attacks

▽ *155-mm M1 howitzers of the U.S. 85th Division are towed across the Reno at Pioppi di Salvaro by tracked prime movers.*
▷ *British infantry rest by a roadside during the closing stages of the Italian campaign. Note the tank destroyers on the road and the weapons carried by the infantry platoon: Lee Enfield rifles, Bren guns and a P.I.A.T. anti-tank weapon.*
▽ ▷ *British infantry bring in two German wounded abandoned by their comrades along the Metauro river.*

by V Corps were broken up and held. Into the confused and unresolved struggle the armoured divisions were ordered forward late on September 4. There had been no breakthrough; the fleeting opportunity, if it had ever existed, had passed. The advance of the armoured brigades was met with a storm of shot and shell and an unbroken defence which now included tanks and self-propelled guns. In their advance towards Coriano, the British armoured brigades lost 65 tanks and many more were still struggling to cross the start line as dusk came.

That night rain began to fall and more German reinforcements (from the 356th Division) reached the front. By September 6 the tracks had turned to mud and air strikes could no longer be guaranteed. Alexander now ordered a regrouping for a set-piece attack (on September 12) to clear the two vital ridges. Now was the time for Clark to launch his attack into the mountains.

Since early August Kesselring's front line troops had been kept short of supplies through the interdiction programme of the Allied air forces. With the Brenner pass frequently blocked, north Italy was virtually isolated from the rest of Europe. There was no direct railway traffic across the Po east of Piacenza and south of the river the railway lines down as far as the Arno had been cut in nearly 100 places. But in spite of every difficulty, sufficient supplies were kept moving forward. Each

night, pontoon bridges were built across the Po and then broken up and hidden by day; and ferries were operating at over 50 points on the river.

The Desert Air Force, which had supported the 8th Army so magnificently at a time when almost all the American air effort had been diverted to the "Dragoon" landing, now switched its whole effort to helping Clark's offensive to get under way. Clark's attack came as no surprise to General Joachim Lemelsen, whose 14th Army had already been milked of three divisions to reinforce Colonel-General Heinrich von Vietinghoff's 10th Army. The latter was now seriously short of infantry, and had been ordered to fall back to the prepared defences in

△ *Local intelligence for an American soldier.*

the mountains. Even after the transfer to his command of the 334th Division from the adjacent LI Mountain Corps, Lemelsen had no reserve and with all his force in the line, each division was on at least a ten mile front. From his post on the "touch-line", as it were, in the quiet and inaccessible Ligurian coastal sector, General von Senger und Etterlin correctly forecast the outcome of this impasse. He later wrote:

"The incessant prodding against [the left wing of] our front across the Futa pass was like jabbing a thick cloth with a sharp spear. The cloth would give way like elastic, but under excessive strain it would be penetrated by the spear."

The 5th Army attack was made by two corps and on a narrow front east of the Il Giogo pass, at the junction of the two German armies, and initially fell on two thinly stretched divisions. Holding the Il Giogo pass was the 4th Parachute Division, which had been made up with very young soldiers with barely three months' training. The pass itself was nothing but a way over a ridge only about 2,900 feet high, but overlooked by some of the highest peaks in the whole moun-

tain range.

Clark used Lieutenant-General Geoffrey Keyes's II Corps of four divisions (U.S. 34th, 85th, 88th, and 91st) as his spearhead against the Il Giogo defences. On the tail of the German withdrawal he launched his offensive on September 13. Once again, Kesselring misread the situation. In spite of the efforts of two U.S. divisions, a considerable artillery concentration, and 2,000 sorties by medium and fighter-bombers, the 4th Parachute Division more than held its ground for the first four days. Meanwhile Kirkman's XIII Corps was attacking on the right flank of the Americans along the parallel routes towards Faenza and Forlì. By September 14 the 8th Indian Division was over the watershed and the following day the British 1st Division took Monte Prefetto and, turning to help its neighbours, attacked the German parachute troops on Monte Pratone. As the pressure mounted on the 4th Parachute Division, the leading American infantry began to make ground, and between September 16 and 18 Monti Altuzzo and Monticelli and the nearby strongholds and peaks were captured.

bog and the otherwise marshy nature of the ground kept the tanks to the main roads.

Having captured Münster, the key to Westphalia, General Dempsey, commanding the British 2nd Army, pushed forward his XXX Corps in the direction of Bremen, XII Corps towards Hamburg, and VIII Corps towards Lübeck.

On the right, VIII Corps (Lieutenant-General Sir Evelyn H. Barker) was momentarily delayed by the *"Clausewitz"* Panzer Division's counter-attack which, as has been mentioned above, was aimed at the point of contact of the 21st and 12th Army Groups. Nonetheless, VIII Corps reached the Elbe opposite Lauenburg on April 19. Here, Montgomery, anxious to move with all possible speed, requested support from Eisenhower and was given the U.S. XVIII

Airborne Corps (8th Division, 5th and 7th Armoured Divisions, and the U.S. 82nd Airborne and British 6th Airborne Divisions). On April 29-30, British and Americans under cover provided by the first R.A.F. jet fighters, Gloster Meteors, forced the Elbe. On May 2, 11th Armoured Division (Major-General Roberts), which was the spearhead of the British VIII Corps, occupied Lübeck and the 6th Airborne Division entered Wismar, 28 miles further east, six hours ahead of Marshal Rokossovsky's leading patrols.

Hamburg and Bremen taken

XII Corps (Lieutenant-General Ritchie) had to sustain one last challenge on April 6 when crossing the Aller, a tributary on the right bank of the Weser. Afterwards, it took advantage of the bridgehead won on the Elbe by VIII Corps and closed in on Hamburg. On

▽ *Infantry of the 3rd Algerian Division cross the Lauter during their advance towards southern Germany and Austria.*

May 2, Lieutenant-General Wolz surrendered the ruins of the great Hanseatic port. Two days later, the 7th Armoured Division (Major-General Lyne) captured intact a bridge over the Kiel Canal at Eckernförde. Ritchie, who was within 35 miles of the town of Flensburg, where Grand-Admiral Dönitz had recently taken over the responsibilities of head of state, had brilliantly avenged the defeat inflicted on him at Tobruk.

In their drive on Bremen, Sir Brian Horrocks and his XXX Corps were held up by a great deal of destruction, and met with altogether fiercer resistance. Before Lingen, what was left of the 7th Parachute Division carried through a hand-to-hand counter-attack with frenetic "Heil Hitler" battle cries.

The 2nd *Kriegsmarine* Division showed the same aggressive spirit in defence, and it needed a pincer movement staged by three divisions to bring about the fall of Bremen on April 26. A few hours before the cease-fire, the Guards Armoured Division occupied Cuxhaven at the mouth of the Elbe.

An historic occasion: General Courtney Hodges, commander of the American 1st Army, greets Colonel-General A.S. Zhadov, commander of the Soviet 5th Guards Army, outside Torgau on the Elbe on April 25. The Eastern and Western Allies had at last linked up, and Germany had been cut in two.
▽ German civilians and their protection against stray bullets.

Canadians in Holland

On April 1, General Crerar, commanding the Canadian 1st Army, recovered his II Corps, reinforced by the British 49th Division, thus bringing his divisions up to six. His mission was twofold: to drive between the Weser and the Zuiderzee with the British XXX Corps in the general direction of Wilhelmshaven and Emden; and to liberate the Dutch provinces still occupied by the enemy. The Canadian II Corps (Lieutenant-General Simonds), which had taken part in the crossing of the Rhine, fulfilled the first of these missions. On April 6, it liberated Zutphen and Almelo, and four days later Groningen and Leeuwarden. In this fine action, it was greatly helped by Dutch resistance while the French 2nd and 3rd Parachute Regiments dropped in the area of Assem and Meppel to open a way for it over the Orange Canal. On German territory, however, General Straube's II Parachute Corps put up a desperate fight, and Crerar had to call on Montgomery for help from the Polish 1st Armoured Division, the Canadian 5th Armoured Division, and the British 3rd Division. With this shot of new blood, the Canadian II Corps accelerated its advance and on May

△ *An incongruous slogan in a town overrun by the Allies: "One People, one Reich, one Leader!"*

wounded, and missing.

Last German high command change

While Field-Marshal Busch had been entrusted with the command of a "Northern Defence Zone", Kesselring was called upon to lead a "Southern Defence Zone" which included the German forces fighting between the Main and the Swiss frontier. So during the final phase of the campaign he found himself facing General Devers, whose 6th Army Group numbered 20 divisions on March 30, 1945, and 22 (13 American and nine French) the following May 8.

More French advances

The task of Lieutenant-General Patch and the American 7th Army was to cross the Rhine upstream of the 3rd Army, then having gained enough ground to the east, turn down towards Munich and make an assault on the "national redoubt", where, according to Eisenhower's Intelligence, Hitler would seek ultimate refuge. But there was no such mission in store for the French 1st Army which, in the initial plans, was ordered to send a corps over the Rhine, following the Americans, to operate in Württemberg, and later a division which would start off from Neuf-Brisach and occupy Baden-Baden.

Neither General de Gaulle nor General de Lattre accepted this view of their intended mission. On March 4, de Gaulle remarked to de Lattre on "reasons of national importance that required his army to advance beyond the Rhine"; and de Lattre expounded the plan he had conceived to this end, which involved moving round the Black Forest via Stuttgart.

While de Gaulle worked on Eisenhower, de Lattre convinced General Devers of his point of view. The operation as conceived by de Lattre required possession of a section of the left bank of the Rhine below Lauterbourg; this was provided by the dexterity with which General de Monsabert managed to extend his II Corps from Lauterbourg to Speyer in the course of Operation "Undertone".

5, 1945, General Maczek's Polish 1st Armoured Division was within nine miles of Wilhelmshaven, and the Canadian 5th Armoured Division on the outskirts of Emden.

The Canadian I Corps (Lieutenant-General C. Foulkes) took Arnhem by an outflanking movement and three days later reached the Zuiderzee at Harderwijk. The Germans responded to this attack by opening the sea-dykes, and Crerar, who was concerned to spare the Dutch countryside the ravages of flooding, agreed to a cease-fire with General von Blumentritt, stipulating in exchange that British and American aircraft be given free passage to provide the Dutch population with food and medical supplies. This dual operation cost the Canadian 1st Army 367 officers and 5,147 N.C.O.s and other ranks killed,

Patch moves south-east

On March 26, XV Corps of the American 7th Army managed without much trouble to cross the Rhine at Gernsheim below Worms. Patch exploited this success by taking Michelstadt then, turning south, he took Mannheim and Heidelberg on March 30. On April 5, having moved up the Neckar as far as Heilbronn, he captured Würzburg in the Main valley. With his left as spearhead, he hurled his forces in the direction Schweinfurt–Bamberg–Nuremberg and on April 19, after some violent fighting, ended all resistance in Munich. With its right wing in contact with the French 1st Army in the Stuttgart area, and the left in touch with the American 3rd, the 7th Army moved in a south-easterly direction. On April 25, it crossed the Danube on an 80 mile front, capturing on the way what was left of XIII Corps with its commanding officer, Lieutenant-General Count d'Oriola.

Berchtesgaden taken

From that moment German resistance in Bavaria collapsed. On May 2, the American XV Corps occupied Munich. Two days later, the French 2nd Armoured Division, once more free for assignment with the Royan pocket liquidated, scaled the slopes of the Obersalzberg and occupied the Berghof, from which *Reichsmarschall* Hermann Göring had just fled. On the same day, the American 3rd Division, which had sped through Innsbruck, crossed the Brenner Pass and met up with the 88th Division of the American 5th Army at Vipiteno. On May 5, General Schulz, last commander of Army Group "G", avoiding capture by the French, surrendered at General Jacob L. Devers's H.Q.

On March 29, General de Gaulle telegraphed de Lattre: "It is essential that you cross the Rhine even if the Americans are against you doing so and even if you cross in boats. It is a matter of the highest national interest. Karlsruhe and Stuttgart are expecting you even if they don't want you."

When he received this message, de Lattre was on his way back from General Devers's H.Q. with the task of sending one corps, of at least three divisions (one of them armoured), across the Rhine to take Karlsruhe, Pforzheim, and Stuttgart. De Lattre had done all in his power to wring this order out of the army group commander. Pierre Lyautey remarks, on seeing him in the H.Q. of the Algerian 3rd Division on March 17, that he was in the process of conceiving "a great German campaign", which would be "full of Napoleonic dash and fury".

In any event, the 1st Army had ceded most of its bridging equipment to the 7th Army to compensate it for similar equipment made over to the 21st Army Group; in addition, in the afternoon of March 30, the French II Corps had barely completed the relief of the American VI Corps at Germersheim and Speyer. Nevertheless, Monsabert, who was down to about 50 motorised and unmotorised boats, was ordered to take two divisions across that very night.

The venture succeeded in conditions of apparently impossible improvisation, and in spite of resistance from the 47th *Volksgrenadier* Division, on March 31. By nightfall, the 3rd Algerian Division (General Guillaume), opposite Speyer, and the 2nd Moroccan Division (General Carpentier), opposite Germersheim, al-

△ An armoured column of the American 3rd Army pushes over the border between Germany and Czechoslovakia. Patton, the army's commander, was typically impetuous in advancing far past his official stop line with "deep patrols".

A German tank factory, considerably damaged by U.S. heavy bombers and then overrun by American ground forces. Note the half-completed *Jagdpanther* tank destroyer on the left. Even though the Germans continued to step up the output of matériel right up to the end of the war, they did not have the fuel to make use of the weapons they already had.

ready had five battalions in Baden-Baden. The next day, the two bridge-heads were connected and the French advanced as far as the Karlsruhe–Frank-furt *Autobahn*, over 12 miles from the right bank. As for the 5th Armoured Division (General de Vernejoul), it crossed the Rhine either by ferrying or with the co-operation of General Brooks, commanding the U.S. VI Corps, "the perfect companion in arms" in de Lattre's words, over the American bridge at Mannheim. Finally, on April 2, the 9th Colonial Division, now under the command of General Valluy, crossed the river in its turn at Leimersheim (six miles south of Germersheim). Two days later, the 1st Army had taken its first objective, Karlsruhe.

As the German 19th Army was resisting fiercely in the Neckar valley and in the hills above Rastatt, making a stand in a strongly fortified position which covered

the Baden-Baden plain, de Lattre shifted the weight of his thrust to the centre. This gave him Pforzheim on April 8, and he then sent his 2nd Moroccan Division, 9th Colonial Division, and 5th Armoured Division deep into the relative wilderness of the Black Forest. On April 10, the fall of Herrenalbon, and the crossing of the Murg allowed Valluy to by-pass Rastatt and open the Kehl bridge to General Béthouart's I Corps.

In the meantime, Monsabert had seized Freudenstadt, the key to the Black Forest, and Horb on the Neckar above Stuttgart, while the American VI Corps was moving up on the capital of Württemberg by way of Heilbronn. On April 20, pushing on from Tübingen, the 5th Armoured Division completed the encirclement of the city. All resistance ceased after 48 hours. The French took 28,000 prisoners, what was left of the four divisions of LXIV

Corps (Lieutenant-General Grimeiss).

The Stuttgart manoeuvre was the third act of this military tragedy, although by April 22, the fourth act, which saw the entrance of I Corps (4th Moroccan Division, 9th Colonial Division, 14th Division, and 1st Armoured Division), was well under way. Béthouart moved on Horb by way of Kehl and Oberkirch, where he turned south up the Neckar, reaching the Swiss frontier in the vicinity of Schaffhausen on the day Stuttgart fell. This led to the cutting off of XVIII S.S. Corps (General Keppler), which comprised four army divisions. These 40,000 Germans attempted to cut their way through the lines of the 4th Moroccan Mountain Division but they were taken in the rear by the 9th Colonial Division and on April 25 all resistance ceased.

The manoeuvre employed here by the 9th Colonial Division was the result of a request made by the Swiss High Command—as is told in the *History of the French 1st Army*—who were understandably not very enthusiastic about disarming and interning thousands of allegedly

△ *An aircraft factory in Hamburg, destroyed by R.A.F. Bomber Command.*

fanatical Germans. Although his plans were slightly put out by this development, de Lattre agreed:

"It is an obligation of another kind to give consideration to the permanent interests of Franco-Swiss friendship, especially when Switzerland, while keeping to its age old principle of neutrality, has always been faithful to this cause.

"The problem confronted me while Valluy was still about to attack the Kaiserstuhl and Lehr's combat command (5th Armoured Division) was still some hours away from Schaffhausen. But my hesitation was only momentary. I had no illusions as to the risks I ran but my inclination was on the side of Franco-Swiss comradeship. This inspired me to issue General Order No. 11 in the night April 20-21, ordering I Corps to 'maintain the drive of the right flank along the Rhine towards Basle, then Waldshut, with simultaneous action from Schaffhausen towards Waldshut so as to link up with the forces coming from Basle', hence ensuring the complete encirclement of the Black Forest and at the same time denying the S.S. divisions any opportunity to force the Swiss-German frontier."

In addition, the alacrity with which General Valluy tackled this new mission without the slightest warning deserves mention, Waldshut being not far short of 90 miles from the Kaiserstuhl via Lorrach.

The fifth and final act of the Rhine–Danube campaign involved the pincer movement carried out by Monsabert and Béthouart on Ulm, the one with the 5th Armoured Division and 2nd Moroccan Division (General de Linarès) to the north of the Danube, the other thrusting his 1st Armoured Division (General Sudre) south of the river along the line of Donaueschingen and Biberach. On April 24 at noon, the tricolour flew above the town which on October 21, 1805, had seen Mack surrender his sword to Napoleon. With the capture of Ulm a new pocket was established, and this yielded 30,000 prisoners.

On April 29, General de Lattre reformed I Corps, putting the 2nd Moroccan Division, the 4th Moroccan Mountain Division, and the 1st and 5th Armoured Divisions under its command, and giving it the task of destroying the German 24th Army, recently formed under General Schmidt with the object of preventing the French from gaining access into the Tyrol and Vorarlberg.

On the next day the 4th Moroccan Mountain Division (General de Hesdin) and the 5th Armoured Division, of which General Schlesser had just assumed command, captured Bregenz in Austria.

Once over the frontier, the French could count on the Austrian resistance to provide guides and information, leading in numerous instances to preventing planned demolition being carried out by the Wehrmacht. At Dornbirn the tanks of the 5th Armoured Division were bombarded with bouquets of lilac; at Bludenz, which was liberated on May 4, General Schlesser was made an honorary

citizen. Meanwhile, the 2nd Moroccan Division and the 1st Armoured Division were moving beyond Ulm up the valley of the Iller; from Oberstdorf General de Linarès's Moroccan troops scaled the snow-covered slopes of the Flexenpass (5,800 feet). Nightfall on May 6 found them at Saint Anton, on the road to the Arlberg, having made contact with the American 44th Division on their left.

On May 7, at 1340 hours, a cease-fire was declared in Austria, following Kesselring's capitulation to General Devers. During its five weeks' campaign, the French 1st Army had brought total destruction on eight German divisions and taken 180,000 prisoners. Among these was Field-Marshal Rommel's son, whom de Lattre, with other considerations than victory in mind, generously released.

▽ *Torpedoes that the Germans never had the chance to use. Although the menace of the conventional U-boat had been beaten by 1945, the Germans had high hopes of their new generation of fast Type XXI and XXIII boats. Post-war Allied evaluation of these new classes proved how dangerous such U-boats would have been.*

CHAPTER 93

BURMA ROAD: CHINA'S LIFELINE

Throughout World War II, the vital problem of transporting supplies into China loomed large. In 1937-39, during the undeclared Sino-Japanese war, the occupation of the coasts of China by the Japanese stimulated intensive efforts to build supply routes from the interior of China to the outside world. Perhaps the most notable of these was the construction by the British and Chinese of the 681-mile road from the Lashio railhead to Muse on the China-Burma border, and on to Kunming. This highway, called the Burma Road, was made passable to motor transport in 1938 by the labours of thousands of Chinese coolies, and for three years, the Burma Road shuddered with the passage of several thousand trucks carrying war supplies to China.

Contemporary Burmese political leaders, however, regarded operations on this road with very little enthusiasm, the desire to keep the doors of Burma shut against foreign intruders being an old theme in Burmese history.

China was dependent on supplies from abroad to enable her to continue in the war against Japan. As well as the Burma Road route, a trickle of supplies also reached China along the narrow-gauge railway from Haiphong, in French Indo-China, to Kunming. With the defeat of France in Europe, though, Japan demanded and received from the Vichy Government the right to land forces in French Indo-China. The Haiphong–Kunming railway was closed in June 1940.

The Japanese followed this by demand-

▽ *Not all caravans were motorised. Here porters with pack mules and balancing poles take a break in their journey.*

The Second Chindit Operation

The four battalions in each L.R.P. brigade were split into and trained to move in eight columns of about 400 men each, comprising a four-platoon infantry company with two 3-inch mortars and two medium machine gun detachments, and supported by R.A.F., sapper, signaller, and medical attachments, all of which were based on mule transport and air supply.

The main object of the Chindit operation in March 1944 was to cut the lines of communications to the Japanese forces facing Stilwell's advance down the Ledo Road and so assist his capture of Mogaung and Myitkyina. In February 1944 the 1st Brigade entered Burma from India on foot, and the five remaining brigades were airlifted out from early March. Two strongholds were established round the airstrips Broadway and Aberdeen and Japanese lines of communications were attacked.

On March 24 Wingate was killed in an air crash, command of the Chindits then passing to Walter Lentaigne. The Chindits' role was changed to supporting Stilwell, who took over direct command on May 17. Myitkyina and Mogaung were captured by Stilwell but, kept in the field too long, the Chindits' effectiveness was radically reduced and they sustained casualties of 3,628 killed.

ing the closure of the Burma Road, and on July 18, 1940, Britain, hard pressed by Germany, reluctantly complied. China was now virtually isolated, but Generalissimo Chiang Kai-shek and the Chinese people remained steadfast.

The Burma Road, fortunately, did not remain closed for long. Britain defeated Germany in the Battle of Britain, and Churchill, with the backing of the United States, which wished to ship Lend-Lease supplies to China, ordered the reopening of the Road on October 18, 1940. This was now the only supply route to China, and large quantities of American Lend-Lease military supplies began to arrive in Rangoon. From here, they travelled by steamer up the Irrawaddy, and by road and rail north through Mandalay to Lashio where they joined the Burma Road.

Air support from the "Flying Tigers"

Air-power is important in any theatre of war, but in Burma it was a dominating factor from the start. In planning at this time, great reliance was placed on the ability of air forces to halt, or at least to delay greatly, the advance of enemy columns. Over the next three years, however, this was shown to be a fallacy. Air attack alone could not stop the movement of either side. Even if it could, the Anglo-American air forces in Burma were not then of a size to attempt it. The air force in Burma consisted of only one R.A.F. squadron, equipped with Buffaloes, and a flight of the Indian Air Force having only a few obsolete machines. The Chinese Air Force also had a handful of antiquated planes. To redeem this situation, the American Volunteer Group (A.V.G.) was formed by Colonel Claire Chennault, Chiang Kai-shek's aeronautics adviser, its major task being to protect the Burma Road, which was extremely vulnerable to air attack. The A.V.G. base was in Kunming, China, but Chiang, realising the importance of Rangoon for the Burma Road, sent the 3rd Squadron of the A.V.G. to R.A.F. Mingaladon, near Rangoon. If the Japanese succeeded in occupying Burma and closing the Road, China's ability to resist Japan would be greatly diminished. The defence of Burma was thus imperative. Without the flow of supplies over the Burma Road, the likelihood that the A.V.G. could continue to function effectively in China was nil.

The A.V.G. was equipped with 100 P-40 Tomahawk aircraft, supplied by America through Lend-Lease, and the airmen were hand-picked volunteers from the American air force. The pilots decorated their planes, which were consequently known as the "Flying Tigers".

The Allied air forces were contending against great odds, however. The Japanese aircraft were superior in number and range, but by February 12, 1942, the Flying Tigers had shot down almost 100 enemy planes for the loss of only 15 of their own, spurred on, no doubt, by a reward of 500 dollars for every Japanese plane downed.

On December 23, 1941, the Japanese launched their first raid on Rangoon. On January 20, 1942, after almost a month of bombing raids against Rangoon and other military installations in Burma, Japanese land forces crossed the Thai border into southern Burma. Their purpose was to cut the link between Rangoon and Kunming and then to capture Burma. Rangoon was captured on March 6, 1942, and Lashio, the southern terminus of the Burma Road, fell on April 29, along with 44,000 tons of Lend-Lease supplies destined for China.

Japanese forces cut the Road

With the closing of the Burma Road, the only land routes to China were the old highway across the Sinkiang province from Russia, and the caravan trails across the Himalayas and through Tibet from India. Neither of these routes was ideal for transporting large quantities of goods to China. The route through Sin-

The War in China

On August 8 1937 Japanese troops had landed in Shanghai, which, due to fierce resistance, was not captured until November 8. Nanking fell to the Japanese on December 13. Chinese forces eventually defeated the Japanese, but the latter continued to advance, seizing Canton in 1938. In 1937 the Chinese Government invited Captain Claire Chennault to be its aeronautics adviser. Chennault enlisted American volunteer pilots to fly P-40 planes, supplied under Lend-Lease, which became known as the "Flying Tigers".

The Japanese suspended their operations in China during 1942. Mao Tse-tung's guerrillas developed an unofficial truce with Japanese occupying forces, allowing the latter more resources to use against the Chinese Nationalist leader Chiang Kai-shek. In 1942 Lieutenant-General Joseph Stilwell arrived in Chungking to head an American military mission. Chiang made Stilwell his chief-of-staff and sent him with 30,000 men to Burma to help the British. The U.S. Air Force set up bases in China and India, but seven of the China-based ones fell into Japanese hands in the winter of 1943 and spring of 1944. Chiang and Stilwell were bitter enemies and Stilwell was relieved of his command on October 18, 1944, to be replaced by Major-General Albert Wedemeyer.

In December 1944 the Japanese advanced towards Kuei-yang, Kunming and Chungking, though Wedemeyer brought in reinforcements from the Burma front to counter-attack and stabilize the position for a period. However, the Japanese renewed their offensives and captured more air bases. After a serious defeat at the hands of the Chinese on May 8, the Japanese withdrew from South China.

kiang was over thousands of miles of over-loaded Russian railways, and although the caravan route through Tibet was a much shorter journey, only pack animals could traverse the mountain trails, which meant that heavy equipment could not be carried.

"The Hump"

The fall of Lashio was therefore a crushing blow to the Chinese, but they survived it through the establishment of the air lift over the "Hump" from India to China.

Pioneers over the Himalayan Hump to China from India were Colonels Old and Tate. After Colonel Old had made the first surveying flight, Colonel Tate proved it was usable by transporting 13,000 Chinese troops to General Stilwell in India during the 1942 monsoon season.

Operating between 16,000 and 22,000 feet with oxygen, the pilots flew through almost all weather, although sometimes monsoon rains and wind delayed the flights for days at a time. When the accident rate became high, Chinese pickets were paid so much for every pilot saved. Although the tonnage carried over the "Hump" was low in the beginning, the Americans stepped up the monthly average to 20,000 tons during 1943.

Even when the planes made their regular journeys, however, there were difficulties in moving the goods from Kunming to the forward bases of the China Air Task Force, which were situated in regions surrounded by Japanese, and defended only by poorly equipped Chinese armies. The China Air Task Force had superseded the A.V.G. in July 1942, and most of the "Hump" supplies were allotted to it as Chiang Kai-shek and Chennault believed that decisive results could be achieved through air-power alone.

For raids against Japanese installations in Burma, China, and Indo-China,

▽ *Indian labourers load bales of cotton on to trucks at Lashio. The road carried commerical as well as military traffic, for Japan controlled China's ports, and consequently the latter was forced to rely on the overland route for imports and exports.*

the China Air Task Force needed a large amount of aviation gasoline. With the closing of the Burma Road, all fuel had to be flown in over the "Hump"; then it had to be carried or rolled by Chinese coolies over hundreds of miles of dirt road to reach the air bases. To carry one day's supply of fuel from Kunming to Kuei-lin took 40 days if carried by cart, and 75 days if rolled by coolies.

On March 10, 1943, the China Air Task Force was enlarged and redesignated the 14th Air Force, still under the command of Chennault. Fuel was in very short supply at this time, not so much because of an insufficient number of planes to ferry goods to China, but due to bottlenecks along the route from Calcutta and Karachi to the airfields in Assam. Indian rail facilities were disorganised and inadequate to convey large quantities of goods quickly. There was also a delay on the part of the British to complete the necessary airfields in Assam on time.

The "Hump" air lift enabled the Chinese to receive supplies to continue in the war. What had happened to the land forces in the meanwhile?

▽ *Lashio railway station. Here the supplies were off-loaded from goods trains and on to trucks for the journey into China. The picture shows the three modes of transport available – human, animal, and motorised.*

△ *Indian and Chinese drivers stop for a wash on the outskirts of Lashio. Their trucks would have been driven from Rangoon, and would be loaded at the dumps at Lashio in preparation for the 1,400-mile drive to Chungking.*

The land force commanders

In the last days of April 1942, the commanders of the Allied forces in Burma and China (Slim, Stilwell, and Alexander) realised that they could no longer hold any line against the Japanese in Burma. The troops therefore withdrew to India, to do so undertaking a 20-day journey of hard foot-slogging through 140 miles of jungle and mountain.

On arriving in Delhi, Stilwell stated that he regarded Burma as a vitally important area for re-entry into China, and that it must be recaptured. Stilwell's determination and implacable will were to be one of the constants during the Allied planning for the return to Burma.

While the British and Chinese forces were struggling through the mountains into Assam, there were still six Chinese divisions in operation in eastern Burma, being vigorously pursued by the enemy. In the middle of May, it appeared that the Japanese were about to launch a major attack up the Burma Road, advance into Yunnan, and capture the terminus of the Road. They did not in fact do this, and later they denied they had any plans to do so, but Chiang and Chennault were convinced that a major attack was imminent. Before the end of April, Japanese units were pushing north from Lashio up the Burma Road with tanks and motorised infantry. Having swept aside Chinese opposition, they reached the gorge of the Salween river. Their advance was halted here, however, when the Chinese destroyed the bridge.

By the end of May the Japanese held

Burma and were in a dominating strategic position. Though temporarily checked by monsoon rains, they were poised to attack either India or China, and could certainly bomb Calcutta, where most of the American and British supplies were concentrated.

Various plans were put forward at this time for the recapture of Burma. The American priority was supplies for China, by road or air, and they therefore wanted the offensive to take place in northern Burma. The Americans also favoured the construction of a new overland route to China, and planned a route for this. The British, too, had a projected road plan, but the American one was chosen, and the building of the road was assigned to the Americans. They possessed the necessary manpower, materials, and engineering experience on a large scale. Stilwell was made responsible for the road. The plans were drawn up by Brigadier-General Raymond Wheeler. American engineers, under the command of Colonel Arrowsmith and later General Pick, commenced work on the road on Christmas Day 1942, cutting the first trace at Milestone Zero, just outside Ledo. They aimed at reaching Shinbwiyang, 103 miles away at the head of the Hukawng valley, within a year.

The Ledo Road project was an ambitious scheme. It aimed at cutting a three-lane highway in gravel from Ledo, the rail-

▽ *Assembled fighters, less their characteristic "Flying Tiger" insignia, wait on an airfield in Burma. Capable of absorbing much battle damage, tractable but slow, the P-40 remains one of the controversial aircraft of the war.*

way terminus in north Assam, through the Patkai hills in north Burma, down the Hukawng valley to Myitkyina, across the Irrawaddy to Bhamo, where it would join up with the old British road from Bhamo to Namkham. It would then go on to the little village of Mong Yaw where it would meet the old Burma Road. The overall distance to the Chinese border was 478 miles. The eventual destination of the convoys, starting from Ledo, was Chung-king, the Nationalist Chinese capital and Chiang Kai-shek's headquarters, nearly 2,000 miles away.

Building the road involved the most complicated engineering and extreme hazards. The uncharted track led through formidable country with cliffs, enormous peaks, hushed forests, and winding rivers. As well as geographical hazards, there were also extremes of temperature, and disease (including malaria, black-water fever, dysentery, and scrub typhus) was rife. Men fought disease by oiling, disinfecting, and spraying the countryside, but even so the sickness rate was high. Fits of depression were also common to the road builders. Yet progress was made in conditions that at any time other than war would have been intolerable. Life was not eased by the frequent infiltration of Japanese behind the Allied lines: balanced in high trees, they sniped at those working on the road, and seriously hampered progress.

American *matériel* paves the way

As the American engineering battalions–composed mostly of negroes with a cadre of white operatives–pushed forward, so the stream of men and *matériel* behind them increased. From America by ship to Karachi and Bombay, then across India by train, came more bulldozers, graders, sifters, caterpillars, medical units, supply units, and transport. From India and the hills, 50,000 coolies came to work on the road.

The monsoon season presented more problems. Rain fell at the rate of up to 15 inches per day, and this led to floods and landslides. Mules and vehicles got bogged down, and bulldozers were lost over collapsing steep banks. The men, wet all the time, slept in waterlogged tents or jungle-hammocks. The soggy jungle became infested with long, purple leeches.

During the monsoon months, though, there was little likelihood of interference from the Japanese north of the Hukawng valley, and the Chinese 38th Division left its Ledo base and was deployed in front of the engineering group as forward protection.

Top priority status allocated

At the "Trident" Conference in May, 1943, the Combined Chiefs-of-Staff urged the importance of operations in northern Burma, and directed that an offensive designed to facilitate the building of the road should begin before the end of the year.

The Ledo Road followed the course of the fighting in Burma through the Hukawng and Mogaung valleys, and on to Myitkyina, which had fallen to Stilwell's Chinese and American troops in the middle of 1944. The road then had to be carried on to Bhamo, from where the Japanese had withdrawn, and then on to Namkham.

The Stilwell Road opens to traffic

On January 31, 1945, a ceremony was held on the Burma-China border at Wan-t'ing chen. With great fanfare and rejoicing, a convoy, largely composed of American journalists out on a spree, and the Chinese 6th Route Army, left for Kunming. The Ledo Road was now officially open.

Chiang Kai-shek proposed that the combined Burma and Ledo roads be renamed the Stilwell Road in honour of the man who had worked so hard to break the land blockade of China.

The value of the Ledo Road was questioned by some who doubted if it would ever repay the expenditure in men and resources devoted to it. Sadly, in November 1946, the Ledo Road was declared "surplus property" by the United States Army after the altogether vital part it had played in keeping China in the war.

CHAPTER 94
THE BRITISH PACIFIC FLEET

by Captain Donald Macintyre

The crucial Allied agreement on how World War II should be conducted was that the war in the Pacific should be subordinated to the defeat of Germany. Nevertheless, when the naval war in European waters had turned decisively in favour of the Allies in September 1943 with the defeat of the U-boat campaign in the Atlantic and the elimination of the Italian fleet in the Mediterranean, Winston Churchill at once offered to President Roosevelt to send a squadron to the Pacific.

The motive behind this offer was two-fold. There was a genuine desire to repay the generous assistance Britain had received from the United States; there was also the need to restore British prestige in the Orient by sharing in the defeat of Japan. A distinct lack of enthusiasm with which this proposal was regarded by the all-powerful head of the U.S. Navy, Admiral Ernest J. King, had a similarly complex source. King's single-minded

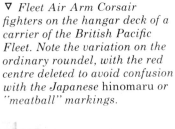

▽ *Fleet Air Arm Corsair fighters on the hangar deck of a carrier of the British Pacific Fleet. Note the variation on the ordinary roundel, with the red centre deleted to avoid confusion with the Japanese* hinomaru *or "meatball" markings.*

devotion to the Navy he served was coloured by a widely-felt and long-standing jealousy of the Royal Navy's erstwhile domination of the oceans of the world. He was determined that its eclipse behind the newly arisen sea power of the United States should be permanent. At the same time he was convinced that the Royal Navy, experienced in and trained and equipped for the relatively short-range warfare in European and Atlantic waters, could not be re-shaped and re-equipped in time to fight effectively in the vast spaces of the Pacific.

King correctly appreciated that the British would find it very difficult to build up the essential logistic organisation. Apart from the establishment of huge stocks of stores and equipment at a main base–in this case Sydney, N.S.W., many thousands of miles from their source–it required the onward transport of such supplies via an advanced base, a further 2,000 miles (in the event it was to be 3,500 miles) to the operational area. In fact, a huge fleet of repair ships, store carriers, ferry carriers, ammunition ships, fast tankers, amenity ships, harbour service craft, the whole known as the "Fleet Train", would have to be procured. The majority of these would be merchant ships. And as, by an early agreement when the United States entered the war, the building of standard merchant ships had been made exclusively a task for American shipyards, while British yards concentrated mainly on warships, and as British merchantmen were for the most part worn out by five hard years of war, ships of the Fleet Train would have to come mainly out of the American building programme.

Nevertheless, by September 1944, Churchill, when offering to place the British main fleet under United States supreme command to operate against the Japanese in the Pacific, felt able to state that an adequate Fleet Train had been assembled. In November of that year the British Pacific Fleet was formed at Colombo with Admiral Sir Bruce Fraser as its Commander-in-Chief. It was to be centred upon a squadron under Rear-Admiral Sir Philip Vian, composed of the fleet carriers *Indefatigable, Illustrious,*

Victorious, and *Indomitable,* to be joined later by the *Formidable* and *Implacable.*

Designed in 1936 with the possibility of war with Germany and Italy in mind, and the likelihood of having to operate within range of superior, shore-based air forces, these ships incorporated a thickly-armoured flight-deck. In the first four to be built this restricted them to a single hangar and to an aircraft complement of about 50, as compared with the 100 aircraft in two hangars in the U.S.S. *Essex* and her numerous sisters, where the flight deck was a light structure with a wooden deck. The *Indefatigable* and *Implacable* were modified to give them an extra half-hangar and a complement of 72 aircraft. British battleships, an essential part of any carrier task force, were slower than American contemporaries.

By this stage of the war a programme of re-equipment of the Fleet Air Arm with American types of carrier aircraft – Hellcat and Corsair fighters and Avenger torpedo-bombers – was in progress. These were to take the place of the Seafires and Sea Hurricanes, unsuitable adaptations of R.A.F. fighters, and the unsuccessful Barracuda torpedo-bombers which were all that the British aircraft industry had been

able to provide. Not only did the British aircraft lack the robustness necessary for deck operation, but their fuel endurance was also less than that of American types. Unfortunately only four of the carriers were to be re-equipped before the B.P.F. joined the 5th Fleet – with consequences which will be discussed later. An escort of battleships, cruisers, and destroyers would support the carriers. As Fraser would be too senior to serve directly under an American fleet commander, he was to fly his flag ashore while Vice-Admiral Sir Bernard Rawlings with his flag in the battleship *King George V* would command the British Pacific Fleet at sea.

This fleet, based on Colombo, was steadily built up and trained through the autumn and winter of 1944. It was "blooded" and trained in a series of carrier strike operations directed at the Japanese-held oil installations in Sumatra and Java. The new methods and tempo of carrier operations which had been evolved in the Pacific War were exercised; and when the fleet reached Sydney on February 10, 1945, it felt ready to operate alongside the U.S. 5th Fleet in the current operations to capture Okinawa. Whether this could be effectively done, however, was

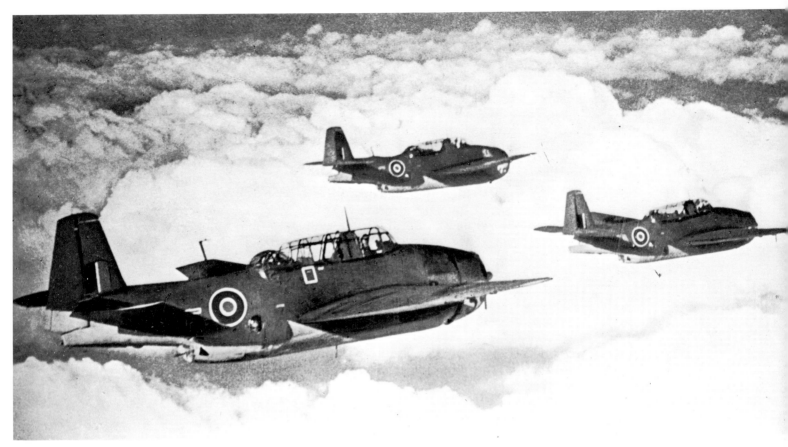

△ *Grumman Avenger torpedo-bombers off on a strike.*

to depend to a crucial degree upon how ready the Fleet Train was to give its essential support. When the B.P.F. moved forward to the advanced base of Manus in the Admiralty Islands, it was to be sadly disappointed in this respect. Out of 69 ships earmarked for the Fleet Train, only 27 had arrived, many of the remainder having been delayed by the chronic labour troubles of the Sydney water-front.

Under these conditions and in the humid heat of a climate for which the British warships were ill-adapted, it was deeply disappointing to be delayed because of an apparently continuing unwillingness of the American allies to welcome them. Admiral King, knowing the B.P.F.'s logistic weakness, was still holding out for it to be used as part of the U.S. 7th Fleet in General MacArthur's South-West Pacific Command in the less-sophisticated naval task involved in the re-conquest of Borneo. Not until March 18 were his objections overborne and, under orders to form part of the U.S. 5th Fleet, the British force sailed from Manus as Task Force 57 on the 23rd. Admiral Vian commanded the carrier squadron with his flag in the 23,000-ton *Indomitable.*

The aircraft complement of the four carriers was as follows:

	Fighters	Bombers
Indefatigable	40 Seafires	20 Avengers
	9 Fireflies	
Illustrious	36 Corsairs	16 Avengers
Indomitable	29 Hellcats	15 Avengers
Victorious	37 Hellcats	14 Avengers

Though the B.P.F. was nominally a Task Force, it was less than equivalent to one of the four Task Groups of which Task Force 58, the 5th Fleet's carrier element, was composed. It was placed under the command of the C.-in-C. 5th Fleet, Admiral Spruance, but its tactical control was reserved to Admiral Rawlings. Combined with the well-founded doubts of the Americans that the less-experienced and, in some ways, less well-equipped British carriers, their speed restricted by the comparatively slow escorting battleships, could operate effectively in close conjunction with their own Task Groups, this resulted in the British force operating at this time independently and against a separate complex of targets. While the main body of the 5th Fleet operated in direct support of the assault on Okinawa, the B.P.F. struck at airfields in the Sakashima group of islands to the southward, which the Japanese used as staging points for their aircraft.

The first strike was flown off at sunrise on March 26, 1945, when 60 Corsairs and Hellcats and 24 Avengers attacked airfields on Miyako Island. Seafires, on account of their poor endurance, were kept airborne over the fleet as Combat Air Patrol; they were to be restricted to this defensive rôle throughout the campaign. With two-day intervals for refuelling at sea (when the lack of experience in all concerned and the unreliable equipment and methods employed were exposed) similar strikes were repeated over the next 26 days.

The targets allocated had proved disappointing; few enemy aircraft were encountered, while the coral airfield runways, cratered during the day, were repaired each night before daylight. On the other hand the ground defences were far from negligible and a number of carrier planes were shot down. And on April 1 the B.P.F. had its first experience of attack by Japanese suicide planes–the *kamikaze*. Early that morning one of these broke through the fighter defence to crash and explode against the base of the *Indefatigable*'s island, killing 14 men and injuring 16 more. The armoured flight

deck now justified itself, preventing crippling damage; within a few hours the ship was again operational. In a second attack on the 6th, this time on the *Illustrious*, the suicide bomber just failed to hit the flight deck, though its wing actually struck the carrier's superstructure as it crashed alongside.

The several *kamikaze* attempts on that day, of which this came nearest to success, were only the back-wash of the first massed attack, or *kikusui*, by some 355 *kamikaze* planes and an equal number of normal bombers on the 5th Fleet. Their attack fell chiefly on the air warning pickets of destroyers maintained at a distance from the fleet. Three of these were sunk as well as three destroyers of the circular screen round the carriers; 18 more were damaged. Other *kikusui* attacks were to follow and would continue until well into June. In that period no less than 27 ships were to be sunk by suicide attacks and 164 damaged, including several American carriers, whose unarmoured flight decks made them very

▽ *Bombs burst along a runway on Ishagaki Island in the Sakishima group during a British carrier strike intended to draw Japanese reinforcements away from the landings on Okinawa.*

vulnerable. As early as the second week in April the American C.-in-C. was having to consider withdrawal of the fleet from the operations.

To assist his defence arrangements, the B.P.F.'s targets were switched on April 12 and 13 to airfields in the northern part of Formosa whence it was believed that many of the most experienced enemy attacks were coming. The raids were successful, with 16 Japanese planes shot down for the loss of only three British. They drew down on the British carriers some determined attacks in return, all of which were defeated by fighters of the C.A.P. or shot down by gunfire. The first period of duty for the B.P.F. should have ended on the 13th, but to relieve the pressure on the 5th Fleet from the massed attacks which went on throughout the 14th, Admiral Rawlings offered to return for a further period after refuelling on the 14th and 15th, an offer which was readily accepted. Finally, on April 20, after gathering in the last returning aircraft, the B.P.F. shaped course for San Pedro Bay, Leyte, for a brief period of rest and replenishment.

There the *Formidable*, carrying six Hellcat and 36 Corsair fighters and 12 Avengers, joined to replace the *Illustrious*, which was by this time in need of a refit and whose fighter squadrons had passed the accepted limit for an operational tour of duty. And on May 1 the B.P.F. sailed again to resume the task of neutralising the Sakishima airfields. Nothing has been said up to now about the two battleships, five cruisers, and 11 destroyers of the fleet. Their functions were almost entirely in support of the carrier squadron, the battleships and cruisers with their anti-aircraft gunfire, the destroyers to guard against submarine attack (which in fact never materialised) and to act as distant air-warning pickets to back up the overcrowded radar information. Now, however, on May 4, Admiral Rawlings brought some fresh interest into the lives of the larger ships by taking the battleships *King George V* and *Howe* and his cruisers to bombard the airfields on Miyako.

While this large proportion of the fleet's anti-aircraft gunnery strength was away, a *kamikaze* attack managed to evade the C.A.P. A Zero fighter and its bombs

▽ *Firefighters at work after a kamikaze has crashed onto a British carrier. It was in such circumstances that the armoured flight decks of the British fleet carriers proved their worth.*

crashed onto the *Formidable,* holing even her stout armoured flight deck: splinters penetrated the ship's central boiler room and her speed was reduced to 18 knots. Eight men were killed and 47 more injured. Eleven aircraft on deck were destroyed. Yet within 90 minutes the *Formidable* was living up to her name, steaming at 24 knots and operating her aircraft. During the same attack another suicide pilot had attempted to do the same to the *Indomitable* but bounced over the side before his bomb exploded, doing only minor damage. Until May 25 Task Force 57 repeated its previous operational pattern with two days delivering strikes on enemy airfields followed by two days of replenishment.

On May 9 the *Formidable* was hit again squarely on her flight deck in the middle of her parked aircraft, 18 of which were destroyed. But 50 minutes later she was ready to operate aircraft. At about the same time a *kamikaze* exploded near the forward lift of the *Victorious.* The deck was holed and a serious fire started. Two minutes later a second bomber crashed the ship but bounced over the side before exploding. The *Victorious* was only out of action for a short while. But both she and the *Formidable* had lost so many aircraft that they had to withdraw for three days to rendezvous with a ferry carrier of the Fleet Train and embark more.

The last strikes by British planes in the Okinawa campaign were delivered on May 25, after which Task Force 57 shaped course for Sydney for repairs and recreation in preparation for the coming assault on the Japanese homeland. As the *Indomitable* was in need of a refit, her place was to be taken by the newly arrived *Implacable,* whose aircraft complement was 48 Seafires, 12 Fireflies, and 15 Avengers. Admiral Vian shifted his flag to the *Formidable.* While the remainder of the fleet was at Sydney, the *Implacable* and three newly-joined cruisers, *Newfoundland,* the New Zealand *Achilles,* and the Canadian *Uganda* were given some operational training and experience in an air strike and bombardment on the Japanese base at Truk in the Carolines on June 14. By the end of the month the B.P.F. had re-assembled at Manus. When they sailed for the operational area on July 6, however, the *Indefatigable* had to be left behind owing to a breakdown of all her air compressors. Thus it was a force of only three carriers,

with one battleship, five cruisers, and 18 destroyers which on July 16, 1945 made rendezvous with the American force, now designated the 3rd Fleet, under Admiral William F. Halsey. This called for a change of the B.P.F.'s Task Force number to 37. A change in the command structure was to take place also. How it came about, the American C.-in-C. reveals in his autobiographical *Admiral Halsey's Story:*

"When I was informed at Pearl Harbor that the British Pacific Fleet would report to me, I naturally assumed that I would have full operational control, but when I re-read the plan at Leyte, I discovered that tactical control had been reserved. This would force me to present Admiral Rawlings with three alternatives and I did so now.

1. Task Force 37 would operate close aboard us as another Task Group in Task Force 38: it would not receive direct orders from me, but it would be privy to the orders I gave Task Force 38. These it would consider as suggestions to be followed to our mutual advantage, thereby assuring us a concentrated force with concentrated weapons.

2. Task Force 37 would operate semi-independently some 60 to 70 miles away, thereby preserving its technical identity at the cost of a divided force. (I stipulated that I would consent to this choice only if the request were put in writing.)

3. Task Force 37 would operate completely independently against soft spots in Japan which we would recommend if so desired.

Rawlings did not hesitate. He said, 'Of course, I'll accept No. 1'. My admiration for him began at that moment."

So, though the arrangement went far beyond what had been agreed at the highest levels, the B.P.F. was virtually absorbed into the U.S. 5th Fleet. No doubt it was inspired by Admiral Spruance's statement at the end of T.F.57's period under his overall command, that "the B.P.F. had gained sufficient experience to form part of the United States First Carrier Force". This was a real compliment to a force which had had to absorb in three months the expertise of carrier warfare over the vastness of the Pacific which the Americans had had more than three years to perfect. The B.P.F. accepted the situation with enthusiasm and strove to operate with

△ *Burial at sea.*

the same slick efficiency as their allies in spite of the very real handicaps of slower ships, of a multiplicity of aircraft types, of the need to fly aircraft on and off at shorter intervals owing to the low endurance of the Seafires, and the slower, less well-equipped tankers which made every refuelling an occasion for contrivance and improvisation followed by a high-speed dash through the night to rejoin the American part of the fleet.

The massed air attacks by the Japanese had petered out by the end of June. Now, until the end of the campaign, though there was still need for a defensive C.A.P. overhead (48 enemy aircraft were shot down over the fleet during July and August), the majority of the B.P.F.'s aircraft joined in the steady pounding of Japanese ports, shipping, and facilities which was intended as preparation for the final invasion. Surviving units of the Japanese fleet were sought out and made the object of special attention until all had been destroyed. On the night of July 18, the *King George V* and two Common-

wealth cruisers joined with American heavy units to hurl some 2,000 tons of shell into a factory area near Tokyo. On July 20 the *Indefatigable* rejoined, having completed repairs.

Meanwhile large reinforcements for the B.P.F. were gathering in Australian waters. They included the battleships *Duke of York* and *Anson*, the new light fleet carriers *Venerable*, *Colossus*, and *Vengeance*, and a number of cruisers and destroyers. They were too late to take an active part in the Pacific War.

On August 6 and 9, respectively, Hiroshima and Nagasaki were destroyed by atomic bombs; but it was not until the 14th that the Japanese capitulation was confirmed and operations ceased. From Task Force 37 a Task Group consisting of the *Indefatigable*, the battleship *Duke of York*, two cruisers, and ten destroyers was formed to remain with the 5th Fleet and be present at the formal Japanese surrender in Tokyo Bay. The remainder returned to Sydney – a first stop on the return journey to England.

▽ *Hellcat fighters line up for take-off.*

CHAPTER 95
VICTORY IN BURMA

△ *Advancing slowly southward through the Kaladan valley, a supply column of the 81st West African Division winds its way along a jungle track.*

There has been a tendency among some historians of the Burma campaign to neglect the Allied fighting forces which operated on either side of their advance and give the impression that it was the 14th Army alone who confronted the Japanese armies when they advanced down from Imphal to Mandalay and Rangoon. This, of course, was not the case and it was the Northern Combat Area Command under Stilwell with his three and then five Chinese divisions, coupled with first the Chindit operations and then the operations of the British 36th Division which first penetrated the plains of north Burma and turned the flank of the Japanese 15th Army facing the 14th Army. The ill-equipped 12 Chinese divisions on the River Salween have been denigrated for their lack of initiative and attacking spirit. But it must be remembered that these particular Chinese divisions each amounted to only a weak British brigade in strength, and from their point of view they were hundreds of miles away in a remote corner of China, facing one of the swiftest and most incalculable rivers in the world, the Salween, while the best armies and technical weapons available were being used to combat the 25

Japanese divisions occupying eastern and central China. Whilst the operations described here were going on, the Japanese, incensed by American air attacks from China on shipping in the South China Sea and as far north as Japan itself, attacked and overran the Chinese provinces of Kwangsi and Hunan, an area about the size of France. It must also be remembered that the objectives given to Mountbatten and Stilwell for 1944, to which Stilwell stuck, was the capture of Mogaung and Myitkyina and an area south sufficient to protect those two towns, so that a road and petrol pipeline could be opened to China and help keep her in the war. Stilwell had responsibilities to China as well as South-East Asia.

General Giffard had judged that the Arakan coastal terrain was an area in which it was uneconomic to operate and had, therefore, decided to stop any further attempt to advance there. But when Mountbatten, who was still without sufficient landing craft to capture Rangoon, was given permission to conquer Burma from the north, he found that he was faced with a big logistic problem. Once the 14th Army, with its 260,000 troops, crossed the Irrawaddy, their communications to a railhead and air bases in Assam lengthened to such an extent that they became uneconomic. It was, therefore, necessary to capture and develop airfields along the coast of Burma which could be supplied easily by sea, so that Slim's 14th Army could in turn be supplied from there by air. Thus plans were made to expand the port and airfields at Chittagong and to capture Akyab and Ramree Islands.

The 14th Army had started to cross the Chindwin early in December 1944 and Major-General T. W. Rees's 19th Indian Division, which had never been in action before, quickly crossed the formidable Zibyu Taungdan Range and made contact at Wuntho on the railway with Festing's British 36th Division.

"Extended Capital"

Lieutenant-General Slim at first imagined that the Japanese would hold a line from Kalewa along the Zibyu Taungdan Range, which was immediately in front of his 14th Army. But Rees's rapid advance and link-up with Festing gave him information that the Japanese were not going to hold any area in force east of

△ Campaigning in the jungle meant using whatever means were available – or capable of coping with conditions. Royal Welch Fusiliers are here crossing the Nanyke Chaung with their pack mules.

the Irrawaddy. Slim had made extensive plans for an operation which he had called "Capital", whose objective was to capture the area west of the Irrawaddy. As soon as he realised that the advance of Stilwell's forces had made the Japanese face two ways, Slim made a new plan.

This new plan was called "Extended Capital". It must be realised here that each successive plan had not only to be devised and approved by both the 11th Army Group and South-East Asia Command planners in Calcutta and Ceylon respectively, but also had to obtain the agreement of first the Chiefs-of-Staff in London and then the Combined Chiefs-of-Staff in Washington, with the hope that Chiang Kai-shek in Chungking would also agree. This complicated planning procedure, although it was necessary to ensure that men, stores, weapons, and equipment were made available and that there would be some co-ordination between the four Supreme Commanders, Mountbatten, Chiang Kai-shek, MacArthur, and Nimitz, fighting the Japanese war, both tended to delay operations and often failed to catch up with events. So Slim carried on ahead of approval.

"Extended Capital", in brief, entailed a fairly direct advance by Lieutenant-General M. G. N. Stopford's XXXIII Corps from Kalewa via Yeu and Monywa onto Mandalay, but included a left-hook with Rees's 19th Division crossing the Irrawaddy and advancing down the left bank on to the town of Mandalay itself. In this way XXXIII Corps could keep in touch with Stilwell's N.C.A.C.

The second and most important part of "Extended Capital" was for IV Corps (Lieutenant-General F. W. Messervy) to move due south down the Gangaw valley towards Pauk and Pakokku below the confluence of the Chindwin and Irrawaddy, cross the Irrawaddy, and advance due east on to the rail, road, and air communications centre of Meiktila. This change of plan meant some swapping of divisions between XXXIII Corps and IV Corps, but this was quickly done on paper.

The 14th Army would now, during the fine weather, be debouching into the dry zone of Burma where the "going" was good for armour and the air forces had good visibility for ground attack on troops and their communications.

A 1,150-foot Bailey bridge was built over the Chindwin at Kalewa and XXXIII Corps, consisting of the British 2nd

A British Stuart light tank moves up for the final assault on Fort Dufferin in Mandalay.
▷△ Two members of the Burma police interrogate villagers during the hunt for Japanese stragglers near Mandalay.
▷▽ A Bailey bridge being assembled in sections, later to be floated to the crossing point for the 14th Army.
▷▽▽ 62nd Motorised Brigade advances along the Myingyan-Meiktila road.
▽ The advance to Mandalay.

Division, the 20th Indian Division, the 254th Indian Tank Brigade, and the 268th Indian Infantry Brigade, advanced with deliberation towards Yeu and Shwebo in the north and Monywa and Myinmu in the south, with the 19th Division, also under command, crossing the Irrawaddy and causing the initial threat to Mandalay.

IV Corps under Messervy decided to make the 28th East African Brigade and the locally recruited "Lushai" Brigade be the vanguard of his corps down the Gangaw valley, with a cover plan that they were another Chindit-type penetration force moving around the Japanese flanks. Behind them would move the hard-hitting 7th and 17th Indian Divisions and the 255th Indian Tank Brigade.

By February 1, 1944, XXXIII Corps was on the right bank of the Irrawaddy. By February 13, IV Corps was reaching its jumping-off positions along the Irrawaddy, south of Myinmu. Meanwhile it would be opportune to review how the Japanese saw the situation and how the operations taking place on both flanks of the 14th Army affected their advance.

After the failure of the "HA-GO" offensive, some changes were made in the Japanese command. Lieutenant-General H. Kimura replaced M. Kawabe as commander of the Burma Area Army. Lieutenant-General S. Katamura took over command of the 15th Army from R. Mutaguchi, who was sent home in disgrace but, in spite of Sato's threat, he was never court-martialled.

Kimura's orders were to cover the strategic areas of Burma as his main job, but, without prejudice to this task, to try to interrupt if possible Allied communications with China. He still had three armies under command and, with the arrival of the 49th Division from Korea, these numbered a total of ten divisions and two independent mixed brigades. But these figures give no indication of the real strength of his force. For instance, the four divisions making up the 15th Army, which had been largely destroyed in north Burma and Imphal, now numbered only 21,400 men. This total was split up between the 53rd Division from Mogaung (4,500), 31st Division (7,000), 33rd Division (5,400), and 15th Division (4,500). These numbers included artillery regiments with less than half their complement of guns, and other ancillary units.

Against this 15th Army strength of 21,000 men, plus a few local reinforce-

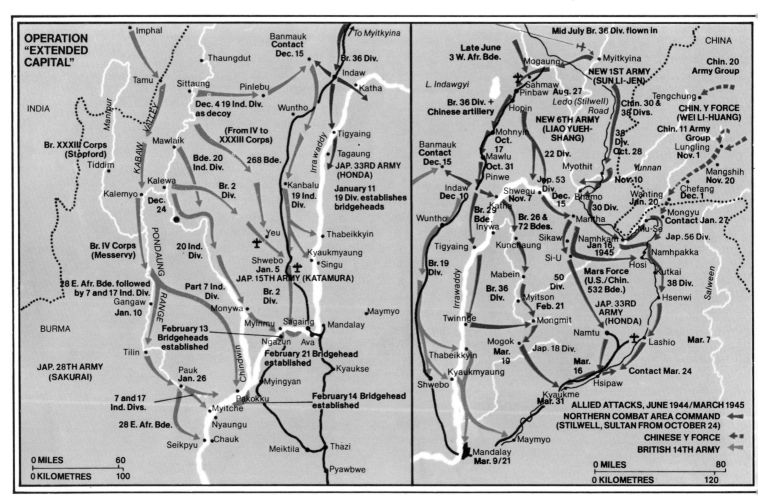

ments and corps and army troops, Slim's 14th Army of six divisions, two independent brigades, plus the lines of communication troops east of the Chindwin and two tank brigades, totalled a ration strength of 260,000 men. With this overwhelming superiority, tactics were not so important for victory as the logistics of manoeuvring such a force into position when so far away from reliable bases.

On the Northern and Salween fronts, Stilwell's five Chinese divisions (kept efficiently up to strength), the British 36th Division, "Mars" Force, (successors to Merrill's Marauders) and the 12 Chinese divisions in Yunnan, were faced by Lieutenant-General M. Honda's 33rd Army, consisting of the 18th, 56th, and 49th Divisions, and the 24th Independent Mixed Brigade. All these formations, except the 49th Division, were also now very much diminished by earlier operations. The 49th Division was Burma Area Army's reserve, of which one regiment was sent to support the 15th Army on the Irrawaddy and the remaining two regiments were deployed behind the 33rd Army on the Burma Road near Maymyo.

The 2nd Division, which had been guarding the coast of south Burma, had been ordered to move to Indo-China where the Japanese had decided to take over complete control from the French colonial government.

Stilwell's forces at this time consisted of the Chinese New 1st Army (30th and 38th Division), the Chinese New 6th Army (14th, 22nd, and 50th Divisions), the British 36th Division, and the "Mars" Task Force (American 475th Infantry and 124th Cavalry Regiments, Chinese 1st Regiment, and American 612th Field Artillery Regiment (Pack)), totalling about 140,000 troops.

On the coast the Japanese 28th Army still had the 54th and 55th Divisions (reinforced by the 72nd Independent Mixed Brigade), whose task was to prevent Christison's XV Corps from advancing over the An and Taungup passes to attack the Japanese communications in the Irrawaddy valley in the rear of the Japanese armies facing north. Opposing these two depleted Japanese divisions were the 25th and 26th Indian Divisions, the 81st and 82nd West African Divisions, and an aggressive and efficient 3rd Commando Brigade, comprising Nos. 1, 5, 42, and 44 Commandos. In all, the forces totalled some 120,000 men. Later an East African brigade was added.

The Allied administrative situation was that the 14th Army could still be supplied as far as the Irrawaddy as long as it was not more than the equivalent of seven divisions totalling 260,000 troops, but after that the numbers must be decreased to a strength of about five divisions. In the latter stages air supply must come from the coastal airfields and not from the Imphal and Agatarla fields. As it happened Akyab was occupied on January 2 and Ramree Island was fully occupied by February 22.

The Allies were again in a dominant position in the air at the beginning of January 1945. They had a first-line strength of 48 fighter and bomber squadrons. These consisted of 17 fighter, 12 fighter-bomber, three fighter-reconnaissance, ten heavy bomber, five medium bomber, and one light bomber squadrons. Together these totalled 4,464 R.A.F. and 186 U.S.A.A.F. aircraft.

Air Command had four troop carrier squadrons and 16 transport squadrons, of which four were R.A.F. and 12 U.S.A.A.F. These were increased to 19 transport squadrons in March and 20 in May, totalling a maximum of 500 transport aircraft. Yet this air transport strength was still insufficient to meet all demands, and the Arakan advance had later to be halted because of the amount of aircraft which had to be diverted to the voracious 14th Army to keep it moving.

Against this air strength the Japanese had a maximum of 66 aircraft, of which only 50 were serviceable by April 1. The Japanese were still using the same type of aircraft as in 1942-3, and their performance could not compare with the modern British and American aircraft of this period.

Command changes

General Stilwell had agreed to serve under the 11th Army Group, but only with the stipulation that when he captured Kamaing he should come under direct command of the Supreme Commander himself. The result was that Mountbatten had now to deal with two army commanders. In order to regulate this position satisfactorily, Mountbatten asked the Chiefs-of-Staff to appoint a Commander-in-Chief Land Forces South-East Asia who had had experience of having satisfactorily commanded American forces in the field. So,

In November 1944, the 11th Army Group was abolished and a new headquarters Allied Land Forces South-East Asia (A.L.F.S.E.A.) was formed to command all land operations against the Japanese in Burma. This meant the departure of General Giffard, who had been the architect and prime mover of the victories in Burma to this date. Lieutenant-General Sir Oliver Leese, who had commanded 8th Army in Italy, was appointed Commander A.L.F.S.E.A.

Shortly afterwards, Christison's XV Corps, which was mainly concerned in combined operations with the navy along the coast, was taken out of Slim's hands and came directly under the command of Leese, who had had much more experience of seaborne operations. At the same time Slim was relieved of the responsibility of his communications back to India so that he could get on with his tactical land battle without having to worry about administrative problems. It was felt that Slim could best serve the Allies by his undoubted great powers of command and example in the field though he had been largely responsible (with his R.A.F. opposite number) in developing the air supply system in Burma.

Messervy's race for Meiktila

Slim's plan was to destroy the Japanese 15th Army between the hammer of Stopford's XXXIII Corps advancing on Mandalay and the armoured anvil of Messervy's IV Corps which was to capture Meiktila.

This plan depended on the speed and secrecy of Messervy's 150-mile advance west of the Irrawaddy, whilst Stopford held the attention of XV Corps near Mandalay. Rees's 19th Division, to the north of Mandalay, was still the main attraction for the Japanese. Stopford's 20th Division started to cross the Irrawaddy at Myinmu on February 12 at a point about 30 miles downstream from Mandalay. This immediately attracted the Japanese, who counter-attacked the bridgehead repeatedly for the next two weeks.

Stopford's British 2nd Division had to wait for the boats and pontoon rafts used by the 20th Division before they could start to cross on February 21 at Ngazun

◁△ *Tied to a boat, two pack mules swim across the Irrawaddy. The entire train made the 500-yard crossing safely.*

◁▽ *A column of men of the 11th East African Division trudges along the road to Kalewa.*

△ *Casualty Clearing Stations operating just behind the front line were a vital link in the chain of medical care for the wounded. After initial treatment, serious cases were flown out in light aircraft to rear areas. The total army casualties suffered by Britain and her Commonwealth in Burma between 1942 and 1945 were 947 officers killed, 1,837 wounded, and 303 missing, British other ranks 5,037, 10,687, and 2,507; Indian other ranks 8,235, 28,873, and 8,786; African other ranks 858, 3,208, and 200; and Burmese other ranks 249, 129, and 3,052. These give a grand total of 15,326 killed, 44,731 wounded, and 14,852 missing. Including the other services, a total of 31,468 British and Commonwealth men died in the war against Japan – 12.4 per cent of the total British and Commonwealth dead.*

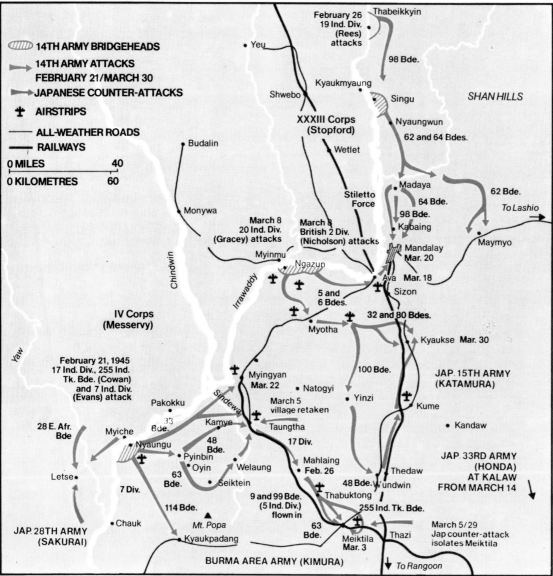

February 26
19 Ind. Div.
(Rees)
attacks
Thabeikkyin

• Yeu

98 Bde.

Kyaukmyaung

Shwebo

Singu   SHAN HILLS

XXXIII Corps
(Stopford)

Nyaungwun

Wetlet

62 and 64 Bdes.

• Budalin

Madaya   62 Bde.

Stiletto
Force

64 Bde.   To Lashio

98 Bde.

• Monywa

Kabaing

March 8
20 Ind. Div.
(Gracey) attacks

March 8
British 2 Div.
(Nicholson) attacks

Mandalay
Mar. 20   Maymyo

Myinmu

Ngazun

Ava Mar. 18

Sizon

5 and
6 Bdes.

IV Corps
(Messervy)

32 and 80 Bdes.

Myotha

Kyaukse Mar. 30

JAP. 15TH ARMY
(KATAMURA)

100 Bde.

February 21, 1945
17 Ind. Div., 255 Ind.
Tk. Bde. (Cowan)
and 7 Ind. Div.
(Evans) attack

Myingyan
Mar. 22   • Natogyi

Kume

Yaw

• Yinzi

Sindewa

Pakokku

March 5
village retaken

• Kandaw

28 E. Afr.
Bde

Myiche

33
Bde.

Kamye

Taungtha

17 Div.

JAP. 33RD ARMY
(HONDA)
AT KALAW
FROM MARCH 14

• Nyaungu

48
Bde.

Mahlaing
• Feb. 26

Thedaw

• Pyinbin

63
Bde.

• Oyin

Welaung

48 Bde. Wundwin

Letse •

7 Div.

• Seiktein

9 and 99 Bde.
(5 Ind. Div.)
flown in

Thabuktong

63
Bde.

255 Ind. Tk. Bde.

March 5/29
Jap counter-attack
isolates Meiktila

114 Bde.

• Chauk

Mt. Popa

Meiktila
Mar. 3   Thazi

JAP. 28TH ARMY
(SAKURAI)

• Kyaukpadang

BURMA AREA ARMY (KIMURA)

To Rangoon

Chindwin

Irrawaddy

△ *Mule-power and man-power bring supplies up from the east bank of the Chindwin, after an unopposed crossing.*
▷ △ *Men of the 4/4th Royal Garrison Rifles and 2nd Royal Berkshire Regiment move around Fort Dufferin as the 8/12th Frontier Force Regiment prepares to make a frontal attack. The fort was one of the last Japanese strongholds within Mandalay.*
▷ *On the 36th Division's front near Pinwe, men of a Chinese Heavy Mortar Regiment fuse 4.2-inch mortar bombs before going into action.*
▷ ▽ *A Priest 105-mm self-propelled howitzer is manned in a hurry.*
◁ *The battles for Meiktila and Mandalay.*

at a point 15 miles from Mandalay. Unfortunately, many of the boats and pontoons had been inadvertently damaged by the 20th Division and the 2nd Division had a difficult crossing. However, these assault crossings achieved the desired strategic effect of attracting the full attention of the tiny Japanese 15th Army, so that when Messervy's 7th Division crossed 90 miles further south on February 13, there was little or no opposition. By the end of February Slim's 14th Army had crossed the 1,000-yard wide swift-flowing Irrawaddy in four places with his northern bridgeheads attracting a violent reaction from the Japanese.

Messervy built up his bridgehead at Nyangu before he made his dash to Meiktila. By February 20 Messervy had got his 17th Division and 255th Tank Brigade across the Irrawaddy into his bridgehead at Nyangu, and was ready to start. Meiktila was 80 miles away across sandy scrub country, broken up by dry river beds. On February 21 Messervy's tanks began to roll. At the same time Major-General G. C. Evans's 7th Division, which had carried out the crossing, was ordered to capture the oil town of Chauk and lead on to Myingyan to the north east. Major-General D. T. Cowan's 17th Division, with its tank brigade, reached the outskirts of Meiktila by the end of February and on March 1, Cowan attacked.

Meiktila fell the following day and its airfield on the eastern edge of the town, which was vital for re-supply and the reinforcement of the defence, was captured on March 3. Cowan did not settle down but immediately sent out fighting patrols of tanks and infantry to seek out and find the enemy.

At this vital juncture Slim flew in with Messervy to visit Cowan and was present to observe a quite severe Japanese counter-attack, in which the British tanks caused many casualties and dispersed the attackers. Two men in the army commander's party were wounded by Japanese artillery fire but Slim, Messervy, and Cowan stood unmoved on the hilltop like Old Testament prophets whilst their men below gained victory.

After a new brigade was flown in Cowan withstood a series of local Japanese counter-attacks. Meanwhile to the north, Stopford, having seen his bridgeheads were secure, made plans for a deliberate advance to capture Mandalay. His plan was that the 19th Division would attack from the north. The 2nd Division would

△ *From their vantage point high on Pagoda Hill, observers look down on the battle raging around Fort Dufferin.*

advance through the old capital of Ava along the Irrawaddy from the west and the 20th Division would sweep round the south to attack Mandalay from the south and the south-east. The 19th Division soon penetrated the town but was held up by defences on Mandalay Hill and the battlements of Fort Dufferin. The 2nd Division was delayed amongst the pagodas of Ava, but the 20th Division made good progress around the south where the opposition was negligible.

As soon as Slim realised that Mandalay was not held in strength, he ordered the 20th Division to send a column south towards Meiktila, leaving the British 2nd Division to surround it from the south.

What was left of the 15th Army in Mandalay was destroyed by heavy bomber attacks. Mandalay became a bomb trap. Meiktila had fallen on March 1 and Mandalay fell on March 20.

At this time the Japanese Intelligence had become completely confused and they did not seem to know what was hitting them and from where. The battles for Meiktila and Mandalay were the death knell of the already depleted 15th Army.

In mid-January the Yunnan Armies at

last began to advance across the Salween. Namkham and Wamting were soon captured. By January 18 the American "Mars" Force was overlooking the Mandalay-Lashio road at Hsenwi and was carrying out guerrilla raids along it. On January 21 the Ledo Road to China via Bhamo, Namkham, Muse, and Wamting was opened, followed by the first convoy to China, which arrived at Kunming on February 4.

This date, February 4, 1945, can be said, therefore, to be the date of the completion of the "Quadrant" plan. However, Chiang Kai-shek made this the occasion to start to withdraw his Yunnan armies back into China for the very sensible reason that he wanted now to retake the huge areas of China which the Japanese had recently overrun. This was naturally supported by the Americans, who required these areas for air bases to support their advance towards the invasion of Japan. But some of the more parochial commanders in A.L.F.S.E.A. tended to denigrate the Chinese for marching away from the "battlefields in Burma", perhaps forgetting that the Chinese had been fighting since 1937.

The final stages

Mandalay may have fallen, but Stilwell's forces were still active. By March 1 the Chinese 30th Division had occupied Hsenwi and the British 36th Division was crossing the Shweli at Myitson and Mongmit against the now 3,000-strong 18th Division. The British received 360 casualties during this crossing.

On March 6 the Chinese 38th Division occupied Lashio and by March 24 the Burma Road from Mandalay to Lashio was in Allied hands. The British 36th Division, having captured the ruby mine town of Mogok on March 19, moved to Mandalay when the Northern Combat Area Command ceased to exist.

The American "Mars" Force, the worthy successors of Merrill's Marauders, was moved to China to be dispersed into training cadres to rebuild the Chinese Army along the same lines as Stilwell's Chinese New Armies.

Thus ended the American army involvement in the war in Burma. It can be said with truth that the few representatives of the American army, Merrill's Marauders and "Mars" Force, gave a very good impression by their fighting capabilities and thrustful initiative to their Allies fighting in Burma.

Parts of the Japanese 33rd Army had been moved from the Lashio Road at the end of the Meiktila battle in a vain attempt to save the town. But even with this last-minute reinforcement, the British forces outnumbered their enemy by about ten to one on the ground and about twenty to one in tanks.

IV Corps casualties from the crossing of the Irrawaddy to the end of March were 835 killed, 3,174 wounded, and 90 missing. The high proportion of wounded was because in the Indian Army, anyone who incurred a wound obtained a pension, and so the smallest wounds were noted, whereas in the British units there was no point in worrying about or recording minor wounds. During these battles IV Corps had 26 tanks destroyed and 44 damaged.

XXXIII Corps, in its capture of Mandalay, lost 1,472 killed and 4,933 wounded, with 120 missing. It had one more division than IV Corps and was in action for six weeks before IV Corps had crossed the Irrawaddy, so that the proportion of casualties is comparable.

No. 221 Group (Air Vice-Marshal S. F. Vincent) was in support throughout and flew 4,360 sorties, of which 2,085 were attacks on Japanese positions or their communications, during which 1,560 tons of bombs were dropped.

The 14th Army was now all set for its dash to capture Rangoon and obtain a port before the monsoon. The opposition to its advance was now negligible from the battered Japanese forces.

The build-up of Allied naval forces resulted in the command of the Indian Ocean and the Bay of Bengal being regained by the Allies by the beginning of 1945. This made possible not only the more rapid reinforcement of India because troopships were able to sail independently without escort, but amphibious operations could now be undertaken along the

△ ◁ On the road to Mandalay, January 1945: British troops dig in at the River Mu weir, anticipating a Japanese counter-attack.
△ Lieutenant-General Sir William Slim, commander of the 14th Army, stands inside Fort Dufferin.
▽ March 1945: the Union Jack flies once more over Fort Dufferin.

△ *Though the end of the war found the Allies still in Burma, they nevertheless moved swiftly to take the surrender of Japanese troops elsewhere in South-East Asia. These officers from the garrison in Kuala Lumpur, Malaya, are laying down their swords under the terms of the surrender.*

▷△ *Improvised gun train in action, carrying a detachment of Rajput gunners escorted by men of the West Yorkshire Regiment.*

▷▽ *D.U.K.W.s carry vital supplies down the Chindwin as the 14th Army continues its advance in Burma.*

coast of Burma without fear of heavy losses to submarines, and without the need for powerful naval covering forces.

Lieutenant-General Sir Philip Christison was given two tasks to carry out. When the 14th Army crossed the Irrawaddy in February 1945 their supply lines to Assam had become uneconomic. It was therefore necessary to capture airfields along the coast of Arakan, from which the 14th Army could be re-supplied during its advance to Meiktila and south to Rangoon. Without these airfields and the necessary sea ports to land stores, the 14th Army could not advance south. Fortunately the Japanese, as a result of the pressure of the 81st West African Division east of them, had evacuated Akyab on December 31 so that Christison's XV Corps landed unopposed on January 2. He immediately arranged to re-open the port of Akyab for supplies.

The total strength of the British portion of A.L.F.S.E.A. (that is not including the Americans and Chinese) was, by the beginning of 1945, 971,828 men, including 127,139 British troops, 581,548 Indians, 44,988 East Africans, 59,878 West Africans, and 158,275 civilian labourers. Of

these, 260,000 were in the 14th Army, including its line of communications troops.

It was calculated, therefore, that in order to supply the 14th Army as well as XV Corps, whose secondary rôle was to try to contain all Japanese forces (including the 54th Division and remnants of the 55th Division) in the area and to try to prevent their being re-deployed in the Irrawaddy valley, it was necessary to open two new ports. The first was at Akyab, and the second at Kyaukpyu on Ramree Island. From these two ports and from Chittagong the divisions of the 14th Army in central Burma, and the formations of XV Corps operating on the Arakan coast could be maintained if the ports could be built up to a capacity sufficient to handle the necessary sea lift tonnage required.

It was calculated that the port of Akyab would have to maintain 46,000 men, as well as the construction stores required for two all-weather airfields and the tonnage necessary to build up a 20,000-ton reserve for the 14th Army. This would require a maximum sea lift of 850 tons a day in February and March 1945, dropping down to 600 tons in May when the un-

necessary formations of XV Corps, having achieved their object, were sent back to India.

In the same manner it was calculated that the port of Kyaukpyu must maintain 36,000 men from February to May and handle stores sufficient to construct two all-weather airfields and build up a stock-pile of 22,000 tons for the 14th Army. The daily sealift required would be 450 tons in February, rising to 650 tons from March to May.

Lieutenant-General M. Kawabe had ordered the 28th Army (Lieutenant-General S. Sakurai) to send its 2nd Division, with a large part of the army's motor transport, to the 33rd Army, which was facing the 14th Army, and to hold with his remaining two divisions (54th and 55th) the Irrawaddy delta and the Arakan coast up to 35 miles north of Kyaukpyu. Later the 2nd Division was to move to Indo-China.

Sakurai was told to hold the offshore islands of Cheduba and Ramree for as long as possible. The removal of the Japanese 2nd Division (on its way to Indo-China), which had previously been responsible for the delta and the remainder of the Burmese coastline further south, meant that Sakurai had to withdraw his 55th Division to protect that area, leaving the 54th Division to face Christison's XV Corps.

Lieutenant-General S. Miyazaki's 54th Division had received orders in December 1944 to protect the rear of the 15th Army in the Irrawaddy valley from any risks of XV Corps cutting their communications between Meiktila and Rangoon. It will be remembered that Miyazaki had carried out the rear guard action of 33rd Division during its wholesale retreat from Kohima brilliantly.

To carry out his orders, Miyazaki had to hold the An and Taungup passes at all costs. As the 81st and then the 82nd West African Division advanced slowly down the Kaladan, Miyazaki decided that he would use a covering force to delay these two divisions for as long as possible whilst basing his main defence in the north at Kangaw, 40 miles east of Akyab. His other strongpoint would be at Taungup itself. Ten miles west of Kangaw lay the Myebon peninsula.

Before Akyab had fallen Christison had already made plans to land on the Myebon peninsula.

XV Corps consisted of the 25th and 26th Indian Divisions, the 81st and 82nd West

African Divisions, and the 3rd Commando Brigade (which was to be increased to four Royal Marine and Army Commandos). Christison now had plenty of landing craft, reinforced with locally constructed craft. Now that the Royal Navy had regained command of the Bay of Bengal and Akyab had fallen, it was possible for XV Corps to advance south. The Myebon peninsula and Ramree Island were held by Japanese outposts covering the main defences on the mainland.

On January 14, the joint force commanders (Rear-Admiral B. C. S. Martin [Flag Officer Force "W"], Lieutenant-General Christison, and Air Vice-Marshal The Earl of Bandon) decided that the 26th Division would assault Ramree on January 21 and the 25th Division (Major-General C. E. N. Lomax) and 3rd Commando Brigade (Brigadier C. R. Hardy) would occupy the Myebon peninsula and strike east towards Kangaw to cut the Japanese 54th Division's communications to the north.

The 3rd Commando Brigade would spearhead the attack on Myebon with the 74th Brigade passing through.

A reconnaissance of the beaches at Myebon by a special boating party found that a line of coconut stakes had been driven in just below the low-water mark about 300 yards offshore. So before the attack, a Combined Operation Piloted Party (part of the special Small Operations Group) went ashore and attached to these stakes explosives timed to go off at zero hour. The anti-boat stakes were thus blown, tearing a gap 25 yards wide for No. 42 (Royal Marine) Commando to land under cover of a smokescreen laid from the air on the morning of January 12.

The Commandos suffered a few casualties from mines on the beach, but quickly formed a beach-head. The landing was supported by the cruiser *Phoebe*, the destroyer *Napier*, the sloops *Narbada* and *Jumna*, and four minesweepers. Forty-nine landing craft of all types (including three L.C.I., five L.C.T., 12 L.C.M., and 18 L.C.A.) landed the commandos.

The Royal Marines found that the beach was too muddy for tanks, vehicles, and stores to land so the Royal Engineers reconnoitred and constructed a new route, using explosives to smooth out a nearby rocky outcrop on which tanks and vehicles could land.

△ *Major-General Wynford Rees, commander of the 19th Indian Division.*

▽ *The drive to Rangoon.*

Shortly afterwards No. 5 Commando landed and passed through No. 42 Commando to widen the beach-head.

Nos. 1 and 44 (Royal Marine) Commandos also inadvertently landed on the same beach and pushed ahead. By this time the tanks belonging to the 19th Lancers were ashore.

The Royal Marines of No. 42 Commando occupied Myebon village on the 13th and the village of Kantha was also captured. At this stage the 74th Brigade (Brigadier J. E. Hirst) took up the advance and overcame the remaining opposition and the Commando Brigade was withdrawn to prepare for the Kangaw operation. By the 17th the whole of the Myebon peninsula was captured.

The 82nd West African Division had relieved 81st Division, which was still in the Kaladan valley. The 82nd Division was now commanded by Major-General H. C. Stockwell, who had previously commanded one of the aggressive British 36th Division's two brigades. Advancing south, Stockwell occupied the ancient capital of Arakan, Myohaung, on January 25 and applied pressure on the Japanese facing him. Christison was anxious to cripple the 54th Division by cutting its communications at Kangaw.

The joint force commanders rather over-insured in the force that they used to overcome opposition on Ramree and Cheduba Islands. But at this time of the war it was common policy for the Allies to deploy as much *matériel* strength as possible to save Allied lives if that *matériel* strength could be easily brought to bear without too much delay.

The naval component of this combined operation included the battleship *Queen Elizabeth*, the cruiser *Phoebe*, the destroyers *Rapid* and *Napier*, the Royal Naval sloop *Flamingo*, and the R.I.N. sloop *Kistna*. No. 224 Group supported the attack with its Thunderbolts and Mitchells. Prior to the attack 85 Liberators of the Strategic Air Command bombarded the beaches and its surrounds.

After the naval and air bombardment, the 71st Brigade (Brigadier R. C. Cottrell-Hill), with a squadron of tanks, a regiment of field artillery, and two companies of the Frontier Force machine gun battalion, landed unopposed at 0942 on January 21 west of the town of Kyaukpyu. The leading motor launch and landing craft both struck mines and were blown up, causing some confusion, but the remainder of the landing proceeded without opposition or further delay.

Next day the 4th Brigade (Brigadier J. F. R. Forman) took over the beachhead and the 71st Brigade moved south.

On January 26 the Royal Marine Commandos landed unopposed on the neighbouring Cheduba Island.

By January 31 Lomax had landed the remainder of his 25th Division on Ramree Island. The opposition from the Japanese outposts increased and the Indian brigades, with tanks, slowly and methodically cleared the island until Ramree town itself was occupied on June 9. On this day, under cover of an attack by the remains of the Japanese 5th Air Division, a Japanese destroyer (accompanied by 20 launches) rushed to the rescue of the Japanese and took off over 500 men. By January 17 resistance on the island ended.

The 22nd East African Brigade, which had come under Christison's command, arrived to garrison Ramree and Cheduba Islands so that the 26th Division would be

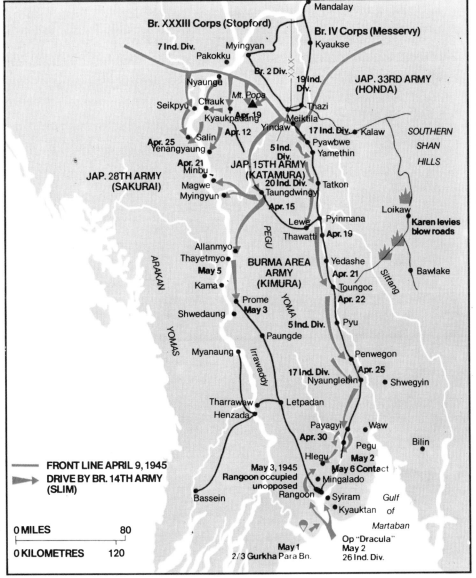

FRONT LINE APRIL 9, 1945
DRIVE BY BR. 14TH ARMY (SLIM)

0 MILES 80
0 KILOMETRES 120

available to land at Toungup.

The fight at Kangaw turned out to be one of the bloodiest and most savage of the Burma campaign. But this fight succeeded in crippling a major part of Miyazaki's 54th Division, which was one of the few divisions in Burma at this time which had not suffered a defeat, was not too depleted, and was still full of fight.

Major-General G. N. Wood's plan for the capture of Kangaw was for the 3rd Commando Brigade (Nos. 1, 5, 42, and 44 Commandos) to seize a bridgehead on the east bank of the Diangbon Chaung two miles south-west of Kangaw. Then his 51st Brigade would pass through the bridgehead and join forces with the 74th Brigade, which was advancing from Kantha across the Min Chaung from the Myebon peninsula. The Japanese would find themselves hemmed in between the two Indian brigades and the West African 82nd Division advancing from the north. Hardy, commanding the 3rd Commando Brigade, wished to go by the indirect route, which he had reconnoitred, and advance up the Diangbon Chaung from

the south and not via the Myebon peninsula, although this meant a trip of 27 miles by boat. On January 21, 50 vessels (including the R.I.N. sloop *Narbada*, a minesweeper, a Landing Craft Tank (carrying a bulldozer and R.E. equipment), four L.C.I.s, 22 L.C.A.s, and some "Z" craft carrying artillery, anchored off the southern entrance of the Diangbon Chaung. The "Z" craft were large but manoeuvrable lighters whose decks had been strengthened with steel so that a troop of 25-pounders could fire from them.

The Diangbon Chaung, as Hardy predicted, had not been mined and the Japanese did not see the approach of the attack. The Royal Navy and R.I.N. bombarded the beaches, supported by the medium bombers of No. 224 Group, which also laid a smokescreen. Surprise was complete and No. 1 Commando pushed on to Hill 170 which was to be the scene of heavy fighting. By nightfall No. 5 Commando had landed, with the next day Nos. 44 (R.M.) and 42 (R.M.) Commandos.

The Japanese on the spot counter-attacked fiercely and efforts to infiltrate

▽ *Patching a damaged bridge with a "scissors" section. Carried on a turretless Covenanter or Valentine tank, this "Scissors Bridge, 30-foot, No. 1" could span a gap of 30 feet and bear a weight of up to 30 tons. They were widely used in the North-West European and Mediterranean theatres, and were particularly useful in Burma, where they made a real contribution to the 14th Army's swift advance.*

the village of Kangaw were rebuffed. The Japanese heavily bombarded the beaches with field artillery on the 24th and 25th, but on the 26th the 51st Brigade (Brigadier R. A. Hutton) landed with a troop of medium tanks followed by the 53rd Brigade (Brigadier B. C. H. Gerty).

As soon as he heard of the landing, General Miyazaki ordered Major-General T. Koba, commanding the "Matsu" Detachment, to repel the invaders and keep open the road. Koba, as a colonel, had commanded the two battalion column which had so successfully driven the 81st West African Division out of the Kaladan in March 1944. The "Matsu" Detachment consisted of the 54th Infantry Group, comprising three infantry battalions and an artillery battalion. Koba arrived on January 31 and immediately launched a heavy attack on Hill 170, which was held by Nos. 1 and 42 Royal Marine Commandos, commanded by Colonel Peter Young, Hardy's second in command.

The Commandos, supported by three tanks, repulsed Koga's most determined assaults. Attack and counter-attack waged around Hill 170 for 36 hours. The "Matsu" Detachment finally launched a pole-charge tank hunting party of en-

▽ *A wounded prisoner escorted by two of his Indian captors.*

gineers. They destroyed two tanks and damaged the third with a loss of 70 of their own men killed. By this time the 74th Brigade was moving in from the north-west: but not before the Commandos had killed over 300 Japanese at a loss to themselves of 66 killed, 15 missing, and 259 wounded. Lieutenant Knowland, of No. 1 Commando, won a posthumous Victoria Cross for his part in the fighting.

As soon as Miyazaki heard that Ramree Island had been occupied he feared that the 26th Division might land in his rear, so he ordered the "Matsu" Detachment to break off the engagement and withdraw to the An Pass, which was vital to the 54th Division's communications. By February 18, the 25th Indian Division had relieved the Commando brigade.

Miyazaki had received heavy casualties but had skillfully avoided the destruction of his force.

It will be remembered that during February IV Corps and XXXIII Corps had crossed the Irrawaddy and by March 1 Meiktila had fallen. Also at this time the Chinese were asking for an air lift of their forces in Burma to take part in the offensive to regain the two provinces that they had lost a few months previously. Transport aircraft, therefore, were at a premium and S.E.A.C. decided that air supply to XV Corps must cease.

Lieutenant-General Sir Oliver Leese (C.-in-C. A.L.F.S.E.A.) therefore decided to withdraw the 25th and 26th Divisions to India. The 26th Division was withdrawn to prepare for a landing at Rangoon. The Commandos had already been withdrawn to train for a landing on the coast of Malaya.

It is an opportune time to consider the effects of the Arakan campaign. Strangely enough, both sides achieved their main objects. The Japanese, with their depleted forces, prevented XV Corps from breaking into the Irrawaddy valley although this was never XV Corps' intention. On the other hand XV Corps captured Akyab without a shot being fired and Ramree Island with trifling loss, although again the Japanese never had any intention of defending them strongly. Without doubt Miyazaki had done very well against the equivalent of five divisions (25th and 26th Indian, 81st and 82nd West African, and 22nd East African Brigade and 3rd Commando Brigade), supported by overwhelming numbers of aircraft and naval ships. As so often occurred in this campaign, XV Corps' main enemy was geography and

the problem of how to apply their superior
forces effectively against a skilful enemy
in difficult terrain. However, it is now
known that Christison had a greater
success than he first realised. Only four
battalions of both the Japanese 54th and
55th Divisions arrived in time to assist the
33rd Army in its operations against 14th
Army. The result was that the 14th Army
had nothing but the remains of divisions
which had already been virtually destroyed to oppose it in its advance south.

During these operations XV Corps lost
5,089 casualties, of which 1,138 were
killed. No. 224 Group (The Earl of Bandon)
lost 78 aircraft, but claimed 63 Japanese
aircraft destroyed. Fortunately there had
never been any serious opposition to the
seaborne landings, but during them the
Royal Navy fired 23,000 rounds varying
from 4-inch to 15-inch calibre. The Navy
had landed in all 54,000 men, 800 animals,
11,000 vehicles, and 14,000 tons of stores.

The final seaborne operation of the
Burma war was the assault on Rangoon,
which started with an airborne attack on
Elephant Point, which covered the en-
trance of the main navigable arm of the
Irrawaddy river leading from the sea to
Rangoon itself. The amphibious operation

for the capture of Rangoon was launched
on April 27, while the 14th Army was held
up at Prome and the Pegu river.

Two naval forces set sail to give long
range protection to the large convoy
during its voyage to the mouth of the
Rangoon river and to intercept any fleeing
Japanese.

The first, under Vice-Admiral Walker,
was directed against the Andaman and
Nicobar Islands, covering Rangoon from
the west. It consisted of the battleships
Queen Elizabeth and *Richelieu*, the
cruisers *Cumberland*, *Suffolk*, *Ceylon*, and
Tromp, the escort carriers *Empress* and
Shah, six destroyers, and two resupply
oil tankers. On the morning of April 30,
Walker bombarded targets in the Nico-
bars and in the evening put in airstrikes
and naval bombardments on to airfields,
docks, and shipping at Port Blair in the
Andamans. Before leaving the area on
May 7, Walker also attacked Victoria
Point and Mergui near to the Malay
border and returned for a second strike at
Port Blair and the Nicobars.

The second naval force consisted of
three destroyers under Commodore A. L.
Poland. On the night of April 29-30
Poland intercepted a convoy of small

ships carrying about 1,000 men and stores from Rangoon to Moulmein. He sank ten craft and picked up some survivors.

At 0230 hours on May 1 a visual control post was dropped as a marker for a parachute landing. Thirty-eight Dakotas dropped a composite battalion of the 50th Gurkha Parachute Brigade at 0545 hours. There were five minor casualties. A further 32 casualties were caused amongst the Gurkhas when some Liberators, aiming at another target, dropped a stick of bombs on the paratroopers. The Gurkhas overcame a small force of 37 Japanese holding Elephant Point itself. The way was then clear for landing craft carrying the assault troops to advance up the river as soon as any mines had been swept.

Aircraft flying over Rangoon saw the words "Japs gone" and "Extract Digit" painted on the roof of Rangoon Jail. Wing-Commander A. E. Saunders (commanding No. 110 Squadron R.A.F.), seeing this well known R.A.F. slang and seeing no signs of the enemy, landed at Mingaladon Airfield, but unfortunately damaged his Mosquito in the craters on the runway. Saunders, having contacted the British prisoners-of-war in Rangoon Jail and hearing that the Japanese had evacuated Rangoon on April 29, went down to the docks and sailed down the Rangoon River in a motor launch to report that the Japanese had gone. Meanwhile, the brigades of the 26th Division moved up the Rangoon river in landing craft and soon occupied Rangoon. It was a tragedy that Colonel Dick Ward, who had been Commander Royal Engineers of the 17th Indian Division from its retreat from Moulmein in 1942 to India and had fought throughout the campaign, was killed when the landing craft in which he was travelling in the van to occupy Rangoon on May 2, 1945 struck a mine.

The battles for Mandalay and Meiktila were over. The Japanese 15th Army which had attacked Kohima/Imphal, and the 33rd Army had both suffered a major defeat. The 33rd Army had been severely mauled by the Chinese and Stilwell's N.C.A.C. (including the British 36th Division). During their counter-attack to recapture Meiktila, their losses were again heavy. The 18th Division also had suffered 1,773 casualties, which was about one-third of its strength and lost about half of their 45 guns. The 49th Division, which (being fairly new in Burma) started with a total strength of 10,000, suffered 6,500 casualties and lost all but three of its 48

guns. Casualties amongst the other divisions were of a similar order. As the official British history states of this period, the Burma Area Army had virtually ceased to exist as a fighting force. Already, by August 1944, the Southern Army had been told that it could expect no further reinforcements in men or *matériel* from Japan, and the divisions were now living on their own fat.

The 28th Army, which was mainly concerned with defending the coast of Burma, had a small force (72nd Independent Mixed Brigade) in the Mount Popa-Chauk-Yenangyaung area but, as related, only four battalions of the 54th and 55th Divisions facing XV Corps were ever deployed in Central Burma to oppose the 14th Army.

General Leese had ordered Slim to reduce the strength of his army to four and two-thirds divisions, which was the maximum number which could be supplied by air during his drive south. XXXIII Corps (Stopford) was to advance down the Irrawaddy valley from Yenanyaung, via Magwe and Allanmyo to the railhead at Prome and on towards Rangoon if it had not already been captured. IV Corps (Messervy) was to use the main road route to Rangoon via Pyabwe, Pyinmana, Toungoo, and Pegu. Each corps would consist of two motorised infantry divisions and one armoured brigade.

The plan was that each corps would move in bounds one division at a time passing through the other, from airfield to airfield, supplied by air-landed stores at each point. Travelling with the divisions would be a large number of airfield construction engineers. As the left flank of Messerby's IV Corps would be in the air, Mountbatten decided to organise the loyal Karens in the hills flanking his advance into levies to protect his eastern flank. Over 3,000 of these fine guerrilla fighters were recruited, and Messervy had then no reason to worry about any unexpected attack from that direction as the Karens were only too glad of the chance to kill Japanese.

Each corps had a distance of 350 miles to go to its objective. XXXIII Corps consisted of the 7th and 20th Indian Divisions and the 268th Indian Infantry Brigade, plus the 254th Indian Tank Brigade. IV Corps consisted of the 5th and 17th Indian Divisions and the 255th Indian Tank Brigade. Each corps had its own artillery component which included two medium regiments with XXXIII Corps

△ *General Slim and Air Marshal Vincent at Government House, Rangoon, May 1945, after the Allied assault and occupation of the city.*

and one medium regiment with IV Corps. There was a special headquarters Royal Engineer Regiment to control the forward airfield engineers and bridging companies with each corps.

A brigade from the 19th Indian Division accompanied IV Corps and garrisoned its communications as it advanced.

Stopford was held up at Pyabwe by the fine defence of the remnants of the famous 18th Division (now only 2,000 strong) which had captured Singapore, had been one of the first divisions to conquer Burma, and had fought for so long on the northern front against Stilwell.

Otherwise there were no hitches except those caused by geography and the weather. Messervy reached Pyinmana on April 19, Toungoo on the 22nd, and Pegu, within 50 miles of Rangoon, on May 1. At Pegu a Japanese improvised brigade, made up of training unit personnel and numbering 1,700 men, delayed his advance. Unseasonable heavy rain on May 2 stopped IV Corps' advance abruptly.

However, the engineers managed to clear 500 mines and to throw a bridge across the Pegu river and at 0930 hours on May 4, IV Corps continued its advance. On May 6 the 1/7th Gurkhas met a column of the Lincolnshire Regiment from the 26th Division, which had advanced northwards from Rangoon.

Meanwhile XXXIII Corps advanced down the Irrawaddy valley. Stopford captured Chauk on April 18 and Magwe and Yenangyaung on April 21, overcoming resistance from the 72nd Independent Mixed Brigade and some battalions from the 28th Army. Allanmyo on the Irrawaddy was captured on April 28 and Stopford entered Prome on May 3. A patrol from XV Corps, advancing from Taungup, contacted him shortly afterwards so that by that date all three corps of Leese's forces were in touch. The Burma victory was now complete.

On June 1, 1945, a 12th Army was formed under command of General Stopford to control mopping-up operations, including the re-establishment of civil government. The 12th Army consisted of IV Corps in the Sittaung valley and the 7th and 20th Indian Divisions and the 268th Brigade in the Irrawaddy valley.

IV Corps consisted of the 5th, 17th, and 19th Indian Divisions, and the 255th Tank Brigade. So with the 7th and 20th Indian Divisions and 268th Brigade, Stopford had five divisions and two brigades under command, with the 26th Division awaiting transport for India. His air support was provided by No. 221 Group R.A.F., but now that the monsoon had broken the R.A.F. was not in a position to give good close support to the troops on the ground. Slim, now promoted General, replaced Leese as Commander Allied Land Forces, South East Asia, and on April 16 took up his command in Kandy, Ceylon.

Stopford's main problem was the Japanese 28th Army which still totalled nearly 30,000 troops.

Sakurai, the army commander, had managed to get the remains of his 54th and 55th Divisions back from the coast and delta over the Irrawaddy and into the Pegu Yomas, a series of jungle-covered hills lying between the Irrawaddy valley on the one hand and the Sittang valley on the other, north of Rangoon. Sakurai's object was to break out and join the remains of the Burma Area Army, which was now regrouping east of the wide flowing and flooded Sittang River. At this time the Sittang was flooded as far north

As their army's organisation disintegrated and their morale crumbled, more and more Japanese soldiers decided it was better to surrender to the enemy than die fighting for the Emperor.
◄ *The first organised party of Japanese to surrender. Men of the 53rd Infantry Division crossed the Sittang river in landing craft to surrender to the 1/10th Gurkhas – who chose the spot where, in 1942, their own division had been defeated by the Japanese.*
◄▽ *Prisoners being brought in for interrogation.*
▽ *Men of the Royal Garhwal Rifles, 26th Indian Division, searching a group of Japanese after the surrender in Malaya.*

△ S.E.A.C. chiefs draw up the surrender terms. From left to right: Slim, Wheeler, Mountbatten, Power, Park, Browning.
▷ Walking from their aircraft to meet their Allied victors – Lieutenant-General Takazo Numato (with glasses) and Rear-Admiral Keigye Chudo.
▽ The formal act of surrender took place in the throne room of Government House, Rangoon.

as Shwegyin, a distance of nearly 50 miles upstream from the Gulf of Martaban. Sakurai decided therefore to advance on a wide 100-mile front between Toungoo and Nyaunglebin, just west of Shwegyin.

It would be tedious here to attempt to describe the numerous small operations which occurred as Sakurai's 28th Army attempted to cross the road in dispersal groups during May and August, all the while being hunted by Stopford's Indian battalions, tanks, and armoured cars. These operations were carried out mainly by junior officers, and were very important to them.

However, a brief resumé of the casualties incurred at that time will indicate the intensity of the fighting and the miserable defeat of the remnants of a once fine army.

On June 28, 1945 the strength of the 28th Army was stated to be 27,764. Three months later, on September 22, the 28th Army's reported strength to the Burma Area Army was as follows: present on duty 7,949; in hospital 1,919; and missing 3,822, some of whom were expected to return.

IV Corps' losses over much the same period were 435 killed, 1,452 wounded, and 42 missing.

Thus in effect ended the war in Burma, where an army of ten Japanese divisions, two Independent Mixed Brigades, and about two Indian National Army divisions were not only defeated, but to all intents and purposes, wiped out as a fighting force.

CHAPTER 96
OKINAWA: THE BATTLE

The Americans began the first phase of the battle for Okinawa on March 18 when carrier-borne planes began pounding Japanese airfields on Kyūshū. On the 19th the Americans switched to the naval bases at Kobe, Kure, and Hiroshima and to Japanese shipping in the Inland Sea. *Kamikazes* and bombers hit back fiercely, damaging *Yorktown, Wasp,* and *Enterprise* and setting *Franklin* ablaze. Task Force 58 began to withdraw on the afternoon of the 19th, and during the next 48 hours was harried by repeated Japanese air attacks. These, however, were fought off by the American fighter pilots, who ran up impressive scores. The tally of Japanese aircraft destroyed between March 18 and 22 was 528, and 16 surface ships were damaged during the same period, including the super-battleship *Yamato.* Mitscher's force had amply fulfilled its rôle. When the main landings went in on Okinawa, the Japanese were unable to throw in a serious air counter-attack for a week.

Next on the schedule was the seizure of the islands of the Kerama Retto group, a task entrusted to the 77th Division under Major-General Andrew D. Bruce. This was a campaign within a campaign, a faithful miniature of the "island-hopping" programme as a whole. A preliminary reconnaissance and bombardment preceded the actual assault, which was launched on the islands of Aka, Geruma, Hokaji, and Zanami on March 26. Initial progress was so rapid that Bruce decided to take Yakabi Island as well, and it fell with minimal resistance on the first day. The Japanese reacted in familiar fashion on Aka and Zanami, pulling back into the interior after conceding the fight for the beaches. The same thing happened the following day when Tokashiki was attacked, together with Amuro and Kuba. The Keramas were declared secure on the 29th, but the Japanese on Aka and Toka-shiki insisted on refusing to surrender

Before Okinawa, American forces captured various small islands in the area.
△ *Raising the flag on Aka.*

The Fire Raids on Japan

On the night of March 9-10, 1945 low-level fire bomb attacks were made on Tokyo by the 21st Bomber Squadron under command of Major-General Curtis E. LeMay. As a result, 15.8 square miles of the city were burnt out, including 18 per cent of the industrial area. Nayoga, Osaka and Kobe were given similar treatment. In March 1,595 sorties had been flown in just 10 days and 9,365 tons of bombs dropped. By May, the Japanese people were pouring into the countryside to avoid the attacks.

Okinawa: The Plans

Operation "Iceberg" was the name of the plan to take Okinawa, as a prelude to the conquest of the Japanese home islands. The defenders of the island were over 100,000 strong. The attack would be carried out by the U.S. 10th Army under General Simon B. Buckner. D-Day was the morning of April 1, 1945.

until the official capitulation of Japan. The occupation of the Keramas was rounded out with the emplacement of two batteries of 155-mm guns on the coral islands of Keise Shima, a mere 11 miles off the Haguchi beaches. These guns would add to the fire-power of the pre-invasion bombardment, and their emplacement on Keise Shima was a repetition of a trick used with great success during the battle for Kwajalein.

Pre-landing bombardment

While the Keramas were still being cleared, the intricate work of preliminary bombardment and minesweeping in the approaches to Okinawa had already been started by Vice-Admiral William H. Blandy's Task Force 52. The first offshore shelling began on March 25, but the job of clearing the dense minefield which the Japanese had laid off the Hagushi beaches was not completed until the evening of the 29th. Blandy himself called it "probably the largest assault sweep operation ever executed". In the week before the assault the American warships pounded the Japanese defences with over 13,000 shells of calibres ranging from 6-inch to 16-inch, while the carrier planes flew 3,095 sorties, covering targets requested by 10th Army. In the last three days, as the offshore obstacles were cleared, the warships steadily shortened the range and intensified their fire. With the method born of experience and the most detailed planning, an intricate naval ballet manoeuvred 1,300 ships into position for the assault on the morning of April 1.

"Land the landing force"

Admiral Turner's order was signalled to the invasion fleet at 0406 hours on the 1st—four and a half hours before the moment scheduled for hitting the beaches with the first wave. As the long ranks of

▽ *Assembling above the beach on Geruma, March 25, 1945.*

landing-craft jockeyed into position for the approach, the terrain behind the beaches shuddered and smoked like a volcano under the shellfire of the bombardment force. The boats moved off at 0800 in perfect conditions and the run-in proceeded as easily as a peace-time manoeuvre. As the bombardment lifted and the gunfire shifted inland the first boats began to ground, almost exactly on schedule, just after 0830. To the troops the actual landing came as an almost ludicrous anti-climax. "Where are the Japs?" was the question every man was asking as the cautious advance into the interior began. Meanwhile the landings continued without a hitch. By the evening of April 1 over 60,000 troops had landed on Okinawa and had pegged out a beach-head over eight miles wide and over two miles deep in places.

"An enemy landing attempt on the eastern coast of Okinawa on Sunday morning was completely foiled, with heavy losses to the enemy." That was how the Japanese boasted of the feint attack made by 2nd Marine Division (Major-General Thomas E. Watson) on the far side of the island from the Hagushi beaches. The Marines had made it look like a genuine attempt, with eight waves of boats dressed in line and covered by bombardment. They moved in simultaneously with the approach to the Hagushi beaches, reversed course precisely at 0830, and headed back to their parent vessels. The same performance was made on the morning of the 2nd and the force was then withdrawn.

Fast progress

On the second and third days the Marines and infantry pushed right across the island and cut it in two, with 96th and 7th Divisions wheeling to the south on the right flank and feeling out the first serious Japanese resistance around Momabaru. By the evening of April 3 interrogated Japanese civilians and liberated P.O.W.s. had informed the advancing troops that the main Japanese forces had pulled back to the south. The puzzle of the non-existent enemy had been solved: the battle for Okinawa had still to begin.

The push to the south was carried out by XXIV Corps: 96th and 7th Divisions, who began the cautious probing of Ushijima's defence outposts. For both divisions, April 5 marked the first day when genuine resistance at last was encountered. The advance continued during the next three days but by April 9 both divisions had been fought to a halt and XXIV Corps had not attained its prescribed objective. On the 9th the 383rd Infantry fought its way on to Kakazu Ridge but were forced to withdraw after a bloody fight. A "powerhouse attack" on April 10 was also repulsed, and the Japanese were still very much in possession of their strongpoint at Kakazu on the 12th. The first round had undoubtedly gone to the Japanese in precisely the sort of battle that Ushijima had planned. American morale was also depressed by President Roosevelt's death, which the Japanese promptly exploited for propaganda. "We must express our deep regret over the death of President Roosevelt," ran one leaflet. "The 'American Tragedy' is now raised here at Okinawa with his death . . Not only the late President but anyone else would die in the excess of worry to hear such an annihilative damage. The dreadful loss that led your late leader to death will make you orphans on this island. The Japanese special assault corps will sink your vessels to the last destroyer. You will witness it realised in the near future."

In the overview the Japanese were whistling in the dark: they certainly had little to boast about as far as naval victories were concerned. On April 7 the "Special Sea Attack Force" had sortied on a one-way mission to Okinawa. It was a suicide run, aimed at sending the super-battleship *Yamato* into the midst of the American invasion fleet and dealing out as much destruction as possible before meeting her inevitable end. But *Yamato* had been sunk by carrier planes before she had even sighted Okinawa. With the grip of the American navy unshaken, it was the Japanese who remained the "orphans of Okinawa", for all the local successes they might win. Much more important was the nature of the battle itself, with the Japanese having to accept the consequences of their defensive strategy. The cost of halting XXIV Corps by April 12 had been grievous: about 5,570 for the Japanese and 451 for the Americans. Despite this twelve-fold imbalance, 32nd Army now went over to the offensive to try to exploit the discomfiture of XXIV Corps by pushing it back to the north.

In two days of intense fighting the Japanese counter-attack, carried out by components of 62nd and 24th Divisions, was repelled at all points. It was a costly deviation from the basic strategy of staying in strongpoints and letting the Americans suffer the losses. By dawn on the 14th stalemate had settled once again over the front line.

Meanwhile Buckner had reversed the original plan of tackling southern Okinawa before clearing the north of the island, and had unleashed Geiger's Marines (6th Marine Division) on April 3. Driving north-eastwards along the nar-

to press ahead with capturing Ieshima, the 5-mile-long oval island 3½ miles off the Motobu Peninsula. The Japanese had built three airstrips on Ie shima and that was Buckner's main objective: to seize the island and use it as a natural aircraft-carrier to intensify the air umbrella over the Okinawa battlefield. Ie shima was a formidable nut to crack. The 2,000 troops on the island had, by exploiting civilian labour, made it a miniature Iwo Jima as far as prepared defence positions were concerned. Major-General Andrew D.

row "neck" of Okinawa, the 6th Marines had reached the sea and cut off the Motobu Peninsula by April 8. But it took them another 12 days to clear the peninsula and they had to exert every effort to crush the main Japanese position at Yae-Take with concentric attacks. Not until the 20th was Japanese resistance in the peninsula broken, and enough Japanese escaped to the hills to begin organised guerrilla warfare.

After changing his plan and clearing northern Okinawa, Buckner also decided

Bruce's 77th Division was earmarked for the capture of Ie shima, and the landings went in on April 16. Despite vigorous resistance, the 77th Division had overrun the western half of the island with its airstrips by the end of the 16th. But the Japanese still held out in Ie town. Five more gruelling days were needed before the island was declared secure, and even then the fighting continued until the 24th. The fight of Ie shima epitomised the bitterness of the Okinawa campaign; commenting on it, General Bruce said

△ *Men of a U.S.A.A.F. liaison squadron rescue one of their Stinson L-5 Sentinels caught in a flash flood on Okinawa. These small planes were invaluable for co-ordinating movements with ground troops.*

that "the last three days of this fighting were the bitterest I ever witnessed".

Surprise attack

Back on the southern front, Buckner was preparing to succeed with stealth where open attacks had failed: a surprise attack on the Shuri defences, pushing yard." The attack of April 19 was a complete failure and cost XXIV Corps 720 casualties. The Japanese fought like furies and held off all the American attempts to slip round their strongpoints. The zones of fire of their artillery and mortars had been carefully drawn and covered all sectors of the front. One regimental commander in the 96th Division commented bitterly after the battle: "You cannot bypass a Jap because a Jap

△ After hurling an explosive into the mouth of a cave, a Marine patrol waits for any surviving Japanese to emerge.

deep into the Japanese lines and by-passing strongpoints such as the Kakazu Ridge. The attack was set for April 19 and was to be launched by a surprise penetration by General Hodge's 27th Division on the 18th. Hodge summed it all up when he said: "It is going to be really tough. There are 65,000 to 70,000 fighting Japs holed up in the south end of the island, and I see no way to get them out except blast them out yard by

does not know when he is bypassed."

Despite their failure in the attack of April 19 the Americans had no choice but to keep up the pressure on the Shuri defences. When the fighting died down with the coming of darkness on the 19th a gap of nearly a mile yawned between 27th and 96th Divisions and General Griner, commander of the 27th, knew that it must be plugged. But the attack of April 20 went the same way as that of the

19th. This time the problem was a Japanese strongpoint which squarely blocked the line of advance west of Gusukuma towards the Machinato airfield – a strongpoint which had got the very best out of the terrain, was heavily manned, and which had to be cleared out, not by-passed. The Americans called it "Item Pocket" and it took them another exhausting week before it fell. Impromptu names for the key landmarks – "Charlie Ridge", "Brewer's Hill", "Dead Horse Gulch" – became feared and hated names during the incessant fighting between April 20 and April 27, when the Pocket was eventually declared secure. Weeks later, however, Japanese were still emerging from the deep bolt-holes and caves which had given the position its strength.

In the meantime the 7th, 27th, and 96th Divisions battered away at the outer Shuri defences on the centre and left of the front. On the latter sector the Japanese had based their defence on "Skyline Ridge", blocking the approach to Unaha and Yonabaru airfield. In the centre, Kakazu Ridge was still in Japanese hands. While the fight for Item Pocket raged on the right flank, the Americans struggled painfully forward until at last, by April 24, they had taken both Kakazu and Skyline Ridges. After three weeks' ordeal the outer shell of the Shuri defences had finally been cracked.

At the end of April, Buckner reshuffled his front-line divisions, many units of which were badly in need of a rest. The 27th Division was relieved by the 1st

Marine Division on April 30, and the 6th Marine also earmarked for a shift south to the front. The fall of Item Pocket on April 27 was followed by an exact replica of the preceding seven days – and then, on May 4, the Japanese unleashed a counter-offensive aimed at smashing the centre of 10th Army and driving its fragments into the sea. It was an ambitious plan, envisaging amphibious landings deep in the rear of the American

positions – but it suffered the same fate as the earlier Japanese attack. The amphibious operation was a total fiasco. Despite a temporary breakthrough in the centre and the recapture of Tanabaru Ridge, the Japanese 24th Division had shot its bolt by the 7th and Ushijima had no choice but to fall back on the defensive, having achieved little but to delay the American advance for just under a week. (During the fighting for the Tanabaru Ridge the

◁▽ *Fighting in the streets of Naha, Okinawa's main city. Many buildings were set on fire by Americans as the only way to flush out Japanese troops.*

△ *V.E. Day on Okinawa – while Europe celebrated, there was no respite for these Marines as the bitter struggle continued. One unit goes in as another pulls back from the fighting in Naha.*

news of the German surrender reached Okinawa. "Well, now," said a colonel of the 17th Infantry Division, as he sniped at the Japanese with an M1 carbine, "if we just had the Japs off the escarpment we'd be all right, wouldn't we?")

Once Ushijima's counter-attack had been safely held, Buckner saw in it a chance for a breakthrough. The attack had drawn the last fresh Japanese reserves into the line, and a prompt resumption of the initiative could well prove decisive. The result was the renewal of the attack on May 10 and its culmination on the 21st with the clearing of a "funnel" on the left flank which enabled the 7th Division to edge forwards into the inner ring of the Shuri defences. In this phase the decisive actions were the clearing of the eastern sides of Conical and Sugar Hills, which bent back the extreme right wing of the Japanese line. Plotted on a map, it seemed that the way was open for the rolling-up of the front from the east—but the Japanese remained in firm control of their positions and no breakthrough came. And now, in the fourth week of May, the elements sided with the Japanese. The rain poured down and the battlefield of Okinawa dissolved in mud.

Transport was paralysed and it was impossible to move heavy equipment through the floods and quagmires—but there was no diminution of the pressure. With the Japanese centre north of Shuri still rock steady, Buckner ordered the flanking divisions to intensify operations and bend back the Japanese wings as far as possible. It was an exhausting and undramatic process. With every day's new advances the "bulge" being formed round Shuri seemed to herald the total envelopment of Ushijima's men—but still the Japanese refused to break and the casualties continued to soar. With the rain and the mud and the pattern of attrition in men's lives (one dead American for every ten dead Japanese by the end of May) the battle of Okinawa was taking on the nature of the most hideous trench-warfare pounding match of World War I—and with as few obvious results.

Yet now at last the persistence of the Americans was rewarded. Even before the ominous constriction of the flanks of the 32nd Army in the last weeks of May, General Ushijima had made the decision to yield the Shuri Line and withdraw to the south after a conference with his staff on May 21. The consensus of opinion had been that to hold on at Shuri would only

mean that the 32nd Army would be destroyed earlier than necessary, without having inflicted sufficient losses on the Americans. The 32nd Army would make its last stand at the southern tip of Okinawa. Supplies and wounded began moving south on the night of May 22-23, heading for the positions previously constructed by the 24th Division.

The Japanese retreat

With the rearguard holding on in front of Shuri, the Japanese pulled out with skill and discipline, and their move was largely completed by the end of May. The Japanese move was helped by the sluicing rains and the lowering overcast, which seriously impeded American aerial reconnaissance. From May 26, however, the long Japanese columns were kept under general surveillance from the air: and a 10th Army staff meeting on the evening of May 30 reached the conclusion that although the Japanese were still holding before Shuri, their line was little but a tough shell. It was widely believed that Ushijima had made his decision too late and that the campaign was all over bar the mopping-up. Once again it was a serious under-estimation of the actual situation. Shuri fell at long last on May 31, but Buckner's divisions did not, as expected, trap the 32nd Army in a pocket and wipe it out. Nor were they able to prevent it from pulling back and forming yet another solid front in the south. For this the Americans could certainly blame the adverse weather conditions: "We had awfully tough luck to get the bad weather at the identical time that things broke," lamented Buckner.

Thus the scene was set for the last round of the battle for Okinawa. The southern end of the island is best described as a downward-pointing arrowhead. The Shuri Line had crossed the shank of the arrowhead above the barbs; and now the 32nd Army had pulled right down into the very tip of the arrow. An amphibious operation coped with the western barb of the arrowhead, the Orotu Peninsula, trapping the remnants of Rear-Admiral Minoru Ota's naval troops and wiping them out by June 15 after a ten-day battle. Meanwhile the first attacks on the main Japanese position behind the Yaeju-Dake Ridge had begun.

It took five murderous days—June 12-

(page 980) ◊ ◊ *Lieutenant-General Simon Bolivar Buckner (left) with Major-General Roy S. Geiger.*
A few days after this picture was taken, Buckner was killed by enemy fire and Geiger succeeded him as commander of the 10th Army.
◊ *On Okinawa an unusually large number of Japanese began to surrender. This officer decided to give himself up after hearing a broadcast from an offshore landing craft.*
▷ *Snatching a well-earned rest, two Marines sleep in a foxhole next to their machine gun.*

17–to crack the Yaeju-Dake position: five days in which the fighting was as intense as ever. The Japanese still had to be blasted and burned from their foxholes, and a new American flame-throwing tactic was to bring up a 200-foot fuel supply hose from which to spray napalm on Japanese positions. By June 17 the survivors of the 32nd Army had been blasted out of their front-line position and compressed into an area eight miles square. After more than two and a half months of superb endurance, the men of the 32nd Army had reached the end of their tether. Between the 18th and the 21st they were split into three independent pockets and it was obvious that the end was near. Buckner sent a personal appeal to Ushijima to see reason and save the lives of his last men. Ushijima received it with vast amusement. He radioed his last message to Tokyo on the evening of the 21st, and he and his chief-of-staff, General Isamu Ota, committed ritual *hara-kiri* the same night. The last organised resistance–on Hill 85, between Medeera and Makabe–was broken on the 21st. Although "Old Glory" was formally raised over Okinawa at the 10th Army headquarters on the morning of the 22nd, mopping-up operations lasted until the end of the month; and the Ryūkyūs campaign was officially declared ended on July 2.

The cost

The Allies had conquered Okinawa and were now only 350 miles from Kyūshū itself. The objective of "Iceberg" had been achieved, but at a terrifying cost. Total American battle casualties were 49,151. The Americans had lost 763 aircraft and 36 ships sunk; another 368 of their ships had been damaged. But the Japanese had lost 110,000 men, including conscripts and drafted civilians, and even this has to be an approximate figure. Only 7,400 Japanese prisoners were taken on Okinawa–most of them in the last days when the 32nd Army was disintegrating. Ten major *kamikaze* attacks had been thrown against Okinawa, using up some 1,465 aircraft; and the total number of suicide sorties was 1,900. The Japanese losses in aircraft were staggering: 7,800. The Imperial Navy lost 16 ships sunk and four damaged.

What did the Okinawa campaign prove?

▽ *Marines move cautiously over "Cemetery Ridge". Enemy snipers keep them pinned down, seeking cover among the gravestones.*

First and foremost, it gave a bitter fore-taste of what the Allies could expect if they ever tried to land on Japanese soil. It was the bloodiest fight of the Pacific war. But above all it proved that nothing could stop the Allies in the Pacific from moving where they wanted, even if it did mean killing every Japanese in their way. And Ushijima himself paid tribute to this in his last message to Tokyo. "Our strategy, tactics, and technics all were used to the utmost and we fought vali-antly," he reported. "But it was as nothing before the material strength of the enemy."

The end of Japan's Navy

After the Battle of Leyte Gulf in October 1944, the Japanese Combined Fleet could no longer be recognised as the proud and efficient fighting force which had gone to war in December 1941. It was a shrivelled husk, largely immobilised by lack of fuel. Never again after Leyte did the Com-bined Fleet concentrate its strength to fight the carrier task forces of the Ameri-can and British Pacific fleets. But the surviving Japanese warships still had a part to play, and they remained high-priority targets for the Allies until the end of the war.

The Midway disaster of 1942 had caused the Japanese to adopt an accelerated and expanded carrier-building programme, but they never made good the losses of Coral Sea and Midway. The programme was a dual affair, including the construction of brand-new carriers from the keel up and the conversion of merchantmen and suitable warship hulls. Typical of the former category was the *Taiho,* lost in her first battle–the last big carrier clash of the Pacific war in the Philippine Sea (June 19, 1944) during the campaign in the Marianas. *Taiho* had actually been laid down before Pearl Harbor, but for months work on her had proceeded at a crawl. She displaced 29,300 tons, com-pared with the 25,675 tons of *Shokaku* and *Zuikaku*. She could achieve 33 knots and carried 74 aircraft (53 of them operational and 21 spare). But the details of her fate reveal the very great changes which had affected the Japanese carrier force between the days of Pearl Harbor and the last year of the war. The American submarine *Albacore* put a torpedo into *Taiho* on the morning of June 19. At first there seemed very little to worry about;

two fuel tanks had been ruptured and the flight-deck elevator jammed shut, but *Taiho* could still maintain full speed. The immediate hazard was the spreading fumes from the liberated oil and aviation spirit. The principal fuel of the vessel in 1944 was crude oil, as a result of overall shortages. The ship's ventilators were put on full blast in an attempt to dispel the fumes – a fatal decision. The fumes were spread throughout the vessel and continued to accumulate. The inevitable end came when a spark on the hangar deck detonated them. The effects were cataclysmic. A tremendous explosion shook *Taiho* from stem to stern, blowing

cannibalised from the uncompleted skeleton of "Hull III", the fourth "Yamato" class super-battleship (significant of the belated swing away from Japan's pre-war obsession with the big battleship as the prime mover of sea power). *Scharnhorst's* original electric turbines were retained; they were in fact only the second set to be used by a ship of the Imperial Navy. In her new guise, *Shinyo* finally joined the fleet in mid-December 1943. She was not present at the Battle of the Philippine Sea but was given a further eight 50-mm A.A. guns after that action, giving her a total of 50. Completely unarmoured, *Shinyo* had a best speed of 22 knots. Her air

out the hangar walls, ripping the flight deck, and perforating the ship's bottom. She sank within minutes, the victim of an elementary hazard of carrier life which had been obvious for years.

As for the second category of the "last generation" of Japanese carriers, a typical example may be cited with *Shinyo*. She started life as the German luxury liner *Scharnhorst*, which had been at Kobe since the outbreak of war in 1939. *Scharnhorst* was purchased by the Japanese Government in the months after Midway; she was renamed *Shinyo*, and her conversion was begun at the Kure Naval Yard in November 1942. Parts were

group consisted of a maximum of 33 planes: 27 operational and six spare. And she fell victim to the far-ranging American submarine arm, being torpedoed by the *Spadefish* in the China Sea on November 17, 1944.

Giant aircraft-carrier

But the biggest conversion job in the Japanese carrier programme was that of the giant *Shinano*, originally the third (after *Yamato* and *Musashi*) of the super-battleships. *Shinano's* whole story was

△ △ *Brigadier-General William J. Wallace* (left), *chief of fighter command, and Major-General Francis P. Mulcahy, commander of the 10th Army's Tactical Air Force, study the latest operations report at Yontan airfield, Okinawa.*

△ ◁ *Two men of the 1st Marines gaze down at a wounded*

one of monstrous error and wasted effort – much like the giant Japanese "I-400" submarines. To start with, argument raged for weeks over what sort of aircraft-carrier she should be: an orthodox carrier or a giant floating depot-ship and mobile base, carrying no aircraft of her own but able to supply and equip – and provide an additional flight-deck for – an entire carrier fleet. The final result was a compromise. *Shinano* would be a carrier supply-ship, but she would also have a few fighters of her own for self-defence and a hangar for storing them. This caused immense difficulties, because *Shinano's* hull had been completed up to the

by 131 feet. She could steam at 27 knots, she bristled with defensive armament, and she could carry 47 aircraft. At last, the backbone of Japan's new carrier fleet was finished – but the carrier fleet did not exist. There were carriers; there were aircraft; but there was little or no fuel for either, and certainly no trained aircrew. *Shinano* was, in fact, an awe-inspiring but thoroughly useless white elephant. And her end was little short of bathos. On November 28, 1944, she left Yokosuka for a brief shake-down cruise, escorted by three destroyers. She had not been at sea 24 hours, let alone moved out of sight of land, when she was caught by

Japanese soldier. At the bottom of the truck is a dead American.
△ *Just north of Naha, two U.S. Marines manhandle their bazooka into position.*
△▷ *With the plasma bottle hooked onto his rifle, a Navy Hospital Corpsman administers blood to a wounded Marine.*

main deck by the time of the decision to convert her. The work crawled along – as slowly, in fact, as did that on Germany's only aircraft-carrier, *Graf Zeppelin* – in a dreary stop-go rhythm. When the builders were finally galvanised into an all-out effort, after the defeat in the Philippine Sea, it was too late. All the reserves of trained aircrew had been whittled away to the point of extinction. Nevertheless, the work on the useless giant moved to completion and *Shinano* was ready for service in November 1944.

She was the biggest aircraft-carrier in the world, and the best protected. Her armoured flight-deck stretched 840 feet

the American submarine *Archerfish,* and hit by a salvo of four torpedoes.

In the Battle of Leyte Gulf, *Shinano's* sister-ship *Musashi* had proved what tremendous punishment the class could take and still stay afloat. *Musashi* had been singled out as the main target for American air attacks as Kurita's battle fleet struggled through the Sibuyan Sea. Plastered by bombs and ripped by repeated torpedo hits, she had refused to sink, and her expert crew kept her afloat by skilful counter-flooding for hours until the end. *Shinano* was not vitally damaged at all by *Archerfish's* torpedoes and could still make 18 knots. But her inexperienced crew neglected practically every damage-control rule in the book. The waters rose and spread from compartment to compartment; she kept on her course at full speed; and her captain would certainly have been court-martialled for gross negligence if he had not gone down with *Shinano*, seven hours after the torpedoing, at 1017 on November 29.

Mobility and hitting-power are the prerequisites of a carrier force, and by 1945 the Japanese carrier force had no fuel and no aircrew. This in turn meant that the surviving units of the Imperial Navy were now finally denuded of their air umbrella and were, from a strategic point of view, little more than floating scrap-iron. The Americans went ahead with the last major offensives of the Pacific war–Luzon, Iwo Jima, and Okinawa–secure in the knowledge that the Japanese Navy would never pose a serious threat to them again.

To the Japanese high command it was unthinkable that the Emperor's last warships should be bombed to destruction in their home ports, or hunted down independently at sea. The *kamikaze* strategy was therefore applied to the Japanese Navy–but, as with the Army and Navy air forces, the problem remained one of *matériel,* not men. There were thousands of eager volunteers willing to show their veneration for their Emperor by immolating themselves on an enemy carrier and taking as many Americans with them as possible. The difficulty was in getting them there. The Navy, as we have seen, developed two main *kamikaze* weapons of its own: *kaiten* and explosive speed-boats. However, the best suicide weapon remained the aircraft, plummeting down on its target from the skies.

Kamikaze mentality

The ambitious "SHO" plan which had thrown the massed strength of the Combined Fleet against the Americans at Leyte had been motivated by the *kamikaze* mentality: to do as much damage as possible with inferior resources. And the same held true of one of the most bizarre episodes in naval history: the suicide sortie of the *Yamato* during the opening phase of the long battle for Okinawa, in April 1945.

Japan's defensive strategy was based on the idea of "Dunkirking" the spearhead troops, once they had got ashore, and disrupting the Allied offensive plan by raising as much havoc as possible. And it was to this end that the "Special Sea Attack Force" was formed. It consisted of the *Yamato* and a light destroyer escort. Using literally the last dregs of the country's fuel oil stocks, the *Yamato* would make straight for the invasion beaches at Okinawa, deal out maximum destruction to the American invasion fleet, then beach herself and fight to the last shell available for her huge 18-inch guns.

Under the command of Vice-Admiral Seiichi Ito, the force sailed from Tokuyama in Japan's Inland Sea on the afternoon of April 6: *Yamato*, surrounded by a ring of eight destroyers and the light cruiser *Yahagi*. The Japanese squadron had barely cleared Japanese territorial waters before it was spotted by American submarines patrolling the Bungo Strait, between the islands of Shikoku and Kyūshū. Once out at sea, Ito altered course to the west, steering into the East China Sea preparatory to a last turn to the south for the final run down to Okinawa, and his ships were sighted at 0822 hours on the 7th by reconnaissance aircraft from Admiral Marc Mitscher's Task Force 58. A mighty strike of 380 dive-bombers and torpedo-bombers took off from Mitscher's carriers at 1000, when the Japanese force was some 250 miles away–just before *Yamato* and her frail ring of escorts swung to the south. Around noon the first contact was made and the final ordeal of the *Yamato* began.

The American pilots were impressed by the massive A.A. fire which came up at them: the Japanese had learned the lesson of air power well, and by the time of her last voyage *Yamato* bristled with no less than 146 25-mm A.A. guns. Most impressive of all, however, were the *San-Shiki* shells fired by her main armament, which may be best described as 18-inch shotgun shells. *Yamato's* main battery was designed for use in the anti-aircraft rôle and the *San-Shiki* shells were crammed with incendiary bullets. The idea was that the shells would be fired into a group of enemy aircraft; the shells would then burst, like a shotgun fired into a flock of birds, mowing down the enemy planes. It was found, however, that the terrifying blast of *Yamato's* 18-inch guns when fired at maximum elevation only served to disrupt the main volume of A.A. fire. The *San-Shiki* shells proved to be a failure, like so many other impressive-sounding Japanese ideas.

The Japanese had the weather–squalls and low clouds–on their side, but little else. The Special Attack Force had no fighter cover whatever and the American bombers were able to make almost unimpeded progress as repeated waves swept in to the attack. The ring of Japanese destroyers soon broke up under the stress of constant manoeuvre to avoid torpedoes. Pounded to a wreck, *Yahagi* sank shortly after 1400 hours; and 25 minutes later came the turn of *Yamato.* She had taken a fearful beating; at least ten torpedoes had hit her, plus seven bombs. Her crew was unable to cope with the inrush of water, or keep her upright by counterflooding. *Yamato* finally capsized and sank at 1425. Admiral Ito and nearly all the ship's company of 2,400 men went down with her. Four of the escorting destroyers were sunk as well, and the battered survivors turned for home.

An era ends

Such was the Battle of the East China Sea on April 7, 1945. It was the end of the Dreadnought age–the last time that a battleship was sunk by enemy action on the high seas. The wheel had indeed come full circle since Pearl Harbor in December 1941, when the superb Japanese carrier arm had proved the vulnerability of the battleship once and for all. *Yamato's* sacrifice was totally useless; she had never even sighted Okinawa, let alone taken any pressure off the gallant Japanese garrison there. On the Japanese side of the ledger there was only one completely insignificant flicker of success: a *kamikaze* hit on the carrier *Hancock.*

The remnants

Cowering in the Japanese home ports lay the remnants of the Imperial Navy. At Yokosuka there was the battleship *Nagato,* in her heyday the strongest battleship in the world with her 16-inch main armament. Her last action had been Leyte Gulf, where she had escaped the holocaust of the battleships. Now in the summer of 1945 she was inoperative, inglorious, with her funnel and foremast removed to assist camouflage. The rump

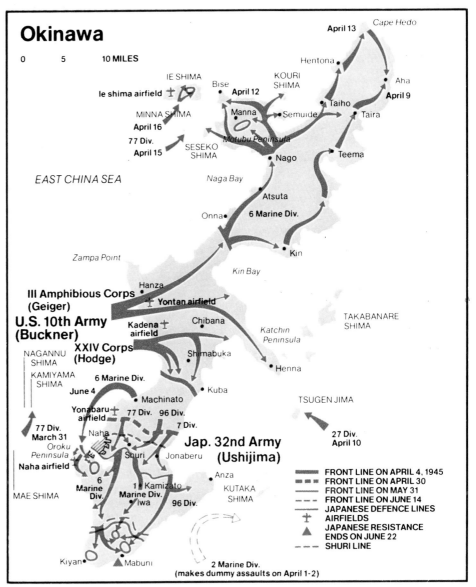

of the battle fleet lay at Kure, Japan's great naval base. There were the *Ise* and *Hyuga,* absurdly converted to seaplane-carriers by the removal of their after turrets. With equal absurdity they had been classified the 4th Carrier Division of the 2nd Fleet in November 1944. In March 1945 they had finally been taken off the active list and now served as A.A. batteries. Also at Kure was the *Haruna,* the last survivor of the "*Kongo*" class battle-cruisers built on the eve of World War I. With the *Kongos* Japanese designers had shown the world that they had seen through the inherent weaknesses of the battle-cruiser concept by specifying their order for fast battleships; and the *Kongos* had been extensively reconstructed between the wars. Another genuine museum-piece at Kure in 1945 was the old target-ship *Settsu,* whose construction had helped place Japan fourth after Britain, the United States, and Germany as a Dreadnought naval power.

△ *The American conquest of the Japanese island of Okinawa.*

△ *The mighty Japanese battleship* Yamato *during her fitting out in 1941.*

The Combined Fleet

There were seven Japanese aircraft-carriers in home waters. First among them was the little *Hosho,* the first carrier in the world to be designed as such from the keel up, which had been launched after World War I. When she served as fleet carrier training ship, most of the Japanese Navy's crack aircrews learned their trade aboard her. She had survived Midway as Yamamoto's last serviceable carrier and was still in service in 1945. The other six carriers—*Ibuki, Amagi, Katsuragi, Kaiyo, Ryuho,* and *Junyo*—represented the losing struggle to restore carrier protection and hitting-power to the Combined Fleet.

Apart from destroyers and submarines still in service, the only other major units of the Combined Fleet in Japanese ports in 1945 were six cruisers.

With American carrier planes now able to range at will over the Japanese homeland, it was only a matter of time before these sorry survivors were singled out for destruction. Admiral Halsey planned it personally: it was to be a formal revenge for Pearl Harbor, an all-American operation without the British Pacific Fleet. It took the form of a fearsome three-day blitz on the Japanese naval bases, concentrating on Kure. Between July 24 and 26, 1945, the American carrier forces struck round the clock. In those hectic days they sank the *Amagi, Ise* and *Hyuga, Haruna, Settsu,* and five cruisers, effectively destroying Japanese hopes of forming a possible suicide squadron from their last heavy warships. If any one date is required for the formal annihilation of the Japanese fleet, it may be set as July 24-26, 1945.

Midget craft

Although the British did not participate in the mass attacks on the Japanese naval bases, they were nevertheless active during this final phase. Ranging over the Inland Sea, British carrier planes sank two frigates and several other small fry, and also claimed a hit on an escort carrier. The biggest feather in the caps of the British, however, was earned thousands of miles away: in a dramatic and successful midget submarine attack on the port of Singapore.

At Singapore lay the Japanese heavy cruisers *Takao* and *Myoko,* both of them marked down for attack by the Submarine Flotilla of the British Pacific Fleet. Two XE-craft – improved versions of the midget submarine which had crippled the German battleship *Tirpitz* in her Arctic lair in late 1943 – were detailed for the job: *XE-1* (Lieutenant J. E. Smart) and *XE-3* (Lieutenant Ian Fraser). On July 30, 1945, the two midgets were on their way to the approaches to Singapore Roads, towed by their parent submarines: *Spark* (*XE-1*) and *Stygian* (*XE-3*).

In the history of submarine warfare this attack is particularly interesting because of the use of the echo depth-finder in navigating to the target. By 0600 hours on July 31 – set as the day for the attack – *XE-3* was manoeuvring up the Johore Strait at 30 feet. The boom — hardly a formidable affair, with a permanent gate some 300 yards wide – was safely passed at 1030 and the target, *Takao,* was sighted at 1250. As *XE-3* closed in on her victim there was a disconcerting moment. As Fraser put it, "I was very upset to see a motor cutter filled with Japanese liberty men only about 30 yards from my periscope." *XE-3,* however, remained undetected as she crawled towards *Takao* across the uneven harbour bottom, fetching up against the hull of the Japanese cruiser with a loud clang at 1442 hours.

With great daring, Fraser decided to make his attack with *XE-3* wedged squarely beneath *Takao's* hull. The attack used two weapons: limpet mines, attached to the enemy hull by the XE-craft's diver, and fused explosive charges, released from the midget's hull from inside. Operating with great difficulty in the murky waters of the harbour, diver Leading-Seaman J. Magennis attached six limpets to *Takao's* bottom. It was a long and exhausting job, for he had to scrape off patches of weed and barnacles to get the limpets to stick. After placing the mines and returning inside *XE-3,* Magennis had to go back outside and release the starboard explosive charge, which refused to detach itself. Tired though he was, Magennis had no hesitation in immediately volunteering for this strenuous and extremely dangerous job. As Fraser's report has it: "He went on oxygen again at 16.25 hrs. and made his exit to the casing with a large spanner in his hand. After seven minutes he managed, by much banging at the carrier and levering at the release pins, to get the carrier away."

With the explosives safely placed in position, Fraser turned to the task of wriggling *XE-3* clear of her victim and retreating to the open sea for the rendezvous with *Stygian.* Despite several harrowing moments the retreat passed off safely. The boom was passed at 1949 hours and at 2100 *XE-3* was able to surface and proceed down the Johore Strait. Rendezvous was safely made with *Stygian* at 2345 hours.

Smart, in *XE-1,* had had bad luck from the start of the approach. One mishap after another had combined to delay his attack so badly that he risked being caught inside the boom if he had pressed on to his own target. Smart therefore took the extremely brave decision to attack Fraser's target as well and take the risk of being blown up by the detonation of *XE-3's* limpets and charges. The possibility of this was heightened by the fact that the detachable charges were fitted with disturbance fuses, and *XE-1* would stand a likely chance of setting them off. But the calculated risk taken by Smart paid off; he dropped his charges and retreated safely. A final mishap was a 24-hour delay in the rendezvous with *Spark.* Fraser and Magennis received the Victoria Cross for their attack, Smart the Distinguished Service Order.

As for the unfortunate *Takao,* left with two sets of explosive charges and six limpet mines, the resultant explosion destroyed her as a fighting ship.

▷ *The end of the* Ise, *awash in Kure harbour after three raids by U.S. bombers. The* Ise *had had two main gun turrets removed for the installation of a flight deck, making her into an unprecedented carrier-battleship. The effectiveness of this combination was never put to the test, however, as the Japanese navy suffered defeat after defeat.*

Inglorious end

The postwar fate of the Japanese warships which survived Halsey's Blitz of July 1945 was inglorious. *Nagato,* last of the battle fleet, was used as a target ship during the Bikini Atoll atom test in 1946, together with the cruiser *Sakawa.* The other cruisers and carriers were either used as targets, scrapped, or sunk at sea by the victors – the Americans in particular sank a hecatomb of surrendered Japanese submarines off Gato Island in April 1946.

The fate of the last vessels of the Imperial Japanese Navy was the grim end to a remarkable story. Japan's emergence as a modern power only dates from the last three decades of the 19th Century. By careful study of the best European models, she built a navy second to none in either *matériel* or fighting spirit in under 30 years. In that period Japanese naval designers not only participated in the birth of the Dreadnought era: they proved again and again that they could lead the world in laying down new concepts for the development of the fighting ship and the evolution of naval warfare.

What went wrong? It is now generally accepted that Japan's decision to go to war in December 1941 was a calculated risk, a gamble which came within an ace of success. But as far as the total defeat of her prime instrument of war in the Pacific – the Combined Fleet – is concerned, several serious errors stand out. The first is that in 1941 the Combined Fleet was a contradiction in terms. Its carrier force was superb but the battle-fleet – the big gun – was still looked to as the weapon which would bring decisive victory. Submarine strategy was totally misguided on the Japanese side, whereas the Americans used their submarines correctly and reaped the rewards. Above all, however, the Japanese naval strategists had to cut their coat according to their cloth: the one thing they could not afford was a war of attrition, and this

they got. The Guadalcanal campaign, for example, cost them the equivalent of an entire peace-time fleet – losses which could never be replaced. The very speed with which the Americans assumed the offensive in the Pacific, never to lose it, showed what a narrow margin the Japanese Navy had.

And the result was an unreal metamorphosis which led the Japanese into building huge white elephants like *Shinano* and the aircraft-carrying *"I-4400"* submarines. It saw the Combined Fleet change from an instrument of the offensive and of victory to a sacrificial victim whose purpose was only to stave off defeat. This process first became dominant at the time of the Marianas campaign in June 1944, and it was the *leitmotif* of the final destruction of the Combined Fleet. That there was great heroism among the men who took *Yamato* out on her last voyage cannot be doubted. But the former cold professionalism which had carried the Japanese Navy to its high tide of victory in the summer of 1942 was gone. In ships, in men, and in men's ideas, too much had been lost in the disastrous naval operations in the Solomon Islands, at Midway, and in the battle of Leyte Gulf.

▽ *A Japanese destroyer is blasted in two by a direct hit from U.S. B-25 bombers. American aircraft finally shattered any hope that the Japanese navy could win the war in the Pacific.*
Overleaf: *Most of the 110,000 Japanese defending Okinawa did so to the death. This naval lieutenant is one of only 7000 who were taken prisoner.*

CHAPTER 97
THE LAST INVASION?

The defeat of Germany took precedence over that of Japan, but within the limits that this imposed, the overall Allied strategy with regard to Japan was to advance by way of the central and south-west Pacific to recapture the Philippines or Formosa with the objective of eventually blockading and possibly invading Japan herself.

When American forces captured the Marianas in June 1944, they breached Japan's inner defence perimeter and brought the Japanese home-land within striking distance of long-range bomber aircraft. At this time too, the greater part of Japan's naval air arm was destroyed in the Battle of the Philippine Sea.

On October 3, 1944, the American Chiefs-of-Staff decided on the strategy to be adopted for the remainder of 1944 and for the following year. MacArthur was ordered to invade Luzon, and Nimitz was to capture one island in the Bonins and one in the Ryukyus, the latter for development into an advanced naval and air base for the invasion of Japan contemplated for the autumn of 1945.

Germany surrendered at the beginning of May 1945, and the American Chiefs-of-Staff turned their attention to ending the war against Japan as quickly as possible. With the end of resistance on Okinawa in June 1945, the American forces were in an even better position to blockade Japan, thus cutting her off from the Asian main-land, and to step up their bombing of Japanese cities and so bring the economic life of Japan to a halt. They were also in a good position to invade Japan if this was considered necessary.

General Curtis LeMay, of the 21st Bomber Command, thought that the war could be ended without invading Japan. He was convinced that with an adequate supply of aircraft and bombs, air power on its own could bring about the Japanese surrender. His own command was due to be enlarged by reinforcements from Europe and India, and he therefore saw no difficulty in stepping up the weight of his offensive after April 1945. LeMay based his assumptions on the results of the five incendiary attacks on Japan in March 1945, and his programme for the defeat of Japan comprised attacks on aircraft factories, industrial cities, oil refineries, storage plants, and in addition, mine-laying to prevent the import to Japan of food and raw materials from Manchuria, Korea, and China.

The American Joint Chiefs, however, did not think that unconditional surrender could be obtained without a successful invasion of Japan. They saw the close sea blockade of Japan and the intensive bombing offensives from Okinawa, Iwo Jima, and the Marianas as preliminaries to the invasion attempt itself. By these means, Japan's industry and communications, and her people's will to resist, would all be considerably weakened.

On April 3, 1945, the Joint Chiefs instructed General Douglas MacArthur (who would lead the invasion) to begin drawing up the plans for the invasion of

▷ *Vice-Admiral Jisaburo Ozawa, commander of the Japanese 3rd Fleet.*
▷▷ *Vice-Admiral Takeo Kurita.*

◁ ◁ *Vice-Admiral Jessie B. Oldendorf, commander of the special strike force, consisting of the large cruisers* Alaska *and* Guam, *set up on July 1, 1945 to make fast surface sweeps through Japanese waters in search of surface shipping.*
◁ *Rear-Admiral Clifton A. F. Sprague, who had distinguished himself in the Battle off Samar, and continued in command of escort-carrier groups for the rest of the war.*

southern Kyūshū in November 1945 to secure forward sea and air bases for the main invasion. This was to take place on the Tokyo plain of Honshū in March 1946.

In readiness for the invasion, the command structure in the Pacific was re-organised. MacArthur was given command of all Army forces and resources, while Admiral Nimitz was to be naval commander. On July 10, a third command, the U.S. Army Strategic Air Force for the Pacific, under General Spaatz, was established to control the air forces involved in the invasion. There was to be no supreme commander in the Pacific, and much was to depend on the ability of MacArthur, Nimitz, and Spaatz to co-operate closely together.

MacArthur's and Nimitz's staffs worked on the plans, and on May 25, MacArthur and Nimitz were officially ordered to undertake the invasion of Kyūshū (Operation "Olympic") on November 1, 1945, and of Honshū (Operation "Coronet") on March 1, 1946. When the Japanese capitulated in August 1945, planning for the invasion had reached an advanced stage.

Prior to the invasion, the Strategic Air Force, based on the Marianas and on Okinawa, would continue its offensive against Japanese industrial centres and lines of communication. To aid this programme, Okinawa and Ie shima were to be developed into a massive air base for some 240 squadrons.

Meanwhile, the Fast Carrier Force would make repeated attacks to destroy Japanese naval and air forces and disrupt land and sea communications.

The Far East Air Force was to neutralise the Japanese air forces in Japan itself and stationed on the Asiatic mainland, harass shipping routes between Asia and Japan, and destroy communications on Kyūshū along with defence installations there.

Operation "Olympic"

Operation "Olympic" had to be undertaken with troops at hand. The bulk of the forces for the invasion of Japan were to be American, although three divisions from the Commonwealth – one from Britain, one from Canada, and one from Australia – were earmarked for later in the Honshū campaign. A small number of Commonwealth air squadrons would participate, in addition to the British Pacific Fleet.

The U.S. 6th Army, comprising some 500,000 men and commanded by General Walter Krueger, was chosen for the initial assault.

Before the actual invasion, a preliminary operation was to be carried out to occupy the islands lying to the west and south of Kyūshū, so that air raid warning facilities, advanced naval anchorages, and sea-plane bases could be established before the landings on Kyūshū.

Three corps, each comprising three divisions, were to land on southern Kyūshū

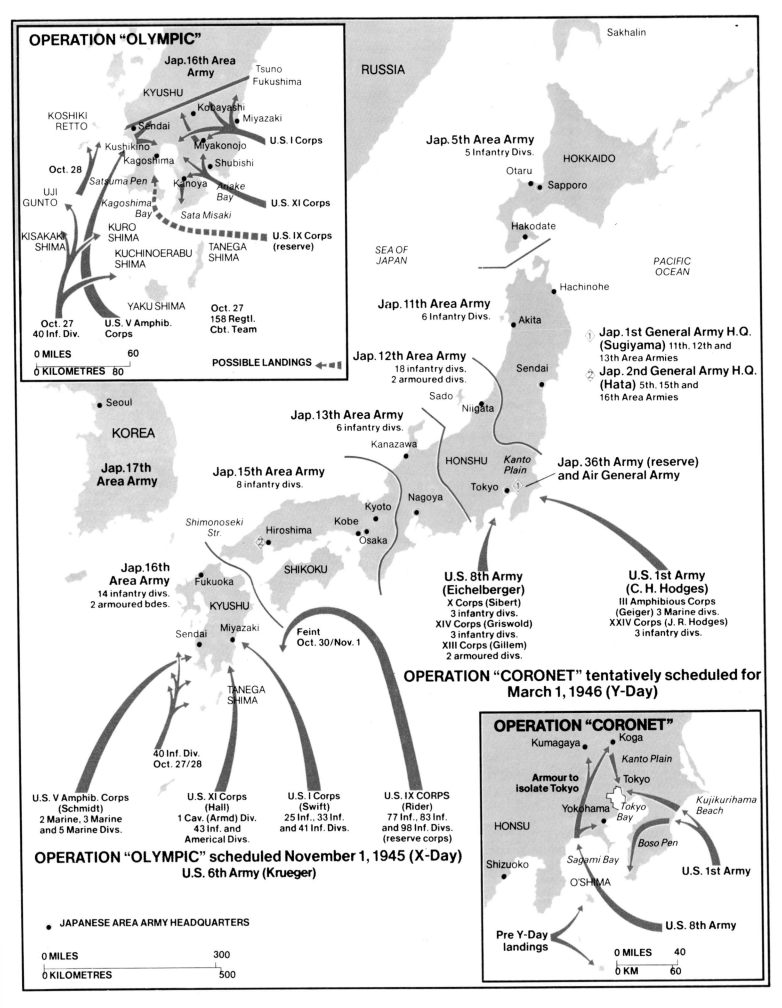

OPERATION "OLYMPIC"

Jap.16th Area Army

Tsuno
Fukushima

KYUSHU

KOSHIKI RETTO

Kobayashi

Sendai

Miyazaki

Kushikino

Kagoshima

Miyakonojo

U.S. I Corps

Oct. 28

Shubishi

Satsuma Pen

Kanoya

Ariake Bay

UJI GUNTO

Kagoshima Bay

Sata Misaki

U.S. XI Corps

KISAKAKI SHIMA

KURO SHIMA

U.S. IX Corps (reserve)

KUCHINOERABU SHIMA

TANEGA SHIMA

YAKU SHIMA

Oct. 27
40 Inf. Div.

U.S. V Amphib. Corps

Oct. 27
158 Regtl. Cbt. Team

0 MILES 60

0 KILOMETRES 80

POSSIBLE LANDINGS ◄◀◂

Sakhalin

RUSSIA

Jap.5th Area Army
5 Infantry Divs.

HOKKAIDO

Otaru

Sapporo

Hakodate

SEA OF JAPAN

PACIFIC OCEAN

Hachinohe

Jap.11th Area Army
6 Infantry Divs.

Akita

① **Jap.1st General Army H.Q. (Sugiyama)** 11th, 12th and 13th Area Armies

Sendai

② **Jap.2nd General Army H.Q. (Hata)** 5th, 15th and 16th Area Armies

Jap.12th Area Army
18 infantry divs.
2 armoured divs.

Sado

Niigata

Seoul

KOREA

Jap.13th Area Army
6 infantry divs.

Kanazawa

HONSHU

Kanto Plain

Tokyo ①

Jap.36th Army (reserve) and Air General Army

Jap.17th Area Army

Jap.15th Area Army
8 infantry divs.

Shimonoseki Str.

②

Hiroshima

Kyoto

Kobe

Nagoya

Osaka

Jap.16th Area Army
14 infantry divs.
2 armoured bdes.

Fukuoka

SHIKOKU

U.S. 8th Army (Eichelberger)
X Corps (Sibert)
3 infantry divs.
XIV Corps (Griswold)
3 infantry divs.
XIII Corps (Gillem)
2 armoured divs.

U.S. 1st Army (C. H. Hodges)
III Amphibious Corps (Geiger) 3 Marine divs.
XXIV Corps (J. R. Hodges)
3 infantry divs.

KYUSHU

Sendai

Miyazaki

Feint
Oct. 30/Nov. 1

OPERATION "CORONET" tentatively scheduled for March 1, 1946 (Y-Day)

TANEGA SHIMA

40 Inf. Div.
Oct. 27/28

U.S. V Amphib. Corps (Schmidt)
2 Marine, 3 Marine and 5 Marine Divs.

U.S. XI Corps (Hall)
1 Cav. (Armd) Div.
43 Inf. and American Divs.

U.S. I Corps (Swift)
25 Inf., 33 Inf. and 41 Inf. Divs.

U.S. IX CORPS (Rider)
77 Inf., 83 Inf. and 98 Inf. Divs. (reserve corps)

OPERATION "OLYMPIC" scheduled November 1, 1945 (X-Day)
U.S. 6th Army (Krueger)

● JAPANESE AREA ARMY HEADQUARTERS

0 MILES 300

0 KILOMETRES 500

OPERATION "CORONET"

Kumagaya

Koga

Kanto Plain

Armour to isolate Tokyo

Tokyo

Yokohama

Tokyo Bay

Kujikurihama Beach

HONSU

Shizuoko

Sagami Bay

O'SHIMA

Boso Pen

U.S. 1st Army

Pre Y-Day landings

U.S. 8th Army

0 MILES 40

0 KM 60

and establish bridgeheads. I Corps would land in the Miya-zaki area, XI Corps in Ariake wan (bay), and V Amphibious Corps in the bay to the south of Kushi-kino. Air attacks were planned to prevent the Japanese bringing up reinforcements to the battle area from the north by road or along the coasts. Within the bridge-heads, work was to begin straightaway on the construction of airfields and bases. Following this, additional areas were to be seized for airfields.

The prime objective of Operation "Olympic" was Kagoshima wan, a 50-mile bay which was to be opened up to Allied shipping and through which would flow most of the men and supplies for the Honshū invasion build-up. Kagoshima wan was also to serve as the navy's advance base.

No advance beyond this would be made, the object of "Olympic" being to secure bases for Operation "Coronet".

If the 14 divisions allotted to the 6th U.S. Army were unable to capture and hold southern Kyūshū, they could be reinforced from December by three divisions per month, intended for Honshū.

The Navy's task in Operation "Olympic" would be to bring reinforcements and supplies to the 6th Army, to cover and support land operations in Kyūshū, to establish a forward base at Kagoshima wan, and to hold island positions necessary for the security of lines of communication.

For Operation "Olympic", Admiral Nimitz divided the American fleet into two – the 3rd and the 5th fleets. The 3rd Fleet, under Admiral William F. Halsey, consisted of a number of fast carrier groups plus supporting battleships, cruisers, and destroyers. Its two main components were Vice-Admiral John Towers's 2nd Carrier Task Force (T.F. 38) and Vice-Admiral H. Bernard Rawlings's British Carrier Task Force (T.F. 37). The 3rd Fleet was to operate against the Kuriles, Hokkaido, and Honshū.

The 5th Fleet, commanded by Admiral Raymond A. Spruance, contained 2,902 vessels, and its main components were the 1st Fast Carrier Force under Vice-Admiral F. C. Sherman (T.F. 58), the Amphibious Force under Admiral Richmond Kelly Turner (T.F. 40), which would land the troops, the Gunfire and Covering Force (T.F. 54) for bombardment and fire support, and T.F. 56, responsible for mine-sweeping operations. The naval bombardment was to begin eight days before the

invasion, and continue until after the launching of the assault.

These were the plans which existed for Operation "Olympic". The second stage of the conquest of the Japanese home islands, Operation "Coronet" – the invasion of Honshū – would have involved even more troops.

◁◁ American plans for the seaborne assault on Japan. If the invasion had been launched, it would have been the largest amphibious attack of all time. ▲▲ and ▲ Japanese civilians under training. In the event of an invasion, Imperial General Headquarters planned to call up most of the male population, arming them with bamboo spears.

Operation "Coronet"

According to the plans that had been drawn up, the troops were to be landed on the Kanto plain, east of Tokyo, a level area with good beaches, which would benefit Allied superiority in armour and mechanisation, and good harbours for the logistic support of the operation. The centre of Japanese political and industrial life was sited in this region, and the American planners felt certain that a defeat here would firmly convince the Japanese that the war was lost.

Only the general outlines of the plan for Operation "Coronet" were fixed when the Japanese capitulated. The final details had still to be settled. However, it is clear that two American armies under MacArthur's command were to take part – the U.S. 1st Army commanded by General Courtney H. Hodges, and comprising XXIV Corps (Lieutenant-General J. R. Hodge) and III Amphibious Corps (Major-General Roy Geiger); and the U.S. 8th Army under General R. L. Eichelberger, comprising X Corps (Major-General F. C. Sibert), XIV Corps (Major-General Oscar Griswold), and XIII Corps (Major-General Alvan Gillem jnr.).

Air support was expected to come from 40 air groups based on Kyūshū, and from a similar force from fields in Iwo Jima, the Marianas, and the Ryūkyūs.

General Eichelberger's 8th Army was to land in Sagami bay and strike north and east to clear the western shore of Tokyo bay as far north as Yokohama. Armoured forces would simultaneously drive north to cut off any Japanese reinforcements. Some of the armour would then be available to assist the 1st Army in the capture of Tokyo, should this prove necessary. At the same time, other divisions would be used to capture Yokohama.

"KETSU-GO" Plan

In April 1945, Imperial General Headquarters of Japan concluded that American forces, already stationed in the Bonins and the Ryūkyūs, were quite likely to invade Kyūshū with between 15 and 20 divisions in October 1945, and then to invade Honshū in March 1946 with up to 30 divisions. They expected the Americans to intensify incendiary bombing attacks and the close blockade in the summer months, and then to concentrate on the destruction of the Japanese air forces. Consequently they decided it would be expedient to decentralise control.

Imperial General H.Q. formulated a plan for the defence of Japan, namely "KETSU-GO", which divided Japan's home islands, plus Korea, into seven

zones, which were all designated certain army areas. The most likely invasion areas, Kyūshū (16th Area Army) and Tokyo (12th Area Army) were allotted 65 infantry divisions, two armoured divisions, 25 independent mixed brigades, three guards brigades, and seven tank brigades – in all, well over half the total of forces available. Arrangements were made for one area to reinforce another if necessary, although it was realised that the individual islands might well be isolated from each other. Continuous defences were to be constructed on the probable landing sites, but out of reach of American naval bombardment. It was hoped that coastal defence divisions would contain the invaders in their beach-head, and that mobile assault divisions would then move up and eliminate the enemy.

△ *A scene that would be all too frequent during the attack on Japan:* kamikaze *attack.*

to secret air bases throughout Japan. Obsolete aircraft were converted to *kamikaze* craft. By the end of June, Kawabe hoped to have 2,000 *kamikazes*, and a further 1,000 by August.

To meet the invasion, it was estimated that, by August, Air General Army would have 800 fighter and bomber aircraft in addition to the *kamikazes*, and approximately 13 million gallons of fuel.

With regard to the navy, there were merely 19 destroyers (with only 3,500 tons of fuel for each one) and 38 submarines to repel the invasion. The destroyers were to be kept in the Inland Sea and used within 180 miles of Kyūshū and Shikoku, and the largest of the submarines were to attack the American advanced naval bases at Ulithi, Leyte, and Okinawa. Medium-sized submarines were to attack convoys on supply routes to the north while the small submarine craft patrolled home waters.

There was also a secondary fleet which, by July 1945, consisted of 3,294 vessels of various types including suicide boats, midget submarines, and human torpedoes. This fleet was organised into eight squadrons, and in deploying these, priority was given firstly to Kyūshū, secondly to the Shikoku coastal area, and finally to the Tokyo coastal area.

The naval air forces had the task of crushing any invasion force whilst it was still at sea. By August 1, 1946, it was estimated that the naval air arm would have approximately 5,145 aircraft. But there would be only two million gallons of fuel for them. Agreements defining the Army and Navy areas of responsibility were drawn up in April, but the proposals were never enacted.

On June 6, 1945, the Chiefs of the Armed Services laid before Japan's Supreme Council a memorandum entitled *The Fundamental Policy to be followed henceforth in the Conduct of the War*, calling for mass mobilisation. To support their proposed policy, they also submitted two subsidiary papers, *Estimates of the World Situation* and *The Present State of National Power*, and these gave no grounds for confidence that the fundamental policy outlined would succeed. The information in the memoranda indicated that Japan would probably not be able to continue the struggle beyond the autumn.

As the Japanese correctly guessed American intentions, so U.S. Intelligence officers deduced Japanese strategy, and American plans henceforth contained

▽ *Cabbage cultivation in the centre of Tokyo, on sites of bomb-destroyed buildings.*

The plan emphasised the need for the government, the people, and the armed forces to be completely united and for the entire nation to be armed and ready to fight for the homeland. Where few regular troops were stationed, guerrilla forces were to be organised and trained.

On April 8, 1945, Air General Army Headquarters were established under General M. Kawabe, to control air defences. Its tasks were to attempt to hamper the Americans' invasion preparations, to counter American air attacks on Japan, Korea, and the China coast, and also to build up the strength of the air force to counter losses already sustained.

General Kawabe formed a number of special *kamikaze* units, as he felt these would be the most effective arm against the invaders. These units were dispersed

▷ *The Japanese heavy cruiser* Tone *(eight 8-inch guns) under air attack in Kure harbour. She was sunk in this raid of July 24, 1945, by aircraft of Task Force 38. In strikes by Task Force 38 on this date and on the 28th, three battleships (*Haruna, Ise, *and* Hyuga*), two heavy cruisers (*Tone *and* Aoba*), and two obsolete cruisers were sunk. The light cruiser* Kitagami, *five destroyers, and many other craft were heavily damaged, and the new carrier* Amagi *was set on fire and later capsized. The carriers* Katsuragi *and* Ryuho *were also put out of action. By the end of the war, virtually all the major units of the Japanese Navy had been lost.*

elaborate provisions to counter *kamikaze* air attacks which could theoretically wipe out the invasion convoys. At Okinawa, overhead fighters had shot down some 60 per cent of attacking *kamikazes*, and anti-aircraft fire accounted for a further 20 per cent. The remaining *kamikazes*, however, had wrought considerable havoc. It was therefore planned that, commencing eight days before the preliminary phase of Operation "Olympic", American aircraft were to locate and attack concealed *kamikaze* bases. Bombing of all known *kamikaze* airstrips within 300 miles of the assault area was to take place in the hope of reducing the *kamikaze* threat by about one-fifth. B-24 and B-32 aircraft were to patrol selected areas containing known Japanese bases, so that early warning could be given of any impending *kamikaze* attack, and so that some aircraft could be destroyed on the ground. Close fighter cover would be provided for convoys to ward off *kamikazes*. Submarines were to give notice of attacks from Korean bases. By these means then, and by the anti-aircraft fire from the ships themselves, it was hoped to reduce the damage done by *kamikazes*. In any case, as they were a wasting asset, the intensity of the attacks was expected to drop as the operation continued. And although the short distances the *kamikazes* would have to fly would make them difficult to intercept, the disruption of communications and the failure of the Japanese to establish a combined air headquarters would be factors working against their success. Also, at this point, the *kamikaze* pilots were no longer all volunteers, the available planes were not

as suitable as earlier *kamikaze* craft, and fuel was in short supply.

As for the water-borne suicide craft, these had not proved highly effective at Okinawa, and with regard to the invasion of Japan, the "Olympic" plan included heavy attacks on their potential bases.

And finally, the raising of the divisions to meet the invasion exhausted all Japan's manpower reserves. Many soldiers expected to fight and resist the invaders were poorly trained and badly equipped. In fact the Japanese encountered such difficulty in providing the Kyūshū defenders with adequate weapons that their ability to resist a landing was imperilled. There was also a serious shortage of experienced officers, and most of the technical units were without experienced tradesmen. There were only enough reserve supplies for a limited period, and both fighting formations and lines of communication were short of transport; much of what was available was animal-drawn. Fuel was in extremely short supply.

In comparison, the U.S. 6th Army comprised fully-equipped and experienced veteran formations. The Allied air forces had air supremacy over Japan and would have had no difficulty in disrupting Japanese communications, and any attempts to move reserves.

However, the Americans realised that the invasion of Kyūshū would quite likely result in such a resurgence of national spirit that the Japanese would be fanatical in their fight to the death to defend every inch of ground, as they had done at Okinawa.

CHAPTER 98
JAPAN SURRENDERS

by Lawson Nagel

In May 1945, the Japanese Army high command was despondent. Germany had surrendered, and it was obvious that the British and Americans were planning to redeploy their military strength for a final assault on the Japanese homeland. Relations with the Soviet Union had grown steadily worse, and there were fears that the Soviets might break their non-aggression pact with Japan and join the Western Allies. The Americans had recently captured Okinawa, only 400 miles from Japan, making it even easier than before for the American bombers to wreak havoc on Japanese cities.

Haunted by the spectre of Allied invasion of the homeland, some members of the high command privately suggested that it was time to consider negotiations. The Navy had admitted in October 1944 that it no longer had enough strength to launch an offensive. In December of the same year, the Americans had completed the Leyte campaign in the Philippines–a campaign which the Japanese premier had said would be decisive. From a strategic standpoint, Japan had already lost the war. Should not the nation surrender now, while retaining some strength and bargaining power, rather than risk total destruction in the invasion?

These fears were not shared by the majority of the high command in May 1945. They agreed that diplomatic attempts to keep the Soviet Union out of the war should be stepped up, but they expressed confidence that any Anglo-American invasion of the Japanese homeland could be repulsed. The main strength of the Army remained intact, and Japan's air force had been dispersed to many airfields to preserve it from destruction by American bombers. Plans to repulse the invaders called for the entire air force to attack the American transports and task forces in waves of *kamikaze* assaults. Army operations would be concentrated on the elimination of the invaders at their debarkation sites. If these operations were not successful, Japanese volunteer reserves would continue operations further inland. Above all, Army leaders said, "what should be remembered in carrying out the general decisive battle is adherence to a vigorous spirit of attack"

to "set the example for 100,000,000 compatriots". The high command felt that a single invasion could be defeated, although they held out no such hope of victory if the Americans launched second or third assaults in quick succession.

The Japanese economy was, in any case, in a state of almost complete collapse. American submarines had isolated the home islands; raw materials were in desperately short supply, and starvation threatened.

Emperor Hirohito himself was soon convinced that it would be necessary to negotiate. His civilian advisers told him that the military situation was hopeless and the war must be ended immediately. Early in July 1945, therefore, while the high command was planning to repulse the invaders and fight to the last man, the diplomats were appealing to the Soviet Union to act as mediator in order to end the war.

The Potsdam Declaration

On July 17, Stalin met with Truman and Churchill at Potsdam. He informed the Western leaders that the Japanese had approached him about peace talks, but seemed unprepared to accept the Allies' demand for unconditional surrender. Truman and Churchill, along with Chiang Kai-shek, issued the Potsdam Proclamation on July 26, reiterating the demand that surrender be unconditional. Otherwise, the proclamation declared, Japan would face "prompt and utter destruction". It did not state that this destruction would be brought about by a new weapon –the atomic bomb.

The debate in top Japanese diplomatic and military circles now revolved around the meaning of the word "unconditional". Did this mean that the nation must surrender, as well as the armed forces? Did it mean that the Emperor would be deposed and the Imperial institution abolished? The Potsdam Proclamation had been silent on this point. Both the diplomats and the high command were determined to support the Emperor, and the generals knew that their men would never accept any agreement which abolished the

Russia's War Against Japan

At midnight on August 8, 1945, the Japanese Ambassador in Moscow received the Soviet declaration of war and ten minutes later 1,500,000 Russian troops were launched against the 1,040,000 men of the Kwantung Army in Manchuria. Despite fierce resistance by the Japanese, Soviet forces took control of Manchuria and were spared a further taste of Japanese resistance by the Japanese capitulation of August 15.

Hiroshima

One hope for enforcing a Japanese surrender, short of invasion, which was discussed at the White House on June 18, 1945, was a prediction of the highly secret U.S. Army Manhattan Engineer District project that two atomic bombs would be available for operational employment by the end of July. The United States Army Air Forces had already provided everything required to drop the atomic bombs when they were ready. The 509th Composite Group had been activated in December 1944 under the command of Colonel Paul W. Tibbets, Jr., and included the 393rd Bombardment Squadron with the most advanced model long-range B-29 bombers – the only American aircraft big enough to carry the first atomic weapons.

On August 6, 1945 at 0245 hours the *Enola Gay* B-29 bomber lifted off from North Field on Tinian Island. At 0815 hours the atomic bomb called "Little Boy" exploded 2,000 feet above the city of Hiroshima, Japan's seventh largest city. Approximately 60,000 out of 90,000 buildings were destroyed or badly damaged. There were an estimated 139,402 casualties, including 71,379 known dead and missing. Among these, were 20,000 school children.

On August 9, a second mission took off bound for Nagasaki with a plutonium bomb called "Fat Man", which exploded 1,750 feet over Nagasaki's industrial sector. Casualties were estimated at 35,000 dead.

▽ *The face of defeat. A group of Japanese officer are given their final orders by their commander before being taken into captivity by the British.*

Imperial institution. In the words of one high-ranking officer, "it would be useless for the people to survive the war if the structure of the State itself were to be destroyed. . . . even if the whole Japanese race were all but wiped out, its determination to preserve the national policy would be forever recorded in the annals of history, but a people who sacrificed will upon the altar of physical existence could never rise again as a nation."

In the midst of this debate, on August 6, the first atomic bomb was dropped on Hiroshima. Three days later a second atomic bomb devastated Nagasaki, and the Soviet Union finally declared war on Japan. A conference of the Emperor and his civilian and military advisers was hastily summoned, and met in an air-raid shelter in the grounds of the Imperial Palace in Tokyo shortly before midnight. In the light of the events of the past three days, even the military authorities agreed now that a surrender was unavoidable. Unlike Foreign Minister Togo, however, who advised surrender on the single condition that the Emperor's rights be preserved, the military leaders asked for three other reservations. First, they wanted to avoid an Allied military occupation of Japan. Second, they wanted to try war criminals themselves. Third, they wanted to disarm their own troops rather than surrender directly to the Allies. War Minister Anami explained that this last proviso could be taken to mean that the Japanese armed forces were not actually defeated, but had decided to stop fighting voluntarily in order to preserve the Japanese land and people from further destruction. When the two sides had expressed their views, the conference was found to be deadlocked. Then the unprecedented happened. The Emperor's advisers actually asked him for his own opinion. Instead of acting according to his advisers' instructions, the Emperor was being asked to advise them. He was to shed the rôle of observer and puppet and make his own decision. Hirohito had already made up his mind, and he soon made it clear that he believed the Foreign Minister's proposal – with only the Emperor's position safeguarded – was more likely to lead to a quick peace settlement and should therefore be accepted. The conference unanimously endorsed the Emperor's decision, and cables were sent within a few hours announcing the Japanese terms.

Later that same day, a reply was re-ceived from U.S. Secretary of State James Byrnes. This note explained that the Allies would not accept anything but an unconditional surrender, and that this meant that the Emperor would be subject to the Supreme Commander for the Allied powers. This statement produced another argument in the Japanese cabinet – what did "subject to" mean? At another meeting on the morning of August 14, it was pointed out that Byrnes' note indicated that the Imperial institution would not be abolished, and in any case the Japanese Emperors had often been "subject to" the power of the shoguns. Once again, Hirohito was asked for his own opinion, and once again he called for immediate acceptance of the Allied demand. The cabinet acceded to the Imperial will, and it was announced over the radio that Japan had surrendered.

That night, the Emperor recorded a message to be broadcast at noon on August 15, calling for all Japanese to accept the surrender. They were warned especially to "beware strictly of any outbursts of emotion" that might create needless complications. In other words, they were to ignore any violent "fight-

△ The surrender signatories aboard the Missouri. They are (in the front row) Minister Mamoru Shigemitsu, to sign for the Emperor, and General Yoshijiro Umezu for the Japanese General Headquarters. In the second row (in top hats) are Katauo Okazaki and Toshikazu Kase, with other service and government representatives behind.

to-the-finish" fanatics. But a small group of officers at the Army headquarters were determined not to surrender, and decided to attempt a *coup d'état*. The Emperor was to be separated from his peace-seeking advisers and persuaded to change his mind and continue the war. On the night of August 14, the conspirators approached General Mori, the commander of the Imperial Guards, at the palace. They asked him to join with them in the *coup* to preserve the honour of the Japanese nation. Mori listened to their arguments, then said that he would go to pray at the Meiji Shrine to help him make up his mind. The conspirators were unwilling to allow any delay, and one of them shot Mori on the spot. Then, using the dead general's seal, they forged orders for the Imperial Guards and began tracking down the Emperor's advisers and the record which was to be broadcast the following day. The whole plot ended in failure when the Eastern Army District commander arrived at the palace, refused to join the rebels, and persuaded them to give up. The officer who had shot General Mori committed *hara-kiri* on the Imperial Plaza. When War Minister Anami heard of the attempted *coup* early in the morning of August 15, he also committed suicide.

In the next few days, several other suicides occurred, but most Japanese accepted the Imperial decision calmly. On August 30, the first American occupation forces (including a small British contingent) landed at Yokosuka. Three days later, at nine o'clock in the morning, Japan's new Foreign Minister, Mamoru Shigemitsu, boarded the *Missouri* in Tokyo Bay. On behalf of the Emperor and the Japanese Government, he signed the official surrender document. General Douglas MacArthur accepted the surrender, a scratchy record of *The Star-Spangled Banner* was played on the ship's speakers, and World War II was over.

▷ *Under the alert gaze of a lone Gurkha, dejected Japanese prisoners await transportation away from the war zone in Burma.*

The War Trials

With the support of the U.S., Great Britain, and 15 other Allied governments, the United Nations War Crimes Commission was established in London on October 7, 1942. On August 8, 1945, the four major victorious powers signed the London Agreement setting up the International Military Tribunal in Nuremberg. The trials began in November 1945 and lasted almost ten months. The defendants were the military, political and economic leaders of the vanquished Nazi Reich: Goring, Ribbentrop, Keitel, Kaltenbrunner, Frank, Frick, Rosenberg, Streicher, Sauckel, Jodl, Seyss-Inquart, Hess, Frunk, Raeder, Schirach, Speer, Neurath, Dönitz, Schacht, Papen and Frizsche. Eleven of the accused received death sentences.

There were a further 12 international trials held at Nuremberg. Twenty eight defendants were tried in Tokyo, seven of whom were sentenced to death by hanging. Orthodox military channels of justice sentenced over 250 defendants to death.

▽ *General of the Army Douglas MacArthur, Supreme Commander for the Allied Powers, signs the surrender document. Behind him are Lieutenant-General Jonathan Wainwright, who surrendered at Corregidor, and Lieutenant-General A.E. Percival, who surrendered at Singapore. They attended the ceremonies on the* Missouri *at the personal invitation of General MacArthur.*

Chronology of Major Events

1938

March 11	Anschluss – German annexation of Austria.
September 29	Munich Agreement signed.
October 5	Germany occupies Sudetenland.
November 9	Kristallnacht – attacks on Jews.

1939

March 14	Slovakia declares its independence.
March 31	Britain and France give guarantee to Poland.
April 7	Italy invades Albania.
May 22	Germany and Italy sign Pact of Steel.
August 23	Molotov-Ribbentrop pact signed between Germany and the Soviet Union.
September 1	Germany invades Poland.
September 1	Britain and France declare war on Germany.
September 17	Soviet Union invades Poland.
November 30	Soviet Union at war with Finland.

1940

March 12	War between Soviet Union and Finland ends.
April 9	Germany invades Norway and Denmark.
April 14	Allied troops land in Norway.
May 10	Fall Gelb, the offensive in the West, is launched by Germany.
May 10	Churchill becomes Prime Minister of Great Britain.
May 14	Dutch Army surrenders.
May 26	Beginning of evacuation of Dunkirk.
May 28	Belgium surrenders.
June 2	Allies withdraw from Norway.
June 4	Dunkirk evacuation complete.
June 10	Italy declares war on Britain and France.
June 14	Germans enter Paris.
June 21	Italy launches offensive against France.
June 22	France and Germany sign armistice.
June 24	France and Italy sign armistice.
July 3	Royal Navy attacks French fleet at Mers el Kebir.
July 10	Beginning of the Battle of Britain.
September 17	Operation Sealion (the invasion of England) postponed by Hitler.
September 21	Italy and Germany sign Tripartite Pact.
September 27	Japan signs Tripartite Pact.
November 20	Hungary signs Tripartite Pact.
November 22	Romania signs Tripartite Pact.
November 23	Slovakia signs Tripartite Pact.

1941

January 19	British launch East African campaign offensive.
January 22	Australian troops take Tobruk.
February 6	British capture Benghazi.
February 11	Rommel arrives in Libya.
March 25	Yugoslavia signs Tripartite Pact.
March 27	Yugoslavia leaves Tripartite Pact after coup d'etat.
March 28	Successful British naval action against Italians off Cape Matapan.
April 6-8	Axis forces invade Yugoslavia and Greece.
April 11	U.S.A. extends its naval neutrality patrols.
April 13	Belgrade falls to Axis forces.
April 14	Yugoslav forces surrender.
April 22	Greek First Army surrenders at Metsovan Pass.
May 16	Italians surrender to British at Amba Alagi.
May 20	Germans land on Crete.
May 24	H.M.S. Hood sunk by Bismarck.
May 27	Bismarck sunk by Royal Navy.
June 1	British withdraw from Crete.
June 2	Germany launches Operation Barbarossa against the Soviet Union.
July 27	Japanese troops invade French Indo-China.
September 19	Germans capture Kiev.
September 28	Three-power Conference in Moscow.
December 6	Britain declares war on Finland, Hungary and Rumania.
December 7	Japanese attack Pearl Harbor.
December 8	U.S.A. and Britain declare war on Japan.
December 8	Japanese invade Malaya and Thailand.
December 11	Germany and Italy declare war on the U.S.A.
December 14	Japanese begin invasion of Burma.
December 25	Japanese take Hong Kong.

1942

February 15	Japanese troops capture Singapore from British.
February 27	Battle of the Java Sea.
February 28	Japanese invade Java.
March 8	Japanese invade New Guinea.
March 17	General MacArthur appointed to command South-West Pacific.
March 27	British raid Saint Nazaire.
April 9	U.S. troops surrender in Bataan.
April 16	George Cross awarded to Island of Malta by H.R.H. King George VI.
April 26	Anglo-Soviet Treaty signed.
May 6	Japanese take Corregidor.
May 7	Battle of the Coral Sea.
May 20	British troops withdraw from Burma.
May 26	Rommel's Afrika Korps attack British at Gazala.
May 30	Royal Air Force launches first thousand-bomber raid on Germany.
June 4	Battle of Midway.
June 21	Rommel's Afrika Korps take Tobruk.
July 1	Sevastopol taken by Germans.
July 1	First Battle of El Alamein.
August 7	U.S. troops land on Guadalcanal.
August 11	PEDESTAL convoy arrives in Malta.

August 19	Raid on Dieppe.
August 31	Battle of Alam Halfa.
October 24	Second Battle of El Alamein.
November 8	Operation TORCH landings in North Africa.
November 11	Germans and Italians occupy Vichy France.
November 27	French fleet scuttled at Toulon.

1943

January 14-24	Allied Conference at Casablanca.
January 23	British troops take Tripoli.
February 2	Germans surrender at Stalingrad.
February 8	Red Army captures Kursk.
February 13	Chindits launch first operation into Burma.
February 19	Battle for the Kasserine Pass.
April 19	First Warsaw rising.
April 19	Bermuda Conference.
May 11-25	TRIDENT conference in Washington.
May 13	Axis forces surrender in North Africa.
May 16	Royal Air Force "Dambuster" raid on Mohne and Eder dams.
May 24	U-boats withdraw from North Atlantic.
July 5	Battle of Kursk.
July 10	Allies land in Sicily.
July 25	Mussolini resigns.
September 3	Allies land on Italian mainland.
September 8	Surrender of Italy announced.
September 9	Allies land at Salerno.
September 10	Germans occupy Rome and Northern Italy.
October 13	Italy declares war on Germany.
November 6	Red Army captures Kiev.
November 23-26	First Allied conference in Cairo.
November 28 -December 1	Allied conference in Teheran.
December 3-7	Second Allied conference in Cairo.
December 24	General Eisenhower promoted to supreme commander for OVERLORD, the Normandy landings.

1944

January 22	Allies land at Anzio.
January 27	Red Army raises Siege of Leningrad.
January 31	U.S. forces land on Marshall Islands.
February 1	Battle for Monte Cassino begins.
March 2	Second Chindit operation into Burma.
May 11	Fourth Battle of Monte Cassino.
June 4	U.S. troops enter Rome.
June 6	Operation OVERLORD – Allied landings in Normandy.
June 19	Battle of the Philippine Sea.
July 1	Breton Woods conference.
July 20	Failed attempt to assassinate Hitler – July Bomb plot.
August 1	Second Warsaw rising.
August 4	Allied troops enter Florence.
August 15	Operation DRAGOON – Allied landings in southern France.

August 25	Germans in paris surrender.
September 4	British troops capture Antwerp.
September 12-16	OCTAGON – Allied conference at Quebec.
September 17	Operation MARKET GARDEN at Arnhem.
September 21	Dumbarton Oaks conference.
October 14	British enter Athens.
October 23	De Gaulle recognised by Britain and U.S.A. as head of French Provisional Government.
October 24	Battle of Leyte Gulf.
December 16	Germans launch campaign in the Ardennes.

1945

January 4-13	Japanese Kamikaze planes sink 17 U.S. ships and damage 50 more.
January 14	Red Army advances into East Prussia.
January 17	Red Army takes Warsaw.
January 30 -February 3	First ARGONAUT Allied conference at Malta.
February 4-11	Second ARGONAUT Allied conference at Malta.
February 6	Allies clear Colmar pocket.
February 19	U.S. forces land on Iwo Jima.
February 26	U.S. 9th Army reaches Rhine.
March 7	U.S. 3rd Army crosses Rhine at Remagen Bridge.
March 20	British capture Mandalay.
March 30	Red Army enters Austria.
April 1	U.S. First and Ninth Armies encircle the Ruhr.
April 1	U.S. forces land on Okinawa.
April 12	President Roosevelt dies and Truman becomes president.
April 13	Red Army takes Vienna.
April 25	U.S. and Soviet forces meet at Torgau.
April 28	Mussolini shot by partisans.
April 29	Germans sign surrender terms for troops in Italy.
April 30	Hitler commits suicide.
May 2	Red Army takes Berlin.
May 3	British enter Rangoon.
May 4	German forces in the Netherlands, northern Germany and Denmark surrender to General Montgomery on Luneburg Heath.
May 5	Germans in Norway surrender.
May 7	General Alfred Jodl signs unconditional surrender of Germany at Reims, to take effect on May 9.
May 8	Victory in Europe Day.
May 10	Red Army takes Prague.
July 17 -August 2	Allied TERMINAL conference held in Potsdam.
July 26	Winston Churchill resigns after being defeated in the general election. Clement Attlee becomes Prime Minister of Great Britain.
August 6	Atomic bomb dropped on Hiroshima.
August 8	Soviet Union declares war on Japan.
August 9	Atomic bomb dropped on Nagasaki.
August 14	Unconditional surrender of Japanese forces announced by Emperor Hirohito.
August 15	Victory in Japan Day.
September 2	Japanese sign surrender aboard U.S.S. Missouri in Tokyo Bay.

INDEX

ACKNOWLEDGEMENTS

The publishers would like to thank the following publishers and agents for permission to quote from the undermentioned books:

A Full Life: Collins Publishers for A Full Life by Lieutenant-General Sir Brian Horrocks.

A Sailor's Odyssey: The Estate of Viscount Cunningham and A.P. Watt & Son for A Sailor's Odyssey by Admiral of the Fleet Viscount Cunningham of Hyndhope.

A Soldier's Story: Hold, Rinehart and Winston Inc. for A Soldier's Story by General of the Army Omar Bradley, " 1951 by Holt, Rinehart and Winston, Inc.

Assignment to Catastrophe: Lady Spears for Assignment to Catastrophe by Major-General Sir Edward Spears, published by William Heinemann.

A Torch to the Enemy: A Fire Raid on Tokyo: Ballantine Books Inc., a Division of Random House, for A Torch to the Enemy, " 1960 by Martin Caidin.

Barbarossa: Alan Clark with the permission of A. D. Peters Co. for Barbarossa. " 1965 by Alan Clark. Berlin Diary: Paul R. Reynolds for Berlin Diary. " 1971 by William Shirer.

Calculated Risk: Harper & Row, Publisher, Inc. For Calculated Risk," 1955 by General Mark Clark.

Ciano Diaries: The Chicago Daily News for the Ciano Diaries by Count Galeazzo Cian, translated by Malcolm Muggeridge, " 1947.

Crusade in Europe: Doubleday & Company, Inc. For excerpt from Crusade in Europe by General of the Army Dwighy D. Eisenhower, " 1948 by Doubleday & Company, Inc.

Defeat in the West: Milton Shulman for Defeat in the West by Milton Shulman, published by Coronet Books.

Full Circle: Ballantine Books Inc.m a Division of Random House, Inc., for Full Circle by Air Vice-Marshal J.E. Johnson, " 1968.

Hitler's War Directives 1939-1945: Sidgwick & Jackson Ltd. for Hitler's War Directives edited by Professor Hugh Trevor-Roper.

I was There: Rear-Admiral William H. Leahy, U.S.N. (Ret'd) for passages from I Was There by Admiral William D. Leahy, published by Brandt and Brandt.

Krieg in Europa: Verlag Kiepenheuer und Witsch for Krieg in Europa by General Friedrich von Senger und Etterlin.

Main Fleet to Singapore: David Higham Associated Ltd. For Main Fleet to Singapore by Russell Grenfell.

Memoirs: Collins Publishers for Memoirs by Field-Marchal Viscount Montgomery of Alamein.

Memoirs of Marshal Mannerheim: E.P. Dutton & Company, Inc., for the Memoirs of Marshal Mannerheim by Marshal Mannerheim, translated by Count Eric Lewenhaupt, " 1954 E. P. Dutton & Company, Inc.

Midway: The Battle that Doomed Japan: The United States Naval Institute, Annapolis, Maryland for Midway: The Battle that Doomed Japan by Mitsuo Fuchida and Masatake Okumiya, " 1955 by United States Naval Institute.

73 North: Peter Janson-Smith for 73 North by Dudley Pope, published by Weidenfeld & Nicolson.

Pacific War Diary 1942-1945: Houghton Mifflin Company, for Pacific War Diary1942-1945 by James Fashey, "1963.

Panzer Leader: Michael Joseph for Panzer Leader by General Heinz Guderian.

Reminiscences: Time Inc. for Reminiscences by General of the Army Douglas MacArthur.

Roosevelt and Hopkins: Harper & Row, Publisher, Inc., for Roosevelt and Hopkins by Robert E. Sherwood, " 1948 and 1950 by Robert E. Sherwood.

Russian at War 1941-1945: E. P. Dutton & Company, Inc. for Russian at War 1941-1945 by Alexander Werth, " by Alexander Werth.

Sixty Days that Shook the West: G. P. Putnam's Sons for Sixty Days that Shook the West by Jacques Benoist-Mechin, translated by Peter Wiles.

Strange Alliance: Viking Press, Inc. for Strange Alliance by General John R. Dean, " 1946 and 1947.

The Battle of the Atlantic: B. T. Batsford for The Battle of the Atlantic by Captain Donald Macintyre.

The Battle of Cassino: Houghton Mifflin Company for The Battle of Cassino by Fred Majdalany.

The Battle of the Mediterranean: B. T. Batsford for The Battle of the Mediterranean by Captain Donald Macintyre.

The Battle for Normandy: B. T. Batsford for The Battle of the Normandy by E. Belfield and General H. Essame.

The Bismarck Episode: Macmillan Publisheing Co., Inc. for The Bismarck Episode by Russell Grenfell.

The Brutal Friendship: Harper & Row, Inc. for The Brutal Friendship by F. W. Deakin, " 1963.

The Coast Watchers: Angus and Robertson (Publishers) Pty Ltd. for The Coast Watchers by Eric Feldt.

The Eden Memoirs: reprinted by permission of The New York Times Company for The Eden Memoirs by the Rt. Hon. The Earl of Avon, " 1960.

The First and the Last: Holt, Rinehart and Winston, Inc. for The First and the Last by General Adolf Galland, " 1955.

The Foxes of the Desert: E. P. Dutton & Company, Inc. for The Foxes of the Desert by Paul Carell, " 1960 in the English translation by Mervyn Savill by E. P. Dutton & Company, Inc.

The Great Sea War: The Story of Naval Action in World War II: Prentic-Hall, Inc. for The Great Sea War: The Story of nval Action in World War II by E. B. Potter and Fleet Admiral Chester W. Nimitz (Editors), " Prentice-Hall , Inc. of Englewood Cliffs, N.J.

The Longest Day: Simon Schuster for The Longest Day by Cornelius Ryan, " 1959.

The Luftwaffe War Diaries: Macdonald & Co. Ltd. for The Luftwaffe War Diaries by Cajus Bekker, " 1964 by Gerhard Stalling Verlag and 1966 in translation by Macdonald & Co. Ltd.

The Marines' War: William Morrow & Co., Inc. for The Marines' War by Fletcher Pratt, "1948.

The Road to Stalingrad: Stalin's war with Germany: Harper and Rowe Publishers Inc. for The Road to Stalingrad: Stalin's war with Germany by Professor John Erickson, " 1975.

The Rommel Papers: Harcourt Brace Jovanovich, Inc.for excerpts from The Rommel Papers, " 1953 by Captain Basil Liddell Hart.

The Stilwell Papers: William Morrow & Co., Inc.for The Stilwell Papers by Arthur Bryant.

Top Secret: Ralph Ingersoll for Top Secret by Ralph Ingersoll, published by Harcourt Brace Jovanovich, " 1946.

Triumph in the West: Collins Publishers for Triumph in the West by Sir Arthur Bryant.

War As I Knew It: Houghton Mifflin Company for War As I Knew It by General George S. Patton, " 1947.

Picture Acknowledgements: The publishers would like to thank the following individuals and organisations:

Agence France-Presse; Aldo Fraccaroli; Associated Press; Belga; Bibliothek fur Zeitgeschichte, Konrad Adenauer; Bibliotheque Nationale; Blitz, British Official Photos; Bundesarchiv, Koblenz; Camera Press; Documentation Francaise; Etablissement Cinematographique et Photographique des Armees; FOT Library; Fox Photos; Fujiphotos; A. Harlingue; Harrisiadis; H. Le Masson; Holmes-Lebel; H.M.S.O.; Imperial War Museum; International News Photos; Keystone; Library of Congress; Musee de la Guerre; Novosti; Picture Press; Popperfoto; Punch; R. Viollet; Rene Dazy; Robert Hunt Library; Sikorski Institute; Staatsbibliothek, Berlin; Suddeutscher Verlag; TRH Pictures; U.S.I.S.; U.S. Airforce; U.S. Army; U.S. Navy; U.S. Marine Corps; United Press; Ullstein; Wiener Library.